W9-BVH-914

American ▬ Civil Liberties

Otis H. Stephens, Jr.
John M. Scheb II

Department of Political Science
University of Tennessee, Knoxville

WEST/WADSWORTH

I(T)P® An International Thomson Publishing Company

Belmont, CA • Albany, NY • Boston • Cincinnati • Johannesburg • London • Madrid • Melbourne
Mexico City • New York • Pacific Grove, CA • Scottsdale, AZ • Singapore • Tokyo • Toronto

Political Science Editor: Clark Baxter
Senior Development Editor: Sharon Adams Poore
Editorial Assistant: Melissa Gleason
Marketing Manager: Jay Hu
Interior and Cover Design: Lois Stanfield
Cover Photograph: David Burnett/Contact Press Images (background flag ©1998 PhotoDisc, Inc.)
Print Buyer: Barbara Britton
Permissions Manager: Susan Walters
Production: Lori Harvey, Carlisle Publishers Services
Compositor: Carlisle Communications, Ltd.
Printer: R.R. Donnelley & Sons

COPYRIGHT © 1999 by Wadsworth Publishing Company
A Division of International Thomson Publishing Inc.
I(T)P   The ITP logo is a registered trademark under license.

Printed in the United States of America
2 3 4 5 6 7 8 9 10

For more information, contact Wadsworth Publishing Company, 10 Davis Drive, Belmont, CA 94002, or electronically at http://www.wadsworth.com

International Thomson Publishing Europe
Berkshire House
168-173 High Holborn
London, WC1V 7AA, United Kingdom

Nelson ITP, Australia
102 Dodds Street
South Melbourne
Victoria 3205 Australia

Nelson Canada
1120 Birchmount Road
Scarborough, Ontario
Canada M1K 5G4

International Thomson Editores
Seneca, 53
Col. Polanco
11560 México D.F. México

International Thomson Publishing Asia
60 Albert Street
#15-01 Albert Complex
Singapore 189969

International Thomson Publishing Japan
Hirakawa-cho Kyowa Building, 3F
2-2-1- Hirakawa-cho Chiyoda-ku
Tokyo 102 Japan

International Thomson Publishing South Africa
Building 18, Constantia Square
138 Sixteenth Road, P.O. Box 2459
Halfway House, 1685 South Africa

All rights reserved. No part of this work covered by the copyright hereon may be reproduced or used in any form or by any means—graphic, electronic, or mechanical, including photocopying, recording, taping, or information storage and retrieval systems—without the written permission of the publisher.

ISBN # 0-534-54954-3

This book is printed on acid-free recycled paper.

PHOTO CREDITS

338 Library of Congress; **339** Corbis-Bettmann; **341** James H. Pickerell/Stock Boston; **377** Historical Pictures/Stock Montage; **383** Collection of the Supreme Court of the United States; **384** Historical Pictures/Stock Montage; **386** Corbis-Bettmann; **389** National Archives; **395** Joseph D. Lavenburg/Collection, The Supreme Court Historical Society; **432** Collection of the Supreme Court of the United States; **434** The New York Times; **436** Library of Congress; **445, 447** AP/Wide World Photos; **448** Collection of the Supreme Court of the United States; **454** Lionel Delevingne/Stock Boston; **455** Michael Grecco/Stock Boston; **537** Corbis-Bettmann; **540** Collection of the Supreme Court of the United States; **583** Historical Pictures/Stock Montage; **595, 604** AP/Wide World Photos; **618, 683, 685, 689** Corbis-Bettmann; **692** Peter Menzel/Stock Boston; **696** AP/Wide World Photos; **738** Historical Pictures/Stock Montage; **743** Corbis-Bettmann; **745** Historical Pictures/Stock Montage; **747** Corbis-Bettmann; **748** AP/Wide World Photos; **756** Corbis-Bettmann; **761, 769** AP/Wide World Photos; **822** Collection of the Supreme Court of the United States

About the Authors

Otis H. Stephens, Jr., is Alumni Distinguished Service Professor of Political Science, Adjunct Professor of Law, and Associate Dean of the College of Arts and Sciences at the University of Tennessee, Knoxville. Professor Stephens holds a Ph.D. in political science from Johns Hopkins University and a J.D. from the University of Tennessee. Professor Stephens is the author of *The Supreme Court and Confessions of Guilt* (1973) and co-author, with Gregory J. Rathjen, of *The Supreme Court and the Allocation of Constitutional Power* (1980) and, with John M. Scheb II, of *American Constitutional Law: Essays and Cases* (1988). He has contributed chapters to *Comparative Human Rights* (1976) and *The Reagan Administration and Human Rights* (1985). He has also authored or co-authored a number of articles in professional journals, including the *Georgetown Law Journal*, the *Journal of Public Law*, the *Tennessee Law Review*, the *Widner Journal of Public Law*, the *Southeastern Political Review*, and the *Criminal Law Bulletin*. Dr. Stephens is also a member of the Tennessee Bar.

John M. Scheb II is Professor of Political Science at the University of Tennessee, Knoxville. He received his Ph.D. from the University of Florida in 1982. Professor Scheb has authored or co-authored numerous articles in professional journals, including the *Journal of Politics*, *American Politics Quarterly*, *Political Research Quarterly*, *Law and Policy*, *Judicature*, *State and Local Government Review*, *Social Science Quarterly*, *Political Behavior*, *Southeastern Political Review*, and the *Tennessee Law Review*. He has also co-authored three other textbooks, *American Constitutional Law: Essays and Cases* (1988), with Otis H. Stephens, Jr.; *Criminal Law and Procedure* 3rd edition (1999), with Judge John M. Scheb; and *American Government: Politics and Political Culture* (1995) with William Lyons and Lilliard E. Richardson, Jr.

Professors Stephens and Scheb regularly teach graduate and undergraduate courses in American government, constitutional law, civil rights and liberties, administrative law, the judicial process, and law in American society.

Dedicated with love
to Mary Stephens
and Sherilyn Scheb

CONTENTS

Preface   viii

Part 2   Civil Rights and Liberties   331

Chapter 6   Constitutional Sources of Civil Rights and Liberties   332
Introduction   332
Rights Recognized in the Original Constitution   333
The Bill of Rights   337
The Fourteenth Amendment   345
Amendments Protecting Voting Rights   351
Standards of Review in Civil Rights and Liberties Cases   353
The Importance of State Constitutions   355
Conclusion   356
Key Terms   356
For Further Reading   356
Internet Resources   357
DeShaney v. Winnebago Social Services (1989)   357
Barron v. Baltimore (1833)   359
Hurtado v. California (1884)   360
Chicago, Burlington and Quincy Railroad Company v. Chicago (1897)   363
Palko v. Connecticut (1937)   364
Adamson v. California (1947)   365
Rochin v. California (1952)   369
Duncan v. Louisiana (1968)   372

Chapter 7   Property Rights and Economic Freedom   376
Introduction   376
The Contract Clause   378
The Rise and Fall of Economic Due Process   382
Equal Protection and Economic Regulation   393
Property Rights and the "Takings" Issue   393
Conclusion   397

Key Terms   398
For Further Reading   398
Internet Resources   399
Dartmouth College v. Woodward (1819)   399
Charles River Bridge Company v. Warren Bridge Company (1837)   401
Home Building and Loan Association v. Blaisdell (1934)   404
The Slaughterhouse Cases (1873)   407
Lochner v. New York (1905)   411
Adkins v. Children's Hospital (1923)   415
West Coast Hotel Company v. Parrish (1937)   420
Ferguson v. Skrupa (1963)   423
Hawaii Housing Authority v. Midkiff (1984)   424
Dolan v. City of Tigard (1994)   426

Chapter 8   Expressive Freedom and the First Amendment   430
Introduction   430
Interpretive Foundations of Expressive Freedom   430
The Prohibition of Prior Restraint   433
The Clear and Present Danger Doctrine   436
Fighting Words, Hate Speech, and Profanity   441
Symbolic Speech and Expressive Conduct   444
Defamation   448
The Intractable Obscenity Problem   451
Expressive Activities in the Public Forum   454
Electronic Media and the First Amendment   460
Commercial Speech   462
Rights of Public Employees and Beneficiaries   464
Freedom of Association   466
Conclusion   468
Key Terms   469
For Further Reading   469
Internet Resources   469
Near v. Minnesota (1931)   470

New York Times Company
  v. United States (1971) — 473
Schenck v. United States (1919) — 477
Brandenburg v. Ohio (1969) — 478
Cohen v. California (1971) — 480
Texas v. Johnson (1989) — 483
Barnes v. Glen Theatre, Inc. (1991) — 487
New York Times Company v. Sullivan (1964) — 490
Miller v. California (1973) — 493
Federal Communications Commission
  v. Pacifica Foundation (1978) — 496
Reno v. American Civil Liberties
  Union (1997) — 500
Edwards v. South Carolina (1963) — 503
Adderley v. Florida (1966) — 505
44 Liquormart, Inc. v. Rhode Island (1996) — 508
National Endowment for the Arts v. Finley (1998) — 512
Hurley v. Irish-American Gay, Lesbian and
  Bisexual Group of Boston (1995) — 515

Chapter 9 Religious Liberty and
Church–State Relations — **521**
Introduction — 521
Religious Belief and the Right to Proselytize — 524
Unconventional Religious Practices — 525
Patriotic Rituals and Civic Duties — 529
Freedom of Religion versus Parens Patriae — 531
The Wall of Separation — 532
Religion and Public Education — 534
Governmental Affirmations of Religious Belief — 540
The Problem of Tax Exemptions — 541
Conclusion — 544
Key Terms — 544
For Further Reading — 544
Internet Resources — 545
West Virginia State Board of Education
  v. Barnette (1943) — 545
Wisconsin v. Yoder (1972) — 548
Employment Division v. Smith (1990) — 553
Church of the Lukumi Babalu Aye,
  Inc. v. City of Hialeah (1993) — 558
Everson v. Board of Education (1947) — 562
Abington School District v. Schempp (1963) — 564
Wallace v. Jaffree (1985) — 567
Edwards v. Aguillard (1987) — 570
Agostini v. Felton (1997) — 573
Marsh v. Chambers (1983) — 576
Lynch v. Donnelly (1984) — 579
Walz v. Tax Commission (1970) — 583

Chapter 10 The Constitution and
Criminal Justice — **586**
Introduction — 586

Search and Seizure — 587
The Exclusionary Rule — 594
Arrest — 598
Police Interrogation and Confessions of Guilt — 599
The Right to Counsel — 603
Bail and Pretrial Detention — 606
Plea Bargaining — 607
Trial by Jury — 609
The Protection Against Double Jeopardy — 613
Incarceration and the Rights of Prisoners — 615
The Death Penalty — 617
Appeal and Postconviction Relief — 621
Juvenile Justice — 625
Conclusion — 626
Key Terms — 627
For Further Reading — 627
Internet Resources — 628
Olmstead v. United States (1928) — 628
Katz v. United States (1967) — 631
Weeks v. United States (1914) — 633
Mapp v. Ohio (1961) — 635
United States v. Leon (1984) — 639
Miranda v. Arizona (1966) — 644
New York v. Quarles (1984) — 647
Powell v. Alabama (1932) — 651
Gideon v. Wainwright (1963) — 654
Batson v. Kentucky (1986) — 656
Kansas v. Hendricks (1997) — 661
Furman v. Georgia (1972) — 665
Gregg v. Georgia (1976) — 670
Payne v. Tennessee (1991) — 671

Chapter 11 Personal Autonomy and the
Constitutional Right of Privacy — **675**
Introduction — 675
Constitutional Foundations of the
  Right of Privacy — 677
Procreation and Birth Control — 679
The Abortion Controversy — 682
The Right of Privacy and Living Arrangements — 690
Privacy and Gay Rights — 691
Other Applications of the Right of Privacy — 693
A Right to Die? — 694
Conclusion — 697
Key Terms — 698
For Further Reading — 698
Internet Resources — 699
Jacobson v. Massachusetts (1905) — 699
Meyer v. Nebraska (1923) — 701
Buck v. Bell (1927) — 702
Poe v. Ullman (1961) — 703
Griswold v. Connecticut (1965) — 709
Roe v. Wade (1973) — 714

Planned Parenthood v. Casey (1992) 719
Bowers v. Hardwick (1986) 727
Washington v. Glucksberg (1997) 731

**Chapter 12 Equal Protection and the
Antidiscrimination Principle** **737**
Introduction 737
Levels of Judicial Scrutiny in Equal
   Protection Cases 738
The Struggle for Racial Equity 741
The Affirmative Action Controversy 749
Gender-Based Discrimination 755
Other Forms of Discrimination 762
The Ongoing Problem of Private Discrimination 768
Conclusion 771
Key Terms 771
For Further Reading 772
Internet Resources 772
The Civil Rights Cases (1883) 773
Plessy v. Ferguson (1896) 776
Brown v. Board of Education of Topeka I (1954) 779
Brown v. Board of Education of Topeka II (1955) 781
Loving v. Virginia (1967) 783
*Swann v. Charlotte-Mecklenburg Board of
   Education* (1971) 785
Missouri v. Jenkins (1995) 788
Adarand Constructors, Inc. v. Peña (1995) 793
Frontiero v. Richardson (1973) 799
United States v. Virgina (1996) 802
Romer v. Evans (1996) 811

**Chapter 13 Elections, Representation,
and Voting Rights** **816**
Introduction 816
Racial Discrimination in Voting Rights 818

The Reapportionment Decisions 827
Political Parties and Electoral Fairness 831
The Problem of Campaign Finance 832
Conclusion 833
Key Terms 834
For Further Reading 834
Internet Resources 835
Smith v. Allwright (1944) 835
Gomillion v. Lightfoot (1960) 837
Mobile v. Bolden (1980) 839
Rogers v. Lodge (1982) 842
Shaw v. Hunt (1996) 847
Reynolds v. Sims (1964) 855
Karcher v. Daggett (1983) 858

Appendix A The Constitution of the United
   States of America A-1

Appendix B Chronology of Justices of the
   United States Supreme Court B-1

Appendix C Supreme Court Justices by
   Appointing President, State Appointed
   From, and Political Party C-1

Appendix D Glossary D-1
Table of Cases T-1
Index I-1

PREFACE

This book examines the constitutional foundations of civil rights and liberties in the United States. It is thus appropriate for either a stand-alone course in civil rights and liberties or the civil rights and liberties components of a course sequence in constitutional law.

This book contains eight chapters covering a broad range of topics in the field of constitutional rights and liberties. We begin with an overview of the Bill of Rights and the other provisions of the Constitution that relate to civil rights and liberties. In this regard, we pay particular attention to the pivotal position of the Fourteenth Amendment. In subsequent chapters we examine property rights and economic freedom, the expressive freedoms protected by the First Amendment, freedom of religion, the rights of persons accused and convicted of crimes, rights of privacy and personal autonomy, equal protection of the law and freedom from discrimination, and voting rights. These topics relate to a panoply of contemporary public policy issues and, in the modern era, represent much of the debate over the meaning of the United States Constitution.

American constitutional law, to paraphrase Charles Evans Hughes, is ultimately what the Supreme Court says it is. But of course it is much more than that. Constitutional law is constantly informed by numerous actors' understandings of the meaning of the United States Constitution. Lawyers, judges, politicians, academicians, and, of course, citizens all contribute to the dialogue that produces constitutional law. Consequently, the Constitution remains a vital part of American public life, continuously woven into the fabric of our history, politics, and culture. Our goal in writing this textbook is to illustrate this premise in the context of those provisions of the Constitution that relate to the core democratic values of freedom and equality.

Each of the chapters in this book includes an extended essay providing the legal, historical, political, and cultural contents for a set of edited decisions of the United States Supreme Court that follows. In selecting and editing these cases, we have emphasized recent trends in major areas of constitutional interpretation. At the same time, we have included many landmark decisions, some of which retain importance as precedents while others illustrate the transient nature of constitutional interpretation.

Although the Supreme Court plays a very important role in American politics, its function is limited to deciding cases that pose legal questions. Accordingly, its political decisions are rendered in legal terms. Because it is both a legal and a political institution, a complete understanding of the Court requires some knowledge of both law and politics. While political discourse is familiar to most college students, the legal world can seem rather bewildering. Terms such as *habeas corpus, ex parte, subpoena duces tecum,* and *certiorari* leave the impression that one must master an entirely new language just to know what is going on, much less achieve a sophisticated understanding. Although we do not believe that a complete mastery of legal terminology is necessary to glean the political from the legal, we recognize that understanding the work of the Supreme Court is a complex task. We have tried to minimize this complexity by deleting as much technical terminology as possible from the judicial opinions excerpted in this book without damaging the integrity of those opinions. Nevertheless, despite our attempts at editing out distracting citations, technical terms, and mere verbiage, the task of understanding Supreme Court decisions remains formidable. It is one that requires concentration, patience, and above all the determination to grasp what may at times seem hopelessly abstruse. We firmly believe that all students of American politics, indeed all citizens, should make the effort.

In completing this project, our efforts have been aided by numerous individuals. Joseph Anderson, a colleague in political science at the University of Tennessee, Knoxville, read several chapters and offered useful criticism. The following students at the University of Tennessee, Knoxville, provided invaluable research assistance and/or read parts of the manuscript and made suggestions for its improvement: Michael Giaimo, Melanie Morris, Hal Watts, and Jay Young. Indeed, we are indebted to our many students in constitutional law, past and present, whose questions and comments sharpened our understanding of the subject of this book.

We wish to express our gratitude to Clark Baxter, our editor at Wadsworth, for his support and encour-agement throughout the project. Thanks are due as well to the entire staff at Wadsworth for their excellent support and assistance. We especially wish to thank Lori Harvey of Carlisle Communications for her excellent work in overseeing copyediting and production.

Thanks are due also to the scholars who reviewed this edition and its predecessor, a list of whom appears on the following page.

Finally, we wish to acknowledge the support provided by our wives, Mary Stephens and Sherilyn Scheb. This book is dedicated to them.

Although many people contributed to the development and production of this book, we, of course, assume full responsibility for any errors that may appear herein.

Otis H. Stephens, Jr.
John M. Scheb II
Knoxville, Tennessee
August 12, 1998

REVIEWERS AND AFFILIATIONS

The authors and publisher wish to thank the following individuals who reviewed the manuscript of this or the previous edition:

Henry Abraham
University of Virginia

Ralph Baker
Ball State University

Paul R. Benson
The Citadel

Robert Bradley
Illinois State University

Saul Brenner
University of North Carolina–Charlotte

Robert V. Burns
South Dakota State University

Larry Elowitz
Georgia College

Philip Fishman
Augsburg College

Marilyn Glater
Tufts University

William Haltom
University of Puget Sound

Sharon Jennings
New Mexico State University—
Grants Campus

William E. Kelly
Auburn University

Kent A. Kirwan
University of Nebraska–Omaha

Mark Landis
Hofstra University

Timothy O. Lenz
Florida Atlantic University

Sarah H. Ludwig
Mary Baldwin College

Connie Mauney
Emporia State University

William P. McLauchlan
Purdue University

R. Christopher Perry
Indiana State University

E.C. Price
California State
University–Northridge

Donald I. Ranish
Antelope Valley College

Wilfred E. Rumble
Vassar College

Elliot E. Slotnick
Ohio State University

John R. Vile
Middle Tennessee State University

Diane E. Wall
Mississippi State University

John Winkle
University of Mississippi

Part 2

CIVIL RIGHTS AND LIBERTIES

6

CONSTITUTIONAL SOURCES OF CIVIL RIGHTS AND LIBERTIES

Chapter Outline

Introduction

Rights Recognized in the Original Constitution

The Bill of Rights

The Fourteenth Amendment

Amendments Protecting and Extending Voting Rights

Standards of Review in Civil Rights and Liberties Cases

The Importance of State Constitutions

Conclusion

Key Terms

For Further Reading

Internet Resources

DeShaney v. Winnebago Social Services (1989)

Barron v. Baltimore (1833)

Hurtado v. California (1884)

Chicago, Burlington and Quincy Railroad Company v. Chicago (1897)

Palko v. Connecticut (1937)

Adamson v. California (1947)

Rochin v. California (1952)

Duncan v. Louisiana (1968)

There is, of course, a sphere within which the individual may assert the supremacy of his own will, and rightfully dispute the authority of any human government, especially of any free government existing under a written constitution, to interfere with the exercise of that will. But it is equally true that in every well-ordered society charged with the duty of conserving the safety of its members, the rights of the individual in respect of his liberty may at times, under the pressure of great dangers, be subjected to such restraint, to be enforced by reasonable regulations, as the safety of the general public may demand.

—JUSTICE JOHN M. HARLAN (THE ELDER), WRITING FOR THE SUPREME COURT IN *JACOBSON V. MASSACHUSETTS* (1905)

INTRODUCTION

One of the principal objectives of the U.S. Constitution, as stated in its preamble, is "to secure the Blessings of Liberty to ourselves and our Posterity." The framers of the Constitution thus recognized the protection of individual liberty as a fundamental goal of constitutional government.

Paraphrasing John Locke, the Declaration of Independence (1776) had declared the **unalienable rights** of man to be "life, liberty and the pursuit of happiness." Other more specific rights, including trial by jury and freedom of speech, were generally embraced by Americans, legacies of the Magna Charta (1215) and the English Bill of Rights (1689). The framers of the Constitution sought to protect these rights by creating a system of government that would be inherently restricted in power and, hence, limited in its ability to transgress the rights of the individual.

The Founders were heavily influenced by the theory of **natural rights,** in which rights are seen as inherently belonging to individuals, not as created by government. According to this view, individuals have the right to do whatever they please unless (1) they interfere with the rights of others or (2) government is constitutionally empowered to act to restrict the exercise of that freedom. The Founders thus conceived of the powers of government as mere islands in a vast sea of individual rights. This was especially true of the newly created national government, which was limited to the exercise of delegated powers. The original Constitution thus contained no provision guaranteeing freedom of religion, because the Constitution gave the federal government no authority to regulate religion. Yet the framers did recognize certain rights, at least indirectly, by enumerating specific limitations on the national government and the states.

During the debate over ratification of the Constitution, a consensus emerged that the Constitution should be more explicit as to the rights of individuals. Reflecting this consensus, the First Congress in 1789 adopted the Bill of Rights, which was ratified in 1791. This prompt response by Congress and the States underscored the strong national commitment to individual freedom.

Liberty, however, is only one aspect of constitutional rights. Equally critical in a constitutional democracy is the ideal of **equality.** Although the framers of the original Constitution were less interested in equality than in liberty, the Constitution has come to be considerably more egalitarian over the years, both through formal amendment and through judicial interpretation. In its constitutional sense, equality means that all citizens are considered to be equal before the law, equal before the state, and equal in their possession of rights. The term **civil rights,** as distinct from **civil liberties,** is generally used to denote citizens' equality claims, as distinct from their liberty claims.

The subject matter of civil rights and liberties is far ranging, touching on most contemporary social, political, and economic issues. School prayer, gay rights, abortion, doctor-assisted suicide, and affirmative action are a few of the more salient policy questions the courts have addressed in recent years in disputes over the meaning of particular civil rights and liberties protections. The Supreme Court's rulings on such issues comprise a major aspect of contemporary American constitutional law and, accordingly, are the subject of Part II of this textbook.

RIGHTS RECOGNIZED IN THE ORIGINAL CONSTITUTION

As noted, the original, unamended Constitution contained few explicit protections of individual rights. This was not because the framers did not value rights but because they thought it unnecessary to deal with them explicitly. Significantly, most of the state constitutions adopted during the American Revolution contained fairly detailed bills of rights placing limits on state and local governments. The framers did not anticipate the growth of a pervasive national government and thus did not regard the extensive enumeration of individual rights in the federal Constitution as critical. They did, however, recognize a few important safeguards in the original Constitution.

Circumscribing the Crime of Treason

The framers of the Constitution, having recently participated in a successful revolution, were understandably sensitive to the prospect that government could employ the crime of **treason** to stifle **political dissent.** Thus, they provided in Article III, Section 3, that "[t]reason against the United States, shall consist only in levying War against them, or in adhering to their enemies, giving them aid and comfort." To protect citizens against unwarranted prosecution for treason, the framers further specified that "[n]o person shall be convicted of Treason unless on the Testimony of two Witnesses to the same overt Act, or on Confession in open Court."

Prohibition of Religious Tests for Public Office

Article VI of the Constitution provides, among other things, that "no religious Test shall ever be required as a Qualification to any Office or Public Trust under the United States." This clause means, in effect, that personal views regarding religion may not officially qualify or disqualify one for public service. The prohibition against **religious tests** reflects the framers' commitment to the idea that government ought to be neutral with respect to matters of religion, a view that was strongly reinforced by adoption of the **Establishment Clause** of the First Amendment (see Chapter 9).

Habeas Corpus

Article I, Section 9, of the Constitution states that "the privilege of the Writ of Habeas Corpus shall not be suspended, unless when in Cases of Invasion or Rebellion the public Safety may require it." Grounded in English common law, the writ of **habeas corpus** gives effect to the all-important right of the individual not to be held in unlawful custody. Specifically, habeas corpus enables a court to review a custodial situation and order the release of an individual who is found to have been illegally incarcerated. This right has many applications, but the most common is in the criminal context, in which an individual is arrested and held in custody but denied due process of law. In adopting the habeas corpus provision of Article I, Section 9, the framers wanted not only to recognize the right but also to limit its suspension to emergency situations. The Constitution is somewhat ambiguous as to which branch of government has the authority to suspend the writ of habeas corpus during emergencies. As noted in Chapter 3, early in the Civil War, President Lincoln authorized military commanders to suspend the writ. Congress ultimately confirmed the president's action through legislation. During the Second World War, the writ of habeas corpus was suspended in the territory of Hawaii.

The writ of habeas corpus is an important element in modern criminal procedure. As a result of legislation passed by Congress in 1867 and subsequent judicial interpretation of that legislation, a person convicted of a crime in a state court and sentenced to state prison may petition a federal district court for habeas corpus relief. This permits a federal court to review the constitutional correctness of the arrest, trial, and sentencing of a state prisoner.

Under Chief Justice Earl Warren, the Supreme Court broadened the scope of federal habeas corpus review of state criminal convictions by permitting prisoners to raise issues in federal court that they did not raise in their state appeals (see, for example, *Fay v. Noia* [1963]). The more conservative Burger and Rehnquist Courts significantly restricted state prisoners' access to federal habeas corpus (see, for example, *Stone v. Powell* [1976] and *McCleskey v. Zant* [1991]). Nevertheless, the continuing controversy over federal habeas corpus review of state criminal convictions prompted Congress to place further restrictions on the availability of the writ.

The Antiterrorism and Effective Death Penalty Act of 1996 curtailed habeas corpus petitions by state prisoners who have already filed such petitions in federal court. Of course, because Congress initially provided this jurisdiction to the federal courts by statute, Congress may modify or abolish this jurisdiction if it so desires. It is unlikely, though, that Congress would eliminate federal habeas review of state criminal cases altogether (for further discussion, see Chapter 10).

Ex Post Facto Laws

Article I, Section 9, of the Constitution prohibits Congress from passing **ex post facto** laws. Article I, Section 10, imposes the same prohibition on state legislatures. *Ex post facto* laws are laws passed after the occurrence of an act that alter the legal status or consequences of that act. In *Calder v. Bull* (1798), the Supreme Court held that the *ex post facto* clauses applied to criminal but not to civil laws. According to Justice Samuel Chase's opinion in that case, impermissible *ex post facto* laws are those that "create or aggravate . . . [a] crime; or increase the punishment, or change the rules of evidence, for the purpose of conviction." Retrospective laws dealing with civil matters are thus not prohibited by the *ex post facto* clauses.

In two cases decided during the late nineteenth century, *Kring v. Missouri* (1883) and *Thompson v. Utah* (1898), the Supreme Court broadened the definition of *ex post facto* laws to prohibit certain changes in criminal procedure that might prove disadvantageous to the accused. However, in *Collins v. Youngblood* (1990), the Supreme Court overruled these precedents and returned to the definition adopted in *Calder v. Bull.* For an act to be invalidated as an *ex post facto* law, two key elements must exist. First, the act must be retroactive—it must apply to events that occurred before its passage. Second, it must seriously disadvantage the accused, not merely by changes in procedure but by means that render conviction more likely or punishment more severe.

Bills of Attainder

Article I, Sections 9 and 10, also prohibit Congress and the states, respectively, from adopting bills of attainder. A **bill of attainder** is a legislative act that imposes punishment on a person without benefit of a trial in a court of law.

Perhaps the best known cases involving bills of attainder are the test oath cases of 1867. In *Ex parte Garland,* the Court struck down an 1865 federal statute forbidding attorneys from practicing before federal courts unless they took an oath that they had not supported the Confederacy during the Civil War. In *Cummings v. Missouri* (1866), the Court voided a provision of the Missouri Constitution that required a similar oath of all persons who wished to be employed in a variety of occupations, including the ministry. Cummings, a Catholic priest, had been fined five hundred dollars for preaching without having taken the oath. The Court found that these laws violated both the bill of attainder and *ex post facto* provisions of Article I.

Since World War II, the Supreme Court has declared only two acts of Congress invalid as bills of attainder. The first instance was *United States v. Lovett* (1946), in which the Court struck down a rider to an appropriations measure that prohibited three named federal employees from receiving compensation from the government. The three individuals had been branded by the House Un-American Activities Committee as "subversives." The Court said that legislative acts "that apply

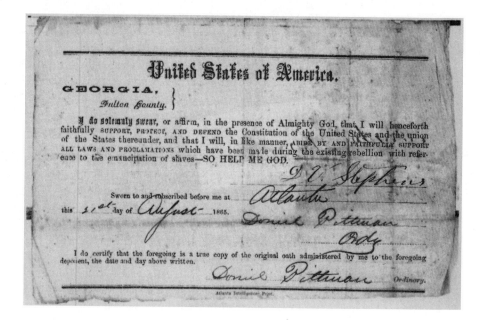

FIGURE 6.1
A Reconstruction Era Loyalty Oath (signed by the great-grandfather of one of the authors of this book)

either to named individuals or to easily ascertainable members of a group in such a way as to inflict punishment on them without a judicial trial are bills of attainder prohibited by the Constitution."

In *United States v. Brown* (1965), the Court invalidated a law that prohibited members of the Communist party from serving as officers in trade unions, saying that Congress had inflicted punishment on "easily ascertainable members of a group." Four justices dissented, however, citing a number of legislative prohibitions on members of the Communist party that the Court had previously upheld (see, for example, *American Communications Association v. Douds* [1950]).

The Supreme Court considered an interesting bill of attainder issue in *Nixon v. Administrator of General Services* (1977). In this case, former President Richard Nixon challenged the Presidential Recordings and Materials Preservation Act of 1974, in which Congress had placed control of Nixon's presidential papers and recordings in the hands of the General Services Administration, an agency of the federal government. Nixon argued that the law singled him out for punishment by depriving him of the traditional right of presidents to control their own presidential papers. The Court ruled 7 to 2 that the act was not a bill of attainder, concluding that Congress's purpose in passing the law was not punitive.

The Contract Clause

After the Revolutionary War, the thirteen states comprising the newly formed Union experienced a difficult period of political and economic instability. Numerous citizens, especially farmers, defaulted on their loans. Many were imprisoned under the harsh debtor laws of the period. Some state legislatures adopted laws to alleviate the plight of debtors. Cheap paper money was made legal tender; bankruptcy laws were adopted; in some states, creditors' access to the courts was restricted; some states prohibited imprisonment for debt. These policies, while commonplace today, were at that time anathema to the wealthy. Members of the creditor class believed that serious steps had to be taken to prevent the states from abrogating debts and interfering with contracts generally.

It is fair to say that one of the motivations behind the Constitutional Convention of 1787 was the desire to secure overriding legal protection for contracts. Thus, Article I, Section 10, prohibits states from passing laws "impairing the obligation of contracts." The **Contract Clause** must be included among the provisions of the original Constitution that protect individual rights—in this case, the right of individuals to be free from governmental interference with their contractual relationships.

By protecting contracts, Article I, Section 10, performed an important function in the early years of American economic development. Historically, the Contract Clause was an important source of litigation in the federal courts. In modern times, it is seldom interpreted to impose significant limits on the states in the field of economic regulation. (The Contract Clause is discussed more fully in Chapter 7.)

 TO SUMMARIZE:

- Apart from the provisions of the first ten amendments, various provisions of Article I, Sections 9 and 10, of the Constitution recognize individual rights by placing restrictions on the federal government and the states, respectively.
- The specific provisions defining and limiting the crime of treason apply only to the federal government, as does the prohibition against religious tests for holding public office.
- The protection of the writ of habeas corpus also applies specifically to the federal government and, in effect, may not be suspended except in cases of national emergency.
- Two provisions of the original Constitution protect certain individual rights against both federal and state encroachment. These are the prohibitions of *ex post facto* laws and bills of attainder.
- The Contract Clause of Article I, Section 10, imposes limitations on state interference with contractual rights and obligations. In the early years of the republic, this provision served as a major basis for federal judicial protection of private property rights.

THE BILL OF RIGHTS

As previously noted, the original Constitution contained little by way of explicit protection of individual rights. In *The Federalist,* No. 84, Alexander Hamilton argued that since the Constitution provided for limited government through enumerated powers, a Bill of Rights was unnecessary. In rebuttal, Anti-Federalists argued that the Necessary and Proper Clause of Article I, Section 8, could be used to justify expansive government power that might threaten individual liberties. As we saw in Chapter 5, the Anti-Federalists were definitely on target.

The omission of a bill of rights from the original Constitution was regarded as a major defect by numerous critics and even threatened to derail ratification in some states. Thomas Jefferson, who had not participated in the Constitutional Convention due to his diplomatic duties in France, was among the most influential critics. In a letter to his close friend James Madison, Jefferson argued, "You must specify

Thomas Jefferson: advocate for the Bill of Rights

your liberties, and put them down on paper." Madison, the acknowledged father of the Constitution, thought it unwise and unnecessary to enumerate individual rights, but Jefferson's view eventually prevailed. Honoring a "gentleman's agreement" designed to secure ratification of the Constitution in several key states, the First Congress considered a proposed bill of rights drafted by Madison.

Madison's original bill of rights called for limitations on the states as well as the federal government, but this proposal was defeated by states' rights advocates in Congress. Twelve amendments to the Constitution were adopted by Congress in September 1789. Although two of these amendments were rejected by the states, the other ten were ratified in November 1791 and were added to the Constitution as the Bill of Rights.

The First Amendment

The **First Amendment** provides a number of crucial guarantees of freedom. The Establishment Clause prohibits Congress from making laws "respecting an establishment of religion," while the **Free Exercise Clause** enjoins the national government from "prohibiting the free exercise thereof." These first two clauses demonstrate the fundamental character of the founders' devotion to freedom of religion. Today, the Religion Clauses remain both important and controversial, involving such emotional issues as prayer and the teaching of "creation science" in the public schools. (The Religion Clauses of the First Amendment are examined in Chapter 9.)

The First Amendment also protects **freedom of speech** and **freedom of the press,** often referred to jointly as **freedom of expression.** One can argue that freedom of expression is the most vital freedom in a democracy, in that it permits the free flow of information between the people and their government. Certainly the framers of the Bill of Rights were aware of its fundamental importance, which is why the freedoms of speech and press were placed in the First Amendment. Finally, the First Amendment protects the "right of the people peaceably to assemble and petition the Government for a redress of grievances." Freedom of assembly remains an important right, and one that is often controversial, such as when an extremist group such as the Ku Klux Klan stages a public rally. The freedom to petition government tends to be less controversial but no less important. Today, it is referred to as "lobbying," the principal activity of interest groups. (The freedoms of speech, press, and assembly are examined in Chapter 8.)

The Second Amendment

Most Americans believe that the Constitution protects their **right to keep and bear arms.** Yet the **Second Amendment** refers not only to the keeping and bearing of arms but also to the need for a **well-regulated militia.** The Second Amendment provides:

> A well-regulated Militia, being necessary to the security of a free state, the right of the people to keep and bear arms shall not be infringed.

In *United States v. Cruikshank* (1875), the Supreme Court held that the Second Amendment guaranteed states the right to maintain militias but did not

The Constitution in action: people expressing their First Amendment rights

guarantee to individuals the right to possess guns. Subsequently, in *United States v. Miller* (1939), the Court upheld a federal law banning the interstate transportation of certain firearms. Miller, who had been arrested for transporting a double-barreled sawed-off shotgun from Oklahoma to Arkansas, sought the protection of the Second Amendment. The Court rejected Miller's argument, asserting that "we cannot say that the Second Amendment guarantees the right to keep and bear such an instrument." In *Lewis v. United States* (1980), the Court reaffirmed the *Miller* precedent. In upholding a federal gun control act, the Court said:

> These legislative restrictions on the use of firearms are neither based on constitutionally suspect criteria, nor do they trench upon any constitutionally protected liberties. . . . [T]he Second Amendment guarantees no right to keep and bear a firearm that does not have "some reasonable relationship to the preservation or efficiency of a well regulated militia."

As currently interpreted, the Second Amendment does not pose a significant constitutional barrier to the enactment or enforcement of gun control laws, whether passed by Congress, state legislatures, or local governments. However, other constitutional provisions may limit Congressional action in this area. See, for example, the discussion of *Printz v. United States* (1997) in Chapter 5. In *Printz,* the Supreme Court struck down provisions of the Brady Handgun Violence Prevention Act requiring state and local law enforcement officers to conduct background checks on prospective handgun purchasers. The Court said these provisions infringed state sovereignty as protected by the Tenth Amendment.

The Third Amendment

The **Third Amendment** prohibits military authorities from quartering troops in citizens' homes without their consent. This was a matter of serious concern to the founders, because English troops had been forcibly billeted in colonists' homes during the Revolutionary War. Today, the Third Amendment is little more than an historical curiosity, since it has not been the subject of any significant litigation.

The Fourth Amendment

The **Fourth Amendment** protects citizens from **unreasonable searches and seizures** conducted by police and other government agents. Reflecting a serious concern of the founders, the Fourth Amendment remains extremely important today, especially in light of the pervasiveness of crime and the national war on drugs. In the twentieth century, the Fourth Amendment has been the source of numerous important Supreme Court decisions and has generated a tremendous and complex body of legal doctrine. For example, in *Katz v. United States* (1967), the Supreme Court under Chief Justice Warren expanded the scope of Fourth Amendment protection to include **wiretapping,** an important tool of modern law enforcement. The Burger and Rehnquist Courts have been decidedly more conservative in this area, facilitating police efforts to ferret out crime. (The Fourth Amendment as it relates to criminal justice is examined in some depth in Chapter 10.)

Drug Testing

The Fourth Amendment is not limited to the areas of law enforcement and criminal justice. In recent years, courts have been called on to interpret the Fourth Amendment in the context of statutes and regulations imposing various **drug testing** requirements. In *Skinner v. Railway Labor Executives' Association* (1989), the United States Supreme Court upheld federal regulations requiring drug and alcohol testing of railroad employees involved in train accidents. The Court has also sustained a Customs Service policy requiring drug tests for persons seeking positions as customs inspectors (see *National Treasury Employees Union v. Von Raab* [1989]). As yet, the Supreme Court has not addressed the issue of general, random drug testing of public employees. It has, however, invalidated a policy under which all political candidates were required to submit to drug testing as a condition of qualifying for the ballot (see *Chandler v. Miller* [1997]).

The Fifth Amendment

The **Fifth Amendment** contains a number of important provisions involving the rights of persons accused of crime. It requires the federal government to obtain an **indictment** from a **grand jury** before trying someone for a major crime. It also prohibits **double jeopardy,** that is, being tried twice for the same offense. Additionally, the Fifth Amendment protects persons against **compulsory self-incrimination,** which is what is commonly meant by the phrase "taking the Fifth." (Fifth Amendment rights of the accused are dealt with in Chapter 10.)

The Fifth Amendment also protects people against arbitrary use of **eminent domain,** the power of government to take private property for public use. The Just Compensation Clause forbids government from taking private property without paying **just compensation** to the owner (see Chapter 7).

Trial by jury: a right guaranteed by the Sixth Amendment

Finally, the Fifth Amendment prohibits the federal government from depriving persons of life, liberty, or property without **due process of law.** A virtually identical clause is found in the **Fourteenth Amendment,** which applies specifically to the states. The Due Process Clauses have implications both for civil and criminal cases, as well as for a variety of relationships between citizen and government. Due process may be the broadest and most basic protection afforded by the Constitution. (The concept of due process is more fully explicated later in this chapter, as part of the discussion of the Fourteenth Amendment.)

The Sixth Amendment

The **Sixth Amendment** is concerned exclusively with the rights of the accused. It requires, among other things, that people accused of crimes be provided a "speedy and public trial, by an impartial jury. . . ." The right of **trial by jury** is one of the most cherished rights in the Anglo-American tradition, predating the Magna Charta of 1215. The Sixth Amendment also grants defendants the right to confront, or cross-examine, witnesses for the prosecution and the right to have "compulsory process" (the power of **subpoena**) to require favorable witnesses to appear in court. Significantly, considering the incredible complexity of the criminal law, the Sixth Amendment guarantees that accused persons have the "Assistance of Counsel" for their defense. The Supreme Court has regarded the **right to counsel** as crucial to a fair trial, holding that defendants who are unable to afford private counsel must be afforded counsel at public expense (*Gideon v. Wainwright* [1963]). (Sixth Amendment rights in the context of criminal justice are examined in Chapter 10.)

The Seventh Amendment

The **Seventh Amendment** guarantees the right to a jury trial in federal civil suits "at common law" where the amount at issue exceeds twenty dollars. Originally, it was widely assumed that the Seventh Amendment required jury trials only in traditional common-law cases, for example, actions for libel, wrongful death, and trespass. But over the years, the Supreme Court expanded the scope of the Seventh Amendment to encompass civil suits seeking enforcement of statutory rights. For example, in *Curtis v. Loether* (1974), an African-American woman brought suit against a number of white defendants, charging them with refusing to rent her an apartment in violation of the Fair Housing Act of 1968. The defendants requested a trial by jury, but the district court ruled that the Seventh Amendment did not apply to lawsuits seeking to enforce the rights created by the Fair Housing Act. In reversing the district court, the Supreme Court said:

> The Seventh Amendment does apply to actions enforcing statutory rights, and requires a jury trial on demand, if the statute creates legal rights and remedies, enforceable in an action for damages in the ordinary courts of law. . . . We recognize . . . the possibility that jury prejudice may deprive a victim of discrimination of the verdict to which he or she is entitled. Of course, the trial judge's power to direct a verdict, to grant judgment notwithstanding the verdict, or to grant a new trial provides substantial protection against this risk. . . .

Although it does apply to suits enforcing statutory rights, the Seventh Amendment does not apply to the adjudication of certain issues by administrative or regulatory agencies. In *Thomas v. Union Carbide* (1985), the Supreme Court said that the Seventh Amendment does not provide the right to a jury trial where Congress "has created a 'private' right that is so closely integrated into a public regulatory scheme as to be a matter appropriate for agency resolution with limited involvement by the Article III judiciary."

Under current interpretation, the Seventh Amendment does not require the traditional common-law twelve-person jury in civil trials. In *Colgrove v. Battin* (1973), the Supreme Court held that a six-person jury was sufficient to try a civil case in federal court. The defendant in the case argued that the Seventh Amendment's reference to "suits at common law" required federal courts to adopt the traditional common-law jury. The Supreme Court, dividing 5 to 4, disagreed. Writing for the Court, Justice William Brennan said:

> Consistently with the historical objective of the Seventh Amendment, our decisions have defined the jury right preserved in cases covered by the Amendment, as "the substance of the common-law right of trial by jury, as distinguished from mere matters of form or procedure. . . ." The Amendment, therefore, does not bind the federal courts to the exact procedural incidents or details of jury trial according to the common law in 1791. . . .

In a lengthy dissent, Justice Thurgood Marshall stressed the need for fidelity to the traditions of the common law:

> Since some definition of "jury" must be chosen, I would . . . rely on the fixed bounds of history which the Framers, by drafting the Seventh Amendment, meant to "preserve. . . ." It may well be that the number 12 is no more than a "historical accident" and is "wholly without significance." . . . But surely there is nothing more significant about the number six, or three or one. The line must be drawn somewhere, and the difference between drawing it in the light of history and drawing it on an *ad hoc* basis is, ultimately, the difference between interpreting a constitution and making it up as one goes along.

The controversy over the appropriate size of the jury in federal civil trials parallels the issue of jury size in criminal cases, a question examined in Chapter 10.

The Eighth Amendment

The **Eighth Amendment** protects persons accused of crimes from being required to post **excessive bail** to secure **pretrial release.** In *Stack v. Boyle* (1951), the Supreme Court held that bail is excessive if it is higher than is necessary to ensure a defendant's appearance for trial. But in *United States v. Salerno* (1987), a case involving the prosecution of an organized crime figure, the Court said that the Eighth Amendment does not require that defendants be released on bail, only that, if the court grants bail, it must not be "excessive." (The issue of **pretrial detention** is discussed more thoroughly in Chapter 10.)

The Eighth Amendment also forbids the imposition of **excessive fines** and the infliction of **cruel and unusual punishments** on persons convicted of crimes. Originally thought to proscribe torture, the Cruel and Unusual Punishments Clause now figures prominently in the ongoing national debate over the death penalty (see Chapter 10). Writing for the Supreme Court in *Trop v. Dulles* (1958), Chief Justice Earl Warren observed that the Cruel and Unusual Punishments Clause "must draw its meaning from the evolving standards of decency that mark the progress of a maturing society." In the *Trop* case, a soldier had lost his citizenship after being found guilty of desertion from the U.S. Army. The Supreme Court restored Trop's citizenship, noting that "[t]he civilized nations of the world are in virtual unanimity that statelessness is not to be imposed as punishment for a crime."

Civil Forfeitures

Federal law provides for forfeiture of the proceeds of a variety of criminal activities. Most controversial are the federal law provisions allowing **forfeiture** of property used in illicit drug activity. Under federal law a "conveyance," which includes aircraft, motor vehicles, and vessels, is subject to forfeiture if it is used to transport controlled substances. Real estate may be forfeited if it is used to commit or facilitate commission of a drug-related felony. Many states have similar statutes. Though technically such forfeitures are civil, and not criminal, sanctions, the Supreme Court has recognized that forfeiture constitutes significant punishment and is thus subject to constitutional limitations under the Eighth Amendment. In *Austin v. United States* (1993), the Court said that forfeiture "constitutes 'payment to a sovereign as punishment for some offense' . . . and, as such, is subject to the limitations of the Eighth Amendment's Excessive Fines Clause." However, the Court left it to state and lower federal courts to determine the tests of "excessiveness" in the context of forfeiture.

The Ninth Amendment

The **Ninth Amendment** was included in the Bill of Rights as a solution to a problem raised by James Madison; namely, that the specification of particular liberties might suggest that individuals possessed only those specified. The Ninth Amendment makes it clear that individuals retain a reservoir of rights and liberties beyond those listed in the Constitution.

> The enumeration in the Constitution, of certain rights, shall not be construed to deny or disparage others retained by the people.

This amendment reflects the dominant thinking of late-eighteenth-century America: Individual rights precede and transcend the power of government; individuals possess all rights except those that have been surrendered to government for the protection of the public good.

Prior to 1965, the Ninth Amendment had little significance in constitutional law. In the words of Justice Potter Stewart,

> [t]he Ninth Amendment, like its companion the Tenth, which this Court has held "states but a truism that all is retained which has not been surrendered, . . ." was framed by James Madison and adopted by the States simply to make clear that the adoption of the Bill of Rights did not alter the plan that the Federal government was to be a government of express and limited powers, and that all rights and powers not delegated to it were retained by the people and the individual States. (*Griswold v. Connecticut* [1965] [dissenting opinion]).

But in *Griswold v. Connecticut* (1965), a Supreme Court majority, in recognizing a constitutional right of privacy (discussed more fully in Chapter 11), relied in part on the Ninth Amendment. Here, the Court invalidated a Connecticut statute that made it a crime to use birth control devices. Justice Stewart, who along with Justice Hugo Black dissented in *Griswold*, expressed dismay that the Court relied on the Ninth Amendment to strike down a state statute:

> . . . [T]he idea that a federal court could ever use the Ninth Amendment to annul a law passed by the elected representatives of the people of the State of Connecticut would have caused James Madison no little wonder.

Although they have seldom relied explicitly on the Ninth Amendment, federal and state courts have over the years recognized a number of rights that Americans take for granted but which are not specifically enumerated in the Constitution. The right to marry, to determine how one's children are to be reared and educated, to choose one's occupation, to start a business, to travel freely across state lines, to sue in the courts, and to be presumed innocent of a crime until proven guilty are all examples of individual rights that have been recognized as "constitutional," despite their absence from the text of the Constitution. Quite often these rights have been recognized under the broad Due Process Clauses of the Fifth and Fourteenth Amendments.

The Tenth Amendment

The Bill of Rights is generally considered to be the first ten amendments to the Constitution. But the Tenth Amendment is of a fundamentally different character than the nine amendments that precede it. The Tenth Amendment provides:

> The powers not delegated to the United States by the Constitution, nor prohibited by it to the States, are reserved to the States respectively, or to the people.

Unlike other provisions of the Bill of Rights, and despite its reference to "the people," the Tenth Amendment recognizes the powers of the states vis-á-vis the federal government and does not directly address individual rights. Accordingly, the Tenth Amendment is largely unrelated to constitutional law in the realm of civil rights and liberties. Rather, it pertains to the area of federalism (see Chapter 5).

TO SUMMARIZE:

- The omission of a more detailed enumeration of rights from the original Constitution was regarded in many quarters as a major deficiency and even threatened to undermine ratification of the Constitution.

- The first ten amendments to the Constitution, known today as the Bill of Rights, were adopted by Congress in 1789 and ratified by the states in 1791. Most of these amendments (the First, Fourth, Fifth, Sixth, Eighth, and Ninth) are of fundamental importance in the field of civil rights and liberties and are discussed in detail in later chapters.
- The Second Amendment protects the "right to keep and bear arms" but does so in the context of a "well-regulated militia." The Supreme Court has never interpreted this amendment as conferring a broad personal right to possess and use firearms. Indeed, the Court has upheld federal statutes regulating the sale, possession, and use of certain weapons.
- The Third Amendment, which prohibits the nonconsensual quartering of troops in private homes, has never been the subject of significant constitutional adjudication.
- The Seventh Amendment, which guarantees the common law right to a jury trial in a civil suit, has been expanded to include civil suits seeking enforcement of statutory rights. Under prevailing interpretation, the Seventh Amendment permits some variation from the use of the traditional twelve-member jury in a civil trial.
- The Tenth Amendment, often referred to as the "states' rights" amendment, applies to matters of federalism and is not directly related to individual rights and liberties.

THE FOURTEENTH AMENDMENT

Without question, the most important amendment to the Constitution outside of the Bill of Rights is the Fourteenth Amendment. Ratified in 1868, the principal objective of the Fourteenth Amendment was to protect the civil rights and liberties of African-Americans. Although slavery had been formally abolished by the **Thirteenth Amendment,** ratified in 1865, questions remained about the legal status of the former slaves. Recall from Chapter 1 that in *Dred Scott v. Sandford* (1857), the Supreme Court not only defended the institution of slavery but indicated that blacks were not citizens of the United States and possessed "no rights or privileges but such as those who held the power and the Government might choose to grant them." Section 1 of the Fourteenth Amendment made clear that *Dred Scott* was no longer the law of the land:

> All persons born or naturalized in the United States, and subject to the jurisdiction thereof, are citizens of the United States and of the State wherein they reside. No state shall make or enforce any law which shall abridge the privileges or immunities of citizens of the United States; nor shall any State deprive any person of life, liberty, or property, without due process of law; nor deny to any person within its jurisdiction the equal protection of the laws.

The federal courts have relied heavily on the **Equal Protection Clause** of Section 1 in advancing the civil rights of African-Americans and other minority groups. The "case of the century," *Brown v. Board of Education* (1954), in which the Supreme Court abolished racial segregation in the public schools, was based squarely on the Equal Protection Clause. The Equal Protection Clause has provided the basis on which the Supreme Court has invalidated a number of state laws discriminating among persons, not only on the basis of race, but on the basis of gender and other characteristics (see Chapter 12).

Section 5 of the Fourteenth Amendment grants to Congress the power to enforce the broad provisions of Section 1 through "appropriate legislation." Congress has relied on Section 5 in passing civil rights legislation, such as the landmark Voting Rights

Act of 1965, which forbids racial discrimination in matters of voting and representation (see Chapter 13).

Although the principal purpose of the Fourteenth Amendment was to protect the rights of African-Americans, it has come to be regarded as a broad shield against actions by state and local governments that would infringe on individual rights and liberties. Of particular importance in this context is the **Due Process Clause.**

Due Process of Law

In its most generic sense, due process refers to the exercise of governmental power under the rule of law with due regard for the rights and interests of individuals. The concept of **procedural due process** embraces government's obligation to provide **fair notice** and a **fair hearing** to individuals before depriving them of "life, liberty or property." Thus, for example, the Supreme Court relied on the Due Process Clause of the Fourteenth Amendment in a landmark decision revolutionizing the juvenile justice system, holding that juveniles must be afforded certain procedural protections before they can be judged "delinquent" and sent to a reformatory (*In re Gault* [1967]). Similarly, the Supreme Court has invoked due process to say that police may not use methods that "shock the conscience" in attempting to gather evidence of criminal wrongdoing (*Rochin v. California* [1952]).

Historically, the concept of due process was extremely important in defending private property rights from government regulation (see Chapter 7). More recently, the courts have recognized government employment and government benefits as "property interests" subject to the requirements of due process. Thus, while there is no constitutional right to receive welfare assistance, government may not terminate a person's welfare benefits without observing certain procedural safeguards (see, for example, *Goldberg v. Kelly* [1970]).

Substantive Due Process

In addition to providing procedural protections against arbitrary and capricious government action, due process has been held to impose substantive limits on government policies as well. Under the concept of **substantive due process,** government is barred from enforcing policies that are irrational, unfair, unreasonable, or unjust, even if such policies do not run counter to other specific constitutional prohibitions.

For almost fifty years (roughly 1890 to 1937), the Supreme Court relied on substantive due process to invalidate a variety of state and federal laws regulating aspects of economic life (see Chapter 7). For example, in *Lochner v. New York* (1905), the Court struck down a state law setting maximum working hours in bakeries. The Court held that the restriction violated both the employer's and the employee's **liberty of contract,** a right not specifically enumerated in the Constitution but held to be embraced within the substantive prohibitions of the Due Process Clause of the Fourteenth Amendment. While the liberty of contract version of substantive due process has been repudiated by the modern Supreme Court, substantive due process lives on under the rubric of the constitutional **right of privacy.**

The Right of Privacy

First recognized in *Griswold v. Connecticut* (1965), the right of privacy is not found in any specific provision of the Bill of Rights. Nevertheless, the Supreme

Court has held that privacy is a **fundamental right** enforceable against the state governments via the Due Process Clause of the Fourteenth Amendment. As previously noted, in *Griswold,* the right of privacy was invoked to invalidate a state law prohibiting the use of birth control devices. Eight years later, in *Roe v. Wade* (1973), the right of privacy was held to be broad enough to include a woman's decision to have an abortion, touching off a constitutional debate that continues to rage. In the popular debate over *Roe,* the issue tends to be the desirability of legalized abortion. Yet the scholarly debate over *Roe v. Wade* focuses to a greater extent on the legitimacy of substantive due process as a constitutional doctrine. (The right of privacy and its application to a variety of issues, including abortion, gay rights, and euthanasia, are discussed in Chapter 11.)

The Fourteenth Amendment and State Action

Normally one thinks of the Fourteenth Amendment, as well as the provisions of the Bill of Rights, as placing constraints on government action. The Supreme Court has said on numerous occasions, the first being in *The Civil Rights Cases* (1883), that the prohibitions of the Fourteenth Amendment apply to **state action** but not to actions by private individuals or corporations. (This important doctrine of constitutional law is discussed at some length in Chapter 12.) However, an action that is ostensibly private in character may be treated as "state action" within the purview of the Fourteenth Amendment if there is a "close nexus" between the state and the private actor. Thus, for example, the Supreme Court in 1944 invalidated the Texas Democratic party's whites-only primary election, even though the party was not, strictly speaking, an agency of the state (see *Smith v. Allwright* [1944], discussed and reprinted in Chapter 13).

Can Inaction Be "State Action"?

In modern times, the doctrine of state action has been criticized as being too restrictive. Indeed, some have argued that the Fourteenth Amendment should be interpreted to impose an affirmative duty on government to protect persons against harm in some circumstances. This argument was made in dramatic form in the 1989 case of *DeShaney v. Winnebago Social Services.* There, the Supreme Court, dividing 6 to 3, held that a social services agency, regardless of its prior knowledge of the danger, did not violate the Fourteenth Amendment by failing to protect a child from his abusive father.

Writing for the majority, Chief Justice Rehnquist noted that the Court had previously recognized a state's constitutional obligation to protect the safety and well-being of those within its custody, including mentally retarded persons in state institutions. But this "affirmative duty to protect" did not arise "from the state's knowledge of [Joshua's] predicament or from its expressions of its intent to help him." Since the state had no constitutional duty to protect Joshua from his father, its failure to do so, although calamitous, did not constitute a violation of the Due Process Clause.

In a dissenting opinion, Justice Harry Blackmun excoriated the Court for its "sterile formalism." Blackmun asserted that the "broad and stirring clauses of the Fourteenth Amendment" were "designed, at least in part, to undo the formalistic legal reasoning that infected antebellum jurisprudence. . . ." Blackmun preferred a "sympathetic reading" of the Fourteenth Amendment that recognized that "compassion need not be exiled from the province of judging."

The Incorporation of the Bill of Rights

One of the most important impacts of the Fourteenth Amendment has been the effective "nationalization" of the Bill of Rights. There is little doubt that, at the time of its ratification in 1791, the Bill of Rights was widely perceived as imposing limitations only on the powers and actions of the national government. This is suggested by the first clause of the First Amendment, which begins, "Congress shall make no law. . . ." The Court held as much in 1833 in the case of *Barron v. Baltimore,* when it refused to permit a citizen to sue a local government for violating his property rights under the Just Compensation Clause of the Fifth Amendment. Speaking for the Court, Chief Justice John Marshall said:

> We are of the opinion, that, the provision in the Fifth Amendment to the Constitution, declaring that private property shall not be taken for public use without just compensation is intended solely as a limitation on the power of the United States, and is not applicable to the legislation of the states.

The ratification of the Fourteenth Amendment in 1868 provided an opportunity for the Supreme Court to reconsider the relationship between the Bill of Rights and state and local governments. As we have seen, Section 1 of the Fourteenth Amendment imposed broad restrictions on state power, requiring the states to provide equal protection of the law to all persons, to respect the "privileges and immunities" of citizens of the United States, and, most importantly, to protect the "life, liberty, and property" of all persons. More to the point, the Fourteenth Amendment enjoined states from depriving persons of these basic rights "without due process of law." Although there is no conclusive evidence that the framers of the Fourteenth Amendment intended for it to "incorporate" the Bill of Rights and thus make the latter applicable to actions of state and local governments, plaintiffs in federal cases began to make this argument fairly soon after the amendment was ratified.

Initially, the Supreme Court was not favorably disposed toward the **doctrine of incorporation.** In *Hurtado v. California* (1884), the Court rejected the argument that the grand jury procedure required in federal criminal cases by the Fifth Amendment was an essential feature of due process and thus required in state criminal cases by the Fourteenth Amendment. Today, the *Hurtado* decision remains good law; states are not required by the federal Constitution to use grand juries to bring criminal charges, although many still do.

Selective Incorporation

The fact that the *Hurtado* decision remains valid indicates that the Supreme Court has never accepted the argument that the Fourteenth Amendment incorporates the Bill of Rights *en toto.* The Court has, however, endorsed a doctrine of **selective incorporation** by which most of the provisions of the Bill of Rights have been extended to limit actions of the state and local governments. The process of selective incorporation began in 1897 in the case of *Chicago, Burlington and Quincy Railroad Company v. Chicago.* There, a conservative Court concerned about protecting private enterprise against a rising tide of government interventionism held that the Due Process Clause of the Fourteenth Amendment imposed on state and local governments the same obligation to respect private property that the Fifth Amendment imposed on the federal government. The Court said that when a state or local government takes private property under its power of eminent domain, it must provide just compensation to the owner. Thus, the Court had "incorporated" the Just Compensation Clause of the Fifth Amendment into the Due Process Clause of the Fourteenth Amendment.

The doctrine of incorporation was next applied to First Amendment freedoms, specifically the freedoms of speech and press. In *Gitlow v. New York* (1925), the Supreme Court said that

> [w]e may and do assume that freedom of speech and of the press—which are protected by the First Amendment from abridgment by Congress—are among the fundamental personal rights and "liberties" protected by the due process clause of the Fourteenth Amendment from impairment by the states. . . .

The dictum in *Gitlow* was soon followed by decisions in which the Court relied on the doctrine of incorporation to invalidate state actions abridging the freedoms of speech and press. In *Fiske v. Kansas* (1927), the Court invalidated a state statute that prohibited mere advocacy of violent action, finding it to be a violation of freedom of speech. Four years later, in *Near v. Minnesota* (1931), the Court struck down a state law that permitted **censorship** of "malicious, scandalous and defamatory" periodicals, finding it to be a clear violation of freedom of the press. In the wake of these and related decisions, state and local policies impinging on freedom of expression became subject to challenge in the courts under the same First Amendment standards that applied to federal legislation.

In *Palko v. Connecticut* (1937), the Supreme Court refused to incorporate the Double Jeopardy Clause of the Fifth Amendment into the Due Process Clause of the Fourteenth. To merit incorporation, said Justice Benjamin N. Cardozo, a provision of the Bill of Rights must be essential to "a scheme of ordered liberty." Cardozo's majority opinion suggested that the First Amendment freedoms that had been previously incorporated represented "the matrix, the indispensable condition, of nearly every other form of freedom." The Double Jeopardy Clause, in Cardozo's view, lay on "a different plane of social and moral values."

Following *Palko v. Connecticut,* the doctrine of incorporation became the subject of an intense debate among the justices of the Supreme Court. In *Cantwell v. Connecticut* (1940), the Court incorporated the Free Exercise of Religion Clause of the First Amendment. Similarly, in *Everson v. Board of Education* (1947), the Court extended the Establishment Clause to the states under the Fourteenth Amendment (for more discussion of both cases and clauses, see Chapter 9). Yet in *Adamson v. California* (1947) and in *Rochin v. California* (1952), the Court refused to extend the Fifth Amendment privilege against compulsory self-incrimination to state criminal trials. The Court's highly selective approach to incorporation of the Bill of Rights drew the particular ire of Justices Hugo Black and William O. Douglas.

In the 1960s, the views of Justices Black and Douglas as to the applicability of the Bill of Rights to state criminal prosecutions came to be supported by a majority of justices on the Supreme Court. Indeed, one of the priorities of the Court under the leadership of Chief Justice Warren was to increase the legal protections afforded to persons accused of crimes, both in state and federal court. In a series of landmark decisions, the Warren Court incorporated nearly all of the relevant provisions of the Bill of Rights into the Due Process Clause of the Fourteenth Amendment and thus made them applicable to state criminal cases (see Table 6.1).

In one of the most significant of these decisions, *Duncan v. Louisiana* (1968), the Court made the ancient right of trial by jury applicable to defendants in state

TABLE 6.1   Chronology of Incorporation of the Bill of Rights

Year	Issue and Amendment Involved	Case
1897	Just compensation (V)	*Chicago, Burlington & Quincy RR v. Chicago*
1927	Speech (I)	*Fiske v. Kansas*
1931	Press (I)	*Near v. Minnesota*
1937	Assembly and petition (I)	*De Jonge v. Oregon*
1940	Free exercise of religion (I)	*Cantwell v. Connecticut*
1947	Separation of church and state (I)	*Everson v. Board of Education*
1948	Public trial (VI)	*In re Oliver*
1949	Unreasonable searches and seizures (IV)	*Wolf v. Colorado*
1962	Cruel and unusual punishment (VIII)	*Robinson v. California*
1963	Right to counsel (VI)	*Gideon v. Wainwright*
1964	Compulsory self-incrimination (V)	*Malloy v. Hogan*
1965	Confrontation of hostile witnesses (VI)	*Pointer v. Texas*
1966	Impartial jury (VI)	*Parker v. Gladden*
1967	Confrontation of favorable witnesses	*Washington v. Texas*
1967	Speedy trial (VI)	*Klopfer v. North Carolina*
1968	Jury trial in nonpetty criminal cases (VI)	*Duncan v. Louisiana*
1969	Double jeopardy (V)	*Benton v. Maryland*

criminal cases. In a concurring opinion joined by Justice Douglas, Justice Black expressed his satisfaction with what the Court had done under the mantle of selective incorporation:

> I believe as strongly as ever that the Fourteenth Amendment was intended to make the Bill of Rights applicable to the States. I have been willing to support the selective incorporation doctrine, however, as an alternative, although perhaps less historically supportable than complete incorporation. . . . [M]ost importantly for me, the selective incorporation process has the virtue of having already worked to make most of the Bill of Rights protections applicable to the States.

The process of selective incorporation of the Bill of Rights may have reached its terminus in 1969. In that year, in *Benton v. Maryland,* the Supreme Court overruled its earlier decision in *Palko v. Connecticut* and decided, after all, that the Double Jeopardy Clause of the Fifth Amendment warranted incorporation into the Fourteenth Amendment. The *Benton* case marks the latest and perhaps last instance of a provision of the Bill of Rights being extended to state action via the Fourteenth Amendment. As of 1998, the only provisions of the Bill of Rights that had not been absorbed into the Fourteenth Amendment were the Second, Third, and Seventh Amendments, the Fifth Amendment grand jury clause, and the Eighth Amendment prohibitions against "excessive fines" and "excessive bail."

The principal thrust of the process of selective incorporation is that today, with few exceptions, policies of state and local government are subject to judicial scrutiny under the same standards that the Bill of Rights imposes on the federal government. Thus, for example, the prohibition of the First Amendment against establishment of religion applies with the same force to a school board in rural Arkansas as it does to the Congress of the United States. Likewise, the Eighth Amendment injunction against cruel and unusual punishments applies equally to high-profile federal prosecutions for treason and to sentences imposed by local courts for violations of city or county ordinances. Note, however, that in a few instances, such as those governed by the Sixth Amendment right to trial by jury, the Supreme Court has been willing to give the states slightly greater latitude than the federal government in complying with Bill of Rights requirements (for further discussion, see Chapter 10).

TO SUMMARIZE:

- Beyond the Bill of Rights, the Fourteenth Amendment (1868) is the most important constitutional amendment in the field of civil rights and liberties. This amendment places broad restrictions on the power of states to infringe on the rights and liberties of citizens.
- The Equal Protection Clause of Section 1 of the Fourteenth Amendment serves as the primary basis for protecting the civil rights of minority groups against discriminatory state action.
- The Due Process Clause of Section 1 is the most far-reaching provision of the Fourteenth Amendment. This clause prohibits states from depriving persons of life, liberty, or property without due process of law. The courts have distinguished between two aspects of due process: procedural and substantive.
- Procedural due process, which embodies the requirements of notice and hearing, requires fundamental fairness in governmental proceedings against individuals.
- Substantive due process prohibits government from enforcing policies that are deemed unreasonable, unfair or unjust, even if they do not violate specific constitutional prohibitions. The right of privacy can be seen as a contemporary manifestation of substantive due process.
- In a long series of cases beginning in the late nineteenth century, the Supreme Court has held that the Due Process Clause of the Fourteenth Amendment incorporates most of the provisions of the Bill of Rights, thus making them applicable to the states.

AMENDMENTS PROTECTING VOTING RIGHTS

While the Fourteenth Amendment is the broadest, and most important, source of protection for civil rights and liberties outside of the Bill of Rights, a number of other constitutional amendments address specific civil rights issues. These amendments (XV, XIX, XXIV, and XXVI) focus on the **right to vote,** which is arguably the most essential right in a democracy. The original Constitution left the matter of voting rights to the states. In 1787, voting in the United States was confined for the most part to "freeholders," that is, white male landowners above the age of twenty-one. As our society has become progressively more democratic, the Constitution has been amended to make the franchise more inclusive.

The Fifteenth Amendment

Like the Thirteenth and Fourteenth Amendments, the **Fifteenth Amendment** (ratified in 1870) was an outgrowth of the Civil War. Unlike the Fourteenth Amendment, however, the Fifteenth Amendment is targeted fairly narrowly, its only concern being the denial of voting rights in state and federal elections on grounds of race. As in the Thirteenth and Fourteenth Amendments, Section 5 of the Fifteenth Amendment grants Congress the power to adopt "appropriate legislation" to enforce its guarantees. In 1965, Congress employed its enforcement powers under Section 5 in adopting the landmark **Voting Rights Act.** Among other things, the act allowed the federal government to supervise actively electoral systems in states where racial discrimination had been pervasive. It also granted individuals the right to sue in federal court to challenge features of state and local elections deemed to be discriminatory. Without question, the Voting Rights Act of 1965 has had an enormous impact on ending racial discrimination in this area. (The issue of voting rights is examined in detail in Chapter 13.)

The Nineteenth Amendment

Like most African-Americans, women were originally excluded from participation in elections in this country. In 1848, a delegation of women, including the famous suffragist Elizabeth Cady Stanton, met at Seneca Falls, New York, to address the "social, civil, and religious conditions and rights of woman." The Seneca Falls Convention adopted a resolution stating that "it is the duty of the women of this country to secure to themselves their sacred right to the elective franchise." Securing the franchise would not be easy. In 1872, Susan B. Anthony was prosecuted for attempting to vote in the presidential election. Three years later, the Supreme Court rebuffed a woman seeking to cast a ballot in a Missouri election, saying that "the Constitution of the United States does not confer the right of suffrage upon anyone" (*Minor v. Happersett* [1875]). In the last decades of the nineteenth century, a few states changed their statutes to permit female suffrage. By 1912, nine states had extended the franchise to include women. In 1918, President Woodrow Wilson took a stand in favor of women's suffrage. Following Wilson's lead, Congress adopted a constitutional amendment granting women the right to vote and submitted it to the states for ratification. In 1920, the **Nineteenth Amendment** was added to the Constitution:

> The right of the citizens of the United States to vote shall not be denied or abridged by the United States or by any State on account of sex. Congress shall have the power, by appropriate legislation, to enforce the provision of this article.

In one fell swoop, the size of the potential electorate was doubled! Political participation by women did not, as some critics feared, radically alter the political system or its public policy outputs.

The Twenty-Fourth Amendment

Although formally granted the right to vote by the Fifteenth Amendment, many African-Americans were still effectively disenfranchised by practices such as **grandfather clauses, literacy tests,** the **"white primary,"** and poll taxes (see Chapter 13). The **poll tax** was a fee required as a condition for voting. Typically, the unpaid fees would accumulate from election to election, posing an ever greater economic impediment to voting. Poll taxes had been common in the United States at the time the Constitution was adopted but fell into disuse by the mid-nineteenth century. They were resurrected after the ratification of the Fifteenth Amendment as a means of preventing African-Americans, most of whom were poor, from voting. In *Breedlove v. Suttles* (1937), the Supreme Court ruled that poll taxes, in and of themselves, did not violate the Fourteenth or Fifteenth Amendments. The *Breedlove* decision gave impetus to a movement to abolish the poll tax, and by 1960, poll taxes existed in only five Southern states. The Twenty-fourth Amendment, ratified in 1964, outlawed poll taxes as a requirement to vote in federal elections. A year later, the Supreme Court extended this policy when it overturned *Breedlove* and struck down poll taxes in state elections as well (*Harper v. Virginia State Board of Elections* [1966]) (see Chapter 13).

The Twenty-Sixth Amendment

During the 1960s, young people, galvanized primarily by the Vietnam War, began to assert themselves politically. Often, political participation by the young was unconventional, taking the form of demonstrations and protests. Many youth leaders argued that if eighteen-year-olds were old enough to be drafted into military service and placed in combat, they were also old enough to cast a ballot. This line of argument was not new; it had persuaded Georgia and Kentucky to lower the minimum voting age to eighteen during the Second World War.

In 1970, Congress passed a measure lowering the voting age from twenty-one to eighteen in both state and federal elections. The Supreme Court, however, declared this measure unconstitutional in *Oregon v. Mitchell* (1970). Dividing 5 to 4, the Court held that, although Congress possessed the authority to lower the voting age in federal elections, it could not by simple statute lower the voting age in state elections. This decision prompted Congress to adopt the **Twenty-sixth Amendment,** which was ratified by the states in record time—five weeks. Unlike women, however, young people have not taken full advantage of the extension of the franchise. People eighteen to twenty-one are considerably less likely to vote than their elders.

TO SUMMARIZE:

- The right to vote, one of the most essential rights in a democracy, has been protected and enlarged by several amendments to the Constitution as interpreted by the Supreme Court.
- The Fifteenth Amendment (1870) prohibits racial discrimination in defining and implementing the right to vote and empowers Congress to enact legislation to achieve this purpose.
- The Nineteenth Amendment (1920) removes gender as a qualification for voting.
- The Twenty-fourth Amendment (1964) prohibits the imposition of a poll tax as a precondition for voting in federal elections. In 1966, the Supreme Court interpreted the Equal Protection Clause of the Fourteenth Amendment to extend this prohibition to state elections as well.
- The Twenty-sixth Amendment (1971) lowered the voting age to eighteen in both state and federal elections.

STANDARDS OF REVIEW IN CIVIL RIGHTS AND LIBERTIES CASES

The Supreme Court has developed several different standards of review in determining the constitutionality of laws affecting civil rights and liberties. These standards can be categorized as **minimal scrutiny, heightened scrutiny,** and **strict scrutiny.**

Minimal Scrutiny: The Rational Basis Test

Minimal scrutiny, the most lenient standard of judicial review, typically involves the application of the **rational basis test.** In *Massachusetts Board of Retirement v. Murgia* (1976), the Supreme Court said that a law that touches on a constitutionally protected interest must, at a minimum, be "rationally related to furthering a legitimate government interest." For example, a state law that prohibits performing surgery without a license impinges on constitutionally protected interests by depriving laypersons of their right to make contracts freely and discriminating against those unable or unwilling to obtain a license. Yet the prohibition is obviously a rational means of advancing the state's legitimate interests in public health and safety. There is no doubt that, if it were challenged, the prohibition would withstand judicial review.

In applying the rational basis test, courts begin with a strong presumption that the challenged law or policy is valid. The burden of proof is on the party making the challenge to show that the law or policy is unconstitutional. To carry this burden, the party must demonstrate that there is no rational basis for the law or policy. Since this is a difficult showing to make, application of the rational basis test usually leads to a judgment sustaining the constitutionality of the challenged law or policy.

Strict Scrutiny: The Compelling Government Interest Test

When a law or policy impinges on a right explicitly protected by the Constitution, such as the right to vote, it is subjected to a more searching judicial scrutiny. This approach also applies in the case of unenumerated rights that the courts have identified as fundamental, such as the right of privacy (see *Roe v. Wade* [1973]) and the right of interstate travel (see *Shapiro v. Thompson* [1969]). Strict judicial scrutiny is also warranted in cases involving forms of discrimination, such as that based on race, that have been held to be "inherently suspect" (see *Korematsu v. United States* [1944]).

Under strict scrutiny, the ordinary **presumption of constitutionality** is reversed, which means, in effect, that the challenged law or policy is presumed to be unconstitutional. The burden shifts to the government (local, state, or federal) to show that the law or policy furthers a **compelling government interest.** Moreover, the government must show that the law is **narrowly tailored** to achieve this interest. This is a heavy burden for the government to carry. Consequently, most laws subjected to strict judicial scrutiny are declared unconstitutional. However, the application of strict scrutiny is not necessarily tantamount to a declaration of unconstitutionality. For example, in *New York v. Ferber* (1982), the Supreme Court upheld a child pornography law that impinged on the First Amendment freedom of expression because, in the view of the Court, the law served a compelling interest in protecting children from the abuse typically associated with the pornography industry.

Intermediate Scrutiny

To further complicate matters, the Supreme Court has developed an intermediate level of review, often referred to as heightened scrutiny. This standard has been most important in reviewing claims of gender-based discrimination under the Equal Protection Clause of the Fourteenth Amendment.

TO SUMMARIZE:

- The Supreme Court utilizes several distinctive standards or review in determining the constitutionality of laws affecting civil rights and liberties.
- The most lenient standard is identified as "minimal scrutiny" or the "rational basis test." Here the ordinary presumption of constitutionality applies, thus placing the burden of persuasion on the party challenging the law. To pass muster under this standard, a law need merely be rationally related to the furtherance of a legitimate government interest.
- The most stringent standard of review, known as "strict scrutiny," applies in cases of racial discrimination and where other fundamental rights are at stake. Here the burden of persuasion rests with the government to show that the law serves a compelling interest and is narrowly tailored to that end.
- The Court has identified an intermediate standard of review, often termed "heightened scrutiny," which has been applied primarily in the area of sex discrimination.

THE IMPORTANCE OF STATE CONSTITUTIONS

In trying to understand constitutional law as it relates to civil rights and liberties, we must not ignore the role of the state constitutions and courts in protecting individual rights. Under our federal system of government, the highest court of each state possesses the authority to interpret with finality its state constitution and statutes. Since every state constitution contains language protecting individual rights and liberties, many state court decisions implicate both state and federal constitutional provisions. Under the relevant language of their constitutions and statutes, state courts are free to recognize greater (but not lesser) protections of individual rights than are provided by the U.S. Constitution as interpreted by the federal courts. For example, in *In re T. W.* (1989), the Florida Supreme Court struck down as a violation of the right of privacy a statute that required parental consent in cases where minors sought abortions. The constitutionality of a similar law had been upheld on federal grounds by the U.S. Supreme Court in *Planned Parenthood v. Ashcroft* (1983). In *T. W.,* the Florida Supreme Court made it clear that it was basing its decision on an amendment to the Florida Constitution that (unlike the federal Constitution) explicitly protects the right of privacy. Similarly, in *State v. Kam* (1988), the Hawaii Supreme Court adopted an interpretation of its state constitution that affords considerably broader protection to pornography than that provided by the U.S. Constitution. These decisions, and many others like them, mean that a study of civil rights and liberties must encompass the provisions of state constitutions that parallel those of the U.S. Constitution.

TO SUMMARIZE:

- Under our system of federalism, the U.S. constitution provides a base level of protection for civil rights and liberties applicable at every level of government.
- Under their respective constitutions, as interpreted by their courts, states may provide higher levels of protection for individual rights than are recognized in the federal Constitution as interpreted by the federal courts.

CONCLUSION

This chapter has provided a broad survey of the constitutional sources of protection for civil rights and liberties. As manifestations of the ideals of liberty and equality, civil rights and liberties are regarded as indispensable features of American democracy. Yet individual rights exist in constant tension with majority rule, another essential feature of democracy. Individual rights must be balanced wisely against compelling societal interests, such as public order, national defense, and the general welfare. The task of achieving this balance rests primarily with the courts, most notably the U.S. Supreme Court. The remaining chapters of this book are devoted to an examination of the Supreme Court's jurisprudence in several key areas of civil rights and liberties.

KEY TERMS

unalienable rights	well-regulated militia	Seventh Amendment	doctrine of incorporation
natural rights	Third Amendment	Eighth Amendment	selective incorporation
liberty	Fourth Amendment	excessive bail	censorship
equality	unreasonable searches and	pretrial release	right to vote
civil rights	seizures	pretrial detention	Fifteenth Amendment
civil liberties	wiretapping	excessive fines	Voting Rights Act
treason	drug testing	cruel and unusual	Nineteenth Amendment
political dissent	Fifth Amendment	punishments	grandfather clause
religious tests	indictment	forfeiture	literacy tests
Establishment Clause	grand jury	Ninth Amendment	white primary
habeas corpus	double jeopardy	Thirteenth Amendment	poll tax
ex post facto laws	compulsory self-incrimination	Equal Protection Clause	Twenty-sixth Amendment
bill of attainder	eminent domain	Due Process Clause	minimal scrutiny
Contract Clause	just compensation	procedural due process	heightened scrutiny
First Amendment	due process of law	fair notice	strict scrutiny
Free Exercise Clause	Fourteenth Amendment	fair hearing	rational basis test
freedom of speech	Sixth Amendment	substantive due process	presumption of
freedom of the press	speedy and public trial	liberty of contract	constitutionality
freedom of expression	trial by jury	right of privacy	compelling government
right to keep and bear arms	subpoena	fundamental right	interest
Second Amendment	right to counsel	state action	narrowly tailored

FOR FURTHER READING

Abraham, Henry J. and Barbara A. Perry. *Freedom and the Court: Civil Rights and Liberties in the United States* (6th ed.). New York: Oxford University Press, 1994.

Barker, Lucius J., and Twiley W. Barker, Jr. *Civil Liberties and the Constitution* (6th ed.). Englewood Cliffs, N.J.: Prentice Hall, 1990.

Biskupic, Joan, and Elder Witt. *The Supreme Court and Individual Rights* (3rd ed.). Washington: Congressional Quarterly Press, 1997.

Dworkin, Ronald. *Taking Rights Seriously*. Cambridge, Mass.: Harvard University Press, 1978.

Morgan, Richard E. *The Law and Politics of Civil Rights and Liberties*. New York: Knopf, 1985.

Perry, Michael. *The Constitution, the Courts, and Human Rights*. New Haven, Conn.: Yale University Press, 1982.

Pritchett, C. Herman. *Constitutional Civil Liberties*. Englewood Cliffs, N.J.: Prentice Hall, 1984.

Sarat, Austin, and Thomas R. Kearns. *Legal Rights: Historical and Philosophical Perspectives*. Ann Arbor, Mich.: The University of Michigan Press, 1996.

Tarr, G. Alan, and Ellis Katz (eds.). *Federalism and Rights*. Lanham, Md.: Rowman & Littlefield, 1996.

INTERNET RESOURCES

Name of Resource	Description	URL (circa 1998)
American Civil Liberties Union	The premier civil rights/civil liberties interest group	http://www.aclu.org/
National Rifle Association	The leading organization dedicated to promoting the right to keep and bear arms	http://www.nra.org/

Case

DeShaney v. Winnebago Social Services

489 U.S. 189; 109 S.Ct. 998; 103 L.Ed. 2d. 249 (1989)
Vote: 6–3

This case dramatizes the tension between law and justice that is inherent in a constitutional system that seeks to "establish justice" and maintain the "rule of law." At issue is whether the failure of a state agency to take action constitutes "state action" for the purposes of the Fourteenth Amendment.

Following his parents' divorce, one-year-old Joshua DeShaney was placed in the custody of his father, who soon established legal residence in Winnebago County, Wisconsin. Two years later, county social workers began to receive reports that the father was physically abusing the child. When Joshua was four years old, his father beat him so severely as to inflict permanent brain damage, leaving the child profoundly retarded and institutionalized for life. Joshua's mother brought suit on her son's behalf under 42 U.S. Code, Section 1983, seeking monetary damages from the state, arguing that the state agency's failure to protect her son constituted an abridgment of his rights under the Fourteenth Amendment.

Chief Justice Rehnquist delivered the opinion of the Court.

. . . The Due Process Clause of the Fourteenth Amendment provides that "[n]o State shall . . . deprive any person of life, liberty, or property, without due process of law." Petitioners contend that the State deprived Joshua of his liberty interest in "free[dom] from . . . unjustified intrusions on personal security," . . . by failing to provide him with adequate protection against his father's violence. The claim is one invoking the substantive rather than procedural component of the Due Process Clause; petitioners do not claim that the State denied Joshua protection without according him appropriate procedural safeguards . . . but that it was categorically obligated to protect him in these circumstances.

But nothing in the language of the Due Process Clause itself requires the State to protect the life, liberty, and property of its citizens against invasion by private actors. The Clause is phrased as a limitation on the State's power to act, not as a guarantee of certain minimal levels of safety and security. It forbids the State itself to deprive individuals of life, liberty, or property without "due process of law," but its language cannot fairly be extended to impose an affirmative obligation on the State to ensure that those interests do not come to harm through other means. Nor does history support such an expansive reading of the constitutional text. Like its counterpart in the Fifth Amendment, the Due Process Clause of the Fourteenth Amendment was intended to prevent government "from abusing [its] power, or employing it as an instrument of oppression. . . ." Its purpose was to protect the people from the State, not to ensure that the State protected them from each other. The Framers were content to leave the extent of governmental obligation in the latter area to the democratic political processes.

Consistent with these principles, our cases have recognized that the Due Process Clauses generally confer no affirmative right to governmental aid, even where such aid may be necessary to secure life, liberty, or property interests of which the government itself may not deprive the individual. . . . If the Due Process Clause does not require the State to provide its citizens with particular protective services, it follows that the State cannot be held liable under the Clause for injuries that could have been averted had it chosen to provide them. As a general matter, then, we conclude that a State's failure to protect an individual against private violence simply does not constitute a violation of the Due Process Clause.

Petitioners contend, however, that even if the Due Process Clause imposes no affirmative obligation on the State to provide the general public with adequate protective services, such a duty may arise out of certain "special relationships" created or assumed by the State with respect to particular individuals. . . . Petitioners argue that such a "special relationship" existed here because the State knew that Joshua faced a special danger of abuse at his father's hands, and specifically proclaimed, by word and by deed, its intention to protect him against that danger. . . . Having actually undertaken to protect Joshua from this danger—which petitioners concede the State played no part in creating—the State acquired an affirmative "duty," enforceable through the Due Process Clause, to do so in a reasonably competent fashion. Its failure to discharge that duty, so the argument goes, was an abuse of governmental power that so "shocks the conscience," . . . as to constitute a substantive due process violation. . . .

We reject this argument. It is true that in certain limited circumstances the Constitution imposes upon the State affirmative duties of care and protection with respect to particular individuals. . . .

. . . While the State may have been aware of the dangers that Joshua faced in the free world, it played no part in their creation, nor did it do anything to render him any more vulnerable to them. That the State once took temporary custody of Joshua does not alter the analysis, for when it returned him to his father's custody, it placed him in no worse position than that in which he would have been had it not acted at all; the State does not become the permanent guarantor of an individual's safety by having once offered him shelter. Under these circumstances, the State had no constitutional duty to protect Joshua. . . .

Judges and lawyers, like other humans, are moved by natural sympathy in a case like this to find a way for Joshua and his mother to receive adequate compensation for the grievous harm inflicted upon them. But before yielding to that impulse, it is well to remember once again that the harm was inflicted not by the State of Wisconsin, but by Joshua's father. The most that can be said of the state functionaries in this case is that they stood by and did nothing when suspicious circumstances dictated a more active role for them. In defense of them it must also be said that had they moved too soon to take custody of the son away from the father, they would likely have been met with charges of improperly intruding into the parent–child relationship. . . .

The people of Wisconsin may well prefer a system of liability which would place upon the State and its officials the responsibility for failure to act in situations such as the present one. They may create such a system, if they do not have it already, by changing the tort law of the State in accordance with the regular law-making process. But they should not have it thrust upon them by this Court's expansion of the Due Process Clause of the Fourteenth Amendment. . . .

Justice Brennan, with whom **Justice Marshall** and **Justice Blackmun** join, dissenting. . . .

Justice Blackmun, dissenting.

Today, the Court purports to be the dispassionate oracle of the law, unmoved by "natural sympathy." But, in this pretense, the Court itself retreats into a sterile formalism which prevents it from recognizing either the facts of the case before it or the legal norms that should apply to those facts. As Justice Brennan demonstrates, the facts here involve not mere passivity, but active state intervention in the life of Joshua DeShaney—intervention that triggered a fundamental duty to aid the boy once the State learned of the severe danger to which he was exposed.

The Court fails to recognize this duty because it attempts to draw a sharp and rigid line between action and inaction. But such formalistic reasoning has no place in the interpretation of the broad and stirring clauses of the Fourteenth Amendment. Indeed, I submit that these clauses were designed, at least in part, to undo the formalistic legal reasoning that infected antebellum jurisprudence, which the late Professor Robert Cover analyzed so effectively in his significant work entitled *Justice Accused* (1975).

Like the antebellum judges who denied relief to fugitive slaves, the Court today claims that its decision, however harsh, is compelled by existing legal doctrine. On the contrary, the question presented by this case is an open one and our Fourteenth Amendment precedents may be read more broadly or narrowly depending upon how one chooses to read them. Faced with the choice, I would adopt a "sympathetic" reading, one which comports with dictates of fundamental justice and recognizes that compassion need not be exiled from the province of judging. . . .

Poor Joshua! Victim of repeated attacks by an irresponsible, bullying, cowardly, and intemperate father, and abandoned by respondents who placed him in a dangerous predicament and who knew or learned what was going on, and yet did essentially nothing except, as the Court revealing observes, . . . "dutifully recorded these incidents in [their] files." It is a sad commentary upon American life, and constitutional principles—so full of late patriotic fervor and proud proclamations about "liberty and justice for all," that this child, Joshua DeShaney, now is assigned to live out the remainder of his life profoundly retarded. Joshua and his mother, as petitioners here, deserve—but now are denied by this Court—the opportunity to have the facts of their case considered in the light of the constitutional protection that 42 U.S.C. Sec. 1983 is meant to provide.

Case

BARRON V. BALTIMORE

7 Pet. (32 U.S.) 243; 8 L.Ed. 672 (1833)
Vote: 7–0

Like the cases that follow in this chapter, Barron v. Baltimore *deals with the issue of whether the protections of the Bill of Rights are applicable to actions of the states and their local subdivisions. The case stemmed from an incident in which the city of Baltimore diverted the flow of certain streams, causing silt to be deposited in front of John Barron's wharf, making it unusable. Barron brought suit in state court, claiming that since the City's action amounted to a taking of private property, he was entitled to "just compensation" under the Fifth Amendment to the U.S. Constitution. The trial court agreed and awarded Barron forty-five hundred dollars. After this judgment was reversed by a state appellate court, Barron appealed to the U.S. Supreme Court on a writ of error.*

Mr. Chief Justice Marshall delivered the Opinion of the Court:

. . . The plaintiff in error [Barron] contends that [this case] comes within that clause in the Fifth Amendment to the Constitution which inhibits the taking of private property for public use without just compensation. He insists that this amendment, being in favor of the liberty of the citizen, ought to be so construed as to restrain the legislative power of a State, as well as that of the United States. If this proposition be untrue, the Court can take no jurisdiction of the cause.

The question thus presented is, we think, of great importance, but not of much difficulty.

The Constitution was ordained and established by the people of the United States for themselves, for their own government, and not for the government of the individual States. Each State established a constitution for itself, and in that constitution provided such limitations and restrictions on the powers of its particular government as its judg-

ment dictated. The people of the United States framed such a government for the United States as they supposed best adapted to their situation, and best calculated to promote their interests. The powers they conferred on this government were to be exercised by itself; and the limitations on power, if expressed in general terms, are naturally, and, we think, necessarily applicable to the government created by the instrument. They are limitations of power granted in the instrument itself; not of distinct governments, framed by different persons and for different purposes.

If this proposition be correct, the Fifth Amendment must be understood as restraining the power of the general government, not as applicable to the States. In their several constitutions they have imposed such restrictions on their respective governments as their own wisdom suggested; such as they deemed most proper for themselves. It is a subject on which they judge exclusively, and with which others interfere no farther than they are supposed to have a common interest.

The counsel for the plaintiff in error insists that the Constitution was intended to secure the people of the several States against the undue exercise of power by their respective State governments; as well as against that which might be attempted by their general government. In support of this argument he relies on the inhibitions contained in the tenth section of the first article.

We think that section affords a strong if not a conclusive argument in support of the opinion already indicated by the Court.

The preceding section contains restrictions which are obviously intended for the exclusive purpose of restraining the exercise of power by the departments of the general government. Some of them use language applicable only to Congress, others are expressed in general terms. The third clause, for example, declares that "no bill of attainder or *ex post facto* law shall be passed." No language can be more general; yet the demonstration is complete that it applies solely to the government of the United States. In addition to the general arguments furnished by the instrument itself, some of which have been already suggested, the succeeding section, the avowed purpose of which is to restrain State legislation, contains in terms the very prohibition. It declares that "no State shall pass any bill of attainder or *ex post facto* law." This provision then, of the ninth section, however comprehensive its language, contains no restriction on State legislation.

The ninth section having enumerated, in the nature of a bill of rights, the limitations intended to be imposed on the powers of the general government, the tenth proceeds to enumerate those which were to operate on the State legislatures. These restrictions are brought together in the same section, and are by express words applied to the States. . . .

. . . It would be tedious to recapitulate the several limitations on the powers of the States which are contained in this section. They will be found, generally, to restrain State legislation on subjects entrusted to the government of the Union, in which the citizens of all the States are interested. In these alone were the whole people concerned. The question of their application to States is not left to construction. It is averred in positive words.

If the original Constitution, in the ninth and tenth sections of the first article, draws this plain and marked line of discrimination between the limitations it imposes on the powers of the general government and on those of the States; if in every inhibition intended to act on State power, words are employed which directly express that intent, some strong reason must be assigned for departing from this safe and judicious course in framing the amendments, before that departure can be assumed.

We search in vain for that reason. . . .

We are of opinion that the provision in the Fifth Amendment to the Constitution, declaring that private property shall not be taken for public use without just compensations, is intended solely as a limitation on the exercise of power by the government of the United States, and is not applicable to the legislation of the States. We are therefore of opinion that there is no repugnancy between the several acts of the General Assembly of Maryland, given in evidence by the defendants at the trial of this cause in the court of that State, and the Constitution of the United States.

This Court, therefore, has no jurisdiction of the cause, and [it] is dismissed.

Case

HURTADO V. CALIFORNIA

110 U.S. 516; 4 S.Ct. 111; 28 L.Ed. 232 (1884)
Vote: 7–1

Here the Court considers whether the grand jury requirement of the Fifth Amendment is applicable to state criminal prosecutions by way of the Fourteenth Amendment. The facts are contained in Justice Matthews's majority opinion.

Mr. Justice Matthews delivered the Opinion of the Court:

The Constitution of the State of California adopted in 1879, in article I, section 8, provides as follows:

Offenses heretofore required to be prosecuted by indictment shall be prosecuted by information after examination and commitment by a magistrate, or by indictment, with or without such examination and commitment, as may be prescribed by law. A grand jury shall be drawn and summoned at least once a year in each county.

Various provisions of the [California] Penal Code regulate proceedings before the examining and committing magistrate in cases of persons arrested and brought before them upon charges of having committed public offenses. These require, among other things, that the testimony of the witnesses shall be reduced to writing in the form of deposition; and section 872 declares that if it appears from the examination that a public offense has been committed, and there is sufficient cause to believe the defendant guilty thereof, the magistrate must indorse on the depositions an order, signed by him, to that effect, describing the general nature of the offense committed, and ordering that the defendant be held to answer thereto. Sec. 809 of the Penal Code is as follows.

When a defendant has been examined and committed, as provided in section 872 of this Code, it shall be the duty of the district attorney, within thirty days thereafter, to file in the superior court of the county in which the offense is triable, an information charging the defendant with such offense. The information shall be in the name of the people of the State of California, and subscribed by the district attorney, and shall be in form like an indictment for the same offense.

In pursuance of the foregoing provision of the Constitution, and of the several sections of the Penal Code of California, the District Attorney of Sacramento County, on the 20th day of February, 1882, made and filed an information against the plaintiff in error, charging him with the crime of murder in the killing of one Jose Antonio Stuardo. Upon this information and without any previous investigation of the cause by any grand jury, the plaintiff in error was arraigned on the 22d day of March, 1882, and pleaded not guilty. A trial of the issue was thereafter had, and on May 7, 1882, the jury rendered its verdict, in which it found the plaintiff in error guilty of murder in the first degree.

On the 5th day of July, 1882, the Superior Court of Sacramento County, in which the plaintiff in error had been tried, rendered its judgment upon said verdict, that the said Joseph Hurtado, plaintiff in error, be punished by the infliction of death, and the day of his execution was fixed for the 20th day of July, 1882. From this judgment an appeal was taken, and the Supreme Court of the State of California affirmed the judgment.

The proposition of law we are asked to affirm is, that an indictment or presentment by a grand jury, as known to the common law of England, is essential to that "due process of law," when applied to prosecutions for felonies, which is secured and guarantied by this provision of the Constitution of the United States, and which accordingly it is forbidden to the States respectively to dispense with in the administration of criminal law.

We are to construe this phrase in the 14th Amendment by the *usus loquendi* of the Constitution itself. The same words are contained in the 5th Amendment. That article makes specific and express provision for perpetuating the institution of the grand jury, so far as relates to prosecutions, for the most aggravated crimes under the laws of the United States. It declares that "[n]o person shall be held to answer for a capital or otherwise infamous crime, unless on a presentment or indictment of a grand jury, except in cases arising in the land or naval forces, or in the militia when in actual service in time of war or public danger; nor shall any person be subject for the same offense to be twice put in jeopardy of life or limb; nor shall he be compelled in any criminal case to be a witness against himself." It then immediately adds: "nor be deprived of life, liberty or property, without due process of law." According to a recognized canon of interpretation, especially applicable to formal and solemn instruments of constitutional law, we are forbidden to assume, without clear reason to the contrary, that any part of this most important Amendment is superfluous. The natural and obvious inference is, that in the sense of the Constitution, "due process of law" was not meant or intended to include, *ex vi termini*, the in-

stitution and procedure of a grand jury in any case. The conclusion is equally irresistible, that when the same phrase was employed in the 14th Amendment to restrain the action of the States, it was used in the same sense and with no greater extent; and that if in the adoption of that Amendment it had been part of its purpose to perpetuate the institution of the grand jury in all the States, it would have embodied, as did the 5th Amendment, express declarations to that effect. Due process of law in the latter refers to that law of the land, which derives its authority from the legislative powers conferred upon Congress by the Constitution of the United States, exercised within the limits therein prescribed, and interpreted according to the principles of the common law. In the 14th Amendment, by parity of reason, it refers to that law of the land in each State, which derives its authority from the inherent and reserved powers of the State, exerted within the limits of those fundamental principles of liberty and justice which lie at the base of all our civil and political institutions, and the greatest security for which resides in the right of the people to make their own laws, and alter them at their pleasure.

For these reasons, finding no error therein, the judgment of the Supreme Court of California is affirmed.

Mr. Justice Harlan, dissenting.

. . . "Due process of law," within the meaning of the national Constitution, does not import one thing with reference to the powers of the States, and another with reference to the powers of the general government. If particular proceedings conducted under the authority of the general government, and involving life, are prohibited, because not constituting that due process of law required by the Fifth Amendment of the Constitution of the United States, similar proceedings, conducted under the authority of a State, must be deemed illegal as not being due process of law within the meaning of the Fourteenth Amendment. What, then, is the meaning of the words, "due process of law" in the latter amendment? . . .

According to the settled usages and modes of proceeding existing under the common and statute law of England at the settlement of this country, information in capital cases was not consistent with the "law of the land," or with "due process of law." Such was the understanding of the patriotic men who established free institutions upon this continent. Almost the identical words of Magna Charta were incorporated into most of the State Constitutions before the adoption of our national Constitution. When they declared, in substance, that no person should be deprived of life, liberty or property, except by the judgment of his peers of the law of the land, they intended to assert his right to the same guaranties that were given in the mother country by the great charter and the laws passed in furtherance of its fundamental principles. . . .

But it is said that the framers of the Constitution did not suppose that due process of law necessarily required for a capital offence the institution and procedure of a grand jury, else they would not in the same amendment prohibiting the deprivation of life, liberty, or property, without due process of law, have made specific and express provision for a grand jury where the crime is capital or otherwise infamous; therefore, it is argued, the requirement by the Fourteenth Amendment of due process of law in all proceedings involving life, liberty, and property, without specific reference to grand juries in any case whatever, was not intended as a restriction upon the power which it is claimed the States previously had, so far as the express restrictions of the national Constitution are concerned, to dispense altogether with grand juries.

This line of argument, it seems to me, would lead to results which are inconsistent with the vital principles of republican government. If the presence in the Fifth Amendment of a specific provision for grand juries in capital cases, alongside the provision for due process of law in proceedings involving life, liberty, or property, is held to prove that "due process of law" did not, in the judgment of the framers of the Constitution, necessarily require a grand jury in capital cases, inexorable logic would require it to be, likewise, held that the right not to be put twice in jeopardy of life and limb for the same offense, nor compelled in a criminal case to testify against one's self—rights and immunities also specifically recognized in the Fifth Amendment—were not protected by that due process of law required by the settled usages and proceedings existing under the common and statute law of England at the settlement of this country. More than that, other amendments of the Constitution proposed at the same time, expressly recognize the right of persons to just compensation for private property taken for public use; their right, when accused of crime, to be informed of the nature and cause of the accusation against them, and to a speedy and public trial, by an impartial jury of the State and district wherein the crime was committed: to be confronted by the witnesses against them; and to have compulsory process for obtaining witnesses in their favor. Will it be claimed that these rights were not secured by the "law of the land" or by "due process of law," as declared and established at the foundation of our government? Are they to be excluded from the enumeration of the fundamental principles of liberty and justice, and, therefore, not embraced by "due process of law?" If the argument of my brethren be sound, those rights—although universally recognized at the establishment of our institutions as secured by that due process of law which for centuries had been the foundation of Anglo-Saxon liberty—were not deemed by our fathers as essential in the due process of law prescribed by our Constitution; because—such seems to be the argument—had they been regarded as involved in due process of law they would not have been specifically and expressly provided for, but left to the protection given by the general clause forbidding the deprivation of life, liberty, or property without due process of law. Further, the reasoning of the opinion indubitably leads to the conclusion that but for the specific provisions made in the Constitution for the security of the personal rights enumerated, the general inhibition against deprivation of life, liberty and property without due process of law would not have prevented Congress from enacting a statute in derogation of each of them. . . .

Mr. Justice Field did not take part in the decision of this case.

Case

CHICAGO, BURLINGTON AND QUINCY RAILROAD COMPANY V. CHICAGO

166 U.S. 226; 17 S.Ct. 581; 41 L.Ed. 979 (1897)
Vote: 7–1

This case arose when the city of Chicago sought to widen Rockwell Street between West Eighteenth and West Nineteenth streets. To obtain the land necessary to widen the street, the city used its power of eminent domain, taking part of the right-of-way owned by the Chicago, Burlington and Quincy Railroad. A state trial court awarded the railroad company a mere one dollar as "just compensation" for the condemned parcels of land. The railroad took the case to the U.S. Supreme Court on a writ of error. Although the Court ruled in favor of the city, its opinion made new law by extending the Just Compensation Clause of the Fifth Amendment to state action under the Fourteenth Amendment.

Mr. Justice Harlan delivered the opinion of the Court.

. . . [A] state may not, by any of its agencies, disregard the prohibitions of the 14th Amendment. Its judicial authorities may keep within the letter of the statute prescribing forms of procedure in the courts and give the parties the fullest opportunity to be heard, and yet it might be that its final action would be inconsistent with that Amendment. In determining what is due process of law, regard must be had to substance, not to form. This court, referring to the 14th Amendment, has said: "Can a state make anything due process of law which, by its own legislation, it chooses to declare such? To affirm this is to hold that the prohibition to the states is of no avail, or has no application where the invasion of private rights is effected under the forms of state legislation. . . ." The same question could be propounded, and the same answer could be made, in reference to judicial proceedings inconsistent with the requirement of due process of law. If compensation for private property taken for public use is an essential element of due process of law as ordained by the 14th Amendment, then the final judgment of a state court, under the authority of which the property is in fact taken, is to be deemed the act of the state within the meaning of that Amendment.

It is proper now to inquire whether the due process of law enjoined by the 14th Amendment requires compensation to be made or adequately secured to the owner of private property taken for public use under the authority of a state.

. . . [A] statute declaring in terms, without more, that the full and exclusive title to a described piece of land belonging to one person should be and is hereby vested in another person, would, if effectual, deprive the former of his property without due process of law, within the meaning of the 14th Amendment. . . . Such an enactment would not receive judicial sanction in any country having a written Constitution distributing the powers of government among three coordinate departments, and committing to the judiciary, expressly or by implication, authority to enforce the provisions of such Constitution. It would be treated, not as an exertion of legislative power, but as a sentence—an act of spoliation. Due protection of the rights of property has been regarded as a vital principle of republican institutions. The requirement that the property shall not be taken for public use without just compensation is but "an affirmance of a great doctrine established by the common law for the protection of private property. It is founded in natural equity, and is laid down as a principle of universal law. Indeed, in a free government almost all other rights would become worthless if the government possessed an uncontrollable power over the private fortune of every citizen." . . .

. . . We have examined all the questions of law arising on the record of which this court may take cognizance, and which, in our opinion, are of sufficient importance to require notice at our hands, and finding no error, the judgment [of the state court] is affirmed.

Mr. Justice Brewer, dissenting:

I dissent from the judgment in this case. I approve that which is said in the first part of the opinion as to the potency of the 14th Amendment to restrain action by a state through either its legislative, executive or judicial departments, which deprives a party of his property rights without due compensation. . . .

It is disappointing after reading so strong a declaration of the protecting reach of the 14th Amendment and the power and duty of this court in enforcing it as against action by a state by any of its officers or agencies, to find sustained a judgment, depriving a party—even though a railroad corporation—of valuable property without any, or, at least only nominal, compensation. . . .

The Chief Justice took no part in the consideration or decision of this case.

Case

PALKO V. CONNECTICUT

302 U.S. 319; 58 S.Ct. 149; 82 L.Ed. 288 (1937)
Vote: 8–1

Here the Court sets forth a test for determining which provisions of the Bill of Rights are applicable to the states via the Fourteenth Amendment.

Mr. Justice Cardozo delivered the opinion of the Court.

A statute of Connecticut permitting appeals in criminal cases to be taken by the state is challenged by appellant as an infringement of the Fourteenth Amendment of the Constitution of the United States. Whether the challenge should be upheld is now to be determined. . . .

The argument for appellant is that whatever is forbidden by the Fifth Amendment is forbidden by the Fourteenth also. The Fifth Amendment, which is not directed to the states, but solely to the federal government, creates immunity from double jeopardy. No person shall be "subject for the same offense to be twice put in jeopardy of life or limb." The Fourteenth Amendment ordains, "nor shall any state deprive any person of life, liberty, or property, without due process of law." To retry a defendant, though under one indictment and only one, subjects him, it is said, to double jeopardy in violation of the Fifth Amendment, if the prosecution is one on behalf of the United States. From this the consequence is said to follow that there is a denial of life or liberty without due process of law, if the prosecution is one on behalf of the People of a State. . . .

We do not find it profitable to mark the precise limits of the prohibition of double jeopardy in federal prosecutions. . . .

We have said that in appellant's view the Fourteenth Amendment is to be taken as embodying the prohibitions of the Fifth. His thesis is even broader. Whatever would be a violation of the original Bill of Rights (Amendments 1 to 8) if done by the federal government is now equally unlawful by force of the Fourteenth Amendment if done by a state. There is no such general rule.

The Fifth Amendment provides, among other things, that no person shall be held to answer for a capital or otherwise infamous crime unless on presentment or indictment of a grand jury. This court has held that, in prosecutions by a state, presentment or indictment by a grand jury may give way to informations at the instance of a public officer. . . . The Fifth Amendment provides also that no person shall be compelled in any criminal case to be a witness against himself. This court has said that, in prosecutions by a state, the exemption will fail if the state elects to end it. . . . The Sixth Amendment calls for a jury trial in criminal cases and the Seventh for a jury trial in civil cases at common law where the value in controversy shall exceed twenty dollars. This court has ruled that consistently with those amendments trial by jury may be modified by a state or abolished altogether. . . .

On the other hand, the Due Process Clause of the Fourteenth Amendment may make it unlawful for a state to abridge by its statutes the freedom of speech which the First Amendment safeguards against encroachment by the Congress . . . or the right of peaceable assembly, without which speech would be unduly trammeled or the right of one accused of crime to the benefit of counsel. . . . In these and other situations immunities that are valid as against the federal government by force of the specific pledges of particular amendments have been found to be implicit in the concept of ordered liberty, and thus, through the Fourteenth Amendment, become valid as against the states.

The line of division may seem to be wavering and broken if there is a hasty catalogue of the cases on the one side and the other. Reflection and analysis will induce a different view. There emerges the perception of a rationalizing principle which gives to discrete instances a proper order and coherence. The right to trial by jury and the immunity from prosecution except as the result of an indictment may have value and importance. Even so, they are not of the very essence of a scheme of ordered liberty. To abolish them is not to violate a "principle of justice so rooted in the traditions and conscience of our people as to be ranked as fundamental. . . ." Few would be so narrow or provincial as to maintain that a fair and enlightened system of justice would be impossible without them. What is true of jury trials and indictments is true also, as the cases show, of the immunity from compulsory self-incrimination. . . . This too might be lost, and justice still be done. Indeed, today as in the past there are students of our penal system who look upon the immunity as a mischief rather than a benefit, and who would limit its scope or destroy it altogether. No doubt there would remain the need to give protection against torture, physical or mental. . . . Justice, however, would not perish if the accused were subject to a duty to respond to orderly inquiry. . . .

We reach a different plane of social and moral values when we pass to the privileges and immunities that have been taken over from the earlier articles of the federal Bill of Rights and brought within the Fourteenth Amendment by a process of absorption. These in their origin were effective against the federal government alone. If the Fourteenth Amendment has absorbed them, the process of absorption has had its source in the belief that neither liberty nor justice would exist if they were sacrificed. . . . This is true, for illustration, of freedom of thought and speech. Of that freedom one may say that it is the matrix, the indispensable condition, of nearly every other form of freedom. With rare aberrations a pervasive recognition of that truth can be traced in our history, political and legal. So it has come about that the domain of liberty, withdrawn by the Fourteenth Amendment from encroachment by the states, has been enlarged by latter-day judgments to include liberty of the mind as well as liberty of action. The extension became, indeed, a logical imperative when once it was recognized, as long ago it was, that liberty is something more than exemption from physical restraint, and that even in the field of substantive rights and duties the legislative judgment, if oppressive and arbitrary, may be overridden by the courts. . . . Fundamental too in the concept of due process, and so in that of liberty, is the thought that condemnation shall be rendered only after trial. . . . The hearing, moreover, must be a real one, not a sham or a pretense. . . . For that reason, ignorant defendants in a capital case were held to have been condemned unlawfully when in truth, though not in form, they were refused the aid of counsel. . . . The decision did not turn upon the fact that the benefit of counsel would have been guaranteed to the defendants by the provisions of the Sixth Amendment if they had been prosecuted in a federal court. The decision turned upon the fact that in the particular situation laid before us in the evidence the benefit of counsel was essential to the substance of a hearing.

Our survey of the cases serves, we think, to justify the statement that the dividing line between them, if not unfaltering throughout its course, has been true for the most part to a unifying principle. On which side of the line the case made out by the appellant has appropriate location must be the next inquiry and the final one. Is that kind of double jeopardy to which the statute has subjected him a hardship so acute and shocking that our polity will not endure it? Does it violate those "fundamental principles of liberty and justice which lie at the base of all our civil and political institutions"? . . . The answer surely must be "no." What the answer would have to be if the state were permitted after a trial free from error to try the accused over again or to bring another case against him, we have no occasion to consider. We deal with the statute before us and no other. The state is not attempting to wear the accused out by a multitude of cases with accumulated trials. It asks no more than this, that the case against him shall go on until there shall be a trial free from the corrosion of substantial legal error. . . . This is not cruelty at all, nor even vexation in any immoderate degree. If the trial had been infected with error adverse to the accused, there might have been review at his instance, and as often as necessary to purge the vicious taint. A reciprocal privilege, subject at all times to the discretion of the presiding judge . . . has now been granted to the state. There is here no seismic innovation. The edifice of justice stands, in its symmetry, to many, greater than before. . . .

The judgment is affirmed.

Mr. Justice Butler dissents.

Case

ADAMSON V. CALIFORNIA

332 U.S. 46; 67 S.Ct. 1672; 91 L.Ed. 1903 (1947)
Vote: 5–4

In Twining v. New Jersey *(1908), the Court held that the Fifth Amendment protection against compulsory self-incrimination did not have to be honored in state criminal trials. The Court revisits this question in the instant case. The student should pay close attention to the different theories of Fourteenth Amendment due process espoused in the various opinions in this case.*

Mr. Justice Reed delivered the opinion of the Court.

The appellant, Adamson, a citizen of the United States, was convicted, without recommendation for mercy, by a jury in a Superior Court of the State of California of murder in the first degree. After considering the same objections to the conviction that are pressed here, the sentence of death was affirmed by the Supreme Court of the state. The provisions of California law which were challenged . . . as invalid under the Fourteenth Amendment . . . permit the failure of a defendant to explain or to deny evidence against him to be commented upon by court and by counsel and to be considered by court and jury. The defendant did not testify. As the trial court gave its instructions and the District Attorney argued the case in accordance with the constitutional and statutory provisions just referred to, we have for decision the question of their constitutionality.

The appellant was charged in the information with former convictions for burglary, larceny and robbery and pursuant to 1025, California Penal Code, answered that he had suffered the previous convictions. This answer barred allusion to these charges of convictions on the trial. Under California's interpretation of Sec. 1025 of the Penal Code and Sec. 2051 of the Code of Civil Procedure, however, if the defendant, after answering affirmative charges alleging prior convictions, takes the witness stand to deny or explain away other evidence that has been introduced "the commission of these crimes could have been revealed to the jury on cross-examination to impeach his testimony." This forces an accused who is a repeat offender to choose between the risk of having his prior offenses disclosed to the jury or having it draw harmful inferences from uncontradicted evidence that can only be denied or explained by the defendant.

In the first place, appellant urges that the provision of the Fifth Amendment that no person "shall be compelled in any criminal case to be a witness against himself" is a fundamental national privilege or immunity protected against state abridgment by the Fourteenth Amendment or a privilege or immunity secured, through the Fourteenth Amendment, against deprivation by state action because it is a personal right, enumerated in the federal Bill of Rights.

Secondly, appellant relies upon the due process of law clause of the Fourteenth Amendment to invalidate the provisions of the California law and as applied (a) because comment on failure to testify is permitted, (b) because appellant was forced to forego testimony in person because of danger of disclosure of his past convictions through cross-examination and (c) because the presumption of innocence was infringed by the shifting of the burden of proof to appellant in permitting comment on his failure to testify.

We shall assume, but without any intention thereby of ruling upon the issue, that permission by law to the court, counsel and jury to comment upon and consider the failure of defendant "to explain or to deny by his testimony any evidence or facts in the case against him" would infringe defendant's privilege against self-incrimination under the Fifth Amendment if this were a trial in a court of the United States under a similar law. Such an assumption does not determine appellant's rights under the Fourteenth Amendment. It is settled law that the clause of the Fifth Amendment, protecting a person against being compelled to be a witness against himself, is not made effective by the Fourteenth Amendment as a protection against state action on the ground that freedom from testimonial compulsion is a right of national citizenship, or because it is a personal privilege or immunity secured by the Federal Constitution as one of the rights of man that are listed in the Bill of Rights.

The reasoning that leads to those conclusions starts with the unquestioned premise that the Bill of Rights, when adopted, was for the protection of the individual against the federal government and its provisions were inapplicable to similar actions done by the states. . . . With the adoption of the Fourteenth Amendment, it was suggested that the dual citizenship recognized by its first sentence, secured for citizens' federal protection for their elemental privileges and immunities of state citizenship. *The Slaughter-House Cases* decided, contrary to the suggestion, that these rights, as privileges and immunities of state citizenship, remained under the sole protection of the state governments. This Court, without the expression of a contrary view upon that phase of the issues before the Court, has approved this determination. The power to free defendants in state trials from self-incrimination was specifically determined to be beyond the scope of the privileges and immunities clause of the Fourteenth Amendment in *Twining v. New Jersey.* . . .

We reaffirm the conclusion of the *Twining* and *Palko* Cases that protection against self-incrimination is not a privilege or immunity of national citizenship.

A right to a fair trial is a right admittedly protected by the due process clause of the Fourteenth Amendment. Therefore, appellant argues, the due process clause of the Fourteenth Amendment protects his privilege against self-incrimination. The due process clause of the Fourteenth Amendment, however, does not draw all the rights of the federal Bill of Rights under its protection. That contention was made and rejected in *Palko v. Connecticut.* . . . It was rejected with citation of the cases excluding several of the rights, protected by the Bill of Rights, against infringement by the National Government. Nothing has been called to our attention that either the framers of the Fourteenth Amendment or the states that adopted it intended its due process clause to draw within its scope the earlier amendments to the Constitution. *Palko* held that such provisions of the Bill of Rights as were "implicit in the concept of ordered liberty," became secure from state interference by the clause. But it held nothing more.

For a state to require testimony from an accused is not necessarily a breach of a state's obligation to give a fair trial. Therefore, we must examine the effect of the California law applied in this trial to see whether the comment on failure to testify violates the protection against state action that the due process clause does grant to an accused. The due process clause forbids compulsion to testify by fear of hurt, torture or exhaustion. So our inquiry is directed, not at the broad question of the constitutionality of compulsory testimony from the accused under the due process clause, but to the constitutionality of the provision of the California law that permits comment upon his failure to testify. It is, of course, logically possible that while an accused might be required, under appropriate penalties, to submit himself as a witness without a violation of due process, comment by judge or jury on inferences to be drawn from his failure to testify, in jurisdictions where an accused's privilege against self-incrimination is protected, might deny due process. For example, a statute might declare that a permitted refusal to testify would compel an acceptance of the truth of the prosecution's evidence.

Generally, comment on the failure of an accused to testify is forbidden in American jurisdictions. This arises from state constitutional or statutory provisions similar in character to the federal provisions. . . . California, however, is one of a few states that permit limited comment upon a defendant's failure to testify. That permission is narrow. The California law authorizes comment by court and counsel upon the "failure of the defendant to explain or to deny by his testimony any evidence or facts in the case against him." This does not involve any presumption, rebuttable or irrebuttable, either of guilt or of the truth of any fact, that is offered in evidence. It allows inferences to be drawn from proven facts. Because of this clause, the court can direct the jury's attention to whatever evidence there may be that a defendant could deny and the prosecution can argue as to inferences that may be drawn from the accused's failure to testify. California has prescribed a method for advising the jury in the search for truth. However sound may be the legislative conclusion that an accused should not be compelled in any criminal case to be a witness against himself, we see no reason why comment should not be made upon his silence. It seems quite natural that when a defendant has opportunity to deny or

explain facts and determines not to do so, the prosecution should bring out the strength of the evidence by commenting upon defendant's failure to explain or deny it. The prosecution evidence may be of facts that may be beyond the knowledge of the accused. If so, his failure to testify would have little if any weight. But the facts may be such as are necessarily in the knowledge of the accused. In that case a failure to explain would point to an inability to explain.

Appellant sets out the circumstances of this case, however, to show coercion and unfairness in permitting comment. The guilty person was not seen at the place and time of the crime. There was evidence, however, that entrance to the place or room where the crime was committed might have been obtained through a small door. It was freshly broken. Evidence showed that six fingerprints on the door were petitioner's. Certain diamond rings were missing from the deceased's possession. There was evidence that appellant, sometime after the crime, asked an unidentified person whether the latter would be interested in purchasing a diamond ring. As has been stated, the information charged other crimes to appellant and he admitted them. His argument here is that he could not take the stand to deny the evidence against him because he would be subjected to a cross-examination as to former crimes to impeach his veracity and the evidence so produced might well bring about his conviction. Such cross-examination is allowable in California. Therefore, appellant contends the California statute permitting comment denies him due process.

It is true that if comment were forbidden, an accused in this situation could remain silent and avoid evidence of former crimes and comment upon his failure to testify. We are of the view, however, that a state may control such a situation in accordance with its own ideas of the most efficient administration of criminal justice. The purpose of due process is not to protect an accused against a proper conviction but against an unfair conviction. When evidence is before a jury that threatens conviction, it does not seem unfair to require him to choose between leaving the adverse evidence unexplained and subjecting himself to impeachment through disclosures of former crimes. Indeed, this is a dilemma with which any defendant may be faced. If facts, adverse to the defendant, are proven by the prosecution, there may be no way to explain them favorably to the accused except by a witness who may be vulnerable to impeachment on cross-examination. The defendant must then decide whether or not to use such a witness. The fact that the witness may also be the defendant makes the choice more difficult but a denial of due process does not emerge from the circumstances. . . .

Mr. Justice Frankfurter, concurring.

. . . [T]he issue is not whether an infraction of one of the specific provisions of the first eight Amendments is disclosed by the record. The relevant question is whether the criminal proceedings which resulted in conviction deprived the accused of the due process of law to which the United States Constitution entitled him. Judicial review of that guaranty of the Fourteenth Amendment inescapably imposes upon this Court an exercise of judgment upon the whole course of the proceedings in order to ascertain whether they offend those canons of decency and fairness which express the notions of justice of English-speaking peoples even toward those charged with the most heinous offenses. These standards of justice are not authoritatively formulated anywhere as though they were prescriptions in a pharmacopoeia. But neither does the application of Due Process Clause imply that judges are wholly at large. The judicial judgment in applying the Due Process Clause must move within the limits of accepted notions of justice and is not to be based upon the idiosyncracies of a merely personal judgment. The fact that judges among themselves may differ whether in a particular case a trial offends accepted notions of justice is not disproof that general rather than idiosyncratic standards are applied. An important safeguard against such merely individual judgment is an alert deference to the judgment of the State court under review.

Mr. Justice Black [joined by Mr. Justice Douglas], dissenting.

This decision reasserts a constitutional theory spelled out in *Twining v. New Jersey*. . . that this Court is endowed by the Constitution with boundless power under "natural law" periodically to expand and contract constitutional standards to conform to the Court's conception of what at a particular time constitutes "civilized decency" and "fundamental liberty and justice." Invoking this *Twining* rule, the Court concludes that although comment upon testimony in a federal court would violate the Fifth Amendment, identical comment in a state court does not violate today's fashion in today's decency and fundamentals and is therefore not prohibited by the Federal Constitution as amended.

The *Twining* Case was the first, and it is the only, decision of this Court, which has squarely held that states were free, notwithstanding the Fifth and Fourteenth Amendments, to extort evidence from one accused of crime. I

agree that if *Twining* be reaffirmed, the result reached might appropriately follow. But I would not reaffirm the *Twining* decision. I think that decision and the "natural law" theory of the Constitution upon which it relies degrade the constitutional safeguards of the Bill of Rights and simultaneously appropriate for this Court a broad power which we are not authorized by the Constitution to exercise.

Whether this Court ever will, or whether it now should, in the light of past decisions, give full effect to what the Amendment was intended to accomplish is not necessarily essential to a decision here. However that may be, our prior decisions, including *Twining*, do not prevent our carrying out that purpose, at least to the extent of making applicable to the states, not a mere part, as the Court has, but the full protection of the Fifth Amendment's provision against compelling evidence from an accused to convict him of crime. And I further contend that the "natural law" formula which the Court uses to reach its conclusion in this case should be abandoned as an incongruous excrescence on our Constitution. I believe that formula to be itself a violation of our Constitution, in that it subtly conveys to courts, at the expense of legislatures, ultimate power over public policies in fields where no specific provision of the Constitution limits legislative power.

I cannot consider the Bill of Rights to be an outworn 18th Century "strait jacket" as the *Twining* opinion did. Its provisions may be thought outdated abstractions by some. And it is true that they were designed to meet ancient evils. But they are the same kind of human evils that have emerged from century to century wherever excessive power is sought by the few at the expense of the many. In my judgment the people of no nation can lose their liberty so long as a Bill of Rights like ours survives and its basic purposes are conscientiously interpreted, enforced and respected so as to afford continuous protection against old, as well as new, devices and practices which might thwart those purposes. I fear to see the consequences of the Court's practice of substituting its own concepts of decency and fundamental justice for the language of the Bill of Rights as its point of departure in interpreting and enforcing that Bill of Rights. If the choice must be between the selective process of the *Palko* decision applying some of the Bill of Rights to the States, or the *Twining* rule applying none of them, I would choose the *Palko* selective process. But rather than accept either of these choices, I would follow what I believe was the original purpose of the Fourteenth Amendment—to extend to all the people of the nation the complete protection of the Bill of Rights. To hold that this Court can determine what, if any provisions of the Bill of Rights will be enforced, and if so to what degree, is to frustrate the great design of a written Constitution.

Conceding the possibility that this Court is now wise enough to improve on the Bill of Rights by substituting natural law concepts for the Bill of Rights, I think the possibility is entirely too speculative to agree to take that course. I would therefore hold in this case that the full protection of the Fifth Amendment's proscription against compelled testimony must be afforded by California. This I would do because of reliance upon the original purpose of the Fourteenth Amendment. . . .

Mr. Justice Murphy, with whom **Mr. Justice Rutledge** concurs, dissenting.

. . . I agree that the specific guarantees of the Bill of Rights should be carried over intact into the first section of the Fourteenth Amendment. But I am not prepared to say that the latter is entirely and necessarily limited by the Bill of Rights. Occasions may arise where a proceeding falls so far short of conforming to fundamental standards of procedure as to warrant constitutional condemnation in terms of a lack of due process despite the absence of a specific provision in the Bill of Rights.

The point, however, need not be pursued here inasmuch as the Fifth Amendment is explicit in its provision that no person shall be compelled in any criminal case to be a witness against himself. That provision, as Mr. Justice Black demonstrates, is a constituent part of the Fourteenth Amendment.

Moreover, it is my belief that this guarantee against self-incrimination has been violated in this case. Under California law, the judge or prosecutor may comment on the failure of the defendant in a criminal trial to explain or deny any evidence or facts introduced against him. As interpreted and applied in this case, such a provision compels a defendant to be a witness against himself in one of two ways:

1. If he does not take the stand, his silence is used as the basis for drawing unfavorable inferences against him as to matters which he might reasonably be expected to explain. Thus he is compelled, through his silence, to testify against himself. And silence can be as effective in this situation as oral statements.

2. If he does take the stand, thereby opening himself to cross-examination, so as to overcome the effects of the provision in question, he is necessarily compelled to testify against himself. In that case, his testimony on cross-examination is the result of the coercive pressure of the provision rather than his own volition.

Much can be said pro and con as to the desirability of allowing comment on the failure of the accused to testify. But policy arguments are to no avail in the face of a clear constitutional command. This guarantee of freedom from self-incrimination is grounded on a deep respect for those who might prefer to remain silent before their accusers. "It is not every one who can safely venture on the witness stand though entirely innocent of the charge against him. Excessive timidity, nervousness when facing others and attempting to explain transactions of a suspicious character, and offenses charged against him, will often confuse and embarrass him to such a degree as to increase rather than remove prejudices against him. It is not every one, however honest, who would, therefore, willingly be placed on the witness stand."

We are obliged to give effect to the principle of freedom from self-incrimination. That principle is as applicable where the compelled testimony is in the form of silence as where it is composed of oral statements. Accordingly, I would reverse the judgment below.

Case

Rochin v. California

342 U.S. 165; 72 S.Ct. 205; 96 L.Ed. 183 (1952)
Vote: 8–0

Here, the Court again considers the meaning of the Due Process Clause of the Fourteenth Amendment and the relationship of the Bill of Rights to the states. Again, the specific issue is that of compulsory self-

incrimination. The facts are contained in Justice Frankfurter's majority opinion.

Mr. Justice Frankfurter delivered the opinion of the Court.

Having "some information that [the petitioner] was selling narcotics," three deputy sheriffs of the County of Los Angeles, on the morning of July 1, 1949, made for the two-story dwelling house in which Rochin lived with his mother, common-law wife, brothers and sisters. Finding the outside door open, they entered and then forced open the door to Rochin's room on the second floor. Inside they found petitioner sitting partly dressed on the side of the bed, upon which his wife was lying. On a "night stand" beside the bed the deputies spied two capsules. When asked "Whose stuff is this?" Rochin seized the capsules and put them in his mouth. A struggle ensued, in the course of which the three officers "jumped upon him" and attempted to extract the capsules. The force they applied proved unavailing against Rochin's resistance. He was handcuffed and taken to a hospital. At the direction of one of the officers a doctor forced an emetic solution through a tube into Rochin's stomach against his will. This "stomach pumping" produced vomiting. In the vomited matter were found two capsules which proved to contain morphine.

Rochin was brought to trial before a California Superior Court, sitting without a jury, on the charge of possessing "a preparation of morphine" in violation of the California Health and Safety Code. . . . Rochin was convicted and sentenced to sixty days' imprisonment. The chief evidence against him was the two capsules. They were admitted over petitioner's objection, although the means of obtaining them was frankly set forth in the testimony by one of the deputies, substantially as here narrated.

On appeal, the District Court of Appeal affirmed the conviction, despite the finding that the officers "were guilty of unlawfully breaking into and entering defendant's room and were guilty of unlawfully assaulting and battering defendant while in the room," and "were guilty of unlawfully assaulting, battering, torturing and falsely imprisoning the defendant at the alleged hospital." . . .

This Court granted certiorari, because a serious question is raised as to the limitations which the Due Process Clause of the Fourteenth Amendment imposes on the conduct of criminal proceedings by the States. . . .

In our federal system the administration of criminal justice is predominantly committed to the care of the States. The power to define crimes belongs to Congress only as an appropriate means of carrying into execution its limited grant of legislative powers. Broadly speaking, crimes in the United States are what the laws of the individual States make them, subject to the limitations of Art. 1 [sec.] 10 [cl. 1], in the original Constitution, prohibiting bills of attainder and ex post facto laws, and of the Thirteenth and Fourteenth Amendments.

These limitations, in the main, concern not restrictions upon the powers of the States to define crime, except in the restricted area where federal authority has preempted the field, but restrictions upon the manner in which the States may enforce their penal codes. Accordingly, in reviewing a State criminal conviction under a claim of right guaranteed by the Due Process Clause of the Fourteenth Amendment, . . . "we must be deeply mindful of the responsibilities of the States for the enforcement of criminal laws, and exercise with due humility our merely negative function in subjecting convictions from state courts to the very narrow scrutiny which the Due Process Clause of the Fourteenth Amendment authorizes." Due process of law is not to be turned into a destructive dogma against the States in the administration of their systems of criminal justice.

However, this Court too has its responsibility. Regard for the requirements of the Due Process Clause "inescapably imposes upon this Court an exercise of judgment upon the whole course of the proceedings [resulting in a conviction] in order to ascertain whether they offend those canons of decency and fairness which express the notions of justice of English-speaking peoples even toward those charged with the most heinous offenses." . . . These standards of justice are not authoritatively formulated anywhere as though they were specifics. Due process of law is a summarized constitutional guarantee of respect for those personal immunities which, as Mr. Justice Cardozo twice wrote for the Court, are "so rooted in the traditions and conscience of our people as to be ranked as fundamental," . . . or are "implicit in the concept of ordered liberty." . . .

The vague contours of the Due Process Clause do not leave judges at large. We may not draw on our merely personal and private notions and disregard the limits that bind judges in their judicial function. Even though the concept of due process of law is not final and fixed, these limits are derived from considerations that are fused in the whole nature of our judicial process. The Due Process Clause places upon this Court the duty of exercising a judgment, within the narrow confines of judicial power in reviewing State convictions, upon interests of society pushing in opposite directions.

Due process of law thus conceived is not to be derided as resort to a revival of "natural law." To believe that this judicial exercise of judgment could be avoided by freezing "due process of law" at some fixed stage of time or thought is to suggest that the most important aspect of constitutional adjudication is a function for inanimate machines and not for judges, for whom the independence safeguarded by Article 3 of the Constitution was designed and who are presumably guided by established standards of judicial behavior. Even cybernetics has not yet made that haughty claim. To practice the requisite detachment and to achieve sufficient objectivity no doubt demands of judges the habit of self-discipline and self-criticism, incertitude that one's own views are incontestable and alert tolerance toward views not shared. They are precisely the qualities society has a right to expect from those entrusted with ultimate judicial power.

Restraints on our jurisdiction are self-imposed only in the sense that there is from our decisions no immediate appeal short of impeachment or constitutional amendment. But that does not make due process of law a matter of judicial caprice. The faculties of the Due Process Clause may be indefinite and vague, but the mode of their ascertainment is not self-willed. In each case "due process of law" requires an evaluation based on a disinterested inquiry pursued in the spirit of science, on a balanced order of facts exactly and fairly stated, on the detached consideration of conflicting claims. . . .

Applying these general considerations to the circumstances of the present case, we are compelled to conclude that the proceedings by which this conviction was obtained do more than offend some fastidious squeamishness or private sentimentalism about combating crime too energetically. This is conduct that shocks the conscience. Illegally breaking into the privacy of the petitioner, the struggle to open his mouth and remove what was there, the forcible extraction of his stomach's contents—this course of proceeding by agents of government to obtain evidence is bound to offend even hardened sensibilities. They are methods too close to the rack and the screw to permit of constitutional differentiation.

It has long since ceased to be true that due process of law is heedless of the means by which otherwise relevant and credible evidence is obtained. This was not true even before the series of recent cases enforced the constitutional principle that the States may not base convictions upon confessions, however much verified, obtained by coercion. These decisions are not arbitrary exceptions to the comprehensive right of States to fashion their own rules of evidence for criminal trials. They are not sports in our constitutional law but applications of a general principle. They are only instances of the general requirement that States in their prosecutions respect certain decencies of civilized conduct. Due process of law, as a historic and generative principle, precludes defining, and thereby confining, these standards of conduct more precisely than to say that convictions cannot be brought about by methods that offend "a sense of justice." It would be a stultification of the responsibility which the course of constitutional history has cast upon this Court to hold that in order to convict a man the police cannot

extract by force what is in his mind but can extract what is in his stomach.

To attempt in this case to distinguish what lawyers call "real evidence" from verbal evidence is to ignore the reasons for excluding coerced confessions. Use of involuntary verbal confessions in State criminal trials is constitutionally obnoxious not only because of their unreliability. They are inadmissible under the Due Process Clause even though statements contained in them may be independently established as true. Coerced confessions offend the community's sense of fair play and decency. So here, to sanction the brutal conduct which naturally enough was condemned by the court whose judgment is before us, would be to afford brutality the cloak of law. Nothing would be more calculated to discredit law and thereby to brutalize the temper of a society.

Mr. Justice Minton took no part in the consideration or decision of this case.

Mr. Justice Black, concurring.

Adamson v. California . . . sets out reasons for my belief that state as well as federal courts and law enforcement officers must obey the Fifth Amendment's command that "No person . . . shall be compelled in any criminal case to be a witness against himself." I think a person is compelled to be a witness against himself not only when he is compelled to testify, but also when as here, incriminating evidence is forcibly taken from him by a contrivance of modern science. . . .

Some constitutional provisions are stated in absolute and unqualified language such, for illustration, as the First Amendment stating that no law shall be passed prohibiting the free exercise of religion or abridging the freedom of speech or press. Other constitutional provisions do require courts to choose between competing policies, such as the Fourth Amendment which, by its terms, necessitates a judicial decision as to what is an "unreasonable" search or seizure. There is, however, no express constitutional language granting judicial power to invalidate every state law of every kind deemed "unreasonable" or contrary to the Court's notion of civilized decencies; yet the constitutional philosophy used by the majority has, in the past, been used to deny a state the right to fix the price of gasoline, and even the right to prevent bakers from palming off smaller for larger loaves of bread. These cases, and others, show the extent to which the evanescent standards of the majority's philosophy have been used to nullify state legislative programs passed to suppress evil economic practices. What paralyzing role this same philosophy will play in the future economic affairs of this country is impossible to predict. Of even graver concern, however, is the use of the philosophy to nullify the Bill of Rights. I long ago concluded that the accordion-like qualities of this philosophy must inevitably imperil all the individual liberty safeguards specifically enumerated in the Bill of Rights. Recent decisions of this Court sanctioning abridgment of the freedom of speech and press have strengthened this conclusion. ˙

Mr. Justice Douglas, concurring.

. . . As an original matter it might be debatable whether the provision in the Fifth Amendment that no person "shall be compelled in any criminal case to be a witness against himself" serves the ends of justice. Not all civilized legal procedures recognize it. But the choice was made by the Framers, a choice which sets a standard for legal trials in this country. The Framers made it a standard of due process for prosecutions by the Federal Government. If it is a requirement of due process for a trial in the federal courthouse, it is impossible for me to say it is not a requirement of due process for a trial in the state courthouse. That was the issue recently surveyed in *Adamson v. California*. . . . The Court rejected the view that compelled testimony should be excluded and held in substance that the accused in a state trial can be forced to testify against himself. I disagree. Of course an accused can be compelled to be present at the trial, to stand, to sit, to turn this way or that, and to try on a cap or a coat. But I think that words taken from his lips, capsules taken from his stomach, blood taken from his veins are all inadmissible provided they are taken from him without his consent. They are inadmissible because of the command of the Fifth Amendment.

That is an unequivocal, definite and workable rule of evidence for state and federal courts. But we cannot in fairness free the state courts from that command and yet excoriate them for flouting the "decencies of civilized conduct" when they admit the evidence. That is to make the rule turn not on the Constitution but on the idiosyncrasies of the judges who sit here. . . .

Case

Duncan v. Louisiana

391 U.S. 145; 88 S.Ct. 1444; 20 L.Ed. 2d. 491 (1968)
Vote: 7–2

This case raises the question of whether, and under what circumstances, the Due Process Clause of the Fourteenth Amendment incorporates the Sixth Amendment guarantee of trial by jury in a criminal case. The facts are set forth in Justice White's majority opinion.

Mr. Justice White delivered the opinion of the Court.

Appellant, Gary Duncan, was convicted of simple battery in the Twenty-fifth Judicial District Court of Louisiana. Under Louisiana law simple battery is a misdemeanor, punishable by a maximum of two years' imprisonment and a $300 fine. Appellant sought trial by jury, but because the Louisiana Constitution grants jury trials only in cases in which capital punishment or imprisonment at hard labor may be imposed, the trial judge denied the request. Appellant was convicted and sentenced to serve 60 days in the parish prison and pay a fine of $150. Appellant sought review in the Supreme Court of Louisiana, asserting that the denial of jury trial violated rights guaranteed to him by the United States Constitution. The Supreme Court, finding "[n]o error of law in the ruling complained of," denied appellant a writ of certiorari. . . . [A]ppellant sought review in this Court, alleging that the Sixth and Fourteenth Amendments to the United States Constitution secure the right to jury trial in state criminal prosecutions where a sentence as long as two years may be imposed. . . .

Appellant was 19 years of age when tried. While driving on Highway 23 in Plaquemines Parish on October 18, 1966, he saw two younger cousins engaged in a conversation by the side of the road with four white boys. Knowing his cousins, Negroes who had recently transferred to a formerly all-white high school, had reported the occurrence of racial incidents at the school, Duncan stopped the car, got out, and approached the six boys. At trial the white boys and white onlooker testified, as did appellant and his cousins. The testimony was in dispute on many points, but the witnesses agreed that appellant and the white boys spoke to each other, that appellant encouraged his cousins to break off the encounter and enter his car, and that appellant was about to enter the car himself for the purpose of driving away with his cousins. The whites testified that just before getting in the car appellant slapped Herman Landry, one of the white boys, on the elbow. The Negroes testified that appellant had not slapped Landry, but had merely touched him. The trial judge concluded that the State had proved beyond a reasonable doubt that Duncan had committed simple battery, and found him guilty. . . .

The Fourteenth Amendment denies the States the power to "deprive any person of life, liberty, or property, without due process of law." In resolving conflicting claims concerning the meaning of this spacious language, the Court has looked increasingly to the Bill of Rights for guidance; many of the rights guaranteed by the first eight Amendments to the Constitution have been held to be protected against state action by the Due Process Clause of the Fourteenth Amendment. That clause now protects the right to compensation for property taken by the State; the rights of speech, press, and religion covered by the First Amendment; the Fourth Amendment rights to be free from unreasonable searches and seizures and to have excluded from criminal trials any evidence illegally seized; the right guaranteed by the Fifth Amendment to be free of compelled self-incrimination; and the Sixth Amendment rights to counsel, to a speedy and public trial, to confrontation of opposing witnesses, and to compulsory process for obtaining witnesses.

The test for determining whether a right extended by the Fifth and Sixth Amendments with respect to federal criminal proceedings is also protected against state action by the Fourteenth Amendment has been phrased in a variety of ways in the opinions of this Court. The question has been asked whether a right is among those "fundamental principles of liberty and justice which lie at the base of all our civil and political institutions," . . . whether it is "basic in our system of jurisprudence," . . . and whether it is "a fundamental right, essential to a fair trial." . . . The claim before us is that the right to trial by jury guaranteed by the Sixth Amendment meets these tests. The position of Louisiana, on the other hand, is that the Constitution imposes upon the States no duty to give a jury trial in any criminal case, regardless of the seriousness of the crime or the size of the punishment which may be imposed. Because we believe that trial by jury in criminal cases is fundamental to the American scheme of justice, we hold that the Fourteenth Amendment guarantees a right of jury trial in all criminal cases which—were they to be tried in a federal court—would come within the Sixth Amendment's guarantee. Since we consider the appeal before us to be such a case, we

hold that the Constitution was violated when appellant's demand for jury trial was refused.

The history of trial by jury in criminal cases has been frequently told. It is sufficient for present purposes to say that by the time our Constitution was written, jury trial in criminal cases had been in existence in England for several centuries and carried impressive credentials traced by many to Magna Charta [1215]. . . .

Jury trial came to America with English colonists, and received strong support from them. Royal interference with the jury trial was deeply resented. . . .

The constitution adopted by the original States guaranteed jury trial. Also, the constitution of every State entering the Union thereafter in one form or another protected the right to jury trial in criminal cases.

Even such skeletal history is impressive support for considering the right to jury in criminal cases to be fundamental to our system of justice, an importance frequently recognized in the opinions of this Court. . . .

Jury trial continues to receive strong support. The laws of every State guarantee a right to jury trial in serious criminal cases; no State has dispensed with it; nor are there significant movements underway to do so. Indeed, the three most recent state constitutional revisions, in Maryland, Michigan, and New York, carefully preserved the right of the accused to have the judgment of a jury when tried for a serious crime.

We are aware of prior cases in this Court in which the prevailing opinion contains statements contrary to our holding today that the right to jury trial in serious criminal cases is a fundamental right and hence must be recognized by the States as part of their obligation to extend due process of law to all persons within their jurisdiction. . . . None of these cases, however, dealt with a State which had purported to dispense entirely with a jury trial in serious criminal cases. . . .

The guarantees of jury trial in the Federal and State Constitutions reflect a profound judgment about the way in which law should be enforced and justice administered. A right to jury trial is granted to criminal defendants in order to prevent oppression by the Government. . . .

The State of Louisiana urges that holding that the Fourteenth Amendment assures a right to jury trial will cast doubt on the integrity of every trial conducted without a jury. Plainly, this is not the import of our holding. Our conclusion is that in the American States, as in the federal judicial system, a general grant of jury trial for serious offenses is a fundamental right, essential for preventing miscarriages of justice and for assuring that fair trials are provided for all defendants. We would not assert, however, that every criminal trial—or any particular trial—held before a judge alone is unfair or that a defendant may never be as fairly treated by a judge as he would be by a jury. Thus we hold no constitutional doubts about the practices, common in both federal and state courts, of accepting waivers of jury trial and prosecuting petty crimes without extending a right to jury trial. However, the fact is that in most places more trials for serious crimes are to juries than to a court alone; a great many defendants prefer the judgment of a jury to that of a court. Even where defendants are satisfied with bench trials, the right to a jury trial very likely serves its intended purpose of making judicial or prosecutorial unfairness less likely.

Louisiana's final contention is that even if it must grant jury trials in serious criminal cases, the conviction before us is valid and constitutional because here the petitioner was tried for simple battery and was sentenced to only 60 days in the parish prison. We are not persuaded. It is doubtless true that there is a category of petty crimes or offenses which is not subject to the Sixth Amendment jury trial provision and should not be subject to the Fourteenth Amendment jury trial requirement here applied to the States. Crimes carrying possible penalties up to six months do not require a jury trial if they otherwise qualify as petty offenses. . . . The question, then, is whether a crime carrying such a penalty is an offense which Louisiana may insist on trying without a jury.

We think not. So-called petty offenses were tried without juries both in England and in the Colonies and have always been held to be exempt from the otherwise comprehensive language of the Sixth Amendment's jury trial provisions. There is no substantial evidence that the Framers intended to depart from this established common-law practice, and the possible consequences to defendants from convictions for petty offenses have been thought insufficient to outweigh the benefits to efficient law enforcement and simplified judicial administration resulting from the availability of speedy and inexpensive nonjury adjudications. These same considerations compel the same result under the Fourteenth Amendment. Of course the boundaries of the petty offense category have always been ill defined, if not ambulatory. . . .

. . . We need not, however, settle in this case the exact location of the line between petty offenses and serious crimes. It is sufficient for our purposes to hold that a crime punishable by two years in prison is, based on past and contemporary standards in this country, a serious crime and not a petty offense. Consequently appellant was entitled to a jury trial and it was error to deny it. . . .

Mr. Justice Fortas, concurring.

. . . [A]lthough I agree with the decision of the Court, I cannot agree with the implication . . . that the tail must go with the hide: that when we hold, influenced by the Sixth Amendment, that "due process" requires that the States accord the right of jury trial for all but petty offenses, we automatically import all of the ancillary rules which have been or may hereafter be developed incidental to the right to jury trial in the federal courts. I see no reason whatever, for example, to assume that our decision today should require us to impose federal requirements such as unanimous verdicts or a jury of 12 upon the States. We may well conclude that these and other features of federal jury practice are by no means fundamental—that they are not essential to due process of law—and that they are not obligatory on the States.

I would make these points clear today. Neither logic nor history nor the intent of the draftsmen of the Fourteenth Amendment can possibly be said to require that the Sixth Amendment or its jury trial provision be applied to the States together with the total gloss that this Court's decisions have supplied. The draftsmen of the Fourteenth Amendment intended what they said, not more or less: that no State shall deprive any person of life, liberty, or property without due process of law. It is ultimately the duty of this Court to interpret, to ascribe specific meaning to this phrase. There is no reason whatever for us to conclude that, in so doing, we are bound slavishly to follow not only the Sixth Amendment but all of its bag and baggage, however securely or insecurely affixed they may be by law and precedent to federal proceedings. To take this course, in my judgment, would be not only unnecessary but mischievous because it would inflict a serious blow upon the principle of federalism. The Due Process Clause commands us to apply its great standard to state court proceedings to assure basic fairness. It does not command us rigidly and arbitrarily to impose the exact pattern of federal proceedings upon the 50 States. On the contrary, the Constitution's command, in my view, is that in our insistence upon state observance of due process, we should, so far as possible, allow the greatest latitude for state differences. It requires, within the limits of the lofty basic standards that it prescribes for the States as well as the Federal Government, maximum opportunity for diversity and minimal imposition of uniformity of methods and detail upon the States. Our Constitution sets up a federal union, not a monolith. . . .

Mr. Justice Black, with whom ***Mr. Justice Douglas*** joins, concurring.

The Court today holds that the right to trial by jury guaranteed defendants in criminal cases in federal courts by Art. III of the United States Constitution and by the Sixth Amendment is also guaranteed by the Fourteenth Amendment to defendants tried in state courts. With this holding I agree for reasons given by the Court. I also agree because of reasons given in my dissent in *Adamson v. California.* . . . I am very happy to support this selective process through which our Court has since the *Adamson* case held most of the specific Bill of Rights' protections applicable to the States to the same extent they are applicable to the Federal Government. Among these are the right to trial by jury decided today, the right against compelled self-incrimination, the right to counsel, the right to compulsory process for witnesses, the right to confront witnesses, the right to a speedy and public trial, and the right to be free from unreasonable searches and seizures. . . .

. . . I believe as strongly as ever that the Fourteenth Amendment was intended to make the Bill of Rights applicable to the States. I have been willing to support the selective incorporation doctrine, however, as an alternative, although perhaps less historically supportable than complete incorporation. The selective incorporation process, if used properly, does limit the Supreme Court in the Fourteenth Amendment field to specific Bill of Rights' protections only and keeps judges from roaming at will in their own notions of what policies outside the Bill of Rights are desirable and what are not. And, most importantly for me, the selective incorporation process has the virtue of having already worked to make most of the Bill of Rights' protections applicable to the States.

Mr. Justice Harlan, whom **Mr. Justice Stewart** joins, dissenting.

. . . The question before us is not whether jury trial is an ancient institution, which it is; nor whether it plays a significant role in the administration of criminal justice, which it does; nor whether it will endure, which it shall. The question in this case is whether the State of Louisiana, which provides trial by jury for all felonies, is prohibited by the Constitution from trying charges of simple battery to the court alone. In my view, the answer to that question, mandated alike by our constitutional history and by the longer history of trial by jury, is clearly "no."

The States have always borne primary responsibility for operating the machinery of criminal justice within their borders, and adapting it to their particular circumstances. In exercising this responsibility, each State is compelled to conform its procedures to the requirements of the Federal Constitution. The Due Process Clause of the Fourteenth Amendment requires that those procedures be fundamentally fair in all respects. It does not, in my view, impose or encourage nationwide uniformity for its own sake; it does not command adherence to forms that happen to be old; and it does not impose on the State the rules that may be in force in the federal courts except where such rules are also found to be essential to basic fairness.

The Court's approach to this case is an uneasy and illogical compromise among the views of various Justices on how the Due Process Clause should be interpreted. The Court does not say that those who framed the Fourteenth Amendment intended to make the Sixth Amendment applicable to the States, and the Court concedes that it finds nothing unfair about the procedure by which the present appellant was tried. Nevertheless, the Court reverses his conviction: it holds, for some reason not apparent to me, that the Due Process Clause incorporates the particular clause of the Sixth Amendment that requires trial by jury in federal criminal cases—including, as I read its opinion, the sometimes trivial accompanying baggage of judicial interpretation in federal contexts. I have raised my voice many times before against the Court's continuing undiscriminating insistence upon fastening on the States federal notions of criminal justice, and I must do so again in this instance. With all respect, the Court's approach and its reading of history are altogether topsy-turvy. . . .

Apart from the approach taken by the absolute incorporationists, I can see only one method of analysis that has any internal logic. That is to start with the words "liberty" and "due process of law" and attempt to define them in a way that accords with American traditions and our system of government. This approach, involving a much more discriminating process of adjudication than does "incorporation," is, albeit difficult, the one that was followed throughout the 19th and most of the present century. It entails a "gradual process of judicial inclusion and exclusion," seeking, with due recognition of constitutional tolerance for state experimentation and disparity, to ascertain those "immutable principles . . . of free government which no member of the Union may disregard." . . .

7

PROPERTY RIGHTS AND ECONOMIC FREEDOM

Chapter Outline

Introduction

The Contract Clause

The Rise and Fall of Economic Due Process

Equal Protection and Economic Regulation

Property Rights and the "Takings" Issue

Conclusion

Key Terms

For Further Reading

Internet Resources

Dartmouth College v. Woodward (1819)

Charles River Bridge Company v. Warren Bridge Company (1837)

Home Building and Loan Association v. Blaisdell (1934)

The Slaughterhouse Cases (1873)

Lochner v. New York (1905)

Adkins v. Children's Hospital (1923)

West Coast Hotel Company v. Parrish (1937)

Ferguson v. Skrupa (1963)

Hawaii Housing Authority v. Midkiff (1984)

Dolan v. City of Tigard (1994)

The great and chief end . . . of Men's uniting into Commonwealths, and putting themselves under Government, is the preservation of their property.

—JOHN LOCKE, *SECOND TREATISE OF GOVERNMENT*

When . . . one devotes his property to a use in which the public has an interest, he, in effect, grants to the public an interest in that use, and must be controlled by the public for the common good, to the extent of the interest he has thus created.

—CHIEF JUSTICE MORRISON WAITE, WRITING FOR THE SUPREME COURT IN *MUNN V. ILLINOIS* (1877)

INTRODUCTION

The twin pillars of any **capitalist economy** are **private property** and **contracts.** For a capitalist system to flourish, it is imperative that there be legal protection for private property and legal enforcement of contracts. Unquestionably, the protection of private property and contractual relationships was particularly important to the framers of the Constitution.

This chapter focuses on historic Supreme Court decisions balancing individual **property rights** and claims of **economic freedom** against the **police power,** both of the states and the national government, to protect the health, safety, and general welfare of the community. The term *property rights* includes the ownership, acquisition, and use of private property. The term *economic freedom* more accurately indicates the cluster of rights associated with private enterprise.

The English philosopher, John Locke. His ideas exerted profound influence on the American Founders

The Influence of John Locke

Americans of the eighteenth century, including those who wrote the Constitution and Bill of Rights, generally accepted the theory of **natural rights** as expounded by the English philosopher John Locke. According to Locke, basic rights to life, liberty, and property were grounded in natural law. As such they were universal and timeless, transcending government and human law. According to Locke and most other **social contract** theorists of the seventeenth and eighteenth centuries, individuals living originally in a "state of nature" (anarchy) subordinated themselves to civil government in exchange for the protection of fundamental rights to life, liberty, and property. Government in turn was limited in the means by which it could interfere with the exercise of individual rights.

Of course, the very existence of social order presumed some loss of personal and economic freedom. To protect individual rights and advance the public good, government might restrict liberty and might even take private property for public use. But in the latter instance, it would have to provide just compensation to the previous owner, and in limiting individual liberty, it would be required to act reasonably. In short, under this social contract theory, governmental restrictions would be balanced against the high priority afforded to individual rights.

This Lockean perspective is reflected in the Contract Clause (Article I, Section 10) of the Constitution. It is also easily recognized in the Due Process Clauses of the Fifth and Fourteenth Amendments, as well as in the Fifth Amendment provision that private property shall not be "taken for public use without just compensation." As with other general provisions of the Constitution, the Supreme Court assumed principal responsibility for interpreting such phrases as "just compensation," "due process of law," and "impairment of the obligation of contracts." The interpretation of these broad phrases defined the central theme of American constitutional lawmaking during roughly the first 150 years of Supreme Court history.

Early Judicial Perspectives

The *ex post facto* law provisions (Article I, Sections 9 and 10) of the original Constitution had the potential to protect property rights against governmental encroachment. But, as noted in Chapter 6, the Supreme Court held in *Calder v. Bull* (1798) that the *ex post facto* limitation applied only to retroactive criminal statutes and not to laws affecting property rights or contractual obligations. Two of the four opinions filed in this case contain important dicta on the sources of individual rights and limitations on government. These opinions, written by Justices Samuel Chase and James Iredell, merit additional attention at this point in our discussion. Without designating any specific constitutuinal limitations, Justice Chase asserted that "certain vital principles in our free republican governments . . . will determine and overrule an apparent and flagrant abuse of legislative power." A legislative act "contrary to the great first principles of the social compact," he continued, "cannot be considered a rightful exercise of legislative authority."

Chase's opinion in *Calder v. Bull* was grounded in natural rights theory. Although this perspective has never achieved dominance on the Supreme Court as a standard for determining the validity of governmental acts, it has occasionally influenced judicial interpretation of the nature and scope of individual rights. By contrast, Justice Iredell's opinion in *Calder* maintained that courts could not invalidate legislation "merely because it is, in their judgment, contrary to the principles of natural justice." If legislatures transgress constitutional boundaries, however, "they violate a fundamental law, which must be our guide, whenever we are called upon, as judges, to determine the validity of a legislative act." Iredell's emphasis on the written Constitution as the ultimate standard for determining the validity of legislation soon became the dominant view among the justices.

The Age of Conservative Activism

Throughout most of the nineteenth century the Supreme Court sought to balance competing public and private interests in its property-related jurisprudence. However, in the face of a rising tide of state and federal economic legislation, the Court of the late nineteenth and early twentieth centuries became more adamant in its defense of what was loosely termed ***laissez-faire* capitalism.** Although the framers of the Constitution attached great importance to the protection of property, it is doubtful that most of them would have subscribed to the doctrines by which the Supreme Court attempted to protect economic individualism. In a series of controversial decisions between the late 1880s and the late 1930s, the Court invoked the constitutional protections of private property and economic freedom to strike down numerous laws designed to regulate economic activity. This period of conservative activism came to an abrupt end with the constitutional revolution of 1937, brought about by a confrontation between the Court and the elected branches over the constitutionality of Roosevelt's New Deal programs (see Chapters 1 and 2).

Modern Judicial Perspectives on Economic Freedom

Since 1937, the Supreme Court has largely deferred to other branches of government in the field of economic regulation. The post–New Deal Court's self-restraint in the economic area has been juxtaposed with a more liberal activism on behalf of cultural, political, or human rights largely outside the field of economic activity. The modern Court, at least until recently, has been much more concerned with matters of free expression, the rights of the accused, personal privacy, and racial and sexual equality (areas of Supreme Court activity discussed in subsequent chapters). Of course, one must recognize that private property and private enterprise are widely shared and deeply held cultural values. Especially in the wake of the decline of communism and socialism around the world, public policy in the United States is unlikely to threaten these established values seriously. Thus, the need for judicial protection of these rights is substantially less now compared to the need in the early days of the Republic or even during the days of the Great Depression. Yet the judicial protection of private property and free enterprise played an extremely important part in the development of American constitutional law and in the institutional history of the Supreme Court.

THE CONTRACT CLAUSE

The **Contract Clause** of Article I, Section 10, forbids states from passing laws "impairing the obligation of contracts." Historically, this clause was extremely important in the protection of economic freedom and private property. Like many important constitutional provisions, the Contract Clause was first given life during the era of Chief Justice John Marshall (1801–1835).

Key Decisions of the Marshall Court

In *Fletcher v. Peck* (1810), the Supreme Court invalidated as a violation of the Contract Clause an act of the Georgia legislature that rescinded the state's sale of land to private investors. To reach this result, it was necessary for Chief Justice Marshall, who wrote the Court's opinion, to conclude that a grant is a contract. In Marshall's view, Georgia's original grant of land carried with it an implied contractual obligation not to assert a right to reclaim the land. Once this land passed into the hands of "innocent third parties" who bought it from the original purchasers, the state could not repeal the original sale, even if it could be proved that the initial grant had been obtained by bribing members of the legislature. As Marshall and his colleagues saw it, "absolute rights" had been established under the contract; that is, they had become "vested" in the subsequent purchasers. But because the state itself was a party to the contract, how could its obligations be enforced? In Marshall's view, Georgia had a moral obligation accorded the status of law, but he was equivocal as to the ultimate source of legal authority. He concluded that Georgia was "restrained" from passing the rescinding act "either by general principles, which are common to our free institutions, or by the particular provisions of the Constitution of the United States." This ambivalence underscores the continuing influence of the "natural rights" approach adopted by Justice Chase in *Calder v. Bull*. Whereas Marshall at least recognized the appropriateness of applying constitutional provisions to protect contractual obligations, Justice William Johnson, in a concurring opinion, opted for the "natural justice" approach exclusively:

> I do not hesitate to declare that a state does not possess the power of revoking its own grants. But I do it on a general principle on the reason and nature of things, a principle which will impose laws even on the deity. . . .

The Dartmouth College Case

Fletcher v. Peck greatly broadened the scope and potential application of the Contract Clause. But the Court's decision nine years later in *Dartmouth College v. Woodward* (1819) had far greater influence on economic development in the nineteenth-century United States. The Court held in essence that a corporate charter was a contract, the terms of which could not be changed materially by the state without violating the Constitution. The charter in question had been issued in 1769 by the British crown for the creation of Dartmouth College. This corporate charter authorized a self-perpetuating twelve-member board of trustees to govern the college. With the American Revolution, the state of New Hampshire succeeded to the rights and obligations of the crown provided by the charter. The college soon became embroiled in state politics, leading to an attempt in 1816 to convert it from a private institution into a state university. This objective was to be accomplished by placing the college under a board of overseers appointed by the governor pursuant to state legislation. The ousted trustees sued to recover the charter, seal, and records of the college and in this way directly challenged the authority of New Hampshire to enact the legislation. Again speaking for the Court, Chief Justice Marshall determined that the charter was a valid contract and that the legislature's attempt to modify the governing structure of the college violated Article I, Section 10, of the Constitution. No specific language in the original charter required this rigid limitation on the state's power to amend it almost half a century after the charter was granted by King George III and at a time when none of the original parties to the contract remained on the scene. Nevertheless, Marshall found that the challenged legislation violated the spirit if not the letter of the Contract Clause. Marshall indicated that any ambiguity in the charter should be construed in favor of "the adventurers" and against the state.

Although Dartmouth College was created as a charitable educational institution, the broad principle that Marshall enunciated in this case was soon applied to profit-seeking corporations. The *Dartmouth College* decision came at a time when business corporations in such fields as insurance, canal building, and road construction were beginning to proliferate. These companies and their financial backers were tangibly aided by an interpretation of the Contract Clause that gave corporate charters firm constitutional protection.

The Marshall Court also interpreted the Contract Clause as a protection of creditor interests against some forms of state regulation. In the same year that it decided the *Dartmouth College* case, the Court, in *Sturges v. Crowninshield* (1819), struck down a New York bankruptcy law under which debtors could obtain relief from financial obligations previously incurred. Speaking through Marshall once again, the Court found that this measure amounted to an impairment of the obligation of contracts. Marshall himself went so far as to assert, eight years later, that the Contract Clause barred state bankruptcy laws that applied to debts incurred *after* their passage. But on this occasion, the legislation was upheld by a majority of his brethren, leaving Marshall to record his only dissenting opinion in a constitutional case (*Ogden v. Saunders,* 1827).

The Contribution of the Taney Court

In spite of the expanded protection of property and business interests through early interpretation of the Contract Clause, the demand for state economic regulation continued to grow. As noted in Chapter 5, the Marshall Court itself began to provide limited recognition to the state police power, and Marshall's successor, Roger B. Taney, significantly extended this recognition. The *Dartmouth College* case logically implied that corporations chartered by the state could conduct their business free of governmental regulation. This *laissez-faire* approach could not survive for long, even in the preindustrial United States of the early nineteenth century. Counterpressures, reflected in the rise of Jacksonian democracy, were too strong to permit the continuation of such limitations on state regulatory power.

The judicial pendulum began to swing back in the other direction with the Taney Court's 1837 decision in the case of *Charles River Bridge Company v. Warren Bridge Company*. In 1785, the Massachusetts legislature had granted a corporate charter to the Charles River Bridge Company that authorized it to build a privately owned bridge between Boston and Charlestown and to collect tolls from persons using the bridge. This highly profitable arrangement, granted for a period of seventy years, was threatened by the legislature's incorporation of the Warren Bridge Company in 1828 with authorization to build a competing bridge nearby. Within a short time, the bridge built by Warren Bridge was to become free to the public as a part of the Massachusetts highway system. The Charles River Bridge Company challenged the 1828 act as a violation of the 1785 charter, which allegedly implied "that the legislature would not authorize another bridge, and especially a free one," alongside the original bridge. Rejecting this contention, Chief Justice Taney construed the language of the charter literally. He concluded that no rights were "taken from the public, or given to the corporation, beyond those which the words of the charter, by their natural and proper construction, [purported] to convey." By contrast with Marshall's approach in the *Dartmouth College* case, Taney was unwilling to restrict legislative authority on the basis of implicit contractual rights. The Court's position was effectively summed up in Taney's assertion that "[w]hile the rights of private property are sacredly guarded, we must not forget that the community also have rights, and that the happiness and well-being of every citizen depends on their faithful preservation."

Later Developments

The decline of the Contract Clause as a bulwark of **vested rights** began with the *Charles River Bridge* case. Some forty years later, in *Stone v. Mississippi* (1880), the Supreme Court refused to extend Contract Clause protection to a chartered lottery company subsequently prohibited from selling lottery tickets in Mississippi. By the late 1880s, the **Due Process Clause of the Fourteenth Amendment** had supplanted the Contract Clause as a source of constitutional restraint on state regulation of business.

The extent of the demise of the Contract Clause in the twentieth century is well illustrated by the decision in the Minnesota mortgage moratorium case (*Home Building and Loan Association v. Blaisdell* [1934]). Here, by a 5-to-4 vote, the Court upheld a state law, passed in 1933 in the depths of the Great Depression, that authorized the postponement of mortgage foreclosures for periods not to extend beyond May 1, 1935. Chief Justice Charles Evans Hughes, writing for the majority, emphasized the qualified nature of the Contract Clause as a limitation on state power. He concluded that "the reservation of the reasonable exercise of the protective power of the state is read into all contracts."

In summary, the Contract Clause figured prominently in the Supreme Court's protection of vested property rights during the early part of the nineteenth century. Although its influence began to be undermined by the expanding doctrine of state police power during the Taney era, the Contract Clause remained a significant weapon in defense of property interests until supplanted by the development of **substantive due process** in the late 1800s. The Supreme Court invoked the Contract Clause in invalidating state legislation in some seventy-five cases prior to 1890. But the Contract Clause has not been a major restraint on state regulatory power for more than a century. Nevertheless, it is not a dead letter and is still occasionally invoked as a constitutional limitation. For example, in 1977, the Court held that a New Jersey statute violated the Contract Clause because it impaired the state's obligation to holders of bonds issued by the Port Authority of New York and New Jersey (*United States Trust Company v. New Jersey*). Similarly, in *Allied Structural Steel Company v. Spannaus* (1978), the Court invalidated under the Contract Clause Minnesota's attempt to regulate a company's pension fund. Writing for a five-member majority, Justice Stewart observed: "If the Contract Clause is to retain any meaning at all, . . . it must be understood to impose *some* limits on the power of a State to abridge existing contractual relationships. . ." [emphasis in the original].

TO SUMMARIZE

- During the Marshall era (1801–1835), the Contract Clause of Article I, Section 10, served as a significant limitation on state interference with private property rights. In particular, John Marshall's opinion for the Court in *Dartmouth College v. Woodward* (1819), which recognized that corporate charters were protected by the Contract Clause, had great influence on nineteenth-century economic development.
- With the rise of the state police power during the Taney era (1836–1864), the Court began to narrow the scope of protection afforded by the Contract Clause. In the pivotal case of *Charles River Bridge Co. v. Warren Bridge Co.* (1837), Chief Justice Taney effectively subordinated traditional contract rights to the interests of the community in a rapidly changing society.
- By the time of the Great Depression, as illustrated by the Court's decision in *Home Building and Loan Association v. Blaisdell* (1934), the Contract Clause no longer stood as a significant impediment to state regulatory power in the economic realm. This remains true today despite occasional recent efforts to resuscitate the more conservative interpretation of the Contract Clause.

THE RISE AND FALL OF ECONOMIC DUE PROCESS

State police power continued to develop through the Civil War and Reconstruction, but the protection of property rights, especially in the context of business activity, remained a prime concern of American judges, including members of the U.S. Supreme Court. Due process as a substantive limitation on governmental authority began to emerge in the 1850s, but its potential was not fully realized until some years after adoption of the Fourteenth Amendment. With the exception of the *Dred Scott* case, in which congressional regulation of slavery in the territories was held to deprive slave owners of property without due process of law (see Chapter 1), the **Fifth Amendment Due Process Clause** was not invoked, prior to the Civil War, as a substantive limitation on federal authority. This is not surprising, since the national government did not play an active role in the field of economic regulation until very late in the nineteenth century.

Origins of Substantive Due Process

It is generally agreed that substantive due process as a limitation on *state* economic regulation originated in an 1856 decision of the New York Court of Appeals (the state's highest court). In *Wynehamer v. New York,* that court held that a state criminal statute prohibiting the sale of liquor curtailed the economic liberty of a Buffalo tavern owner who had been prosecuted for violating its provisions. The court of appeals held that the state police power could not be used to deprive the tavern owner of his liberty to practice his livelihood, a liberty protected by the due process clause of the New York constitution.

Following adoption of the Fourteenth Amendment, lawyers representing business interests in opposition to growing state regulation began to emphasize substantive due process arguments. These arguments drew heavily on an influential legal treatise entitled *Constitutional Limitations,* written by a Michigan judge, Thomas M. Cooley. First published in 1868, the year in which the Fourteenth Amendment was ratified, Cooley's treatise went through several editions in the late

Stephen J. Field: Associate
Justice, 1863—1897

1800s and had a significant impact on the constitutional jurisprudence of the *laissez-faire* era.

As noted in previous chapters, substantive due process focuses on the reasonableness of legislation. By contrast with the more familiar procedural aspect, which emphasizes such elements as notice and the right to a fair hearing (in other words, *how* government should operate in relation to the individual), substantive due process stresses *what* government may or may not do.

Early Supreme Court Resistance to Economic Due Process

For a number of years following the adoption of the Fourteenth Amendment, most members of the Supreme Court resisted the **economic due process** approach. Thus, in *The Slaughter-house Cases* (1873), a narrowly divided Court upheld Louisiana's grant of a monopoly in the slaughtering business in and around New Orleans. Although officially designated as "An Act to Protect the Health of the City of New Orleans," the law was not in any meaningful sense a health measure. Its only apparent effect was to deprive more than a thousand persons of their right to engage in the slaughtering trade. A number of these persons filed suit, maintaining that the state had conferred "odious and exclusive privileges upon a small number of persons at the expense of the great body of the community of New Orleans."

In rejecting this contention, the Supreme Court, in an opinion by Justice Samuel F. Miller, narrowly interpreted Fourteenth Amendment restrictions on state authority. Miller virtually read out of the Fourteenth Amendment the provision that says: "No state shall make or enforce any law which shall abridge the privileges or immunities of citizens of the United States. . . ." This language, he said, extended only to rights held by Americans as citizens of the nation, as distinguished from their rights as state citizens.

In addition to this restrictive view of the Privileges and Immunities Clause, Justice Miller also found no deprivation of rights under the Due Process and Equal Protection Clauses. He identified the central purpose of the Fourteenth Amendment as the protection of the civil rights of former slaves, although he was unwilling to say that no one else was entitled to this protection. In a strong dissenting opinion, Justice Stephen J. Field took issue with Miller's narrow interpretation of the Privileges and Immunities Clause: "The privileges and immunities designated," he maintained, "are those which of right belong to the citizens of all free governments." To this day, however, the Court has not been willing to accept the broader interpretation of the Privileges and Immunities Clause that Miller gave it in *The Slaughter-house Cases*. Such an interpretation, as a number of scholars have suggested, might have enabled the Court to develop a more plausible basis for protecting property rights than that provided by the Due Process Clause. Of more immediate relevance in light of subsequent developments is the dissenting opinion of Justice Joseph L. Bradley. While agreeing with Field's position regarding the broad protection that should be afforded by the Privileges and Immunities Clause, Bradley went one important step further, by expressing the view that

a law which prohibits a large class of citizens from adopting a lawful employment previously adopted, does deprive them of liberty as well as property, without due process of law. Their right of choice is a portion of their liberty; their occupation is their property.

Morrison Waite: Chief Justice, 1874–1888

"Business Affected with a Public Interest"

Four years later, the Court again sustained a broad exercise of the state police power, in this instance an act of the Illinois legislature fixing maximum storage rates charged by grain elevators and public warehouses and requiring licenses to operate these facilities. This legislation grew out of the granger movement, in which thousands of farmers sought protection against excessive freight rates charged by railroads and other businesses involved in the distribution of agricultural commodities. Chief Justice Morrison R. Waite, writing for a seven-member majority in *Munn v. Illinois* (1877), sustained the rate regulation under the English common law doctrine of **business affected with a public interest.** Like common carriers, innkeepers, and other persons directly serving the public, Waite reasoned, the owners of grain elevators were equally subject to regulation under this standard. Sounding a note that aroused the anger of business leaders, Waite acknowledged that such regulatory power was subject to abuse but admonished that, in such instances, "the people must resort to the polls, and not to the courts."

Dissenting in *Munn,* Justice Field contended that the regulation violated due process. He maintained that under our system of government, the legislature lacked power "to fix the price which anyone shall receive for his property of any kind." He also argued that "there is hardly any enterprise or business engaging the attention and labor of any considerable portion of the community in which the public has not an interest in the sense in which that term is used by the Court." This was a prescient observation in view of the Court's rejection, almost half a century later, of the distinction between "private" businesses and those "affected with a public interest" (*Nebbia v. New York* [1934]).

Ironically, once the concept of substantive due process came to be recognized by a court majority as a basis for invalidating economic legislation, the Court began to apply Waite's rationale negatively. For example, regulations of labor-management disputes, theater ticket scalping, and the rates charged by private employment agencies were ruled unconstitutional on the ground that the businesses involved were not "affected with a public interest" (see, for example, *Charles Wolff Packing Company v. Court of Industrial Relations* [1923], *Tyson v. Banton* [1927], and *Ribnik v. McBride* [1928]).

The Court Reflects Growing Corporate Influence

Powerful corporate interests reacted sharply and decisively to the *Munn* decision. In fact, the American Bar Association was organized for the immediate purpose of leading the counterattack. In 1882, former Senator Roscoe Conkling, in an argument before the Supreme Court, unveiled his "conspiracy theory" of the Fourteenth Amendment. Conkling had participated as a member of the joint congressional committee that drafted the Fourteenth Amendment in 1866. Referring selectively to a previously undisclosed journal of committee proceedings, Conkling maintained in essence that those who drafted the amendment intended for the word "person," as used in the Equal Protection and Due Process clauses, to include corporations. Later research established that Conkling's "conspiracy theory" was of dubious validity, if not an outright fraud. But in the 1880s, the theory was eagerly received and widely supported by those who sought to justify the protection of economic rights under the Fourteenth Amendment. In 1886, the Supreme Court announced without discussion that the Equal Protection Clause did apply to corporations (*Santa Clara County v. Southern Pacific Railroad*). This conclusion extended logically to the Due Process Clause as well.

Changes in Supreme Court personnel also influenced the shift toward economic due process. Chief Justice Waite, who had written the majority opinion in the *Munn* case, died in 1888 and was succeeded by Melville W. Fuller. In 1890, David J. Brewer, a nephew of Justice Field, took the seat on the high bench vacated by Justice Stanley Matthews. These and other appointees, drawn largely from the ranks of corporation lawyers, were receptive to the limited government approach implicit in substantive due process. During this period, under the leadership of Chief Justice Fuller, the Court significantly curtailed national authority through a restrictive interpretation of the commerce and taxing powers (see Chapter 2). Theories of economic individualism, especially the **social Darwinism** of Herbert Spencer and William Graham Sumner, were very much in vogue during the period and obviously had some impact on the justices.

The Court's changing mood was signaled clearly by Justice John Marshall Harlan (the elder) in 1887. Writing for the Court in upholding a Kansas law prohibiting the sale of certain alcoholic beverages, he warned that not all exercises of the state police power would be automatically approved: "The Courts are not bound by mere forms, nor are they to be misled by mere pretenses. They are at liberty—indeed, are under a solemn duty—to look at the substance of things" (*Mugler v. Kansas* [1887]).

Economic Due Process Comes of Age

The first major shift in the Court's position came in 1890 with the decision that a state legislature could not authorize a commission to set railroad rates with finality. Such rate making, the Court concluded, must be subject to judicial review (*Chicago, Milwaukee, & St. Paul Railway Company v. Minnesota*). In 1897, the Court invalidated Louisiana's effort to regulate out-of-state insurance companies transacting business in the state. Writing for the Court, Justice Rufus Peckham found this regulation to be an infringement of the **liberty of contract** protected by the Fourteenth Amendment Due Process Clause (*Allgeyer v. Louisiana* [1897]). ("Liberty of contract," as used by the Court in this and many subsequent due process cases, should not be confused with the Contract Clause of Article I, Section 10, discussed earlier in this chapter.)

Lochner v. New York: The Apotheosis of Economic Due Process

Justice Peckham used the same rationale eight years later in what has become the best known case of the early twentieth century: *Lochner v. New York* (1905). In *Lochner,* the Court, dividing 5 to 4, struck down a state law specifying a maximum sixty-hour workweek for bakery employees. Seven years earlier, the Court had upheld, as a proper exercise of the police power, an act of the Utah legislature establishing an eight-hour workday for employees in "mines . . . smelters and all other institutions for the reduction or refining of ores or metals. . ." (*Holden v. Hardy* [1898]). The Utah statute was recognized as a reasonable health measure, but the

During the late nineteenth and early twentieth centuries, workers often labored for long hours at low wages under oppressive conditions

majority in *Lochner* found no such justification for limiting working hours "in the occupation of a baker." "To the common understanding," Peckham opined, "the trade of a baker has never been regarded as an unhealthy one." However, the Court's fundamental objection to the legislation was that it was a "meddlesome interference" with business. The majority gave no consideration to the relative bargaining power of employers and employees in the baking industry. They simply regarded the law as an unjustified infringement on "the right to labor, and with the right of free contract on the part of the individual, either as employer or employee."

Justice Harlan and his celebrated colleague Oliver Wendell Holmes, Jr., filed powerful dissenting opinions in the *Lochner* case. While Harlan pursued a conventional line of analysis, Justice Holmes attacked the majority for reading *laissez-faire* theory into the Constitution:

> This case is decided upon an economic theory which a large part of the country does not entertain. If it were a question whether I agreed with that theory, I should desire to study it further and long before making up my mind. But I do not conceive that to be my duty, because I strongly believe that my agreement or disagreement has nothing to do with the right of a majority to embody their opinions in law. . . . The Fourteenth Amendment does not enact Mr. Herbert Spencer's *Social Statics*.

The Heyday of Economic Due Process

Although the philosophical perspective underlying the *Lochner* ruling remained influential for a number of years, its practical effect was short-lived. In 1908, the Court upheld an Oregon act limiting the workday to ten hours for women in designated occupational fields (*Muller v. Oregon*). In this case, attorney (later Associate Justice) Louis D. Brandeis submitted a novel brief in support of the legislation, presenting extensive sociological and medical data in support of the state's contention that the limitation of working hours was directly related to the promotion of the health and welfare of women. The **Brandeis brief,** which added a new dimension to constitutional argumentation, underscored the relationship between legal principles and research in the social and biological sciences. Following the *Muller* precedent, the Court in 1917 sustained the constitutionality of a maximum-hours limitation for men as well as women employed in mills and factories (*Bunting v. Oregon*). This decision amounted to the *de facto* overruling of *Lochner*, but the Court did not specifically refer to the latter case.

The Court's willingness to sustain maximum-hours laws did not carry over into other areas of labor legislation. A federal law outlawing **yellow dog contracts** (employment contracts in which workers agree not to join unions) was invalidated in 1908 as a violation of the Due Process Clause of the Fifth Amendment (*Adair v. United States*). Seven years later, in *Coppage v. Kansas* (1915), the Court voided a similar state provision as a violation of the freedom of contract protected by the Fourteenth Amendment. In these cases, the Court seemed unconcerned with the blatant inequality in the bargaining positions of individual nonunion employees and corporate employers. Indeed, in the Court's view, it was unreasonable for the legislature to interfere with the "natural order" of inequalities, no matter how great the resulting disparities between employer and employee.

Wages proved to be as invulnerable to legislative regulation as yellow dog contracts. Thus, in 1923 a divided Court struck down a congressional measure authorizing the setting of minimum wages for women and minors employed in the District of Columbia (*Adkins v. Children's Hospital*). The stated purposes of the minimum wage were to provide women with " 'the necessary cost of living,' . . . to maintain them in good health and to protect their morals." As in *Lochner*, the government's perceived interference with liberty of contract was held to violate due process—in this instance, the Fifth Amendment's restriction on federal authority. Writing for the majority, Justice George Sutherland noted that the law was demeaning to women, especially in light of the drive toward political equality that had resulted, shortly before this decision, in ratification of the Nineteenth Amendment, which removed sex as a qualification for voting. But the real object of Sutherland's concern is unmistakably apparent from the following excerpt from his majority opinion:

> The law takes account of the necessities of only one party to the contract. It ignores the necessities of the employer by compelling him to pay not less than a certain sum, not only whether the employee is capable of earning it, but irrespective of the ability of his business to sustain the burden, generously leaving him, of course, the privilege of abandoning his business as an alternative of going on at a loss. . . .

During the 1920s, Chief Justice William Howard Taft often supported the Court's limitation of regulatory authority by way of substantive due process (see, for example, his majority opinion in *Charles Wolff Packing Company v. Court of Industrial Relations* [1923]). However, Taft dissented in the *Adkins* case. In an opinion supported by Justice Edward T. Sanford, Taft expressed his belief that because no meaningful distinction could be drawn between minimum-wage and maximum-hours legislation and since the latter had been upheld in the *Muller* and *Bunting* cases, the Washington, D.C., minimum wage should be sustained. This view was further supported, he maintained, by the fact that the law upheld in *Bunting* contained a time-and-a-half provision for overtime pay. He emphasized, moreover, that "it is not the function of this Court to hold congressional acts invalid simply because they are passed to carry out economic views which the Court believes to be unwise or unsound."

Justice Holmes wrote a separate dissenting opinion, asserting that the power of Congress to enact minimum-wage legislation seemed "absolutely free from doubt." Holmes criticized sharply the Court's development of what he called the "dogma" of liberty of contract. The word *contract,* he pointed out, is not mentioned in the Due Process Clause. Holmes viewed contract merely as "an example of doing what you want to do, embodied in the word liberty. But pretty much all law," he added, "consists in forbidding men to do some things that they want to do, and contract is no more exempt from law than other acts."

Substantive due process as a restriction on economic legislation continued to flourish through the 1920s and into the 1930s. It was an integral part of the Supreme Court's intellectual defense of business interests in general. This judicial philosophy also produced a number of rulings limiting the application of the antitrust acts as restrictions on corporate behavior while extending these restrictions to such labor practices as strikes and secondary boycotts (see, for example, *Loewe v. Lawlor* [1908], *Duplex Printing Company v. Deering* [1921], and *Bedford Cut Stone Company v. Journeymen Stone Cutters' Association* [1927]). The Court strongly resisted efforts during this period to restrict child labor and to regulate agricultural and industrial production. Apparently economic liberties, although not officially designated as "preferred freedoms," were accorded paramount importance and often prevailed over countervailing demands for socioeconomic regulation.

Patterns of Supreme Court decision making, especially in complex areas of constitutional law, often do not follow unwavering lines of analytical precision or logical consistency. As we have noted, during the period marked by such decisions as *Lochner* and *Adkins,* the Court did not always invalidate challenged regulatory legislation. The Court still adhered (officially, at least) to the principle of the presumptive validity of legislation and, as a result, many regulatory measures were upheld during the heyday of economic due process. Nevertheless, enough state and federal measures were invalidated to retard serious efforts at economic and social reform.

The Decline of Economic Due Process

The Great Depression of the 1930s, with its crippling effect on employment, industrial production, and the economic well-being of millions of people, forced the Supreme Court to rethink its constitutional commitment to limited government in the field of economic policy. It did so in a variety of issue areas between the mid-1930s and the early 1940s. With this reappraisal came the Court's repudiation of substantive due process as a restriction on the regulation of business.

This fundamental change in the Court's posture was signaled by two key decisions in 1934. As previously indicated, in that year, the Court upheld the Minnesota Mortgage Moratorium Act, finding that its provisions did not violate the Contract Clause (*Home Building and Loan Association v. Blaisdell*). Although this decision did not turn on the meaning of due process, its implications for the Court's interpretation of liberty of contract under the Fifth and Fourteenth Amendments were unmistakable.

The due process issue was confronted directly in *Nebbia v. New York* (1934), in which the Court upheld by a 5-to-4 margin the power of a state to regulate the retail price of milk. Concluding that this price regulation did not violate due process, Justice Owen J. Roberts emphasized the breadth of legislative power in relation to economic matters: "It is clear that there is no closed class or category of businesses

A Depression-era soup line

affected with a public interest." Since the *Munn* case, the Court had gradually narrowed the category of businesses thus "affected" and had established a substantial constitutional barrier against state regulation in a number of areas. In fact, during the decade or so immediately prior to the *Nebbia* decision, very few businesses other than public utilities and places of public accommodation were subject to price control with full judicial approval. Consequently, the Court's obliteration of the category of "business affected with a public interest" represented a significant turning point in constitutional development. In effect, the Court was saying in *Nebbia* that all businesses, irrespective of their supposed relationship to the public interest, are subject to regulation.

This stern repudiation of judicial activism in the field of economic liberties drew a scathing dissent from Justice James C. McReynolds, supported by Justices Willis Van Devanter, George Sutherland, and Pierce Butler. The fixing of retail prices as a means of stabilizing production was, in McReynolds's view, "not regulation, but management, control, dictation," amounting to "deprivation of the fundamental right which one has to conduct his own affairs honestly and along customary lines." He strongly suggested that the Court's decision amounted to a declaration that "rights guaranteed by the Constitution exist only so long as supposed public interest does not require their extinction." McReynolds asserted that adoption of this view "would put an end to liberty under the Constitution."

The "end to liberty" feared by Justice McReynolds was postponed in the field of economic rights for another three years. In fact, in 1936, the Court reaffirmed its controversial *Adkins* ruling by striking down a New York minimum-wage law for women (*Morehead v. New York ex rel. Tipaldo*). In this decision, the majority simply reiterated the "liberty of contract" rationale, but the decision was given added significance because it coincided with the Court's invalidation of major New Deal legislation (see, for example, *United States v. Butler* [1936] and *Carter v. Carter*

Coal Company [1936], which is discussed and reprinted in Chapter 2). In seeking Supreme Court review of a New York Court of Appeals decision invalidating this minimum-wage statute, attorneys failed to ask specifically for reconsideration of the *Adkins* precedent. Rather, they sought to distinguish the New York minimum-wage law from the congressional act invalidated in *Adkins*. Writing for a five-member majority, Justice Butler seized on this omission and considered only the question of whether the two cases were distinguishable. He found that they were not and thus struck down the New York law.

In dissenting opinions, Chief Justice Charles Evans Hughes and Justice Harlan Fiske Stone (supported by Justices Brandeis and Benjamin Cardozo) maintained that the two laws were, in fact, distinguishable. More significantly, however, they criticized the Court for its refusal to reconsider the validity of *Adkins*, especially in light of the country's experience during the Great Depression. Justice Stone chastised his colleagues in the majority for reading their own economic views into the Constitution.

It is not for the courts to resolve doubts about whether the remedy by wage regulation is as efficacious as many believe, or is better than some other, or is better even than the blind operation of uncontrolled economic forces. The legislature must be free to choose unless government is to be rendered impotent. The Fourteenth Amendment has no more embedded in the Constitution our preference for some particular set of economic beliefs than it has adopted, in the name of liberty, the system of theology that we may happen to approve.

West Coast Hotel Company v. Parrish: A Sudden Turnaround

Ten months later, the Supreme Court, again by a 5-to-4 vote (Justice Roberts having changed sides), dramatically overruled the *Adkins* and *Tipaldo* decisions in *West Coast Hotel Company v. Parrish* (1937). Although the votes of the justices had occurred in conference several weeks before President Franklin Roosevelt unveiled his controversial Court-packing plan on February 5, 1937, most political observers and the public in general regarded the *Parrish* decision, announced on March 29, as a clear indication that the Court had caved in to pressure from a popular presidential administration. Justice Roberts later claimed he had voted with the majority in *Tipaldo* simply because he believed that the only question presented in that case was whether the New York minimum-wage law could be distinguished from the provision struck down in *Adkins*. Whatever the true motivations of Justice Roberts, his change of position in this and several other major constitutional decisions in the spring of 1937 figured prominently in the constitutional revolution that to this day marks the single most important transition in Supreme Court history.

In *West Coast Hotel Company v. Parrish*, the Court considered the constitutionality of a Washington State minimum-wage law enacted in 1913. Chief Justice Hughes delivered the majority opinion. He noted that in upholding the minimum wage, the Washington Supreme Court had "refused to regard the decision in the *Adkins* case as determinative." Such a ruling, Hughes declared, "demands on our part a reexamination" of the *Adkins* case. This reexamination began with the dismantling of the liberty of contract doctrine on which *Adkins* was based. Hughes pointed out that this freedom is not absolute. Moreover, "the liberty safeguarded is liberty in a social organization which requires the protection of law against the evils which menace the health, safety, morals, and welfare of the people." Thus, constitutional liberty is "necessarily subject to the restraints of due process, and regulation which is reasonable in relation to its subject and is adopted in the interests of the community is due process."

Hughes enumerated a wide array of state laws in the field of employer–employee relations previously upheld by the Supreme Court. Then, after quoting approvingly from the dissenting opinions of Chief Justice Taft and Justice Holmes in *Adkins,* he branded that decision as "a departure from the true application of the principles governing the regulation by the state of the relation of employer and employed."

In further support of the formal overruling of *Adkins* and in repudiation of the philosophy it represented, Hughes took judicial notice of "the unparalleled demands for relief" arising during the Great Depression and still very much in evidence at the time of this decision. Interestingly, no Brandeis brief had been filed in the *Parrish* case, primarily because this approach had failed in the *Tipaldo* case the previous year. Acknowledging the absence in the record of statistical data establishing the need for minimum-wage legislation, Hughes nevertheless had no doubt, based on "common knowledge," that the state of Washington had "encountered the same social problem . . . present elsewhere." The state, he concluded, was free to correct the abusive practices of "unconscionable employers" who selfishly disregard the public interest.

West Coast Hotel Company v. Parrish marked the end of an era in American constitutional law. Although the fact might not have been fully recognized at the time, substantive due process as a limitation on governmental power in the field of economic regulation was dead. Justice Sutherland, the author of the *Adkins* majority opinion, sounded a defensive, subdued note in a dissenting opinion. For him, the Constitution had a fixed meaning that did not change "with the ebb and flow of economic events." He attempted, with little success, to distinguish between the "judicial function" of constitutional interpretation and "the power of amendment under the guise of interpretation." "To miss the point of difference between the two," he said, "is to miss all that the phrase 'supreme law of the land' stands for and to convert what was intended as inescapable and enduring mandates into mere moral reflections." That was precisely what the critics of the *Lochner-Adkins-Tipaldo* approach charged that the Court had been doing. But Sutherland insisted that

> [i]f the Constitution, intelligently and reasonably construed in the light of these principles, stands in the way of desirable legislation, the blame must rest upon that instrument, and not upon the Court for enforcing it according to its terms.

Personnel changes, beginning only a few months after announcement of the *Parrish* decision, soon resulted in the replacement of all four dissenting justices in that case. The newly constituted "Roosevelt Court" continued the trend begun in *Parrish* and in other 1937 decisions upholding far-reaching economic and social legislation (see, for example, *National Labor Relations Board v. Jones & Laughlin Steel Corporation* [1937] and *Steward Machine Company v. Davis* [1937], both of which are discussed and reprinted in Chapter 2). In 1939, the Court upheld the second Agricultural Adjustment Act (*Mulford v. Smith*), and in 1941, it sustained sweeping federal regulatory power in the areas of employer–employee relations by sustaining the Fair Labor Standards Act (*United States v. Darby,* reprinted in Chapter 2). The constitutional revolution begun by the *Parrish* case in 1937 thus applied directly not only to due process interpretation but also to other key provisions of the Constitution, including the Commerce Clause, the taxing and spending power, and the Tenth Amendment.

The Court Gives Carte Blanche to Legislatures in the Economic Regulation Field

For more than half a century, no significant state or federal regulation of business or labor-management relations has been struck down on due process grounds. The 1963 decision in *Ferguson v. Skrupa* is representative of the modern approach in this area. Here, the Supreme Court, in an opinion by Justice Hugo Black, upheld the validity of a Kansas statute conferring a virtual monopoly on the legal profession to engage in the business of "debt adjusting." Black noted that the doctrine prevailing in the *Lochner-Coppage-Adkins* line of cases authorizing courts to invalidate laws because of a belief that the legislature acted unwisely "has long since been discarded." The Court, he continued, had "returned to the original constitutional proposition that courts do not substitute their social and economic beliefs for the judgment of legislative bodies, who are elected to pass laws." Once again, we see how the "original" meaning of the Constitution can mean diametrically opposing things to various Supreme Court justices. In any event, for Justice Black, objections to the law on grounds of social utility should be addressed by the legislature, not the courts. "Whether the legislature takes for its textbook Adam Smith, Herbert Spencer, Lord Keynes, or some other," Black concluded, "is no concern of ours." He also found no violation of the Equal Protection Clause of the Fourteenth Amendment in the legislative decision to provide lawyers a monopoly in the field of debt adjusting.

For the most part, the Supreme Court during the last four decades has followed the approach taken in the *Skrupa* case. Substantive due process has virtually disappeared as a barrier to economic policy making by Congress and state legislatures. However, as a constitutional doctrine, substantive due process is anything but dead. It lives on in recent Court decisions recognizing various noneconomic rights under the Fifth and Fourteenth Amendments, especially the constitutional right of privacy (see Chapter 11).

TO SUMMARIZE:

- In the late nineteenth century, as the Supreme Court came under the influence of social Darwinism and the economic doctrine of *laissez-faire*, the Due Process Clause of the Fourteenth Amendment served as the basis for invalidating state economic regulation. The Court developed a substantive interpretation of due process in which "liberty of contract" prevailed over competing claims based on state police power. In the leading case of *Lochner v. New York* (1905), a sharply divided Court followed this approach in striking down a New York law limiting working hours in bakeries. Critics of this decision argued that the Court was merely reading its own economic theory into the Constitution.
- After three decades in which the Court used the liberty of contract doctrine to invalidate numerous state laws dealing with conditions of employment and related matters, the Court finally yielded to political pressures stemming from the Great Depression and the New Deal. In *West Coast Hotel Company v. Parrish* (1937), the Court overturned precedent in upholding a state law establishing a minimum wage for working women.
- Since 1937 the Supreme Court has steadfastly refused to invoke the Due Process Clause as a substantive limitation on the power of government to regulate the economy.

EQUAL PROTECTION AND ECONOMIC REGULATION

Our discussion has thus far focused on the substantive interpretation of due process in the protection of private enterprise. Note, however, that during the heyday of economic due process, the Court occasionally read similar protections into the **Equal Protection Clause** of the Fourteenth Amendment. For example, in *Yick Wo v. Hopkins* (1886), the Court invalidated a San Francisco ordinance requiring owners of laundries housed in wooden buildings to obtain permission from the Board of Supervisors to continue operation of their businesses. The Court found that the ordinance was being administered to the serious detriment of Chinese immigrants. Whereas all of the affected Chinese laundry owners were denied licenses by the Board of Supervisors, nearly all non-Chinese applicants were granted licenses. Writing for the Court, Justice Stanley Matthews observed: "No reason whatever, except the will of the Supervisors, is assigned why they [the Chinese laundry owners] should not be permitted to carry on, in the accustomed manner, their harmless and useful occupation, on which they depend for a livelihood."

Similarly, in 1915, the Court struck down an Arizona law requiring that a minimum of 80 percent of any company's workforce had to consist of American citizens (*Truax v. Raich*). In these cases, the Court was especially concerned with the adverse impact of discriminatory legislation on the conduct of business.

Equal protection, like due process, disappeared as an important limitation on state economic regulatory power after the mid-1930s. It was used, however, in the late 1950s, to strike down a provision of an Illinois law exempting the American Express Company from the requirement that any firm selling or issuing money orders in the state obtain a license and submit to state regulation (*Morey v. Doud* [1957]). The effect of the discrimination here was not reasonably related to the underlying regulatory purpose of the statute. This ruling is an isolated exception to the modern Court's unwillingness to invalidate economic regulation on Fourteenth Amendment grounds.

TO SUMMARIZE:

- During the age of conservative activism, the Court on occasion also used the Equal Protection Clause of the Fourteenth Amendment to limit state economic regulation. In the post–New Deal era, equal protection, like due process, has virtually disappeared as a restraint on state regulatory power in this area.

PROPERTY RIGHTS AND THE "TAKINGS" ISSUE

The final provision of the Fifth Amendment states "nor shall private property be taken for public use without just compensation." In *Barron v. Baltimore* (1833), the Supreme Court held that the **Just Compensation Clause,** like the other provisions of the Bill of Rights, was applicable only to the acts and policies of the national government. However, in 1897, this clause became the first provision of the Bill of Rights to be incorporated into the Fourteenth Amendment and thus made applicable to the states (*Chicago, Burlington, & Quincy Railroad v. Chicago*). (For further discussion of the **incorporation doctrine** and these important cases, see Chapter 6.) The salient legal questions raised by the Just Compensation Clause are these: (1) What constitutes a "taking" of private property? (2) What constitutes a "public use"? and (3) What constitutes "just compensation"?

Although the "takings" concept has sometimes been interpreted literally to refer only to a physical appropriation of private property by the government, there are circumstances in which a regulation may be so severe as to constitute a **taking.** The basic problem is to determine the point at which a regulation goes beyond the legitimate scope of the police power and becomes an exercise of the power of **eminent domain.** The dominant view is that the distinction between a valid regulation and the taking of property is one of degree. Justice Holmes stated this rule in the 1922 case of *Pennsylvania Coal Company v. Mahon.* Under a duly executed deed, the coal company claimed rights to mine coal under the land on which Mahon's dwelling was located. Mahon claimed, however, that irrespective of the deed, these rights were superseded by a Pennsylvania statute preventing the mining of coal in such a way as to cause the subsidence of specified types of improved land, including that on which his house was located. The issue was whether this exercise of the state's police power amounted to a "taking" of the coal company's property without just compensation. Writing for the Court, Holmes concluded that it did, and that the company was entitled to compensation. "The general rule," he declared, "is that while property may be regulated to a certain extent, if regulation goes too far it will be recognized as a taking."

Although the general concept remains valid, the value of the *Mahon* case as a precedent has been substantially diminished by the Supreme Court's decision in *Keystone Bituminous Coal Association v. DeBenedictis* (1987). Dividing 5 to 4, the Court held that a more recent Pennsylvania law designed to prevent subsidence damage from coal mining did not on its face violate either the Takings Clause or the Contract Clause.

As the *Keystone* case suggests, the modern Court tends to give a narrow interpretation to the rights protected by the Takings Clause. Thus, in *Hawaii Housing Authority v. Midkiff* (1984), the Court ruled unanimously that the state of Hawaii had not violated the Public Use Clause by adopting a policy for the redistribution of land as a means of reducing the high concentration of ownership by a small number of individuals. After extensive hearings, the legislature had discovered in the mid-1960s that, whereas the state and federal governments owned almost 49 percent of the land in Hawaii, 47 percent of the total was in the hands of seventy-two private landowners. On the heavily populated island of Oahu, twenty-two landowners held 72.5 percent of the **fee simple** titles. The legislature concluded that such concentrated land ownership was responsible for skewing the state's real estate market in the area of home ownership, that it inflated land prices, and that it was detrimental to the public welfare.

Writing for the Supreme Court, Justice Sandra Day O'Connor found ample precedent for the exercise of such regulatory power. O'Connor acknowledged that there had to be a legitimate public purpose for taking land, even where, as here, compensation was provided. "But where the exercise of the eminent domain power is rationally related to a conceivable public purpose, the Court has never held a compensated taking to be proscribed by the Public Use Clause." O'Connor concluded that on this basis, the Hawaii land reform policy was clearly constitutional. The regulation of oligopoly and "the evils associated with it is a classic exercise of a state's police powers." The Court would inquire only as to the rationality of the act, not its wisdom or desirability as public policy. O'Connor concluded that the legislature passed this act "not to benefit a particular class of identifiable individuals, but to at-

Antonin Scalia: Associate
Justice, 1986–

tack certain perceived evils of concentrated property ownership in Hawaii—a legitimate public purpose."

The Takings Issue Under the Rehnquist Court

In a move generally applauded by conservatives, the Rehnquist Court has shown renewed interest in the Takings Clause as a basis for protecting property rights. For example, in *First English Evangelical Lutheran Church v. County of Los Angeles* (1987), the Court reviewed an ordinance that prohibited the reconstruction of privately owned buildings destroyed by a flood. The prohibition applied to a parcel of land owned by the Evangelical Lutheran Church, which filed a lawsuit seeking compensation for the loss it would sustain in not being able to continue to use its land as a campground. Dividing 6 to 3, the Court found that the ordinance at issue "denied appellant all use of its property for a considerable period of years" and held that "invalidation of the ordinance without payment of fair value for the use of the property during this period of time would be a constitutionally insufficient remedy."

In another California case, the Supreme Court considered a state agency ruling that required owners of beachfront property to grant an **easement** to allow public beach access as a condition for obtaining a building permit. In *Nollan v. California Coastal Commission* (1987), the Court struck down this requirement by a 5-to-4 vote. Speaking through Justice Antonin Scalia, the Court said that the state's justification for the law was

> simply an expression of the . . . [state's] belief that the public interest will be served by a continuous strip of publicly accessible beach along the coast. The [Coastal] Commission may well be right that it is a good idea, but that does not establish that the Nollans (and other coastal residents) alone can be compelled to contribute to its realization. Rather, California is free to advance its 'comprehensive program,' if it wishes, by using its power of eminent domain. . . , but if it wants an easement across the Nollans' property, it must pay for it.

In a bitter dissent, Justice William Brennan castigated the Court's "narrow view" of the case, saying that its "reasoning is hardly suited to the complex reality of natural resource protection in the 20th century." Brennan concluded by expressing hope "that today's decision is an aberration, and that a broader vision ultimately prevails."

In another important decision involving eminent domain, the Court in 1994 held that state and local governments that refuse to allow land development unless an owner dedicates part of the land for public use must prove that the required conditions are related to the impact of the proposed development. In *Dolan v. City of Tigard*, the Court split 5 to 4 in holding that a city had taken private property without just compensation where the city was unwilling to grant a development permit because the owner refused to dedicate part of the land to a public use. According to Chief Justice Rehnquist's majority opinion, government must show a rough proportionality between the required set-aside of land and the harm that will be caused by the new development. Rehnquist observed that the Takings Clause of the Fifth Amendment should no longer be "relegated to the status of a poor relation" among the provisions of the Bill of Rights. Dissenting from the decision were the Court's liberals: Justices Blackmun, Stevens, Souter, and Ginsburg.

The decisions in *Nollan* and *Tigard* were warmly welcomed by advocates of renewed judicial protection for property rights. On the other hand, these decisions were severely criticized by environmentalists, planners, and others who believe in regulation of private property for the general welfare. Yet several of its decisions suggest that the Rehnquist Court is not committed to a wholesale rejuvenation of private property rights. For example, in *Pennell v. City of San Jose* (1988), the Court rejected a challenge to a local rent control ordinance. The following year, in *Duquesne Light Co. v. Barasch* (1989), the Court upheld a state law forbidding utilities from passing along to consumers costs associated with abandoned nuclear reactors. The Court rejected a utility's claim that the restriction amounted to an uncompensated taking of property. Similarly, in *Preseault v. Interstate Commerce Commission* (1990), the Court sustained an ICC ruling on the transfer of a railroad right-of-way and said that the Fifth Amendment did not demand that compensation be paid prior to or simultaneously with a government taking of private property. It would seem, then, that the Rehnquist Court is committed to steering a moderate course in this area. President Clinton's appointments of Ruth Ginsburg and Stephen Breyer will help keep the Court on a moderate course.

The *PruneYard* Case: Freedom of Expression Versus Private Control of Property

The decision in *PruneYard Shopping Center v. Robins* (1980) illustrates how property rights may be at odds with the freedom of expression and how, in such instances, the modern Court is likely to strike a balance in favor of the latter. Our discussion of this case leads logically into the examination of freedom of expression in Chapter 8. The privately owned PruneYard Shopping Center in Campbell, California, had a policy prohibiting on its premises all "expressive activity" not directly related to its commercial purposes. In accordance with this policy, the shopping center had excluded several high school students who were seeking signatures for a petition opposing a United Nations resolution against Zionism. The California Supreme Court interpreted a state constitutional provision as granting the students a right to engage in this activity on the shopping center's property. In an opinion by Justice Rehnquist, the U.S. Supreme Court rejected the shopping center owner's allegations that his federally protected property rights and freedom of speech had been violated. The Court found no violation of the constitutional guarantee against the taking of private property without just compensation. Although Rehnquist recognized that "one of the essential sticks in the bundle of property rights is the right to exclude others," he found "nothing to suggest that preventing [the shopping center] from prohibiting this activity will unreasonably impair the value or use of [the] property as a shopping center." The students were orderly and had limited their activities to the "common area" of the shopping center. PruneYard had failed to show that its "right to exclude others" was "so essential to the use or economic value of [its] property that the state-authorized limitation of it amounted to a 'taking.' " In addition, Rehnquist found that the state constitutional provision granting the right of access satisfied the test of rationality established in such cases as *Nebbia v. New York* (1934). Moreover, the state could reasonably conclude that recognizing a right of access furthered its "asserted interest in promoting more expansive rights of free speech and petition than [those] conferred by the Federal Constitution." This opinion, written by one of the most conservative justices, underscores the extent to which the modern Court defers to state policies limiting economic freedom.

TO SUMMARIZE:

- The Takings Clause of the Fifth Amendment, enforceable against the states through the Fourteenth Amendment, restricts government's use of the power of eminent domain. Government can take private property only for a "public use" and only with "just compensation" to the previous owner. The "taking" of private property is not limited to its physical appropriation, but includes regulatory measures that effectively deprive the owner of the enjoyment, use, or control of the property.
- Throughout most of the twentieth century, the Takings Clause has not served as a significant limitation on governmental power. However, in recent years the Court has found occasion to remind public policy makers, especially at the local level, that this constitutional guarantee retains some practical force.

CONCLUSION

For almost a century and a half, the U.S. Supreme Court extended significant constitutional protection to property rights and economic freedom. The balance between these rights and the exercise of the police power shifted to some extent from period to period. The Marshall Court, primarily through the Contract Clause, erected major safeguards for "vested rights." Coincident with the subsequent rise of Jacksonian democracy, these rights began to give way to the state police power. This trend continued from the beginning of the Taney era in the late 1830s into the 1880s. With significant personnel changes on the Court and the rising influence of corporate business interests, the Court began to interpret various provisions of the Constitution, particularly the Due Process Clauses of the Fifth and Fourteenth Amendments, as substantive limitations on economic legislation. This orientation, with its emphasis on "liberty of contract," became more pronounced around the turn of the century and, despite growing criticism from dissenting justices and legal commentators, continued to have a powerful influence on constitutional interpretation until the Supreme Court's confrontation with the Great Depression and the New Deal.

Because private property and free enterprise are deeply ingrained cultural values, there is little need for heightened judicial protection of these institutions. Nevertheless, it should be recognized that American judges at all levels continue to accord great weight to the protection of private property and contractual rights. Congress, the state legislatures, and local governments are unlikely to enact measures that seriously undermine economic freedom. At the same time, substantial political support exists for economic policy measures that regulate the economy "around the margins." A strong consensus exists in support of public policy designed to foster competition, reduce inequalities, stabilize the business cycle, and protect the environment, the consumer, and the worker. Facing a political consensus, the modern Supreme Court has generally acceded to these departures from *laissez-faire* capitalism.

During the 1980s, conservative theorists displeased with the policies of the modern regulatory state, most notably Bernard Seigan and Richard Epstein, urged the Supreme Court to resurrect its former commitment to private property and private enterprise. As yet, there is little evidence that the Court is interested in moving very far in that direction. For now, battles over government regulation of the economy appear to be more in the province of the constitutional historian than the constitutional lawyer. Of course, given the vicissitudes of American constitutional politics, nothing in the law should be considered settled once and for all.

The Modern Concern for Noneconomic Rights

As the last vestiges of *laissez-faire* disappeared from the Court's majority opinions, the justices began to give significantly greater attention to the protection of cultural and political freedoms, especially as exercised by members of racial and religious minorities outside the mainstream of American life. Consistent with this reorientation, the Court also began to recognize broader constitutional safeguards for persons accused of crime.

To a greater or lesser degree, the Court has continued to emphasize individual rights largely outside the economic sphere. Some observers have criticized the Court for having withdrawn so completely from the defense of property interests, but even the Court's most conservative members seem disinclined to reassert the *laissez-faire*–oriented judicial activism of the 1920s. Of course, the Supreme Court cannot successfully pursue a course of constitutional interpretation far removed from the prevailing national political consensus. At the same time, the Court should not be expected to relinquish its position of coequality as a branch of the national government. During the past half century, it has found ample opportunity to shape constitutional interpretation in many areas directly affecting the lives of the American people. The remaining chapters of this book will examine the Court's performance in the most important of these areas.

KEY TERMS

capitalist economy

private property

contracts

property rights

economic freedom

police power

natural rights

social contract

laissez-faire capitalism

Contract Clause

vested rights

Due Process Clause of the
    Fourteenth Amendment

substantive due process

Fifth Amendment Due
    Process Clause

economic due process

business affected with a
    public interest

social Darwinism

liberty of contract

Brandeis brief

yellow dog contracts

Equal Protection Clause

Just Compensation Clause

incorporation doctrine

taking

eminent domain

fee simple

easement

FOR FURTHER READING

Ackerman, Bruce. *Private Property and the Constitution.* New Haven, Conn.: Yale University Press, 1977.

Conant, Michael. *The Constitution and Capitalism.* St. Paul, Minn.: West, 1974.

Corwin, Edward S. *Liberty Against Government.* Baton Rouge, La.: Louisiana State University Press, 1948.

Dorn, James A., and Henry G. Manne (eds.). *Economic Liberties and the Judiciary.* Fairfax, Va.: George Mason University Press, 1987.

Ely, James W., Jr. (ed.). *Property Rights in American History,* 6 vols. New York: Garland, 1997.

Epstein, Richard A. *Takings: Private Property and the Power of Eminent Domain.* Cambridge, Mass.: Harvard University Press, 1985.

Gillman, Howard. *The Constitution Besieged: The Rise and Decline of Lochner Era Police Powers Jurisprudence.* Durham, N.C.: Duke University Press, 1993.

Kens, Paul. *Judicial Power and Reform Politics: The Anatomy of Lochner v. New York.* Lawrence, Kans.: University of Kansas Press, 1990.

Keynes, Edward. *Liberty, Property, and Privacy: Toward a Jurisprudence of Substantive Due Process.*

University Park, Pa.: Pennsylvania State University Press, 1996.

Mendelson, Wallace. *Capitalism, Democracy, and the Supreme Court.* New York: Appleton-Century-Crofts, 1960.

Nedelsky, Jennifer. *Private Property and the Limits of American Constitutionalism: The Madisonian Framework and Its Legacy.* Chicago: University of Chicago Press, 1990.

Seigan, Bernard H. *Economic Liberties and the Constitution.* Chicago: University of Chicago Press, 1980.

Wright, Benjamin F. *The Contract Clause of the Constitution.* Cambridge, Mass.: Harvard University Press, 1938.

INTERNET RESOURCES

Name of Resource	Description	URL (circa 1998)
Center for Democratic Values	Think tank sponsored by the Democratic Socialists of America	http://www.igc.org/cdv/
American Enterprise Institute	Conservative policy research organization that emphasizes economic issues	http://www.aei.org/
Cato Institute	A leading libertarian think tank	http://www.cato.org/
Defenders of Property Rights	A legal foundation devoted to protecting private property rights	http://www.defendersproprights.org/
American Land Rights Association	An organization dedicated to protecting private property rights, especially in rural areas	http://www.landrights.org/
Public Citizen	A proconsumer, prodemocracy group founded by Ralph Nader	http://www.citizen.org/

Case

DARTMOUTH COLLEGE V. WOODWARD

4 Wheat. (17 U.S.) 518; 4 L.Ed. 629 (1819)
Vote: 6–1

Dartmouth College was originally chartered by King George III in 1769. Under the royal charter, the trustees of the College were "forever" granted the right to govern the institution as they saw fit. However, in 1816, the New Hampshire legislature attempted to take control of the college, believing its royal charter was no longer valid. Naturally, the trustees turned to the courts for protection. Failing in the state judiciary, they appealed to the Supreme Court on a writ of error.

The opinion of the Court was delivered by *[Chief Justice Marshall].*

. . . It can require no argument to prove, that the circumstances of this case constitute a contract. An application is made to the crown for a charter to incorporate a religious and literary institution. In the application, it is stated, that large contributions have been made for the object, which will be conferred on the corporation, as soon as it shall be created. The charter is granted, and on its faith the property is conveyed. Surely, in this transaction every ingredient of a complete and legitimate contract is to be found. The points for consideration are, 1. Is this contract protected by the Constitution of the United States? 2. Is it impaired by the acts under which the defendant holds? . . .

. . . [I]t appears that Dartmouth College is an eleemosynary institution, incorporated for the purpose of perpetuating the application of the bounty of the donors to the specified objects of that bounty; that its trustees or governors were originally named by the founder, and invested with the power of perpetuating themselves; that they are not public officers, nor is it a civil institution, participating in the administration of government; but a charity school, or a seminary of education, incorporated for the preservation of its property, and the perpetual application of that property to the objects of its creation. . . .

This is plainly a contract to which the donors, the trustees, and the Crown (to whose rights and obligations New Hampshire succeeds) were the original parties. It is a contract made on a valuable consideration. It is a contract on the faith of which real and personal estate has been conveyed to the corporation. It is then a contract within the letter of the Constitution, and within its spirit also, unless the fact that the property is invested by the donors in trustees, for the promotion of religion and education, for the benefit of persons who are perpetually changing, though the objects remain the same, shall create a particular exception, taking this case out of the prohibition contained in the Constitution.

It is more than possible that the preservation of rights of this description was not particularly in the view of the framers of the Constitution, when the clause under consideration was introduced into that instrument. It is probable that interferences of more frequent recurrence, to which the temptation was stronger, and of which the mischief was more extensive, constituted the great motive for imposing this restriction on the state legislatures. But although a particular and a rare case may not, in itself, be of sufficient magnitude to induce a rule, yet it must be governed by the rule, when established, unless some plain and strong reason for excluding it can be given. It is not enough to say, that this particular case was not in the mind of the Convention when the article was framed, nor of the American people when it was adopted. It is necessary to go further, and to say that, had this particular case been suggested, the language would have been so varied as to exclude it, or it would have been made a special exception. The case being within the words of the rule, must be within its operation likewise, unless there be something in the literal construction so obviously absurd or mischievous, or repugnant to the general spirit of the instrument, as to justify those who expound the Constitution in making it an exception.

On what safe and intelligible ground can this exception stand? There is no expression in the Constitution, no sentiment delivered by its contemporaneous expounders, which would justify us in making it. In the absence of all authority of this kind, is there, in the nature and reason of the case itself, that which would sustain a construction of the Constitution not warranted by its words? Are contracts of this description of a character to excite so little interest that we must exclude them from the provisions of the Constitution, as being unworthy of the attention of those who framed the instrument? Or does public policy so imperiously demand their remaining exposed to legislative alteration as to compel us, or rather permit us to say, that these words, which were introduced to give stability to contracts, and which in their plain import comprehend this contract, must yet be so construed as to exclude it? . . .

If the insignificance of the object does not require that we should exclude contracts respecting it from the protection of the Constitution, neither, as we conceive,

is the policy of leaving them subject to legislative alteration so apparent, as to require a forced construction of that instrument, in order to effect it. These eleemosynary institutions do not fill the place, which would otherwise be occupied by government, but that which would otherwise remain vacant. They are complete acquisitions to literature. They are donations to education; donations, which any government must be disposed rather to encourage than to discountenance. It requires no very critical examination of the human mind, to enable us to determine, that one great inducement to these gifts is the conviction felt by the giver, that the disposition he makes of them is immutable. It is probable, that no man was, and that no man ever will be, the founder of a college, believing at the time, that an act of incorporation constitutes no security for the institution; believing, that it is immediately to be deemed a public institution, whose funds are to be governed and applied, not by the will of the donor, but by the will of the legislature. All such gifts are made in the pleasing, perhaps delusive hope, that the charity will flow forever in the channel which the givers have marked out for it. If every man finds in his own bosom strong evidence of the universality of this sentiment, there can be but little reason to imagine, that the framers of our Constitution were strangers to it, and that, feeling the necessity and policy of giving permanence and security to contracts, of withdrawing them from the influence of legislative bodies, whose fluctuating policy and repeated interferences, produced the most perplexing and injurious embarrassments, they still deemed it necessary to leave these contracts subject to those interferences. The motives for such an exception must be very powerful, to justify the construction which makes it. . . .

We next proceed to the inquiry, whether its obligation has been impaired by those acts of the legislature of New Hampshire, to which the special verdict refers? . . .

It has been already stated, that the act "to amend the charter, and enlarge and improve the corporation of Dartmouth College," increases the number of trustees to twenty-one, gives the appointment of the additional members to the executive of the state, and creates a board of overseers, to consist of twenty-five persons, of whom twenty-one are also appointed by the executive of New Hampshire, who have power to inspect and control the most important acts of the trustees.

On the effect of this law [of 1816], two opinions cannot be entertained. Between acting directly, and acting through the agency of trustees and overseers, no essential difference is perceived. The whole power of governing the college is transferred from trustees appointed according to the will of the founder, expressed in the charter, to the executive of New Hampshire. The management and application of the funds of this eleemosynary institution, which are placed by the donors in the hands of trustees named in the charter, and empowered to perpetuate themselves, are placed by this act under the control of the government of the state. The will of the state is substituted for the will of the donors, in every essential operation of the college. This is not an immaterial change. The founders of the college contracted, not merely for the perpetual application of the funds which they gave, to the objects for which those funds were given; they contracted, also, to secure that application by the Constitution of the corporation. They contracted for a system which should, as far as human foresight can provide, retain forever the government of the literary institution they had formed, in the hands of persons approved by themselves. This system is totally changed. The charter of 1769 exists no longer. It is reorganized; and reorganized in such a manner as to convert a literary institution, moulded according to the will of its founders, and placed under the control of private literary men, into a machine entirely subservient to the will of government. This may be for the advantage of literature in general; but it is not according to the will of the donors, and is subversive of that contract on the faith of which their property was given. . . .

It results from this opinion, that the acts of the legislature of New Hampshire, which are stated in the special verdict found in this cause, are repugnant to the Constitution of the United States; and that the judgment on this special verdict ought to have been for the plaintiffs. The judgment of the State Court must therefore be reversed.

Mr. Justice Duvall dissented.

Case

CHARLES RIVER BRIDGE COMPANY V. WARREN BRIDGE COMPANY

11 Pet. (36 U.S.) 420; 9 L.Ed. 773 (1837)
Vote: 5–2

This decision was one of the Taney Court's most important contributions to American constitutional development. The case grew out of a dispute involving rival companies in the business of building and operating bridges. The constitutional issue stemmed from the fact that both companies were operating under charters granted them by a state legislature. In 1785, the Massachusetts legislature incorporated the Charles River Bridge Company for forty years, for the purpose of building and operating a toll bridge over the Charles River between Boston and Cambridge. In 1792, the legislature extended the term of the charter to seventy years. In 1828, the legislature chartered another company, the Warren Bridge Company, and authorized it to build another bridge three hundred yards from the Charles River Bridge. The Charles River Bridge Company then brought suit, arguing that the legislature had implicitly granted it an exclusive right to operate a bridge in the area throughout the life of its charter. According to the Charles River Bridge Company, the grant of the charter to the Warren Bridge Company was an im- *pairment of the obligation of contracts, forbidden by Article I, Section 10, of the Constitution. The state courts rejected this argument, and the Supreme Court took the case on a writ of error.*

Mr. Chief Justice Taney delivered the opinion of the Court.

. . . This brings us to the act of the legislature of Massachusetts, of 1785, by which the plaintiffs were incorporated by the name of "The Proprietors of the Charles River Bridge"; and it is here, and in the law of 1792, prolonging their charter, that we must look for the extent and nature of the franchise conferred upon the plaintiffs.

Much has been said in the argument of the principles of construction by which this law is to be expounded, and what undertakings, on the part of the state, may be implied. The Court think[s] there can be no serious difficulty on that head. It is the grant of certain franchises by the public to a private corporation, and in a matter where the public interest is concerned. The rule of construction in such cases is well settled, both in England and by the decisions of our own tribunals. . . . In the case of the *Proprietors of the Stourbridge Canal v. Wheely* and others, the Court say[s], "The canal having been made under an act of Parliament, the rights of the plaintiffs are derived entirely from that act. This, like many other cases, is a bargain between a company of adventurers and the public, the terms of which are expressed in the statute; and the rule of construction, in all such cases, is now fully established to be this; that any ambiguity in the terms of the contract must operate against the adventurers, and in favor of the public, and the plaintiffs can claim nothing that is not clearly given them by the act." And the doctrine thus laid down is abundantly sustained by the authorities referred to in this decision. . . .

. . . The argument in favour of the proprietors of the Charles River bridge, is . . . that the power claimed by the state, if it exists, may be so used as to destroy the value of the franchise they have granted to the corporation. . . . The existence of the power does not, and cannot depend upon the circumstance of its having been exercised or not.

. . . [T]he object and end of all government is to promote the happiness and prosperity of the community by which it is established, and it can never be assumed, that the government intended to diminish its power of accomplishing the end for which it was created. And in a country like ours, free, active, and enterprising, continually advancing in numbers and wealth, new channels of communication are daily found necessary, both for travel and trade; and are essential to the comfort, convenience and prosperity of the people. A state ought never to be presumed to surrender this power, because, like the taxing power, the whole community have an interest in preserving it undiminished. And when a corporation alleges that a state has surrendered, for seventy years, its power of improvement and public accommodation, in a great and important line of travel, along which a vast number of its citizens must daily pass, the community have a right to insist, in the language of this court above quoted, "that its abandonment ought not to be presumed in a case in which the deliberate purpose of the state to abandon it does not appear." The continued existence of a government would be of no great value, if by implications and presumptions it was disarmed of the powers necessary to accomplish the ends of its creation, and the functions it was designed to perform, transferred to the hands of privileged corporations. The rule of construction announced by the court was not confined to the taxing power; nor is it so limited in the opinion delivered. On the contrary, it was distinctly placed on the ground that the interests of the community were concerned in preserving, undiminished, the power then in question; and whenever any power of the state is said to be surrendered and diminished, whether it be the taxing power or any other affecting the public interest, the same principle applies, and the rule of construction must be the same. No one will question that the interests of the great body of the people of the state would, in this instance, be affected by the surrender of this great line of travel to a single corporation, with the right to exact toll, and exclude competition for seventy years. While the rights of private property are sacredly guarded, we must not forget that the community also have rights, and that the happiness and well-being of every citizen depends on their faithful preservation.

Adopting the rule of construction above stated as the settled one, we proceed to apply it to the charter of 1785, to the proprietors of the Charles River bridge. This act of incorporation is in the usual form, and the privileges such as are commonly given to corporations of that kind. It confers on them the ordinary faculties of a corporation, for the purpose of building the bridge; and establishes certain rates of toll, which the company are authorized to take. This is the whole grant. There is no exclusive privilege given to them over the waters of Charles River, above or below their bridge; no right to erect another bridge themselves, nor to prevent other persons from erecting one. No engagement from the state, that another shall not be erected; and no undertaking not to sanction competition, nor to make improvements that may diminish the amount of its income. Upon all these subjects, the charter is silent, and nothing is said in it about a line of travel, so much insisted on in the argument, in which they are to have exclusive privileges. . . .

. . . In short, all the franchises and rights of property, enumerated in the charter, and there mentioned to have been granted to it, remain unimpaired. But its income is destroyed by the Warren bridge; which, being free, draws off the passengers and property which would have gone over it, and renders their franchise of no value. This is the gist of the complaint. For it is not pretended, that the erection of the Warren bridge would have done them any injury, or in any degree affected their right of property, if it had not diminished the amount of their tolls. In order, then, to entitle themselves to relief, it is necessary to show, that the legislature contracted not to do the act of which they complain; and that they impaired, or in other words, violated, that contract by the erection of the Warren bridge.

The inquiry, then, is, does the charter contain such a contract on the part of the state? Is there any such stipulation to be found in that instrument? It must be admitted on all hands, that there is none; no words that even relate to another bridge, or to the [diminution] of their tolls, or to the line of travel. If a contract on that subject can be gathered from the charter, it must be by implication; and cannot be found in the words used. Can such an agreement be implied? The rule of construction before stated is an answer to the question; in charters of this description, no rights are taken from the public, or given to corporations, beyond those which the words of the charter, by their natural and proper construction, purport to convey. There are no words which import such a contract as the plaintiffs in error contend for, and none can be implied. . . .

Indeed, the practice and usage of almost every state in the Union, old enough to have commenced the work of internal improvement, is opposed to the doctrine contended for on the part of the plaintiffs in error. Turnpike roads have been made in succession, on the same line of travel; the later ones interfering materially with the profits of the first. These corporations have, in some instances, been utterly ruined by the introduction of newer and better modes of transportation and travelling. In some cases, railroads have rendered the turnpike roads on the same line of travel so entirely useless, that the franchise of the turnpike corporation is not worth preserving. Yet in none of these cases have the corporations supposed that their privileges were invaded, or any contract violated on the part of the state. Amid the multitude of cases which have occurred, and have been daily occurring for the last forty or fifty years, this is the first instance in which such an implied contract has been contended for, and this court called upon to infer it, from an ordinary act of incorporation, containing nothing more than the usual stipulations and provisions to be found in every such law. The absence of any such controversy, when there must have been so many occasions to give rise to it, proves that neither states, nor individuals, nor corporations, ever imagined that such a contract could be implied from such charters. It shows, that the men who voted for these laws never imagined that they were forming such a contract; and if we maintain that they have made it, we must create it by a legal fiction, in opposition to the truth of the fact, and the obvious intention of the party. We cannot deal thus with the rights reserved to the states; and by legal intendments and mere technical reasoning, take away from them any portion of that power over their own internal police and improvement, which is not necessary to their well-being and prosperity.

And what would be the fruits of this doctrine of implied contracts, on the part of the states, and of property in a line of travel by a corporation if it should now be sanctioned by this court? To what results would it lead us? If it is to be found in the charter to this bridge, the same process of reasoning must dis-

cover it, in the various acts which have been passed, within the last forty years, for turnpike companies. And what is to be the extent of the privileges of exclusion on the different sides of the road? The counsel who have so ably argued this case, have not attempted to define it by any certain boundaries. How far must the new improvement be distant from the old one? How near may you approach, without invading its rights in the privileged line? If this court should establish the principles now contented for, what is to become of the numerous railroads established on the same line of travel with turnpike companies; and which have rendered the franchises of the turnpike corporations of no value? Let it once be understood, that such charters carry with them these implied contracts, and give this unknown and undefined prosperity in a line of travelling; and you will soon find the old turnpike corporations awakening from their sleep and calling upon this court to put down the improvements which have taken their place. The millions of property which have been invested in railroads and canals, upon lines of travel which had been before occupied by turnpike corporations, will be put in jeopardy. We shall be thrown back to the improvements of the last century, and obliged to stand still, until the claims of the old turnpike corporations shall be satisfied; and they shall consent to permit these states to avail themselves of the lights of modern science, and to partake of the benefit of those improvements which are now adding to the wealth and prosperity, and the convenience and comfort, of every other part of the civilized word. Nor is this all. This court will find itself compelled to fix, by some kind of arbitrary rule, the width of this new kind of property in a line of travel; for if such a right of property exists, we have no lights to guide us in marking out its extent, unless, indeed, we resort to the old feudal grants, and to the exclusive rights of ferries, by prescription, between towns; and are prepared to decide that when a turnpike road from one town to another, had been made, no railroad or canal, between these two points, could afterwards be established. This court are not prepared to sanction principles which must lead to such results. . . .

The judgment of the supreme judicial court of the commonwealth of Massachusetts, dismissing the plaintiffs' bill, must therefore, be affirmed with costs.

Mr. Justice McLean delivered an opinion [concurring in the judgment] holding that the case should be dismissed for want of jurisdiction.

Mr. Justice Story, dissenting. . . .

. . . Upon the whole, my judgment is that the act of the legislature of Massachusetts granting the charter of Warren Bridge, is an act impairing the obligation of the prior contract and grant to the proprietors of Charles River bridge; and, by the Constitution of the United States, it is, therefore, utterly void. I am for reversing the decree of the state court for further proceedings. . . .

Mr. Justice Thompson concurred in this [dissenting] opinion. . . .

Case

HOME BUILDING AND LOAN ASSOCIATION V. BLAISDELL

290 U.S. 398; 54 S.Ct. 231; 78 L.Ed. 413 (1934)
Vote: 5–4

In 1933, the Minnesota legislature adopted an act designed to prevent the foreclosure of mortgages on real estate during the economic emergency produced by the Great Depression. The Mortgage Moratorium Act authorized courts to extend the redemption periods of mortgages in order to prevent foreclosures. The act was to remain in effect only during the emergency period and in no case beyond May 1, 1935.

Mr. Chief Justice Hughes delivered the opinion of the Court.

. . . The state court upheld the statute as an emergency measure. Although conceding that the obligations of the mortgage contract were impaired, the court decided that what it thus described as an impairment was, notwithstanding the contract clause of the Federal Constitution, within the police power of the state as that power was called into exercise by the public economic emergency which the legislature had found to exist. . . .

In determining whether the provision for this temporary and conditional relief exceeds the power of the state by reason of the clause in the Federal Constitution prohibiting impairment of the obligations of contracts, we must consider the relation of emergency to constitutional power, the historical setting of the contract clause, the development of the jurisprudence of this Court in the construction of that clause, and the principles of construction which we may consider to be established.

Emergency does not create power. Emergency does not increase granted power or remove or diminish the restrictions imposed upon power granted or reserved. The Constitution was adopted in a period of grave emergency. Its grants of power to the Federal Government and its limitations of the power of the states were determined in the light of emergency, and they are not altered by emergency. What power was thus granted and what limitations were thus imposed are questions which have always been, and always will be, the subject of close examination under our constitutional system.

While emergency does not create power, emergency may furnish the occasion for the exercise of power. "Although an emergency may not call into life a power which has never lived, nevertheless emergency may afford a reason for the exertion of a living power already enjoyed." . . . The constitutional question presented in the light of an emergency is whether the power possessed embraces the particular exercise of it in response to particular conditions. Thus, the war power of the federal government is not created by the emergency of war, but it is a power to wage war successfully, and thus it permits the harnessing of the entire energies of the people in a supreme co-operative effort to preserve the nation. But even the war power does not remove constitutional limitations safeguarding essential liberties. When the provisions of the Constitution, in grant or restriction, are specific, so particularized as not to admit a state to have more than two Senators in the Congress, or permit the election of a President by a general popular vote without regard to the number of electors to which the states are respectively entitled, or permit the states to "coin money" or to "make anything but gold and silver coin a tender in payment of debts." But, where constitutional grants and limitations of power are set forth in general clauses, which afford a broad outline, the process of construction is essential to fill in the details. That is true of the contract clause. . . .

In the construction of the contract clause, the debates in the Constitutional Convention are of little aid. But the reasons which led to the adoption of that clause, and of the other prohibitions of Section 10 of Article I, are not left in doubt, and have frequently been described with eloquent emphasis. The widespread distress following the revolutionary period, and the plight of debtors had called forth in the state an ignoble array of legislative schemes for the defeat of creditors and the invasion of contractual obligations. Legislative interferences had been so numerous and extreme that the confidence essential to prosperous trade had been undermined and the utter destruction of credit was threatened. "The sober people of America" were convinced that some "thorough reform" was needed which would "inspire a general prudence and industry, and give a regular course to the business of society." . . .

The inescapable problems of construction have been: What is a contract? What are the obligations of contracts? What constitutes impairment of these obligations? What residuum of power is there still in the states, in relation to the operation of contracts, to protect the vital interests of the community? Questions of this character, "of no small nicety and intricacy, have vexed the legislative halls, as well as the judicial tribunals, with an uncounted variety and frequency of litigation and speculation." . . .

It is manifest . . . that there has been a growing appreciation of public needs and of the necessity of finding ground for a rational compromise between individual rights and public welfare. . . . Pressure of a constantly increasing density of population, the interrelation of the activities of our people and the complexity of our economic interests, have inevitably led to an increased use of the organization of society in order to protect the very bases of individual opportunity. Where, in earlier days, it was thought that only the concerns of individuals or of classes were involved, and that those of the state itself were touched only remotely, it has later been found that the fundamental interests of the state are directly affected; and that the question is no longer merely that of one party to a contract as against another, but of the use of reasonable means to safeguard the economic structure upon which the good of all depends.

It is no answer to say that this public need was not apprehended a century ago, or to insist that what the provision of the Constitution meant to the vision of that day it must mean to the vision of our time. If by the statement that what the Constitution meant at the time of its adoption it means today, it is intended to say that the great clauses of the Constitution must be confined to the interpretation which the framers, with the conditions and outlook of their time, would have placed upon them, the statement carries its own refutation. It was to guard against such a narrow conception that Chief Justice Marshall uttered the memorable warning: "We must never forget, that it is a *constitution* we are expounding"; . . . "a constitution intended to endure for ages to come, and, consequently, to be adapted to the various *crises* of human affairs." . . . When we are dealing with the words of

the Constitution, . . . "we must realize that they have called into life a being the development of which could not have been foreseen completely by the most gifted of its begetters. . . . The case before us must be considered in the light of our whole experience and not merely in that of what was said a hundred years ago." . . .

Nor is it helpful to attempt to draw a fine distinction between the intended meaning of the words of the Constitution and their intended application. When we consider the contract clause and the decisions which have expounded it in harmony with the essential reserved power of the states to protect the security of their peoples, we find no warrant for the conclusion that the clause has been warped by these decisions from its proper significance or that the founders of our government would have interpreted the clause differently had they had occasion to assume that responsibility in the conditions of the later day. The vast body of law which has been developed was unknown to the fathers, but it is believed to have preserved the essential content and the spirit of the Constitution. With a growing recognition of public needs and the relation of individual right to public security, the Court has sought to prevent the perversion of the clause through its use as an instrument to throttle the capacity of the states to protect their fundamental interests. . . .

We are of the opinion that the Minnesota statute as here applied does not violate the contract clause of the Federal Constitution. Whether the legislation is wise or unwise as a matter of policy is a question with which we are not concerned. . . .

Mr. Justice Sutherland, dissenting.

Few questions of greater moment than that just decided have been submitted for judicial inquiry during this generation. He simply closes his eyes to the necessary implications of the decision who fails to see in it the potentiality of future gradual but ever-advancing encroachments upon the sanctity of private and public contracts. The effect of the Minnesota legislation, though serious enough in itself, is of trivial significance compared with the far more serious and dangerous inroads upon the limitations of the Constitution which are almost certain to ensue as a consequence naturally following any step beyond the boundaries fixed by that instrument. And those of us who are thus apprehensive of the effect of this decision would, in a matter so important, be neglectful of our duty should we fail to spread upon the permanent records of the court the reasons which move us to the opposite view.

A provision of the Constitution, it is hardly necessary to say, does not admit of two distinctly opposite interpretations. It does not mean one thing at one time and an entirely different thing at another time. If the Contract Impairment Clause, when framed and adopted, meant that the terms of a contract for the payment of money could not be altered . . . by a state statute enacted for the relief of hardly pressed debtors to the end and with the effect of postponing payment or enforcement during and because of an economic or financial emergency, it is but to state the obvious to say that it means the same now. This view, at once so rational in its application to the written word, and so necessary to the stability of constitutional principles, though from time to time challenged, has never, unless recently, been put within the realm of doubt by the decisions of this Court. . . .

The provisions of the federal Constitution, undoubtedly, are pliable in the sense that in appropriate cases they have the capacity of bringing within their grasp every new condition which falls within their meaning. But their *meaning* is changeless; it is only their *application* which is extensible. . . . Constitutional grants of power and restrictions upon the exercise of power are not flexible as the doctrines of the common law are flexible. These doctrines, upon the principles of the common law itself, modify or abrogate themselves whenever they are or whenever they become plainly unsuited to different or changed conditions. . . .

The whole aim of construction, as applied to a provision of the Constitution, is to discover the meaning, to ascertain and give effect to the intent, of its framers and the people who adopted it. . . . And if the meaning be at all doubtful, the doubt should be resolved, wherever reasonably possible to do so, in a way to forward the evident purpose with which the provision was adopted. . . .

An application of these principles to the question under review removes any doubt, if otherwise there would be any, that the Contract Impairment Clause denies to the several states the power to mitigate hard consequences resulting to debtors from financial or economic exigencies by an impairment of the obligation of contracts of indebtedness. A candid consideration of the history and circumstances which led up to and accompanied the framing and adoption of this clause will demonstrate conclusively that it was framed and adopted with the specific and studied purpose of preventing legislation designed to relieve debtors especially in time of financial distress. Indeed, it is not probable that any other purpose was definitely in the minds of those who composed the framers' convention or the ratifying state conventions which followed, although the restriction has been given a wider application upon principles clearly stated by Chief Justice Marshall in the Dartmouth College Case. . . .

The present exigency is nothing new. From the beginning of our existence as a nation, periods of depression, of industrial failure, of financial distress, of unpaid and unpayable indebtedness, have alternated with years of plenty. The vital lesson that expenditure beyond income begets poverty, that public or private extravagance, financed by promises to pay, either must end in complete or partial repudiation or the promises be fulfilled by self-denial and painful effort, though constantly taught by bitter experience, seems never to be learned; and the attempt by legislative devices to shift the misfortune of debtor to the shoulders of the creditor without coming into conflict with the Contract Impairment Clause has been persistent and oft-repeated.

The defense of the Minnesota law is made upon grounds which were discountenanced by the makers of the Constitution and have many times been rejected by this court. That defense should not now succeed, because it constitutes an effort to overthrow the constitutional provision by an appeal to facts and circumstances identical with those which brought it into existence. With due regard for the process of logical thinking, it legitimately cannot be urged that conditions which produced the rule may now be invoked to destroy it.

. . . The opinion concedes that emergency does not create power, or increase granted power, or remove or diminish restrictions upon power granted or reserved. It then proceeds to say, however, that while emergency does not create power, it may furnish the occasion for the exercise of power. I can only interpret what is said on that subject as meaning that while an emergency does not diminish a restriction upon power it furnishes an occasion for diminishing it; and this, as it seems to me, is merely to say the same thing by the use of another set of words, with the effect of affirming that which has just been denied.

It is quite true that an emergency may supply the occasion for the exercise of power, depending upon the nature of the power and the intent of the Constitution with respect thereto. The emergency of war furnishes an occasion for the exercise of certain of the war powers. This the Constitution contemplates, since they cannot be exercised upon any other occasion. The existence of another kind of emergency authorizes the United States to protect each of the states of the Union against domestic violence. . . . But we are here dealing not with a power granted by the federal Constitution, but with the state policy power, which exists in its own right. Hence the question is not whether an emergency furnishes the occasion for the exercise of that state power, but whether an emergency furnishes an occasion for the relaxation of the restrictions upon the power imposed by the Contract Impairment Clause, and the difficulty is that the Contract Impairment Clause forbids state action under any circumstances, if it have the effect of impairing the obligation of contracts. That clause restricts every state power in the particular specified, no matter what may be the occasion. It does not contemplate that an emergency shall furnish an occasion for softening the restriction or making it any the less a restriction upon state action in that contingency than it is under strictly normal conditions.

The Minnesota statute either impairs the obligation of contracts or it does not. If it does not, the occasion to which it relates becomes immaterial, since then the passage of the statute is the exercise of a normal, unrestricted, state power and requires no special occasion to render it effective. If it does, the emergency no more furnishes a proper occasion for its exercise than if the emergency were nonexistent. And so, while, in form, the suggested distinction seems to put us forward in a straight line, in reality it simply carries us back in a circle, like bewildered travelers lost in a wood, to the point where we parted company with the view of the state court. . . .

I quite agree with the opinion of the Court that whether the legislation under review is wise or unwise is a matter with which we have nothing to do. Whether it is likely to work well or work ill presents a question entirely irrelevant to the issue. The only legitimate inquiry we can make is whether it is constitutional. If it is not, its virtues, if it have any, cannot save it; if it is, its faults cannot be invoked to accomplish its destruction. If the provisions of the Constitution be not upheld when they pinch as well as when they comfort, they may as well be abandoned. Being unable to reach any other conclusion than that the Minnesota statute infringes the constitutional restrictions under review, I have no choice but to say so.

I am authorized to say that **Mr. Justice Van Devanter, Mr. Justice McReynolds** and **Mr. Justice Butler** concur in this opinion.

Case

THE SLAUGHTERHOUSE CASES

16 Wall. (83 U.S.) 36; 21 L.Ed. 394 (1873)
Vote: 5–4

In 1869, the Louisiana legislature granted to a slaughterhouse company a monopoly for the city of New Orleans. A number of independent butchers sought injunctions against the monopoly. Unable to secure injunctions in the state courts, they turned to the Supreme Court, which granted review pursuant to a writ of error.

Mr. Justice Miller . . . delivered the opinion of the Court.

The plaintiffs . . . allege that the statute is a violation of the Constitution of the United States in these several particulars:

That it creates an involuntary servitude forbidden by the thirteenth article of amendment;

That it abridges the privileges and immunities of citizens of the United States;

That it denies to the plaintiffs the equal protection of the laws; and,

That it deprives them of their property without due process of law; contrary to the provisions of the first section of the fourteenth article of amendment.

This court is thus called upon for the first time to give construction to these articles.

. . . On the most casual examination of the language of [the Thirteenth, Fourteenth, and Fifteenth] amendments, no one can fail to be impressed with the one pervading purpose found in them all, lying at the foundation of each, and without which none of them would have been even suggested; we mean the freedom of the slave race, the security and firm establishment of that freedom, and the protection of the newly-made freeman and citizen from the oppressions of those who had formerly exercised unlimited dominion over him. It is true that only the Fifteenth Amendment, in terms, mentions the negro by speaking of his color and his slavery. But it is just as true that each of the other articles was addressed to the grievances of that race, and designed to remedy them as the Fifteenth.

We do not say that no one else but the negro can share in this protection. Both the language and spirit of these articles are to have their fair and just weight in any question of construction. Undoubtedly while negro slavery alone was in the mind of the congress which proposed the thirteenth article, it forbids any other kind of slavery, now or hereafter. If Mexican peonage or the Chinese cooly labor system shall develop slavery of the

Mexican or Chinese race within our territory, this amendment may safely be trusted to make it void. And so if other rights are assailed by the States which properly and necessarily fall within the protection of these articles, that protection will apply, though the party interested may not be of African descent. But what we do say, and what we wish to be understood is, that in any fair and just construction of any section or phrase of these amendments, it is necessary to look to the purpose which we have said was the pervading spirit of them all, the evil which they were designed to remedy, and the process of continued addition to the Constitution, until that purpose was supposed to be accomplished, as far as constitutional law can accomplish it. . . .

The next observation is more important in view of the arguments of counsel in the present case. It is, that the distinction between citizenship of the United States and citizenship of a State is clearly recognized and established. Not only may a man be a citizen of the United States without being a citizen of a State, but an important element is necessary to convert the former into the latter. He must reside within the State to make him a citizen of it, but it is only necessary that he should be born or naturalized in the United States to be a citizen of the Union.

It is quite clear, then, that there is a citizenship of the United States, and a citizenship of a State, which are distinct from each other, and which depend upon different characteristics of circumstance in the individual.

We think this distinction and its explicit recognition in this amendment of great weight in this argument, because the next paragraph of this same section, which is the one mainly relied on by the plaintiffs in error, speaks only of privileges and immunities of citizens of the United States, and does not speak of those of citizens of the several States. The argument, however, in favor of the plaintiffs rests wholly on the assumption that the citizenship is the same, and the privileges and immunities guaranteed by the clause are the same.

The language is, "No State shall make or enforce any law which shall abridge the privileges or immunities of citizens of the United States." It is a little remarkable, if this clause was intended as a protection to the citizen of a State against the legislative power of his own State, that the [words] *citizen of the State* should be left out when it is so carefully used, and used in contradistinction to citizens of the United States, in the very sentence which precedes it. It is too clear for argument that the change in phraseology was adopted understandingly and with a purpose.

Of the privileges and immunities of the citizen of the United States, and of the privileges and immunities of the citizen of the States, and what they respectively are, we will presently consider; but we wish to state here that it is only the former which are placed by this clause under the protection of the Federal Constitution, and that the latter, whatever they may be, are not intended to have any additional protection by this paragraph of the amendment.

If, then, there is a difference between the privileges and immunities belonging to a citizen of the United States as such, and those belonging to the citizen of the State as such the latter must rest for their security and protection where they have heretofore rested; for they are not embraced by this paragraph of the amendment. . . .

Fortunately we are not without judicial construction of this clause of the Constitution, the first and the leading case on the subject is that of *Corfield v. Coryell,* . . . decided by Mr. Justice Washington in the Circuit Court for the District of Pennsylvania in 1823. "The inquiry," he says, is,

> [W]hat are the privileges and immunities of citizens of the several States? We feel no hesitation in confining these expressions to those privileges and immunities which are fundamental; which belong of right to the citizens of all free governments, and which have at all times been enjoyed by citizens of the several States which compose this Union, from the time of their becoming free, independent, and sovereign. What these fundamental principles are, it would be more tedious than difficult to enumerate. They may all, however, be comprehended under the following general heads: protection by the government, with the right to acquire and possess property of every kind, to such restraints as the government may prescribe for the general good of the whole. . . .

It would be the vainest show of learning to attempt to prove by citations of authority, that up to the adoption of the recent amendments, no claim or pretense was set up that those rights depended on the Federal government for their existence or protection, beyond the very few express limitations which the Federal Constitution imposed upon the States—such, for instance, as the prohibition against *ex post facto* laws, bills of attainder, and laws impairing the obligation of contracts. But with the exception of these and a few other restrictions, the entire domain of the privileges and immunities of the citizens of the States, and without that of the Federal government. Was it the purpose of the Fourteenth Amendment, by the simple declaration that no States should make or enforce any law which abridge the privileges and immunities of citizens of the United States, to transfer the security and protection of all the civil rights which we have mentioned, from the states to the Federal government? And where it is declared that Congress shall have the power to enforce that article, was it intended to bring within the power of Congress the entire domain of civil rights heretofore belonging exclusively to the States?

All this and more must follow, if the proposition of the plaintiffs in error be sound. For not only are these rights subject to the control of Congress whenever in its discretion any of them are supposed to be abridged by State legislation, but that body may also pass laws in advance, limiting and restricting the exercise of legislative power of the States, in their most ordinary and usual functions, as in its judgment it may think proper on all such subjects. And still further, such a construction followed by the reversal of the judgments of the Supreme Court of Louisiana in these cases, would constitute this court a perpetual censor upon all legislation of the States, on the civil rights of their own citizens, with authority to nullify such as it did not approve as consistent with those rights, as they existed at the time of the adoption of this amendment. The argument we admit is not always the most conclusive which is drawn from the consequences urged against the adoption of a particular construction of an instrument. But when, as in the case before us, these consequences are so serious, so far-reaching and pervading, so great a departure from the structure and spirit of our institutions; when the effect is to fetter and degrade the State governments by subjecting them to the control of Congress, in the exercise of powers heretofore universally conceded to them of the most ordinary and fundamental character; when in fact it radically changes the whole theory of the relations of the State and Federal governments to each other and of both of these governments to the people; the argument has a force that is irresistible, in the absence of language which expresses such a purpose too clearly to admit of doubt.

We are convinced that no such results were intended by the Congress which proposed these amendments, nor by the legislatures of the States which ratified them.

Having shown that the privileges and immunities relied on in the argument are those which belong to citizens of the States as such, and that they are left to the State governments for security and protection, and not by this article placed under the special care of the Federal government, we may hold ourselves excused from defining the privileges and immunities of citizens of the United States which no State can abridge, until some case involving those privileges may make it necessary to do so.

But lest it be said that no such privileges and immunities are to be found if those we have been considering are excluded, we venture to suggest some which owe their existence to the Federal government, its National character, its Constitution, or its laws.

One of these is well described in the case of *Crandall v. Nevada*. . . . It is said to be the right of the citizens of this great country, protected by implied guarantees of its Constitution, "to come to the seat of government to assert any claim he may have upon that government, to transact any business he may have with it, to seek its protection, to share its offices, to engage in administering its functions. He has the right of free access to its seaports, through which all operations of foreign commerce are conducted, to the subtreasuries, land offices, and courts of justice in the several States." And quoting from the language of Chief Justice Taney in another case, it is said "that for all the great purposes for which the Federal government was established, we are one people, with one common country, we are all citizens of the United States"; and it is, as such citizens, that their rights are supported in this court in *Crandall v. Nevada*. . . .

The argument has not been much pressed in these cases that the defendant's charter deprives the plaintiffs of their property without due process of law, or that it denies to them the equal protection of the law. The first of these paragraphs has been in the Constitution since the adoption of the fifth amendment, as a restraint upon the Federal power. It is also to be found in some form of expression in the constitutions of nearly all the States, as a restraint upon the power of the States. This law, then, has practically been the same as it now is during the existence of the government, except so far as the present amendment may place the restraining power over the States in this matter in the hands of the Federal government.

We are not without judicial interpretation, therefore, both State and National, of the meaning of this clause. And it is sufficient to say that under no construction of that provision that we have ever seen, or any that we deem admissible, can the restraint imposed by the state of Louisiana upon the exercise of their trade by the butchers of New Orleans be held to be a deprivation of property within the meaning of that provision.

"Nor shall any State deny to any person within its jurisdiction the equal protection of the laws."

In the light of the history of these amendments, and the pervading purpose of them, which we have already discussed, it is not difficult to give a meaning to this clause. The existence of laws in the states where the newly emancipated negroes resided, which discriminated with gross injustice and hardship against them as a class, was the evil to be remedied by this clause, and by it such laws are forbidden.

If, however, the states did not conform their laws to its requirements, then by the fifth section of the article of amendment Congress was authorized to enforce it by suitable legislation. We doubt very much whether any action of a State not directed by way of discrimination against the negroes as a class, or on account of their race, will ever be held to come within the purview of this provision. It is so clearly a provision for that race and that emergency, that a strong case would be necessary for its application to any other. But as it is a State that is to be dealt with, and not alone the validity of its laws, we may safely leave that matter until congress shall have exercised its power, or some case of State oppression, by denial of equal justice in its courts, shall have claimed a decision at our hands. We find no such case in the one before us, and do not deem it necessary to go over the argument again, as it may have relation to this particular clause of the amendment. . . .

The judgments of the Supreme Court of Louisiana in these cases are affirmed.

Mr. Justice Field, dissenting:

. . . The question presented is . . . one of the gravest importance, not merely to the parties here, but to the whole country. It is nothing less than the question whether the recent amendments to the Federal Constitution protect the citizens of the United States against the deprivation of their common rights by State legislation. In my judgment the Fourteenth Amendment does afford such protection, and was so intended by the Congress which framed and the States which adopted it.

The amendment does not attempt to confer any new privileges or immunities upon citizens, or to enumerate or define those already existing. It assumes that there are such privileges and immunities which belong of right to citizens as such, and ordains that they shall not be abridged by State legislation. If this inhibition has no reference to privileges and immunities of this character, but only refers, as held by the majority of the court in their opinion, to such privileges and immunities as were before its adoption specially designated in the Constitution or necessarily implied as belonging to citizens of the United States, it was a vain and idle enactment, which accomplished nothing, and most unnecessarily excited Congress and the people on its passage. With privileges and immunities thus designated or implied no State could ever have interfered by its laws and no new constitutional provision was required to inhibit such interference. The supremacy of the Constitution and the laws of the United States always controlled any State legislation of that char-

acter. But if the amendment refers to the natural and inalienable rights which belong to all citizens, the inhibition has a profound significance and consequence.

What, then, are the privileges and immunities which are secured against abridgment by State legislation? . . .

The terms, privileges and immunities, are not new in the Amendment; they were in the Constitution before the Amendment was adopted. They are found in the second section of the fourth article, which declares that "the citizens of each State shall be entitled to all privileges and immunities of citizens in the several States," and they have been the subject of frequent consideration in judicial decisions. . . . The privileges and immunities designated are those which of right belong to the citizens of all free governments. Clearly among these must be placed the right to pursue a lawful employment in a lawful manner, without other restraint than such as equally affects all persons. . . .

This equality of right, with exemption from all disparaging and partial enactments, in the lawful pursuits of life, throughout the whole country, is the distinguishing privilege of citizens of the United States. To them, everywhere, all pursuits, all professions, all avocations are open without other restrictions than such as are imposed equally upon all others of the same age, sex, and condition. The State may prescribe such regulations for every pursuit and calling of life as will promote the public health, secure the good order and advance the general prosperity of society, but when once prescribed, the pursuit or calling must be free to be followed by every citizen who is within the conditions designated, and will conform to the regulations. This is the fundamental idea upon which our institutions rest, and unless adhered to in the legislation of the country our government will be a republic only in name. The Fourteenth Amendment, in my judgment, makes it essential to the validity of the legislation of every State that this equality of right should be respected. How widely this equality has been departed from, how entirely rejected and trampled upon by the act of Louisiana, I have already shown. And it is to me a matter of profound regret that its validity is recognized by a majority of this court, for by it the right of free labor, one of the most sacred and imprescriptible rights of man, is violated. . . .

I am authorized by the **Chief Justice, Mr. Justice Swayne,** and **Mr. Justice Bradley,** to state that they concur with me in this dissenting opinion.

Mr. Justice Bradley, dissenting.

. . . The right of a State to regulate the conduct of its citizens is undoubtedly a very broad and extensive one, and not to be lightly restricted. But there are certain fundamental rights which this right of regulation cannot infringe. It may prescribe the manner of their exercise, but it cannot subvert the rights themselves. . . .

The granting of monopolies, or exclusive privileges to individuals or corporations, is an invasion of the right of another to choose a lawful calling, and an infringement of personal liberty. It was so felt by the English nation as far back as the reigns of Elizabeth and James. A fierce struggle for the suppression of such monopolies, and for abolishing the prerogative of creating them, was made and was successful. . . . And ever since that struggle no English-speaking people have ever endured such an odious badge of tyranny. . . .

Can the Federal courts administer relief to citizens of the United States whose privileges and immunities have been abridged by a State? Of this I entertain no doubt. Prior to the Fourteenth Amendment this could not be done, except in a few instances, for the want of the requisite authority. . . .

Admitting, therefore, that formerly the States were not prohibited from infringing any fundamental privileges and immunities of citizens of the United States, except in a few specified cases, that cannot be said now, since the adoption of the Fourteenth Amendment. In my judgment, it was the intention of the people of this country in adopting that amendment to provide National security against violation by the States of the fundamental rights of the citizen. . . .

In my view, a law which prohibits a large class of citizens from adopting a lawful employment, or from following a lawful employment previously adopted, does deprive them of liberty as well as property, without due process of law. Their right of choice is a portion of their liberty; their occupation is their property. Such a law also deprives those citizens of the equal protection of the laws, contrary to the last clause of the section. . . .

Mr. Justice Swayne, dissenting. . . .

Case

LOCHNER V. NEW YORK

198 U.S. 45; 25 S.Ct. 539; 49 L.Ed. 937 (1905)
Vote: 5–4

Joseph Lochner, a bakery owner in Utica, New York, was fined $50 for violating a state law that limited employment in bakeries to ten hours a day and sixty hours a week. After the state appellate courts upheld his conviction, Lochner obtained review in the U.S. Supreme Court on a writ of error.

Mr. Justice Peckham delivered the opinion of the Court.

The indictment . . . charges that the plaintiff in error violated . . . the labor law of the state of New York, in that he wrongfully and unlawfully required and permitted an employee working for him to work more than sixty hours in one week. . . . The mandate of the statute, that "no employee shall be required or permitted to work," is the substantial equivalent of an enactment that "no employee shall contract or agree to work," more than ten hours per day; and, as there is no provision for special emergencies, the statute is mandatory in all cases. It is not an act merely fixing the number of hours which shall constitute a legal day's work, but an absolute prohibition upon the employer permitting, under any circumstances, more than ten hours work to be done in his establishment. The employee may desire to earn the extra money which would arise from his working more than the prescribed time, but this statute forbids the employer from permitting the employee to earn it.

The statute necessarily interferes with the right of contract between the employer and employees, concerning the number of hours in which the latter may labor in the bakery of the employer. The general right to make a contract in relation to his business is part of the liberty of the individual protected by the 14th Amendment of the Federal Constitution. . . . Under that provision no state can deprive any person of life, liberty, or property without due process of law. The right to purchase or to sell labor is part of the liberty protected by this amendment, unless there are circumstances which exclude the right. There are, however, certain powers, existing in the sovereignty of each state in the Union, somewhat vaguely termed police powers, the exact description and limitation which have not been attempted by the courts. Those powers, broadly stated, and without, at present, any attempt at a more specific limitation, relate to the safety, health, morals, and general welfare of the public. Both property and liberty are held on such reasonable conditions as may be imposed by the governing power of the state in the exercise of those powers, and with such conditions the 14th Amendment was not designed to interfere. . . .

The state, therefore, has power to prevent the individual from making certain kinds of contracts, and in regard to them the Federal Constitution offers no protection. If the contract be one which the state, in the legitimate exercise of its police power, has the right to prohibit, it is not prevented from prohibiting it by the 14th Amendment. Contracts in violation of a statute, for immoral purposes, or to do any other unlawful act, could obtain no protection from the Federal Constitution, as coming under the liberty of person or of free contract. Therefore, when the state, by its legislature, in the assumed exercise of its police powers, has passed an act which seriously limits the right to labor or the right of contract in regard to their means of livelihood between persons who are *sui juris* (both employer and employee), it becomes of great importance to determine which shall prevail—the right of the individual to labor for such time as he may choose, or the right of the state to prevent the individual from laboring, or from entering into any contract to labor, beyond a certain time prescribed by the state.

This court has recognized the existence and upheld the exercise of the police powers of the states in many cases which might fairly be considered as border ones, and it has, in the course of its determination of questions regarding the asserted invalidity of such statutes, on the ground of their violation of the rights secured by the Federal Constitution, been guided by rules of a very liberal nature, the application of which has resulted, in numerous instances, in upholding the validity of state statutes thus assailed. Among the later cases where the state law has been upheld by this court is that of *Holden v. Hardy.* . . . A provision in the act of the legislature of Utah was there under consideration, the act limiting the employment of workmen in all underground mines or workings, to eight hours per day, "except in cases of emergency, where life or property is in imminent danger." It also limited the hours of labor in smelting and other institutions for the reduction or refining of ores or metals to eight hours per day, except in like cases of emergency. The act was held to be a valid exercise of the police powers of the state. . . .

It must, of course, be conceded that there is a limit to the valid exercise of the police power by the state. There is no dispute concerning this general proposition. Otherwise the 14th Amendment would have no efficacy and the legislatures of the states would have unbounded

power, and it would be enough to say that any piece of legislation was enacted to conserve the morals, the health, or the safety of the people; such legislation would be valid, no matter how absolutely without foundation the claim might be. The claim of the police power would be a mere pretext—become another and delusive name for the supreme sovereignty of the state to be exercised free from constitutional restraint. This is not contended for. In every case that comes before this court, therefore, where legislation of this character is concerned, and where the protection of the Federal Constitution is sought, the question necessarily arises. Is this a fair, reasonable, and appropriate exercise of the police power of the state, or is it an unreasonable, unnecessary, and arbitrary interference with the right of the individual to his personal liberty, or to enter into those contracts in relation to labor which may seem to him appropriate or necessary for the support of himself and his family? Of course the liberty of contract relating to labor includes both parties to it. The one has as much right to purchase as the other to sell labor.

This is not a question of substituting the judgment of the court for that of the legislature. If the act be within the power of the state it is valid, although the judgment of the court might be totally opposed to the enactment of such a law. But the question would still remain: Is it within the police power of the state? And that question must be answered by the court.

The question whether this act is valid as a labor law, pure and simple, may be dismissed in a few words. There is no reasonable ground for interfering with the liberty of person or the right of free contract, by determining the hours of labor, in the occupation of a baker. There is no contention that bakers as a class are not equal in intelligence and capacity to men in other trades or manual occupations, or that they are not able to assert their rights and care for themselves without the protecting arm of the state, interfering with their independence of judgment and of action. They are in no sense wards of the state. Viewed in the light of a purely labor law, with no reference whatever to the question of health, we think that a law like the one before us involves neither the safety, the morals, nor the welfare, of the public, and that interest of the public is not in the slightest degree affected by such an act. The law must be upheld, if at all, as a law pertaining to the health of the individual engaged in the occupation of a baker. It does not affect any other portion of the public than those who are engaged in that occupation. Clean and wholesome bread does not depend upon whether the baker works but ten hours per day or only sixty hours a week. The limitation of the hours of labor does not come within the police power on that ground.

It is a question of which of two powers or rights shall prevail—the power of the state to legislate or the right of the individual to liberty of person and freedom of contract. The mere assertion that the subject relates, though but in a remote degree, to the public health, does not necessarily render the enactment valid. The act must have a more direct relation, as a means to an end, and the end itself must be appropriate and legitimate, before an act can end, and the end itself must be appropriate and legitimate, before an act can be held to be valid which interferes with the general right of an individual to be free in his person and in his power to contract in relation to his own labor. . . .

We think the limit of the police power has been reached and passed in this case. There is, in our judgment, no reasonable foundation for holding this to be necessary or appropriate as a health law to safeguard the public health, or the health of the individuals who are following the trade of a baker. If this statute be valid, and if, therefore, a proper case is made out in which to deny the right of an individual, *sui juris,* as employer or employee, to make contracts for the labor of the latter under the protection of the provisions of the Federal Constitution, there would seem to be no length to which legislation of this nature might not go. . . .

We think that there can be no fair doubt that the trade of a baker, in and of itself, is not an unhealthy one to that degree which would authorize the legislature to interfere with the right to labor, and with the right of free contract on the part of the individual, either as employer or employee. In looking through statistics regarding all trades and occupations, it may be true that the trade of a baker does not appear to be as healthy as some other trades, and is also vastly more healthy than still others. To the common understanding the trade of a baker has never been regarded as an unhealthy one. Very likely physicians would not recommend the exercise of that or of any other trade as a remedy for ill health. Some occupations are more healthy than others, but we think there are none which might not come under the power of the legislature to supervise and control the hours of working therein, if the mere fact that the occupation is not absolutely and perfectly healthy is to confer that right upon the legislative department of the government. . . .

. . . Statutes of the nature of that under review, limiting the hours in which grown and intelligent men may labor to earn their living, are mere meddlesome interferences with the rights of the individual, and they are not saved from condemnation by the claim that they are

passed in the exercise of the police power and upon the subject of the health of the individual whose rights are interfered with, unless there be some fair ground, reasonable in and of itself, to say that there is material danger to the public health or to the health of the employees if the hours of labor are not curtailed. If this be not clearly the case, the individuals whose rights are thus made the subject of legislative interference are under the protection of the Federal Constitution regarding their liberty of contract as well as of person, and the legislature of the State has no power to limit their right as proposed in this statute. All that it could properly do has been done by it with regard to the conduct of bakeries, as provided for in the other sections of the act above set forth. These several sections provide for the inspection of the premises where the bakery is carried on, with regard to furnishing proper wash-rooms and water-closets, apart from the bake-room, also with regard to providing proper drainage, plumbing and painting; the sections, in addition, provide for the height of the ceiling, the cementing or tiling of floors, where necessary in the opinion of the factory inspector, and for other things of that nature; alterations are also provided for and are to be made where necessary in the opinion of the inspector, in order to comply with the provisions of the statute. These various sections may be wise and valid regulations, and they certainly go to the full extent of providing for the cleanliness and the healthiness, so far as possible, of the quarters in which bakeries are to be conducted. Adding to all these requirements a prohibition to enter into any contract of labor in a bakery for more than a certain number of hours a week is, in our judgment, so wholly beside the matter of a proper, reasonable and fair provision as to run counter to that liberty of person and of free contract provided for in the Federal Constitution.

It is impossible for us to shut our eyes to the fact that many of the laws of this character, while passed under what is claimed to be the police power for the purpose of protecting the public health or welfare, are, in reality, passed from other motives. We are justified in saying so when, from the character of the law and the subject upon which it legislates, it is apparent that the public health or welfare bears but the most remote relation to the law. The purpose of a statute must be determined from the natural and legal effect of the language employed; and whether it is or is not repugnant to the Constitution of the United States must be determined from the natural effect of such statutes when put into operation, and not from their proclaimed purpose. . . .

It is manifest to us that the limitation of the hours of labor as provided for in this section of the statute under which the indictment was found, and the plaintiff in error convicted, has no such direct relation to, and no such substantial effect upon, the health of the employee, as to justify us in regarding the section as really a health law. It seems to us that the real object and purpose were simply to regulate the hours of labor between the master and his employees . . . in a private business, not dangerous in any degree to morals, or in any real and substantial degree to the health of the employees. Under such circumstances the freedom of master and employee to contract with each other in relation to their employment, and in defining the same, cannot be prohibited or interfered with, without violating the Federal Constitution.

The judgment of the Court of Appeals of New York, as well as that of the Supreme Court and of the County Court of Oneida County, must be reversed and the case remanded to County Court for further proceedings not inconsistent with this opinion.

Reversed.

Mr. Justice Harlan [with whom **Mr. Justice White** and **Mr. Justice Day** concurred], dissenting:

. . . It is plain that this statute was enacted in order to protect the physical well-being of those who work in bakery and confectionery establishments. It may be that the statute had its origin, in part, in the belief that employers and employees in such establishments were not upon an equal footing, and that the necessities of the latter often compelled them to submit to such exactions as unduly taxed their strength. Be this as it may, the statute must be taken as expressing the belief of the people of New York that, as a general rule, and in the case of the average man, labor in excess of sixty hours during a week in such establishments may endanger the health of those who thus labor. Whether or not this be wise legislation it is not the province of the court to inquire. Under our system of government the courts are not concerned with the wisdom or policy of legislation. So that, in determining the question of power to interfere with liberty of contract, the court may inquire whether the means devised by the state are germane to an end which may be lawfully accomplished and have a real or substantial relation to the protection of health, as involved in the daily work of the persons, male and female, engaged in bakery and confectionery establishments. But when this inquiry is entered upon I find it impossible, in view of common experience, to say that there is here no real or substantial relation between the means employed by the state and the end sought to be accomplished by its legislation. Nor can I say that the statute has no ap-

propriated or direct connection with that protection to health which each state owes to her citizens; or that it is not promotive of the health of the employees in question; or that the regulation prescribed by the state is utterly unreasonable and extravagant or wholly arbitrary. Still less can I say that the statute is, beyond question, a plain, palpable invasion of rights secured by the fundamental law. Therefore I submit that this court will transcend its functions if it assumes to annul the statute of New York. It must be remembered that this statute does not apply to all kinds of business. It applies only to work in bakery and confectionery establishments, in which, as all know, the air constantly breathed by workmen is not as pure and healthful as that to be found in some other establishments or out of doors. . . .

. . . [T]he state is not amenable to the judiciary, in respect of its legislative enactments, unless such enactments are plainly, palpably, beyond all question, inconsistent with the Constitution of the United States. We are not to presume that the state of New York has acted in bad faith. Nor can we assume that its legislature acted without due deliberation, or that it did not determine this question upon the fullest attainable information and for the common good. We cannot say that the state has acted without reason, nor ought we to proceed upon the theory that its action is a mere sham. Our duty, I submit, is to sustain the statute as not being in conflict with the Federal Constitution, for the reason—and such is an all-sufficient reason—it is not shown to be plainly and palpably inconsistent with that instrument. Let the state alone in the management of its purely domestic affairs, so long as it does not appear beyond all question that it has violated the Federal Constitution. This view necessarily results from the principle that the health and safety of the people of a state are primarily for the state to guard and protect.

I take leave to say that the New York statute, in the particulars here involved, cannot be held to be in conflict with the 14th Amendment, without enlarging the scope of the amendment far beyond its original purpose, and without bringing under the supervision of this court matters which have been supposed to belong exclusively to the legislative departments of the several states . . . to guard the health and safety of their citizens. . . .

Mr. Justice Holmes, dissenting:

. . . This case is decided upon an economic theory which a large part of the country does not entertain. If it were a question whether I agreed with that theory, I should desire to study it further and long before making up my mind. But I do not conceive that to be my duty, because I strongly believe that my agreement or disagreement has nothing to do with the right of a majority to embody their opinions in law. It is settled by various decisions of this court that . . . state laws may regulate life in many ways which are as legislators might think as injudicious, or if you like as tyrannical, as this, and which, equally with this, interfere with the liberty to contract. Sunday laws and usury laws are ancient examples. A more modern one is the prohibition of lotteries. The liberty of the citizen to do as he likes so long as he does not interfere with the liberty of others to do the same, which has been a shibboleth for some well-known writers, is interfered with by school laws, by the post office, by every state or municipal institution which takes his money for purposes thought desirable, whether he likes it or not. The 14th Amendment does not enact Mr. Herbert Spencer's *Social Statics*. . . . But a Constitution is not intended to embody a particular economic theory, whether of paternalism and the organic relation of the citizen to the state or of laissez faire. It is made for people of fundamentally differing views, and the accident of finding certain opinions natural and familiar, or novel, and even shocking, ought not to conclude our judgment upon the question whether statutes embodying them conflict with the Constitution of the United States.

General propositions do not decide concrete cases. The decision will depend on a judgment or intuition more subtle than any articulate major premise. But I think that the proposition just stated, if it is accepted, will carry us far toward the end. Every opinion tends to become a law. I think that the word "liberty," in the 14th Amendment, is perverted when it is held to prevent the natural outcome of a dominant opinion, unless it can be said that a rational and fair man necessarily would admit that the statute proposed would infringe fundamental principles as they have been understood by the traditions of our people and our law. It does not end research to show that no such sweeping condemnation can be passed upon the statute before us. A reasonable man might think it a proper measure on the score of health. Men whom I certainly could not pronounce unreasonable would uphold it as a first installment of a general regulation of the hours of work. Whether in the latter aspect it would be open to the charge of inequality I think it unnecessary to discuss.

Case

ADKINS V. CHILDREN'S HOSPITAL

261 U.S. 525; 43 S.Ct. 394; 67 L.Ed. 785 (1923)
Vote: 5–3

In 1918, Congress created a board and empowered it to set minimum wages for women and children working in the District of Columbia. Children's Hospital obtained an injunction to prevent Adkins and other board members from enforcing the minimum wage. Adkins et al. appealed to the Supreme Court.

Mr. Justice Sutherland delivered the opinion of the Court.

. . . The judicial duty of passing upon the constitutionality of an act of Congress is one of great gravity and delicacy. The statute here in question has successfully borne the scrutiny of the legislative branch of the government, which, by enacting it, has affirmed its validity; and that determination must be given great weight. This Court, by an unbroken line of decisions from Chief Justice Marshall to the present day, has steadily adhered to the rule that every possible presumption is in favor of the validity of an act of Congress until overcome beyond rational doubt. But if, by clear and indubitable demonstration, a statute be opposed to the Constitution, we have no choice but to say so. The Constitution, by its own terms, is the supreme law of the land, emanating from the people, the repository of ultimate sovereignty under our form of government. A congressional statute, on the other hand, is the act of an agency of this sovereign authority, and, if it conflict with the Constitution, must fall; for that which is not supreme must yield to that which is. . . .

The statute now under consideration is attacked upon the ground that it authorizes an unconstitutional interference with the freedom of contract included within the guarantees of the due process clause of the Fifth Amendment. That the right to contract about one's affairs is a part of the liberty of the individual protected by this clause is settled by the decisions of this Court, and is no longer open to question. . . . Within this liberty are contracts of employment of labor. In making such contracts, generally speaking, the parties have an equal right to obtain from each other the best terms they can as the result of private bargaining. . . .

There is, of course, no such thing as absolute freedom of contract. It is subject to a great variety of restraints. But freedom of contract is, nevertheless, the general rule and restraint the exception; and the exercise of legislative authority to abridge it can be justified only by the existence of exceptional circumstances. Whether these circumstances exist in the present case constitutes the question to be answered. . . .

In the *Muller* Case the validity of an Oregon statute, forbidding the employment of any female in certain industries more than ten hours during any one day, was upheld. The decision proceeded upon the theory that the difference between the sexes may justify a different rule respecting hours of labor in the case of women than in the case of men. It is pointed out that these consist in differences of physical structure, especially in respect of the maternal functions, and also in the fact that historically woman has always been dependent upon man, who has established his control by superior physical strength. . . . But the ancient inequality of the sexes, otherwise than physical as suggested in the *Muller* Case has continued "with diminishing intensity." In view of the great—not to say revolutionary—changes which have taken place since that utterance, in the contractual, political, and civil status of women, culminating in the Nineteenth Amendment, it is not unreasonable to say that these differences have now come almost, if not quite, to the vanishing point. In this aspect of the matter, while the physical differences must be recognized in appropriate cases, and legislation fixing hours or conditions of work may properly taken them into account, we cannot accept the doctrine that women of mature age, *sui juris,* require or may be subjected to restrictions upon their liberty of contract which could not lawfully be imposed in the case of men under similar circumstances. To do so would be to ignore all the implications to be drawn from the present-day trend of legislation, as well as that of common thought and usage, by which woman is accorded emancipation from the old doctrine that she must be given special protection or be subjected to special restraint in her contractual and civil relationships. In passing, it may be noted that the instant statute applies in the case of a woman employer contracting with a woman employee as it does when the former is a man.

The essential characteristics of the statute now under consideration, which differentiate it from the laws fixing hours of labor, will be made to appear as we proceed. It is sufficient now to point out that the latter . . . deal with incidents of the employment having no neces-

sary effect upon the heart of the contract; that is, the amount of wages to be paid and received. A law forbidding work to continue beyond a given number of hours leaves the parties free to contract about wages and thereby equalize whatever additional burdens may be imposed upon the employer as a result of the restrictions as to hours, by an adjustment in respect of the amount of wages. Enough has been said to show that the authority to fix hours of labor cannot be exercised except in respect of those occupations where work of long-continued duration is detrimental to health. This Court has been careful in every case where the question has been raised, to place its decision upon this limited authority of the legislature to regulate hours of labor, and to disclaim any purpose to uphold the legislation as fixing wages, thus recognizing an essential difference between the two. It seems plain that these decisions afford no real support for any form of law establishing minimum wages.

If now, in the light furnished by the foregoing exceptions to the general rule forbidding legislative interference with freedom of contract, we examine and analyze the statute in question, we shall see that it differs from them in every material respect. . . . It is simply and exclusively a price-fixing law, confined to adult women (for we are not now considering the provisions relating to minors), who are legally as capable of contracting for themselves as men. It forbids two parties having lawful capacity under penalties as to the employer to freely contract with one another in respect of the price for which one shall render service to the other in a purely private employment where both are willing, perhaps anxious, to agree, even though the consequences may be to oblige one to surrender a desirable engagement, and the other to dispense with the services of a desirable employee. . . .

The standard furnished by the statute for the guidance of the board is so vague as to be impossible of practical application with any reasonable degree of accuracy. What is sufficient to supply the necessary cost of living for a woman worker and maintain her in good health and protect her morals is obviously not a precise or unvarying sum—not even approximately so. The amount will depend upon a variety of circumstances: The individual temperament, habits of thrift, care, ability to buy necessaries intelligently, and whether the woman lives alone or with her family. To those who practice economy, a given sum will afford comfort, while to those of contrary habit the same sum will be wholly inadequate. The cooperative economies of the family group are not taken into account, though they constitute an important consideration in estimating the cost of living, for it is obvious that the individual expense will be less in the case of a member of a family than in the case of one living alone. The relation between earnings and morals is not capable of standardization. It cannot be shown that well-paid women safeguard their morals more carefully than those who are poorly paid. Morality rests upon other considerations than wages; and there is, certainly, no such prevalent connection between the two as to justify a broad attempt to adjust the latter with reference to the former. . . .

The law takes account of the necessities of only one party to the contract. It ignores the necessities of the employer by compelling him to pay not less than a certain sum, not only whether the employee is capable of earning it, but irrespective of the ability of his business to sustain the burden, generously leaving him, of course, the privilege of abandoning his business as an alternative for going on at a loss. Within the limits of the minimum sum, he is precluded, under penalty of fine and imprisonment, from adjusting compensation to the differing merits of his employees. It compels him to pay at least the sum fixed in any event, because the employee needs it, but requires no service of equivalent value from the employee. . . . To the extent that the sum fixed exceeds the fair value of the services rendered, it amounts to a compulsory exaction from the employer for the support of a partially indigent person, for whose condition there rests upon him no peculiar responsibility, and therefore, in effect, arbitrarily shifts to his shoulders a burden which, if it belongs to anybody, belongs to society as a whole.

The feature of this statute which, perhaps more than any other, puts upon it the stamp of invalidity is that it exacts from the employer an arbitrary payment for a purpose and upon a basis having no causal connection with his business, or the contract, or the work the employee engages to do. . . . The ethical right of every worker, man or woman, to a living wage, may be conceded. One of the declared and important purposes of trade organizations is to secure it. And with that principle and with every legitimate effort to realize it in fact, no one can quarrel; but the fallacy of the proposed method of attaining it is that it assumes that every employer is bound, at all events to furnish it. The moral requirement, implicit in every contract of employment, *viz.,* that the amount to be paid and the service to be rendered shall bear to each other some relation of just equivalence, is completely ignored. . . . Certainly the employer, by paying a fair equivalent for the service rendered, though not sufficient to support the employee, has neither caused nor contributed to her poverty. On the contrary, to the extent of what he pays, he has re-

lieved it. In principle, there can be no difference between the case of selling labor and the case of selling goods. If one goes to the butcher, the baker, or grocer to buy food, he is morally entitled to obtain the worth of his money, but he is not entitled to more. If what he gets is worth what he pays, he is not justified in demanding more simply because he needs more; and the shopkeeper, having dealt fairly and honestly in that transaction, is not concerned in any peculiar sense with the question of his customer's necessities. . . . But a statute which prescribes payment without regard to any of these things, and solely with relation to circumstances apart from the contract of employment, the business affected by it, and the work done under it, is so clearly the product of a naked, arbitrary exercise of power, that it cannot be allowed to stand under the Constitution of the United States.

We are asked, upon the one hand, to consider the fact that several states have adopted similar statutes, and we are invited, upon the other hand, to give weight to the fact that three times as many states, presumably as well informed and as anxious to promote the health and morals of their people, have refrained from enacting such legislation. We have also been furnished with a large number of printed opinions approving the policy of the minimum wage, and our own reading has disclosed a large number to the contrary. These are all proper enough for the consideration of the lawmaking bodies, since their tendency is to establish the desirability or undesirability of the legislation; but they reflect no legitimate light upon the question of its validity, and that is what we are called upon to decide. The elucidation of that question cannot be aided by counting heads.

It is said that great benefits have resulted from the operation of such statutes, not alone in the District of Columbia, but in the several states where they have been in force. A mass of reports, opinions of special observers and students of the subject, and the like, has been brought before us in support of this statement, all of which we have found interesting but only mildly persuasive. That the earnings of women now are greater than they were formerly, and that conditions affecting women have become better in other respects, may be conceded; but convincing indications of the logical relation of these desirable changes to the law in question are significantly lacking. They may be, and quite probably are, due to other causes. . . .

Finally, it may be said that if, in the interest of the public welfare, the police power may be invoked to justify the fixing of a minimum wage, it may, when the public welfare is thought to require it, be invoked to justify a maximum wage. The power to fix high wages connotes, by like course of reasoning, the power to fix low wages. If, in the face of the guarantees of the Fifth Amendment, this form of legislation shall be legally justified, the field for the operation of the police power will have been widened to a great and dangerous degree. If, for example, in the opinion of future lawmakers, wages in the building trades shall become so high as to preclude people of ordinary means from building and owning homes, an authority which sustains the minimum wage will be invoked to support a maximum wage for building laborers and artisans, and the same argument which has been here urged to strip the employer of his constitutional liberty of contract in one direction will be utilized to strip the employee of his constitutional liberty of contract in the opposite direction. A wrong decision does not end with itself: it is a precedent, and, with the swing of sentiment, its bad influence may run from one extremity of the arc to the other.

It has been said that legislation of the kind now under review is required in the interest of social justice, for whose ends freedom of contract may lawfully be subjected to restraint. The liberty of the individual to do as he pleases, even in innocent matters, is not absolute. It must frequently yield to the common good, and the line beyond which the power of interference may not be pressed is neither definite nor unalterable, but may be made to move, within limits not well defined, with changing need and circumstance. Any attempt to fix a rigid boundary would be unwise as well as futile. But, nevertheless, there are limits to the power, and when these have been passed, it becomes the plain duty of the courts, in the proper exercise of their authority, to so declare. To sustain the individual freedom of action contemplated by the Constitution is not to strike down the common good, but to exalt it; for surely the good of society as a whole cannot be better served than by the preservation against arbitrary restraint of the liberties of its constituent members.

It follows from what has been said that the act in question passes the limit prescribed by the Constitution, and, accordingly, the decrees of the court below are affirmed.

Mr. Justice Brandeis took no part in the consideration or decision of these cases.

Mr. Chief Justice Taft, dissenting.

. . . The boundary of the police power, beyond which its exercise becomes an invasion of the guaranty of liberty under the Fifth and Fourteenth Amendments to the Constitution, is not easy to mark. Our Court has been laboriously engaged in pricking out a line in successive cases. We must be careful, it seems to me, to follow that line as well as we can, and not to depart from it by suggesting a distinction that is formal rather than real.

Legislatures, in limiting freedom of contract between employee and employer by a minimum wage, proceed on the assumption that employees in the class receiving least pay are not upon a full level of equality of choice with their employer, and in their necessitous circumstances are prone to accept pretty much anything that is offered. They are peculiarly subject to the overreaching of the harsh and greedy employer. The evils of the sweating system and of the long hours and low wages which are characteristic of it are well known. Now, I agree that it is a disputable question in the field of political economy how far a statutory requirement of maximum hours or minimum wages may be a useful remedy for these evils, and whether it may not make the case of the oppressed employee worse than it was before. But it is not the function of this Court to hold congressional acts invalid simply because they are passed to carry out economic views which the Court believes to be unwise or unsound. . . .

The right of the legislature under the Fifth and Fourteenth Amendments to limit the hours of employment on the score of the health of the employee, it seems to me, has been firmly established. As to that, one would think, the line had been pricked out so that it has become a well-formulated rule. . . . In [*Bunting v. Oregon*] . . . this Court sustained a law limiting the hours of labor of any person, whether man or woman, working in any mill, factory, or manufacturing establishment, to ten hours a day, with a proviso as to further hours [allowing limited overtime at one and one-half times the regular wage]. . . . The law covered the whole field of industrial employment, and certainly covered the case of persons employed in bakeries. Yet the opinion in the *Bunting* Case does not mention the *Lochner* Case. No one can suggest any constitutional distinction between employment in a bakery and one in any other kind of a manufacturing establishment which should make a limit of hours in the one invalid, and the same limit in the other permissible. It is impossible for me to reconcile the *Bunting* Case and the *Lochner* Case, and I have always supposed that the *Lochner* Case was thus overruled *sub silentio*. Yet the opinion of the Court herein in support of its conclusion quotes from the opinion in the *Lochner* Case as one which has been sometimes distinguished, but never overruled. Certainly there was no attempt to distinguish it in the *Bunting* Case.

However, the opinion herein does not overrule the *Bunting* Case in express terms, and therefore I assume that the conclusion in this case rests on the distinction between a minimum of wages and a maximum of hours in the limiting of liberty to contract. I regret to be at variance with the court as to the substance of this distinction. In absolute freedom of contract the one term is as important as the other, for both enter equally into the consideration given and received; a restriction as to one is not any greater in essence than the other, and is of the same kind. One is the multiplier and the other the multiplicand.

If it be said that long hours of labor have a more direct effect upon the health of the employee than the low wage, there is very respectable authority from those observers, disclosed in the record and in the literature on the subject, quoted at length in the briefs, that they are equally harmful in this regard. Congress took this view, and we cannot say it was not warranted in so doing. . . .

I am authorized to say that **Mr. Justice Sanford** concurs in this opinion.

Mr. Justice Holmes, dissenting.

The question in this case is the broad one, whether Congress can establish minimum rates of wages for women in the District of Columbia, with due provision for special circumstances, or whether we must say that Congress has no power to meddle with the matter at all. To me, notwithstanding the deference due to the prevailing judgment of the Court, the power of Congress seems absolutely free from doubt. The end—to remove conditions leading to ill health, immorality, and the deterioration of the race—no one would deny to be within the scope of constitutional legislation. The means are means that have the approval of Congress, of many states, and of those governments from which we have learned our greatest lessons. When so many intelligent persons, who have studied the matter more than any of us can, have thought that the means are effective and are worth the price, it seems to me impossible to deny that the belief reasonably may be held by reasonable men. If the law encountered no other objection than that the means bore no relation to the end, or that they cost too much, I do not suppose that anyone would venture to say that it was bad. I agree, of course, that a law answering the foregoing requirements might be invalidated by specific provisions of the Constitution. For instance, it might take private property without just compensation. But, in the present instance, the only objection that can be urged is found within the vague contours of the Fifth Amendment, prohibiting the depriving any person of liberty or property without due process of law. To that I turn.

The earlier decisions upon the same words in the Fourteenth Amendment began within our memory, and went no farther than an unpretentious assertion of the liberty to follow the ordinary callings. Later that innocuous generality was expanded into the dogma, Liberty of Contract. Contract is not specifically mentioned in the text that we have to construe. It is merely an example of doing what you want to do, embodied in the word "liberty." But pretty much all law consists in forbidding men to do some things that they want to do, and contract is no more exempt from law than other acts. Without enumerating all the restrictive laws that have been upheld, I will mention a few that seem to me to have interfered with liberty of contract quite as seriously and directly as the one before us. Usury laws prohibit contracts by which a man receives more than so much interest for the money that he lends. Statutes of frauds restrict many contracts to certain forms. Some Sunday laws prohibit practically all contracts during one-seventh of our whole life. Insurance rates may be regulated. Finally, women's hours of labor may be fixed. . . . And the principle was extended to men, with the allowance of a limited overtime, to be paid for "at the rate of time and one half of the regular wage," in *Bunting v. Oregon*. . . .

I confess that I do not understand the principle on which the power to fix a minimum for the wages of women can be denied by those who admit the power to fix a maximum for their hours of work. I fully assent to the proposition that here, as elsewhere, the distinctions of the law are distinctions of degree; but I perceive no difference in the kind or degree of interference with liberty, the only matter with which we have any concern, between the one case and the other. The bargain is equally affected whichever half you regulate. *Muller v. Oregon* [1908], I take it, is as good law today as it was in 1908. It will need more than the Nineteenth Amendment to convince me that there are no differences between men and women, or that legislation cannot take those differences into account. I should not hesitate to take them into account if I thought it necessary to sustain this act. . . . But after *Bunting v. Oregon* . . . I had supposed that it was not necessary, and that *Lochner v. New York* . . . would be allowed a deserved repose. . . .

Case

WEST COAST HOTEL COMPANY V. PARRISH

300 U.S. 379; 57 S.Ct. 578; 81 L.Ed. 703 (1937)

Vote: 5–4

In May 1935, Elsie Parrish was discharged from her job as a chambermaid at the Cascadian Hotel (owned by the West Coast Hotel Company) in Wenatchee, Washington. She had originally been employed in the late summer of 1933 at a wage rate of twenty-two cents per hour. At the time of her dismissal, Parrish was being paid twenty-five cents an hour, still well below the $14.50 weekly minimum set by the Industrial Welfare Committee pursuant to a state minimum-wage law passed in 1913. Elsie Parrish and her husband, Ernest, promptly sued the West Coast Hotel Company for $216.19, the amount by which the minimum wage exceeded her actual earnings during the period of her employment. Although the Parrishes lost at the trial level (the judge held that the case was controlled by Adkins v. Children's Hospital*), they appealed to the state supreme court which, in spite of* Adkins*, sustained the Washington minimum-wage statute. The U.S. Supreme Court agreed to review their case in the late fall of 1936.*

Mr. Chief Justice Hughes delivered the opinion of the Court.

This case presents the question of the constitutional validity of the minimum wage law of the state of Washington. . . . It provides:

Sec. 1. The welfare of the State of Washington demands that women and minors be protected from conditions of labor which have a pernicious effect on their health and morals. The State of Washington, therefore, exercising herein its police and sovereign power declares that inadequate wages and unsanitary conditions of labor exert such pernicious effect.

Sec. 2. It shall be unlawful to employ women or minors in any industry or occupation within the State of Washington under conditions of labor detrimental to their health or morals; and it shall be unlawful to employ women workers in any industry within the State of Washington at wages which are not adequate for their maintenance.

Sec. 3. There is hereby created a commission to be known as the "Industrial Welfare Commission" for the State of Washington, to establish such standards of wages and conditions of labor for women and minors employed within the State of Washington, as shall be held hereunder to be reasonable and not detrimental to health and morals, and which shall be sufficient for the decent maintenance of women. . . .

The appellant conducts a hotel. The appellee Elsie Parrish was employed as a chambermaid and (with her husband) brought this suit to recover the difference between the wages paid her and the minimum wage fixed pursuant to the state law. The minimum wage was $14.50 per week of 48 hours. The appellant challenged the act as repugnant to the due process clause of the Fourteenth Amendment of the Constitution of the United States. The Supreme Court of the State, reversing the trial court, sustained the statute and directed judgment for the plaintiffs. . . .

The appellant relies upon the decision of the Court in *Adkins v. Children's Hospital* . . . which held invalid the District of Columbia Minimum Wage Act, which was attacked under the Due Process Clause of the Fifth Amendment. On the argument at bar, counsel for the appellees attempted to distinguish the *Adkins* case upon the ground that the appellee was employed in a hotel and that the business of an innkeeper was affected with a public interest. That effort at distinction is obviously futile, as it appears that in one of the cases ruled by the *Adkins* opinion the employee was a woman employed as an elevator operator in a hotel. . . .

The recent case of *Morehead v. New York ex rel. Tipaldo* . . . came here on certiorari to the New York court, which had held the New York minimum wage act for women to be invalid. A minority of this Court thought that the New York statute was distinguishable in a material feature from that involved in the *Adkins* case, and that for that and other reasons the New York statute should be sustained. But the Court of Appeals of New York had said that it found no material difference between the two statutes, and this Court held that the "meaning of the statute" as fixed by the decision of the state court "must be accepted here as if the meaning had been specifically expressed in the enactment." . . . That view led to the affirmance by this Court of the judgment in the Morehead case, as the Court considered that the only question before it was whether the *Adkins* case was distinguishable and that reconsideration of that decision had not been sought. . . .

We think that the question which was not deemed to be open in the *Morehead* case is open and is necessarily presented here. The Supreme Court of Washington has upheld the minimum wage statute of that State. It has decided that the statute is a reasonable exercise of the police power of the State. In reaching that conclusion the state court has invoked principles long established by this Court in the application of the Fourteenth Amendment. The state court has refused to regard the decision in the *Adkins* case as determinative and has pointed to our decisions both before and since that case as justifying its position. We are of the opinion that this ruling of the state court demands on our part a reexamination of the *Adkins* case. The importance of the question, in which many States having similar laws are concerned, the close division by which the decision in the *Adkins* case was reached, and the economic conditions which have supervened, and in the light of which the reasonableness of the exercise of the protective power of the State must be considered, make it not only appropriate, but we think imperative, that in deciding the present case the subject should receive fresh consideration. . . .

The principle which must control our decision is not in doubt. The constitutional provision invoked is the due process clause of the Fourteenth Amendment governing the States, as the due process clause invoked in the *Adkins* case governed Congress. In each case the violation alleged by those attacking minimum wage regulation for women is deprivation of freedom of contract. What is this freedom? The Constitution does not speak of freedom of contract. It speaks of liberty and prohibits the deprivation of liberty without due process of law. In prohibiting that deprivation the Constitution does not recognize an absolute and uncontrollable liberty. Liberty in each of its phases has its history and connotation. But the liberty safeguarded is liberty in a social organization which requires the protection of law against the evils which menace the health, safety, morals and welfare of the people. Liberty under the Constitution is thus necessarily subject to the restraints of due process, and regulation which is reasonable in relation to its subject and is adopted in the interests of the community is due process.

This essential limitation of liberty in general governs freedom of contract in particular. More than twenty-five years ago we set forth the applicable principle in these words, after referring to the cases where the liberty guaranteed by the Fourteenth Amendment had been broadly described:

But it was recognized in the cases cited, as in many others, that freedom of contract is a qualified and not an absolute right. There is no absolute freedom to do as one wills or to contract as one chooses. The guaranty of liberty does not withdraw from legislative supervision that wide department of activity which consists of the making of contracts, or deny to government the power to provide restrictive safeguards. Liberty implies the absence of arbitrary restraint, not immunity from reasonable regulations and prohibitions imposed in the interests of the community. . . .

This power under the Constitution to restrict freedom of contract has had many illustrations. That it may be exercised in the public interest with respect to contracts between employer and employee is undeniable. . . .

The point that has been strongly stressed that adult employees should be deemed competent to make their own contracts was decisively met nearly forty years ago in *Holden v. Hardy* . . . where we pointed out the inequality in the footing of the parties. We said:

The legislature has also recognized the fact, which the experience of legislators in many States has corroborated, that the proprietors of these establishments and their operatives do not stand upon an equality, and that their interests are, to a certain extent, conflicting. The former naturally desire to obtain as much labor as possible from their employees, while the latter are often induced by the fear of discharge to conform to regulations which their judgment, fairly exercised, would pronounce to be detrimental to their health or strength. In other words, the proprietors lay down the rules and the laborers are practically constrained to obey them. In such cases self-interest is often an unsafe guide, and the legislature may properly interpose its authority.

And we added that the fact "that both parties are of full age and competent to contract does not necessarily deprive the state of the power to interfere where the parties do not stand upon an equality, or where the public health demands that one party to the contract shall be protected against himself." . . .

It is manifest that this established principle is peculiarly applicable in relation to the employment of women in whose protection the State has a special interest. That phase of the subject received elaborate consideration in *Muller v. Oregon* . . . where the constitutional authority of the State to limit the working hours of women was sustained. We emphasized the consideration that "woman's physical structure and the performance of maternal functions place her at a disadvantage in the struggle for subsistence" and that her physical well-being "becomes an object of public interest and care in order to preserve the strength and vigor of the race." We emphasized the need of protecting women against oppression despite her possession of contractual rights. We said that "though limitations upon personal and contractual rights may be removed by legislation, there is that in her disposition and habits of life which will operate against a full assertion of those rights. She will still be where some legislation to protect her seems necessary to secure a real equality of right." Hence she was "properly placed in a class by herself, and legislation designed for her protection may be sustained even when like legislation is not necessary for men and could not be sustained." We concluded that the limitations which the statute there in question "placed upon her contractual powers, upon her right to agree with her employer as to the time she shall labor" were "not imposed solely for her benefit, but also largely for the benefit of all." . . .

. . . [T]he dissenting Justices in the *Adkins* case [argued] that the minimum wage statute [should] be sustained. The validity of the distinction made by the Court between a minimum wage and a maximum of hours in limiting liberty of contract was especially challenged. . . . That challenge persists and is without any satisfactory answer. As Chief Justice Taft observed: "In absolute freedom of contract the one term is as important as the other, for both enter equally into the consideration given and received, a restriction as to the one is not greater in essence than the other and is of the same kind. One is the multiplier and the other the multiplicand." And Mr. Justice Holmes, while recognizing that "the distinctions of the law are distinctions of degree," could "perceive no difference in the kind or degree of interference with liberty, the only matter with which we have any concern, between the one case and the other. The bargain is equally affected whichever half you regulate." . . .

The minimum wage to be paid under the Washington statute is fixed after full consideration by representatives of employers, employees and the public. It may be assumed that the minimum wage is fixed in consideration of the services that are performed in the particular occupations under normal conditions. Provision is made for special licenses at less wages in the case of women who are incapable of full service. . . .

The statement of Mr. Justice Holmes in the *Adkins* case is pertinent:

> This statute does not compel anybody to pay anything. It simply forbids employment at rates below those fixed as the minimum requirement of health and right living. It is safe to assume that women will not be employed at even the lowest wages allowed unless they earn them, or unless the employer's business can sustain the burden. In short the law in its character and operation is like hundreds of so-called police laws that have been upheld. . . .

And Chief Justice Taft forcibly pointed out the consideration which is basic in a statute of this character:

> Legislatures which adopt a requirement of maximum hours or minimum wages may be presumed to believe that when sweating employers are prevented from paying unduly low wages by positive law they will continue their business, abating that part of their profits, which were wrung from the necessities of their employees, and will concede the better terms required by the law; and that while in individual cases hardship may result, the restriction will enure to the benefit of the general class of employees in whose interest the law is passed and so to that of the community at large. . . .

We think that the views thus expressed are sound and that the decision in the *Adkins* case was a departure from the true application of the principles governing the regulation by the State of the relation of employer and employed. . . .

With full recognition of the earnestness and vigor which characterize the prevailing opinion in the *Adkins* case, we find it impossible to reconcile that ruling with these well-considered declarations. What can be closer to the public interest than the health of women and their protection from unscrupulous and overreaching employers? And if the protection of women is a legitimate end of the exercise of state power, how can it be said that the requirement of the payment of a minimum wage fairly fixed in order to meet the very necessities of existence is not an admissible means to that end? The legislature of the State was clearly entitled to consider the situation of women in employment, the fact that they are in the class receiving the least pay, that their bargaining power is relatively weak, and that they are the ready victims of those who would take advantage of their necessitous circumstances. The legislature was entitled to adopt measures to reduce the evils of the "sweating system," the exploiting of workers at wages so low as to be insufficient to meet the bare cost of living, thus making their very helplessness the occasion of a most injurious competition. The legislature had the right to consider that its minimum wage requirements would be an important aid in carrying out its policy of protection. The adoption of similar requirements by many States evidences a deep-seated conviction both as to the presence of the evil and as to the means adapted to check it. Legislative response to that conviction cannot be regarded as arbitrary or capricious, and that is all we have to decide. Even if the wisdom of the policy be regarded as debatable and its effects uncertain, still the legislature is entitled to its judgment. . . .

Affirmed.

Mr. Justice Sutherland [joined by Justices *Van Devanter, McReynolds* and *Butler*], dissenting.

The principles and authorities relied upon to sustain the judgment, were considered in *Adkins v. Children's Hospital* and *Morehead v. New York ex rel. Tipaldo*; and their lack of application to cases like the one in hand was pointed out. A sufficient answer to all that is now said will be found in the opinions of the Court in those cases. Nevertheless, in the circumstances, it seems well to restate our reasons and conclusions. . . .

It is urged that the question involved should now receive fresh consideration, among other reasons, because of "the economic conditions which have supervened"; but the meaning of the Constitution does not change with the ebb and flow of economic events. We frequently are told in more general words that the Constitution must be construed in the light of the present. If by that it is meant that the Constitution is made up of living words that apply to every new condition which they include, the statement is quite true. But to say, if that be intended, that the words of the Constitution mean today what they did not mean when written—that is, that they do not apply to a situation now to which they would have applied then—is to rob that instrument of the essential element which continues it in force as the people have made it until they, and not their official agents, have made it otherwise. . . .

The judicial function is that of interpretation; it does not include the power of amendment under the guise of interpretation. To miss the point of difference between the two is to miss all that the phrase "supreme law of the land" stands for and to convert what was intended as inescapable and enduring mandates into mere moral reflections.

If the Constitution, intelligently and reasonably construed in the light of these principles, stands in the way of desirable legislation, the blame must rest upon that instrument, and not upon the Court for enforcing it according to its terms. The remedy in that situation—and the only true remedy—is to amend the Constitution. . . .

Coming, then, to a consideration of the Washington statute, it first is to be observed that it is in every substantial respect identical with the statute involved in the *Adkins* case. Such vices as existed in the latter are present in the former. And if the *Adkins* case was properly decided, as we who join in this opinion think it was, it necessarily follows that the Washington statute is invalid. . . .

Case

FERGUSON V. SKRUPA

372 U.S. 726; 83 S.Ct. 1028; 10 L.Ed. 2d. 93 (1963)
Vote: 9–0

In this case the Court repudiates substantive due process as a barrier to economic regulation. The pertinent facts and issues are contained in Justice Black's opinion for the Court.

Mr. Justice Black delivered the opinion of the Court.

In this case . . . we are asked to review the judgment of a three-judge District Court enjoining, as being in violation of the Due Process Clause of the Fourteenth Amendment, a Kansas statute making it a misdemeanor for any person to engage "in the business of debt adjusting" except as an incident to "the lawful practice of law in this state." The statute defines "debt adjusting" as "the making of a contract, express, or implied with a particular debtor whereby the debtor agrees to pay a certain amount of money periodically to the person engaged in the debt adjusting business who shall for a consideration distribute the same among certain specified creditors in accordance with a plan agreed upon."

The complaint, filed by appellee Skrupa doing business as "Credit Advisor," alleged that Skrupa was engaged in the business of "debt adjusting" as defined by the statute, that his business was a "useful and desirable" one, that his business activities were not "inherently immoral or dangerous" or in any way contrary to the public welfare, and that therefore the business could not be "absolutely prohibited" by Kansas. The three-judge court heard evidence by Skrupa tending to show the usefulness and desirability of his business and evidence by the state officials tending to show that "debt adjusting" lends itself to grave abuses against distressed debtors, particularly in the lower income brackets, and that these abuses are of such gravity that a number of States have strictly regulated "debt adjusting" or prohibited it altogether. The court found that Skrupa's business did fall within the Act's proscription and concluded, one judge dissenting, that the Act was prohibitory, not regulatory, but that even if construed in part as regulatory it was an unreasonable regulation of a "lawful business," which the court held amounted to a violation of the Due Process Clause of the Fourteenth Amendment. The court accordingly enjoined enforcement of the statute.

Under the system of government created by the Constitution, it is up to legislatures, not courts, to decide on the wisdom and utility of legislation. There was a time then the Due Process Clause was used by this Court to strike down laws which were thought unreasonable, that is, unwise or incompatible with some particular economic or social philosophy. In this manner the Due Process Clause was used, for example, to nullify laws prescribing maximum hours for work in bakeries, *Lochner v. New York,* . . . outlawing "yellow dog" contracts, *Coppage v. Kansas,* . . . setting minimum wages for women, *Adkins v. Children's Hospital,* . . . and fixing the weight of loaves of bread, *Jay Burns Baking Co. v. Bryan.* . . . This intrusion by the judiciary into the realm of legislative value judgments was strongly objected to at the time, particularly by Mr. Justice Holmes and Mr. Justice Brandeis. . . .

The doctrine that prevailed in *Lochner, Coppage, Adkins, Burns,* and like cases—that due process authorizes courts to hold laws unconstitutional when they believe the legislature has acted unwisely—has long since been discarded. We have returned to the original constitutional proposition that courts do not substitute their social and economic beliefs for the judgment of legislative bodies, who are elected to pass laws. As this Court stated in a unanimous opinion in 1941, "We are not concerned . . . with the wisdom, need, or appropriateness of the legislation." Legislative bodies have broad scope to experiment with economic problems, and this Court does not sit to "subject the State to an intolerable supervision hostile to the basic principles of our Government and wholly beyond the protection which the general clause of the Fourteenth Amendment was intended to secure." It is now settled that States "have power to legislate against what are found to be injurious practices in their internal commercial and business affairs, so long as their laws do not run afoul of some specific federal constitutional prohibition or of some valid federal law."

. . . We conclude that the Kansas Legislature was free to decide for itself that legislation was needed to deal with the business of debt adjusting. Unquestionably, there are arguments showing that the business of debt adjusting has social utility, but such arguments are properly addressed to the legislature, not to us. We refuse to sit as a "superlegislature to weigh the wisdom of legislation," and we emphatically refuse to go back to the time when courts used the Due Process Clause "to strike down state laws, regulatory of business and industrial conditions, because they may be unwise, improvident, or out of harmony with a particular school of thought." Nor are we able or willing to draw lines by calling a law "prohibitory" or "regulatory." Whether the legislature takes for its textbook Adam Smith, Herbert Spencer, Lord Keynes, or some other is no concern of ours. The Kansas debt adjusting statute may be wise or unwise. But relief, if any be needed, lies not with us but with the body constituted to pass laws for the State of Kansas.

Nor is the statute's exception of lawyers a denial of equal protection of the laws to nonlawyers. Statutes create many classifications which do not deny equal protection; it is only "invidious discrimination" which offends the Constitution. If the State of Kansas wants to limit debt adjusting to lawyers, the Equal Protection Clause does not forbid. We also find no merit in the contention that the Fourteenth Amendment is violated by the failure of the Kansas statute's title to be as specific as appellee thinks it ought to be under the Kansas constitution.

Reversed.

Mr. Justice Harlan concurs in the judgment on the ground that this state measure bears a rational relation to a constitutionally permissible objective. . . .

Case

HAWAII HOUSING AUTHORITY V. MIDKIFF

467 U.S. 229; 104 S.Ct. 2321; 81 L.Ed. 2d. 186 (1984)
Vote: 8–0

In this case the Court considers whether the state of Hawaii may use its power of eminent domain to redistribute land previously held by a small minority of large landowners. The constitutional question is whether the state's "taking" is justified by a valid "public use."

Justice O'Connor delivered the opinion of the Court.

. . . The starting point for our analysis of the Act's constitutionality is the Court's decision in *Berman v. Parker*

[1954]. . . . In *Berman,* the Court held constitutional the District of Columbia Redevelopment Act of 1945. That Act provided both for the comprehensive use of the eminent domain power to redevelop slum areas and for the possible sale or lease of the condemned lands to private interests. In discussing whether the takings authorized by that Act were for a "public use," . . . the Court stated

We deal, in other words, with what traditionally has been known as the police power. An attempt to define its reach or trace its outer limits is fruitless, for each case must turn on its own facts. The definition is essentially the product of legislative determinations addressed to the purposes of government, purposes neither abstractly nor historically capable of complete definition. Subject to specific constitutuinal limitations, when the legislature has spoken, the public interest has been declared in terms well-nigh conclusive. In such cases the legislature, not the judiciary, is the main guardian of the public needs to be served by social legislation, whether it be Congress legislating concerning the District of Columbia . . . or the States legislating concerning local affairs. . . . This principle admits of no exception merely because the power of eminent domain is involved. . . .

The "public use" requirement is thus coterminous with the scope of a sovereign's police powers.

There is, of course, a role for courts to play in reviewing a legislature's judgment of what constitutes a public use, even when the eminent domain power is equated with the police power. But the Court in *Berman* made clear that it is "an extremely narrow" one. The Court in *Berman* cited with approval the Court's decision in *Old Dominion Co. v. United States* [1925], . . . which held that deference to the legislature's "public use" determination is required "until it is shown to involve an impossibility." The *Berman* Court also cited to *United States ex rel. TVA v. Welch* [1946], . . . which emphasized that "[a]ny departure from this judicial restraint would result in courts deciding on what is and is not a governmental function and in their invalidating legislation on the basis of their view on that question at the moment of decision, a practice which has proved impracticable in other fields." In short, the Court has made clear that it will not substitute its judgment for a legislature's judgment as to what constitutes a public use "unless the use be palpably without reasonable foundation." . . .

To be sure, the Court's cases have repeatedly stated that "one person's property may not be taken for the benefit of another private person without a justifying public purpose, even though compensation be paid." . . . Thus, in *Missouri Pacific R. Co. v. Nebraska* [1896], . . . where

the "order in question was not, and was not claimed to be, . . . a taking of private property for a public use under the right of eminent domain," . . . the Court invalidated a compensated taking of property for lack of a justifying public purpose. But where the exercise of the eminent domain power is rationally related to a conceivable public purpose, the Court has never held a compensated taking to be proscribed by the Public Use Clause. . . .

On this basis, we have no trouble concluding that the Hawaii Act is constitutional. The people of Hawaii have attempted, much as the settlers of the original 13 Colonies did, to reduce the perceived social and economic evils of a land oligopoly traceable to their monarchs. The land oligopoly has, according to the Hawaii Legislature, created artificial deterrents to the normal functioning of the State's residential land market and forced thousands of individual homeowners to lease, rather than buy, the land underneath their homes. Regulating oligopoly and the evils associated with it is a classic exercise of a State's police powers. . . . We cannot disapprove of Hawaii's exercise of this power.

Nor can we condemn as irrational the Act's approach to correcting the land oligopoly problem. The Act presumes that when a sufficiently large number of persons declare that they are willing but unable to buy lots at fair prices the land market is malfunctioning. When such a malfunction is signaled, the Act authorizes HHA to condemn lots in the relevant tract. The Act limits the number of lots any one tenant can purchase and authorizes HHA to use public funds to ensure that the market dilution goals will be achieved. This is a comprehensive and rational approach to identifying and correcting market failure.

Of course, this Act, like any other, may not be successful in achieving its intended goals. But "whether in fact the provision will accomplish its objectives is not the question: the [constitutional requirement] is satisfied if . . . the . . . [state] Legislature rationally could have believed that the [Act] would promote its objective." . . . When the legislature's purpose is legitimate and its means are not irrational, our cases make clear that empirical debates over the wisdom of takings—no less than debates over the wisdom of other kinds of socioeconomic legislation—are not to be carried out in the federal courts. Redistribution of fees simple to correct deficiencies in the market determined by the state legislature to be attributable to land oligopoly is a rational exercise of the eminent domain power. Therefore, the Hawaii statute must pass the scrutiny of the Public Use Clause. . . .

The State of Hawaii has never denied that the Constitution forbids even a compensated taking of property when executed for no reason other than to confer a private benefit on a particular private party. A purely private taking could not withstand the scrutiny of the public use requirement; it would serve no legitimate purpose of government and would thus be void. But no purely private taking is involved in this case. The Hawaii Legislature enacted its Land Reform Act not to benefit a particular class of identifiable individuals but to attack certain perceived evils of concentrated property ownership in Hawaii—a legitimate public purpose. Use of the condemnation power to achieve this purpose is not irrational. Since we assume for purposes of this appeal that the weighty demand of just compensation has been met, the requirements of the Fifth and Fourteenth Amendments have been satisfied. Accordingly, we reverse the judgment of the Court of Appeals, and remand these cases for further proceedings in conformity with this opinion. . . .

Justice Marshall took no part in the consideration or decision of these cases.

Case

DOLAN V. CITY OF TIGARD

512 U.S. 374, 114 S.Ct. 2309, 129 L.Ed. 2d. 304 (1994)
Vote: 5–4

In this case the Supreme Court addresses a city's refusal to grant a building permit unless the property owner agreed to dedicate a portion of her land for flood control and traffic improvements. In deciding the case, the Court considers a question left open in Nollan v. California Coastal Commission (1987) regarding the relationship between the impact of proposed development and the conditions imposed by government on such development.

Chief Justice Rehnquist delivered the opinion of the Court.

. . . The State of Oregon enacted a comprehensive land use management program in 1973. . . . The program required all Oregon cities and counties to adopt new comprehensive land use plans that were consistent with the statewide planning goals. . . . The plans are implemented by land use regulations which are part of an integrated hierarchy of legally binding goals, plans, and regulations. . . . Pursuant to the State's requirements, the city of Tigard, a community of some 30,000 residents on the southwest edge of Portland, developed a comprehensive plan and codified it in its Community Development Code (CDC). The CDC requires property owners in the area zoned Central Business District to comply with a 15% open space and landscaping requirement, which limits total site coverage, including all structures and paving parking to 85% of the parcel. . . . After the completion of a transportation study that identified congestion in the Central Business District as a particular problem, the city adopted a plan for a pedestrian/bicycle pathway intended to encourage alternatives to automobile transportation for short trips. The CDC requires that new development facilitate this plan by dedicating land for pedestrian pathways where provided for in the pedestrian/bicycle pathway plan.

The city also adopted a Master Drainage Plan (Drainage Plan). The Drainage Plan noted that flooding occurred in several areas along Fanno Creek, including areas near petitioner's property. . . . The Drainage Plan also established that the increase in impervious surfaces associated with continued urbanization would exacerbate these flooding problems. To combat these risks, the Drainage Plan suggested a series of improvements to the Fanno Creek Basin, including channel excavation in the area next to petitioner's property. . . . Other recommendations included ensuring that the floodplain remains free of structures and that it be preserved as greenways to minimize flood damage to structures. . . . The Drainage Plan concluded that the cost of these improvements should be shared based on both direct and indirect benefits, with property owners along the waterways paying more due to the direct benefit that they would receive. . . .

Petitioner Florence Dolan owns a plumbing and electric supply store located on Main Street in the Central Business District of the city. The store covers approximately 9,700 square feet on the eastern side of a 1.67 acre parcel, which includes a gravel parking lot. Fanno Creek flows through the southwestern corner of the lot and along its western boundary. The year-round flow of the creek renders the area within the creek's 100-year floodplain virtually unusable for commercial development. The city's comprehensive plan includes the Fanno Creek floodplain as part of the city's greenway system.

Petitioner applied to the city for a permit to redevelop the site. Her proposed plans called for nearly doubling the size of the store to 17,600 square feet, and paving a 39-space parking lot. The existing store, located on the opposite side of the parcel, would be razed in sections as construction progressed on the new building. In the second phase of the project, petitioner proposed to build an additional structure on the northeast side of the site for complementary businesses, and to provide more parking. The proposed expansion and intensified use are consistent with the city's zoning scheme in the Central Business District. . . .

The City Planning Commission granted petitioner's permit application subject to conditions imposed by the city's CDC. The CDC establishes the following standard for site development review approval: "Where landfill and/or development is allowed within and adjacent to the 100-year floodplain, the city shall require the dedication of sufficient open land area for greenway adjoining and within the floodplain. This area shall include portions at a suitable elevation for the construction of a pedestrian/bicycle pathway within the floodplain in accordance with the adopted pedestrian/bicycle plan." . . .

Thus, the Commission required that petitioner dedicate the portion of her property lying within the 100-year floodplain for improvement of a storm drainage system along Fanno Creek and that she dedicate an additional 15-foot strip of land adjacent to the floodplain as a pedestrian/bicycle pathway. The dedication required by that condition encompasses approximately 7,000 square feet, or roughly 10% of the property. In accordance with city practice, petitioner could rely on the dedicated property to meet the 15% open space and landscaping requirement mandated by the city's zoning scheme. . . . The city would bear the cost of maintaining a landscaped buffer between the dedicated area and the new store. . . .

Petitioner requested variances from the CDC standards. Variances are granted only where it can be shown that, owing to special circumstances related to a specific piece of the land, the literal interpretation of the applicable zoning provisions would cause "an undue or unnecessary hardship" unless the variance is granted. . . . Rather than posing alternative mitigating measures to offset the expected impacts of her proposed development, as allowed under the CDC, petitioner simply argued that her proposed development would not conflict with the policies of the comprehensive plan. . . . The Commission denied the request.

The Commission made a series of findings concerning the relationship between the dedicated conditions and the projected impacts of petitioner's project. First, the Commission noted that "[i]t is reasonable to assume that customers and employees of the future uses of this site could utilize a pedestrian/bicycle pathway adjacent to this development for their transportation and recreational needs." . . . The Commission noted that the site plan has provided for bicycle parking in a rack in front of the proposed building and "[i]t is reasonable to expect that some of the users of the bicycle parking provided for by the site plan will use the pathway adjacent to Fanno Creek if it is constructed." . . . In addition, the Commission found that creation of a convenient, safe pedestrian/bicycle pathway system as an alternative means of transportation "could offset some of the traffic demand on [nearby] streets and lessen the increase in traffic congestion." . . . The Commission went on to note that the required floodplain dedication would be reasonably related to petitioner's request to intensify the use of the site given the increase in the impervious surface. The Commission stated that the "anticipated increased stormwater flow from the subject property to an already strained creek and drainage basin can only add to the public need to manage the stream channel and floodplain for drainage purposes." . . . Based on this anticipated increased stormwater flow, the Commission concluded that "the requirement of dedication of the floodplain area on the site is related to the applicant's plan to intensify development on the site." . . . The Tigard City Council approved the Commission's final order. . . .

Petitioner appealed to the Land Use Board of Appeals (LUBA) on the ground that the city's dedication requirements were not related to the proposed development, and, therefore, those requirements constituted an uncompensated taking of their property under the Fifth Amendment. . . . [This appeal was unsuccessful.]

The Oregon Court of Appeals affirmed, rejecting petitioner's contention that in *Nollan v. California Coastal Commission* . . . we had abandoned the "reasonable relationship" test in favor of a stricter "essential nexus" test. . . . The court decided that both the pedestrian/bicycle pathway condition and the storm drainage dedication had an essential nexus to the development of the proposed site. . . . Therefore, the court found the conditions to be reasonably related to the impact of the expansion of petitioner's business. . . . We granted certiorari . . . because of an alleged conflict between the Oregon Supreme Court's decision and our decision in *Nollan*.

The Takings Clause of the Fifth Amendment . . . provides: "[N]or shall private property be taken for public use, without just compensation." One of the principal purposes of the Takings Clause is "to bar Government from forcing some people alone to bear public burdens which, in all fairness and justice, should be borne by the public as a whole." . . . Without question, had the city simply required petitioner to dedicate a strip of land along Fanno

Creek for public use, rather than conditioning the grant of her permit to redevelop her property on such a dedication, a taking would have occurred. . . . Such public access would deprive petitioner of the right to exclude others, "one of the most essential sticks in the bundle of rights that are commonly characterized as property." . . .

. . . Under the well-settled doctrine of "unconstitutional conditions," the government may not require a person to give up a constitutional right—the right to receive just compensation when property is taken for a public use—in exchange for a discretionary benefit conferred by the government where the property sought has little or no relationship to the benefit. . . .

Petitioner contends that the city has forced her to choose between the building permit and her right under the Fifth Amendment to just compensation for the public easements. Petitioner does not quarrel with the city's authority to exact some forms of dedication as a condition for the grant of a building permit, but challenges the showing made by the city to justify these exactions. She argues that the city has identified "no special benefits" conferred on her, and has not identified any "special quantifiable burdens" created by her new store that would justify the particular dedications required from her which are not required from the public at large.

In evaluating petitioner's claim, we must first determine whether the "essential nexus" exists between the "legitimate state interest" and the permit condition exacted by the city. . . . If we find that a nexus exists, we must then decide the required degree of connection between the exactions and the projected impact of the proposed development. We were not required to reach this question in Nollan, because we concluded that the connection did not meet even the loosest standard. . . . Here, however, we must decide this question. . . .

. . . Undoubtedly, the prevention of flooding along Fanno Creek and the reduction of traffic congestion in the Central Business District qualify as the type of legitimate public purposes we have upheld. . . . It seems equally obvious that a nexus exists between preventing flooding along Fanno Creek and limiting development within the creek's 100-year floodplain. Petitioner proposes to double the size of her retail store and to pave her now-gravel parking lot, thereby expanding the impervious surface on the property and increasing the amount of stormwater run-off into Fanno Creek.

The same may be said for the city's attempt to reduce traffic congestion by providing for alternative means of transportation. In theory, a pedestrian/bicycle pathway provides a useful alternative means of transportation for workers and shoppers . . . .

The second part of our analysis requires us to determine whether the degree of the exactions demanded by the city's permit conditions bear the required relationship to the projected impact of petitioner's proposed development. . . .

The city required that the petitioner dedicate "to the city as greenway all portions of the site that fall within the existing 100-year floodplain . . . and all property 15 feet above [the floodplain] boundary." In addition, the city demanded that the retail store be designed so as not to intrude into the greenway area. The city relies on the Commission's rather tentative findings that increased stormwater flow from petitioner's property "can only add to the public need to manage the [floodplain] for drainage purposes" to support its conclusion that the "requirement of dedication of the floodplain area on the site is related to the applicant's plan to intensify development on the site." . . .

The city made the following specific findings relevant to the pedestrian/bicycle pathway: "In addition, the proposed expanded use of this site is anticipated to generate additional vehicular traffic thereby increasing congestion on nearby collector and arterial streets. Creation of a convenient, safe pedestrian/bicycle pathway system as an alternative means of transportation could offset some of the traffic demand on these nearby streets and lessen the increase in traffic congestion." . . .

The question for us is whether these findings are constitutionally sufficient to justify the conditions imposed by the city on petitioner's building permit. Since state courts have been dealing with this question a good deal longer than we have, we turn to representative decisions made by them.

In some States, very generalized statements as to the necessary connection between the required dedication and the proposed development seem to suffice. . . . We think this standard is too lax to adequately protect petitioner's right to just compensation if her property is taken for a public purpose. . . .

A number of state courts have taken an intermediate position, requiring the municipality to show a "reasonable relationship" between the required dedication and the impact of the proposed development. . . .

We think the "reasonable relationship" test adopted by a majority of the state courts is closer to the federal constitutional norm than either of those previously discussed. But we do not adopt it as such, partly because the term "reasonable relationship" seems confusingly similar to the term "rational basis" which describes the minimal level of scrutiny under the Equal Protection Clause of the Fourteenth Amendment. We think a term such as "rough proportionality" best encapsulates what we hold to be the requirement of the Fifth Amendment. No precise mathematical calculation is required, but the city must make some sort of individualized determination that the required dedication is related both in nature and extent to the impact of the proposed development. . . .

It is axiomatic that increasing the amount of impervious surface will increase the quantity and rate of stormwater flow from petitioner's property. . . . Therefore, keeping the floodplain open and free from development would likely confine the pressures on Fanno Creek created by petitioner's development. . . .

. . . As we have noted, [the] right to exclude others is "one of the most essential sticks in the bundle of rights that are commonly characterized as property." . . . It is difficult to see why recreational visitors trampling along petitioner's floodplain easement are sufficiently related to the city's legitimate interest in reducing flooding problems along Fanno Creek, and the city has not attempted to make any individualized determination to support this part of its request. . . .

Admittedly, petitioner wants to build a bigger store to attract members of the public to her property. She also wants, however, to be able to control the time and manner in which they enter. . . . [T]he city wants to impose a permanent recreational easement upon petitioner's property that borders Fanno Creek. Petitioner would lose all rights to regulate the time in which the public entered onto the Greenway, regardless of any interference it might pose with her retail store. Her right to exclude would not be regulated, it would be eviscerated.

If petitioner's proposed development had somehow encroached on existing greenway space in the city, it would have been reasonable to require petitioner to provide some alternative greenway space for the public either on her property or elsewhere. . . . But that is not the case here. We conclude that the findings upon which the city relies do not show the required reasonable relationship between the floodplain easement and the petitioner's proposed new building.

With respect to the pedestrian/bicycle pathway, we have no doubt that the city was correct in finding that the larger retail sales facility proposed by petitioner will increase traffic on the streets of the Central Business District. The city estimates that the proposed development would generate roughly 435 additional trips per day. Dedications for streets, sidewalks, and other public ways are generally reasonable exactions to avoid excessive congestion from a proposed property use. But on the record before us, the city has not met its burden of demonstrating that the additional number of vehicle and bicycle trips generated by the petitioner's development reasonably relate to the city's requirement for a dedication of the pedestrian/bicycle pathway easement. The city simply found that the creation of the pathway "could offset some of the traffic demand . . . and lessen the increase in traffic congestion."

. . . No precise mathematical calculation is required, but the city must make some effort to quantify its findings in support of the dedication for the pedestrian/bicycle pathway beyond the conclusory statement that it could offset some of the traffic demand generated.

Cities have long engaged in the commendable task of land use planning, made necessary by increasing urbanization particularly in metropolitan areas such as Portland. The city's goals of reducing flooding hazards and traffic congestion, and providing for public greenways, are laudable, but there are outer limits to how this may be done. . . .

Justice Stevens, with whom **Justice Blackmun** and **Justice Ginsburg** join, dissenting.

. . . If the Court proposes to have the federal judiciary micromanage state decisions of this kind, it is indeed extending its welcome mat to a significant new class of litigants. Although there is no reason to believe that state courts have failed to rise to the task, property owners have surely found a new friend today.

The Court has made a serious error by abandoning the traditional presumption of constitutionality and imposing a novel burden of proof on a city implementing an admittedly valid comprehensive land use plan. Even more consequential than its incorrect disposition of this case, however, is the Court's resurrection of a species of substantive due process analysis that it firmly rejected decades ago. . . .

In our changing world one thing is certain: uncertainty will characterize predictions about the impact of new urban developments on the risks of floods, earthquakes, traffic congestion, or environmental harms. When there is doubt concerning the magnitude of those impacts, the public interest in averting them must outweigh the private interest of the commercial entrepreneur. If the government can demonstrate that the conditions it has imposed in a land-use permit are rational, impartial and conducive to fulfilling the aims of a valid land-use plan, a strong presumption of validity should attach to those conditions. The burden of demonstrating that those conditions have unreasonably impaired the economic value of the proposed improvement belongs squarely on the shoulders of the party challenging the state action's constitutionality. That allocation of burdens has served us well in the past. The Court has stumbled badly today by reversing it. . . .

Justice Souter, dissenting. . . .

8

EXPRESSIVE FREEDOM AND THE FIRST AMENDMENT

Chapter Outline

Introduction
Interpretive Foundations of Expressive Freedom
The Prohibition of Prior Restraint
The Clear and Present Danger Doctrine
Fighting Words, Hate Speech, and Profanity
Symbolic Speech and Expressive Conduct
Defamation
The Intractable Obscenity Problem
Expressive Activities in the Public Forum
Electronic Media and the First Amendment
Commercial Speech
Rights of Public Employees and Beneficiaries
Freedom of Association
Conclusion
Key Terms
For Further Reading
Internet Resources
Near v. Minnesota (1931)
New York Times Company v. U. S. (1971)
Schenck v. United States (1919)
Brandenburg v. Ohio (1969)
Cohen v. California (1971)
Texas v. Johnson (1989)
Barnes v. Glen Theatre, Inc. (1991)
New York Times Company v. Sullivan (1964)
Miller v. California (1973)
Federal Communications Commission v. Pacifica Foundation (1978)
Reno v. American Civil Liberties Union (1997)
Edwards v. South Carolina (1963)
Adderley v. Florida (1966)
44 Liquormart, Inc. v. Rhode Island (1996)
National Endowment for the Arts v. Finley (1988)
Hurley v. Irish-American Gay, Lesbian and Bisexual Group of Boston (1995)

Freedom to speak and write about public questions is as important to the life of our government as is the heart to the human body. In fact, this privilege is the heart of our government. If that heart be weakened, the result is debilitation; if it be stilled, the result is death.

—JUSTICE HUGO BLACK, *MILK WAGON DRIVERS UNION V. MEADOWMOOR DAIRIES* (1941)

INTRODUCTION

This chapter examines the Supreme Court's development of constitutional doctrine effectively defining **freedom of expression,** which encompasses both **freedom of speech** and **freedom of the press.** To a lesser extent, the chapter deals with **freedom of assembly,** which is an explicit component of the First Amendment, and **freedom of association,** which the courts have recognized as an implicit First Amendment right. We deal separately with the First Amendment freedom of religion in the following chapter. As important as freedom of religion was to the founders of the Republic, one can argue that freedom of expression is *the* fundamental freedom in a democracy. Accordingly, our examination of specific civil liberties begins with the expressive freedoms of the First Amendment.

INTERPRETIVE FOUNDATIONS OF EXPRESSIVE FREEDOM

The idea of free speech is a decidedly modern concept that correlates with the emergence of democracy. To the ancient and medieval world, freedom of speech was unthinkable, especially in religious and political matters. In England, the idea of freedom of speech emerged gradually coincident with the development of parliamentary government. The importance of free speech in galvanizing the American Revolution resulted in specific protections of freedom of speech being incorporated into the constitutions of the new American states.

The constitutional commitment to freedom of the press also has its roots in English history and in American colonial experience, especially during the decades immediately preceding the American Revolution. The mass media of that period, consisting of small independent newspaper and pamphlet publishers, played a vital role in facilitating political debate and in disseminating information. It is worth recalling in this context that the ratification of the Constitution was vigorously debated not only in the state ratifying conventions but in the press as well. The collection of essays known as *The Federalist Papers* first appeared as a series of newspaper articles analyzing and endorsing the new Constitution. Anti-Federalists also made wide use of newspapers to express opposition to ratification.

Despite the obvious importance of freedoms of speech and press in the establishment of American democracy, the U.S. Supreme Court did not pay major attention to these values during the early days of the Republic. For a brief period during the administration of President John Adams, the national government sought to suppress public criticism through enforcement of the Sedition Act, passed by Congress in 1798. The Sedition Act prohibited "any false, scandalous and malicious" writing against the national government. A few of Thomas Jefferson's partisans were prosecuted under this statute, and it may have had a **chilling effect** on criticism of the government. Nevertheless, the provision expired on March 3, 1801, just before Jefferson and his newly victorious party took power. Jefferson pardoned those convicted under the statute, and no occasion arose for the Supreme Court to determine its constitutionality.

During the Civil War, a number of limits were imposed on freedom of expression. These included newspaper censorship and the prosecution of some of the more vociferous critics of the Lincoln administration. However, no constitutional challenges raising First Amendment issues reached the Supreme Court.

Incorporation of the Freedoms of Speech and Press

The principal reason that First Amendment controversies did not reach the Supreme Court during the nineteenth century was that, by design, the First Amendment did not apply to the state and local governments. Not until *Gitlow v. New York* (1925) did the Supreme Court recognize that the First Amendment freedoms of speech and press were applicable to the states via the Fourteenth Amendment. In addition to the **incorporation** of the First Amendment, changes in the national political environment brought questions of freedom of speech to the forefront. The national government's efforts to deal with political dissent in the early decades of the twentieth century produced a series of cases that required the Court to interpret the scope of First Amendment protection. By the 1920s, the First Amendment emerged as an important field of constitutional interpretation.

Preferred Freedoms?

In the wake of the constitutional revolution of the late 1930s, the Supreme Court moved away from the protection of private property rights and toward the enhancement of personal freedoms. The First Amendment figured prominently in the Court's newfound emphasis. Writing for the Court in *Palko v. Connecticut* (1937), Justice Benjamin Cardozo characterized freedom of speech as "the matrix, the in-

Hugo Black: Associate Justice, 1937–1971

dispensable condition, of nearly every other form of freedom." During the 1940s several members of the Supreme Court went so far as to suggest that the First Amendment freedoms of speech and press enjoy a "preferred position" in relation to other constitutional guarantees (see, for example, Justice William O. Douglas's majority opinion in *Murdock v. Pennsylvania* [1943]).

Although the Court soon abandoned the **preferred freedoms** language, freedom of expression was accorded high priority during the Warren Court era (1953–1969). The Warren Court established a number of important precedents in this area, and the more conservative Burger and Rehnquist Courts have, for the most part, adhered to these precedents. Clearly, First Amendment questions of increasing complexity and difficulty continue to be among the most important concerns of the Court.

Are the Protections of the First Amendment Absolute?

Although the First Amendment begins with the seemingly absolute injunction, "Congress shall make *no* law . . ." [emphasis added], the Supreme Court has never taken the view that First Amendment protections are absolute in character. Indeed, only a few justices who have served on the Court have argued for an absolutist interpretation. Hugo Black, the best known and most forceful of the First Amendment absolutists, believed that all speech and writing, regardless of its purpose, content, or impact, should be absolutely protected against **censorship** or sanction. Thus Black believed that criminal laws prohibiting **obscenity, profanity,** and **seditious speech** were inherently unconstitutional. Justice Black also believed that laws that permitted civil suits for **libel** or **slander** could not be reconciled with the First Amendment.

In Black's view, the First Amendment gives everyone the right to say or write anything, regardless of its impact on other individuals or society in general. However, Justice Black believed that the protections of the First Amendment were limited to **pure speech** and pure writing. In his view, **picketing** and other forms of **expressive conduct** were not covered by the First Amendment.

Although Hugo Black wrote a number of important opinions for the Court on questions of freedom of speech and freedom of the press, most of his colleagues and most of the justices who came after him refused to accept Black's **First Amendment absolutism.** The Court has never taken the position that the protections of the First Amendment are absolute. Indeed, the Court has recognized that certain types of expression, including obscenity, **fighting words,** and **defamation,** are outside the scope of the First Amendment. It has also held that speech that is normally protected by the Constitution might not be protected depending on the circumstances in which it takes place.

On the other hand, the Court has recognized that the protections of the First Amendment are not limited to pure speech and writing. Rather, the First Amendment potentially protects communication of any kind. Protests, demonstrations, performances, advertisements, artistic endeavors—all of these are within the ambit of expression. So too are records, films, videos, software, e-mail, broadcasts, cablecasts, and sites on the Internet. In short, the First Amendment protects communication, regardless of its nature or medium. Whether specific instances of expression merit First Amendment protection or may be censored or sanctioned by government depends on a number of factors that we will examine in this chapter.

Government can infringe on freedom of expression in two ways. It can prevent a specific instance of expression from reaching the public—a practice known as censorship. Alternatively, it can punish someone after the fact, usually through criminal prosecution. We begin our examination of First Amendment doctrine with the principle that limits government censorship prior to expression or publication—the rule against **prior restraint.**

TO SUMMARIZE:

- Constitutional freedoms of expression came of age in the twentieth century. In the 1920s and 1930s, the Supreme Court incorporated freedoms of speech, press, and assembly into the Fourteenth Amendment, thus making them fully applicable to the states as well as the federal government.
- Although a majority of the Court has never regarded the First Amendment freedoms as absolute, they have come to be regarded as fundamental rights essential to the preservation of a constitutional democracy.

THE PROHIBITION OF PRIOR RESTRAINT

The framers of the Bill of Rights saw the need for the First Amendment because common law, which this nation inherited from England, provided little protection to freedom of expression. However, one common-law doctrine has been grafted onto the First Amendment through judicial interpretation. This is the rule against prior restraint. In *Commentaries on the Laws of England,* Vol. IV (1769), William Blackstone stated the rule against prior restraint in the context of freedom of the press: "The liberty of the press is indeed essential to the nature of a free state; but this consists in laying no previous restraints upon publications, and not in freedom from censure for criminal matter when published." In this country, the concept of prior restraint has been of great importance to the Supreme Court in defining both freedom of the press and freedom of speech under the First Amendment. The concept was first discussed by the Court, however, in the context of a dispute over publication of a newspaper.

The Court Adopts the Rule Against Prior Restraint

In *Near v. Minnesota* (1931), the Court struck down a state law that permitted public officials to seek an injunction to stop publication of any "malicious, scandalous and defamatory newspaper, magazine or other periodical." The statute was invoked to suppress publication of a small Minneapolis newspaper, the *Saturday Press,* which had strong anti-Semitic overtones and maligned local political officials, particularly the chief of police. The state law provided that once a newspaper was enjoined, further publication was punishable as contempt of court. Writing for the Court in *Near,* Chief Justice Hughes characterized this mode of suppression as "the essence of censorship" and declared it unconstitutional. Note also that with its decision in *Near v. Minnesota,* the Court specifically incorporated the First Amendment freedom of the press into the Due Process Clause of the Fourteenth Amendment, thus making it fully applicable to the states.

In commenting with general approval on the rule against prior restraint, Chief Justice Hughes acknowledged that this restriction is not absolute. It would not, for

In June, 1971, the New York Times began a series of stories based on the Pentagon Papers

example, prevent the government in time of war from prohibiting publication of "the sailing dates of transports or the number and location of troops." In these and related situations, national security interests are almost certain to prevail over freedom of the press. But where is the line to be drawn? How far can the "national security" justification be extended in suppressing publication?

The Pentagon Papers Case

The Court revisited the question of prior restraint on the press in the much-heralded Pentagon papers case of 1971 (*New York Times Company v. United States*). Here, the federal government attempted to prevent the *New York Times* and the *Washington Post* from publishing excerpts from a classified study titled "History of U.S. Decision-Making Process on Viet Nam Policy" (the Pentagon papers). By a 6-to-3 vote, the Supreme Court, in a brief *per curiam* opinion, held that the government's effort to block publication of this material amounted to an unconstitutional prior restraint. The majority was simply not convinced that such publication—several years after the events and decisions discussed in the Pentagon papers—constituted a significant threat to national security. The furor produced by this highly publicized case and the great pressure brought to bear on the Court for a speedy decision help explain why no detailed majority opinion was produced. The justices in fact wrote nine separate opinions, advancing a wide variety of rationales for and against application of the prior restraint concept. Excerpts from each of these opinions are reprinted in the Jurisprudence section of this chapter, and it is important to consider the constitutional implications of the various arguments.

May the Government Prevent Publication of How to Make a Hydrogen Bomb?

The issue of prior restraint arose again in 1979 in connection with the publication of a magazine article purporting to describe the process of making a hydrogen bomb. The federal government obtained a preliminary injunction against *The Progressive* blocking publication of the article pending a hearing. In the meantime, however, another magazine published a similar article, with no apparent damage to national security. As a result, the case against *The Progressive* was dismissed and the injunction lifted (see *United States v. Progressive* [1979]). *The Progressive*'s hydrogen bomb article was ultimately published in November 1979. In light of the Pentagon papers and *Progressive* cases, we could conclude that, although national security may justify a departure from the rule against prior restraint, in the real world of American constitutional law, such departures tend to be rare and short-lived.

Does the Prior Restraint Doctrine Apply to Student Newspapers?

One notable exception to the protection of press freedom against prior restraint involves the publication of student-operated school newspapers. In *Hazelwood School District v. Kuhlmeier* (1988), the Supreme Court voted 5 to 3 to uphold a public school principal's decision to excise certain controversial material from the school newspaper. The principal objected to certain articles dealing with divorce and teenage pregnancy on the grounds that they were written in such a way as to permit students to identify classmates who had encountered such difficulties. The student newspaper staff hired a lawyer and challenged the principal's action in federal court. Writing for the majority, Justice Byron White concluded that "educators do not offend the First Amendment by exercising editorial control over the style and content of student speech in school-sponsored expressive activities so long as their actions are reasonably related to legitimate pedagogical concerns." Dissenting, Justice William Brennan accused the majority of eviscerating *Tinker v. Des Moines Independent Community School District* (1969), in which the Court had accorded First Amendment protection to certain expressive activities by students in public schools. According to Brennan, the majority opinion in *Hazelwood* "denudes high school students of much of the First Amendment protection that *Tinker* itself prescribed."

The controversy in *Hazelwood* centered around a student newspaper at a public high school. Would the federal courts permit officials at a state college or university to censor student-run campus newspapers? Could "legitimate pedagogical concerns" at this level ever justify such interference? Most observers doubt the Courts would permit this type of censorship.

TO SUMMARIZE:

- The prohibition of prior restraint has evolved from a technical common-law rule regarding the licensing of publications into a broad First Amendment principle that restricts government censorship of expression prior to its utterance.
- The Supreme Court applied the rule against prior restraint most prominently in the Pentagon papers case of 1971. In this case, the Court refused to allow the federal government to bar newspapers from publishing classified documents dealing with the Vietnam War.

Oliver Wendell Holmes, Jr.:
Associate Justice, 1902–1932

THE CLEAR AND PRESENT DANGER DOCTRINE

Even though a specific instance of expression may not be censored prior to its utterance or publication, it may still be subject to sanctions after the fact. Individuals may be subjected to criminal prosecution or civil suit for instances of expression that violate specific legal prohibitions. Whether such instances of expression are protected by the First Amendment depends on a number of factors including the nature of the expression and context in which it takes place.

In *Schenck v. United States* (1919), the first major Supreme Court decision interpreting the scope of free speech, the Court made plain that there are instances in which speech that is normally subject to constitutional protection may be suppressed by the government. Writing for the Court, Justice Oliver Wendell Holmes, Jr., flatly rejected an absolutist interpretation of the First Amendment. In what has become a stock phrase in the American political lexicon, Holmes observed that "the most stringent protection of free speech would not protect a man in falsely shouting fire in a theater, and causing a panic." Holmes went on to articulate the famous **clear and present danger test,** saying that "the question in every case is whether the words used are used in such circumstances and are of such a nature as to create a clear and present danger that they will bring about the substantive evils that Congress has a right to prevent." For example, government has a right, indeed an obligation, to protect the national security. If an instance of expression creates a clear and present danger to national security, then government has the right to prohibit the speech or punish the speaker.

In the *Schenck* case, an official of the Socialist party was convicted for conspiring to print and circulate leaflets urging resistance to the military draft. The leaflets urged resistance to the draft on the grounds that it violated the Thirteenth Amendment of the Constitution. Although sharply critical of the war effort, Schenck's message was confined to the advocacy of peaceful measures, such as petition for repeal of the draft. Nevertheless, a unanimous Supreme Court believed that Schenck's activities amounted to a clear and present danger. One must remember, though, that Schenck's prosecution occurred during World War I. As Justice Holmes observed, "when a nation is at war many things that might be said in time of peace are such a hindrance to its effort that their utterance will not be endured so long as men fight, and that no court could regard them as protected by any constitutional right."

It is also noteworthy that the Court's decision came down at a time when there was widespread concern about the specter of international communism. For the next four decades, the clear and present danger doctrine competed with other approaches to First Amendment interpretation in the area of political dissent.

The "Bad Tendency" Test

The standard that Justice Holmes articulated in the *Schenck* case was ignored by a Court majority some eight months later in *Abrams v. United States* (1919). Here, the Court affirmed the convictions of Jacob Abrams, a self-styled "anarchist-Socialist," and several associates for distributing leaflets in New York City urging the "workers of the world" to resist, among other things, American intervention in Russia against the newly formed Bolshevik government. For Justice John H. Clarke, the Court's majority spokesman, it was enough that Abrams was advocating a general strike "in the greatest port of our land" for the purpose of "curtailing the production of ordnance and munitions necessary and essential to the prosecution of the war. . . ." In effect, Clarke was reverting to the traditional common-law **bad tendency test,** according little importance to the free speech question and focusing on the possibility that Abrams's circular might in some way hinder the war effort.

In a powerful dissenting opinion, Justice Holmes, joined by Justice Louis D. Brandeis, again resorted to the clear and present danger test, but this time he used it as a basis for challenging, rather than endorsing, governmental interference with free speech:

> [T]he ultimate good desired is better reached by free trade in ideas. . . . I think that we should be eternally vigilant against attempts to check the expression of opinions that we loathe and believe to be fraught with death, unless they so imminently threaten immediate interference with the lawful and pressing purposes of the law that an immediate check is required to save the country.

Through the 1920s, a Court majority continued to adhere to the bad tendency test, while Holmes and Brandeis further developed the clear and present danger doctrine as a rationale in support of freedom of expression and association. In *Gitlow v. New York* (1925), the Court upheld a conviction under New York's Criminal Anarchy Act that prohibited advocacy of the overthrow of government "by force or violence." Prior to this decision, the Court had addressed issues of freedom of expression arising from the states strictly on the basis of the Due Process Clause of the Fourteenth Amendment, without specific reference to the First Amendment. In fact, as late as 1922 the Court observed that "the Constitution of the United States imposes upon the States no obligation to convey upon those within their jurisdiction . . . the right of free speech . . ." (*Prudential Insurance Company v. Cheek*).

In 1923, the Court invalidated on due process grounds a Nebraska law prohibiting the teaching of the German language in primary schools (*Meyer v. Nebraska*). Similarly, in *Pierce v. Society of Sisters* (1925), the Court struck down an amendment to the Oregon constitution aimed at prohibiting parents from sending their children to private schools. In the *Meyer* and *Pierce* cases, the Court focused on the deprivation of liberty and property rights protected by the Fourteenth Amendment Due Process Clause. In the *Gitlow* case, however, Justice Edward T. Sanford, writing for the majority, stated without elaboration: "For present purposes we may and do assume that freedom of speech and of the press—which are protected by the First Amendment from abridgment by Congress—are among the fundamental personal rights and 'liberties' protected by the Due Process Clause of the Fourteenth Amendment from impairment by the states." (The Court first invalidated a state law on First Amendment freedom of speech grounds two years later in *Fiske v. Kansas* [1927].)

The incident giving rise to the *Gitlow* case was publication of the "Left Wing Manifesto," a statement of beliefs held by what the Court characterized as the most radical section of the Socialist party. In essence, the manifesto called for the destruction of established government and its replacement by a "revolutionary dictatorship of the proletariat." In affirming the conviction of Benjamin Gitlow, business manager of *The Revolutionary Age,* the Socialist party paper that published the "Left Wing Manifesto," Justice Sanford stated the essence of the bad tendency test:

> That a state, in the exercise of its police power, may punish those who abuse [freedom of speech and press] by utterances inimical to the public welfare, tending to corrupt public morals, incite to crime, or disturb the public peace, is not open to question. . . .

Sanford continued:

> . . . The state cannot reasonably be required to measure the danger from every such utterance in the nice balance of a jeweler's scale. A single revolutionary spark may kindle a fire that, smoldering for a time, may burst into a sweeping and destructive conflagration. It cannot be said that the state is acting arbitrarily or unreasonably when, in the exercise of its judgment as to the measures necessary to protect the public peace and safety, it seeks to extinguish the spark without waiting until it has enkindled the flame or blazed into the conflagration.

Again, Justices Holmes and Brandeis dissented. They could find no clear and present danger of an effort "to overthrow the government by force on the part of the admittedly small minority who shared the defendant's views." In response to the contention that the "Left Wing Manifesto" was an incitement, Holmes asserted that:

> Every idea is an incitement. It offers itself for belief and if believed it is acted on unless some other belief outweighs it or some failure of energy stifles the movement at its birth. The only difference between the expression of an opinion and an incitement in the narrower sense is the speaker's enthusiasm for the result. Eloquence may set fire to reason. But whatever may be thought of the redundant discourse before us it had no chance of starting a present conflagration. If in the long run the beliefs expressed in proletarian dictatorship are destined to be accepted by the dominant forces of the community, the only meaning of free speech is that they should be given their chance and have their way.

This ringing endorsement of the concept of a **free marketplace of ideas** contrasts sharply with Holmes's earlier deference, in the *Schenck* case, to governmental control of dissident expression. As we have seen in connection with judicial review of economic regulation (in Chapter 7), Holmes was inclined to give wide latitude to legislative discretion in matters of public policy. But his dissent in *Gitlow,* like his dissent in *Abrams v. United States,* reflected a decided shift in emphasis where First Amendment values were concerned. This change was probably influenced by Holmes's association on the Court with Justice Brandeis, a dedicated and articulate defender of civil rights and liberties, and his acquaintance with Harvard University law professor Zechariah Chafee, Jr., a widely recognized authority on the First Amendment.

Brandeis himself had occasion to discuss the clear and present danger formula in a concurring opinion in *Whitney v. California* (1927). In this case, the majority, speaking again through Justice Sanford, adhered to the bad tendency test in affirming the conviction of Charlotte Anita Whitney (a niece of Justice Stephen J. Field) for violating California's Criminal Syndicalism Act. The statute defined "criminal syndicalism" as "any doctrine or precept advocating, teaching or aiding and abetting the commission of crime, sabotage . . . or unlawful acts of force and violence or unlawful methods of terrorism as a means of accomplishing a change in industrial ownership or control, or effecting any political change." Whitney's conviction was based on her participation in the organizing convention of the Communist Labor party of California. The jury rejected her contention that at this meeting she advocated lawful, non-violent political reform. She maintained that her conviction was a deprivation of liberty without due process of law, but she did not contend specifically that her participation in organizing the Communist Labor party constituted no clear and present danger. Sanford rejected the view that the act, as applied in this case, was an unreasonable or arbitrary exercise of the police power of the state, unwarrantably infringing any right of free speech, assembly, or association, or that those persons are protected by the Due Process Clause who abuse such rights by joining and furthering an organization . . . menacing the peace and welfare of the state.

Because Whitney did not raise the clear and present danger issue, Brandeis and Holmes felt compelled to concur. The jury was presented with evidence of a conspiracy and under the circumstances, they concluded, its verdict should not be disturbed. Nevertheless, Brandeis took sharp issue with the majority's narrow view of the constitutional protection that should be afforded political dissent. The crux of the Brandeis—Holmes position is contained in the following excerpts:

> Those who won our independence believed that the final end of the state was to make men free to develop their faculties; and that in its government the deliberative forces should prevail over the arbitrary. They valued liberty both as an end and as a means. They believed liberty to be the secret of happiness and courage to be the secret of liberty. They believed that . . . public discussion is a political duty; and that this should be a fundamental principle of the American government. . . .

> . . . To justify suppression of free speech there must be reasonable ground to fear that serious evil will result if free speech is practiced. There must be reasonable ground to believe that the danger apprehended is imminent. There must be reasonable ground to believe that the evil to be presented is a serious one.

A Supreme Court majority first used the clear and present danger test in defense of free speech in the 1937 case of *Herndon v. Lowry.* This decision reversed a conviction for violation of a Georgia statute prohibiting "any attempt, by persuasion or otherwise," to incite insurrection. Following this decision, the Court began to apply the clear and present danger test not only to "seditious" speech but to other First Amendment issues as well.

Clear and Probable Danger

The Cold War, which had begun after World War II, deepened after the United States became embroiled in the Korean conflict, and by the early 1950s, McCarthyism, with its emphasis on the "communist menace," had achieved substantial national influence. Against this background of Cold War paranoia, the Supreme Court reviewed and affirmed the convictions of eleven leaders of the American Communist party in *Dennis v. United States* (1951). Eugene Dennis and his ten codefendants had been convicted after a highly publicized nine-month federal trial for violation of the Internal Security Act of 1940, more commonly known as the Smith Act.

The Smith Act made it a crime "to knowingly or willfully advocate, abet, advise, or teach the duty, necessity, desirability, or propriety of overthrowing or destroying any government in the United States by force or violence. . . ." In essence, the defendants' convictions resulted from their activities in organizing and furthering the purposes of the Communist party in the United States.

The Court of Appeals for the Second Circuit upheld these convictions. In his opinion for that court, Chief Judge Learned Hand substituted a more limited defense of First Amendment freedoms than that of clear and present danger. This doctrine, popularly known as the **clear and probable danger test,** was adopted by Chief Justice Frederick M. Vinson in a plurality opinion announcing the Supreme Court's judgment affirming the convictions. The new standard that Hand articulated required courts in each case to "ask whether the gravity of the 'evil,' discounted by its improbability, justifies such invasion of free speech as is necessary to avoid the danger."

Two members of the *Dennis* majority, Justices Felix Frankfurter and Robert Jackson, wrote separate concurring opinions, neither of which endorsed Hand's formula or the clear and present danger test. Frankfurter maintained that the Court should defer to the legislative balancing of competing interests in the free speech area no less than in other areas of policy making. Jackson differentiated between isolated, localized protest and what he saw as a highly organized conspiracy of international dimensions aimed at subverting American government. He regarded the clear and present danger test as an inadequate standard for assessing a conspiracy of this magnitude. Jackson found "no constitutional right to 'gang up' on the Government."

Justice Black, who dissented along with Justice Douglas, expressed the hope that "in calmer times, when present pressures, passions and fears subside, this or some later Court will restore the First Amendment liberties to the high preferred place where they belong in a free society."

Changes in public opinion and in Supreme Court personnel did in fact result in a gradual movement away from the restrictive First Amendment interpretation symbolized by the *Dennis* decision. Although, as previously indicated, the Court did not resurrect the phrase "preferred position" and did not formally overrule *Dennis,* it narrowed the scope of the Smith Act and offered greater protection to advocacy of ideas, including the forcible overthrow of government. The Court raised evidentiary standards for Smith Act prosecutions and confined its "membership clause" to "active" as distinguished from "nominal" membership in an organization advocating forcible overthrow of the government (see, for example, *Yates v. United States* [1957], *Scales v. United States* [1961], *Noto v. United States* [1961], and *Communist Party v. Subversive Activities Control Board* [1961]).

Ad Hoc Balancing

In the aftermath of *Dennis,* the Court moved away from the clear and present danger test and relied instead on ***ad hoc* balancing** to determine the limits of First Amendment protection in the area of internal security. This weighing of "competing private and public interests," as Justice Harlan phrased it, emphasized the particular circumstances of each case (see *Barenblatt v. United States* [1959], reprinted in Chapter 2). Thus *ad hoc* balancing in practice amounted to a process of decision making, rather than a clear interpretive doctrine. However, it is doubtful that a standard such as clear and present danger is, on close analysis, any more definite.

The Imminent Lawless Action Standard

In the early twentieth century, many states had adopted statutes prohibiting **criminal syndicalism,** which was, in essence, the crime of advocating political change through violent means. As discussed earlier, in *Whitney v. California* (1927), the

Supreme Court had upheld one such law, but by the 1960s the Warren Court was ready to revisit the issue. Thus, in *Brandenburg v. Ohio* (1969), the Court invalidated a criminal syndicalism statute and explicitly overruled *Whitney v. California.* In reversing the conviction of a local Ku Klux Klan leader who had conducted a televised rally near Cincinnati, the Court held that "the constitutional guarantees of free speech and free press do not permit a State to forbid or proscribe advocacy of the use of force or of law violation except where such advocacy is directed to inciting or producing **imminent lawless action** and is likely to incite or produce such action."

The *Brandenburg* standard, with emphasis on imminent lawless action, reaffirmed and expanded the old clear and present danger test as articulated by Justice Holmes. The Burger Court firmly adhered to this standard in the 1970s and 1980s, as seen in *Hess v. Indiana* (1973), *Communist Party of Indiana v. Whitcomb* (1974), and *National Association for the Advancement of Colored People v. Claiborne Hardware Co.* (1982). The Rehnquist Court has not extensively discussed the imminent lawless action standard, but has not given any indication of moving away from it. To the contrary, the Court has indicated a clear willingness to protect political dissent (see, for example, *Texas v. Johnson* [1989], reprinted in this chapter).

TO SUMMARIZE:

- In *Schenck v. United States* (1919), the Supreme Court, speaking through Justice Holmes, first articulated the famous clear and present danger doctrine. Under this doctrine government may punish expression if it creates a clear and present danger of bringing about conditions that government has authority to prevent. Although the doctrine was first used as a rationale for upholding restrictions on radical political expression, in later years it came to be used as basis for protecting dissent.
- In the decades following the *Schenck* ruling the Court occasionally opted for more restrictive approaches to the First Amendment, including the bad tendency, clear and probable danger, and *ad hoc* balancing tests. In *Brandenburg v. Ohio* (1969), however, the Court reaffirmed the essential concept of the clear and present danger doctrine but limited its application to expression in situations where there is "imminent lawless action."

FIGHTING WORDS, HATE SPEECH, AND PROFANITY

Does the First Amendment protect expression that is uncivil, vulgar, hateful, or profane? Prior to the 1960s, the Supreme Court took the view that offensive speech was beyond the pale of the First Amendment. In *Chaplinsky v. New Hampshire* (1942), the Court observed that

> [t]here are certain well defined and narrowly limited classes of speech, the prevention and punishment of which have never been thought to raise any constitutional problem. These include the lewd and obscene, the profane, the libelous, and the insulting or "fighting" words—those which by their very utterance inflict injury or tend to incite an immediate breach of the peace. It has been well observed that such utterances are no essential part of any exposition of ideas, and are of such slight social

value as a step to truth that any benefit that may be derived from them is clearly outweighed by the social interest in order and morality.

Fighting Words

The preceding quotation from *Chaplinsky v. New Hampshire* provides the original statement of the fighting words doctrine. Under *Chaplinsky,* speech could be punished if it inflicted injury or created a danger that the person addressed would resort to violence. The Court probably underestimated the social value of what some would regard as fighting words, and no consideration was given to the question of whether police should be expected to exercise more restraint than the average person in responding to such epithets. For several decades, state courts routinely used the fighting words doctrine and the *Chaplinsky* precedent to justify prosecutions of intemperate street-corner orators for incitement to riot or breach of the peace.

In 1971 the Court significantly narrowed the fighting words exception. In *Cohen v. California* (1971), the Court refused to classify as fighting words the message "Fuck the Draft" emblazoned on the back of a jacket worn by Paul Robert Cohen in the corridors of the Los Angeles County Courthouse. Reversing Cohen's conviction for breach of the peace, the Court, through Justice Harlan, reasoned as follows:

> While the four-letter word displayed by Cohen in relation to the draft is not uncommonly employed in a personally provocative fashion, in this instance it was clearly not "directed to the person of the hearer." . . . No individual actually or likely to be present could reasonably have regarded the words on appellant's jacket as a direct personal insult. Nor do we have here an instance of the exercise of the State's police power to prevent a speaker from intentionally provoking a given group to hostile reaction.

Although the Court still gives formal recognition to the fighting words exception, it has not in recent years found any specific instances of expression to qualify as fighting words.

Hate Speech

During the 1980s, a number of communities adopted laws aimed at protecting African-Americans and other minority groups from so-called **hate crimes,** crimes motivated by racial or other group-related hatred. One such ordinance was enacted by the city of St. Paul, Minnesota:

> Whoever places on public or private property a symbol, object, appellation, characterization or graffiti, including, but not limited to, a burning cross or Nazi swastika, which one knows or has reasonable grounds to know arouses anger, alarm or resentment in others on the basis of race, color, creed, religion or gender commits disorderly conduct and shall be guilty of a misdemeanor.

In the widely publicized case of *R.A.V. v. St. Paul* (1992), the Supreme Court declared the ordinance unconstitutional. Justice Scalia summarized the rationale of the majority as follows:

> Assuming *arguendo,* that all of the expression reached by the ordinance is proscribable under the "fighting words" doctrine, we nonetheless conclude that the ordinance is facially unconstitutional in that it prohibits otherwise permitted speech solely on the basis of the subjects the speech addresses.

The Court's decision in *R.A.V.* raised serious questions as to whether hate crimes legislation can be made to conform to constitutional standards. Nevertheless, states and communities have a number of legal means at their disposal for combating hate crimes. For example, an individual who burns a cross on someone else's front lawn may be charged with criminal trespass and possibly with malicious mischief or vandalism.

Another approach to deterring hate crimes is enhancing or extending criminal penalties based on characteristics of the crime or the victim. In *Wisconsin v. Mitchell* (1993), the U.S. Supreme Court upheld a Wisconsin statute that increases the severity of punishment if a crime victim is chosen on the basis of race or other designated characteristics. Stressing the fact that the statute was aimed at conduct rather than belief, the Court held that increasing punishment because the defendant targeted the victim on the basis of his race does not infringe the defendant's freedom of conscience protected by the First Amendment. Many commentators, however, thought that *Wisconsin v. Mitchell* could not be squared with the Court's earlier decision in *R.A.V.*

Profanity

Although in *Chaplinsky v. New Hampshire* (1942) the Supreme Court specifically enumerated profanity as being among those categories of speech so lacking in value as not to merit First Amendment protection, this view no longer prevails. As we discussed earlier, in *Cohen v. California* the Supreme Court overturned the conviction of a man who entered a courthouse wearing a jacket emblazoned with the slogan "Fuck the Draft." Speaking for the Court, Justice Harlan opined that

> while the particular four-letter-word being litigated here is perhaps more distasteful than others of its genre, it is nevertheless often true that one man's vulgarity is another's lyric. Indeed, we think it is largely because government officials cannot make principled distinctions in this area that the Constitution leaves matters of taste and style so largely to the individual.

Despite the Supreme Court's decision in *Cohen v. California,* most states and many cities retain laws proscribing profanity. But these laws are seldom enforced and even more rarely challenged in court.

TO SUMMARIZE:

- In the early 1940s, the Court recognized that "fighting words," utterances that are inherently likely to produce a violent reaction, are outside the scope of First Amendment protection. In recent times, the fighting words doctrine has been honored more in the breach than in the observance.
- A more recent problem is posed by "hate speech" directed at members of targeted groups such as women and minorities. Unless a particular instance of hate speech can be identified with fighting words, defamation, or imminent lawless action, it is likely to be accorded First Amendment protection. Of course, an instance of hate speech that involves criminal conduct such as trespass or assault may be subject to criminal prosecution.
- Although profanity was once recognized as falling outside the scope of First Amendment protection, this view has eroded to the point where profanity is now considered part of ordinary speech thus entitling it to constitutional protection.

SYMBOLIC SPEECH AND EXPRESSIVE CONDUCT

As *Cohen v. California* and *R.A.V. v. St. Paul* make clear, the protection of the First Amendment is not limited to pure speech. The term **symbolic speech** is applied to a wide range of nonverbal communication that is subject to First Amendment protection. Of course, not every symbol is entitled to constitutional protection; it depends on the circumstances in which the symbol is displayed.

The Flag Salute Controversy

An early example of the modern Court's willingness to protect symbolic speech is provided by the flag salute cases of *Minersville School District v. Gobitis* (1940) and *West Virginia State Board of Education v. Barnette* (1943). (These cases, which also implicate freedom of religion, are discussed more fully in Chapter 9.) In the first of these cases, the Court upheld a local school board directive requiring public school students to salute the American flag as part of the daily class routine. In one of the most dramatic turnabouts in its history, the Court overruled this precedent three years later in the second flag salute case. In *Barnette,* a six-member majority recognized the right of school children who were members of Jehovah's Witnesses to refrain from participation in the flag salute ritual. Writing for the Court, Justice Robert Jackson observed that "no official, high or petty, can prescribe what shall be orthodox in politics, nationalism, religion, or other matters of opinion or force citizens to confess by word or act their faith therein."

Symbolic Speech in the Vietnam Era

Protests against the Vietnam War produced a number of controversies over symbolic speech. For example, in *United States v. O'Brien* (1968), the Court rejected the First Amendment claim of a Vietnam War protester that publicly burning his draft card was a form of constitutionally protected symbolic speech. David Paul O'Brien, who had burned his Selective Service registration certificate on the steps of the South Boston Courthouse in the presence of a "sizable crowd," was convicted for violation of a federal law providing that an offense was committed by any person "who forges, alters, knowingly destroys, knowingly mutilates, or in any manner changes any such certificate. . . ." Chief Justice Earl Warren, writing for a seven-member majority, determined that Congress had ample constitutional authority to prohibit the destruction or mutilation of draft cards. The card, after all, belonged to the government, not to Mr. O'Brien.

A less defiant form of symbolic speech in opposition to the Vietnam War was afforded First Amendment protection in *Tinker v. Des Moines Independent Community School District* (1969). High school students John Tinker and Christopher Eckhardt, along with Tinker's sister Mary Beth, wore black armbands to school to protest American involvement in the Vietnam War. Anticipating this protest, school officials had adopted a policy that students refusing to remove such armbands would be suspended until they agreed to return to school without them. The Tinkers and Eckhardt refused to remove their armbands when requested and were sent home under suspension. They then brought suit to recover nominal damages and to enjoin school officials from enforcing the regulation. The case eventually reached the Supreme Court, which rejected the lower court's view that the action of school officials was "reasonable" because it was based on fear that a disturbance would result from the wearing of armbands. Writing for the majority, Justice Abe Fortas concluded that the wearing of armbands in this instance "was divorced from actual or potential disruptive conduct . . ." and as such was "closely akin to 'pure speech' which . . . is entitled to comprehensive protection under the First Amendment. . . ." For public school officials to justify prohibiting the "particular expression of opinion," Fortas asserted, they must be able to show that such action "was caused by something more than a mere desire to avoid the discomfort and unpleasantness that always accompany an unpopular viewpoint."

Flag Burning

During the same year in which it decided the *Tinker* case, the Court had an opportunity to address the question of whether burning the American flag is entitled to constitutional protection as symbolic speech (*Street v. New York* [1969]). The Court focused on the element of verbal expression also presented in this case, however, and effectively avoided the symbolic speech issue. After learning of the assassination attempt against civil rights leader James Meredith in Mississippi, Sidney Street burned his American flag on a Brooklyn street corner. The arresting officer testified that he heard Street say to a small crowd of onlookers: "We don't need no damn flag." Street was convicted of "malicious mischief" in violation of a New York state statute making it a misdemeanor to "publicly mutilate, deface, defile, or defy, trample upon or cast contempt upon, either by words or act [any flag of the United States]." Because a general verdict was rendered by the trial court, the Supreme Court, in an opinion by Justice Harlan, observed that Street might have been punished for his speech as well as for burning the flag. The Court concluded that under the circumstances, he could not be constitutionally punished for his words alone.

Protestors burning American flags. A form of free speech?

Harlan emphasized that the Court was not ruling on the question of whether Street could be punished for flag burning, "even though the burning was an act of protest."

The Warren Court's decision left open the question of whether flag burning *per se* was a form of symbolic speech protected by the First Amendment. The Rehnquist Court, surprising many observers, answered that question in the affirmative in the highly publicized case of *Texas v. Johnson* (1989). After publicly burning the American flag outside the 1984 Republican National Convention in Dallas, Gregory Johnson was prosecuted under a Texas law prohibiting flag desecration. Johnson was convicted at trial, but his conviction was reversed by the Texas Court of Criminal Appeals, which held that Johnson's conduct was protected by the First Amendment. In an extremely controversial decision, the U.S. Supreme Court agreed, splitting 5 to 4. Perhaps most surprising to Court watchers was the fact that two Reagan appointees, Justices Antonin Scalia and Anthony Kennedy, joined the majority. On the other hand, Justice John Paul Stevens, generally considered a liberal on civil liberties issues, was among the dissenters.

Writing for the Court in *Johnson,* Justice William Brennan observed that "[t]he expressive, overtly political nature of [Johnson's] conduct was both intentional and overwhelmingly apparent." In Brennan's view,

> Johnson was convicted for engaging in expressive conduct. The State's interest in preventing breaches of the peace does not support his conviction because Johnson's conduct did not threaten to disturb the peace. Nor does the State's interest in preserving the flag as a symbol of nationhood and national unity justify his criminal conviction for engaging in political expression.

Dissenting, Chief Justice William Rehnquist challenged the majority's conclusion that Johnson's act of flag burning was a form of political speech, saying that "flag burning is the equivalent of an inarticulate grunt or roar that . . . is most likely to be indulged in not to express any particular idea, but to antagonize others. . . ." Rehnquist stressed the "unique position" of the flag "as the symbol of our Nation, a uniqueness that justifies a governmental prohibition against flag burning. . . ." But for Justice Brennan and the majority, "[t]he way to preserve the flag's special role is not to punish those who feel differently. . . ."

In the wake of the *Johnson* decision, conservatives called for a constitutional amendment to place flag burning beyond the pale of First Amendment protection. In an attempt to address the issue by less drastic means, Congress passed the Federal Flag Protection Act of 1989, making flag burning a federal crime. In *United States v. Eichman* (1990), the Court struck down the Flag Protection Act as applied to flag burning as a means of political protest.

Are Nude Performances a Form of Symbolic Speech?

Every state has a prohibition against indecent exposure. Generally, these statutes are applied in situations where individuals expose themselves in public or private to unwilling viewers. But what if the exposure takes place by mutual consent, such as in a night club that features nude dancing? Although there is certainly no First Amendment protection for public nudity generally, nudity may acquire constitutional protection in certain contexts. As a part of a play or performance that is not legally obscene, nudity may be considered symbolic speech protected under the First Amendment. In *Doran v. Salem Inn* (1975), the Supreme Court said that "although the customary 'barroom' type of nude dancing may involve only the barest

Is nude dancing a form of free expression under the First Amendment?

minimum of constitutional protection, . . . this form of entertainment might be entitled to First and Fourteenth Amendment protection under some circumstances."

The Court faced the nude dancing issue squarely in *Barnes v. Glen Theatre, Inc.* (1991). This case involved a constitutional challenge to an Indiana statute requiring that night club dancers wear "pasties" and "G-strings." The Court rejected the challenge, splitting 5 to 4. Speaking for a plurality, Chief Justice Rehnquist recognized that nude dancing was "expressive conduct within the outer perimeters of the First Amendment" but held that the state's interest in fostering order and morality justified the minimal burden on free expression associated with requiring dancers to wear pasties and G-strings. Justice Scalia's opinion concurring in the judgment was even more conservative in refusing to recognize any First Amendment protection for such activities.

Justice David Souter's concurrence was more narrowly drawn. Like Rehnquist, Souter recognized the applicability of the First Amendment but concluded that the state's interest in eliminating "harmful secondary effects, including the crime associated with adult entertainment," justified the limited restriction on freedom of expression.

The four dissenting justices in *Glen Theatre* (White, Marshall, Blackmun, and Stevens) found the nude dancing at issue in the case to be "communicative activity" squarely within the protection of the First Amendment, saying that "nudity is itself an expressive component of the dance, not merely incidental 'conduct.' " The dissenters quoted approvingly from the Court's previous decision in *Doran v. Salem Inn,* which observed that "while the entertainment afforded by a nude ballet at Lincoln Center to those who can pay the price may differ vastly in content (as viewed by judges) or in quality (as viewed by critics), it may not differ in substance from the dance viewed by the person who . . . wants some 'entertainment' with his beer or shot of rye."

In the wake of the Supreme Court's decision in *Glen Theatre,* states, cities, and counties around the country where nude dancing has been permitted began to consider ordinances to restrict this activity. A number of communities adopted laws prohibiting all-nude dancing in establishments that serve alcohol. How far such restrictions may go remains uncertain.

TO SUMMARIZE:

- Symbolic speech refers to nonverbal communication that is deemed entitled to First Amendment protection.
- The determination of whether a particular symbol is accorded constitutional protection depends on the circumstances surrounding its display.
- The Supreme Court has accorded First Amendment protection to the burning of the American flag as a form of nonviolent political protest.
- Although public nudity in general is not recognized as symbolic speech, nudity as a form of artistic expression may under some circumstances be granted this constitutionally protected status.

DEFAMATION

Defamation of character consists of injuring someone's reputation by making false public statements about that person. Defamation is not a crime, but a tort. The appropriate remedy is a civil suit for damages. Defamation may take two forms. The verbal form is called *slander;* the written form is known as *libel.* From a legal and constitutional perspective, this distinction matters little. As a practical matter, most of the litigation in this area has involved libel, usually alleged to have been committed by newspapers.

As the Court observed in *Chaplinsky v. New Hampshire* (1942), libelous publications have traditionally been outside the scope of First Amendment protection. However, since the mid-1960s, the Supreme Court has in effect made it easier for defendants in libel suits brought by "public persons" to avoid libel judgments. In so doing, the Court has substantially expanded First Amendment freedom in an area traditionally controlled by principles of tort law. This development reflects what Justice Brennan described as "a profound national commitment to the principle that debate on public issues should be uninhibited, robust, and wide-open" (*New York Times Company v. Sullivan* [1964]).

Actual Malice

Prior to the Supreme Court's decision in *New York Times v. Sullivan,* the primary defense in a libel action was proof that the published material was true. The *Sullivan* decision substituted a new rule that afforded far greater protection to published criticism of official conduct. As stated by Justice Brennan, this standard "prohibits a public official from recovering damages for a defamatory falsehood relating to his official conduct unless he proves that the statement was made with '**actual malice**'—that is, with knowledge that it was false or with reckless disregard of whether it was false or not." As long as there is an "absence of

William Brennan: Associate Justice, 1956–1990

malice" on the part of the press, public officials are barred from recovering damages for the publication of false statements about them.

The *Sullivan* case emerged out of the civil rights struggle of the 1960s. L. B. Sullivan, a city commissioner in Montgomery, Alabama, brought suit against the *New York Times* for its publication of a paid advertisement in which civil rights leaders chastised Montgomery officials for police responses to civil rights demonstrations. The *Sullivan* decision, which broadened protection of the press against libel actions, thus reflected the Warren Court's commitment to protecting free expression by minority groups facing a politically hostile environment.

Libel Suits Brought by "Public Persons"

Although *New York Times v. Sullivan* applied only to cases where public officials sued for libel, the principle was soon expanded to cover a broader category designated as **public figures** (see *Curtis Publishing Company v. Butts* [1967]). This category includes prominent (and not so prominent) public figures, as well as persons who thrust themselves into the glare of publicity. The theory underlying this doctrine is that public figures have sufficient access to the media to defend themselves against false charges and thus do not require the assistance of libel suits. In *Gertz v. Robert Welch, Inc.* (1974), the Supreme Court stated that "public officials and public figures usually enjoy significantly greater access to the channels of effective communication and hence have a more realistic opportunity to counteract false statements than private individuals normally enjoy." The Court went on to discuss the concept of a "public figure":

> In some instances an individual may achieve such pervasive fame or notoriety that he becomes a public figure for all purposes and in all contexts. More commonly, an individual voluntarily injects himself or is drawn into a particular public controversy and thereby becomes a public figure for a limited range of issues. In either case, such persons assume special prominence in the resolution of public questions.

The concept of "public person" has been difficult to apply, but the Supreme Court has made it clear that publicity does not necessarily make a private citizen a public figure for purposes of libel law. For example, in *Time, Inc. v. Firestone* (1976), the Court rejected an attempt by a defendant in a libel suit to characterize Dorothy Firestone, a wealthy Palm Beach socialite, as a public figure merely because she was involved in a highly publicized divorce case. Speaking for the Court, Justice William Rehnquist said that for a plaintiff in a libel suit to be considered a public figure, the alleged defamation must involve a public controversy, not merely a private dispute that has been publicized in the press. While Firestone's divorce may have generated widespread public interest, it did not involve questions of vital public concern. Moreover, Firestone had not sought public attention; it was thrust upon her by an inquiring press.

Reverend Jerry Falwell Takes on *Hustler* Magazine

In one of its more colorful recent cases, *Hustler Magazine v. Falwell* (1988), the Supreme Court reaffirmed the *Sullivan-Gertz* rules. In its November 1983 issue, *Hustler* ran a fictional advertisement entitled "Jerry Falwell talks about his first time." The ad, which was a spoof on the popular ad campaign for Campari liqueur, portrayed Rev. Falwell as a hypocritical drunkard whose "first time" involved sex with his mother in an outhouse. At the bottom of the page, in fine print, was the disclaimer "Ad Parody—Not to be Taken Seriously." Nevertheless, Rev. Falwell took the ad very seriously, and brought a federal lawsuit alleging libel and intentional infliction of emotional distress. Given the outrageous nature of the parody, which no reasonable person could have believed to be true, the jury found for *Hustler* on the libel claim. But the jury did rule in Rev. Falwell's favor on the claim of infliction of emotional distress and awarded substantial monetary damages against *Hustler.* In a unanimous decision, the Supreme Court reversed the judgment, holding that Falwell, as a public figure, could not recover damages for infliction of emotional distress without showing that *Hustler* had published a false statement of fact with actual malice. Writing for the Court, Chief Justice Rehnquist observed that

> in the world of debate about public affairs, many things done with motives that are less than admirable are protected by the First Amendment. . . . Thus while such a bad motive may be deemed controlling for purposes of tort liability in other areas of the law, we think the First Amendment prohibits such a result in the area of public debate about public figures.

Invasions of Privacy

Closely related to libel is the concept of invasion of privacy. Many jurisdictions have laws permitting private individuals to sue the press for unwarranted invasions of their privacy. Following its decision in *New York Times Company v. Sullivan,* the Supreme Court began to restrict such lawsuits. The first major decision came in *Time, Inc. v. Hill* (1967). There, the Court set aside a judgment in an **invasion of privacy** suit brought against *Life* magazine. *Life* had published a story about a family that had been held hostage by escaped prisoners. Unfortunately, not all of the statements made in the magazine story were true. Under New York law, family members could sue regardless of whether the story constituted libel. In setting aside the verdict for the plaintiffs, the Supreme Court said that the First Amendment "preclude[s] the application of the New York statute to redress false reports of matters of public interest in the absence of proof that the defendant published the report with knowledge of its falsity or in reckless disregard of the truth."

In a similar vein, the Supreme Court has blocked efforts to restrict the press from reporting the identities of crime victims. In *Cox Broadcasting v. Cohn* (1975), the Court reversed a judgment for the plaintiff in a case in which a television station reported the name of a rape victim. The Court emphasized the fact that the name had been contained in the indictment and was thus a part of the public record. Similarly, in *The Florida Star v. B.J.F.* (1989), the Court overturned a verdict against a newspaper that reported the name of a rape victim. The newspaper had obtained the victim's name from a police report that had been released in violation of state law and the established policy of the police department. The *Cox Broadcasting* and *Florida Star* decisions reflect a commitment to the principle that the press has the right to report information that it lawfully obtains.

TO SUMMARIZE:

- The tort of libel is outside the scope of First Amendment protection. However, the Supreme Court has since the mid-1960s extended First Amendment safeguards to defendants in libel suits brought by "public persons," thus expanding freedom of expression in a field traditionally controlled by principles of tort law.

- Under the rule adopted in *New York Times v. Sullivan* (1964) a public official (a term later expanded to include all "public persons") cannot recover damages for a "defamatory falsehood" relating to official conduct unless it is proved that the statement in question "was made with 'actual malice'—that is, with knowledge that it was false or with reckless disregard of whether it was false or not."
- In general the press is accorded freedom to publish any material lawfully obtained, even though publication may seriously invade the privacy of individuals.

THE INTRACTABLE OBSCENITY PROBLEM

In recent decades sexually explicit magazines, books, videotapes and films have become increasingly available in the marketplace. To locate such materials, one does not need to go to an "adult bookstore." Soft-core pornography like *Hustler* is readily available at most convenience stores and magazine stands. Many cable and satellite television companies also provide adult entertainment in varying degrees of explicitness. Even **hard-core pornography** is easily obtained in the back rooms of many local video rental stores. The commercial success of such ventures obviously indicates a degree of social acceptance, but many critics continue to regard pornography as an evil that should be curtailed if not eliminated altogether.

Of course, anyone accused of producing or selling obscene materials will argue that the First Amendment protects his or her right to engage in such activities. One of the most difficult tasks the Supreme Court has undertaken in recent decades is that of determining the degree to which the First Amendment protects pornography.

Prior to the Supreme Court's entry into this field in 1957, most American courts adhered to a legal definition of obscenity derived from the 1868 English case of *Regina v. Hicklin.* The *Hicklin* test was "whether the tendency of the matter charged as obscenity is to deprave and corrupt those whose minds are open to such immoral influences, and into whose hands a publication of this sort may fall." By the mid-twentieth century, this standard was widely regarded as unduly restrictive of artistic and literary expression. The principal objection to the *Hicklin* test was that it sought to measure obscenity with reference to its supposed impact on the most vulnerable members of society.

The Prurient Interest Test

In *Roth v. United States* (1957), the Supreme Court handed down new legal guidelines for obscenity. Writing for the majority, Justice Brennan expressed the view that obscenity is "utterly without redeeming social importance" and thus entitled to no First Amendment protection. Rejecting the essence of the *Hicklin* standard, he stated the new test as "whether to the average person, applying contemporary community standards, the dominant theme of the material taken as a whole appeals to a prurient interest."

Roth v. United States, a federal case, was consolidated with the state case of *Alberts v. California,* thus making the new test applicable to every level of government in the country. But in spite of its uniform applicability and apparent simplicity, the *Roth-Alberts* test drew the Court into an interpretive quagmire from which it has not yet emerged. Virtually every term contained in the new obscenity test proved elusive. The Court could never reach full agreement on what constitutes a **prurient interest.** The term **redeeming social importance** also failed to generate consensus. A majority of the Court, in the years immediately following *Roth,* could not even agree on whether the term "community" referred to the nation as a whole or to individual states or localities. Although most of the justices believed that hard-core pornography was not entitled to First Amendment protection, they were unable to define its meaning. Justice Potter Stewart's well-known remark "I know it when I see it" (see *Jacobellis v. Ohio* [1964], concurring opinion) points up the difficulty of precise definition in this area.

The *Miller* Test

Partly because of the complexity of the problem and partly as a result of the refusal of Justices Hugo Black and William O. Douglas to recognize the legitimacy of *any* limitations on expression in the obscenity field, the Warren Court was unable to muster a clear majority in support of all aspects of the *Roth-Alberts* test during the 1960s. The Burger Court was also sharply divided but ultimately achieved a bare majority in restating the constitutional test of obscenity. Writing for the Court in *Miller v. California* (1973), Chief Justice Burger stated that "the basic guidelines for the trier of fact" in obscenity cases are as follows:

> (a) whether "the average person, applying contemporary community standards" would find that the work, taken as a whole, appeals to the prurient interest, . . .
> (b) whether the work depicts or describes, in a patently offensive way, sexual conduct specifically defined by the applicable state law, and (c) whether the work, taken as a whole, lacks serious literary, artistic, political, or scientific value.

The *Miller* test was somewhat more restrictive of free expression than was the original *Roth-Alberts* test as embellished and applied by the Warren Court. The Burger Court explicitly rejected the "utterly without redeeming social value" standard advanced by a minority of justices in the 1960s (see *Memoirs v. Massachusetts* [1966]). Nevertheless, the new guidelines were far from clear. Exactly what is **patently offensive** material? Precisely how does a prurient interest in sex differ from a normal, healthy interest? What constitutes serious literary, artistic, political, or scientific value? And, perhaps most importantly, whose standards are to prevail in making these determinations?

In *Miller* the Court indicated that the applicable **community standards** under the new test were local or at most statewide standards. But when authorities in Albany, Georgia, purportedly applying "community standards," attempted to ban the movie *Carnal Knowledge,* the Court ruled that the test had been improperly applied. Only material showing "patently offensive hard core sexual conduct" could be proscribed under the new rules (*Jenkins v. Georgia* [1974]).

In 1987, a 5-to-4 majority of the Court modified the "contemporary community standards" yardstick. Writing for the majority in *Pope v. Illinois,* Justice White declared that "the proper inquiry is not whether an ordinary member of any given community would find serious literary, artistic, political and scientific value in allegedly obscene material, but whether a reasonable person would find such value in the material, taken as a whole." Whether this "reasonable person" alternative represents a liberalization of the obscenity test or fosters "intolerable orthodoxy," as Justice John Paul Stevens predicted in a dissenting opinion, it is clear that First Amendment issues in the field of obscenity are far from resolved.

Pornography on the Internet

As a practical matter, one must recognize that pornography has become much more widely available in recent years. This is due to several factors. Most fundamentally, society's attitudes in this area have become more permissive. Second, prosecutions in this area have become increasingly rare. In the absence of a public outcry, prosecutors tend to avoid this area in favor of more "ordinary" types of crime. Finally, one must recognize the effect of the Internet, which has made pornography easily accessible to people who might not wish to enter an adult bookstore or place an order from the back of an adult magazine. The World Wide Web has thousands of sites devoted to "adult entertainment," many of which feature extremely graphic, hardcore pornography. One of the principal concerns about pornography on the Internet is its availability to children.

In 1996, Congress passed the Communications Decency Act, which made it a crime to display "indecent" material on the Internet in a manner that might make it available to minors. In *Reno v. American Civil Liberties Union* (1997), the Court declared this statute unconstitutional on First Amendment grounds. Writing for the Court, Justice Stevens concluded that, with respect to cyberspace, "the interest in encouraging freedom of expression in a democratic society outweighs any theoretical but unproven benefit of censorship." The Court's opinion in *Reno* left open the possibility that a more narrowly tailored statute, that is, one limited to prohibiting *obscenity* as distinct from *indecency,* might pass constitutional muster.

Child Pornography

It is now well established that government may criminalize the production and distribution of material depicting children engaged in sexual activities, irrespective of whether the material meets the legal test of obscenity. In *New York v. Ferber* (1982), the Court held that a state has a compelling interest in protecting children from sexual abuse and found a close connection between such abuse and the use of children in the production of pornographic materials. In 1990, the Rehnquist Court went beyond the *Ferber* decision in upholding a state law prohibiting the possession and viewing of child pornography (*Osborne v. Ohio*). Justices Brennan, Marshall, and Stevens, all of whom had concurred in the *Ferber* case, dissented in *Osborne.* Justice Brennan found the law to be "overly broad" and criticized the Court for departing from its earlier decision in *Stanley v. Georgia* (1969). Together, the *Ferber* and *Osborne* decisions provide a clear indication that the Supreme Court is not sympathetic to any First Amendment claim that would protect from criminal prosecution those who produce, distribute, or consume child pornography.

An interesting question arose in Oklahoma City in 1997 when a state judge found the feature film *The Tin Drum* to be in violation of the state's child pornography law. An R-rated film from the 1970s, *The Tin Drum* depicts life in the Netherlands during the Nazi occupation as seen through the eyes of a teenage boy. The critically acclaimed film contains a scene in which a young boy performs oral sex on a teenage girl. The scene is not explicit and clearly the film does not meet the legal test of obscenity. But it may violate Oklahoma's strict prohibition against depiction of sexual conduct by persons actually or represented to be under eighteen. At the time this book was being written, that question was still in litigation in the federal courts.

TO SUMMARIZE:

- The Supreme Court has said that the First Amendment does not protect expression determined to be obscene. The Court has made it clear that obscenity refers only to hard-core pornography that meets a specific legal test.
- Under *Miller v. California* (1973), the definition of obscenity is (a) whether "the average person, applying contemporary community standards" would find that the work, taken as a whole, appeals to the prurient interest, . . . (b) whether the work depicts or describes, in a patently offensive way, sexual conduct specifically defined by the applicable state law, and (c) whether the work, taken as a whole, lacks serious literary, artistic, political, or scientific value.
- In striking down the Communications Decency Act of 1996, the Supreme Court refused to accept the government's argument that "indecent" material on the Internet is subject to regulations similar to those upheld for the broadcast media. Thus the Court recognized the Internet as a form of communication comparable to the printed page.
- It is now well established that government may criminalize the production and distribution of material depicting children engaged in sexual activities, regardless of whether the material meets the legal test of obscenity.

EXPRESSIVE ACTIVITIES IN THE PUBLIC FORUM

Although the Supreme Court has recognized legitimate community interests that may, under some conditions, justify limitations on speech and assembly, it has tended to favor the First Amendment right of groups to assemble and express themselves in the **public forum,** especially for the purpose of communicating a political message. Such expressive activities in the public forum are an essential part of the democratic process.

The Constitution in action: Freedom of assembly in the Nation's capital

Civil Rights Demonstrations of the 1960s

Organized public protest against racial segregation in southern and border states was a critical component of the **Civil Rights movement** of the 1950s and 1960s. In many instances these protests resulted in arrests. Several of these cases reached the Supreme Court. In *Edwards v. South Carolina* (1963), for example, the Court reversed breach-of-the-peace convictions of 187 African-American college students who had participated in a peaceful civil rights demonstration on the grounds of the state capitol in Columbia, South Carolina. The Court held that in "arresting, convicting and punishing" these students, South Carolina had infringed their "constitutionally protected rights of free speech, free assembly, and freedom to petition for redress of their grievances." In his opinion for the majority, Justice Potter Stewart observed that "the Fourteenth Amendment does not permit a state to make criminal the peaceful expression of unpopular views."

In a similar case, *Cox v. Louisiana* (1965), the Court reversed convictions for breach of the peace, obstructing "public passages," and picketing near a courthouse. In this case Rev. B. Elton Cox led two thousand African-American college students in a peaceful demonstration protesting the jailing of twenty-three fellow students who had been picketing segregated lunch counters in Baton Rouge, Louisiana. When the students refused to comply with a police order to disperse, tear gas was used to break up the demonstration. In *Cox*, the Court held that the convictions for breach of the peace and for obstructing the sidewalk violated Cox's First Amendment freedoms of speech and assembly. The picketing conviction was reversed on due process grounds.

A similar factual pattern was presented in the 1966 case of *Adderley v. Florida,* but this time the Court affirmed the conviction of African-American students who were protesting local practices of racial segregation. Like the situation in *Cox,* the demonstrators were also denouncing the arrests of other students, in this instance students from Florida A & M University who had attempted to integrate movie theaters in Tallahassee. During their demonstration, Harriet Louise Adderley and other students had allegedly blocked a jail driveway not normally used by the public.

Members of the Ku Klux Klan exercising their First Amendment rights

When they ignored requests to leave this area, they were arrested and charged with violating a state law that prohibited trespass "committed with a malicious and mischievous intent."

In justifying defendants' convictions, Justice Black, writing for a majority of five, found that nothing in the Constitution prevented Florida from "even-handed enforcement of its general trespass statute. . . ." Emphasizing the use of the driveway for vehicles providing service to the jail and playing down the symbolic significance of a civil rights protest at the place of incarceration, Black insisted: "The State, no less than a private owner of property, has power to preserve the property under its control for the use to which it is lawfully dedicated."

The *Adderley* decision may be viewed as marking the Warren Court's outer limit of tolerance for public protest. But *Adderley* is perhaps more accurately seen as a concession to public opinion. The decision was rendered at a time of great public concern over a rising tide of crime and violence in America's cities. Perhaps certain justices on the Court saw the *Adderley* case as a good opportunity to make a statement in favor of "law and order," a value that the Warren Court was seldom credited with stressing.

The Civil Rights and antiwar movements of the 1960s were characterized by frequent demonstrations, most of which stayed within constitutional parameters, others of which pressed the limits of constitutional tolerance for public protest. The relatively tranquil decades of the 1970s, 1980s, and 1990s produced fewer cases involving large-scale demonstrations.

Anti-Abortion Demonstrations

The issue that has consistently produced the most turmoil in the public forum in recent decades has been abortion. "Pro-choice" and "pro-life" activists have often clashed in the streets, screaming at one another and sometimes resorting to violence. Pro-life forces have been particularly aggressive in their public demonstrations, often congregating outside abortion clinics and sometimes harassing women seeking to enter these clinics. On occasion, operators of abortion clinics have gone to court to obtain injunctions limiting pro-lifers' protest activities.

In *Madsen v. Women's Health Center* (1994) the Court upheld a Florida court's injunction that prohibited anti-abortion protesters from coming within a thirty-six-foot buffer zone around the entrances to an abortion clinic. The state judge had found that protesters were impeding access to the clinic and harassing clients. In addition to creating a buffer zone that included a section of the public street and sidewalk, the judge banned "singing, chanting, whistling, shouting, yelling, use of bullhorns, auto horns, sound amplification equipment or other sounds or images observable to or within earshot of the patients inside the clinic" between the hours of 7:30 A.M. and noon on Mondays through Saturdays. The injunction was similar to many others that had been issued by state judges around the country to protect abortion clinics and their patrons from the activities of protesters. Judy Madsen, a member of Operation Rescue who had participated in the demonstrations, challenged the constitutionality of the injunction on First Amendment grounds. The Florida Supreme Court upheld the injunction, but in a separate case, the Eleventh Circuit Court of Appeals in Atlanta struck it down. By a 6-to-3 vote, the Supreme Court sided with Florida's highest court.

Writing for the majority, Chief Justice Rehnquist concluded that the thirty-six-foot buffer zone "burdens no more speech than necessary to accomplish the governmental interest at stake." Rehnquist noted the state's interests in ensuring public safety and order, promoting the free flow of traffic along streets and sidewalks, protecting a woman's freedom to seek abortion and other pregnancy-related services, and protecting the property rights of all citizens. The Court also upheld the noise restrictions contained in the injunction, noting that "the First Amendment does not demand that patients at a medical facility undertake Herculean efforts to escape the cacophony of political protests." But the Court invalidated other parts of the injunction, holding that the state judge had gone too far in limiting expression. In a stinging dissent, joined by Justices Thomas and Kennedy, Justice Scalia asserted that the entire injunction "departs so far from the established course of our jurisprudence that in any other context it would have been regarded as a candidate for summary reversal."

Six years later, in *Schenck v. Pro-Choice Network* (1997), the Court applied its *Madsen* rationale in upholding an injunction designed to keep demonstrators at least fifteen feet from the doorways and driveways of clinics. Consistent with *Madsen,* the Court, however, struck down a provision of the injunction creating a "floating buffer zone" around clients and staff entering and exiting abortion clinics.

What Constitutes a Public Forum?

A key issue for the Court in the last several decades has been defining the concept of public forum. The Supreme Court has recognized that the term *public forum* includes not only streets and parks but any property that government "has opened for use by the public as a place for expressive activity" (*Perry Educational Association v. Perry Local Educators' Association* [1983]). In *United States v. Grace* (1983), the Court recognized that the sidewalks surrounding the Court's own building in Washington, D.C., qualified as a public forum and struck down the federal law forbidding use of that space for picketing or handing out leaflets.

Not every place open to the public constitutes a public forum for purposes of the First Amendment. For example, a privately owned shopping center is not considered a public forum. In *Lloyd Corporation v. Tanner* (1972), the Supreme Court observed that a privately owned shopping center does not "lose its private character merely because the public is generally invited to use it for designated purposes. . . ." On the other hand, the Court let stand a California Supreme Court ruling that recognized shopping centers as public forums under the California Constitution (see *PruneYard Shopping Center v. Robins* [1980]). The *PruneYard* decision points up the ability of state courts and state constitutions to grant civil liberties claims transcending those recognized under the federal constitution.

Is an Airport a Public Forum?

The Supreme Court has struggled with the problem of whether an airport is a public forum for the purposes of soliciting, proselytizing, and distributing literature. In *Board of Airport Commissioners v. Jews for Jesus* (1987) and *Lee v. International Society for Krishna Consciousness* (1992), the Court struck down policies that restricted such activities in public airport terminals. Although it relied in both decisions on First Amendment considerations, the Court was unable to reach agreement, however, as to whether an airport is a public forum. Given the prevalence of expressive activities in airports, it is unlikely that the Court will be unable to avoid this question forever.

Time, Place, and Manner Regulations

It is well-established that reasonable **time, place, and manner regulations** can justify the restriction of First Amendment activities in the public forum. The general rule is that such regulations must be reasonable, narrowly drawn, and **content-neutral.** Applying this standard, the Supreme Court struck down, as unconstitutional on its face, a local ordinance that gave unlimited discretion to the chief of police in forbidding or permitting the use of sound amplification devices, such as loudspeakers on trucks (*Saia v. New York* [1948]). A year later, in *Kovacs v. Cooper,* the Court upheld a narrowly interpreted ordinance prohibiting vehicles on the public streets from operating amplifiers or other instruments emitting "loud and raucous noises."

The requirement of content neutrality is not absolute, but government cannot depart from it without meeting a heavy burden of justification. The Court is likely to invalidate a regulation of this kind unless the government can show that it is necessary to serve a compelling interest and is narrowly drawn to achieve that purpose. The Court applied this standard in declaring unconstitutional the previously noted restriction on picketing on the sidewalks surrounding the Supreme Court building (*United States v. Grace* [1983]).

In *Boos v. Barry* (1988), the Supreme Court struck down a District of Columbia regulation that prohibited the display of signs within five hundred feet of a foreign embassy if the message displayed on the signs brought the embassy's government into "disrepute." At the same time, the Court sustained the regulation permitting police to disperse assemblies within five hundred feet of embassies. The former regulation was a restriction on the content of a political message; the latter, if applied evenhandedly, was regarded as a legitimate time, place, and manner regulation.

The Special Problem of Zoning Regulations

Time, place, and manner restrictions often take the form of local **zoning** requirements that have the effect of limiting freedom of expression. In the continuing process of First Amendment line drawing, the Supreme Court has had occasion to look closely at a number of these restrictions. In *Heffron v. International Society for Krishna Consciousness (ISKCON)* (1981), a majority of five justices upheld a Minnesota "zoning" restriction limiting solicitation at the state fair, as applied to an organization wishing to distribute and sell religious literature and request donations from fair patrons. The regulation, which applied to nonprofit, charitable, and commercial enterprises alike, confined solicitation activities to booths rented on a first-come, first-served basis. ISKCON maintained that this restriction violated the First and Fourteenth Amendments by interfering with one of its sacred rituals, *sankirtan,* which required the faithful to distribute and sell religious literature and to solicit contributions. Writing for the majority, Justice White left no doubt that he was unimpressed by this line of argument:

> None of our cases suggest that the inclusion of peripatetic solicitation as part of a church ritual entitles church members to solicitation rights in a public forum superior to those members of other religious groups who raise money but do not purport to ritualize the process.

In the majority's view, the regulation at issue was content-neutral and nondiscriminatory in application. Moreover, it served a significant governmental interest, that of maintaining crowd control on the congested state fairgrounds. Justice Brennan, speaking for the four dissenters, saw the First Amendment issue quite differently:

> As soon as a proselytizing member of ISKCON hands out a free copy of the Bhagavad-Gita to an interested listener, or a political candidate distributes his campaign brochure to a potential voter, he becomes subject to arrest and removal from the fairgrounds. This constitutes a significant restriction on First Amendment rights.

Five years later, the Court upheld a zoning ordinance passed by the city of Renton, Washington, prohibiting the location of "adult theaters" within one thousand feet of residential, church, park, or school property (*Renton v. Playtime Theatres, Inc.* [1986]). Writing for a majority of seven, Justice Rehnquist found that the ordinance was "content-neutral," that it served a "substantial governmental interest," and that it permitted reasonable alternative "avenues of communication." He asserted that the ordinance was a "valid governmental response to the 'admittedly serious problems' created by adult theaters." The city had not used its zoning power as a "pretext for suppressing expression" but had made areas available for adult theaters and their patrons while "preserving the quality of life in the community at large." Rehnquist concluded: "This, after all, is the essence of zoning."

Again Justice Brennan filed a dissenting opinion, this time supported only by Justice Marshall. Brennan flatly rejected the central premise of the majority opinion when he asserted that ". . . the circumstances here strongly suggest that the ordinance was designed to suppress expression, even that constitutionally protected, and thus was not to be analyzed as a content-neutral time, place and manner restriction." From Justice Brennan's criticism of the Court's analysis in this case, it is clear that the initial characterization of a law, for First Amendment purposes, is all-important. Regulations are not automatically classified as reasonable time, place, and manner restrictions simply because the legislative body enacting them uses that rationale. Ultimately, in matters touching freedom of expression, judges must determine whether a given law is to be viewed as primarily a content-neutral time, place, and manner restriction or as a deliberate attempt, under the guise of this rationale, to limit freedom of expression. The Court may apply neat verbal formulas and strive for analytical consistency, but ultimately the question comes down to one of judgment in which intuition and ideology are often decisive factors.

TO SUMMARIZE:

- Because expressive activities in the public forum are an essential part of the democratic process, the Supreme Court has accorded broad First Amendment protection to groups desiring to assemble and express themselves in the public forum.
- Since the 1930s the Supreme Court has had numerous opportunities to interpret the First Amendment in the context of political and social protests. Most notable among these are the civil rights demonstrations of the 1950s and 1960s and the public protests on both sides of the abortion issue since the 1970s.
- The Supreme Court has recognized that the term *public forum* includes not only streets and parks but any property that government "has opened for use by the public as a place for expressive activity."

- Although the Court strongly resists governmental efforts to control the content of expression in the public forum, the justices have repeatedly upheld reasonable "time, place, and manner" regulations on such expression.

ELECTRONIC MEDIA AND THE FIRST AMENDMENT

The framers of the First Amendment could not have foreseen the invention of radio and television, let alone the prevalence of **electronic media** in contemporary society. Nevertheless, because television and radio are used to express ideas in the public forum, most observers would agree that these electronic media deserve First Amendment protection, at least to some extent. Yet since their inception, radio and television have been regulated extensively by the federal government.

To operate a television or radio station, one must obtain a license from the Federal Communications Commission (FCC); to broadcast without a license from the FCC is a federal crime (as operators of "pirate" radio stations have often discovered). In granting licenses, the FCC is authorized to regulate the station's frequency, wattage, and hours of transmission. To a lesser extent, it also has the power to regulate the content of broadcasts. For example, the FCC has developed regulations to keep the airwaves free of "obscene" or "indecent" programming. Moreover, station licenses come up for renewal every three years, and the FCC is invested with tremendous discretion to determine whether a given station has been operating "in the public interest."

Clearly, government regulations that apply to the electronic media would be unconstitutional if applied to books, newspapers, and magazines. The more permissive approach to government regulation of television and radio was originally predicated on the **scarcity theory,** which held that due to the limited number of available broadcast channels, the government must allocate this scarce resource in the public interest. The proliferation of cable TV and radio has undermined the controlling influence of the scarcity doctrine. Moreover, changing societal norms have led to a relaxation of earlier restrictions on sexual content and profanity on radio and TV. Nevertheless, the Supreme Court continues to recognize the FCC's authority to impose restrictions on broadcast media that would not be tolerated if they were applied to the print medium.

Restrictions of "Indecent" Programming on Television and Radio

In a broad regulation that would almost certainly be declared unconstitutional if applied to a magazine or newspaper, the FCC has prohibited radio and television stations, whether public or private, from broadcasting "indecent" or "obscene" programs. In April 1987, the FCC made national news when it threatened not to renew the licenses of certain radio stations in New York and California. These stations were engaged in so-called "shock radio," which featured talk programs that were intentionally tasteless and given to heavy doses of profanity and frequent sexual references. Although the FCC's threats made headlines, there was little talk of litigation to challenge the agency's regulations. The Supreme Court had previously upheld restrictions on indecent broadcasting in *FCC v. Pacifica Foundation* (1978). In that case, the Court reviewed FCC regulations as applied to a radio broadcast of a monologue by comedian George Carlin that examined "seven dirty words you can't say on the radio." Attorneys for the Pacifica Foundation argued that the monologue in question did not meet the legal test of obscenity and therefore could not be banned from the radio by the FCC. Writing for the Court, Justice Stevens disagreed, observing that "when the Commission finds that a pig has entered the parlor, the exercise of its regulatory power does not depend on proof that the pig is obscene."

Indecent Programming on Cable Television

The so-called "Helms Amendment" to the Cable Television Consumer Protection and Competition Act of 1992 required cable systems that lease channels to commercial providers of "patently offensive" programming to scramble the signals of those channels and make them available only to subscribers who specifically request access. In *Denver Area Educational Telecommunications Consortium v. Federal Communications Commission* (1996), the Court struck down this provision. Writing for the Court, Justice Breyer observed that the provision was not carefully drafted, failed to consider less intrusive alternatives, and was not a "narrowly or reasonably tailored effort to protect children." In Breyer's view, the provision was "overly restrictive, 'sacrific[ing]' important First Amendment interests for too 'speculative a gain.' " In dissent, Justice Thomas (joined by Scalia and Rehnquist) argued that the requirement that indecent programming be scrambled was supported by the government's compelling interest in protecting children. In Thomas's view, the provision at issue was in keeping with "precedents [which] establish that government may support parental authority to direct the moral upbringing of their children. . . ."

Some commentators were disappointed that the Court failed in the *Denver Consortium* decision to articulate a coherent general theory of the First Amendment as it relates to new technology and media. Indeed, the various opinions produced by the justices manifested uncertainty, even confusion, as to the fundamental First Amendment issues involved. This is often the case when the law is confronted by rapid technological change. By 1997, however, the Court achieved greater clarity in addressing the question of whether government could regulate "indecency" on the Internet (see previous discussion of *Reno v. ACLU* [1997]). While recognizing the government's legitimate role in shielding children from inappropriate expression, the Court insisted that this objective cannot justify limiting adults' access to the Internet only to material that is appropriate for children.

Editorializing by Public Television and Radio Stations

Public radio and television, as distinguished from commercial stations and networks, have long been subject to more restrictive government regulations on editorializing. Based on a 1967 act of Congress, the FCC prohibited public radio and television stations from engaging in editorializing altogether. However, in *FCC v. League of Women Voters* (1984), the Supreme Court declared this ban unconstitutional. Writing for a sharply divided Court, Justice Brennan concluded that the ban failed to meet a **least restrictive means test.** In Brennan's view, the ban "far exceeds what is necessary to protect against the risk of governmental interference or to prevent the public from assuming that editorials by public broadcasting stations represent the official view of government."

The Court's general expansion of freedom of expression in the latter half of the twentieth century is reflected not only in areas of political, social, and cultural dialogue, but in the Court's growing awareness that we live in an information age. The emergence and dynamic growth of electronic media, most recently the Internet, have stimulated the Court's development of a First Amendment jurisprudence that elevates communication to an almost hallowed status.

TO SUMMARIZE:

- Traditionally the Supreme Court has tolerated more extensive regulation of electronic media than of books, newspapers, and periodicals. This was originally justified by the scarcity theory, an idea that has since been undermined by the proliferation of cable TV and radio.
- The Court has approved the FCC's prohibition against "indecent" content on radio and TV broadcasts, but has resisted the application of such restrictions to cable TV and to the Internet.
- The trend of modern Court decisions is away from governmental control of the content of expression in the media. This is exemplified by the Court's invalidation of an FCC ban on editorializing by public television and radio stations.

COMMERCIAL SPEECH

Prior to the mid-1970s, the Supreme Court regarded the regulation of **commercial speech** (a broad category including but not limited to the advertising of products and services) as simply an aspect of economic regulation, entitled to no special First Amendment protection. In an important 1976 decision, however, the Court struck down Virginia's ban on the advertisement of prescription drug prices (*Virginia State Board of Pharmacy v. Virginia Citizens Consumer Council*). Writing for the Court, Justice Harry Blackmun stated that although reasonable time, place, and manner restrictions on commercial speech are legitimate and although the state is free to proscribe "false and misleading" advertisements, consumers have a strong First Amendment interest in the free flow of information about goods and services available in the marketplace.

A Test for Judging Regulations of Commercial Speech

In his opinion for the Court in *Central Hudson Gas and Electric Corporation v. Public Service Commission of New York* (1980), Justice Lewis Powell articulated the general rationale for First Amendment protection in this area:

> Commercial expression not only serves the economic interest of the speaker, but also assists consumers and furthers the societal interest in the fullest possible dissemination of information. In applying the First Amendment to this area, we have rejected the "highly paternalistic" view that government has complete power to suppress or regulate commercial speech.

In the same opinion, Justice Powell outlined a four-part test for evaluating regulations of commercial speech. To begin with, commercial speech must "concern lawful activity and not be misleading" if it is to be protected under the First Amendment. If this prerequisite is met, then three additional questions must be considered: (1) Is the "asserted governmental interest" in regulation substantial? (2) Does the regulation directly advance the asserted governmental interest? (3) Finally, is the regulation more extensive than is necessary to serve that purpose? This test is an attempt to balance the need for consumer protection on one hand with the value of a free marketplace of ideas on the other.

Conflicting Applications of the Test

In an important decision in 1986, a narrowly divided Supreme Court opted for consumer protection over the free marketplace of ideas. In *Posadas De Puerto Rico Associates v. Tourism Company,* the Court upheld a law prohibiting advertisements inviting residents of the territory of Puerto Rico to gamble legally in local casinos. In his majority opinion, Justice Rehnquist emphasized Puerto Rico's substantial interest in reducing the demand for casino gambling among its citizens and noted that the regulation at issue directly advanced this objective. He maintained that the legislature of Puerto Rico "surely could have prohibited casino gambling by the residents of Puerto Rico altogether." He concluded that this "greater power to completely ban casino gambling necessarily includes the lesser power to ban advertising of casino gambling."

In a strongly worded dissent, Justice Stevens contended that Puerto Rico had not merely banned the advertising of casino gambling, it had "blatantly" discriminated in punishing speech "depending on the publication, audience and words employed." In his view, the challenged prohibition established "a regime of prior restraint" and articulated a "hopelessly vague and unpredictable" standard.

Commercial Advertising of Alcoholic Beverages

Under the Twenty-first Amendment, states have broad authority to regulate the sale of alcoholic beverages. Does this authority extend to the ban of advertising in this area? In *44 Liquormart, Inc. v. Rhode Island* (1996) the Court struck down Rhode Island's "statutory prohibition against advertisements that provide the public with accurate information about retail prices of alcoholic beverages. . . ." Speaking for a unanimous Court, Justice Stevens concluded that "such an advertising ban is an abridgment of speech protected by the First Amendment and . . . is not shielded from constitutional scrutiny by the Twenty-first Amendment." In a concurring opinion, Justice Thomas wrote that "[a]ll attempts to dissuade legal choices by citizens by keeping them ignorant are impermissible."

Attorney Advertising and Solicitation

Until the late 1970s attorneys were prohibited by their state bar associations from advertising. These prohibitions reflected a desire by the elite elements of the bar to maintain lawyering as a noble and learned profession. But critics of the prohibition, including many newly licensed attorneys, viewed it as an unwarranted restriction on the dissemination of important information in the marketplace. In *Bates v. State Bar of Arizona* (1977), the Supreme Court sided with the critics, and extended First Amendment protection to attorney advertising. As a consequence, it is now common to see ads for legal services on TV, in newspapers, and on buses.

Despite the relaxation of the ban on attorney advertising, many states still maintain restrictions on solicitation by lawyers. For example, the Florida Bar, a state-sanctioned organization, prohibits lawyers from sending targeted direct-mail solicitations to personal injury victims and their relatives for thirty days following an accident or disaster. The rule was challenged by a number of personal injury lawyers who argued that it violated the First Amendment. In *Florida Bar v. Went For It, Inc.* (1995), the Court divided 5 to 4 in upholding the challenged restriction. Justice O'Connor delivered the opinion of the Court, concluding that the Florida Bar "has substantial interest both in protecting injured Floridians from invasive conduct by lawyers and in preventing the erosion of confidence in the profession that such repeated invasions have engendered." In an unusually caustic dissent, Justice Kennedy attacked the majority opinion as "a serious departure, not only from our prior decisions involving attorney advertising, but also from the principles that govern the transmission of commercial speech." Kennedy accused the majority of unsettling precedents "at the expense of those victims most in need of legal assistance."

In spite of the somewhat restrictive (some would say paternalistic) ruling in *Florida Bar v. Went For It,* it is clear that a great many commercial messages today are entitled to First Amendment protection that was nonexistent two decades ago. This enlargement of freedom of expression in the commercial realm underscores the recognition that First Amendment freedoms are by no means limited to the traditional categories of political debate and social protest, important as these concerns are in a constitutional democracy.

TO SUMMARIZE:

- Until the mid-1970s, the Supreme Court accorded little if any First Amendment protection to commercial speech. Since that time, however, the Court has not only recognized the First Amendment's application in this area, but has generally narrowed the gap between commercial speech and traditional areas of constitutionally protected expression.
- Under prevailing doctrine, commercial speech must "concern lawful activity and not be misleading" if it is to be protected under the First Amendment. If this prerequisite is met, then three additional questions must be considered: (1) Is the "asserted governmental interest" in regulation substantial? (2) Does the regulation directly advance the asserted governmental interest? (3) Finally, is the regulation more extensive than is necessary to serve that purpose?
- The Twenty-first Amendment, which gives states broad authority to regulate the sale of alcoholic beverages, has not been interpreted to override First Amendment protections of commercial speech as they relate to advertising in this area.

RIGHTS OF PUBLIC EMPLOYEES AND BENEFICIARIES

Government employment, government grants and contracts, even government programs such as Social Security are not constitutional rights but benefits that government may eliminate altogether or deny to particular individuals, as long as it provides due process of law. Can government make the enjoyment of such benefits contingent on the surrender of constitutional rights, in particular those rights guaranteed by the First Amendment?

Under the Federal Lobbying (Hatch) Act, federal civil servants are barred from actively participating in political campaigns. The Supreme Court upheld this prohibition in *United States v. Harris* (1954) and again in *United States Civil Service*

Commission v. National Association of Letter Carriers (1973). Writing for the Court in the latter decision, Justice White asserted that it was essential that the political influence of federal government workers be limited in order to maintain the concept of a merit-based civil service.

The Court's recent jurisprudence shows greater solicitude for the First Amendment rights of public employees. For example, in *Branti v. Finkel* (1980) the Court said that the First Amendment bars the firing of public prosecutors merely for expressing their political sentiments. Similarly, in *Rankin v. McPherson* (1987), the Court held that a newly hired deputy constable could not be terminated merely for making an intemperate remark about the president. Upon learning of John Hinckley's unsuccessful attempt to assassinate President Reagan in 1981, Ardith McPherson was overheard saying, "If they go for him again, I hope they get him." McPherson, who was at the time a probationary employee, was summarily discharged for making this statement. Writing for the Supreme Court, Justice Thurgood Marshall remarked that "[v]igilance is necessary to ensure that public employers do not use authority over employees to silence discourse, not because it hampers public functions but simply because superiors disagree with the content of employees' speech."

In *United States v. National Treasury Employees Union* (1995), the Court struck down a provision of the Ethics in Government Act that barred federal civil service employees from accepting honoraria for speeches and articles. Although the ban was content-neutral, it applied to all honoraria, even those received for speeches and writings having nothing to do with civil servants' jobs. Writing for the Court, Justice Stevens quoted approvingly from *Pickering v. Board of Education* (1968): "Even though respondents work for the Government, they have not relinquished 'the First Amendment rights they would otherwise enjoy as citizens to comment on matters of public interest.' " The vote was 6 to 3, with Chief Justice Rehnquist and Justices Scalia and Thomas in dissent. Writing for the dissenters, Chief Justice Rehnquist complained that the majority's "application of the First Amendment understates the weight which should be accorded to the governmental justifications for the honoraria ban and overstates the amount of speech which actually will be deterred."

First Amendment Rights of Government Contractors

In *O'Hare Trucking Service v. Northlake* (1996) the Court split 7 to 2 (Scalia and Thomas dissenting) in ruling that independent contractors who do business with government agencies have the same free-speech rights as government employees. Writing for the majority, Justice Kennedy stated that "government officials may indeed terminate at-will [contractual] relationships . . . without cause; but it does not follow that this discretion can be exercised to impose conditions on expressing, or not expressing, specific political views." Given the sheer volume of federal, state, and local contracts, and the fact that political favoritism often plays a role in determining which companies obtain contracts, the decision is apt to spawn considerable litigation.

Restricting Abortion Counseling

The decision in *Rust v. Sullivan* (1991) suggests a different perspective on issues in this area. In *Rust*, the Court sustained a federal regulation barring private birth control clinics that receive federal funds from counseling their clients regarding abortion. The Department of Health and Human Services imposed this restriction in 1987 at the direction of the Reagan administration. When the Court upheld the restriction in

June 1991, abortion rights activists were not the only ones to protest. Civil libertarians, members of the medical profession, and even some supporters of the Bush administration expressed opposition to what they perceived as an attack on free speech.

Critics of the *Rust* decision pointed out that if government could make the receipt of federal funds conditional upon the surrender of First Amendment rights, then all government benefits might be used as devices to limit constitutional rights. For example, people who live in public housing could be asked to surrender their Fourth Amendment rights or face eviction; public defenders could be limited in the defenses they provide to their indigent clients; students could have their choice of occupations dictated by conditions imposed on student loans. The most serious implication of the *Rust* ruling is that public employees, including teachers, might be prohibited from addressing controversial issues or face losing their jobs. The precedential value of *Rust* is open to question, however, given the close division among the justices and subsequent changes in Court personnel.

The NEA Funding Controversy

Since the late 1980s, controversy has surrounded National Endowment for the Arts (NEA) funding of provocative works of art that offend the religious and sexual sensibilities of many people. In 1990, Congress directed the NEA to consider "general standards of decency" in making its funding decisions. During the early stages of the 1992 presidential election campaign, President George Bush intensified the dispute by firing NEA Chairman John Frohnmeyer. Is it legitimate for the federal government to censor works of art that it subsidizes through a granting agency like the NEA? In a speech to the National Press Club on March 23, 1992, Frohnmeyer argued that "when the government does support free expression, it must do so with a level playing field—no blacklists and no ideological preconceptions." On the other hand, conservative critics of the NEA argued that the taxpayers have no obligation to support works of art that many people find offensive. In *NEA v. Finley* (1998) the Supreme Court upheld the decency requirement, construing the statute as more of an exhortation than a restriction on expression.

TO SUMMARIZE:

- Traditionally, public employees (especially in the federal civil service) have operated under a number of constraints on their political activities. Consistent with its expanding recognition of constitutionally protected expression, however, the Supreme Court in recent years has shown greater solicitude for the right of public employees to express themselves on political issues.
- The Court has said that government contractors enjoy the same rights of free expression as those accorded to public employees.
- There is continuing controversy over the extent to which government can condition the provision of benefits on the surrender of First Amendment rights.

FREEDOM OF ASSOCIATION

Although the Constitution makes no explicit reference to freedom of association, the Supreme Court has long recognized association as a "penumbral" or "implicit" constitutional right. Different provisions of the Constitution have been identified as sources for the protection of various types of association, and some associational freedoms are given more protections than others. Intimate associations—for example, those between husband and wife or parent and child—are extensively protected by the constitutional right of privacy (see Chapter 11). On the other hand, economic associations, like property rights, are afforded more limited protection under the Due Process Clauses of the Fifth and Fourteenth Amendments. The right to associate with others for purposes of worship or devotion is obviously implied by the Free Exercise of Religion Clause of the First Amendment (see Chapter 9). Similarly, the First Amendment freedoms of speech, assembly, and petition implicitly protect the right of individuals to associate for political purposes.

Political Association

Political association, like political expression, occupies a high place in the Supreme Court's scheme of constitutional values. But, like political expression, freedom of political association is far from absolute. Thus, in *Scales v. United States* (1961), the Supreme Court was willing to place its stamp of approval on Section 2 of the Smith Act, which impinged on freedom of association by making it a crime merely to belong to the Communist party. The majority saved the constitutionality of Section 2 by interpreting it narrowly so as to apply only to "active" members of the Communist party who had a "specific intent" to bring about the violent overthrow of the United States government. Four members of the Court (Douglas, Black, Warren, and Brennan) dissented, claiming that the majority had in effect legalized guilt by association.

The constitutional controversy over communism and government efforts to rid the country of the "red menace" greatly diminished during the 1960s. On the other hand, the Civil Rights movement was at that time reaching its apogee. In the struggle for civil rights, the National Association for the Advancement of Colored People (NAACP) was one of the most significant political organizations. The NAACP had aroused tremendous hostility in the South and had occasionally been the target of state government attempts at intimidation and suppression. In *NAACP v. Alabama* (1958), the Supreme Court found that the state of Alabama had unconstitutionally infringed the NAACP's freedom of association by selectively enforcing a law requiring organizations based outside Alabama to register members' names and addresses with state authorities.

In ruling in favor of the NAACP, the Supreme Court had to distinguish a precedent that cut the other way. In 1928, it had upheld a New York law under which the Ku Klux Klan was forced to disclose its membership list. In that case, *Bryant v. Zimmerman,* the Court had justified the state policy by stressing the violent and unlawful tactics of the Klan. In *NAACP v. Alabama,* the Court stressed the fact that the NAACP used lawful means in seeking its political objectives.

Freedom of Association and the Problem of Discrimination

In the 1990s, there is very little controversy about the rights of minorities to organize for purposes of litigation and political action. Today, many states use their legislative powers on behalf of minority groups and women seeking integration into the economic and cultural mainstream. Public accommodations laws have been used to force civic groups and social clubs to extend membership to women and minorities. Freedom of association has often been raised as a constitutional objection to such efforts.

In *Roberts v. United States Jaycees* (1984), a unanimous Supreme Court found that Minnesota's interest in eradicating sex discrimination was sufficiently compelling to justify a decision of its human rights commission requiring local chapters of the Jaycees to admit women. Writing for the Court, Justice Brennan recognized a political dimension to the Jaycees' activities but nevertheless held that the organization's freedom of political association must give way to the superior state interest in abolishing sex discrimination. In *Rotary International v. Rotary Club of Duarte* (1987), the Court extended its decision in the *Jaycees* case to encompass the Rotary Club as well. In 1988, the Court upheld a city ordinance requiring large all-male social clubs to admit women (*New York State Club Association v. City of New York*). The Court's decisions dealing with "private" clubs suggest that freedom of association in that context must yield to the societal interest in eradicating racial and sexual inequality.

Freedom of Association Versus Gay Rights

In *Hurley v. Irish-American Gay, Lesbian and Bisexual Group of Boston* (1995), the Court held that the state of Massachusetts could not prohibit a private organization from excluding a gay rights group from its annual St. Patrick's Day parade. The Massachusetts Supreme Court had ruled against the South Boston Allied War Veterans Council, which organized the parade and refused to permit gay rights groups from participating. The state court held that gay rights groups could not be excluded under Massachusetts' long-standing and broadly construed public accommodations statute. In a unanimous decision, the Supreme Court reversed, saying that the state could not compel the parade's organizers to promote a message of which they disapproved. Writing for the Court, Justice Souter insisted that the decision "rests not on any particular view about the Council's message but on the Nation's commitment to protect freedom of speech." One wonders whether the decision would have been the same had the parade's organizers sought to exclude women or African-Americans.

TO SUMMARIZE:

- Although the Constitution does not explicitly provide for freedom of association, the Supreme Court has long recognized association as an implied First Amendment right.
- The Court has balanced the right of individuals to associate freely against legitimate government interests such as the protection of national security and the promotion of social equality. In general, freedom of association will be protected unless the government advances a very strong justification for abridging it.

CONCLUSION

The preceding discussion of major issues involving freedom of expression, assembly, and association, although necessarily selective, underscores several important First Amendment themes. The Supreme Court recognizes no absolutes in this area, but it does operate on the assumption that First Amendment freedoms are of fundamental importance in a democratic society. As a result, the Court generally imposes high standards in determining the constitutionality of legislation challenged on First Amendment grounds. In recent years, a majority of the justices have resisted easy generalizations and uncritical application of neat doctrinal tests in this particularly complex area of constitutional interpretation. In deciding difficult First Amendment cases, the Court attempts to accommodate legitimate governmental interests in maintaining peace, order, security, decency, and overall quality of life with an open society's vital interest in maintaining a free marketplace of ideas.

KEY TERMS

freedom of expression	slander	clear and probable danger	patently offensive
freedom of speech	pure speech	test	community standards
freedom of the press	picketing	*ad hoc* balancing	public forum
freedom of assembly	expressive conduct	criminal syndicalism	Civil Rights movement
freedom of association	First Amendment	imminent lawless action	time, place, and manner
chilling effect	absolutism	hate crimes	regulations
incorporation	fighting words	symbolic speech	content-neutral
preferred freedoms	defamation	actual malice	zoning
censorship	prior restraint	public figures	electronic media
obscenity	clear and present danger	invasion of privacy	scarcity theory
profanity	test	hard-core pornography	least restrictive means test
seditious speech	bad tendency test	prurient interest	commercial speech
libel	free marketplace of ideas	redeeming social importance	

FOR FURTHER READING

Berns, Walter. *The First Amendment and the Future of American Democracy*. New York: Basic Books, 1976.

Bollinger, Lee. *The Tolerant Society: Freedom of Speech and Extremist Speech in America*. New York: Oxford University Press, 1986.

Downs, D. A. *Nazis in Skokie: Freedom, Communication and the First Amendment*. South Bend, Ind.: Notre Dame University Press, 1985.

Fortas, Abe. *Concerning Dissent and Civil Disobedience*. New York: New American Library, 1968.

Irons, Peter. *May It Please the Court: The First Amendment*. New York: The New Press, 1997.

Kalven, Harry, Jr. *A Worthy Tradition: Freedom of Speech in America*. New York: Harper and Row, 1988.

Konefsky, Samuel J. *The Legacy of Holmes and Brandeis: A Study in the Influence of Ideas*. New York: Macmillan, 1956.

Lowenthal, David. *No Liberty for License: The Forgotten Logic of the First Amendment*. Spence Publishing Co., 1997.

Polenberg, Richard. *Fighting Faiths: The Abrams Case, the Supreme Court and Free Speech*. New York: Viking Press, 1987.

Walker, Sam. *Hate Speech: The History of an American Controversy*. Lincoln, Nebr.: University of Nebraska Press, 1994.

INTERNET RESOURCES

Name of Resource	Description	URL (circa 1998)
The Freedom Forum	A nonpartisan foundation dedicated to freedoms of speech and press	http://www.freedomforum.org/
First Amendment Lawyers Association	An organization of lawyers dedicated to the defense of the First Amendment	http://www.fala.org/
The Thomas Jefferson Center for the Protection of Free Expression	A nonprofit organization located in Charlottesville, Virginia, and devoted to the defense of free expression in all its forms	http://www.tjcenter.org/

Case

NEAR V. MINNESOTA

283 U.S. 697; 51 S.Ct. 625; 75 L.Ed. 1357 (1931)
Vote: 5–4

In this seminal case the Court interprets the First Amendment as imposing a broad prohibition against prior restraints on publication.

Mr. Chief Justice Hughes delivered the opinion of the Court.

Chapter 285 of the Sessions Laws of Minnesota for the year 1925 provides for the abatement, as a public nuisance, of a "malicious, scandalous and defamatory newspaper, magazine or other periodical." . . .

Under this statute . . . the county attorney of Hennepin County brought this action to enjoin the publication of what was described as a "malicious, scandalous and defamatory newspaper, magazine and periodical," known as "The Saturday Press," published by the defendants in the city of Minneapolis. The complaint alleged that the defendants, on September 24, 1927, and on eight subsequent dates in October and November, 1927, published and circulated editions of that periodical which were "largely devoted to malicious, scandalous and defamatory articles" concerning [various public officials and others]. . . .

The district court . . . found in general terms that the editions in question were "chiefly devoted to malicious, scandalous and defamatory articles," concerning the individuals named. The court further found that the defendants through these publications "did engage in the business of regularly and customarily producing, publishing and circulating a malicious, scandalous and defamatory newspaper," and that "the said publication . . . constitutes a public nuisance under the laws of the state." Judgment was thereupon entered adjudging that "the newspaper, magazine and periodical known as The Saturday Press, as a public nuisance, be and is hereby abated. . . ."

The defendant Near appealed from this judgment to the supreme court of the state, . . . asserting his right under the Federal Constitution, and the judgment was affirmed upon the authority of the former decision. . . .

From the judgment as thus affirmed, the defendant Near appeals to this Court.

This statute, for the suppression as a public nuisance of a newspaper or periodical, is unusual, if not

unique, and raises questions of grave importance transcending the local interests involved in the particular action. It is no longer open to doubt that the liberty of the press and of speech is within the liberty safeguarded by the Due Process Clause of the Fourteenth Amendment from invasion by state action. It was found impossible to conclude that this essential personal liberty of the citizen was left unprotected by the general guaranty of fundamental rights of persons and property. . . . Liberty of speech and of the press is not an absolute right, and the state may punish its abuse. Liberty, in each of its phases, has its history and connotation and, in the present instance, the inquiry is as to the historic conception of the liberty of the press and whether the statute under review violates the essential attributes of that liberty. . . .

If we cut through mere details of procedure, the operation and effect of the statute in substance is that public authorities may bring the owner or publisher of a newspaper or periodical before a judge upon a charge of conducting a business of publishing scandalous and defamatory matter—in particular that the matter consists of charges against public officers of official dereliction—and unless the owner or publisher is able and disposed to bring competent evidence to satisfy the judge that the charges are true and are published with good motives and for justifiable ends, his newspaper or periodical is suppressed and further publication is made punishable as a contempt. This is of the essence of censorship.

The question is whether a statute authorizing such proceedings in restraint of publication is consistent with the conception of the liberty of the press as historically conceived and guaranteed. In determining the extent of the constitutional protection, it has been generally, if not universally, considered that it is the chief purpose of the guaranty to prevent previous restraints upon publication. The struggle in England, directed against the legislative power of the licenser, resulted in renunciation of the censorship of the press. The liberty deemed to be established was thus described by Blackstone:

The liberty of the press is indeed essential to the nature of a free state; but this consists in laying no previous restraints upon publications, and not in freedom from censure for criminal matter when published. Every freeman has an undoubted right to lay what sentiments he pleases before the public; to forbid this, is to destroy the freedom of the press; but if he publishes what is improper, mischievous or illegal, he must take the consequences of his own temerity. . . .

The criticism upon Blackstone's statement has not been because immunity from previous restraint upon publication has not been regarded as deserving of special emphasis, but chiefly because that immunity cannot be deemed to exhaust the conception of the liberty guaranteed by state and Federal constitutions. The point of criticism has been "that the mere exemption from previous restraints cannot be all that is secured by the constitutional provisions;" and that "the liberty of the press might be rendered a mockery and a delusion, and the phrase itself a by-word, if, while every man was at liberty to publish what he pleased, the public authorities might nevertheless punish him for harmless publications." . . .

The objection has also been made that the principle as to immunity from previous restraint is stated too broadly, if every such restraint is deemed to be prohibited. That is undoubtedly true; the protection even as to previous restraint is not absolutely unlimited. But the limitation has been recognized only in exceptional cases. "When a nation is at war many things that might be said in time of peace are such a hindrance to its effort that their utterance will not be endured so long as men fight and that no court could regard them as protected by any constitutional right." . . . No one would question but that a government might prevent actual obstruction to its recruiting service or the publication of the sailing dates of transports or the number and location of troops. On similar grounds, the primary requirements of decency may be enforced against obscene publications. The security of the community life may be protected against incitements to acts of violence and the overthrow by force of orderly government.

The constitutional guaranty of free speech does not "protect a man from an injunction against uttering words that may have all the effect of force. . . ."

The exceptional nature of its limitations places in a strong light the general conception that liberty of the press, historically considered and taken up by the Federal Constitution, has meant, principally, although not exclusively, immunity from previous restraints or censorship. The conception of the liberty of the press in this country has broadened with the exigencies of the colonial period and with the efforts to secure freedom from oppressive administration. That liberty was especially cherished for the immunity it afforded from previous restraint of the publication of censure of public officers and charges of official misconduct. . . .

The fact that for approximately one hundred and fifty years there has been almost an entire absence of attempts to impose previous restraints upon publications relating to the malfeasance of public officers is significant of the deep-seated conviction that such restraints would violate constitutional rights. Public officers, whose character and conduct remain open to debate and free discussion in the press, find their remedies for false accusations in actions under libel laws providing for redress and punishment, and not in proceedings to restrain the publication of newspapers and periodicals. . . .

The importance of this immunity has not lessened. While reckless assaults upon public men, and efforts to bring obloquy upon those who are endeavoring faithfully to discharge official duties, exert a baleful influence and deserve the severest condemnation in public opinion, it cannot be said that this abuse is greater, and it is believed to be less, than that which characterized the period in which our institutions took shape. Meanwhile, the administration of government has become more complex, the opportunities for malfeasance and corruption have multiplied, crime has grown to most serious proportions, and the danger of its protection by unfaithful officials and of the impairment of the fundamental security of life and property by criminal alliances and official neglect, emphasizes the primary need of a vigilant and courageous press, especially in great cities. The fact that the liberty of the press may be abused by miscreant purveyors of scandal does not make any the less necessary the immunity of the press from previous restraint in dealing with official misconduct. Subsequent punishment for such abuses as may exist is the appropriate remedy, consistent with constitutional privilege. . . .

The statute in question cannot be justified by reason of the fact that the publisher is permitted to show, before injunction issues, that the matter published is true, and is published with good motives and for justifiable ends. If such a statute, authorizing suppression and injunction on such a basis, is constitutionally valid, it would be equally permissible for the legislature to provide that at any time the publisher of any newspaper could be brought before a court, or even an administrative officer (as the constitutional protection may not be regarded as resting on mere procedural details) and required to produce proof of the truth of his publication, or of what he intended to publish, and of his motives, or stand enjoined. If this can be done, the legislature may provide machinery for determining in the complete exercise of its discretion what are justifiable ends and restrain publication accordingly. And it would be but a step to a complete system of censorship. The recognition of authority to impose previous restraint upon publication in order to protect the community against the circulation of charges of misconduct, and especially of official misconduct, necessarily would carry with it the admission of the authority of the censor against which the constitutional barrier was erected. The preliminary freedom, by virtue of the very reason for its existence, does not depend, as this court has said, on proof of truth. . . .

Equally unavailing is the insistence that the statute is designed to prevent the circulation of scandal which tends to disturb the public peace and to provoke assaults and the commission of crime. Charges of reprehensible conduct, and in particular of official malfeasance, unquestionably create a public scandal, but the theory of the constitutional guaranty is that even a more serious public evil would be caused by authority to prevent publication.

For these reasons we hold the statute, so far as it authorized the proceedings in this action under clause (b) of section one, to be an infringement of the liberty of the press guaranteed by the Fourteenth Amendment. We should add that this decision rests upon the operation and effect of the statute, without regard to the question of the truth of the charges contained in the particular periodical. The fact that the public officers named in this case, and those associated with the charges of official dereliction, may be deemed to be impeccable, cannot affect the conclusion that the statute imposes an unconstitutional restraint upon publication.

Judgment reversed.

Mr. Justice Butler, dissenting:

The decision of the Court in this case declares Minnesota and every other state powerless to restrain by injunction the business of publishing and circulating among the people malicious, scandalous and defamatory periodicals that in due course of judicial procedure has been adjudged to be a public nuisance. It gives to freedom of the press a meaning and a scope not heretofore recognized and construes "liberty" in the Due Process Clause of the Fourteenth Amendment to put upon the states a Federal restriction that is without precedent. . . .

The Minnesota statute does not operate as a previous restraint on publication within the proper meaning of that phrase. It does not authorize administrative control in advance such as was formerly exercised by the licensers and censors but prescribes a remedy to be enforced by a suit in equity. In this case there was previous publication made in the course of the business of regularly producing malicious, scandalous and defamatory periodicals. The business and publications unquestionably constitute an abuse of the right of free press. The statute denounces the things done as a nuisance on the ground, as stated by the state supreme court, that they threaten morals, peace and good order. There is no question of the power of the state to denounce such transgressions. The restraint authorized is only in respect of continuing to do what has been duly adjudged to constitute a nuisance. . . . There is nothing in the statute purporting to prohibit publications that have not been adjudged to constitute a nuisance. It is fanciful to suggest similarity between the granting or enforcement of the decree authorized by this statute to prevent further publication of malicious, scandalous and defamatory articles and the previous restraint upon the press by licensers as referred to by Blackstone and described in the history of the times to which he alludes. . . .

It is well known, as found by the state supreme court, that existing libel laws are inadequate effectively to suppress evils resulting from the kind of business and publications that are shown in this case. The doctrine that measures such as the one before us are invalid because they operate as previous restraints to infringe freedom of press exposes the peace and good order of every community and the business and private affairs of every individual to the constant and protracted false and malicious assaults of any insolvent publisher who may have purpose and sufficient capacity to contrive and put into effect a scheme or program for oppression, blackmail or extortion.

The judgment should be affirmed.

Mr. Justice Van Devanter, Mr. Justice McReynolds, and Mr. Justice Sutherland, concur in this opinion.

Case

NEW YORK TIMES COMPANY V. UNITED STATES (THE PENTAGON PAPERS CASE)

403 U.S. 713; 91 S.Ct. 2140; 29 L.Ed. 2d. 822 (1971)
Vote: 6–3

In June 1971 Daniel Ellsberg, a disaffected Pentagon employee, turned over to the New York Times *a 7000-page top secret study entitled "History of U.S. Decision-Making Process on Viet Nam Policy." Excerpts from the study, popularly known as the Pentagon Papers, appeared in the* New York Times *beginning on June 13, 1971. After the* Times *refused a request to cease publishing excerpts from the study, the Justice Department filed a motion for an injunction in federal court. On Tuesday, June 16, 1971, Judge Harold Gurfein issued the first federal court injunction against a newspaper in this nation's history. Three days later, a federal district court in Washington, D.C., refused to issue a similar injunction against the* Washington Post. *Thereupon, Judge Gurfein lifted the injunction against the* New York Times. *On appeal to the circuit courts, the injunctions were quickly reinstated. The Supreme Court granted certiorari and heard the case immediately.*

PER CURIAM. We granted certiorari in these cases in which the United States seeks to enjoin the *New York Times* and the *Washington Post* from publishing the contents of a classified study entitled "History of U.S. Decision-Making Process on Viet Nam Policy."

"Any system of prior restraints of expression comes to this Court bearing a heavy presumption against its constitutional validity." . . . The Government "thus carries a heavy burden of showing justification for the imposition of such a restraint." . . . The District Court for the Southern District of New York in the *New York Times* case and the District Court for the District of Columbia and the Court of Appeals for the District of Columbia Circuit in the *Washington Post* case held that the Government had not met that burden. We agree.

The judgment of the Court of Appeals for the District of Columbia Circuit is therefore affirmed. The order of the Court of Appeals for the Second Circuit is reversed and the case is remanded with directions to enter a judg-

ment affirming the judgment of the District Court for the Southern District of New York. The stays entered June 25, 1971, by the Court are vacated. The judgments shall issue forthwith.

So ordered.

Mr. Justice Black, with whom *Mr. Justice Douglas* joins, concurring.

. . . I believe that every moment's continuance of the injunctions against these newspapers amounts to a flagrant, indefensible, and continuing violation of the First Amendment. . . . In my view it is unfortunate that some of my Brethren are apparently willing to hold that the publication of news may sometimes be enjoined. Such a holding would make a shambles of the First Amendment. . . .

In seeking injunctions against these newspapers and in its presentation to the Court, the Executive Branch seems to have forgotten the essential purpose and history of the First Amendment. . . .

In the First Amendment the Founding Fathers gave the free press the protection it must have to fulfill its essential role in our democracy. The press was to serve the governed, not the governors. The Government's power to censor the press was abolished so that the press would remain forever free to censure the Government. The press was protected so that it could bare the secrets of government and inform the people. Only a free and unrestrained press can effectively expose deception in government. And paramount among the responsibilities of a free press is the duty to prevent any part of the government from deceiving the people and sending them off to distant lands to die of foreign fevers and foreign shot and shell. In my view, far from deserving condemnation for their courageous reporting, the *New York Times*, the *Washington Post*, and other newspapers should be commended for serving the purpose that the Founding Fathers saw so clearly. In revealing the workings of government that led to the Vietnam war, the newspapers nobly did precisely that which the Founders hoped and trusted they would do. . . .

. . . [W]e are asked to hold that despite the First Amendment's emphatic command, the Executive Branch, the Congress, and the Judiciary can make laws enjoining publication of current news and abridging freedom of the press in the name of "national security." The Government does not even attempt to rely on any act of Congress. Instead it makes the bold and dangerously far-reaching contention that the courts should take it upon themselves to "make" a law abridging freedom of the press in the name of equity, presidential power, and national security, even when the representatives of the people in Congress have adhered to the command of the First Amendment and refused to make such a law. . . . To find that the President has "inherent power" to halt the publication of news by resort to the courts would wipe out the First Amendment and destroy the fundamental liberty and security of the very people the Government hopes to make "secure." No one can read the history of the adoption of the First Amendment without being convinced beyond any doubt that it was injunctions like those sought here that Madison and his collaborators intended to outlaw in this Nation for all time.

The word "security" is a broad, vague generality whose contours should not be invoked to abrogate the fundamental law embodied in the First Amendment. The guarding of military and diplomatic secrets at the expense of informed representative government provides no real security for our Republic. The Framers of the First Amendment, fully aware of both the need to defend a new nation and the abuses of the English and colonial Governments, sought to give this new society strength and security by providing that freedom of speech, press, religion, and assembly should not be abridged. . . .

Mr. Justice Douglas, with whom **Mr. Justice Black** joins, concurring.

. . . The Government says that it has inherent powers to go into court and obtain an injunction to protect the national interest, which in this case is alleged to be national security. *Near v. Minnesota* [1931] . . . repudiated that expansive doctrine in no uncertain terms.

The dominant purpose of the First Amendment was to prohibit the widespread practice of governmental suppression of embarrassing information. It is common knowledge that the First Amendment was adopted against the widespread use of the common law of seditious libel to punish the dissemination of material that is embarrassing to the powers-that-be. . . . The present cases will, I think, go down in history as the most dramatic illustration of that principle. A debate of large proportions goes on in the Nation over our posture in Vietnam. That debate antedated the disclosure of the contents of the present documents. The latter are highly relevant to the debate in progress.

Secrecy in government is fundamentally antidemocratic, perpetuating bureaucratic errors. Open debate and discussion of public issues are vital to our national health. On public questions there should be "uninhibited, robust, and wide-open" debate. . . .

Mr. Justice Brennan, concurring.

. . . I write separately in these cases only to emphasize what should be apparent: that our judgments in the present cases may not be taken to indicate the propriety, in the future, of issuing temporary stays and restraining orders to block the publication of material sought to be suppressed by the Government. So far as I can determine, never before has the United States sought to enjoin a newspaper from publishing information in its possession. The relative novelty of the question presented, the necessary haste with which decisions were reached, the magnitude of the interests asserted, and the fact that all the parties have concentrated their arguments upon the question whether permanent restraints were proper may have justified at least some of the restraints heretofore imposed in these cases. Certainly it is difficult to fault the several courts below for seeking to assure that the issues here involved were preserved for ultimate review by this Court. But even if it be assumed that some of the interim restraints were proper in the two cases before us, that assumption has no bearing upon the propriety of similar judicial action in the future. To begin with, there has now been ample time for reflection and judgment; whatever values there may be in the preservation of novel questions for appellate review may not support any restraints in the future. More important, the First Amendment stands as an absolute bar to the imposition of judicial restraints in circumstances of the kind presented by these cases. . . .

The error that has pervaded these cases from the outset was the granting of any injunctive relief whatsoever, interim or otherwise. The entire thrust of the Government's claim throughout these cases has been that publication of the material sought to be enjoined "could," or "might," or "may" prejudice the national interest in various ways. But the First Amendment tolerates absolutely no prior judicial restraints of the press predicated upon surmise or conjecture that untoward consequences may result. . . .

Mr. Justice Stewart, with whom **Mr. Justice White** joins, concurring.

In the governmental structure created by our Constitution, the Executive is endowed with enormous power in the two related areas of national defense and international relations. This power, largely unchecked by the

Legislative and Judicial branches, has been pressed to the very hilt since the advent of the nuclear missile age. For better or for worse, the simple fact is that a President of the United States possesses vastly greater constitutional independence in these two vital areas of power than does, say, a prime minister of a country with a parliamentary form of government.

In the absence of the governmental checks and balances present in other areas of our national life, the only effective restraint upon executive policy and power in the areas of national defense and international affairs may lie in an enlightened citizenry—in an informal and critical public opinion which alone can here protect the values of democratic government. For this reason, it is perhaps here that a press that is alert, aware, and free most vitally serves the basic purpose of the First Amendment. For without an informed and free press there cannot be an enlightened people.

Yet it is elementary that the successful conduct of international diplomacy and the maintenance of an effective national defense require both confidentiality and secrecy. Other nations can hardly deal with this Nation in an atmosphere of mutual trust unless they can be assured that their confidences will be kept. And within our own executive departments, the development of considered and intelligent international policies would be impossible if those charged with their formulation could not communicate with each other freely, frankly, and in confidence. In the area of basic national defense the frequent need for absolute secrecy is, of course, self-evident.

I think there can be but one answer to this dilemma, if dilemma it be. The responsibility must be where the power is. If the Constitution gives the Executive a large degree of unshared power in the conduct of foreign affairs and the maintenance of our national defense, then under the Constitution the Executive must have the largely unshared duty to determine and preserve the degree of internal security necessary to exercise that power successfully. It is an awesome responsibility, requiring judgment and wisdom of a high order. I should suppose that moral, political, and practical considerations would dictate that a very first principle of that wisdom would be an insistence upon avoiding secrecy for its own sake. For when everything is classified, then nothing is classified, and the system becomes one to be disregarded by the cynical or the careless, and to be manipulated by those intent on self-protection or self-promotion. I should suppose, in short, that the hallmark of a truly effective internal security system would be the maximum possible disclosure, recognizing that secrecy can best be preserved

only when credibility is truly maintained. But be that as it may, it is clear to me that it is the constitutional duty of the Executive—as a matter of sovereign prerogative and not as a matter of law as the courts know law—through the promulgation and enforcement of executive regulations, to protect the confidentiality necessary to carry out its responsibilities in the fields of international relations and national defense.

This is not to say that Congress and the courts have no role to play. Undoubtedly Congress has the power to enact specific and appropriate criminal laws to protect government property and preserve government secrets. Congress has passed such laws, and several of them are of very colorable relevance to the apparent circumstances of these cases. And if a criminal prosecution is instituted, it will be the responsibility of the courts to decide the applicability of the criminal law under which the charge is brought. Moreover, if Congress should pass a specific law authorizing civil proceedings in this field, the courts would likewise have the duty to decide the constitutionality of such a law as well as its applicability to the facts proved.

But in the cases before us we are asked neither to construe specific regulations nor to apply specific laws. We are asked, instead, to perform a function that the Constitution gave to the Executive, not the Judiciary. We are asked, quite simply, to prevent the publication by two newspapers of material that the Executive Branch insists should not, in the national interest, be published. I am convinced that the Executive is correct with respect to some of the documents involved. But I cannot say that disclosure of any of them will surely result in direct, immediate, and irreparable damage to our Nation or its people. That being so, there can under the First Amendment be but one judicial resolution of the issues before us. I join the judgments of the Court.

Mr. Justice White, with whom **Mr. Justice Stewart** joins, concurring.

I concur in today's judgments, but only because of the concededly extraordinary protection against prior restraints enjoyed by the press under our constitutional system. I do not say that in no circumstances would the First Amendment permit an injunction against publishing information about government plans or operations. Nor, after examining the materials the Government characterizes as the most sensitive and destructive, can I deny that revelation of these documents will do substantial damage to public interests. Indeed, I am confident that their disclosure will have that result. But I nevertheless agree that the United States has not satisfied the very heavy burden that it must meet to warrant an injunction against publication in these cases, at least in the absence of express and appropriately limited congressional authorization for prior restraints in circumstances such as these. . . .

Mr. Justice Marshall, concurring.

. . . It would . . . be utterly inconsistent with the concept of separation of powers for this Court to use its power of contempt to prevent behavior that Congress has specifically declined to prohibit. There would be a similar damage to the basic concept of these coequal branches of Government if when the Executive Branch has adequate authority granted by Congress to protect "national security" it can choose instead to invoke the contempt power of a court to enjoin the threatened conduct. The Constitution provides that Congress shall make laws, the President execute laws, and courts interpret laws. It did not provide for government by injunction in which the courts and the Executive Branch can "make law" without regard to the action of Congress. It may be more convenient for the Executive Branch if it need only convince a judge to prohibit conduct rather than ask the Congress to pass a law, and it may be more convenient to enforce a contempt order than to seek a criminal conviction in a jury trial. Moreover, it may be considered politically wise to get a court to share the responsibility for arresting those who the Executive Branch has probable cause to believe are violating the law. But convenience and political considerations of the moment do not justify a basic departure from the principles of our system of government. . . .

Mr. Chief Justice Burger, dissenting.

. . . I suggest . . . these cases have been conducted in unseemly haste. . . . [T]he chronology of events demonstrat[es] the hectic pressures under which these cases have been processed and I need not restate them. The prompt setting of these cases reflects our universal abhorrence of prior restraint. But prompt judicial action does not mean unjudicial haste.

Here, moreover, the frenetic haste is due in large part to the manner in which the *Times* proceeded from the date it obtained the purloined documents. It seems reasonably clear now that the haste precluded reasonable and deliberate judicial treatment of these cases and was not warranted. The precipitate action of this Court aborting trials not yet completed is not the kind of judicial conduct that ought to attend the disposition of a great issue.

The newspapers make a derivative claim under the First Amendment; they denominate this right as the public "right to know"; by implication, the *Times* asserts a sole trusteeship of that right by virtue of its journalistic "scoop." The right is asserted as an absolute. Of course, the First Amendment right itself is not an absolute, as Justice Holmes so long ago pointed out in his aphorism concerning the right to shout "fire" in a crowded theater if there was no fire. There are other exceptions, some of which Chief Justice Hughes mentioned by way of example in *Near v. Minnesota.* There are no doubt other exceptions no one has had occasion to describe or discuss. Conceivably such exceptions may be lurking in these cases and would have been flushed had they been properly considered in the trial courts, free from unwarranted deadlines and frenetic pressures. An issue of this importance should be tried and heard in a judicial atmosphere conducive to thoughtful, reflective deliberation, especially when haste, in terms of hours, is unwarranted in light of the long period the *Times,* by its own choice, deferred publication.

It is not disputed that the *Times* has had unauthorized possession of the documents for three to four months, during which it has had its expert analysts studying them, presumably digesting them and preparing the material for publication. During all of this time, the *Times* presumably in its capacity as trustee of the public's "right to know," had held up publication for purposes it considered proper and thus public knowledge was delayed. No doubt this was for a good reason; the analysis of 7,000 pages of complex material drawn from a vastly greater volume of material would inevitably take time and the writing of good news stories takes time. But why should the United States Government, from whom this information was illegally acquired by someone, along with all the counsel, trial judges, and appellate judges be placed under needless pressure? After these months of deferral, the alleged "right to know" has somehow and suddenly become a right that must be vindicated instanter.

Would it have been unreasonable since the newspaper could anticipate the Government's objections to release of secret material, to give the Government an opportunity to review the entire collection and determine whether agreement could be reached on publication? Stolen or not, if security was not in fact jeopardized, much of the material could no doubt have been declassified, since it spans a period ending in 1968. With such an approach—one that great newspapers have in the past practiced and stated editorially to be the duty of an honorable press—the newspapers and Government might well have narrowed the area of disagreement as to what was and was not publishable, leaving the remainder to be resolved in orderly litigation, if necessary. To me it is hardly believable that a newspaper long regarded as a great institution in American life would fail to perform one of the basic and simple duties of every citizen with respect to the discovery or possession of stolen property or secret government documents. That duty, I had thought—perhaps naively—was to report forthwith, to responsible public officers. This duty rests on taxi drivers, Justices and the *New York Times.* The course followed by the *Times,* whether so calculated or not, removed any possibility of orderly litigation of the issues. If the action of the judges up to now has been correct, that result is sheer happenstance. . . .

Mr. Justice Harlan, with whom the ***Chief Justice*** and ***Mr. Justice Blackmun*** join, dissenting.

. . . Pending further hearings in each case conducted under the appropriate ground rules, I would continue the restraints on publication. I cannot believe that the doctrine prohibiting prior restraints reaches to the point of preventing courts from maintaining the status quo long enough to act responsibly in matters of such national importance as those involved here. . . .

Mr. Justice Blackmun, dissenting.

. . . The First Amendment, after all, is only one part of an entire Constitution. Article II of the great document vests in the Executive Branch primary power over the conduct of foreign affairs and places in that branch the responsibility for the Nation's safety. Each provision of the Constitution is important, and I cannot subscribe to a doctrine of unlimited absolutism for the First Amendment at the cost of downgrading other provisions. . . .

Case

SCHENCK V. UNITED STATES

249 U.S. 47; 39 S.Ct. 247; 63 L.Ed. 470 (1919)
Vote: 9–0

Charles T. Schenck, general secretary of the Socialist party, was convicted of "causing and attempting to cause insubordination in the military and naval forces of the United States," in violation of the Espionage Act of 1917. The conviction stemmed from the Socialist party's activities in printing and distributing leaflets attacking American participation in the First World War and urging young men to oppose the military draft.

Mr. Justice Holmes delivered the opinion of the Court:

This is an indictment in three counts. The first charges a conspiracy to violate the Espionage Act of June 15, 1917, . . . by causing and attempting to cause insubordination, etc., in the military and naval forces of the United States, and to obstruct the recruiting and enlistment service of the United States, when the United States was at war with the German Empire; to wit, that the defendant wilfully conspired to have printed and circulated to men who had been called and accepted for military service, a document set forth and alleged to be calculated to cause such insubordination and obstruc-

tion. The court alleges overt acts in pursuance of the conspiracy, ending in the distribution of the document set forth. The second count alleges a conspiracy to commit an offense against the United States; to wit, to use the mails for the transmission of matter declared to be non-mailable, . . . to wit, the above-mentioned document, with an averment of the same overt acts. The third count charges an unlawful use of the mails for the transmission of same matter and otherwise as above. The defendants were found guilty on all the counts. They set up the First Amendment to the Constitution, forbidding Congress to make any law abridging the freedom of speech or of the press. . . .

According to the testimony Schenck said he was general secretary of the Socialist party and had charge of the Socialist headquarters from which the documents were sent. He identified a book found there as the minutes of the executive committee of the party. The book showed a resolution of August 13, 1917, that 15,000 leaflets should be printed . . . to be mailed to men who had passed exemption boards, and for distribution. Schenck personally attended to the printing. On August 20 the general secretary's report said, "Obtained new leaflets from the printer and started work addressing envelopes," etc.; and there was a resolve that Comrade Schenck be allowed $125 for sending leaflets through the mail. He said that he had about fifteen or sixteen thousand printed. There were files of the circular in question in the inner office. . . . Copies were proved to have been sent through the mails to drafted men. Without going into confirmatory details that were proved, no reasonable man could doubt that the defendant Schenck was largely instrumental in sending the circulars about. . . .

The document in question, upon its first printed side, recited the 1st section of the Thirteenth Amendment, said that the idea embodied in it was violated by the Conscription Act, and that a conscript is little better than a convict. In impassioned language it intimated that conscription was despotism in its worst form and a monstrous wrong against humanity, in the interest of Wall Street's chosen few. It said: "Do not submit to intimidation"; but in form at least confined itself to peaceful measures, such as a petition for the repeal of the act. The other and later printed side of the sheet was headed, "Assert Your Rights." It stated reasons for alleging that anyone violated the Constitution when he refused to recognize "your right to assert your opposition to the draft," and went on: "If you do not assert and support your rights, you are helping to deny or disparage rights which it is the solemn duty of all citizens and residents of the United States to retain." It described the arguments on the other side as coming from cunning politicians and a mercenary capitalist press, and even silent consent to the Conscription Law as helping to support an infamous conspiracy. It denied the power to send our citizens away to foreign shores to shoot up the people of other lands, and added that words could not express the condemnation such cold-blooded ruthlessness deserves, etc., etc., winding up, "You must do your share to maintain, support, and uphold the rights of the people of this country." Of course the document would not have been sent unless it had been intended to have some effect, and we do not see what effect it could be expected to have upon persons subject to the draft except to influ-

ence them to obstruct the carrying of it out. The defendants do not deny that the jury might find against them on this point.

But it is said, suppose that that was the tendency of this circular, it is protected by the First Amendment to the Constitution. Two of the strongest expressions are said to be quoted respectively from well-known public men. It well may be that the prohibition of laws abridging the freedom of speech is not confined to previous restraints, although to prevent them may have been the main purpose. . . . We admit that in many places and in ordinary times the defendants, in saying all that was said in the circular, would have been within their constitutional rights. But the character of every act depends upon the circumstances in which it is done. . . . The most stringent protection of free speech would not protect a man in falsely shouting fire in a theater, and causing a panic. It does not even protect a man from an injunction against uttering words that may have all the effect of force. . . . The question in every case is whether the words used are used in such circumstances and are of such a nature as to create a clear and present danger that they will bring about the substantive evils that Congress has a right to prevent. It is a question of proximity and degree. When a nation is at war many things that might be said in time of peace are such a hindrance to its effort that their utterance will not be endured so long as men fight, and that no court could regard them as protected by any constitutional right. It seems to be admitted that if an actual obstruction of the recruiting service were proved, liability for words that produced that effect might be enforced. The Statute of 1917 punishes conspiracies to obstruct as well as actual obstruction. If the act (speaking, or circulating a paper), its tendency and the intent with which it is done, are the same, we perceive no ground for saying that success alone warrants making the act a crime. . . .

Case

BRANDENBURG V. OHIO

395 U.S. 444; 89 S.Ct. 1827; 23 L.Ed. 2d. 430 (1969)
Vote: 9–0

In Whitney v. California *(1927), the Court upheld a state criminal syndicalism statute. Here the Court reconsiders the constitutionality of such laws. The* *court also reconsiders the formulation of the clear and present danger test.*

PER CURIAM. The appellant, a leader of a Ku Klux Klan group, was convicted under the Ohio Criminal Syndicalism statute for "advocat[ing] . . . the duty, necessity, or propriety of crime, sabotage, violence, or unlawful methods of terrorism as a means of accomplishing industrial or political reform" and for "voluntarily assembl[ing] with any society, group, or assemblage of persons formed to teach or advocate the doctrines of criminal syndicalism." . . . He was fined $1,000 and sentenced to one to 10 years' imprisonment. The appellant challenged the constitutionality of the criminal syndicalism statute under the First and Fourteenth Amendments to the United States Constitution, but the intermediate appellate court of Ohio affirmed his conviction without opinion. The Supreme Court of Ohio dismissed his appeal. . . . It did not file an opinion or explain its conclusions. Appeal was taken to this Court, and we noted probable jurisdiction. . . . We reverse.

The record shows that a man, identified at trial as the appellant, telephoned an announcer-reporter on the staff of a Cincinnati television station and invited him to come to a Ku Klux Klan "rally" to be held at a farm in Hamilton County. With the cooperation of the organizers, the reporter and a cameraman attended the meeting and filmed the events. Portions of the films were later broadcast on the local station and on a national network.

The prosecution's case rested on the films and on testimony identifying the appellant as the person who communicated with the reporter and who spoke at the rally. The State also introduced into evidence several articles appearing in the film, including a pistol, a rifle, a shotgun, ammunition, a Bible, and a red hood worn by the speaker in the films.

One film showed 12 hooded figures, some of whom carried firearms. They were gathered around a large wooden cross, which they burned. No one was present other than the participants and the newsmen who made the film. Most of the words uttered during the scene were incomprehensible when the film was projected, but scattered phrases could be understood that were derogatory of Negroes and, in one instance, of Jews. Another scene on the same film showed the appellant, in Klan regalia, making a speech. The speech, [in part], was as follows:

> . . . We're not a revengent organization, but if our President, our Congress, our Supreme Court, continues to suppress the white, Caucasian race, it's possible that there might have to be some revengeance taken.

The second film showed six hooded figures, one of whom, later identified as the appellant, repeated a speech very similar to that recorded on the first film. The reference to the possibility of "revengeance" was omitted, and one sentence was added: "Personally, I believe the nigger should be returned to Africa, the Jew re-

turned to Israel." Though some of the figures in the films carried weapons, the speaker did not.

The Ohio Criminal Syndicalism Statute was enacted in 1919. From 1917 to 1920, identical or quite similar laws were adopted by 20 States and two territories. . . . In 1927, this Court sustained the constitutionality of California's Criminal Syndicalism Act, the text of which is quite similar to that of the laws of Ohio. . . . The Court upheld that statute on the ground that, without more, "advocating" violent means to effect political and economic change involves such danger to the security of the State that the State may outlaw it. . . . But [this view] has been thoroughly discredited by later decisions. . . . These later decisions have fashioned the principle that the constitutional guarantees of free speech and free press do not permit a State to forbid or proscribe advocacy of the use of force or of law violation except where such advocacy is directed to inciting or producing imminent lawless action and is likely to incite or produce such action. As we said in *Noto v. United States*, . . . "the mere abstract teaching . . . of the moral propriety or even moral necessity for a resort to force and violence, is not the same as preparing a group for violent action and steeling it to such action." . . . A statute which fails to draw this distinction impermissibly intrudes upon the freedoms guaranteed by the First and Fourteenth Amendments. It sweeps within its condemnation speech which our Constitution has immunized from governmental control. . . .

Measured by this test, Ohio's Criminal Syndicalism Act cannot be sustained. The Act punishes persons who "advocate or teach the duty, necessity, or propriety" of violence "as a means of accomplishing industrial or political reform"; or who publish or circulate or display any book or paper containing such advocacy; or who "justify" the commission of violent acts "with intent to exemplify, spread or advocate the propriety of the doctrines of criminal syndicalism"; or who "voluntarily assemble" with a group formed "to teach or advocate the doctrines of criminal syndicalism." . . .

. . . [W]e are here confronted with a statute which, by its own words and as applied, purports to punish mere advocacy and to forbid, on pain of criminal punishment, assembly with others merely to advocate the described type of action. Such a statute falls within the condemnation of the First and Fourteenth Amendments. The contrary teaching of *Whitney v. California* . . . cannot be supported and that decision is therefore overruled. . . .

Mr. Justice Black, concurring. . . .

Mr. Justice Douglas, concurring.

. . . I see no place in the regime of the First Amendment for any "clear and present danger" test, whether strict and tight as some would make it, or freewheeling. . . .

The line between what is permissible and not subject to control and what may be made impermissible and subject to regulation is the line between ideas and overt acts.

The example usually given by those who would punish speech is the case of one who falsely shouts fire in a crowded theatre.

This is, however, a classic case where speech is brigaded with action. . . . They are indeed inseparable and a prosecution can be launched for the overt acts actually caused. Apart from rare instances of that kind, speech is, I think, immune from prosecution. Certainly there is no constitutional line between advocacy of abstract ideas . . . and advocacy of political action. . . . The quality of advocacy turns on the depth of the conviction; and government has no power to invade that sanctuary of belief and conscience.

Case

COHEN V. CALIFORNIA

403 U.S. 15; 91 S.Ct. 1780; 29 L.Ed. 2d. 284 (1971)
Vote: 5–4

Paul Robert Cohen was convicted in Los Angeles Municipal Court of "maliciously and willfully disturb[ing] the peace" by "offensive conduct" and was sentenced to thirty days in jail. The constitutional question is whether Cohen's conduct constitutes speech as protected by the First Amendment.

Mr. Justice Harlan delivered the opinion of the Court.

. . . On April 26, 1968, the defendant was observed in the Los Angeles County Courthouse in the corridor outside the division 20 of the municipal court wearing a jacket bearing the words "Fuck the Draft" which were plainly visible. There were women and children present in the corridor. The defendant was arrested. The defendant testified that he wore the jacket knowing that the words were on the jacket as a means of informing the public of the depth of his feelings against the Vietnam War and the draft.

The defendant did not engage in, nor threaten to engage in, nor did anyone as the result of his conduct in fact commit or threaten to commit any act of violence. The defendant did not make any loud or unusual noise, nor was there any evidence that he uttered any sound prior to his arrest. . . .

In affirming the conviction the Court of Appeal held that "offensive conduct" means "behavior which has a tendency to provoke others to acts of violence or to in turn disturb the peace," and that the State had proved this element because, on the facts of this case, "[i]t was

certainly reasonably foreseeable that such conduct might cause others to rise up to commit a violent act against the person of the defendant or attempt to forcibly remove his jacket." . . .

I

In order to lay hands on the precise issue which this case involves, it is useful first to canvass various matters which this record does not present.

The conviction quite clearly rests upon the asserted offensiveness of the words Cohen used to convey his message to the public. The only "conduct" which the State sought to punish is the fact of communication. Thus, we deal here with a conviction resting solely upon "speech," . . . not upon any separately identifiable conduct which allegedly was intended by Cohen to be perceived by others as expressive of particular views but which, on its face, does not necessarily convey any message and hence arguably could be regulated without effectively repressing Cohen's ability to express himself. . . . Further, the State certainly lacks power to punish Cohen for the underlying content of the message the inscription conveyed. At least so long as there is no showing of an intent to incite disobedience to or disruption of the draft, Cohen could not, consistently with the First and Fourteenth Amendments, be punished for asserting the evident position on the inutility or immorality of the draft his jacket reflected. . . .

Appellant's conviction, then, rests squarely upon his exercise of the "freedom of speech" protected from arbitrary governmental interference by the Constitution and can be justified, if at all, only as a valid regulation of the manner in which he exercised that freedom, not as a permissible prohibition on the substantive message it conveys. This does not end the inquiry, of course, for the First and Fourteenth Amendments have never been thought to give absolute protection to every individual to speak whenever or wherever he pleases, or to use any form of address in any circumstances that he chooses. In this vein, too, however, we think it important to note that several issues typically associated with such problems are not presented here. . . .

In the first place, Cohen was tried under a statute applicable throughout the entire State. Any attempt to support this conviction on the ground that the statute seeks to preserve an appropriately decorous atmosphere in the courthouse where Cohen was arrested must fall in the absence of any language in the statute that would have put appellant on notice that certain kinds of otherwise permissible speech or conduct would nevertheless, under California law, not be tolerated in certain places. . . .

In the second place, as it comes to us, this case cannot be said to fall within those relatively few categories of instances where prior decisions have established the power of government to deal more comprehensively with certain forms of individual expression simply upon a showing that such a form was employed. This is not, for example, an obscenity case. Whatever else may be necessary to give rise to the States' broader power to prohibit obscene expression, such expression must be, in some significant way, erotic. . . . It cannot plausibly be maintained that this vulgar allusion to the Selective Service System would conjure up such psychic stimulation in anyone likely to be confronted with Cohen's crudely defaced jacket.

This Court has also held that the States are free to ban the simple use, without a demonstration of additional justifying circumstances, of so-called "fighting words," those personally abusive epithets which, when addressed to the ordinary citizen, are, as a matter of common knowledge, inherently likely to provoke violent reaction. . . . While the four-letter word displayed by Cohen in relation to the draft is not uncommonly employed in a personally provocative fashion, in this instance it was clearly not "directed to the person of the hearer." . . . No individual actually or likely to be present could reasonably have regarded the words on appellant's jacket as a direct personal insult. Nor do we have here an instance of the exercise of the State's police power to prevent a speaker from intentionally provoking a given group to hostile reaction. . . . There is, as noted above, no showing that anyone who saw Cohen was in fact violently aroused or that appellant intended such a result.

Finally, in arguments before this Court much has been made of the claim that Cohen's distasteful mode of expression was thrust upon unwilling or unsuspecting viewers, and that the State might therefore legitimately act as it did in order to protect the sensitive from otherwise unavoidable exposure to appellant's crude form of protest. Of course, the mere presumed presence of unwitting listeners or viewers does not serve automatically to justify curtailing all speech capable of giving offense. . . . While this Court has recognized that government may properly act in many situations to prohibit intrusion into the privacy of the home of unwelcome views and ideas which cannot be totally banned from the public dialogue, . . . we have at the same time consistently stressed that "we are often 'captives' outside the sanctuary of the home and subject to objectionable speech." . . . The ability of government, consonant with the Constitution, to shut off discourse solely to protect others from hearing it is, in other words, dependent upon a showing that substantial privacy interests are being invaded in an essentially intolerable manner. Any broader view of this authority would effectively empower a majority to silence dissidents simply as a matter of personal predilections.

In this regard, persons confronted with Cohen's jacket were in a quite different posture than, say, those subjected to the raucous emissions of sound trucks blaring outside their residences. Those in the Los Angeles courthouse could effectively avoid further bombardment of their sensibilities simply by averting their eyes. And, while it may be that one has a more substantial claim to a recognizable privacy interest when walking through a courthouse corridor than, for example, strolling through Central Park, surely it is nothing like the interest in being free from unwanted expression in the confines of one's own home. Given the subtlety and complexity of the factors involved, if Cohen's "speech" was otherwise entitled to constitutional protection, we do not think the fact that some unwilling "listeners" in a public building may have been briefly exposed to it can serve to justify this breach of the peace conviction where, as here, there was no evidence that persons powerless to avoid appellant's conduct did in fact object to it, and where that portion of the statute upon which Cohen's conviction rests evinces no concern, either on its face or as construed by the California courts, with the special plight of the captive auditor, but, instead, indiscriminately sweeps within its prohibitions all "offensive conduct" that disturbs "any neighborhood or person." . . .

Against this background, the issue flushed by this case stands out in bold relief. It is whether California can excise, as "offensive conduct," one particular scurrilous epithet from the public discourse, either upon the theory of the court below that its use is inherently likely to cause violent reaction or upon a more general assertion that the States, acting as guardians of public morality, may properly remove this offensive word from the public vocabulary.

The rationale of the California court is plainly untenable. At most it reflects an "undifferentiated fear or apprehension of disturbance [which] is not enough to overcome the right to freedom of expression." . . . We have been shown no evidence that substantial numbers of citizens are standing ready to strike out physically at whoever may assault their sensibilities with execrations like that uttered by Cohen. There may be some persons about with such lawless and violent proclivities, but that is an insufficient base upon which to erect, consistently with constitutional values, a governmental power to force persons who wish to ventilate their dissident views into avoiding particular forms of expression. The argument amounts to little more than the self-defeating proposition that to avoid physical censorship of one who has not sought to provoke such a response by a hypothetical coterie of the violent and lawless, the State may more appropriately effectuate that censorship themselves. . . .

Admittedly, it is not so obvious that the First and Fourteenth Amendments must be taken to disable the States from punishing public utterance of this unseemly expletive in order to maintain what they regard as a suitable level of discourse within the body politic. We think, however, that examination and reflection will reveal the shortcomings of a contrary viewpoint.

. . . [W]e cannot overemphasize that, in our judgment, most situations where the State has a justifiable interest in regulating speech will fall within one or more of the various established exceptions, discussed above but not applicable here, to the usual rule that governmental bodies may not prescribe the form or content of individual expression. Equally important to our conclusion is the constitutional backdrop against which our decision must be made. The constitutional right of free expression is powerful medicine in a society as diverse and populous as ours. It is designed and intended to remove governmental restraints from the arena of public discussion, putting the decision as to what views shall be voiced largely into the hands of each of us, in the hope that use of such freedom will ultimately produce a more capable citizenry and more perfect polity and in the belief that no other approach would comport with the premise of individual dignity and choice upon which our political system rests. . . .

To many, the immediate consequence of this freedom may often appear to be only verbal tumult, discord, and even offensive utterance. These are, however, within established limits, in truth necessary side effects of the broader enduring values which the process of open debate permits us to achieve. That the air may at times seem filled with verbal cacophony is, in this sense, not a sign of weakness but of strength. We cannot lose sight of the fact that, in what otherwise might seem a trifling and annoying instance of individual distasteful abuse of a privilege, these fundamental societal values are truly implicated. That is why "[w]holly neutral futilities . . . come under the protection of free speech as fully as do Keats' poems or Donne's sermons," . . . and why "so long as the means are peaceful, the communication need not meet standards of acceptability." . . .

Against this perception of the constitutional policies involved, we discern certain more particularized considerations that peculiarly call for reversal of this conviction. First, the principle contended for by the State seems inherently boundless. How is one to distinguish this from any other offensive word? Surely the State has no right to cleanse public debate to the point where it is grammatically palatable to the most squeamish among us. Yet no readily ascertainable general principle exists for stopping short of that result were we to affirm the judgment below. For, while the particular four-letter word being litigated here is perhaps more distasteful than most others of its genre, it is nevertheless often true that one man's vulgarity is another's lyric. Indeed, we think it is largely because governmental officials cannot make principled distinctions in this area that the Constitution leaves matter of taste and style so largely to the individual.

Additionally, we cannot overlook the fact, because it is well illustrated by the episode involved here, that much linguistic expression serves a dual communicative function: it conveys not only ideas capable of relatively precise detached explication, but otherwise inexpressible emotions as well. In fact, words are often chosen as much for their emotive as their cognitive force. We cannot sanction the view that the Constitution, while solicitous of the cognitive content of individual speech, has little or no regard for that emotive function which, practically speaking, may often be the more important element of the overall message sought to be communicated. Indeed, as Mr. Justice Frankfurter has said, "[o]ne of the prerogatives of American citizenship is the right to criticize public men and measures—and that means not only informed and responsible criticism but the freedom to speak foolishly and without moderation." . . .

Finally, and in the same vein, we cannot indulge the facile assumption that one can forbid particular words without also running a substantial risk of suppressing ideas in the process. Indeed, governments might soon seize upon the censorship of particular words as a convenient guise for banning the expression of unpopular views. We have been able, as noted above, to discern little social benefit that might result from running the risk of opening the door to such grave results.

It is, in sum, our judgment that, absent a more particularized and compelling reason for its actions, the State may not, consistently with the First and Fourteenth Amendments, make the simple public display

here involved of this single four-letter expletive a criminal offense. . . .

Reversed.

Mr. Justice Blackmun, with whom the **Chief Justice** and **Mr. Justice Black** join, dissenting.

. . . Cohen's absurd and immature antic, in my view, was mainly conduct and little speech. . . . The California Court of Appeal appears so to have described it, . . . and I cannot characterize it otherwise. Further, the case appears to me to be well within the sphere of *Chaplinsky v. New Hampshire,* . . . where Mr. Justice Murphy, a known champion of First Amendment freedoms, wrote for a unanimous bench. As a consequence, this Court's agonizing over First Amendment values seems misplaced and unnecessary. . . .

Mr. Justice White [dissenting]. . . .

Case

Texas v. Johnson

491 U.S. 397, 109 S.Ct. 2533, 105 L.Ed. 2d. 342 (1989)
Vote: 5–4

After burning an American flag as part of a public protest, Gregory Lee Johnson was convicted of desecrating a flag in violation of Texas law. The Texas Court of Criminal Appeals reversed the conviction, holding that the statute under which Johnson was convicted was unconstitutional as applied to his particular conduct.

Justice Brennan delivered the opinion of the Court.

. . . We must first determine whether Johnson's burning of the flag constituted expressive conduct, permitting him to invoke the First Amendment in challenging his conviction. . . . If his conduct was expressive, we next decide whether the State's regulation is related to the suppression of free expression. . . . If the State's regulation is not related to expression, then the less stringent standard we announced in *United States v. O'Brien* [1968] for regulations of noncommunicative conduct controls. . . . If it is, then we are outside of *O'Brien's* test, and we must ask whether this interest justifies Johnson's conviction under a more demanding standard. . . . A third possibility is that the State's asserted interest is

simply not implicated on these facts, and in that event the interest drops out of the picture. . . .

The First Amendment literally forbids the abridgement only of "speech," but we have long recognized that its protection does not end at the spoken or written word. While we have rejected "the view that an apparently limitless variety of conduct can be labeled 'speech' whenever the person engaging in the conduct intends thereby to express an idea," . . . we have acknowledged that conduct may be "sufficiently imbued with elements of communication to fall within the scope of the First and Fourteenth Amendments." . . .

In deciding whether particular conduct possesses sufficient communicative elements to bring the First Amendment into play, we have asked whether "[a]n intent to convey a particularized message was present, and [whether] the likelihood was great that the message was present, and [whether] the likelihood was great that the message would be understood by those who viewed it." Hence, we have recognized the expressive nature of students' wearing of black armbands to protest American military involvement in Vietnam, . . . of the wearing of American military uniforms in a dramatic presentation criticizing American involvement in Vietnam, . . . and of picketing about a wide variety of causes. . . .

Especially pertinent to this case are our decisions recognizing the communicative nature of conduct relating to flags. Attaching a peace sign to the flag, . . . saluting the flag, . . . and displaying a red flag, . . . we have held, all may find shelter under the First Amendment. . . . That we have had little difficulty identifying an expressive element in conduct relating to flags should not be surprising. The very purpose of a national flag is to serve as a symbol of our country; it is, one might say, "the one visible manifestation of two hundred years of nationhood." . . . Pregnant with expressive content, the flag as readily signifies this Nation as does the combination of letters found in "America."

We have not automatically concluded, however, that any action taken with respect to our flag is expressive. Instead, in characterizing such action for First Amendment purposes, we have considered the context in which it occurred.

The State of Texas conceded for purposes of its oral argument in this case that Johnson's conduct was expressive conduct. . . . Johnson burned an American flag as part—indeed, as the culmination—of a political demonstration that coincided with the convening of the Republican Party and its renomination of Ronald Reagan for President. The expressive, overtly political nature of this conduct was both intentional and overwhelmingly apparent. . . .

The government generally has a freer hand in restricting expressive conduct than it has in restricting the written or spoken word. . . . It may not, however, proscribe particular conduct because it has expressive elements. . . . It is, in short, not simply the verbal or nonverbal nature of the expression, but the governmental interest at stake, that helps to determine whether a restriction on that expression is valid. . . .

In order to decide whether *O'Brien*'s test applies here, therefore we must decide whether Texas has asserted an interest in support of Johnson's conviction that is unrelated to the suppression of expression. If we find that an interest asserted by the State is simply not implicated on the facts before us, we need not ask whether *O'Brien*'s test applies. . . . The State offers two separate interests to justify this conviction: preventing breaches of the peace, and preserving the flag as a symbol of nationhood and national unity. We hold that the first interest is not implicated on this record and that the second is related to the suppression of expression. . . .

Texas claims that its interest in preventing breaches of the peace justifies Johnson's conviction for flag desecration. However, no disturbance of the peace actually occurred or threatened to occur because of Johnson's burning of the flag. Although the State stresses the disruptive behavior of the protestors during their march toward City Hall, . . . it admits that no actual breach of the peace "occurred at the time of the flag burning or in response to the flag burning." The State's emphasis on the protestors' disorderly actions prior to arriving at City Hall is not only somewhat surprising given that no charges were brought on the basis of this conduct, but it also fails to show that a disturbance of the peace was a likely reaction to Johnson's conduct. The only evidence offered by the State at trial to show the reaction to Johnson's actions was the testimony of several persons who had been seriously offended by the flag burning.

The State's position, therefore, amounts to a claim that an audience that takes serious offense at particular expression is necessarily likely to disturb the peace and that the expression may be prohibited on this basis. Our precedents do not countenance such a presumption. On the contrary, they recognize that a principal "function of free speech under our system of government is to invite dispute. It may indeed best serve its high purpose when it induces a condition of unrest, creates dissatisfaction with conditions as they are, or even stirs people to anger." . . .

. . . Johnson's expressive conduct [does not] fall within that small class of "fighting words" that are "likely to provoke the average person to retaliation, and thereby cause a breach of the peace." . . . No reasonable onlooker would have regarded Johnson's generalized expression of dissatisfaction with the policies of the Federal Government as a direct personal insult or an invitation to exchange fisticuffs.

We thus conclude that the State's interest in maintaining order is not implicated on these facts. The State need not worry that our holding will disable it from preserving the peace. We do not suggest that the First Amendment forbids a State to prevent "imminent lawless action." . . .

The State also asserts an interest in preserving the flag as a symbol of nationhood and national unity. . . . The State, apparently, is concerned that . . . [flag burning] will lead people to believe either that the flag does not stand for nationhood and national unity, but instead reflects other, less positive concepts, or that the concepts reflected in the flag do not in fact exist, that is, we do not enjoy unity as a Nation. These concerns blossom only when a person's treatment of the flag communicates some message, and thus are related "to the suppression of free expression" within the meaning of *O'Brien*. We are thus outside of *O'Brien*'s test altogether.

It remains to consider whether the State's interest in preserving the flag as a symbol of nationhood and national unity justifies Johnson's conviction.

. . . Johnson was not . . . prosecuted for the expression of just any idea; he was prosecuted for his expression of dissatisfaction with the policies of this country, expression situated at the core of our First Amendment values. . . .

Moreover, Johnson was prosecuted because he knew that his politically charged expression would cause "serious offense." If he had burned the flag as a means of disposing of it because it was dirty or torn, he would not have been convicted of flag desecration under this Texas law: federal law designates burning as the preferred means of disposing of a flag "when it is in such condition that it is no longer a fitting emblem for display," . . . and Texas has no quarrel with this means of disposal. The Texas law is thus not aimed at protecting the physical integrity of the flag in all circumstances, but is designed instead to protect it only against impairments that would cause serious offense to others. . . .

Whether Johnson's treatment of the flag violated Texas law thus depended on the likely communicative impact of his expressive conduct. . . . [T]his restriction on Johnson's expression is content-based.

. . . Johnson's political expression was restricted because of the content of the message he conveyed. We must therefore subject the State's asserted interest in preserving the special symbolic character of the flag to "the most exacting scrutiny." . . .

If there is a bedrock principle underlying the First Amendment, it is that Government may not prohibit the expression of an idea simply because society finds the idea itself offensive or disagreeable. . . .

. . . [N]othing in our precedents suggests that a State may foster its own view of the flag by prohibiting expressive conduct relating to it. . . .

There is, moreover, no indication—either in the text of the Constitution or in our cases interpreting it—that a separate judicial category exists for the American flag alone. Indeed, we would not be surprised to learn that the persons who framed our Constitution and wrote the Amendment that we now construe were not known for their reverence for the Union Jack. The First Amendment does not guarantee that other concepts virtually sacred to our Nation as a whole—such as the principle that discrimination on the basis of race is odious and destructive—will go unquestioned in the marketplace of ideas. . . . We decline, therefore to create for the flag an exception to the joust of principles protected by the First Amendment.

It is not the State's ends, but its means, to which we object. It cannot be gainsaid that there is a special place reserved for the flag in this Nation, and thus we do not doubt that the Government has a legitimate interest in making efforts to "preserv[e] the national flag as an unalloyed symbol of our country." . . . Congress has, for example, enacted precatory regulations describing the proper treatment of the flag . . . and we cast no doubt on the legitimacy of its interest in making such recommendations. To say that the Government has an interest in encouraging proper treatment of the flag, however, is not to say that it may criminally punish a person for burning a flag as a means of political protest. . . .

We are tempted to say . . . that the flag's deservedly cherished place in our community will be strengthened, not weakened, by our holding today. Our decision is a reaffirmation of the principles of freedom and inclusiveness that the flag best reflects, and of the conviction that our toleration of criticism such as Johnson's is a sign and source of our strength.

The way to preserve the flag's special role is not to punish those who feel differently about these matters. It is to persuade them that they are wrong.

. . . [P]recisely because it is our flag that is involved, one's response to the flag-burners may exploit the uniquely persuasive power of the flag itself. We can imagine no more appropriate response to burning a flag than waving one's own, no better way to counter a flag-burner's message than by saluting the flag that burns, no surer means of preserving the dignity even of the flag that burned than by—as one witness here did—according its remains a respectful burial. We do not consecrate the flag by punishing its desecration, for in doing so we dilute the freedom that this cherished emblem represents. . . .

The judgment of the Texas Court of Criminal Appeals is . . . affirmed.

Justice Kennedy, concurring. . . .

Chief Justice Rehnquist, with whom ***Justice White*** and ***Justice O'Connor*** join, dissenting.

In holding this Texas statute unconstitutional, the Court ignores Justice Holmes' familiar aphorism that "a page of history is worth a volume of logic." . . . For more than 200 years, the American flag has occupied a unique position as the symbol of our Nation, a uniqueness that justifies a governmental prohibition against flag burning in the way respondent Johnson did here. . . .

Here it may equally well be said that the public burning of the American flag by Johnson was no essential part of any exposition of ideas, and at the same time it had a tendency to incite a breach of the peace. Johnson was free to make any verbal denunciation of the flag that he wished; indeed, he was free to burn the flag in private. He could publicly burn other symbols of the Government or effigies of political leaders. He did lead a march through the streets of Dallas, and conducted a rally in front of the Dallas City Hall. He engaged in a "die-in" to protest nuclear weapons. He shouted out various slogans during the march, including: "Reagan, Mondale which will it be? Either one means World War III"; "Ronald Reagan, killer of the hour, perfect example of US power"; and "red, white and blue, we spit on you, you stand for plunder, you will go under." . . . For none of these acts was he arrested or prosecuted; it was only when he proceeded to burn publicly an American flag stolen from its rightful owner that he violated the Texas statute. . . .

The Court concludes its opinion with a regrettably patronizing civics lecture, presumably addressed to the Members of both Houses of Congress, the members of the 48 state legislatures that enacted prohibitions against flag burning, and the troops fighting under that flag in Vietnam who objected to its being burned: "The way to preserve the flag's special role is not to punish those who feel differently about these matters. It is to persuade them that they are wrong." . . . The Court's role as the final expositor of the Constitution is well established, but its role as a platonic guardian admonishing those responsible to public opinion as if they were truant school children has no similar place in our system of government. The cry of "no taxation without representation" animated those who revolted against the English Crown to found our Nation—the idea that those who submitted to government should have some say as to what kind of laws would be passed. Surely one of the high purposes of a democratic society is to legislate against conduct that is regarded as evil and profoundly offensive to the majority of people—whether it be murder, embezzlement, pollution, or flag burning.

Our Constitution wisely places limits on powers of legislative majorities to act, but the declaration of such limits by this Court "is, at all times, a question of much delicacy which ought seldom, if ever, to be decided in the affirmative, in a doubtful case." . . . Uncritical extension of constitutional protection to the burning of the flag risks the frustration of the very purpose for which organized governments are instituted. The Court decides that the American flag is just another symbol, about which not only must opinions pro and con be tolerated, but for which the most minimal public respect may not be enjoined. The government may conscript

men into the Armed Forces where they must fight and perhaps die for the flag, but the government may not prohibit the public burning of the banner under which they fight. I would uphold the Texas statute as applied in this case.

Justice Stevens, dissenting.

. . . A country's flag is a symbol of more than "nationhood and national unity." . . . It also signifies the ideas that characterize the society that has chosen that emblem as well as the special history that has animated the growth and power of those ideas. The fleur-de-lis and the tricolor both symbolized "nationhood and national unity," but they had vastly different meanings. The message conveyed by some flags—the swastika, for example—may survive long after it has outlived its usefulness as a symbol of regimented unity in a particular nation.

So it is with the American flag. It is more than a proud symbol of the courage, the determination, and the gifts of nature that transformed 13 fledgling Colonies into a world power. It is a symbol of freedom, of equal opportunity, of religious tolerance, and of goodwill for other peoples who share our aspirations. The symbol carries its message to dissidents both at home and abroad who may have no interest at all in our national unity or survival.

The value of the flag as a symbol cannot be measured. Even so, I have no doubt that the interest in preserving that value for the future is both significant and legitimate. Conceivably that value will be enhanced by the Court's conclusion that our national commitment to free expression is so strong that even the United States as ultimate guarantor of that freedom is without power to prohibit the desecration of its unique symbol. But I am unpersuaded. The creation of a federal right to post bulletin boards and graffiti on the Washington Monument might enlarge the market for free expression, but at a cost I would not pay. . . .

The Court is . . . quite wrong in blandly asserting that respondent "was prosecuted for his expression of dissatisfaction with the policies of this country, expression situated at the core of our First Amendment values." . . . Respondent was prosecuted because of the method he chose to express his dissatisfaction with those policies. Had he chosen to spray paint—or perhaps convey with a motion picture projector—his message of dissatisfaction on the facade of the Lincoln Memorial, there would be no question about the power of the Government to prohibit his means of expression. The prohibition would be supported by the legitimate interest in preserving the quality of an important national asset. Though the asset at stake in this case is intangible, given its unique value, the same interest supports a prohibition on the desecration of the American flag.

The ideas of liberty and equality have been an irresistible force in motivating leaders like Patrick Henry, Susan B. Anthony, and Abraham Lincoln, schoolteachers like Nathan Hale and Booker T. Washington, the Philippine Scouts who fought at Bataan, and the soldiers who scaled the bluff at Omaha Beach. If those ideas are worth fighting for—and our history demonstrates that they are—it cannot be true that the flag that uniquely symbolizes their power is not itself worthy of protection from unnecessary desecration.

I respectfully dissent.

Case

BARNES V. GLEN THEATRE, INC.

501 U.S. 560; 111 S.Ct. 2456; 115 L.Ed. 2d. 504 (1991)
Vote: 5–4

Two South Bend, Indiana, establishments that featured all-nude dancing brought suit in the U.S. District Court for the Northern District of Indiana seeking an injunction against enforcement of an Indiana statute prohibiting complete nudity in public places. The district court dismissed the case, concluding that "the type of dancing these plaintiffs wish to perform is not expressive activity protected by the Constitution of the United States." On appeal, the Court of Appeals for the Seventh Circuit reversed, holding that the nude dancing at issue was "expressive conduct protected by the First Amendment." The Supreme Court granted certiorari.

Chief Justice Rehnquist . . . [announced the judgment of the Court and delivered an opinion joined by Justices O'Connor and Kennedy].

. . . The Kitty Kat Lounge, Inc. (Kitty Kat) is located in the city of South Bend. It sells alcoholic beverages and presents "go-go dancing." Its proprietor desires to present "totally nude dancing," but an applicable Indiana statute regulating public nudity requires that the dancers wear "pasties" and a "G-string" when they dance. The dancers are not paid an hourly wage, but work on commission. They receive a 100 percent commission on the first $60 in drink sales during their performances. Darlene Miller, one of the respondents in the action, had worked at the Kitty Kat for about two years at the time this action was brought. Miller wishes to dance nude because she believes she would make more money doing so.

Respondent Glen Theatre, Inc. is an Indiana corporation with a place of business in South Bend. Its primary business is supplying so-called adult entertainment through written and printed materials, movie showings, and live entertainment at the "bookstore" consists of nude and seminude performances and showings of the female body through glass panels. Customers sit in a booth and insert coins into a timing mechanism that permits them to observe the live nude and seminude dancers for a period of time. One of Glen Theatre's dancers, Gayle Ann Marie Sutro, has danced, modeled, and acted professionally for more than 15 years, and in addition to her performances at the Glen Theatre, can be seen in a pornographic movie at a nearby theater. . . .

Several of our cases contain language suggesting that nude dancing of the kind involved here is expressive conduct protected by the First Amendment. In *Doran v. Salem Inn, Inc.* . . . (1975), we said: "[A]lthough the customary 'barroom' type of nude dancing may involve only the barest minimum of protected expression, we recognized in *California v. LaRue* . . . (1972), that this form of entertainment might be entitled to First and Fourteenth Amendment protection under some circumstances." In *Schad v. Borough of Mount Ephraim* . . . (1981), we said that "[f]urthermore, as the state courts in this case recognized, nude dancing is not without its First Amendment protections from official regulation" (citations omitted). These statements support the conclusion of the Court of Appeals that nude dancing of the kind sought to be performed here is expressive conduct within the outer perimeters of the First Amendment, though we view it as only marginally so. This, of course, does not end our inquiry. We must determine the level of protection to be afforded to the expressive conduct at issue, and must determine whether the Indiana statute is an impermissible infringement of that protected activity.

Indiana, of course, has not banned nude dancing as such, but has proscribed public nudity across the board. The Supreme Court of Indiana has construed the Indiana statute to preclude nudity in what are essentially places of public accommodation such as the Glen Theatre and the Kitty Kat Lounge. In such places, respondents point out, minors are excluded and there are no non-consenting viewers. Respondents contend that while the state may license establishments such as the ones involved here, and limit the geographical area in which they do business, it may not in any way limit the performance of the dances within them without violating the First Amendment. The petitioner contends, on the other hand, that Indiana's restriction on nude dancing is a valid "time, place or manner" restriction under cases such as *Clark v. Community for Creative Non-Violence* . . . (1984).

The "time, place, or manner" test was developed for evaluating restriction on expression taking place on the public property which had been dedicated as a "public forum," . . . although we have on at least one occasion applied it to conduct occurring on private property. . . . In *Clark* we observed that this test has been interpreted to embody much the same standards as those set forth in *United States v. O'Brien* . . . (1968), and we turn, therefore, to the rule enunciated in *O'Brien*. . . .

This Court has held that when "speech" and "nonspeech" elements are combined in the same course of conduct, a sufficiently important governmental interest in regulating the nonspeech element can justify incidental limitation on First Amendment freedoms. To characterize the quality of the governmental interest which must appear, the Court has employed a variety of descriptive terms: compelling; substantial; subordinating; paramount; cogent; strong. Whatever imprecision inheres in these terms, we think it clear that a government regulation is sufficiently justified if it is within the constitutional power of the Government; if it furthers an important or substantial governmental interest; if the governmental interest is unrelated to the suppression of free expression; and if the incidental restriction on alleged First Amendment freedoms is no greater than essential to the furtherance of that interest. . . .

Applying the four-part *O'Brien* test enunciated above, we find that Indiana's public indecency statute is justified despite its incidental limitations on some expressive activity. The public indecency statute is clearly within the constitutional power of the State and furthers substantial governmental interests. It is impossible to discern, other than from the text of the statute, exactly what governmental interest the Indiana legislators had in mind when they enacted this statute, for Indiana does not record legislative history, and the state's highest court has not shed additional light on the statute's pur-

pose. Nonetheless, the statute's purpose of protecting societal order and morality is clear from its text and history. Public indecency statutes of this sort are of ancient origin, and presently exist in at least 47 States. Public indecency, including nudity, was a criminal offense at common law, and this Court recognized the common-law roots of the offense of "gross and open indecency" in *Winters v. New York* . . . (1948). Public nudity was considered an act *malum en se*. . . . Public indecency statutes such as the one before us reflect moral disapproval of people appearing in the nude among strangers in public places.

This public indecency statute follows a long line of earlier Indiana statutes banning all public nudity. The history of Indiana's public indecency statute shows that it predates barroom nude dancing and was enacted as a general prohibition. At least as early as 1831, Indiana has a statute punishing "open and notorious lewdness, or . . . any grossly scandalous and public indecency." . . . A gap during which no statute was in effect was filled by the Indiana Supreme Court in *Ardery v. State* . . . (1877), which held that the court could sustain a conviction for exhibitions of "privates" in the presence of others. The court traced the offense to the Bible story of Adam and Eve. . . . In 1881, a statute was enacted that would remain essentially unchanged for nearly a century:

> Whoever, being over fourteen years of age, makes an indecent exposure of his person in a public place, or in any place where there are other persons to be offended or annoyed thereby, . . . is guilty of public indecency. . . .

The language quoted above remained unchanged until it was simultaneously repealed and replaced with the present statute in 1976. . . .

This and other public indecency statutes were designed to protect morals and public order. The traditional police power of the States is defined as the authority to provide for the public health, safety, and morals, and we have upheld such a basis for legislation. . . .

. . . In *Bowers v. Hardwick* . . . (1986), we said: "The law, however, is constantly based on notion of morality, and if all laws representing essentially moral choices are to be invalidated under the Due Process Clause, the courts will be very busy indeed."

Thus, the public indecency statute furthers a substantial government interest in protecting order and morality.

This interest is unrelated to the suppression of free expression. Some may view restricting nudity on moral grounds as necessarily related to expression. We disagree. It can be argued, of course, that almost limitless types of conduct—including appearing in the nude in public—are "expressive," and in one sense of the word this is true. People who go about in the nude in public may be expressing something about themselves by so doing. But the Court rejected this expansive notion of "expressive conduct" in *O'Brien*, saying:

We cannot accept the view that an apparently limitless variety of conduct can be labelled "speech" whenever the person engaging in the conduct intends thereby to express an idea. . . .

Respondents contend that even though prohibiting nudity in public generally may not be related to suppressing expression, prohibiting the performance of nude dancing is related to expression because the state seeks to prevent its erotic message. Therefore, they reason that the application of the Indiana statute to the nude dancing in this case violates the First Amendment, because it fails the third part of the *O'Brien* test, viz: the governmental interest must be unrelated to the suppression of free expression.

But we do not think that when Indiana applies its statute to the nude dancing in these nightclubs it is proscribing nudity because of the erotic message conveyed by the dancers. Presumably numerous other erotic performances are presented at these establishments and similar clubs without any interference from the state, so long as the performers wear a scant amount of clothing. Likewise the requirement that the dancers don pasties and a G-string does not deprive the dance of whatever erotic message it conveys; it simply makes the message slightly less graphic. The perceived evil that Indiana seeks to address is not erotic dancing, but public nudity. The appearance of people of all shapes, sizes and ages in the nude at a beach, for example, would convey little if any erotic message, yet the state still seeks to prevent it. Public nudity is the evil the state seeks to prevent, whether or not it is combined with expressive activity.

This conclusion is buttressed by a reference to the facts of *O'Brien*. An act of Congress provided that anyone who knowingly destroyed a selective service registration certificate committed an offense. O'Brien burned his certificate on the steps of the South Boston Courthouse to influence others to adopt his anti-war beliefs. The Court upheld his conviction, reasoning that the continued availability of issued certificates served a legitimate and substantial purpose in the administration of the selective service system. O'Brien's deliberate destruction of his certificate frustrated this purpose and "for this non-communicative aspect of his conduct, and for nothing else, he was convicted." . . . It was assumed that *O'Brien*'s act in burning the certificate had a communicative element in it sufficient to bring into play the First Amendment, . . . but it was for the non-communicative element that he was prosecuted. So here with the Indiana statute; while the dancing to which it was applied had a communicative element, it was not the dancing that was prohibited, but simply its being done in the nude.

The fourth part of the *O'Brien* test requires that the incidental restriction on First Amendment freedom be no greater than is essential to the furtherance of the governmental interest. As indicated in the discussion above, the governmental interest served by the text of the prohibition is societal disapproval of nudity in public places and among strangers. The statutory prohibition is not a means to some greater end, but an end in itself. It is without cavil that the public indecency statute is "narrowly tailored"; Indiana's requirement that the dancers wear at least pasties and a G-string is modest, and the bare minimum necessary to achieve the state's purpose.

The judgment of the Court of Appeals accordingly is . . . reversed.

Justice Scalia, concurring in the judgment. . . .

Justice Souter, concurring in the judgment. . . .

Justice White, with whom **Justice Marshall, Justice Blackmun,** and **Justice Stevens** join, dissenting.

. . . We are told by the Attorney General of Indiana that . . . the Indiana Supreme Court [has] held that the statute at issue here cannot and does not prohibit nudity as part of some larger form of expression meriting protection when the communication of ideas is involved. . . . Petitioners also state that the evils sought to be avoided by applying the statute in this case would not obtain in the case of theatrical productions such as *Salome* or *Hair.* Neither is there any evidence that the State has attempted to apply the statute to nudity in performances such as plays, ballets or operas. "No arrests have ever been made for nudity as part of a play or ballet." . . .

Thus, the Indiana statute is not a general prohibition of the type that we have upheld in prior cases. As a result, the Court's and Justice Scalia's simple references to the State's general interest in promoting societal order and morality [are] not sufficient justification for a statute which concededly reaches a significant amount of expressive activity. Instead of applying the *O'Brien* test, we are obligated to carefully examine the reasons the State has chosen to regulate this expressive conduct in a less than general statute. In other words, when the State enacts a law which draws a line between expressive conduct of the same type which is regulated and nonexpressive conduct which is not regulated, *O'Brien* places the burden on the State to justify the distinctions it has made. Closer inquiry as to the purpose of the statute is surely appropriate.

Legislators do not just randomly select certain conduct for proscription; they have reasons and those reasons illuminate the purpose of the law that is passed. Indeed, a law may have multiple purposes. The purpose of forbidding people from appearing nude in parks, beaches, hot dog stands, and like public places is to protect others from offense. But that could not possibly be the purpose of preventing nude dancing in theaters and barrooms since the viewers are exclusively consenting adults who pay money to see these dances. The purpose of the proscription in these contexts is to protect the viewers from what the State believes is the harmful message that nude dancing communicates. . . .

That the performances in the Kitty Kat Lounge may not be high art, to say the least, and may not appeal to the Court, is hardly an excuse for distorting and ignoring settled doctrine. The Court's assessment of the artistic merits of nude dancing performances should not be the determining factor in deciding this case. In the words of Justice Harlan, "it is largely because governmental officials cannot make principled decisions in this area that the Constitution leaves matters of taste and style so largely to the individual." . . . "[W]hile the entertainment afforded by a nude ballet at Lincoln Center to those who can pay the price may differ vastly in content (as viewed by judges) or in quality (as viewed by critics), it may not differ in substance from the dance viewed by the person who . . . wants some 'entertainment' with his beer or shot of rye." . . .

As I see it, our cases require us to affirm absent a compelling state interest supporting the statute. Neither the Court nor the State suggest that the statute could withstand scrutiny under that standard. . . .

Accordingly, I would affirm the judgment of the Court of Appeals, and dissent from this Court's judgment.

Case

NEW YORK TIMES COMPANY V. SULLIVAN

376 U.S. 254; 84 S.Ct. 710; 11 L.Ed. 2d. 686 (1964)
Vote: 9–0

In this case the Court determines the extent to which the First Amendment limits a state's power to award damages in a libel suit brought by a public official against critics of his official conduct.

Mr. Justice Brennan delivered the opinion of the Court.

. . . Respondent L. B. Sullivan is one of the three elected Commissioners of the City of Montgomery, Alabama. He testified that he was "Commissioner of Public Affairs and the duties are supervision of the Police Department, Fire Department, Department of Cemetery and Department of Scales." He brought this civil libel action against the four individual petitioners, who are Negroes and Alabama clergymen, and against petitioner the New York Times Company, a New York corporation which publishes the *New York Times,* a daily newspaper. A jury in the Circuit Court of Montgomery County awarded him damages of $500,000, the full amount claimed, against all the petitioners and the Supreme Court of Alabama affirmed. . . .

Respondent's complaint alleged that he had been libeled by statements in a full-page advertisement that was carried in the *New York Times* on March 29, 1960. Entitled "Heed Their Rising Voices," the advertisement began by stating that "As the whole world knows by now, thousands of Southern Negro students are engaged in widespread nonviolent demonstrations in positive affirmation of the right to live in human dignity as guaranteed by the U.S. Constitution and the Bill of Rights." It went on to charge that "in their efforts to uphold these guarantees, they are being met by an unprecedented wave of terror by those who would deny and negate that document which the whole world looks upon as setting the pattern for modern freedom. . . ." Succeeding paragraphs purported to illustrate the "wave of terror" by describing certain alleged events. The text concluded with an appeal for funds for three purposes: support of the student movement, "the struggle for the right-to-vote," and the legal defense of Dr. Martin Luther King, Jr., leader of the movement, against a perjury indictment then pending in Montgomery.

The text appeared over the names of 64 persons, many widely known for their activities in public affairs, religion, trade unions, and the performing arts. Below these names, and under a line reading "We in the south who are struggling daily for dignity and freedom warmly endorse this appeal," appeared the names of the four individual petitioners and of 16 other persons, all but two of whom were identified as clergymen in various Southern cities. The advertisement was signed at the bottom of the page by the "Committee to Defend Martin Luther King and the Struggle for Freedom in the South," and the officers of the Committee were listed.

Of the 10 paragraphs of text in the advertisement, the third and a portion of the sixth were the basis of respondent's claim of libel. They read as follows:

Third paragraph:

In Montgomery, Alabama, after students sang "My Country, 'Tis of Thee" on the State Capitol steps, their leaders were expelled from school, and truckloads of police armed with shotguns and tear-gas ringed the Alabama State College Campus. When the entire student body protested to state authorities by refusing to re-register, their dining hall was padlocked in an attempt to starve them into submission.

Sixth paragraph:

Again and again the Southern violators have answered Dr. King's peaceful protests with intimidation and violence. They have bombed his home almost killing his wife and child. They have assaulted his person. They have arrested him seven times—for "speeding," "loitering" and similar "offenses." And now they have charged him with "perjury"—a felony under which they could imprison him for ten years. . . .

Although neither of these statements mentions respondent by name, he contended that the word "police" in the third paragraph referred to him as the Montgomery Commissioner who supervised the Police Department, so that he was being accused of "ringing" the campus with police. He further claimed that the paragraph would be read as imputing to the police, and hence to him, the padlocking of the dining hall in order to starve the students into submission. As to the sixth paragraph, he contended that since arrests are ordinarily made by the police, the statement "They have arrested [Dr. King] seven times" would be read as referring to him; he further contended that the "They" who did the arresting would be equated with the "They" who

committed the other described acts and with the "Southern violators." Thus, he argued, the paragraph would be read as accusing the Montgomery police, and hence him, of answering Dr. King's protests with "intimidation and violence," bombing his home, assaulting his person, and charging him with perjury. Respondent and six other Montgomery residents testified that they read some of all of the statements as referring to him in his capacity as Commissioner.

It is uncontroverted that some of the statements contained in the two paragraphs were not accurate descriptions of events which occurred in Montgomery. Although Negro students staged a demonstration on the State Capitol steps, they sang the National Anthem and not "My Country, 'Tis of Thee." Although nine students were expelled by the State Board of Education, this was not for leading the demonstration at the Capitol, but for demanding service at a lunch counter in the Montgomery County Courthouse on another day. Not the entire student body, but most of it, had protested the expulsion, not by refusing to register, but by boycotting classes on a single day; virtually all the students did register for the ensuing semester. The campus dining hall was not padlocked on any occasion, and the only students who may have been barred from eating there were the few who had neither signed a preregistration application nor requested temporary meal tickets. Although the police were deployed near the campus in large numbers on three occasions, they did not at any time "ring" the campus, and they were not called to the campus in connection with the demonstration on the State Capitol steps, as the third paragraph implied. Dr. King had not been arrested seven times, but only four; and although he claimed to have been assaulted some years earlier in connection with his arrest for loitering outside a courtroom, one of the officers who made the arrest denied that there was such an assault.

On the premise that the charges in the sixth paragraph could be read as referring to him, respondent was allowed to prove that he had not participated in the events described. Although Dr. King's home had in fact been bombed twice when his wife and child were there, both of these occasions antedated respondent's tenure as Commissioner, and the police were not only not implicated in the bombings, but had made every effort to apprehend those who were. Three of Dr. King's four arrests took place before respondent became Commissioner. Although Dr. King had in fact been indicted (he was subsequently acquitted) on two counts of perjury, each of which carried a possible five-year sentence, respondent had nothing to do with procuring the indictment. . . .

Because of the importance of the constitutional issues involved, we granted the separate petitions for certiorari of the individual petitioners and of the *Times*. . . . We reverse the judgment. We hold that the rule of law applied by the Alabama courts is constitutionally deficient for failure to provide the safeguards for freedom of speech and of the press that are required by the First and Fourteenth Amendments in a libel action brought by a public official against critics of his official conduct. We further hold that under the proper safeguards the evidence presented in this case is constitutionally insufficient to support the judgment for respondent. . . .

Under Alabama law as applied in this case, a publication is "libelous per se" if the words "tend to injure a person . . . in his reputation" or to "bring [him] into public contempt"; the trial court stated that the standard was met if the words are such as to "injure him in his public office, or impute misconduct to him in his office, or want of official integrity, or want of fidelity to a public trust. . . ." The jury must find that the words were published "of and concerning" the plaintiff, but where the plaintiff is a public official his place in the governmental hierarchy is sufficient evidence to support a finding that his reputation has been affected by statements that reflect upon the agency of which he is in charge. Once "libel per se" has been established, the defendant has no defense as to stated facts unless he can persuade the jury that they were true in all their particulars. . . . His privilege of "fair comment" for expressions of opinion depends on the truth of the facts upon which the comment is based. . . . Unless he can discharge the burden of proving truth, general damages are presumed, and may be awarded without proof of pecuniary injury. A showing of actual malice is apparently a prerequisite to recovery of punitive damages, and the defendant may in any event forestall a punitive award by a retraction meeting the statutory requirements. Good motives and belief in truth do not negate an inference of malice, but are relevant only in mitigation of punitive damages if the jury chooses to accord them weight. . . .

The question before us is whether this rule of liability, as applied to an action brought by a public official against critics of his official conduct, abridges the freedom of speech and of the press that is guaranteed by the First and Fourteenth Amendments.

Respondent relies heavily, as did the Alabama courts, on statements of this Court to the effect that the Constitution does not protect libelous publications. Those statements do not foreclose our inquiry here. None of the cases sustained the use of libel laws to impose sanctions upon expression critical of the official conduct of public officials. . . . Like insurrection, contempt, advocacy of unlawful acts, breach of the peace, obscenity, solicitation of legal business, and the various other formulae for the repression of expression that have been challenged in this Court, libel can claim no talismanic immunity from constitutional limitations. It must be measured by standards that satisfy the First Amendment. . . .

[W]e consider this case against the background of a profound national commitment to the principle that debate on public issues should be uninhibited, robust, and wide-open, and that it may well include vehement, caustic, and sometimes unpleasantly sharp attacks on government and public officials. . . .

A rule compelling the critic of official conduct to guarantee the truth of all his factual assertions—and to do so on pain of libel judgments virtually unlimited in amount—leads to a comparable "self-censorship." Allowance of the defense of truth, with the burden of proving it on the defendant, does not mean that only false speech will be deterred. Even courts accepting this defense as an adequate safeguard have recognized the difficulties of adducing legal proofs that the alleged libel was true in all its factual particulars. . . . Under such a rule, would-be critics of official conduct may be deterred from voicing their criticism, even though it is believed to be true and even though it is in fact true, because of doubt whether it can be proved in court or fear of the expense of having to do so. They tend to make only statements which "steer far wider of the unlawful zone." . . . The rule thus dampens the vigor and limits the variety of public debate. It is inconsistent with the First and Fourteenth Amendments.

The constitutional guarantees require, we think, a federal rule that prohibits a public official from recovering damages for a defamatory falsehood relating to his official conduct unless he proves that the statement was made with "actual malice"—that is, with knowledge that it was false or with reckless disregard of whether it was false or not. . . .

Such a privilege for criticism of official conduct is appropriately analogous to the protection accorded a public official when he is sued for libel by a private citizen. . . . The reason for the official privilege is said to be that the threat of damage suits would otherwise "inhibit the fearless, vigorous, and effective administration of policies of government" and "dampen the ardor of all but the most resolute, or the most irresponsible, in the unflinching discharge of their duties." . . . Analogous considerations support the privilege for the citizen-critic of government. It is as much his duty to criticize as it is the official's duty to administer. . . . It would give public servants an unjustified preference over the public they serve, if critics of official conduct did not have a fair equivalent of the immunity granted to the officials themselves. . . .

We hold today that the Constitution delimits a State's power to award damages for libel in actions brought by public officials against critics of their official conduct. Since this is such an action, the rule requiring proof of actual malice is applicable. While Alabama law apparently requires proof of actual malice for an award of punitive damages, where general damages are concerned malice is "presumed." Such a presumption is inconsistent with the federal rule. . . . Since the trial judge did not instruct the jury to differentiate between general and punitive damages, it may be that the verdict was wholly an award of one or the other. But it is impossible to know, in view of the general verdict returned. Because of this uncertainty, the judgment must be reversed and the case remanded. . . .

Mr. Justice Black, with whom **Mr. Justice Douglas** joins, concurring.

. . . I base my vote to reverse on the belief that the First and Fourteenth Amendments not merely "delimit" a State's power to award damages to "public officials against critics of their official conduct" but completely prohibit a State from exercising such a power. The Court goes on to hold that a State can subject such critics to damages if "actual malice" can be proved against them. "Malice," even as defined by the Court, is an elusive, abstract concept, hard to prove and hard to disprove. The requirement that malice be proved provides at best an evanescent protection for the right critically to discuss public affairs and certainly does not measure up to the sturdy safeguard embodied in the First Amendment. Unlike the Court, therefore, I vote to reverse exclusively on the ground that the *Times* and the individual defendants had an absolute, unconditional constitutional right to publish in the *Times* advertisement their criticisms of the Montgomery agencies and officials. . . .

Case

MILLER V. CALIFORNIA
413 U.S. 15; 93 S.Ct. 2607; 37 L.Ed. 2d. 419 (1973)
Vote: 5–4

In this case the Supreme Court sets forth the constitutional standards for determining obscenity. The defendant, Miller, was convicted in the Orange County Superior Court of "knowingly distributing obscene matter," a misdemeanor under California law. The appellate court affirmed his conviction without opinion.

Mr. Chief Justice Burger delivered the opinion of the Court.

. . . Appellant conducted a mass mailing campaign to advertise the sale of illustrated books, euphemistically called "adult" material. After a jury trial, he was convicted of violating California Penal Code [Section] 311.2 (a), a misdemeanor, by knowingly distributing obscene matter, and the Appellate Department, Superior Court of California, County of Orange, summarily affirmed the judgment without opinion. Appellant's conviction was specifically based on his conduct in causing five unsolicited advertising brochures to be sent through the mail in an envelope addressed to a restaurant in Newport Beach, California. The envelope was opened by the manager of the restaurant and his mother. They had not requested the brochures; they complained to the police.

The brochures advertise four books entitled "Intercourse," "Man-Woman," "Sex Orgies Illustrated," and "An Illustrated History of Pornography," and a film entitled "Marital Intercourse." While the brochures contain some descriptive printed material, primarily they consist of pictures and drawings very explicitly depicting men and women in groups of two or more engaging in a variety of sexual activities, with genitals often prominently displayed. . . .

. . . This much has been categorically settled by the Court, that obscene material is unprotected by the First Amendment. . . . "The First and Fourteenth Amendments have never been treated as absolutes." . . . We acknowledge, however, the inherent dangers of undertaking to regulate any form of expression. State statutes designed to regulate obscene materials must be carefully limited. . . . As a result, we now confine the permissible scope of such regulation to works which depict or describe sexual conduct. That conduct must be specifically defined by the applicable state law, as written or authoritatively construed. A state office must also be limited to works which, taken as a whole, appeal to the prurient interest in sex, which portray sexual conduct in a patently offensive way, and which, taken as a whole, do not have serious literary, artistic, political, or scientific value.

The basic guidelines for the trier of fact must be: (a) whether "the average person, applying contemporary community standards" would find that the work, taken as a whole, appeals to the prurient interest, . . . (b) whether the work depicts or describes, in a patently offensive way, sexual conduct specifically defined by the applicable state law, and (c) whether the work, taken as a whole, lacks serious literary, artistic, political, or scientific value. We do not adopt as a constitutional standard the "*utterly* without redeeming social value" test of *Memoirs v. Massachusetts;* . . . that concept has never commanded the adherence of more than three Justices at one time. . . . If a state law that regulates obscene material is thus limited, as written or construed, the First Amendment values applicable to the States through the Fourteenth Amendment are adequately protected by the ultimate power of appellate courts to conduct an independent review of constitutional claims when necessary. . . .

We emphasize that it is not our function to propose regulatory schemes for the States. That must await their concrete legislative efforts. It is possible, however, to give a few plain examples of what a state statute could define for regulation under the second part (b) of the standard announced in this opinion *supra:*

(a) Patently offensive representations or descriptions of ultimate sexual acts, normal or perverted, actual or simulated.

(b) Patently offensive representations or descriptions of masturbation, excretory functions, and lewd exhibition of the genitals.

Sex and nudity may not be exploited without limit by films or pictures exhibited or sold in places of public accommodation any more than live sex and nudity can be exhibited or sold without limit in such public places. At a minimum, prurient, patently offensive depiction or description of sexual conduct must have serious literary, artistic, political, or scientific value to merit First Amendment protection. . . .

Under the holdings announced today, no one will be subject to prosecution for the sale or exposure of obscene materials unless these materials depict or describe patently offensive "hard core" sexual conduct specifically defined by the regulating state law, as written or construed. We are satisfied that these specific prerequisites will provide fair notice to a dealer in such materials that his public and commercial activities may bring prosecution. . . .

It is certainly true that the absence, since *Roth v. United States* of a single majority view of this Court as to proper standards for testing obscenity has placed a strain on both state and federal courts. But today, for the first time since *Roth* was decided in 1957, a majority of this Court has agreed on concrete guidelines to isolate "hard core" pornography from expression protected by the First Amendment. . . .

This may not be an easy road, free from difficulty. But no amount of "fatigue" should lead us to adopt a convenient "institutional" rationale—an absolutist, "anything goes" view of the First Amendment—because it will lighten our burdens. "Such an abnegation of judicial supervision in this field would be inconsistent with our duty to uphold the constitutional guarantees." . . . Nor should we remedy "tension between state and federal courts" by arbitrarily depriving the States of a power reserved to them under the Constitution, a power which they have enjoyed and exercised continuously from before the adoption of the First Amendment to this day. . . .

Under a national Constitution, fundamental First Amendment limitations on the powers of the States do not vary from community to community, but this does not mean that there are, or should or can be, fixed, uniform national standards of precisely what appeals to the "prurient interest" or is "patently offensive." These are essentially questions of fact, and our nation is simply too big and too diverse for this Court to reasonably expect that such standards could be articulated for all 50 States in a single formulation, even assuming the prerequisite consensus exists. When triers of fact are asked to decide whether "the average person, applying contemporary community standards" would consider certain materials "prurient," it would be unrealistic to require that the answer be based on some abstract formulation. The adversary system, with lay jurors as the usual ultimate factfinders in criminal prosecution, has historically permitted triers-of-fact to draw on the standards of their community, guided always by limiting instructions on the law. To require a State to structure obscenity proceedings around evidence of a national "community standard" would be an exercise in futility. . . .

It is neither realistic nor constitutionally sound to read the First Amendment as requiring that the people of Maine or Mississippi accept public depiction of conduct found tolerable in Las Vegas, or New York City. . . . People in different States vary in their tastes and attitudes, and this diversity is not to be strangled by the absolutism of imposed uniformity. . . .

The dissenting Justices sound the alarm of repression. But, in our view, to equate the free and robust exchange of ideas and political debate with commercial exploitation of obscene material demeans the grand conception of the First Amendment and its high purposes in the historic struggle for freedom. It is a "misuse of the great guarantees of free speech and free press." . . . The First Amendment protects works which, taken as a whole, have serious literary, artistic, political or scientific value, regardless of whether the government or a majority of the people approve the ideas these works represent. "The protection given speech and press was fashioned to assure unfettered interchange of *ideas* for the bringing about of political and social changes desired by the people." . . . But the public portrayal of hard core sexual conduct for its own sake, and for the ensuing commercial gain, is a different matter.

One can concede that the "sexual revolution" of recent years may have had useful byproducts in striking layers of prudery from a subject long irrationally kept from needed ventilation. But it does not follow that no regulation of patently offensive "hard core" materials is needed or permissible; civilized people do not allow unregulated access to heroin because it is a derivative of medicinal morphine. . . .

Mr. Justice Douglas, dissenting.

. . . Today the Court retreats from the earlier formulations of the constitutional test and undertakes to make new definitions. This effort, like the earlier ones, is earnest and well-intentioned. The difficulty is that we do not deal with constitutional terms, since "obscenity" is not mentioned in the Constitution or Bill of Rights. And the First Amendment makes no such exception from "the press" which it undertakes to protect nor, as I have said on other occasions, is an exception necessarily implied, for there was no recognized exception to the free press at the time the Bill of Rights was adopted which treated "obscene" publications differently from other types of papers, magazines, and books. So there are no constitutional guidelines for deciding what is and what is not "obscene." The Court is at large because we deal with tastes and standards of literature. What shocks me

may be sustenance for my neighbor. What causes one person to boil up in rage over one pamphlet or movie may reflect only his neurosis, not shared by others. We deal here with problems of censorship which, if adopted, should be done by constitutional amendment after full debate by the people.

Obscenity cases usually generate tremendous emotional outbursts. They have no business being in the courts. If a constitutional amendment authorized censorship, the censor would probably be an administrative agency. Then criminal prosecutions could follow as, if and when publishers defied the censor and sold their literature. Under that regime a publisher would know when he was on dangerous ground. Under the present regime—whether the old standards or the new ones are used—the criminal law becomes a trap. A brand new test would put a publisher behind bars under a new law improvised by the courts after the publication. . . .

My contention is that until a civil proceeding has placed a tract beyond the pale, no criminal prosecution should be sustained. For no more vivid illustration of vague and uncertain laws could be designed than those we have fashioned. As Mr. Justice Harlan has said:

The upshot of all this divergence in viewpoint is that anyone who undertakes to examine the Court's decisions since *Roth* which have held particular material obscene or not obscene would find himself in utter bewilderment. . . .

. . . The idea that the First Amendment permits government to ban publications that are "offensive" to some people puts an ominous gloss on freedom of the press. That test would make it possible to ban any paper or any journal or magazine in some benighted place. The First Amendment was designed "to invite dispute," to induce "a condition of unrest," to "create dissatisfactions with conditions as they are," and even to stir "people to anger." . . . The idea that the First Amendment permits punishment for ideas that are "offensive" to the particular judge or jury sitting in judgment is astounding. No greater leveler of speech or literature has ever been designed. To give the power to the censor, as we do today, is to make a sharp and radical break with the traditions of a free society. The First Amendment was not fashioned as a vehicle for dispensing tranquilizers to the people. Its prime function was to keep debate open to "offensive" as well as to "staid" people. The tendency throughout history has been to subdue the individual and to exalt the power of government. The use of the standard "offensive" gives authority to government that cuts the very vitals out of the First Amendment. As is intimated by the Court's opinion, the materials before us may be garbage. But so is much of what is said in political campaigns, in the daily press, on TV or over the radio. By reason of the First Amendment—and solely because of it—speakers and publishers have not been threatened or subdued because their thoughts and ideas may be "offensive" to some. . . .

Mr. Justice Brennan, with whom ***Mr. Justice Stewart*** and ***Mr. Justice Marshall*** join, dissenting. . . .

Case

FEDERAL COMMUNICATIONS COMMISSION V. PACIFICA FOUNDATION

438 U.S. 726; 98 S.Ct. 3026; 57 L.Ed. 2d. 1073 (1978)
Vote: 5–4

On Tuesday, October 30, 1973, at about 2 p.m., a New York radio station owned by the Pacifica Foundation broadcast a George Carlin monologue on the "seven dirty words you can't say on the radio." Before airing the recording, the station warned listeners of the strong content. The station received no complaints directly from listeners. Several weeks later, a man who claimed that he had heard the monologue while driving in his car with his young son filed a complaint with the Federal Communications Commission. Although it imposed no formal sanctions, the FCC indicated that the complaint would be "associated with the station's license file, and in the event that subsequent complaints are received, the Commission will then decide whether it should utilize any of the available sanctions it has been granted by Congress." Pacifica Foundation appealed the agency's action to the U.S. Court of Appeals, which reversed the FCC.

Justice Stevens delivered the opinion of the Court . . .

. . . Obscene materials have been denied the protection of the First Amendment because their content is so offensive to contemporary moral standards. . . . But the fact that society may find speech offensive is not a sufficient reason for suppressing it. Indeed, if it is the speaker's opinion that gives offense, that consequence is a reason for according it constitutional protection. For it is a central tenet of the First Amendment that the government must remain neutral in the marketplace of ideas. If there were any reason to believe that the Commission's characterization of the Carlin monologue as of-fensive could be traced to its political content—or even to the fact that it satirized contemporary attitudes about four-letter words—First Amendment protection might be required. But that is simply not this case. These words offend for the same reasons that obscenity offends. This place in the hierarchy of First Amendment values was aptly sketched by Justice Murphy when he said: "Such utterances are no essential part of any exposition of ideas, and are of such slight social value as a step to truth that any benefit that may be derived from them is clearly outweighed by the social interest in order and morality." . . .

Although these words ordinarily lack literary, political, or scientific value, they are not entirely outside the protection of the First Amendment. Some uses of even the most offensive words are unquestionably protected. . . . Indeed, we may assume, *arguendo,* that this monologue would be protected on other contexts. Nonetheless, the constitutional protection accorded to a communication containing such patently offensive sexual and excretory language need not be the same in every context. It is a characteristic of speech such as this that both its capacity to offend and its "social value," to use Justice Murphy's term, vary with the circumstances. Words that are commonplace in one setting are shocking in another. To paraphrase Justice Harlan, one man's lyric is another's vulgarity. . . .

In this case it is undisputed that the content of Pacifica's broadcast was "vulgar," "offensive," and "shocking." Because content of that character is not entitled to absolute constitutional protection under all circumstances, we must consider its context in order to determine whether the Commission's action was constitutionally permissible.

We have long recognized that each medium of expression presents special First Amendment problems. And of all forms of communication, it is broadcasting that has received the most limited First Amendment protection. Thus, although other speakers cannot be licensed except under laws that carefully define and narrow official discretion, a broadcaster may be deprived of his license and his forum if the Commission decides that such an action would serve "the public interest, convenience, and necessity." . . . Similarly, although the First Amendment protects newspaper publishers from being required to print the replies of those whom they criticize, . . . it affords no such protection to broadcasters; on the contrary, they must give free time to the victims of their criticism. . . .

The reasons for these distinctions are complex, but two have relevance to the present case. First, the broadcast media have established a uniquely pervasive presence in the lives of all Americans. Patently offensive, indecent material presented over the airwaves confronts the citizen, not only in public, but also in the privacy of the home, where the individual's right to be left alone plainly outweighs the First Amendment rights of an intruder. . . . Because the broadcast audience is constantly tuning in and out, prior warnings cannot completely protect the listener or viewer from unexpected program content. To say that one may avoid further offense by turning off the radio when he hears indecent language is like saying that the remedy for an assault is to run away after the first blow. One may hang up on an indecent phone call, but that option does not give the caller a constitutional immunity or avoid a harm that has already taken place.

Second, broadcasting is uniquely accessible to children, even those too young to read. . . . Pacifica's broadcast could have enlarged a child's vocabulary in an instant. Other forms of offensive expression may be withheld from the young without restricting the expression at its source. Bookstores and motion picture theaters, for example, may be prohibited from making indecent material available to children. We held in *Ginsberg v. New York* . . . [1968], that the government's interest in the "well-being of its young" and in supporting "parents' claim to authority in their own household" justified the regulation of otherwise protected expression. The ease with which children may obtain access to broadcast material, coupled with the concerns recognized in *Ginsberg,* amply justify special treatment of indecent broadcasting.

It is appropriate, in conclusion, to emphasize the narrowness of our holding. This case does not involve a two-way radio conversation between a cab driver and a dispatcher, or a telecast of an Elizabethan comedy. We have not decided that an occasional expletive in either setting would justify any sanction, or, indeed, that this broadcast would justify a criminal prosecution. The Commission's decision rested entirely on a nuisance rationale under which context is all-important. The concept requires consideration of a host of variables. The time of day was emphasized by the Commission. The content of the program in which the language is used will also affect the composition of the audience, and differences between radio, television, and perhaps closed-circuit transmissions, may also be relevant. As Justice Sutherland wrote, a "nuisance may be merely a right thing in the wrong place—like a pig in the parlor instead of the barnyard." . . . We simply hold that when the Commission finds that a pig has entered the parlor, the exercise of its regulatory power does not depend on proof that the pig is obscene.

The judgment of the Court of Appeals is reversed.

Justice Powell, with whom **Justice Blackmun** joins, concurring in part.

The issue . . . is whether the Commission may impose civil sanctions on a licensee radio station for broadcasting the monologue at two o'clock in the afternoon. The Commission's primary concern was to prevent the broadcast from reaching the ears of unsupervised children who were likely to be in the audience at that hour. In essence, the Commission sought to "channel" the monologue to hours when the fewest unsupervised children would be exposed to it. In my view, this consideration provides strong support for the Commission's holding.

The Court has recognized society's right to "adopt more stringent controls on communicative materials available to youths than on those available to adults." . . . This recognition stems in large part from the fact that "a child . . . is not possessed of that full capacity for individual choice which is the presupposition of First Amendment guarantees." . . . At the same time, such speech may have a deeper and more lasting negative effect on a child than on an adult. . . . The Commission properly held that the speech from which society may attempt to shield its children is not limited to that which appeals to the youthful prurient interest. The language involved in this case is as potentially degrading and harmful to children as representations of many erotic acts.

In most instances, the dissemination of this kind of speech to children may be limited without also limiting willing adults' access to it. Sellers of printed and recorded matter and exhibitors of motion pictures and live performances may be required to shut their doors to children, but such a requirement has no effect on adults' access. The difficulty is that such a physical separation of the audience cannot be accomplished in the broadcast media. . . .

In my view, the Commission was entitled to give substantial weight to this difference in reaching its decision in this case.

A second difference, not without relevance, is that broadcasting—unlike most other forms of communication—comes directly into the home, the one place where people ordinarily have the right not to be assaulted by uninvited and offensive sights and sounds. . . . The Commission also was entitled to give this factor appropriate weight in the circumstances of the instant case. This is not to say, however, that the Commission has an unrestricted license to decide what speech, protected in other media, may be banned from the airwaves in order to protect unwilling adults from momentary exposure to it in their homes. Making the sensitive judgments required in these cases is not easy. But this responsibility has been reposed initially in the Commission, and its judgment is entitled to respect. . . .

In short, I agree that on the facts of this case, the Commission's order did not violate respondent's First Amendment rights. . . .

In my view, the result in this case does not turn on whether Carlin's monologue, viewed as a whole, or the words that constitute it, have more or less "value" than a candidate's campaign speech. This is a judgment for each person to make, not one for the judges to impose upon him.

The result turns instead on the unique characteristics of the broadcast media, combined with society's right to protect its children from speech generally agreed to be inappropriate for their years, and with the interest of unwilling adults in not being assaulted by such offensive speech in their homes. Moreover, I doubt whether today's decision will prevent any adult who wishes to receive Carlin's message in Carlin's own words from doing so, and from making for himself a value judgment as to the merit of the message and words.

Justice Brennan, with whom ***Justice Marshall*** joins, dissenting.

Without question, the privacy interests of an individual in his home are substantial and deserving of significant protection. In finding these interests sufficient to justify the content regulation of protected speech, however, the Court commits two errors. First, it misconceives the nature of the privacy interest involved where an individual voluntarily chooses to admit radio communications into his home. Second, it ignores the constitutionally protected interests of both those who wish to transmit and those who desire to receive broadcasts that

many—including the FCC and this Court—might find offensive. . . .

Even if an individual who voluntarily opens his home to radio communications retains privacy interests of sufficient moment to justify a ban on protected speech if those interests are "invaded in an essentially intolerable manner," . . . the very fact that those interests are threatened only by a radio broadcast precludes any intolerable invasion of privacy; for unlike other intrusive modes of communication, such as sound trucks, "[t]he radio can be turned off," . . . —and with a minimum of effort. . . . Whatever the minimal discomfort suffered by a listener who inadvertently tunes into a program he finds offensive during the brief interval before he can simply extend his arm and switch stations or flick the "off" button, it is surely worth the candle to preserve the broadcaster's right to send, and the right of those interested to receive, a message entitled to full First Amendment protection. . . .

The Court's balance, of necessity, fails to accord proper weight to the interests of listeners who wish to hear broadcasts the FCC deems offensive. It permits majoritarian tastes completely to preclude a protected message from entering the home of a receptive, unoffended minority. No decision of this Court supports such a result. Where the individuals constituting the offended majority may freely choose to reject the material being offered, we have never found their privacy interests of such moment to warrant the suppression of speech on privacy grounds. . . .

Most parents will undoubtedly find understandable as well as commendable the Court's sympathy with the FCC's desire to prevent offensive broadcasts from reaching the ears of unsupervised children. Unfortunately, the facial appeal of this justification for radio censorship masks its constitutional insufficiency. . . .

Because the Carlin monologue is obviously not an erotic appeal to the prurient interests of children, the Court, for the first time, allows the government to prevent minors from gaining access to materials that are not obscene, and are therefore protected, as to them. It thus ignores our recent admonition that "[s]peech that is neither obscene as to youths nor subject to some other legitimate proscription cannot be suppressed solely to protect the young from ideas or images that a legislative body thinks unsuitable for them." . . . The Court's refusal to follow its own pronouncements is especially lamentable since it has the anomalous subsidiary effect, at least in the radio context at issue here, of making completely unavailable to adults material which may not constitutionally be kept even from children. This result violates in spades the principle of *Butler v. Michigan* . . . (1957). *Butler* involved a challenge to a Michigan statute that forbade the publication, sale, or distribution of printed material "tending to incite minors to violent or depraved or immoral acts, manifestly tending to the corruption of the morals of youth." Although *Roth v. United States* . . . (1957) had not yet been decided, it is at least arguable that the material the statute in *Butler* was designed to suppress could have been constitutionally denied to children. Nevertheless, this Court found the statute unconstitutional. . . .

Where, as here, the government may not prevent the exposure of minors to the suppressed material, the principle of *Butler* applies *a fortiori.* . . .

[N]either . . . the intrusive nature of radio [nor] the presence of children in the listening audience . . . can . . . support the FCC's disapproval of the Carlin monologue. These two asserted justifications are further plagued by a common failing: the lack of principled limits on their use as a basis for FCC censorship. No such limits come readily to mind, and neither of the opinions constituting the Court serve to clarify the extent to which the FCC may assert the privacy and children-in-the-audience rationales as justification for expunging from the airways protected communications the Commission finds offensive. Taken to their logical extreme, these rationales would support the cleansing of public radio of any "four-letter words" whatsoever, regardless of their context. The rationales could justify the banning from radio of a myriad of literary works, novels, poems, and plays by the likes of Shakespeare, Joyce, Hemingway, Ben Jonson, Henry Fielding, Robert Burns, and Chaucer; they could support the suppression of a good deal of political speech, such as the Nixon tapes; and they could even provide the basis for imposing sanctions for the broadcast of certain portions of the Bible. . . .

To insure that the FCC's regulation of protected speech does not exceed these bounds, my Brother Powell is content to rely upon the judgment of the Commission while my Brother Stevens deems it prudent to rely on this Court's ability accurately to assess the worth of various kinds of speech. For my own part, even accepting that this case is limited to its facts, I would place the responsibility and the right to weed worthless and offensive communications from the public airways where it belongs and where, until today, it resided: in a public free to choose those communications worthy of its attention from a marketplace unsullied by the censor's hand. . . .

[T]here runs throughout the opinions of my Brothers Powell and Stevens another vein I find equally disturbing: a depressing inability to appreciate that in our land of cultural pluralism, there are many who think, act, and talk differently from the Members of this Court, and who do not share their fragile sensibilities. It is only an acute ethnocentric myopia that enables the Court to approve the censorship of communications solely because of the words they contain. . . .

Today's decision will thus have its greatest impact on broadcasters desiring to reach, and listening audiences composed of, persons who do not share the Court's view as to which words or expressions are acceptable and who, for a variety of reasons, including a conscious desire to flout majoritarian conventions, express themselves using words that may be regarded as offensive by those from different socio-economic backgrounds. In this context, the Court's decision may be seen for what, in the broader perspective, it really is: another of the dominant culture's inevitable efforts to force those groups who do not share its mores to conform to its way of thinking, acting, and speaking.

Justice Stewart, with whom **Justice Brennan, Justice White,** and **Justice Marshall** join, dissenting.

I think that "indecent" should properly be read as meaning no more than "obscene." Since the Carlin monologue concededly was not "obscene," I believe that the Commission lacked statutory authority to ban it. Under this construction of the statute, it is unnecessary to address the difficult and important issue of the Commission's constitutional power to prohibit speech that would be constitutionally protected outside the context of electronic broadcasting. . . .

Case

RENO V. AMERICAN CIVIL LIBERTIES UNION

___ U.S. ___, 117 S.Ct. 2329, 138 L.Ed. 2d. 874 (1997)
Vote: 7–2

In this widely publicized case, the Court considers the constitutionality of the Communications Decency Act, federal legislation enacted to protect minors from "indecent" and "patently offensive" communications on the Internet.

Justice Stevens delivered the opinion of the Court.

. . . Notwithstanding the legitimacy and importance of the congressional goal of protecting children from harmful materials, we agree with the three judge District Court that the statute abridges "the freedom of speech" protected by the First Amendment. . . .

. . . In its appeal, the Government argues that the District Court erred in holding that the CDA violated both the First Amendment because it is overbroad and the Fifth Amendment because it is vague. While we discuss the vagueness of the CDA because of its relevance to the First Amendment overbreadth inquiry, we conclude that the judgment should be affirmed without reaching the Fifth Amendment issue. We begin our analysis by reviewing the principal authorities on which the Government relies. Then, after describing the overbreadth of the CDA, we consider the Government's specific contentions, including its submission that we save portions of the statute either by severance or by fashioning judicial limitations on the scope of its coverage.

In arguing for reversal, the Government contends that the CDA is plainly constitutional under three of our prior decisions: (1) *Ginsberg v. New York* . . . (1968); (2) *FCC v. Pacifica Foundation* . . . (1978); and (3) *Renton v. Playtime Theatres, Inc.,* . . . (1986). A close look at these cases, however, raises—rather than relieves—doubts concerning the constitutionality of the CDA. . . . [*Justice Stevens proceeds to discuss these precedents.*]

These precedents . . . surely do not require us to uphold the CDA and are fully consistent with the application of the most stringent review of its provisions.

In *Southeastern Promotions, Ltd. v. Conrad* . . . (1975), we observed that "[e]ach medium of expression . . . may present its own problems." Thus, some of our cases have recognized special justifications for regulation of the broadcast media that are not applicable to other speakers, see *Red Lion Broadcasting Co. v. FCC* . . . (1969); *FCC v. Pacifica Foundation* . . . (1978). In these cases, the Court relied on the history of extensive government regulation of the broadcast medium; the scarcity of available frequencies at its inception; and its "invasive" nature.

Those factors are not present in cyberspace. Neither before nor after the enactment of the CDA have the vast democratic fora of the Internet been subject to the type of government supervision and regulation that has attended the broadcast industry. Moreover, the Internet is not as "invasive" as radio or television. The District Court specifically found that "[c]ommunications over the Internet do not 'invade' an individual's home or appear on one's computer screen unbidden. Users seldom encounter content 'by accident.'" It also found that "[a]lmost all sexually explicit images are preceded by warnings as to the content," and cited testimony that " 'odds are slim' that a user would come across a sexually explicit sight by accident." . . .

Finally, unlike the conditions that prevailed when Congress first authorized regulation of the broadcast spectrum, the Internet can hardly be considered a "scarce" expressive commodity. It provides relatively unlimited, low cost capacity for communication of all kinds. The Government estimates that "[a]s many as 40 million people use the Internet today, and that figure is expected to grow to 200 million by 1999." This dynamic, multifaceted category of communication includes not only traditional print and news services, but also audio, video, and still images, as well as interactive, real time dialogue. Through the use of chat rooms, any person with a phone line can become a town crier with a voice that resonates farther than it could from any soapbox. Through the use of Web pages, mail exploders, and newsgroups, the same individual can become a pamphleteer. As the District Court found, "the content on the Internet is as diverse as human thought." . . . We agree with its conclusion that our cases provide no basis for qualifying the level of First Amendment scrutiny that should be applied to this medium.

Regardless of whether the CDA is so vague that it violates the Fifth Amendment, the many ambiguities concerning the scope of its coverage render it problematic for purposes of the First Amendment. For instance, each of the two parts of the CDA uses a different linguistic form. The first uses the word "indecent," . . . while the second speaks of material that "in context, depicts or describes, in terms patently offensive as measured by contemporary community standards, sexual or excretory activities or organs." Given the absence of a definition of either term, this difference in language will provoke uncertainty among speakers about how the two standards relate to each other and just what they mean. Could a speaker confidently assume that a serious discussion about birth control practices, homosexuality, the First Amendment issues raised by the Appendix to our *Pacifica* opinion, or the consequences of prison rape would not violate the CDA? This uncertainty undermines the likelihood that the CDA has been carefully tailored to the congressional goal of protecting minors from potentially harmful materials.

The vagueness of the CDA is a matter of special concern for two reasons. First, the CDA is a content based regulation of speech. The vagueness of such a regulation raises special First Amendment concerns because of its obvious chilling effect on free speech. . . . Second, the CDA is a criminal statute. In addition to the opprobrium and stigma of a criminal conviction, the CDA threatens violators with penalties including up to two years in prison for each act of violation. The severity of criminal sanctions may well cause speakers to remain silent rather than communicate even arguably unlawful words, ideas, and images. . . . As a practical matter, this increased deterrent effect, coupled with the "risk of discriminatory enforcement" of vague regulations, poses greater First Amendment concerns. . . .

In contrast to *Miller* [*v. California*] and our other previous cases, the CDA . . . presents a greater threat of censoring speech that, in fact, falls outside the statute's scope. Given the vague contours of the coverage of the statute, it unquestionably silences some speakers whose messages would be entitled to constitutional protection. That danger provides further reason for insisting that the statute not be overly broad. The CDA's burden on protected speech cannot be justified if it could be avoided by a more carefully drafted statute.

We are persuaded that the CDA lacks the precision that the First Amendment requires when a statute regulates the content of speech. In order to deny minors access to potentially harmful speech, the CDA effectively suppresses a large amount of speech that adults have a constitutional right to receive and to address to one another. That burden on adult speech is unacceptable if less restrictive alternatives would be at least as effective in achieving the legitimate purpose that the statute was enacted to serve.

In evaluating the free speech rights of adults, we have made it perfectly clear that "[s]exual expression which is indecent but not obscene is protected by the First Amendment." . . . Indeed, *Pacifica* itself admonished that "the fact that society may find speech offensive is not a sufficient reason for suppressing it." . . .

It is true that we have repeatedly recognized the governmental interest in protecting children from harmful materials. . . . But that interest does not justify an unnecessarily broad suppression of speech addressed to adults. As we have explained, the Government may not "reduc[e] the adult population . . . to . . . only what is fit for children." . . .

In arguing that the CDA does not so diminish adult communication, the Government relies on the incorrect factual premise that prohibiting a transmission whenever it is known that one of its recipients is a minor would not interfere with adult to adult communication. The findings of the District Court make clear that this premise is untenable.

Given the size of the potential audience for most messages, in the absence of a viable age verification process, the sender must be charged with knowing that one or more minors will likely view it. Knowledge that, for instance, one or more members of a 100 person chat group will be minor—and therefore that it would be a crime to send the group an indecent message—would surely burden communication among adults.

The District Court found that at the time of trial existing technology did not include any effective method for a sender to prevent minors from obtaining access to its communications on the Internet without also denying access to adults. The Court found no effective way to determine the age of a user who is accessing material through e mail, mail exploders, newsgroups, or chat rooms. As a practical matter, the Court also found that it would be prohibitively expensive for noncommercial—as well as some commercial—speakers who have web sites to verify that their users are adults. . . . These limitations must inevitably curtail a significant amount of adult communication on the Internet. By contrast, the District Court found that "[d]espite its limitations, currently available user based software suggests that a reasonably effective method by which parents can prevent their children from accessing sexually explicit and other material which parents may believe is inappropriate for their children will soon be widely available." . . .

The breadth of the CDA's coverage is wholly unprecedented. . . . [T]he scope of the CDA is not limited to commercial speech or commercial entities. Its open ended prohibitions embrace all nonprofit entities and individuals posting indecent messages or displaying them on their own computers in the presence of minors. The general, undefined terms "indecent" and "patently offensive" cover large amounts of nonpornographic material with serious educational or other value. Moreover, the "community standards" criterion as applied to the Internet means that any communication available to a nation wide audience will be judged by the standards of the community most likely to be offended by the message. The regulated subject matter includes any of the seven "dirty words" used in the Pacifica monologue, the use of which the Government's expert acknowledged could constitute a felony. . . . It may also extend to discussions about prison rape or safe sexual practices, artistic images that include nude subjects, and arguably the card catalogue of the Carnegie Library. . . .

The breadth of this content based restriction of speech imposes an especially heavy burden on the Government to explain why a less restrictive provision would not be as effective as the CDA. It has not done so. The arguments in this Court have referred to possible alternatives such as requiring that indecent material be "tagged" in a way that facilitates parental control of material coming into their homes, making exceptions for messages with artistic or educational value, providing some tolerance for parental choice, and regulating some portions of the Internet—such as commercial web sites—differently than others, such as chat rooms. Particularly in the light of the absence of any detailed findings by the Congress, or even hearings addressing the special problems of the CDA, we are persuaded that the CDA is not narrowly tailored if that requirement has any meaning at all. . . .

We agree with the District Court's conclusion that the CDA places an unacceptably heavy burden on protected speech, and that the defenses do not constitute the sort of "narrow tailoring" that will save an otherwise patently invalid unconstitutional provision. . . . The CDA, casting a far darker shadow over free speech, threatens to torch a large segment of the Internet community. . . .

In this Court, though not in the District Court, the Government asserts that—in addition to its interest in protecting children—its "[e]qually significant" interest in fostering the growth of the Internet provides an independent basis for upholding the constitutionality of the CDA. . . . The Government apparently assumes that the unregulated availability of "indecent" and "patently offensive" material on the Internet is driving countless citizens away from the medium because of the risk of exposing themselves or their children to harmful material.

We find this argument singularly unpersuasive. The dramatic expansion of this new marketplace of ideas contradicts the factual basis of this contention. The record demonstrates that the growth of the Internet has been and continues to be phenomenal. As a matter of constitutional tradition, in the absence of evidence to the contrary, we presume that governmental regulation of the content of speech is more likely to interfere with the free exchange of ideas than to encourage it. The interest in encouraging freedom of expression in a democratic society outweighs any theoretical but unproven benefit of censorship.

For the foregoing reasons, the judgment of the district court is affirmed.

Justice O'Connor, with whom the ***Chief Justice*** joins, concurring in the judgment in part and dissenting in part.

. . . I view the Communications Decency Act of 1996 (CDA) as little more than an attempt by Congress to create "adult zones" on the Internet. Our precedent indicates that the creation of such zones can be constitutionally sound. Despite the soundness of its purpose, however, portions of the CDA are unconstitutional because they stray from the blueprint our prior cases have developed for constructing a "zoning law" that passes constitutional muster. . . .

. . . [T]o prevail in a facial challenge, it is not enough for a plaintiff to show "some" overbreadth. Our cases require a proof of "real" and "substantial" overbreadth, . . . and appellees have not carried their burden in this case. In my view, the universe of speech constitutionally protected as to minors but banned by the CDA—i.e., the universe of material that is "patently offensive," but which nonetheless has some redeeming value for minors or does not appeal to their prurient interest—is a very small one. Appellees cite no examples of speech falling within this universe and do not attempt to explain why that universe is substantial "in relation to the statute's plainly legitimate sweep." . . . That the CDA might deny minors the right to obtain material that has some "value," . . . is largely beside the point. While discussions about prison rape or nude art . . . may have some redeeming education value for adults, they do not necessarily have any such value for minors, and . . . minors only have a First Amendment right to obtain patently offensive material that has "redeeming social importance for minors." . . . There is also no evidence in the record to support the contention that "many [e] mail transmissions from an adult to a minor are conversations between family members," . . . and no support for the legal proposition that such speech is absolutely immune from regulation. Accordingly, in my view, the CDA does not burden a substantial amount of minors' constitutionally protected speech.

. . . [T]he constitutionality of the CDA as a zoning law hinges on the extent to which it substantially interferes with the First Amendment rights of adults. Because the rights of adults are infringed only by the "display" provision and by the "indecency transmission" and "specific person" provisions as applied to communications involving more than one adult, I would invalidate the CDA only to that extent. Insofar as the "indecency transmission" and "specific person" provisions prohibit the use of indecent speech in communications between an adult and one or more minors, however, they can and should be sustained. The Court reaches a contrary conclusion, and from that holding that I respectfully dissent.

Case

EDWARDS V. SOUTH CAROLINA
372 U.S. 229; 83 S.Ct. 680; 9 L.Ed. 2d. 697 (1963)
Vote: 8–1

In this case the Court considers the issues of freedom of assembly and freedom of speech in the public forum in the context of a civil rights demonstration on the grounds of a state capitol.

Mr. Justice Stewart delivered the opinion of the Court.

The petitioners, 187 in number, were convicted in a magistrate's court in Columbia, South Carolina, of the common-law crime of breach of the peace. . . .

There was no substantial conflict in the trial evidence. Late in the morning of March 2, 1961, the petitioners, high school and college students of the Negro race, met at the Zion Baptist Church in Columbia. From there, at about noon, they walked in separate groups of about 15 to the South Carolina State House grounds, an area of two city blocks open to the general public. Their purpose was "to submit a protest to the citizens of South Carolina, along with the Legislative Bodies of South Carolina, our feelings and our dissatisfaction with the present condition of discriminatory actions against Negroes, in general, and to let them know that we were dissatisfied and that we would like for the laws which prohibited Negro privileges in this State to be removed."

Already on the State House grounds when the petitioners arrived were 30 or more law enforcement officers, who had advance knowledge that the petitioners were coming. Each group of petitioners entered the grounds through a driveway and parking area known in the record as the "horseshoe." As they entered, they were told by the law enforcement officials that "they had a right, as a citizen, to go through the State House grounds, as any other citizen has, as long as they were peaceful." During the next half hour or 45 minutes, the petitioners, in the same small groups, walked single file or two abreast in an orderly way through the grounds, each group carrying placards bearing such messages as "I am proud to be a Negro" and "Down with segregation."

During this time a crowd of some 200 to 300 onlookers had collected in the horseshoe area and on the adjacent sidewalks. There was no evidence to suggest that these onlookers were anything but curious, and no evidence at all of any threatening remarks, hostile gestures, or offensive language on the part of any member of the crowd. The City Manager testified that he recognized some of the onlookers, whom he did not identify, as "possible trouble makers," but his subsequent testimony made clear that nobody among the crowd actually caused or threatened any trouble. There was no obstruction of pedestrian or vehicular traffic within the State House grounds. No vehicle was prevented from entering or leaving the horseshoe area. Although vehicular traffic at a nearby street intersection was slowed down somewhat, an officer was dispatched to keep traffic moving. There were a number of bystanders on the public sidewalks adjacent to the State House grounds, but they all moved on when asked to do so, and there was no impediment of pedestrian traffic. Police protection at the scene was at all times sufficient to meet any foreseeable possibility of disorder.

In the situation and under the circumstances thus described, the police authorities advised the petitioners that they would be arrested if they did not disperse within 15 minutes. Instead of dispersing, the petitioners engaged in what the City manager described as "boisterous," "loud," and "flamboyant" conduct, which, as his later testimony made clear, consisted of listening to a "religious harangue" by one of their leaders, and loudly singing "The Star Spangled Banner" and other patriotic and religious songs, while stamping their feet and clapping their hands. After 15 minutes had passed, the police arrested the petitioners and marched them off to jail.

Upon this evidence the state trial court convicted the petitioners of breach of the peace, and imposed sentences ranging from a $10 fine or five days in jail, to a $100 fine or 30 days in jail. In affirming the judgments, the Supreme Court of South Carolina said that under the law of that State the offense of breach of the peace "is not susceptible for exact definition," but that the "general definition of the offense" is as follows:

In general terms, a breach of the peace is a violation of public order, a disturbance of the public tranquility, by any act or conduct inciting to violence . . . , it includes any violation of any law enacted to preserve peace and good order. It may consist of an act of violence or an act likely to produce violence. It is not necessary that the peace be actually broken to lay the foundation for a prosecution for this offense. If what is done is unjustifiable and unlawful, tending with sufficient directness to break the peace, no more is required. Nor is actual personal violence an essential element in the offense. . . .

By "peace," as used in the law in this connection, is meant the tranquility enjoyed by citizens of a municipality or community where good order reigns among its members, which is the natural right of all persons in political society. . . .

. . . It has long been established that these First Amendment freedoms are protected by the Fourteenth Amendment from invasion by the States. . . . The circumstances in this case reflect an exercise of these basic constitutional rights in their most pristine and classic form. The petitioners felt aggrieved by laws of South Carolina which allegedly "prohibited Negro privileges in this State." They peaceably assembled at the site of the State Government and there peaceably expressed their grievances "to the citizens of South Carolina, along with the Legislative Bodies of South Carolina." Not until they were told by police officials that they must disperse on pain of arrest did they do more. Even then, they but sang patriotic and religious songs after one of their leaders had delivered a "religious harangue." There was no violence or threat of violence on their part, or on the part of any member of the crowd watching them. Police protection was "ample."

This, therefore, was a far cry from the situation in *Feiner v. New York* [1951], . . . where two policemen were faced with a crowd which was "pushing, shoving, and milling around," . . . where at least one member of the crowd "threatened violence if the police did not act," . . . where "the crowd was pressing closer around petitioner and the officer," . . . and where "the speaker passes the bounds of argument or persuasion and undertakes incitement to riot." . . . And the record is barren of any evidence of "fighting words." . . .

We do not review in this case criminal convictions resulting from the even-handed application of a precise and narrowly drawn regulatory statute evincing a legislative judgment that certain specific conduct be limited or proscribed. If, for example, the petitioners had been convicted upon evidence that they had violated a law regulating traffic, or had disobeyed a law reasonably limiting the periods during which the State House grounds were open to the public, this would be a different case. . . . These petitioners were convicted of an offense so generalized as to be, in the words of the South Carolina Supreme Court, "not susceptible of exact definition." And they were convicted upon evidence which showed no more than that the opinions which they were peaceably expressing were sufficiently opposed to the views of the majority of the community to attract a crowd and necessitate police protection. . . .

Mr. Justice Clark, dissenting.

. . . Beginning, as did the South Carolina courts, with the premise that the petitioners were entitled to assemble and voice their dissatisfaction with segregation, the enlargement of constitutional protection for the conduct here is as fallacious as would be the conclusion that free speech necessarily includes the right to broadcast from a sound truck in the public street. . . . Here the petitioners were permitted without hindrance to exercise their rights of free speech and assembly. Their arrests occurred only after a situation arose in which the law-enforcement officials on the scene considered that a dangerous disturbance was imminent. The County Court found that "[t]he evidence is clear that the officers were motivated solely by a proper concern for the preservation of order and prevention of further interference with traffic upon the public streets and sidewalks." . . .

. . . [I]n *Feiner v. New York* . . . (1951), we upheld a conviction for breach of the peace in a situation no more dangerous than that found here. There the demonstration was conducted by only one person and the crowd was limited to approximately 80, as compared with the present lineup of some 200 demonstrators and 300 onlookers. There the petitioner was "endeavoring to arouse the Negro people against the whites, urging that they rise up in arms and fight for equal rights." . . . Only one person—in a city having an entirely different historical background—was exhorting adults. Here 200 youthful Negro demonstrators were being aroused to a "fever pitch" before a crowd of some 300 people who undoubtedly were hostile. Perhaps their speech was not so animated but in this setting their actions, their placards reading "You may jail our bodies but not our souls" and their chanting of "I Shall Not Be Moved," accompanied by stamping feet and clapping hands, created a much greater danger of riot and disorder. It is my belief that anyone conversant with the almost spontaneous combustion in some Southern communities in such a situation will agree that the [city's] action may well have averted a major catastrophe.

The gravity of the danger here surely needs no further explication. The imminence of that danger has been emphasized at every stage of this proceeding, from the complaints charging that the demonstrations "tended directly to immediate violence" to the State Supreme Court's affirmance on the authority of *Feiner*. . . . This record, then, shows no steps backward from a standard of "clear and present danger." But to say that the police may not intervene until the riot has occurred is like keeping out the doctor until the patient dies. I cannot subscribe to such a doctrine. . . .

Case

ADDERLEY V. FLORIDA

385 U.S. 39; 87 S.Ct. 242; 17 L.Ed. 2d. 149 (1966)
Vote: 5–4

In this case the Court reviews the convictions of thirty-two college students who marched onto the premises of the county jail in Tallahassee, Florida, to protest the arrest of other students the previous day. Are the premises of a county jail a public forum?

Mr. Justice Black delivered the opinion of the Court.

Petitioners, Harriett Louise Adderley and 31 other persons, were convicted by a jury in a joint trial in the County Judge's Court of Leon County, Florida, on a charge of "trespass with a malicious and mischievous intent" upon the premises of the county jail contrary to 821.18 of the Florida statutes set out below. Petitioners, apparently all students of the Florida A. & M. University in Tallahassee, had gone from the school to the jail about a mile away, along with many other students, to "demonstrate" at the jail their protests of arrests of other protesting students the day before, and perhaps to protest more generally against state and local policies and practices of racial segregation, including segregation of the jail. The county sheriff, legal custodian of the jail and jail grounds, tried to persuade the students to leave the jail grounds. When this did not work, he notified them that they must leave, that if they did not leave he would arrest them for trespassing, and that if they resisted he would charge them with that as well. Some of the students left but others, including petitioners, remained and they were arrested. On appeal the convictions were affirmed by the Florida Circuit Court and then by the Florida District Court of Appeal. . . . That being the highest state court to which they could appeal, petitioners applied to us for certiorari contending that, in view of petitioners' purpose to protest against jail and other segregation policies, their conviction denied them "rights of free speech, assembly, petition, due process of law and equal protection of the laws as guaranteed by the Fourteenth Amendment to the Constitution of the United States." On this "Question Presented" we granted certiorari. . . .

Petitioners have insisted from the beginning of this case that it is controlled by and must be reversed because of our prior cases of *Edwards v. South Carolina* . . . and *Cox v. Louisiana*. . . . We cannot agree. . . .

Petitioners argue that "petty criminal statutes may not be used to violate minorities' constitutional rights." This of course is true but this abstract proposition gets us nowhere in deciding this case. . . .

Petitioners here contend that "Petitioners' convictions are based on a total lack of relevant evidence." If true, this would be a denial of due process . . . Both in the petition for certiorari and in the brief on the merits petitioners state that their summary of the evidence "does not conflict with the facts contained in the Circuit Court's opinion" which was in effect affirmed by the District Court of Appeal. . . . That statement is correct and petitioners' summary of facts, as well as that of the Circuit Court, shows an abundance of facts to support the jury's verdict of guilty in this case.

In summary both these statements show testimony ample to prove this: Disturbed and upset by the arrest of their schoolmates the day before, a large number of Florida A. & M. students assembled on the school grounds and decided to march down to the county jail. Some apparently wanted to be put in jail too, along with the students already there. A group of around 200 marched from the school and arrived at the jail singing and clapping. They went directly to the jail-door entrance where they were met by a deputy sheriff, evidently surprised by their arrival. He asked them to move back, claiming they were blocking the entrance to the jail and fearing that they might attempt to enter the jail. They moved back part of the way, where they stood or sat, singing, clapping and dancing, on the jail driveway and on an adjacent grassy area upon the jail premises. This particular jail entrance and driveway were not normally used by the public, but by the sheriff's department for transporting prisoners to and from the courts several blocks away and by commercial concerns for servicing the jail. Even after their partial retreat, the demonstrators continued to block vehicular passage over this driveway up to the entrance of the jail. Someone called the sheriff who was at the moment apparently conferring with one of the state court judges about incidents connected with prior arrests for demonstrations. When the sheriff returned to the jail, he immediately inquired if all was safe inside the jail and was told it was. He then engaged in a conversation with two of the leaders. He told them that they were trespassing upon jail property and that he would give them 10 minutes to leave or he would arrest them. Neither of the leaders did anything to disperse the crowd, and one of them told the sheriff that they wanted to get arrested. A local minister talked with some of the demonstrators and told them not to enter the jail, because they could not arrest themselves, but just to remain where they were. After about 10 minutes, the sheriff, in a voice loud enough to be heard by all, told the demonstrators that he was the legal custodian of the jail and its premises, that they were trespassing on county property in violation of the law, that they should all leave forthwith or he would arrest them, and that if they attempted to resist arrest, he would charge them with that as a separate offense. Some of the group then left. Others, including all petitioners, did not leave. Some of them sat down. In a few minutes, realizing that the remaining demonstrators had no intention of leaving, the sheriff ordered his deputies to surround those remaining on jail premises and placed them, 107 demonstrators, under arrest. The sheriff unequivocally testified that he did not arrest any persons other than those who were on the jail premises. Of the three petitioners testifying, two insisted that they were arrested before they had a chance to leave, had they wanted to, and one testified that she did not intend to leave. The sheriff again explicitly testified that he did not arrest any person who was attempting to leave.

Under the foregoing testimony the jury was authorized to find that the State had proven every essential element of the crime, as it was defined by the state court. That interpretation is, of course, binding on us, leaving only the question of whether conviction of the state offense, thus defined, unconstitutionally deprives petitioners of their rights to freedom of speech, press, assembly or petition. We hold it does not. The sheriff, as jail custodian, had power, as the state courts have here held, to direct that this large crowd of people get off the grounds. There is not a shred of evidence in this record that this power was exercised, or that its exercise was sanctioned by the lower courts, because the sheriff objected to what was being sung or said by the demonstrators or because he disagreed with the objectives of their protest. The record reveals that he objected only to their presence on that part of the jail grounds reserved for jail uses. There is no evidence at all that on any other occasion had similarly large groups of the public been permitted to gather on this portion of the jail grounds for any purpose. Nothing in the Constitution of the United States prevents Florida from even-handed enforcement of its general trespass statute against those refusing to obey the sheriff's order to remove themselves from what amounted to the curtilage of the jailhouse. The State, no less than a private owner of property, has power to preserve the property under its control for the use to which it is lawfully dedicated. For this reason there is no merit to the petitioners' argument that they had a constitutional right to stay on the property, over the jail custodian's objections, because this "area chosen for the peaceful civil rights demonstration was not only 'reasonable' but also particularly appropriate. . . ." Such an argument has as its major unarticulated premise the assumption that people who want to propagandize protests or views have a constitutional right to do so whenever and however and wherever they please. That concept of constitutional law was vigorously and forthrightly rejected in . . . *Cox v. Louisiana*. . . . We reject it again. . . .

Mr. Justice Douglas, with whom the **Chief Justice, Mr. Justice Brennan,** and **Mr. Justice Fortas** concur, dissenting.

. . . The jailhouse, like an executive mansion, a legislative chamber, a courthouse, or the statehouse itself . . . is one of the seats of government, whether it be the Tower of London, the Bastille, or a small county jail. And when it houses political prisoners or those who many think are unjustly held, it is an obvious center for protest. The right to petition for the redress of grievances has an ancient history and is not limited to writing a letter or sending a telegram to a congressman; it is not confined to appearing before the local city council, or writing letters to the President or Governor or Mayor. . . .

Conventional methods of petitioning may be, and often have been, shut off to large groups of our citizens. Legislators may turn deaf ears; formal complaints may be routed endlessly through a bureaucratic maze; courts may let the wheels of justice grind very slowly. Those who do not control television and radio, those who cannot afford to advertise in newspapers or circulate elaborate pamphlets may have only a more limited type of access to public officials. Their methods should not be condemned as tactics of obstruction and harassment as long as the assembly and petition are peaceable, as these were.

There is no question that petitioners had as their purpose a protest against the arrest of Florida A. & M. students for trying to integrate public theatres. The sheriff's testimony indicates that he well understood the purpose of the rally. The petitioners who testified unequivocally stated that the group was protesting the arrests, and state and local policies of segregation, including segregation of the jail. This testimony was not contradicted or even questioned. The fact that no one gave a formal speech, that no elaborate handbills were distributed, and that the group was not laden with signs would seem to be immaterial. Such methods are not the *sine qua non* of petitioning for the redress of grievances. The group did sing "freedom" songs. And history shows that a song can be a powerful tool of protest. . . . There was no violence; no threat of violence; no attempted jail break; no storming of a prison; no plan or plot to do anything but protest. The evidence is uncontradicted that the petitioners' conduct did not upset the jailhouse routine; things went on as they normally would. None of the group entered the jail. Indeed, they moved back from the entrance as they were instructed. There was no shoving, no pushing, no disorder or threat of riot. It is said that some of the group blocked part of the driveway leading to the jail entrance. The chief jailer, to be sure, testified that vehicles would not have been able to use the driveway. Never did the students locate themselves so as to cause interference with persons or vehicles going to or coming from the jail. Indeed, it is undisputed that the sheriff and deputy sheriff, in separate cars, were able to drive up the driveway to the parking places near the entrance and that no one obstructed their path. Further, it is undisputed that the entrance to the jail was not blocked. And whenever the students were requested to move they did so. If there was congestion, the solution was a further request to move to lawns or parking areas, not complete ejection and arrest. The claim is made that a tradesman waited inside the jail because some of the protestants were sitting around and leaning on his truck. The only evidence supporting such a conclusion is the testimony of a deputy sheriff that the tradesman "came to the door . . . and then did not leave." His remaining is just as consistent with a desire to satisfy his curiosity as it is with a restraint. Finally, the fact that some of the protestants may have felt their cause so just that they were willing to be arrested for making their protest outside the jail seems wholly irrelevant. A petition is nonetheless a petition, though its futility may make martyrdom attractive.

We do violence to the First Amendment when we permit this "petition for redress of grievances" to be turned into a trespass action. It does not help to analogize this problem to the problem of picketing. Picketing is a form of protest usually directed against private interests. I do not see how rules governing picketing in general are relevant to this express constitutional right to assemble and to petition for redress of grievances. In the first place the jailhouse grounds were not marked with "no trespassing!" signs, nor does respondent claim that the public was generally excluded from the grounds. Only the sheriff's fiat transformed lawful conduct into an unlawful trespass. To say that a private owner could have done the same if the rally had taken place on private property is to speak of a different case, as an assembly and a petition for redress of grievances run to government, not to private proprietors.

The Court forgets that prior to this day our decisions have drastically limited the application of state statutes inhibiting the right to go peacefully on public property to exercise First Amendment rights. . . .

There may be some public places which are so clearly committed to other purposes that their use for the airing of grievances is anomalous. There may be some instances in which assemblies and petitions for redress of grievances are not consistent with other necessary purposes of public property. A noisy meeting may be out of keeping with the serenity of the statehouse or the quiet of the courthouse. No one, for example, would suggest that the Senate gallery is the proper place for a vociferous protest rally. And in other cases it may be necessary to adjust the right to petition for redress of grievances to the other interests inhering in the uses to which the public property is normally put. . . . But this is quite different from saying that all public places are off limits to people with grievances. . . .

Today a trespass law is used to penalize people for exercising a constitutional right. Tomorrow a disorderly conduct statute, a breach-of-the-peace statute, a vagrancy statute will be put to the same end. It is said that the sheriff did not make the arrests because of the views which petitioners espoused. That excuse is usually given,

as we know from the many cases involving arrests of minority groups for breaches of the peace, unlawful assemblies, and parading without a permit. The charge against William Penn, who preached a nonconformist doctrine in a street in London, was that he caused "a great concourse and tumult of people" in contempt of the King and "to the great disturbance of his peace." . . . That was in 1670. In modern times, also such arrests are usually sought to be justified by some legitimate function of government. Yet by allowing these orderly and civilized protests against injustice to be suppressed, we only increase the forces of frustration which the conditions of second-class citizenship are generating amongst us.

Case

44 LIQUORMART, INC. V. RHODE ISLAND

517 U.S. 484, 116 S.Ct. 1495, 134 L.Ed. 2d. 711 (1996)
Vote: 9–0

In this case the Court reviews two Rhode Island statutes regulating advertising of alcoholic beverages. One of the statutes banned any and all advertising of the prices of alcoholic beverages. The other specifically prohibited advertisements of liquor prices. State officials imposed sanctions on 44 Liquormart, Inc., for violating the advertising ban. 44 Liquormart and several other plaintiffs challenged the ban on First Amendment grounds. A federal district judge invalidated the ban, but the circuit court reversed. The Supreme Court granted cert.

Justice Stevens announced the judgment of the Court. . . .

Last Term we held that a federal law abridging a brewer's right to provide the public with accurate information about the alcoholic content of malt beverages is unconstitutional. *Rubin v. Coors Brewing Co.* (1995). We now hold that Rhode Island's statutory prohibition against advertisements that provide the public with accurate information about retail prices of alcoholic beverages is also invalid. Our holding rests on the conclusion that such an advertising ban is an abridgment of speech protected by the First Amendment and that it is not shielded from constitutional scrutiny by the Twenty-first Amendment.

. . . In accord with the role that commercial messages have long played, the law has developed to ensure that advertising provides consumers with accurate information about the availability of goods and services. In the early years, the common law, and later, statutes, served the consumers' interest in the receipt of accurate information in the commercial market by prohibiting fraudulent and misleading advertising. It was not until the 1970's, however, that this Court held that the First Amendment protected the dissemination of truthful and nonmisleading commercial messages about lawful products and services.

In *Bigelow v. Virginia* (1975), we held that it was error to assume that commercial speech was entitled to no First Amendment protection or that it was without value in the marketplace of ideas. The following Term in *Virginia Bd. of Pharmacy v. Virginia Citizens Consumer Council, Inc.*, we expanded on our holding in Bigelow and held that the State's blanket ban on advertising the price of prescription drugs violated the First Amendment.

Virginia Pharmacy Bd. reflected the conclusion that the same interest that supports regulation of potentially misleading advertising, namely the public's interest in receiving accurate commercial information, also supports an interpretation of the First Amendment that provides constitutional protection for the dissemination of accurate and nonmisleading commercial messages. . . . The opinion further explained that a State's paternalistic assumption that the public will use truthful, nonmisleading commercial information unwisely cannot justify a decision to suppress it. . . .

On the basis of these principles, our early cases uniformly struck down several broadly based bans on truthful, nonmisleading commercial speech, each of which served ends unrelated to consumer protection. . . .

At the same time, our early cases recognized that the State may regulate some types of commercial advertising more freely than other forms of protected speech. Specifically, we explained that the State may require commercial messages to "appear in such a form, or include such additional information, warnings, and disclaimers, as are necessary to prevent its being deceptive," . . . and that it may restrict some forms of aggressive sales practices that have the potential to exert "undue influence" over consumers. . . .

Virginia Pharmacy Bd. attributed the State's authority to impose these regulations in part to certain "commonsense differences" that exist between commercial messages and other types of protected expression. . . .

In *Central Hudson Gas & Elec. Corp. v. Public Serv. Comm'n of N. Y.* (1980), we took stock of our developing commercial speech jurisprudence. In that case, we considered a regulation "completely" banning all promotional advertising by electric utilities. Our decision acknowledged the special features of commercial speech but identified the serious First Amendment concerns that attend blanket advertising prohibitions that do not protect consumers from commercial harms.

Five Members of the Court recognized that the state interest in the conservation of energy was substantial, and that there was "an immediate connection between advertising and demand for electricity." Nevertheless, they concluded that the regulation was invalid because the Commission had failed to make a showing that a more limited speech regulation would not have adequately served the State's interest.

. . . [T]he Court concluded that "special care" should attend the review of such blanket bans, and it pointedly remarked that "in recent years this Court has not approved a blanket ban on commercial speech unless the speech itself was flawed in some way, either because it was deceptive or related to unlawful activity." . . .

. . . When a State regulates commercial messages to protect consumers from misleading, deceptive, or aggressive sales practices, or requires the disclosure of beneficial consumer information, the purpose of its regulation is consistent with the reasons for according constitutional protection to commercial speech and therefore justifies less than strict review. However, when a State entirely prohibits the dissemination of truthful, nonmisleading commercial messages for reasons unrelated to the preservation of a fair bargaining process, there is far less reason to depart from the rigorous review that the First Amendment generally demands. . . .

Precisely because bans against truthful, nonmisleading commercial speech rarely seek to protect consumers from either deception or overreaching, they usually rest solely on the offensive assumption that the public will respond "irrationally" to the truth. The First Amendment directs us to be especially skeptical of regulations that seek to keep people in the dark for what the government perceives to be their own good. . . .

In this case, there is no question that Rhode Island's price advertising ban constitutes a blanket prohibition against truthful, nonmisleading speech about a lawful product. There is also no question that the ban serves an end unrelated to consumer protection. Accordingly, we must review the price advertising ban with "special care," . . . mindful that speech prohibitions of this type rarely survive constitutional review.

The State argues that the price advertising prohibition should nevertheless be upheld because it directly advances the State's substantial interest in promoting temperance, and because it is no more extensive than necessary. . . . Although there is some confusion as to what Rhode Island means by temperance, we assume that the State asserts an interest in reducing alcohol consumption. . . .

We can agree that common sense supports the conclusion that a prohibition against price advertising, like a collusive agreement among competitors to refrain from such advertising, will tend to mitigate competition and maintain prices at a higher level than would prevail in a completely free market. . . . However, without any findings of fact, or indeed any evidentiary support whatsoever, we cannot agree with the assertion that the price advertising ban will significantly advance the State's interest in promoting temperance.

. . . [T]he State has presented no evidence to suggest that its speech prohibition will significantly reduce marketwide consumption. . . .

The State also cannot satisfy the requirement that its restriction on speech be no more extensive than necessary. It is perfectly obvious that alternative forms of regulation that would not involve any restriction on speech would be more likely to achieve the State's goal of promoting temperance. As the State's own expert conceded, higher prices can be maintained either by direct regulation or by increased taxation. Per capita purchases could be limited as is the case with prescription drugs. Even educational campaigns focused on the problems of excessive, or even moderate, drinking might prove to be more effective.

As a result, even under the less than strict standard that generally applies in commercial speech cases, the State has failed to establish a "reasonable fit" between its abridgment of speech and its temperance goal. It necessarily follows that the price advertising ban cannot survive the more stringent constitutional review that *Central Hudson* itself concluded was appropriate for the complete suppression of truthful, nonmisleading commercial speech. . . .

The State responds by arguing that it merely exercised appropriate "legislative judgment" in determining that a price advertising ban would best promote temperance. Relying on the *Central Hudson* analysis set forth in *Posadas de Puerto Rico Associates v. Tourism Co.* . . . (1986) and *United States v. Edge Broadcasting Co.* (1993), Rhode Island first argues that, because expert opinions as to the effectiveness of the price advertising ban "go both ways," the Court of Appeals correctly concluded that the ban constituted a "reasonable choice" by the legislature. The State next contends that precedent requires us to give particular deference to that legislative choice because the State could, if it chose, ban the sale of alcoholic beverages outright. Finally, the State argues that deference is appropriate because alcoholic beverages are so-called "vice" products. We consider each of these contentions in turn. . . .

Given our longstanding hostility to commercial speech regulation of this type, *Posadas* clearly erred in concluding that it was "up to the legislature" to choose suppression over a less speech-restrictive policy. The *Posadas* majority's conclusion on that point cannot be reconciled with the unbroken line of prior cases striking down similarly broad regulations on truthful, nonmisleading advertising when non-speech-related alternatives were available.

Because the 5-to-4 decision in *Posadas* marked such a sharp break from our prior precedent, and because it concerned a constitutional question about which this Court is the final arbiter, we decline to give force to its highly deferential approach. Instead, in keeping with our prior holdings, we conclude that a state legislature does not have the broad discretion to suppress truthful, nonmisleading information for paternalistic purposes that the *Posadas* majority was willing to tolerate.

We also cannot accept the State's second contention. . . . The text of the First Amendment makes clear that the Constitution presumes that attempts to regulate speech are more dangerous than attempts to

regulate conduct. That presumption accords with the essential role that the free flow of information plays in a democratic society. As a result, the First Amendment directs that government may not suppress speech as easily as it may suppress conduct, and that speech restrictions cannot be treated as simply another means that the government may use to achieve its ends. . . .

Finally, we find unpersuasive the State's contention that . . . the price advertising ban should be upheld because it targets commercial speech that pertains to a "vice" activity. . . . The respondents misread our precedent. Our decision last Term striking down an alcohol-related advertising restriction effectively rejected the very contention respondents now make. . . .

From 1919 until 1933, the Eighteenth Amendment to the Constitution totally prohibited "the manufacture, sale, or transportation of intoxicating liquors" in the United States and its territories. Section 1 of the Twenty-first Amendment repealed that prohibition, and 2 delegated to the several States the power to prohibit commerce in, or the use of, alcoholic beverages. . . .

As is clear, the text of the Twenty-first Amendment supports the view that, while it grants the States authority over commerce that might otherwise be reserved to the Federal Government, it places no limit whatsoever on other constitutional provisions. Nevertheless, Rhode Island argues, and the Court of Appeals agreed, that in this case the Twenty-first Amendment tilts the First Amendment analysis in the State's favor. . . .

[A]lthough the Twenty-first Amendment limits the effect of the dormant Commerce Clause on a State's regulatory power over the delivery or use of intoxicating beverages within its borders, "the Amendment does not license the States to ignore their obligations under other provisions of the Constitution." . . . That general conclusion reflects our specific holdings that the Twenty-first Amendment does not in any way diminish the force of the Supremacy Clause, . . . the Establishment Clause, . . . or the Equal Protection Clause. . . . We see no reason why the First Amendment should not also be included in that list. Accordingly, we now hold that the Twenty-first Amendment does not qualify the constitutional prohibition against laws abridging the freedom of speech embodied in the First Amendment. The Twenty-first Amendment, therefore, cannot save Rhode Island's ban on liquor price advertising.

Because Rhode Island has failed to carry its heavy burden of justifying its complete ban on price advertising, we conclude that [the challenged statutes] abridge speech in violation of the First Amendment as made applicable to the States by the Due Process Clause of the Fourteenth Amendment. The judgment of the Court of Appeals is therefore reversed. . . .

Justice Thomas, concurring in part and concurring in the judgment.

In cases such as this, in which the government's asserted interest is to keep legal users of a product or service ignorant in order to manipulate their choices in the marketplace, the balancing test adopted in *Central Hudson Gas & Elec. Corp. v. Public Serv. Comm'n of N. Y.* (1980) should not be applied, in my view. Rather, such an "interest" is per se illegitimate and can no more justify regulation of "commercial" speech than it can justify regulation of "noncommercial" speech. . . .

I do not join the principal opinion's application of the *Central Hudson* balancing test because I do not believe that such a test should be applied to a restriction of "commercial" speech, at least when, as here, the asserted interest is one that is to be achieved through keeping would-be recipients of the speech in the dark. Application of the advancement-of-state-interest prong of *Central Hudson* makes little sense to me in such circumstances. Faulting the State for failing to show that its price advertising ban decreases alcohol consumption "significantly," as Justice Stevens does, seems to imply that if the State had been more successful at keeping consumers ignorant and thereby decreasing their consumption, then the restriction might have been upheld. This contradicts *Virginia Pharmacy Bd.*'s rationale for protecting "commercial" speech in the first instance. . . .

Although the Court took a sudden turn away from *Virginia Pharmacy Bd.* in *Central Hudson,* it has never explained why manipulating the choices of consumers by keeping them ignorant is more legitimate when the ignorance is maintained through suppression of "commercial" speech than when the same ignorance is maintained through suppression of "noncommercial" speech. The courts, including this Court, have found the *Central Hudson* "test" to be, as a general matter, very difficult to apply with any uniformity. This may result in part from the inherently nondeterminative nature of a case-by-case balancing "test" unaccompanied by any categorical rules, and the consequent likelihood that individual judicial preferences will govern application of the test. . . . Rather than continuing to apply a test that makes no sense to me when the asserted state interest is of the type involved here, I would return to the reasoning and holding of *Virginia Pharmacy Bd.* Under that decision, these restrictions fall.

Justice O'Connor, with whom the **Chief Justice, Justice Souter,** and **Justice Breyer** join, concurring in the judgment.

Rhode Island prohibits advertisement of the retail price of alcoholic beverages, except at the place of sale. The State's only asserted justification for this ban is that it promotes temperance by increasing the cost of alcoholic beverages. I agree with the Court that Rhode Island's price-advertising ban is invalid. I would resolve this case more narrowly, however, by applying our established *Central Hudson* test to determine whether this commercial-speech regulation survives First Amendment scrutiny.

Under that test, we first determine whether the speech at issue concerns lawful activity and is not misleading, and whether the asserted governmental interest is substantial. If both these conditions are met, we must decide whether the regulation "directly advances the governmental interest asserted, and whether it is not more extensive than is necessary to serve that interest." . . .

Given the means by which this regulation purportedly serves the State's interest, our conclusion is plain: Rhode Island's regulation fails First Amendment scrutiny.

Both parties agree that the first two prongs of the *Central Hudson* test are met. Even if we assume *arguendo* that Rhode Island's regulation also satisfies the requirement that it directly advance the governmental interest, Rhode Island's regulation fails the final prong; that is, its ban is more extensive than necessary to serve the State's interest.

As we have explained, in order for a speech restriction to pass muster under the final prong, there must be a fit between the legislature's goal and method, "a fit that is not necessarily perfect, but reasonable; that represents not necessarily the single best disposition but one whose scope is in proportion to the interest served." . . . While the State need not employ the least restrictive means to accomplish its goal, the fit between means and ends must be "narrowly tailored." The scope of the restriction on speech must be reasonably, though it need not be perfectly, targeted to address the harm intended to be regulated. . . . The State's regulation must indicate a "carefu[l] calculat[ion of] the costs and benefits associated with the burden on speech imposed by its prohibition." . . . The availability of less burdensome alternatives to reach the stated goal signals that the fit between the legislature's ends and the means chosen to accomplish those ends may be too imprecise to withstand First

Amendment scrutiny. . . . If alternative channels permit communication of the restricted speech, the regulation is more likely to be considered reasonable.

Rhode Island offers one, and only one, justification for its ban on price advertising. Rhode Island says that the ban is intended to keep alcohol prices high as a way to keep consumption low. . . .

The fit between Rhode Island's method and this particular goal is not reasonable. If the target is simply higher prices generally to discourage consumption, the regulation imposes too great, and unnecessary, a prohibition on speech in order to achieve it. The State has

other methods at its disposal—methods that would more directly accomplish this stated goal without intruding on sellers' ability to provide truthful, nonmisleading information to customers. . . .

Rhode Island's prohibition on alcohol-price advertising, as a means to keep alcohol prices high and consumption low, cannot survive First Amendment scrutiny. The Twenty-first Amendment cannot save this otherwise invalid regulation. While I agree with the Court's finding that the regulation is invalid, I would decide that issue on narrower grounds. I therefore concur in the judgment.

Case

NATIONAL ENDOWMENT FOR THE ARTS V. FINLEY

WL 332991(U.S.) (June 25, 1998)
Vote: 8–1

Here the Court considers a statutory requirement that the National Endowment for the Arts take into account "general standards of decency" in deciding which artistic endeavors will receive public support. In a case brought by performance artist Karen Finley, a federal district judge in California declared the provision unconstitutional under the First Amendment. The Ninth Circuit Court of Appeals affirmed.

Justice O'Connor delivered the opinion of the Court.

The National Foundation on the Arts and Humanities Act, as amended in 1990, requires the Chairperson of the National Endowment for the Arts (NEA) to ensure that "artistic excellence and artistic merit are the criteria by which [grant] applications are judged, taking into consideration general standards of decency and respect for the diverse beliefs and values of the American public." 20 U.S.C. § 954(d)(1). . . .

Since 1965, the NEA has distributed over three billion dollars in grants to individuals and organizations, funding that has served as a catalyst for increased state, corporate, and foundation support for the arts. Congress has recently restricted the availability of federal funding for individual artists, confining grants primarily to qualifying organizations and state arts agencies, and constraining sub-granting. . . . By far the largest portion of the grants distributed in fiscal year 1998 were awarded directly to state arts agencies. In the remaining cate-

gories, the most substantial grants were allocated to symphony orchestras, fine arts museums, dance theater foundations, and opera associations. . . .

Throughout the NEA's history, only a handful of the agency's roughly 100,000 awards have generated formal complaints about misapplied funds or abuse of the public's trust. Two provocative works, however, prompted public controversy in 1989 and led to congressional revaluation of the NEA's funding priorities and efforts to increase oversight of its grant-making procedures. The Institute of Contemporary Art at the University of Pennsylvania had used $30,000 of a visual arts grant it received from the NEA to fund a 1989 retrospective of photographer Robert Mapplethorpe's work. The exhibit, entitled The Perfect Moment , included homoerotic photographs that several Members of Congress condemned as pornographic. . . . Members also denounced artist Andres Serrano's work Piss Christ, a photograph of a crucifix immersed in urine. . . . Serrano had been awarded a $15,000 grant from the Southeast Center for Contemporary Art, an organization that received NEA support.

When considering the NEA's appropriations for fiscal year 1990, Congress reacted to the controversy surrounding the Mapplethorpe and Serrano photographs by eliminating $45,000 from the agency's budget, the precise amount contributed to the two exhibits by NEA grant recipients. Congress also enacted an amendment providing that no NEA funds "may be used to promote, disseminate, or produce materials which in the judgment of [the NEA] may be considered obscene, including but not limited to, depictions of sadomasochism, homoeroticism, the sexual exploitation of children, or individuals engaged in sex acts and which, when taken as a whole, do not have serious literary, artistic, political, or scientific value." . . . The NEA implemented Congress' mandate by instituting a requirement that all grantees certify in writing that they would not utilize federal funding to engage in projects inconsistent with the criteria in the 1990 appropriations bill. That certification requirement was subsequently invalidated as unconstitutionally vague by a Federal District Court . . . and the NEA did not appeal the decision.

In the 1990 appropriations bill, Congress also agreed to create an Independent Commission of constitutional law scholars to review the NEA's grant-making procedures and assess the possibility of more focused standards for public arts funding. The Commission's report, issued in September 1990, concluded that there is no constitutional obligation to provide arts funding, but also recommended that the NEA rescind the certification requirement and cautioned against legislation setting forth any content restrictions. Instead, the Commission suggested procedural changes to enhance the role of advisory panels and a statutory reaffirmation of "the high place the nation accords to the fostering of mutual respect for the disparate beliefs and values among us." . . .

Informed by the Commission's recommendations, and cognizant of pending judicial challenges to the funding limitations in the 1990 appropriations bill, Congress debated several proposals to reform the NEA's grant-making process when it considered the agency's reauthorization in the fall of 1990. . . . Ultimately, Congress adopted . . . a bipartisan compromise between Members opposing any funding restrictions and those favoring some guidance to the agency. In relevant part, [this compromise] became § 954(d)(1). . . .

. . . Respondents raise a facial constitutional challenge to § 954(d)(1), and consequently they confront "a heavy burden" in advancing their claim. . . . Facial invalidation "is, manifestly, strong medicine" that "has been employed by the Court sparingly and only as a last resort." . . . To prevail, respondents must demonstrate a substantial risk that application of the provision will lead to the suppression of speech. . . .

Respondents argue that the provision is a paradigmatic example of viewpoint discrimination because it rejects any artistic speech that either fails to respect mainstream values or offends standards of decency. The premise of respondents' claim is that § 954(d)(1) constrains the agency's ability to fund certain categories of artistic expression. The NEA, however, reads the provision as merely hortatory, and contends that it stops well short of an absolute restriction. Section 954(d)(1) adds "considerations" to the grant-making process; it does not preclude awards to projects that might be deemed

"indecent" or "disrespectful," nor place conditions on grants, or even specify that those factors must be given any particular weight in reviewing an application. . . .

Furthermore, like the plain language of § 954(d), the political context surrounding the adoption of the "decency and respect" clause is inconsistent with respondents' assertion that the provision compels the NEA to deny funding on the basis of viewpoint discriminatory criteria. The legislation was a bipartisan proposal introduced as a counterweight to amendments aimed at eliminating the NEA's funding or substantially constraining its grant-making authority. . . .

That § 954(d)(1) admonishes the NEA merely to take "decency and respect" into consideration, and that the legislation was aimed at reforming procedures rather than precluding speech, undercut respondents' argument that the provision inevitably will be utilized as a tool for invidious viewpoint discrimination. In cases where we have struck down legislation as facially unconstitutional, the dangers were both more evident and more substantial. . . .

. . . Thus, we do not perceive a realistic danger that § 954(d)(1) will compromise First Amendment values. As respondents' own arguments demonstrate, the considerations that the provision introduces, by their nature, do not engender the kind of directed viewpoint discrimination that would prompt this Court to invalidate a statute on its face.

Respondents' claim that the provision is facially unconstitutional may be reduced to the argument that the criteria in § 954(d)(1) are sufficiently subjective that the agency could utilize them to engage in viewpoint discrimination. Given the varied interpretations of the criteria and the vague exhortation to "take them into consideration," it seems unlikely that this provision will introduce any greater element of selectivity than the determination of "artistic excellence" itself. And we are reluctant, in any event, to invalidate legislation "on the basis of its hypothetical application to situations not before the Court." . . .

Finally, although the First Amendment certainly has application in the subsidy context, we note that the Government may allocate competitive funding according to criteria that would be impermissible were direct regulation of speech or a criminal penalty at stake. So long as legislation does not infringe on other constitutionally protected rights, Congress has wide latitude to set spending priorities. . . .

Section 954(d)(1) merely adds some imprecise considerations to an already subjective selection process. It does not, on its face, impermissibly infringe on First or Fifth Amendment rights. Accordingly, the judgment of the Court of Appeals is reversed and the case is remanded for further proceedings consistent with this opinion.

Justice Scalia, with whom **Justice Thomas** joins, concurring in the judgment.

"The operation was a success, but the patient died." What such a procedure is to medicine, the Court's opinion in this case is to law. It sustains the constitutionality of § 954(d)(1) by gutting it. The most avid congressional opponents of the provision could not have asked for more. I write separately because, unlike the Court, I think that § 954(d)(1) must be evaluated as written, rather than as distorted by the agency it was meant to control. By its terms, it establishes content and viewpoint-based criteria upon which grant applications are to be evaluated. And that is perfectly constitutional. . . .

The nub of the difference between me and the Court is that I regard the distinction between "abridging" speech and funding it as a fundamental divide, on this side of which the First Amendment is inapplicable. The Court, by contrast, seems to believe that the First Amendment, despite its words, has some ineffable effect upon funding, imposing constraints of an indeterminate nature which it announces (without troubling to enunciate any particular test) are not violated by the statute here-or, more accurately, are not violated by the quite different, emasculated statute that it imagines. "[T]he Government," it says, "may allocate competitive funding according to criteria that would be impermissible were direct regulation of speech or a criminal penalty at stake." . . . The government, I think, may allocate both competitive and noncompetitive funding ad libitum, insofar as the First Amendment is concerned. Finally, what is true of the First Amendment is also true of the constitutional rule against vague legislation: it has no application to funding. Insofar as it bears upon First Amendment concerns, the vagueness doctrine addresses the problems that arise from government regulation of expressive conduct, . . . not government grant programs. In the former context, vagueness produces an abridgment of lawful speech; in the latter it produces, at worst, a waste of money. I cannot refrain from observing, however, that if the vagueness doctrine were applicable, the agency charged with making grants under a statutory standard of "artistic excellence"-and which has itself thought that standard met by everything from the playing of Beethoven to a depiction of a crucifix immersed in urine-would be of more dubious constitutional validity than the "decency" and "respect" limitations that respondents (who demand to be judged on the same strict standard of "artistic excellence") have the humorlessness to call too vague.

In its laudatory description of the accomplishments of the NEA, . . . the Court notes with satisfaction that "only a handful of the agency's roughly 100,000 awards have generated formal complaints." . . . The Congress that felt it necessary to enact § 954(d)(1) evidently thought it much more noteworthy that any money exacted from American taxpayers had been used to produce a crucifix immersed in urine, or a display of homoerotic photographs. It is no secret that the provision was prompted by, and directed at, the funding of such offensive productions. Instead of banning the funding of such productions absolutely, which I think would have been entirely constitutional, Congress took the lesser step of requiring them to be disfavored in the evaluation of grant applications. The Court's opinion today renders even that lesser step a nullity. For that reason, I concur only in the judgment.

Justice Souter, dissenting.

. . . The decency and respect proviso mandates viewpoint-based decisions in the disbursement of government subsidies, and the Government has wholly failed to explain why the statute should be afforded an exemption from the fundamental rule of the First Amendment that viewpoint discrimination in the exercise of public authority over expressive activity is unconstitutional. . . .

"If there is a bedrock principle underlying the First Amendment, it is that the government may not prohibit the expression of an idea simply because society finds the idea itself offensive or disagreeable." . . . Because this principle applies not only to affirmative suppression of speech, but also to disqualification for government favors, Congress is generally not permitted to pivot discrimination against otherwise protected speech on the offensiveness or unacceptability of the views it expresses. . . .

It goes without saying that artistic expression lies within this First Amendment protection. . . . The constitutional protection of artistic works turns not on the political significance that may be attributable to such productions, though they may indeed comment on the political, but simply on their expressive character, which falls within a spectrum of protected "speech" extending outward from the core of overtly political declarations. Put differently, art is entitled to full protection because our "cultural life," just like our native politics, "rests upon [the] ideal" of governmental viewpoint neutrality. . . . When called upon to vindicate this ideal, we characteristically begin by asking "whether the government has adopted a regulation of speech because of disagreement with the message it conveys. The government's purpose is the controlling consideration." . . . The answer in this case is damning. One need do nothing more than read the text of the statute to conclude that Congress's purpose in imposing the decency and respect criteria was to prevent the funding of art that conveys an offensive message; the decency and respect provision on its face is quintessentially viewpoint based, and quotations from the Congressional Record merely confirm the obvious legislative purpose. In the words of a cosponsor of the bill that enacted the proviso, "[w]orks which deeply offend the sensibilities of significant portions of the public ought not to be supported with public funds." . . . Another supporter of the bill observed that

"the Endowment's support for artists like Robert Mapplethorpe and Andre[s] Serrano has offended and angered many citizens," behooving "Congress . . . to listen to these complaints about the NEA and make sure that exhibits like [these] are not funded again." . . . Indeed, if there were any question at all about what Congress had in mind, a definitive answer comes in the succinctly accurate remark of the proviso's author, that the bill "add[s] to the criteria of artistic excellence and artistic merit, a shell, a screen, a viewpoint that must be constantly taken into account." . . .

Since the [challenged legislation] is substantially overbroad and carries with it a significant power to chill artistic production and display, it should be struck down on its face.

Case

HURLEY V. IRISH-AMERICAN GAY, LESBIAN AND BISEXUAL GROUP OF BOSTON

515 U.S. 557, 115 S.Ct. 2338, 132 L.Ed. 2d. 487 (1995)
Vote: 9–0

The issue here is whether the state of Massachusetts can require organizers of the annual St. Patrick's Day parade in Boston to include a "gay pride" group in the parade.

Justice Souter delivered the opinion of the Court.

. . . March 17 is set aside for two celebrations in South Boston. As early as 1737, some people in Boston observed the feast of the apostle to Ireland, and since 1776 the day has marked the evacuation of royal troops and Loyalists from the city, prompted by the guns captured at Ticonderoga and set up on Dorchester Heights under General Washington's command. . . . Although the General Court of Massachusetts did not officially designate March 17 as Evacuation Day until 1938, . . . the City Council of Boston had previously sponsored public celebrations of Evacuation Day, including notable commemorations on the centennial in 1876, and on the 125th anniversary in 1901, with its parade, salute, concert, and fireworks display. . . .

The tradition of formal sponsorship by the city came to an end in 1947, however, when Mayor James Michael

Curley himself granted authority to organize and conduct the St. Patrick's Day–Evacuation Day Parade to the petitioner South Boston Allied War Veterans Council, an unincorporated association of individuals elected from various South Boston veterans groups. Every year since that time, the Council has applied for and received a permit for the parade, which at times has included as many as 20,000 marchers and drawn up to 1 million watchers. No other applicant has ever applied for that permit. . . . Through 1992, the city allowed the Council to use the city's official seal, and provided printing services as well as direct funding.

1992 was the year that a number of gay, lesbian, and bisexual descendants of the Irish immigrants joined together with other supporters to form the respondent organization, GLIB, to march in the parade as a way to express pride in their Irish heritage as openly gay, lesbian, and bisexual individuals, to demonstrate that there are such men and women among those so descended, and to express their solidarity with like individuals who sought to march in New York's St. Patrick's Day Parade. . . . Although the Council denied GLIB's application to take part in the 1992 parade, GLIB obtained a state-court order to include its contingent, which marched— uneventfully—among that year's 10,000 participants and 750,000 spectators. . . .

In 1993, after the Council had again refused to admit GLIB to the upcoming parade, the organization and some of its members filed this suit . . . alleging violations of the State and Federal Constitutions and of the state public accommodations law, which prohibits "any distinction, discrimination or restriction on account of . . . sexual orientation . . . relative to the admission of any person to, or treatment in any place of public accommodation, resort or amusement." . . . After finding that "[f]or at least the past 47 years, the Parade has traveled the same basic route along the public streets of South Boston, providing entertainment, amusement, and recreation to participants and spectators alike," the state trial court ruled that the parade fell within the statutory definition of a public accommodation, which includes "any place . . . which is open to and accepts or solicits the patronage of the general public and, without limiting the generality of this definition, whether or not it be . . . (6) a boardwalk or other public highway [or] . . . (8) a place of public amusement, recreation, sport, exercise or entertainment." . . . The court found that the Council had no written criteria and employed no particular procedures for admission, voted on new applications in batches, had occasionally admitted groups who simply showed up at the parade without having submitted an application, and did "not generally inquire into the specific messages or views of each applicant." . . .

The court consequently rejected the Council's contention that the parade was "private" (in the sense of being exclusive), holding instead that "the lack of genuine selectivity in choosing participants and sponsors demonstrates that the Parade is a public event." . . . It found the parade to be "eclectic," containing a wide variety of "patriotic, commercial, political, moral, artistic, religious, athletic, public service, trade union, and eleemosynary themes," as well as conflicting messages. . . . While noting that the Council had indeed excluded the Ku Klux Klan and ROAR (an antibusing group), . . . it attributed little significance to these facts, concluding ultimately that "[t]he only common theme among the participants and sponsors is their public involvement in the Parade." . . . The court rejected the Council's assertion that the exclusion of "groups with sexual themes merely formalized [the fact] that the Parade expresses traditional religious and social values," . . . and found the Council's "final position [to be] that GLIB would be excluded because of its values and its message, i.e., its members' sexual orientation." . . . This position, in the court's view, was not only violative of the public accommodations law but "paradoxical" as well, since "a proper celebration of St. Patrick's and Evacuation Day requires diversity and inclusiveness." . . . The court rejected the notion that GLIB's admission would trample on the Council's First Amendment rights since

the court understood that constitutional protection of any interest in expressive association would "requir[e] focus on a specific message, theme, or group" absent from the parade. . . . "Given the [Council's] lack of selectivity in choosing participants and failure to circumscribe the marchers' message," the court found it "impossible to discern any specific expressive purpose entitling the Parade to protection under the First Amendment." . . . It concluded that the parade is "not an exercise of [the Council's] constitutionally protected right of expressive association," but instead "an open recreational event that is subject to the public accommodations law." . . .

The court held that because the statute did not mandate inclusion of GLIB but only prohibited discrimination based on sexual orientation, any infringement on the Council's right to expressive association was only "incidental" and "no greater than necessary to accomplish the statute's legitimate purpose" of eradicating discrimination. . . . Accordingly, it ruled that "GLIB is entitled to participate in the Parade on the same terms and conditions as other participants." . . .

The Supreme Judicial Court of Massachusetts affirmed, seeing nothing clearly erroneous in the trial judge's findings that GLIB was excluded from the parade based on the sexual orientation of its members, that it was impossible to detect an expressive purpose in the parade, that there was no state action, and that the parade was a public accommodation within the meaning of [the law]. . . . Turning to petitioners' First Amendment claim that application of the public accommodations law to the parade violated their freedom of speech (as distinguished from their right to expressive association, raised in the trial court), the court's majority held that it need not decide on the particular First Amendment theory involved "because, as the [trial] judge found, it is 'impossible to discern any specific expressive purpose entitling the parade to protection under the First Amendment.' " . . . The defendants had thus failed at the trial level "to demonstrate that the parade truly was an exercise of . . . First Amendment rights," . . . and on appeal nothing indicated to the majority of the Supreme Judicial Court that the trial judge's assessment of the evidence on this point was clearly erroneous. . . . The court rejected petitioners' further challenge to the law as overbroad, holding that it does not, on its face, regulate speech, does not let public officials examine the content of speech, and would not be interpreted as reaching speech. . . . Finally, the court rejected the challenge that the public accommodations law was unconstitutionally vague, holding that this case did not present an issue of speech and that the law gave persons of ordinary intelligence a reasonable opportunity to know what was prohibited. . . .

We granted certiorari to determine whether the requirement to admit a parade contingent expressing a message not of the private organizers' own choosing violates the First Amendment. . . . We hold that it does and reverse.

II

Given the scope of the issues as originally joined in this case, it is worth noting some that have fallen aside in the course of the litigation, before reaching us. Although the Council presents us with a First Amendment claim, respondents do not. Neither do they press a claim that the Council's action has denied them equal protection of the laws in violation of the Fourteenth Amendment. While the guarantees of free speech and equal protection guard only against encroachment by the government and "erec[t] no shield against merely private conduct," . . . respondents originally argued that the Council's conduct was not purely private, but had the character of state action. The trial court's review of the city's involvement led it to find otherwise, however, and although the Supreme Judicial Court did not squarely address the issue, it appears to have affirmed the trial court's decision on that point as well as the others. In any event, respondents have not brought that question up either in a crosspetition for certiorari or in their briefs filed in this Court. When asked at oral argument whether they challenged the conclusion by the Massachusetts' courts that no state action is involved in the parade, respondents' counsel answered that they "do not press that issue here". . . . In this Court, then, their claim for inclusion in the parade rests solely on the Massachusetts public accommodations law.

There is no corresponding concession from the other side, however, and certainly not to the state courts' characterization of the parade as lacking the element of expression for purposes of the First Amendment. Accordingly, our review of petitioners' claim that their activity is indeed in the nature of protected speech carries with it a constitutional duty to conduct an independent examination of the record as a whole, without deference to the trial court. . . . The "requirement of independent appellate review . . . is a rule of federal constitutional law," . . . which does not limit our deference to a trial court on matters of witness credibility, . . . but which generally requires us to "review the finding of facts by a State court . . . where a conclusion of law as to a Federal right and a

finding of fact are so intermingled as to make it necessary, in order to pass upon the Federal question, to analyze the facts." . . . This obligation rests upon us simply because the reaches of the First Amendment are ultimately defined by the facts it is held to embrace, and we must thus decide for ourselves whether a given course of conduct falls on the near or far side of the line of constitutional protection. . . . Even where a speech case has originally been tried in a federal court, subject to the provision of Federal Rule of Civil Procedure 52(a) that "[f]indings of fact . . . shall not be set aside unless clearly erroneous," we are obliged to make a fresh examination of crucial facts. Hence, in this case, though we are confronted with the state courts' conclusion that the factual characteristics of petitioners' activity place it within the vast realm of non-expressive conduct, our obligation is to " 'make an independent examination of the whole record,' . . . so as to assure ourselves that th[is] judgment does not constitute a forbidden intrusion on the field of free expression." . . .

III

A

If there were no reason for a group of people to march from here to there except to reach a destination, they could make the trip without expressing any message beyond the fact of the march itself. Some people might call such a procession a parade, but it would not be much of one. Real "[p]arades are public dramas of social relations, and in them performers define who can be a social actor and what subjects and ideas are available for communication and consideration." . . . Hence, we use the word "parade" to indicate marchers who are making some sort of collective point, not just to each other but to bystanders along the way. Indeed a parade's dependence on watchers is so extreme that nowadays, as with Bishop Berkeley's celebrated tree, "if a parade or demonstration receives no media coverage, it may as well not have happened." . . . Parades are thus a form of expression, not just motion, and the inherent expressiveness of marching to make a point explains our cases involving protest marches. . . .

The protected expression that inheres in a parade is not limited to its banners and songs, however, for the Constitution looks beyond written or spoken words as mediums of expression. Noting that "[s]ymbolism is a primitive but effective way of communicating ideas," . . . our cases have recognized that the First Amendment shields such acts as saluting a flag (and refusing to do so), . . . wearing an arm band to protest a war, . . . displaying a red flag, . . . and even "[m]arching, walking or parading" in uniforms displaying the swastika. . . . As some of these examples show, a narrow, succinctly articulable message is not a condition of constitutional protection. . . .

Not many marches, then, are beyond the realm of expressive parades, and the South Boston celebration is not one of them. Spectators line the streets; people march in costumes and uniforms, carrying flags and banners with all sorts of messages. . . ; marching bands and pipers play, floats are pulled along, and the whole show is broadcast over Boston television. . . . To be sure, we agree with the state courts that in spite of excluding some applicants, the Council is rather lenient in admitting participants. But a private speaker does not forfeit constitutional protection simply by combining multifarious voices, or by failing to edit their themes to isolate an exact message as the exclusive subject matter of the speech. Nor, under our precedent, does First Amendment protection require a speaker to generate, as an original matter, each item featured in the communication. Cable operators, for example, are engaged in protected speech activities even when they only select programming originally produced by others. . . . For that matter, the presentation of an edited compilation of speech generated by other persons is a staple of most newspapers' opinion pages, which, of course, fall squarely within the core of First Amendment security, . . . as does even the simple selection of a paid noncommercial advertisement for inclusion in a daily paper. . . . The selection of contingents to make a parade is entitled to similar protection.

Respondents' participation as a unit in the parade was equally expressive. GLIB was formed for the very purpose of marching in it, as the trial court found, in order to celebrate its members' identity as openly gay, lesbian, and bisexual descendants of the Irish immigrants, to show that there are such individuals in the community, and to support the like men and women who sought to march in the New York parade. . . . The organization distributed a fact sheet describing the members' intentions, . . . and the record otherwise corroborates the expressive nature of GLIB's participation. . . . In 1993, members of GLIB marched behind a shamrock-strewn banner with the simple inscription "Irish American Gay, Lesbian and Bisexual Group of Boston." GLIB understandably seeks to communicate its ideas as part of the existing parade, rather than staging one of its own.

B

The Massachusetts public accommodations law under which respondents brought suit has a venerable history. At common law, innkeepers, smiths, and others who "made profession of a public employment," were prohibited from refusing, without good reason, to serve a customer. . . . As one of the 19th century English judges put it, the rule was that "[t]he innkeeper is not to select his guests[;] [h]e has no right to say to one, you shall come into my inn, and to another you shall not, as every one coming and conducting himself in a proper manner has a right to be received; and for this purpose innkeepers are a sort of public servants." . . .

After the Civil War, the Commonwealth of Massachusetts was the first State to codify this principle to ensure access to public accommodations regardless of race. . . . In prohibiting discrimination "in any licensed inn, in any public place of amusement, public conveyance or public meeting," . . . the original statute already expanded upon the common law, which had not conferred any right of access to places of public amusement. . . . As with many public accommodations statutes across the Nation, the legislature continued to broaden the scope of legislation, to the point that the law today prohibits discrimination on the basis of "race, color, religious creed, national origin, sex, sexual orientation . . . , deafness, blindness or any physical or mental disability or ancestry" in "the admission of any person to, or treatment in any place of public accommodation, resort or amusement." . . . Provisions like these are well within the State's usual power to enact when a legislature has reason to believe that a given group is the target of discrimination, and they do not, as a general matter, violate the First or Fourteenth Amendments. . . . Nor is this statute unusual in any obvious way, since it does not, on its face, target speech or discriminate on the basis of its content, the focal point of its prohibition being rather on the act of discriminating against individuals in the provision of publicly available goods, privileges, and services on the proscribed grounds.

C

In the case before us, however, the Massachusetts law has been applied in a peculiar way. Its enforcement does not address any dispute about the participation of openly gay, lesbian, or bisexual individuals in various units admitted to the parade. The petitioners disclaim any intent to exclude homosexuals as such, and no individual member of GLIB claims to have been excluded from parading as a member of any group that the Council has approved to march. Instead, the disagreement goes to the admission of GLIB as its own parade unit carrying its own banner. . . . Since every participating unit affects the message conveyed by the private organizers, the state courts' application of the statute produced an order essentially requiring petitioners to alter the expressive content of their parade. Although the state courts spoke of the parade as a place of public accommodation, . . . at, once the expressive character of both the parade and the marching GLIB contingent is understood, it becomes apparent that the state courts' application of the statute had the effect of declaring the sponsors' speech itself to be the public accommodation. Under this approach any contingent of protected individuals with a message would have the right to participate in petitioners' speech, so that the communication produced by the private organizers would be shaped by all those protected by the law who wished to join in with some expressive demonstration of their own. But this use of the State's power violates the fundamental rule of protection under the First Amendment, that a speaker has the autonomy to choose the content of his own message.

"Since all speech inherently involves choices of what to say and what to leave unsaid," . . . one important manifestation of the principle of free speech is that one who chooses to speak may also decide "what not to say." . . . Although the State may at times "prescribe what shall be orthodox in commercial advertising" by requiring the dissemination of "purely factual and uncontroversial information," . . . outside that context it may not compel affirmance of a belief with which the speaker disagrees. . . . Indeed this general rule, that the speaker has the right to tailor the speech, applies not only to expressions of value, opinion, or endorsement, but equally to statements of fact the speaker would rather avoid, . . . subject, perhaps, to the permissive law of defamation. . . . Nor is the rule's benefit restricted to the press, being enjoyed by business corporations generally and by ordinary people engaged in unsophisticated expression as well as by professional publishers. Its point is simply the point of all speech protection, which is to shield just those choices of content that in someone's eyes are misguided, or even hurtful. . . .

Petitioners' claim to the benefit of this principle of autonomy to control one's own speech is as sound as the South Boston parade is expressive. Rather like a composer, the Council selects the expressive units of the parade from potential participants, and though the score may not produce a particularized message, each contin-

gent's expression in the Council's eyes comports with what merits celebration on that day. Even if this view gives the Council credit for a more considered judgment than it actively made, the Council clearly decided to exclude a message it did not like from the communication it chose to make, and that is enough to invoke its right as a private speaker to shape its expression by speaking on one subject while remaining silent on another. The message it disfavored is not difficult to identify. Although GLIB's point (like the Council's) is not wholly articulate, a contingent marching behind the organization's banner would at least bear witness to the fact that some Irish are gay, lesbian, or bisexual, and the presence of the organized marchers would suggest their view that people of their sexual orientations have as much claim to unqualified social acceptance as heterosexuals and indeed as members of parade units organized around other identifying characteristics. The parade's organizers may not believe these facts about Irish sexuality to be so, or they may object to unqualified social acceptance of gays and lesbians or have some other reason for wishing to keep GLIB's message out of the parade. But whatever the reason, it boils down to the choice of a speaker not to propound a particular point of view, and that choice is presumed to lie beyond the government's power to control.

Respondents argue that any tension between this rule and the Massachusetts law falls short of unconstitutionality, citing the most recent of our cases on the general subject of compelled access for expressive purposes. . . . Respondents contend on this authority that admission of GLIB to the parade would not threaten the core principle of speaker's autonomy because the Council, like a cable operator, is merely "a conduit for the speech of participants in the parade "rather than itself a speaker." . . . But this metaphor is not apt here, because GLIB's participation would likely be perceived as having resulted from the Council's customary determination about a unit admitted to the parade, that its message was worthy of presentation and quite possibly of support as well. . . . Thus, when dissemination of a view contrary to one's own is forced upon a speaker intimately connected with the communication advanced, the speaker's right to autonomy over the message is compromised. . . .

Parades and demonstrations, in contrast, are not understood to be so neutrally presented or selectively viewed. Unlike the programming offered on various channels by a cable network, the parade does not consist of individual, unrelated segments that happen to be transmitted together for individual selection by members of the audience. Although each parade unit generally identifies itself, each is understood to contribute something to a common theme, and accordingly there is no customary practice whereby private sponsors disavow "any identity of viewpoint" between themselves and the selected participants. Practice follows practicability here, for such disclaimers would be quite curious in a moving parade. . . . Without deciding on the precise significance of the likelihood of misattribution, it nonetheless becomes clear that in the context of an expressive parade, as with a protest march, the parade's overall message is distilled from the individual presentations along the way, and each unit's expression is perceived by spectators as part of the whole. . . .

The [Massachusetts public accommodations] statute is a piece of protective legislation that announces no purpose beyond the object both expressed and apparent in its provisions, which is to prevent any denial of access to (or discriminatory treatment in) public accommodations on proscribed grounds, including sexual orientation. On its face, the object of the law is to ensure by statute for gays and lesbians desiring to make use of public accommodations what the old common law promised to any member of the public wanting a meal at the inn, that accepting the usual terms of service, they will not be turned away merely on the proprietor's exercise of personal preference. When the law is applied to expressive activity in the way it was done here, its apparent object is simply to require speakers to modify the content of their expression to whatever extent beneficiaries of the law choose to alter it with messages of their own. But in the absence of some further, legitimate end, this object is merely to allow exactly what the general rule of speaker's autonomy forbids.

It might, of course, have been argued that a broader objective is apparent: that the ultimate point of forbidding acts of discrimination toward certain classes is to produce a society free of the corresponding biases. Requiring access to a speaker's message would thus be not an end in itself, but a means to produce speakers free of the biases, whose expressive conduct would be at least neutral toward the particular classes, obviating any future need for correction. But if this indeed is the point of applying the state law to expressive conduct, it is a decidedly fatal objective. Having availed itself of the public thoroughfares "for purposes of assembly [and] communicating thoughts between citizens," the Council is engaged in a use of the streets that has "from ancient times, been a part of the privileges, immunities, rights, and liberties of citizens." . . . Our tradition of free speech commands that a speaker who takes to the street corner to express his views in this way should be free from interference by the State based on the content of what he says. . . . The very idea that a noncommercial speech restriction be used to produce thoughts and statements acceptable to some groups or, indeed, all people, grates on the First Amendment, for it amounts to nothing less than a proposal to limit speech in the service of orthodox expression. The Speech Clause has no more certain antithesis. . . . While the law is free to promote all sorts of conduct in place of harmful behavior, it is not free to interfere with speech for no better reason than promoting an approved message or discouraging a disfavored one, however enlightened either purpose may strike the government. . . .

[In *New York State Club Association v. City of New York* (1988)] . . . we turned back a facial challenge to a state antidiscrimination statute on the assumption that the expressive associational character of a dining club with over 400 members could be sufficiently attenuated to permit application of the law even to such a private organization, but we also recognized that the State did not prohibit exclusion of those whose views were at odds with positions espoused by the general club memberships. . . . In other words, although the association provided public benefits to which a State could ensure equal access, it was also engaged in expressive activity; compelled access to the benefit, which was upheld, did not trespass on the organization's message itself. If we were to analyze this case strictly along those lines, GLIB would lose. Assuming the parade to be large enough and a source of benefits (apart from its expression) that would generally justify a mandated access provision, GLIB could nonetheless be refused admission as an expressive contingent with its own message just as readily as a private club could exclude an applicant whose manifest views were at odds with a position taken by the club's existing members.

IV

Our holding today rests not on any particular view about the Council's message but on the Nation's commitment to protect freedom of speech. Disapproval of a private speaker's statement does not legitimize use of the Commonwealth's power to compel the speaker to alter the message by including one more acceptable to others. Accordingly, the judgment of the Supreme Judicial Court is reversed and the case remanded for proceedings not inconsistent with this opinion. . . .

9

RELIGIOUS LIBERTY AND CHURCH–STATE RELATIONS

Chapter Outline

Introduction
Religious Belief and the Right to
    Proselytize
Unconventional Religious Practices
Patriotic Rituals and Civic Duties
Freedom of Religion Versus *Parens*
    Patriae
The Wall of Separation
Religion and Public Education
Governmental Affirmations of Religious
    Belief
The Problem of Tax Exemptions
Conclusion
Key Terms
For Further Reading
Internet Resources
West Virginia State Board of Education
    v. Barnette (1943)
Wisconsin v. Yoder (1972)
Employment Division v. Smith (1990)
Church of the Lukumi Babalu Aye, Inc.
    v. City of Hialeah (1993)
Everson v. Board of Education (1947)
Abington School District v. Schempp
    (1963)
Wallace v. Jaffree (1985)
Edwards v. Aguillard (1987)
Agostini v. Felton (1997)
Marsh v. Chambers (1983)
Lynch v. Donnelly (1984)
Walz v. Tax Commission (1970)

We are a people whose institutions presuppose a Supreme Being.

—JUSTICE WILLIAM O. DOUGLAS, WRITING FOR THE COURT IN *ZORACH V. CLAUSON* (1952)

[O]ne of the mandates of the First Amendment is to promote a viable, pluralistic society and to keep government neutral, not only between sects, but also between believers and nonbelievers.

—JUSTICE WILLIAM O. DOUGLAS, DISSENTING IN *WALZ V. TAX COMMISSION* (1970)

INTRODUCTION

Religion is one of the hallmarks of American society. Americans are more likely than people in other Western democracies to hold religious beliefs, affiliate with religious denominations, and attend religious services. Another distinguishing feature of American social life is the great diversity of religious beliefs and practices that coexist peacefully. No other society on earth has such a wide array of creeds and denominations. Despite obvious differences in doctrine and styles of worship, most religions are united by their common belief in a Supreme Being and their commitment to standards of right and wrong. Nevertheless, history teaches us that human beings are given to zealotry, intolerance, persecution, and even warfare in the name of God. Peaceful coexistence among competing religious groups is one of the major accomplishments of modern democracy.

The framers of the Bill of Rights were well aware of the excesses that can result when one denomination is established as the official religion and recognized and supported by government. Indeed, a profound thirst for the freedom to worship God in one's own way, without coercion or persecution by government, was one of the principal motivations in the formation of the American colonies. However, nine of the thirteen original American colonies set up official churches and provided them with financial support. In fact, at the time the Bill of Rights was ratified in 1791, Connecticut, Massachusetts, and New Hampshire continued to recognize the Congregational Church as the official, state-sponsored denomination. Nevertheless, opposition to officially established religion ultimately prevailed. The First Amendment to the Constitution provides that "Congress shall make no law respecting an establishment of religion, or prohibiting the free exercise thereof. . . ."

That the protection of religious freedom was of fundamental importance to the framers is underscored by the fact that the Religion Clauses are listed first among the safeguards contained in the Bill of Rights. These clauses not only reflect the strong desire for religious freedom held by eighteenth-century Americans, they also protect and foster the religious diversity that exists in America today.

Widespread agreement exists regarding the abstract value of the **Religion Clauses of the First Amendment.** Nevertheless, there is equally broad disagreement about what these clauses specifically require, permit, and forbid. Some of the Supreme Court's least popular decisions are in the realm of government involvement with religion, specifically in the area of **school prayer.** Note, however, that these decisions are often as misunderstood as they are unpopular. This chapter attempts to clarify and explain what the Supreme Court has said in some of its many decisions interpreting the Religion Clauses of the First Amendment. Sadly, too often those who are given to strong opinions on the subject of religion are unwilling or unable to understand clearly what has been decided by the courts. While informed debate over judicial decisions is to be encouraged, criticism based on ignorance is counterproductive.

The Incorporation of the Religion Clauses

In his original draft of the Bill of Rights, James Madison proposed that state as well as federal establishments of religion be prohibited. The First Congress rejected Madison's suggestion in this respect, preferring to allow states to make their own determinations in this area. Thus, the First Amendment proscribed establishments of religion by the national government only. By the late 1940s, the Supreme Court had ruled, however, that the Religion Clauses of the First Amendment were of sufficient importance in a "scheme of ordered liberty" to warrant their application to the states through the Due Process Clause of the Fourteenth Amendment (for a discussion of the doctrine of incorporation, see Chapter 6). The **Free Exercise Clause** was definitively applied to the states in *Cantwell v. Connecticut* (1940); arguably, it had been incorporated in the 1934 case of *Hamilton v. Regents of the University of California.* The **Establishment Clause** was incorporated in *Everson v. Board of Education* (1947). Thus, all levels of government, from local school boards to the U.S. Congress, are now required to abide by the strictures of the Religion Clauses of the First Amendment.

What Constitutes Religion for First Amendment Purposes?

Before one can define "establishment of religion" or "the free exercise thereof," one must understand what is meant by the term *religion.* It comes from the Latin *religare,* which means "to tie down" or "to restrain." Since its appearance in the English language at the beginning of the thirteenth century, the term *religion* has had a distinctly theological connotation. *Webster's Third New International Dictionary of the English Language* (1986) offers seven definitions of the term. The first is "the personal commitment to and serving of God or a god with worshipful devotion. . . ." It goes on to define religion as "a personal awareness or conviction of the existence of a supreme being or of supernatural powers or influences controlling one's own, humanity's, or all nature's destiny. . . ."

In the 1890 case of *Davis v. Beason,* the Supreme Court first had occasion to define religion. In a majority opinion authored by Justice Stephen J. Field, the Court stated that "the term 'religion' has reference to one's view of his relations to his Creator, and to the obligations they impose of reverence for His being and character, and obedience to His will." This conception of religion was strictly theistic, which no doubt mirrored popular attitudes circa 1890. By the 1960s, however, American society had become much more religiously diverse, and nontheistic creeds from Asia, such as Buddhism and Taoism, were beginning to find adherents in this country.

Religion Broadly Defined

In 1965, the Supreme Court attempted to define religion in a fashion broad enough to respect the diversity of creeds that coexist in modern America. The definitional problem arose in *United States v. Seeger* (1965), a case involving four men who claimed **conscientious objector** status in refusing to serve in the Vietnam War. In the Universal Military Training and Service Act of 1940, Congress exempted from combat duty anyone "who, by reason of religious training and belief, is conscientiously opposed to participation in war in any form." The act defined "religious training and belief" as training or belief "in a relation to a Supreme Being involving duties superior to those arising from any human relation." Although some organized religions (such as the Quakers) do not approve of participation in war, Daniel Seeger was not a member of any such group. Nevertheless, he sought conscientious objector status on religious grounds. When specifically asked about his belief in a Supreme Being, Seeger stated that "you could call [it] a belief in the Supreme Being or God. These just do not happen to be the words that I use." Forest Peter, another man whose refusal to serve in Vietnam was before the Supreme Court in *Seeger,* claimed that after considerable meditation and reflection "on values derived from the Western religious and philosophical tradition," he determined that it would be "a violation of his moral code to take human life and that he considered this belief superior to any obligation to the state." In deciding the *Seeger* case, the Court avoided a constitutional question by interpreting the statutory definition of religion broadly. Writing for the Court, Justice Tom C. Clark held that

> Congress, in using the expression "Supreme Being" rather than the designation "God," was merely clarifying the meaning of religious tradition and belief so as to embrace all religions and to exclude essentially political, sociological, or philosophical views [and] the test of belief "in a relation to a Supreme Being" is whether a given belief that is sincere and meaningful occupies a place in the life of its possessor parallel to the orthodox belief in God.

Apparently the Court was persuaded that Seeger, Peter, and the others whose refusal to serve in Vietnam was before the Court possessed such a belief and recognized them as conscientious objectors on religious grounds.

A Working Definition of Religion

Subsequent decisions in both federal and state tribunals have expanded the definition of religion adopted by the Supreme Court in the *Seeger* case. Essentially, a creed must meet four criteria to qualify as a religion as this term is used in the First Amendment. First, as noted earlier, there must be a belief in God or some parallel belief that occupies a central place in the believer's life. Second, the religion must involve a moral code that transcends individual belief—it cannot be purely subjective. Third, some associational ties must be involved. That is, there must be some community of people united by common beliefs. Fourth, there must be a demonstrable sincerity of belief. Under these criteria, even nontheistic creeds, such as Taoism or Zen Buddhism, qualify as religions. But frivolous or ridiculous beliefs, such as Stanley Oscar Brown's professed "faith" in Kozy Kitten Cat Food (see *Brown v. Pena* [1977]), fail to meet any of the four criteria. Of course, there is a long continuum between ludicrous beliefs such as Brown's and conventional religions.

RELIGIOUS BELIEF AND THE RIGHT TO PROSELYTIZE

The First Amendment provides virtually absolute protection with respect to individual religious convictions and beliefs. The government may never question a person's beliefs or impose penalties or disabilities based solely on those beliefs. Thus, in *Torasco v. Watkins* (1961), the Court unanimously struck down a state law requiring persons wishing to run for public office to take an oath declaring their belief in God. Likewise, in *McDaniel v. Paty* (1978), the Court was unanimous in holding that states may not bar priests and ministers from serving as delegates to state constitutional conventions.

The Free Exercise Clause obviously protects more than belief—it carries over into the realm of action. But here the protections are somewhat attenuated. Whether specific actions are protected by the First Amendment depends on the character of those actions and the government's rationale for trying to regulate them.

Religious Solicitation

The highest degree of protection is accorded to **religious speech** and other **expressive religious conduct.** Thus, in *Cantwell v. Connecticut* (1940), the Court struck down a state law that prohibited door-to-door solicitation for any religious or charitable cause without prior approval of a state agency. The law was challenged by Newton Cantwell, a member of the Jehovah's Witnesses, a sect committed to active proselytizing. Cantwell and his sons routinely went from door to door or stopped people on the street in order to communicate a message that was highly critical of the Roman Catholic Church and other organized religions. Eventually they were arrested and charged with failure to obtain approval for solicitation under the state law, as well as with common law breach of the peace. The Court reversed the breach-of-the-peace conviction and invalidated the state statute:

> In the realm of religious faith, and in that of political belief, sharp differences arise. In both fields the tenets of one man may seem the rankest error to his neighbor. To persuade others to his point of view, the pleader, as we know, resorts to exaggeration, to vilification of men who have been, or are, prominent in church or state, and

even to false statement. But the people of this nation have ordained in the light of history, that, in spite of the probability of excesses and abuses, these liberties are, in the long view, essential to enlightened opinion and right conduct on the part of citizens of a democracy.

Three years later, the Court in *Douglas v. City of Jeanette* (1943) held that police could not prohibit members of the Jehovah's Witnesses from peaceable and orderly proselytizing on Sundays merely because other citizens complained. In another 1943 case involving the Jehovah's Witnesses, *Murdock v. Pennsylvania*, the Court held that a state law requiring the payment of a tax for the privilege of solicitation could not be constitutionally applied to cases of religious solicitation. Writing for the Court, Justice William O. Douglas observed that "a person cannot be compelled to purchase . . . a privilege freely granted by the Constitution."

In still another case involving members of the Jehovah's Witnesses, *Niemotko v. Maryland* (1951), the Supreme Court held unconstitutional a city council's denial of a permit to the Jehovah's Witnesses to use the city park for a public meeting. The city council had refused to grant the permit because the Jehovah's Witnesses' answers to questions about Catholicism, military service, and other issues were "unsatisfactory." A unanimous Supreme Court regarded this denial of the public forum to an unpopular religious group as blatant censorship.

Time, Place, and Manner Regulations

As we saw in the preceding chapter, the First Amendment does not guarantee the right to communicate one's views at all times and places or in any manner that may be desired. Religious expression in the **public forum** is subject to reasonable **time, place, and manner regulations.** Airports, courthouses, and other public buildings may be declared off-limits to all First Amendment activities, as long as particular groups are not singled out. Similarly, religious proselytizing in congested areas may be limited to certain areas so as to maintain the safe and orderly flow of pedestrian and vehicular traffic (see, for example, *Heffron v. Int'l Society for Krishna Consciousnesss* [1981]).

TO SUMMARIZE:

- The First Amendment affords virtually unlimited protection to freedom of belief.
- The actions of believers in proselytizing and soliciting contributions are also highly protected by the First Amendment, but are subject to reasonable time, place, and manner restrictions.

UNCONVENTIONAL RELIGIOUS PRACTICES

Although the Supreme Court has consistently defended the right of unpopular religious groups to meet, canvass, solicit, and proselytize in the public forum, it has generally rejected arguments that the Free Exercise Clause allows religious groups to engage in activities that are proscribed as detrimental to public health, safety, or morality. Thus, in 1975, the Court refused to review a lower court decision upholding Tennessee's law prohibiting the handling of poisonous snakes in religious ceremonies (see *State ex rel. Swann v. Pack*). In *Employment Division v. Smith* (1990), the Supreme Court rejected a claim made by members of the Native American Church that their ritualistic use of peyote constituted free exercise of religion.

The Mormon Polygamy Case

The first major pronouncement from the Supreme Court on the subject of **unconventional religious practices** came in *Reynolds v. United States* (1879). In this landmark case, the Court upheld application of the federal antipolygamy statute to a Mormon who claimed it was his religious duty to have several wives. The federal law in question merely adopted the long-standing common-law prohibition against bigamy (the crime of having more than one spouse). Although the law applied to everyone regardless of religion, it is clear from the congressional debates surrounding this legislation that the law was aimed at the Mormons, which had become highly controversial in nineteenth-century America.

The *Reynolds* decision was based on a sharp distinction between belief and conduct. According to Chief Justice Morrison R. Waite, "Congress was deprived of all legislative power over mere opinion, but was left free to reach actions which were in violation of social duties or subversive of good order." Although the Supreme Court has occasionally reiterated the distinction between religious belief and conduct, it has largely repudiated the position taken in *Reynolds* that religious conduct is beyond the pale of the Free Exercise Clause. After all, few if any government policies infringe religious belief *per se;* rather, they are aimed at particular kinds of actions deemed socially undesirable.

The Warren Court Establishes the Compelling Interest Test

In its post–New Deal expansion of civil liberties, the Court markedly increased the degree of judicial protection of religiously motivated conduct, but this did not mean that religious activity received absolute immunity from government regulation. The Court remained willing to uphold public policies that infringed on religious practices if the government could point to an important secular justification for such infringement. In *Sherbert v. Verner* (1963), the Court said that freedom of religion is a **fundamental right** that could be abridged only if necessary to protect a **compelling governmental interest.** Although the justices often disagreed over precisely which government interests should be viewed as compelling, this general standard established a strong presumption in favor of the free exercise of religion.

The Oregon Peyote Case

Throughout the 1970s and 1980s, the Supreme Court continued to apply the rationale established in *Sherbert v. Verner* (see, for example, *Thomas v. Review Board* [1981] and *Hobbie v. Unemployment Appeals Division* [1987]). These cases stood for the proposition that, in the absence of a compelling justification, a state could not withhold unemployment compensation from an employee who resigned or was discharged due to unwillingness to depart from religious practices or beliefs that conflicted with job requirements. In 1990, however, a sharply divided Court, in *Employment Division v. Smith,* departed dramatically from this approach and imposed potentially serious limits on the scope of religious freedom protected by the First Amendment.

In *Smith,* a state's interest in prohibiting the use of illicit drugs came into conflict with well-established practices of the Native American Church, a sect outside the Judeo-Christian mainstream of American religion. Two members of this church, Alfred Smith and Galen Black, worked as drug rehabilitation counselors for a private social service agency in Oregon. Along with other church members, Smith and Black ingested peyote, a hallucinogenic drug, at a sacramental ceremony practiced by Native Americans for hundreds of years. Citing their use of peyote as "job-related misconduct," the social service agency fired Smith and Black. Recognizing no exception, even for sacramental purposes, Oregon's controlled substances statute made the possession of peyote a criminal offense. Although Smith and Black were not charged with violation of this law, its existence figured prominently in the Supreme Court's ultimate resolution of the free exercise issue in this case.

Shortly after they were fired, Smith and Black applied for unemployment compensation. The Oregon Employment Appeals Board denied their applications, accepting the employer's explanation that Smith and Black had been discharged for job-related misconduct. The former counselors successfully challenged this administrative ruling in the Oregon Court of Appeals, thus initiating a lengthy and complex judicial struggle that generated several state court decisions and two rulings by the U.S. Supreme Court. On remand from the first of these rulings, the Oregon Supreme Court held that the controlled substance law, as applied in this case, violated the Free Exercise Clause of the First Amendment and that Smith and Black were thus entitled to unemployment compensation.

Reviewing the case for a second time and finally reaching the basic constitutional issue, the U.S. Supreme Court reversed. Justice Antonin Scalia, writing for the majority, ruled that "if prohibiting the exercise of religion . . . is . . . merely the incidental effect of a generally applicable and otherwise valid [criminal] law, the First Amendment has not been offended." According to this reasoning, the Free Exercise Clause would be violated only if a particular religious practice were singled out for proscription. In supporting this holding, Scalia relied heavily on *Reynolds v. United States* (1879), in effect equating Oregon's drug prohibition with the federal antipolygamy statute. He contended that "[t]o make an individual's obligation to obey such a law contingent upon the law's coincidence with his religious beliefs except where the state's interest is compelling . . . contradicts both constitutional tradition and common sense." The legislature, Scalia maintained, is free to make accommodations for religious practices. Such accommodations, however, are not required, no matter how "central" a particular practice might be to one's religious beliefs.

As Justice Sandra Day O'Connor's concurring opinion indicates, Scalia's rejection of the compelling governmental interest test was the most controversial aspect of this decision. Although she supported the Court's judgment that the Free Exercise Clause had not been violated, O'Connor sharply criticized the majority opinion as a dramatic departure "from well-settled First Amendment jurisprudence . . . and . . . [as] incompatible with our Nation's fundamental commitment to individual religious liberty." This part of O'Connor's opinion was supported by Justices Brennan, Marshall, and Blackmun, who dissented from the Court's decision. "The compelling interest test," O'Connor asserted, "effectuates the First Amendment's command that religious liberty is an independent liberty, that it occupies a preferred position, and that the Court will not permit encroachments upon this liberty, whether direct or indirect, unless required by clear and compelling governmental interests 'of the highest order.' "

In a separate dissenting opinion, Justice Harry Blackmun, joined by Justices Brennan and Marshall, charged the majority with "mischaracterizing" precedents and "overturning . . . settled law concerning the Religion Clauses of our Constitution." With evident sarcasm, Blackmun expressed the hope that the Court was "aware of the consequences" and that the result was not a "product of overreaction to the serious problems the country's drug crisis [had] generated." He pointed out that the Native American Church restricted and supervised the sacramental use of peyote. The state thus had no significant health or safety justification for regulating this form of drug use. Blackmun also noted that Oregon had not attempted to prosecute Smith and Black or, for that matter, any other Native Americans for the sacramental use of peyote. He concluded that "Oregon's interest in enforcing its drug laws against religious use of peyote [was] not sufficiently compelling to outweigh respondents' right to the free exercise of their religion."

The Religious Freedom Restoration Act

Negative public reaction, especially from the religious community, to the Court's decision in *Smith* convinced a majority in Congress to enact the **Religious Freedom Restoration Act (RFRA)** of 1993. The RFRA prohibited government at all levels from substantially burdening a person's free exercise of religion, even if such burden resulted from a generally applicable rule, unless the government could demonstrate a compelling interest and that the rule constituted the least restrictive means of furthering that interest. In passing the RFRA, Congress sought to restore the *status quo ante*—to return the law in this area to what it was prior to the *Smith* decision. In adopting this statute, Congress relied on its broad powers under Section 5 of the Fourteenth Amendment.

In *City of Boerne v. Flores* (1997) the Supreme Court, dividing 6 to 3, declared the RFRA unconstitutional. While conceding that Congress has broad power to enforce the provisions of the Fourteenth Amendment, Justice Kennedy, writing for the majority, concluded that "RFRA contradicts vital principles necessary to maintain separation of powers and the federal balance." In this decision the Court stressed the primacy of its role as interpreter of the Constitution. It was firm and unequivocal in rejecting, on broad institutional grounds, a direct congressional challenge of final judicial authority on a question of constitutional interpretation.

Is Animal Sacrifice "Free Exercise of Religion"?

In 1987, the city of Hialeah, a Miami suburb, passed an ordinance making it a crime to "unnecessarily kill, torment, torture, or mutilate an animal in a public or private ritual or ceremony not for the primary purpose of food consumption." The ordinance came in response to local concern over the sacrificial practices associated with Santeria, a blend of Roman Catholicism and West African religions brought to the Caribbean by East African slaves. Santeria, which literally means "worship of the saints," involves occasional sacrifices of live animals, usually goats or chickens. According to some estimates, there are as many as 70,000 devotees of Santeria in the Miami area, and perhaps as many as one million nationwide. Ernesto Pichardo, a Santeria priest, challenged the Hialeah law as a violation of the First Amendment.

In *Church of the Lukumi Babalu Aye v. City of Hialeah* (1993), the Justices unanimously invalidated the Hialeah ordinance. Writing for the Supreme Court, Justice Kennedy observed that "the laws in question were enacted by officials who did not understand, failed to perceive, or chose to ignore the fact that their official actions violated the Nation's essential commitment to religious freedom." Justice Kennedy was careful to point out that the ordinance in question was not a generally applicable criminal prohibition, but rather singled out practitioners of Santeria in that it forbade animal slaughter only insofar as it took place within the context of religious rituals. Thus, the decision in *Lukumi Babalu Aye* is consistent with the Court's decision in *Employment Division v. Smith*.

TO SUMMARIZE:

- In contrast to proselytizing and solicitation of contributions, unconventional religious practices such as polygamy and use of illicit drugs receive far less protection under the Free Exercise Clause.
- Although generally applicable prohibitions that incidentally burden religion are likely to be upheld, prohibitions that single out particular religious groups are less likely to survive constitutional challenge.

PATRIOTIC RITUALS AND CIVIC DUTIES

Some religious groups prefer to live largely in isolation from the mainstream of modern society, pursuing lifestyles and embracing virtues reminiscent of the early nineteenth century. For the most part, they are uninterested in things political, preferring to concentrate on their families' moral and spiritual development. They are generally unwilling to serve in the armed forces, since they are opposed to war in any form. They also avoid displays of nationalism or even citizenship. Sometimes, they refuse to school their children formally beyond the primary grades. To what extent does the First Amendment protect such groups from being forced to observe patriotic rituals and civic duties that are readily observed by most Americans?

The Flag Salute Cases

In *Minersville School District v. Gobitis* (1940), the Supreme Court upheld a local school board requirement that all public school students participate in a daily flag salute program. The requirement had been challenged by a member of the Jehovah's Witnesses whose children were being forced to salute the American flag in violation of their religious training, which held the flag salute to be the worship of a "graven image" (see Exodus 20:4–5). In a dramatic turnabout, the *Gobitis* decision was overruled three years later in *West Virginia State Board of Education v. Barnette* (1943). In the *Gobitis* decision, Justice Felix Frankfurter had justified the compulsory flag salute as an appropriate means for the attainment of national unity, which he viewed as "the basis of national security." Writing for the Court that overruled Frankfurter's position, Justice Robert Jackson stated that "compulsory unification of opinion leads only to the unanimity of the graveyard," obviously referring to the situation in Europe in 1943. For Justice Jackson, "to believe that patriotism will not flourish if patriotic ceremonies are voluntary and spontaneous instead of a compulsory routine is to make an unflattering estimate of the appeal of our institutions to free minds."

Nothing that the Supreme Court has decided since *Barnette* indicates that government has any justification for forcing citizens to make professions of patriotism. The Court has even gone as far as to prohibit the state of New Hampshire from requiring that an automobile display a license plate inscribed with the State's motto "Live Free or Die" if such motto offends the religious sensibilities of the car's owner (see *Wooley v. Maynard* [1977]). Although the Court has not faced the question since 1931 (see *United States v. Bland*), it is interesting to speculate as to whether the current Court would require a religious pacifist who wishes to become a citizen to swear that he or she would "defend the Constitution and the laws of the United States against all enemies, foreign or domestic," which is the oath required of all naturalized citizens. The Court upheld the oath requirement in 1931. Would it do so today?

Free Exercise of Religion and Military Service

Another interesting constitutional question involves conscientious objection to military service, alluded to earlier in the discussion of the *Seeger* case. Although Congress has provided an exemption from military service for religiously motivated conscientious objectors, is such an exemption required by the Free Exercise Clause? In other words, would the Supreme Court permit religiously motivated refusal to serve in combat on constitutional grounds if there were no act of Congress providing such an exemption? On the other hand, is it not possible to argue that, in granting an exemption only to those whose refusal to serve is based on religion, Congress has run afoul of the Establishment Clause? The Court has never squarely addressed these questions.

One of the most controversial Supreme Court decisions in the area of free exercise of religion deals with military regulations that were alleged to infringe First Amendment rights. In *Goldman v. Weinberger* (1986), the Court upheld an Air Force dress code requirement against the challenge of an Orthodox Jew who was disciplined for wearing a yarmulke while in uniform. Stressing the need for discipline and uniformity in the military, the Court rejected the challenge by a vote of 5 to 4. Writing for the sharply divided Court, Justice William Rehnquist maintained that "when evaluating whether military needs justify a particular restriction on religiously motivated conduct, courts must give great deference to the professional judgment of military authorities concerning the relative importance of a particular military interest."

In *Goldman,* the Supreme Court thus reiterated the position taken five years before that "[j]udicial deference . . . is at its apogee when legislative action under the congressional authority to raise and support armies and make rules and regulations for their governance is challenged" (*Rostker v. Goldberg* [1981]). Constitutional rights enjoyed by American citizens are to a large extent sacrificed during military service.

TO SUMMARIZE:

- The First Amendment prohibits government from compelling individuals to make public affirmations of belief, whether religious or political.
- Because Congress has created a statutory basis for conscientious objection to military service, the Supreme Court has not faced the issue of whether exemptions for conscientious objectors are required by the Free Exercise Clause.

▪ The Court tends to be deferential to military regulations such as dress codes that impinge upon the free exercise of religion by persons in military service, as long as such regulations do not single out or discriminate against particular religions.

FREEDOM OF RELIGION VERSUS PARENS PATRIAE

Our legal traditions recognize government as ***parens patriae,*** meaning literally "parent of the country." This term refers to the role of government as guardian of persons who are not legally competent to make their own decisions, for example, children, the severely retarded, and the mentally ill. Occasionally, the state uses this power to take custody of children who are the victims of neglect or abuse. The state's role as *parens patriae* has sometimes come into conflict with the Free Exercise Clause when parents refuse on religious grounds to allow their children to receive medical treatment. Some devoutly religious persons believe that medical science is blasphemous—that true faith is all that is necessary to promote healing. For example, in a 1983 Tennessee case that attracted wide attention, a fundamentalist preacher refused to allow a hospital to treat his young daughter for cancer. The state intervened as *parens patriae* and secured a court order requiring medical treatment (see *In the Matter of Hamilton* [1983]).

Although some state and federal court decisions have recognized a competent adult's **right to refuse medical treatment** on religious and/or privacy grounds, courts are generally disinclined to uphold such free exercise claims where the health of children is involved. Judges generally assume that children are not sufficiently mature to make rational choices regarding medical treatment and, in some instances, must be protected against the consequences of their parents' unusual religious convictions.

In *Prince v. Massachusetts* (1944), the Supreme Court upheld a child labor law against an attack based on the Free Exercise Clause. The law prohibited boys under twelve and girls under eighteen from selling newspapers on the streets. The law was challenged by a member of the Jehovah's Witnesses whose children normally assisted her in the sale and distribution of religious literature. Dividing 8 to 1, the Court held that the state's role as *parens patriae* in protecting the safety of children overrode Prince's free exercise claim.

Compulsory School Attendance

In *Wisconsin v. Yoder* (1972), the Supreme Court held that a state's compulsory high school attendance law could not be constitutionally applied to members of the Old Order Amish faith, which does not permit secular education beyond the eighth grade. Writing for the Court, Chief Justice Warren E. Burger placed great stress on the fact that the education of the Amish teenager continued in the home, with emphasis on practical skills as well as religious and moral values. Based on Burger's opinion in *Yoder,* it seems unlikely that the Court would grant the Amish an exemption from compulsory primary education. Nor would it grant an exemption to members of a "religion" that strikes the Court as silly, faddish, or insincere.

One wonders whether the Amish would prevail if their case came before the current Supreme Court. After all, compulsory school attendance laws are generally applicable rules. In *Minnesota v. Hershberger* (1990), the Court vacated a state supreme court decision exempting the Amish from compliance with state traffic laws. On the other hand, the Court has long recognized the rights of parents in matters pertaining to the education of their children (see, for example, *Meyer v. Nebraska* [1923]). One can make good arguments for the current court deciding the compulsory school attendance issue either way.

TO SUMMARIZE:

- Courts have recognized the right of competent adults to refuse medical treatment on religious grounds, but generally do not permit parents to refuse life-saving medical treatment for their minor children.
- The Supreme Court has held that the Free Exercise Clause exempts members of the Old Order Amish faith from compliance with state laws requiring children to attend school beyond the eighth grade. The Court recognized the exceptional circumstances under which this exemption was granted, making it clear that a mere claim of religious liberty is not enough to warrant such special treatment.

THE WALL OF SEPARATION

The Establishment Clause of the First Amendment was adopted in contradiction to the practice, prevalent not only in Europe but among the American colonies, of having official churches supported by taxation. Indeed, as previously noted, some states maintained their established churches well into the nineteenth century. Thus, the concept of "a wall of separation between church and state," as Thomas Jefferson referred to it, was an American invention whose application remained to be worked out in practice. In *Everson v. Board of Education* (1947), the Supreme Court adopted Jefferson's metaphor as encapsulating the meaning of the Establishment Clause.

Competing Interpretations of the Establishment Clause

In the two centuries since the Establishment Clause went into effect, Americans both on and off the Supreme Court have disagreed sharply over the meaning of the clause. One view is that it merely forbids the establishment of an official, state-supported religion. According to this restrictive interpretation, Congress does not run afoul of the First Amendment as long as it refrains from selecting one denomination as the official or preferred religion. However, even the literal language of the First Amendment suggests a broader prohibition than this, however. It does not say that Congress shall make no law establishing an official religion; rather, it states that "Congress shall make no law *respecting an establishment of religion*" [emphasis added]. This general language indicates a broader restriction than mere prohibition of an established church. For the most part, the Supreme Court has opted for this broader interpretation.

When polled, most Americans respond approvingly to the abstract concept of **separation of church and state.** Yet there is no consensus on how high or how thick the wall of separation should be. Thus, the Supreme Court's decisions applying this concept to particular situations have been even more controversial than its decisions under the Free Exercise Clause. Many of these controversial decisions involve education, notably prayer in public schools and state aid to private religious schools.

Traditional Government Practices

Potential Establishment Clause questions are implicit in many traditional government practices. For example, consider the practice of Congress and every state legislature of paying a chaplain, usually of a particular Protestant denomination, to lead our representatives in public prayer (see *Marsh v. Chambers* [1983]). What about the inscription "In God We Trust" on American currency? Or the Supreme Court's time-honored practice of opening oral argument with the invocation "God save the United States and this honorable Court"? Or the recognition of America as "one nation under God" in the official pledge of allegiance to the flag? These and other common practices indicate the degree to which religion figures prominently in the public life of this nation. Although many Americans no doubt approve of such official endorsement and invocation of religion, what about the rights of nonbelievers? How far does the First Amendment allow the government to go in recognizing, endorsing, or accommodating religious beliefs? As the controversial Supreme Court decisions interpreting the Establishment Clause demonstrate, the answer to this question is far from clear.

The *Lemon* Test

In 1971, the Court laid down a three-pronged test for determining the constitutionality of policies challenged under the Establishment Clause (see *Lemon v. Kurtzman*). The so-called **Lemon** *test* synthesized various elements of the Court's Establishment Clause jurisprudence as it had evolved during the 1950s and 1960s. Although controversial from its inception, the *Lemon* test has been applied to a broad range of issues involving separation of church and state. Under the *Lemon* test, a challenged policy must meet the following criteria in order to pass muster under the Establishment Clause: (1) it must have a "secular purpose"; (2) it must not have the principal or primary effect of "inhibiting or advancing religion"; and (3) it must avoid an "excessive government entanglement with religion."

It should go without saying that the *Lemon* test does not contain hard and fast criteria for judicial decision making. Rather, like all judicial doctrines, it is subject to some degree of manipulation by those who are predisposed to a particular result. For example, how can the "purpose" of a challenged law be determined with certainty by the courts? How does one distinguish the "principal" or "primary" effects of a law from its secondary or tertiary effects? Finally, how much entanglement between religion and government is "excessive"? During the 1970s and 1980s, the Court was often criticized for inconsistency in its application of the *Lemon* test, leading some scholars to question the value of the test altogether. In the 1990s, the Court has moved away from a strict application of the *Lemon* test, but has stopped short of repudiating it altogether (see, for example, *Agostini v. Felton* [1997], discussed below and excerpted at the end of the chapter.)

TO SUMMARIZE:

- The Supreme Court has adopted Thomas Jefferson's metaphor of a "wall of separation between church and state" as capturing the essential meaning of the Establishment Clause. Since its first decision in this area, however, the Court has sought to balance the idea of separation of church and state with the equally important constitutional commitment to free exercise of religion.

- In *Lemon v. Kurtzman* (1971), the Court fashioned a three-part test for determining whether a particular policy constitutes an establishment of religion. To survive challenge, the policy must have a secular purpose, its principal effect must not be to advance or inhibit religion, and it must avoid excessive entanglement between government and religion.
- The Court has moved away from a strict application of the *Lemon* test but has stopped short of repudiating it altogether.

RELIGION AND PUBLIC EDUCATION

In *Everson v. Board of Education* (1947), the first case in which the Supreme Court applied the Establishment Clause to the states via the Fourteenth Amendment, the issue was whether a local school board could reimburse parents for expenses they incurred in transporting their children to and from Catholic schools. The payments to parents of children in parochial schools were part of a general program under which all parents of children in public schools and nonprofit private schools, regardless of religious affiliation, were entitled to reimbursement for transportation costs. However, it is worth noting that the overwhelming number of children attending nonprofit private schools in this New Jersey school district were enrolled in Catholic schools. Writing for a sharply divided Court, Justice Hugo Black justified the challenged payments on the theory that the school board was merely furthering the state's legitimate interest in getting children, "regardless of their religion, safely and expeditiously to and from accredited schools."

Justice Wiley Rutledge, joined by Justices Felix Frankfurter, Robert Jackson, and Harold Burton, dissented vigorously. Professing sympathy for the economic hardships involved in sending one's children to private, religious schools, Justice Rutledge nevertheless asserted:

> Like St. Paul's freedom, religious liberty with a great price must be bought. And for those who exercise it most fully, by insisting upon religious education for their children mixed with secular, by the terms of our Constitution the price is greater than for others.

The **child benefit theory** articulated in *Everson* has for the most part been maintained. Thus, for example, in *Board of Education v. Allen* (1968), the Supreme Court upheld a New York statute requiring local public school districts to lend textbooks on secular subjects to students in private and parochial schools. And in *Meek v. Pittenger* (1975), the Court reaffirmed this position.

Released Time Programs and Equal Access Policies

To accommodate the religious beliefs of public school students, the Court has upheld **released-time programs,** which allow students to leave campus to attend religious exercises. Distinguishing a 1948 decision in which it struck down an on-campus released-time program (*McCollum v. Board of Education*), the Court in *Zorach v. Clauson* (1952) upheld a New York policy under which public school students who received parental permission left campus to attend religious services while other students attended study hall. Writing for the Court,

Justice Douglas stressed the need for governmental accommodation of religious practices, a position from which he would later retreat.

Released-time programs, although constitutionally permissible under *Zorach v. Clauson,* are not in widespread use in public schools today. More common today are policies under which religiously oriented student groups are permitted **equal access** to school facilities. In *Widmar v. Vincent* (1981), the Supreme Court said that public school facilities that have been designated an open forum may not be placed off-limits to religious groups. In *Board of Education v. Mergens* (1990), the Court upheld the Equal Access Act of 1984, in which Congress prohibited public secondary schools that receive federal funds from disallowing meetings of student groups on the basis of "religious, political, philosophical or other content of the speech at such meetings."

Government Efforts to Assist Religious Schools

In *Lemon v. Kurtzman* (1971), the Court struck down Pennsylvania and Rhode Island policies providing publicly funded salary supplements to teachers in parochial schools as fostering "excessive entanglement." Similarly, in *Committee for Public Education v. Nyquist* (1973), the Court used the three-pronged test in striking down a New York law that provided various forms of economic aid to parochial schools. Although the released-time programs approved in *Zorach* have not been recently litigated before the Supreme Court, it is highly unlikely such programs could survive a rigorous application of the *Lemon* test.

The Supreme Court reinforced its holdings in *Lemon* and *Nyquist* in two significant decisions of the mid-1980s. In *Aguilar v. Felton* (1985), the Court struck down a New York City program that used federal funds to supplement the salaries of public school teachers who taught remedial courses on the premises of religious schools. Similarly, in *Grand Rapids School District v. Ball* (1985), the Court invalidated a program in which supplementary classes for students in sectarian schools were taught by public school teachers at public expense. Writing for the Court in the *Grand Rapids* case, Justice Brennan observed that "the symbolic union of church and state inherent in the provision of secular, state-provided instruction in the religious school buildings threatens to convey a message of state support for religion to students and to the general public."

Justice Byron White used the occasion to dissent not only from the Court's *Grand Rapids* holding but from the entire thrust of the Court's decisions in the area of state aid to religious schools:

> I am firmly of the belief that the Court's decisions in these cases, like its decisions in *Lemon* and *Nyquist,* are not required by the First Amendment and [are] contrary to the long-range interest of the country. . . . I am satisfied that what the States have sought to do in these cases is well within their authority and is not forbidden by the Establishment Clause.

In 1994 the Court reaffirmed its decisions in *Aguilar* and *Grand Rapids* by striking down a New York law that created a new special school district in a community occupied exclusively by Hassidic Jews. Virtually all of the community's children were being educated in private schools. The new district was established for the purpose of enabling the community to avail itself of public funds for the education of children with disabilities. Under *Aguilar* and *Grand Rapids,* this kind of assistance could not be provided directly to the community's private schools, thus explaining the creation of a new public school district. In *Kiryas Joel School District v. Grumet* (1994), the Court found this arrangement to be an unconstitutional establishment of religion. In this case the Court conspicuously avoided relying on the *Lemon* test, leading commentators to wonder whether this three-pronged formulation was being phased out. Recalling Justice White's dissent in *Grand Rapids,* Justice Scalia, joined by Chief Justice Rehnquist and Justice Thomas, was sharply critical of the Court's decision and indeed of its general approach in this area.

By 1997 a Court majority was willing to give ground in the area of aid to parochial schools. Thus, in *Agostini v. Felton,* a bare majority of justices voted to overturn *Aguilar v. Felton* and corresponding portions of *Grand Rapids School District v. Ball.* In her majority opinion, Justice O'Connor maintained that *Aguilar* was inconsistent with the Court's later Establishment Clause decisions. O'Connor stressed the neutrality of the federally funded remedial instruction and the procedural safeguards surrounding the program. She also noted that this program could not "reasonably be viewed as an endorsement of religion." With the concurrence of Chief Justice Rehnquist and Justices Scalia, Kennedy, and Thomas, Justice O'Connor therefore concluded that "*Aguilar,* as well as the portion of *Ball* addressing Grand Rapids' 'shared time' program, are no longer good law." In dissent, Justices Stevens, Souter, Ginsburg, and Breyer continued to express concern about the difficulty of limiting government assistance in this area to purely secular objectives.

The Continuing School Prayer Controversy

Few decisions of the modern Supreme Court have been criticized more intensely than the **school prayer decisions** of the early 1960s. In *Engel v. Vitale* (1962), the Court invalidated a New York Board of Regents policy that established the voluntary recitation of a brief generic prayer by children in the public schools at the start of each school day. Justice Black wrote the opinion for the majority, saying that "in this country it is no part of the business of government to compose official prayers for any group of the American people to recite as part of a religious program carried on by government."

Justice Potter Stewart, the lone dissenter in *Engel v. Vitale,* compared the recitation of the regents' prayer to other official recognitions of God and religion, such as the pledge of allegiance to the flag, the president's oath of office, and the invocation said prior to oral argument in the Supreme Court:

> I do not believe that this Court, or the Congress, or the President has by the actions and practices I have described established an "official religion" in violation of the Constitution. And I do not believe the State of New York has done so in this case. What each has done has been to recognize and to follow the deeply entrenched and highly cherished spiritual traditions of our Nation.

In 1963, the Court reinforced the *Engel* decision in the companion cases of *Abington School District v. Schempp* and *Murray v. Curlett* by striking down the practice of Bible reading and the recitation of the Lord's prayer in the Pennsylvania and Maryland public schools. Again, only Justice Stewart dissented.

The reaction to the Court's school prayer decisions came fast and furious and, indeed, has still not disappeared. The Court was roundly condemned by religious leaders and conservative members of Congress and through resolutions passed by several state legislatures. Polls have consistently shown that a majority of Ameri-

Free exercise of religion or a violation of separation of church and state? An organized prayer session in a public school classroom

cans oppose the Court's ban on school prayer. Even today, the public has lower regard for the Court's work in this area than in other policy areas (see Table 9.1).

On several occasions, constitutional amendments have been introduced in Congress aimed specifically at overturning the school prayer decisions. In November 1971, one such proposal in the House of Representatives fell only twenty-eight votes short of the two-thirds majority required for constitutional amendments. In the election of 1980, Ronald Reagan capitalized on public sentiment about school prayer by advocating the "school prayer amendment." However, once in office, President Reagan was either unwilling or unable to push this proposal through Congress.

Negative public reaction and widespread noncompliance notwithstanding, the Supreme Court has maintained, although by a shrinking majority, the position articulated in the school prayer cases. For example, in *Stone v. Graham* (1980), the Court invalidated a Kentucky law requiring that the Ten Commandments be posted in all public school classrooms. In *Wallace v. Jaffree* (1985) the Court struck down an Alabama law that required public school students to observe a **moment of silence** "for the purpose of meditation or voluntary prayer" at the start of each school day. In *Lee v. Wesiman* (1992) the Court held unconstitutional the practice of

TABLE 9.1   The Public Evaluates the Work of the Supreme Court in Three Policy Areas

Policy Area	Excellent %	Good %	Fair %	Poor %	Not Sure %
Matters dealing with civil rights, such as affirmative action	3	32	36	17	12
Matters dealing with religion, such as school prayer	3	19	30	42	7
Matters dealing with criminal justice, such as the death penalty	4	28	32	25	11

Source: National telephone survey of 658 randomly selected adults conducted October 6–16, 1997, by the Social Science Research Institute at the University of Tennessee, Knoxville.

inviting a member of the clergy to deliver a nonsectarian prayer at a public school graduation ceremony.

Note that in no case has the Court held that it is unconstitutional for a student to pray voluntarily in the public school classroom, although some school officials have interpreted the Court's position this way. What the Court has said is that it is unconstitutional for the state schools to require, endorse, or sanction prayer, either directly or indirectly. One might think that if this were better understood, some of the public hostility toward the Court's decisions would abate. On the other hand, given the nature and intensity of feelings on this issue, it is unlikely that an accurate public perception of the Court's holdings would diminish the public opprobrium.

The Evolution–Creationism Conflict

With the rapid expansion of public education in the early twentieth century, especially in rural areas dominated by fundamentalist Protestantism, a controversy erupted over the teaching of evolution in the public schools. The controversy achieved national prominence in 1925 when John T. Scopes, a high school biology teacher in Dayton, Tennessee, was prosecuted for teaching evolution in violation of a state law that had been passed earlier that year. Amidst a carnival-like atmosphere, the "Monkey Trial," as it was caricatured in the press, pitted famous politician and orator William Jennings Bryan against celebrated lawyer Clarence Darrow in a battle royal in the courtroom. Although Darrow outsmarted Bryan in a much-publicized debate over biblical literalism, Scopes was nevertheless convicted of violating the state statute. The Tennessee Supreme Court reversed the conviction on technical grounds, however, preventing the U.S. Supreme Court from having to consider what was potentially the most explosive constitutional question of that decade.

In the wake of the **Scopes trial,** two states, Arkansas and Mississippi, enacted legislation similar to the Tennessee antievolution law. Yet it was not until 1965 that one of these laws was challenged in court. In that year, Susan Epperson, a high school biology teacher in Little Rock, filed a lawsuit challenging the Arkansas statute. Although the Arkansas trial court ruled in favor of Epperson and struck down the antievolution law, the state supreme court reversed and reinstated the statute. On certiorari, the U.S. Supreme Court reversed (*Epperson v. Arkansas* [1968]). Writing for the Court, Justice Abe Fortas asserted that Arkansas could not "prevent its teachers from discussing the theory of evolution because it is contrary to the belief of some that the Book of Genesis must be the exclusive source of doctrine as to the origins of man."

The *Epperson* decision put to rest the issue of whether states could prohibit the teaching of evolution in their public schools. But two decades later, the evolution–creationism conflict resurfaced in Louisiana. This time, the question was whether the state could mandate that creationism, or **creation science,** be given equal time in the classroom along with the theory of evolution. In *Edwards v. Aguillard* (1987), the Supreme Court answered this question in the negative. Writing for a majority of seven, Justice Brennan averred that "the primary purpose" of the Louisiana Creationism Act was "to endorse a particular religious doctrine," rather than further the legitimate interests of the state in fostering different points of view in the classroom.

In the wake of such decisions as *Edwards v. Aguillard* and *Epperson v. Arkansas,* as well as the school prayer decisions discussed previously, fundamentalist Christians began to argue that, in its attempt to expunge religious teaching and symbols from the public schools, the Supreme Court had fostered a "religion" of **secular humanism.** According to its detractors, secular humanism is a philosophy emphasizing the view that morality is a human invention and that moral choices are largely matters of personal values. In the view of some fundamentalists, the pervasiveness of secular humanism in public school curricula was highly corrosive to traditional values and institutions.

In 1987, a federal district court barred the use of certain widely used history, social studies, and home economics textbooks in the public schools of Mobile County, Alabama. In essence, the district judge held that these books advanced the "religion" of secular humanism. In embracing this philosophy, the textbooks allegedly ignored or understated the historical and contemporary significance of traditional religion in American life, thus abridging the Free Exercise rights of students holding theistic beliefs. The "teaching" of secular humanism amounted to "a sweeping fundamental belief that must not be promoted by the public schools." Such promotion, the court concluded, was a violation of the Establishment Clause of the First Amendment. The Court of Appeals for the Eleventh Circuit promptly overruled this novel decision, finding that the "purpose" for using the textbooks in question was "purely secular" (see *Smith v. Board of School Commissioners of Mobile County* [1987]).

In a similar case initiated in 1986, fundamentalist parents in Hawkins County, Tennessee, sued their county school board over the reading curriculum in the local public schools, complaining of the humanist perspective embodied in the curriculum. Although plaintiffs won at trial, the judgment was overruled on appeal by the Court of Appeals for the Sixth Circuit. The Supreme Court declined to review the case (*Mozert v. Hawkins County Public Schools* [1988]), thus letting the appeals court's decision stand.

Discrimination Against Religious Expression in Public Educational Arena

If a public school or university subsidizes a variety of student newspapers, can it withhold funds from a particular paper solely because it "promotes or manifests a particular belief in or about a deity or an ultimate reality"? This was the issue before the Court in *Rosenberger v. University of Virginia* (1995). The university denied a subsidy to "Wide Awake: A Christian Perspective at the University of Virginia." The student-publisher of the paper went to court. The Supreme Court found the denial of support violative of free speech, in that the University was discriminating against the paper based on its content. Moreover, the Court rejected the argument that to subsidize the paper, the University would be breaching the wall of separation between church and state. Four justices (Souter, Stevens, Ginsburg, and Breyer) dissented, claiming that for the university to provide the subsidy in question would constitute a clear violation of the Establishment Clause. Some observers regarded Justice O'Connor's concurring opinion as somewhat equivocal, leading them to speculate that in a similar case O'Connor might be persuaded to go the other way. It is possible that the *Rosenberger* decision will be limited to its rather unique facts.

TO SUMMARIZE:

- The Supreme Court has struggled with the question of whether various kinds of governmental support for education extending to private, parochial schools can be justified under a general "child benefit" theory or must be barred as a violation of the Establishment Clause.

- The Court has aroused deep and protracted controversy with its persistent efforts to proscribe officially sponsored religious exercises in the public schools. From its school prayer decisions of the early 1960s through its "moment of silence" ruling in 1985 to its 1992 holding regarding commencement exercises, the Court has steadfastly applied a principle of strict separation in this area.
- The Court has also applied the principle of separation of church and state in thwarting state efforts dating from the 1920s to forbid the teaching of evolution and later attempts to promote the teaching of "creation science" in the public schools.

GOVERNMENTAL AFFIRMATIONS OF RELIGIOUS BELIEF

In a religious society such as ours, it is inevitable (and, many would say, desirable) for there to be numerous public affirmations of belief. The Court's decision in *Abington v. Schempp* suggests, however, that government sponsorship of such affirmations may be unconstitutional. Nevertheless, the Supreme Court has been unwilling to hold government-sponsored displays or affirmations of belief to the same standard of **strict neutrality** that underlies the school prayer decisions. For example, in *McGowan v. Maryland* (1961) the Court upheld laws that prohibited certain businesses from operating on Sunday, despite the obvious religious underpinnings of such restrictions. In the Court's view, these **Sunday closing laws** had a secular purpose in that they represented the community's desire for a day of rest and relaxation, independent of any religious significance. The fact that this day of rest happened to be the day of worship for most Christians was merely incidental. Writing for the Court in *McGowan,* Chief Justice Earl Warren noted that

> it is common knowledge that the first day of the week has come to have special significance as a rest day in this country. People of all religions and people with no religion regard Sunday as a time for family activity, for visiting friends and relatives, for late sleeping, for passive and active entertainments, for dining out, and the like.

Warren E. Burger: Chief Justice, 1969–1986

Perhaps the best example of the Court's unwillingness to extend the holding of *Abington v. Schempp* to its logical conclusion came in *Marsh v. Chambers* (1983). Here, the Court refused to invalidate Nebraska's policy of beginning legislative sessions with prayers offered by a Protestant chaplain retained at the taxpayers' expense. Writing for the Court, Chief Justice Burger made no pretense of applying the strict three-part test laid down in his own majority opinion in *Lemon v. Kurtzman.* Instead, Burger's opinion relied heavily on history and the need for accommodation of popular religious beliefs. In a caustic dissent, Justice Brennan observed that "if any group of law students were asked to apply the principles of *Lemon* to the question of legislative prayer, they would nearly unanimously find the practice to be unconstitutional."

The decision in *Marsh v. Chambers* suggested to some observers that the Supreme Court was prepared to abandon the strict tripartite *Lemon* test for determining establishment of religion. To others, *Marsh* was a mere aberration, based on the pragmatic realization that the Court would inevitably be embarrassed if it were to attempt to strike down a practice that occurs in nearly every legislature in the United States, including the U.S. Congress. This case provides a good illustration of the practical limits of judicial power.

Christmas Displays on Public Property

The decision in *Lynch v. Donnelly* (1984) suggests that *Marsh* was more than a mere aberration. In *Lynch,* the Court upheld a city-sponsored nativity scene in Pawtucket, Rhode Island. Chief Justice Burger's majority opinion barely mentioned the *Lemon* test. Again Burger relied on history and the fact that the créche had become for many a "neutral harbinger of the holiday season," rather than a symbol of Christianity.

Five years later, in the Pennsylvania case of *County of Allegheny v. American Civil Liberties Union* (1989), the Court reexamined the constitutional question posed by traditional holiday displays on public property. Here, the justices considered two separate displays: a créche prominently situated on the grand staircase inside the county courthouse and an arrangement featuring a Christmas tree and a Hanukkah menorah placed just outside the nearby city–county building. A sign bearing the mayor's name and entitled "Salute to Liberty" was placed at the foot of the Christmas tree. Justice Blackmun, for a majority of the Court, maintained that the display of the créche inside the courthouse, with the accompanying words "Gloria in Excelsis Deo," clearly conveyed a religious message. By authorizing the display, the county had, in Blackmun's view, indicated its endorsement of that message. Such endorsement, he concluded, was a violation of the Establishment Clause. By contrast, the Christmas tree and menorah display, in tandem with the mayor's message, was not in the Court's view "an endorsement of religious faith, but simply a recognition of cultural diversity." The overall display conveyed a predominantly secular message and thus did not violate the Establishment Clause.

The Supreme Court's decisions in *Marsh* and *Lynch* indicate that the Burger Court retreated from the strict neutrality of the Warren Court in favor of an approach that might be labeled **accommodation** or **benevolent neutrality.** The *Allegheny County* decision suggested, however, that the Rehnquist Court was seeking a middle ground in this area.

TO SUMMARIZE:

- With respect to the issue of governmental affirmation of popular religious beliefs, the Court has sought a middle ground in which considerations of tradition and established practice are balanced against the principle of church–state separation.

THE PROBLEM OF TAX EXEMPTIONS

Traditionally, church properties have been exempt from local property taxes and church incomes have been exempt from federal and state income taxes. Such exemptions generally are not limited to churches but extend to various private, nonprofit organizations that can be classified as charitable institutions. The existence of **tax exemptions** for churches and religious schools raises questions under both the Establishment and Free Exercise Clauses of the First Amendment. On the one hand, it can be argued that a tax exemption is an indirect subsidy. Arguably, for government to exempt churches and church schools from paying taxes is to subsidize them in violation of the requirement of separation of church and state. On the other hand, one can argue that failure to exempt churches from taxation amounts to an infringement of the Free Exercise Clause, since, as Chief Justice John Marshall pointed out in *M'Culloch v. Maryland* (1819), "the power to tax involves the power to destroy."

The Supreme Court considered the constitutionality of property tax exemptions for churches in the case of *Walz v. Tax Commission* (1970). Frederick Walz brought suit against the New York City Tax Commission, arguing that the commission's grant of property tax exemptions to churches (as allowed by state law) required him to subsidize those churches indirectly. Relying heavily on the long-standing practice of religious tax exemptions and the Court's traditional deference to legislative bodies with regard to the taxing power, the Court found no constitutional violation. Writing for a majority of eight, Chief Justice Burger noted that

> [f]ew concepts are more deeply embedded in the fabric of our national life, beginning with pre-Revolutionary colonial times, than for the government to exercise . . . this kind of benevolent neutrality toward churches and religious exercise generally so long as none was favored over others and none suffered interference.

Dissenting vigorously, Justice Douglas argued for strict government neutrality toward religion as distinct from the Chief Justice's "benevolent neutrality" approach:

> If believers are entitled to public financial support, so are nonbelievers. A believer and nonbeliever under the present law are treated differently because of the articles of their faith. Believers are doubtless comforted that the cause of religion is being fostered by this legislation. Yet one of the mandates of the First Amendment is to promote a viable, pluralistic society and to keep government neutral, not only between sects, but also between believers and nonbelievers.

It is interesting to compare Justice Douglas's dissent in *Walz* with his majority opinion in *Zorach v. Clauson.* In 1952, Douglas had written, apparently in earnest, about the importance of governmental accommodation of religion. In concurring opinions in the school prayer decisions of 1962 and 1963, Douglas indicated that he was reconsidering his position on the Establishment Clause generally. By 1970, his stance had shifted from accommodation to strict neutrality. Justice Douglas's forceful dissent in *Walz* to the contrary notwithstanding, it is unlikely that the Supreme Court would ever invalidate religious tax exemptions. There is simply too much public support for these long-standing policies.

To take advantage of tax exemptions for religious property, a small minority of unscrupulous individuals have established "churches" in their homes after obtaining inexpensive "doctor of divinity" degrees through the mail. For example, in the late 1970s in one small town in New York, nearly 85 percent of the residents became "ministers" and claimed tax-exempt status for their homes. This subterfuge was finally ended through state legislation that was upheld by a later court decision. The U.S. Supreme Court dismissed the appeal, thus allowing the state court decision to stand (*Hardenbaugh v. New York* [1981]).

One of the most controversial Supreme Court decisions of the early 1980s dealt with the question of whether tax-exempt status could be withdrawn from religious schools that practice race discrimination. In *Bob Jones University v. United States* (1983), the Court held that such institutions could indeed be denied their federal income tax exemptions by the Internal Revenue Service (IRS). Prior to 1975, Bob Jones University, a fundamentalist Christian college in South Carolina, had refused to admit African-Americans. After 1975, African-Americans were admitted, but interracial dating and marriage were strictly prohibited. The IRS formally revoked the school's long-standing tax exemption in 1976. Then, in 1982, the Reagan administration announced that the IRS was restoring tax-exempt status to all segregated private schools, claiming that the IRS lacked the authority to remove tax exemptions without specific authorizing legislation from Congress. The Court's 8-to-1 decision in *Bob Jones* repudiated the Reagan administration's view that the IRS lacked authority to revoke the tax-exempt status of religious schools that practice racial discrimination. With regard to the First Amendment issue, the Court held that

> [t]he governmental interest at stake here is compelling. . . . The government has a fundamental, overriding interest in eradicating racial discrimination in education. . . . That governmental interest substantially outweighs whatever burden denial of tax benefits places on petitioners' exercise of their religious beliefs.

The Court's decision in *Bob Jones* implies that tax exemptions for religious enterprises are not a matter of constitutional entitlement—they are granted through governmental benevolence and can be withdrawn for reasons of public policy.

Tuition Tax Credits

A number of states have considered the idea of providing tax credits to parents of children in private and parochial schools. Indeed, in 1982, President Reagan proposed **tuition tax credits** of five hundred dollars per child for parents whose children attend private and parochial schools. Although the proposal did not obtain congressional approval, serious questions were raised about its constitutionality. In *Committee for Public Education v. Nyquist* (1973), the Supreme Court had struck down a state tax deduction for parents of children in parochial schools. However, the Court may be moving away from the *Nyquist* decision, at least insofar as it dealt with tax benefits. In 1983, in *Mueller v. Allen,* the Court upheld a Minnesota law that allowed parents of children in private and parochial schools to deduct as much as seven hundred dollars of school expenses from their incomes subject to state income tax. Given the conservatism of the Rehnquist Court it is unlikely that the justices will raise serious constitutional objections to tax credits or vouchers that benefit parochial schools, as long as parochial schools do not receive *selective* benefits.

TO SUMMARIZE:

- While state and local governments are not constitutionally required to provide tax exemptions for religious institutions, such exemptions have been upheld so long as they extend to all nonprofit charitable entities.
- The Supreme Court has permitted the Internal Revenue Service to revoke tax-exempt status from private schools that engage in racial discrimination in clear violation of fundamental public policy commitments.
- In light of the Court's diverse opinions in the area of governmental aid to parochial schools, it is an open question whether the Court would approve tuition tax credits to parents of children attending such schools.

CONCLUSION

Although the United States is a decidedly religious nation, much more so than other advanced democracies, it is also committed to **secular government** and religious freedom. These competing values create tensions that can never be fully resolved. Inevitably, constitutional law on the subject of religious liberty remains unsettled, reflecting the evolving views of a maturing society.

The Supreme Court of the 1990s appears to accord legitimacy to governmental efforts to accommodate traditional religious practices. In this respect, it has followed the initiatives of the Burger Court in such cases as *Widmar v. Vincent* (1981) and *Lynch v. Donnelly* (1984). The Court has been less receptive to unorthodox religious practices, especially if they are perceived to be in conflict with the imperatives of law enforcement (see, for example, *Employment Division v. Smith* [1990]). The ideological impact on the Court resulting from appointments made by Presidents Nixon, Reagan, and Bush is apparent in this area. In addition to the influence of partisan judicial appointments, we see the Court responding to a conservative trend in society's attitudes with respect to religion, crime, and deviance. The following chapter examines the changing response of the Supreme Court to constitutional questions dealing specifically with crime and punishment.

KEY TERMS

Religion Clauses of the First Amendment

school prayer

Free Exercise Clause

Establishment Clause

conscientious objector

religious speech

expressive religious conduct

public forum

time, place, and manner regulations

unconventional religious practices

fundamental right

compelling governmental interest

Religious Freedom Restoration Act (RFRA)

parens patriae

right to refuse medical treatment

separation of church and state

Lemon test

child benefit theory

released-time programs

equal access

school prayer decisions

moment of silence

Scopes trial

creation science

secular humanism

strict neutrality

Sunday closing laws

accommodation

benevolent neutrality

tax exemptions

tuition tax credits

secular government

FOR FURTHER READING

Bellah, Robert, et al. *The Good Society.* New York: Knopf, 1991.

Carter, Lief. *An Introduction to Constitutional Interpretation: Cases in Law and Religion.* New York: Longman, 1991.

Curry, Thomas J. *The First Freedoms.* New York: Oxford University Press, 1986.

Howe, Mark DeWolfe. *The Garden and the Wilderness: Religion and Government in American Constitutional History.* Chicago: University of Chicago Press, 1985.

Irons, Peter. *The Courage of Their Convictions: Sixteen Americans Who Fought Their Way to the Supreme* *Court.* New York: Penguin Books, 1990. See, in particular, Chapters 1, 7, 9, and 15.

Kauper, Paul. *Religion and the Constitution.* Baton Rouge: Louisiana State University Press, 1964.

Levy, Leonard. *The Establishment Clause: Religion and the First Amendment.* New York: Macmillan, 1986.

Manwaring, David. *Render Unto Caesar: The Flag Salute Controversy.* Chicago: University of Chicago Press, 1962.

Miller, William Lee. *The First Liberty: Religion and the American Republic.* New York: Knopf, 1986.

Oaks, Dallin (ed.). *The Wall Between Church and State.* Chicago: University of Chicago Press, 1963.

Pfeffer, Leo. *God, Caesar and the Constitution.* Boston: Beacon Press, 1975.

Sorauf, Frank. *The Wall of Separation: The Constitutional Politics of Church and State.* Princeton, N.J.: Princeton University Press, 1976.

Stokes, Anson, and Leo Pfeffer. *Church and State in the United States.* New York: Harper and Row, 1965.

Tussman, Joseph. *The Supreme Court on Church and State.* New York: Oxford University Press, 1962.

INTERNET RESOURCES

Name of Resource	Description	URL (circa 1998)
Catholic League for Religious and Civil Rights	Site promoting the nation's largest Catholic civil rights organization	http://www.catholicleague.org/
The Christian Coalition	A political organization dedicated to public policies informed by conservative Christian ideas	http://www.cc.org/
Americans United for Separation of Church and State	A site maintained by one of the best known anti-establishmentarian organizations	http://www.au.org/
The Secular Web	A web site devoted to promoting secular humanism	http://www.secular.org/

Case

WEST VIRGINIA STATE BOARD OF EDUCATION V. BARNETTE

319 U.S. 624; 63 S.Ct. 1178; 87 L. Ed. 1628 (1943)
Vote: 6–3

In Minersville School District v. Gobitis *(1940), the Supreme Court, in an 8-to-1 decision, upheld a local school board directive in Minersville, Pennsylvania, requiring public school students and teachers to participate in a flag salute ceremony conducted as a regular part of the daily classroom schedule. This requirement had been challenged by Walter Gobitis, a member of the Jehovah's Witnesses sect, whose children, Lillian and William (ages twelve and ten), were expelled from school for refusing to salute the flag. In upholding the flag salute requirement, the Court rejected Gobitis's contention that it violated First Amendment principles of religious liberty as applied to the states through the Due Process Clause of the Fourteenth Amendment.*

Three years later, in a dramatic and highly publicized reversal of its position, the Supreme Court, by a 6-to-3 margin, overruled the Gobitis *case by striking down a virtually identical flag salute requirement imposed by the West Virginia Board of Education. The board was acting under authority of a statute passed by the West Virginia legislature in the immediate aftermath of the* Gobitis *decision. This law required all schools in the state to offer classes in civics, history, and the federal and state constitutions "for the purpose of teaching, fostering, and perpetuating the ideals, principles, and spirit of Americanism, and increasing the knowledge of the organization and machinery of the Government."*

Walter Barnette and two other Jehovah's Witnesses, all of whom had children in the public schools, filed suit to enjoin the compulsory flag salute on grounds that it violated a constitutionally protected religious precept contained in the Old Testament (Exod. 20:4–5) forbidding the worship of "any graven image." Under their reading of the Scriptures, the flag salute constituted such forbidden worship.

Because this decision represents such a swift and decisive overruling of constitutional precedent, it is interesting to compare the alignments of the justices in Gobitis *and* Barnette. *Justice Frankfurter wrote the majority opinion in the* Gobitis *case, with only Justice Stone dissenting. Justice Jackson, who along with Justice Rutledge joined the Court after that decision was announced, wrote the majority opinion in* Barnette. *Justices Black, Douglas, and Murphy, all of whom had supported Frankfurter's original majority position, switched sides and supported the majority opinion in* Barnette. *Justices Frankfurter, Reed, and Roberts dissented in the latter case.*

Mr. Justice Jackson delivered the opinion of the Court.

. . . National unity as an end which officials may foster by persuasion and example is not in question. The problem is whether under our Constitution compulsion as here employed is a permissible means for its achievement.

Struggles to coerce uniformity of sentiment in support of some end thought essential to their time and country have been waged by many good as well as by evil men. Nationalism is a relatively recent phenomenon but at other times and places the ends have been racial or territorial security, support of a dynasty or regime, and particular plans for saving souls. As first and moderate methods to attain unity have failed, those bent on its accomplishment must resort to an ever increasing severity. As governmental pressure toward unity becomes greater, so strife becomes more bitter as to whose unity it shall be. Probably no deeper division of our people could proceed from any provocation than from finding it necessary to choose what doctrine and whose program public educational officials shall compel youth to unite in embracing. Ultimate futility of such attempts to compel coherence is the lesson of every such effort from the Roman drive to stamp out Christianity as a disturber of its pagan unity, the Inquisition, as a means to religious and dynastic unity, the Siberian exiles as a means to Russian unity, down to the fast failing efforts of our present totalitarian enemies. Those who begin coercive elimination of dissent soon find themselves exterminating dissenters. Compulsory unification of opinion achieves only the unanimity of the graveyard.

It seems trite but necessary to say that the First Amendment to our Constitution was designed to avoid these ends by avoiding these beginnings. There is no mysticism in the American concept of the State or of the nature or origin of its authority. We set up government by consent of the governed, and the Bill of Rights denies those in power any legal opportunity to coerce that consent. Authority here is to be controlled by public opinion, not public opinion by authority.

The case is made difficult not because the principles of its decision are obscure but because the flag involved is our own. Nevertheless, we apply the limitations of the Constitution with no fear that freedom to be intellectually and spiritually diverse or even contrary will disintegrate the social organization. To believe that patriotism will not flourish if patriotic ceremonies are voluntary and spontaneous instead of a compulsory routine is to make an unflattering estimate of the appeal of our institutions to free minds. We can have intellectual individualism and the rich cultural diversities that we owe to exceptional minds only at the price of occasional eccentricity and abnormal attitudes. When they are so harmless to others or to the State as those we deal with here, the price is not too great. But freedom to differ is not limited to things that do not matter much. That would be a mere shadow of freedom. The test of its substance is the right to differ as to things that touch the heart of the existing order.

If there is any fixed star in our constitutional constellation, it is that no official, high or petty, can prescribe what shall be orthodox in politics, nationalism, religion, or other matters of opinion or force citizens to confess by word or act their faith therein. If there are any circumstances which permit an exception, they do not now occur to us.

We think the action of the local authorities in compelling the flag salute and pledge transcends constitutional limitations on their power and invades the sphere of intellect and spirit which it is the purpose of the First Amendment to our Constitution to reserve from all official control.

The decision of this Court in *Minersville School Dist. v. Gobitis* and the holdings of those few *per curiam* decisions which preceded and foreshadowed it are overruled, and the judgment enjoining enforcement of the West Virginia Regulation is affirmed.

Mr. Justice Roberts and **Mr. Justice Reed** adhere to the views expressed by the Court in *Minersville School Dist. v. Gobitis,* . . . and are of the opinion that the judgment below should be reversed.

Mr. Justice Black and **Mr. Justice Douglas,** concurring.

We are substantially in agreement with the opinion just read, but since we originally joined with the Court in the *Gobitis* case, it is appropriate that we make a brief statement of reasons for our change of view.

Reluctance to make the Federal Constitution a rigid bar against state regulation of conduct thought inimical to the public welfare was the controlling influence which moved us to consent to the *Gobitis* decision. Long reflection convinced us that although the principle is sound, its application in the particular case was wrong. . . . We believe that the statute before us fails to accord full scope to the freedom of religion secured to the appellees by the First and Fourteenth Amendments. . . .

No well ordered society can leave to the individuals an absolute right to make final decisions, unassailable by the State, as to everything they will or will not do. The First Amendment does not go so far. Religious faiths, honestly held, do not free individuals from responsibility to conduct themselves obediently to laws which are either imperatively necessary to protect society as a whole from grave and pressingly imminent dangers or which, without any general prohibition, merely regulate time, place or manner of religious activity. Decisions as to the constitutionality of particular laws which strike at the substance of religious tenets and practices must be made by this Court. The duty is a solemn one, and in meeting it we cannot say that a failure, because of religious scruples, to assume a particular physical position and to repeat the words of a patriotic formula creates a grave danger to the nation. Such a statutory exaction is a form of test oath, and the test oath has always been abhorrent in the United States.

Words uttered under coercion are proof of loyalty to nothing but self-interest. Love of country must spring from willing hearts and free minds, inspired by a fair administration of wise laws enacted by the people's elected representatives within the bounds of express constitutional prohibitions. These laws must, to be consistent with the First Amendment, permit the widest toleration of conflicting viewpoints consistent with a society of free men.

Neither our domestic tranquility in peace nor our martial effort in war depend on compelling little children to participate in a ceremony which ends in nothing for them but a fear of spiritual condemnation. If, as we think, their fears are groundless, time and reason are the proper antidotes for their errors. The ceremonial, when enforced against conscientious objectors, more likely to defeat than to serve its high purpose, is a handy implement for disguised religious persecution. As such, it is inconsistent with our Constitution's plan and purpose.

Mr. Justice Murphy, concurring:

. . . Without wishing to disparage the purposes and intentions of those who hope to inculcate sentiments of loyalty and patriotism by requiring a declaration of allegiance as a feature of public education, or unduly belittle the benefits that may accrue therefrom, I am impelled to conclude that such a requirement is not essential to the maintenance of effective government and orderly society. To many it is deeply distasteful to join in a public chorus of affirmation of private belief. By some, including the members of this sect, it is apparently regarded as incompatible with a primary religious obligation and therefore a restriction on religious freedom. Official compulsion to affirm what is contrary to one's religious beliefs is the antithesis of freedom of worship which, it is well to recall, was achieved in this country only after what Jefferson characterized as the "severest contests in which I have ever been engaged." . . .

Mr. Justice Frankfurter, dissenting.

One who belongs to the most vilified and persecuted minority in history is not likely to be insensible to the freedoms guaranteed by our Constitution. Were my purely personal attitude relevant I should wholeheartedly associate myself with the general libertarian views in the Court's opinion, representing as they do the thought and action of a lifetime. But as judges we are neither Jew nor Gentile, neither Catholic nor agnostic. We owe equal attachment to the Constitution and are equally bound by our judicial obligations whether we derive our citizenship from the earliest or the latest immigrants to these shores. As a member of this Court I am not justified in writing my private notions of policy into the Constitution, no matter how deeply I may cherish them or how mischievous I may deem their disregard. The duty of a judge who must decide which of two claims before the Court shall prevail, that of a State to enact and enforce laws within its general competence or that of an individual to refuse obedience because of the demands of his conscience, is not that of the ordinary person. It can never be emphasized too much that one's own opinion about the wisdom or evil of a law should be excluded altogether when one is doing one's duty on the bench. The only opinion of our own even looking in that direction that is material is our opinion whether legislators could in reason have enacted such a law. In the light of all the circumstances, including the history of this question in this Court, it would require more daring than I possess to deny that reasonable legislators could have taken the action which is before us for review. Most unwillingly, therefore, I must differ from my brethren with regard to legislation like this. I cannot bring my mind to believe that the "liberty" secured by the Due Process Clause gives this Court authority to deny to the State of West Virginia the attainment of that which we all recognize as a legitimate legislative end, namely, the promotion of good citizenship, by employment of the means here chosen. . . .

Of course patriotism cannot be enforced by the flag salute. But neither can the liberal spirit be enforced by judicial invalidation of illiberal legislation. Of constant preoccupation with the constitutionality of legislation rather than with its wisdom tends to preoccupation of the American mind with a false value. The tendency of focusing attention on constitutionality is to make constitutionality synonymous with wisdom, to regard a law as all right if it is constitutional. Such an attitude is a great enemy of liberalism. Particularly in legislation affecting freedom of thought and freedom of speech much which should offend a free-spirited society is constitutional. Reliance for the most precious interests of civilization, therefore, must be found outside of their vindication in courts of law. Only a persistent positive translation of the faith of a free society into the convictions and habits and actions of a community is the ultimate reliance against unabated temptations to fetter the human spirit.

Case

WISCONSIN V. YODER

406 U.S. 205; 92 S.Ct. 1526; 32 L. Ed. 2d 15 (1972)
Vote: 6–1

Here the Court considers whether members of the Old Order Amish have a constitutional right to refuse to comply with a state's compulsory high school attendance law.

Mr. Chief Justice Burger delivered the opinion of the Court.

. . . Respondents Jonas Yoder and Wallace Miller are members of the Old Order Amish religion, and respondent Adin Yutzy is a member of the Conservative Amish Mennonite Church. They and their families are residents of Green County, Wisconsin. Wisconsin's compulsory school-attendance law required them to cause their children to attend public or private school until . . . age 16 but the respondents declined to send their children, ages 14 and 15, to public school after they completed the eighth grade. The children were not enrolled in any private school, or within any recognized exception to the compulsory-attendance law, and they are conceded to be subject to the Wisconsin statute.

On complaint of the school district administrator for the public schools, respondents were charged, tried, and convicted of violating the compulsory-attendance law in Green County Court and were fined the sum of $5 each. Respondents defended on the ground that the application of the compulsory-attendance law violated their rights under the First and Fourteenth Amendments. The trial testimony showed that respondents believed, in accordance with the tenets of Old Order Amish communities generally, that their children's attendance at high school, public or private, was contrary to the Amish religion and way of life. They believed that by sending their children to high school, they would not only expose themselves to the danger of the censure of the church community, but, as found by the county court, also endanger their own salvation and that of their children. The State stipulated that respondents' religious beliefs were sincere.

In support of their position, respondents presented as expert witnesses scholars on religion and education whose testimony is uncontradicted. They expressed their opinions on the relationship of the Amish belief concerning school attendance to the more general tenets of their religion, and described the impact that compulsory high school attendance could have on the continued survival of Amish communities as they exist in the United States today. The history of the Amish sect was given in some detail, beginning with the Swiss Anabaptists of the 16th century who rejected institutionalized churches and sought to return to the early, simple, Christian life de-emphasizing material success, rejecting the competitive spirit, and seeking to insulate themselves from the modern world. As a result of their common heritage, Old Order Amish communities today are characterized by a fundamental belief that salvation requires life in a church community separate and apart from the world and worldly influence. This concept of life aloof from the world and its values is central to their faith. . . .

Amish objection to formal education beyond the eighth grade is firmly grounded in these central religious concepts. They object to the high school, and higher education generally, because the values they teach are in marked variance with Amish values and the Amish way of life; they view secondary school education as an impermissible exposure of their children to a "worldly" influence in conflict with their beliefs. The high school tends to emphasize intellectual and scientific accomplishments, self-distinction, competitiveness, worldly success, and social life with other students. Amish society emphasizes informal learning-through-doing; a life of "goodness," rather than a life of intellect; wisdom, rather than technical knowledge, community welfare, rather than competition; and separation from, rather than integration with, contemporary worldly society. . . .

The Amish do not object to elementary education through the first eight grades as a general proposition because they agree that their children must have basic skills in the "three R's" in order to read the Bible, to be good farmers and citizens, and to be able to deal with non-Amish people when necessary in the course of daily affairs. They view such a basic education as acceptable because it does not significantly expose their children to worldly values or interfere with their development in the Amish community during the crucial adolescent period. While Amish accept compulsory elementary education generally, wherever possible they have established their own elementary schools in many respects like the small local schools of the past. In the Amish belief higher learning tends to develop values they reject as influences that alienate man from God. . . .

Although the trial court in its careful findings determined that the Wisconsin compulsory school-attendance law "does interfere with the freedom of the Defendants to act in accordance with their sincere religious belief" it also concluded that the requirement of high school attendance until age 16 was a "reasonable and constitutional" exercise of governmental power, and therefore denied the motion to dismiss the charges. The Wisconsin Circuit Court affirmed the convictions. The Wisconsin Supreme Court, however, sustained respondents' claim under the Free Exercise Clause of the First Amendment and reversed the convictions. A majority of the court was of the opinion that the State had failed to make an adequate showing that its interest in "establishing and maintaining an educational system overrides the defendants' right to the free exercise of their religion." . . .

There is no doubt as to the power of a State, having a high responsibility for education of its citizens, to impose reasonable regulations for the control and duration of basic education. See, e.g., *Pierce v. Society of Sisters* . . . (1925). Providing public schools ranks at the very apex of the function of a State. Yet even this paramount responsibility was, in *Pierce,* made to yield to the right of parents to provide an equivalent education in a privately operated system. There the Court held that Oregon's statute compelling attendance in a public school from age eight to age 16 unreasonably interfered with the interest of parents in directing the rearing of their offspring, including their education in church-operated schools. As that case suggests, the values of parental direction of the religious upbringing and education of their children in their early and formative years have a high place in our society. . . . Thus, a State's interest in universal education, however highly we rank it, is not totally free from a balancing process when it impinges on fundamental rights and interests, such as those specifically protected by the Free Exercise Clause of the First Amendment, and the traditional interest of parents with respect to the religious upbringing of their children so long as they, in the words of *Pierce,* "prepare [them] for additional obligations." . . .

It follows that in order for Wisconsin to compel school attendance beyond the eighth grade against a claim that such attendance interferes with the practice of a legitimate religious belief, it must appear either that the State does not deny the free exercise of religious belief by its requirement, or that there is a state interest of sufficient magnitude to override the interest claiming protection under the Free Exercise Clause. Long before there was general acknowledgment of the need for universal formal education, the Religion Clauses had specially and firmly fixed the right to free exercise of religious beliefs, and buttressing this fundamental right was an equally firm, even if less explicit, prohibition against the establishment of any religion by government. The values underlying these two provisions relating to religion have been zealously protected, sometimes even at the expense of other interests of admittedly high social importance. The invalidation of financial aid to parochial schools by government grants for a salary subsidy for teachers is but one example of the extent to which courts have gone in this regard, notwithstanding that such aid programs were legislatively determined to be in the public interest and the service of sound educational policy by States and by Congress. . . .

The essence of all that has been said and written on the subject is that only those interests of the highest order and those not otherwise served can overbalance legitimate claims to the free exercise of religion. We can accept it as settled, therefore, that, however strong the State's interest in universal compulsory education, it is by no means absolute to the exclusion or subordination of all other interests. . . .

We come then to the quality of the claims of the respondents concerning the alleged encroachment of Wisconsin's compulsory school-attendance statute on their rights and the rights of their children to the free exercise of the religious beliefs they and their forebears have adhered to for almost three centuries. In evaluating those claims we must be careful to determine whether the Amish religious faith and their mode of life are, as they claim, inseparable and interdependent. A way of life, however virtuous and admirable, may not be interposed as a barrier to reasonable state regulation of education if it is based on purely secular considerations; to have the protection of the Religion Clauses, the claims must be rooted in religious belief. Although a determination of what is a "religious" belief or practice entitled to constitutional protection may present a most delicate question, the very concept of ordered liberty precludes allowing every person to make his own standards on matters of conduct in which society as a whole has important interests. . . .

. . . [T]he record in this case abundantly supports the claim that the traditional way of life of the Amish is not merely a matter of personal preference, but one of deep religious conviction, shared by an organized group, and intimately related to daily living. . . .

The impact of the compulsory-attendance law on respondents' practice of the Amish religion is not only severe, but inescapable, for the Wisconsin law affirmatively compels them, under threat of criminal sanction, to perform acts undeniably at odds with fundamental tenets of their religious beliefs. : . . Nor is the impact of the compulsory-attendance law confined to grave interference with important Amish religious tenets from a subjective point of view. It carries with it precisely the kind of objective danger to the free exercise of religion that the First Amendment was designed to prevent. As the record shows, compulsory school attendance to age 16 for Amish children carries with it a very real threat of undermining the Amish community and religious practice as they exist today; they must either abandon belief and be assimilated into society at large, or be forced to migrate to some other and more tolerant region.

In sum, the unchallenged testimony of acknowledged experts in education and religious history, almost 300 years of consistent practice, and strong evidence of a sustained faith pervading and regulating respondents' entire mode of life support the claim that enforcement of the State's requirement of compulsory formal education after the eighth grade would gravely endanger if not destroy the free exercise of respondents' religious beliefs.

Neither the findings of the trial court nor the Amish claims as to the nature of their faith are challenged in this Court by the State of Wisconsin. Its position is that the State's interest in universal compulsory formal secondary education to age 16 is so great that it is paramount to the undisputed claims of respondents that their mode of preparing their youth for Amish life, after the traditional elementary education, is an essential part of their religious belief and practice. Nor does the State undertake to meet the claim that the Amish mode of life and education is inseparable from and a part of the basic tenets of their religion—indeed, as much a part of their religious belief and practices as baptism, the confessional, or a Sabbath may be for others.

Wisconsin concedes that under the Religion Clauses religious beliefs are absolutely free from the State's control, but it argues that "actions," even though religiously grounded, are outside the protection of the First Amendment. But our decisions have rejected the idea that religiously grounded conduct is always outside the protection of the Free Exercise Clause. It is true that activities of individuals, even when religiously based, are often subject to regulation by the States in the exercise of their undoubted power to promote the health, safety, and general welfare, or the Federal government in the exercise of its delegated powers. . . . But to agree that religiously grounded conduct must often be subject to the broad police power of the State is not to deny that there are areas of conduct protected by the Free Exercise Clause of the First Amendment and thus beyond the power of the State to control, even under regulations of general applicability. . . . This case, therefore, does not become easier because respondents were convicted for their "actions" in refusing to send their children to the public high school; in this context belief and action cannot be neatly confined in logic-tight compartments. . . .

Nor can this case be disposed of on the grounds that Wisconsin's requirement for school attendance to age 16 applies uniformly to all citizens of the State and does not, on its face, discriminate against religions or a particular religion, or that it is motivated by legitimate secular concerns. A regulation neutral on its face may, in its application, nonetheless offend the constitutional requirement for governmental neutrality if it unduly burdens the free exercise of religion. . . . The Court must not ignore the danger that an exception from a general obligation of citizenship on religious grounds may run afoul of the Establishment Clause, but that danger cannot be allowed to prevent any exception no matter how vital it may be to the protection of values promoted by the right of free exercise. . . .

We turn, then, to the State's broader contention that its interest in its system of compulsory education is so compelling that even the established religious practices of the Amish must give way. Where fundamental claims of religious freedom are at stake, however, we cannot accept such a sweeping claim; despite its admitted validity in the generality of cases, we must searchingly examine the interests that the State seeks to promote by its requirement for compulsory education to age 16, and the impediment to those objectives that would flow from recognizing the claimed Amish exemption. . . .

The State advances two primary arguments in support of its system of compulsory education. It notes, as Thomas Jefferson pointed out early in our history, that some degree of education is necessary to prepare citizens to participate effectively and intelligently in our open political system if we are to preserve freedom and independence. Further, education prepares individuals to be self-reliant and self-sufficient participants in society. We accept these propositions.

However, the evidence adduced by the Amish in this case is persuasively to the effect that an additional one or two years of formal high school for Amish children in place of their long-established program of informal vocational education would do little to serve those interests. Respondents' experts testified at trial, without challenge, that the value of all education must be assessed in terms of its capacity to prepare the child for life. It is one thing to say that compulsory education for a year or two beyond the eighth grade may be necessary when its goal is the preparation of the child for life in modern society as the majority live, but is quite another if the goal of education be viewed as the preparation of the child for life in the separated agrarian community that is the keystone of the Amish faith. . . .

The State attacks respondents' position as one fostering "ignorance" from which the child must be protected by the State. No one can question the State's duty to protect children from ignorance but this argument does not square with the facts disclosed in the record. Whatever their idiosyncrasies as seen by the majority, this record strongly shows that the Amish community has been a highly successful social unit within our society, even if apart from the conventional "mainstream." Its members are productive and very law-abiding members of society; they reject public welfare in any of its usually modern forms. The Congress itself recognized their self-sufficiency by authorizing exemption of such groups as the Amish from the obligation to pay social security taxes.

It is neither fair nor correct to suggest that the Amish are opposed to education beyond the eighth grade level. What this record shows is that they are opposed to conventional formal education of the type provided by a certified high school because it comes at the child's crucial adolescent period of religious development. . . .

We must not forget that in the Middle Ages important values of the civilization of the Western World were preserved by members of religious orders who isolated themselves from all worldly influences against great obstacles. There can be no assumption that today's majority is "right" and the Amish and others like them are "wrong." A way of life that is odd or even erratic but interferes with no rights or interests of others is not to be condemned because it is different.

The State, however, supports its interest in providing an additional one or two years of compulsory high school education to Amish children because of the possibility that some such children will choose to leave the Amish community, and that if this occurs they will be ill-equipped for life. The State argues that if Amish children leave their church they should not be in the position of making their way in the world without the education available in the one or two additional years the State requires. However, on this record, that argument is highly speculative. There is no specific evidence of the loss of Amish adherents by attrition, nor is there any showing that upon leaving the Amish community Amish children, with their practical agricultural training and habits of industry and self-reliance, would become burdens on society because of educational shortcomings. Indeed, this argument of the State appears to rest primarily on the State's mistaken assumption, already noted, that the Amish do not provide any education for their children beyond the eighth grade, but allow them to grow in "ignorance." To the contrary, not only do the Amish accept the necessity for formal schooling through the eighth grade level, but continue to provide what has been characterized by the undisputed testimony of expert educators as an "ideal" vocational education for their children in the adolescent years.

There is nothing in this record to suggest that the Amish qualities of reliability, self-reliance, and dedication to work would fail to find ready markets in today's society. Absent some contrary evidence supporting the State's position, we are unwilling to assume that persons possessing such valuable vocational skills and habits are doomed to become burdens on society should they determine to leave the Amish faith, nor is there any basis in the record to warrant a finding that an additional one or two years of formal school education beyond the eighth grade would serve to eliminate any such problem that might exist.

Insofar as the State's claim rests on the view that a brief additional period of formal education is imperative to enable the Amish to participate effectively and intelligently in our democratic process, it must fall. The Amish alternative to formal secondary school education has enabled them to function effectively in their day-to-day life under self-imposed limitations on relations with the world, and to survive and prosper in contemporary society as a separate, sharply identifiable and highly self-sufficient community for more than 200 years in this country. In itself this is strong evidence that they are capable of fulfilling the social and political responsibilities of citizenship without compelled attendance beyond the eighth grade at the price of jeopardizing their free exercise of religious belief. When Thomas Jefferson emphasized the need for education as a bulwark of a free people against tyranny, there is nothing to indicate he had in mind compulsory education through any fixed age beyond a basic education. Indeed, the Amish communities singularly parallel and reflect many of the virtues of Jefferson's ideal of the "sturdy yeoman" who would form the basis of what he considered as the ideal of a democratic society. Even their idiosyncratic separateness exemplifies the diversity we profess to admire and encourage.

The requirement for compulsory education beyond the eighth grade is a relatively recent development in our history. Less than 60 years ago, the educational requirements of almost all of the States were satisfied by completion of the elementary grades, at least where the child was regularly and lawfully employed. The independence and successful social functioning of the Amish community for a period approaching almost three centuries and more than 200 years in this country are strong evidence that there is at best a speculative gain, in terms of meeting the duties of citizenship, from an additional one or two years of compulsory formal education. Against this background it would require a more particularized showing from the State on this point to justify the severe interference with religious freedom such additional compulsory attendance would entail. . . .

Finally, the State . . . argues that a decision exempting Amish children from the State's requirement fails to recognize the substantive right of the Amish child to a secondary education, and fails to give due regard to the power of the State as *parens patriae* to extend the benefit of secondary education to children regardless of the wishes of their parents. . . .

The State's argument proceeds without reliance on any actual conflict between the wishes of parents and children. It appears to rest on the potential that exemption of Amish parents from the requirements of the compulsory-education law might allow some parents to act contrary to the best interests of their children by foreclosing their opportunity to make an intelligent choice between the Amish way of life and that of the outside world. The same argument could, of course, be made with respect to all church schools short of college. There is nothing in the record or in the ordinary course of human experience to suggest that non-Amish parents generally consult with children of ages 14–16 if they are placed in a church school of the parents' faith.

Indeed it seems clear that if the State is empowered, as *parens patriae,* to "save" a child from himself or his Amish parents by requiring an additional two years of compulsory formal high school education, the State will in large measure influence, if not determine, the religious future of the child. [T]his case involves the fundamental interest of parents, as contrasted with that of the State, to guide the religious future and education of their children. The history and culture of Western civilization reflect a strong tradition of parental concern for the nurture and upbringing of their children. This primary role of the parents in the upbringing of their children is now established beyond debate as an enduring American tradition.

For the reasons stated we hold, with the Supreme Court of Wisconsin, that the First and Fourteenth Amendments prevent the State from compelling respondents to cause their children to attend formal high school to age 16. . . .

Nothing we hold is intended to undermine the general applicability of the State's compulsory school-attendance statutes or to limit the power of the State to promulgate reasonable standards that, while not impairing the free exercise of religion, provide for continuing agricultural vocational education under parental and church guidance by the Old Order Amish or others similarly situated. The States have had a long history of amicable and effective relationships with church-sponsored schools, and there is no basis for assuming that, in this related context, reasonable standards cannot be established concerning the content of the continuing vocational education of Amish children under parental guidance, provided always that state regulations are not inconsistent with what we have said in this opinion.

Affirmed.

Mr. Justice Powell and *Mr. Justice Rehnquist* took no part in the consideration or decision of this case.

Mr. Justice Stewart, with whom *Mr. Justice Brennan* joins, concurring. . . .

Mr. Justice Douglas, dissenting in part.

I agree with the Court that the religious scruples of the Amish are opposed to the education of their children beyond the grade schools, yet I disagree with the Court's conclusion that the matter is within the dispensation of parents alone. The Court's analysis assumes that the only interests at stake in the case are those of the Amish parents on the one hand, and those of the State on the other. The difficulty with this approach is that, despite the Court's claim, the parents are seeking to vindicate not only their own free exercise claims, but also those of their high-school-age children. . . .

. . . Our opinions are full of talk about the power of the parents over the child's education. . . . And we have in the past analyzed similar conflicts between parent and State with little regard for the views of the child. . . . Recent cases, however, have clearly held that the children themselves have constitutionally protectible interests. . . .

On this important and vital matter of education, I think the children should be entitled to be heard. While the parents, absent dissent, normally speak for the entire family, the education of the child is a matter on which the child will often have decided views. He may want to be a pianist or an astronaut or an oceanographer. To do so he will have to break from the Amish tradition.

It is the future of the student, not the future of the parents, that is imperiled by today's decision. If a parent keeps his child out of school beyond the grade school, then the child will be forever barred from entry into the new and amazing world of diversity that we have today. The child may decide that that is the preferred course, or he may rebel. It is the student's judgment, not his parents', that is essential if we are to give full meaning to what we have said about the Bill of Rights and of the right of students to be masters of their own destiny. If he is harnessed to the Amish way of life by those in authority over him and if his education is truncated, his entire life may be stunted and deformed. The child, therefore, should be given an opportunity to be heard before the State gives the exemption which we honor today.

The views of the two children in question were not canvassed by the Wisconsin courts. The matter should be explicitly reserved so that new hearings can be held on remand of the case. . . .

Case

EMPLOYMENT DIVISION V. SMITH

494 U.S. 872; 110 S.Ct. 1595; 108 L. Ed.2d 876 (1990)
Vote: 6–3

Alfred Smith and Galen Black, both members of the Native American Church, were fired from their jobs as drug rehabilitation counselors on the grounds that they had used peyote during a religious ritual. They were subsequently denied unemployment benefits because they had been discharged for "misconduct." The question before the U.S. Supreme Court is whether the refusal of the state to grant unemployment benefits in this situation constitutes an abridgement of rights under the Free Exercise Clause of the First Amendment.

Justice Scalia delivered the opinion of the Court.

. . . Respondents' claim for relief rests on our decisions in *Sherbert v. Verner* . . . [1963]; *Thomas v. Review Board* . . . [1981]; and *Hobbie v. Unemployment Appeals Comm'n of Florida* . . . [1987], in which we held that a State could not condition the availability of unemployment insurance on an individual's willingness to forego conduct required by his religion. . . . [H]owever, the conduct at issue in those cases was not prohibited by law. . . . [T]hat distinction [is] critical, for "if Oregon does prohibit the religious use of peyote, and if that prohibition is consistent with the Federal Constitution, there is no federal right to engage in that conduct in Oregon," and "the State is free to withhold unemployment compensation from respondents for engaging in work-related misconduct, despite its religious motivation." . . . Now that the Oregon Supreme Court has confirmed that Oregon does prohibit the religious use of peyote, we proceed to consider whether that prohibition is permissible under the Free Exercise Clause. . . .

The free exercise of religion means, first and foremost, the right to believe and profess whatever religious doctrine one desires. Thus, the First Amendment obviously excludes all "governmental regulation of religious beliefs as such." . . .

But the "exercise of religion" often involves not only belief and profession but the performance of (or abstention from) physical acts: assembling with others for a worship service, participating in sacramental use of bread and wine, proselytizing, abstaining from certain foods or certain modes of transportation. It would be true, we think (though no case of ours has involved the point), that a state would be "prohibiting the free exercise [of religion]" . . . if it sought to ban such acts or abstentions only when they are engaged in for religious reasons, or only because of the religious belief that they display. It would doubtless be unconstitutional, for example, to ban the casting of "statues that are to be used for worship purposes," . . . or to prohibit bowing down before a golden calf.

Respondents in the present case, however, seek to carry the meaning of "prohibiting the free exercise [of religion]" one large step further. They contend that their religious motivation for using peyote places them beyond the reach of a criminal law that is not specifically directed at their religious practice, and that is concededly constitutional as applied to those who use the drug for other reasons. They assert, in other words, that "prohibiting the free exercise [of religion]" includes requiring any individual to observe a generally applicable law that requires (or forbids) the performance of an act that his religious belief forbids (or requires). As a textual matter, we do not think the words must be given that meaning. It is no more necessary to regard the collection of a general tax, for example, as "prohibiting the free exercise [of religion]" by those citizens who believe support of organized government to be sinful, than it is to regard the same tax as "abridging the freedom . . . of the press" of those publishing companies that must pay the tax as a condition of staying in business. It is a permissible reading of the text, in the one case as in the other, to say that if prohibiting the exercise of religion (or burdening the activity of printing) is not the object of the tax but merely the incidental effect of a generally applicable and otherwise valid provision, the First Amendment has not been offended. . . .

Our decisions reveal that the latter reading is the correct one. We have never held that an individual's religious beliefs excuse him from compliance with an otherwise valid law prohibiting conduct that the State is free to regulate. . . .

The only decisions in which we have held that the First Amendment bars application of a neutral, generally applicable law to religiously motivated action have involved not the Free Exercise Clause alone, but the Free Exercise Clause in conjunction with other constitutional protections, such as freedom of speech and of the press. . . .

The present case does not present such a hybrid situation, but a free exercise claim unconnected with any communicative activity or parental right. Respondents urge us to hold, quite simply, that when otherwise prohibitable conduct is accompanied by religious convictions, not only the convictions but the conduct itself must be free from governmental regulation. . . .

Respondents argue that even though exemption from generally applicable criminal laws need not automatically be extended to religiously motivated actors, at least the claim for a religious exemption must be evaluated under the balancing test set forth in *Sherbert v. Verner* [1963]. . . . Under the *Sherbert* test, governmental actions that substantially burden a religious practice must be justified by a compelling governmental interest. . . . Applying that test we have, on three occasions, invalidated state unemployment compensation rules that conditioned the availability of benefits upon an applicant's willingness to work under conditions forbidden by his religion. . . . We have never invalidated any governmental action on the basis of the *Sherbert* test except the denial of unemployment compensation. . . .

Even if we were inclined to breathe into *Sherbert* some life beyond the unemployment compensation field, we would not apply it to require exemptions from a generally applicable criminal law. . . .

We conclude today that the sounder approach, and the approach in accord with the vast majority of our precedents, is to hold the test inapplicable to such challenges. The government's ability to enforce generally applicable prohibitions of socially harmful conduct, like its ability to carry out other aspects of public policy, "cannot depend on measuring the effects of a governmental action on a religious objector's spiritual development." . . . To make an individual's obligation to obey such a law contingent upon the law's coincidence with his religious beliefs, except where the State's interest is "compelling"—permitting him, by virtue of his beliefs, "to become a law unto himself," . . . —contradicts both constitutional tradition and common sense.

The "compelling government interest" requirement seems benign, because it is familiar from other fields. But using it as the standard that must be met before the government may accord different treatment on the basis of race, . . . is not remotely comparable to using it for the purpose asserted here. What it produces in those other fields—equality of treatment, and an unrestricted flow of contending speech—are constitutional norms; what it would produce here—a private right to ignore generally applicable laws—is a constitutional anomaly.

Nor is it possible to limit the impact of respondents' proposal by requiring a "compelling state interest" only when the conduct prohibited is "central" to the individual's religion. It is no more appropriate for judges to determine the "centrality" of religious beliefs before applying a "compelling interest" test in the free exercise field, than it would be for them to determine the "importance" of ideas before applying the "compelling interest" test in the free speech field. What principle of law or logic can be brought to bear to contradict a believer's assertion that a particular act is "central" to his personal faith? . . .

If the "compelling interest" test is to be applied at all, then, it must be applied across the board, to all actions thought to be religiously commanded. Moreover, if "compelling interest" really means what it says (and watering it down here would subvert its rigor in the other fields where it is applied), many laws will not meet the test. Any society adopting such a system would be courting anarchy, but that danger increases in direct proportion to the society's diversity of religious beliefs, and its determination to coerce or suppress none of them. . . .

Values that are protected against government interference through enshrinement in the Bill of Rights are not thereby banished from the political process. Just as a society that believes in the negative protection accorded to the press by the First Amendment is likely to enact laws that affirmatively foster the dissemination of the printed word, so also a society that believes in the negative protection accorded to religious belief can be expected to be solicitous of that value in its legislation as well. It is therefore not surprising that a number of States have made an exception to their drug laws for sacramental peyote use. But to say that a nondiscriminatory religious-practice exemption is permitted, or even that it is desirable, is not to say that it is constitutionally required, and that the appropriate occasions for its creation can be discerned by the courts. It may fairly be said that leaving accommodation to the political process will place at a relative disadvantage those religious practices that are not widely engaged in; but that unavoidable consequence of democratic government must be preferred to a system in which each conscience is a law unto itself or in which judges weigh the social importance of all law against the centrality of all religious beliefs. . . .

Because respondent's ingestion of peyote was prohibited under Oregon law, and because that prohibition is constitutional, Oregon may, consistent with the Free Exercise Clause, deny respondents unemployment compensation when their dismissal results from use of the drug. The decision of the Oregon Supreme Court is accordingly reversed.

It is so ordered.

Justice O'Connor . . . [concurring in the judgment only].

Although I agree with the result the Court reaches in this case, I cannot join its opinion. In my view, today's holding dramatically departs from well-settled First Amendment jurisprudence, appears unnecessary to resolve the question presented, and is incompatible with our Nation's fundamental commitment to individual religious liberty. . . .

The Court today extracts from our long history of free exercise precedents the single categorical rule that "if prohibiting the exercise of religion . . . is . . . merely the incidental effect of a generally applicable and otherwise valid provision, the First Amendment has not been offended." . . . Indeed, the Court holds that where the law is a generally applicable criminal prohibition, our usual free exercise jurisprudence does not even apply. To reach this sweeping result, however, the Court must not only give a strained reading of the First Amendment but must also disregard our consistent application of free exercise doctrine to cases involving generally applicable regulations that burden religious conduct. . . .

The Court today . . . interprets the Clause to permit the government to prohibit, without justification, conduct mandated by an individual's religious beliefs, so long as that prohibition is generally applicable. But a law that prohibits certain conduct—conduct that happens to be an act of worship for someone—manifestly does prohibit that person's free exercise of his religion. A person who is barred from engaging in religiously motivated conduct is barred from freely exercising his religion regardless of whether the law prohibits the conduct only when engaged in for religious reasons, only by members of that religion, or by all persons. It is difficult to deny that a law that prohibits religiously motivated conduct, even if the law is generally applicable, does not at least implicate First Amendment concerns.

The Court responds that generally applicable laws are "one large step" removed from laws aimed at specific religious practices. The First Amendment, however, does not distinguish between laws that are generally applicable and laws that target particular religious practices. Indeed, few States would be so naive as to enact a law directly prohibiting or burdening a religious practice as such. Our free exercise cases have all concerned generally applicable laws that had the effect of significantly burdening a religious practice. If the First Amendment is to have any vitality, it ought not be construed to cover only the extreme and hypothetical situation in which a State directly targets a religious practice. . . .

To say that a person's right to free exercise has been burdened, of course, does not mean that he has an absolute right to engage in the conduct. Under our established First Amendment jurisprudence, we have recognized that the freedom to act, unlike the freedom to believe, cannot be absolute. Instead, we have respected both the First Amendment's express textual mandate and the governmental interest in regulation of conduct by requiring the Government to justify any substantial burden on religiously motivated conduct by a compelling state interest and by means narrowly tailored to achieve that interest. . . .

The compelling interest test effectuates the First Amendment's command that religious liberty is an independent liberty, that it occupies a preferred position, and that the Court will not permit encroachments upon this liberty, whether direct or indirect, unless required by clear and compelling governmental interests "of the highest order." . . .

In my view, however, the essence of a free exercise claim is relief from a burden imposed by government on religious practices or beliefs, whether the burden is imposed directly through laws that prohibit or compel specific religious practices, or indirectly through laws that, in effect, make abandonment of one's own religion or conformity to the religious beliefs of others the price of an equal place in the civil community. . . .

Indeed, we have never distinguished between cases in which a State conditions receipt of a benefit on conduct prohibited by religious beliefs and cases in which a State affirmatively prohibits such conduct. The *Sherbert* compelling interest test applies in both kinds of cases. . . .

Finally, the Court today suggests that the disfavoring of minority religions is an "unavoidable consequence" under our system of government and that accommodation of such religions must be left to the political process. . . . In my view, however, the First Amendment was enacted precisely to protect the rights of those whose religious practices are not shared by the majority and may be viewed with hostility. The history of our free exercise doctrine amply demonstrates the harsh impact majoritarian rule has had on unpopular or emerging religious groups such as the Jehovah's Witnesses and the Amish. . . .

The Court's holding today not only misreads settled First Amendment's precedent; it appears to be unnecessary to this case. I would reach the same result applying our established free exercise jurisprudence. . . .

[T]he critical question in this case is whether exempting respondents from the State's general criminal prohibition "will unduly interfere with fulfillment of the governmental interest." . . . Although the question is close, I would conclude that uniform application of Oregon's criminal prohibition is "essential to accomplish" its overriding interest in preventing the physical harm caused by the use of a Schedule I controlled substance. Oregon's criminal prohibition represents that State's judgment that the possession and use of controlled substances, even by only one person, is inherently harmful and dangerous. Because the health effects caused by the use of controlled substances exist regardless of the motivation of the user, the use of such substances, even for religious purposes, violates the very purpose of the law that prohibits them. . . .

For these reasons, I believe that granting a selective exemption in this case would seriously impair Oregon's compelling interest in prohibiting possession of peyote by its citizens. Under such circumstances, the Free Exercise Clause does not require the State to accommodate respondents' religiously motivated conduct. . . .

I would therefore adhere to our established free exercise jurisprudence and hold that the State in this case has a compelling interest in regulating peyote use by its citizens and that accommodating respondents' religiously motivated conduct "will unduly interfere with fulfillment of the governmental interest." . . . Accordingly, I concur in the judgment of the Court.

Justice Blackmun, with whom **Justice Brennan** and **Justice Marshall** join, dissenting.

This Court over the years painstakingly has developed a consistent and exacting standard to test the constitutionality of a state statute that burdens the free exercise of religion. Such a statute may stand only if the law in general, and the State's refusal to allow a religious exemption in particular, are justified by a compelling interest that cannot be served by less restrictive means.

Until today, I thought this was a settled and inviolate principle of this Court's First Amendment jurisprudence. The majority, however, perfunctorily dismisses it as a "constitutional anomaly." As carefully detailed in Justice O'Connor's concurring opinion . . . the majority is able to arrive at this view only by mischaracterizing this Court's precedents. The Court discards leading free exercise cases such as *Cantwell v. Connecticut* . . . (1940), and *Wisconsin v. Yoder* (1972), as "hybrid." . . . The Court views traditional free exercise analysis as somehow inapplicable to criminal prohibitions (as opposed to conditions on the receipt of benefits), and to state laws of general applicability (as opposed, presumably, to laws that expressly single out religious practices). The Court cites cases in which, due to various exceptional circumstances, we found strict scrutiny inapposite, to hint that the Court is aware of the consequences, and that its result is not a product of overreaction to the serious problems the country's drug crisis has generated.

This distorted view of our precedents leads the majority to conclude that strict scrutiny of a state law burdening the free exercise of religion is a "luxury" that a well-ordered society cannot afford, and that the repression of minority religions is an "unavoidable consequence of democratic government." . . . I do not believe the Founders thought their dearly bought freedom from religious persecution a "luxury," but an essential element of liberty—and they could not have thought religious intolerance "unavoidable," for they drafted the Religion Clauses precisely in order to avoid that intolerance.

For these reasons, I agree with Justice O'Connor's analysis of the applicable free exercise doctrine. . . . As she points out, "the critical question in this case is whether exempting respondents from the State's general criminal prohibition: 'will unduly interfere with fulfillment of the governmental interest.' " . . . I do disagree, however, with her specific answer to that question.

The State's interest in enforcing its prohibition, in order to be sufficiently compelling to outweigh a free exercise claim, cannot be merely abstract or symbolic. The State cannot plausibly assert that unbending application of a criminal prohibition is essential to fulfill any compelling interest, if it does not, in fact, attempt to enforce that prohibition. In this case, the State actually has not evinced any concrete interest in enforcing its drug laws against religious users of peyote. Oregon has never sought to prosecute respondents, and does not claim that it has made significant enforcement efforts against other religious users of peyote. The State's asserted interest thus amounts only to the symbolic preservation of an unenforced prohibition. . . .

The State proclaims an interest in protecting the health and safety of its citizens from the dangers of unlawful drugs. It offers, however, no evidence that the religious use of peyote has ever harmed anyone. . . .

The fact that peyote is classified as a Schedule I controlled substance does not, by itself, show that any and all uses of peyote, in any circumstance, are inherently harmful and dangerous. The Federal Government, which created the classifications of unlawful drugs from which Oregon's drug laws are derived, apparently does not find peyote so dangerous as to preclude an exemption for religious use. . . .

The carefully circumscribed ritual context in which respondents used peyote is far removed from the irresponsible and unrestricted recreational use of unlawful drugs. The Native American Church's internal restrictions on, and supervision of, its members' use of peyote substantially obviate the State's health and safety concerns. . . .

Moreover, just as in *Yoder*, the values and interests of those seeking a religious exemption in this case are congruent, to a great degree, with those the State seeks to promote through its drug laws. . . . Not only does the Church's doctrine forbid nonreligious use of peyote; it also generally advocates self-reliance, familial responsibility, and abstinence from alcohol. . . . Far from promoting the lawless and irresponsible use of drugs, Native American Church members' spiritual code exemplifies values that Oregon's drug laws are presumably intended to foster. . . .

Finally, although I agree with Justice O'Connor that courts should refrain from delving into questions of whether, as a matter of religious doctrine, a particular practice is "central" to the religion, I do not think this means that the courts must turn a blind eye to the severe impact of a State's restrictions on the adherents of a minority religion. . . .

If Oregon can constitutionally prosecute them for this act of worship, they, like the Amish, may be "forced to migrate to some other and more tolerant region." *Yoder*. This potentially devastating impact must be viewed in light of the federal policy—reached in reaction to many years of religious persecution and intolerance—of protecting the religious freedom of Native Americans. . . .

The American Indian Religious Freedom Act, in itself, may not create rights enforceable against government action restricting religious freedom, but this Court must scrupulously apply its free exercise analysis to the religious claims of Native Americans, however unorthodox they may be. Otherwise, both the First Amendment and the stated policy of Congress will offer to Native Americans merely an unfulfilled and hollow promise.

For these reasons, I conclude that Oregon's interest in enforcing its drug laws against religious use of peyote is not sufficiently compelling to outweigh respondents' right to the free exercise of their religion. Since the State could not constitutionally enforce its criminal prohibition against respondents, the interests underlying the State's drug laws cannot justify its denial of unemployment benefits. Absent such justification, the State's regulatory interest in denying benefits for religiously motivated "misconduct," is indistinguishable from the state interests this Court has rejected. . . . The State of Oregon cannot, consistently with the Free Exercise Clause, deny respondents unemployment benefits. . . .

Case

CHURCH OF THE LUKUMI BABALU AYE, INC. V. CITY OF HIALEAH

508 U.S. 520, 113 S.Ct. 2217, 124 L.Ed. 2d. 472 (1993)
Vote: 9–0

In this case the Court considers a challenge to a set of local ordinances prohibiting animal sacrifice in religious rituals.

Justice Kennedy delivered the opinion of the Court.

. . . This case involves practices of the Santeria religion, which originated in the nineteenth century. When hundreds of thousands of members of the Yoruba people were brought as slaves from eastern Africa to Cuba, their traditional African religion absorbed significant elements of Roman Catholicism. The resulting syncretion, or fusion, is Santeria, "the way of the saints." The Cuban Yoruba express their devotion to spirits, called orishas, through the iconography of Catholic saints. . . .

. . . The basis of the Santeria religion is the nurture of a personal relation with the orishas, and one of the principal forms of devotion is an animal sacrifice. . . .

. . . Sacrifices are performed at birth, marriage, and death rites, for the cure of the sick, for the initiation of new members and priests, and during an annual celebration. Animals sacrificed in Santeria rituals include chickens, pigeons, doves, ducks, guinea pigs, goats, sheep, and turtles. The animals are killed by the cutting of the carotid arteries in the neck. The sacrificed animal is cooked and eaten, except after healing and death rituals. . . .

Petitioner Church of the Lukumi Babalu Aye, Inc. (Church), is a not-for-profit corporation organized under Florida law in 1973. The Church and its congregants practice the Santeria religion. The president of the Church is petitioner Ernesto Pichardo, who is also the Church's priest and holds the religious title of Italero, the second highest in the Santeria faith. In April 1987, the Church leased land in the City of Hialeah, Florida, and announced plans to establish a house of worship as well as a school, cultural center, and museum. Pichardo indicated that the Church's goal was to bring the practice of the Santeria faith, including its ritual of animal sacrifice, into the open. The Church began the process of obtaining utility service and receiving the necessary licensing, inspection, and zoning approvals. Although the Church's efforts at obtaining the necessary licenses and permits were far from smooth, . . . it appears that it received all needed approvals by early August 1987.

The prospect of a Santeria church in their midst was distressing to many members of the Hialeah community, and the announcement of the plans to open a Santeria church in Hialeah prompted the city council to hold an emergency public session on June 9. . . .

In September 1987, the city council adopted three substantive ordinances addressing the issue of religious animal sacrifice. Ordinance 87-52 defined "sacrifice" as "to unnecessarily kill, torment, torture, or mutilate an animal in a public or private ritual or ceremony not for the primary purpose of food consumption," and prohibited owning or possessing an animal "intending to use such animal for food purposes." It restricted application of this prohibition, however, to any individual or group that "kills, slaughters or sacrifices animals for any type of ritual, regardless of whether or not the flesh or blood of the animal is to be consumed." The ordinance contained an exemption for slaughtering by "licensed establishment[s]" of animals "specifically raised for food purposes." Declaring, moreover, that the city council "has determined that the sacrificing of animals within the city limits is contrary to the public health, safety, welfare and morals of the community," the city council adopted Ordinance 87-71. That ordinance defined sacrifice as had Ordinance 87-52, and then provided that "[i]t shall be unlawful for any person, persons, corporations or associations to sacrifice any animal within the corporate limits of the City of Hialeah, Florida." The final Ordinance, 87-72, defined "slaughter" as "the killing of animals for food" and prohibited slaughter outside of areas zoned for slaughterhouse use. The ordinance provided an exemption, however, for the slaughter or processing for sale of "small numbers of hogs and/or cattle per week in accordance with an exemption provided in state law." All ordinances and resolutions passed the city council by unanimous vote. Violations of each of the four ordinances were punishable by fines not exceeding $500 or imprisonment not exceeding 60 days, or both.

Following enactment of these ordinances, the Church and Pichardo filed this action pursuant to 42 U.S.C. § 1983 in the United States District Court for the Southern District of Florida. . . .

Balancing the competing governmental and religious interests, the District Court concluded the compelling governmental interests "fully justify the absolute prohibition on ritual sacrifice" accomplished by the ordinances. . . . The court also concluded that an exception to the sacrifice prohibition for religious conduct would "unduly interfere with fulfillment of the governmental interest" because any more narrow restrictions—e.g., regulation of disposal of animal carcasses—would be unenforceable as a result of the secret nature of the Santeria religion. . . . A religious exemption from the city's ordinances, concluded the court, would defeat the city's compelling interests in enforcing the prohibition. . . .

The Court of Appeals for the Eleventh Circuit affirmed. . . .

II

. . . In addressing the constitutional protection for free exercise of religion, our cases establish the general proposition that a law that is neutral and of general applicability need not be justified by a compelling governmental interest even if the law has the incidental effect of burdening a particular religious practice. . . . Neutrality and general applicability are interrelated, and, as becomes apparent in this case, failure to satisfy one requirement is a likely indication that the other has not been satisfied. A law failing to satisfy these requirements must be justified by a compelling governmental interest and must be narrowly tailored to advance that interest. . . .

At a minimum, the protections of the Free Exercise Clause pertain if the law at issue discriminates against some or all religious beliefs or regulates or prohibits conduct because it is undertaken for religious reasons. . . . Indeed, it was "historical instances of religious persecution and intolerance that gave concern to those who drafted the Free Exercise Clause." . . . These principles, though not often at issue in our Free Exercise Clause cases, have played a role in some. . . .

Although a law targeting religious beliefs as such is never permissible, . . . if the object of a law is to infringe upon or restrict practices because of their religious motivation, the law is not neutral; . . . and it is invalid unless it is justified by a compelling interest and is narrowly tailored to advance that interest. . . .

The record in this case compels the conclusion that suppression of the central element of the Santeria worship service was the object of the ordinances. First, though use of the words "sacrifice" and "ritual" does not compel a finding of improper targeting of the Santeria religion, the choice of these words is support for our conclusion. There are further respects in which the text of the city council's enactments discloses the improper attempt to target Santeria. . . . No one suggests, and on this record it cannot be maintained, that city officials had in mind a religion other than Santeria.

It becomes evident that these ordinances target Santeria sacrifice when the ordinances' operation is considered. Apart from the text, the effect of a law in its real operation is strong evidence of its object. To be sure, adverse impact will not always lead to a finding of impermissible targeting. For example, a social harm may have been a legitimate concern of government for reasons quite apart from discrimination. . . . The subject at hand does implicate, of course, multiple concerns unrelated to religious animosity, for example, the suffering or mistreatment visited upon the sacrificed animals, and health hazards from improper disposal. But the ordinances when considered together disclose an object remote from these legitimate concerns. The design of these laws accomplishes instead a "religious gerrymander," . . . an impermissible attempt to target petitioners and their religious practices.

It is a necessary conclusion that almost the only conduct subject to [the] Ordinances . . . is the religious exercise of Santeria church members. The tests show that they were drafted in tandem to achieve this result. . . .

The legitimate governmental interests in protecting the public health and preventing cruelty to animals could be addressed by restrictions stopping far short of a flat prohibition of all Santeria sacrificial practice. If improper disposal, not the sacrifice itself, is the harm to be prevented, the city could have imposed a general regulation on the disposal of organic garbage. It did not do so. Indeed, counsel for the city conceded at oral argument that, under the ordinances, Santeria sacrifices would be illegal even if they occurred in licensed, inspected, and zoned slaughterhouses. . . . Thus, these broad ordinances prohibit Santeria sacrifice even when it does not threaten the city's interest in the public health. The District Court accepted the argument that narrower regulation would be unenforceable because of the secrecy in the Santeria rituals. . . . It is difficult to understand, however, how a prohibition of the sacrifices themselves, which occur in private, is enforceable if a ban on improper disposal, which occurs in public, is not. The neutrality of a law is suspect if First Amendment freedoms are curtailed to prevent isolated collateral harms not themselves prohibited by direct regulation. . . .

Under similar analysis, a narrow regulation would achieve the city's interest in preventing cruelty to animals. . . .

Ordinance 87-72—unlike the three other ordinances—does appear to apply to substantial nonreligious conduct and not to be overbroad. For our purposes here, however, the four substantive ordinances may be treated as a group for neutrality purposes. . . .

That the ordinances were enacted " 'because of,' not merely 'in spite of,' " their suppression of Santeria religious practice is revealed by the events preceding enactment of the ordinances. Although respondent claimed at oral argument that it had experienced significant problems resulting from the sacrifice of animals within the city before the announced opening of the Church, the city council made no attempt to address the supposed problem before its meeting in June 1987, just weeks after the Church announced plans to open. The minutes and taped excerpts of the June 9 session, both of which are in the record, evidence significant hostility exhibited by residents, members of the city council, and other city officials toward the Santeria religion and its practice of animal sacrifice. The public crowd that attended the June 9 meetings interrupted statements by council members critical of Santeria with cheers and the brief comments of Pichardo with taunts. When Councilman Martinez, a supporter of the ordinances, stated that in prerevolutionary Cuba "people were put in jail for practicing this religion," the audience applauded.

Other statements by members of the city council were in a similar vein. For example, Councilman Martinez, after noting his belief that Santeria was outlawed in Cuba, questioned, "if we could not practice this [religion] in our homeland [Cuba], why bring it to this country?" Councilman Cardoso said that Santeria devotees at the Church "are in violation of everything this country stands for." Councilman Mejides indicated that he was "totally against the sacrificing of animals" and distinguished Kosher slaughter because it had a "real purpose." The "Bible says we are allowed to sacrifice an animal for consumption," he continued, "but for any other purposes, I don't believe that the Bible allows that." The president of the city council, Councilman Echevarria, asked "What can we do to prevent the Church from opening?" . . .

In sum, the neutrality inquiry leads to one conclusion: The ordinances had as their object the suppression of religion. The pattern we have recited discloses animosity to Santeria adherents and their religious practices; the ordinances by their own terms target this religious exercise; the texts of the ordinances were gerrymandered with care to proscribe religious killings of animals but to exclude almost all secular killings, and the ordinances suppress much more religious conduct than is necessary in order to achieve the legitimate ends asserted in their defense. . . .

We turn next to a second requirement of the Free Exercise Clause, the rule that laws burdening religious practice must be of general applicability. . . . All laws are selective to some extent, but categories of selection are of paramount concern when a law has the incidental effect of burdening religious practice. The Free Exercise Clause "protect[s] religious observers against unequal treatment," . . . and inequality results when a legislature decides that the governmental interests it seeks to advance are worthy of being pursued only against conduct with a religious motivation.

The principle that government, in pursuit of legitimate interests, cannot in a selective manner impose burdens only on conduct motivated by religious belief is essential to the protection of the rights guaranteed by the Free Exercise Clause. The principle underlying the general applicability requirement has parallels in our First Amendment jurisprudence. . . . In this case we need not define with precision the standard used to evaluate whether a prohibition is of general application, for these ordinances fall well below the minimum standard necessary to protect First Amendment rights.

Respondents claim that Ordinances 87-40, 87-52, and 87-71 advance two interests: protecting the public health and preventing cruelty to animals. The ordinances are underinclusive for those ends. They fail to prohibit non-religious conduct that endangers these interests in a similar or greater degree than Santeria sacrifice does. The underinclusion is substantial, not inconsequential. Despite the city's proffered interest in preventing cruelty to animals, the ordinances are drafted with care to forbid few killings but those occasioned by religious sacrifice. . . .

We conclude . . . that each of Hialeah's ordinances pursues the city's governmental interests only against conduct motivated by religious belief. The ordinances "ha[ve] every appearance of a prohibition that society is prepared to impose upon [Santeria worshippers] but not upon itself." . . . This precise evil is what the requirement of general applicability is designed to prevent.

III

A law burdening religious practice that is not neutral or not of general application must undergo the most rigorous of scrutiny. To satisfy the commands of the First Amendment, a law restrictive of religious practice must " 'interests of the highest order' " and must be narrowly tailored in pursuit of those interests. . . . A law that targets religious conduct for distinctive treatment or advances legitimate governmental interests only against conduct with a religious motivation will survive strict scrutiny only in rare cases. It follows from what we have already said that these ordinances cannot withstand this scrutiny.

First, even were the governmental interests compelling, the ordinances are not drawn in narrow terms to accomplish those interests. As we have discussed, . . . all four ordinances are overbroad or underinclusive in substantial respects. The proffered objectives are not pursued with respect to analogous non-religious conduct, and those interests could be achieved by narrower ordinances that burdened religion to a far lesser degree. The absence of narrow tailoring suffices to establish the invalidity of the ordinances. . . .

Respondent has not demonstrated, moreover, that, in the context of these ordinances, its governmental interests are compelling. Where government restricts only conduct protected by the First Amendment and fails to enact feasible measures to restrict other conduct producing substantial harm or alleged harm of the same sort, the interest given in justification of the restriction is not compelling. It is established in our strict scrutiny jurisprudence that "a law cannot be regarded as protecting an interest 'of the highest order' . . . when it leaves appreciable damage to that supposedly vital interest unprohibited." . . . As we show above, . . . the ordinances are underinclusive to a substantial extent with respect to each of the interests that respondent has asserted, and it is only conduct motivated by religious conviction that bears the weight of the governmental restrictions. There can be no serious claim that those interests justify the ordinances.

IV

The Free Exercise Clause commits government itself to religious tolerance, and upon even slight suspicion that proposals for state intervention stem from animosity to religion or distrust of its practices, all officials must pause to remember their own high duty to the Constitution and to the rights it secures. Those in office must be resolute in resisting importunate demands and must en-

sure that the sole reasons for imposing the burdens of law and regulation are secular. Legislators may not devise mechanisms, overt or disguised, designed to persecute or oppress a religion or its practices. The laws here in question were enacted contrary to these constitutional principles, and they are void.

Reversed.

Justice Scalia, with whom the **Chief Justice** joins, concurring in part and concurring in the judgment. . . .

Justice Souter, concurring in part and concurring in the judgment. . . .

Justice Blackmun, with whom **Justice O'Connor** joins, concurring in the judgment. . . .

The Court holds today that the city of Hialeah violated the First and Fourteenth Amendments when it passed a set of restrictive ordinances explicitly directed at petitioners' religious practice. With this holding I agree. I write separately to emphasize that the First Amendment's protection of religion extends beyond those rare occasions on which the government explicitly targets religion (or a particular religion) for disfavored treatment, as is done in this case. In my view, a statute that burdens the free exercise of religion "may stand only if the law is general, and the State's refusal to allow a religious exemption in particular, are justified by a compelling interest that cannot be served by less restrictive means." *Employment Div., Oregon Dept. of Human Resources v. Smith* . . . (1990) (dissenting opinion). The Court, however, applies a different test. It applies the test announced in *Smith,* under which "a law that is neutral and of general applicability need not be justified by a compelling governmental interest even if the law has the incidental effect of burdening a particular religious practice." . . . I continue to believe that *Smith* was wrongly decided, because it ignored the value of religious freedom as an affirmative individual liberty and treated the Free Exercise Clause as no more than an antidiscrimination principle. . . . Thus, while I agree with the result the Court reaches in this case, I arrive at that result by a different route. . . .

Case

EVERSON V. BOARD OF EDUCATION

330 U.S. 1; 67 S.Ct. 504; 91 L.Ed. 711 (1947)
Vote: 5–4

In this case, the seminal decision in the Court's Establishment Clause jurisprudence, the issue is whether the First Amendment prohibits a local school board from reimbursing parents for costs incurred as a result of transporting their children to and from parochial schools.

Mr. Justice Black delivered the opinion of the Court.

A New Jersey statute authorizes its local school districts to make rules and contracts for the transportation of children to and from schools. The appellee, a township board of education, acting pursuant to this statute, authorized reimbursement to parents of money expended by them for the bus transportation of their children on regular buses operated by the public transportation system. Part of this money was for the payment of transportation of some children in the community to Catholic parochial schools. These church schools give their students, in addition to secular education, regular religious instruction conforming to the religious tenets and modes of worship of the Catholic Faith. The superintendent of these schools is a Catholic priest.

The appellant, in his capacity as a district taxpayer, filed suit in a state court challenging the right of the Board to reimburse parents of parochial school students. He contended that the statute and the resolution passed pursuant to it violated both the State and the Federal Constitutions. That court held that the legislature was without power to authorize such payment under the state constitution. . . . The New Jersey Court of Errors and Appeals reversed, holding that neither the statute nor the resolution passed pursuant to it was in conflict with the State constitution or the provisions of the Federal Constitution in issue. . . .

Since there has been no attack on the statute on the ground that a part of its language excludes children attending private schools operated for profit from enjoying State payment for their transportation, we need not consider this exclusionary language; it has no relevancy to any constitutional question here presented. Furthermore, if the exclusion clause had been properly challenged, we do not know whether New Jersey's highest court would construe its statutes as precluding payment of the school transportation of any group of pupils, even those of a private school run for profit. Consequently, we put to one side the question as to the validity of the statute against the claim that it does not authorize payment for the transportation generally of school children in New Jersey. . . .

The New Jersey statute is challenged as a "law respecting the establishment of religion." The First Amendment, as made applicable to the states by the Fourteenth, . . . commands that a state "shall make no law respecting an establishment of religion, or prohibiting the free exercise thereof. . . ." These words of the First Amendment reflected in the minds of early Americans a vivid mental picture of conditions and practices which they fervently wished to stamp out in order to preserve liberty for themselves and for their posterity. Doubtless their goal has not been entirely reached; but so far has the Nation moved toward it that the expression "law respecting the establishment of religion," probably does not so vividly remind present-day Americans of the evils, fears, and political problems that caused that expression to be written into our Bill of Rights. . . .

The meaning and scope of the First Amendment, preventing establishment of religion or prohibiting the free exercise thereof, in the light of its history and the evils it was designed forever to suppress, have been several times elaborated by the decisions of this Court prior to the application of the First Amendment to the states by the Fourteenth. The broad meaning given the Amendment by these earlier cases has been accepted by this Court in its decisions concerning an individual's religious freedom rendered since the Fourteenth Amendment was interpreted to make the prohibitions of the First applicable to state action abridging religious freedom. There is every reason to give the same application and broad interpretation to the "establishment of religion" clause. . . .

The "establishment of religion" clause of the First Amendment means at least this: Neither a state nor the Federal Government can set up a church. Neither can pass laws which aid one religion, aid all religions, or prefer one religion over another. Neither can force nor influence a person to go to or to remain away from church against his will or force him to profess a belief or disbelief in any religion. No person can be punished for entertaining or professing religious beliefs or disbeliefs, for church attendance or nonattendance. No tax in any amount, large or small, can be levied to support any religious activities or institutions, whatever they may be called, or whatever form they may adopt to teach or practice religion. Neither a state nor the Federal Government can, openly or secretly, participate in the affairs of any religious organizations or groups and vice versa. In the words of Jefferson, the clause against establishment of religion by law was intended to erect "a wall of separation between church and State." . . .

We must consider the New Jersey statute in accordance with the foregoing limitations imposed by the First Amendment. But we must not strike that state statute down if it is within the State's constitutional power even though it approaches the verge of that power. . . . New Jersey cannot consistently with the "establishment of religion" clause of the First Amendment contribute tax-raised funds to the support of an institution which teaches the tenets and faith of any church. On the other hand, other language of the amendment commands that New Jersey cannot hamper its citizens in the free exercise of their own religion. Consequently, it cannot exclude individual Catholics, Lutherans, Mohammedans, Baptists, Jews, Methodists, Non-believers, Presbyterians, or the members of any other faith, because of their faith, or lack of it, from receiving the benefits of public welfare legislation. While we do not mean to intimate that a state could not provide transportation only to children attending public schools, we must be careful in protecting the citizens of New Jersey against state-established churches, to be sure that we do not inadvertently prohibit New Jersey from extending its general state law benefits to all its citizens without regard to their religious belief.

Measured by these standards, we cannot say that the First Amendment prohibits New Jersey from spending tax-raised funds to pay the bus fares of parochial school pupils as a part of a general program under which it pays the fares of pupils attending public and other schools. It is undoubtedly true that children are helped to get to church schools. There is even a possibility that some of the children might not be sent to the church schools if the parents were compelled to pay their children's bus fares out of their own pockets when transportation to a public school would have been paid for by the State. The same possibility exists where the state requires a local transit company to provide reduced fares to school children including those attending parochial schools, or where a municipally owned transportation system undertakes to carry all school children free of charge. Moreover, state-paid policemen, detailed to protect children going to and from church schools from the very real hazards of traffic, would serve much the same purpose and accomplish much the same result as state provisions intended to guarantee free transportation of a kind which the state

deems to be best for the school children's welfare. And parents might refuse to risk their children to the serious danger of traffic accidents going to and from parochial schools, the approaches to which were not protected by policemen. Similarly, parents might be reluctant to permit their children to attend schools which the state had cut off from such general government services as ordinary police and fire protection, connections for sewage disposal, public highways and sidewalks. Of course, cutting off church schools from these services, so separate and so indisputably marked off from the religious function, would make it far more difficult for the schools to operate. But such is obviously not the purpose of the First Amendment. That Amendment requires the state to be a neutral in its relations with groups of religious believers and non-believers; it does not require the state to be their adversary. State power is no more to be used so as to handicap religions than it is to favor them.

This Court has said that parents may, in the discharge of their duty under state compulsory education laws, send their children to a religious rather than a public school if the school meets the secular educational requirements which the state has power to impose. . . . It appears that these parochial schools meet New Jersey's requirements. The State contributes no money to the schools. It does not support them. Its legislation, as applied, does no more than provide a general program to help parents get their children, regardless of their religion, safely and expeditiously to and from accredited schools.

The First Amendment has erected a wall between church and state. That wall must be kept high and impregnable. We could not approve the slightest breach. New Jersey has not breached it here.

Affirmed.

Mr. Justice Jackson, dissenting.

I find myself, contrary to first impressions, unable to join in this decision. I have a sympathy, though it is not ideological, with Catholic citizens who are compelled by law to pay taxes for public schools, and also feel constrained by conscience and discipline to support other schools for their own children. Such relief to them as this case involves is not in itself a serious burden to taxpayers and I had assumed it to be as little serious in principle. Study of this case convinces me otherwise. The Court's opinion marshals every argument in favor of state aid and puts the case in its most favorable light, but much of its reasoning confirms my conclusions that there are no good grounds upon which to support the present legislation. In fact, the undertones of the opinion, advocating complete and uncompromising separation of Church from State, seem utterly discordant with its conclusion yielding support to their commingling in educational matters. The case which irresistibly comes to mind as the most fitting precedent is that of Julia who, according to Byron's reports, "whispering 'I will ne'er consent,'—consented." . . .

This policy of our Federal Constitution has never been wholly pleasing to most religious groups. They all are quick to invoke its protections; they are all irked when they feel its restraints. This Court has gone a long way, if not an unreasonable way, to hold that public business of such paramount importance as maintenance of public order, protection of the privacy of the home, and taxation may not be pursued by a state in a way that even indirectly will interfere with religious proselyting. . . .

But we cannot have it both ways. Religious teaching cannot be a private affair when the state seeks to impose regulations which infringe on it indirectly, and a public affair when it comes to taxing citizens of one faith to aid another, or those of no faith to aid all. If these principles seem harsh in prohibiting aid to Catholic education, it must not be forgotten that it is the same Constitution that alone assures Catholics the right to maintain these schools at all when predominant local sentiment would forbid them. . . . Nor should I think that those who have done so well without this aid would want to see this separation between Church and State broken down. If the state may aid these religious schools, it may therefore regulate them. Many groups have sought aid from tax funds only to find that it carried political controls with it. Indeed this Court has declared that "It is hardly lack of due process for the Government to regulate that which it subsidizes." . . .

But in any event, the great purposes of the Constitution do not depend on the approval or convenience of those they restrain. I cannot read the history of the struggle to separate political from ecclesiastical affairs, well summarized in the opinion of Mr. Justice Rutledge in which I generally concur, without a conviction that the Court today is unconsciously giving the clock's hands a backward turn.

Mr. Justice Frankfurter joins in this opinion.

Mr. Justice Rutledge, with whom *Mr. Justice Frankfurter, Mr. Justice Jackson* and *Mr. Justice Burton* agree, dissenting.

. . . No one conscious of religious values can be unsympathetic toward the burden which our constitutional separation puts on parents who desire religious instruction mixed with secular for their children. They pay taxes for others' children's education, at the same time the added cost of instruction for their own. Nor can one happily see benefits denied to children which others receive, because in conscience they or their parents for them desire a different kind of training others do not demand.

But if those feelings should prevail, there would be an end to our historic constitutional policy and command. No more unjust or discriminatory in fact is it to deny attendants at religious schools the cost of their transportation than it is to deny them tuitions, sustenance for their teachers, or any other educational expense which others receive at public cost. . . .

. . . [I]t is only by observing the prohibition rigidly that the state can maintain its neutrality and avoid partisanship in the dissensions inevitable when sect opposes sect over demands for public moneys to further religious education, teaching or training in any form or degree, directly or indirectly. Like St. Paul's freedom, religious liberty with a great price must be bought. And for those who exercise it most fully, by insisting upon religious education for their children mixed with secular, by the terms of our Constitution the price is greater than for others. . . .

Case

ABINGTON SCHOOL DISTRICT V. SCHEMPP

374 U.S. 203; 83 S.Ct. 1560; 10 L.Ed. 2d. 844 (1963)
Vote: 8–1

This is one of the controversial school prayer decisions handed down by the Warren Court.

Mr. Justice Clark delivered the opinion of the Court.

. . . The appellees Edward Lewis Schempp, his wife Sidney, and their children, Roger and Donna, are of the Unitarian faith and are members of the Unitarian Church in Germantown, Philadelphia, Pennsylvania, where they, as well as another son, Ellory, regularly attend religious services. The latter was originally a party but having graduated from the school system . . . was voluntarily dismissed from the action. The other children attend the Abington Senior High School, which is a public school operated by appellant district.

On each school day at the Abington Senior High School . . . opening exercises are conducted pursuant to [state law]. The exercises are broadcast into each room in the school building through an intercommunications system and are conducted under the supervision of a teacher by students attending the school's radio and television workshop. Selected students from this course gather each morning in the school's workshop studio for the exercises, which include readings by one of the students of 10 verses of the Holy Bible, broadcast to each room in the building. This is followed by the recitation of the Lord's Prayer, likewise over the intercommunications system, but also by the students in the various classrooms, who are asked to stand and join in repeating the prayer in unison. The exercises are closed with the flag salute and such pertinent announcements as are of interest to the students. Participation in the opening exercises, as directed by the statute, is voluntary. The student reading the verses from the Bible may select the passages and read from any version he chooses, although the only copies furnished by the school are the King James version, copies of which were circulated to each teacher by the school district. During the period in which the exercises have been conducted the King James, the Douay and the Revised Standard versions of the Bible have been used, as well as the Jewish Holy Scriptures. There are no prefatory statements, no questions asked or solicited, no comments or explanations made and no interpretations given at or during the exercises. The students and parents are advised that the student may absent himself from the classroom or, should he elect to remain, not participate in the exercises. . . .

The wholesome "neutrality" of which this Court's cases speak . . . stems from a recognition of the teachings of history that powerful sects or groups might bring about a fusion of governmental and religious functions or a concert or dependency of one upon the other to the end that official support of the State or Federal Government would be placed behind the tenets of one or of all orthodoxies. This the Establishment Clause prohibits. And a further reason for neutrality is found in the Free Exercise Clause, which recognizes the value of religious training, teaching and observance and, more particularly, the right of every person to freely choose his own course with reference thereto, free of any compulsion from the state. This the Free Exercise Clause guarantees. Thus, the two clauses may overlap. . . . [T]he Establishment Clause has been directly considered by this Court eight times in the past score of years and, with only one Justice dissenting on the point, it has consis-

tently held that the clause withdrew all legislative power respecting religious belief or the expression thereof. The test may be stated as follows: what are the purpose and the primary effect of the enactment? If either is the advancement or inhibition of religion then the enactment exceeds the scope of legislative power as circumscribed by the Constitution. That is to say that to withstand the strictures of the Establishment Clause there must be a secular legislative purpose and a primary effect that neither advances nor inhibits religion. . . . The Free Exercise Clause, likewise considered many times here, withdraws from legislative power, state and federal, the exertion of any restraint on the free exercise of religion. Its purpose is to secure religious liberty in the individual by prohibiting any invasions thereof by civil authority. Hence it is necessary in a free exercise case for one to show the coercive effect of the enactment as it operates against him in the practice of his religion. The distinction between the two clauses is apparent—a violation of the Free Exercise Clause is predicated on coercion while the Establishment Clause violation need not be so attended.

Applying the Establishment Clause principles to the cases at bar we find that the States are requiring the selection and reading at the opening of the school day of verses from the Holy Bible and the recitation of the Lord's Prayer by the students in unison. These exercises are prescribed as part of the curricular activities of students who are required by law to attend school. They are held in the school buildings under the supervision and with the participation of teachers employed in those schools. . . . The trial court . . . has found that such an opening exercise is a religious ceremony and was intended by the State to be so. We agree with the trial court's finding as to the religious character of the exercises. Given that finding, the exercises and the law requiring them are in violation of the Establishment Clause. . . .

The conclusion follows that the laws require religious exercises and such exercises are being conducted in direct violation of the rights of the appellees and petitioners. Nor are these required exercises mitigated by the fact that individual students may absent themselves upon parental request, for that fact furnishes no defense to a claim of unconstitutionality under the Establishment Clause. . . . Further, it is no defense to urge that the religious practices here may be relatively minor encroachments on the First Amendment. The breach of neutrality that is today a trickling stream may all too soon become a raging torrent and, in the words of Madison, "it is proper to take alarm at the first experiment on our liberties." . . .

It is insisted that unless these religious exercises are permitted a "religion of secularism" is established in the schools. We agree of course that the State may not establish a "religion of secularism" in the sense of affirmatively opposing or showing hostility to religion, thus "preferring those who believe in no religion over those who do believe." . . . We do not agree, however, that this decision in any sense has that effect. In addition, it might well be said that one's education is not complete without a study of comparative religion or the history of religion and its relationship to the advancement of civilization. It certainly may be said that the Bible is worthy of study for its literary and historic qualities. Nothing we have said here indicates that such study of the Bible or of religion, when presented objectively as part of a secular program of education, may not be effected consistently with the First Amendment. But the exercises here do not fall into those categories. They are religious exercises, required by the State in violation of the command of the First Amendment that the Government maintain strict neutrality, neither aiding nor opposing religion.

Finally, we cannot accept that the concept of neutrality, which does not permit a State to require a religious exercise even with the consent of the majority of those affected, collides with the majority's right to free exercise of religion. While the Free Exercise Clause clearly prohibits the use of state action to deny the rights of free exercise to anyone, it has never meant that a majority could use the machinery of the State to practice its beliefs. . . .

The place of religion in our society is an exalted one, achieved through a long tradition of reliance on the home, the church and the inviolable citadel of the individual heart and mind. We have come to recognize through bitter experience that it is not within the power of government to invade that citadel, whether its purpose or effect be to aid or oppose, to advance or retard. In the relationship between man and religion, the State is firmly committed to a position of neutrality. Though the application of that rule requires interpretation of a delicate sort, the rule itself is clearly and concisely stated in the words of the First Amendment. Applying that rule to the facts of these cases, we affirm. . . .

Mr. Justice Douglas, concurring. . . .

Mr. Justice Goldberg, with whom **Mr. Justice Harlan** joins, concurring. . . .

Mr. Justice Stewart, dissenting.

I think the records in the two cases before us are so fundamentally deficient as to make impossible an informed or responsible determination of the constitutional issues presented. Specifically, I cannot agree that on these records we can say that the Establishment Clause has necessarily been violated. But I think there exist serious questions under both that provision and the Free Exercise Clause—insofar as each is imbedded in the Fourteenth Amendment—which require the remand of these cases for the taking of additional evidence. . . .

What our Constitution indispensably protects is the freedom of each of us, be he Jew or Agnostic, Christian or Atheist, Buddhist or Freethinker, to believe or disbelieve, to worship or not worship, to pray or keep silent, according to his own conscience, uncoerced and unrestrained by government. It is conceivable that these school boards, or even all school boards, might eventually find it impossible to administer a system of religious exercises during school hours in such a way as to meet this constitutional standard—in such a way as completely to free from any kind of official coercion those who do not affirmatively want to participate. But I think we must not assume that school boards so lack the qualities of inventiveness and good will as to make impossible the achievement of that goal.

I would remand both cases for further hearings.

Case

WALLACE V. JAFFREE

472 U.S. 38; 105 S.Ct. 2479; 86 L.Ed. 2d. 29 (1985)
Vote: 6–3

In 1978, the Alabama legislature passed a law that provided: "At the commencement of the first class each day in the first through the sixth grades in all public schools . . . a period of silence, not to exceed one minute in duration, shall be observed for meditation, and during any such period silence shall be maintained and no activities engaged in." In 1981, this law was amended to authorize the period of silence "for meditation or voluntary prayer." The amended version of the Alabama "moment of silence law" is before the Supreme Court in this case.

Justice Stevens delivered the opinion of the Court.

. . . [T]he narrow question for decision is whether [the challenged law], which authorizes a period of silence for "meditation or voluntary prayer," is a law respecting the establishment of religion within the meaning of the First Amendment.

Appellee Ishmael Jaffree is a resident of Mobile County, Alabama. On May 28, 1982, he filed a complaint on behalf of three of his minor children; two of them were second-grade students and the third was then in kindergarten. The complaint named members of the Mobile County School Board, various school officials, and the minor plaintiffs' three teachers as defendants. The complaint alleged that the appellees brought the action "seeking principally a declaratory judgment and an injunction restraining the Defendants and each of them from maintaining or allowing the maintenance of regular religious prayer services or other forms of religious observances in the Mobile County Public Schools in violation of the First Amendment as made applicable to states by the Fourteenth Amendment to the United States Constitution." The complaint further alleged that two of the children had been subjected to various acts of religious indoctrination "from the beginning of the school year in September, 1981"; that the defendant teachers had "on a daily basis" led their classes in saying certain prayers in unison; that the minor children were exposed to ostracism from their peer group class members if they did not participate; and that Ishmael Jaffree had re-

peatedly but unsuccessfully requested that the devotional services be stopped. The original complaint made no reference to any Alabama statute. . . .

Jaffree's complaint was later amended to challenge the revised "moment of silence" statute. The U.S. district court dismissed the challenge to the statute holding that "the Establishment Clause of the First Amendment to the U.S. Constitution does not prohibit the state from establishing a religion." The U.S. court of appeals reversed, finding the challenged law to be in violation of the First Amendment.

When the court has been called upon to construe the breadth of the Establishment Clause, it has examined the criteria developed over a period of many years. Thus, in *Lemon v. Kurtzman,* . . . we wrote:

> Every analysis in this area must begin with consideration of the cumulative criteria developed by the Court over many years. Three such tests may be gleaned from our cases. First, the statute must have a secular legislative purpose; second, its principal or primary effect must be one that neither advances nor inhibits religion, . . . finally, the statute must not foster "an excessive government entanglement with religion." . . .

It is the first of these three criteria that is most plainly implicated by this case. As the District Court correctly recognized, no consideration of the second or third criteria is necessary if a statute does not have a clearly secular purpose. For even though a statute that is motivated in part by a religious purpose may satisfy the first criterion, . . . the First Amendment requires that a statute must be invalidated if it is entirely motivated by a purpose to advance religion.

In applying the purpose test, it is appropriate to ask "whether government's actual purpose is to endorse or disapprove of religion." In this case, the answer to that question is dispositive. For the record not only provides us with an unambiguous affirmative answer, but it also reveals that the enactment of [the amended statute] was not motivated by any clearly secular purpose—indeed, the statute had *no* secular purpose.

The sponsor of the bill that became [the challenged law], Senator Donald Holmes, inserted into the legislative record—apparently without dissent—a statement indicating that the legislation was an "effort to return voluntary prayer" to the public schools. Later Senator Holmes confirmed this purpose before the District Court. In response to the question whether he had any purpose for the legislation other than returning voluntary prayer to public schools, he stated, "No, I did not have no other purpose in mind." The State did not present evidence of *any* secular purpose. . . .

The legislative intent to return prayer to the public schools is, of course, quite different from merely protecting every student's right to engage in voluntary prayer during an appropriate moment of silence during the school day. The 1978 statute already protected that right, containing nothing that prevented any student from engaging in voluntary prayer during a silent minute of meditation. Appellants have not identified any secular purpose that was not fully served by [the original statute] before the enactment of [the amendment]. Thus, only two conclusions are consistent with the text . . . (1) the statute was enacted to convey a message of State endorsement and promotion of prayer; or (2) the statute was enacted for no purpose. No one suggests that the statute was nothing but a meaningless or irrational act.

We must, therefore, conclude that the Alabama Legislature intended to change existing law and that it was motivated by the same purpose that the Governor's Answer to the Second Amended Complaint expressly admitted; that the statement inserted in the legislative history revealed; and that Senator Holmes' testimony frankly described. The Legislature enacted [the challenged statute] for the sole purpose of expressing the State's endorsement of prayer activities for one minute at the beginning of each school day. The addition of "or voluntary prayer" indicates that the State intended to characterize prayer as a favored practice. Such an endorsement is not consistent with the established principle that the Government must pursue a course of complete neutrality toward religion.

The importance of that principle does not permit us to treat this as an inconsequential case involving nothing more than a few words of symbolic speech on behalf of the political majority. For whenever the State itself speaks on a religious subject, one of the questions that we must ask is "whether the Government intends to convey a message of endorsement or disapproval of religion." The well-supported concurrent findings of the District Court and the Court of Appeals—that [the challenged law] was intended to convey a message of State-approval of prayer activities in the public schools—make it unnecessary, and indeed inappropriate, to evaluate the practical significance of the addition of the words "or

voluntary prayer" to the statute. Keeping in mind, as we must, "both the fundamental place held by the Establishment Clause in our constitutional scheme and the myriad, subtle ways in which Establishment Clause values can be eroded," we conclude that [the challenged statute] violates the First Amendment.

The judgment of the Court of Appeals is affirmed.

Justice Powell, concurring. . . .

Justice O'Connor, concurring in the judgment.

Nothing in the United States Constitution as interpreted by this Court or in the laws of the State of Alabama prohibits public school students from voluntarily praying at any time before, during, or after the school day. Alabama has facilitated voluntary silent prayers of students who are so inclined by enacting [the 1978 law] which provides a moment of silence in appellees' schools each day. The parties to these proceedings concede the validity of this enactment. At issue in these appeals is the constitutional validity of an additional and subsequent Alabama statute, . . . which both the District Court and the Court of Appeals concluded was enacted solely to officially encourage prayer during the moment of silence. I agree with the judgment of the Court that, in light of the findings of the Courts below and the history of its enactment, [the challenged law] violates the Establishment Clause of the First Amendment. In my view, there can be little doubt that the purpose and likely effect of this subsequent enactment is to endorse and sponsor voluntary prayer in the public schools. I write separately to identify the peculiar features of the Alabama law that render it invalid, and to explain why moment of silence laws in other States do not necessarily manifest the same infirmity. I also write to explain why neither history nor the Free Exercise Clause of the First Amendment validate the Alabama law struck down by the Court today. . . .

After an extensive discussion of Supreme Court decisions interpreting the religion clauses of the First Amendment, Justice O'Connor concludes:

The Court does not hold that the Establishment Clause is so hostile to religion that it precludes the States from affording schoolchildren an opportunity for voluntary silent prayer. To the contrary, the moment of silence statutes of many States should satisfy the Establishment Clause standard we have here applied. The Court holds only that Alabama has intentionally crossed the line between creating a quiet moment during which those so inclined may pray, and affirmatively endorsing the particular religious practice of prayer. This line may be a fine one, but our precedents and the principles of religious liberty require that we draw it. In my view, the judgment of the Court of Appeals must be affirmed.

Chief Justice Burger, dissenting.

Some who trouble to read the opinions in this case will find it ironic—perhaps even bizarre—that on the very day we heard arguments in this case, the Court's session opened with an invocation for Divine protection. Across the park a few hundred yards away, the House of Representatives and the Senate regularly open each session with a prayer. These legislative prayers are not just one minute in duration, but are extended, thoughtful invocations and prayers for Divine guidance. They are given, as they have been since 1789, by clergy appointed as official Chaplains and paid from the Treasury of the United States. Congress has also provided chapels in the Capitol, at public expense, where Members and others may pause for prayer, meditation—or a moment of silence.

Inevitably some wag is bound to say that the Court's holding today reflects a belief that the historic practice of the Congress and this Court is justified because members of the Judiciary and Congress are more in need of Divine guidance than are schoolchildren. Still others will say that all this controversy is "much ado about nothing," since no power on earth—including this Court and Congress—can stop any teacher from opening the school day with a moment of silence for pupils to meditate, to plan their day—or to pray if they voluntarily elect to do so. . . .

Justice White, dissenting.

. . . As I read the filed opinions, a majority of the Court would approve statutes that provided for a moment of silence but did not mention prayer. But if a student asked whether he could pray during that moment, it is difficult to believe that the teacher could not answer in the affirmative. If that is the case, I would not invalidate a statute that at the outset provided the legislative answer to the question "May I pray?" This is so even if the Alabama statute is infirm, which I do not believe it is, because of its peculiar legislative history.

I appreciate Justice Rehnquist's explication of the history of the Religion Clauses of the First Amendment. Against that history, it would be quite understandable if we undertook to reassess our cases dealing with these clauses, particularly those dealing with the Establishment Clause. Of course, I have been out of step with many of the Court's decisions dealing with this subject matter, and it is thus not surprising that I would support a basic reconsideration of our precedents.

Justice Rehnquist, dissenting.

. . . The true meaning of the Establishment Clause can only be seen in its history. . . . As drafters of our Bill of Rights, the framers inscribed the principles that control today. Any deviation from their intentions frustrates the permanence of that Charter and will only lead to the type of unprincipled decisionmaking that has plagued our Establishment Clause cases since *Everson.*

The Framers intended the Establishment Clause to prohibit the designation of any church as a "national" one. The Clause was also designed to stop the Federal Government from asserting a preference for one religious denomination or sect over others. Given the "incorporation" of the Establishment Clause as against the States via the Fourteenth Amendment in *Everson,* States are prohibited as well from establishing a religion or discriminating between sects. As its history abundantly shows, however, nothing in the Establishment Clause requires government to be strictly neutral between religion and irreligion, nor does that Clause prohibit Congress or the States from pursuing legitimate secular ends through nondiscriminatory sectarian means.

The Court strikes down the Alabama statute . . . because the State wished to "endorse prayer as a favored practice." . . . It would come as much of a shock to those who drafted the Bill of Rights as it will to a large number of thoughtful Americans today to learn that the Constitution, as construed by the majority, prohibits the Alabama Legislature from "endorsing" prayer. George Washington himself, at the request of the very Congress which passed the Bill of Rights, proclaimed a day of "public thanksgiving and prayer, to be observed by acknowledging with grateful hearts the many and signal favors of Almighty God." History must judge whether it was the father of his country in 1789, or a majority of the Court today, which has strayed from the meaning of the Establishment Clause.

The State surely has a secular interest in regulating the manner in which public schools are conducted. Nothing in the Establishment Clause of the First Amendment, properly understood, prohibits any such generalized "endorsement" of prayer. I would therefore reverse the judgment of the Court of Appeals. . . .

Case

EDWARDS V. AGUILLARD

482 U.S. 578; 107 S.Ct. 2573; 96 L.Ed. 2d. 510 (1987)
Vote: 7–2

The teaching of evolution in the public schools has long been controversial. Indeed, some states have attempted to ban the teaching of evolution altogether. Such a prohibition was struck down in Epperson v. Arkansas *(1968). More recently, states have attempted to balance the teaching of evolution with the teaching of "creation science." Whether this is a legitimate secular requirement for public school curricula or an attempt to instruct public school students in the biblical account of creation is the issue before the Supreme Court in this case.*

Justice Brennan delivered the opinion of the Court.

The question for decision is whether Louisiana's "Balanced Treatment for Creation-Science and Evolution-Science in Public School Instruction" Act (Creationism Act) . . . is facially invalid as violative of the Establishment Clause of the First Amendment.

The Creationism Act forbids the teaching of the theory of evolution in public schools unless accompanied by instruction in "creation science." . . . No school is required to teach evolution or creation science. If either is taught, however, the other must also be taught. . . . The theories of evolution and creation science are statutorily defined as "the scientific evidences for [creation or evolution] and inferences from those scientific evidences." . . .

Appellees, who include parents of children attending Louisiana public schools, Louisiana teachers, and religious leaders, challenged the constitutionality of the Act in District Court, seeking an injunction and declaratory relief. Appellants, Louisiana officials charged with implementing the Act, defended on the ground that the purpose of the Act is to protect a legitimate secular interest, namely, academic freedom. Appellees attacked the Act as facially invalid because it violated the Establishment Clause and made a motion for summary judgment. The District Court granted the motion. . . . The court held that there can be no valid secular reason for prohibiting the teaching of evolution, a theory historically opposed by some religious denominations. The court further concluded that "the teaching of 'creation-science' and 'creationism,' as contemplated by the

statute, involves teaching 'tailored to the principles' of a particular religious sect or group of sects." . . . The District Court therefore held that the Creationism Act violated the Establishment Clause either because it prohibited the teaching of evolution or because it required the teaching of creation science with the purpose of advancing a particular religious doctrine.

The Court of Appeals affirmed. . . . The court observed that the statute's avowed purpose of protecting academic freedom was inconsistent with requiring, upon risk of sanction, the teaching of creation science whenever evolution is taught. . . . The court found that the Louisiana legislature's actual intent was "to discredit evolution by counterbalancing its teaching at every turn with the teaching of creationism, a religious belief." . . . Because the Creationism Act was thus a law furthering a particular religious belief, the Court of Appeals held that the Act violated the Establishment Clause. A suggestion for rehearing *en banc* was denied over a dissent. . . . We noted probable jurisdiction, . . . and now affirm.

The Establishment Clause forbids the enactment of any law "respecting an establishment of religion." The Court has applied a three-pronged test to determine whether legislation comports with the Establishment Clause. First, the legislature must have adopted the law with a secular purpose. Second, the statute's principal or primary effect must be one that neither advances nor inhibits religion. Third, the statute must not result in an excessive entanglement of government with religion. *Lemon v. Kurtzman* . . . (1971). State action violates the Establishment Clause if it fails to satisfy any of these prongs. . . .

Lemon's first prong focuses on the purpose that animated adoption of the Act. "The purpose prong of the *Lemon* test asks whether government's actual purpose is to endorse or disapprove of religion." . . . A governmental intention to promote religion is clear when the State enacts a law to serve a religious purpose. This intention may be evidenced by promotion of religion in general, . . . or by advancement of a particular religious belief. . . . If the law was enacted for the purpose of endorsing religion, "no consideration of the second or third criteria [of *Lemon*] is necessary." . . . In this case, the petitioners had identified no clear secular purpose for the Louisiana Act.

True, the Act's stated purpose is to protect academic freedom. . . . This phrase might, in common parlance, be understood as referring to enhancing the freedom of teachers to teach what they will. The Court of Appeals, however, correctly concluded that the Act was not designed to further that goal. We find no merit in the State's argument that the "legislature may not [have] use[d] the terms 'academic freedom' in the correct legal sense. They might have [had] in mind, instead, a basic concept of fairness: teaching all of the evidence." . . . Even if "academic freedom" is read to mean "teaching all of the evidence" with respect to the origin of human beings, the Act does not further this purpose. The goal of providing a more comprehensive science curriculum is not furthered either by outlawing the teaching of evolution or by requiring the teaching of creation science.

While the Court is normally deferential to a State's articulation of a secular purpose, it is required that the statement of such purpose be sincere and not a sham. . . .

It is clear from the legislative history that the purpose of the legislative sponsor, Senator Bill Keith, was to narrow the science curriculum. During the legislative hearings, Senator Keith stated: "My preference would be that neither [creationism nor evolution] be taught." . . . Such a ban on teaching does not promote—indeed, it undermines—the provision of a comprehensive scientific education.

It is equally clear that requiring schools to teach creation science with evolution does not advance academic freedom. The Act does not grant teachers a flexibility that they did not already possess to supplant the present science curriculum with the presentation of theories, besides evolution, about the origin of life. Indeed, the Court of Appeals found that no law prohibited Louisiana public schoolteachers from teaching any scientific theory. . . . As the president of the Louisiana Science Teachers Association testified, "[a]ny scientific concept that's based on established fact can be included in our curriculum already, and no legislation allowing this is necessary." . . . The Act provides Louisiana schoolteachers with no new authority. Thus the stated purpose is not furthered by it. . . .

Furthermore, the goal of basic "fairness" is hardly furthered by the Act's discriminatory preference for the teaching of creation science and against the teaching of evolution. While requiring that curriculum guides be developed for creation science, the Act says nothing of comparable guides for evolution. . . . Similarly, research services are supplied for creation science but not for evolution. . . . Only "creation scientists" can serve on the panel that supplies the resource services. . . . The Act forbids school boards to discriminate against anyone who "chooses to be a creation-scientist" or to teach

"creationism," but fails to protect those who choose to teach evolution or any other noncreation science theory, or who refuse to teach creation science. . . .

If the Louisiana legislature's purpose was solely to maximize the comprehensiveness and effectiveness of science instruction, it would have encouraged the teaching of all scientific theories about the origins of humankind. But under the Act's requirements, teachers who were once free to teach any and all facets of this subject are now unable to do so. Moreover, the Act fails even to ensure that creation science will be taught, but instead requires the teaching of this theory only when the theory of evolution is taught. Thus we agree with the Court of Appeals' conclusion that the Act does not serve to protect academic freedom, but has the distinctly different purpose of discrediting "evolution by counterbalancing its teaching at every turn with the teaching of creation science." . . .

. . . [W]e need not be blind in this case to the legislature's preeminent religious purpose in enacting this statute. There is a historic and contemporaneous link between the teachings of certain religious denominations and the teaching of evolution. It was this link that concerned the Court in *Epperson v. Arkansas* [1968], . . . which also involved a facial challenge to a statute regulating the teaching of evolution. In that case, the Court reviewed an Arkansas statute that made it unlawful for an instructor to teach evolution or to use a textbook that referred to this scientific theory. Although the Arkansas antievolution law did not explicitly state its predominate religious purpose, the Court could not ignore that "[t]he statute was a product of the upsurge of 'fundamentalist' religious fervor" that has long viewed this particular scientific theory as contradicting the literal interpretation of the Bible. . . . After reviewing the history of antievolution statutes, the Court determined that "there can be no doubt that the motivation for the [Arkansas] law was the same [as other antievolution statutes]: to suppress the teaching of a theory which, it was thought, 'denied' the divine creation of man." . . . The Court found that there can be no legitimate state interest in protecting particular religions from scientific views "distasteful to them," . . . and concluded "that the First Amendment does not permit the State to require that teaching and learning must be tailored to the principles or prohibitions of any religious sect or dogma." . . .

These same historic and contemporaneous antagonisms between the teachings of certain religious denominations and the teaching of evolution are present in this case. The preeminent purpose of the Louisiana legislature was clearly to advance the religious viewpoint that a supernatural being created humankind. The term "creation science" was defined as embracing this particular religious doctrine by those responsible for the passage of the Creationism Act. Senator Keith's leading expert on creation science, Edward Boudreaux, testified at the legislative hearings that the theory of creation science included belief in the existence of a supernatural creator. . . . Senator Keith also cited testimony from other experts to support the creation-science view that "a creator [was] responsible for the universe and everything in it." . . . The legislative history therefore reveals that the term "creation science," as contemplated by the legislature that adopted this Act, embodies the religious belief that a supernatural creator was responsible for the creation of humankind.

Furthermore, it is not happenstance that the legislature required the teaching of a theory that coincided with this religious view. The legislative history documents that the Act's primary purpose was to change the science curriculum of public schools in order to provide persuasive advantage to a particular religious doctrine that rejects the factual basis of evolution in its entirety. The sponsor of the Creationism Act, Senator Keith, explained during the legislative hearings that his disdain for the theory of evolution resulted from the support that evolution supplied to views contrary to his own religious beliefs. According to Senator Keith, the theory of evolution was consonant with the "cardinal principle[s] of religious humanism, secular humanism, theological liberalism, aetheistism [sic]." . . . The state senator repeatedly stated that scientific evidence supporting his religious views should be included in the public school curriculum to redress the fact that the theory of evolution incidentally coincided with what he characterized as religious beliefs antithetical to his own. The legislation therefore sought to alter the science curriculum to reflect endorsement of a religious view that is antagonistic to the theory of evolution.

In this case, the purpose of the Creationism Act was to restructure the science curriculum to conform with a particular religious viewpoint. Out of many possible science subjects taught in the public schools, the legislature chose to affect the teaching of the one scientific theory that historically has been opposed by certain religious sects. As in *Epperson,* the legislature passed the Act to give preference to those religious groups which have as one of their tenets the creation of humankind by a divine creator. The "overriding fact" that confronted the Court in *Epperson* was "that Arkansas' law selects

from the body of knowledge a particular segment which it proscribes for the sole reason that it is deemed to conflict with . . . a particular interpretation of the Book of Genesis by a particular religious group." . . . Similarly, the Creationism Act is designed either to promote the theory of creation science which embodies a particular religious tenet by requiring that creation science be taught whenever evolution is taught or to prohibit the teaching of a scientific theory disfavored by certain religious sects by forbidding the teaching of evolution when creation science is not also taught. The Establishment Clause, however, "forbids alike the preference of a religious doctrine or the prohibition of theory which is deemed antagonistic to a particular dogma." . . . Because the primary purpose of the Creationism Act is to advance a particular religious belief, the Act endorses religion in violation of the First Amendment.

We do not imply that a legislature could never require that scientific critiques of prevailing scientific theories be taught. Indeed, the Court acknowledged in *Stone* that its decision forbidding the posting of the Ten Commandments did not mean that no use could ever be made of the Ten Commandments, or that the Ten Commandments played an exclusively religious role in the history of Western civilization. . . . In a similar way, teaching a variety of scientific theories about the origins of humankind to schoolchildren might be validly done with the clear secular intent of enhancing the effectiveness of science instruction. But because the primary purpose of the Creationism Act is to endorse a particular religious doctrine, the Act furthers religion in violation of the Establishment Clause. . . .

Justice Powell, with whom **Justice O'Connor** joins, concurring. . . .

Justice White, concurring in the judgment. . . .

Justice Scalia, with whom the **Chief Justice** joins, dissenting.

Even if I agreed with the questionable premise that legislation can be invalidated under the Establishment Clause on the basis of its motivation alone, without regard to its effects, I would still find no justification for today's decision. The Louisiana legislators who passed the "Balanced Treatment for Creation-Science and Evolution-Science Act" (Balanced Treatment Act), . . . each of whom had sworn to support the Constitution, were well aware of the potential Establishment Clause problems and considered that aspect of the legislation with great care. After seven hearings and several months of study, resulting in substantial revision of the original proposal, they approved the Act overwhelmingly and specifically articulated the secular purpose they meant it to serve. Although the record contains abundant evidence of the sincerity of that purpose (the only issue pertinent to this case), the Court today holds, essentially on the basis of "its visceral knowledge regarding what must have motivated the legislators," . . . that the members of the Louisiana Legislature knowingly violated their oaths and then lied about it. I dissent. Had requirements of the Balanced Treatment Act that are not apparent on its face been clarified by an interpretation of the Louisiana Supreme Court, or by the manner of its implementation, the Act might well be found unconstitutional; but the question of its constitutionality cannot rightly be disposed of on the gallop, by impugning the motives of its supporters. . . .

Given the many hazards involved in assessing the subjective intent of governmental decisionmakers, the first prong of *Lemon [v. Kurtzman]* is defensible, I think, only if the text of the Establishment Clause demands it. That is surely not the case. The Clause states that "Congress shall make no law respecting an establishment of religion." One could argue, I suppose, that any time Congress acts with the intent of advancing religion, it has enacted a "law respecting an establishment of religion"; but far from being an unavoidable reading, it is quite an unnatural one. I doubt, for example, that the Clayton Act . . . could reasonably be described as a "law respecting an establishment of religion" if bizarre new historical evidence revealed that it lacked a secular purpose, even though it has no discernible nonsecular effect. It is, in short, far from an inevitable reading of the Establishment Clause that it forbids all governmental action intended to advance religion; and if not inevitable, any reading with such untoward consequences must be wrong.

In the past we have attempted to justify our embarrassing Establishment Clause jurisprudence on the ground that it "sacrifices clarity and predictability for flexibility." . . . One commentator had aptly characterized this as "a euphemism . . . for . . . the absence of any principled rationale." . . . I think it time that we sacrifice some "flexibility" for "clarity and predictability." Abandoning *Lemon*'s purpose test—a test which exacerbates the tension between the Free Exercise and Establishment Clause, has no basis in the language or history of the amendment, and, as today's decision shows, has wonderfully flexible consequences—would be a good place to start.

Case

AGOSTINI V. FELTON

521 U.S. ___, 117 S.Ct. 1997, 138 L.Ed. 2d. 391 (1997)
Vote: 5–4

Here the Court reconsiders its decision in Aguilar v. Felton *(1985), which held that the Establishment Clause prohibited a city from sending public school teachers into parochial schools to provide remedial education.*

Justice O'Connor delivered the opinion of the Court.

. . . Petitioners maintain that *Aguilar* cannot be squared with our intervening Establishment Clause jurisprudence and ask that we explicitly recognize what our more recent cases already dictate: *Aguilar* is no longer good law. We agree with petitioners that *Aguilar* is not consistent with our subsequent Establishment Clause decisions. . . .

In order to evaluate whether *Aguilar* has been eroded by our subsequent Establishment Clause cases, it is necessary to understand the rationale upon which *Aguilar*, as well as its companion case, *School Dist. of Grand Rapids v. Ball*, 473 U.S. 373 (1985), rested. . . .

Our more recent cases have undermined the assumptions upon which *Ball* and *Aguilar* relied. To be sure, the general principles we use to evaluate whether government aid violates the Establishment Clause have not changed since *Aguilar* was decided. For example, we continue to ask whether the government acted with the purpose of advancing or inhibiting religion, and the nature of that inquiry has remained largely unchanged. . . . Likewise, we continue to explore whether the aid has the "effect" of advancing or inhibiting religion. What has changed since we decided *Ball* and *Aguilar* is our understanding of the criteria used to assess whether aid to religion has an impermissible effect. . . .

. . . New York City's Title I program does not run afoul of any of three primary criteria we currently use to evaluate whether government aid has the effect of advancing religion: it does not result in governmental indoctrination; define its recipients by reference to religion; or create an excessive entanglement. We therefore hold that a federally funded program providing supplemental, remedial instruction to disadvantaged children on a neutral basis is not invalid under the Establishment Clause when such instruction is given on the premises of sectarian schools by government employees pursuant to a program containing safeguards such as those present here. The same considerations that justify this holding require us to conclude that this carefully constrained program also cannot reasonably be viewed as an endorsement of religion. . . . Accordingly, we must acknowledge that *Aguilar,* as well as the portion of *Ball* addressing Grand Rapids' Shared Time program, are no longer good law.

The doctrine of *stare decisis* does not preclude us from recognizing the change in our law and overruling *Aguilar* and those portions of *Ball* inconsistent with our more recent decisions. . . . That policy is at its weakest when we interpret the Constitution because our interpretation can be altered only by constitutional amendment or by overruling our prior decisions. . . . Thus, we have held in several cases that *stare decisis* does not prevent us from overruling a previous decision where there has been a significant change in or subsequent development of our constitutional law. . . . As discussed above, our Establishment Clause jurisprudence has changed significantly since we decided *Ball* and *Aguilar,* so our decision to overturn those cases rests on far more than "a present doctrinal disposition to come out differently from the Court of [1985]." Casey, supra, at 864. We therefore overrule *Ball* and *Aguilar* to the extent those decisions are inconsistent with our current understanding of the Establishment Clause. . . .

We . . . conclude that our Establishment Clause law has "significant[ly] change[d]" since we decided *Aguilar.* . . . We are only left to decide whether this change in law entitles petitioners to relief under Rule 60(b)(5). We conclude that it does. Our general practice is to apply the rule of law we announce in a case to the parties before us. . . . We adhere to this practice even when we overrule a case. . . .

We do not acknowledge, and we do not hold, that other courts should conclude our more recent cases have, by implication, overruled an earlier precedent. We reaffirm that "if a precedent of this Court has direct application in a case, yet appears to rest on reasons rejected in some other line of decisions, the Court of Appeals should follow the case which directly controls, leaving to this Court the prerogative of overruling its own decisions." . . . Adherence to this teaching by the District Court and Court of Appeals in this case does not insulate a legal principle on which they relied from our review to determine its continued vitality. The trial court acted within its discretion in entertaining the motion with supporting allegations, but it was also correct to recognize that the motion had to be denied unless and until this Court reinterpreted the binding precedent. . . .

. . . [O]ur decision today is intimately tied to the context in which it arose. This litigation involves a party's request under Rule 60(b)(5) to vacate a continuing injunction entered some years ago in light of a bona fide, significant change in subsequent law. The clause of Rule 60(b)(5) that petitioners invoke applies by its terms only to "judgment[s] hav[ing] prospective application." Intervening developments in the law by themselves rarely constitute the extraordinary circumstances required for relief under Rule 60(b)(6), the only remaining avenue for relief on this basis from judgments lacking any prospective component. . . . Our decision will have no effect outside the context of ordinary civil litigation where the propriety of continuing prospective relief is at issue. . . . Given that Rule 60(b)(5) specifically contemplates the grant of relief in the circumstances presented here, it can hardly be said that we have somehow warped the Rule into a means of "allowing an 'anytime' rehearing." . . .

Respondents further contend that "[p]etitioners' [p]roposed [u]se of Rule 60(b) [w]ill [e]rode the [i]nstitutional [i]ntegrity of the Court." Brief for Respondents 26. Respondents do not explain how a proper application of Rule 60(b)(5) undermines our legitimacy. Instead, respondents focus on the harm occasioned if we were to overrule *Aguilar.* But as discussed above, we do no violence to the doctrine of *stare decisis* when we recognize bona fide changes in our decisional law. And in those circumstances, we do no violence to the legitimacy we derive from reliance on that doctrine. . . .

As a final matter, we see no reason to wait for a "better vehicle" in which to evaluate the impact of subsequent cases on *Aguilar*'s continued vitality. To evaluate the Rule 60(b)(5) motion properly before us today in no way undermines "integrity in the interpretation of procedural rules" or signals any departure from "the responsive, non agenda setting character of this Court." . . . Indeed, under these circumstances, it would be particularly inequitable for us to bide our time waiting for another case to arise while the city of New York labors under a continuing injunction forcing it to spend millions of dollars on mobile instructional units and leased sites when it could instead be spending that money to give economically disadvantaged children a better chance at success in life by means of a program that is perfectly consistent with the Establishment Clause.

For these reasons, we reverse the judgment of the Court of Appeals and remand to the District Court with instructions to vacate its September 26, 1985, order.

Justice Souter, with whom **Justice Stevens** and **Justice Ginsburg** join, and with whom **Justice Breyer** joins as to Part II, dissenting.

In this novel proceeding, petitioners seek relief from an injunction the District Court entered 12 years ago to implement our decision in *Aguilar v. Felton*. . . .[T]he Court's holding that petitioners are entitled to relief under Rule 60(b) is seriously mistaken. The Court's misapplication of the rule is tied to its equally erroneous reading of our more recent Establishment Clause cases, which the Court describes as having rejected the underpinnings of *Aguilar* and portions of *Aguilar*'s companion case, *School Dist. of Grand Rapids v. Ball*, 473 U.S. 373 (1985). The result is to repudiate the very reasonable line drawn in *Aguilar* and *Ball*, and to authorize direct state aid to religious institutions on an unparalleled scale, in violation of the Establishment Clause's central prohibition against religious subsidies by the government. . . .

. . . I believe *Aguilar* was a correct and sensible decision, and my only reservation about its opinion is that the emphasis on the excessive entanglement produced by monitoring religious instructional content obscured those facts that independently called for the application of two central tenets of Establishment Clause jurisprudence. The State is forbidden to subsidize religion directly and is just as surely forbidden to act in any way that could reasonably be viewed as religious endorsement. . . .

These principles were violated by the programs at issue in *Aguilar* and *Ball*, as a consequence of several significant features common to both Title I, as implemented in New York City before *Aguilar*, and the Grand Rapids Shared Time program: each provided classes on the premises of the religious schools, covering a wide range of subjects including some at the core of primary and secondary education, like reading and mathematics; while their services were termed "supplemental," the programs and their instructors necessarily assumed responsibility for teaching subjects that the religious schools would otherwise have been obligated to provide; the public employees carrying out the programs had broad responsibilities involving the exercise of consider-

able discretion; while the programs offered aid to nonpublic school students generally (and Title I went to public school students as well), participation by religious school students in each program was extensive; and, finally, aid under Title I and Shared Time flowed directly to the schools in the form of classes and programs, as distinct from indirect aid that reaches schools only as a result of independent private choice. . . .

What, therefore, was significant in *Aguilar* and *Ball* about the placement of state paid teachers into the physical and social settings of the religious schools was not only the consequent temptation of some of those teachers to reflect the schools' religious missions in the rhetoric of their instruction, with a resulting need for monitoring and the certainty of entanglement. . . . What was so remarkable was that the schemes in issue assumed a teaching responsibility indistinguishable from the responsibility of the schools themselves. The obligation of primary and secondary schools to teach reading necessarily extends to teaching those who are having a hard time at it, and the same is true of math. Calling some classes remedial does not distinguish their subjects from the schools' basic subjects, however inadequately the schools may have been addressing them.

What was true of the Title I scheme as struck down in *Aguilar* will be just as true when New York reverts to the old practices with the Court's approval after today. There is simply no line that can be drawn between the instruction paid for at taxpayers' expense and the instruction in any subject that is not identified as formally religious. While it would be an obvious sham, say, to channel cash to religious schools to be credited only against the expense of "secular" instruction, the line between "supplemental" and general education is likewise impossible to draw. If a State may constitutionally enter the schools to teach in the manner in question, it must in constitutional principle be free to assume, or assume payment for, the entire cost of instruction provided in any ostensibly secular subject in any religious school. . . .

. . . [T]he object of Title I is worthy without doubt, and the cost of compliance is high. In the short run there is much that is genuinely unfortunate about the administration of the scheme under *Aguilar*'s rule. But constitutional lines have to be drawn, and on one side of every one of them is an otherwise sympathetic case that provokes impatience with the Constitution and with the line. But constitutional lines are the price of constitutional government.

Justice Ginsburg, with whom **Justice Stevens, Justice Souter,** and **Justice Breyer** join, dissenting.

The Court today finds a way to rehear a legal question decided in respondents' favor in this very case some 12 years ago. . . . Subsequent decisions, the majority says, have undermined *Aguilar* and justify our immediate reconsideration. This Court's Rules do not countenance the rehearing here granted. For good reason, a proper application of those rules and the Federal Rules of Civil Procedure would lead us to defer reconsideration of *Aguilar* until we are presented with the issue in another case. . . .

Unlike the majority, I find just cause to await the arrival of . . . another case in which our review appropriately may be sought, before deciding whether *Aguilar* should remain the law of the land. That cause lies in the maintenance of integrity in the interpretation of procedural rules, preservation of the responsive, non agenda setting character of this Court, and avoidance of invitations to reconsider old cases based on "speculat[ions] on chances from changes in [the Court's membership]." . . .

Case

Marsh v. Chambers

463 U.S. 783; 103 S.Ct. 3330; 77 L.Ed. 2d. 1019 (1983)
Vote: 6–3

Here the Court considers whether a state legislature's practice of opening each legislative day with a prayer by a chaplain paid from public funds violates the Establishment Clause.

Chief Justice Burger delivered the opinion of the Court.

. . . The Nebraska Legislature begins each of its sessions with a prayer offered by a chaplain who is chosen biennially by the Executive Board of the Legislative Council and paid out of public funds. Robert E. Palmer, a Presbyterian minister, has served as chaplain since 1965 at a salary of $319.75 per month for each month the legislature is in session.

Ernest Chambers is a member of the Nebraska Legislature and a taxpayer of Nebraska. Claiming that the Nebraska Legislature's chaplaincy practice violates the Establishment Clause of the First Amendment, he brought this action . . . seeking to enjoin enforcement of the practice. After denying a motion to dismiss on the ground of legislative immunity, the District Court held that the Establishment Clause was not breached by the prayers, but was violated by paying the chaplain from public funds. . . . It therefore enjoined the legislature from using public funds to pay the chaplain; it declined to enjoin the policy of beginning sessions with prayers. . . .

Applying the three-part test of *Lemon v. Kurtzman,* . . . the [Court of Appeals] held that the chaplaincy practice violated all three elements of the test: the purpose and primary effect of selecting the same minister for 16 years and publishing his prayers was to promote a particular religious expression; use of state money for compensation and publication led to entanglement. . . . Accordingly, the Court of Appeals modified the District Court's injunction and prohibited the State from engaging in any aspect of its established chaplaincy practice.

We granted certiorari limited to the challenge to the practice of opening sessions with prayers by a state-employed clergyman, . . . and we reverse.

The opening of sessions of legislative and other deliberative public bodies with prayer is deeply embedded in the history and tradition of this country. From colonial times through the founding of the Republic and ever since, the practice of legislative prayer has coexisted with the principles of disestablishment and religious freedom. In the very courtrooms in which the United States District Judge and later three Circuit Judges heard and decided this case, the proceedings opened with an announcement that concluded, "God save the United States and this Honorable Court." The same invocation occurs at all sessions of this Court.

The tradition in many of the colonies was, of course, linked to an established church, but the Continental Congress, beginning in 1774, adopted the traditional procedure of opening its sessions with a prayer offered by a paid chaplain. . . . Although prayers were not offered during the Constitutional Convention, the First Congress, as one of its early items of business, adopted the policy of selecting a chaplain to open each session with prayer. Thus on April 7, 1789, the Senate appointed a committee "to take under consideration the manner of electing Chaplains." . . . An April 9, 1789, a similar committee was appointed by the House of Representatives. On April 25, 1789, the Senate elected its first chaplain, . . . the House followed suit on May 1, 1789. . . . A statute providing for the payment of these chaplains was enacted into law on Sept. 22, 1789. . . .

On Sept. 25, 1789, three days after Congress authorized the appointment of paid chaplains, final agreement was reached on the language of the Bill of Rights. . . . Clearly the men who wrote the First Amendment Religion Clauses did not view paid legislative chaplains and opening prayers as a violation of that Amendment, for the practice of opening sessions with prayer has continued without interruption ever since that early session of Congress. It has also been followed consistently in most of the states, including Nebraska, where the institution of opening legislative sessions with prayer was adopted even before the State attained statehood. . . .

Standing alone, historical patterns cannot justify contemporary violations of constitutional guarantees, but there is far more here than simply historical patterns. In this context, historical evidence sheds light not only on what the draftsmen intended the Establishment Clause to mean, but also on how they thought that clause applied to the practice authorized by the First Congress— their actions reveal their intent. . . .

In *Walz v. Tax Comm'n.* [1970], . . . we considered the weight to be accorded to history:

> It is obviously correct that no one acquires a vested or protected right in violation of the Constitution by long use, even when that span of time covers our entire national existence and indeed predates it. Yet an unbroken practice . . . is not something to be lightly cast aside.

No more is Nebraska's practice of over a century, consistent with two centuries of national practice, to be cast aside. . . . In applying the First Amendment to the states through the Fourteenth Amendment, . . . it would be incongruous to interpret that clause as imposing more stringent First Amendment limits on the States than the draftsmen imposed on the Federal Government.

This unique history leads us to accept the interpretation of the First Amendment draftsmen who saw no real threat to the Establishment Clause arising from a practice of prayer similar to that now challenged. . . .

In light of the unambiguous and unbroken history of more than 200 years, there can be no doubt that the practice of opening legislative sessions with prayer has become part of the fabric of our society. To invoke Divine guidance on a public body entrusted with making the laws is not, in these circumstances, an "establishment" of religion or a step toward establishment; it is simply a tolerable acknowledgement of beliefs widely held among the people of this country. As Justice Douglas observed, "[w]e are a religious people whose institutions presuppose a Supreme Being." . . .

We turn then to the question of whether any features of the Nebraska practice violate the Establishment Clause. Beyond the bare fact that a prayer is offered, three points have been made: first, that a clergyman of only one denomination—Presbyterian— has been selected for 16 years; second, that the chaplain is paid at public expense; and third, that the prayers are in the Judeo-Christian tradition. Weighed against the historical background, these factors do not serve to invalidate Nebraska's practice.

The Court of Appeals was concerned that Palmer's long tenure has the effect of giving preference to his religious views. We, no more than Members of Congresses of this century, can perceive any suggestion that choosing a clergyman of one denomination advances the beliefs of a particular church. To the contrary, the evidence indicates that Palmer was reappointed because his performance and personal qualities were acceptable to the body appointing him. Palmer was not the only clergyman heard by the Legislature; guest chaplains have officiated at the request of various legislators and as substitutes during Palmer's absences. . . . Absent proof that the chaplain's reappointment stemmed from an impermissible motive, we conclude that his long tenure does not in itself conflict with the Establishment Clause.

Nor is the compensation of the chaplain from public funds a reason to invalidate the Nebraska Legislature's chaplaincy; remuneration is grounded in historic practice initiated . . . by the same Congress that adopted the Establishment Clause of the First Amendment. . . . The content of the prayer is not of concern to judges where, as here, there is no indication that the prayer opportunity has been exploited to proselytize or advance any one, or to disparage any other, faith or belief. That being so, it is not for us to embark on a sensitive evaluation or to parse the content of a particular prayer.

We do not doubt the sincerity of those, who like respondent, believe that to have prayer in this context risks the beginning of the establishment the Founding Fathers feared. But this concern is not well founded. . . . The unbroken practice for two centuries in the National Congress, for more than a century in Nebraska and in many other states, gives abundant assurance that there is no real threat "while this Court sits." . . .

The judgment of the Court of Appeals is reversed.

Justice Brennan, with whom ***Justice Marshall*** joins, dissenting.

. . . [D]isagreement with the Court requires that I confront the fact that some twenty years ago, in a concurring opinion in one of the cases striking down official prayer and ceremonial Bible reading in the public schools, I came very close to endorsing essentially the result reached by the Court today. Nevertheless, after much reflection, I have come to the conclusion that I was wrong then and that the Court is wrong today. I now believe that the practice of official invocational prayer, as it exists in Nebraska and most other State Legislatures, is unconstitutional. It is contrary to the doctrine as well the underlying purposes of the Establishment Clause, and it is not saved either by its history or by any of the other considerations suggested in the Court's opinion.

I respectfully dissent.

The Court makes no pretense of subjecting Nebraska's practice of legislative prayer to any of the formal "tests" that have traditionally structured our inquiry under the Establishment Clause. That it fails to do so is, in a sense, a good thing, for it simply confirms that the Court is carving out an exception to the Establishment Clause rather than reshaping Establishment Clause doctrine to accommodate legislative prayer. For my purposes, however, I must begin by demonstrating what should be obvious: that, if the Court were to judge legislative prayer through the unsentimental eye of our settled doctrine, it would have to strike it down as a clear violation of the Establishment Clause.

The most commonly cited formulation of prevailing Establishment Clause doctrine is found in *Lemon v. Kurtzman* [1971]: . . .

Every analysis in this area must begin with consideration of the cumulative criteria developed by the Court over many years. Three such tests may be gleaned from our cases. First, the statute [at issue] must have a secular legislative purpose; second, its principal or primary effect must be one that neither advances nor inhibits religion; finally, the statute must not foster "an excessive government entanglement with religion." . . .

That the "purpose" of legislative prayer is preeminently religious rather than secular seems to me to be self-evident. "To invoke Divine guidance on a public body entrusted with making the laws," . . . is nothing but a religious act. Moreover, whatever secular functions legislative prayer might play—formally opening the legislative session, getting the members of the body to quiet down, and imbuing them with a sense of seriousness and high purpose—could so plainly be performed in a purely nonreligious fashion that to claim a secular purpose for the prayer is an insult to the perfectly honorable individuals who instituted and continue the practice.

The "primary effect" of legislative prayer is also clearly religious. As we said in the context of officially sponsored prayers in the public schools, "prescribing a particular form of religious worship," even if the individuals involved have the choice not to participate, places "indirect coercive pressure upon religious minorities to conform to the prevailing officially approved religion. . . ." . . . More importantly, invocations in Nebraska's legislative halls explicitly link religious belief and the prestige of the State. "[T]he mere appearance of a joint exercise of legislative authority by Church and State provides a significant symbolic benefit to religion in the minds of some by reason of the power conferred." . . .

Finally, there can be no doubt that the practice of legislative prayer leads to excessive "entanglement" between the State and religion. *Lemon* pointed out that "entanglement" can take two forms: First, a state statute or program might involve the state impermissibly in monitoring and overseeing religious affairs. . . . In the case of legislative prayer, the process of choosing a "suitable" chaplain, whether on a permanent or rotating basis, and insuring that the chaplain limits himself to "suitable" prayers, involves precisely the sort of supervision that agencies of government should if at all possible avoid.

Second, excessive "entanglement" might arise out of "the divisive political potential" of a state statute or program. . . . In this case, this second aspect of entanglement is also clear. The controversy between Senator Chambers and his colleagues, which had reached the stage of difficulty and rancor long before this lawsuit was brought, has split the Nebraska Legislature precisely on issues of religion and religious conformity. . . . The record in this case also reports a series of instances, involving legislators other than Senator Chambers, in which invocations by Reverend Palmer and others led to controversy along religious lines. And in general, the history of legislative prayer has been far more eventful—and divisive—than a hasty reading of the Court's opinion might indicate.

In sum, I have no doubt that, if any group of law students were asked to apply the principles of *Lemon* to the question of legislative prayer, they would nearly unanimously find the practice to be unconstitutional. . . .

The argument is made occasionally that a strict separation of religion and state robs the nation of its spiritual identity. I believe quite the contrary. It may be true that individuals cannot be "neutral" on the question of religion. But the judgment of the Establishment Clause is that neutrality by the organs of government on questions of religion is both possible and imperative. . . .

Justice Stevens, dissenting.

In a democratically elected legislature, the religious beliefs of the chaplain tend to reflect the faith of the majority of the lawmakers' constituents. Prayers may be said by a Catholic priest in the Massachusetts Legislature and by a Presbyterian minister in the Nebraska Legislature, but I would not expect to find a Jehovah's Witness or a disciple of Mary Baker Eddy or the Reverend Moon serving as the official chaplain in any state legislature. Regardless of the motivation of the majority that exercises the power to appoint the chaplain, it seems

plain to me that the designation of a member of one religious faith to serve as the sole official chaplain of a state legislature for a period of 16 years constitutes the preference of one faith over another in violation of the Establishment Clause of the First Amendment.

The Court declines to "embark on a sensitive evaluation or to parse the content of a particular prayer." . . . Perhaps it does so because it would be unable to explain away the clearly sectarian content of some of the prayers given by Nebraska's chaplain. Or perhaps the Court is unwilling to acknowledge that the tenure of the chaplain must inevitably be conditioned on the acceptability of that content to the silent majority.

I would affirm the judgment of the Court of Appeals.

Case

Lynch v. Donnelly

465 U.S. 668; 104 S.Ct. 1355; 79 L.Ed. 2d. 604 (1984)
Vote: 5–4

In this case the Court decides whether the Establishment Clause prohibits a city from including a nativity scene in its annual Christmas display.

The Chief Justice delivered the opinion of the Court.

. . . Each year, in cooperation with the downtown retail merchants' association, the City of Pawtucket, Rhode Island, erects a Christmas display as part of its observance of the Christmas holiday season. The display is situated in a park owned by a nonprofit organization and located in the heart of the shopping district. The display is essentially like those to be found in hundreds of towns or cities across the Nation—often on public grounds—during the Christmas season. The Pawtucket display comprises many of the figures and decorations traditionally associated with Christmas, including, among other things, a Santa Claus house, reindeer pulling Santa's sleigh, candy-striped poles, a Christmas tree, carolers, cutout figures representing such characters as a clown, an elephant, and a teddy bear, hundreds of colored lights, a large banner that reads "seasons greetings," and the crèche at issue here. All components of this display are owned by the city.

The crèche, which has been included in the display for 40 or more years, consists of the traditional figures, including the Infant Jesus, Mary and Joseph, angels,

shepherds, kings, and animals, all ranging in height from 5" to 5'. In 1973, when the present crèche was acquired, it cost the City $1,365; it now is valued at $200. The erection and dismantling of the crèche costs the City about $20 per year; nominal expenses are incurred in lighting the crèche. No money has been expended on its maintenance for the past 10 years.

Respondents, Pawtucket residents and individual members of the Rhode Island affiliate of the American Civil Liberties Union, and the affiliate itself, brought this action in the United States District Court for Rhode Island, challenging the City's inclusion of the crèche in the annual display. The District Court held that the City's inclusion of the crèche in the display violates the Establishment Clause, . . . which is binding on the states through the Fourteenth Amendment. The District Court found that, by including the crèche in the Christmas display, the City has "tried to endorse and promulgate religious beliefs," . . . and that "erection of the crèche has the real and substantial effect of affiliating the City with the Christian beliefs that the crèche represents." . . . This "appearance of official sponsorship," it believed, "confers more than a remote and incidental benefit on Christianity." . . . Last, although the court acknowledged the absence of administrative entanglement, it found that excessive entanglement has been fostered as a result of the political divisiveness of including the crèche in the celebration. . . . The City was permanently enjoined from including the crèche in the display.

A divided panel of the Court of Appeals for the First Circuit affirmed. . . . We granted certiorari, . . . and we reverse.

. . . The Court has sometimes described the Religion Clause as erecting a "wall" between church and state. . . . The concept of a "wall" of separation is a useful figure of speech probably deriving from views of Thomas Jefferson. The metaphor has served as a reminder that the Establishment Clause forbids an established church or anything approaching it. But the metaphor itself is not a wholly accurate description of the practical aspects of the relationship that in fact exists between church and state.

No significant segment of our society and no institution within it can exist in a vacuum or in total or absolute isolation from all the other parts, much less from government. "It has never been thought either possible or desirable to enforce a regime of total separation. . . ." . . . Nor does the Constitution require complete separation of church and state; it affirmatively mandates accommodation, not merely tolerance, of all religions, and forbids hostility toward any. . . . Anything less would require the "callous indifference" we have said was never intended by the Establishment Clause. . . . Indeed, we have observed, such hostility would bring us into "war with our national tradition as embodied in the First Amendment's guaranty of the free exercise of religion." . . .

Our history is replete with official references to the value and invocation of Divine guidance in deliberations and pronouncements of the Founding Fathers and contemporary leaders. Beginning in the early colonial period long before Independence, a day of Thanksgiving was celebrated as a religious holiday to give thanks for the bounties of Nature as gifts from God. President Washington and his successors proclaimed Thanksgiving, with all its religious overtones, a day of national celebration and Congress made it a National Holiday more than a century ago. . . . That holiday has not lost its theme of expressing thanks for Divine aid any more than has Christmas lost its religious significance.

Executive Orders and other official announcements of Presidents and the Congress have proclaimed both Christmas and Thanksgiving National Holidays in religious terms. And, by Acts of Congress, it has long been the practice that federal employees are released from duties on these National Holidays, while being paid from the same public revenues that provide the compensation of the Chaplains of the Senate and the House and the military services. Thus, it is clear that Government has long recognized—indeed it has subsidized—holidays with religious significance.

Other examples of reference to our religious heritage are found in the statutorily prescribed national motto "In God We Trust," . . . which Congress and the President mandated for our currency, . . . and in the language "One nation under God," as part of the Pledge of Allegiance to the American flag. That pledge is recited by thousands of public school children—and adults—every year.

Art galleries supported by public revenues display religious paintings of the 15th and 16th centuries, predominantly inspired by one religious faith. The National Gallery in Washington, maintained with Government support, for example, has long exhibited masterpieces with religious messages, notably the Last Supper, and paintings depicting the Birth of Christ, the Crucifixion, and the Resurrection, among many others with explicit Christian themes and messages. The very chamber in which oral arguments on this case were heard is decorated with a notable and permanent—not seasonal—symbol of religion: Moses with Ten Commandments. Congress has long provided chapels in the Capitol for religious worship and meditation.

There are countless other illustrations of the Government's acknowledgment of our religious heritage and governmental sponsorship of graphic manifestations of that heritage. Congress has directed the President to proclaim a National Day of Prayer each year "on which [day] the people of the United States may turn to God in prayer and meditation at churches, in groups, and as individuals." . . . Our Presidents have repeatedly issued such Proclamations. Presidential Proclamations and messages have also issued to commemorate Jewish Heritage Week, . . . and the Jewish High Holy Days. . . . One cannot look at even this brief resume without finding that our history is pervaded by expressions of religious beliefs. . . . Equally pervasive is the evidence of accommodation of all faiths and all forms of religious expression, and hostility toward none. . . .

. . . This history may help explain why the Court consistently has declined to take a rigid, absolutist view of the Establishment Clause. We have refused "to construe the Religion Clauses with a literalness that would undermine the ultimate constitutional objective as illuminated by history." . . . In our modern, complex society, whose traditions and constitutional underpinnings rest on and encourage diversity and pluralism in all areas, an absolutist approach in applying the Establishment Clause is simplistic and has been uniformly rejected by the Court. . . .

In each case, the inquiry calls for line drawing; no fixed, per se rule can be framed. The Establishment Clause like the Due Process Clauses is not a precise, detailed provision in a legal code capable of ready application. The purpose of the Establishment Clause "was to state an objective, not to write a statute." . . . The line between permissible relationships and those barred by the Clause can no more be straight and unwavering than due process can be defined in a single stroke or phrase or test. The Clause erects a "blurred, indistinct, and variable barrier depending on all the circumstances of a particular relationship." . . .

In the line-drawing process we have often found it useful to inquire whether the challenged law or conduct has a secular purpose, whether its principal or primary effect is to advance or inhibit religion, and whether it creates an excessive entanglement of government with religion. . . . But, we have repeatedly emphasized our unwillingness to be confined to any single test or criterion in this sensitive area. . . .

In this case, the focus of our inquiry must be on the crèche in the context of the Christmas season. . . . Focus exclusively on the religious component of any activity would inevitably lead to its invalidation under the Establishment Clause. . . .

The narrow question is whether there is a secular purpose for Pawtucket's display of the crèche. The display is sponsored by the City to celebrate the Holiday and to depict the origins of that Holiday. These are legitimate secular purposes. The District Court's inference, drawn from the religious nature of the crèche, that the City has no secular purpose was, on this record, clearly erroneous.

The District Court found that the primary effect of including the crèche is to confer a substantial and impermissible benefit on religion in general and on the Christian faith in particular. Comparisons of the relative benefits to religion of different forms of governmental support are elusive and difficult to make. But to conclude that the primary effect of including the crèche is to advance religion in violation of the Establishment Clause would require that we view it as more beneficial to and more an endorsement of religion, for example, than expenditure of large sums of public money for textbooks supplied throughout the country to students attending church-sponsored schools, . . . expenditure of public funds for transportation of students to church-sponsored schools, . . . federal grants for college buildings of church-sponsored institutions of higher education combining secular and religious education, . . . noncategorical grants to church-sponsored colleges and universities, . . . and tax exemptions for church properties. . . .

We are unable to discern a greater aid to religion deriving from inclusion of the crèche than from these benefits and endorsements previously held not violative of the Establishment Clause. . . .

Entanglement is a question of kind and degree. In this case, however, there is no reason to disturb the District Court's finding on the absence of administrative entanglement. There is no evidence of contact with church authorities concerning the content or design of the exhibit prior to or since Pawtucket's purchase of the crèche. No expenditures for maintenance of the crèche have been necessary; and since the City owns the crèche, now valued at $200, the tangible material it contributes is *de minimis.* In many respects the display requires far less ongoing, day-to-day interaction between church and state than religious paintings in public galleries. . . .

The Court of Appeals correctly observed that this Court has not held that political divisiveness alone can serve to invalidate otherwise permissible conduct. And we decline to so hold today. This case does not involve a direct subsidy to church-sponsored schools or colleges, or other religious institutions, and hence no inquiry into potential political divisiveness is even called for. . . . In any event, apart from this litigation there is no evidence of political friction or divisiveness over the crèche in the 40-year history of Pawtucket's Christmas celebration. The District Court stated that the inclusion of the crèche for the 40 years has been "marked by no apparent dissension" and that the display has had a "calm history." . . . Curiously, it went on to hold that the political divisiveness engendered by this lawsuit was evidence of excessive entanglement. A litigant cannot, by the very act of commencing a lawsuit, however, create the appearance of divisiveness and then exploit it as evidence of entanglement.

We are satisfied that the city has a secular purpose for including the crèche, that the city has not impermissibly advanced religion, and that including the crèche does not create excessive entanglement between religion and government. . . .

. . . Accordingly, the judgment of the Court of Appeals is reversed.

Justice O'Connor, concurring. . . .

Justice Brennan, with whom **Justice Marshall, Justice Blackmun** and **Justice Stevens** join, dissenting.

. . . As we have sought to meet new problems arising under the Establishment Clause, our decisions, with few exceptions, have demanded that a challenged governmental practice satisfy the following criteria:

First the [practice] must have a secular legislative purpose; second, its principal or primary effect must be one that neither advances nor inhibits religion; finally, [it] must not foster 'an excessive government entanglement with religion.' . . .

This well-defined three-part test expresses the essential concerns animating the Establishment Clause. Thus, the test is designed to ensure that the organs of government remain strictly separate and apart from religious affairs, for "a union of government and religion tends to destroy government and degrade religion." . . . And it seeks to guarantee that government maintains a position of neutrality with respect to religion and neither advances nor inhibits the promulgation and practice of religious beliefs. . . . In this regard, we must be alert in our examination of any challenged practice not only for an official establishment of religion, but also for those other evils at which the Clause was aimed—"sponsorship, financial support, and active involvement of the sovereign in religious activity." . . .

. . . Under our constitutional scheme, the role of safeguarding our "religious heritage" and of promoting religious beliefs is reserved as the exclusive prerogative of our nation's churches, religious institutions and spiritual leaders. Because the Framers of the Establishment Clause understood that "religion is too personal, too sacred, too holy to permit its 'unhallowed perversion' by civil [authorities]," . . . the Clause demands that government play no role in this effort. The Court today brushes aside these concerns by insisting that Pawtucket has done nothing more than include a "traditional" symbol of Christmas in its celebration of this national holiday, thereby muting the religious content of the créche. . . . But the city's action should be recognized for what it is: a coercive, though perhaps small, step toward establishing the sectarian preferences of the majority at the expense of the minority, accomplished by placing public facilities and funds in support of the religious symbolism and theological tidings that the créche conveys. As Justice Frankfurter, writing in *McGowan v. Maryland,* observed, the Establishment Clause "withdr[aws] from the sphere of legitimate legislative concern and competence a specific,

but comprehensive area of human conduct: man's belief or disbelief in the verity of some transcendental idea and man's expression in action of that belief or disbelief." . . . That the Constitution sets this realm of thought and feeling apart from the pressures and antagonisms of government is one of its supreme achievements. Regrettably, the Court today tarnishes that achievement.

I dissent.

Justice Blackmun, with whom ***Justice Stevens*** joins, dissenting.

. . . Not only does the Court's resolution of this controversy make light of our precedents, but also, ironically, the majority does an injustice to the créche and the message it manifests. While certain persons, including the Mayor of Pawtucket, undertook a crusade to "keep 'Christ' in Christmas," . . . the Court today has declared that presence virtually irrelevant. The majority urges that the display, "with or without a créche," "recall[s] the religious nature of the Holiday," and "engenders a friendly community spirit of goodwill in keeping with the season." . . . Before the District Court, an expert witness for the city made a similar, though perhaps more candid, point, stating that Pawtucket's display invites people "to participate in the Christmas spirit, brotherhood, peace, and let loose with their money." . . . The créche has been relegated to the role of a neutral harbinger of the holiday season, useful for commercial purposes, but devoid of any inherent meaning and incapable of enhancing the religious tenor of a display of which it is an integral part. The city has its victory—but it is a Pyrrhic one indeed.

The import of the Court's decision is to encourage use of the créche in a municipally sponsored display, a setting where Christians feel constrained in acknowledging its symbolic meaning and non-Christians feel alienated by its presence. Surely, this is a misuse of a sacred symbol. Because I cannot join the Court in denying either the force of our precedents or the sacred message that is at the core of the créche, I dissent and join Justice Brennan's opinion.

Case

WALZ V. TAX COMMISSION

397 U.S. 664; 90 S.Ct. 1409; 25 L.Ed. 2d. 697 (1970)
Vote: 8–1

In this case the Court considers whether a property tax exemption for religious organizations constitutes a violation of the Establishment Clause.

Mr. Chief Justice Burger delivered the opinion of the Court.

. . . Appellant, owner of real estate in Richmond County, New York, sought an injunction in the New York courts to prevent the New York City Tax Commission from granting property tax exemptions to religious organizations for religious properties used solely for religious worship. The exemption from state taxes is authorized by Art. 16, Sec. 1, of the New York Constitution, which provides in relevant part:

> Exemptions from taxation may be granted only by general laws. Exemptions may be altered or repealed except those exempting real or personal property used exclusively for religious, educational or charitable purposes as defined by law and owned by any corporation or association organized or conducted exclusively for one or more of such purposes and not operating for profit.

The essence of appellant's contention was that the New York City Tax Commission's grant of an exemption to church property indirectly requires the appellant to make a contribution to religious bodies and thereby violates provisions prohibiting establishment of religion under the First Amendment which under the Fourteenth Amendment is binding on the States.

Appellee's motion for summary judgment was granted and the Appellate Divisions of the New York Supreme Court, and the New York Court of Appeals affirmed. We noted probable jurisdiction . . . and affirm.

Prior opinions of this Court have discussed the development and historical background of the First Amendment in detail. . . . It would therefore serve no useful purpose to review in detail the background of the Establishment and Free Exercise Clauses of the First Amendment or to restate what the Court's opinions have reflected over the years. . . .

The course of constitutional neutrality in this area cannot be an absolutely straight line; rigidity could well defeat the basic purpose of these provisions, which is to insure that no religion be sponsored or favored, none commanded, and none inhibited. The general principle deducible from the First Amendment and all that has been said by the Court is this: that we will not tolerate either governmentally established religion or governmental interference with religion. Short of those expressly proscribed governmental acts there is room for play in the joints productive of a benevolent neutrality which will permit religious exercise to exist without sponsorship and without interference.

Each value judgment under the Religion Clauses must therefore turn on whether particular acts in question are intended to establish or interfere with religious beliefs and practices or have the effect of doing so. Adherence to the policy of neutrality that derives from an accommodation of the Establishment and Free Exercise Clauses has prevented the kind of involvement that would tip the balance toward government control of churches or governmental restraint on religious practice. Adherents of particular faiths and individual churches frequently take strong positions on public issues including . . . vigorous advocacy of legal or constitutional positions. Of course, churches as much as secular bodies and private citizens have that right. No perfect or absolute separation is really possible; the very existence of the Religion Clauses is an involvement of sorts—one that seeks to mark boundaries to avoid excessive entanglement. . . .

The legislative purpose of a property tax exemption is neither the advancement nor the inhibition of religion; it is neither sponsorship nor hostility. New York, in common with the other States, has determined that certain entities that exist in a harmonious relationship to the community at large, and that foster its "moral or mental improvement," should not be inhibited in their activities by property taxation or the hazard of loss of those properties for nonpayment of taxes. It has not singled out one particular church or religious group or even churches as such; rather, it has granted exemption to all houses of religious worship within a broad class of property owned by nonprofit, quasi-public corporations which include hospitals, libraries, playgrounds, scientific, professional, historical, and patriotic groups. The State has an affirmative policy that considers these groups as beneficial and stabilizing influences in community life and finds this classification useful, desirable, and in the public interest. Qualification for tax exemption is not perpetual or immutable; some tax-exempt groups lose that status when their activities take them outside the classification and new entities can come into being and qualify for exemption.

Governments have not always been tolerant of religious activity, and hostility toward religion has taken many shapes and forms—economic, political, and sometimes harshly oppressive. Grants of exemption historically reflect the concern of authors of constitutions and statutes as to the latent dangers inherent in the imposition of property taxes; exemption constitutes a reasonable and balanced attempt to guard against those dangers. The limits of permissible state accommodation to religion are by no means coextensive with the noninterference mandated by the Free Exercise Clause. To equate the two would be to deny a national heritage with roots in the Revolution itself. . . . We cannot read New York's statute as attempting to establish religion; it is simply sparing the exercise of religion from the burden of property taxation levied on private profit institutions. . . .

Granting tax exemptions to churches necessarily operates to afford an indirect economic benefit and also gives rise to some, but yet a lesser, involvement than taxing them. In analyzing either alternative the questions are whether the involvement is excessive, and whether it is a continuing one calling for official and continuing surveillance leading to an impermissible degree of entanglement. Obviously a direct money subsidy would be a relationship pregnant with involvement and, as with most governmental grant programs, could encompass sustained and detailed administrative relationships for enforcement of statutory or administrative standards, but that is not this case. The hazards of churches supporting government are hardly less in their potential than the hazards of government supporting churches, each relationship carries some involvement rather than the desired insulation and separation. We cannot ignore the instances in history when church support of government led to the kind of involvement we seek to avoid.

The grant of a tax exemption is not sponsorship since the government does not transfer part of its revenue to churches but simply abstains from demanding that the church support the state. No one has ever suggested that tax exemption has converted libraries, art galleries, or hospitals into arms of the state or put employees "on the public payroll." There is no genuine nexus between tax exemption and establishment of religion. As Mr. Justice Holmes commented in a related context "a page of history is worth a volume of logic." . . . The exemption creates only a minimal and remote involvement between church and state and far less than taxation of churches. It restricts the fiscal relationship between church and state, and tends to complement and reinforce the desired separation insulating each from the other.

Separation in this context cannot mean absence of all contact; the complexities of modern life inevitably produce some contact and the fire and police protection received by houses of religious worship are no more than incidental benefits accorded all persons or institutions within a State's boundaries, along with many other exempt organizations. The appellant has not established even an arguable quantitative correlation between the payment of an *ad valorem* property tax and the receipt of these municipal benefits.

All of the 50 States provide for tax exemption of places of worship, most of them doing so by constitutional guarantees. For so long as federal income taxes have had any potential impact on churches—over 75 years—religious organizations have been expressly exempt from the tax. Such treatment is an "aid" to churches no more and no less in principle than the real estate tax exemption granted by States. Few concepts are more deeply embedded in the fabric of our national life, beginning with pre-Revolutionary colonial times, than for the government to exercise at the very least this kind of benevolent neutrality toward churches and religious exercise generally so long as none was favored over others and none suffered interference. . . .

It is obviously correct that no one acquires a vested or protected right in violation of the Constitution by long use, even when that span of time covers our entire national existence and indeed predates it. Yet an unbroken practice of according the exemption to churches, openly and by affirmative state action, not covertly or by state inaction, is not something to be lightly cast aside. Nearly 50 years ago Mr. Justice Holmes stated:

"If a thing has been practiced for two hundred years by common consent, it will need a strong case for the Fourteenth Amendment to affect it. . . ." . . . Nothing in this national attitude toward religious tolerance and two centuries of uninterrupted freedom from taxation has given the remotest sign of leading to an established church or religion and on the contrary it has operated affirmatively to help guarantee the free exercise of all forms of religious belief. Thus, it is hardly useful to suggest that tax exemption is but the "foot in the door" or the "nose of the camel in the tent" leading to an established church. If tax exemption can be seen as this first step toward "establishment" of religion, as Mr. Justice Douglas fears, the second step has been long in coming. . . .

The argument that making "fine distinctions" between what is and what is not absolute under the Constitution is to render us a government of men, not laws, gives too little weight to the fact that it is an essential part of adjudication to draw distinctions, including fine ones, in the process of interpreting the Constitution. We must frequently decide, for example, what are "reasonable" searches and seizures under the Fourth Amendment. Determining what acts of government tend to establish or interfere with religion falls well within what courts have long been called upon to do in sensitive areas.

It is interesting to note that while the precise question we now decide has not been directly before the Court previously, the broad question was discussed by the Court in relation to real estate taxes assessed nearly a century ago on land owned by and adjacent to a church in Washington, D.C. At that time Congress granted real estate tax exemptions to buildings devoted to art, to institutions of public charity, libraries, cemeteries, and "church buildings, and grounds actually occupied by such buildings." In denying tax exemption as to land owned by but not used for the church, but rather to produce income, the Court concluded:

> In the exercise of this [taxing] power, Congress, like any State legislature unrestricted by constitutional provisions, may at its discretion wholly exempt certain classes of property from taxation, or may tax them at a lower rate than other property. . . .

It appears that at least up to 1885 this Court, reflecting more than a century of our history and uninterrupted practice, accepted without discussion the proposition that federal or state grants of tax exemption to churches were not a violation of the Religion Clauses of the First Amendment. As to the New York statute, we now confirm that view.

Affirmed.

Mr. Justice Brennan, concurring. . . .

. . . ***Mr. Justice Harlan*** [concurring]. . .

Mr. Justice Douglas, dissenting.

. . . [There] is a major difference between churches on the one hand and the rest of the nonprofit organizations on the other. Government could provide or finance operas, hospitals, historical societies, and all the rest because they represent social welfare programs within the reach of the police power. In contrast, government may not provide or finance worship because of the Establishment Clause any more than it may single out "atheistic" or "agnostic" centers or groups and create or finance them.

The Brookings Institution, writing in 1933, before the application of the Establishment Clause of the First Amendment to the States, said about tax exemptions of religious groups:

> Tax exemption, no matter what its form, is essentially a government grant or subsidy. Such grants would seem to be justified only if the purpose for which they are made is one for which the legislative body would be equally willing to make a direct appropriation from public funds equal to the amount of the exemption. This test would not be met except in the case where the exemption is granted to encourage certain activities of private interests, which, if not thus performed, would have to be assumed by the government at an expenditure at least as great as the value of the exemption. . . .

If believers are entitled to public financial support, so are nonbelievers. A believer and nonbeliever under the present law are treated differently because of the articles of their faith. Believers are doubtless comforted that the cause of religion is being fostered by this legislation. Yet one of the mandates of the First Amendment is to promote a viable, pluralistic society and to keep government neutral, not only between sects, but also between believers and nonbelievers. The present involvement of government in religion may seem *de minimis*. But it is, I fear, a long step down the Establishment path. Perhaps I have been misinformed. But as I have read the Constitution and its philosophy, I gathered that independence was the price of liberty.

I conclude that this tax exemption is unconstitutional.

10 THE CONSTITUTION AND CRIMINAL JUSTICE

Chapter Outline:

Introduction
Search and Seizure
The Exclusionary Rule
Arrest
Police Interrogation and Confessions of
    Guilt
The Right to Counsel
Bail and Pretrial Detention
Plea Bargaining
Trial by Jury
The Protection Against Double Jeopardy
Incarceration and the Rights of
    Prisoners
The Death Penalty
Appeal and Postconviction Relief
Juvenile Justice
Conclusion
Key Terms
For Further Reading
Internet Resources
Olmstead v. United States (1928)
Katz v. United States (1967)
Weeks v. United States (1914)
Mapp v. Ohio (1961)
United States v. Leon (1984)
Miranda v. Arizona (1966)
New York v. Quarles (1984)
Powell v. Alabama (1932)
Gideon v. Wainwright (1963)
Batson v. Kentucky (1986)
Kansas v. Hendricks (1997)
Furman v. Georgia (1972)
Gregg v. Georgia (1976)
Payne v. Tennessee (1991)

We could, of course, facilitate the process of administering justice to those who violate criminal laws by ignoring . . . the entire Bill of Rights—but it is the very purpose of the Bill of Rights to identify values that may not be sacrificed to expediency. In a just society those who govern, as well as those who are governed, must obey the law.

—JUSTICE JOHN P. STEVENS, DISSENTING IN UNITED STATES V. LEON (1984)

INTRODUCTION

Protecting citizens against crime is one of the fundamental obligations of any government. In the United States, of course, government must perform the function of crime control while respecting the constitutional rights of individuals. Balancing the public interest in crime control against the values of individual liberty and privacy is, without question, the most common problem facing trial and appellate courts today. Many of the nation's courts, especially in major metropolitan areas, are flooded with criminal cases, many of which raise vexing questions of constitutional law. This chapter examines the development of constitutional standards in this extremely important area of the law.

Relevant Constitutional Provisions

The most obvious source of constitutional protection for persons suspected, accused, or convicted of crimes is the Bill of Rights. Numerous provisions of the Bill of Rights bear directly on the administration of criminal justice in the United States. Several restrictions in the original Constitution, together with guarantees in the Fourth, Fifth, Sixth, and Eighth Amendments, were designed to prevent government from subjecting individuals to arbitrary arrest, prosecution, and punishment. Both the national government and the states are prohibited from enacting ***ex post facto*** **laws** and **bills of attainder** (Article I, Sections 9 and 10). By contrast, the **habeas corpus** guarantee (Article I, Section 9) applies only to the national government, leaving the preservation of this right in state jurisdictions up to the states themselves. Most provisions of the Bill of Rights, including those pertaining to criminal justice, have been incorporated into the Due Process Clause of the Fourteenth Amendment, thereby making them applicable to the states as well as the national government. (For a discussion of *ex post facto* laws, bills of attainder, habeas corpus, and "selective incorporation" of the Bill of Rights, see Chapter 6.)

SEARCH AND SEIZURE

The Fourth Amendment recognizes a right of personal privacy entitling the American people to protection against arbitrary intrusions by law enforcement officers. The framers of the Bill of Rights were acutely sensitive to the need to insulate people from unlimited governmental powers of **search and seizure.** One of the chief complaints of the American colonists was the power of police and customs officials to conduct "general" searches under the dreaded writs of assistance authorized by Parliament in 1662. In 1761, James Otis reviled the writs of assistance as "the worst instrument of arbitrary power, the most destructive of English liberty and the fundamental principles of law, that was ever found in an English law book" (quoted in *Boyd v. United States* [1886]).

When the First Congress considered the Bill of Rights, most state constitutions already contained limitations on government powers in this area. Thus, there was little objection in Congress to the search and seizure amendment contained in James Madison's proposal for a Bill of Rights. After minor changes in language, the Fourth Amendment was adopted:

> The right of the people to be secure in their persons, houses, papers and effects, against unreasonable searches and seizures, shall not be violated, and no warrants shall issue, but upon probable cause, supported by Oath or Affirmation, and particularly describing the place to be searched, and the persons or things to be seized.

Like many of the broad provisions of the Constitution, the Fourth Amendment raises as many questions as it answers. It is clear that government cannot subject people to unreasonable searches and seizures, but what is meant by "unreasonable"? What exactly is a search? What is the precise meaning of **probable cause?** In our legal system, these are questions for the Supreme Court to answer. Unfortunately for the student, the police on the street, the criminal suspect, and the ordinary, law-abiding citizen, the answers to these questions can be very complicated and confusing.

"Reasonable Expectations of Privacy"

One of the most difficult problems in applying the eighteenth-century language of the Fourth Amendment to modern conditions is determining the scope of the privacy to be protected. Obviously, the Amendment prohibits unreasonable searches of one's dwelling. But what about the search of an individual's automobile, motorhome, or boat? What about one's telephone conversations, fax transmissions, or electronic mail? Are such communications protected by the Fourth Amendment?

In *Olmstead v. United States* (1928), the Supreme court took a very strict view of the scope of the Fourth Amendment. Roy Olmstead, a suspected bootlegger, was charged with conspiracy to violate the National Prohibition Act. The government's evidence consisted of transcripts of Olmstead's telephone conversations obtained through a wiretap placed outside his property. The agents had obtained no warrant authorizing the wiretap. Although there was no search or seizure of his person or physical property, Olmstead maintained that the Fourth Amendment had been violated. The term *effects,* as used in the Fourth Amendment, could have been interpreted to include telephone conversations, but the Court opted for a narrower construction. Writing for the majority, Chief Justice William Howard Taft stated:

> The reasonable view is that one who installs in his house a telephone instrument with connecting wires intends to project his voice to those quite outside, and that the wires beyond his house, and messages passing over them, are not within the protection of the Fourth Amendment.

Justice Louis Brandeis, along with three of his colleagues, dissented. In one of his most forward-looking opinions, he asserted the need to keep the Constitution relevant to changing technological conditions:

> The progress of science in furnishing the government with means of espionage is not likely to stop with wiretapping. Ways may some day be developed by which the government, without removing papers from secret drawers, can reproduce them in court, and by which it will be enabled to expose to a jury the most intimate occurrences of the home. . . . Can it be that the Constitution affords no protection against such invasions of individual security?

In 1928, the telephone was in fairly wide use; today, it is virtually omnipresent. Perhaps it was this reality that motivated the Supreme Court in 1967 to overturn *Olmstead* in the landmark decision of *Katz v. United States.* Here, the Court reversed a conviction in which government agents, acting without a warrant, attached a "bug," or listening device, to the outside of a public telephone booth from which Charles Katz, a suspected bookie, often placed calls. Writing for the Court, Justice Potter Stewart stated that "the Fourth Amendment protects people—not places."

Adhering to Justice John M. Harlan's concurrence in *Katz,* the Supreme Court has since held that the Fourth Amendment extends to any place or any thing in which an individual has a **reasonable expectation of privacy.** The Court has demonstrated a willingness to consider hotel rooms, garages, offices, automobiles, sealed letters, suitcases, and other closed containers as protected by the Fourth Amendment. On the other hand, the Court has held that there is no Fourth Amendment protection for abandoned or discarded property or for **open fields** (see *Oliver v. United States* [1984]).

Probable Cause

The fundamental requirement imposed by the Fourth Amendment is that searches and seizures must be *reasonable.* The amendment presupposes that searches will be authorized by warrants, and that warrants will not be issued without probable cause. The Supreme Court has recognized exceptions to the **warrant requirement,** but has for the most part viewed the probable cause requirement as an indispensable precondition of a valid search.

Probable cause is a term of art that does not have any precise meaning. The Supreme Court has observed that "probable cause is a fluid concept—turning on the assessment of probabilities in particular factual contexts—not readily, or even usefully, reduced to a neat set of legal rules" (*Illinois v.* Gates [1983]). As interpreted by the Court, probable cause means in effect that for a search to be valid, a police officer must have good reason to believe that the search will produce evidence of crime. According to the Court's decision in *Brinegar v. United States* (1949), officers have probable cause when "the facts and circumstances within their knowledge, and of which they had reasonably trustworthy information, [are] sufficient in themselves to warrant a man of reasonable caution in the belief that an offense has been or is being committed."

The Warrant Requirement

A **search warrant** is simply an order issued by a judge or magistrate that authorizes a search. To obtain a search warrant, a law enforcement officer must take an oath or sign an affidavit attesting to certain facts that, if true, constitute probable cause to support the issuance of a warrant.

In *Coolidge v. New Hampshire* (1971), the Supreme Court invalidated a warrant that was issued by the state's attorney general, rather than a judicial officer. Thus, the Court places great importance on the role of the **neutral and detached magistrate** in maintaining the integrity of the Fourth Amendment. This amendment also requires that search warrants describe with particularity "the place to be searched, and the persons or things to be seized." This provision reflects the framers' distaste for the **general warrants** used in colonial America. In *Stanford v. Texas* (1965), the Supreme Court reaffirmed this long-standing distaste for "dragnet" searches when it invalidated a five-hour search of a Communist party headquarters resulting in the seizure of some five thousand items, including books by Justice Hugo Black and Pope John XXIII.

Confidential and Anonymous Informants

One of the most controversial questions concerning the issuance of search warrants involves the use of **confidential or anonymous informants.** Police often use tips provided by confidential informants to obtain search warrants that lead to the discovery of incriminating evidence. In *Aguilar v. Texas* (1963), police obtained a warrant simply by swearing that they "had received reliable information from a credible person" that illegal drugs would be found at a certain location. The Supreme Court ultimately invalidated the warrant, holding that an affidavit must inform the magistrate of

> the underlying circumstances from which the informant concluded that the narcotics were where he claimed they were, and some of the underlying circumstances from which the officer concluded that the informant, whose identity need not be disclosed, . . . was "credible" or his information "reliable."

Five years later, the Court reaffirmed this two-pronged test in the case of *Spinelli v. United States* (1969). The so-called *Aguilar–Spinelli* test made it more difficult for police to obtain warrants based on tips from confidential informants. Accordingly, on this issue, as on several others, the Warren Court was much criticized for "handcuffing the police." In 1983, a more conservative Supreme Court under Chief Justice Warren E. Burger abandoned the rigorous *Aguilar–Spinelli* test in favor of a **totality of circumstances** approach that makes it easier for police to get search warrants. In *Illinois v. Gates,* Justice William Rehnquist asserted that the *Aguilar–Spinelli* test could not "avoid seriously impeding the task of law enforcement" because "anonymous tips seldom could survive a rigorous application of either of the *Spinelli* prongs." Dissenting, Justice William Brennan argued that

> the Court [gave] virtually no consideration to the value of insuring that findings of probable cause are based on information that a magistrate can reasonably say has been obtained in a reliable way by an honest or credible person. I . . . fear that the Court's rejection of *Aguilar* and *Spinelli* . . . "may foretell an evisceration of the probable cause standard."

In 1984, the Court held that the totality of circumstances standard announced in the *Gates* decision was to be given a broad interpretation by lower courts (*Massachusettes v. Upton*). Subsequently, the Court moved beyond *Gates* and manifested an even greater level of permissiveness toward police reliance on anonymous tips (see, for example, *Alabama v. White* [1990]). Critics of these decisions argue that the Court's interest in facilitating law enforcement is eclipsing its traditional concern for the privacy of citizens subjected to police searches.

Execution of Search Warrants

Under federal law an officer is required to **knock and announce** upon arrival at the place to be searched. The purpose of the knock-and-announce requirement is to reduce the potential for violence and protect the right of privacy of the occupants. In *Wilson v. Arkansas* (1995), the Court decided unanimously that the Fourth Amendment requires police, absent a threat of physical violence or other exigent circumstances, to knock and announce when serving a search warrant at a home. The most striking aspect of the Court's decision was that the opinion was authored by Justice Thomas, who generally takes a pro-law enforcement position in criminal cases. In keeping with his adherence to the doctrine of original intent, Thomas examined the state of the common law at the time the Fourth Amendment was adopted. He concluded that "[a]t the time of the framing, the common law of search and seizure recognized a law enforcement officer's authority to break open the doors of a dwelling, but generally indicated that he first ought to announce his presence and authority. . . ." Thomas concluded that the framers of the Bill of Rights intended for the common-law knock-and-announce requirement to be part and parcel of the Fourth Amendment. *Wilson* resolved a conflict among lower courts as to whether the federal Constitution requires officers to knock and announce, a requirement that many states already observed under their respective constitutions, statutes, or judicial decisions.

One of the reasons police officers resist compliance with the knock-and-announce requirement is that by announcing their presence, officers risk losing evidence that is easily destroyed or disposed of. In *Wilson,* the Court said that officers facing exigent circumstances could dispense with the knock-and-announce requirement. But in *Richards v. Wisconsin* (1997), the Court ruled unanimously that states may not create a blanket "drug exception" to the requirement that police officers knock and announce prior to executing a search warrant.

Warrantless Searches

Although the Fourth Amendment clearly indicates a preference for search warrants, the Supreme Court has held that, under **exigent circumstances,** a **warrantless search** may nevertheless be "reasonable." One example of a legitimate warrantless search is the **search incidental to a lawful arrest.** In *Chimel v. California* (1969), Justice Stewart's majority opinion stated:

> When an arrest is made, it is reasonable for the arresting officer to search the person arrested in order to remove any weapons that the latter might seek to use in order to resist arrest or effect his escape. . . . In addition, it is entirely reasonable for the arresting officer to search for and seize any evidence on the arrestee's person in order to prevent its concealment or destruction.

Consent Searches

An obvious example of a legitimate warrantless search is one based on the consent of the individual whose privacy is to be invaded. It is an elementary principle of law that individuals may waive their constitutional rights; Fourth Amendment protections are no exception. In *Schneckloth v. Bustamonte* (1973), the Supreme Court upheld a **search based on consent** even though the police failed to advise the individual that he was not obligated to consent to the police request. In *Florida v. Bostick,* a highly publicized 1991 decision, the Court upheld the controversial police practice of boarding interstate buses in big-city terminals, approaching persons matching a **drug courier profile,** and asking them for permission to search their belongings. More recently, in *Ohio v. Robinette* (1996), the Court held that police are not required to inform motorists who are stopped for other reasons that they are "free to go" before asking them to consent to a search of their automobile. To determine whether consent was given voluntarily, and knowingly, the Court looks to the totality of circumstances surrounding the search.

Other Justifications for Warrantless Searches

Other accepted justifications for warrantless searches include plain view (see *Coolidge v. New Hampshire* [1971]), **hot pursuit** (see *Warden v. Hayden* [1967]), **evanescent evidence** (see *Schmerber v. California* [1966]), and **emergency searches** (see *Michigan v. Tyler* [1978]). In each of these examples, compelling exigencies make the warrant requirement itself unreasonable, at least in the view of the nation's highest court.

Automobile Searches

One of the most interesting—and most problematic—exceptions to the warrant requirement is the **automobile search.** In *Carroll v. United States* (1925), the Supreme Court upheld the warrantless search of an automobile believed to be carrying illegal liquor. The Court stressed, however, that probable cause was essential to justify a warrantless automobile search. Indiscriminately stopping and searching passing motorists in an effort to discover evidence of crime could never be constitutionally justified.

The case of *Arkansas v. Sanders* (1979) presented the Court with an interesting question. Can warrantless searches of automobiles extend to all the contents of said vehicles, or do police still need a warrant to search luggage taken from the trunk? In *Sanders,* the Court disallowed the search of the luggage, suggesting to some observers that the automobile exception was "in trouble." However, in *United*

States v. Ross (1982), the Supreme Court demonstrated otherwise. In a 6-to-3 decision, the Court upheld a warrantless search of a paper bag and a leather pouch found in the locked trunk of a stopped automobile, a search that produced thirty-two hundred dollars in cash and a sizable quantity of heroin. Writing for the Court, Justice John Paul Stevens clarified the legitimate scope of a warrantless automobile search as that "no greater than a magistrate could have authorized by issuing a warrant based on the probable cause that justified the search." Dissenting vehemently in *Ross,* Justice Thurgood Marshall assailed the majority position as "flatly inconsistent . . . with established Fourth Amendment principles. . . ." In 1991, the Court went one step further and formally overruled *Arkansas v. Sanders* (see *California v. Acevedo*), removing any lingering doubts about judicial distinctions between searches of automobiles and closed containers found therein. Thus, under current interpretation of the Fourth Amendment, the legitimate scope of a warrantless search, whether of an automobile or any other place, is determined more by the nature of the object of the search than by the nature of the space being searched.

Stop and Frisk

One of the most controversial forms of police search is the **stop and frisk.** This type of limited search occurs when police confront suspicious persons in an effort to prevent a crime from taking place. The seminal case in this area is *Terry v. Ohio* (1968). Here, an experienced plainclothes officer observed three men acting suspiciously. The officer concluded that they were preparing to rob a nearby store and approached them. He identified himself as a police officer and asked for their names. Unsatisfied with their mumbled responses, he then subjected one of the trio to a **pat-down search,** which produced a gun for which the individual had no permit. In this instance, the police officer had no warrant; indeed, he did not have probable cause in its traditional sense. The Court nevertheless allowed the pat-down search on the basis of **reasonable suspicion.** However, given that the "sole justification of the search . . . is the protection of the police officer and others nearby," the Court limited the frisk to "an intrusion reasonably designed to discover guns, knives, clubs or other hidden instruments for the assault of the police officer."

Of course, if police discover contraband or other evidence of crime in the process of performing the pat-down for weapons, such evidence is admissible under a theory analogous to the plain view doctrine. For example, if a pat-down reveals an object in a jacket pocket that the officer believes to be a knife, the officer may retrieve the object. If the object turns out to be a vial of cocaine, that contraband has been lawfully seized. But may an officer retrieve an object that does not appear to be a weapon but does have the characteristics of contraband or containers used to carry contraband? In *Minnesota v. Dickerson* (1993), the Supreme Court answered this question in the affirmative, saying that "the suspect's privacy interests are not advanced by a categorical rule barring the seizure of contraband plainly detected through the sense of touch."

Investigatory Detention

The type of police encounter upheld in *Terry v. Ohio* and numerous subsequent court decisions has come to be known as **investigatory detention** or the "*Terry* stop." Police may stop and question suspicious persons, pat them down for weapons, and even subject them to nonintrusive search procedures, such as the use of metal detectors and drug-sniffing dogs. While a suspect is being detained, a computer search can be performed to determine if the suspect is wanted for crimes in other jurisdictions. If so, then he or she may be arrested and a search conducted incident to that arrest.

Investigatory detention has become extremely important in the highly publicized "war on drugs," as police officers have been given the power to detain, question, and investigate suspected drug couriers. In *United States v. Sokolow* (1989), the Supreme Court upheld a search and seizure that stemmed from a *Terry* stop conducted at an international airport. The defendant in the case aroused the suspicions of federal Drug Enforcement Administration (DEA) agents by conforming to a controversial drug courier profile developed by the DEA.

United States v. Sokolow is consistent with a host of judicial decisions affording law enforcement officers wide latitude to investigate and detain suspected drug smugglers at international airports. In one widely publicized case, such a suspect was held for sixteen hours while airport security officers obtained a court order permitting a rectal examination of the suspect. During the exam, officers retrieved a plastic balloon filled with cocaine and placed the suspect under arrest. Over the next few days, the suspect passed eighty-eight similar balloons! The Supreme Court upheld the long detention, even though security personnel lacked probable cause to make the initial stop. As in *Terry v. Ohio,* the Court found that there was reasonable suspicion to justify the original detention (*United States v. Montoya de Hernandez* [1985]).

Detention of an Automobile Based on an Anonymous Tip

The Supreme Court has become increasingly permissive as to what constitutes reasonable suspicion for purposes of investigatory detention. For example, in *Alabama v. White* (1990), the Court upheld a *Terry* stop of an automobile based solely on an anonymous tip that described a certain car that would be at a specific location. Police went to the location, located the vehicle, and detained the driver, Vanessa White. The encounter led ultimately to the discovery of marijuana and cocaine in the automobile. Writing for the Court, Justice Byron White noted that "[a]lthough it is a close case, we conclude that under the totality of the circumstances, the anonymous tip, as corroborated, exhibited sufficient indicia of reliability to justify the investigatory stop of respondent's car." In a dissenting opinion joined by Justices Brennan and Marshall, Justice Stevens observed that under *Alabama v. White,* "every citizen is subject to being seized and questioned by any officer who is prepared to testify that the warrantless stop was based on an anonymous tip predicting whatever conduct the officer had just observed." Clearly, the Court's willingness to permit the detention in *Alabama v. White* stands in sharp contrast to the Warren Court's carefully drawn stop-and-frisk policy delineated in *Terry v. Ohio.*

John Paul Stevens:
Associate Justice, 1975–

Can Police Require People to Exit Their Car during an Automobile Stop?

During automobile stops police routinely request that drivers exit their cars. Sometimes they also request passengers to exit. These practices are justified by the police by the need to protect officers from weapons that might be concealed inside the passenger compartment of a stopped vehicle. In *Maryland v. Wilson* (1997), the Supreme Court noted that in 1994 eleven police officers were killed and more than five thousand officers were assaulted during traffic stops. Of course, when drivers and passengers are required to exit their automobiles, police often discover contraband or observe behavior indicative of intoxication. Such was the case in *Maryland v. Wilson,* in which a passenger who had been ordered to exit a vehicle dropped a quantity of crack cocaine onto the ground. This evidence was used to secure a conviction for possession with intent to distribute and, ultimately, the conviction was sustained by the Supreme Court.

TO SUMMARIZE:

- The Fourth Amendment recognizes a right of personal privacy entitling the American people to protection against arbitrary intrusions by law enforcement officers.
- The Supreme Court has held that the Fourth Amendment extends to any place or any thing in which an individual has a reasonable expectation of privacy.
- The fundamental requirement imposed by the Fourth Amendment is that searches and seizures must be reasonable. The amendment presupposes that searches will be authorized by warrants, and that warrants will not be issued without probable cause.
- The Supreme Court has recognized exceptions to the warrant requirement, but has for the most part viewed the probable cause requirement as indispensable.
- Examples of legitimate warrantless searches include searches incidental to a lawful arrest, searches based on consent, seizures of evidence in plain view, searches for evanescent evidence, searches conducted during "hot pursuit," and emergency searches.
- Police often use tips provided by confidential or anonymous informants to obtain search warrants that lead to the discovery of incriminating evidence. Such tips may or may not constitute probable cause, depending on the "totality of circumstances."
- The Supreme Court has said that, in the absence of exigent circumstances, police officers must "knock and announce" prior to executing a search warrant at a private residence.
- The Court has permitted police officers to subject persons to a "stop and frisk" as long as there is "reasonable suspicion" (a less demanding standard than probable cause) that criminal activity is afoot. This principle also applies to automobile stops and brief investigatory detentions of drivers and passengers.

THE EXCLUSIONARY RULE

In addition to the difficult questions involving police methods of obtaining incriminating evidence, we must also consider the controversial issue of how violations of the Fourth Amendment are to be remedied and deterred. As far back as 1886, in *Boyd v. United States,* the Supreme Court suggested that evidence obtained in violation of the Fourth Amendment should be excluded from trial. In *Weeks v. United States* (1914) the Court made this dictum a formal requirement of criminal procedure in federal courts. Writing for the Court in *Weeks,* Justice William R. Day suggested that the **exclusionary rule,** as it came to be known, was implicit in the requirements of the Fourth Amendment. Day also argued that to allow illegally obtained evidence to be used in a criminal trial would be an affront to the integrity of the judiciary.

In *Wolf v. Colorado* (1949), the Supreme Court held first that the Fourth Amendment is incorporated within the Due Process Clause of the Fourteenth Amendment and is therefore applicable to state criminal justice systems. However, the Court refused to apply the exclusionary rule to the state courts, preferring instead to view the rule as a procedural device that the Supreme Court imposed on federal criminal cases by virtue of its **supervisory power** over the lower federal courts. According to Justice Felix Frankfurter's opinion for the Court, considerations of federalism and judicial restraint prohibited the Court from imposing the exclusionary rule on the states.

The Warren Court Expands the Exclusionary Rule

Under *Wolf v. Colorado,* states were free to adopt or ignore the *Weeks* exclusionary rule. Some adopted the rule; most did not. The discrepancy between the rules applicable to state and federal courts gave rise to the **silver platter doctrine.** Federal authorities could (and did) provide illegally obtained evidence to prosecutors in states that did not have the exclusionary rule. Moreover, because the *Weeks* decision applied only to illegal seizures by *federal* authorities, federal prosecutors could use evidence obtained illegally by state and local law enforcement agencies.

In *Mapp v. Ohio* (1961) the Court overturned *Wolf v. Colorado* and extended the exclusionary rule to state criminal prosecutions by way of the Fourteenth Amendment. Writing for the Court, Justice Tom Clark made clear that the exclusionary rule was "an essential ingredient of the Fourth Amendment" which was "vouchsafed against the states by the Due Process Clause" of the Fourteenth Amendment. In dissent, Justice Harlan accused the Court of forgetting its sense of judicial restraint and failing to show due regard for *stare decicis.*

The *Mapp* decision was certainly one of the Warren Court's major contributions to the law of criminal procedure and, accordingly, it remains a very controversial holding. Those who believe the exclusionary rule is merely a judicially created rule

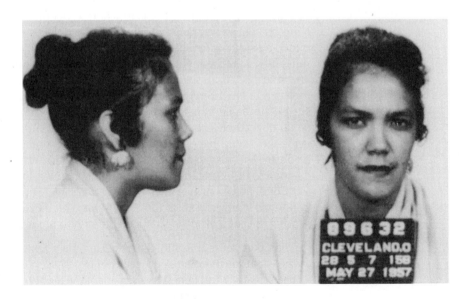

Dollree Mapp

have criticized the Supreme Court for extending its supervisory power to the state courts. On the other hand, if the exclusionary rule is implicit in the Fourth Amendment and if the Fourth Amendment is made applicable to the states through the Fourteenth Amendment (see *Wolf v. Colorado* [1949]), then it follows that the exclusionary rule must be respected in state criminal prosecutions.

The Burger Court Curtails the Exclusionary Rule

The Supreme Court under Chief Justice Burger substantially curtailed the application of the exclusionary rule. In *United States v. Calandra* (1974), the Burger Court made its philosophy quite clear: "the rule is a judicially created remedy designed to safeguard Fourth Amendment Rights generally through its deterrent effect, rather than a personal constitutional right of the party aggrieved."

The Court's current approach to cases involving the exclusionary rule is to weigh the perceived costs of its application against the potential benefits of deterring police misconduct. Using this approach, the Court has refused to extend the exclusionary rule to grand jury proceedings (*United States v. Calandra* [1974]) and to federal civil proceedings where evidence was obtained unlawfully by state agents (*United States v. Janis* [1976]). A majority on the current Supreme Court evidently agree with Chief Justice Burger's assessment (dissenting in *Bivens v. Six Unknown Named Federal Narcotics Agents* [1971]) of the social costs of suppressing otherwise valid evidence:

> Some clear demonstration of the benefits and effectiveness of the exclusionary rule is required to justify it in view of the high price it extracts from society—the release of countless guilty criminals. . . . But there is no empirical evidence to support the claim that the rule actually deters illegal conduct of law enforcement officials.

The Good-Faith Exception

Without question, the most important Burger Court decisions on the exclusionary rule were the companion cases of *United States v. Leon* and *Massachusetts v. Sheppard* (1984). In these cases, the Court adopted a limited **good-faith exception** to the exclusionary rule where officers seize evidence in good faith, relying on search warrants later held to be defective. In *Leon,* police officers obtained a search warrant acting on a tip from a confidential informant of unproven reliability. A subsequent search of a residence turned up a substantial amount of illegal drugs. At an evidentiary hearing prior to trial, a judge ruled that the warrant had been wrongly issued and that there was insufficient information to constitute probable cause. The Supreme Court ultimately held that the evidence could nevertheless be admitted against the defendants, because to exclude such evidence would have no deterrent effect on police misconduct. The error was made by the magistrate who issued the warrant, not by the police who were deemed to be acting in good faith. In like manner, in *Massachusetts v. Sheppard,* the Court held that use of the wrong warrant form as authorization for a search in a murder investigation did not render the seized evidence inadmissible. Dissenting in the *Leon* case, Justice Brennan exploded:

> The Court seeks to justify this result on the ground that the "costs" of adhering to the exclusionary rule . . . exceed the "benefits." But . . . it is clear that we have not been treated to an honest assessment of the merits of the exclusionary rule but have instead been drawn into a curious world where the "costs" of excluding illegally ob-

tained evidence loom to exaggerated heights and where the "benefits" of such exclusion are made to disappear with a mere wave of the hand.

It is clear that the intense intra-Court conflict in *Leon* and *Sheppard* stemmed from basic differences of opinion as to the constitutional foundations of the exclusionary rule. If one agrees with Justice Brennan that suppression of illegally obtained evidence is a personal right under the Fourth Amendment, then clearly the exclusionary rule cannot be sacrificed on the altar of cost–benefit analysis. On the other hand, if the rule is nothing more than a judicially created rule of evidence or procedure designed to deter future police misconduct, then the Court is free to apply or dispense with the rule depending on its perceived utility.

The Rehnquist Court reaffirmed the good-faith exception in 1995. In *Arizona v. Evans* (1995) the Arizona supreme court had ruled that evidence seized by a police officer who acted in reliance on a police record indicating the existence of an outstanding arrest warrant—a record that was later determined to be erroneous—had to be suppressed regardless of the source of the error. In fact, the error had been committed by the court clerk's office. The Supreme Court reversed by a 7-to-2 vote. Chief Justice Rehnquist wrote for the Court, saying that the exclusionary rule need apply only where the error is attributable to the police. The *Evans* decision was based squarely on *Leon,* and did not represent a major innovation.

The controversy over the exclusionary rule is far from over. It remains to be seen whether the Rehnquist Court will extend the good-faith exception to warrantless searches involving unintended violations of constitutionally protected privacy.

Civil Suits to Enforce the Fourth Amendment

One alternative to the exclusionary rule is filing a civil suit for damages against the officers who performed the illegal search. This remedy is especially appealing to persons who are the victims of illegal searches or seizures but are not prosecuted for any crime. Such persons have no real alternative to filing a civil suit to obtain redress for the wrongs perpetrated against them. In *Malley v. Briggs* (1986), the Supreme Court allowed civil suits under 42 U.S. Code Section 1983 against police officers who "knowingly violate the law" or act in a fashion that "no reasonably competent officer" would consider to be legal in conducting arrests, searches, and seizures. In the *Malley* case, a Rhode Island state trooper obtained a warrant for the arrest of a prominent couple who were charged with "conspiring to possess marijuana." The warrant was based on a suggestion overheard by police wiretappers that the couple had hosted a marijuana party some three months earlier. The couple was taken into custody, but no physical evidence of any crime was discovered. Consequently, the grand jury refused to hand down an indictment. Not satisfied with this after-the-fact vindication, the couple filed a civil suit for damages against the police officer. The federal district court dismissed the case, holding that a police officer could not be held liable for actions based on a warrant issued by a magistrate. Ultimately, however, the Supreme Court disagreed, underscoring its previous recognition of civil suits as means of enforcing Fourth Amendment rights.

The civil remedy was advanced as an alternative to the exclusionary rule by Justice Felix Frankfurter in the 1949 case of *Wolf v. Colorado.* In a strongly worded dissenting opinion in *Wolf,* Justice Frank Murphy cast grave doubt on the viability of the civil remedy as a realistic alternative. The Warren Court, as reflected in its decisions on the exclusionary rule, apparently agreed with Murphy's assessment. But the civil liability approach was resurrected by Chief Justice Burger in his dissent in the *Bivens* case.

Finally, in *Malley,* a majority of the Court found occasion to apply the civil remedy in the context of an outrageous Fourth Amendment violation.

TO SUMMARIZE:

- In *Weeks v. United States* (1914) the Court held that evidence obtained in violation of the Fourth Amendment may not be used in federal criminal trials. In *Mapp v. Ohio* (1961) the Court extended this Fourth Amendment exclusionary rule to state criminal prosecutions by way of the Fourteenth Amendment.
- The Supreme Court under Chief Justice Burger and Chief Justice Rehnquist has substantially curtailed the application of the exclusionary rule. The Court's current approach is to weigh the perceived costs of the rule's application against the potential benefits of deterring police misconduct.
- The Court has adopted a limited good-faith exception to the exclusionary rule in which officers can seize evidence in good faith, relying on search warrants later held to be defective.

ARREST

An **arrest** entails the deprivation of one's liberty by a law enforcement officer or other person with legal authority. Normally, an arrest occurs when someone suspected of having committed a crime is taken into custody by a police officer. Because an arrest is, in effect, a "seizure," it must conform to the probable cause and warrant requirements of the Fourth Amendment. In *Ker v. California* (1963), the Supreme Court held that the legality of arrests by state and local officers should be determined by the same standards applicable to federal law enforcement officials.

Use of Force by Police in Making Arrests

Since suspects often resist arrest, police on occasion must use force to take a person into custody. The courts have generally recognized that the Fourth Amendment permits police to use only such force as is "reasonable" and "necessary" in effectuating an arrest. In *Tennessee v. Garner* (1985), the Supreme Court held that police officers may use *deadly* force only when necessary to apprehend a fleeing felon and only when "the officer has probable cause to believe that the suspect poses a significant threat of death or physical injury to the officer or others." While most police officers take care to exercise force responsibly, police have committed acts of brutality in numerous instances. In such cases, police officers are subject not only to internal departmental sanctions but also to civil suit and even criminal prosecution under applicable state and federal statutes.

The Arrest Warrant

Arrests are often made pursuant to warrants based on preliminary investigations. An **arrest warrant,** like a search warrant, is issued by a judge or magistrate upon a showing of probable cause. Under some circumstances, however, warrantless arrests are permissible. The most common of these is where police observe someone committing a crime or have direct knowledge of criminal activity. Whether or not it is made pursuant to a warrant, an arrest must be based on probable cause.

The Probable Cause Hearing

As the warrant requirement of the Fourth Amendment implies, the legality of detention after arrest also depends on the existence of probable cause. It follows logically that a person arrested *without* a warrant must be brought *promptly* before a judicial officer for a **probable cause hearing.** This principle had in fact emerged in English common law by the late seventeenth century, long before ratification of the Fourth Amendment in 1791. It was not until 1975 that the Supreme Court, in *Gerstein v. Pugh,* explicitly recognized the probable cause hearing as a Fourth Amendment requirement in cases of **warrantless arrest.** This decision, however, did not specify the maximum time that a person could be held in custody prior to a probable cause determination. In *County of Riverside v. McLaughlin* (1991), the Rehnquist Court adopted a permissive interpretation of the probable cause hearing requirement. In this controversial 5-to-4 decision, the majority, speaking through Justice Sandra Day O'Connor, held that an individual could be detained for as long as forty-eight hours prior to a probable cause hearing without necessarily violating the Fourth Amendment.

In the *McLaughlin* case, the Court balanced Fourth Amendment rights against state interests in administrative convenience and local autonomy. In a sharply worded dissent, Justice Antonin Scalia, generally favorable to law enforcement claims, criticized the majority for going far beyond the Court's prevailing concern that criminals not go unpunished. He argued that the Court had improperly applied the *Gerstein* precedent, repudiating one of the "core applications" of the Fourth Amendment "so that the presumptively innocent may be left in jail." By definition, the failure to find probable cause points to the innocence of the arrestee. According to the many critics of the *McLaughlin* decision, the majority lost sight of this consideration in its apparent zeal to accommodate the practical demands of law enforcement.

TO SUMMARIZE:

- Because an arrest is, in effect, a "seizure," it must conform to the probable cause and warrant requirements of the Fourth Amendment.
- The courts have generally recognized that the Fourth Amendment permits police to use only such force as is "reasonable" and "necessary" in effectuating an arrest.
- Arrests are often made pursuant to warrants based on preliminary investigations. An arrest warrant, like a search warrant, is issued by a judge or magistrate upon a showing of probable cause. Under some circumstances warrantless arrests, like warrantless searches, are permissible assuming there is probable cause.
- A person arrested *without* a warrant must be brought *promptly* before a judicial officer for a probable cause hearing.

POLICE INTERROGATION AND CONFESSIONS OF GUILT

Another of the Warren Court's controversial contributions to the criminal process was its enlargement of protection for criminal suspects subjected to **custodial interrogation.** Clearly, police must have the authority to question suspects in order to solve crimes. But the Supreme Court held as far back as 1897 (*Bram v. United States*) that a coerced confession violates the Self-Incrimination Clause of the Fifth Amendment. Of course, the Self-Incrimination Clause was not incorporated into the Fourteenth Amendment until well into the 1960s. Prior to incorporation, the Court's scrutiny of police interrogation in the states was limited to a broad due process inquiry that examined the totality of circumstances in each case with one eye on the fairness of the defendant's trial and the other on methods of police interrogation.

The traditional test used by the Court was whether a challenged confession could reasonably be deemed to have been voluntary. **Subjective voluntariness,** however, is extremely difficult to discern, even through direct observation, let alone through appellate hindsight years later. Consequently, the Supreme Court's decisions in this area were often unclear and inconsistent. For example, in the 1944 case of *Ashcraft v. Tennessee,* the Court overturned a murder conviction on grounds that the defendant's alleged confession was coerced because it had been preceded by a thirty-six-hour period of continuous police interrogation. Writing for a six-member majority, Justice Black made no attempt to weigh the effect of this long and intense period of questioning on the suspect. Black simply concluded that thirty-six hours of questioning was "inherently coercive" and that use of the confession violated the Due Process Clause of the Fourteenth Amendment. Justice Robert H. Jackson dissented sharply, pointing out that coerciveness could not be measured simply by reference to the clock. Just over a month later, in *Lyons v. Oklahoma* (1944), the Court, dividing 5 to 4, held to be "voluntary" a confession repeated some twelve hours after the suspect, during incommunicado detention in the dead of night, had been forced to hold in his lap a pan containing the charred bones of his alleged murder victims.

By the 1960s, many believed that another approach to the law governing police interrogation was necessary. The Court's decision in *Malloy v. Hogan* (1964) to incorporate the Self-Incrimination Clause paved the way for a stricter attitude toward interrogation by state law enforcement personnel. A sharp break with the voluntariness approach came in 1964 when the Supreme Court decided *Escobedo v. Illinois*. Here, the Court held that once a police interrogation

> has begun to focus on a particular suspect, the suspect has been taken into custody, the police carry out a process of interrogations that lends itself to incriminating statements, the suspect has requested and been denied an opportunity to consult with his lawyer, and the police have not effectively warned him of his absolute constitutional right to remain silent . . . no statement elicited by the police during the interrogation may be used against him during the criminal trial.

In effect, *Escobedo* adopted an exclusionary rule similar to that of *Mapp v. Ohio* but applied to enforce Fifth and Sixth Amendment rights. Two years later, in *Miranda v. Arizona* (1966), the Court elaborated on the need for constitutional safeguards to protect citizens from "inherently coercive" police interrogation.

It is obvious that such an interrogation environment is created for no purpose other than to subjugate the individual to the will of his examiner. This atmosphere carries its own badge of intimidation. To be sure this is not physical intimidation, but it is equally destructive to human dignity. The current practice of incommunicado interrogation is at odds with one of our nation's most cherished principles—that the individual may not be compelled to incriminate himself.

The *Miranda* Warnings

To safeguard the immunity against self-incrimination, the Court developed the well-known ***Miranda* warnings.** Unless police inform suspects of their rights to remain silent and have an attorney present during questioning and unless police obtain voluntary waivers of these rights, suspects' confessions and other statements are inadmissible at trial. When the *Miranda* decision came down in 1966, the Court was harshly criticized, especially by the law enforcement community, for "coddling criminals" and "hamstringing the police." However, the practice of "Mirandizing" suspects soon became standard operating procedure in law enforcement. Today, many in law enforcement support the *Miranda* decision as a means of professionalizing police conduct and, perhaps more importantly, protecting legitimate confessions from later challenges. As long as the police provide suspects with the warning and avoid coercion, anything said by the suspect can be used against him or her in a court of law. Whereas, prior to *Miranda,* there was something of a presumption against the admissibility of a confession, today the presumption is clearly in favor of admitting confessions as evidence as long as the requirements of *Miranda* have been observed by the police.

Although the Supreme Court has reaffirmed the *Miranda* decision, it has substantially narrowed the scope of its requirements. For example, in *Harris v. New York* (1971), the Court ruled that confessions excluded from trial under *Miranda* could nevertheless be used to impeach the credibility of a defendant who takes the stand to testify in his or her own behalf. Writing for the Court, Chief Justice Burger pointed out that the privilege against compulsory self-incrimination "cannot be construed to include the right to commit perjury."

The Public Safety Exception to *Miranda*

In 1984, the Supreme Court created the public safety exception to the requirement that *Miranda* warnings be given before any questioning of the suspect takes place. In *New York v. Quarles,* the Court examined an interesting factual situation. Two New York City police officers were approached by a woman who claimed she had just been raped and that her assailant had gone into a nearby grocery store. The police were informed that the assailant was carrying a gun. The officers proceeded to the store and immediately spotted Benjamin Quarles, who matched the description given by the victim. Upon seeing the police, Quarles turned and ran. One of the police officers drew his service revolver and ordered Quarles to freeze. Quarles complied with the officer's request. The officer frisked Quarles and discovered an empty shoulder holster. Before reading Quarles the *Miranda* warnings, the officer asked where the gun was. Quarles nodded in the direction of some empty boxes and said, "The gun is over there."

He was then placed under arrest and given the *Miranda* warnings. Later, Quarles moved to have his statement suppressed from evidence since it was made prior to the *Miranda* warnings. He also moved for suppression of the gun under the **fruit of the poisonous tree doctrine.** Under this doctrine, evidence that is derived from illegally obtained evidence is itself tainted (see *Wong Sun v. United States* [1963]). The Supreme Court allowed both pieces of evidence to be used against Quarles, notwithstanding the delay in the *Miranda* warnings. Obviously, the Court felt that the officers were justified in locating a discarded weapon prior to Mirandizing Quarles. In so holding, the Court created the **public safety exception** to *Miranda.*

The Inevitable Discovery Exception

Another exception to the *Miranda* exclusionary rule is based on inevitable discovery of physical evidence that is challenged as the fruit of the poisonous tree. In a macabre case decided in 1984 (*Nix v. Williams*), the Court allowed evidence to be admitted even though it was obtained through the statement of a suspect who had indicated his desire to remain silent until he could meet with his attorney. After one of the police officers involved made a speech emphasizing the need for a "Christian burial" for the victim, the suspect led police to the body of a young girl he had kidnapped and murdered. In allowing the body to be used as evidence, the Court reasoned that the body was not the fruit of a poisonous tree since a search underway in the area would eventually have located the body anyway. Hence, the Court created an **inevitable discovery exception** to the fruit of the poisonous tree doctrine.

Police Deception

The Court has refused to expand the scope of custodial interrogation beyond an actual arrest or significant "deprivation of freedom." In *Oregon v. Mathiason* (1977), the Court allowed the use of a confession obtained by police during voluntary interrogation of a suspect who was not at the time under arrest. An interesting fact in the *Mathiason* case is that the police officer who obtained the confession lied to the suspect about his fingerprints being found at the scene of the crime. Only after this deception did Mathiason confess. Nevertheless, he was not under formal arrest at the time and had even come to the station house unescorted to talk to police. In the Court's view, this was a "noncustodial" situation; hence, *Miranda* did not apply.

In another controversial decision involving **police deception,** *Moran v. Burbine* (1986), the Court further delimited the scope of the *Miranda* rule. Police arrested Burbine for burglary and later obtained information that linked him to an unsolved murder. Burbine's sister, unaware of the possible murder charge, retained an attorney to represent her brother. The attorney telephoned the police, who assured her that Burbine was not to be questioned until the next day but failed to tell her of a possible murder charge against her client. Despite their assurances to the contrary, the police then interrogated Burbine, failing to tell him that an attorney had been obtained for him and had attempted to contact him. Burbine waived his rights to counsel and to remain silent and eventually confessed to the killing. The Supreme Court found no constitutional violation, holding that Burbine had knowingly, intelligently, and voluntarily waived his rights.

In one of the most significant decisions in this area, *Arizona v. Fulminante* (1991), the Supreme Court disallowed the use of a confession that was obtained by a prisoner who was also a confidential Federal Bureau of Investigation (FBI) informant. Oreste Fulminante, who was suspected of murdering his eleven-year-old stepdaughter Jeneane, was incarcerated in federal prison on an unrelated charge. He was befriended by Anthony Sarivola, a former police officer serving time for extortion. Sarivola led Fulminante to believe that he had organized-crime connections and could protect Fulminante from other prisoners who had heard that Fulminante was suspected of killing his stepdaughter. Sarivola insisted, however, that Fulminante tell him what really happened to his stepdaughter. Fulminante then confided in Sarivola that he had indeed taken his stepdaughter on his motorcycle into the desert where, in the words of Justice White, "he choked her, sexually assaulted her, and made her beg for her life, before shooting her twice in the head." Sarivola gave this information to the FBI, which, in turn, passed it along to Arizona authorities. After being released from prison, Fulminante was indicted for the murder of his stepdaughter. Denying his motion to suppress, the Arizona trial court allowed the confession to be introduced and subsequently found Fulminante guilty of first-degree murder. In reviewing this conviction, the Supreme Court found that Fulminante's confession had been coerced. However, the most significant aspect of the Court's decision was its holding that a coerced confession is subject to **harmless error analysis.** Prior to this holding, a defendant was automatically entitled to reversal of his or her conviction if a coerced confession had been introduced into evidence at trial. Under the *Fulminante* decision, an appellate court is permitted to affirm a conviction if it determines that the defendant would have been convicted on other evidence even in the absence of the coerced confession. Note that the Supreme Court found that the use of Fulminante's confession was not harmless error and therefore reversed his conviction. Irrespective of this result, the *Fulminante* decision has been criticized as a further erosion of the constitutional protection against coerced confessions.

TO SUMMARIZE:

- The Supreme Court has long held that a coerced confession violates the Self-Incrimination Clause of the Fifth Amendment as well as the due process requirements of the Fifth and Fourteenth Amendments.
- The traditional test used by the Court was whether a challenged confession could reasonably be deemed to have been voluntary.
- To safeguard the immunity against self-incrimination, the Court developed the well-known *Miranda* warnings. Unless police inform suspects of their rights to remain silent and have an attorney present during questioning and unless police obtain voluntary waivers of these rights, suspects' confessions and other statements are inadmissible at trial.
- Although the Supreme Court has reaffirmed the *Miranda* decision, it has substantially narrowed the scope of its application. The Court has refused to expand the scope of custodial interrogation beyond an actual arrest or significant "deprivation of freedom." The Court has also recognized a number of exceptions to *Miranda,* including the public safety and inevitable discovery exceptions.

THE RIGHT TO COUNSEL

Historically, the Sixth Amendment right to counsel in "all criminal prosecutions" meant no more than that the government could not prevent a person accused of a crime from hiring a lawyer if he or she could afford to do so. The Supreme Court moved significantly away from this traditional view in the celebrated Scottsboro case. Here, the Court reversed the convictions of a group of young African-American men who had been sentenced to death in an Alabama court for allegedly raping two white women. During the rushed investigation and trial, conducted in an atmosphere of extreme racial animosity, the defendants were not represented by counsel in any meaningful sense. In *Powell v. Alabama* (1932), the Supreme Court found that the defendants had been denied due process of law in violation of the Fourteenth Amendment. Justice George Sutherland's majority opinion placed great

Some of the defendants who challenged their convictions in Powell v. Alabama

importance on the failure of the trial judge to ensure effective representation and adequate time to prepare a defense.

The *Gideon* Decision

Under Chief Justice Earl Warren, the Supreme Court placed enormous stress on the need for professional representation of persons suspected or accused of crimes. In its *Escobedo* and *Miranda* decisions, for example, the Warren Court

Clarence Earl Gideon

was obviously concerned about the absence of defense counsel during custodial police interrogation. In *Gideon v. Wainwright* (1963), the Court overruled precedent and held that the Sixth Amendment **right to counsel** as applied to the states via the Due Process Clause of the Fourteenth Amendment requires states to provide counsel to defendants who cannot afford to hire attorneys on their own. The *Gideon* Court recognized that "in our adversary system of criminal justice, any person haled into court, who is too poor to hire a lawyer, cannot be assured a fair trial unless counsel is provided for him."

In a related case decided the same day as *Gideon* (*Douglas v. California* [1963]), the Court held that a state must provide counsel to an indigent defendant who has a right under state law to appeal a conviction to a higher court. (However, in *Pennsylvania v. Finley* [1987], the Court made clear what had been only implicit in *Douglas v. California*, namely, that "the right to appointed counsel extends to the first appeal . . . and no further.")

Because *Gideon* was made retroactive, it had a tremendous impact on the criminal justice system. For example, in Florida, where the *Gideon* case originated, the state was required to retry hundreds of convicted felons who had not been represented by counsel at their first trials. In many cases, the key witnesses were no longer available, and the state was forced to drop its charges. In the wake of *Gideon,* many states decided it would be more economical in the long run to set up permanent offices to handle indigent defense rather than to have judges appoint counsel *ad hoc.* Most states now have public defenders to make good on the state's responsibility under the Due Process Clause of the Fourteenth Amendment. Although many state judges, legislators, governors, and law enforcement officers resented the Court's "meddling" in their affairs, the *Gideon* decision has come, like so many other Supreme Court rulings, to be accepted and even praised by state officials.

For the most part, the Burger Court maintained this commitment to providing counsel to indigent defendants. In *Argersinger v. Hamlin* (1972), the Court extended the *Gideon* ruling to cover misdemeanor trials (*Gideon* applied only to felonies). The *Argersinger* decision was ambiguous, however, on the issue of whether misdemeanor defendants were entitled to counsel if they faced possible jail terms or only if their convictions *actually resulted in* incarceration. In *Scott v. Illinois* (1979), the Supreme Court clarified the situation, holding that counsel had to be provided to indigent misdemeanants only if conviction would actually result in imprisonment. Writing for the Court, Justice Rehnquist thus opted for a narrow interpretation of *Argersinger,* arguing that "any extension would create confusion and impose unpredictable, but necessarily substantial costs on fifty quite diverse states."

Effectiveness of Appointed Counsel

One of the most elusive contemporary issues in the right to counsel area is that of **ineffective representation.** As the Court recognized in *Powell v. Alabama* (1932), the right to counsel is useless unless one is competently represented. Until recently, most federal courts followed the **mockery of justice test** in determining the competency of appointed counsel. The question was whether the attorney was so ineffective as to constitute "a farce or mockery of justice" (see, for example, *Edwards v. United States* [1958]). This permissive standard was rapidly adopted by most of the state supreme courts. However, the federal circuit courts adopted different standards of varying strictness. In 1984, the Supreme Court finally standardized the test that courts must follow to comply with the Sixth Amendment. In *Strickland v. Washington,* the Court held that an indigent appellant must show (1) that his or her trial lawyer was less than reasonably effective and (2) that there is a reasonable probability that the outcome of the trial would have been different had counsel been more effective. Obviously, this is a difficult test to meet, allowing for reversal only in cases of egregious incompetence.

Self-Representation

Although decisions such as *Powell v. Alabama* and *Gideon v. Wainwright* stressed the importance of counsel in ensuring a fair trial, the Supreme Court has made it quite clear that a defendant has a constitutional right to refuse counsel, as long as the waiver is made "knowingly and intelligently." In *Faretta v. California* (1975), the Court decided a case in which Faretta, accused of grand theft, requested permission from the trial court to represent himself, arguing that the public defender's office was too busy to provide him with effective representation. The trial judge refused the request and appointed an assistant public defender to represent him.

Faretta's conviction was ultimately vacated by the Supreme Court by a 6-to-3 vote. The majority asserted that "[t]he language and spirit of the Sixth Amendment contemplate that counsel, like the other defense tools guaranteed by the Amendment, shall be an aid to a willing defendant—not an organ of the state interposed between an unwilling defendant and his right to defend himself personally."

Although the *Faretta* decision did not produce a rash of *pro se* defenses (those in which the defendant conducts his or her own defense), occasionally a defendant will "go it alone" in the courtroom. One noteworthy example of **self-representation** occurred in the trial of serial killer Ted Bundy in Florida in the early 1980s. Bundy, a former law student, insisted on representing himself, although the trial judge appointed a lawyer to serve as standby counsel. Although most observers believed that Bundy did a reasonably effective job in representing himself, he still claimed on appeal that his conviction was invalid because he had ineffective representation at trial. Not surprisingly, the appellate court was unmoved by this attempt to have it both ways!

TO SUMMARIZE:

- Historically, the Sixth Amendment right to counsel in "all criminal prosecutions" meant no more than that the government could not prevent a person accused of a crime from hiring a lawyer if he or she could afford to do so.
- In *Gideon v. Wainwright* (1963), the Court overruled precedent and held that the Sixth Amendment right to counsel as applied to the states via the Due Process Clause of the Fourteenth Amendment requires states to provide counsel to felony defendants who cannot afford to hire attorneys on their own.
- For the most part, the Burger and Rehnquist Courts have maintained this commitment to providing counsel to indigent defendants.
- The Court has made it quite clear that a defendant has a constitutional right to refuse to be represented by appointed counsel, as long as the waiver is made "knowingly and intelligently."

BAIL AND PRETRIAL DETENTION

Since persons accused of crime are presumed innocent until proven guilty, it is customary for defendants to be released from custody prior to **arraignment** and trial. Ordinarily, courts require defendants to post **bail** (a sum of money), which is forfeited if the defendant flees to escape prosecution. The Eighth Amendment prohibits "excessive bail." The Supreme Court has recognized that the purpose of bail is not to inflict punishment but to ensure that a defendant appears in court. In *Stack v. Boyle* (1951), the Court said that "[b]ail set at a figure higher than an amount reasonably calculated to fulfill this purpose is 'excessive' under the Eighth Amendment." However, the Court has never held that the Excessive Bail Clause is incorporated by the Fourteenth Amendment, leaving the issue of excessive bail in state criminal prosecutions to state constitutions, legislatures, and courts.

It has been a long-standing practice for courts to deny bail to defendants who are deemed especially dangerous or pose an unusual likelihood of fleeing to avoid prosecution. This raises the question of whether the Eighth Amendment implies a right to pretrial release. In *United States v. Salerno* (1987), the Supreme Court answered this question in the negative. Here, the Court upheld the Bail Reform Act of 1984, which permits **pretrial detention** in federal cases where a court determines that the release of a defendant would pose a serious threat to public safety. Writing for the Court, Chief Justice Rehnquist agreed that "a primary function of bail is to safeguard the courts' role in adjudicating the guilt or innocence of defendants" but rejected "the proposition that the Eighth Amendment categorically prohibits the government from pursuing other admittedly compelling interests through the regulation of pretrial release."

The Court's decision in *Salerno,* while applying formally only to federal criminal cases, suggests the validity of state laws denying bail to persons accused of violent felonies, especially where such persons have a record of violent crimes. It is doubtful that the Supreme Court would approve a policy of long-term pretrial detention for defendants accused of nonviolent crimes.

TO SUMMARIZE:

- Because persons accused of crime are presumed innocent until proven guilty, it is customary for defendants to be released from custody prior to arraignment and trial.
- The Supreme Court has upheld the common practice for courts to deny bail to defendants who are deemed especially dangerous or pose an unusual likelihood of fleeing to avoid prosecution.

PLEA BARGAINING

Most books dealing with the rights of the accused focus on problems associated with the criminal trial, such as jury selection, jury verdicts, the "public trial" controversy, and so on. It must be recognized, however, that only a small proportion of criminal cases ever gets to trial. In a typical jurisdiction, only about 5 percent of felony arrests result in trials. Many cases are dropped by the prosecution after key evidence has been suppressed on Fourth, Fifth, or Sixth Amendment grounds. Other cases must be dropped because key witnesses cannot be located or made to testify. But the main reason that criminal cases do not often result in trials is the existence of **plea bargaining.** Plea bargaining results in an agreement by the accused to plead guilty in exchange for some concession from the prosecution. This concession might be a reduction in the severity or number of the charges brought, or it might simply be a promise by the prosecutor not to seek the maximum sentence allowed by law.

Conventional wisdom holds that plea bargaining occurs because of the scarce resources allocated to the processing of criminal cases. The criminal trial can be a protracted process. There simply are not enough prosecutors, public defenders, and judges to try all the criminal cases coming into the system. Nor does the public or its elected representatives seem inclined to provide the necessary resources. Even if such resources were miraculously furnished, there is reason to believe plea bargaining would still occur. The evidence indicates that plea bargaining occurs in those jurisdictions where scarce resources are really not a problem. In addition, an incentive to plea bargain may be built into the very nature of the criminal justice process. We know that organizations generally try to minimize uncertainties associated with their activities. The defense counsel group is probably no different. Lawyers especially dislike the uncertainty inherent in a trial governed by due process. The legal technicalities associated with proving guilt and the unpredictability of juries make the criminal trial a very uncertain enterprise. Many prosecutors and defense lawyers would rather settle on a plea bargain that is certain than to go into the courtroom and take their chances on losing the case. This suggests that plea bargaining is here to stay.

Plea bargaining has been and will continue to be an object of criticism. Some are offended by what they perceive to be insufficient penalties meted out to criminals through plea bargains. Others are concerned that our historic commitment to due process of law is being sacrificed on the altar of expediency.

The Supreme Court has addressed the issue of plea bargaining in several cases dating from the late 1960s (see, for example, *Jackson v. United States* [1968], *Boykin v. Alabama* [1969], *Brady v. United States* [1970], and *Santobello v. New York* [1971]). Basically, the Court has manifested concern over plea bargaining but nevertheless has recognized its practicality, if not its inevitability. However, the Court has stated emphatically that a trial judge must ascertain that the defendant has made a **knowing and intelligent waiver** of the right to a trial before accepting the defendant's plea of guilty. As the Court noted in *Boykin v. Alabama,*

> a plea of guilty is more than an admission of conduct, it is a conviction. Ignorance, incomprehension, coercion, terror, inducements, subtle or blatant threats might be a cover-up of unconstitutionality.

One of the more difficult cases decided by the Court in the area of plea bargaining was *Bordenkircher v. Hayes* (1978). Paul Hayes was indicted by a Kentucky grand jury for writing a bad check. It was not his first offense. The prosecutor informed Hayes that if he did not plead guilty, he (the prosecutor) would return to the grand jury to seek a tougher indictment based on the state's habitual offender statute. The defendant refused to "cop a plea," and the prosecutor carried out his threat. The grand jury handed down the more serious indictment. Hayes was tried, convicted, and sentenced to life imprisonment. Was this threat by the prosecutor constitutionally permissible? Dividing 5 to 4, the Supreme Court ruled that it was, since Hayes was "properly chargeable" under the recidivist statute from the start. Dissenting, Justice Harry Blackmun refused to approve what he perceived as "prosecutorial vindictiveness." In Blackmun's view, Hayes was being punished for the exercise of constitutional rights. The sharp division in *Bordenkircher* underscores the fact that reasonable people, including those trained in the law, can disagree on what offends the "fundamental fairness" required by due process.

TO SUMMARIZE:

- Plea bargaining refers to an agreement by the accused to plead guilty in exchange for some concession from the prosecution.
- The Supreme Court has approved the practice of plea bargaining but has stated emphatically that a trial judge must ascertain that the defendant has made a knowing and intelligent waiver of the right to a trial before accepting his or her plea of guilty.

TRIAL BY JURY

In spite of the pervasiveness of plea bargaining, the **jury trial** still plays a prominent role not only in American legal mythology but also in the day-to-day operation of the criminal justice process. Trial by jury is recognized as a federal constitutional right in criminal and civil cases. Reference to jury trial appears once in the original Constitution and twice in the Bill of Rights. Article III provides: "The trial of all Crimes, except in Cases of Impeachment, shall be by Jury. . . ." The Seventh Amendment requires that "the right of trial by jury shall be preserved" in civil suits. Most pertinent to our concerns is the Sixth Amendment, which states: "In all criminal prosecutions, the accused shall enjoy the right to a speedy and public trial by an impartial jury. . . ." Of course, prior to the incorporation of this provision into the Fourteenth Amendment in 1968 (see *Duncan v. Louisiana*), "all criminal prosecutions" meant all *federal* criminal prosecutions. Ever since *Duncan,* defendants in both state and federal criminal cases have had a constitutional right to trial by jury. The only exception to the right to jury trial involves misdemeanor trials where defendants face incarceration for less than six months.

The Problem of Pretrial Publicity

Even before the Sixth Amendment right to trial by jury was incorporated into the Fourteenth Amendment, the Supreme Court had occasion to reverse jury verdicts in state criminal cases where the fairness of the trial was prejudiced by excessive publicity. In so doing, the Court used the **fair trial doctrine** under the Fourteenth Amendment, rather than the Sixth Amendment jury trial provision. *Sheppard v. Maxwell* (1966) is an excellent case in point. There, the Court reversed a murder conviction reached in a trial conducted against a backdrop of sensationalistic publicity. The circumstances surrounding the *Sheppard* case are almost comical in retrospect. Local officials allowed Dr. Sam Sheppard's murder trial to degenerate into a circus. The jurors in the case were constantly exposed to the intense media coverage of the case right up until the time at which they began their deliberations. Under these circumstances, the guilty verdict was virtually a foregone conclusion. Concluding that fundamental fairness had been denied, the Supreme Court reversed Sheppard's conviction.

Sheppard v. Maxwell leads one to wonder just what steps can be legitimately taken to insulate a trial jury from prejudicial publicity in a sensational case. One possibility is to take extreme care in the jury selection process, possibly by increasing the number of peremptory challenges available to the defense and the prosecution (such challenges, while limited in number, do not ordinarily require an explanation by counsel or a ruling by the trial judge). Another common step is to sequester the jury during the course of the trial. Another frequent measure is to postpone the trial until the publicity dies down. A less common approach is a **change of venue**—moving the trial to a locale less affected by the **pretrial publicity.** Although there is no question about the propriety of these measures, considerable doubt remains as to their efficacy.

Some judges have attempted more drastic means of protecting the defendant's right to a fair trial. One of these is to impose **gag orders** on the press, prohibiting the reportage of certain facts or incidents related to a sensational crime. In *Nebraska Press Association v. Stuart* (1976), the Supreme Court invalidated a gag order imposed by a trial judge to safeguard the rights of a man accused of a brutal mass murder. The Court viewed the order as a prior restraint in violation of the First Amendment's protection of the freedom of the press. The *Nebraska Press* case vividly illustrates the head-on conflict of two cherished constitutional principles: freedom of the press and the right to a fair trial. Although the Court was unanimous in striking down the gag order, Chief Justice Burger's majority opinion left open the possibility that such orders might be permissible under extreme circumstances.

Closure of Judicial Proceedings

Another more drastic means of protecting the defendant's right to a fair trial is **closure of pretrial proceedings.** In *Gannet v. DePasquale* (1979), the Court allowed the closure of a pretrial hearing to determine the admissibility of evidence with the consent of both the prosecution and the defense. Writing for a divided Court, Justice Stewart stated that the right to a "public trial" guaranteed by the Sixth Amendment is personal to the defendant, not a general right of public access. Stewart went on to say that any First Amendment right of access by the press was outweighed by the right of the accused to receive a fair trial. In 1980, the Court appeared to alter its position somewhat. In *Richmond Newspapers v. Virginia,* the Court voted 7 to 1 to disallow the closure of a criminal trial. Although there was no majority opinion, the justices seemed to have agreed that the First Amendment prohibits trial closure. The very next year, in *Chandler v. Florida* (1981), the Court allowed television coverage of criminal trials, suggesting that *Richmond Newspapers* was no anomaly. The Court's decision in *Waller v. Georgia* (1984) also suggests a strong commitment to the value of a public trial. In *Waller,* the Court refused to allow closure of a pretrial suppression hearing that had been granted by the trial court over the objection of the accused. Although the Court in *Waller* suggested that extreme circumstances might allow the closure of a pretrial proceeding despite the objection of the defendant, the Court adopted a test that makes it very difficult to justify closure.

Jury Size

Historically, trial juries in the United States were composed of twelve persons, all of whom had to agree in order to convict a defendant. Although this is still the case in most states, some jurisdictions allow for six-person juries in noncapital cases. And four states (Oregon, Louisiana, Oklahoma, and Texas) no longer require juries to be unanimous to convict defendants, at least in some noncapital cases. In *Williams v. Florida* (1970), the Supreme Court approved Florida's use of six-person juries in noncapital cases. Justice White's opinion for the Court discussed the relationship between jury size and the Sixth Amendment:

> [T]he fact that the jury at common law was composed of precisely twelve is a historical accident, unnecessary to effect the purposes of the jury system and wholly without significance. . . . To read the Sixth Amendment as forever codifying a feature so incidental to the real purpose of the Amendment is to ascribe a blind formalism to the Framers. . . .

Serious questions exist about the factual assertions made by the Court in the *Williams* case. Is it true, as the Court asserted, that "neither currently available evidence nor theory suggests that the twelve-member jury is necessarily more advantageous to the defendant . . . "? Some experts on jury behavior have concluded otherwise. However, in *Ballew v. Georgia* (1978), the Court drew the line on jury size when it refused to permit the use of five-person juries. The Court cited studies to show that "the purpose and functioning of the jury . . . is seriously impaired . . . by a reduction in size to below six members." Thus, state legislatures are free to specify the number of persons to serve on juries in noncapital cases as long as they observe the constitutional minimum of six.

The Unanimity Principle

In *Johnson v. Louisiana* (1972) and its companion case *Apodaca v. Oregon* (1972), the Supreme Court surprised many observers by allowing state criminal trials to depart from the historic **unanimity rule.** In *Johnson,* the state of Louisiana passed a law allowing for convictions by nine votes on twelve-person juries in noncapital cases. Writing for a sharply divided Court, Justice White tried to reconcile nonunanimity with the **reasonable doubt standard** required by due process:

> Of course, the State's proof could be regarded as more certain if it had convinced all 12 jurors instead of only nine; it would have been even more compelling if it had . . . convinced 24 or 36 jurors. But the fact remains that nine jurors—a substantial majority of the jury—were convinced by the evidence. In our view disagreement of three jurors does not alone establish reasonable doubt.

One can argue, as Justice Marshall did in his dissent, that the refusal of three presumably reasonable jurors to sanction a guilty verdict might in and of itself indicate a reasonable doubt as to the guilt of the accused:

> The juror whose dissenting voice is unheard may be a spokesman, but simply for himself—and that, in my view, is enough. The doubts of a single juror are in my view evidence that the government has failed to carry its burden of proving guilt beyond a reasonable doubt.

The Court's decisions in *Williams v. Florida* and *Johnson v. Louisiana* left many observers wondering whether the Court would permit **nonunanimous verdicts** by six-member juries. In *Burch v. Louisiana* (1979), the Court allayed the fears of those who thought it was going too far to facilitate criminal convictions. Justice Rehnquist wrote the opinion for a unanimous Court:

> We agree . . . that the question presented is a "close" one. Nevertheless, we believe that conviction by a nonunanimous six-member jury in a state criminal trial for a non-petty offense deprives an individual of his constitutional right to trial by jury.

Exclusion of Minorities from Juries

Another problem that has beset the courts with respect to trial juries is the exclusion of women, African-Americans, and other minority groups from juries, especially when the defendants are members of such groups. Although the Court has quite clearly stated that there is no constitutional right of a defendant to have on the jury individuals of his or her gender or ethnic identity, it has also held that the systematic exclusion of such groups is unconstitutional under the Fourteenth Amendment (see *Strauder v. West Virginia* [1879] and *Swain v. Alabama* [1965]). The Court has recognized that a jury should, at least ideally, represent a cross-section of the community in order to be completely fair and just to the accused.

One of the more difficult issues in jury selection is the use of the **peremptory challenge** to eliminate prospective jurors on the grounds of race. In *Batson v. Kentucky* (1986), the Supreme Court held that a prosecutor's use of peremptory challenges to exclude African-Americans from a jury trying an African-American defendant constituted a basis for reversal on appeal. Consequently, today in the trial of an African-American defendant, the exclusion of a single African-American juror can be the basis for the trial court to deny the use of a peremptory challenge, if the judge is persuaded that the challenge is racially motivated. In 1991, the *Batson* rule was broadened so that a defendant need not be of the same race as the excluded juror to successfully challenge that juror's exclusion (Powers v. Ohio). In the same year, the Supreme Court extended the *Batson* rule to encompass civil trials as well *(Edmondson v. Leesville Concrete Company).*

In *Georgia v. McCollum* (1992), the Court revisited this area of the law and extended the *Batson* rule by holding that a defendant's exercise of peremptory challenges was state action, and that the Equal Protection Clause also prohibits defendants from engaging in purposeful discrimination on the ground of race. As a result of the pronouncements in *Batson, Powers,* and *McCollum,* federal and state courts have reevaluated their views on the exercise of peremptory challenges. In general, trial judges are still vested with broad discretion in reviewing **racially motivated peremptory challenges,** but many trial lawyers have expressed concern that peremptory challenges may become relics in our system of jurisprudence.

Gender-Based Peremptory Challenges

The view that peremptory challenges are on the way out was reinforced by a trend in the late 1980s and early 1990s to restrict **gender-based peremptory challenges.** By 1993 federal appellate courts had issued disparate rulings on the issue. Finally, in *J.E.B. v. Alabama ex rel. T.B.* (1994), the Supreme Court resolved that conflict and held that the Equal Protection Clause of the Fourteenth Amendment prohibits gender-based peremptory challenges. Writing for the majority, Justice Blackmun emphasized the relationship between racially based and gender-based peremptory challenges when he observed that "[f]ailing to provide jurors the same protection against gender discrimination as race discrimination could frustrate the purpose of *Batson* itself."

There may be reason to believe that the Court is retreating somewhat from the *Batson* decision. In *Purkett v. Elem* (1995), the Court held in effect that judges are not required to disallow a peremptory challenge, even if the lawyer making the challenge gives an implausible nonracial explanation for why the juror was excluded.

TO SUMMARIZE:

- Defendants in both state and federal criminal cases have a constitutional right to trial by jury, except in misdemeanor cases where defendants face incarceration for less than six months.
- Trial judges have at their disposal several means of protecting a defendant's right to a fair trial against potentially prejudicial media coverage. These include a change of venue, sequestration of the jury, and postponement of the trial.
- On rare occasions the Supreme Court has invoked the "fair trial doctrine" to limit media coverage of judicial proceedings. However, the Court tends to give the widest possible latitude to freedom of the press in this regard.

- Historically, trial juries have been composed of twelve persons, all of whom had to agree in order to convict a defendant. In recent decades, however, the Supreme Court has upheld state-level variations from the traditional size and unanimity requirements in noncapital cases.
- Although a defendant has no constitutional right to have on the jury individuals of his or her gender or ethnic identity, the Supreme Court has held that the systematic exclusion of such persons is unconstitutional. Since the mid-1980s, the Court has restricted the use of peremptory challenges in accordance with this principle.

THE PROTECTION AGAINST DOUBLE JEOPARDY

The Fifth Amendment provides that no person "shall . . . be subject for the same offense to be twice put in jeopardy of life or limb." This protection against double jeopardy has deep roots in the soil of the common law. To allow the government to continue to prosecute a defendant on the same charge, using the same evidence that had previously resulted in acquittal, would seem to violate "fundamental canons of decency and fairness." Yet, in *Palko v. Connecticut* (1937), the Supreme Court held otherwise in refusing to incorporate the Double Jeopardy Clause into the Fourteenth Amendment. This holding has been overruled (see *Benton v. Maryland* [1969]), and the Double Jeopardy Clause has taken its place among those protections deemed "essential to a scheme of ordered liberty." However, the question of what exactly constitutes **double jeopardy** remains open. Essentially, the clause prevents the government from attempting to convict the accused of an illegal act after it has once failed to do so. However, there are a number of exceptions to this general rule.

Successive State and Federal Prosecutions

Given our system of federalism, it is possible for one set of actions to lead to separate criminal prosecutions in the state and federal courts. A good example of this is provided by the case of the Los Angeles police officers involved in the videotaped beating of African-American motorist Rodney King in 1992. A state court's verdict that found the police officers not guilty of criminal misconduct was followed by considerable outrage and large-scale destructive rioting in Los Angeles. Despite the officers' acquittal on state charges, the federal government brought new charges against them for violating King's civil rights. On appeal, the officers argued that the new federal charges were barred by the double jeopardy clause. In *United States v. Koon* (1994), the Ninth circuit rejected this claim, saying that "there is no evidence that the federal prosecution was a 'sham' or a 'cover' for the state prosecution." Ultimately, the defendants were convicted and served time in federal prison.

Mistrials

Another legitimate deviation from the double jeopardy principle occurs in the case of a **mistrial** granted on the request of the defense. Judges often declare a mistrial if some extraordinary event occurs, such as the death of a juror or attorney; if some prejudicial error cannot be corrected; or if a **hung jury** (that is, a jury unable to reach a verdict) results. The declaration of a mistrial, at least on the motion of the defendant, has the effect of "wiping the slate clean," of declaring that no trial took place. Thus, the state's renewal of its prosecution of the accused does not violate the Double Jeopardy Clause.

Confinement of Sexual Predators in Mental Institutions

In *Kansas v. Hendricks* (1997) the Court upheld the Kansas Sexually Violent Predator Act, which permits the state to continue to institutionalize certain sex offenders after they have completed their prison sentences. The Court concluded that the law, which provides for involuntary confinement in mental institutions, did not inflict "punishment" and was therefore beyond the pale of the Double Jeopardy Clause. Justice Thomas wrote the Opinion of the Court, joined by Chief Justice Rehnquist and Justices O'Connor, Kennedy and Scalia. Dissenting, Justice Breyer (joined by Stevens, Souter, and Ginsburg) argued that the confinement amounted to an unconstitutional *ex post facto* law. The Court, however, rejected this argument on the grounds that the confinement resulted from a civil commitment proceeding, not a criminal prosecution. Ever since *Calder v. Bull* (1798), the *Ex Post Facto* Clause has been limited to criminal punishments. Technically, civil confinement is not criminal punishment, although the result may be indistinguishable from the point of view of the person who loses his freedom.

Civil Forfeitures, Double Jeopardy, and Excessive Fines

Federal law provides for the **forfeiture** of real estate and other property used in illegal drug trafficking. In *United States v. Ursery* (1996), the Court held that such forfeitures do not constitute "punishment" for purposes of the Double Jeopardy Clause. Two federal circuit courts had held that the Double Jeopardy Clause prohibits both punishing a defendant for a criminal offense and forfeiting his property for that same offense in a separate civil proceeding. The Supreme Court reversed, with Chief Justice Rehnquist noting that "Congress long has authorized the Government to bring parallel criminal proceedings and civil forfeiture proceedings, and this Court consistently has found civil forfeitures not to constitute punishment under the Double Jeopardy Clause." In a lone dissent, Justice Stevens relied on the Court's prior decisions in *Austin v. United States* (1993) and *Department of Revenue of Montana v. Kurth Ranch* (1994). In *Austin,* the Court decided that a property forfeiture stemming from a drug crime is subject to limitation under the Eighth Amendment. In *Kurth Ranch,* the Court invoked the Double Jeopardy Clause in striking down a state tax imposed on a quantity of marijuana when the taxpayer had already been convicted of possessing the same contraband. In Stevens's view, these decisions dictated "a far different conclusion" than that reached by the Court.

TO SUMMARIZE:

- Essentially, the Double Jeopardy Clause prevents the government from attempting to convict the accused of an illegal act after it has once failed to do so. However, there are a number of exceptions to this general rule.
- Given our system of federalism, it is possible for one episode of criminal misconduct to lead to separate criminal prosecutions in the state and federal courts.

- The renewal of a prosecution after the declaration of a mistrial does not constitute Double Jeopardy.
- The Supreme Court has held that civil confinement of violent sexual predators after completion of their criminal sentences does not violate the double jeopardy prohibition.

INCARCERATION AND THE RIGHTS OF PRISONERS

The framers of the Bill of Rights were well aware of the sordid history of torture that characterized criminal punishment in pre-Revolutionary Europe. In *O'Neil v. Vermont* (1892), the Supreme Court said that the Eighth Amendment prohibition of **cruel and unusual punishments** was directed to "punishments which inflict torture, such as the rack, the thumb-screw, the iron boot, the stretching of limbs and the like, which are attended with acute pain and suffering." Yet the Court recognized that the Eighth Amendment also proscribed "punishments which by their excessive length or severity are greatly disproportionate to the offense charged."

Torture is no longer a significant legal issue in this country. Indeed, corporal punishment has been abolished as a penalty for criminal acts. Yet the question of proportionality of punishments and crimes remains a viable problem for contemporary courts of law. In *Robinson v. California* (1962), the Supreme Court held that state courts were bound by the Cruel and Unusual Punishments Clause. Since then, there have been numerous challenges to state sentencing policies as well as the conditions of state prisons.

Mandatory Life Imprisonment

Can imprisonment alone constitute cruel and unusual punishment? The answer to this general question depends on the circumstances of individual cases and the makeup of the Supreme Court at any given time. For example, in *Rummel v. Estelle* (1980), the Court upheld a **mandatory life sentence** imposed on a man who had committed three nonviolent felonies. In three separate cases over a period of years, Rummel had been convicted of the fraudulent use of a credit card, forging a check, and obtaining money under false pretenses. Under Texas law, he was adjudged a **habitual offender** and sentenced to life in prison. In a similar case three years later, the Court struck down a South Dakota statute that authorized life imprisonment for habitual felons (see *Solem v. Helm* [1983]). Because the South Dakota law did not provide for release on parole, the Court distinguished this case from *Rummel v. Estelle*. In 1991, the Supreme Court, in *Harmelin v. Michigan*, upheld a life sentence without possibility of parole imposed on an individual for possessing 772 grams of cocaine. Michigan law required the automatic imposition of this sentence on anyone convicted of possessing 650 grams or more of any mixture containing cocaine. In all three of the aforementioned cases, the Court divided 5 to 4, indicating the absence of consensus in this area.

Prisoners' Rights

Because they have been convicted of serious crimes, the inmates in our nation's crowded prison system have lost many of the rights we take for granted. In *Price v. Johnson* (1948), the Supreme Court held that lawful incarceration necessarily requires suspension or limitation of rights. In *Hudson v. Palmer* (1984), the Court reiterated this position, stating that "the curtailment of certain rights is necessary as a practical matter, to accommodate a myriad of institutional needs and objectives of prison facilities, chief among them which is internal security. . . ." The Court further observed that "these restrictions or retractions also serve, incidentally, as reminders that, under our system of justice, deterrence and retribution are factors in addition to correction."

By definition, prisoners have forfeited their right to live in civil society, to move about freely, to associate with whom they choose, and to make decisions about everyday matters such as eating, sleeping, recreation, and work. Under state and federal laws, many prisoners have also forfeited their right to vote or to hold public office. But they have not been stripped of all constitutional rights and protections. Just which of the many constitutional rights are retained by those confined to prison is still unclear. Judicial restraint dictates that such questions be left open until raised in specific controversies; the Court has yet to decide more than a handful of cases in this area.

Prior to the 1960s, courts appeared indifferent to **prisoners' rights.** The main reason for this was that so few cases were ever filed; for the most part, prisoners were denied access to counsel and the courts. As a result of favorable Supreme Court decisions of the 1950s and early 1960s, however, prisoners began to obtain access to the federal judiciary, using petitions for writs of habeas corpus. Then, in the 1970s, their cases began to reach the level of the Supreme Court. Today, several pronouncements from the High Court guide lower court judges, legislators, and prison officials in dealing with the legal aspects of prison confinement (see, for example, *Cruz v. Beto* [1972], *Procunier v. Martinez* [1974], and *Baxter v. Palmigiano* [1976]).

In *Hutto v. Finney* (1978), the Supreme Court upheld a federal court order imposing a thirty-day limit on the use of **punitive isolation** by a state prison. The case, which began in 1969 under the name *Holt v. Sarver,* involved an Eighth Amendment challenge to the conditions of confinement in the Arkansas prison system, particularly the notorious Cummins Farm. The challenged conditions included corporal punishment and torture; abysmal sanitation, diet, and health care; and an overall atmosphere of violence. The conditions that prevailed at Cummins Farm were not altogether atypical of conditions in maximum security state prisons at the time the litigation began. Today, as a result of increased judicial oversight, such conditions are rare exceptions.

In 1992, the Supreme Court demonstrated continuing solicitude toward prisoners subjected to inhumane treatment. In *Hudson v. McMillian,* the Court held that a prisoner who is beaten maliciously by guards may bring a civil suit to recover damages under a claim of cruel and unusual punishment, even if the injuries sustained are not serious. In one of his first dissenting opinions on the High Court, Justice Clarence Thomas (joined by Justice Scalia) expressed the view that nonserious injury to a prisoner does not rise to the level of cruel and unusual punishment.

Many people, especially prison officials, regard judicial oversight of prisons with disdain. Few observers beyond prisoners themselves and a few groups representing their interests are prepared to lavish praise on the federal courts for their involvement in this area. As a group, prisoners have very little political power and even less public support. Nevertheless, some argue that one of the most important functions of the judiciary is to protect **discrete and insular minorities** who have no effective means of representing themselves in the political process. Certainly prisoners are such a minority. And although they may well deserve harsh punishment, they are nevertheless persons and, as such, are entitled to the applicable protections of the Constitution.

TO SUMMARIZE:

- By definition, persons serving terms of imprisonment forfeit many of their civil and constitutional rights. The Supreme Court has recognized, however, that prisoners retain a few basic substantive and procedural rights. These include access to the courts and to legal counsel and protection against cruel and unusual punishment.
- In recent years the Supreme Court has shown less solicitude for the rights of prisoners and more concern for prison discipline and security.

THE DEATH PENALTY

Although already in decline, the **death penalty** was in widespread use when the Constitution was adopted—not only for murder but also for an array of lesser offenses. The Due Process Clauses of the Fifth and Fourteenth Amendments explicitly recognize, although they do not necessarily endorse, the death penalty: "no person shall be deprived of *life,* liberty or property without due process of law" [emphasis added]. In *Trop v. Dulles* (1958), however, Chief Justice Warren indicated that the Cruel and Unusual Punishments Clause "must draw its meaning from the **evolving standards of decency** that mark the progress of a maturing society." By the 1960s, it was clear that public support for the death penalty had diminished substantially. By 1966, public opinion polls were finding that a majority of Americans opposed capital punishment. Reflecting this change in societal attitudes, only two persons were executed in the United States between 1967 and the Supreme Court's decision in *Furman v. Georgia* (1972), which struck down the Georgia death penalty law.

The *Furman* Case

In *Furman v. Georgia,* five justices voted to strike down Georgia's death penalty statute. There was, however, only a brief *per curiam* opinion announcing the judgment of the Court. For the majority's rationale, one had to look at five separate concurring opinions. Two of the five justices—Brennan and Marshall—held that the death penalty itself was cruel and unusual punishment, given the "evolving standards of decency." Throughout their subsequent tenure on the Court, Brennan and Marshall steadfastly maintained the position that the death penalty is inherently unconstitutional (Justice Brennan retired in 1990; Justice Marshall followed suit in 1991).

If evolving standards of decency have anything to do with public opinion, then the Brennan–Marshall position on the death penalty is difficult to defend. Since the late 1960s, probably as a result of the increasing salience of the crime problem, the level of support for the death penalty has risen steadily, to 69 percent in 1977. It is thus difficult to make the evolving-standards argument unless one is talking about one's own standards! However, it is generally considered unacceptable for judges to impose their personal standards of morality on public policy under the aegis of the Constitution. Thus, Justice Marshall, dissenting in *Gregg v. Georgia* (1976), took

The death penalty: Just deserts or "cruel and unusual punishment"?

the position that "the American people, fully informed as to the purposes of the death penalty and its liabilities, would in my view reject it as morally unacceptable." Justice Marshall's statement was regarded by many critics as arrogant, but it should be admitted that we simply do not know whether Marshall's assertion was correct. His hypothesis is possibly testable through empirical or experimental research; unfortunately, such research has yet to reach fruition.

Of the five justices who voted to invalidate the death penalty in the *Furman* case, Justice Stewart's opinion seems to have been the most influential. For Stewart, the problem with the death penalty was not the punishment itself but the manner in which it was being administered. Trial juries were being left with virtually unfettered discretion in deciding when to impose capital punishment. The result, according to Stewart, was that the death penalty was "wantonly and . . . freakishly imposed." Although Stewart explicitly linked his objection to the Cruel and Unusual Punishment Clause, it seems as though he was making a due process argument: The death penalty was invalid because it was being administered in an arbitrary and capricious fashion.

Gregg v. Georgia: The Court Reinstates the Death Penalty

In the wake of the *Furman* decision, some thirty-five state legislatures rewrote their death penalty laws. Georgia's revamped death penalty statute was before the Supreme Court in the *Gregg* case of 1976. The revised Georgia law requires a bifurcated trial for capital crimes: In the first stage, guilt is determined in the usual manner; the second stage deals with the appropriate sentence. For the jury to impose the death penalty, it has to find at least one of several statutorily pre-scribed **aggravating factors.** Automatic appeal to the state supreme court is also provided. The appellate review must consider not only the procedural regularity of the trial but also whether the evidence supports the finding of the aggravating factor and whether the death sentence is disproportionate to the penalty imposed in similar cases.

The Court had little difficulty upholding the new Georgia statute, with only Justices Brennan and Marshall dissenting. Thus, after a hiatus of four years, the death penalty was effectively reinstated. Although Justice Stewart's opinion in *Gregg* makes much of the procedural safeguards required by the Georgia law, one suspects that the marked increase in public support for the death penalty that occurred during the four years after *Furman* had something to do with the Court's decision to uphold Georgia's revised law. In this, as in other areas, the Court seldom strays far from a clear national consensus. Fortunately for the Court, the restraint demonstrated by several of the justices in *Furman* (by deciding the case on fairly narrow grounds) facilitated the reinstatement of the death penalty in *Gregg* four years later without the necessity of overruling a recent precedent.

Is the Death Penalty an Appropriate Punishment for Lesser Crimes than Murder?

Although the Court now recognizes the death penalty, it has refused to allow states to execute criminals convicted of lesser crimes than first-degree murder. In *Coker v. Georgia* (1977), the Court invalidated an attempt to execute a man convicted of rape. Writing for a plurality, Justice White characterized the death sentence for rape as "disproportionate" and "excessive."

Later Burger Court Decisions on the Death Penalty

Later decisions of the Burger Court indicated an increasingly permissive stance toward imposition of capital punishment. For the most part, the Burger Court was unsympathetic to challenges to the legal sufficiency of procedures used to impose the death penalty. For example, in *Lockhart v. McCree* (1986), the Court facilitated the use of capital punishment by ruling that potential jurors could be excluded before trial if their opposition to the death penalty was so intense that it would impair their ability to perform as impartial jurors. One departure from this trend came in the summer of 1986. In *Ford v. Wainwright,* the Supreme Court held that the Eighth Amendment prohibits the execution of a prisoner who is insane. Invoking the "evolving standards of decency" test, the Court asserted that "the intuition that such an execution . . . offends humanity is shared across this Nation." Three years later, though, in *Penny v. Lynaugh* (1989), the Court held that mild mental retardation, in and of itself, is not a sufficient basis to bar the imposition of the death penalty.

Death Penalty Jurisprudence of the Rehnquist Court

In terms of the death penalty, the Rehnquist Court picked up where the Burger Court left off. For example, In *McCleskey v. Kemp* (1987), the Court upheld the death sentence imposed on Warren McCleskey, an African-American defendant who relied on a thorough statistical study in contending that capital punishment in Georgia was infected by pervasive racial discrimination. The Court took the view that, even assuming the statistical validity of the study, McCleskey had not shown that his sentence was the result of racial discrimination.

The Court Rejects Vagueness Challenges to Capital Punishment Statutes

In *Walton v. Arizona* (1990), the Court upheld a state law permitting the trial judge, rather than the jury, to determine the existence of aggravating and **mitigating circumstances.** In this case, the Court also concluded that Arizona's characterization of "heinous, cruel or depraved" conduct as an aggravating factor was sufficiently specific to meet the requirements of the Eighth Amendment.

Similarly, in *Proctor v. California* (1994), the Court upheld California's death penalty statute against the challenge that it was excessively vague. The 8-to-1 decision, with only Justice Blackmun in dissent, came as a major disappointment to the 383 men awaiting execution on California's death row. Many of these inmates would have been able to challenge their sentences had the Supreme Court decided the case differently. The challenge was brought by William Proctor, who was sentenced to death in 1982 for the murder of a woman whom he also robbed and raped. Proctor argued that California law failed to give juries adequate guidance in considering the factors that determine whether a given crime should merit a death sentence. In rejecting Proctor's challenge, the Court, speaking through Justice Kennedy, found that the law had a "common-sense core of meaning that criminal juries should be capable of understanding." (see *Tuilaepa v. California* [1994].)

Victim Impact Evidence

In the late 1980s, growing concern for the rights of crime victims led some states to enact laws permitting the introduction of **victim impact statements** at the penalty phase of capital trials. Such statements related to personal characteristics of murder victims and to the impact of their murders on family members. In *Booth v. Maryland* (1987) and *South Carolina v. Gathers* (1989), the Supreme Court declared that the introduction of such "victim-impact evidence" violated the Eighth Amendment. In a dramatic reversal of this position, a more conservative Court in 1991 held that "the Eighth Amendment erects no *per se* bar" to "the admission of victim impact evidence and prosecutorial argument on that subject . . . " (*Payne v. Tennessee*). While victims' rights advocates praised this decision, civil libertarians and defense attorneys objected sharply to what they perceived as an invitation to infuse excessive emotion into the criminal process. In one of the last opinions he wrote before retiring, Justice Marshall, dissenting, delivered a broadside against the Rehnquist Court's disregard of precedent:

> In dispatching *Booth* and *Gathers* to their graves, today's majority ominously suggests that an even more extensive upheaval of this Court's precedents may be in store. . . . The majority today sends a clear signal that scores of established constitutional liberties are now ripe for reconsideration. . . .

The Federal Death Penalty

In August 1997, Timothy McVeigh was sentenced to death by lethal injection for his role in the bombing of the federal office building in Oklahoma City in 1995. In his federal trial, McVeigh was convicted of twenty-eight counts of murder of a federal law enforcement agent on active duty. Under federal law, executions are carried out in the state where the defendant was sentenced, unless that state has no death penalty, in which case the prisoner is transferred to another state for execution. As of 1999, the federal government had not executed anyone since 1963, but many observers expected the McVeigh conviction to spur the federal government to renew executions.

The Federal Anti-Drug Abuse Act of 1988 allows the death penalty for so-called "drug kingpins" who control "continuing criminal enterprises" whose members intentionally kill or procure others to kill in furtherance of the enterprise. Moreover, the Violent Crime Control and Law Enforcement Act of 1994, better known as the Federal Crime Bill, dramatically increased the number of federal crimes eligible for the death penalty. Capital punishment is now authorized for dozens of federal crimes, including treason, murder of a federal law enforcement official, and kidnapping, carjacking, child abuse, and bank robbery that result in death. It remains to be seen whether the federal courts will permit the death penalty for nonhomicidal crimes. *Coker v. Georgia* (1977) would suggest otherwise.

TO SUMMARIZE:

- The Court has said that the Cruel and Unusual Punishments Clause "must draw its meaning from the evolving standards of decency that mark the progress of a maturing society." Consistent with this perspective, the Court in 1972 in effect invalidated capital punishment as it existed throughout the United States, but left the door open for states to revise their death penalty statutes. In 1976, the Court upheld several such revised statutes, thus effectively reinstating the death penalty.
- Since the late 1970s, the Court has found occasion to set aside particular death sentences, but in general has shown increasing deference to the states in the implementation of capital punishment. An example of this trend is seen in the Court's willingness to allow the use of "victim impact statements" in the sentencing stage of capital trials.

APPEAL AND POSTCONVICTION RELIEF

The federal Constitution makes no mention of a defendant's right to appeal from a criminal conviction, although one could argue that such a right is implicit in the concept of procedural due process. In *McKane v. Durston* (1894), the Supreme Court held that there is no such constitutional right. Given the expansiveness of modern notions of due process, it is likely that the Supreme Court would reconsider *McKane v. Durston* but for the fact that Congress and all fifty state legislatures have created statutory rights of appeal. Indeed, a federal defendant's right of appeal is of fairly ancient vintage, having first been granted by the Judiciary Act of 1789. The so-called **appeal by right** granted by federal and state statutes applies to defendants who are convicted over their pleas of "not guilty." The only situation in which a defendant who pleads guilty retains the right of appeal is where such a provision is made pursuant to a plea bargain. The prosecution is never permitted to appeal from the acquittal of the defendant but may appeal certain pretrial rulings resulting in the dismissal of the case.

The appeal by right is an important means whereby defendants assert constitutional rights alleged to have been violated in their apprehension or the investigation, prosecution, or trial of their case. The appeal by right thus permits appellate courts to perform the important function of **error correction.** Of course, not all errors constitute the basis for reversal on appeal. Only those errors deemed prejudicial to the accused necessitate reversal; other mistakes are referred to as **harmless errors** (see *Chapman v. California* [1967]).

In 1991, the Supreme Court made news when it decided that, under certain circumstances, the use of an involuntary confession as evidence at trial constitutes a harmless error (see *Arizona v. Fulminante,* discussed earlier). Previously, the use of an illegally obtained confession was considered a sufficient basis for reversal of a conviction, regardless of the strength of the other evidence against the accused.

Beyond the right to one appeal, defendants may petition higher courts to review their convictions, but such review is granted at the discretion of the higher court. In the U.S. Supreme Court and most state supreme courts, **discretionary review** involves the issuance of a writ of certiorari. In essence, the writ of certiorari is issued to the lower court, directing it to provide the record in a given case so that the higher court may conduct its review. The use of this type of discretionary review is usually limited to new and important issues of law, especially where the lower appellate courts are in conflict.

Federal Habeas Corpus Review of State Criminal Cases

A state prisoner who has exhausted his or her appeals in the state courts may petition a federal district court for a writ of habeas corpus. The power of federal courts to issue habeas corpus in state cases can be traced to an act of Congress adopted just after the Civil War (see *Ex parte McCardle* [1869], discussed and reprinted in Chapter 1). Rarely used prior to the 1950s, in the modern era, this aspect of federal jurisdiction has played an important role in the development of constitutional law as it relates to the criminal process. In *Brown v. Allen* (1953), the Supreme Court held that state prisoners could readjudicate issues on federal habeas review that had already been addressed in state proceedings. Then in *Fay v. Noia* (1963), the Warren Court further expanded federal habeas corpus by deciding that state prisoners could raise issues in their federal habeas corpus petitions that they failed to raise in state appeals. Moreover, unless it was found that they deliberately abused the writ, there was no limit on the number of habeas corpus petitions that state prisoners could file in federal district courts (see *Sanders v. United States* [1963]).

The Warren Court's decision to expand federal habeas corpus helped fuel the "criminal justice revolution" of the 1960s. Federal district courts could look at and correct the state courts' failures to implement the pronouncements of the High Court in such key areas as search and seizure, confessions, double jeopardy, and the right to counsel. Accordingly, one of the strategies of the Burger and Rehnquist Courts' "counterrevolution" in the criminal process area has been to restrict federal habeas corpus review of state criminal convictions.

Judicial Limitations on Federal Habeas Corpus Review

The first significant limitation on federal habeas corpus came in *Stone v. Powell* (1976). There, the Burger Court decided that state prisoners could not use federal habeas corpus petitions to raise Fourth Amendment issues where they had been provided "a full and fair opportunity" to litigate those issues in the state courts. Subsequently, in *Engle v. Isaac* (1982), the Court refused to allow a state prisoner to use federal habeas corpus to challenge a questionable jury instruction to which he failed to object during trial. Other decisions of the Burger Court chipped away at the Warren Court's expansive interpretations of federal habeas corpus relief (see, for example, *Kuhlmann v. Wilson* [1986] and *Straight v. Wainwright* [1986]).

The Rehnquist Court has continued the trend toward limiting access to federal habeas corpus. In 1991, the Court barred Warren McCleskey, still on death row in Georgia, from filing a second federal habeas corpus petition, holding that he had "abused the writ" (see *McCleskey v. Zant*). In the *McCleskey* case, the Court held that a state need not prove that a petitioner deliberately abandoned a constitutional claim in his or her first habeas corpus petition for the petitioner to be barred from raising the claim in a subsequent petition. The Court thus moved away from the "deliberate abandonment" standard the Warren Court had articulated in *Sanders v. United States* (1963). In another bitter dissent, Justice Marshall blasted the Court for departing from precedent, saying that "whatever 'abuse of the writ' today's decision is designed to avert pales in comparison with the majority's own abuse of the norms that inform the proper judicial function."

In *Keeney v. Tamayo-Reyes* (1992), the Court overturned *Townsend v. Sain* (1963), in which the Warren Court had held that state prisoners had the right to seek federal habeas corpus relief unless they had deliberately bypassed the state courts.

The Supreme Court's decisions in *McCleskey v. Zant* and *Keeney v. Tamayo-Reyes* came at a time when many in Congress were calling for legislative restrictions on federal habeas corpus. Both the Supreme Court and Congress were responding to a widespread perception that state prisoners were being afforded excessive opportunities to challenge their convictions in federal courts. Indeed, some conservative commentators questioned the need for federal postconviction review of state criminal cases altogether. While federal habeas corpus has been subject to abuse by state prisoners, eliminating this aspect of federal jurisdiction altogether would remove some of the pressure that has led to an increased awareness of and appreciation for defendants' rights in the state courts. Indeed, in the *McCleskey* case the Supreme Court expressed a commitment to the continued efficacy of habeas corpus to prevent miscarriages of justice in the state courts.

In 1993, the Supreme Court handed down two decisions restricting federal habeas corpus review of state criminal convictions. In *Herrera v. Collins,* the Court held that a belated claim of innocence does not entitle a state prisoner on death row to a federal district court hearing prior to his execution. In *Brecht v. Abrahamson,* the Court ruled that federal district courts may not overturn state criminal convictions unless the petitioner can show that he or she suffered "actual prejudice" from the errors cited in the habeas corpus petition. Previously, the state carried the burden of proving beyond a reasonable doubt that any constitutional error committed during or prior to trial was "harmless," that is, not prejudicial to the defendant. *Brecht v. Abrahamson* had the effect of shifting the burden of proof from the state to the petitioner in a federal habeas corpus hearing.

Congress Modifies the Federal Habeas Corpus Procedure

On April 24, 1996, President Clinton signed into law the Antiterrorism and Effective Death Penalty Act of 1996. One of the provisions of this statute curtails second habeas corpus petitions by state prisoners who have already filed such petitions in federal court. Under the new statute, any second or subsequent habeas petition must meet a particularly high standard and must pass through a "gatekeeping" function exercised by the U.S. Courts of Appeals. A circuit court must grant a motion giving the inmate permission to file the petition in a district court; denial of this motion is not appealable to the Supreme Court. In *Felker v. Turpin* (1996), an inmate awaiting execution in Georgia challenged the constitutionality of this provision, posing two constitutional objections: (1) that the new law amounted to an unconstitutional "suspension" of the writ of habeas corpus and (2) that the prohibition against Supreme Court review of a circuit court's denial of permission to file a subsequent habeas petition is an unconstitutional interference with the Supreme Court's jurisdiction as defined in Article III of the Constitution.

In a unanimous decision rendered less than one month after the case was argued, the Supreme Court rejected these challenges and upheld the statute. In a "saving construction" of the statute, the Court interpreted the law in such a way as to preserve the right of state prisoners to file habeas petitions directly in the Supreme Court. The Court stated, however, that it would exercise this jurisdiction only in "exceptional circumstances." According to Chief Justice Rehnquist, who spoke for a unanimous bench, the fact that habeas corpus relief remains available by direct petition to the Supreme Court "obviates any claim by petitioner under the Exceptions Clause of Article III, Section 2, of the Constitution." Turning to the argument that Congress had, in effect, improperly suspended the writ of habeas corpus, Rehnquist observed that "[t]he new restrictions on successive petitions constitute a . . . restraint on what is called in habeas corpus practice 'abuse of the writ.' " Noting the evolving body of judicial decisions attempting to limit abuses of habeas corpus, the Chief Justice concluded that "[t]he added restrictions . . . on second habeas petitions are well within the compass of this evolutionary process. . . ."

Interestingly, in *Felker v. Turpin,* the Court managed to sustain what Congress had done while at the same time reaffirming its own statutory and constitutional powers. Note, however, that the provision at issue in *Felker* was but one of several restrictions on habeas corpus petitions embodied in the Antiterrorism Act. Indeed, other challenges to various sections of the law are working their way through the lower federal courts. The Supreme Court will likely address these issues in the near future. The enactment of " habeas corpus reform," fully supported by the Clinton administration, and the Court's refusal to invalidate it, indicates the existence of a clear consensus in the national government that "abuse of the writ" of habeas corpus must be curtailed.

TO SUMMARIZE:

- Although there is no constitutional right of appeal in a criminal case, federal and state statutes provide this right to persons who are convicted after having pleaded not guilty.
- Federal law permits federal courts to grant writs of habeas corpus to review state court convictions after all state appellate remedies have been exhausted. The

Warren Court expanded this form of postconviction relief, but in recent years Congress and the Court have significantly curtailed federal habeas corpus review.

JUVENILE JUSTICE

At the time of the founding of the United States, children were treated essentially as adults for the purposes of criminal justice. It was not uncommon for teenagers to be hanged, flogged, or placed in the public pillory as punishment for their crimes. Toward the end of the nineteenth century, public outcry against such treatment led to the establishment of a separate justice system for juveniles. Reformatories and specialized courts were created to deal with young offenders not as hardened criminals but as misguided youth in need of special care. This special treatment was legally justified by the ***parens patriae*** concept: that the state is responsible for caring for those incapable of caring for themselves. The newly created juvenile courts were usually separate from the regular tribunals; often the judges or referees that presided over these courts did not have formal legal training. There was little procedural regularity or even opportunity for the juvenile offender to confront his or her accusers.

The abuses that came to be associated with **juvenile courts** were addressed by the Supreme Court in the landmark case *In re Gault* (1967). Along with *Mapp v. Ohio, Gideon v. Wainwright,* and *Miranda v. Arizona, Gault* is considered to be one of the "four horsemen" of the Warren Court's revolution in the criminal justice area. In *Gault,* the Court essentially made the juvenile courts adhere to standards of due process, applying most of the basic procedural safeguards enjoyed by adults accused of crimes. Moreover, *Gault* held that juvenile courts must respect the right of counsel, the freedom from compulsory self-incrimination, and the right to confront (cross-examine) hostile witnesses.

For the most part, the Supreme Court has reaffirmed the *Gault* decision (see, for example, *Breed v. Jones* [1975]). In *McKeiver v. Pennsylvania* (1971), however, the Court refused to extend the right to trial by jury to juvenile proceedings. Writing for a plurality, Justice Blackmun concluded that juries are not indispensable "to fair and equitable juvenile proceedings." Thirteen years later, in *Schall v. Martin* (1984), the Court upheld a pretrial detention program for juveniles that might well have been found violative of due process had it applied to adults. Writing for the Court, Justice Rehnquist stressed that "the Constitution does not mandate elimination of all differences in the treatment of juveniles." At this point, it appears likely that the Supreme Court will maintain the requirements imposed in *Gault* and a few subsequent cases. But further expansion of juvenile due process seems unlikely.

Capital Punishment of Juveniles

One of the most difficult issues facing the courts in the area of juvenile justice is whether, and under what circumstances, persons below the age of legal majority (but who are tried as adults in regular criminal courts) should face the death penalty when convicted of capital crimes. In *Eddings v. Oklahoma* (1982), the Supreme Court voted 5 to 4 to vacate the death sentence of a sixteen-year-old boy. In 1988, the Court divided 6 to 3 in ruling that the Constitution forbids execution of juveniles who are fifteen or younger at the time they committed their capital crimes

(*Thompson v. Oklahoma*). One year later, in *Stanford v. Kentucky* (1989), the Court split 5 to 4 in deciding that juveniles sixteen and older at the time of their crimes may be sentenced to death. According to Justice O'Connor's controlling opinion in *Stanford,* "it is sufficiently clear that no national consensus forbids the imposition of capital punishment on 16 or 17-year-old capital murderers." Thus, for the time being, the line appears to be drawn at sixteen years; juveniles who were, at the time of their crimes, sixteen or older may be subject to the death penalty without offending the current Court's interpretation of the Eighth Amendment. This line, of course, is subject to alteration as the membership of the Court and national opinion change.

TO SUMMARIZE:

- Persons under the age of legal majority who engage in criminal conduct are typically within the jurisdiction of specialized juvenile courts.
- Although juvenile courts need not conform to all of the procedural requirements that apply to adult criminal prosecutions (e.g., trial by jury), the Supreme Court has held that they must respect the right of counsel, the freedom from compulsory self-incrimination, and the right to confront hostile witnesses.
- One of the most difficult issues in this area is whether juveniles who are tried as adults should face the death penalty when convicted of capital crimes. The Supreme Court has, in effect, permitted imposition of the death penalty on persons who were over the age of 16 at the time they committed capital crimes.

CONCLUSION

This chapter has summarized the development of constitutional standards in the field of criminal justice. Here, as in much of its First Amendment jurisprudence, the Supreme Court has attempted to balance legitimate interests of public safety and public order with equally legitimate interests in individual liberty and privacy. In seeking to protect the constitutional rights of persons suspected, accused, or convicted of crimes, the Court has often challenged established law enforcement methods. This tendency began in the 1930s and was most pronounced in the areas of search and seizure, police interrogation, and the right to counsel. Sharp criticism resulted from Supreme Court efforts to "police the police" and to upgrade standards of criminal procedure in the courts. Such criticism was particularly strong toward the end of the Warren era in the late 1960s.

Reflecting strong currents of change in public opinion, as well as the impact of the Nixon, Reagan, and Bush appointments, the Supreme Court since the 1970s has been decidedly more sympathetic to law enforcement than was the Warren Court. By refusing to extend or in some cases overturning Warren Court precedents, the Burger and Rehnquist Courts opened themselves to the charge of insensitivity to the rights of individuals. This criticism has been particularly strident with respect to decisions in the area of search and seizure.

The reason the framers of the Bill of Rights imposed constraints on law enforcement was not that the framers were opposed to law and order. Rather, they were deeply distrustful of power; they feared what well-meaning but overzealous officials might do if not constrained by the rule of law. Certainly there was ample historical evidence to support their fears. Consequently, they gave us a Bill of Rights that makes it more difficult for government to investigate, prosecute, and punish crime.

But what we as a society lose in our ability to control crime, we gain in increased liberty and privacy. It is hard to have it both ways, but, of course, most of us would like to! The great challenge to courts, especially the Supreme Court, is to strike a delicate balance between society's need for crime control and our equally strong desires for individual privacy and freedom.

KEY TERMS

ex post facto laws
bills of attainder
habeas corpus
search and seizure
probable cause
reasonable expectation of
   privacy
open fields
warrant requirement
search warrant
neutral and detached
   magistrate
general warrants
confidential or anonymous
   informants
totality of circumstances
knock and announce
exigent circumstances
warrantless search
search incidental to a lawful
   arrest
search based on consent
drug courier profile
hot pursuit
evanescent evidence

emergency searches
automobile search
stop and frisk
pat-down search
reasonable suspicion
investigatory detention
exclusionary rule
supervisory power
silver platter doctrine
good-faith exception
arrest
arrest warrant
probable cause hearing
warrantless arrest
custodial interrogation
subjective voluntariness
Miranda warnings
fruit of the poisonous tree
   doctrine
public safety exception
inevitable discovery
   exception
police deception
harmless error analysis
right to counsel

ineffective representation
mockery of justice test
self-representation
arraignment
bail
pretrial detention
plea bargaining
knowing and intelligent
   waiver
jury trial
fair trial doctrine
change of venue
pretrial publicity
gag orders
closure of pretrial
   proceedings
unanimity rule
reasonable doubt standard
nonunanimous verdicts
peremptory challenge
racially motivated
   peremptory challenges
gender-based peremptory
   challenges

double jeopardy
mistrial
hung jury
forfeiture
cruel and unusual
   punishments
mandatory life sentence
habitual offender
prisoners' rights
punitive isolation
discrete and insular
   minorities
death penalty
evolving standards of
   decency
aggravating factors
mitigating circumstances
victim impact statements
appeal by right
error correction
harmless errors
discretionary review
parens patriae
juvenile courts

FOR FURTHER READING

Amar, Akhil Reed. *The Constitution and Criminal Procedure: First Principles*. New Haven: Yale University Press, 1997.

Baker, Liva. *Miranda: Crime, Law and Politics*. New York: Atheneum Press, 1983.

Bedau, Hugo Adam (ed.). *The Death Penalty in America* (3rd ed.). New York: Oxford University Press, 1982.

Berns, Walter. *For Capital Punishment*. New York: Basic Books, 1979.

Black, Charles, Jr. *Capital Punishment: The Inevitability of Caprice and Mistake*. New York: Norton, 1974.

Dershowitz, Alan M. *The Best Defense*. New York: Random House, 1982.

Eisenstein, James, Roy B. Fleming, and Peter F. Nardulli. *The Contours of Justice: Communities and Their Courts*. Boston: Little, Brown, 1988.

Heumann, Milton. *Plea Bargaining: The Experiences of Prosecutors, Judges and Defense Attorneys.* Chicago: University of Chicago Press, 1978.

Jacob, Herbert. *Law and Politics in the United States.* Boston: Little, Brown, 1986.

Kalven, Harry, and Hans Zeisel. *The American Jury.* Chicago: University of Chicago Press, 1966.

Landynski, Jacob W. *Search and Seizure and the Supreme Court.* Baltimore, Md.: Johns Hopkins University Press, 1978.

Levy, Leonard W. *Against the Law: The Nixon Court and Criminal Justice.* New York: Harper and Row, 1974.

Lewis, Anthony. *Gideon's Trumpet.* New York: Vintage, 1964.

Miller, Leonard G. *Double Jeopardy and the Federal System.* Chicago: University of Chicago Press, 1968.

Packer, Herbert L. *The Limits of the Criminal Sanction.* Stanford, Calif.: Stanford University Press, 1968.

Scheb, John M., and John M. Scheb, II. *Criminal Law and Procedure* (3rd ed.). Belmont, Calif.: West/Wadsworth, 1999.

Scheingold, Stuart A. *The Politics of Law and Order: Street Crime and Public Policy.* New York: Longman, 1984.

Schlesinger, Stephen. *Exclusionary Injustice.* New York: Dekker, 1977.

Sigler, Jay. *Double Jeopardy: The Development of a Legal and Social Policy.* Ithaca, N.Y.: Cornell University Press, 1969.

Stephens, Otis H., Jr. *The Supreme Court and Confessions of Guilt.* Knoxville: University of Tennessee Press, 1973.

Way, H. Frank. *Criminal Justice and the American Constitution.* Belmont, Calif.: Duxbury Press, 1980.

White, Welsh. *The Death Penalty in the Eighties.* Ann Arbor: University of Michigan Press, 1988.

Zalman, Marvin, and Larry J. Siegel. *Criminal Procedure* (2nd ed.). Belmont, Calif.: West/Wadsworth, 1997.

INTERNET RESOURCES

Name of Resource	Description	URL (circa 1998)
Bureau of Justice Statistics	Agency with the U.S. Department of Justice responsible for collecting and disseminating data dealing with crime and the justice system	http://www.ojp.usdoj.gov/bjs/
Federal Bureau of Investigation (FBI)	The premier federal law enforcement agency	http://www.fbi.gov/
Federal Bureau of Prisons (BOP)	Federal agency responsible for running the federal government's prison system	http://www.bop.gov/
U.S. Sentencing Commission	The federal agency responsible for promulgating federal sentencing guidelines	http://www.ussc.gov/
Court TV	Good source for news on crime, courts, and the legal system	http://www.courttv.com/

Case

OLMSTEAD V. UNITED STATES

277 U.S. 438; 48 S.Ct. 564; 72 L.Ed. 944 (1928)
Vote: 5–4

In this decision, which has since been overturned, the Court considers the admissibility of evidence obtained through wiretapping conducted without prior judicial authorization.

Mr. Chief Justice Taft delivered the opinion of the Court.

These cases are here by certiorari from the Circuit Court of Appeals for the Ninth Circuit. They were granted with the distinct limitation that the hearing should be confined to the single question whether the use of evidence of private telephone conversations between the defendants and others, intercepted by means of wire tapping, amounted to a violation of the 4th and 5th Amendments.

The petitioners were convicted in the District Court for the Western District of Washington of a conspiracy to violate the National Prohibition Act by unlawfully possessing, transporting and importing intoxicating liquors and maintaining nuisances, and by selling intoxicating liquors. Seventy-two others in addition to the petitioners were indicted. Some were not apprehended, some were acquitted, and others pleaded guilty.

The evidence in the records discloses a conspiracy of amazing magnitude to import, possess and sell liquor unlawfully. It involved the employment of not less than fifty persons, of two seagoing vessels for the transportation of liquor to British Columbia, of smaller vessels for coastwise transportation to the state of Washington, the purchase and use of a ranch beyond the suburban limits of Seattle, with a large underground cache for storage and a number of smaller caches in that city, the maintenance of a central office manned with operators, the employment of executives, salesmen, deliverymen, dispatchers, scouts, bookkeepers, collectors and an attorney. In a bad month sales amounted to $176,000; the aggregate for a year must have exceeded two millions of dollars.

Olmstead was the leading conspirator and the general manager of the business. He made a contribution of $10,000 to the capital; eleven others contributed $1,000 each. The profits were divided one-half to Olmstead and the remainder to the other eleven. Of the several offices in Seattle the chief one was in a large office building. In this there were three telephones on three different lines. There were telephones in an office of the manager in his own home, at the homes of his associates, and at other places in the city. Communication was had frequently with Vancouver, British Columbia. Times were fixed for the deliveries of the "stuff," to places along Puget Sound near Seattle, and from there the liquor was removed and deposited in the caches already referred to. One of the chief men was always on duty at the main office to receive orders by the telephones and to direct their filing by a corps of men stationed in another room—the "bull pen." The call numbers of the telephones were given to those known to be likely customers. At times the sales amounted to 200 cases of liquor per day.

The information which led to the discovery of the conspiracy and its nature and extent was largely obtained by intercepting messages on the telephones of the conspirators by four Federal prohibition officers. Small wires were inserted along the ordinary telephone wires from the residences of four of the petitioners and those leading from the chief office. The insertions were made without trespass upon any property of the defendants. They were made in the basement of the large office building. The taps from house lines were made in the streets near the houses.

The gathering of evidence continued for many months. Conversations of the conspirators, of which refreshing stenographic notes were currently made, were testified to by the government witnesses. They revealed the large business transactions of the partners and their subordinates. Men at the wires heard the orders given for liquor by customers, and the acceptances; they became auditors of the conversations between the partners. All this disclosed the conspiracy charged in the indictment. Many of the intercepted conversations were not merely reports but parts of the criminal acts. The evidence also disclosed the difficulties to which the conspirators were subjected, the reported news of the capture of vessels, the arrest of their men and the seizure of cases of liquor in garages and other places. It showed the dealing by Olmstead, the chief conspirator, with members of the Seattle police, the messages to them which secured the release of arrested members of the conspiracy, and also direct promises to officers of payments as soon as opportunity offered. . . .

The well-known historical purpose of the 4th Amendment, directed against general warrants and writs of assistance, was to prevent the use of governmental force to search a man's house, his person, his papers, and his effects, and to prevent their seizure against his will. . . .

The Amendment itself shows that the search is to be of material things—the person, the house, his papers or his effects. The description of the warrant necessary to make the proceeding lawful is that it must specify the place to be searched and the person or things to be seized. . . .

. . . The 4th Amendment may have proper application to a sealed letter in the mail because of the constitutional provision for the Post Office Department and the relations between the government and those who pay to secure protection of their sealed letters. . . . It is plainly within the words of the Amendment to say that the unlawful rifling by a government agent of a sealed letter is a search and seizure of the sender's papers or effects. The letter is a paper, an effect, and in the custody of a government that forbids carriage except under its protection.

The United States takes no such care of telegraph or telephone messages as of mailed sealed letters. The Amendment does not forbid what was done here. There was no searching. There was no seizure. The evidence was secured by the use of the sense of hearing and that only. There was no entry of the house or offices of the defendants.

By the invention of the telephone fifty years ago, and its application for the purpose of extending communications, one can talk with another at a far distant place.

The language of the Amendment can not be extended and expanded to include telephone wires reaching to the whole world from the defendant's house or office. The intervening wires are not part of his house or office, any more than are the highways along which they are stretched. . . .

"The 4th Amendment is to be construed in the light of what was deemed an unreasonable search and seizure when it was adopted and in a manner which will conserve public interests as well as the interests and rights of individual citizens." . . .

Congress may, of course, protect the secrecy of telephone messages by making them, when intercepted, inadmissible in evidence in Federal criminal trials, by direct legislation, and thus depart from the common law of evidence. But the courts may not adopt such a policy by attributing an enlarged and unusual meaning to the 4th Amendment. The reasonable view is that one who installs in his house a telephone instrument with connecting wires intends to project his voice to those quite outside, and that the wires beyond his house and messages while passing over them are not within the protection of the 4th Amendment. Here those who intercepted the projected voices were not in the house of either party to the conversation. . . .

We think, therefore, that the wire tapping here disclosed did not amount to a search or seizure within the meaning of the 4th Amendment. . . .

Mr. Justice Holmes [dissenting]. . . .

Mr. Justice Brandeis, dissenting:

. . . The government makes no attempt to defend the methods employed by its officers. Indeed, it concedes that if wire-tapping can be deemed a search and seizure within the 4th Amendment, such wire-tapping as was practiced in the case at bar was an unreasonable search and seizure, and that the evidence thus obtained was inadmissible. But it relies on the language of the Amendment; and it claims that the protection given thereby cannot properly be held to include a telephone conversation. . . .

Time and again, this court, in giving effect to the principle underlying the 4th Amendment, has refused to place an unduly literal construction upon it. . . .

The protection guaranteed by the Amendments is much broader in scope. The makers of our Constitution undertook to secure conditions favorable to the pursuit of happiness. They recognized the significance of man's spiritual nature, of his feelings and of his intellect. They knew that only a part of the pain, pleasure and satisfactions of life are to be found in material things. They sought to protect Americans in their beliefs, their thoughts, their emotions and their sensations. They conferred, as against the government, the right to be let alone—the most comprehensive of rights and the right most valued by civilized men. To protect that right, every unjustifiable intrusion by the government upon the privacy of the individual, whatever the means employed, must be deemed a violation of the 4th Amendment. . . .

. . .[T]he defendants' objections to the evidence obtained by a wiretapping must, in my opinion, be sustained. It is, of course, immaterial where the physical connection with the telephone wires leading into the defendants' premises was made. And it is also immaterial that the intrusion was in aid of law enforcement. Experience should teach us to be most on our guard to protect liberty when the government's purposes are beneficent. Men born to freedom are naturally alert to repel invasion of their liberty by evil-minded rulers. The greatest dangers to liberty lurk in insidious encroachment by men of zeal, well-meaning, but without understanding. . . .

Decency, security, and liberty alike demand that government officials shall be subjected to the same rules of conduct that are commands to the citizen. In a government of laws, existence of the government will be imperilled if it fails to observe the law scrupulously. Our government is the potent, the omnipresent, teacher. For good or for ill, it teaches the whole people by its example. Crime is contagious. If the government becomes a law-breaker, it breeds contempt for law; it invites every man to become a law unto himself; it invites anarchy. To declare that in the administration of the criminal law the end justifies the means—to declare that the government may commit crimes in order to secure the conviction of a private criminal—would bring terrible retribution. Against that pernicious doctrine this court should resolutely set its face.

Mr. Justice Butler, dissenting. . . .

Mr. Justice Stone, dissenting. . . .

Case

KATZ V. UNITED STATES

389 U.S. 347; 88 S.Ct. 507; 19 L.Ed. 2d. 576 (1967)
Vote: 7–1

In this case the Court overturns its earlier ruling in Olmstead v. United States *and adopts a broad view of the scope of Fourth Amendment protection.*

Mr. Justice Stewart delivered the opinion of the Court.

The petitioner was convicted in the District Court for the Southern District of California under an eight-count indictment charging him with transmitting wagering information by telephone from Los Angeles to Miami and Boston in violation of a federal statute. At trial the Government was permitted, over the petitioner's objection, to introduce evidence of the petitioner's end of telephone conversations, overheard by FBI agents who had attached an electronic listening and recording device to the outside of the public telephone booth from which he had placed his calls. In affirming his conviction, the Court of Appeals rejected the contention that the recordings had been obtained in violation of the Fourth Amendment, because "[t]here was no physical entrance into the area occupied by [the petitioner]." We granted certiorari in order to consider the constitutional questions thus presented. . . .

. . . [T]he parties have attached great significance to the characterization of the telephone booth from which the petitioner placed his calls. The petitioner has strenuously argued that the booth was a "constitutionally protected area." The Government has maintained with equal vigor that it was not. But this effort to decide whether or not a given "area," viewed in the abstract, is "constitutionally protected" deflects attention from the problem presented by this case. For the Fourth Amendment protects people, not places. What a person knowingly exposes to the public, even in his own home or office, is not a subject of Fourth Amendment protection. But what he seeks to preserve as private, even in an area accessible to the public, may be constitutionally protected.

The Government stresses the fact that the telephone booth from which the petitioner made his calls was constructed partly of glass, so that he was as visible after he entered it as he would have been if he had remained out-side. But what he sought to exclude when he entered the booth was not the intruding eye—it was the uninvited ear. He did not shed his right to do so simply because he made his calls from a place where he might be seen. No less than an individual in a business office, in a friend's apartment, or in a taxicab, a person in a telephone booth may rely upon the protection of the Fourth Amendment. One who occupies it, shuts the door behind him, and pays the toll that permits him to place a call is surely entitled to assume that the words he utters into the mouthpiece will not be broadcast to the world. To read the Constitution more narrowly is to ignore the vital role that the public telephone has come to play in private communication.

The Government contends, however, that the activities of its agents in this case should not be tested by Fourth Amendment requirements, for the surveillance technique they employed involved no physical penetration of the telephone booth from which the petitioner placed his calls. It is true that the absence of such penetration was at one time thought to foreclose further Fourth Amendment inquiry, . . . for that Amendment was thought to limit only searches and seizures of tangible property. But "[t]he premise that property interests control the right of the Government to search and seize has been discredited." Thus, although a closely divided Court supposed in *Olmstead* that surveillance without any trespass and without the seizure of any material object fell outside the ambit of the Constitution, we have since departed from the narrow view on which that decision rested. Indeed, we have expressly held that the Fourth Amendment governs not only the seizure of tangible items, but extends as well to the recording of oral statements overheard without any "technical trespass under . . . local property law." Once this much is acknowledged, and once it is recognized that the Fourth Amendment protects people—and not simply "areas"—against unreasonable searches and seizures it becomes clear that the reach of the Amendment cannot turn upon the presence or absence of a physical intrusion into any given enclosure.

We conclude that the underpinnings of . . . [*Olmstead v. United States*] . . . have been so eroded by our subsequent decisions that the "trespass" doctrine there enunciated can no longer be regarded as controlling. The Government's activities in electronically listening to and recording the petitioner's words violated the privacy upon which he justifiably relied while using the telephone booth and thus constituted a "search and seizure" within the meaning of the Fourth Amendment. The fact that the electronic device employed to achieve that end did not happen to penetrate the wall of the booth can have no constitutional significance.

The question remaining for decision, then, is whether the search and seizure conducted in this case complied with constitutional standards. In that regard, the Government's position is that its agents acted in an entirely defensible manner. They did not begin their electronic surveillance until investigation of the petitioner's activities had established a strong probability that he was using the telephone in question to transmit gambling information to persons in other States, in violation of federal law. Moreover, the surveillance was limited, both in scope and in duration, to the specific purpose of establishing the contents of the petitioner's unlawful telephone communications. The agents confined their surveillance to the brief periods during which he used the telephone booth, and they took great care to overhear only the conversations of the petitioner himself.

Accepting this account of the Government's actions as accurate, it is clear that this surveillance was so narrowly circumscribed that a duly authorized magistrate, properly notified of the need for such investigation, specifically informed of the basis on which it was to proceed, and clearly apprised of the precise intrusion it would entail, could constitutionally have authorized, with appropriate safeguards, the very limited search and seizure that the Government asserts in fact took place. . . .

. . . The government agents here ignored "the procedure of antecedent justification . . . that is central to the Fourth Amendment," . . . a procedure that we hold to be a constitutional precondition of the kind of electronic surveillance involved in this case. Because the surveillance here failed to meet that condition, and because it led to the petitioner's conviction, the judgment must be reversed. . . .

Mr. Justice Marshall took no part in the consideration or decision of this case.

Mr. Justice Douglas, with whom **Mr. Justice Brennan** joins, concurring. . . .

Mr. Justice Harlan, concurring.

. . . As the Court's opinion states, "the Fourth Amendment protects people, not places." The question, however, is what protection it affords to those people. Generally, as here, the answer to that question requires reference to a "place." My understanding of the rule that has emerged from prior decisions is that there is a twofold requirement, first that a person have exhibited an actual (subjective) expectation of privacy and, second, that the expectation be one that society is prepared to recognize as "reasonable." Thus a man's home is, for most purposes, a place where he expects privacy, but objects, activities, or statements that he exposes to the "plain view" of outsiders are not "protected" because no intention to keep them to himself has been exhibited. On the other hand, conversations in the open would not be protected against being overheard, for the expectation of privacy under the circumstances would be unreasonable.

The critical fact in this case is that "[o]ne who occupies it [a telephone booth], shuts the door behind him, and pays the toll that permits him to place a call is surely entitled to assume" that his conversation is not being intercepted. The point is not that the booth is "accessible to the public" at other times, but that it is a temporarily private place whose momentary occupants' expectations of freedom from intrusion are recognized as reasonable. . . .

Mr. Justice White, concurring. . . .

Mr. Justice Black, dissenting.

My basic objection is twofold: (1) I do not believe that the words of the Amendment will bear the meaning given them by today's decision, and (2) I do not believe that it is the proper role of this Court to rewrite the Amendment in order "to bring it into harmony with the times" and thus reach a result that many people believe to be desirable.

While I realize that an argument based on the meaning of words lacks the scope, and no doubt the appeal, of broad policy discussions and philosophical discourses on such nebulous subjects as privacy, for me the language of the Amendment is the crucial place to look in construing a written document such as our Constitution. . . .

The first clause [of the Fourth Amendment] protects "persons, houses, papers, and effects, against unreasonable searches and seizures. . . ." These words connote the idea of tangible things with size, form, and weight, things capable of being searched, seized, or both. The second clause of the Amendment still further established its Framers' purpose to limit its protection to tangible things by providing that no warrants shall issue but those "particularly describing the place to be searched, and the persons or things to be seized." A conversation overheard by eavesdropping, whether by plain snooping or wire-tapping, is not tangible and, under the normally accepted meanings of the words, can neither be searched nor seized. In addition the language of the second clause indicates that the Amendment refers not only to something tangible so it can be seized but to something already in existence so it can be described. Yet the Court's interpretation would have the Amendment apply to overhearing future conversations which by their very nature are nonexistent until they take place. How can one "describe" a future conversation, and, if one cannot, how can a magistrate issue a warrant to eavesdrop one in the future? It is argued that information showing what is expected to be said is sufficient to limit the boundaries of what later can be admitted into evidence; but does such general information really meet the specific language of the Amendment which says "particularly describing"? Rather than using language in a completely artificial way, I must conclude that the Fourth Amendment simply does not apply to eavesdropping. . . .

Since I see no way in which the words of the Fourth Amendment can be construed to apply to eavesdropping, that closes the matter for me. In interpreting the Bill of Rights, I willingly go as far as a liberal construction of the language takes me, but I simply cannot in good conscience give a meaning to words which they have never before been thought to have and which they certainly do not have in common ordinary usage. I will not distort the words of the Amendment in order to "keep the Constitution up to date" or "to bring it into harmony with the time." It was never meant that this Court have such power, which in effect would make us a continuously functioning constitutional convention.

Case

WEEKS V. UNITED STATES
232 U.S. 383; 34 S.Ct. 341; 58 L.Ed. 652 (1914)
Vote: 9–0

In this case the Court first establishes the Fourth Amendment exclusionary rule, although the ruling applies only to criminal trials in federal courts.

Mr. Justice Day delivered the opinion of the Court:

An indictment was returned against the plaintiff in error, defendant below, and herein so designated, in the District Court of the United States for the Western District of Missouri, containing nine counts. The seventh count, upon which a conviction was had, charged the use of the mails for the purpose of transporting certain coupons or tickets representing chances or shares in a lottery . . . in violation of the Criminal Code. Sentence of fine and imprisonment was imposed. This writ of error is to review that judgment.

The defendant was arrested by a police officer, so far as the record shows, without warrant, at the Union Station in Kansas City, Missouri, where he was employed by an express company. Other police officers had gone to the house of the defendant, and being told by a neighbor where the key was kept, found it and entered the house. They searched the defendant's room and took possession of various papers and articles found there, which were afterwards turned over to the United States marshal. Later in the same day police officers returned with the marshal, who thought he might find additional evidence, and, being admitted by someone in the house, probably a boarder, in response to a rap, the marshal searched the defendant's room and carried away certain letters and envelopes found in the drawer of a chiffonier. Neither the marshal nor the police officers had a search warrant.

The defendant filed in the cause before time for trial . . . [a] . . . Petition to Return Private Papers, Books, and Other Property.

Upon consideration of the petition the court entered an order directing the return of such property as was not pertinent to the charge against the defendant, but denied the petition as to pertinent matter, reserving the right to pass upon the pertinency at a later time. In obedience to the order the district attorney returned part of the property taken, and retained the remainder, concluding a list of the latter with the statement that, "all of which last above described property is to be used in evidence in the trial of the above-entitled cause, and pertains to the alleged sale of lottery tickets of the company above named."

After the jury had been sworn and before any evidence had been given, the defendant again urged his petition for the return of his property, which was denied by the court. Upon the introduction of such papers during the trial, the defendant objected on the ground that the papers had been obtained without a search warrant, and by breaking into his home, in violation of the 4th and 5th Amendments to the Constitution of the United States, which objection was overruled by the court. Among the papers retained and put in evidence were a number of lottery tickets and statements with reference to the lottery, taken at the first visit of the police to the defendant's room, and a number of letters written to the defendant in respect to the lottery, taken by the marshal upon his search of defendant's room.

The defendant assigns error, among other things, in the court's refusal to grant his petition for the return of his property, and in permitting the papers to be used at the trial.

It is thus apparent that the question presented involves the determination of the duty of the court with reference to the motion made by the defendant for the return to certain letters, as well as other papers, taken from his room by the United States marshal, who, without authority of process, if any such could have been illegally issued, visited the room of the defendant for the declared purpose of obtaining additional testimony to support the charge against the accused, and, having gained admission to the house, took from the drawer of a chiffonier there found certain letters written to the defendant, tending to show his guilt. These letters were placed in the control of the district attorney, and were subsequently produced by him and offered in evidence against the accused at the trial. The defendant contends that such appropriation of his private correspondence was in violation of rights secured to him by the 4th and 5th Amendments to the Constitution of the United States. We shall deal with the 4th Amendment. . . .

The history of this Amendment is given with particularity in the opinion of Mr. Justice Bradley, speaking for the court in *Boyd v. United States* [1884]. . . . As was there shown, it took its origin in the determination of the framers of the Amendments to the Federal Constitution to provide for that instrument a Bill of Rights, securing to the American people, among other things, those safeguards which had grown up in England to protect the people from unreasonable searches and seizures, such as were permitted under the general warrants issued under authority of the government, by which there had been invasions of the home and privacy of the citizens, and the seizure of their private papers in support of charges, real or imaginary, made against them. Such practices had also received sanction under warrants and seizures under the so-called writs of assistance, issued

in the American colonies. Resistance to these practices had established the principle which was enacted into the fundamental law in the 4th Amendment, that a man's house was his castle, and not to be invaded by any general authority to search and seize his goods and papers.

The effect of the 4th Amendment is to put the courts of the United States and Federal officials, in the exercise of their power and authority, under limitations and restraints as to the exercise of such power and authority, and to forever secure the people, their persons, houses, papers, and effects, against all unreasonable searches and seizures under the guise of law. This protection reaches all alike, whether accused of crime or not, and the duty of giving to it force and effect is obligatory upon all intrusted under our Federal system with the enforcement of the laws. The tendency of those who execute the criminal laws of the country to obtain conviction by means of unlawful seizures and enforced confessions, the latter often obtained after subjecting accused persons to unwarranted practices destructive of rights secured by the Federal Constitution, should find no sanction in the judgments of the courts, which are charged at all times with the support of the Constitution, and to which people of all conditions have a right to appeal for the maintenance of such fundamental rights.

What, then, is the present case? Before answering that inquiry specifically, it may be well by a process of exclusion to state what it is not. It is not an assertion of the right on the part of the government, always recognized under English and American law, to search the person of the accused when legally arrested, to discover and seize the fruits or evidences of crime. Nor is it the case of testimony offered at a trial where the court is asked to stop and consider the illegal means by which proofs, otherwise competent, were obtained—of which we shall have occasion to treat later in this opinion. Nor is it the case of burglar's tools or other proofs of guilt found upon his arrest within the control of the accused.

The case in the aspect in which we are dealing with it involves the right of the court in a criminal prosecution to retain for the purposes of evidence the letters and correspondence of the accused, seized in his house in his absence and without his authority, by a United States marshal holding no warrant for his arrest and none for the search of his premises. If letters and private documents can thus be seized and held and used in evidence against a citizen accused of an offense, the protection of the 4th Amendment, declaring his right to be secure against such searches and seizures, is of no value, and, so far as those thus placed are concerned, might as well be stricken from the Constitution. The efforts of the courts and their officials to bring the guilty to punishment, praise-worthy as they are, are not to be aided by the sacrifice of those great principles established by years of endeavor and suffering which have resulted in their embodiment in the fundamental law of the land. The United States marshal could only have invaded the house of the accused when armed with a warrant issued as required by the Constitution, upon sworn information, and describing with reasonable particularity the thing for which the search was to be made. Instead, he acted without sanction of law, doubtless prompted by the desire to bring further proof to the aid of the government, and under color of his office undertook to make a seizure of private papers in direct violation of the constitutional prohibition against such action. Under such circumstances, without sworn information and particular description, not even an order of court would

have justified such procedure; much less was it within the authority of the United States marshal to thus invade the house and privacy of the accused.

We therefore reach the conclusion that the letters in question were taken from the house of the accused by an official of the United States, acting under color of his office, in direct violation of the constitutional rights of the defendant; that having made a seasonable application for their return, which was heard and passed upon by the court, there was involved in the order refusing the application of denial of the constitutional rights of the accused, and that the court should have restored these letters to the accused. In holding them and permitting their use upon the trial, we think prejudicial error was committed. . . .

It results that the judgment of the court below must be reversed, and the case remanded for further proceedings in accordance with this opinion.

Reversed.

Case

Mapp v. Ohio

367 U.S. 643; 81 S.Ct. 1684; 6 L.Ed. 2d. 1081 (1961)
Vote: 6–3

In this case the Court extends the Fourth Amendment exclusionary rule to state criminal trials.

Mr. Justice Clark delivered the opinion of the Court.

Appellant stands convicted of knowingly having had in her possession and under her control certain lewd and lascivious books, pictures, and photographs in violation of . . . Ohio's Revised Code. . . . [T]he Supreme Court of Ohio found that her conviction was valid though "based primarily upon the introduction in evidence of lewd and lascivious books and pictures unlawfully seized during an unlawful search of defendant's home. . . ."

On May 23, 1957, three Cleveland police officers arrived at appellant's residence in that city pursuant to information that "a person [was] hiding out in the home, who was wanted for questioning in connection with a recent bombing, and that there was a large amount of policy [gambling] paraphernalia being hidden in the home." Miss Mapp and her daughter by a former marriage lived on the top floor of the two-family dwelling. Upon their arrival at that house, the officers knocked on the door and demanded entrance but appellant, after telephoning

her attorney, refused to admit them without a search warrant. They advised their headquarters of the situation and undertook a surveillance of the house.

The officers again sought entrance some three hours later when four or more additional officers arrived on the scene. When Miss Mapp did not come to the door immediately at least one of the several doors to the house was forcibly opened and the policemen gained admittance. Meanwhile Miss Mapp's attorney arrived, but the officers, having secured their own entry, and continuing in their defiance of the law, would permit him neither to see Miss Mapp nor to enter the house. It appears that Miss Mapp was halfway down the stairs from the upper floor to the front door when the officers, in this high-handed manner, broke into the hall. She demanded to see the search warrant. A paper, claimed to be a warrant, was held up by one of the officers. She grabbed the "warrant" and placed it in her bosom. A struggle ensued in which the officers recovered the piece of paper and as a result of which they handcuffed appellant because she had been "belligerent" in resisting their official rescue of the "warrant" from her person. Running roughshod over appellant, a policeman "grabbed" her, "twisted [her] hand," and she "yelled [and] pleaded with him" because "it was hurting." Appellant, in handcuffs, was then forcibly taken upstairs to her bedroom where the officers searched a dresser, a chest of drawers, a closet and some suitcases. They also looked into a photo album and through personal papers belonging to the appellant. The search spread to the rest of the second floor including the child's bedroom, the living room, the kitchen and a dinette. The basement of the building and a trunk found therein were also searched. The obscene materials for possession of which she was ultimately convicted were discovered in the course of that widespread search.

At the trial no search warrant was produced by the prosecution, nor was the failure to produce one explained or accounted for. At best, "There is, in the record, considerable doubt as to whether there ever was any warrant for the search of defendant's home." . . .

The State says that even if the search were made without authority, or otherwise unreasonably, it is not prevented from using the unconstitutionally seized evidence at trial, citing *Wolf v. Colorado* [1949], in which this Court did indeed hold "that in a prosecution in a State court for a State crime the Fourteenth Amendment does not forbid the admission of evidence obtained by an unreasonable search and seizure." . . . On this appeal, of which we have noted probable jurisdiction, . . . it is urged once again that we review that holding. . . .

[I]n the year 1914, in the *Weeks* Case, this Court "for the first time" held that, "in a federal prosecution the Fourth Amendment barred the use of evidence secured through an illegal search and seizure." . . . This Court has ever since required of federal law officers a strict adherence to that command which this Court has held to be a clear, specific, and constitutionally required—even if judicially implied—deterrent safeguard without insistence upon which the Fourth Amendment would have been reduced to "a form of words." . . . It meant, quite simply, that "conviction by means of unlawful seizures and enforced confessions . . . should find no sanction in the judgments of the courts. . . ." . . .

There are in the cases of this Court some passing references to the *Weeks* rule as being one of evidence. But the plain and unequivocal language of *Weeks*—and its later paraphrase in *Wolf*—to the effect that the *Weeks* rule is of constitutional origin, remains entirely undisturbed. In *Byars v. United States* . . . (1927), a unanimous Court declared that "the doctrine [cannot] . . . be tolerated under our constitutional system, that evidences of crime discovered by a federal officer in making a search without lawful warrant may be used against the victim of the unlawful search where a timely challenge has been interposed." . . .

In 1949, 35 years after *Weeks* was announced, this Court, in *Wolf v. Colorado* for the first time discussed the effect of the Fourth Amendment upon the States through the operation of the Due Process Clause of the Fourteenth Amendment. It said: "[W]e have no hesitation in saying that were a State affirmatively to sanction such police incursion into privacy it would run counter to the guaranty of the Fourteenth Amendment." . . . Nevertheless, after declaring that the "security of one's privacy against arbitrary intrusion by the police" is "implicit in 'the concept of ordered liberty' and as such enforceable against the States through the Due Process Clause," and announcing that it "stoutly adhere[d]" to the *Weeks* decision, the Court decided that the *Weeks* exclusionary rule would not then be imposed upon the States as "an essential ingredient of the right." . . . The Court's reasons for not considering essential to the right to privacy, as a curb imposed upon the States by the Due Process Clause, that which decades before had been posited as part and parcel of the Fourth Amendment's limitation upon federal encroachment of individual privacy, were bottomed on factual considerations.

While they are not basically relevant to a decision that the exclusionary rule is an essential ingredient of the Fourth Amendment as the right it embodies is vouchsafed against the States by the Due Process Clause, we will consider the current validity of the factual grounds upon which *Wolf* was based.

The Court in *Wolf* first stated that "[t]he contrariety of views of the States" on the adoption of the exclusionary rule of *Weeks* was "particularly impressive"; . . . and, in this connection that it could not "brush aside the experience of States which deem the incidence of such conduct by the police too slight to call for a deterrent remedy . . . by overriding the [States'] relevant rules of evidence." . . . While in 1949, prior to the *Wolf* Case, almost two-thirds of the States were opposed to the use of the exclusionary rule, now, despite the *Wolf* Case, more than half of those since passing upon it, by their own legislative or judicial decision, have wholly or partly adopted or adhered to the *Weeks* rule. . . . Significantly, among those now following the rule is California, which, according to its highest court, was "compelled to reach that conclusion because other remedies have completely failed to secure compliance with the constitutional provisions. . . ." . . . The experience of California that such other remedies have been worthless and futile is buttressed by the experience of other States. The obvious futility of relegating the Fourth Amendment to the protection of other remedies has, moreover, been recognized by this Court since *Wolf*. . . .

Likewise, time has set its face against what *Wolf* called the "weighty testimony" of *People v. Defore* . . .

(1926). There Justice (then Judge) Cardozo, rejecting adoption of the *Weeks* exclusionary rule in New York, had said that "[t]he Federal rule as it stands is either too strict or too lax." . . . However, the force of that reasoning has been largely vitiated by later decisions of this Court. These include the recent discarding of the "silver platter" doctrine which allowed federal judicial use of evidence seized in violation of the Constitution by state agents; . . . the relaxation of the formerly strict requirements as to standing to challenge the use of evidence, thus seized, so that now the procedure of exclusion, "ultimately referable to constitutional safeguards," is available to anyone even "legitimately on [the] premises" unlawfully searched; . . . and, finally, the formulation of a method to prevent state use of evidence unconstitutionally seized by federal agents. . . . Because there can be no fixed formula, we are admittedly met with "recurring questions of the reasonableness of searches," but less is not to be expected when dealing with a Constitution, and, at any rate, "[r]easonableness is in the first instance for the [trial court] . . . to determine." . . .

It, therefore, plainly appears that the factual considerations supporting the failure of the *Wolf* Court to include the *Weeks* exclusionary rule when it recognized the enforceability of the right to privacy against the States in 1949, while not basically relevant to the constitutional consideration, could not, in any analysis, now be deemed controlling. . . .

Since the Fourth Amendment's right of privacy has been declared enforceable against the States through the Due Process Clause of the Fourteenth, it is enforceable against them by the same sanction of exclusion as is used against the Federal Government. Were it otherwise, then just as without the *Weeks* rule the assurance against unreasonable federal searches and seizures would be "a form of words," valueless and undeserving of mention in a perpetual charter of inestimable human liberties, so too, without that rule the freedom from state invasions of privacy would be so ephemeral and so neatly severed from its conceptual nexus with the freedom from all brutish means of coercing evidence as not to merit this Court's high regard as a freedom "implicit in the concept of ordered liberty." At the time that the Court held in *Wolf* that the Amendment was applicable to the States through the Due Process Clause, the cases of this Court, as we have seen, had steadfastly held that as to federal officers the Fourth Amendment included the exclusion of the evidence seized in violation of its provisions. Even *Wolf* "stoutly adhered" to that proposition. The right to privacy, when conceded operatively

enforceable against the States, was not susceptible of destruction by avulsion of the sanction upon which its protection and enjoyment had always been deemed dependent under the *Boyd*, *Weeks* and *Silverthorne* cases. Therefore, in extending the substantive protections of due process to all constitutionally unreasonable searches—state or federal—it was logically and constitutionally necessary that the exclusion doctrine—an essential part of the right to privacy—be also insisted upon as an essential ingredient of the right newly recognized by the *Wolf* case. In short, the admission of the new constitutional right by *Wolf* could not consistently tolerate denial of its most important constitutional privilege, namely, the exclusion of the evidence which an accused had been forced to give by reason of the unlawful seizure. To hold otherwise is to grant the right but in reality to withhold its privilege and enjoyment. Only last year the Court itself recognized that the purpose of the exclusionary rule "is to deter—to compel respect for the constitutional guaranty in the only effectively available way—by removing the incentive to disregard it." . . .

Moreover, our holding that the exclusionary rule is an essential part of both the Fourth and Fourteenth Amendments is not only the logical dictate of prior cases, but it also makes very good sense. There is no war between the Constitution and common sense. Presently, a federal prosecutor may make no use of evidence illegally seized, but a State's attorney across the street may, although he supposedly is operating under the enforceable prohibitions of the same Amendment. Thus the State, by admitting evidence unlawfully seized, serves to encourage disobedience to the Federal Constitution which it is bound to uphold. Moreover, . . . "[t]he very essence of a healthy federalism depends upon the avoidance of needless conflict between state and federal courts." . . .

Federal-state cooperation in the solution of crime under constitutional standards will be promoted, if only by recognition of their now mutual obligation to respect the same fundamental criteria in their approaches. "However much in a particular case insistence upon such rules may appear as a technicality that inures to the benefit of a guilty person, the history of the criminal law proves that tolerance of shortcut methods in law enforcement impairs its enduring effectiveness." . . . Denying shortcuts to only one of two cooperating law enforcement agencies tends naturally to breed legitimate suspicion of "working arrangements" whose results are equally tainted. . . .

There are those who say, as did Justice (then Judge) Cardozo, that under our constitutional exclusionary doctrine "[t]he criminal is to go free because the constable has blundered." . . . In some cases this will undoubtedly be the result. But, . . . "there is another consideration—the imperative of judicial integrity." . . . The criminal goes free, if he must, but it is the law that sets him free. Nothing can destroy a government more quickly than its failure to observe its own laws, or worse, its disregard of the charter of its own existence. As Mr. Justice Brandeis, dissenting, said in *Olmstead v. United States*: "Our Government is the potent, the omnipresent teacher. For good or for ill, it teaches the whole people by its example. . . . If the Government becomes a lawbreaker, it breeds contempt for law; it invites every man to become a law unto himself; it invites anarchy." . . . Nor can it lightly be assumed that, as a practical matter, adoption of the exclusionary rule fetters law enforcement. Only last year this Court expressly considered that contention and found that "pragmatic evidence of a sort" to the contrary was not wanting. . . .

The ignoble shortcut to conviction left open to the State tends to destroy the entire system of constitutional restraints on which the liberties of the people rest. Having once recognized that the right to privacy embodied in the Fourth Amendment is enforceable against the States, and that the right to be secure against rude invasions of privacy by state officers is, therefore, constitutional in origin, we can no longer permit that right to remain an empty promise. Because it is enforceable in the same manner and to like effect as other basic rights secured by the Due Process Clause, we can no longer permit it to be revocable at the whim of any police officer who, in the name of law enforcement itself, chooses to suspend its enjoyment. Our decision, founded on reason and truth, gives to the individual no more than that which the Constitution guarantees him, to the police officer no less than that to which honest law enforcement is entitled, and, to the courts, that judicial integrity so necessary in the true administration of justice.

The judgment of the Supreme Court of Ohio is reversed and the case remanded for further proceedings not inconsistent with this opinion.

Reversed and remanded.

Mr. Justice Black, concurring.

I am still not persuaded that the Fourth Amendment, standing alone, would be enough to bar the introduction into evidence against an accused of papers and effects seized from him in violation of its commands. For the Fourth Amendment does not itself contain any provision expressly precluding the use of such evidence, and I am

extremely doubtful that such a provision could properly be inferred from nothing more than the basic command against unreasonable searches and seizures. Reflection on the problem, however, in the light of cases coming before the Court since *Wolf*, has led me to conclude that when the Fourth Amendment's ban against unreasonable searches and seizures is considered together with the Fifth Amendment's ban against compelled self-incrimination, a constitutional basis emerges which not only justifies but actually requires the exclusionary rule. . . .

Mr. Justice Douglas, concurring. . . .

Mr. Justice Harlan, whom Mr. Justice Frankfurter and Mr. Justice Whittaker join, dissenting.

In overruling the *Wolf* case the Court, in my opinion, has forgotten the sense of judicial restraint which, with due regard for *stare decisis*, is one element that should enter into deciding whether a past decision of this Court should be overruled. Apart from that I also believe that the *Wolf* rule represents sounder Constitutional doctrine than the new rule which now replaces it.

From the Court's statement of the case one would gather that the central, if not controlling, issue on this appeal is whether illegally state-seized evidence is Constitutionally admissible in a state prosecution, an issue which would of course face us with the need for re-examining *Wolf*. However, such is not the situation. For, although that question was indeed raised here and below among appellant's subordinate points, the new and pivotal issue brought to the Court by this appeal is whether section 2905.34 of the Ohio Revised Code making criminal the mere knowing possession or control of obscene material, and under which appellant has been convicted, is consistent with the rights of free thought and expression assured against state action by the Fourteenth Amendment. That was the principal issue which was decided by the Ohio Supreme Court, which was tendered by appellant's Jurisdictional Statement, and which was briefed and argued in this Court.

In this posture of things, I think it fair to say that five members of this Court have simply "reached out" to overrule *Wolf*. With all respect for the views of the majority, and recognizing that *stare decisis* carries different weight in Constitutional adjudication than it does in nonconstitutional decision, I can perceive no justification for regarding this case as an appropriate occasion for re-examining *Wolf*. . . .

I would not impose upon the States this federal exclusionary remedy. The reasons given by the majority for now suddenly turning its back on *Wolf* seem to me notably unconvincing.

First, it is said that "the factual grounds upon which *Wolf* was based" have since changed, in that more States now follow the *Weeks* exclusionary rule than was so at the time *Wolf* was decided. While that is true, a recent survey indicates that at present one-half of the States still adhere to the common-law non-exclusionary rule, and one, Maryland, retains the rule as to felonies. . . . But in any case surely all this is beside the point, as the majority itself indeed seems to recognize. Our concern here, as it was in *Wolf*, is not with the desirability of that rule but only with the question whether the States are constitutionally free to follow it or not as they may themselves determine, and the relevance of the disparity of views among the States on this point lies simply in the fact that the judgment involved is a debatable one. Moreover, the very fact on which the majority relies, instead of lending support to what is now

being done, points away from the need of replacing voluntary state action with federal compulsion.

The preservation of a proper balance between state and federal responsibility in the administration of criminal justice demands patience on the part of those who might like to see things move faster among the States in this respect. . . .

Memorandum of *Mr. Justice Stewart.*

Agreeing fully with Part I of Mr. Justice Harlan's dissenting opinion, I express no view as to the merits of the constitutional issue which the Court today decides. I would, however, reverse the judgment in this case, because I am persuaded that the provision . . . upon which the petitioner's conviction was based is, in the words of Mr. Justice Harlan, not "consistent with the rights of free thought and expression assured against state action by the Fourteenth Amendment."

Case

UNITED STATES V. LEON

468 U.S. 897; 104 S.Ct. 3405; 82 L.Ed. 2d. 677 (1984)
Vote: 6–3

In this case the Court recognizes a limited good-faith exception to the Fourth Amendment exclusionary rule.

Justice White delivered the opinion of the Court.

This case presents the question whether the Fourth Amendment exclusionary rule should be modified so as not to bar the use in the prosecution's case-in-chief of evidence obtained by officers acting in reasonable reliance on a search warrant issued by a detached and neutral magistrate but ultimately found to be unsupported by probable cause. To resolve this question, we must consider once again the tension between the sometimes competing goals of, on the one hand, deterring official misconduct and removing inducements to unreasonable invasions of privacy and, on the other, establishing procedures under which criminal defendants are "acquitted or convicted on the basis of all the evidence which exposes the truth." . . .

In August 1981, a confidential informant of unproven reliability informed an officer of the Burbank Police Department that two persons known to him as "Armando" and "Patsy" were selling large quantities of cocaine and

methaqualone from their residence at 620 Price Drive in Burbank, Cal. The informant also indicated that he had witnessed a sale of methaqualone by "Patsy" at the residence approximately five months earlier and had observed at that time a shoebox containing a large amount of cash that belonged to "Patsy." He further declared that "Armando" and "Patsy" generally kept only small quantities of drugs at their residence and stored the remainder at another location in Burbank.

On the basis of this information, the Burbank police initiated an extensive investigation focusing first on the Price Drive residence and later on two other residences as well. Cars parked at the Price Drive residence were determined to belong to respondents Armando Sanchez, who had previously been arrested for possession of marihuana, and Patsy Stewart, who had no criminal record. During the course of the investigation, officers observed an automobile belonging to respondent Ricardo Del Castillo, who had previously been arrested for possession of 50 pounds of marihuana, arrive at the Price residence. The driver of that car entered the house, exited shortly thereafter carrying a small paper sack, and drove away. A check of Del Castillo's probation records led the officers to respondent Alberto Leon, whose telephone number Del Castillo had listed as his employer's. Leon had been arrested in 1980 on drug charges, and a companion had informed the police at that time that Leon was heavily involved in the importation of drugs into this country. Before the current investigation began, the Burbank officers had learned that an informant had told a Glendale police officer that Leon stored a large quantity of methaqualone at his residence in Glendale. During the course of this investigation, the Burbank officers learned that Leon was living at 716 South Sunset Canyon in Burbank.

Subsequently, the officers observed several persons, at least one of whom had prior drug involvement, arriving at the Price Drive residence and leaving with small packages; observed a variety of other material activity at the two residences as well as at a condominium at 7902 Via Magdalena; and witnessed a variety of relevant activity involving respondents' automobiles. The officers also observed respondents Sanchez and Stewart board separate flights for Miami. The pair later returned to Los Angeles together, consented to a search of their luggage that revealed only a small amount of marihuana, and left the airport. Based on these and other observations summarized in the affidavit, Officer Cyril Rombach of the Burbank Police Department, an experienced and well-trained narcotics investigator, prepared an application for a warrant to search 620 Price Drive, 716 South Sunset Canyon, 7902 Via Magdalena, and automobiles registered to each of the respondents for an extensive list of items believed to be related to respondent's drug-trafficking activities. Officer Rombach's extensive application was reviewed by several Deputy District Attorneys.

A facially valid search warrant was issued in September 1981 by a State Superior Court Judge. The ensuing searches produced large quantities of drugs at the Via Magdalena and Sunset Canyon addresses and a small quantity at the Price Drive residence. Other evidence was discovered at each of the residences and in Stewart's and Del Castillo's automobiles. . . .

The respondents then filed motions to suppress the evidence seized pursuant to the warrant. The District Court . . . concluded that the affidavit was insufficient to establish probable cause, but did not suppress all of the evidence as to all of the respondents because none of the respondents had standing to challenge all of the searches. In response to a request from the Government, the court made clear that Officer Rombach had acted in good faith, but it rejected the Government's suggestion that the Fourth Amendment exclusionary rule should not apply where evidence is seized in reasonable, good-faith reliance on a search warrant. . . .

The Fourth Amendment contains no provision expressly precluding the use of evidence obtained in violation of its commands, and an examination of its origin and purposes makes clear that the use of fruits of a past unlawful search or seizure "work[s] no new Fourth Amendment wrong." . . . The wrong condemned by the Amendment is "fully accomplished" by the unlawful search or seizure itself, . . . and the exclusionary rule is neither intended nor able to "cure the invasion of the defendant's rights which he has already suffered." . . . The rule thus operates as "a judicially created remedy designed to safeguard Fourth Amendment rights generally through its deterrent effect, rather than a personal constitutional right of the person aggrieved." . . .

Whether the exclusionary sanction is appropriately imposed in a particular case, our decisions make clear, is "an issue separate from the question whether the Fourth Amendment rights of the party seeking to invoke the rule were violated by police conduct." . . . Only the former question is currently before us, and it must be resolved by weighing the costs and benefits of preventing the use in the prosecution's case-in-chief of inherently trustworthy tangible evidence obtained in reliance on a search warrant issued by a detached and neutral magistrate that ultimately is found to be defective.

The substantial social costs exacted by the exclusionary rule for the vindication of Fourth Amendment rights have long been a source of concern. "Our cases have consistently recognized that unbending application of the exclusionary sanction to enforce ideals of government rectitude would impede unacceptably the truth-finding functions of judge and jury." . . . An objectionable collateral consequence of this interference with the criminal justice system's truth-finding function is that some guilty defendants may go free or receive reduced sentences as a result of favorable plea bargains. Particularly when law enforcement officers have acted in objective good faith or their transgressions have been minor, the magnitude of the benefit conferred on such guilty defendants offends basic concepts of the criminal justice system. . . . Indiscriminate application of the exclusionary rule, therefore, may well "generat[e] disrespect for the law and the administration of justice." . . . Accordingly, "[a]s with any remedial device, the application of the rule has been restricted to those areas where its remedial objectives are thought most efficaciously served." . . .

. . . The Court has, to be sure, not seriously questioned, "in the absence of a more efficacious sanction, the continued application of the rule to suppress evidence from the [prosecution's] case where a Fourth Amendment violation has been substantial and deliberate. . . ." . . . Nevertheless, the balancing approach that has evolved in various contexts—including criminal trial—"forcefully suggest[s] that the exclusionary rule be more generally modified to permit the introduction of evidence obtained in the reasonable good-faith belief that a search or a seizure was in accord with the Fourth Amendment." . . .

As cases considering the use of unlawfully obtained evidence in criminal trials themselves make clear, it does not follow from the emphasis on the exclusionary rule's deterrent value that "anything which deters illegal searches is thereby commanded by the Fourth Amendment." . . . In determining whether persons aggrieved solely by the introduction of damaging evidence unlawfully obtained from their co-conspirators or co-defendants could seek suppression, for example, we found that the additional benefits of such an extension of the exclusionary rule would not outweigh its costs. . . . Standing to invoke the rule has thus been limited to cases in which the prosecution seeks to use the fruits of an illegal search or seizure against the victim of police misconduct. . . .

Because a search warrant "provides the detached scrutiny of a neutral magistrate, which is a more reliable safeguard against improper searches than the hurried judgment of a law enforcement officer 'engaged in the often competitive enterprise of ferreting out crime,' " . . . we have expressed a strong preference for warrants and declared that "in a doubtful or marginal case a search under a warrant may be sustainable where without one it would fall." . . . Reasonable minds frequently may differ on the question whether a particular affidavit establishes probable cause, and we have thus concluded that the preference for warrants is most appropriately effectuated by according "great deference" to a magistrate's determination. . . .

Deference to the magistrate, however, is not boundless. It is clear, first, that the deference accorded to a magistrate's finding of probable cause does not preclude inquiry into the knowing or reckless falsity of the affidavit on which that determination was based. . . . Second, the courts must also insist that the magistrate purport to "perform his 'neutral and detached' function and not serve merely as a rubber stamp for the police." . . .

Third, reviewing courts will not defer to a warrant based on an affidavit that does not "provide the magistrate with a substantial basis for determining the existence of probable cause." . . . Even if the warrant application was supported by more than a "bare bones" affidavit, a reviewing court may properly conclude that,

notwithstanding the deference that magistrates deserve, the warrant was invalid because the magistrate's probable-cause determination reflected an improper analysis of the totality of the circumstances, . . . or because the form of the warrant was improper in some respect.

Only in the first of these three situations, however, has the Court set forth a rationale for suppressing evidence obtained pursuant to a search warrant; in the other areas, it has simply excluded such evidence without considering whether Fourth Amendment interests will be advanced. To the extent that proponents of exclusion rely on its behavioral effects on judges and magistrates in these areas, their reliance is misplaced. First, the exclusionary rule is designed to deter police misconduct rather than to punish the errors of judges and magistrates. Second, there exists no evidence suggesting that judges and magistrates are inclined to ignore or subvert the Fourth Amendment or that lawlessness among those actors requires application of the extreme sanction of exclusion.

Third, and most important, we discern no basis, and are offered none, for believing that exclusion of evidence seized pursuant to a warrant will have a significant deterrent effect on the issuing judge or magistrate. . . . Judges and magistrates are not adjuncts to the law enforcement team; as neutral judicial officers, they have no stake in the outcome of particular criminal prosecutions. The threat of exclusion thus cannot be expected significantly to deter them. Imposition of the exclusionary sanction is not necessary meaningfully to inform judicial officers of their errors, and we cannot conclude that admitting evidence obtained pursuant to a warrant while at the same time declaring that the warrant was somehow defective will in any way reduce judicial officers' professional incentives to comply with the Fourth Amendment, encourage them to repeat their mistakes, or lead to the granting of all colorable warrant requests.

If exclusion of evidence obtained pursuant to a subsequently invalidated warrant is to have any deterrent effect, therefore, it must alter the behavior of individual law enforcement officers or the policies of their departments. . . .

We have frequently questioned whether the exclusionary rule can have any deterrent effect when the offending officers acted in the objectively reasonable belief that their conduct did not violate the Fourth Amendment. "No empirical researcher, proponent or opponent of the rule, has yet been able to establish with any assurance whether the rule has a deterrent effect. . . ." . . . But even assuming that the rule effectively deters some police misconduct and provides incentives for the law enforcement profession as a whole to conduct itself in accord with the Fourth Amendment, it cannot be expected, and should not be applied, to deter objectively reasonable law enforcement activity. . . .

We conclude that the marginal or nonexistent benefits produced by suppressing evidence obtained in objectively reasonable reliance on a subsequently invalidated search warrant cannot justify the substantial costs of exclusion. . . .

When the principles we have enunciated today are applied to the facts of this case, it is apparent that the judgment of the Court of Appeals cannot stand. The Court of Appeals applied the prevailing legal standards to Officer Rombach's warrant application and concluded that the application could not support the magistrate's probable-cause determination. In so doing, the court clearly informed the magistrate that he had erred in issuing the challenged warrant. This aspect of the court's judgment is not under attack in this proceeding.

Having determined that the warrant should not have issued, the Court of Appeals understandably declined to adopt a modification of the Fourth Amendment exclusionary rule that this court had not previously sanctioned. Although the modification finds strong support in our previous cases, the Court of Appeals' commendable self-restraint is not to be criticized. We have now reexamined the purposes of the exclusionary rule and the propriety of its application in cases where officers have relied on a subsequently invalidated search warrant. Our conclusion is that the rule's purposes will only rarely be served by applying it in such circumstances. . . .

Accordingly, the judgment of the Court of Appeals is reversed.

Justice Blackmun, concurring. . . .

Justice Brennan, with whom *Justice Marshall* joins, dissenting.

Ten years ago in *United States v. Calandra* . . . (1974), I expressed the fear that the Court's decision "may signal that a majority of my colleagues have positioned themselves to reopen the door [to evidence secured by official lawlessness] still further and abandon altogether the exclusionary rule in search-and-seizure cases." . . . Since then, in case after case, I have witnessed the Court's gradual but determined strangulation of the rule. It now appears that the Court's victory over the Fourth Amendment is complete. . . .

The Court seeks to justify this result on the ground that the "costs" of adhering to the exclusionary rule in cases like those before us exceed the "benefits." But the language of deterrence and of cost/benefit analysis, if used indiscriminately, can have a narcotic effect. It creates an illusion of technical precision and ineluctability. It suggests that not only constitutional principle but also empirical data supports the majority's result. When the Court's analysis is examined carefully, however, it is clear that we have not been treated to an honest assessment of the merits of the exclusionary rule, but have instead been drawn into a curious world where the "costs" of excluding illegally obtained evidence loom to exaggerated heights and where the "benefits" of such exclusion are made to disappear with a mere wave of the hand.

The majority ignores the fundamental constitutional importance of what is at stake here. While the machinery of law enforcement and indeed the nature of crime itself have changed dramatically since the Fourth Amendment became part of the Nation's fundamental law in 1791, what the Framers understood then remains true today—that the task of combating crime and convicting the guilty will in every era seem of such critical and pressing concern that we may be lured by the temptations of expediency into forsaking our commitment to protecting individual liberty and privacy. It was for that very reason that the Framers of the Bill of Rights insisted that law enforcement efforts be permanently and unambiguously restricted in order to preserve personal freedoms. In the constitutional scheme they ordained, the sometimes unpopular task of ensuring that the government's enforcement efforts remain within the strict boundaries fixed by the Fourth Amendment was entrusted to the courts. . . . If those independent tribunals lose their resolve, however, as the Court has done today, and give way to the seductive call of expediency, the vital guarantees of the Fourth Amendment are reduced to nothing more than a "form of words." . . .

A proper understanding of the broad purposes sought to be served by the Fourth Amendment demonstrates that the principles embodied in the exclusionary rule rest upon a far firmer constitutional foundation than the shifting sands of the Court's deterrence rationale. But even if I were to accept the Court's chosen method of analyzing the question posed by these cases, I would still conclude that the Court's decision cannot be justified. . . .

At bottom, the Court's decision turns on the proposition that the exclusionary rule is merely a "judicially created remedy designed to safeguard Fourth Amendment rights generally through its deterrent effect, rather than a personal constitutional right." . . . The germ of that idea is found in *Wolf v. Colorado,* . . . and although I had thought that such a narrow conception of the rule had been forever put to rest by our decision in *Mapp v. Ohio,* . . . it has been revived by the present Court and reaches full flower with today's decision. The essence of this view, as expressed initially in the *Calandra* opinion and as reiterated today, is that the sole "purpose of the Fourth Amendment is to prevent unreasonable governmental intrusions into the privacy of one's person, house, papers, or effects. The wrong condemned is the unjustified governmental invasion of these areas of an individual's life. That wrong . . . is *fully* accomplished by the original search without probable cause." . . . This reading of the Amendment implies that its proscriptions are directed solely at those government agents, who may actually invade an individual's constitutionally protected privacy. The courts are not subject to any direct constitutional duty to exclude illegally obtained evidence, because the question of the admissibility of such evidence is not addressed by the Amendment. This view of the scope of the Amendment relegates the judiciary to the periphery. Because the only constitutionally cognizable injury has already been "fully accomplished" by the police by the time a case comes before the courts, the Constitution is not itself violated if the judge decides to admit the tainted evidence. Indeed, the most the judge *can* do is wring his hands and hope that perhaps by excluding such evidence he can deter future transgressions by the police.

Such a reading appears plausible, because, as critics of the exclusionary rule never tire of repeating, the Fourth Amendment makes no express provision of the exclusion of evidence secured in violation of its commands. A short answer to this claim, of course, is that many of the Constitution's most vital imperatives are stated in general terms and the task of giving meaning to these precepts is therefore left to subsequent judicial decisionmaking in the context of concrete cases. The nature of our Constitution, as Chief Justice Marshall long ago explained, "requires that only its great outlines should be marked, its important objects designated, and the minor ingredients which compose those objects be deduced from the nature of the objects themselves." . . .

A more direct answer may be supplied by recognizing that the Amendment, like other provisions of the Bill of Rights, restrains the power of the government as a whole; it does not specify only a particular agency and exempt all others. The judiciary is responsible, no less than the executive, for ensuring that constitutional rights are respected. . . .

. . . It is difficult to give any meaning at all to the limitations imposed by the Amendment if they are read to proscribe only certain conduct by the police but to allow other agents of the same government to take advantage of evidence secured by the police in violation of its requirements. The Amendment therefore must be read to condemn not only the initial unconstitutional invasion of privacy—which is done, after all, for the purpose of securing evidence—but also the subsequent use of any evidence so obtained.

The Court evades this principle by drawing an artificial line between the constitutional rights and responsibilities that are engaged by actions of the police and those that are engaged when a defendant appears before the courts. According to the Court, the substantive protections of the Fourth Amendment are wholly exhausted at the moment when police unlawfully invade an individual's privacy and thus no substantive force remains to those protections at the time of trial when the government seeks to use evidence obtained by the police.

I submit that such a crabbed reading of the Fourth Amendment casts aside the teaching of those Justices who first formulated the exclusionary rule, and rests ultimately on an impoverished understanding of judicial responsibility in our constitutional scheme. For my part, "[t]he right of the people to be secure in their persons, houses, papers and effects, against unreasonable searches and seizures" comprises a personal right to exclude all evidence secured by means of unreasonable searches and seizures. The right to be free from the initial invasion of privacy and the right of exclusion are coordinate components of the central embracing right to be free from unreasonable searches and seizures. . . .

Justice Stevens, dissenting. . . .

Case

Miranda v. Arizona

384 U.S. 436; 86 S.Ct. 1602; 16 L.Ed. 2d. 694 (1966)
Vote: 5–4

In one of the most important criminal justice decisions of the Warren era, the Court imposes procedural safeguards on custodial police interrogations.

Mr. Chief Justice Warren delivered the opinion of the Court.

The cases before us raise questions which go to the roots of our concepts of American criminal jurisprudence: the restraints society must observe consistent with the Federal Constitution in prosecuting individuals for crime. More specifically, we deal with the admissibility of statements obtained from an individual who is subjected to custodial police interrogation and the necessity for procedures which assure that the individual is accorded his privilege under the Fifth Amendment to the Constitution not to be compelled to incriminate himself.

We dealt with certain phases of this problem recently in *Escobedo v. Illinois* . . . (1964). We start here, as we did in *Escobedo,* with the premise that our holding is not an innovation in our jurisprudence, but is an application of principles long recognized and applied in other settings. We have undertaken a thorough re-examination of the *Escobedo* decision and the principles it announced, and we reaffirm it. That case was but an explication of basic rights that are enshrined in our Constitution—that "No person . . . shall be compelled in any criminal case to be a witness against himself," and that "the accused shall . . . have the Assistance of Counsel"—rights which were put in jeopardy in that case through official overbearing. These precious rights were fixed in our Constitution only after centuries of persecution and struggle. And in the words of Chief Justice Marshall, they were secured "for ages to come, and . . . designed to approach immortality as nearly as human institutions can approach it."
. . .

Our holding will be spelled out with some specificity in the pages which follow but briefly stated it is this: the prosecution may not use statements, whether exculpatory or inculpatory, stemming from custodial interrogation of the defendant unless it demonstrates the use of procedural safeguards effective to secure the privilege against self-incrimination. By custodial interrogation, we mean questioning initiated by law enforcement officers after a person has been taken into custody or otherwise deprived of his freedom of action in any significant way. As for the procedural safeguards to be employed, unless other fully effective means are devised to inform accused persons of their right of silence and to assure a continuous opportunity to exercise it, the following measures are required. Prior to any questioning, the person must be warned that he has a right to remain silent, that any statement he does make may be used as evidence against him, and that he has a right to the presence of an attorney, either retained or appointed. The defendant may waive effectuation of these rights, provided the waiver is made voluntarily, knowingly and intelligently. If, however, he indicates in any manner and at any stage of the process that he wishes to consult with an attorney before speaking there can be no questioning. Likewise, if the individual is alone and indicates in any manner that he does not wish to be interrogated, the police may not question him. The mere fact that he may have answered some questions or volunteered some statements on his own does not deprive him of the right to refrain from answering any further inquiries until he has consulted with an attorney and thereafter consents to be questioned.

The constitutional issue we decide . . . is the admissibility of statements obtained from a defendant questioned while in custody or otherwise deprived of his freedom of action in any significant way. In each, the defendant was questioned by police officers, detectives, or a prosecuting attorney in a room in which he was cut off from the outside world. In none of these cases was the defendant given a full and effective warning of his rights at the outset of the interrogation process. In all the cases, the questioning elicited oral admissions, and in three of them, signed statements as well which were admitted at their trials. They all thus share salient features—*incommunicado* interrogation of individuals in a police-dominated atmosphere, resulting in self-incriminating statements without full warnings of constitutional rights.

An understanding of the nature and setting of this in-custody interrogation is essential to our decisions today. The difficulty in depicting what transpires at such interrogations stems from the fact that in this country they have largely taken place *incommunicado*. From extensive factual studies undertaken in the early 1930's, including the famous Wickersham Report to Congress by a Presidential Commission, it is clear that police violence and the "third degree" flourished at that time. In a series of cases decided by this Court long after these studies, the police resorted to physical brutality—beating, hanging, whipping—and to sustained and protracted questioning *incommunicado* in order to extort confessions. The Commission on Civil Rights in 1961 found much evidence to indicate that "some policemen still resort to physical force to obtain confessions." The use of physical brutality and violence is not, unfortunately, relegated to the past or to any part of the country. Only recently in Kings County, New York, the police brutally beat, kicked and placed lighted cigarette butts on the back of a potential witness under interrogation for the purpose of securing a statement incriminating a third party. . . .

The examples given above are undoubtedly the exception now, but they are sufficiently widespread to be the object of concern. Unless a proper limitation upon custodial interrogation is achieved—such as these decisions will advance—there can be no assurance that practices of this nature will be eradicated in the foreseeable future.

Again we stress that the modern practice of in-custody interrogation is psychologically rather than physically oriented. Interrogation still takes place in privacy. Privacy results in secrecy and this in turn results in a gap in our knowledge as to what in fact goes on in the interrogation rooms. A valuable source of information about present police practices, however, may be found in various police manuals and texts which document procedures employed with success in the past, and which recommended various other effective tactics. These texts are used by law enforcement agencies themselves as guides. It should be noted that these texts professedly present the most enlightened and effective means presently used to obtain statements through custodial interrogation. By considering these texts and other data, it is possible to describe procedures observed and noted around the country.

Even without employing brutality, the "third degree" or the specific stratagems described above, the very fact of custodial interrogation exacts a heavy toll on individual liberty and trades on the weakness of individuals.

In the cases before us today, given this background, we concern ourselves primarily with this interrogation atmosphere and the evils it can bring.

In these cases, we might not find the defendants' statements to have been involuntary in traditional terms. Our concern for adequate safeguards to protect precious Fifth Amendment rights is, of course, not lessened in the slightest. In each of the cases, the defendant was thrust into an unfamiliar atmosphere and run through menacing police interrogation procedures. The potentiality for compulsion is forcefully apparent, for example, in *Miranda*, where the indigent Mexican defendant was a seriously disturbed individual with pronounced sexual fantasies. . . .

It is obvious that such an interrogation environment is created for no purpose other than to subjugate the individual to the will of his examiner. This atmosphere carries its own badge of intimidation. . . . The current practice of *incommunicado* interrogation is at odds with one of our Nation's most cherished principles—that the individual may not be compelled to incriminate himself. Unless adequate protective devices are employed to dispel the compulsion inherent in custodial surroundings, no statement obtained from the defendant can truly be the product of his free choice.

From the foregoing, we can readily perceive an intimate connection between the privilege against self-incrimination and police custodial questioning. It is fitting to turn to history and precedent underlying the Self-Incrimination Clause to determine its applicability in this situation.

We sometimes forget how long it has taken to establish the privilege against self-incrimination, the sources from which it came and the fervor with which it was defended. Its roots go back into ancient times.

As a "noble principle often transcends its origins," the privilege has come rightfully to be recognized in part as an individual's substantive right, a "right to a private enclave where he may lead a private life. That right is the hallmark of our democracy." . . . We have recently noted that the privilege against self-incrimination—the essential mainstay of our adversary system—is founded on a complex of values. . . . All these policies point to one overriding thought: the constitutional foundation underlying the privilege is the respect a government—state or federal—must accord to the dignity and integrity of its citizens.

We are satisfied that all the principles embodied in the privilege apply to informal compulsion exerted by law-enforcement officers during in-custody questioning. An individual swept from familiar surroundings into police custody, surrounded by antagonistic forces, and subjected to the techniques of persuasion described above cannot be otherwise than under compulsion to speak. As a practical matter, the compulsion to speak in the isolated setting of the police station may well be greater than in courts or other official investigations, where there are often impartial observers to guard against intimidation or trickery.

The presence of counsel, in all the cases before us today, would be the adequate protective device necessary to make the process of police interrogation conform to the dictates of the privilege. His presence would insure that statements made in the government-established atmosphere are not the product of compulsion.

It is impossible for us to foresee the potential alternatives for protecting the privilege which might be devised by Congress or the States in the exercise of their creative rulemaking capacities. Therefore we cannot say that the Constitution necessarily requires adherence to any particular solution for the inherent compulsions of the interrogation process as it is presently conducted. Our decision in no way creates a constitutional straitjacket which will handicap sound efforts at reform, nor is it intended to have this effect. We encourage Congress and the States to continue their laudable search for increasingly effective ways of protecting the rights of the individual while promoting efficient enforcement of our criminal laws.

A recurrent argument made in these cases is that society's need for interrogation outweighs the privilege. This argument is not unfamiliar to this Court. . . .

In announcing these principles, we are not unmindful of the burdens which law enforcement officials must bear, often under trying circumstances. We also fully recognize the obligation of all citizens to aid in enforcing the criminal laws. This Court, while protecting individual rights, has always given ample latitude to law enforcement agencies in the legitimate exercise of their duties. The limit we have placed on the interrogation process should not constitute an undue interference with a proper system of law enforcement. As we have noted, our decision does not in any way preclude police from carrying out their traditional investigatory functions. Although confessions may play an important role in some convictions, the cases before us present graphic examples of the overstatement of the "need" for confessions.

Therefore, in accordance with the foregoing, the judgment of the Supreme Court of Arizona . . . [is] reversed. . . .

Mr. Justice Harlan, whom **Mr. Justice Stewart** and **Mr. Justice White** join, dissenting. . . .

Mr. Justice White, with whom **Mr. Justice Harlan** and **Mr. Justice Stewart** join, dissenting.

. . . The obvious underpinning of the Court's decision is a deep-seated distrust of all confessions. As the Court declares that the accused may not be interrogated without counsel present, absent a waiver of the right to counsel, and as the Court all but admonishes the lawyer to advise the accused to remain silent, the result adds up to a judicial judgment that evidence from the accused should not be used against him in any way, whether compelled or not. This is the not so subtle overtone of the opinion—that it is inherently wrong for the police to gather evidence from the accused himself. And this is precisely the nub of this dissent. I see nothing wrong or immoral, and certainly nothing unconstitutional, in the police's asking a suspect whom they have reasonable cause to arrest whether or not he killed his wife or in confronting him with the evidence on which the arrest was based, at least where he has been plainly advised that he may remain completely silent. . . .

The rule announced today will measurably weaken the ability of the criminal law to perform these tasks. It is a deliberate calculus to prevent interrogations, to reduce the incidence of confessions and pleas of guilty and to increase the number of trials. . . .

In some unknown number of cases the Court's rule will return a killer, a rapist or other criminal to the streets and to the environment which produced him, to repeat his crime whenever it pleases him. As a consequence, there will not be a gain, but a loss, in human dignity. The real concern is not the unfortunate consequences of this new decision on the criminal law as an abstract, disembodied series of authoritative proscriptions, but the impact on those who rely on the public authority for protection and who without it can only engage in violent self-help with guns, knives and the help of their neighbors similarly inclined. There is, of course, a saving factor: the next victims are uncertain, unnamed and unrepresented in this case.

Nor can this decision do other than have a corrosive effect on the criminal law as an effective device to prevent crime. A major component in its effectiveness in this regard is its swift and sure enforcement. The easier it is to get away with rape and murder, the less the deterrent effect on those who are inclined to attempt it. This is still good common sense. If it were not, we should posthaste liquidate the whole law enforcement establishment as a useless, misguided effort to control human conduct.

And what about the accused who has confessed or would confess in response to simple, noncoercive questioning and whose guilt could not otherwise be proved?

Is it so clear that release is the best thing for him in every case? Has it so unquestionably been resolved that in each and every case it would be better for him not to confess and to return to his environment with no attempt whatsoever to help him? I think not. It may well be that in many cases it will be no less than a callous disregard for his own welfare as well as for the interests of his next victim.

Much of the trouble with the Court's new rule is that it will operate indiscriminately in all criminal cases, regardless of the severity of the crime or the circumstances involved. It applies to every defendant, whether the professional criminal or one committing a crime of momentary passion who is not part and parcel of organized crime. It will slow down the investigation and the apprehension of confederates in those cases where time is of the essence, such as kidnapping, those involving the national security, and some of those involving organized crime. In the latter context the lawyer who arrives may also be the lawyer for the defendant's colleagues and can be relied upon to insure that no breach of the organization's security takes place even though the accused may feel that the best thing he can do is to cooperate.

At the same time, the Court's *per se* approach may not be justified on the ground that it provides a "bright line" permitting the authorities to judge in advance whether interrogation may safely be pursued without jeopardizing the admissibility of any information obtained as a consequence. Nor can it be claimed that judicial time and effort, assuming that is a relevant consideration, will be conserved because of the ease of application of the new rule. Today's decision leaves open such questions as whether the accused was in custody, whether his statements were spontaneous or the product of interrogation, whether the accused has effectively waived his rights, and whether nontestimonial evidence introduced at trial is the fruit of statements made during a prohibited interrogation, all of which are certain to prove productive of uncertainty during investigation and litigation during prosecution. For all these reasons, if further restrictions on police interrogation are desirable at this time, a more flexible approach makes much more sense than the Court's constitutional straitjacket which forecloses more discriminating treatment by legislative or rule-making pronouncements. . . .

Mr. Justice Clark, dissenting. . . .

Case

NEW YORK V. QUARLES

467 U.S. 649; 104 S.Ct. 2626; 81 L.Ed.2d. 550 (1984)
Vote: 5–4

In this case the Court recognizes a public safety exception to Miranda v. Arizona.

Justice Rehnquist delivered the opinion of the Court.

Respondent Benjamin Quarles was charged in the New York trial court with criminal possession of a weapon. The trial court suppressed the gun in question, and a statement made by respondent, because the statement was obtained by police before they read respondent his "*Miranda* rights." That ruling was affirmed on appeal through the New York Court of Appeals. We granted certiorari, . . . and we now reverse. We conclude that under the circumstances involved in this case, overriding considerations of public safety justify the officer's failure to provide *Miranda* warnings before he asked questions devoted to locating the abandoned weapon.

On September 11, 1980, at approximately 12:30 A.M., Officer Frank Kraft and Officer Sal Scarring were on road patrol in Queens, New York, when a young woman approached their car. She told them that she had just been raped by a black male, approximately six feet tall, who was wearing a black jacket with the name "Big Ben" printed in yellow letters on the back. She told the officers that the man had just entered an A & P supermarket located nearby and that the man was carrying a gun.

The officers drove the woman to the supermarket, and Officer Kraft entered the store while Officer Scarring radioed for assistance. Officer Kraft quickly spotted respondent, who matched the description given by the woman, approaching a checkout counter. Apparently upon seeing the officer, respondent turned and ran toward the rear of the store, and Officer Kraft pursued him with a drawn gun. When respondent turned the corner at the end of an aisle, Officer Kraft lost sight of him for several seconds, and upon regaining sight of respondent, ordered him to stop and put his hands over his head.

Although more than three other officers had arrived on the scene by that time, Officer Kraft was the first to reach respondent. He frisked him and discovered that he was wearing a shoulder holster which was then empty. After handcuffing him, Officer Kraft asked him where the gun was. Respondent nodded in the direction of some empty cartons and responded, "the gun is over there." Officer Kraft thereafter retrieved a loaded .38 caliber revolver from one of the cartons, formally placed respondent under arrest, and read him his *Miranda* rights from a printed card. Respondent indicated that he would be willing to answer questions without an attorney present. Officer Kraft then asked respondent if he owned the gun and where he had purchased it. Respondent answered that he did own it and that he had purchased it in Miami, Florida.

In the subsequent prosecution of respondent for criminal possession of a weapon, the judge excluded the statement, "the gun is over there," and the gun because the officer had not given respondent the warnings required by our decision in *Miranda v. Arizona,* . . . before asking him where the gun was located. The judge excluded the other statements about respondent's ownership of the gun and the place of purchase, as evidence tainted by the prior *Miranda* violation. The Appellate Division of the Supreme Court of New York affirmed without opinion.

The Court of Appeals . . . concluded that respondent was in "custody" within the meaning of *Miranda* during all questioning and rejected the state's argument that the exigencies of the situation justified Officer Kraft's failure to read respondent his *Miranda* rights until after he had located the gun. The court declined to recognize an exigency exception to the usual requirements of *Miranda* because it found no indication from Officer Kraft's testimony at the suppression hearing that his subjective motivation in asking the question was to protect his own safety or the safety of the public. . . . For the reasons which follow, we believe that this case presents a situation where concern for public safety must be paramount to adherence to the literal language of the prophylactic rules enunciated in *Miranda.* . . .

In this case we have before us no claim that respondent's statements were actually compelled by police conduct which overcame his will to resist. . . . Thus the only issue before us is whether Officer Kraft was justified in failing to make available to respondent the procedural safeguards associated with the privilege against compulsory self-incrimination since *Miranda.*

The New York Court of Appeals was undoubtedly correct in deciding that the facts of this case come within the ambit of the *Miranda* decision as we have subsequently interpreted it. We agree that respondent was in police custody because we have noted that "the ultimate inquiry is simply whether there is a 'formal arrest or restraint on freedom of movement' of the degree associated with a formal arrest." . . . Here Quarles was surrounded by at least four police officers and was handcuffed when the questioning at issue took place. As the New York Court of Appeals observed, there was nothing to suggest that any of the officers were any longer concerned for their safety. The New York Court of Appeals' majority declined to express an opinion as to whether there might be an exception to the *Miranda* rule if the police had been acting to protect the public, because the lower courts in New York had made no factual determination that the police had acted with that motive. . . .

We hold that on these facts there is a "public safety" exception to the requirement that *Miranda* warnings be given before a suspect's answers may be admitted into evidence, and the availability of that exception does not depend upon the motivation of the individual officers involved. In a kaleidoscopic situation such as the one confronting these officers, where spontaneity rather than adherence to a police manual is necessarily the order of the day, the application of the exception which we recognize today should not be made to depend on *post hoc* findings at a suppression hearing concerning the subjective motivation of the arresting officer. Undoubtedly most police officers, if placed in Officer Kraft's position, would act out of a host of different, instinctive, and largely unverifiable motives—their own safety, the safety of others, and perhaps as well the desire to obtain incriminating evidence from the suspect.

Whatever the motivation of individual officers in such a situation, we do not believe that the doctrinal underpinnings of *Miranda* required that it be applied in all its rigor to a situation in which police officers ask questions reasonably prompted by a concern for the public safety. The *Miranda* decision was based in large part on this Court's view that the warnings which it required police to give to suspects in custody would reduce the likelihood that the suspects would fall victim to constitutionally impermissible practices of police interrogation in the presumptively coercive environment of the station house. . . . The dissenters warned that the requirement of *Miranda* warnings would have the effect of decreasing the number of suspects who respond to police questioning. . . . The *Miranda* majority, however, apparently felt that whatever the cost to society in terms of fewer convictions of guilty suspects, that cost would simply have to be borne in the interest of enlarged protection for the Fifth Amendment privilege.

The police in this case, in the very act of apprehending a suspect, were confronted with the immediate necessity of ascertaining the whereabouts of a gun which they had every reason to believe the suspect had just removed from his empty holster and discarded in the supermarket. So long as the gun was concealed somewhere in the supermarket, with its actual whereabouts unknown, it obviously posed more than one danger to the public safety: an accomplice might make use of it, a customer or employee might later come upon it.

In such a situation, if the police are required to recite the familiar *Miranda* warnings before asking the whereabouts of the gun, suspects in Quarles' position might well be deterred from responding. Procedural safeguards which deter a suspect from responding were deemed acceptable in *Miranda* in order to protect the Fifth Amendment privilege; when the primary social cost of those added protections is the possibility of fewer convictions, the *Miranda* majority was willing to bear that cost. Here, had *Miranda* warnings deterred Quarles from responding to Officer Kraft's question about the whereabouts of the gun, the cost would have been something more than merely the failure to obtain evidence useful in convicting Quarles but to insure that further danger to the public did not result from the concealment of the gun in a public area.

We conclude that the need for answers to questions in a situation posing a threat to the public safety outweighs the need for the prophylactic rule protecting the Fifth Amendment's privilege against self-incrimination. We decline to place officers such as Officer Kraft in the untenable position of having to consider, often in a matter of seconds, whether it best serves society for them to ask the necessary questions without the *Miranda* warnings and render whatever probative evidence they uncover inadmissible, or for them to give the warnings in order to preserve the admissibility of evidence they might uncover but possibly damage or destroy their ability to obtain that evidence and neutralize the volatile situation confronting them.

In recognizing a narrow exception to the *Miranda* rule in this case, we acknowledge that to some degree we lessen the desirable clarity of that rule. At least in part in order to preserve its clarity, we have over the years refused to sanction attempts to expand our *Mi-*

randa holding. . . .But as we have pointed out, we believe that the exception which we recognize today lessens the necessity of that on-the-scene balancing process. The exception will not be difficult for police officers to apply because in each case it will be circumscribed by the exigency which justifies it. We think police officers can and will distinguish almost instinctively between questions necessary to secure their own safety or the safety of the public and questions designed solely to elicit testimonial evidence from a suspect.

The facts of this case clearly demonstrate that distinction and an officer's ability to recognize it. Officer Kraft asked only the question necessary to locate the missing gun before advising respondent of his rights. It was only after securing the loaded revolver and giving the warnings that he continued with investigatory questions about the ownership and place of purchase of the gun. The exception which we recognize today, far from complicating the thought processes and the on-the-scene judgments of police officers, will simply free them to follow their legitimate instincts when confronting situations presenting a danger to the public safety.

We hold that the Court of Appeals in this case erred in excluding the statement, "the gun is over there," and the gun because of the officer's failure to read respondent his *Miranda* rights before attempting to locate the weapon. Accordingly we hold that it also erred in excluding the subsequent statements as illegal fruits of a *Miranda* violation. We therefore reverse and remand for further proceedings not inconsistent with this opinion.

Justice O'Connor, concurring in part in the judgment and dissenting in part.

. . . Were the Court writing from a clean slate, I could agree with its holding. But *Miranda* is now the law and, in my view, the Court has not provided sufficient justification for departing from it or for blurring its now clear strictures. Accordingly, I would require suppression of the initial statement taken from respondent in this case. On the other hand, nothing in *Miranda* or the privilege itself requires exclusion of nontestimonial evidence derived from informal custodial interrogation, and I therefore agree with the Court that admission of the gun in evidence is proper. . . .

Justice Marshall, with whom **Justice Brennan** and **Justice Stevens** join, dissenting.

The police in this case arrested a man suspected of possessing a firearm in violation of New York law. Once the suspect was in custody and found to be unarmed, the arresting officer initiated an interrogation. Without being advised of his right not to respond, the suspect incriminated himself by locating the gun. The majority concludes that the State may rely on this incriminating statement to convict the suspect of possessing a weapon. I disagree. The arresting officers had no legitimate reason to interrogate the suspect without advising him of his rights to remain silent and to obtain assistance of counsel. By finding on these facts justification for unconsented interrogation, the majority abandons the clear guidelines enunciated in *Miranda v. Arizona* . . . and condemns the American judiciary to a new era of *post hoc* inquiry into the propriety of custodial interrogations. More significantly and in direct conflict with this Court's long-standing interpretation of the Fifth Amendment, the majority has endorsed the introduction of coerced self-incriminating statements in criminal prosecutions. I dissent. . . .

The majority's entire analysis rests on the factual assumption that the public was at risk during Quarles' interrogation. This assumption is completely in conflict with the facts as found by New York's highest court. Before the interrogation began, Quarles had been "reduced to a condition of physical powerlessness." . . . Contrary to the majority's speculations, . . . Quarles was not believed to have, nor did he in fact have, an accomplice to come to his rescue. When the questioning began, the arresting officers were sufficiently confident of their safety to put away their guns. As Officer Kraft acknowledged at the suppression hearing, "the situation was under control." . . . Based on Officer Kraft's testimony, the New York Court of Appeals found: "Nothing suggests that any of the officers was by that time concerned for his own physical safety." . . . The Court of Appeals also determined that there was no evidence that the interrogation was prompted by the arresting officers' concern for the public's safety. . . .

The majority's treatment of the legal issues presented in this case is no less troubling than its abuse of the facts. Before today's opinion, the Court had twice concluded that, under *Miranda v. Arizona,* police officers conducting custodial interrogations must advise suspects of their rights before any questions concerning the whereabouts of incriminating weapons can be asked. . . . Now the majority departs from these cases and rules that police may withhold *Miranda* warnings whenever custodial interrogations concern matters of public safety.

The majority contends that the law, as it currently stands, places police officers in a dilemma whenever they interrogate a suspect who appears to know of some threat to the public's safety. If the police interrogate the suspect without advising him of his rights, the suspect may reveal information that the authorities can use to defuse the threat, but the suspect's statements will be inadmissible at trial. If, on the other hand, the police advise the suspect of his rights, the suspect may be deterred from responding to the police's questions, and the risk to the public may continue unabated. According to the majority, the police must now choose between establishing the suspect's guilt and safeguarding the public from danger.

The majority proposes to eliminate this dilemma by creating an exception to *Miranda v. Arizona* for custodial interrogations concerning matters of public safety. . . . Under the majority exception, police would be permitted to interrogate suspects about such matters before the suspects have been advised of their constitutional rights. Without being "deterred" by the knowledge that they have a constitutional right not to respond, these suspects will be likely to answer the questions. Should the answers also be incriminating, the State would be free to introduce them as evidence in a criminal prosecution. Through this "narrow exception to the *Miranda* rule," . . . the majority proposes to protect the safety without jeopardizing the prosecution of criminal defendants. I find in this reasoning an unwise and unprincipled departure from our Fifth Amendment precedents.

Before today's opinion, the procedures established in *Miranda v. Arizona* had "the virtue of informing police and prosecutors with specificity as to what they may do in conducting custodial interrogation, and of informing courts under what circumstances statements obtained during such interrogations are not admissible." . . . In a chimerical quest for public safety, the majority has abandoned the rule that brought eighteen years of doctrinal tranquillity to the field of custodial interrogations. As the majority candidly concedes, a public-safety exception destroys forever the clarity of *Miranda* for both law enforcement officers and members of the judiciary. The Court's candor cannot mask what a serious loss the administration of justice has incurred.

This case is illustrative of the chaos the "public-safety" exception will unleash. The circumstances of Quarles' arrest have never been in dispute. After the benefit of briefing and oral argument, the New York Court of Appeals concluded that there was "no evidence in the record before us that there were exigent circumstances posing a risk to the public safety." Upon reviewing the same facts and hearing the same arguments, a majority of this Court has come to precisely the opposite conclusion: "So long as the gun was concealed somewhere in the supermarket, with its actual whereabouts unknown, it obviously posed more than one danger to the public safety. . . ." . . .

If after plenary review two appellate courts so fundamentally differ over the threat to public safety presented by the simple and uncontested facts of this case, one must seriously question how law enforcement officers will respond to the majority's new rule in the confusion and haste of the real world. . . . Not only will police officers have to decide whether the objective facts of an arrest justify an unconsented custodial interrogation; they will also have to remember to interrupt the interrogation and read the suspect his *Miranda* warnings once the focus of the inquiry shifts from protecting the public's

safety to ascertaining the suspect's guilt. Disagreements of the scope of the "public-safety" exception and mistakes in its application are inevitable. . . .

Though unfortunate, the difficulty of administering the "public-safety" exception is not the most profound flaw in the majority's decision. The majority has lost sight of the fact that *Miranda v. Arizona* and our earlier custodial-interrogation cases all implemented a constitutional privilege against self-incrimination. The rules established in these cases were designed to protect criminal defendants against prosecutions based on coerced self-incriminating statements. The majority today turns its back on these constitutional considerations, and invites the government to prosecute through the use of what necessarily are coerced statements. . . .

Case

POWELL V. ALABAMA

287 U.S. 45; 53 S.Ct. 55; 77 L.Ed. 158 (1932)
Vote: 7–2

Here, the Court reviews the convictions of eight young African-American men who had been sentenced to death by an Alabama court for allegedly raping two white women.

Mr. Justice Sutherland delivered the opinion of the Court.

. . . The record shows that on the day when the offense is said to have been committed, these defendants, together with a number of other negroes, were upon a freight train on its way through Alabama. On the same train were seven white boys and two white girls. A fight took place between the negroes and the white boys, in the course of which the white boys, with the exception of one named Gilley, were thrown off the train. A message was sent ahead, reporting the fight and asking that every negro be gotten off the train. The participants in the fight, and the two girls, were in an open gondola car. The two girls testified that each of them was assaulted by six different negroes in turn, and they identified the seven defendants as having been among the number. None of the white boys was called to testify, with the exception of Gilley, who was called in rebuttal.

Before the train reached Scottsboro, Alabama, a sheriff's posse seized the defendants and two other negroes. Both girls and the negroes then were taken to Scottsboro, the county seat. Word of their coming and of the alleged assault had preceded them, and they were met at Scottsboro by a large crowd. It does not sufficiently appear that the defendants were seriously threatened with, or that they were actually in danger of, mob violence; but it does appear that the attitude of the community was one of great hostility. The sheriff thought it necessary to call for the militia to assist in safeguarding the prisoners. Chief Justice Anderson pointed out in his opinion that every step taken from the arrest and arraignment to the sentence was accompanied by the military. Soldiers took the defendants to Gadsden for safekeeping, brought them back to Scottsboro for arraignment, returned them to Gadsden for safekeeping while awaiting trial, escorted them to Scottsboro for trial a few days later, and guarded the courthouse and grounds at every stage of the proceedings. It is perfectly apparent that the proceedings, from beginning to end, took place in an atmosphere of tense, hostile and excited public sentiment. During the entire time, the defendants were closely confined or were under military guard. The record does not disclose their ages, except that one of them was nineteen; but the record clearly indicates that most, if not all, of them were youthful, and they are constantly referred to as "the boys." They were ignorant and illiterate. All of them were residents of other states, where alone members of their families or friends resided.

However guilty defendants, upon due inquiry might prove to have been, they were, until convicted, presumed to be innocent. It was the duty of the court having their cases in charge to see that they were denied no necessary incident of a fair trial. With any error of the state court involving alleged contravention of the state statutes or constitution we, of course, have nothing to do. The sole inquiry which we are permitted to make is whether the federal Constitution was contravened . . . and as to that, we confine ourselves, as already suggested, to the inquiry whether the defendants were in substance denied the right to counsel, and if so, whether such denial infringes the Due Process Clause of the Fourteenth Amendment.

First. The record shows that immediately upon the return of the indictment defendants were arraigned and pleaded not guilty. Apparently they were not asked whether they had, or were able to employ, counsel, or wished to have counsel appointed; or whether they had friends or relatives who might assist in that regard if communicated with. . . .

It is hardly necessary to say that the right to counsel being conceded, a defendant should be afforded a fair opportunity to secure counsel of his own choice. Not only was that not done here, but such designation of counsel as was attempted was either so indefinite or so close upon the trial as to amount to a denial of effective and substantial aid in that regard. This will be amply demonstrated by a brief review of the record.

April 6, six days after indictment, the trial began. When the first case was called, the court inquired whether the parties were ready for trial. The state's attorney replied that he was ready to proceed. No one answered for the defendants or appeared to represent or defend them. Mr. Roddy, a Tennessee lawyer, not a member of the local bar, addressed the court, saying that he had not been employed, but that people who were interested had spoken to him about the case. He was asked by the court whether he intended to appear for the defendants, and answered that he would like to appear along with counsel that the court might appoint. The record then proceeds:

> The Court: If you appear for these defendants, then I will not appoint counsel; if local counsel are willing to appear and assist you under the circumstances all right, but I will not appoint them.
>
> Mr. Roddy: Your Honor has appointed counsel, is that correct?
>
> The Court: I appointed all the members of the bar for the purpose of arraigning the defendants and then of course

I anticipated them to continue to help them if no counsel appears.

> Mr. Roddy: Then I don't appear then as counsel but I do want to stay in and not be ruled out in this case.
>
> The Court: Of course I would not do that—
>
> Mr. Roddy: I just appear here through the courtesy of Your Honor.
>
> The Court: Of course I give you that right; . . .

. . . [T]his action of the trial judge in respect of appointment of counsel was little more than an expansive gesture, imposing no substantial or definite obligation upon any one . . . during perhaps the most critical period of the proceedings against these defendants, that is to say, from the time of their arraignment until the beginning of their trial, when consultation, thorough-going investigation and preparation were vitally important, the defendants did not have the aid of counsel in any real sense, although they were as much entitled to such aid during that period as at the trial itself. . . .

Nor do we think the situation was helped by what occurred on the morning of the trial. At that time, as appears from the colloquy printed above, Mr. Roddy stated to the court that he did not appear as counsel, but that he would like to appear along with counsel that the court might appoint; that he had not been given an opportunity to prepare the case; that he was not familiar with the procedure in Alabama, but merely came down as a friend of the people who were interested; that he thought the boys would be better off if he should step entirely out of the case. Mr. Moody, a member of the local bar, expressed a willingness to help Mr. Roddy in anything he would do under the circumstances. To this the court responded, "All right, all the lawyers that will; of course I would not require a lawyer to appear if—." And Mr. Moody continued, "I am willing to do that for him as a member of the bar; I will go ahead and help do anything I can do." With this dubious understanding, the trials immediately proceeded. The defendants, young, ignorant, illiterate, surrounded by hostile sentiment, haled back and forth under guard of soldiers, charged with an atrocious crime regarded with especial horror in the community where they were to be tried, were thus put in peril of their lives within a few moments after counsel for the first time charged with any degree of responsibility began to represent them.

It is not enough to assume that counsel thus precipitated into the case thought there was no defense, and exercised their best judgment in proceeding to trial without preparation. Neither they nor the court could say what a prompt and thorough-going investigation might disclose as to the facts. No attempt was made to investigate. No opportunity to do so was given. Defendants were immediately hurried to trial. Chief Justice Anderson, after disclaiming any intention to criticize harshly counsel who attempted to represent defendants at the trials, said: " . . . The record indicates that the appearance was rather *pro forma* than zealous and active. . . ." Under the circumstances disclosed, we hold that defendants were not accorded the right of counsel in any substantial sense. To decide otherwise, would simply be to ignore actualities. . . .

The prompt disposition of criminal cases is to be commended and encouraged. But in reaching that result a defendant, charged with a serious crime, must not be stripped of his right to have sufficient time to advise with counsel and prepare his defense. To do that is not to proceed promptly in the calm spirit of regulated justice but to go forward with the haste of the mob. . . .

Second. The Constitution of Alabama provides that in all criminal prosecutions the accused shall enjoy the right to have the assistance of counsel; and a state statute requires the court in a capital case, where the defendant is unable to employ counsel, to appoint counsel for him. The state supreme court held that these provisions had not been infringed. . . . The question, however, which it is our duty, and within our power, to decide, is whether the denial of the assistance of counsel contravenes the Due Process Clause of the Fourteenth Amendment to the federal Constitution.

If recognition of the right of a defendant charged with a felony to have the aid of counsel depended upon the existence of a similar right at common law as it existed in England when our Constitution was adopted, there would be great difficulty in maintaining it as necessary to due process. Originally, in England, a person charged with treason or felony was denied the aid of counsel, except in respect of legal questions which the accused himself might suggest. At the same time parties in civil cases and persons accused of misdemeanors were entitled to the full assistance of counsel. After the revolution of 1688, the rule was abolished as to treason, but was otherwise steadily adhered to until 1836, when by act of Parliament the full right was granted in respect of felonies generally. . . .

An affirmation of the right to the aid of counsel in petty offenses, and its denial in the case of crimes of the gravest character, where such aid is most needed, is so outrageous and so obviously a perversion of all sense of

proportion that the rule was constantly, vigorously and sometimes passionately assailed by English statesmen and lawyers. As early as 1758, Blackstone, although recognizing that the rule was settled at common law, denounced it as not in keeping with the rest of the humane treatment of prisoners by the English law. "For upon what face of reason," he says, "can that assistance be denied to save the life of a man, which yet is allowed him in prosecutions for every petty trespass?" . . . One of the grounds upon which Lord Coke defended the rule was that in felonies the court itself was counsel for the prisoner. . . . But how can a judge, whose functions are purely judicial, effectively discharge the obligations of counsel for the accused? He can and should see to it that in the proceedings before the court the accused shall be dealt with justly and fairly. He cannot investigate the facts, advise and direct the defense, or participate in those necessary conferences between counsel and accused which sometimes partake of the inviolable character of the confessional. . . .

In light of the facts outlined in the forepart of this opinion—the ignorance and illiteracy of the defendants, their youth, the circumstances of public hostility, the imprisonment and the close surveillance of the defendants by the military forces, the fact that their friends and families were all in other states and communication with them necessarily difficult, and above all that they stood in deadly peril of their lives—we think the failure of the trial court to give them reasonable time and opportunity to secure counsel was a clear denial of due process.

But passing that, and assuming their inability, even if opportunity had been given, to employ counsel, as the trial court evidently did assume, we are of opinion that, under the circumstances just stated, the necessity of counsel was so vital and imperative that the failure of the trial court to make an effective appointment of counsel was likewise a denial of due process within the meaning of the Fourteenth Amendment. Whether this would be so in other criminal prosecutions, or under other circumstances, we need not determine. All that it is necessary now to decide, as we do decide, is that in a capital case, where the defendant is unable to employ counsel, and is incapable adequately of making his own defense because of ignorance, feeble-mindedness, illiteracy, or the like, it is the duty of the court, whether requested or not, to assign counsel for him as a necessary requisite of due process of law; and that duty is not discharged by an assignment at such a time or under such circumstances as to preclude the giving of effective aid in the preparation and trial of the case. To hold otherwise would be to ignore the fundamental postulate, already adverted to, "that there are certain immutable principles of justice which inhere in the very idea of free government which no member of the Union may disregard." . . . In a case such as this, whatever may be the rule in other cases, the right to have counsel appointed, when necessary, is a logical corollary from the constitutional right to be heard by counsel. . . .

The judgments must be reversed and the causes remanded for further proceedings not inconsistent with this opinion.

Mr. Justice Butler, dissenting.

If correct, the ruling that the failure of the trial court to give petitioners time and opportunity to secure counsel was denial of due process is enough, and with this the opinion should end. But the Court goes on to declare that "the failure of the trial court to make an effective appointment of counsel was likewise a denial of due process within the meaning of the Fourteenth Amendment." This is an extension of federal authority into a field hitherto occupied exclusively by the several States. Nothing before the Court calls for a consideration of the point. It was not suggested below and petitioners do not ask for its decision here. The Court, without being called upon to consider it, adjudges without a hearing an important constitutional question concerning criminal procedure in state courts.

It is a wise rule firmly established by a long course of decisions here that constitutional questions—even when properly raised and argued—are to be decided only when necessary for a determination of the rights of the parties in controversy before it. . . .

The record wholly fails to reveal that petitioners have been deprived of any right guaranteed by the Federal Constitution, and I am of opinion that the judgment should be affirmed.

Mr. Justice McReynolds concurs in this opinion.

Case

GIDEON V. WAINWRIGHT

372 U.S. 335; 83 S.Ct. 792; 9 L.Ed. 2d. 799 (1963)
Vote: 9–0

Here the Court considers whether state courts must as a matter of course appoint counsel to represent indigent defendants accused of felonies.

Mr. Justice Black delivered the opinion of the Court.

Petitioner was charged in a Florida state court with having broken and entered a poolroom with intent to commit a misdemeanor. This offense is a felony under Florida law. Appearing in court without funds and without a lawyer, petitioner asked the court to appoint counsel for him, whereupon the following colloquy took place:

> The Court: Mr. Gideon, I am sorry, but I cannot appoint Counsel to represent you in this case. Under the laws of the State of Florida, the only time the Court can appoint Counsel to represent a Defendant is when that person is charged with a capital offense. I am sorry, but I will have to deny your request to appoint Counsel to defend you in this case.
>
> The Defendant: The United States Supreme Court says I am entitled to be represented by Counsel.

Put to trial before a jury, *Gideon* conducted his defense about as well as could be expected from a layman. He made an opening statement to the jury, cross-examined the State's witnesses, presented witnesses in his own defense, declined to testify himself, and made a short argument "emphasizing his innocence to the charge contained in the Information filed in this case." The jury returned a verdict of guilty, the petitioner was sentenced to serve five years in the state prison. Later, petitioner filed in the Florida Supreme Court this habeas corpus petition attacking his conviction and sentence on the ground that the trial court's refusal to appoint counsel for him denied him rights "guaranteed by the Constitution and the Bill of Rights by the United States Government." Treating the petition for habeas corpus as properly before it, the State Supreme Court, "upon consideration thereof" but without an opinion, denied all relief. Since 1942, when *Betts v. Brady,* . . . was decided by a divided Court, the problem of a defendant's federal constitutional right to counsel in a state court has been a continuing source of controversy and litigation in both state and federal courts. To give this problem another review here, we granted certiorari. Since *Gideon* was proceeding *in forma pauperis,* we appointed counsel to represent him and requested both sides to discuss in their briefs and oral arguments the following: "Should this Court's holding in *Betts v. Brady* be reconsidered?"

Since the facts and circumstances of the two cases are so nearly indistinguishable, we think the *Betts v. Brady* holding if left standing would require us to reject Gideon's claim that the Constitution guarantees him the assistance of counsel. Upon full reconsideration we conclude that *Betts v. Brady* should be overruled.

The facts upon which Betts claimed that he had been unconstitutionally denied the right to have counsel appointed to assist him are strikingly like the facts upon which *Gideon* here bases his federal constitutional claim. The Sixth Amendment provides, "In all criminal prosecutions, the accused shall enjoy the right . . . to have the Assistance of Counsel for his defense." We have construed this to mean that in federal courts counsel must be provided for defendants unable to employ counsel unless the right is competently and intelligently waived. Betts argued that this right is extended to indigent defendants in state courts by the Fourteenth Amendment. In response the Court stated that, while the Sixth Amendment laid down "no rule for the conduct of the states, the question recurs whether the constraint laid by Amendment upon the national courts expresses a rule so fundamental and essential to a fair trial, and so, to due process of law, that it is made obligatory upon the States by the Fourteenth Amendment." In order to decide whether the Sixth Amendment's guarantee of counsel is of this fundamental nature, the Court in *Betts* set out and considered "[r]elevant data on the subject . . . afforded by constitutional and statutory provisions subsisting in the colonies and the States prior to the inclusion of the Bill of Rights in the national Constitution, and in the constitutional, legislative, and judicial history of the States to the present date." . . . On the basis of this historical data the Court concluded that "appointment of counsel is not a fundamental right, essential to a fair trial." . . . It was for this reason the *Betts* Court refused to accept the contention that the Sixth Amendment's guarantee of counsel for indigent federal defendants was extended to or, in the words of that Court, "made obligatory upon the States by the Fourteenth Amendment." . . . Plainly, had the Court concluded that appointment of counsel for an indigent criminal defendant was "a fundamental right, essential to a fair trial," . . . it would have held that the Fourteenth Amendment requires appointment of counsel in a state court, just as the Sixth Amendment requires in a federal court.

We think the Court in *Betts* had ample precedent for acknowledging that those guarantees of the Bill of Rights which are fundamental safeguards of liberty immune from federal abridgment are equally protected against state invasion by the Due Process Clause of the Fourteenth Amendment. This same principle was recognized, explained, and applied in *Powell v. Alabama,* . . . a case upholding the right of counsel, where the Court held that despite sweeping language to the contrary in *Hurtado v. California,* . . . the Fourteenth Amendment "embraced" those " 'fundamental principles of liberty and justice which lie at the base of all our civil and political institutions,' " even though they had been "specifically dealt with in another part of the federal Constitution." . . . In many cases other than *Powell* and *Betts,* this Court has looked to the fundamental nature of original Bill of Rights guarantees to decide whether the Fourteenth Amendment makes them obligatory on the States.

In light of these and many other prior decisions of this Court, it is not surprising that the *Betts* Court, when faced with the contention that "one charged with crime, who is unable to obtain counsel, must be furnished counsel by the State," . . . conceded that "[e]xpressions in the opinions of this court lend color to the argument. . . ." . . . The fact is that in deciding as it did—that "appointment of counsel is not a fundamental right, essential to a fair trial" . . . —the Court in *Betts v. Brady* made an abrupt break with its own well-considered precedents. In returning to these old precedents, sounder we believe than the new, we but restore constitutional principles established to achieve a fair system of justice. Not only these precedents but also reason and reflection require us to recognize that in our adversary system of criminal justice, any person haled into court, who is too poor to hire a lawyer, cannot be assured a fair trial unless counsel is provided for him. This seems to us to be an obvious truth. Governments, both state and federal, quite properly spend vast sums of money to establish machinery to try defendants accused of crime. Lawyers to prosecute are everywhere deemed essential to protect the public's interest in an orderly society. Similarly, there are few defendants charged with crime, few indeed, who fail to hire the best lawyers they can get to prepare and present their defenses. That government hires lawyers to prosecute and defendants who have the money hire lawyers to defend are the strongest indications of the widespread belief that lawyers in criminal courts are necessities, not luxuries. The right of one charged with crime to counsel may not be deemed fundamental and essential to fair trials in some countries, but it is in ours. From the very beginning, our state and national constitutions and laws have laid great emphasis on procedural and substantive safeguards designed to assure fair trials before impartial tribunals in which every defendant stands equal before the law. This noble ideal cannot be realized if the poor man charged with crime has to face his accusers without a lawyer to assist him.

The Court in *Betts v. Brady* departed from the sound wisdom upon which the Court's holding in *Powell v. Alabama* rested. Florida, supported by two other States, has asked that *Betts v. Brady* be left intact. Twenty-two States, as friends of the Court, argue that *Betts* was "an anachronism when handed down" . . . and that it should now be overruled. We agree.

The judgment is reversed and the cause is remanded to the Supreme Court of Florida for further action not inconsistent with this opinion.

Mr. Justice Douglas, concurring. . . .

Mr. Justice Clark, concurring in the result. . . .

Mr. Justice Harlan, concurring. . . .

Case

BATSON V. KENTUCKY

476 U.S. 79; 106 S.Ct. 1712; 90 L.Ed. 2d. 69 (1986)
Vote: 7–2

In this case the Court reexamines the practice of using peremptory challenges to exclude members of the defendant's race from the jury.

Justice Powell delivered the opinion of the Court.

. . . Petitioner, a black man, was indicted in Kentucky on charges of second-degree burglary and receipt of stolen goods. On the first day of trial in Jefferson Circuit Court, the judge conducted voir dire examination of the venire, excused certain jurors for cause, and permitted the parties to exercise peremptory challenges. The prosecutor used his peremptory challenges to strike all four black persons on the venire, and a jury composed only of white persons was selected. Defense counsel moved to discharge the jury before it was sworn on the ground that the prosecutor's removal of the black veniremen violated petitioner's rights under the Sixth and Fourteenth Amendments to a jury drawn from a cross-section of the community, and under the Fourteenth Amendment to equal protection of the laws. Counsel requested a hearing on his motion. Without expressly ruling on the request for a hearing, the trial judge observed that the parties were entitled to use their peremptory challenges to "strike anybody they want to." The judge then denied petitioner's motion, reasoning that the cross-section requirement applies only to selection of the venire and not to selection of the petit jury itself.

The jury convicted petitioner on both counts. . . .

The Supreme Court of Kentucky affirmed. . . . We granted certiorari . . . and now reverse.

In *Swain v. Alabama* [1965], this Court recognized that a "State's purposeful or deliberate denial to Negroes on account of race of participation as jurors in the administration of justice violates the Equal Protection Clause." . . . This principle has been "consistently and repeatedly" reaffirmed, . . . in numerous decisions of this Court both preceding and following *Swain.* We reaffirm the principle today.

More than a century ago, the Court decided that the State denies a black defendant equal protection of the laws when it puts him on trial before a jury from which members of his race have been purposefully excluded. *Strauder v. West Virginia,* . . . (1880). That decision laid the foundation for the Court's unceasing efforts to eradicate racial discrimination in the procedures used to select the venire from which individual jurors are drawn. In *Strauder,* the Court explained that the central concern of the recently ratified Fourteenth Amendment was to put an end to governmental discrimination on account of race. . . . Exclusion of black citizens from service as jurors constitutes a primary example of the evil the Fourteenth Amendment was designed to cure.

In holding that racial discrimination in jury selection offends the Equal Protection Clause, the Court in *Strauder* recognized, however, that a defendant has no right to a "petit jury composed in whole or in part of persons of his own race." . . . "The number of our races and nationalities stands in the way of evolution of such a conception" of the demand of equal protection. . . . But the defendant does have the right to be tried by a jury whose members are selected pursuant to nondiscriminatory criteria. . . . The Equal Protection Clause guarantees the defendant that the State will not exclude members of his race from the jury venire on account of race, . . . or on the false assumption that members of his race as a group are not qualified to serve as jurors. . . .

Purposeful racial discrimination in selection of the venire violates a defendant's right to equal protection because it denies him the protection that a trial by jury is intended to secure. "The very idea of a jury is a body . . . composed of the peers or equals of the person whose rights it is selected or summoned to determine; that is, of his neighbors, fellows, associates, persons having the same legal status in society as that which he holds." . . . The petit jury has occupied a central position in our system of justice by safeguarding a person accused of crime against the arbitrary exercise of power by prosecutor or judge. . . . Those on the venire must be "indifferently chosen" to secure the defendant's right under the Fourteenth Amendment to "protection of life and liberty against race or color prejudice." . . .

Racial discrimination in selection of jurors harms not only the accused whose life or liberty they are summoned to try. Competence to serve as a juror ultimately depends on an assessment of individual qualifications and ability impartially to consider evidence presented at a trial. . . . A person's race simply "is unrelated to his fitness as a juror." . . . As long ago as *Strauder*, therefore, the Court recognized that by denying a person participation in jury service on account of his race, the State unconstitutionally discriminated against the excluded juror. . . .

The harm from discriminatory jury selection extends beyond that inflicted on the defendant and the excluded juror to touch the entire community. Selection procedures that purposefully exclude black persons from juries undermine public confidence in the fairness of our system of justice. . . . Discrimination within the judicial system is most pernicious because it is "a stimulant to that race prejudice which is an impediment to securing to [black citizens] that equal justice which the law aims to secure to all others." . . .

In *Strauder*, the Court invalidated a state statute that provided that only white men could serve as jurors. . . . We can be confident that no state now has such a law. The Constitution requires, however, that we look beyond the face of the statute defining juror qualifications and also consider challenged selection practices to afford "protection against action of the State through its administrative officers in effecting the prohibited discrimination." . . . Thus, the Court has found a denial of equal protection where the procedures implementing a neutral statute operated to exclude persons from the

venire on racial grounds, and has made clear that the Constitution prohibits all forms of purposeful racial discrimination in selection of jurors. While decisions of this Court have been concerned largely with discrimination during selection of the venire, the principles announced there also forbid discrimination on account of race in selection of the petit jury. Since the Fourteenth Amendment protects an accused throughout the proceedings bringing him to justice, . . . the State may not draw up its jury lists pursuant to neutral procedures but then resort to discrimination at "other stages in the selection process." . . .

Accordingly, the component of the jury selection process at issue, here, the State's privilege to strike individual jurors through peremptory challenges, is subject to the commands of the Equal Protection Clause. Although a prosecutor ordinarily is entitled to exercise permitted peremptory challenges "for any reason at all, as long as that reason is related to his view concerning the outcome" of the case to be tried, . . . the Equal Protection Clause forbids the prosecutor to challenge potential jurors solely on account of their race or on the assumption that black jurors as a group will be unable impartially to consider the State's case against a black defendant.

The principles announced in *Strauder* never have been questioned in any subsequent decision of this Court. Rather, the Court has been called upon repeatedly to review the application of those principles to particular facts. A recurring question in these cases, as in any case alleging a violation of the Equal Protection Clause, was whether the defendant had met his burden of proving purposeful discrimination on the part of the State. . . . That question also was at the heart of the portion of *Swain v. Alabama* we reexamine today.

Swain required the Court to decide, among other issues, whether a black defendant was denied equal protection by the State's exercise of peremptory challenges to exclude members of his race from the petit jury. . . . The record in *Swain* showed that the prosecutor had used the State's peremptory challenges to strike the six black persons included on the petit jury venire. . . . While rejecting the defendant's claim for failure to prove purposeful discrimination, the Court nonetheless indicated that the Equal Protection Clause placed some limits on the State's exercise of peremptory challenges. . . .

The Court sought to accommodate the prosecutor's historical privilege of peremptory challenge free of judicial control, . . . and the constitutional prohibition on exclusion of persons from jury service on account of race. . . . While the Constitution does not confer a right to peremptory challenges, . . . those challenges traditionally have been viewed as one means of assuring the selection of a qualified and unbiased jury. . . . To preserve the peremptory nature of the prosecutor's challenge, the Court in *Swain* declined to scrutinize his actions in a particular case by relying on a presumption that he properly exercised the State's challenges. . . .

The Court went on to observe, however, that a state may not exercise its challenges in contravention of the Equal Protection Clause. It was impermissible for a prosecutor to use his challenges to exclude blacks from the jury "for reasons wholly unrelated to the outcome of the particular case on trial" or to deny to blacks "the same right and opportunity to participate in the administration of justice enjoyed by the white population." . . . Accordingly, a black defendant could make out a prima facie case of purposeful discrimination on proof that the peremptory challenge system was "being perverted" in that manner. For example, an inference of purposeful discrimination would be raised on evidence that a prosecutor, "in case after case, whatever the circumstances, whatever the crime and whoever the defendant or the victim may be, is responsible for the removal of Negroes who have been selected as qualified jurors by the jury commissioners and who have survived challenges for cause, with the result that no Negroes ever serve on petit juries." . . . Evidence offered by the defendant in *Swain* did not meet that standard. While the defendant showed that prosecutors in the jurisdiction had exercised their strikes to exclude blacks from the jury, he offered no proof of the circumstances under which prosecutors were responsible for striking black jurors beyond the facts of his own case. . . .

A number of lower courts following the teaching of *Swain* reasoned that proof of repeated striking of blacks over a number of cases was necessary to establish a violation of the Equal Protection Clause. Since this interpretation of *Swain* has placed on defendants a crippling burden of proof, prosecutors' peremptory challenges are now largely immune from constitutional scrutiny. For reasons that follow, we reject this evidentiary formulation as inconsistent with standards that have been developed since *Swain* for assessing a prima facie case under the Equal Protection Clause. . . .

As in any equal protection case, the "burden is, of course," on the defendant who alleges discriminatory selection of the venire "to prove the existence of purposeful discrimination." . . . In deciding if the defendant has carried his burden of persuasion, a court must under-

take "a sensitive inquiry into such circumstantial and direct evidence of intent as may be available." . . . Circumstantial evidence of invidious intent may include proof of disproportionate impact. . . . We have observed that under some circumstances proof of discriminatory impact "may for all practical purposes demonstrate unconstitutionality because in various circumstances the discrimination is very difficult to explain on nonracial grounds." . . . For example, "total or seriously disproportionate exclusion of Negroes from jury venires is itself such an 'unequal application of the law . . . as to show intentional discrimination.' " . . .

Moreover, since *Swain*, we have recognized that a black defendant alleging that members of his race have been impermissibly excluded from the venire may make out a prima facie case of purposeful discrimination by showing that the totality of the relevant facts gives rise to an inference of discriminatory purpose. . . . Once the defendant makes the requisite showing, the burden shifts to the State to explain adequately the racial exclusion. . . . The State cannot meet this burden on mere general assertions that its officials did not discriminate or that they properly performed their official duties. . . . Rather, the State must demonstrate that "permissible racially neutral selection criteria and procedures have produced the monochromatic result." . . .

The showing necessary to establish a prima facie case of purposeful discrimination in selection of the venire may be discerned in this Court's decisions. . . . The defendant initially must show that he is a member of a racial group capable of being singled out for differential treatment. . . . In combination with the evidence, a defendant may then make a prima facie case by proving that in the particular jurisdiction members of his race have not been summoned for jury service over an extended period of time. . . . Proof of systematic exclusion from the venire raises an inference of purposeful discrimination because the "result bespeaks discrimination." . . .

Since the ultimate issue is whether the State has discriminated in selecting the defendant's venire, however, the defendant may establish a prima facie case "in other ways than by evidence of long-continued unexplained absence" of members of his race "from many panels." . . . In cases involving the venire, this Court has found a prima facie case on proof that members of the defendant's race were substantially underrepresented on the venire from which his jury was drawn, and that the venire was selected under a practice providing "the opportunity for discrimination." . . . This combination of factors raises the necessary inference of purposeful discrimination because the Court has declined to attribute to chance the absence of black citizens on a particular jury array where the selection mechanism is subject to abuse. When circumstances suggest the need, the trial court must undertake a "factual inquiry" that "takes into account all possible explanatory factors" in the particular case. . . .

Thus, since the decision in *Swain*, this Court has recognized that a defendant may make a *prima facie* showing of purposeful racial discrimination in selection of the venire by relying solely on the facts concerning its selection in his case. These decisions are in accordance with the proposition . . . that "a consistent pattern of official racial discrimination" is not "a necessary predicate to a violation of the Equal Protection Clause. A single invidiously discriminatory governmental act" is not "immunized by the absence of such discrimination in the making of the comparable decisions." . . . For evidentiary requirements to dictate that "several must suffer discrimination" before one could object, . . . would be inconsistent with the promise of equal protection to all.

The standards for assessing a prima facie case in the context of discriminatory selection of the venire have been fully articulated since *Swain.* . . . These principles support our conclusion that a defendant may establish a prima facie case of purposeful discrimination in selection of the petit jury solely on evidence concerning the prosecutor's exercise of peremptory challenges at the defendant's trial. To establish such a case, the defendant first must show that he is a member of a cognizable racial group, . . . and that the prosecutor has exercised peremptory challenges to remove from the venire members of the defendant's race. Second, the defendant is entitled to rely on the fact, as to which there can be no dispute, that peremptory challenges constitute a jury selection practice that permits "those to discriminate who are of a mind to discriminate." . . . Finally, the defendant must show that these facts and any other relevant circumstances raise an inference that the prosecutor used that practice to exclude the veniremen from the petit jury on account of their race. This combination of factors in the empanelling of the petit jury, as in the selection of the venire, raises the necessary inference of purposeful discrimination.

In deciding whether the defendant has made the requisite showing, the trial court should consider all relevant circumstances. For example, a "pattern" of strikes against black jurors included in the particular venire might give rise to an inference of discrimination. Similarly, the prosecutor's questions and statements during voir dire examination and in exercising his challenges may support or refute an inference of discriminatory purpose. These examples are merely illustratives. We have confidence that trial judges, experienced in supervising voir dire, will be able to decide if the circumstances concerning the prosecutor's use of peremptory challenges creates a prima facie case of discrimination against black jurors.

Once the defendant makes a *prima facie* showing, the burden shifts to the State to come forward with a neutral explanation for challenging black jurors. Though this requirement imposes a limitation in some cases on the full peremptory character of the historic challenge, we emphasize that the prosecutor's explanation need not rise to the level justifying exercise of a challenge for cause. But the prosecutor may not rebut the defendant's prima facie case of discrimination by stating merely that he challenged jurors of the defendant's race on the assumption—or his intuitive judgment—that they would be partial to the defendant because of their shared race. . . . Just as the Equal Protection Clause forbids the States to exclude black persons from the venire on the assumption that blacks as a group are unqualified to serve as jurors, . . . so it forbids the States to strike black veniremen on the assumption that they will be biased in a particular case simply because the defendant is black. The core guarantee of equal protection, ensuring citizens that their State will not discriminate on account of race, would be meaningless were we to approve the exclusion of jurors on the basis of such assumptions, which arise solely from the jurors' race. Nor may the prosecutor rebut the defendant's case merely by denying that he had a discriminatory motive or "affirming his good faith in individual selections." . . . If these general assertions were accepted as rebutting a defendant's prima facie case, the Equal Protection Clause "would be but a vain and illusory requirement." . . . The prosecutor therefore must articulate a neutral explanation related to the particular case to be tried. The trial court then will have the duty to determine if the defendant has established purposeful discrimination.

The State contends that our holding will eviscerate the fair trial values served by the peremptory challenge. Conceding that the Constitution does not guarantee a right to peremptory challenges and that *Swain* did state that their use ultimately is subject to the strictures of equal protection, the State argues that the privilege of unfettered exercise of the challenge is of vital importance to the criminal justice system.

While we recognize, of course, that the peremptory challenge occupies an important position in our trial procedures, we do not agree that our decision today will undermine the contribution the challenge generally makes to the administration of justice. The reality of practice, amply reflected in many state and federal court opinions, shows that the challenge may be, and unfortunately at times has been, used to discriminate against black jurors. By requiring trial courts to be sensitive to the racially discriminatory use of peremptory challenges, our decision enforces the mandate of equal protection and furthers the ends of justice. In view of the heterogeneous population of our nation, public respect for our criminal justice system and the rule of law will be strengthened if we ensure that no citizen is disqualified from jury service because of his race.

Nor are we persuaded by the State's suggestion that our holding will create serious administrative difficulties. In those states applying a version of the evidentiary standard we recognize today, courts have not experienced serious administrative burdens, and the peremptory challenge system has survived. We decline, however, to formulate particular procedures to be followed upon a defendant's timely objection to a prosecutor's challenges.

In this case, petitioner made a timely objection to the prosecutor's removal of all black persons on the venire. Because the trial court flatly rejected the objection without requiring the prosecutor to give an explanation for his action, we remand this case for further proceedings. If the trial court decides that the facts establish, prima facie, purposeful discrimination and the prosecutor does not come forward with a neutral explanation for his action, our precedents require that petitioner's conviction be reversed. . . .

Justice White, concurring. . . .

Justice Marshall, concurring. . . .

Justice Stevens, with whom **Justice Brennan** joins, concurring. . . .

Justice Rehnquist, with whom the **Chief Justice** joins, dissenting.

. . . I cannot subscribe to the Court's unprecedented use of the Equal Protection Clause to restrict the historic scope of the peremptory challenge, which has been described as "a necessary part of trial by jury." . . . In my view, there is simply nothing "unequal" about the State using its peremptory challenges to strike blacks from the jury in cases involving black defendants, so long as such challenges are also used to exclude whites in cases involving white defendants, Hispanics in cases involving Hispanic defendants, Asians in cases involving Asian defendants, and so on. This case-specific use of peremptory challenges by the State does not single out blacks, or members of any other race for that matter, for discriminatory treatment. Such use of peremptories is at best based upon seat-of-the-pants instincts, which are undoubtedly crudely stereotypical and may in many cases be hopelessly mistaken. But as long as they are applied across the board to jurors of all races and nationalities, I do not see—and the Court most certainly has not explained—how their use violates the Equal Protection Clause.

Nor does such use of peremptory challenges by the State infringe upon any other constitutional interests. The Court does not suggest that exclusion of blacks from the jury through the State's use of peremptory challenges results in a violation of either the fair cross-section or impartiality component of the Sixth Amendment. . . . And because the case-specific use of peremptory challenges by the State does not deny blacks the right to serve as jurors in cases involving non-black defendants, it harms neither the excluded jurors nor the remainder of the community.

The use of group affiliations, such as age, race, or occupation, as a "proxy" for potential juror partiality, based on the assumption or belief that members of one group are more likely to favor defendants who belong to the same group, has long been accepted as a legitimate basis for the State's exercise of peremptory challenges. . . . Indeed, given the need for reasonable limitations on the time devoted to voir dire, the use of such "proxies" by both the State and the defendant may be extremely useful in eliminating from the jury persons who might be biased in one way or another. The Court today holds that the State may not use its peremptory challenges to strike black prospective jurors on this basis without violating the Constitution. But I do not believe there is anything in the Equal Protection Clause, or any other Constitutional provision, that justifies such a departure. . . . Petitioner in the instant case failed to make a sufficient showing to overcome the presumption announced in *Swain* that the State's use of peremptory challenges was related to the context of the case. I would therefore affirm the judgment of the court below.

KANSAS V. HENDRICKS

___ U.S. ___, 117 S.Ct. 2072, 138 L.Ed.2d. 501 (1997)

Vote: 5–4

In this case the Court considers the constitutionality of state legislation that permits violent sexual predators to be confined even after their prison sentences are completed.

Justice Thomas delivered the opinion of the Court.

In 1994, Kansas enacted the Sexually Violent Predator Act, which establishes procedures for the civil commitment of persons who, due to a "mental abnormality" or a "personality disorder," are likely to engage in "predatory acts of sexual violence." . . . The State invoked the Act for the first time to commit Leroy Hendricks, an inmate who had a long history of sexually molesting children, and who was scheduled for release from prison shortly after the Act became law. Hendricks challenged his commitment on . . . "substantive" due process, double jeopardy, and ex post-facto grounds. The Kansas Supreme Court invalidated the Act, holding that its pre-commitment condition of a "mental abnormality" did not satisfy what the court perceived to be the "substantive" due process requirement that involuntary civil commitment must be predicated on a finding of "mental illness." . . . The State of Kansas petitioned for certiorari. Hendricks subsequently filed a cross petition in which he reasserted his federal double jeopardy and ex post-facto claims. We granted certiorari . . . and now reverse the judgment below. . . .

. . . Although freedom from physical restraint "has always been at the core of the liberty protected by the Due Process Clause from arbitrary governmental action," . . . that liberty interest is not absolute. The Court has recognized that an individual's constitutionally protected interest in avoiding physical restraint may be overridden even in the civil context. . . .

Accordingly, States have in certain narrow circumstances provided for the forcible civil detainment of people who are unable to control their behavior and who thereby pose a danger to the public health and safety. . . . We have consistently upheld such involuntary commitment statutes provided the confinement takes place pursuant to proper procedures and evidentiary standards. . . . It thus cannot be said that the involuntary civil confinement of a limited subclass of dangerous persons is contrary to our understanding of ordered liberty. . . .

The challenged Act unambiguously requires a finding of dangerousness either to one's self or to others as a prerequisite to involuntary confinement. Commitment proceedings can be initiated only when a person "has been convicted of or charged with a sexually violent offense," and "suffers from a mental abnormality or personality disorder which makes the person likely to engage in the predatory acts of sexual violence." . . . The statute thus requires proof of more than a mere predisposition to violence; rather, it requires evidence of past sexually violent behavior and a present mental condition that creates a likelihood of such conduct in the future if the person is not incapacitated. As we have recognized, "[p]revious instances of violent behavior are an important indicator of future violent tendencies." . . . A finding of dangerousness, standing alone, is ordinarily not a sufficient ground upon which to justify indefinite involuntary commitment. We have sustained civil commitment statutes when they have coupled proof of dangerousness with the proof of some additional factor, such as a "mental illness" or "mental abnormality." . . . These added statutory requirements serve to limit involuntary civil confinement to those who suffer from a volitional impairment rendering them dangerous beyond their control. The Kansas Act is plainly of a kind with these other civil commitment statutes: It requires a finding of future dangerousness, and then links that finding to the existence of a "mental abnormality" or "personality disorder" that makes it difficult, if not impossible, for the person to control his dangerous behavior. . . . The pre-commitment requirement of a "mental abnormality" or "personality disorder" is consistent with the requirements of these other statutes that we have upheld in that it narrows the class of persons eligible for confinement to those who are unable to control their dangerousness.

Hendricks nonetheless argues that our earlier cases dictate a finding of "mental illness" as a prerequisite for civil commitment, citing *Foucha,* and *Addington.* He then asserts that a "mental abnormality" is not equivalent to a "mental illness" because it is a term coined by the Kansas Legislature, rather than by the psychiatric community. Contrary to Hendricks' assertion, the term "mental illness" is devoid of any talismanic significance. Not only do "psychiatrists disagree widely and frequently on what constitutes mental illness," . . . but the Court itself has used a variety of expressions to describe the mental condition of those properly subject to civil confinement. . . .

Indeed, we have never required State legislatures to adopt any particular nomenclature in drafting civil commitment statutes. Rather, we have traditionally left to legislators the task of defining terms of a medical nature that have legal significance. . . . As a consequence, the States have, over the years, developed numerous specialized terms to define mental health concepts. Often, those definitions do not fit precisely with the definitions employed by the medical community. The legal definitions of "insanity" and "competency," for example, vary substantially from their psychiatric counterparts. . . . Legal definitions, however, which must "take into account such issues as individual responsibility . . . and competency," need not mirror those advanced by the medical profession. . . .

To the extent that the civil commitment statutes we have considered set forth criteria relating to an individual's inability to control his dangerousness, the Kansas Act sets forth comparable criteria and Hendricks' condition doubtless satisfies those criteria. The mental health professionals who evaluated Hendricks diagnosed him as suffering from pedophilia, a condition the psychiatric profession itself classifies as a serious mental disorder. . . . Hendricks even conceded that, when he becomes "stressed out," he cannot "control the urge" to molest children. . . . This admitted lack of volitional control, coupled with a prediction of future dangerousness, adequately distinguishes Hendricks from other dangerous persons who are perhaps more properly dealt with exclusively through criminal proceedings. Hendricks' diagnosis as a pedophile, which qualifies as a "mental abnormality" under the Act, thus plainly suffices for due process purposes.

We granted Hendricks' cross petition to determine whether the Act violates the Constitution's double jeopardy prohibition or its ban on ex post-facto lawmaking. The thrust of Hendricks' argument is that the Act establishes criminal proceedings; hence confinement under it necessarily constitutes punishment. He contends that where, as here, newly enacted "punishment" is predicated upon past conduct for which he has already been convicted and forced to serve a prison sentence, the Constitution's Double Jeopardy and Ex Post-Facto Clauses are violated. We are unpersuaded by Hendricks' argument that Kansas has established criminal proceedings.

The categorization of a particular proceeding as civil or criminal "is first of all a question of statutory construction." . . . We must initially ascertain whether the legislature meant the statute to establish "civil" proceedings. If so, we ordinarily defer to the legislature's stated intent. Here, Kansas' objective to create a civil proceeding is evidenced by its placement of the Sexually Violent Predator Act within the Kansas probate code, instead of the criminal code, as well as its description of the Act as creating a "civil commitment procedure." . . . Nothing on the face of the statute suggests that the legislature sought to create anything other than a civil commitment scheme designed to protect the public from harm.

Although we recognize that a "civil label is not always dispositive," . . . we will reject the legislature's manifest intent only where a party challenging the statute provides "the clearest proof" that "the statutory scheme [is] so punitive either in purpose or effect as to negate [the State's] intention" to deem it "civil." . . . In those limited circumstances, we will consider the statute to have established criminal proceedings for constitutional purposes. Hendricks, however, has failed to satisfy this heavy burden.

As a threshold matter, commitment under the Act does not implicate either of the two primary objectives of criminal punishment: retribution or deterrence. The Act's purpose is not retributive because it does not affix culpability for prior criminal conduct. Instead, such conduct is used solely for evidentiary purposes, either to demonstrate that a "mental abnormality" exists or to support a finding of future dangerousness. We have previously concluded that an Illinois statute was nonpunitive even though it was triggered by the commission of a sexual assault, explaining that evidence of the prior criminal conduct was "received not to punish past misdeeds, but primarily to show the accused's mental condition and to predict future behavior." . . . In addition, the Kansas Act does not make a criminal conviction a prerequisite for commitment—persons absolved of criminal responsibility may nonetheless be subject to confinement under the Act. . . . An absence of the necessary criminal responsibility suggests that the State is not seeking retribution for a past misdeed. Thus, the fact that the Act may be "tied to criminal activity" is "insufficient to render the statut[e] punitive." . . .

Moreover, unlike a criminal statute, no finding of scienter is required to commit an individual who is found to be a sexually violent predator; instead, the commitment determination is made based on a "mental abnormality" or "personality disorder" rather than on one's criminal intent. The existence of a scienter requirement is customarily an important element in distinguishing criminal from civil statutes. . . . The absence of such a requirement here is evidence that confinement under the statute is not intended to be retributive.

Nor can it be said that the legislature intended the Act to function as a deterrent. Those persons committed under the Act are, by definition, suffering from a "mental abnormality" or a "personality disorder" that prevents them from exercising adequate control over their behavior. Such persons are therefore unlikely to be deterred by the threat of confinement. And the conditions surrounding that confinement do not suggest a punitive purpose on the State's part. The State has represented that an individual confined under the Act is not subject to the more restrictive conditions placed on state prisoners, but instead experiences essentially the same conditions as any involuntarily committed patient in the state mental institution. . . . Because none of the parties argues that people institutionalized under the Kansas general civil commitment statute are subject to punitive conditions, even though they may be involuntarily confined, it is difficult to conclude that persons confined under this Act are being "punished."

Although the civil commitment scheme at issue here does involve an affirmative restraint, "the mere fact that a person is detained does not inexorably lead to the conclusion that the government has imposed punishment." . . . The State may take measures to restrict the freedom of the dangerously mentally ill. This is a legitimate nonpunitive governmental objective and has been historically so regarded. . . .The Court has, in fact, cited the confinement of "mentally unstable individuals who present a danger to the public" as one classic example of nonpunitive detention. . . . If detention for the purpose of protecting the community from harm necessarily constituted punishment, then all involuntary civil commitments would have to be considered punishment. But we have never so held.

Hendricks focuses on his confinement's potentially indefinite duration as evidence of the State's punitive intent. That focus, however, is misplaced. Far from any punitive objective, the confinement's duration is instead linked to the stated purposes of the commitment, namely, to hold the person until his mental abnormality no longer causes him to be a threat to others. . . . If, at any time, the confined person is adjudged "safe to be at large," he is statutorily entitled to immediate release. . . .

Furthermore, commitment under the Act is only potentially indefinite. The maximum amount of time an in-

dividual can be incapacitated pursuant to a single judicial proceeding is one year. . . . If Kansas seeks to continue the detention beyond that year, a court must once again determine beyond a reasonable doubt that the detainee satisfies the same standards as required for the initial confinement. . . . This requirement again demonstrates that Kansas does not intend an individual committed pursuant to the Act to remain confined any longer than he suffers from a mental abnormality rendering him unable to control his dangerousness.

Hendricks next contends that the State's use of procedural safeguards traditionally found in criminal trials makes the proceedings here criminal rather than civil. . . . The numerous procedural and evidentiary protections afforded here demonstrate that the Kansas Legislature has taken great care to confine only a narrow class of particularly dangerous individuals, and then only after meeting the strictest procedural standards. That Kansas chose to afford such procedural protections does not transform a civil commitment proceeding into a criminal prosecution.

Finally, Hendricks argues that the Act is necessarily punitive because it fails to offer any legitimate "treatment." Without such treatment, Hendricks asserts, confinement under the Act amounts to little more than disguised punishment. Hendricks' argument assumes that treatment for his condition is available, but that the State has failed (or refused) to provide it. The Kansas Supreme Court, however, apparently rejected this assumption, explaining:

> "It is clear that the overriding concern of the legislature is to continue the segregation of sexually violent offenders from the public. Treatment with the goal of reintegrating them into society is incidental, at best. The record reflects that treatment for sexually violent predators is all but nonexistent. The legislature concedes that sexually violent predators are not amenable to treatment under [the existing Kansas involuntary commitment statute]. If there is nothing to treat under [that statute], then there is no mental illness. In that light, the provisions of the Act for treatment appear somewhat disingenuous." . . .

It is possible to read this passage as a determination that Hendricks' condition was untreatable under the existing Kansas civil commitment statute, and thus the Act's sole purpose was incapacitation. Absent a treatable mental illness, the Kansas court concluded, Hendricks could not be detained against his will.

Accepting the Kansas court's apparent determination that treatment is not possible for this category of individuals does not obligate us to adopt its legal conclusions. We have already observed that, under the appropriate circumstances and when accompanied by proper procedures, incapacitation may be a legitimate end of the civil law. . . . Accordingly, the Kansas court's determination that the Act's "overriding concern" was the continued "segregation of sexually violent offenders" is consistent with our conclusion that the Act establishes civil proceedings, . . . especially when that concern is coupled with the State's ancillary goal of providing treatment to those offenders, if such is possible. While we have upheld state civil commitment statutes that aim both to incapacitate and to treat, . . . we have never held that the Constitution prevents a State from civilly detaining those for whom no treatment is available, but who nevertheless pose a danger to others. A State could hardly be seen as furthering a "punitive" purpose by involuntarily confining persons afflicted with an untreatable, highly contagious disease. . . . Similarly, it would be of little value to require treatment as a precondition for civil confinement of the dangerously insane when no acceptable treatment existed. To conclude otherwise would obligate a State to release certain confined individuals who were both mentally ill and dangerous simply because they could not be successfully treated for their afflictions. . . .

Alternatively, the Kansas Supreme Court's opinion can be read to conclude that Hendricks' condition is treatable, but that treatment was not the State's "overriding concern," and that no treatment was being provided (at least at the time Hendricks was committed). . . . Even if we accept this determination that the provision of treatment was not the Kansas Legislature's "overriding" or "primary" purpose in passing the Act, this does not rule out the possibility that an ancillary purpose of the Act was to provide treatment, and it does not require us to conclude that the Act is punitive. Indeed, critical language in the Act itself demonstrates that the Secretary of Social and Rehabilitation Services, under whose custody sexually violent predators are committed, has an obligation to provide treatment to individuals like Hendricks. . . . Other of the Act's sections echo this obligation to provide treatment for committed persons. . . . Thus . . . "the State has a statutory obligation to provide 'care and treatment for [persons adjudged sexually dangerous] designed to effect recovery,' " . . . and we may therefore conclude that "the State has . . . provided for the treatment of those it commits."

Although the treatment program initially offered Hendricks may have seemed somewhat meager, it must be remembered that he was the first person committed under the Act. That the State did not have all of its treatment procedures in place is thus not surprising. What is significant, however, is that Hendricks was placed under the supervision of the Kansas Department of Health and Social and Rehabilitative Services, housed in a unit segregated from the general prison population and operated not by employees of the Department of Corrections, but by other trained individuals. And, before this Court, Kansas declared "[a]bsolutely" that persons committed under the Act are now receiving in the neighborhood of "31.5 hours of treatment per week." . . .

Where the State has "disavowed any punitive intent"; limited confinement to a small segment of particularly dangerous individuals; provided strict procedural safeguards; directed that confined persons be segregated from the general prison population and afforded the same status as others who have been civilly committed; recommended treatment if such is possible; and permitted immediate release upon a showing that the individual is no longer dangerous or mentally impaired, we cannot say that it acted with punitive intent. We therefore hold that the Act does not establish criminal proceedings and that involuntary confinement pursuant to the Act is not punitive. Our conclusion that the Act is nonpunitive thus removes an essential prerequisite for both Hendricks' double jeopardy and ex post-facto claims.

The Double Jeopardy Clause provides: "[N]or shall any person be subject for the same offence to be twice put in jeopardy of life or limb." Although generally understood to preclude a second prosecution for the same offense, the Court has also interpreted this prohibition to prevent the State from "punishing twice, or attempting a second time to punish criminally, for the same offense." . . . Hendricks argues that, as applied to him, the Act violates double jeopardy principles because his confinement under the Act, imposed after a conviction and a term of incarceration, amounted to both a second prosecution and a second punishment for the same offense. We disagree.

Because we have determined that the Kansas Act is civil in nature, initiation of its commitment proceedings does not constitute a second prosecution. . . . Moreover, as commitment under the Act is not tantamount to "punishment," Hendricks' involuntary detention does not violate the Double Jeopardy Clause, even though that confinement may follow a prison term. . . . If an individual otherwise meets the requirements for involuntary civil commitment, the State is under no obligation to release that individual simply because the detention would follow a period of incarceration.

Hendricks also argues that even if the Act survives the "multiple punishments" test, it nevertheless fails the "same elements" test of *Blockburger v. United States* . . . (1932). Under *Blockburger,* "where the same act or transaction constitutes a violation of two distinct statutory provisions, the test to be applied to determine whether there are two offenses or only one, is whether each provision requires proof of a fact which the other does not." The *Blockburger* test, however, simply does not apply outside of the successive prosecution context. A proceeding under the Act does not define an "offense," the elements of which can be compared to the elements of an offense for which the person may previously have been convicted. Nor does the Act make the commission of a specified "offense" the basis for invoking the commitment proceedings. Instead, it uses a prior conviction (or previously charged conduct) for evidentiary purposes to determine whether a person suffers from a "mental abnormality" or "personality disorder" and also poses a threat to the public. Accordingly, we are unpersuaded by Hendricks' novel application of the *Blockburger* test and conclude that the Act does not violate the Double Jeopardy Clause.

Hendricks' ex post-facto claim is similarly flawed. The Ex Post-Facto Clause, which " 'forbids the application of any new punitive measure to a crime already consummated,' " has been interpreted to pertain exclusively to penal statutes. . . . As we have previously determined, the Act does not impose punishment; thus, its application does not raise ex post-facto concerns. Moreover, the Act clearly does not have retroactive effect. Rather, the Act permits involuntary confinement based upon a determination that the person currently both suffers from a "mental abnormality" or "personality disorder" and is likely to pose a future danger to the public. To the extent that past behavior is taken into account, it is used, as noted above, solely for evidentiary purposes. Because the Act does not criminalize conduct legal before its enactment, nor deprive Hendricks of any defense that was available to him at the time of his crimes, the Act does not violate the Ex Post-Facto Clause.

We hold that the Kansas Sexually Violent Predator Act comports with due process requirements and neither runs afoul of double jeopardy principles nor constitutes an exercise in impermissible ex post-facto lawmaking. Accordingly, the judgment of the Kansas Supreme Court is reversed.

It is so ordered.

Justice Kennedy, concurring. . . .

Justice Breyer, [joined by Justices Stevens, Souter and Ginsburg] dissenting.

I agree with the majority that the Kansas Act's "definition of 'mental abnormality' " satisfies the "substantive" requirements of the Due Process Clause. . . . Kansas, however, concedes that Hendricks' condition is treatable; yet the Act did not provide Hendricks (or others like him) with any treatment until after his release date from prison and only inadequate treatment thereafter. These, and certain other, special features of the Act convince me that it was not simply an effort to commit Hendricks civilly, but rather an effort to inflict further punishment upon him. The Ex Post-Facto Clause therefore prohibits the Act's application to Hendricks, who committed his crimes prior to its enactment. . . .

The statutory provisions before us do amount to punishment primarily because . . . the legislature did not tailor the statute to fit the nonpunitive civil aim of treatment, which it concedes exists in Hendricks' case. The Clause in these circumstances does not stand as an obstacle to achieving important protections for the public's safety; rather it provides an assurance that, where so significant a restriction of an individual's basic freedoms is at issue, a State cannot cut corners. Rather, the legislature must hew to the Constitution's liberty protecting line. . . .

Case

FURMAN V. GEORGIA

408 U.S. 238, 92 S.Ct. 2726, 33 L.Ed. 2d. 346 (1972)
Vote: 5–4

In this landmark decision, the U.S. Supreme Court invalidates Georgia's death penalty statute. This decision represents three death penalty cases that were *consolidated on appeal. All three defendants were African-American. One of them was convicted for murder; two were found guilty of rape. All three were sentenced to death by juries.*

PER CURIAM.   The Court holds that the imposition and carrying out of the death penalty in these cases constitutes cruel and unusual punishment in violation of the

Eighth and Fourteenth Amendments. The judgment in each case is therefore reversed insofar as it leaves undisturbed the death sentence imposed, and the cases are remanded for further proceedings.

Mr. Justice Douglas, Mr. Justice Brennan, Mr. Justice Stewart, Mr. Justice White, and Mr. Justice Marshall have filed separate opinions in support of the judgments. The Chief Justice, Mr. Justice Blackmun, Mr. Justice Powell, and Mr. Justice Rehnquist have filed separate dissenting opinions.

Mr. Justice Douglas concurring.

. . . In each [of these cases] the determination of whether the penalty should be death or a lighter punishment was left by the State to the discretion of the judge or of the jury. . . . I vote to vacate each judgment, believing that the exaction of the death penalty does violate the Eighth and Fourteenth Amendments. . . .

The words "cruel and unusual" certainly include penalties that are barbaric. But the words, at least when read in light of the English proscription against selective and irregular use of penalties, suggest that it is "cruel and unusual" to apply the death penalty—or any other penalty selectively to minorities whose numbers are few, who are outcasts of society, and who are unpopular, but whom society is willing to see suffer though it would not countenance general application of the same penalty across the board. . . .

. . . [W]e deal with a system of law and of justice that leaves to the uncontrolled discretion of judges or juries the determination whether defendants committing these crimes should die or be imprisoned. Under these laws no standards govern the selection of the penalty. People live or die, dependent on the whim of one man or of 12. In a Nation committed to equal protection of the laws there is no permissible "caste" aspect of law enforcement. Yet we know that the discretion of judges and juries in imposing the death penalty enables the penalty to be selectively applied, feeding prejudices against the accused if he is poor and despised, lacking political clout, or if he is a member of a suspect or unpopular minority, and saving those who by social position may be in a more protected position. . . .

The high service rendered by the "cruel and unusual" punishment clause of the Eighth Amendment is to require legislatures to write penal laws that are evenhanded, nonselective, and nonarbitrary, and to require judges to see to it that general laws are not applied sparsely, selectively, and spottily to unpopular groups.

. . . [T]hese discretionary statutes are unconstitutional in their operation. They are pregnant with discrimination and discrimination is an ingredient not compatible with the idea of equal protection of the laws that is implicit in the ban on "cruel and unusual" punishments.

Mr. Justice Brennan, concurring.

Ours would indeed be a simple task were we required merely to measure a challenged punishment against those that history has long condemned. That narrow and unwarranted view of the Clause, however, was left behind with the 19th century. Our task today is more complex. We know "that the words of the [Clause] are not precise and that their scope is not static." We know, therefore, that the Clause "must draw its meaning from the evolving standards of decency that mark the progress of a maturing society." That knowledge, of course, is but the beginning of the inquiry.

. . . [T]he question is whether [a] penalty subjects the individual to a fate forbidden by the principle of civilized treatment guaranteed by the [Clause]." It was also said that a challenged punishment must be examined "in light of the basic prohibition against inhuman treatment" embodied in the Clause.

. . . "The basic concept underlying the [Clause] is nothing less than the dignity of man. While the State has the power to punish, the [Clause] stands to assure that this power be exercised within the limits of civilized standards." At bottom, then, the Cruel and Unusual Punishment Clause prohibits the infliction of uncivilized and inhuman punishments. The State, even as it punishes, must treat its members with respect for their intrinsic worth as human beings. A punishment is "cruel and unusual," therefore, if it does not comport with human dignity. . . .

. . . [T]he punishment of death is inconsistent with . . . four principles: Death is an unusually severe and degrading punishment; there is a strong probability that it is inflicted arbitrarily; its rejection by contemporary society is virtually total; and there is no reason to believe that it serves any penal purpose more effectively than the less severe punishment of imprisonment. The function of these principles is to enable a court to determine whether a punishment comports with human dignity. Death, quite simply, does not. . . .

Mr. Justice Stewart, concurring.

. . . Legislatures—state and federal—have sometimes specified that the penalty of death shall be the mandatory punishment for every person convicted of engaging in certain designated criminal conduct.

If we were reviewing death sentences imposed under these or similar laws, we would be faced with the need to decide whether capital punishment is unconstitutional for all crimes and under all circumstances. We would need to decide whether a legislature—state or federal—could constitutionally determine that certain criminal conduct is so atrocious that society's interest in deterrence and retribution wholly outweighs any considerations of reform or rehabilitation of the perpetrator, and that, despite the inconclusive empirical evidence, only the automatic penalty of death will provide maximum deterrence.

On that score I would say only that I cannot agree that retribution is a constitutionally impermissible ingredient in the imposition of punishment. The instinct for retribution is part of the nature of man, and channeling that instinct in the administration of criminal justice serves an important purpose in promoting the stability of a society governed by law. When people begin to believe that organized society is unwilling or unable to impose upon criminal offenders the punishment they "deserve," then there are sown the seeds of anarchy—of self-help, vigilante justice and lynch law.

The constitutionality of capital punishment in the abstract is not, however, before us in these cases. For the Georgia and Texas Legislatures have not provided that the death penalty shall be imposed upon all those who are found guilty of forcible rape. And the Georgia Legislature has not ordained that death shall be the automatic punishment for murder.

Instead, the death sentences now before us are the product of a legal system that brings them, I believe, within the very core of the Eighth Amendment's guarantee against cruel and unusual punishments, a guarantee applicable against the States through the Fourteenth Amendment. In the first place, it is clear that these sentences are "cruel" in the sense that they excessively go beyond, not in degree but in kind, the punishments that the state legislatures have determined to be necessary. In the second place, it is equally clear that these sentences are "unusual" in the sense that the penalty of death is infrequently imposed for murder, and that its imposition for rape is extraordinarily rare. But I do not rest my conclusion upon these two propositions alone.

These death sentences are cruel and unusual in the same way that being struck by lightning is cruel and unusual. For, of all the people convicted of rapes and murders in 1967 and 1968, many just as reprehensible as these, the petitioners are among a capriciously selected random handful upon whom the sentence of death has

in fact been imposed. My concurring Brothers have demonstrated that, if any basis can be discerned for the selection of these few to be sentenced to die, it is the constitutionally impermissible basis of race. But racial discrimination has not been proved, and I put it to one side. I simply conclude that the Eighth and Fourteenth Amendments cannot tolerate the infliction of a sentence of death under legal systems that permit this unique penalty to be so wantonly and so freakishly imposed.

Mr. Justice White, concurring.

. . . The narrow question to which I address myself concerns the constitutionality of capital punishment statutes under which (1) the legislature authorizes the imposition of the death penalty for murder or rape; (2) the legislature does not itself mandate the penalty in any particular class or kind of case (that is, legislative will is not frustrated if the penalty is never imposed), but delegates to judges or juries the decisions as to those cases, if any, in which the penalty will be utilized; and (3) judges and juries have ordered the death penalty with such infrequency that the odds are now very much against imposition and execution of the penalty with respect to any convicted murderer or rapist. It is in this context that we must consider whether the execution of these petitioners would violate the Eighth Amendment.

. . . [L]ike my Brethren, I must arrive at judgment; and I can do no more than state a conclusion based on 10 years of almost daily exposure to the facts and circumstances of hundreds and hundreds of federal and state criminal cases involving crimes for which death is the authorized penalty. That conclusion, as I have said, is that the death penalty is exacted with great infrequency even for the most atrocious crimes and that there is no meaningful basis for distinguishing the few cases in which it is imposed from the many cases in which it is not. The short of it is that the policy of vesting sentencing authority primarily in juries—a decision largely motivated by the desire to mitigate the harshness of the law and to bring community judgment to bear on the sentence as well as guilt or innocence—has so effectively achieved its aims that capital punishment within the confines of the statutes now before us has for all practical purposes run its course. . . .

Mr. Justice Marshall, concurring.

. . . Perhaps the most important principle in analyzing "cruel and unusual" punishment questions is one that is reiterated again and again in the prior opinions of the Court: i.e., the cruel and unusual language "must draw its meaning from the evolving standards of decency that mark the progress of a maturing society." Thus, a penalty that was permissible at one time in our Nation's history is not necessarily permissible today. . . .

In judging whether or not a given penalty is morally acceptable, most courts have said that the punishment is valid unless "it shocks the conscience and sense of justice of the people."

While a public opinion poll obviously is of some assistance in indicating public acceptance or rejection of a specific penalty, its utility cannot be very great. This is because whether or not a punishment is cruel and unusual depends, not on whether its mere mention "shocks the conscience and sense of justice of the people," but on whether people who were fully informed as to the purposes of the penalty and its liabilities would find the penalty shocking, unjust, and unacceptable.

In other words, the question with which we must deal is not whether a substantial proportion of American citizens would today, if polled, opine that capital punishment is barbarously cruel, but whether they would find it to be so in the light of all information presently available.

This information would almost surely convince the average citizen that the penalty was unwise, but a problem arises as to whether it would convince him that the penalty was morally reprehensible. This problem arises from the fact that the public's desire for retribution, even though this is a goal that the legislature cannot constitutionally pursue as its sole justification for capital punishment, might influence the citizenry's view of the morality of capital punishment. The solution to the problem lies in the fact that no one has ever seriously advanced retribution as a legitimate goal of our society. Defenses of capital punishment are always mounted on deterrent or other similar theories. This should not be surprising. It is the people of this country who have urged in the past that prisons rehabilitate as well as isolate offenders, and it is the people who have injected a sense of purpose into our penology. I cannot believe that at this stage in our history, the American people would ever knowingly support purposeless vengeance. Thus, I believe that the great mass of citizens would conclude on the basis of the material already considered that the death penalty is immoral therefore unconstitutional.

In striking down capital punishment, this Court does not malign our system of government. On the contrary, it pays homage to it. Only in a free society could right triumph in difficult times, and could civilization record its magnificent advancement. In recognizing the humanity of our fellow beings, we pay ourselves the highest tribute.

We achieve "a major milestone in the long road up from barbarism" and join the approximately 70 other jurisdictions in the world which celebrate their regard for civilization and humanity by shunning capital punishment.

Mr. Chief Justice Burger, with whom ***Mr. Justice Blackmun,*** and ***Mr. Justice Rehnquist,*** join, dissenting.

. . . If we were possessed of legislative power, I would either join with Mr. Justice Brennan and Mr. Justice Marshall or, at the very least, restrict the use of capital punishment to a small category of the most heinous crimes. Our constitutional inquiry, however, must be divorced from personal feelings as to the morality and efficacy of the death penalty, and be confined to the meaning and applicability of the uncertain language of the Eighth Amendment. There is no novelty in being called upon to interpret a constitutional provision that is less than self-defining, but, of all our fundamental guarantees, the ban on "cruel and unusual punishments" is one of the most difficult to translate into judicially manageable terms. The widely divergent views of the Amendment expressed in today's opinions reveals the haze that surrounds this constitutional command. Yet it is essential to our role as a court that we not seize upon the enigmatic character of the guarantee as an invitation to enact our personal predilections into law.

Although the Eighth Amendment literally reads as prohibiting only those punishments that are both "cruel" and "unusual," history compels the conclusion that the Constitution prohibits all punishments of extreme and barbarous cruelty, regardless of how frequently or infrequently imposed.

But where, as here, we consider a punishment well known to history, and clearly authorized by legislative enactment, it disregards the history of the Eighth Amendment and all the judicial comment that has followed to rely on the term "unusual" as affecting the outcome of these cases. Instead, I view these cases as turning on the single question whether capital punishment is "cruel" in the constitutional sense. The term "unusual" cannot be read as limiting the ban on "cruel" punishments or as somehow expanding the meaning of the term "cruel." For this reason I am unpersuaded by the facile argument that since capital punishment has always been cruel in the everyday sense of the word, and has become unusual due to decreased use, it is, therefore, now "cruel and unusual." . . .

Mr. Justice Blackmun, dissenting.

. . . Cases such as these provide for me an excruciating agony of the spirit. I yield to no one in the depth of my distaste, antipathy, and, indeed, abhorrence, for the death penalty, with all its aspects of physical distress and fear and of moral judgment exercised by finite minds. That distaste is buttressed by a belief that capital punishment serves no useful purpose that can be demonstrated. For me, it violates childhood's training and life's experiences, and is not compatible with the philosophical convictions I have been able to develop. It is antagonistic to any sense of "reverence for life." Were I a legislator, I would vote against the death penalty for the policy reasons argued by counsel for the respective petitioners and expressed and adopted in the several opinions filed by the Justices who vote to reverse these convictions.

Although personally I may rejoice at the Court's result, I find it difficult to accept or to justify as a matter of history, of law, or of constitutional pronouncement. I fear the Court has overstepped. It has sought and has achieved an end.

Mr. Justice Powell, with whom the **Chief Justice, Mr. Justice Blackmun,** and **Mr. Justice Rehnquist** join, dissenting.

. . . The Court granted certiorari in these cases to consider whether the death penalty is any longer a permissible form of punishment. It is the judgment of five Justices that the death penalty, as customarily prescribed and implemented in this country today, offends the constitutional prohibition against cruel and unusual punishments. The reasons for that judgment are stated in five separate opinions, expressing as many separate rationales. In my view, none of these opinions provides a constitutionally adequate foundation for the Court's decision. . . .

Mr. Justice Rehnquist, with whom the **Chief Justice, Mr. Justice Blackmun,** and **Mr. Justice Powell** join, dissenting.

. . . Whatever its precise rationale, today's holding necessarily brings into sharp relief the fundamental question of the role of judicial review in a democratic society. How can government by the elected representatives of the people co-exist with the power of the federal judiciary, whose members are constitutionally insulated from responsiveness to the popular will, to declare invalid laws duly enacted by the popular branches of government?

Sovereignty resides ultimately in the people as a whole and, by adopting through their States a written Constitution for the Nation and subsequently adding amendments to that instrument, they have both granted certain powers to the National Government, and denied other powers to the National and the State Governments. Courts are exercising no more than the judicial function conferred upon them by Art. III of the Constitution when they assess, in a case before them, whether or not a particular legislative enactment is within the authority granted by the Constitution to the enacting body, and whether it runs afoul of some limitation placed by the Constitution on the authority of that body. For the theory is that the people themselves have spoken in the Constitution, and therefore its commands are superior to the commands of the legislature, which is merely an agent of the people.

The Founding Fathers thus wisely sought to have the best of both worlds, the undeniable benefits of both democratic self-government and individual rights protected against possible excesses of that form of government.

The very nature of judicial review, as pointed out by Justice Stone in his dissent in the Butler case, makes the courts the least subject to Madisonian check in the event that they shall, for the best of motives, expand judicial authority beyond the limits contemplated by the Framers. It is for this reason that judicial self-restraint is surely an implied, if not an expressed, condition of the grant of authority of judicial review. The Court's holding in these cases has been reached, I believe, in complete disregard of that implied condition.

Case

GREGG V. GEORGIA

428 U.S. 153, 96 S.Ct. 2909, 49 L.Ed. 2d. 859 (1976)
Vote: 7–2

Here the Supreme Court effectively reinstates the death penalty by sustaining a revised Georgia death penalty law. The petitioner, Troy Gregg, was convicted of armed robbery and murder and was sentenced to death. In accordance with Georgia's death penalty law revised after Furman v. Georgia, *the trial was conducted in two stages, a guilt stage and a sentencing stage.*

Judgment of the Court, and opinion of **Mr. Justice Stewart, Mr. Justice Powell,** and **Mr. Justice Stevens,** announced by **Mr. Justice Stewart.**

. . . There is no question that death as a punishment is unique in its severity and irrevocability. When defendant's life is at stake, the Court has been particularly sensitive to insure that every safeguard is observed. But we are concerned here only with the imposition of capital punishment for the crime of murder, and when a life has been taken deliberately by the offender, we cannot say that the punishment is invariably disproportionate to the crime. It is an extreme sanction, suitable to the most extreme of crimes.

We hold that the death penalty is not a form of punishment that may never be imposed, regardless of the circumstances of the offense, regardless of the character of the offender, and regardless of the procedure followed in reaching the decision to impose it.

We now turn to consideration of the constitutionality of Georgia's capital-sentencing procedures. In the wake of *Furman,* Georgia amended its capital punishment statute, but chose not to narrow the scope of its murder provisions. Thus, now as before *Furman,* in Georgia "[a] person commits murder when he unlawfully and with malice aforethought, either express or implied, causes the death of another human being." All persons convicted of murder "shall be punished by death or by imprisonment for life."

Georgia did act, however, to narrow the class of murderers subject to capital punishment by specifying 10 statutory aggravating circumstances, one of which must be found by the jury to exist beyond a reasonable doubt before a death sentence can ever be imposed. In addition, the jury is authorized to consider any other appropriate aggravating or mitigating circumstances. The jury is not required to find any mitigating circumstance in order to make a recommendation of mercy that is binding on the trial court, but it must find a statutory aggravating circumstance before recommending a sentence of death.

These procedures require the jury to consider the circumstances of the crime and the criminal before it recommends sentence. No longer can a Georgia jury do as *Furman*'s jury did: reach a finding of the defendant's guilt and then, without guidance or direction, decide whether he should live or die. Instead, the jury's attention is directed to the specific circumstances of the crime: Was it committed in the course of another capital felony? Was it committed for money? Was it committed upon a peace officer or judicial officer? Was it committed in a particularly heinous way or in a manner that endangered the lives of many persons? In addition, the jury's attention is focused on the characteristics of the person who committed the crime: Does he have a record of prior convictions for capital offenses? Are there any special facts about this defendant that mitigate against imposing capital punishment (e.g., his youth, the extent of his cooperation with the police, his emotional state at the time of the crime). As a result, while some jury discretion still exists, "the discretion to be exercised is controlled by clear and objective standards so as to produce non-discriminatory application."

As an important additional safeguard against arbitrariness and caprice, the Georgia statutory scheme provides for automatic appeal of all death sentences to the State's Supreme Court. That court is required by statute to review each sentence of death and determine whether it was imposed under the influence of passion or prejudice, whether the evidence supports the jury's finding of a statutory aggravating circumstance, and whether the sentence is disproportionate compared to those sentences imposed in similar cases.

In short, Georgia's new sentencing procedures require as a prerequisite to the imposition of the death penalty, specific jury findings as to the circumstances of the crime or the character of the defendant. Moreover to guard further against a situation comparable to that presented in *Furman,* the Supreme Court of Georgia compares each death sentence with the sentences imposed on similarly situated defendants to ensure that the sentence of death in a particular case is not disproportionate. On their face these procedures seem to satisfy the concerns of *Furman.* No longer should there be "no meaningful basis for distinguishing the few cases in which [the death penalty] is imposed from the many cases in which it is not."

The basic concern of *Furman* centered on those defendants who were being condemned to death capriciously and arbitrarily. Under the procedures before the Court in that case, sentencing authorities were not directed to give attention to the nature or circumstances of the crime committed or to the character or record of the defendant. Left unguided, juries imposed the death sentence in a way that could only be called freakish. The new Georgia sentencing procedures, by contrast, focus the jury's attention on the particularized nature of the crime and the particularized characteristics of the individual defendant. While the jury is permitted to consider any aggravating or mitigating circumstances, it must find and identify at least one statutory aggravating factor before it may impose a penalty of death. In this way the jury's discretion is channeled. No longer can a jury wantonly and freakishly impose the death sentence; it is always circumscribed by the legislative guidelines. In addition, the review function of the Supreme Court of Georgia affords additional assurance that the concerns that prompted our decision in *Furman* are not present to any significant degree in the Georgia procedure applied here.

Mr. Justice White, with whom the **Chief Justice** and **Mr. Justice Rehnquist** join, concurring in the judgment. . . .

Mr. Justice Blackmun, concurring in the judgment. . . .

Mr. Justice Marshall, dissenting.

In *Furman v. Georgia,* I set forth at some length my views on the basic issue presented to the Court in these cases. The death penalty, I concluded, is a cruel and unusual punishment prohibited by the Eighth and Fourteenth Amendments. That continues to be my view.

In *Furman* I concluded that the death penalty is constitutionally invalid for two reasons. First, the death penalty is excessive. And second, the American people, fully informed as to the purposes of the death penalty and its liabilities, would in my view reject it as morally unacceptable. . . .

The mere fact that the community demands the murderer's life in return for the evil he has done cannot sustain the death penalty, for as the plurality reminds us, "the Eighth Amendment demands more than that a challenged punishment be acceptable to contemporary society." To be sustained under the Eighth Amendment, the death penalty must "[comport] with the basic concept of human dignity at the core of the Amendment." . . . Under these standards, the taking of life "because the wrongdoer deserves it" surely must fall, for such a punishment has as its very basis the total denial of the wrongdoer's dignity and worth.

The death penalty, unnecessary to promote the goal of deterrence or to further any legitimate notion of retribution, is an excessive penalty forbidden by the Eighth and Fourteenth Amendments. I respectfully dissent from the Court's judgment upholding the sentences of death imposed upon the petitioners in these cases.

Mr. Justice Brennan, dissenting. . . .

Case

PAYNE V. TENNESSEE
501 U.S. 808, 111 S.Ct. 2597, 115 L.Ed. 2d. 720 (1991)
Vote: 6–3

In this case the Supreme Court overturns its decisions in Booth v. Maryland *(1987), and* South Carolina v. Gathers (1989), *barring the admission of victim impact evidence during the sentencing phase of a capital trial.*

Chief Justice Rehnquist delivered the opinion of the Court.

. . . The petitioner, Pervis Tyrone Payne, was convicted by a jury on two counts of first-degree murder and

one count of assault with intent to commit murder in the first degree. He was sentenced to death for each of the murders, and to 30 years in prison for the assault.

The victims of Payne's offenses were 28-year-old Charisse Christopher, her 2-year-old daughter Lacie, and her 3-year-old son Nicholas. The three lived together in an apartment in Millington, Tennessee, across the hall from Payne's girlfriend, Bobbie Thomas. On Saturday, June 27, 1987, Payne visited Thomas' apartment several times in expectation of her return from her mother's house in Arkansas, but found no one at home. On one visit, he left his overnight bag, containing clothes and other items for his weekend stay, in the hallway outside Thomas' apartment. With the bag were three cans of malt liquor.

Payne passed the morning and early afternoon injecting cocaine and drinking beer. Later, he drove around the town with a friend in the friend's car, each of them taking turns reading a pornographic magazine. Sometime around 3 P.M., Payne returned to the apartment complex, entered the Christophers' apartment, and began making sexual advances towards Charisse. Charisse resisted and Payne became violent. A neighbor who resided in the apartment directly beneath the Christophers, heard Charisse screaming, "'Get out, get out' as if she were telling the children to leave." The noise briefly subsided and then began "horribly loud." The neighbor called the police after she heard a "blood curdling scream" from the Christopher apartment. . . .

When the first police officer arrived at the scene, he immediately encountered Payne who was leaving the apartment building, so covered with blood that he appeared to be "sweating blood." The officer confronted Payne, who responded, "I'm the complainant." . . . When the officer asked, "What's going on up there?" Payne struck the officer with the overnight bag, dropped his tennis shoes, and fled.

Inside the apartment, the police encountered a horrifying scene. Blood covered the walls and floor throughout the unit. Charisse and her children were lying on the floor in the kitchen. Nicholas, despite several wounds inflicted by a butcher knife that completely penetrated through his body from front to back, was still breathing. Miraculously, he survived, but not until after undergoing seven hours of surgery and a transfusion of 1700 cc's of blood—400 to 500 cc's more than his estimated normal blood volume. Charisse and Lacie were dead.

Charisse's body was found on the kitchen floor on her back, her legs fully extended. She had sustained 42 direct knife wounds and 42 defensive wounds on her arms and hands. The wounds were caused by 41 separate thrusts of a butcher knife. None of the 84 wounds inflicted by Payne were individually fatal; rather, the cause of death was most likely bleeding from all of the wounds.

Lacie's body was on the kitchen floor near her mother. She had suffered stab wounds to the chest, abdomen, back, and head. The murder weapon, a butcher knife, was found at her feet. Payne's baseball cap was snapped on her arm near her elbow. Three cans of malt liquor bearing Payne's fingerprints were found on a table near her body, and a fourth empty one was on the landing outside the apartment door.

Payne was apprehended later that day hiding in the attic of the home of a former girlfriend. As he descended the stairs of the attic, he stated to the arresting officers,

"Man, I ain't killed no woman." According to one of the officers, Payne had "a wild look about him. His pupils were contracted. He was foaming at the mouth, saliva. He appeared to be very nervous. He was breathing real rapid." He had blood on his body and clothes and several scratches across his chest. It was later determined that the blood stains matched the victims' blood types. A search of his pockets revealed a packet containing cocaine residue, a hypodermic syringe wrapper, and a cap from a hypodermic syringe. His overnight bag, containing a bloody white shirt, was found in a nearby dumpster.

At trial, Payne took the stand and, despite the overwhelming and relatively uncontroverted evidence against him, testified that he had not harmed any of the Christophers. Rather, he asserted that another man had raced by him as he was walking up the stairs to the floor where the Christophers lived. He stated that he had gotten blood on himself when, after hearing moans from the Christopher's apartment, he had tried to help the victims. According to his testimony, he panicked and fled when he heard police sirens and noticed the blood on his clothes. The jury returned guilty verdicts against Payne on all counts.

During the sentencing phase of the trial, Payne presented the testimony of four witnesses: his mother and father, Bobbie Thomas, and Dr. John T. Huston, a clinical psychologist specializing in criminal court evaluation work. Bobbie Thomas testified that she met Payne at church, during a time when she was being abused by her husband. She stated that Payne was a very caring person, and that he devoted much time and attention to her three children, who were being affected by her marital difficulties. She said that the children had come to love him very much and would miss him and that he "behaved just like a father that loved his kids." She asserted that he did not drink, nor did he use drugs, and that it was generally inconsistent with Payne's character to have committed these crimes.

Dr. Huston testified that based on Payne's low score on an IQ test, Payne was "mentally handicapped." Huston also said that Payne was neither psychotic nor schizophrenic, and that Payne was the most polite prisoner he had ever met. Payne's parents testified that their son had no prior criminal record and had never been arrested. They also stated that Payne had no history of alcohol or drug abuse, he worked with his father as a painter, he was good with children, and that he was a good son.

The State presented the testimony of Charisse's mother, Mary Zvolanek. When asked how Nicholas had been affected by the murders of his mother and sister, she responded:

He cries for his mom. He doesn't seem to understand why she doesn't come home. And he cries for his sister Lacie. He comes to me many times during the week and asks me, Grandmama, do you miss my Lacie. And I tell him yes. He says, I'm worried about my Lacie. . . .

In arguing for the death penalty during closing argument, the prosecutor commented on the continuing effects of Nicholas' experience, stating:

But we do know that Nicholas was alive. And Nicholas was in the same room. Nicholas was still conscious. His eyes were open. He responded to the paramedics. He was able to follow their directions. He was able to hold his intestines in as he was carried to the ambulance. So he knew what happened to his mother and baby sister. . . .

There is nothing you can do to ease the pain of any of the families involved in this case. There is nothing you can do to ease the pain of Bernice or Carl Payne, and that's a tragedy. There is nothing you can do basically to ease the pain of Mr. and Mrs. Zvolanek, and that's a tragedy. They will have to live with it the rest of their lives. There is obviously nothing you can do for Charisse and Lacie Jo. But there is something that you can do for Nicholas.

Somewhere down the road Nicholas is going to grow up, hopefully. He's going to want to know what happened. And he is going to know what happened to his baby sister and his mother. He is going to want to know what type of justice was done. He is going to want to know what happened. With your verdict, you will provide the answer. . . .

In the rebuttal to Payne's closing argument, the prosecutor stated:

You saw the videotape this morning. You saw what Nicholas Christopher will carry in his mind forever. When you talk about cruel, when you talk about atrocious, and when you talk about heinous, that picture will always come into your mind, probably throughout the rest of your lives.

. . . No one will ever know about Lacie Jo because she never had the chance to grow up. Her life was taken from her at the age of two years old. So, no, there won't be a high school principal to talk about Lacie Jo Christopher, and there won't be anybody to take her to her high school prom. And there won't be anybody there—there won't be her mother there or Nicholas' mother there to kiss him at night. His mother will never kiss him good night or pat him as he goes off to bed, or hold him and sing him a lullaby.

[Petitioner's attorney] wants you to think about a good reputation, people who love the defendant and things about him. He doesn't want you to think about the people who love Charisse Christopher, her mother and daddy who loved her. The people who loved little Lacie Jo, the grandparents who are still here. The brother who mourns for her every single day and wants to know where his best little playmate is. He doesn't have anybody to watch cartoons with him, a little one. These are the things that go into why it is especially cruel, heinous, and atrocious, the burden that that child will carry forever. . . .

The jury sentenced Payne to death on each of the murder counts.

The Supreme Court of Tennessee affirmed the convictions and sentence. The court rejected Payne's contention that the admission of the grandmother's testimony and the State's closing argument constituted prejudicial violations of his rights under the Eighth Amendment. . . .

We granted certiorari . . . to reconsider our holdings in *Booth* [*v. Maryland*] and [*South Carolina v.*] *Gathers.* . . .

We are now of the view that a State may properly conclude that for the jury to assess meaningfully the defendant's moral culpability and blameworthiness, it should have before it at the sentencing phase evidence of the specific harm caused by the defendant. "[T]he State has a legitimate interest in counteracting the mitigating evidence which the defendant is entitled to put in, by reminding the sentencer that just as the murderer should be considered as an individual, so too the victim is an individual whose death represents a unique loss to society and in particular to his family." . . . *Booth* deprives the State of the full moral force of its evidence and may prevent the jury from having before it all the information necessary to determine the proper punishment for a first-degree murder.

The present case is an example of the potential for such unfairness. The capital sentencing jury heard testimony from Payne's girlfriend that they met at church, that he was affectionate, caring, kind to her children, that he was not an abuser of drugs or alcohol, and that it was inconsistent with his character to have committed the murder. Payne's parents testified that he was a good son, and a clinical psychologist testified that Payne was an extremely polite prisoner and suffered from a low IQ. None of this testimony was related to the circumstances of Payne's brutal crimes. In contrast, the only evidence of the impact of Payne's offenses during the sentencing phase was Nicholas' grandmother's description—in response to a single question—that the child misses his mother and baby sister. Payne argues that the Eighth Amendment commands that the jury's death sentence must be set aside because the jury heard this testimony. But the testimony illustrated quite poignantly some of the harm that Payne's killing had caused; there is nothing unfair about allowing the jury to bear in mind that harm at the same time as it considers the mitigating evidence introduced by the defendant. The Supreme Court of Tennessee in this case obviously felt the unfairness of the rule pronounced by *Booth* when it said "[i]t is an affront to the civilized members of the human race to say that at sentencing in a capital case, a parade of witnesses may praise the background, character and good deeds of Defendant (as was done in this case) without limitation as to relevancy, but nothing may be said that bears upon the character of, or the harm imposed, upon the victims." . . .

We thus hold that if the State chooses to permit the admission of victim impact evidence and prosecutorial argument on that subject, the Eighth Amendment erects no *per se* bar. A State may legitimately conclude that evidence about the victim and about the impact of the murder on the victim's family is relevant to the jury's decision as to whether or not the death penalty should be imposed. There is no reason to treat such evidence differently than other relevant evidence is treated. . . . Reconsidering these decisions now, we conclude for the reasons heretofore stated, that they were wrongly decided and should be, and now are,

overruled. We accordingly affirm the judgment of the Supreme Court of Tennessee.

Justice O'Connor, with whom *Justice White* and *Justice Kennedy* join, concurring. . . .

Justice Scalia, with whom *Justice O'Connor* and *Justice Kennedy* join [in part], concurring. . . .

Justice Souter, with whom *Justice Kennedy* joins, concurring. . . .

Justice Marshall, with whom *Justice Blackmun* joins, dissenting. . . .

Justice Stevens, with whom *Justice Blackmun* joins, dissenting.

. . . Until today our capital punishment jurisprudence has required that any decision to impose the death penalty be based solely on evidence that tends to inform the jury about the character of the offense and the character of the defendant. Evidence that serves no purpose other than to appeal to the sympathies or emotions of the jurors has never been considered admissible. Thus, if a defendant, who had murdered a convenience store clerk in cold blood in the course of an armed robbery, offered evidence unknown to him at the time of the crime about the immoral character of his victim, all would recognize immediately that the evidence was irrelevant and inadmissible. Even-handed justice requires that the same constraint be imposed on the advocate of the death penalty. . . .

11

PERSONAL AUTONOMY AND THE CONSTITUTIONAL RIGHT OF PRIVACY

Chapter Outline

Introduction

Constitutional Foundations of the Right of Privacy

Procreation and Birth Control

The Abortion Controversy

The Right of Privacy and Living Arrangements

Privacy and Gay Rights

Other Applications of the Right of Privacy

A Right to Die?

Conclusion

Key Terms

For Further Reading

Internet Resources

Jacobson v. Massachusetts (1905)

Meyer v. Nebraska (1923)

Buck v. Bell (1927)

Poe v. Ullman (1961)

Griswold v. Connecticut (1965)

Roe v. Wade (1973)

Planned Parenthood v. Casey (1992)

Bowers v. Hardwick (1986)

Washington v. Glucksberg (1997)

. . . [T]here is a sphere of action in which society, as distinguished from the individual, has, if any, only an indirect interest; comprehending all that portion of a person's life and conduct which affects only himself, or if it also affects others, only with their free, voluntary and undeceived consent and participation.

—JOHN STUART MILL, *On Liberty* (1859)

INTRODUCTION

The **constitutional right of privacy** protects the individual from unwarranted government interference in intimate personal relationships or activities. As it has taken shape since the mid-1960s, the right of privacy includes the freedom of the individual to make fundamental choices involving sex, reproduction, family life, and other intimate personal relationships.

Of the various constitutional rights addressed in this book, the right of privacy remains the most intensely disputed. The controversy stems in part from the absence of any specific reference to privacy in the Constitution. Some scholars and judges still adhere to Justice Hugo Black's view that a right of privacy cannot reasonably be inferred from the language of the original Constitution or any of its amendments. However, it is clear that this is a minority position in the late 1990s. Among recent Supreme Court nominees, only Judge Robert Bork has rejected the interpretive foundation of the right of privacy. For most Americans, the debate over privacy has less to do with competing theories of constitutional interpretation than with the profound implications of the privacy principle for divisive social and moral questions, such as **abortion, gay rights,** and **euthanasia.**

In *Roe v. Wade* (1973), the Supreme Court held that the right of privacy "is broad enough to encompass a woman's decision whether or not to terminate her pregnancy." As the ongoing protest against legal abortion makes clear, abortion is hardly an ordinary issue of public policy. Nor was *Roe v. Wade* a run-of-the-mill Supreme Court decision. Unlike most constitutional decisions, *Roe* aroused deep philosophical conflict and even deeper political and emotional turmoil. *Roe v. Wade* drew the Supreme Court into a firestorm of political controversy that continues unabated after two decades. This controversy has dominated public discussion of the Court, often eclipsing other important issues and likewise influencing the debate surrounding nominations to the Supreme Court.

Although abortion is the focal point of the debate over the right of privacy, the viability of the right of privacy is not based solely on the continued vitality of *Roe v. Wade*. Even if *Roe* were to be overturned, the right of privacy would still exist as an independent constitutional right, albeit somewhat circumscribed. The right of privacy is now well established in both federal and state constitutional law and has application to numerous questions of public policy beyond abortion. This chapter examines some of the more salient ones.

Philosophical Foundations of the Right of Privacy

When the Supreme Court invoked the right of privacy to effectively legalize abortion within stated limits, it was giving expression to a sense of **moral individualism** that is deeply rooted in American culture. However, countervailing notions of traditional morality are also deeply ingrained in American society, as the relentless and widespread attacks on *Roe v. Wade* demonstrate. In no other area of constitutional law are individualism and traditional morality so sharply antagonistic as in the area of privacy rights.

The moral individualism underlying the constitutional right of privacy was conceived in the political liberalism of the Age of Enlightenment. This classical liberalism gained ascendancy in the nineteenth century. Today, it is most closely approximated by the philosophy of **libertarianism,** which holds that individual freedom is the highest good and that law should be interpreted to maximize the scope of liberty.

During and after the 1960s, the libertarian perspective became increasingly widespread among Americans, especially younger people. In the late 1960s and throughout the 1970s, a large number of people began to question the authority of government to regulate the private lives of individuals in the name of traditional morality. In the libertarian view, the legitimate role of government is protection of individuals from one another, not from their own vices. Thus, libertarians often object to laws regulating sexual conduct, living arrangements, and the private use of drugs—and even to laws mandating that motorcycle riders wear helmets. Perhaps the ultimate libertarian position is opposition to the criminal law against suicide. In the libertarian view, the individual has the right to make basic decisions regarding his or her own life—or death.

The countervailing position, which might be dubbed **classical conservatism,** holds that individuals must often be protected against their own vices. Classical conservatives not only defend traditional morality but the embodiment of that morality in the law. On the contemporary Supreme Court, Justice Antonin Scalia has endorsed the classical conservative view of law and morality. In *Barnes v. Glen Theatre, Inc.* (1991) (the "nude dancing" decision discussed and reprinted in Chapter 8), Scalia wrote:

> Our society prohibits, and all human societies have prohibited, certain activities not because they harm others but because they are considered . . . immoral. In American society, such prohibitions have included, for example, sadomasochism, cockfighting,

bestiality, suicide, drug use, prostitution and sodomy. While there might be a great diversity of views on whether various of these prohibitions should exist, . . . there is no doubt that absent specific constitutional protection for the conduct involved, the Constitution does not prohibit them simply because they regulate "morality."

The debate over the constitutional right of privacy is ultimately a debate between two sharply divergent views of the law. In the libertarian view, the law exists to protect individuals from one another. In this view, morality is not in and of itself a legitimate basis for law. The classical conservative view, on the other hand, sees law and morality as inseparable and holds that the maintenance of societal morality is one of the essential functions of the legal system.

CONSTITUTIONAL FOUNDATIONS OF THE RIGHT OF PRIVACY

Although libertarianism has roots in the liberalism of the Enlightenment, it is doubtful that any of the framers of the Constitution were libertarians in the modern sense of the term. Certainly the framers believed in individual freedom, but most did not conceive of freedom as including the right to flout traditional principles of conduct embodied in the common law. Yet the right of privacy, in essence the constitutionalization of libertarianism, has been "found" by the Supreme Court to emanate from various provisions of the Bill of Rights (see *Griswold v. Connecticut* [1965]).

Several provisions of the Bill of Rights were adopted to protect individuals from unreasonable invasions of privacy. The Third Amendment explicitly protects the privacy of the home in peacetime from soldiers seeking quarters. The Fourth Amendment protects individuals from unreasonable searches and seizures where they have a "reasonable expectation of privacy" (*Katz v. United States* [1967], Harlan, J., concurring). The Fifth Amendment prohibits compulsory self-incrimination, thus protecting the privacy of an accused individual's thoughts. The First Amendment ensures freedom of conscience in both political and religious matters, again recognizing the autonomy of the individual. Finally, the First Amendment's implicit guarantee of freedom of association protects one's right to choose one's friends, one's spouse, one's business partners, and so on. In *Griswold v. Connecticut* (1965), the Supreme Court interpreted these protections as embodying a right to be free of those government intrusions into the realm of intimate personal decisions.

Proponents of a constitutional right of privacy often cite the Ninth Amendment, which guarantees rights "retained by the people" even though they are not enumerated in the Constitution. Indeed, historically, the courts have recognized a variety of unenumerated constitutional rights. The right to marry, to choose one's spouse, to select an occupation, to travel freely within the country, and to enter into contracts are all examples of long-standing rights retained by the people although they are not explicitly provided for in the Constitution. They have achieved constitutional status by virtue of the fact that they are elements of the "liberty" protected by the Due Process Clauses of the Fifth and Fourteenth Amendments.

Dissenting in *Olmstead v. United States* (1928), Justice Louis Brandeis wrote:

The makers of our Constitution undertook to secure conditions favorable to the pursuit of happiness. They recognized the significance of man's spiritual nature, of his feelings and his intellect. They knew that only a part of his pain, pleasure, and satisfactions of life are to be found in material things. They sought to protect Americans in their beliefs, their thoughts, their emotions and their sensations. They conferred, as against the Government, the right to be let alone—the most comprehensive of rights and the right most valued by civilized men.

These words were written by way of dissent in a case dealing with the scope of the Fourth Amendment's protection against wiretapping (see Chapter 10). Yet they may be interpreted as foreshadowing the modern right of privacy, which is, in essence, the **right to be let alone.**

Substantive Due Process

To understand the emergence of the constitutional right of privacy, one must return to the era of economic due process (see Chapter 7). In a landmark decision in 1905, the Supreme Court broadly interpreted the Due Process Clause of the Fourteenth Amendment to impose a restriction on the power of state legislatures to engage in economic regulation. In *Lochner v. New York,* the Court held that the "liberty of contract" protected by the Fourteenth Amendment had been infringed when the state of New York adopted a law restricting the working hours of bakery employees. Although *Lochner* and related decisions were concerned exclusively with the protection of individual property rights (see Chapter 7), they paved the way for the creation of the right of privacy by giving a substantive (as distinct from a strictly procedural) interpretation to the Due Process Clause of the Fourteenth Amendment. Under the **substantive due process** formula, courts can "discover" in the Fourteenth Amendment rights that are "fundamental" or "implicit in a scheme of ordered liberty." Again, the Ninth Amendment's recognition of rights "retained by the people" provides additional justification for the substantive interpretation of the Fourteenth Amendment.

In the first two decades of the twentieth century, substantive due process was by and large confined to the protection of economic liberties from government regulation. Just two months before the Court handed down its controversial decision in *Lochner,* it refused to find in the Due Process Clause a prohibition against compulsory vaccination laws (*Jacobson v. Massachusetts* [1905]). Nevertheless, Justice John M. Harlan's majority opinion did recognize that "[t]here is, of course, a sphere within which the individual may assert the supremacy of his own will and rightfully dispute the authority of any human government, especially of any free government existing under a written constitution, to interfere with the exercise of that will."

For Justice Harlan and most of his brethren, the state's interest in promoting the public health through compulsory vaccination was superior to the individual "exercise of will." Nevertheless, in *Jacobson,* the Court suggested that the Fourteenth Amendment might protect certain noneconomic aspects of individual autonomy.

The expansion of substantive due process to include noneconomic rights took a quantum leap in 1923. In that year, the Court recognized that citizens have the right to study foreign languages in private schools, state statutes to the contrary notwithstanding (*Meyer v. Nebraska*). Two years later, the Court emphasized the right to a private education by striking down an Oregon law that required parents to send their children to public schools (*Pierce v. Society of Sisters* [1925]).

TO SUMMARIZE:

- The right of privacy, aptly defined by Justice Brandeis as "the right to be let alone," can be viewed as a constitutional expression of libertarianism, the doctrine that elevates individual freedom above all other values.

- Although nowhere mentioned explicitly in the Constitution, the right of privacy is generally viewed as implicit in the protections of the Bill of Rights or the broad guarantee of "liberty" found in the Due Process Clauses of the Fifth and Fourteenth Amendments.
- Proponents of the right of privacy often invoke the Ninth Amendment, which guarantees rights "retained by the people" even though they are not enumerated in the Constitution.
- To the extent that judicial recognition of the right of privacy relies on the Due Process Clauses of the Fifth and Fourteenth Amendments, it may be viewed as a modern application of the doctrine of substantive due process.

PROCREATION AND BIRTH CONTROL

The slowly emerging right of privacy experienced a temporary setback in *Buck v. Bell* (1927). There, the Court refused to find in the Fourteenth Amendment an immunity against **compulsory sterilization** for mentally retarded persons. Carrie Buck, a young woman crassly characterized by the Court as "feeble minded," was committed to a state institution, where her mother was also confined. Pursuant to state law, the director of the institution sought to have Carrie Buck sterilized after she had given birth to a mentally retarded child. Carrie Buck's attorneys immediately challenged the constitutionality of the statute, but the Supreme Court, in an 8-to-1 decision, upheld the sterilization law. Writing for the Court, Justice Oliver Wendell Holmes, Jr., declared that the principle announced in *Jacobson v. Massachusetts* was "broad enough to cover cutting the Fallopian tubes." In one of his more memorable (and most gratuitous) lines, Holmes went on to write that "[t]hree generations of imbeciles are enough."

Although *Buck v. Bell* has never been formally overruled, it is unlikely that it would command a majority today. In 1942, the Court struck down a state law providing for the compulsory sterilization of criminals (*Skinner v. Oklahoma*). Although the decision was based on the Equal Protection Clause of the Fourteenth Amendment, rather than on substantive due process, *Skinner* in effect recognized a constitutional right of procreation. The Court characterized the right to procreate as "one of the basic civil rights of man." The Court's decisions in *Meyer v. Nebraska*, *Pierce v. Society of Sisters*, and *Skinner v. Oklahoma* paved the way for the landmark 1965 decision in *Griswold v. Connecticut* recognizing an independent constitutional right of privacy.

The Connecticut Birth Control Controversy

The Griswold case involved a challenge to an 1879 Connecticut law that made the sale and possession of birth control devices a misdemeanor. The law also forbade anyone from assisting, abetting, or counseling another in the use of birth control devices.

In *Poe v. Ullman* (1961) the Supreme Court voted 5 to 4 to dismiss a challenge to the Connecticut law. The challenge stemmed not from a criminal prosecution but from a lawsuit brought by a married couple and their physician who complained of state interference in the doctor–patient relationship. Writing for a four-member plurality, Justice Felix Frankfurter said that there was no real "case or controversy" and that the issue was unripe for judicial review. Frankfurter alluded to a "tacit agreement" whereby the birth control law would no longer be enforced. In a forceful dissent, Justice William O. Douglas pointed out that an earlier criminal prosecution had effectively prevented birth control clinics from operating in the state. Douglas not only asserted that the case was properly before the Court but characterized the statute as "an invasion of the privacy implicit in a free society." Douglas's sharp dissent in *Poe v. Ullman* anticipated the Court's decision in *Griswold* four years later.

Estelle Griswold was the director of Planned Parenthood in Connecticut. Just three days after Planned Parenthood opened a clinic in New Haven, Griswold was arrested. Reportedly, she had given detectives a tour of the clinic, pointing out contraceptives that the clinic was dispensing. After a short trial, Griswold was convicted and fined one hundred dollars. As expected, the Connecticut courts upheld her conviction, rejecting the contention that the state law was unconstitutional. Also as expected, Griswold's attorneys filed a petition for certiorari in the U.S. Supreme Court. When the Court agreed to take the case, it was clear that the justices were going to rule on the constitutionality of the Connecticut law.

Griswold's attorneys argued that the birth control law infringed a right of privacy implicit in the Bill of Rights, as embodied in the concept of personal liberty protected by the Fourteenth Amendment. Moreover, they maintained that the Connecticut statute lacked a reasonable relationship to a legitimate legislative purpose. The state of Connecticut responded by emphasizing its broad police powers, arguing that the birth control law was a rational means of promoting the welfare of Connecticut's people. Interestingly, however, Connecticut's brief failed to state the particular legislative purpose behind the birth control law. Rather, the brief was designed chiefly to persuade the justices that they should not second-guess the wisdom or desirability of social legislation.

On June 7, 1965, the Supreme Court announced its decision striking down the Connecticut birth control law. The vote was 7 to 2. Justice Douglas was given the task of writing the majority opinion. After a disclaimer that "we do not sit as a super-legislature to determine the wisdom, need and propriety of laws . . . ," Douglas proceeded to explain why, in his view, the Connecticut law ran afoul of the Constitution. As an advocate of "total incorporation" (see Chapter 6), Justice Douglas sought to identify an implicit right of privacy in the Bill of Rights, rather than in the vague notions of "liberty" that the Court had in the past attached to the Due Process Clause of the Fourteenth Amendment.

In what has become frequently quoted language, Douglas asserted that "specific guarantees in the Bill of Rights have penumbras, formed by emanations from those guarantees that help give them life and substance." Douglas reasoned that the explicit language of the Bill of Rights, specifically the First, Third, Fourth, Fifth, and Ninth Amendments, when considered along with their "emanations" and "penumbras" as defined by previous decisions of the Court, add up to a general, independent right of privacy. In Douglas's view, this general right was infringed by the state of Connecticut when it outlawed birth control. In the sharpest language of the majority opinion, Douglas wrote:

> Would we allow the police to search the sacred precincts of marital bedrooms for telltale signs of the use of contraceptives? The very idea is repulsive to the notions of privacy surrounding the marriage relationship.

While the prospect of the police searching one's bedroom for evidence of contraception is no doubt repulsive to many, the question is whether the law allowing such a search is constitutional. Obviously, Justices John Harlan and Byron White, who voted to strike down the Connecticut law, were not altogether persuaded by

Justice Douglas's discovery of a general right of privacy in the Bill of Rights. In their separate opinions concurring in the judgment, Harlan and White maintained that the Connecticut law infringed the "liberty" protected by the Fourteenth Amendment, a liberty that, in their view, transcends the particular protections of the Bill of Rights. In taking this course, Justices Harlan and White were not embarking on uncharted jurisprudential waters; they were merely using the substantive due process approach that had been employed in *Meyer v. Nebraska, Pierce v. Society of Sisters,* and the numerous cases in which the Court had used "liberty of contract" to invalidate economic legislation.

Dissenting sharply, Justice Black criticized what he perceived as a blatant attempt to amend the Constitution through loose interpretation. Justice Black never hesitated to urge invalidation of a legislative act if he believed it ran afoul of a specific provision of the Constitution. Consequently, he and Justice Douglas often found themselves voting together in civil liberties cases, thus earning the label "judicial activists." But, as one who preferred to adhere strictly to the text of the Constitution, Black refused in *Griswold* to go along with what he regarded as a discredited approach to constitutional interpretation:

> I cannot rely on the Due Process Clause or the Ninth Amendment or any mysterious and uncertain natural law concept as a reason for striking down this state law. . . . I had thought that we had laid that formula, as a means of striking down state legislation, to rest once and for all.

The debate over modes of constitutional interpretation is certainly a legitimate one. Cogent jurisprudential arguments can be made for and against the Court's decision in *Griswold.* However, it must be recognized that the Court's decision was not based on a radical departure from traditional jurisprudence, as a few extreme critics have claimed. Rather, there is ample precedent for the broad interpretation of the Constitution in general (for example, *Marbury v. Madison*), and the substantive due process formula in particular, in the rich history of the Court's constitutional decision making.

Although *Griswold* was sharply criticized by commentators who shared Justice Black's view of constitutional interpretation and by a few staunch social conservatives, the Court's decision was not subjected to the kind of public outcry occasioned by the desegregation decisions of the 1950s or the school prayer decisions of the early 1960s. Obviously, the average person is not particularly concerned with the legal aspects of a Supreme Court decision; he or she is much more likely to focus on the Court's substantive policy output. As a matter of public policy, *Griswold* was quite well received.

A Gallup Poll conducted in 1965 found that 81 percent of the American public agreed with the statement that "birth control information should be available to anyone who wants it." There can be little doubt that changing societal attitudes about sex, procreation, and contraception had more to do with the Court's decision in *Griswold* than did "emanations" from the Bill of Rights!

Beyond the Marital Bedroom

In the *Griswold* case, the Court was careful to invalidate the Connecticut law only insofar as it invaded marital privacy, thus leaving open the question of whether states could prohibit the use of birth control devices by unmarried persons. In *Eisenstadt v. Baird* (1972), the Court faced a challenge to a Massachusetts law that prohibited unmarried persons from obtaining and using contraceptives. William Baird, a former medical student, was arrested after he delivered a lecture on birth control at Boston University during which he provided some contraceptive foam to a female student. In reversing Baird's conviction and striking down the Massachusetts law, the Court established the right of privacy as an individual right, not a right enjoyed solely by married couples. As Justice William Brennan's opinion for the Court stated,

> [t]he marital couple is not an independent entity with a mind and heart of its own, but an association of two individuals each with separate intellectual and emotional makeup. If the right of privacy means anything, it is the right of the individual, married or single, to be free from unwarranted governmental intrusion into matters so fundamentally affecting a person as the decision whether or not to beget a child.

Having thus articulated an independent right of privacy protecting individual decisions in the area of sex and procreation, *Eisenstadt v. Baird* paved the way for the most controversial decision the Supreme Court was to make during the Chief Justiceship of Warren Burger: *Roe v. Wade.*

TO SUMMARIZE:

- The right of privacy was first invoked in the area of procreation and birth control. In *Griswold v. Connecticut* (1965) the Court struck down a state statute prohibiting the use of birth control devices insofar as the statute applied to married couples. Later, the Court made clear that because the right of privacy is an individual right, laws forbidding the use of contraceptives by unmarried adults are likewise invalid.
- Justice William O. Douglas's opinion for the Court in *Griswold* attempted to justify the right of privacy in terms of "emanations" from the Bill of Rights. Dissenting justices criticized the majority for loosely interpreting the Constitution.
- The *Griswold* case set the stage for the most controversial decision of the Court's modern era: *Roe v. Wade* (1973).

THE ABORTION CONTROVERSY

Norma McCorvey, also known as Jane Roe, was a twenty-five-year-old unmarried Texas woman who was faced with an unwanted pregnancy resulting from an alleged gang rape that she later admitted never occurred. After her doctor informed her that abortion was illegal in Texas, she went to see an attorney. That attorney, Linda Coffee, introduced McCorvey to Sarah Weddington, a young woman just out of law school, who ultimately argued the case before the Supreme Court. Weddington expressed her view that the Constitution allows a woman to control her own body, including the decision to terminate an unwanted pregnancy. Shortly thereafter, Coffee and Weddington filed suit in federal district court against Dallas District Attorney Henry Wade, seeking to enjoin him from enforcing what was claimed to be an unconstitutional law. The suit was filed as a class action, that is, not only on behalf of Jane Roe but on behalf of all women "similarly situated." The district court declared the Texas law unconstitutional but refused to issue the injunction, invoking the doctrine of abstention (see Chapter 1). As permitted in cases of this kind, Jane Roe appealed directly to the Supreme Court.

Norma McCorvey, a.k.a.
"Jane Roe"

The Supreme Court Decides *Roe v. Wade*

On January 22, 1973, the Supreme Court handed down a 7-to-2 decision striking down the Texas law. Justice Harry A. Blackmun wrote the majority opinion. After determining that the case was properly before the Court, Blackmun reviewed prior decisions on the right of privacy. In what is perhaps the best known statement from his opinion in *Roe,* Blackmun concluded that the right of privacy "is broad enough to encompass a woman's decision whether or not to terminate her pregnancy." Yet Blackmun's analysis did not end with this pronouncement, because the right of privacy, like all constitutional rights, may be limited if there is a sufficiently strong justification to do so by the state. Specifically, because the Court identified privacy as a **fundamental right,** the state of Texas had to demonstrate a **compelling interest** to justify regulating or prohibiting abortion. The Court recognized a compelling interest in protecting maternal health that justifies "reasonable" state regulations of abortions performed after the first trimester of pregnancy.

However, the state of Texas sought not only to regulate but also to proscribe abortion altogether and claimed a compelling state interest in protecting unborn human life. The Court recognized this interest as legitimate but held that it does not become compelling until that point in pregnancy when the fetus becomes "viable," that is, capable of "meaningful life outside the mother's womb." Beyond the point of **viability,** according to the Court, the state may prohibit abortion, except in cases where it is necessary to preserve the life or health of the mother.

The Court summarily rejected the argument that a fetus is a "person" as that term is used in the Constitution and thus possessed of a right to life, holding that the term "has application only postnatally." If a fetus is regarded as a person from the point of conception, then any abortion is certainly homicide. If that were the case, then states could not allow abortions even in cases of rape or where the pregnancy endangers the life of the mother (as the Texas law challenged in *Roe* allowed). Nor would intrauterine devices or "morning after" pills, both of which prevent implantation after conception, be permissible. Like abortion, these forms of birth control, which are regarded by most as morally acceptable, would be tantamount to murder. Clearly, the Court was not inclined to make such a pronouncement. Nor was it prepared to assert that the woman's right to obtain an abortion is absolute—"that she is entitled to terminate at whatever time, in whatever way and for whatever reason she alone chooses. . . ." The Court tried to steer a middle course, to accommodate what it regarded as legitimate interests on both sides of the issue.

Roe v. Wade was the product of sharp conflict, bargaining, and compromise within the Supreme Court. Although the Court's decision attempted to strike a reasonable balance between the state's interest in protecting unborn life and a woman's interest in controlling her own body, the abortion decision was not viewed by the "pro-life" forces as an acceptable compromise. The hostile reaction to *Roe v. Wade* was immediate and intense. Justices of the Supreme Court, especially Harry Blackmun, received hate mail and even death threats. The 1980s saw frequent public demonstrations, harassment of women entering abortion clinics, and even the occasional bombing of such facilities. Militant confrontation between pro-life and pro-choice forces continues in the late 1990s.

Since the *Roe* decision came down in 1973, public opinion has remained sharply divided on the abortion question. This sharp division was reflected in the U.S. Senate, which, in 1983, defeated by one vote a proposed constitutional amendment that would have provided that "[t]he right to an abortion is not secured by this Constitution." Although it is difficult to say with certainty which side of the issue is favored by public opinion, it was clear until recently that the anti-abortion forces manifest greater intensity in their opposition to abortion than the pro-choice forces do in their support. In politics, intensity may count for as much as numbers. In constitutional law, neither is supposed to matter; but there is considerable evidence that both do!

Regulation of Abortion in the Wake of *Roe v. Wade*

In the wake of *Roe v. Wade,* many state and local governments enacted regulations governing the performance of abortions. As previously noted, the Court in *Roe* allowed for "reasonable" regulation of abortions to effectuate the state's legitimate interest in protecting maternal health. However, many state statutes and local ordinances affecting abortion were not intended to promote maternal health at all but to deter women from obtaining abortions.

In *Planned Parenthood of Central Missouri v. Danforth* (1976), the Court struck down a Missouri law that required minors to obtain the consent of their husbands or parents before obtaining an abortion. Three years later, in *Bellotti v. Baird* (1979), the Court struck down a similar law passed by the state of Massachusetts. This law required an unmarried pregnant minor to obtain parental consent for an abortion or, if parental consent was not given, to obtain authorization from a judge who was to determine whether the abortion was in the minor's best interest. Taken together, the decisions in *Bellotti* and *Danforth* emphasized the personal nature of the abortion decision. Other parties, whether one's spouse, parents, or the state, cannot be given a veto over the exercise of one's constitutional rights.

In 1983, the Court appeared to back away from the strong position taken in *Bellotti* and *Danforth.* In *Planned Parenthood v. Ashcroft,* the Court upheld a Missouri law that required parental consent for "unemancipated" minors but apparently only because the law provided a mechanism whereby exceptionally mature minors could obtain abortions by seeking judicial intervention.

The same day *Ashcroft* came down, the Court announced its decision in *Akron v. Akron Center for Reproductive Health* (1983). In this case, the Court struck down a city ordinance that, in addition to requiring parental consent for minors' abortions, required (1) that all abortions be performed in hospitals; (2) a twenty-four-hour waiting period before abortions could be performed; (3) that physicians make certain specified statements to the woman seeking abortion to ensure that her decision is truly an informed one; and (4) that all fetal remains be disposed of in a manner that is both humane and sanitary. The Court found that these requirements imposed significant burdens on a woman's exercise of her constitutional rights without substantially furthering the state's legitimate interests. The "humane and sanitary" disposal requirement was invalidated as "impermissibly vague" in obliquely suggesting an intention on the part of the city to "mandate some sort of 'decent burial' of the embryo at the earliest stages of formation."

Restrictions on Public Funding of Abortions

One of the more successful legislative assaults on abortion involves the exemption of abortions not deemed to be medically necessary from medical welfare programs. As a matter of public policy, this exemption is highly questionable. For one thing, it

The Constitution in action: A "pro-life" demonstration

creates a double standard for rich and poor. Moreover, it seems likely to increase the numbers of future dependents on food stamps, welfare, and Medicaid. However, as the Supreme Court has frequently observed, the wisdom of a particular public policy and the constitutionality thereof are separate questions. In *Maher v. Roe* (1977), the Court voted 6 to 3 to uphold a Connecticut welfare regulation that denied Medicaid benefits to indigent women seeking to have abortions, unless their attending physicians certified their abortions as "medically necessary." The Court's decision was based on the "new due process-equal protection" analysis developed by the Court during the last two decades (see Chapter 12). In a nutshell, the Court held that the denial of Medicaid benefits to poor women seeking elective abortions neither discriminated against a "suspect class" of persons nor unduly burdened the exercise of fundamental rights. Therefore, the Court judged the Connecticut regulation to be permissible under both the Equal Protection and Due Process Clauses of the Fourteenth Amendment.

Three years later, in *Harris v. McRae* (1980), the Court upheld a provision of federal law, commonly known as the **Hyde Amendment,** forbidding the use of federal funds to support nontherapeutic abortions. Writing for a sharply divided Court, Justice Potter Stewart concluded that

> [i]t simply does not follow that a woman's freedom of choice carries with it a constitutional entitlement to the financial resources to avail herself of the full range of protected choices. . . . Although government may not place obstacles in the path of a woman's exercise of her freedom of choice, it need not remove those not of its own creation. Indigency falls in the latter category.

The Hyde Amendment restricted federal funding of abortions, leaving states to decide whether to impose similar restrictions on the use of state funds. As noted, the U.S. Supreme Court upheld Connecticut's restriction on abortion funding in *Maher v. Roe* (1977). Yet several state supreme courts have invalidated similar restrictions under their state constitutions (see, for example, *Committee to Defend Reproductive Rights v. Myers* [Cal. S.Ct. 1981], *Moe v. Secretary of Administration* [Mass. S.Jud.Ct. 1981], and *Right to Choose v. Byrne* [N.J. S.Ct. 1982]).

Eroding Support for *Roe v. Wade* on the Supreme Court in the 1980s

By the early 1980s, the bloc of justices supportive of *Roe v. Wade* had begun to erode. In the *Akron Center* decision of 1983, the Court had explicitly reaffirmed *Roe* but by one less vote than the *Roe* majority of 1973. While Potter Stewart had voted with the majority in *Roe,* his successor on the Court, Sandra Day O'Connor, dissented in the *Akron* case. In one of her most significant early opinions, Justice O'Connor expressed considerable dissatisfaction with the **trimester framework** adopted by the Court in *Roe v. Wade.* O'Connor's *Akron* dissent went well beyond a critique of the particular formulation adopted by the Court in *Roe,* however. Her opinion suggested that a state has a sufficiently compelling interest in protecting potential life to allow it to ban abortion at any stage of pregnancy. O'Connor's apparent dissent from the *Roe* decision did not necessarily indicate that she opposed legalized abortion. It did suggest that O'Connor believed that the state legislature (not a court of law) is the proper forum for resolving the abortion issue. Again, quoting from her dissent in *Akron v. Akron Center,* "[i]t is . . . difficult to believe that this Court, without the resources available to those bodies entrusted with making legislative choices, believes itself competent to make these inquiries."

Substantial support exists, even among those who favor some form of legalized abortion, for the position adopted by Justice O'Connor. Some would argue that the question of abortion is simply not one that courts should decide. These critics would call for judicial restraint, for deference to the legislative judgment. While many state legislators have criticized the Supreme Court for usurping the role of the legislature in deciding *Roe v. Wade,* others have expressed relief that the judiciary has "taken the heat" on the abortion issue. Few legislators relish the prospect of voting on the abortion question. On both sides of the issue are powerful interest groups, and a middle ground on abortion is difficult to locate, much less defend.

The Supreme Court reaffirmed *Roe v. Wade* again in *Thornburgh v. American College of Obstetricians and Gynecologists* (1986). However, in *Thornburgh,* the vote in favor of a constitutional right to abortion was 5 to 4, because Chief Justice Burger switched sides and joined the dissenters. Although Burger retired after the 1985 term, his departure did not strengthen the position of *Roe v. Wade.* President

Ronald Reagan elevated Associate Justice William Rehnquist to the position of chief justice and appointed Antonin Scalia, a conservative, to fill the vacancy.

In 1987, it appeared that the opponents of legalized abortion were only one vote away from overturning *Roe v. Wade*. In that year, Justice Lewis Powell, a member of the *Roe* majority, retired from the Court. It looked as if the Court would be divided 4 to 4 on the abortion issue, possibly making the next appointee to the Court the swing vote on whether to overrule *Roe v. Wade*. To a great extent, this fact explains the furor surrounding President Reagan's nomination of conservative federal judge Robert Bork to fill the vacancy left by Justice Powell. A well-known critic of *Roe* and of the right of privacy generally, Bork entered a firestorm of political controversy when he appeared before the Senate Judiciary Committee. The Senate, controlled by the Democrats, ultimately rejected Bork, in no small measure due to his stand on the right of privacy. Eventually, the Senate confirmed Reagan's nomination of another federal judge, Anthony Kennedy. In his confirmation hearing, Kennedy was asked repeatedly about his views on abortion. He replied, "If I had a . . . fixed view . . . I might be obliged to disclose that to you. I don't have such a view." The nation would have to wait two years for Kennedy to register his opinion in the abortion debate.

The *Webster* Decision

Without question, the most significant abortion case of the 1980s was *Webster v. Reproductive Health Services* (1989). Many thought the *Webster* case would be the one in which the Supreme Court would overturn *Roe v. Wade*. Those who favored such an outcome were disappointed by the decision. Yet those who supported legalized abortion found cause for alarm in what they perceived as a significant departure from the philosophy of *Roe*.

The *Webster* case involved a challenge to a Missouri statute containing a number of restrictions on abortions. Most worrisome from the pro-choice perspective was the statement in the preamble of the law that "the life of each human being begins at conception." In its various provisions, the law forbade state employees from performing, assisting in, or counseling women to have abortions. It also prohibited the use of any state facilities for these purposes. Finally, it required all doctors who would perform abortions to conduct viability tests on fetuses at or beyond twenty weeks' gestation.

The Supreme Court, splitting 5 to 4, sustained the constitutionality of the Missouri statute. Yet in deciding the issues in *Webster,* the Supreme Court could not agree on a majority opinion. A plurality (Chief Justice Rehnquist and Associate Justices White, Kennedy, and O'Connor) expressed the view that the legislation could be sustained without overruling *Roe v. Wade*. In her separate concurrence, Justice O'Connor stressed the "fundamental rule of judicial restraint," which dictates that courts not decide major issues unless absolutely necessary. Only Justice Scalia, in a separate concurrence, called for the explicit overruling of *Roe* and chided his colleagues in the majority for not facing the issue squarely: "Of the four courses we might have chosen today—to reaffirm *Roe,* to overrule it explicitly, to overrule it *sub silentio,* or to avoid the question—the last is the least responsible." Justice Blackmun, the author of the Court's opinion in *Roe v. Wade,* accused the plurality of undermining *Roe:*

> With feigned restraint, the plurality announces that its analysis leaves *Roe* "undisturbed," albeit "modif[ied] and narrow[ed]." . . . But this disclaimer is totally meaningless. The plurality opinion is filled with winks, and nods, and knowing glances to those who would do away with *Roe* explicitly, but turns a stone face to anyone in

search of what the plurality conceives as the scope of a woman's right under the Due Process Clause to terminate a pregnancy free from the coercive and brooding influence of the State.

Rust v. Sullivan: Restricting Information About Abortion

Supporters of legalized abortion were dealt another setback during the spring of 1991. In *Rust v. Sullivan,* the Supreme Court upheld a federal regulation that barred birth control clinics that received federal funds from providing information about abortion services to their clients. The regulation had been imposed in 1987 by the Department of Health and Human Services (HHS) at the direction of the Reagan administration, which opposed legalized abortion. The Supreme Court found the regulation to be a legitimate condition imposed on the receipt of financial assistance from the government. In the Court's view, the regulation was neither an invasion of privacy rights nor of freedom of speech, as plaintiffs in the lawsuit alleged. Congress, with broad public support, passed a measure designed to overturn the HHS regulation. However, this act was vetoed by President George Bush, and Congress was unable to muster the two-thirds vote necessary to override the veto.

The Court Reaffirms *Roe v. Wade*

In *Rust v. Sullivan,* as in the *Webster* decision two years earlier, the Court did not face squarely the question of whether *Roe v. Wade* should be maintained as the law of the land. Yet these decisions did send a strong signal that the Court was prepared to tolerate greater restrictions on legalized abortion. On January 21, 1992, on the eve of the nineteenth anniversary of its landmark decision in *Roe v. Wade,* the Supreme Court announced that it would hear a case challenging a Pennsylvania law that contained a series of restrictions on abortion (*Planned Parenthood v. Casey* [1992]). Among other things, the law required spousal notification, parental consent in cases of minors, and a twenty-four-hour waiting period before an abortion could be performed. Identical requirements had been declared invalid by the Supreme Court in previous decisions, but the Third Circuit Court of Appeals in Philadelphia upheld most of the provisions of the Pennsylvania statute. The appellate court based its ruling largely on the Supreme Court's 1989 *Webster* decision, which it interpreted as a significant retreat from the "strict scrutiny" to which abortion regulations had been subjected.

On April 22, 1992, the Supreme Court heard oral arguments in *Planned Parenthood v. Casey.* Ernest Preate, Jr., attorney general of Pennsylvania, defended the constitutionality of the statute, contending, among other things, that "*Roe* did not establish an absolute right to abortion on demand, but rather a limited right subject to reasonable State regulations. . . ." Attacking the statute, Kathryn Kolbert, counsel for the American Civil Liberties Union, characterized Pennsylvania's regulations not only as unreasonable but as "cruel and oppressive." U.S. Solicitor General Kenneth W. Starr, speaking on behalf of the Bush administration, urged the Court to abandon the "compelling state interest" test and adopt a more lenient "rational basis test" for determining the constitutionality of statutes in this area. When asked by Justice White whether the adoption of such a test would lead to a conclusion that the Pennsylvania law should be upheld, Starr replied, "Exactly."

The Supreme Court handed down its much anticipated decision in *Planned Parenthood v. Casey* on June 29, 1992, the last day of the Court's 1991 term. To the surprise of many observers, the Court reaffirmed by a 5-to-4 vote the essential holding in *Roe v. Wade* that the constitutional right of privacy is broad enough to include a woman's decision to terminate her pregnancy. The Court was highly fragmented, however, producing five opinions. Two justices, Blackmun and Stevens, took the position that *Roe v. Wade* should be reaffirmed and that all of the challenged provisions of the Pennsylvania statute should be declared invalid. Four justices, Rehnquist, Scalia, White, and Thomas, took the view that *Roe* should be overruled and all of the Pennsylvania restrictions upheld. Adopting an extremely unusual method of presentation underscoring the gravity of the case, Justices O'Connor, Kennedy, and Souter jointly authored the controlling opinion of the Court. This lengthy joint opinion thoroughly reexamined *Roe v. Wade*, its underlying rationale and formulation, and the line of cases it spawned. While joining Justices Blackmun and Stevens in explicitly reaffirming *Roe*, the joint opinion abandoned the trimester framework and declared a new "undue burden" test for judging regulations of abortion. Applying this test, the joint opinion upheld the parental consent, waiting period, and record-keeping and reporting provisions but invalidated the spousal notification requirement.

The *Casey* decision was greeted with dismay and derision from both pro-life and pro-choice groups. Pro-choice groups expressed alarm that the Court was willing to overturn recent precedent (*Akron v. Akron Center for Reproductive Health* [1983] and *Thornburgh v. American College of Obstetricians and Gynecologists* [1986]) and uphold Pennsylvania's restrictions on abortion. Pro-life advocates were disappointed that two Reagan appointees (Kennedy and O'Connor) and one Bush appointee (Souter) voted to reaffirm *Roe v. Wade*.

In their separate opinions in *Casey*, Chief Justice Rehnquist and Justice Scalia, supported by Justices White and Thomas, made it clear that four members of the Court are fully prepared to overrule *Roe v. Wade*. However, with the replacement of Justice White by Justice Ruth Bader Ginsburg in 1993, the anti-*Roe* bloc on the Court has been diminished. In 1994, Justice Blackmun, the author of the *Roe* opinion, resigned from the Court. His replacement by Justice Stephen G. Breyer, the second Clinton appointee to the Court, is not likely to weaken support of the *Roe* precedent.

The Constitution in action: A "pro-choice" demonstration

Abortion Rights Under State Constitutions

Even if the Court were to overrule *Roe v. Wade,* this would by no means result in the immediate recriminalization of abortion. If *Roe* were overruled, state legislatures would be free, just as they were prior to 1973, to determine their own policies in this area. Moreover, state courts would have to determine the scope of abortion rights under their respective state constitutions. It is quite conceivable that some state supreme courts would take this position. For example, Florida is one of four states whose constitutions contain explicit recognition of the right of privacy (the others are Alaska, California, and Montana). The Florida Supreme Court has said that "[s]ince the people of this state exercised their prerogative and enacted an amendment to the Florida Constitution which expressly and succinctly provides for a strong right of privacy. . . , it can only be concluded that the right is much broader in scope than that of the federal constitution" (*Winfield v. Division of PariMutuel Wagering* [Fla. S.Ct. 1985]). That court has also indicated quite clearly that a woman's right to choose abortion is protected by the privacy amendment to the state constitution (see *In re T.W.* [Fla. S.Ct. 1989]). Thus, even if the Supreme Court were to overturn *Roe v. Wade,* it would not *ipso facto* return the abortion issue to the exclusive domain of the state legislatures.

The abortion issue is *the* constitutional question of our time. But it is far more complex than most observers of American law and politics realize, going well beyond the domain of the U.S. Supreme Court and the fate of *Roe v. Wade.* It will be many years before this question is finally resolved.

TO SUMMARIZE:

- In *Roe v. Wade* (1973), the Court relied on the right of privacy in striking down a Texas statute criminalizing most abortions. In *Roe,* the Court held that the state's interest in protecting the fetus becomes compelling only at the point of fetal viability outside the womb. States may thus prohibit only those abortions that are performed after the point of viability.
- In the next two decades, the Court reviewed a number of cases in which state and local governments imposed various restrictions on abortion. During the 1970s, most of these restrictions were declared unconstitutional. In the 1980s, however, an increasingly conservative Supreme Court began to view such restrictions more favorably.
- By the late 1980s, it appeared that *Roe v. Wade* might be overturned. In *Planned Parenthood v. Casey* (1992), however, the Court reaffirmed its basic holding in *Roe* but in so doing gave states broader latitude in regulating access to abortion.
- Even if the Court were to overturn *Roe v. Wade,* state courts would be free to determine whether their own states' restrictions on abortion violate relevant provisions of their state constitutions.

THE RIGHT OF PRIVACY AND LIVING ARRANGEMENTS

While Supreme Court decisions in the area of reproductive freedom receive most of the public attention, the Court's decisions applying the constitutional right of privacy are by no means confined to contraception and abortion. The right of privacy has also been applied in reviewing city ordinances governing residential occupancy. In *Belle Terre v. Boraas* (1974), the Supreme Court upheld a village ordinance that limited residential land use to one-family dwellings. A couple who had leased a house to six unrelated college students challenged the law on the ground that it "trenche[d] on the newcomers' rights of privacy." The Court, adopting the traditional rational basis test, found the ordinance to be a valid exercise of the police power. Justice Thurgood Marshall dissented, maintaining that fundamental rights of privacy and association were infringed and that the village failed to demonstrate a compelling justification for this infringement.

In *Moore v. City of East Cleveland* (1977), the Court struck down an ordinance that limited the occupancy of residences to members of single families. However, the East Cleveland ordinance defined "family" in such a way as to prohibit a grandmother from cohabiting with her two grandsons. Distinguishing the ordinance from the one upheld in *Belle Terre,* which primarily affected unrelated individuals, the Court stressed the "freedom of choice in matters of marriage and family life."

> Our decisions teach that the Constitution protects the sanctity of the family precisely because the institution of the family is deeply rooted in our history and tradition. [Ours] is by no means a tradition limited to respect for [the] nuclear family. The tradition of uncles, aunts, cousins, and especially grandparents sharing a household along with parents and children has roots equally venerable and equally deserving of constitutional recognition.

In a rather caustic concurrence, Justice Brennan noted that "in today's America, the nuclear family is the pattern so often found in much of white suburbia" but that "the Constitution cannot tolerate the imposition by government upon the rest of us of white suburbia's preference in patterns of family living."

TO SUMMARIZE:

- While Supreme Court decisions in the area of reproductive freedom receive most of the public attention, the Court's decisions applying the constitutional right of privacy are by no means confined to contraception and abortion.
- Stressing "freedom of choice in matters of marriage and family life," the Court has used the right of privacy to scrutinize ordinances limiting residential living arrangements.

PRIVACY AND GAY RIGHTS

In *Eisenstadt v. Baird* (1972), the Supreme Court tacitly acknowledged the right of an unmarried adult to engage in heterosexual activity. If this right is based on the premise that one may decide what to do with his or her own body without interference by the state, how can laws that prohibit private, consensual homosexual conduct be justified? What is the compelling interest on the part of the state that could be advanced to justify such prohibitions? The question has been raised in federal court. In *Doe v. Commonwealth's Attorney* (1976), the Supreme Court summarily affirmed a federal district court decision that upheld Virginia's **sodomy** law. The district court, dividing 2 to 1, cited Justice Harlan's dissent in the 1961 case of *Poe v. Ullman,* which, although supportive of sexual privacy within marriage, suggested that homosexual conduct could be prosecuted even if practiced privately. The Supreme Court, in refusing to hear the appeal in *Doe v. Commonwealth's Attorney,* in effect endorsed Justice Harlan's position.

A "gay rights" march in San Francisco

In *Bowers v. Hardwick* (1986), the Supreme Court reached the merits of a case challenging the application of Georgia's sodomy law to homosexual activity. Michael Hardwick, an admitted homosexual, was charged with committing sodomy with a consenting male adult in the privacy of his home. Although the state prosecutor decided not to take the case to the grand jury, Hardwick brought suit in federal court, seeking a declaration that the statute was unconstitutional. The district court dismissed the case, but the appeals court reversed, remanding the suit for trial. The Supreme Court granted the state's petition for certiorari and reversed the court of appeals.

In arguing his case before the Supreme Court, Hardwick relied on *Griswold v. Connecticut* and *Roe v. Wade,* as well as on the Court's 1969 decision in *Stanley v. Georgia.* In *Stanley,* the Court held that the First Amendment prohibits a state from punishing a person merely for the private possession of obscene materials. Although ostensibly a First Amendment case, the *Stanley* decision suggested that the home was a sanctuary from prosecution for acts that might well be criminal outside the home.

Dividing 5 to 4 in *Hardwick,* the Court upheld the Georgia law, refusing to recognize "a fundamental right to engage in homosexual sodomy." Writing for the Court, Justice White stressed the traditional legal and moral prohibitions against sodomy. Responding to the libertarian argument that the state has no right to legislate solely on the basis of morality, White wrote that "law . . . is constantly based on notions of morality, and if all laws representing essentially moral choices are to be invalidated . . . , the Courts will be very busy indeed."

Dissenting, Justice Blackmun disputed the Court's characterization of the issue. For Blackmun and three of his colleagues, the case was not about a "fundamental right to engage in homosexual sodomy" but the more general right of an adult, homosexual or heterosexual, to engage in consensual sexual acts with another adult. Striking a libertarian chord, Justice John Paul Stevens wrote that "the fact that the governing majority in a State has traditionally viewed a practice as immoral is not a sufficient reason for upholding a law prohibiting the practice. . . ."

Whether the Supreme Court would uphold a sodomy law as applied to heterosexual activity remains to be seen. If the Supreme Court were to strike down sodomy laws as applied to married couples, there would probably be little criticism of the Court. If, however, the Court were to invalidate sodomy laws as applied to unmarried persons, whether heterosexual or homosexual, then questions might be raised regarding the constitutionality of laws against prostitution, incest, and polygamy. In *Hardwick,* Justice White averred that the Court was "reluctant to start down that road."

Interestingly, retired Supreme Court Justice Lewis Powell, one of the members of the *Hardwick* majority, has expressed reservations about his vote in that case. In talking to a group of law students at New York University in October 1990, Justice Powell said, "I think I probably made a mistake in that one." In a subsequent interview, Powell said that the case was a "close call" and that his decision to support the majority was based in part on the fact that the sodomy law had been largely unenforced. Powell minimized the importance of the case, referring to it as "frivolous" and suggesting that it had been filed "just to see what the court would do . . ." (*Washington Post,* October 26, 1990, p. A-3).

Is *Bowers v. Hardwick* Still Good Law?

The Court's decision in *Romer v. Evans* (1996) calls into question the precedential value of *Bowers v. Hardwick.* In what the American Civil Liberties Union hailed as a "transforming moment in the fight for equality for lesbians and gay men," the Court struck down a Colorado constitutional amendment that barred state and local government from providing various legal protections for gays and lesbians. In dissent, Justice Scalia argued that "if it is constitutionally permissible for a State to make homosexual conduct criminal, surely it is constitutionally permissible for a State to enact other laws merely disfavoring homosexual conduct." Although the Court did not reconsider *Bowers v. Hardwick* in *Romer v. Evans,* it is doubtful that *Hardwick* would command a majority if it came before the Court today. However, because people are rarely prosecuted for consensual sodomy, the Court may not have another occasion to reconsider *Hardwick.*

TO SUMMARIZE:

- Gay rights activists and most libertarians generally argue that laws prohibiting homosexual conduct violate the right of privacy and that traditional morality is an insufficient basis for upholding such legislation.
- In *Bowers v. Hardwick* (1986) the Supreme Court narrowly upheld a Georgia anti-sodomy law as applied to homosexual conduct. It is doubtful whether this position would command a majority if the issue were revisited by the current Court.

OTHER APPLICATIONS OF THE RIGHT OF PRIVACY

Controversy has long surrounded the so-called **victimless crimes** of gambling, use of "recreational" drugs, prostitution, and so forth. Libertarians argue that the state has no business criminalizing conduct where no individual claims to have been injured. Individuals charged with such offenses have sometimes invoked the right of privacy by way of defense.

The Private Use of "Recreational" Drugs

In a widely publicized decision in 1975, *Ravin v. State,* the Alaska Supreme Court held that the right of privacy under both the federal and Alaska constitutions was broad enough to encompass the right to possess marijuana for personal use. In its opinion, the court noted the strong libertarian orientation of Alaskans. To date, the Alaska Supreme Court decision has not been emulated by the federal courts or by the courts of other states. Of course, even if the U.S. Supreme Court were to rule that the right of privacy under the Constitution did not protect the private use of marijuana, the Alaska decision would still be valid on independent state constitutional grounds. The Alaska Supreme Court is the authoritative interpreter of the Alaska constitution. Interestingly, the Alaska constitution contains an explicit right of privacy, unlike the U.S. Constitution and the constitutions of most states. Of course, this explicit right of privacy did not prevent Alaska voters in 1990 from approving a constitutional amendment in effect overruling *Ravin v. State*. Like the U.S. Supreme Court, a state supreme court is the final authority on matters of constitutional interpretation unless and until the constitution is amended. In 1990, amidst the widespread public concern over the problem of drug abuse, Alaskans decided through a referendum that their state constitution should not condone even the private use of illicit drugs.

Helmet and Seat Belt Laws

Another application of the right of privacy is in the area of safety laws, as exemplified by laws requiring motorcyclists to wear protective helmets and drivers to wear seat belts. Again, the libertarian thesis would be that the government has no right to protect the individual from him- or herself. In *State v. Albertson* (1970), the Idaho Supreme Court rejected a privacy-based challenge to that state's motorcycle helmet law, citing an important public safety interest. In all likelihood, most state courts would find sufficient public safety interests to uphold helmet laws, as well as mandatory seat belt laws.

TO SUMMARIZE:

- The right of privacy has been used with limited success at the state court level in attacking the constitutionality of laws prohibiting the recreational use of drugs and other "victimless crimes." The Supreme Court has shown little interest in this area.

A RIGHT TO DIE?

Since the mid-1970s, the right of privacy has been successfully asserted as a basis for refusing medical treatment. For example, in *Superintendent of Belchertown State School v. Saikewicz* (Mass. 1977), the Massachusetts Supreme Judicial Court permitted the guardian of an elderly, retarded man to assert his ward's right of privacy and refuse chemotherapy treatment for the elderly man's leukemia. Under the right of privacy, courts have also authorized the discontinuation of artificial means of life support, even if it results in the immediate death of the patient. For example, in the case of *Guardianship of Andrew Barry* (1984), a Florida appellate court allowed the removal of a respirator that was maintaining the life of a comatose infant. Andrew Barry was one of twins, the other of whom died at birth. Andrew had a serious brain defect that kept him comatose and unable to breathe without mechanical assistance. After it became clear that Andrew would never achieve a "sapient existence" and would spend his life on the ventilator, his parents asked the hospital to remove the machine. Not surprisingly, the hospital refused to do so without a court order.

The Karen Quinlan Case

In both *Saikewicz* and *Barry,* courts relied on the doctrine of "substituted judgment" whereby legal guardians are permitted to exercise the rights of persons under their authority. The best known case involving the doctrine of substituted judgment in relation to the so-called right to die is *In re Quinlan* (N.J. 1976). Karen Quinlan was a healthy young woman who became permanently comatose after she ingested large quantities of drugs and alcohol. In this condition, she was unable to maintain normal breathing without a ventilator. After it became clear that Karen Quinlan would not regain consciousness, her parents asked her physicians to remove the respirator. The physicians refused, no doubt concerned about possible criminal prosecution or civil liability. The Quinlans went to court and obtained an order allowing removal of the life-support machine. According to the New Jersey Supreme Court, the right of privacy was "broad enough to encompass [Karen Quinlan's] decision to decline medical treatment under certain circumstances, in much the same way as it is broad enough to encompass a woman's decision to terminate pregnancy. . . ." Of course, Karen Quinlan, lying comatose in the hospital, was unable to communicate her intentions to exercise this aspect of the right of privacy. According to the Court's opinion, the "only practical way to prevent destruction of [Karen Quinlan's] right is to permit the guardian and family . . . to render their best judgment as to whether she would exercise [the right to decline treatment] in these circumstances."

After Karen Quinlan was taken off the breathing machine, she lived for nine years in a coma, taking food and water through a nasogastric tube. Her parents never asked that this feeding be discontinued, but therein lies another troubling question. Does the right of privacy empower a terminally ill patient to refuse food and water provided through a nasogastric tube? In *Bouvia v. Superior Court* (Cal. 1986), the California Supreme Court answered this question in the affirmative in a case involving a young woman who, although competent, was suffering the terrible effects of an advanced degenerative illness.

A Right to Commit Suicide?

Court decisions such as *Quinlan* and *Bouvia* have led to a national debate over the **right to die.** In what circumstances and by what means does a person have a right to bring about his or her own demise? Critics of the right to die argue that it is a "slippery slope" leading inexorably to the legal recognition of "mercy killing" and suicide. If the right of privacy allows an individual to make "fundamental life choices" and to decide what happens to his or her body, then how can laws that forbid suicide (or aiding and abetting suicide) be constitutional? In 1991, the public debate over the right to die took an eerie turn when Dr. Jack Kevorkian was prosecuted after assisting several people to commit suicide. Kevorkian, an advocate of euthanasia, had developed a "suicide machine" by which individuals could self-administer lethal injections of drugs and thereby achieve painless death. The case of Dr. Kevorkian and his suicide machine raises troubling questions, one that the courts will be grappling with in the years to come.

Dr. Jack Kevorkian and his "suicide machine"

The Nancy Cruzan Case

The U.S. Supreme Court's only significant decision to date involving the right to die is the 1990 case of *Cruzan v. Missouri Health Department*. When the case reached the Supreme Court, Nancy Cruzan had for six years been confined to a hospital bed in a state of unconsciousness. Her condition was the result of extreme brain damage that occurred in an automobile accident. When it became apparent that Cruzan's condition was irreversible, her parents asked the hospital to remove the nasogastric tube that was keeping her alive. The hospital refused absent a court order. The trial court issued the order, but the Missouri Supreme Court reversed, citing the state's "policy strongly favoring the preservation of life." The Missouri Supreme Court said that since Nancy Cruzan was unable to communicate, there would have to be clear and convincing evidence of her desire to have the feeding tube removed. Dividing 5 to 4, the U.S. Supreme Court upheld the Missouri Supreme Court's decision. Writing for the Court, Chief Justice Rehnquist held that, although Nancy Cruzan had a right to terminate life-prolonging treatment, it was reasonable for the state to impose the clear and convincing evidence standard as a means of guarding against potential abuse of the "substituted judgment" doctrine.

Critics of the right to die, many of whom also oppose legalized abortion, hailed the *Cruzan* decision as a victory for the pro-life movement. It remains to be seen, however, whether the *Cruzan* decision represents a turnaround in the development of the right to die or merely the fine-tuning of a right that is now well established in American jurisprudence. It is likely that state, rather than federal, courts will continue to take the lead in developing this important new area of the law.

Doctor-Assisted Suicide

The courts have recognized a sharp distinction between termination of life-support systems and the active administration of means designed to end a person's life. But recently this distinction between passive and active euthanasia has been called into question. There are those in the medical community who believe that physicians should be able to provide active assistance to terminally ill patients who wish to hasten their own demise. There are those who argue that doctor-assisted suicide is well within the scope of privacy protected by the Constitution. But such views have yet to be accepted by the mainstreams of the medical and legal communities.

To prevent assisted suicide in the state of Washington, the legislature enacted a law providing that "A person is guilty of promoting a suicide attempt when he knowingly causes or aids another person to attempt suicide." "Promoting a suicide attempt" is a felony punishable by up to five years' imprisonment and up to a $10,000 fine. In 1994, a federal judge ruled that Washington's statute banning assisted suicide was unconstitutional. Hearing the case *en banc,* the Ninth Circuit concluded that the State's assisted suicide ban was unconstitutional as applied to "terminally ill competent adults who wish to hasten their deaths with medication prescribed by their physicians."

In *Washington v. Glucksberg* (1997), the Supreme Court reversed the Ninth Circuit's decision. Writing for a unanimous Court, Chief Justice Rehnquist discussed the historical and cultural background of laws prohibiting assisted suicide. He pointed out that in almost every state it is a crime to assist in a suicide, and that the statutes banning assisted suicide are long-standing expressions of the states' commitment to the protection and preservation of all human life. Rehnquist analyzed the interests that come into play in determining whether a statute banning assisted suicide passes constitutional muster. He rejected any parallel between a person's right to terminate medical treatment and the "right" to have assistance in committing suicide. The Court's decision in *Glucksberg* recognized that a serious debate was taking place throughout the nation about the morality and legality of assisted suicide—a debate that the Court's decision permitted to continue. It is likely, though, that the Court will revisit this issue in the not too distant future.

TO SUMMARIZE:

- Since the mid-1970s, the right of privacy has been successfully asserted in state courts as a basis for competent adults to refuse medical treatment. It has been extended to allow the termination of artificial life-support systems in cases where patients are found to be in a persistent vegetative state resulting from injury or illness.
- The courts have generally rejected a thoroughgoing "right to die" that would allow any competent adult to commit suicide under any conditions.
- In 1990 the Supreme Court recognized that terminally ill patients have the right to order removal of life-support systems, but permitted states to impose a requirement that there be clear and convincing evidence of patients' desire that such systems be removed.
- In 1997 the Court entered the debate over physician-assisted suicide, holding that there is no constitutional right to engage in such conduct. This decision effectively permits states to regulate in this area, although state courts can play a significant role under the relevant provisions of state constitutions.

CONCLUSION

The modern Supreme Court has fashioned a general, independent constitutional right of privacy by drawing on the Fourteenth Amendment and on various provisions of the Bill of Rights. While the legal logic underlying the right of privacy is debatable, the right is now firmly established in American constitutional law. The right of privacy has been recognized by the courts of most states, and several state constitutions now even contain explicit protections of the right of privacy.

It is unclear whether, and how far, the courts will further extend the right of privacy. In 1965, when the Supreme Court decided *Griswold v. Connecticut*, public sentiment had become decidedly more liberal in the area of sex and reproduction. The 1973 abortion decision did not meet with the same extent of popular approbation, and the opposition to abortion has been much more intense than the opposition to the use of devices that prevent conception. The so-called right to die, if it is limited to the withholding of extraordinary means of life prolongation, seems to be socially acceptable. But there would be considerable opposition to the legalization of active euthanasia or suicide. At this time, prevailing social norms do not condone homosexual conduct or the private use of "recreational" drugs. For courts to assert constitutional protections for such activities would be a bold move indeed, possibly leading to political retaliation. One certainly would not expect the U.S. Supreme Court, which has become steadily more conservative in recent years, to adopt such libertarian positions in the near future. The evolution of the right of privacy thus illustrates the "give and take" of American constitutional law. It also dramatizes the fact that constitutional rights do not exist in a social, political, or moral vacuum.

KEY TERMS

constitutional right of privacy	moral individualism	compulsory sterilization	trimester framework
abortion	libertarianism	fundamental right	sodomy
gay rights	classical conservatism	compelling interest	victimless crimes
euthanasia	right to be let alone	viability	right to die
	substantive due process	Hyde Amendment	doctor-assisted suicide

FOR FURTHER READING

Barnett, Randy (ed.). *The Rights Retained by the People: The History and Meaning of the Ninth Amendment.* Fairfax, Va.: George Mason University Press, 1989.

Breckenridge, Adam Carlyle. *The Right to Privacy.* Lincoln, Nebr.: University of Nebraska Press, 1970.

Johnson, Charles A., and Bradley C. Canon. *Judicial Policies: Implementation and Impact.* Washington, D.C.: Congressional Quarterly Press, 1984.

Luker, Kristin. *Abortion and the Politics of Motherhood.* Berkeley, Calif.: University of California Press, 1980.

McClellan, Grant S. (ed.). *The Right to Privacy.* New York: H. W. Wilson, 1976.

Miller, Arthur R. *The Assault on Privacy.* Ann Arbor, Mich.: University of Michigan Press, 1971.

Neeley, G. Steven. *The Constitutional Right to Suicide: A Legal and Philosophical Examination.* New York: Peter Lang Publishing, 1994.

O'Brien, David M. *Privacy, Law and Public Policy.* New York: Praeger, 1979.

O'Connor, Karen. *No Neutral Ground? Abortion Politics in an Age of Absolutes.* Boulder, Colo.: Westview Press, 1996.

Rubin, Eva R. *Abortion, Politics and the Courts:* Roe v. Wade *and Its Aftermath.* New York: Greenwood Press, 1987.

Shattuck, John H. F. *Rights of Privacy.* Skokie, Ill.: National Textbook Company, 1977.

Steiner, Gilbert Y. (ed.). *The Abortion Dispute and the American System.* Washington, D.C.: Brookings Institution, 1983.

Tribe, Laurence. *Abortion: The Clash of Absolutes.* New York: Norton, 1990.

Westin, Alan F. *Privacy and Freedom.* New York: Atheneum, 1970.

INTERNET RESOURCES

Name of Resource	Description	URL (circa 1998)
National Abortion Rights Action League	An interest group dedicated to maintaining legalized abortion.	http://www.naral.org/
Operation Rescue	An anti-abortion interest group.	http://www.orn.org/
The Hemlock Society	An organization supporting the "right to die" and legalization of physician-assisted suicide.	http://www2.privatei.com/hemlock/index.html
Compassion in Dying	Another organization supporting the "right to die."	http://www.compassionindying.org/
Not Dead Yet	A national organization of people with disabilities who oppose the legalization of physician-assisted suicide.	http://acils.com/notdeadyet/

Case

JACOBSON V. MASSACHUSETTS

197 U.S. 11; 25 S.Ct. 358; 49 L.Ed. 643 (1905)
Vote: 7–2

Acting under authority of state law, the board of health of Cambridge, Massachusetts, adopted a regulation requiring that, with certain exceptions, inhabitants of the city be vaccinated against smallpox. State law imposed a five-dollar fine for violation of the vaccination requirement. Henning Jacobson, a resident of Cambridge, refused to comply with the regulation. As a result, charges were filed against him: He was convicted, and the fine was imposed. Jacobson appealed his conviction, contending that the compulsory vaccination law and implementing regulation violated his rights under the Fourteenth Amendment. The state, in response, argued that the statute was a legitimate exercise of its police power. The Massachusetts Supreme Judicial Court sustained the constitutionality of the law, and Jacobson obtained review by the U.S. Supreme Court.

Mr. Justice Harlan delivered the opinion of the Court:

This case involves the validity, under the Constitution of the United States, of certain provisions in the statutes of Massachusetts relating to vaccination. . . .

Is the statute . . . inconsistent with the liberty which the Constitution of the United States secures to every person against deprivation by the state?

The authority of the state to enact this statute is to be referred to what is commonly called the police power—a power which the state did not surrender when becoming a member of the Union under the Constitution. Although this court has refrained from any attempt to define the limits of that power, yet it has "health laws of every description;" indeed, all laws that relate to matters completely within its territory and which do not by their necessary operation affect the people of other states. According to settled principles, the police power of a state must be held to embrace, at least, such reasonable regulations established directly by legislative enactment as will protect the public health and the public safety. . . .

We come, then, to inquire whether any right given or secured by the Constitution is invaded by the statute as interpreted by the state court. The defendant insists that his liberty is invaded when the state subjects him to fine or imprisonment for neglecting or refusing to submit to vaccination; that a compulsory vaccination law is unreasonable, arbitrary, and oppressive, and, therefore, hostile to the inherent right of every freeman to care for his own body and health in such a way as to him seems best; and that the execution of such a law against one who objects to vaccination, no matter for what reason, is nothing short of an assault upon his person. But the liberty secured by the Constitution of the United States to every person within its jurisdiction does not import an absolute right in each person to be, at all times and in all circumstances, wholly freed from restraint. There are manifold restraints to which every person is necessarily subject for the common good. On any other basis organized society could not exist with safety to its members. Society based on the rule that each one is a law unto himself would soon be confronted with disorder and anarchy. Real liberty for all could not exist under the operation of a principle which recognizes the right of each individual person to use his own, whether in respect of his person or his property, regardless of the injury that may be done to others. . . .

Applying these principles to the present case, it is to be observed that the legislature of Massachusetts required the inhabitants of a city or town to be vaccinated only when, in the opinion of the board of health, that was necessary for the public health or the public safety. The authority to determine for all what ought to be done in such an emergency must have been lodged somewhere or in some body; and surely it was appropriate for the legislature to refer that question, in the first instance, to a board of health composed of persons residing in the locality affected, and appointed, presumably, because of their fitness to determine such questions. To invest such a body with authority over such matters was not an unusual, nor an unreasonable or arbitrary, requirement. Upon the principle of self-defense, of paramount necessity, a community has the right to protect itself against an epidemic of disease which threatens the safety of its members. . . .

There is, of course, a sphere within which the individual may assert the supremacy of his own will, and rightfully dispute the authority of any human government, especially of any free government existing under a written constitution, to interfere with the exercise of that will. But it is equally true that in every well-ordered society charged with the duty of conserving the safety of its members the rights of the individual in respect of his liberty may at times, under the pressure of great dangers, be subjected to such restraint, to be enforced by reasonable regulations, as the safety of the general public may demand. . . .

Whatever may be thought of the expediency of this statute, it cannot be affirmed to be, beyond question, in palpable conflict with the Constitution. Nor, in view of the methods employed to stamp out the disease of smallpox, can anyone confidently assert that the means prescribed by the state to that end has no real or substantial relation to the protection of the public health and the public safety? Such an assertion would not be consistent with the experience of this and other countries whose authorities have dealt with the disease of smallpox. And the principle of vaccination as a means to prevent the spread of smallpox has been enforced in many states by statutes making the vaccination of children a condition of their right to enter or remain in public school. . . .

We are not prepared to hold that a minority, residing or remaining in any city or town where smallpox is prevalent, and enjoying the general protection afforded by an organized local government, may thus defy the will of its constituted authorities, acting in good faith for all, under the legislative sanction of the state. If such be the privilege of a minority, then a like privilege would belong to each individual of the community, and the spectacle would be presented of the welfare and safety of an entire population being subordinated to the notions of a single individual who chooses to remain a part of that population. We are unwilling to hold it to be an element in the liberty secured by the Constitution of the United States that one person, or a minority of persons, residing in any community and enjoying the benefits of its local government, should have the power thus to dominate the majority when supported in their action by the authority of the state. While this court should guard with firmness every right appertaining to life, liberty, or property as secured to the individual by the supreme law of the land, it is of the last importance that it should not invade the domain of local authority except when it is plainly necessary to do so in order to enforce that law. The safety and the health of the people of Massachusetts are, in the first instance, for that commonwealth to guard and protect. They are matters that do not ordinarily concern the national government. So far as they can be reached by any government, they depend, primarily, upon such action as the state, in its wisdom, may take; and we do not perceive that this legislation has invaded any right secured by the Federal Constitution. . . .

We now decide only that the statute covers the present case, and that nothing clearly appears that would justify this Court in holding it to be unconstitutional and inoperative in its application to the plaintiff in error.

The judgment of the court below must be affirmed.

Mr. Justice Brewer and **Mr. Justice Peckham** dissent.

Case

MEYER V. NEBRASKA

262 U.S. 390; 43 S.Ct. 625; 67 L.Ed. 1042 (1923)
Vote: 7–2

Here the Court reviews a state law that forbids teaching foreign languages to children.

Mr. Justice McReynolds delivered the opinion of the Court.

Plaintiff in error was tried and convicted in the District Court for Hamilton County, Nebraska, under an information which charged that on May 25, 1920, while an instructor in Zion Parochial School, he unlawfully taught the subject of reading in the German language to Raymond Parpart, a child of ten years, who had not attained and successfully passed the eighth grade. The information is based upon "An act relating to the teaching of foreign languages in the State of Nebraska," approved April 9, 1919. . . .

The following excerpts from the opinion [of the Supreme Court of Nebraska] sufficiently indicate the reasons advanced to support [its] conclusion.

> The salutary purpose of the statute is clear. The legislature had seen the baneful effects of permitting foreigners, who had taken residence in this country, to rear and educate their children in the language of their native land. The result of that condition was found to be inimical to our own safety. To allow the children of foreigners, who had emigrated here, to be taught from early childhood the language of the country of their parents was to rear them with that language as their mother tongue. It was to educate them so that they must always think in that language, and, as a consequence, naturally inculcate in them the ideas and sentiments foreign to the best interests of this country. The statute, therefore, was intended not only to require that the education of all children be conducted in the English language, but that, until they had grown into that language and until it had become a part of them, they should not in the schools be taught any other language. The obvious purpose of this statute was that the English language should become the mother tongue of all children reared in this state. The enactment of such a statute comes reasonably within the police power of the state. . . .

While this Court has not attempted to define with exactness the liberty [guaranteed by the Fourteenth Amendment], the term has received much consideration and some of the included things have been definitely stated. Without doubt, it denotes not merely freedom from bodily restraint but also the right of the individual to contract, to engage in any of the common occupations of life, to acquire useful knowledge, to marry, establish a home and bring up children, to worship God according to the dictates of his own conscience, and generally to enjoy those privileges long recognized at common law as essential to the orderly pursuit of happiness by free men. . . . The established doctrine is that this liberty may not be interfered with, under the guise of protecting the public interest, by legislative action which is arbitrary or without reasonable relation to some purpose within the competency of the State to effect. Determination by the legislature of what constitutes proper exercise of police power is not final or conclusive but is subject to supervision by the courts. . . .

Corresponding to the right of control, it is the natural duty of the parent to give his children education suitable to their station in life; and nearly all the States, including Nebraska, enforce this obligation by compulsory laws.

Practically, education of the young is only possible in schools conducted by especially qualified persons who devote themselves thereto. The calling always has been regarded as useful and honorable, essential, indeed, to the public welfare. Mere knowledge of the German language cannot reasonably be regarded as harmful. Heretofore it has been commonly looked upon as helpful and desirable. Plaintiff in error taught this language in school as part of his occupation. His right thus to teach and the right of parents to engage him so to instruct their children, we think, are within the liberty of the Amendment.

The challenged statute forbids the teaching in school of any subject except in English; also the teaching of any other language until the pupil has attained and successfully passed the eighth grade, which is not usually accomplished before the age of twelve. The Supreme Court of the State has held that "the so-called ancient or dead languages" are not "within the spirit or the purpose of the act." . . . Latin, Greek, Hebrew are not proscribed; but German, French, Spanish, Italian and every other alien speech are within the ban. Evidently the legislature has attempted materially to interfere with the calling of modern language teachers, with the opportunities of pupils to acquire knowledge, and with the power of parents to control the education of their own. . . .

Mr. Justice Holmes [with whom **Justice Sutherland** concurred], dissenting.

We all agree, I take it, that it is desirable that all the citizens of the United States should speak a common tongue, and therefore that the end aimed at by the statute is a lawful and proper one. The only question is whether the means adopted deprive teachers of the liberty secured to them by the Fourteenth Amendment. It is with hesitation and unwillingness that I differ from my brethren with regard to a law like this but I cannot bring my mind to believe that in some circumstances, and circumstances existing it is said in Nebraska, the statute might not be regarded as a reasonable or even necessary method of reaching the desired result. The part of the act with which we are concerned deals with the teaching of young children. Youth is the time when familiarity with a language is established and if there are sections in the State where a child would hear only Polish or French or German spoken at home I am not prepared to say that it is unreasonable to provide that in his early years he shall hear and speak only English at school. But if it is reasonable it is not an undue restriction of the liberty either of teacher or scholar. No one would doubt that a teacher might be forbidden to teach many things, and the only criterion of his liberty under the Constitution that I can think of is "whether, considering the end in view, the statute passes the bounds of reason and assumes the character of a merely arbitrary fiat." . . . I think I appreciate the objection to the law but it appears to me to present a question upon which men reasonably might differ and therefore I am unable to say that the Constitution of the United States prevents the experiment being tried. . . .

Case

BUCK V. BELL

274 U.S. 200; 47 S.Ct. 584; 71 L.Ed. 1000 (1927)
Vote: 8–1

In this notorious case, the Court considers whether the Constitution permits a state to order the sterilization of a "mentally defective" person who is in state custody.

Mr. Justice Holmes delivered the opinion of the Court.

This is a writ of error to review a judgment of the Supreme Court of Appeals of the State of Virginia, affirming a judgment of the Circuit Court of Amherst County, by which the defendant in error [Dr. J. H. Bell], the superintendent of the State Colony for Epileptics and Feeble Minded, was ordered to perform the operation of salpingectomy upon Carrie Buck, the plaintiff in error, for the purpose of making her sterile. . . . The case comes here upon the contention that the statute authorizing the judgment is void under the Fourteenth Amendment as denying to the plaintiff in error due process of law and the equal protection of the laws.

Carrie Buck is a feeble minded white woman who was committed to the State Colony above mentioned in due form. She is the daughter of a feeble-minded mother in the same institution, and the mother of an illegitimate feeble-minded child. She was eighteen years old at the time of the trial of her case in the Circuit Court, in the latter part of 1924. An Act of Virginia, approved March 20, 1924, recites that the health of the patient and the welfare of society may be promoted in certain cases by the sterilization of mental defectives, under careful safeguard. . . .

The attack is not upon the procedure but upon the substantive law. . . . In view of the general declarations of the legislature and the specific findings of the Court, obviously we cannot say as matter of law that the grounds do not exist, and if they exist they justify the result. . . . It is better for all the world, if instead of waiting to execute degenerate offspring for crime, or to let them starve for their imbecility, society can prevent those who are manifestly unfit from continuing their kind. The principle that sustains compulsory vaccination is broad enough to cover cutting the Fallopian tubes. Three generations of imbeciles are enough.

But, it is said, however it might be if this reasoning were applied generally, it fails when it is confined to the small number who are in the institutions named and is not applied to the multitudes outside. It is the usual last resort of constitutional arguments to point out shortcomings of this sort. But the answer is that the law does all that is needed when it does all that it can, indicates a policy, applies it to all within the lines, and seeks to bring within the lines all similarly situated so far and so fast as its means allow. Of course so far as the operations enable those who otherwise must be kept confined to be returned to the world, and thus open the asylum to others, the equality aimed at will be more nearly reached.

Judgment affirmed.

Mr. Justice Butler dissents.

Case

POE V. ULLMAN

367 U.S. 497; 81 S.Ct. 1752; 6 L.Ed. 2d. 989 (1961)
Vote: 5–4

In this case, the Supreme Court considers the constitutionality of state laws forbidding the use of artificial means of birth control. The Court dismisses the case as unripe for judicial review. However, Justice Harlan's dissenting opinion is noteworthy for its conceptualization of the constitutional right of privacy.

Mr. Justice Frankfurter announced the judgment of the Court and an opinion in which the **Chief Justice** [Warren], **Mr. Justice Clark** and **Mr. Justice Whittaker** join.

These appeals challenge the constitutionality, under the Fourteenth Amendment, of Connecticut statutes which, as authoritatively construed by the Connecticut Supreme Court of Errors, prohibit the use of contraceptive devices and the giving of medical advice in the use of such devices. In proceedings seeking declarations of law, not on review of convictions for violation of the statutes, that court has ruled that these statutes would be applicable in the case of married couples and even under claim that conception would constitute a serious threat to the health or life of the female spouse.

. . . The [first] complaint . . . alleges that the plaintiffs, Paul and Pauline Poe, are a husband and wife, thirty and twenty-six years old respectively, who live together and have no children. Mrs. Poe has had three consecutive pregnancies terminating in infants with multiple congenital abnormalities from which each died shortly after birth. Plaintiffs have consulted Dr. Buxton, an obstetrician and gynecologist of eminence, and it is Dr. Buxton's opinion that the cause of the infants' abnormalities is genetic, although the underlying "mechanism" is unclear. In view of the great emotional stress already suffered by plaintiffs, the probable consequence of another pregnancy is psychological strain extremely disturbing to the physical and mental health of both husband and wife. . . . [I]t is Dr. Buxton's opinion that the best and safest medical treatment which could be prescribed for their situation is advice in methods of preventing conception. Dr. Buxton knows of drugs, medicinal articles and instruments which can be safely used to effect contraception.

Medically, the use of these devices is indicated as the best and safest preventive measure necessary for the protection of plaintiffs' health. Plaintiffs, however, have been unable to obtain this information for the sole reason that its delivery and use may or will be claimed by the defendant State's Attorney (appellee in this Court) to constitute offenses against Connecticut law. The State's Attorney . . . claims that the giving of contraceptive advice and the use of contraceptive devices would be offenses forbidden by Conn. Gen. Stat. Rev. 1958, Sections 53–32 and 54–196. . . . [Paul and Pauline Poe] ask a declaratory judgment that sections 53–32 and 54–196 are unconstitutional, in that they deprive the plaintiffs of life and liberty without due process of law.

The second action . . . is brought by Jane Doe, a twenty-five-year-old housewife. Mrs. Doe, it is alleged, lives with her husband, they have no children; Mrs. Doe recently underwent a pregnancy which induced in her a critical physical illness—two weeks' unconsciousness and a total of nine weeks' acute sickness which left her with partial paralysis, marked impairment of speech, and emotional instability. Another pregnancy would be exceedingly perilous to her life. She, too, has consulted Dr. Buxton, who believes that the best and safest treatment for her is contraceptive advice. The remaining allegations of Mrs. Doe's complaint, and the relief sought, are similar to those in the case of Mr. and Mrs. Poe.

Appellants' complaints in these declaratory judgment proceedings do not clearly, and certainly do not in terms, allege that appellee Ullman threatens to prosecute them for use of, or for giving advice concerning, contraceptive devices. The allegations are merely that, in the course of his public duty, he intends to prosecute any offenses against Connecticut law, and that he claims that use of and advice concerning contraceptives would constitute offenses. The lack of immediacy of the threat described by these allegations might alone raise serious questions of non-justiciability of appellants' claims. . . . But even were we to read the allegations to convey a clear threat of imminent prosecutions, we are not bound to accept as true all that is alleged on the face of the complaint and admitted, technically, by demurrer, any more than the Court is bound by stipulation of the parties. . . . Formal agreement between parties that collides with plausibility is too fragile a foundation for indulging in constitutional adjudication.

The Connecticut law prohibiting the use of contraceptives has been on the State's books since 1879. . . . During the more than three-quarters of a century since its enactment, a prosecution for its violation seems never to have been initiated, save in *State v. Nelson*. . . . The circumstances of that case, decided in 1940, only prove the abstract character of what is before us. There, a test case was brought to determine the constitutionality of the Act as applied against two doctors and a nurse who had allegedly disseminated contraceptive information. After the Supreme Court of Errors sustained the legislation on appeal from a demurrer to the information, the State moved to dismiss the information. Neither counsel nor our own researchers have discovered any other attempt to enforce the prohibition of distribution or use of contraceptive devices by criminal process. . . .

. . . It is clear that the mere existence of a state penal statute would constitute insufficient grounds to support a federal court's adjudication of its constitutionality in proceedings brought against the State's prosecuting officials if real threat of enforcement is wanting. . . . If the prosecutor expressly agrees not to prosecute, a suit against him for declaratory and injunctive relief is not such an adversary case as will be reviewed here. . . . Eighty years of Connecticut history demonstrate a similar, albeit tacit agreement. The fact that Connecticut has not chosen to press to enforcement of this statute deprives these controversies of the immediacy which is an indispensable condition of constitutional adjudication. This Court cannot be umpire to debates concerning harmless, empty shadows. To find it necessary to pass on these statutes now, in order to protect appellants from the hazards of prosecution, would be to close our eyes to reality. . . .

Justiciability is of course not a legal concept with a fixed content or susceptible of scientific verification. Its utilization is the result of many subtle pressures, including the appropriateness of the issues for decision by this Court and the actual hardship to the litigants of denying them the relief sought. Both these factors justify withholding adjudication of the constitutional issue raised under the circumstances and in the manner in which they are now before the Court.

Dismissed.

Mr. Justice Black dissents because he believes that the constitutional questions should be reached and decided.

Mr. Justice Brennan, concurring in the judgment. . . .

Mr. Justice Stewart, dissenting. . . .

Mr. Justice Douglas, dissenting. . . .

Mr. Justice Harlan, dissenting.

I am compelled, with all respect, to dissent from the dismissal of these appeals. In my view the course which the Court has taken does violence to established concepts of "justiciability," and unjustifiably leaves these appellants under the threat of unconstitutional prosecution. . . . Between them these suits seek declaratory relief against the threatened enforcement of Connecticut's antibirth-control laws making criminal the use of contraceptives, insofar as such laws relate to the use of contraceptives by married persons and the giving of advice to married persons in their use. The appellants, a married couple, a married woman, and a doctor, ask that it be adjudged, contrary to what the Connecticut courts have held, that such laws, as threatened to be applied to them in circumstances described in the opinion announcing the judgment of the Court violate the Fourteenth Amendment, in that they deprive appellants of life, liberty, or property without due process. . . .

I consider that this Connecticut legislation, as construed to apply to these appellants, violates the Fourteenth Amendment. I believe that a statute making it a criminal offense for married couples to use contraceptives is an intolerable and unjustifiable invasion of privacy and in the conduct of the most intimate concerns of an individual's personal life. I reach this conclusion, even though I find it difficult and unnecessary at this juncture to accept appellants' other argument that the judgment of policy behind the statute, so applied, is so arbitrary and unreasonable as to render the enactment invalid for that reason alone. Since both the contentions draw their basis from no explicit language of the Constitution, and have yet to find expression in any decision of this Court, I feel it desirable at the outset to state the framework of Constitutional principles in which I think the issue must be judged.

In reviewing state legislation, whether considered to be in the exercise of the State's police powers, or in provision for the health, safety, morals or welfare of its people, it is clear that what is concerned are "the powers of government inherent in every sovereignty." . . . Only to the extent that the Constitution so requires may this Court interfere with the exercise of this plenary power of government. . . . But precisely because it is the Constitution alone which warrants judicial interference in sovereign operations of the State, the basis of judgment as to the Constitutionality of state action must be a rational one, approaching the text which is the only commission for our power not in a literalistic way, as if we had a tax statute before us, but as the basic charter of our society, setting out in spare but meaningful terms the principles of government. But as inescapable as is the rational process in Constitutional adjudication in general, nowhere is it more so than in giving meaning to the prohibitions of the Fourteenth Amendment and, where the Federal Government is involved, the Fifth Amendment, against the deprivation of life, liberty or property without due process of law.

It is but a truism to say that this provision of both Amendments is not self-explanatory. As to the Fourteenth, which is involved here, the history of the Amendment also sheds little light on the meaning of the provision. . . . It is important to note, however, that two views of the Amendment have not been accepted by this Court as delineating its scope. One view, which was ably and insistently argued in response to what were felt to be abuses by this Court of its reviewing power, sought to limit the provision to a guarantee of procedural fairness. . . . The other view which has been rejected would have it that the Fourteenth Amendment, whether by way of the Privileges and Immunities Clause or the Due Process Clause, applied against the States only and precisely those restraints which had prior to the Amendment been applicable merely to federal action. However, "due process" in the consistent view of this Court has ever been a broader concept than the first view and more flexible than the second.

Were due process merely a procedural safeguard it would fail to reach those situations where the deprivation of life, liberty or property was accomplished by legislation which by operating in the future could, given even the fairest possible procedure in application to individuals, nevertheless destroy the enjoyment of all three. . . .

However it is not the particular enumeration of rights in the first eight Amendments which spells out the reach of Fourteenth Amendment due process, but rather, as was suggested in another context long before the adoption of that Amendment, those concepts which are considered to embrace those rights "which are fundamental, which belong to the citizens of all free governments," . . . for "the purposes [of securing] which men enter into society." . . . Again and again this Court has resisted the notion that the Fourteenth Amendment is no more than a shorthand reference to what is explicitly set out elsewhere in the Bill of Rights. . . . Indeed the fact that an identical provision limiting federal action is found among the first eight Amendments, applying to the Federal Government, suggests that due process is a discrete concept which subsists as an independent guaranty of liberty and procedural fairness, more general and inclusive than the specific prohibitions. . . .

Due process has not been reduced to any formula; its content cannot be determined by reference to any code. The best that can be said is that through the course of this Court's decisions it has represented the balance which our Nation, built upon postulates of respect for the liberty of the individual has struck between that liberty and the demands of organized society. If the supplying of content to this Constitutional concept has of necessity been a rational process, it certainly has not been one where judges have felt free to roam where unguided speculation might take them. The balance of which I speak is the balance struck by this country, having regard to what history teaches are the traditions from which it developed as well as the traditions from which it broke. That tradition is a living thing. A decision of this Court which radically departs from it could not long survive, while a decision which builds on what has survived is likely to be sound. No formula could serve as a substitute, in this area, for judgment and restraint.

It is this outlook which has led the Court continuingly to perceive distinctions in the imperative character of Constitutional provisions, since that character must be discerned from a particular provision's larger context. And inasmuch as this context is not one of words, but of history and purposes, the full scope of the liberty guaranteed by the Due Process Clause cannot be found in or limited by the precise terms of the specific guarantees elsewhere provided in the Constitution. This "liberty" is not a series of isolated points pricked out in terms of the taking of property; the freedom of speech, press, and religion; the right to keep and bear arms; the freedom from unreasonable searches and seizures; and so on. It is a rational continuum which, broadly speaking, includes a freedom from all substantial arbitrary impositions and purposeless restraints . . . and which also recognizes, what a reasonable and sensitive judgment must, that certain interests require particularly careful scrutiny of the state needs asserted to justify their abridgment.

Each new claim to Constitutional protection must be considered against a background of Constitutional purposes, as they have been rationally perceived and historically developed. Though we exercise limited and sharply restrained judgment, yet there is no "mechanical yardstick," no "mechanical answer." The decision of an apparently novel claim must depend on grounds which follow closely on well-accepted principles and criteria. The new decision must take "its place in relation to what went before and further [cut] a channel for what is to come." . . .

On these premises I turn to the particular Constitutional claim in this case.

Appellants contend that the Connecticut statute deprives them, as it unquestionably does, of a substantial measure of liberty in carrying on the most intimate of all personal relationships, and that it does so arbitrarily and without any rational, justifying purpose. The State, on the other hand, asserts that it is acting to protect the moral welfare of its citizenry, both directly, in that it considers the practice of contraception immoral in itself, and instrumentally, in that the availability of contraceptive materials tends to minimize "the disastrous consequence of dissolute action," that is fornication and adultery.

It is argued by appellants that the judgment, implicit in this statute—that the use of contraceptives by married couples is immoral—is an irrational one, that in effect it subjects them in a very important matter to the arbitrary whim of the legislature, and that it does so for no good purpose. Where, as here, we are dealing with what must be considered "a basic liberty," . . . "[t]here are limits to the extent to which the presumption of constitutionality can be pressed," . . . and at the mere assertion that the action of the State finds justification in the controversial realm of morals cannot justify alone any and every restriction it imposes. . . .

Yet the very inclusion of the category of morality among state concerns indicates that society is not limited in its objects only to the physical well-being of the community, but has traditionally concerned itself with the moral soundness of its people as well. Indeed to attempt a line between public behavior and that which is purely consensual or solitary would be to withdraw from community concern a range of subjects with which every society in civilized times has found it necessary to deal. The laws regarding marriage which provide both when the sexual powers may be used and the legal and societal context in which children are born and brought up, as well as laws forbidding adultery, fornication and homosexual practices which express the negative of the proposition, confining sexuality to lawful marriage, form a pattern so deeply pressed into the substance of our social life that any Constitutional doctrine in this area must build upon that basis. . . .

It is in this area of sexual morality, which contains many proscriptions of consensual behavior having little or no direct impact on others, that the State of Connecticut has expressed its moral judgment that all use of contraceptives is improper. Appellants cite an impressive list of authorities who, from a great variety of points of view, commend the considered use of contraceptives by married couples. What they do not emphasize is that not too long ago the current of opinion was very probably quite the opposite and that even today the issue is not free of controversy. Certainly, Connecticut's judgment is no more demonstrably correct or incorrect than are the varieties of judgment, expressed in law, on marriage and divorce, on adult consensual homosexuality, abortion, and sterilization, or euthanasia and suicide. If we had a case before us which required us to decide simply, and in abstraction, whether the moral judgment implicit in the application of the present statute to married couples was a sound one, the very controversial nature of these questions would, I think, require us to hesitate long before concluding that the Constitution precluded Connecticut from choosing as it has among these various views. . . .

But, as might be expected, we are not presented simply with this moral judgment to be passed on as an abstract proposition. The secular state is not an examiner of consciences: it must operate in the realm of behavior, of overt actions, and where it does so operate, not only the underlying, moral purpose of its operations, but also the choice of means becomes relevant to any Constitutional judgment on what is done. The moral presupposition on which appellants ask us to pass judgment could form the basis of a variety of legal rules and administrative choices, each presenting a different issue for adjudication. For example, one practical expression of the moral view propounded here might be the rule that a marriage in which only contraceptive relations had taken place had never been consummated and could be annulled. . . . Again, the use of contraceptives might be made a ground for divorce, or perhaps tax benefits and subsidies could be provided for large families. Other examples also readily suggest themselves.

Precisely what is involved here is this: the State is asserting the right to enforce its moral judgment by intruding upon the most intimate details of the marital relation with the full power of the criminal law. Potentially, this could allow the deployment of all the incidental machinery of the criminal law, arrests, searches and seizures; inevitably it must mean at the very least the lodging of criminal charges, a public trial, and testimony as to the *corpus delicti.* Nor could any imaginable elaboration of presumptions, testimonial privileges, or other safeguards, alleviate the necessity for testimony as to the mode and manner of the married couples' sexual relations, or at least the opportunity for the accused to make denial of the charges. In sum, the statute allows the State to enquire into, prove and punish married people for the private use of their marital intimacy.

This, then, is the precise character of the enactment whose Constitutional measure we must take. The statute must pass a more rigorous Constitutional test than that of going merely to the plausibility of its underlying rationale. . . . This enactment involves what, by common understanding throughout the English-speaking world, must be granted to be a most fundamental aspect of "liberty," the privacy of the home in its most basic sense, and it is this which requires that the statute be subjected to "strict scrutiny." . . .

That aspect of liberty which embraces the concept of the privacy of the home receives explicit Constitutional protection at two places only. These are the Third Amendment, relating to the quartering of soldiers, and the Fourth Amendment, prohibiting unreasonable searches and seizures. While these Amendments reach only the Federal Government, this Court has held in the strongest terms, and today again confirms, that the concept of "privacy" embodied in the Fourth Amendment is part of the "ordered liberty" assured against state action by the fourteenth Amendment. . . .

It is clear, of course, that this Connecticut statute does not invade the privacy of the home in the usual sense, since the invasion involved here may, and doubtless usually would, be accomplished without any physical intrusion whatever into the home. What the statute undertakes to do, however, is to create a crime which is grossly offensive to this privacy, while the Constitution refers only to methods of ferreting out substantive wrongs, and the procedure it requires presupposes that substantive offenses may be committed and sought out in the privacy of the home. But such an analysis forecloses any claim to Constitutional protection against this form of deprivation of privacy, only if due process in this respect is limited to what is explicitly provided in the Constitution, divorced from the rational purposes, historical roots, and subsequent developments of the relevant provisions. . . .

I think the sweep of the Court's decisions, under both the Fourth and Fourteenth Amendments, amply shows that the Constitution protects the privacy of the home against all unreasonable intrusion of whatever character. "[These] principles . . . affect the very essence of constitutional liberty and security. They reach farther than [a] concrete form of the case . . . before the court, with its adventitious circumstances; they apply to all invasions on the part of the government and its employees of the sanctity of a man's home and the privacies of life." . . . "The security of one's privacy against arbitrary intrusion by the police—which is at the core of the Fourth Amendment—is basic to a free society." . . .

It would surely be an extreme instance of sacrificing substance to form were it to be held that the Constitutional principle of privacy against arbitrary official intrusion comprehends only physical invasions by the police. To be sure, the times presented the framers with two particular threats to that principle, the general warrant, . . . and the quartering of soldiers in private homes. But though "[l]egislation, both statutory and constitutional, is enacted, . . . from an experience of evils . . . its general language should not, therefore, be necessarily confined to the form that evil had theretofore taken. . . . [A] principle, to be vital, must be capable of wider application than the mischief which gave it birth." . . .

Although the form of intrusion here—the enactment of a substantive offense—does not, in my opinion, preclude the making of a claim based on the right of privacy embraced in the "liberty" of the Due Process Clause, it must be acknowledged that there is another sense in which it could be argued that this intrusion on privacy differs from what the Fourth Amendment, and the similar concept of the Fourteenth, were intended to protect; here we have not an intrusion into the home so much as on the life which characteristically has its place in the home. But to my mind such a distinction is so insubstantial as to be captious: if the physical curtilage of the home is protected, it is surely as a result of solicitude to protect the privacies of the life within. Certainly the safeguarding of the home does not follow merely from the sanctity of property rights. The home derives its preeminence as the seat of family life. And the integrity of that life is something so fundamental that it has been found to draw to its protection the principles of more than one explicitly granted Constitutional right. . . .

Of this whole "private realm of family life" it is difficult to image what is more private or more intimate than a husband and wife's marital relations. We would indeed be straining at a gnat and swallowing a camel were we to show concern for the niceties of property law involved in our recent decision, under the Fourth Amendment, . . . and yet fail at least to see any substantial claim here.

Of course, just as the requirement of a warrant is not inflexible in carrying out searches and seizures, . . . so there are countervailing considerations at this more fundamental aspect of the right involved. "[T]he family . . . is not beyond regulation," . . . and it would be an absurdity to suggest either that offenses may not be committed in the bosom of the family or that the home can be made a sanctuary for crime. The right of privacy most manifestly is not an absolute. Thus, I would not suggest that adultery, homosexuality, fornication and incest are immune from criminal enquiry, however privately practiced. So much has been explicitly recognized in acknowledging the State's rightful concern for its people's moral welfare. . . . But not to discriminate between what is involved in this case and either the traditional offenses against good morals or crimes which, though they may be committed anywhere, happen to have been committed or concealed in the home, would entirely misconceive the argument that is being made.

Adultery, homosexuality and the like are sexual intimacies which the State forbids altogether, but the intimacy of husband and wife is necessarily an essential and accepted feature of the institution of marriage, an institution which the State not only must allow, but which always and in every age it has fostered and protected. It is one thing when the State exerts its power either to forbid extra-marital sexuality altogether, or to say who may marry, but it is quite another when, having acknowledged a marriage and the intimacies inherent in it, it undertakes to regulate by means of the criminal law the details of that intimacy.

In sum, even though the State has determined that the use of contraceptives is as iniquitous as any act of extra-marital sexual immorality, the intrusion of the whole machinery of the criminal law into the very heart of marital privacy, requiring husband and wife to render account before a criminal tribunal of their uses of that intimacy, is surely a very different thing indeed from punishing those who establish intimacies which the law has always forbidden and which can have no claim to social protection.

In my view the appellants have presented a very pressing claim for Constitutional protection. Such difficulty as the claim presents lies only in evaluating it against the State's countervailing contention that it be allowed to enforce, by whatever means it deems appropriate, its judgment of the immorality of the practice this law condemns. In resolving this conflict a number of factors compel me to conclude that the decision here must most emphatically be for the appellants. Since, as it appears to me, the statute marks an abridgment of important fundamental liberties protected by the Fourteenth Amendment, it will not do to urge in justification of that abridgement simply that the statute is rationally related to the effectuation of a proper state purpose. A closer scrutiny and stronger justification than that are required. . . .

Though the State has argued the Constitutional permissibility of the moral judgment underlying this statute, neither its brief, not its argument, nor anything in any of the opinions of its highest court in these or other cases even remotely suggests a justification for the obnoxiously intrusive means it has chosen to effectuate that policy. To me the very circumstance that Connecticut has not chosen to press the enforcement of this statute against individual users, while it nevertheless persists in asserting its right to do so at any time—in effect a right to hold this statute as an imminent threat to the privacy of the households of the State—conduces to the inference either that it does not consider the policy of the statute a very important one, or that it does not regard the means it has chosen for its effectuation as appropriate or necessary.

But conclusive, in my view, is the utter novelty of this enactment. Although the Federal Government and many States have at one time or other had on their books statutes forbidding or regulating the distribution of contraceptives, none, so far as I can find, has made the use of contraceptives a crime. Indeed, a diligent search has revealed that no nation, including several which quite evidently share Connecticut's moral policy, has seen fit to effectuate that policy by the means presented here.

Though undoubtedly the States are and should be left free to reflect a wide variety of policies and should be allowed broad scope in experimenting with various means of promoting those policies, I must agree with Mr. Justice Jackson that "[t]here are limits to the extent to which a legislatively represented majority may conduct . . . experiments at the expense of the dignity and personality" of the individual. . . . In this instance these limits are, in my view, reached and passed. . . .

Case

GRISWOLD V. CONNECTICUT

381 U.S. 479; 85 S.Ct. 1678; 14 L.Ed. 2d. 510 (1965)
Vote: 7–2

In this landmark case the Court considers the constitutionality of a state statute criminalizing the use of birth control devices.

Mr. Justice Douglas delivered the opinion of the Court.

Appellant Griswold is Executive Director of the Planned Parenthood League of Connecticut. Appellant Buxton is a licensed physician and a professor at the Yale Medical School who served as Medical Director for the League at its Center in New Haven—a center open and operating from November 1 to November 10, 1961, when appellants were arrested.

They gave information, instruction and medical advice to *married* persons as to the means of preventing conception. They examined the wife and prescribed the best contraceptive device or material for her use. Fees were usually charged, although some couples were serviced free.

The statutes whose constitutionality is involved in this appeal [provide]:

Any person who uses any drug, medicinal article or instrument for the purpose of preventing conception shall be fined not less than fifty dollars or imprisoned not less than sixty days nor more than one year or be both fined and imprisoned.

Any person who assists, abets, counsels, causes, hires or commands another to commit any offense may be prosecuted and punished as if he were the principal offender.

The appellants were found guilty as accessories and fined $100 each, against the claim that the accessory statute as so applied violated the Fourteenth Amendment. The Appellate Division of the Circuit Court affirmed. The Supreme Court of Errors affirmed that judgment. . . .

We think that appellants have standing to raise the constitutional rights of the married people with whom they had a professional relationship. . . . Certainly the accessory should have standing to assert that the offense which he is charged with assisting is not, or cannot constitutionally be, a crime. . . .

Coming to the merits, we are met with a wide range of questions that implicate the Due Process Clause of the Fourteenth Amendment. Overtones of some arguments suggest that *Lochner v. New York,* . . . should be our guide. But we decline that invitation. . . . We do not sit as a super-legislature to determine the wisdom, need, and propriety of laws that touch economic problems, business affairs, or social conditions. This law, however, operates directly on an intimate relation of husband and wife and their physician's role in one aspect of that relation.

The association of people is not mentioned in the Constitution nor in the Bill of Rights. The right to educate a child in a school of the parents' choice—whether public or private or parochial—is also not mentioned. Nor is the right to study any particular subject or any foreign language. Yet the First Amendment has been construed to include certain of those rights.

By *Pierce v. Society of Sisters,* the right to educate one's children as one chooses is made applicable to the States by the force of the First and Fourteenth Amendments. By *Meyer v. Nebraska,* the same dignity is given the right to study the German language in a private school. In other words, the State may not, consistently with the spirit of the First Amendment, contract the spectrum of available knowledge. The right of freedom of speech and press includes not only the right to utter or to print, but the right to distribute, the right to receive, the right to read . . . and freedom of inquiry, freedom of thought, and freedom to teach . . . indeed the freedom of the entire university community. . . . Without those peripheral rights the specific rights would be less secure. And so we reaffirm the principle of the *Pierce* and the *Meyer* cases.

In *NAACP v. Alabama,* . . . we protected the "freedom to associate and privacy in one's associations," noting that freedom of association was a peripheral First Amendment right. Disclosure of membership lists of a constitutionally valid association, we held, was invalid "as entailing the likelihood of a substantial restraint upon the exercise by petitioner's members of their right to freedom of association." In other words, the First Amendment has a penumbra where privacy is protected from governmental intrusion. In like context, we have protected forms of "association" that are not political in the customary sense but pertain to the social, legal, and economic benefit of the members. . . .

[Previous] . . . cases suggest that specific guarantees in the Bill of Rights have penumbras, formed by emanations from those guarantees that help give them life and substance. Various guarantees create zones of privacy. The right of association contained in the penumbra of the First Amendment is one, as we have seen. The Third Amendment in its prohibition against the quartering of soldiers "in any house" in time of peace without the consent of the owner is another facet of that privacy. The Fourth Amendment explicitly affirms the "right of the people to be secure in their persons, houses, papers, and effects, against unreasonable searches and seizures." The Fifth Amendment in its Self-Incrimination Clause enables the citizen to create a zone of privacy which government may not force him to surrender to his detriment. The Ninth Amendment provides: "The enumeration in the Constitution, of certain rights, shall not be construed to deny or disparage others retained by the people."

The Fourth and Fifth Amendments were described in *Boyd v. United States* . . . as protection against all governmental invasions "of the sanctity of a man's home and the privacies of life." We recently referred in *Mapp v. Ohio* . . . to the Fourth Amendment as creating a "right to privacy, no less important than any other right carefully and particularly reserved to the people." . . .

We have had many controversies over these penumbral rights of "privacy and repose." . . . These cases bear witness that the right of privacy which presses for recognition here is a legitimate one.

The present case, then, concerns a relationship lying within the zone of privacy created by several fundamental constitutional guarantees. And it concerns a law which, in forbidding the *use* of contraceptives rather than regulating their manufacture or sale, seeks to achieve its goals by means having a maximum destructive impact upon that relationship. Such a law cannot stand in light of the familiar principle, so often applied by this Court, that a "governmental purpose to control or prevent activities constitutionally subject to state regulation may not be achieved by means which sweep unnecessarily broadly and thereby invade the area of protected freedoms." . . . Would we allow the police to search the sacred precincts of marital bedrooms for telltale signs of the use of contraceptives? The very idea is repulsive to the notions of privacy surrounding the marriage relationship. . . .

Mr. Justice Goldberg, whom the **Chief Justice** and **Mr. Justice Brennan** join, concurring.

I agree with the Court that Connecticut's birth-control law unconstitutionally intrudes upon the right of marital privacy, and I join in its opinion and judgment. Although

I have not accepted the view that "due process" as used in the Fourteenth Amendment incorporates all of the first eight Amendments, . . . I do agree that the concept of liberty protects those personal rights that are fundamental, and is not confined to the specific terms of the Bill of Rights. My conclusion that the concept of liberty is not so restricted and that it embraces the right of marital privacy though that right is not mentioned explicitly in the Constitution is supported both by numerous decisions of this Court, referred to in the Court's opinion, and by the language and history of the Ninth Amendment. . . . In reaching the conclusion that the right of marital privacy is protected, as being within the protected penumbra of specific guarantees of the Bill of Rights, the Court refers to the Ninth Amendment, . . . I add these words to emphasize the relevance of that Amendment to the Court's holding. . . .

The Ninth Amendment reads, "The enumeration in the Constitution, of certain rights, shall not be construed to deny or disparage others retained by the people." The Amendment is almost entirely the work of James Madison. It was introduced in Congress by him and passed the House and Senate with little or no debate and virtually no change in language. It was proffered to quiet expressed fears that a bill of specifically enumerated rights could not be sufficiently broad to cover all essential rights and that the specific mention of certain rights would be interpreted as a denial that others were protected. . . .

. . . The Ninth Amendment to the Constitution may be regarded by some as a recent discovery and may be forgotten by others, but since 1791 it has been a basic part of the Constitution which we are sworn to uphold. To hold that a right so basic and fundamental and so deep-rooted in our society as the right of privacy in marriage may be infringed because that right is not guaranteed in so many words by the first eight amendments to the Constitution is to ignore the Ninth Amendment and to give it no effect whatsoever. Moreover, a judicial construction that this fundamental right is not protected by the Constitution because it is not mentioned in explicit terms by one of the first eight amendments or elsewhere in the Constitution would violate the Ninth Amendment. . . .

A dissenting opinion suggests that my interpretation of the Ninth Amendment somehow "broaden[s] the powers of this Court." . . . With all due respect, I believe that it misses the import of what I am saying. I do not take the position of my Brother Black in his dissent in *Adamson v. California* . . . that the entire Bill of Rights is incorporated in the Fourteenth Amendment, and I do not mean to imply that the Ninth Amendment is applied against the States by the Fourteenth. Nor do I mean to state that the Ninth Amendment constitutes an independent source of rights protected from infringement by either the States or the Federal Government. Rather, the Ninth Amendment shows a belief of the Constitution's authors that fundamental rights exist that are not expressly enumerated in the first eight amendments and an intent that the list of rights included there not be deemed exhaustive. As any student of this Court's opinions knows, this Court has held, often unanimously, that the Fifth and Fourteenth Amendments protect certain fundamental personal liberties from abridgment by the Federal Government or the States. . . . The Ninth Amendment simply shows the intent of the Constitution's authors that other fundamental personal rights should not be denied such protection or disparaged in any other way simply because they are not specifically listed in the first eight constitutional amendments. I do not see how this broadens the authority of the Court; rather it serves to support what this Court has been doing in protecting fundamental rights.

Nor am I turning somersaults with history in arguing that the Ninth Amendment is relevant in a case dealing with a *State's* infringement of a fundamental right. While the Ninth Amendment—and indeed the entire Bill of Rights—originally concerned restrictions upon *federal* power, the subsequently enacted Fourteenth Amendment prohibits the States as well from abridging fundamental personal liberties. And, the Ninth Amendment, in indicating that not all such liberties are specifically mentioned in the first eight amendments, is surely relevant in showing the existence of other fundamental personal rights, now protected from state, as well as federal, infringement. In sum, the Ninth Amendment simply lends strong support to the view that the "liberty" protected by the Fifth and Fourteenth Amendments from infringement by the Federal Government or the States is not restricted to rights specifically mentioned in the first eight amendments. . . .

In determining which rights are fundamental, judges are not left at large to decide cases in light of their personal and private notions. Rather, they must look to the "traditions and [collective] conscience of our people" to determine whether a principle is "so rooted [there] . . . as to be ranked as fundamental." . . . The inquiry is whether a right involved "is of such a character that it cannot be denied without violating those 'fundamental principles of liberty and justice which lie at the base of all our civil and political institutions.' " . . .

The entire fabric of the Constitution and the purposes that clearly underlie its specific guarantees demonstrate that the rights to marital privacy and to marry and raise a family are of similar order and magnitude as the fundamental rights specifically protected.

Although the Constitution does not speak in so many words of the right of privacy in marriage, I cannot believe that it offers these fundamental rights no protection. The fact that no particular provision of the Constitution explicitly forbids the State from disrupting the traditional relation of the family—a relation as old and as fundamental as our entire civilization—surely does not show that the Government was meant to have the power to do so. Rather, as the Ninth Amendment expressly recognizes, there are fundamental personal rights such as this one, which are protected from abridgment by the Government though not specifically mentioned in the Constitution. . . .

The logic of the dissents would sanction federal or state legislation that seems to me even more plainly unconstitutional than the statute before us. Surely the Government, absent a showing of a compelling subordinating state interest, could not decree that all husbands and wives must be sterilized after two children have been born to them. Yet by their reasoning such an invasion of marital privacy would not be subject to constitutional challenge because, while it might be "silly," no provision of the Constitution specifically prevents the Government from curtailing the marital right to bear children and raise a family. While it may shock some of my Brethren that the Court today holds that the Constitution protects the right of marital privacy, in my view it is far more shocking to believe that the personal liberty guaranteed by the Constitution does not include protection against such totalitarian limitation of family size, which is at complete variance with our constitutional concepts. Yet, if upon a showing of a slender basis of rationality, a law outlawing voluntary birth control by married persons is valid, then, by the same reasoning, a law requiring compulsory birth control also would seem to be valid. In my view, however, both types of law would unjustifiably intrude upon rights of marital privacy which are constitutionally protected.

In a long series of cases this Court has held that where fundamental personal liberties are involved, they may not be abridged by the States simply on a showing that a regulatory statute has some rational relationship to the effectuation of a proper state purpose. . . .

Although the Connecticut birth-control law obviously encroaches upon a fundamental personal liberty, the State does not show that the law serves any "subordinating [state] interest which is compelling" or that it is "necessary . . . to the accomplishment of a permissible state policy." The State, at most, argues that there is some rational relation between this statute and what is admittedly a legitimate subject of state concern—the discouraging of extra-marital relations. It says that preventing the use of birth-control devices by married persons helps prevent the indulgence by some in such extra-marital relations. The rationality of this justification is dubious, particularly in light of the admitted widespread availability to all persons in the State of Connecticut, unmarried as well as married, of birth-control devices for the prevention of disease, as distinguished from the prevention of conception. . . . But, in any event, it is clear that the state interest in safeguarding marital fidelity can be served by a more discriminately tailored statute, which does not, like the present one, sweep unnecessarily broadly, reaching far beyond the evil sought to be dealt with and intruding upon the privacy of all married couples. . . .

Finally, it should be said of the Court's holding today that it in no way interferes with a State's proper regulation of sexual promiscuity or misconduct. . . .

In sum, I believe that the right of privacy in the marital relation is fundamental and basic—a personal right "retained by the people" within the meaning of the Ninth Amendment. Connecticut cannot constitutionally abridge this fundamental right, which is protected by the Fourteenth Amendment from infringement by the States. I agree with the Court that petitioners' convictions must therefore be reversed.

Mr. Justice Harlan, concurring in the judgment.

I fully agree with the judgment of reversal, but find myself unable to join the Court's opinion. The reason is that it seems to me to evince an approach to this case very much like that taken by my Brothers Black and Stewart in dissent, namely: the Due Process Clause of the Fourteenth Amendment does not touch this Connecticut statute unless the enactment is found to violate some right assured by the letter or penumbra of the Bill of Rights.

In other words, what I find implicit in the Court's opinion is that the "incorporation" doctrine may be used to *restrict* the reach of Fourteenth Amendment Due Process. For me this is just as unacceptable constitutional doctrine as is the use of the "incorporation" approach to *impose* upon the States all the requirements of the Bill of Rights as found in the provisions of the first eight amendments and in the decisions of this court interpreting them. . . .

In my view, the proper constitutional inquiry in this case is whether this Connecticut statute infringes the Due Process Clause of the Fourteenth Amendment because the enactment violates basic values "implicit in the concept of ordered liberty." . . . For reasons stated at length in my dissenting opinion in *Poe v. Ullman,* I believe that it does. While the relevant inquiry may be aided by resort to one or more of the provisions of the Bill of Rights, it is not dependent on them or any of their radiations. The Due Process Clause of the Fourteenth Amendment stands, in my opinion, on its own bottom. . . .

While I could not more heartily agree that judicial "self restraint" is an indispensable ingredient of sound constitutional adjudication, I do submit that the formula suggested for achieving it is more hollow than real. "Specific" provisions of the Constitution, no less than "due process," lend themselves as readily to "personal" interpretations by judges whose constitutional outlook is simply to keep the Constitution in supposed "tune with the times." . . .

Judicial self-restraint will not, I suggest, be brought about in the "due process" area by the historically unfounded incorporation formula long advanced by my Brother Black, and now in part espoused by my Brother Stewart. It will be achieved in this area, as in other constitutional areas, only by continual insistence upon respect for the teachings of history, solid recognition of the basic values that underlie our society, and wise appreciation of the great roles that the doctrines of federalism and separation of powers have played in establishing and preserving American freedoms. . . . Adherence to these principles will not, of course, obviate all constitutional differences of opinion among judges, nor should it. Their continued recognition will, however, go farther toward keeping most judges from roaming at large in the constitutional field than will the interpolation into the Constitution of an artificial and largely illusory restriction on the content of the Due Process Clause.

Mr. Justice White, concurring in the judgment.

In my view this Connecticut law as applied to married couples deprives them of "liberty" without due process of law, as that concept is used in the Fourteenth Amendment. I therefore concur in the judgment of the Court reversing these convictions under the Connecticut aiding and abetting statute. . . .

Mr. Justice Black, with whom **Mr. Justice Stewart** joins, dissenting.

I agree with my Brother Stewart's dissenting opinion. And like him I do not to any extent whatever base my view that this Connecticut law is constitutional on a belief that the law is wise or that its policy is a good one. In order that there may be no room at all to doubt why I vote as I do, I feel constrained to add that the law is every bit as offensive to me as it is to my Brethren of the majority and my Brothers Harlan, White and Goldberg who, reciting reasons why it is offensive to them, hold it unconstitutional. There is no single one of the graphic and eloquent strictures and criticisms fired at the policy of this Connecticut law either by the Court's opinion or by those of my concurring brethren to which I cannot subscribe—except their conclusion that the evil qualities they see in the law make it unconstitutional.

. . . I get nowhere in this case by talk about a constitutional "right of privacy" as an emanation from one or more constitutional provisions. I like my privacy as well as the next one, but I am nevertheless compelled to admit that government has a right to invade it unless prohibited by some specific constitutional provision. For these reasons I cannot agree with the Court's judgment and the reasons it gives for holding this Connecticut law unconstitutional. . . .

I realize that many good and able men have eloquently spoken and written, sometimes in rhapsodical strains, about the duty of this Court to keep the Constitution in tune with the times. The idea is that the Constitution must be changed from time to time and that this Court is charged with a duty to make those changes. For myself, I must with all deference reject that philosophy. The Constitution makers knew the need for change and provided for it. Amendments suggested by the people's elected representatives can be submitted to the people or their selected agents for ratification. That method of change was good enough for our Fathers, and being somewhat old-fashioned I must add it is good enough for me. And so, I cannot rely on the Due Process Clause or the Ninth Amendment or any mysterious and uncertain natural law concept as a reason for striking down this state law. The Due Process Clause with an "arbitrary and capricious" or "shocking to the conscience" formula was liberally used by this Court to strike down economic legislation in the early decades of this century, threatening, many people thought, the tranquility and stability of the Nation. . . . That formula, based on subjective considerations of "natural justice," is no less dangerous when used to enforce this Court's views about personal rights than those about economic rights. I had thought that we had laid that formula, as a means for striking down state legislation, to rest once and for all. . . .

Mr. Justice Stewart, whom **Mr. Justice Black** joins, dissenting.

Since 1879 Connecticut has had on its books a law which forbids the use of contraceptives by anyone. I think this is an uncommonly silly law. As a practical matter, the law is obviously unenforceable, except in the oblique context of the present case. As a philosophical matter, I believe the use of contraceptives in the relationship of marriage should be left to personal and private choice, based upon the individual's moral, ethical, and religious beliefs. As a matter of social policy, I think professional counsel about methods of birth control should be available to all, so that each individual's choice can be meaningfully made. But we are not asked in this case to say whether we think this law is unwise, or even asinine. We are asked to hold that it violates the United States Constitution. And that I cannot do.

In the course of its opinion the Court refers to no less than six Amendments to the Constitution: the First, the Third, the Fourth, the Fifth, the Ninth, and the Fourteenth. But the Court does not say which of these Amendments, if any, it thinks is infringed by this Connecticut law.

We are told that the Due Process Clause of the Fourteenth Amendment is not, as such, the "guide" in this case. With that much I agree. There is no claim that this law, duly enacted by the Connecticut Legislature, is unconstitutionally vague. There is no claim that the appellants were denied any of the elements of procedural due process at their trial, so as to make their convictions constitutionally invalid. And, as the Court says, the day has long passed since the Due Process Clause was regarded as a proper instrument for determining "the wisdom, need, and propriety" of state laws. . . . My Brothers Harlan and White to the contrary, "[w]e have returned to the original constitutional proposition that courts do not substitute their social and economic beliefs for the judgment of legislative bodies, who are elected to pass laws." . . .

As to the First, Third, Fourth, and Fifth Amendments, I can find nothing in any of them to invalidate this Connecticut law, even assuming that all those Amendments are fully applicable against the States. It has not even been argued that this is a law "respecting an establishment of religion, or prohibiting the free exercise thereof." And surely, unless the solemn process of constitutional adjudication is to descend to the level of a play on words, there is not involved here any abridgment of "the freedom of speech, or of the press; or the right of the people peaceably to assemble, and to petition the Government for a redress of grievances." No soldier has been quartered in any house. There has been no search, and no seizure. Nobody has been compelled to be a witness against himself.

The Court also quotes the Ninth Amendment, and my Brother Goldberg's concurring opinion relies heavily upon it. But to say that the Ninth Amendment has anything to do with this case is to turn somersaults with history. The Ninth Amendment, like its companion the Tenth, which this Court held "states but a truism that all is retained which has not been surrendered," . . . was framed by James Madison and adopted by the States simply to make clear that the adoption of the Bill of Rights did not alter the plan that the Federal Government was to be a government of express and limited powers, and that all rights and powers not delegated to it were retained by the people and the individual States. Until today no member of this Court has ever suggested that the Ninth Amendment meant anything else, and the idea that a federal court could ever use the Ninth

Amendment to annul a law passed by the elected representatives of the people of the State of Connecticut would have caused James Madison no little wonder.

What provision of the Constitution, then, does make this state law invalid? The Court says it is the right of privacy "created by several fundamental constitutional guarantees." With all deference, I can find no such general right of privacy in the Bill of Rights, in any other part of the Constitution, or in any case ever before decided by this Court.

At the oral argument in this case we were told that the Connecticut law does not "conform to current community standards." But it is not the function of this Court to decide cases on the basis of community standards. We are here to decide cases "agreeably to the Constitution and laws of the United States." It is the essence of judicial duty to subordinate our own personal views, our own ideas of what legislation is wise and what is not. If, as I should surely hope, the law before us does not reflect the standards of the people of Connecticut, the people of Connecticut can freely exercise their true Ninth and Tenth Amendment rights to persuade their elected representative to repeal it. That is the constitutional way to take this law off the books.

Case

ROE V. WADE

410 U.S. 113; 93 S.Ct. 705; 35 L.Ed. 2d. 147 (1973)
Vote: 7–2

In what is perhaps the most controversial judicial decision of the modern era, the Supreme Court reviews a Texas law criminalizing abortion.

Mr. Justice Blackmun delivered the opinion of the Court.

. . . The Texas statutes that concern us here . . . make it a crime to "procure an abortion," as therein defined, or to attempt one, except with respect to "an abortion procured or attempted by medical advice for the purpose of saving the life of the mother." Similar statutes are in existence in a majority of the States.

Texas first enacted a criminal abortion statute in 1854. . . . This was soon modified into language that has remained substantially unchanged to the present time. . . .

Jane Roe, a single woman who was residing in Dallas County, Texas, instituted this federal action in March

1970 against the District Attorney of the county. She sought a declaratory judgment that the Texas criminal abortion statutes were unconstitutional on their face, and an injunction restraining the defendant from enforcing the statutes.

Roe alleged that she was unmarried and pregnant; that she wished to terminate her pregnancy by an abortion "performed by a competent, licensed physician, under safe, clinical conditions"; that she was unable to get a "legal" abortion in Texas because her life did not appear to be threatened by the continuation of her pregnancy; and that she could not afford to travel to another jurisdiction in order to secure a legal abortion under safe conditions. She claimed that the Texas statutes were unconstitutionally vague and that they abridged her right of personal privacy, protected by the First, Fourth, Fifth, Ninth, and Fourteenth Amendments. By an amendment to her complaint Roe purported to sue "on behalf of herself and all other women" similarly situated. . . .

The principal thrust of appellant's attack on the Texas statutes is that they improperly invade a right, said to be possessed by the pregnant woman, to choose to terminate her pregnancy. Appellant would discover this right in the concept of personal "liberty" embodied in the Fourteenth Amendment's Due Process Clause; or in personal, marital, familial, and sexual privacy said to be protected by the Bill of Rights or its penumbras, . . . or among those rights reserved to the people by the Ninth Amendment. . . . Before addressing this claim, we feel it desirable briefly to survey, in several aspects, the history of abortion, for such insight as that history may afford us, and then to examine the state purposes and interests behind the criminal abortion laws. . . .

Three reasons have been advanced to explain historically the enactment of criminal abortion laws in the 19th century and to justify their continued existence.

It has been argued occasionally that these laws were the product of a Victorian social concern to discourage illicit sexual conduct. Texas, however, does not advance this justification in the present case, and it appears that no court or commentator has taken the argument seriously. . . .

A second reason is concerned with abortion as a medical procedure. When most criminal abortion laws were first enacted, the procedure was a hazardous one for the woman. This was particularly true prior to the development of antisepsis. Antiseptic techniques, of course, were based on discoveries by Lister, Pasteur, and others first announced in 1867, but were not generally accepted and employed until about the turn of the century. Abortion mortality was high. Even after 1900, and perhaps until as late as the development of antibiotics in the 1940s, standard modern techniques such as dilation and curettage were not nearly so safe as they are today. Thus, it has been argued that a State's real concern in enacting a criminal abortion law was to protect the pregnant woman, that is, to restrain her from submitting to a procedure that placed her life in serious jeopardy.

Modern medical techniques have altered this situation. Mortality rates for women undergoing early abortions, where the procedure is legal, appear to be as low as or lower than the rates for normal childbirth. Consequently, any interest of the State in protecting the woman from an inherently hazardous procedure, except when it would be equally dangerous for her to forgo it, has largely disappeared. Of course, important state interests in the area of health and medical standards do remain. . . .

The third reason is the State's interest—some phrase it in terms of duty—in protecting prenatal life. Some of the argument for this justification rests on the theory that a new human life is present from the moment of conception. The State's interest and general obligation to protect

life then extends, it is argued, to prenatal life. Only when the life of the pregnant mother herself is at stake, balanced against the life she carries within her, should the interest of the embryo or fetus not prevail. Logically, of course, a legitimate state interest in this area need not stand or fall on acceptance of the belief that life begins at conception or at some other point prior to live birth. In assessing the State's interest, recognition may be given to the less rigid claim that as long as at least potential life is involved, the State may assert interests beyond the protection of the pregnant woman alone. . . .

The Constitution does not explicitly mention any right of privacy. In a line of decisions, . . . the Court has recognized that a right of personal privacy or a guarantee of certain areas or zones of privacy, does exist under the Constitution. . . .

This right of privacy, whether it be founded in the Fourteenth Amendment's concept of personal liberty and restrictions upon state action, as we feel it is, or, as the District Court determined, in the Ninth Amendment's reservation of rights to the people, is broad enough to encompass a woman's decision whether or not to terminate her pregnancy. The detriment that the State would impose upon the pregnant woman by denying this choice altogether is apparent. Specific and direct harm medically diagnosable even in early pregnancy may be involved. Maternity, or additional offspring, may force upon the woman a distressful life and future. Psychological harm may be imminent. Mental and physical health may be taxed by child care. There is also the distress, for all concerned, associated with the unwanted child, and there is the problem of bringing a child into a family already unable, psychologically and otherwise, to care for it. In other cases, as in this one, the additional difficulties and continuing stigma of unwed motherhood may be involved. All these are factors the woman and her responsible physician necessarily will consider in consultation.

On the basis of elements such as these, appellant and some *amici* argue that the woman's right is absolute and that she is entitled to terminate her pregnancy at whatever time, in whatever way, and for whatever reason she alone chooses. With this we do not agree. Appellant's arguments that Texas either has no valid interest at all in regulating the abortion decision, or no interest strong enough to support any limitation upon the woman's sole determination, is unpersuasive. The Court's decisions recognizing a right of privacy also acknowledge that some state regulation in areas protected by the right is appropriate. As noted above, a State may properly assert important interests in safeguarding health, in maintaining medical standards, and in protecting potential life. At some point in pregnancy, these respective interests become sufficiently compelling to sustain regulation of the factors that govern the abortion decision. The privacy right involved, therefore, cannot be said to be absolute. . . .

We, therefore, conclude that the right of personal privacy includes the abortion decision, but that this right is not unqualified and must be considered against important state interests in regulation.

We note that those federal and state courts that have recently considered abortion law challenges have reached the same conclusion. A majority, in addition to the District Court in the present case, have held state laws unconstitutional, at least in part, because of vagueness or because of overbreadth and abridgment of rights. . . .

Although the results are divided, most of these courts have agreed that the right of privacy, however based, is broad enough to cover the abortion decision; that the right, nonetheless, is not absolute and is subject to some limitations; and that at some point the state interests as to protection of health, medical standards, and prenatal life, become dominant. We agree with this approach.

Where certain "fundamental rights" are involved, the Court has held that regulation limiting these rights may be justified only by a "compelling state interest," . . . and that legislative enactments must be narrowly drawn to express only the legitimate state interests at stake. . . .

The District Court held that the appellee failed to meet his burden of demonstrating that the Texas statute's infringement upon Roe's rights was necessary to support a compelling state interest, and that, although the appellee presented "several compelling justifications for state presence in the area of abortions," the statutes outstripped these justifications and swept "far beyond any areas of compelling state interest." Appellant and appellee both contest that holding. Appellant, as has been indicated, claims an absolute right that bars any state imposition of criminal penalties in the area. Appellee argues that the State's determination to recognize and protect prenatal life from and after conception constitutes a compelling state interest. As noted above, we do not agree fully with either formulation.

The appellee and certain *amici* argue that the fetus is a "person" within the language and meaning of the Fourteenth Amendment. In support of this, they outline at length and in detail the well-known facts of fetal development. If this suggestion of personhood is established, the appellant's case, of course, collapses, for the fetus' right to life is then guaranteed specifically by the Amendment. The appellant conceded as much on reargument. On the other hand, the appellee conceded on reargument that no case could be cited that holds that a fetus is a person within the meaning of the Fourteenth Amendment.

The Constitution does not define "person" in so many words. Section 1 of the Fourteenth Amendment contains three references to "person." The first, in defining "citizens," speaks of "persons born or naturalized in the United States." The word also appears both in the Due Process Clause and in the Equal Protection Clause. "Person" is used in other places in the Constitution. . . . But in nearly all these instances, the use of the word is such that it has application only postnatally. None indicates, with any assurance, that it has any possible prenatal application.

All this, together with our observation, that throughout the major portion of the 19th century prevailing legal abortion practices were far freer than they are today, persuades us that the word "person," as used in the Fourteenth Amendment, does not include the unborn.

This conclusion, however, does not of itself fully answer the contentions raised by Texas, and we pass on to other considerations.

The pregnant woman cannot be isolated in her privacy. She carries an embryo and, later, a fetus, if one accepts the medical definitions of the developing young in the human uterus. The situation there is inherently different from marital intimacy, or bedroom possession of obscene material, or marriage, or procreation, or education. . . . As we have intimated above, it is reasonable and appropriate for a State to decide that at some point in time another interest, that of the health of the mother or that of potential human life, becomes significantly involved. The woman's privacy is no longer sole and any right of privacy she possesses must be measured accordingly.

Texas urges that, apart from the Fourteenth Amendment, life begins at conception and is present throughout pregnancy, and that, therefore, the State has a compelling interest in protecting that life from and after conception. We need not resolve the difficult question of when life begins. When those trained in the respective disciplines of medicine, philosophy, and theology are unable to arrive at any consensus, the judiciary, at this point in the development of man's knowledge, is not in a position to speculate as to the answer.

It should be sufficient to note briefly the wide divergence of thinking on this most sensitive and difficult question. There has always been strong support for the view that life does not begin until live birth. This was the belief of the Stoics. It appears to be the predominant, though not the unanimous, attitude of the Jewish faith. It may be taken to represent also the position of a large segment of the Protestant community, insofar as that can be ascertained; organized groups that have taken a formal position on the abortion issue have generally regarded abortion as a matter for the conscience of the individual and her family. As we have noted, the common law found greater significance in quickening. Physicians and their scientific colleagues have regarded that event with less interest and have tended to focus either upon conception, upon live birth, or upon the interim point at which the fetus becomes "viable," that is, potentially able to live outside the mother's womb, albeit with artificial aid. Viability is usually placed at about seven months (28 weeks) but may occur earlier, even at 24 weeks. The Aristotelian theory of "mediate animation," that held sway throughout the Middle Ages and the Renaissance in Europe, continued to be official Roman Catholic dogma until the 19th century, despite opposition to this "ensoulment" theory from those in the Church who would recognize the existence of life from the moment of conception. The latter is now, of course, the official belief of the Catholic Church. As one of the briefs *amicus* discloses, this is a view strongly held by many non-Catholics as well, and by many physicians. Substantial problems for precise definition of this view are posed, however, by new embryological data that purport to indicate that conception is a "process" over time, rather than an event, and by new medical techniques such as menstrual extraction, the "morning-after" pill, implantation of embryos, artificial insemination, even artificial wombs.

In areas other than criminal abortion, the law has been reluctant to endorse any theory that life, as we recognize it, begins before live birth or to accord legal rights to the unborn except in narrowly defined situations and except when the rights are contingent upon live birth. For example, the traditional rule of tort law denied recovery for prenatal injuries even though the child was born alive. That rule has been changed in almost every jurisdiction. In most States, recovery is said to be permitted only if the fetus was viable, or at least quick, when the injuries were sustained, though few courts have squarely so held. In a recent development, generally opposed by the commentators, some States permit the parents of a stillborn child to maintain an action for wrongful death because of prenatal injuries. Such an action, however, would appear to be one to vindicate the parents' interest and is thus consistent with the view that the fetus, at most, represents only the potentiality

of life. Similarly, unborn children have been recognized as acquiring rights or interests by way of inheritance or other devolution of property, and have been represented by guardians *ad litem*. Perfection of the interests involved, again, has generally been contingent upon live birth. In short, the unborn have never been recognized in the law as persons in the whole sense.

In view of all this, we do not agree that, by adopting one theory of life, Texas may override the rights of the pregnant woman that are at stake. We repeat, however, that the State does have an important and legitimate interest in preserving and protecting the health of the pregnant woman, whether she be a resident of the State or a nonresident who seeks medical consultation and treatment there, and that it has still another important and legitimate interest in protecting the potentiality of human life. These interests are separate and distinct. Each grows in substantiality as the woman approaches term and, at a point during pregnancy, each becomes "compelling."

With respect to the State's important and legitimate interest in the health of the mother, the "compelling" point, in the light of present medical knowledge, is at approximately the end of the first trimester. This is so because of the now-established medical fact that until the end of the first trimester mortality in abortion may be less than mortality in normal childbirth. It follows that, from and after this point, a State may regulate the abortion procedure to the extent that the regulation reasonably relates to the preservation and protection of maternal health. Examples of permissible state regulation in this area are requirements as to the qualifications of the person who is to perform the abortion; as to the licensure of that person; as to the facility in which the procedure is to be performed, that is, whether it must be a hospital or may be a clinic or some other place of less-than-hospital status; as to the licensing of the facility; and the like.

This means, on the other hand, that for the period of pregnancy prior to this "compelling" point, the attending physician, in consultation with his patient, is free to determine, without regulation by the State, that, in his medical judgment, the patient's pregnancy should be terminated. If that decision is reached, the judgment may be effectuated by an abortion free of interference by the State.

With respect to the State's important and legitimate interest in potential life, the "compelling" point is at viability. This is so because the fetus then presumably has the capability of meaningful life outside the mother's womb. State regulation protective of fetal life after viability thus has both logical and biological justifications. If the State is interested in protecting fetal life after viability, it may go so far as to proscribe abortion during that period, except when it is necessary to preserve the life or health of the mother.

Measured against these standards, the Texas Penal Code, in restricting legal abortions to those "procured or attempted by medical advice for the purpose of saving the life of the mother," sweeps too broadly. The statute makes no distinction between abortions performed early in pregnancy and those performed later, and it limits to a single reason, "saving" the mother's life, the legal justification for the procedure. The statute, therefore, cannot survive the constitutional attack made upon it here.

To summarize and to repeat:

1. A state criminal abortion statute of the current Texas type, that excepts from criminality only a life-saving procedure on behalf of the mother, without regard to pregnancy stage and without recognition of the other interests involved, is violative of the Due Process Clause of the Fourteenth Amendment.

    (a) For the stage prior to approximately the end of the first trimester, the abortion decision and its effectuation must be left to the medical judgment of the pregnant woman's attending physician.

    (b) For the stage subsequent to approximately the end of the first trimester, the State, in promoting its interest in the health of the mother, may, if it chooses, regulate the abortion procedure in ways that are reasonably related to maternal health.

    (c) For the stage subsequent to viability, the State in promoting its interest in the potentiality of human life may, if it chooses, regulate, and even proscribe, abortion except where it is necessary, in appropriate medical judgment, for the preservation of the life or health of the mother.

This holding, we feel, is consistent with the relative weights of the respective interests involved, with the lessons and examples of medical and legal history, with the lenity of the common law, and with the demands of the profound problems of the present day. The decision leaves the State free to place increasing restrictions on abortion as the period of pregnancy lengthens, so long as those restrictions are tailored to the recognized state in-

terests. The decision vindicates the right of the physician to administer medical treatment according to his professional judgment up to the points where important state interests provide compelling justifications for intervention. Up to those points, the abortion decision in all its aspects is inherently, and primarily, a medical decision, and basic responsibility for it must rest with the physician. If an individual practitioner abuses the privilege of exercising proper medical judgment, the usual remedies, judicial and intraprofessional, are available. . . .

Mr. Chief Justice Burger, concurring.

. . . I do not read the Court's holdings today as having the sweeping consequences attributed to them by dissenting Justices; the dissenting views discount the reality that the vast majority of physicians observe the standards of their profession, and act only on the basis of carefully deliberated medical judgments relating to life and health. Plainly, the Court today rejects any claim that the Constitution requires abortion on demand.

Mr. Justice Douglas, concurring. . . .

Mr. Justice Stewart, concurring. . . .

Mr. Justice White, with whom **Mr. Justice Rehnquist** joins, dissenting.

At the heart of the controversy in these cases are those recurring pregnancies that pose no danger whatsoever to the life or health of the mother but are, nevertheless, unwanted for any one or more of a variety of reasons—convenience, family planning, economics, dislike of children, the embarrassment of illegitimacy, etc. The common claim before us is that for any one of such reasons, or for no reason at all, and without asserting or claiming any threat to life or health, any woman is entitled to an abortion at her request if she is able to find a medical advisor willing to undertake the procedure.

The Court for the most part sustains this position: During the period prior to the time the fetus becomes viable, the Constitution of the United States values the convenience, whim, or caprice of the putative mother more than the life or potential life of the fetus; the Constitution, therefore, guarantees the right to an abortion as against any state law or policy seeking to protect the fetus from an abortion not prompted by more compelling reasons of the mother.

With all due respect, I dissent. I find nothing in the language or history of the Constitution to support the Court's judgment. The Court simply fashions and announces a new constitutional right for pregnant mothers and, with scarcely any reason or authority for its action, invests that right with sufficient substance to override most existing state abortion statutes. The upshot is that the people and the legislatures of the 50 States are constitutionally disentitled to weigh the relative importance of the continued existence and development of the fetus, on the one hand, against a spectrum of possible impacts on the mother, on the other hand. As an exercise of raw judicial power, the Court perhaps has authority to do what it does today; but in my view its judgment is an improvident and extravagant exercise of the power of judicial review that the Constitution extends to this Court. . . .

Mr. Justice Rehnquist, dissenting.

. . . The Due Process Clause of the Fourteenth Amendment undoubtedly does place a limit, albeit a broad one, on legislative power to enact laws such as this. If the Texas statute were to prohibit an abortion even where the mother's life is in jeopardy, I have little doubt that such a statute would lack a rational relation to a valid state objective. . . . But the Court's sweeping invalidation of any restrictions on abortion during the first trimester is impossible to justify under that standard, and the conscious weighing of competing factors that the Court's opinion apparently substitutes for the established test is far more appropriate to a legislative judgment than to a judicial one.

The Court eschews the history of the Fourteenth Amendment in its reliance on the "compelling state interest" test. But the Court adds a new wrinkle to this test by transposing it from the legal considerations associated with the Equal Protection Clause of the Fourteenth Amendment to this case arising under the Due Process Clause of the Fourteenth Amendment. Unless I misapprehend the consequences of this transplanting of the "compelling state interest test," the Court's opinion will accomplish the seemingly impossible feat of leaving this area of the law more confused than it found it.

. . . While the Court's opinion quotes from the dissent of Mr. Justice Holmes in *Lochner v. New York,* the result it reaches is more closely attuned to the majority opinion of Mr. Justice Peckham in that case. As in *Lochner* and similar cases applying substantive due process standards to economic and social welfare legislation, the adoption of the compelling state interest standard will inevitably require this Court to examine the legislative policies and pass on the wisdom of these policies in the very process of deciding whether a particular state interest put forward may or may not be "compelling." The decision here to break pregnancy into three distinct terms and to outline the permissible restrictions the State may impose in each one, for example, partakes more of judicial legislation than it does of a determination of the intent of the drafters of the Fourteenth Amendment.

The fact that a majority of the States reflecting, after all, the majority sentiment in those States, have had restrictions on abortions for at least a century is a strong indication, it seems to me, that the asserted right to an abortion is not "so rooted in the traditions and conscience of our people as to be ranked as fundamental. . . ." Even today, when society's views on abortion are changing, the very existence of the debate is evidence that the "right" to an abortion is not so universally accepted as the appellants would have us believe. . . .

Case

PLANNED PARENTHOOD V. CASEY

505 U.S. 833; 112 S.Ct. 2791; 120 L.Ed. 2d. 674 (1992)
Vote: 5–4 / 7–2

In this case, Planned Parenthood of Southeastern Pennsylvania brought suit against Pennsylvania Governor Robert Casey to challenge the constitutionality of a series of provisions of the Pennsylvania Abortion Control Act of 1982 as amended in 1988 and 1989. The act required a woman seeking an abortion to give her informed consent prior to the abortion procedure, and specified that she be provided with certain information at least twenty-four hours before the abortion is performed. For a minor to obtain an abortion, the Act required the informed consent of one of her parents, but provided for a "judicial bypass" option if the minor did not wish to or could not obtain a parent's consent.

Another provision of the Act required that, with some exceptions, a married woman seeking an abortion must sign a statement indicating that she has notified her husband of her intended abortion. The act exempted compliance with these three requirements in the event of a medical emergency. Finally, the act imposed certain reporting requirements on facilities that provide abortion services. After a trial, the federal district court declared all of these provisions unconstitutional. The Court of Appeals for the Third Circuit reversed in part, upholding all of the requirements with the exception of the spousal notification provision.

A fragmented Supreme Court upheld all of the statutory provisions with the exception of the spousal notification requirement. The Court produced five opinions. Two justices, Blackmun and Stevens, took the position (in separate opinions concurring in part and dissenting in part) that Roe v. Wade should be reaffirmed and that all of the statutory provisions should be declared invalid. Four justices, Rehnquist, Scalia, White, and Thomas, took the view that Roe should be overruled and that all of the Pennsylvania restrictions should be upheld. The controlling opinion, coauthored by Justices O'Connor, Kennedy, and Souter, joined Justices Blackmun and Stevens in explicitly reaffirming Roe v. Wade. However, the "joint opinion" abandoned the Roe trimester framework and declared a new "unduly burdensome" test for judging regulations of abortion. Applying this test, the joint opinion upheld the parental consent and informed consent provisions but invalidated the spousal notification requirement. Thus, the vote on the Court was 5 to 4 to reaffirm Roe v. Wade and invalidate the spousal notification requirement and 7 to 2 to uphold the other statutory provisions.

Justice O'Connor, Justice Kennedy, and **Justice Souter** . . . delivered the opinion of the Court. . . .

. . . Liberty finds no refuge in a jurisprudence of doubt. Yet 19 years after our holding that the Constitution protects a woman's right to terminate her pregnancy in its early stages, *Roe v. Wade* . . . (1973), that definition of liberty is still questioned. Joining the respondents as *amicus curiae,* the United States, as it has done in five other cases in the last decade, again asks us to overrule *Roe.* . . .

After considering the fundamental constitutional questions resolved by *Roe,* principles of institutional integrity, and the rule of *stare decisis,* we are led to conclude this: the essential holding of *Roe v. Wade* should be retained and once again reaffirmed. . . .

II

. . . Men and women of good conscience can disagree, and we suppose some always shall disagree, about the profound moral and spiritual implications of terminating a pregnancy, even in its earliest stage. Some of us as individuals find abortion offensive to our most basic principles of morality, but that cannot control our decision. Our obligation is to define the liberty of all, not to mandate our own moral code. The underlying constitutional issue is whether the state can resolve these philosophic questions in such a definitive way that a woman lacks all choice in the matter, except perhaps in those rare circumstances in which the pregnancy is itself a danger to her own life or health, or is the result of rape or incest.

It is conventional constitutional doctrine that where reasonable people disagree the Government can adopt one position or the other. . . . That theorem, however, assumes a state of affairs in which the choice does not intrude upon a protected liberty. Thus, while some people might disagree about whether or not the flag should be saluted, or disagree about the proposition that it may not be defiled, we have ruled that a state may not compel or enforce one view or the other. . . .

. . . Our cases recognize "the right of the individual, married or single, to be free from unwarranted governmental intrusion into matters so fundamentally affecting a person as the decision whether to bear or beget a child." . . . Our precedents "have respected the private realm of family life which the state cannot enter." . . . These matters, involving the most intimate and personal choices a person may make in a lifetime, choices central to personal dignity and autonomy, are central to the liberty protected by the Fourteenth Amendment. At the heart of liberty is the right to define one's own concept of existence, of meaning, of the universe, and of the mystery of human life. Beliefs about these matters could not define the attributes of personhood were they formed under compulsion of the State.

These considerations begin our analysis of the woman's interest in terminating her pregnancy but cannot end it, for this reason: though the abortion decision may originate within the zone of conscience and belief, it is more than a philosophic exercise. Abortion is a unique act. It is an act fraught with consequences for others: for the woman who must live with the implications of her decision; for the persons who perform and assist in the procedure; for the spouse, family, and society which must confront the knowledge that these procedures exist, procedures some deem nothing short of an act of violence against innocent human life; and, depending on one's beliefs, for the life or potential life that is aborted. Though abortion is conduct, it does not follow that the State is entitled to proscribe it in all instances. That is because the liberty of the woman is at stake in a sense unique to the human condition and so unique to the law. . . .

III

. . . [W]hen this Court reexamines a prior holding, its judgment is customarily informed by a series of prudential and pragmatic considerations designed to test the consistency of overruling a prior decision with the ideal of the rule of law, and to gauge the respective costs of reaffirming and overruling a prior case. Thus, for example, we may ask whether the rule has proved to be intolerable simply in defying practical workability, . . . whether the rule is subject to a kind of reliance that would lend a special hardship to the consequences of overruling and add inequity to the cost of repudiation, . . . whether related principles of law have so far developed as to have left the old rule no more than a remnant of abandoned doctrine, . . . or whether facts have so changed or come to be seen so differently, as to have robbed the old rule of significant application or justification. . . .

Although *Roe* has engendered opposition, it has in no sense proven "unworkable," . . . representing as it does a simple limitation beyond which a state law is unenforceable. While *Roe* has, of course, required judicial assessment of state laws affecting the exercise of the choice guaranteed against government infringement, and although the need for such review will remain as a consequence of today's decision, the required determinations fall within judicial competence.

. . . [F]or two decades of economic and social developments, people have organized intimate relationships and made choices that define their views of themselves and their places in society, in reliance on the availability of abortion in the event that contraception should fail. The ability of women to participate equally in the economic and social life of the nation has been facilitated by their ability to control their reproductive lives. . . . The Constitution serves human values, and while the effect of reliance on *Roe* cannot be exactly measured, neither can the certain cost of overruling *Roe* for people who have ordered their thinking and living around that case be dismissed.

No evolution of legal principle has left *Roe*'s doctrinal footings weaker than they were in 1973. No development of constitutional law since the case was decided has implicitly or explicitly left *Roe* behind as a mere survivor of obsolete constitutional thinking. . . .

We have seen how time has overtaken some of *Roe*'s factual assumptions: advances in maternal health care

allow for abortions safe to the mother later in pregnancy than was true in 1973, . . . and advances in neonatal care have advanced viability to a point somewhat earlier. . . . But these facts go only to the scheme of time limits on the realization of competing interests, and the divergences from the factual premises of 1973 have no bearing on the validity of *Roe*'s central holding, that viability marks the earliest point at which the state's interest in fetal life is constitutionally adequate to justify a legislative ban on nontherapeutic abortions.

The soundness or unsoundness of that constitutional judgment in no sense turns on whether viability occurs at approximately 28 weeks, as was usual at the time of *Roe*, at 23 to 24 weeks, as it sometimes does today, or at some moment even slightly earlier in pregnancy, as it may if fetal respiratory capacity can somehow be enhanced in the future. Whenever it may occur, the attainment of viability may continue to serve as the critical fact, just as it has done since *Roe* was decided; which is to say that no change in *Roe*'s factual underpinning has left its central holding obsolete, and none supports an argument for overruling it.

The sum of the precedential inquiry to this point shows *Roe*'s underpinnings unweakened in any way affecting its central holding. While it has engendered disapproval, it has not been unworkable. An entire generation has come of age free to assume *Roe*'s concept of liberty in defining the capacity of women to act in society, and to make reproductive decisions; no erosion of principle going to liberty or personal autonomy has left *Roe*'s central holding a doctrinal remnant; *Roe* portends no developments at odds with other precedent for the analysis of personal liberty; and no changes of fact have rendered viability more or less appropriate as the point at which the balance of interests tips. Within the bounds of normal *stare decisis* analysis, then, and subject to the considerations on which it customarily turns, the stronger argument is for affirming *Roe*'s central holding, with whatever degree of personal reluctance any of us may have, not for overruling it. . . .

The Court's duty in the present case is clear. In 1973, it confronted the already-divisive issue of governmental power to limit personal choice to undergo abortion, for which it provided a new resolution based on the due process guaranteed by the Fourteenth Amendment. Whether or not a new social consensus is developing on that issue, its divisiveness is no less today than in 1973, and pressure to overrule the decision, like pressure to retain it, has grown only more intense. A decision to overrule *Roe*'s essential holding under the existing circumstances would address error, if error there was, at the cost of both profound and unnecessary damage to the Court's legitimacy, and to the Nation's commitment to the rule of law. It is therefore imperative to adhere to the essence of *Roe*'s original decision, and we do so today.

IV

From what we have said so far it follows that it is a constitutional liberty of the woman to have some freedom to terminate her pregnancy. We conclude that the basic decision in *Roe* was based on a constitutional analysis which we cannot now repudiate. The woman's liberty is not so unlimited, however, that from the outset the State cannot show its concern for the life of the unborn, and at a later point in fetal development the state's interest in life has sufficient force so that the right of the woman to terminate the pregnancy can be restricted. . . .

Yet it must be remembered that *Roe v. Wade* speaks with clarity in establishing not only the woman's liberty but also the state's "important and legitimate interest in potential life." . . . That portion of the decision in *Roe* has been given too little acknowledgement and implementation by the Court in its subsequent cases. Those cases decided that any regulation touching upon the abortion decision must survive strict scrutiny, to be sustained only if drawn in narrow terms to further a compelling state interest. . . . Not all of the cases decided under that formulation can be reconciled with the holding in *Roe* itself that the state has legitimate interests in the health of the woman and in protecting the potential life within her. In resolving this tension, we choose to rely upon *Roe,* as against the later cases.

. . . Regulations which do no more than create structural mechanisms by which the state, or the parent or guardian of a minor, may express profound respect for the life of the unborn are permitted, if they are not a substantial obstacle to the woman's exercise of the right to choose. . . . Unless it has that effect on her right of choice, a state measure designed to persuade her to choose childbirth over abortion will be upheld if reasonably related to that goal. Regulations designed to foster the health of a woman seeking an abortion are valid if they do not constitute an undue burden.

Even when jurists reason from shared premises, some disagreement is inevitable. . . . That is to be expected in the application of any legal standard which must accommodate life's complexity. We do not expect it to be otherwise with respect to the undue burden standard. We give this summary:

(a) To protect the central right recognized by *Roe v. Wade* while at the same time accommodating the state's profound interest in potential life, we will employ the undue burden analysis. . . . An undue burden exists, and therefore a provision of law is invalid, if its purpose or effect is to place a substantial obstacle in the path of a woman seeking an abortion before the fetus attains viability.

(b) We reject the rigid trimester framework of *Roe v. Wade.* To promote the state's profound interest in potential life, throughout pregnancy the state may take measures to ensure that the woman's choice is informed, and measures designed to advance this interest will not be invalidated as long as their purpose is to persuade the woman to choose childbirth over abortion. The measures must not be an undue burden on the right.

(c) As with any medical procedure, the state may enact regulations to further the health or safety of a woman seeking an abortion. Unnecessary health regulations that have the purpose or effect of presenting a substantial obstacle seeking an abortion impose an undue burden on the right.

(d) Our adoption of the undue burden analysis does not disturb the central holding of *Roe v. Wade,* and we reaffirm that holding. Regardless of whether exceptions are made for particular circumstances, a State may not prohibit any woman from making the ultimate decision to terminate her pregnancy before viability.

(e) We also reaffirm *Roe*'s holding that "subsequent to viability, the State in promoting its interest in the potentiality of human life may, if it chooses, regulate, and even proscribe, abortion except where it is necessary, in appropriate medical judgment, for the preservation of the life or health of the mother." . . .

V

The Court of Appeals applied what it believed to be the undue burden standard and upheld each of the provisions [of the Pennsylvania law] except for the husband notification requirement. We agree generally with this conclusion, but refine the undue burden analysis in accordance with the principles articulated above. We now consider the separate statutory sections at issue.

A

Because it is central to the operation of other requirements, we begin with the statute's definition of medical emergency. Under the statute, a medical emergency is "[t]hat condition which, on the basis of the physician's good faith clinical judgment, so complicates the medical condition of a pregnant woman as to necessitate the immediate abortion of her pregnancy to avert her death or for which a delay will create serious risk of substantial and irreversible impairment of a major bodily function." . . .

. . . [T]he Court of Appeals . . . stated: "we read the medical emergency exception as intended by the Pennsylvania legislature to assure that compliance with its abortion regulations would not in any way pose a significant threat to the life or health of a woman." . . . Normally, . . . we defer to the construction of a state statute given it by the lower federal courts. Indeed, we have said that we will defer to lower court interpretations of state law unless they amount to "plain" error. . . . We adhere to that course today, and conclude that, as construed by the Court of Appeals, the medical emergency definition imposes no undue burden on a woman's abortion right.

B

We next consider the informed consent requirement. . . . Except in a medical emergency, the statute requires that at least 24 hours before performing an abortion a physician inform the woman of the nature of the procedure, the health risks of the abortion and of childbirth, and the "probable gestational age of the unborn child." . . . The physician or a qualified nonphysician must inform the woman of the availability of printed materials published by the State describing the fetus and providing information about medical assistance for childbirth, information about child support from the father, and a list of agencies which provide adoption and other services as alternatives to abortion. An abortion may not be performed unless the woman certifies in writing that she has been informed of the availability of these printed materials and has been provided them if she chooses to view them.

. . . Petitioners challenge the statute's definition of informed consent because it includes the provision of specific information by the doctor and the mandatory 24-hour waiting period. The conclusions reached by a majority of the Justices in the separate opinions filed today and the undue burden standard adopted in this opinion require us to overrule in part some of the Court's past decisions, decisions driven by the trimester framework's prohibition of all pre-viability regulations designed to further the State's interest in fetal life.

The Court then proceeds to overrule portions of *Akron v. Akron Center for Reproductive Health* (1983), *Thornburgh v. American College of Obstetricians and Gynecologists* (1986), and *Planned Parenthood of Central Missouri v. Danforth* (1976).

. . . [O]n the record before us, and in the context of this facial challenge, we are not convinced that the 24-hour waiting period constitutes an undue burden.

We are left with the argument that the various aspects of the informed consent required are unconstitutional because they place barriers in the way of abortion on demand. Even the broadest reading of *Roe,* however, has not suggested that there is a constitutional right to abortion on demand. . . . Rather, the right protected by *Roe* is a right to decide to terminate a pregnancy free of undue interference by the State. Because the informed consent requirement facilitates the wise exercise of that right it cannot be classified as an interference with the right *Roe* protects. The informed consent requirement is not an undue burden on that right.

C

. . . Pennsylvania's abortion law provides, except in cases of medical emergency, that no physician shall perform an abortion on a married woman without receiving a signed statement from the woman that she has notified her spouse that she is about to undergo an abortion. The woman has the option of providing an alternative signed statement certifying that her husband is not the man who impregnated her; that her husband could not be located; that the pregnancy is the result of spousal sexual assault which she has reported; or that the woman believes that notifying her husband will cause him or someone else to inflict bodily injury upon her. A physician who performs an abortion on a married woman without receiving the appropriate signed statement will have his or her license revoked, and is liable to the husband for damages. . . .

. . . In well-functioning marriages, spouses discuss important intimate decisions such as whether to bear a child. But there are millions of women in this country who are the victims of regular physical and psychological abuse at the hands of their husbands. Should these women become pregnant, they may have very good reasons for not wishing to inform their husbands of their decision to obtain an abortion. . . .

The spousal notification requirement is thus likely to prevent a significant number of women from obtaining an abortion. It does not merely make abortions a little more difficult or expensive to obtain; for many women, it will impose a substantial obstacle. We must not blind ourselves to the fact that the significant number of women who fear for their safety and the safety of their children are likely to be deterred from procuring an abortion as surely as if the Commonwealth had outlawed abortion in all cases. . . . It is an undue burden, and therefore invalid.

This conclusion is in no way inconsistent with our decisions upholding parental notification or consent requirements. . . . Those enactments, and our judgment that they are constitutional, are based on the quite reasonable assumption that minors will benefit from consultation with their parents and that children will often not realize that their parents have their best interests at heart. We cannot adopt a parallel assumption about adult women. . . .

D

We next consider the parental consent provision. Except in a medical emergency, an unemancipated young woman under 18 may not obtain an abortion unless she and one of her parents (or guardian) provides informed consent. . . . If neither a parent nor a guardian provides consent, a court may authorize the performance of an abortion upon a determination that the young woman is mature and capable of giving informed consent and has in fact given her informed consent, or that an abortion would be in her best interests.

We have been over most of this ground before. Our cases establish, and we reaffirm today, that a State may require a minor seeking an abortion to obtain the consent of a parent or guardian, provided that there is an adequate judicial bypass procedure. . . . Under these precedents, in our view, the one-parent consent requirement and judicial bypass procedure are constitutional. . . .

E

Under the record keeping and reporting requirements of the statute, every facility which performs abortions is required to file a report stating its name and address as well as the name and address of any related entity, such as controlling or subsidiary organization. In the case of state-funded institutions, the information becomes public.

For each abortion performed, a report must be filed identifying: the physician (and the second physician where required); the facility; the referring physician or agency; the woman's age; the number of prior pregnancies and prior abortions she has had; gestational age; the type of abortion procedure; the date of the abortion;

whether there were any pre-existing medical conditions which would complicate pregnancy; medical complications with the abortion; where applicable, the basis for the determination that the abortion was medically necessary; the weight of the aborted fetus; and whether the woman was married, and if so, whether notice was provided or the basis for the failure to give notice. Every abortion facility must also file quarterly reports showing the number of abortions performed broken down by trimester. . . . In all events, the identity of each woman who has had an abortion remains confidential.

In [*Planned Parenthood v.*] *Danforth,* . . . we held that record keeping and reporting provisions "that are reasonably directed to the preservation of maternal health and that properly respect a patient's confidentiality and privacy are permissible." We think that under this standard all the provisions at issue here except that relating to spousal notice are constitutional. Although they do not relate to the State's interest in informing the woman's choice, they do relate to health. The collection of information with respect to actual patients is a vital element of medical research, and so it cannot be said that the requirements serve no purpose other than to make abortions more difficult. Nor do we find that the requirements impose a substantial obstacle to a woman's choice. At most they might increase the cost of some abortions by a slight amount. While at some point increased cost could become a substantial obstacle, there is no such showing on the record before us.

Subsection (12) of the reporting provision requires the reporting of, among other things, a married woman's "reason for failure to provide notice" to her husband. . . . This provision in effect requires women, as a condition of obtaining an abortion, to provide the Commonwealth with the precise information we have already recognized that many women have pressing reasons not to reveal. Like the spousal notice requirement itself, this provision places an undue burden on a woman's choice, and must be invalidated for that reason. . . .

Justice Stevens, concurring in part and dissenting in part.

. . . The Court is unquestionably correct in concluding that the doctrine of *stare decisis* has controlling significance in a case of this kind, notwithstanding an individual justice's concerns about the merits. The central holding of *Roe v. Wade,* . . . has been a "part of our law" for almost two decades. It was a natural sequel to the protection of individual liberty established in *Griswold v. Connecticut.* . . . The societal costs of overruling *Roe* at this late date would be enormous. *Roe* is an integral part of a correct understanding of both the concept of liberty and the basic equality of men and women. . . .

In my opinion, the principles established in [the] long line of cases [since *Roe v. Wade*] . . . should govern our decision today. Under these principles, [the informed consent provisions] of the Pennsylvania statute are unconstitutional. Those sections require a physician or counselor to provide the woman with a range of materials clearly designed to persuade her to choose not to undergo the abortion. . . .

The 24-hour waiting period raises even more serious concerns. . . . Part of the constitutional liberty to choose is the equal dignity to which each of us is entitled. A woman who decides to terminate her pregnancy is entitled to the same respect as a woman who decides to carry the fetus to term. The mandatory waiting period denies women that equal respect. . . .

Justice Blackmun, concurring in part and dissenting in part.

Three years ago, in *Webster v. Reproductive Health Services,* . . . four members of this Court appeared poised to "cas(t) into darkness the hopes and visions of every woman in this country" who had come to believe that the Constitution guaranteed her the right to reproductive choice. . . . All that remained between the promise of *Roe* and the darkness of the plurality was a single, flickering flame. Decisions since *Webster* gave little reason to hope that this flame would cast much light. But now, just when so many expected the darkness to fall, the flame has grown bright.

I do not underestimate the significance of today's joint opinion. Yet I remain steadfast in my belief that the right to reproductive choice is entitled to the full protection afforded by the Court before *Webster.* And I fear for the darkness as four Justices anxiously await the single vote necessary to extinguish the light. . . .

Make no mistake, the joint opinion of Justices O'Connor, Kennedy, and Souter is an act of personal courage and constitutional principle. In contrast to previous decisions in which Justices O'Connor and Kennedy postponed reconsideration of *Roe v. Wade,* . . . the authors of the joint opinion today join Justice Stevens and me in concluding that "the essential holding of *Roe* should be retained and once again reaffirmed." . . . In brief, five members of this Court today recognize that "the Constitution protects a woman's right to terminate her pregnancy in its early stages." . . .

A fervent view of individual liberty and the force of *stare decisis* have led the Court to this conclusion. . . .

In one sense, the Court's approach is worlds apart from that of the Chief Justice and Justice Scalia. And yet, in another sense, the distance between the two approaches is short—the distance is but a single vote. I am 83 years old. I cannot remain on this Court forever, and when I do step down, the confirmation process for my successor well may focus on the issue before us today. That, I regret, may be exactly where the choice between the two worlds will be made.

Chief Justice Rehnquist, with whom **Justice White, Justice Scalia,** and **Justice Thomas** join, concurring in part and dissenting in part.

The joint opinion, following its newly-minted variation on *stare decisis,* retains the outer shell of *Roe v. Wade,* but beats a wholesale retreat from the substance of that case. We believe that *Roe* was wrongly decided, and that it can and should be overruled consistently with our traditional approach to *stare decisis* in constitutional cases. We would adopt the approach of the plurality in *Webster v. Reproductive Health Services* . . . and uphold the challenged provisions of the Pennsylvania statute in their entirety. . . .

The joint opinion of Justices O'Connor, Kennedy, and Souter cannot bring itself to say that *Roe* was correct as an original matter, but the authors are of the view that "the immediate question is not the soundness of *Roe's* resolution of the issue, but the precedential force that must be accorded to its holding." . . .

Instead of claiming that *Roe* was correct as a matter of original constitutional interpretation, the opinion therefore contains an elaborate discussion of *stare decisis.* . . .

In our view, authentic principles of *stare decisis* do not require that any portion of the reasoning in *Roe* be kept intact. "*Stare decisis* is not . . . a universal, inexorable command," . . . especially in cases involving the interpretation of the Federal Constitution. Erroneous decisions in such constitutional cases are uniquely durable, because correction through legislation action, save for constitutional amendment, is impossible. It is therefore our duty to reconsider constitutional interpretations that "depart(t) from a proper understanding" of the Constitution. . . .

The Judicial Branch derives its legitimacy, not from following public opinion, but from deciding by its best lights whether legislative enactments of the popular branches of Government comport with the Constitution. The doctrine of *stare decisis* is an adjunct of this duty, and should be no more subject to the vagaries of public opinion than is the basic judicial task. . . .

The decision in *Roe* has engendered large demonstrations, including repeated marches on this Court and on Congress, both in opposition to and in support of that opinion. A decision either way on *Roe* can therefore be perceived as favoring one group or the other. But this perceived dilemma arises only if one assumes, as the joint opinion does, that the Court should make its decisions with a view toward speculative public perceptions. . . .

The sum of the joint opinion's labors in the name of *stare decisis* and "legitimacy" is this: *Roe v. Wade* stands as a sort of judicial Potemkin Village, which may be pointed out to passers by as a monument to the importance of adhering to precedent. But behind the facade, an entirely new method of analysis, without any roots in constitutional law, is imported to decide the constitutionality of state laws regulating abortion. Neither *stare decisis* nor "legitimacy" are truly served by such an effort. . . .

Justice Scalia, with whom the **Chief Justice, Justice White,** and **Justice Thomas** join, concurring in part and dissenting in part.

My views on this matter are unchanged. . . . The states may, if they wish, permit abortion-on-demand, but the Constitution does not require them to do so.

The permissibility of abortion, and the limitations upon it, are to be resolved like most important questions in our democracy: by citizens trying to persuade one another and then voting. As the Court acknowledges, "where reasonable people disagree the government can adopt one position or the other." . . .

The Court is correct in adding the qualification that this "assumes a state of affairs in which the choice does not intrude upon a protected liberty," . . . but the crucial part of that qualification is the penultimate word. A State's choice between two positions on which reasonable people can disagree is constitutional even when (as is often the case) it intrudes upon a "liberty" in the absolute sense.

Laws against bigamy, for example—which entire societies of reasonable people disagree with—intrude upon men and women's liberty to marry and live with one another. But bigamy happens not to be a liberty specially "protected" by the Constitution.

That is, quite simply, the issue in this case: not whether the power of a woman to abort her unborn child is a "liberty" in the absolute sense; or even whether it is a liberty of great importance to many women. Of course it is both. The issue is whether it is a liberty protected by the Constitution of the United States. I am sure it is not.

I reach that conclusion not because of anything so exalted as my views concerning the "concept of existence, of meaning, of the universe, and of the mystery of life." . . . Rather, I reach it for the same reason that bigamy is not constitutionally protected—because of two simple facts: (1) the Constitution says absolutely nothing about it, and (2) the longstanding traditions of American society have permitted it to be legally proscribed. . . .

The Court's description of the place of *Roe* in the social history of the United States is unrecognizable. Not only did *Roe* not, as the Court suggests, resolve the deeply divisive issue of abortion; it did more than anything else to nourish it, by elevating it to the national level where it is infinitely more difficult to resolve.

National politics were not plagued by abortion protests, national abortion lobbying, or abortion marches on Congress, before *Roe v. Wade* was decided. Profound disagreement existed among our citizens over the issue—as it does over other issues, such as the death penalty—but that disagreement was being worked out at the state level. As with many other issues, the division of sentiment within each State was not as closely balanced as it was among the population of the Nation as a whole, meaning not only that more people would be satisfied with the results of state-by-state resolution, but also that those results would be more stable. Pre-*Roe,* moreover, political compromise was possible.

Roe's mandate for abortion-on-demand destroyed the compromises of the past, rendered compromises impossible for the future, and required the entire issue to be resolved, uniformly, at the national level. At the same time, *Roe* created a vast new class of abortion consumers and abortion proponents by eliminating the moral opprobrium that had attached to the act ("If the Constitution guarantees abortion, how can it be bad?"—not an accurate line of thought, but a natural one).

Many favor all of those developments, and it is not for me to say that they are wrong. But to portray *Roe* as the statesmanlike "settlement" of a divisive issue, a jurisprudential Peace of Westphalia that is worth preserving, is nothing less than Orwellian. . . .

Case

BOWERS V. HARDWICK

478 U.S. 186; 106 S.Ct. 2841; 92 L.Ed. 2d. 140 (1986)
Vote: 5–4

In this case the Court considers the constitutionality of a state sodomy statute as applied to homosexual conduct.

Justice White delivered the opinion of the Court.

In August 1982, respondent was charged with violating the Georgia statute criminalizing sodomy by committing that act with another adult male in the bedroom of respondent's home. After a preliminary hearing, the District Attorney decided not to present the matter to grand jury unless further evidence developed.

Respondent then brought suit in the Federal District Court, challenging the constitutionality of the statute insofar as it criminalized consensual sodomy. He asserted that he was a practicing homosexual, that the Georgia sodomy statute, as administered by the defendants, placed him in imminent danger of arrest, and that the statute for several reasons violates the Federal Constitution. The District Court granted the defendants' motion to dismiss [relying on *Doe v. Commonwealth's Attorney* (1976)]. . . .

A divided panel of the Court of Appeals for the Eleventh Circuit reversed.. . . Relying on our decisions in *Griswold v. Connecticut*, . . . *Eisenstadt v. Baird*, . . . *Stanley v. Georgia*, . . . and *Roe v. Wade*, . . . the court went on to hold that the Georgia statute violated respondent's fundamental rights because his homosexual activity is a private and intimate association that is beyond the reach of the state regulation by reason of the Ninth Amendment and the Due Process Clause of the Fourteenth Amendment. The case was remanded for trial, at which, to prevail, the State would have to prove that the statute is supported by a compelling interest and is the most narrowly drawn means of achieving that end.

Because other Courts of Appeals have arrived at judgments contrary to that of the Eleventh Circuit in this case, we granted the State's petition for certiorari. . . .

This case does not require a judgment on whether laws against sodomy between consenting adults in general, or between homosexuals in particular, are wise or desirable. It raises no question about the right or propriety of state legislative decisions to repeal their laws that criminalize homosexual sodomy, or of state court decisions invalidating those laws on state constitutional grounds. The issue presented is whether the Federal Constitution confers a fundamental right upon homosexuals to engage in sodomy and hence invalidates the laws of the many States that still make such conduct illegal and have done so for a very long time. The case also calls for some judgment about the limits of the Court's role in carrying out its constitutional mandate.

We first register our disagreement with the Court of Appeals and with respondent that the Court's prior cases have construed the Constitution to confer a right of privacy that contends to homosexual sodomy and for all intents and purposes have decided this case. . . .

Accepting the decisions in these cases and the above description of them, we think it evident that none of the rights announced in those cases bears any resemblance to the claimed constitutional right of homosexuals to engage in acts of sodomy, that is asserted in this case. No connection between family, marriage, or procreation on the one hand and homosexual activity on the other has been demonstrated, either by the Court of Appeals or by respondent. Moreover, any claim that these cases nevertheless stand for the proposition that any kind of private sexual conduct between consenting adults is constitutionally insulated from state proscription is unsupportable. Indeed, the Court's opinion in *Carey* [*v. Population Services*] twice asserted that the privacy right, which the *Griswold* line of cases found to be one of the protections provided by the Due Process Clause, did not reach so far. . . .

Precedent aside, however, respondent would have us announce, as the Court of Appeals did, a fundamental right to engage in homosexual sodomy. This we are quite unwilling to do. It is true that despite the language of the Due Process Clauses of the Fifth and Fourteenth Amendments, which appears to focus only on the processes by which life, liberty, or property is taken, the cases are legion in which Clauses have been interpreted to have substantive content, subsuming rights that to a great extent are immune from federal or state regulation or proscription. Among such cases are those recognizing rights that have little or no textual support in the constitutional language. . . .

Striving to assure itself and the public that announcing rights not readily identifiable in the constitution's text involves much more than the imposition of the Justices' own choice of values on the States and the Federal Government, the Court has sought to identify the nature of the rights qualifying for heightened judicial protection. In *Palko v. Connecticut* . . . (1937), it was said that this category includes those fundamental liberties that are "implicit in the concept of the record liberty," such that "neither liberty nor justice would exist if [they] were sacrificed." A different description of fundamental liberties appeared in *Moore v. East Cleveland* . . . where they are characterized [by Justice Powell] as those liberties that are "deeply rooted in this Nation's history and tradition."

It is obvious to us that neither of these formulations would extend a fundamental right to homosexuals to engage in acts of consensual sodomy. Proscriptions against that conduct have ancient roots. . . . Sodomy was a criminal offense at common law and was forbidden by the laws of the original thirteen States when they ratified the Bill of Rights. In 1868, when the Fourteenth Amendment was ratified, all but 5 of the 37 States in the Union had criminal sodomy laws. In fact, until 1961, all States outlawed sodomy, and today, 24 States and the District of Columbia continue to provide criminal penalties for sodomy performed in private and between consenting adults. . . . Against this background, to claim that a right to engage in such conduct is "deeply rooted in this Nation's history and tradition" or "implicit in the concept of ordered liberty" is, at best, facetious. . . .

Nor are we inclined to take a more expansive view of our authority to discover new fundamental rights imbedded in the Due Process Clause. The Court is most vulnerable and comes nearest to illegitimacy when it deals with judge-made constitutional law having little or no cognizable roots in the language or design of the Constitution. That this is so was painfully demonstrated by the face-off between the Executive and the Court in the 1930's, which resulted in the repudiation of much of the substantive gloss that the Court had placed on the Due Process Clause of the Fifth and Fourteenth Amendments. There should be therefore, great resistance to expand the substantive reach of those Clauses, particularly if it requires redefining the category of rights deemed to be fundamental. Otherwise, the Judiciary necessarily takes to itself further authority to govern the country without express constitutional authority. The claimed right pressed on us today falls far short of overcoming this resistance.

Respondent, however, asserts that the result should be different where the homosexual conduct occurs in the privacy of the home. He relies on *Stanley v. Georgia* . . . (1969), where the Court held that the First Amendment prevents conviction for possessing and reading obscene material in the privacy of his home: "If the First Amendment means anything, it means that a State has no business telling a man, sitting alone in his house, what books he may read or what films he may watch." . . .

Stanley did protect conduct that would not have been protected outside the home, and it partially prevented the enforcement of state obscenity laws; but the decision was firmly grounded in the First Amendment. The right pressed upon us here has no similar support in the text of the Constitution, and it does not qualify for recognition under the prevailing principles for construing the Fourteenth Amendment. Its limits are also difficult to discern. Plainly enough, otherwise illegal conduct is not always immunized whenever it occurs in the home. Victimless crimes, such as the possession and use of illegal drugs, do not escape the law where they are committed at home. *Stanley* itself recognized that its holding offered no protection for the possession in the home of drugs, firearms, or stolen goods. . . . And if respondent's submission is limited to the voluntary sexual conduct between consenting adults, it would be difficult, except by fiat, to limit the claimed right to homosexual conduct while leaving exposed to prosecution adultery, incest, and other sexual crimes even though they are committed in the home. We are unwilling to start down that road.

Even if the conduct at issue here is not a fundamental right, respondent asserts that there must be a rational basis for the law and that there is none in this case other than the presumed belief of a majority of the electorate in Georgia that homosexual sodomy is immoral and unacceptable. This is said to be an inadequate rationale to support the law. The law, however, is constantly based on notions of morality, and if all laws representing essentially moral choices are to be invalidated under the Due Process Clause, the courts will be very busy indeed. Even respondent makes no such claim, but insists that majority sentiments about the morality of homosexuality should be declared inadequate. We do not agree, and are unpersuaded that the sodomy laws of some 25 States should be invalidated on this basis. . . .

Accordingly, the judgment of the Court of Appeals is reversed.

Chief Justice Burger, concurring.

I join the Court's opinion, but I write separately to underscore my view that in constitutional terms there is no such thing as a fundamental right to commit homosexual sodomy.

As the Court notes, . . . the proscriptions against sodomy have very "ancient roots." Decisions of individuals relating to homosexual conduct have been subject to state intervention throughout the history of Western Civilization. Condemnation of those practices is firmly rooted in Judeo-Christian moral and ethical standards. Homosexual sodomy was a capital crime under Roman law. . . . During the English Reformation when powers of the ecclesiastical courts were transferred to the King's Courts, the first English statute criminalizing sodomy was passed. . . . Blackstone described "the infamous crime against nature" as an offense of "deeper malignity" than rape, an heinous act "the very mention of which is a disgrace to human nature," and "a crime not fit to be named." . . . The common law of England, including its prohibition of sodomy, became the received law of Georgia and the other Colonies. In 1816 the Georgia Legislature passed the statute at issue here, and that statute has been continuously in force in one form or another since that time. To hold that the act of homosexual sodomy is somehow protected as a fundamental right would be to cast aside millennia of moral teaching.

This is essentially not a question of personal "preferences" but rather that of the legislative authority of the State. I find nothing in the Constitution depriving a State of the power to enact the statute challenged here.

Justice Powell, concurring. . . .

Justice Blackmun, with whom **Justice Brennan, Justice Marshall,** and **Justice Stevens** join, dissenting.

This case . . . is about "the most comprehensive of rights and the right most valued by civilized men," namely, "the right to be let alone." . . .

The statute at issue denies individuals the right to decide for themselves whether to engage in particular forms of private, consensual sexual activity. The Court concludes that [it] is valid essentially because "the laws of . . . many States . . . still make such conduct illegal and have done so for a very long time." . . . But the fact that the moral judgments expressed by statutes like [such] may be "natural and familiar . . . ought not to conclude our judgment upon the question whether statutes embodying them conflict with the Constitution of the United States." . . .

I believe that "[i]t is revolting to have not better reason for a rule of law than that so it was laid down in the time of Henry IV. It is still more revolting if the grounds upon which it was laid down have vanished long since, and the rule simply persists from blind imitation of the

past." . . . I believe we must analyze respondent's claim in the light of the values that underlie the constitutional right to privacy. If that right means anything, it means that, before Georgia can prosecute its citizens for making choices about the most intimate aspects of their lives, it must do more than assert that the choice they have made is an "abominable crime not fit to be named among Christians." . . .

In its haste to reverse the Court of Appeals and hold that the Constitution does not "confe[r] a fundamental right upon homosexuals to engage in sodomy," the Court relegates the actual statute being challenged to a footnote and ignores the procedural posture of the case before it. A fair reading of the statute and of the complaint clearly reveals that the majority has distorted the question this case presents.

First, the Court's almost obsessive focus on homosexual activity is particularly hard to justify in light of the broad language Georgia has used. Unlike the Court, the Georgia Legislature has not proceeded on the assumption that homosexuals are so different from other citizens that their lives may be controlled in a way that would not be tolerated if it limited the choices of those other citizens. . . . Rather, Georgia has provided that "[a] person commits the offense of sodomy when he performs or submits to any sexual act involving the sex organs of one person and the mouth or anus of another." . . . The sex or status of the persons who engage in the act is irrelevant as a matter of state law. In fact, to the extent I can discern a legislative purpose for Georgia's 1968 enactment . . . that purpose seems to have been to broaden the coverage of the law to reach heterosexual as well as homosexual activity. I therefore see no basis for the Court's decision to treat this case as an "as applied" challenge to Sec. 16-6-2, . . . or for Georgia's attempt, both in its brief and at oral argument, to defend Sec. 16-6-2 solely on the grounds that it prohibits homosexual activity. Michael Hardwick's standing may rest in significant part on Georgia's apparent willingness to enforce against homosexuals a law it seems not to have any desire to enforce against heterosexuals. . . . But his claim that Sec. 16-6-2 involves an unconstitutional intrusion into his privacy and his right of intimate association does not depend . . . on his sexual orientation.

Until 1968, Georgia defined sodomy as "the carnal knowledge and connection against the order of nature, by man with man, or in the same unnatural manner with woman." . . . In *Thompson v. Aldredge* . . . (1939), the Georgia Supreme Court held that [the law] did not prohibit lesbian activity. And in *Riley v. Garrett* . . . (1963), the

Georgia Supreme Court held that [the law] did not prohibit heterosexual cunnilingus. Georgia passed the act-specific statute currently in force "perhaps in response to the restrictive court decisions such as *Riley.*" . . .

Second, I disagree with the Court's refusal to consider whether [the sodomy law] runs afoul of the Eighth or Ninth Amendments or the Equal Protection Clause of the Fourteenth Amendment. . . . Respondent's complaint expressly invoked the Ninth Amendment, . . . and he relied heavily before this Court on *Griswold v. Connecticut* . . . (1965), which identifies that Amendment as one of the specific constitutional provisions giving "life and substance" to our understanding of privacy. . . . More importantly, the procedural posture of the case requires that we affirm the Court of Appeals' judgment if there is any ground on which respondent may be entitled to relief. . . .

Despite historical views of homosexuality, it is no longer viewed by mental health professionals as a "disease" or disorder. . . . But, obviously, neither is it simply a matter of deliberate personal election. Homosexual orientation may well form part of the very fiber of an individual's personality. Consequently, . . . the Eighth Amendment may pose a constitutional barrier to sending an individual to prison for acting on that attraction regardless of the circumstances. An individual's ability to make constitutionally protected "decisions concerning sexual relations," . . . is rendered empty indeed if he or she is given no real choice but a life without any physical intimacy.

With respect to the Equal Protection Clause's applicability to [the challenged law], I note that Georgia's exclusive stress before this Court on its interest in prosecuting homosexual activity despite the gender-neutral terms of the statute may arise serious questions of discriminatory enforcement, questions that cannot be disposed of before the Court on a motion to dismiss. . . . The legislature having decided that the sex of the participants is irrelevant to the legality of the acts, I do not see why the State can defend [the law] on the ground that individuals singled out for prosecution are of the same sex as their partners. Thus, under the circumstances of this case, a claim under the Equal Protection Clause may well be available without having to reach the more controversial question whether homosexuals are a suspect class. . . .

The Court concludes today that none of our prior cases dealing with various decisions that individuals are entitled to make free of governmental interference "bears any resemblance to the claimed constitutional right of homosexuals to engage in acts of sodomy that is asserted in this case." . . . While it is true that these cases may be characterized by their connection to protection of the family, . . . the Court's conclusion that they extend no further than this boundary ignores the warning in *Moore v. East Cleveland,* . . . against "clos[ing] our eyes to the basic reasons why certain rights associated with the family have been accorded shelter under the Fourteenth Amendment's Due Process Clause." We protect those rights not because they contribute, in some direct and material way, to the general public welfare, but because they form so central a part of an individual's life. "[T]he concept of privacy embodies the 'moral fact that a person belongs to himself and not others nor to society as a whole.' " . . .

. . . The Court claims that its decision today merely refuses to recognize a fundamental right to engage in homosexual sodomy; what the Court really has refused to recognize is the fundamental interest all individuals have in controlling the nature of their intimate associations with others.

The behavior for which Hardwick faces prosecution occurred in his own home, a place to which the Fourth Amendment attaches special significance. The Court's treatment of this aspect of the case is symptomatic of its overall refusal to consider the broad principles that have informed our treatment of privacy in specific cases. Just as the right to privacy is more than the mere aggregation of a number of entitlements to engage in specific behavior, so too, protecting the physical integrity of the home is more than merely a means of protecting specific activities that often take place there. . . .

Indeed, the right of an individual to conduct intimate relationships in the intimacy of his or her own home seems to me to be the heart of the Constitution's protection of privacy. . . .

Justice Stevens, with whom **Justice Brennan** and **Justice Marshall** join, dissenting. . . .

Case

WASHINGTON V. GLUCKSBERG

521 U.S. ___, 117 S.Ct. 2258, 138 L.Ed. 2d. 772 (1997)
Vote: 9–0

In this case the Court reviews a state statute prohibiting doctor-assisted suicide.

Chief Justice Rehnquist delivered the opinion of the Court.

The question presented in this case is whether Washington's prohibition against "caus[ing]" or "aid[ing]" a suicide offends the Fourteenth Amendment to the United States Constitution. We hold that it does not.

It has always been a crime to assist a suicide in the State of Washington. In 1854, Washington's first Territorial Legislature outlawed "assisting another in the commission of self murder." Today, Washington law provides: "A person is guilty of promoting a suicide attempt when he knowingly causes or aids another person to attempt suicide." . . . "Promoting a suicide attempt" is a felony, punishable by up to five years' imprisonment and up to a $10,000 fine. . . . At the same time, Washington's Natural Death Act, enacted in 1979, states that the "withholding or withdrawal of life sustaining treatment" at a patient's direction "shall not, for any purpose, constitute a suicide." . . .

Petitioners in this case are the State of Washington and its Attorney General. Respondents Harold Glucksberg, M. D., Abigail Halperin, M. D., Thomas A. Preston, M. D., and Peter Shalit, M. D., are physicians who practice in Washington. These doctors occasionally treat terminally ill, suffering patients, and declare that they would assist these patients in ending their lives if not for Washington's assisted suicide ban. In January 1994, respondents, along with three gravely ill, pseudonymous plaintiffs who have since died and Compassion in Dying, a nonprofit organization that counsels people considering physician assisted suicide, sued in the United States District Court, seeking a declaration that [the statute] is, on its face, unconstitutional. . . .

The plaintiffs asserted "the existence of a liberty interest protected by the Fourteenth Amendment which extends to a personal choice by a mentally competent, terminally ill adult to commit physician assisted suicide." . . . Relying primarily on *Planned Parenthood v. Casey* . . . (1992), and *Cruzan v. Director, Missouri*

Dept. of Health . . . (1990), the District Court agreed, . . . and concluded that Washington's assisted suicide ban is unconstitutional because it "places an undue burden on the exercise of [that] constitutionally protected liberty interest." . . . The District Court also decided that the Washington statute violated the Equal Protection Clause's requirement that " 'all persons similarly situated . . . be treated alike.' " . . .

A panel of the Court of Appeals for the Ninth Circuit reversed, emphasizing that "[i]n the two hundred and five years of our existence no constitutional right to aid in killing oneself has ever been asserted and upheld by a court of final jurisdiction." . . . The Ninth Circuit reheard the case *en banc,* reversed the panel's decision, and affirmed the District Court. . . . Like the District Court, the *en banc* Court of Appeals emphasized our *Casey* and *Cruzan* decisions. . . . The court also discussed what it described as "historical" and "current societal attitudes" toward suicide and assisted suicide, . . . and concluded that "the Constitution encompasses a due process liberty interest in controlling the time and manner of one's death—that there is, in short, a constitutionally recognized 'right to die.' " . . . After "[w]eighing and then balancing" this interest against Washington's various interests, the court held that the State's assisted suicide ban was unconstitutional "as applied to terminally ill competent adults who wish to hasten their deaths with medication prescribed by their physicians." . . . The court did not reach the District Court's equal protection holding. . . . We granted certiorari. . . . and now reverse.

We begin, as we do in all due process cases, by examining our Nation's history, legal traditions, and practices. . . . In almost every State—indeed, in almost every western democracy—it is a crime to assist a suicide. The States' assisted suicide bans are not innovations. Rather, they are longstanding expressions of the States' commitment to the protection and preservation of all human life. . . . Indeed, opposition to and condemnation of suicide—and, therefore, of assisting suicide—are consistent and enduring themes of our philosophical, legal, and cultural heritages. . . .

More specifically, for over 700 years, the Anglo American common law tradition has punished or otherwise disapproved of both suicide and assisting suicide. . . .

. . . [C]olonial and early state legislatures and courts did not retreat from prohibiting assisting suicide. . . .

And the prohibitions against assisting suicide never contained exceptions for those who were near death. . . .

The earliest American statute explicitly to outlaw assisting suicide was enacted in New York in 1828 . . . and many of the new States and Territories followed New York's example. . . . In this century, the Model Penal Code also prohibited "aiding" suicide, prompting many States to enact or revise their assisted suicide bans. The Code's drafters observed that "the interests in the sanctity of life that are represented by the criminal homicide laws are threatened by one who expresses a willingness to participate in taking the life of another, even though the act may be accomplished with the consent, or at the request, of the suicide victim." . . .

Though deeply rooted, the States' assisted suicide bans have in recent years been reexamined and, generally, reaffirmed. Because of advances in medicine and technology, Americans today are increasingly likely to die in institutions, from chronic illnesses. . . . Public concern and democratic action are therefore sharply focused on how best to protect dignity and independence at the end of life, with the result that there have been many significant changes in state laws and in the attitudes these laws reflect. Many States, for example, now permit "living wills," surrogate health care decision making, and the withdrawal or refusal of life sustaining medical treatment. . . .At the same time, however, voters and legislators continue for the most part to reaffirm their States' prohibitions on assisting suicide.

The Washington statute at issue in this case. . . . was enacted in 1975 as part of a revision of that State's criminal code. Four years later, Washington passed its Natural Death Act, which specifically stated that the "withholding or withdrawal of life sustaining treatment . . . shall not, for any purpose, constitute a suicide" and that "[n]othing in this chapter shall be construed to condone, authorize, or approve mercy killing. . . ." . . . In 1991, Washington voters rejected a ballot initiative which, had it passed, would have permitted a form of physician assisted suicide. Washington then added a provision to the Natural Death Act expressly excluding physician assisted suicide. . . .

California voters rejected an assisted suicide initiative similar to Washington's in 1993. On the other hand, in 1994, voters in Oregon enacted, also through ballot initiative, that State's "Death With Dignity Act," which legalized physician assisted suicide for competent, terminally ill adults. Since the Oregon vote, many proposals to legalize assisted suicide have been and continue to be introduced in the States' legislatures, but none has been enacted. And just last year, Iowa and Rhode Island

joined the overwhelming majority of States explicitly prohibiting assisted suicide. . . .

Thus, the States are currently engaged in serious, thoughtful examinations of physician assisted suicide and other similar issues. For example, New York State's Task Force on Life and the Law—an ongoing, blue ribbon commission composed of doctors, ethicists, lawyers, religious leaders, and interested laymen—was convened in 1984 and commissioned with "a broad mandate to recommend public policy on issues raised by medical advances." . . . Over the past decade, the Task Force has recommended laws relating to end of life decisions, surrogate pregnancy, and organ donation. . . . After studying physician assisted suicide, however, the Task Force unanimously concluded that "[l]egalizing assisted suicide and euthanasia would pose profound risks to many individuals who are ill and vulnerable. . . . [T]he potential dangers of this dramatic change in public policy would outweigh any benefit that might be achieved." . . .

Attitudes toward suicide itself have changed . . . but our laws have consistently condemned, and continue to prohibit, assisting suicide. Despite changes in medical technology and notwithstanding an increased emphasis on the importance of end of life decision making, we have not retreated from this prohibition. Against this backdrop of history, tradition, and practice, we now turn to respondents' constitutional claim. . . .

The Due Process Clause guarantees more than fair process, and the "liberty" it protects includes more than the absence of physical restraint. . . . The Clause also provides heightened protection against government interference with certain fundamental rights and liberty interests. . . . In a long line of cases, we have held that, in addition to the specific freedoms protected by the Bill of Rights, the "liberty" specially protected by the Due Process Clause includes the rights to marry, . . . to have children, . . . to direct the education and upbringing of one's children, . . . to marital privacy, . . . to use contraception, . . . to bodily integrity, . . . and to abortion. . . . We have also assumed, and strongly suggested, that the Due Process Clause protects the traditional right to refuse unwanted lifesaving medical treatment. . . .

But we "ha[ve] always been reluctant to expand the concept of substantive due process because guideposts for responsible decision making in this uncharted area are scarce and open ended." . . . By extending constitutional protection to an asserted right or liberty interest, we, to a great extent, place the matter outside the arena of public debate and legislative action. We must therefore "exercise the utmost care whenever we are asked to break new ground in this field," . . . lest the liberty protected by the Due Process Clause be subtly transformed into the policy preferences of the members of this Court. . . .

Our established method of substantive due process analysis has two primary features: First, we have regularly observed that the Due Process Clause specially protects those fundamental rights and liberties which are, objectively, "deeply rooted in this Nation's history and tradition," . . . and "implicit in the concept of ordered liberty," such that "neither liberty nor justice would exist if they were sacrificed." . . . Second, we have required in substantive due process cases a "careful description" of the asserted fundamental liberty interest. . . . Our Nation's history, legal traditions, and practices thus provide the crucial "guideposts for responsible decision making," . . . that direct and restrain our exposition of the Due Process Clause. As we stated recently. . . ., the Fourteenth Amendment "forbids the government to infringe . . . 'fundamental' liberty interests at all, no matter what process is provided, unless the infringement is narrowly tailored to serve a compelling state interest." . . .

. . . The Washington statute at issue in this case prohibits "aid[ing] another person to attempt suicide," . . . and, thus, the question before us is whether the "liberty" specially protected by the Due Process Clause includes a right to commit suicide which itself includes a right to assistance in doing so.

. . . [W]e are confronted with a consistent and almost universal tradition that has long rejected the asserted right, and continues explicitly to reject it today, even for terminally ill, mentally competent adults. To hold for respondents, we would have to reverse centuries of legal doctrine and practice, and strike down the considered policy choice of almost every State. . . .

Respondents contend, however, that the liberty interest they assert is consistent with this Court's substantive due process line of cases, if not with this Nation's history and practice. Pointing to *Casey* and *Cruzan,* respondents read our jurisprudence in this area as reflecting a general tradition of "self sovereignty," Brief of Respondents 12, and as teaching that the "liberty" protected by the Due Process Clause includes "basic and intimate exercises of personal autonomy." . . . According to respondents, our liberty jurisprudence, and the broad, individualistic principles it reflects, protects the "liberty of competent, terminally ill adults to make end of life decisions free of undue government interference." Brief for Respondents 10. The question presented in this case, however, is whether the

protections of the Due Process Clause include a right to commit suicide with another's assistance. . . .

The history of the law's treatment of assisted suicide in this country has been and continues to be one of the rejection of nearly all efforts to permit it. That being the case, our decisions lead us to conclude that the asserted "right" to assistance in committing suicide is not a fundamental liberty interest protected by the Due Process Clause. The Constitution also requires, however, that Washington's assisted suicide ban be rationally related to legitimate government interests. . . . This requirement is unquestionably met here. As the court below recognized, . . . Washington's assisted suicide ban implicates a number of state interests. . . .

First, Washington has an "unqualified interest in the preservation of human life." . . . The State's prohibition on assisted suicide, like all homicide laws, both reflects and advances its commitment to this interest. . . .

Respondents admit that "[t]he State has a real interest in preserving the lives of those who can still contribute to society and enjoy life." . . .

Relatedly, all admit that suicide is a serious public health problem, especially among persons in otherwise vulnerable groups. . . .

Those who attempt suicide—terminally ill or not—often suffer from depression or other mental disorders. . . . Research indicates, however, that many people who request physician assisted suicide withdraw that request if their depression and pain are treated. . . . [B]ecause depression is difficult to diagnose, physicians and medical professionals often fail to respond adequately to seriously ill patients' needs. . . . Thus, legal physician assisted suicide could make it more difficult for the State to protect depressed or mentally ill persons, or those who are suffering from untreated pain, from suicidal impulses.

The State also has an interest in protecting the integrity and ethics of the medical profession. . . . [T]he American Medical Association, like many other medical and physicians' groups, has concluded that "[p]hysician assisted suicide is fundamentally incompatible with the physician's role as healer." . . .

Next, the State has an interest in protecting vulnerable groups—including the poor, the elderly, and disabled persons—from abuse, neglect, and mistakes. . . . If physician assisted suicide were permitted, many might resort to it to spare their families the substantial financial burden of end of life health care costs.

The State's interest here goes beyond protecting the vulnerable from coercion; it extends to protecting disabled and terminally ill people from prejudice, negative and inaccurate stereotypes, and "societal indifference." . . . The State's assisted suicide ban reflects and reinforces its policy that the lives of terminally ill, disabled, and elderly people must be no less valued than the lives of the young and healthy, and that a seriously disabled person's suicidal impulses should be interpreted and treated the same way as anyone else's. . . .

Finally, the State may fear that permitting assisted suicide will start it down the path to voluntary and perhaps even involuntary euthanasia. . . . [W]hat is couched as a limited right to "physician assisted suicide" is likely, in effect, a much broader license, which could prove extremely difficult to police and contain. Washington's ban on assisting suicide prevents such erosion.

This concern is further supported by evidence about the practice of euthanasia in the Netherlands. The Dutch government's own study revealed that in 1990, there were 2,300 cases of voluntary euthanasia (defined as "the deliberate termination of another's life at his request"), 400 cases of assisted suicide, and more than 1,000 cases of euthanasia without an explicit request. In addition to these latter 1,000 cases, the study found an additional 4,941 cases where physicians administered lethal morphine overdoses without the patients' explicit consent. . . . This study suggests that, despite the existence of various reporting procedures, euthanasia in the Netherlands has not been limited to competent, terminally ill adults who are enduring physical suffering, and that regulation of the practice may not have prevented abuses in cases involving vulnerable persons, including severely disabled neonates and elderly persons suffering from dementia. . . .

We need not weigh exactly the relative strengths of these various interests. They are unquestionably important and legitimate, and Washington's ban on assisted suicide is at least reasonably related to their promotion and protection. We therefore hold that [the challenged statute] does not violate the Fourteenth Amendment, either on its face or "as applied to competent, terminally ill adults who wish to hasten their deaths by obtaining medication prescribed by their doctors." . . .

Throughout the Nation, Americans are engaged in an earnest and profound debate about the morality, legality, and practicality of physician assisted suicide. Our holding permits this debate to continue, as it should in a democratic society. The decision of the *en banc* Court of Appeals is reversed, and the case is remanded for further proceedings consistent with this opinion.

Justice O'Connor, concurring. . . .

Justice Stevens, concurring in the judgments.

The Court ends its opinion with the important observation that our holding today is fully consistent with a continuation of the vigorous debate about the "morality, legality, and practicality of physician assisted suicide" in a democratic society. . . . I write separately to make it clear that there is also room for further debate about the limits that the Constitution places on the power of the States to punish the practice.

The morality, legality, and practicality of capital punishment have been the subject of debate for many years. In 1976, this Court upheld the constitutionality of the practice in cases coming to us from Georgia, Florida, and Texas. In those cases we concluded that a State does have the power to place a lesser value on some lives than on others; there is no absolute requirement that a State treat all human life as having an equal right to preservation. Because the state legislatures had sufficiently narrowed the category of lives that the State could terminate, and had enacted special procedures to ensure that the defendant belonged in that limited category, we concluded that the statutes were not unconstitutional on their face. In later cases coming to us from each of those States, however, we found that some applications of the statutes were unconstitutional.

Today, the Court decides that Washington's statute prohibiting assisted suicide is not invalid "on its face," that is to say, in all or most cases in which it might be applied. That holding, however, does not foreclose the possibility that some applications of the statute might well be invalid. . . .

. . . [J]ust as our conclusion that capital punishment is not always unconstitutional did not preclude later decisions holding that it is sometimes impermissibly cruel, so is it equally clear that a decision upholding a general statutory prohibition of assisted suicide does not mean that every possible application of the statute would be valid. A State, like Washington, that has authorized the death penalty and thereby has concluded that the sanctity of human life does not require that it always be preserved, must acknowledge that there are situations in which an interest in hastening death is legitimate. Indeed, not only is that interest sometimes legitimate, I am also convinced that there are times when it is entitled to constitutional protection. . . .

There remains room for vigorous debate about the outcome of particular cases that are not necessarily resolved by the opinions announced today. How such cases may be decided will depend on their specific facts. In my judgment, however, it is clear that the so called "unqualified interest in the preservation of human life,"

. . . is not itself sufficient to outweigh the interest in liberty that may justify the only possible means of preserving a dying patient's dignity and alleviating her intolerable suffering.

Justice Souter, concurring in the judgment.

. . . Legislatures [in contrast to courts] have superior opportunities to obtain the facts necessary for a judgment about the present controversy. Not only do they have more flexible mechanisms for fact finding than the Judiciary, but their mechanisms include the power to experiment, moving forward and pulling back as facts emerge within their own jurisdictions. There is, indeed, good reason to suppose that in the absence of a judgment for respondents here, just such experimentation will be attempted in some of the States. . . .

. . . Sometimes a court may be bound to act regardless of the institutional preferability of the political branches as forums for addressing constitutional claims. . . . Now, it is enough to say that our examination of legislative reasonableness should consider the fact that the Legislature of the State of Washington is no more obviously at fault than this Court is in being uncertain about what would happen if respondents prevailed today. We therefore have a clear question about which institution, a legislature or a court, is relatively more competent to deal with an emerging issue as to which facts currently unknown could be dispositive. The answer has to be, for the reasons already stated, that the legislative process is to be preferred. There is a closely related further reason as well.

One must bear in mind that the nature of the right claimed, if recognized as one constitutionally required, would differ in no essential way from other constitutional rights guaranteed by enumeration or derived from some more definite textual source than "due process." An unenumerated right should not therefore be recognized, with the effect of displacing the legislative ordering of things, without the assurance that its recognition would prove as durable as the recognition of those other rights differently derived. To recognize a right of lesser promise would simply create a constitutional regime too uncertain to bring with it the expectation of finality that is one of this Court's central obligations in making constitutional decisions. . . .

Legislatures, however, are not so constrained. The experimentation that should be out of the question in constitutional adjudication displacing legislative judgments is entirely proper, as well as highly desirable, when the legislative power addresses an emerging issue like assisted suicide. The Court should accordingly stay its hand to allow reasonable legislative consideration. While I do not decide for all time that respondents' claim should not be recognized, I acknowledge the legislative institutional competence as the better one to deal with that claim at this time

Justice Ginsburg, concurring in the judgments. . . .

Justice Breyer, concurring in the judgments.

. . . I agree with the Court . . . that the articulated state interests justify the distinction drawn between physician assisted suicide and withdrawal of life support. I also agree with the Court that the critical question in both of the cases before us is whether "the 'liberty' specially protected by the Due Process Clause includes a right of the sort that the respondents assert. *Washington v. Glucksberg,* ante, at 19. I do not agree, however, with the Court's formulation of that claimed "liberty" interest. The Court describes it as a "right to commit suicide with another's assistance." Ante, at 20. But I would not reject the respondents' claim without considering a different formulation, for which our legal tradition may provide greater support. That formulation would use words roughly like a "right to die with dignity." But irrespective of the exact words used, at its core would lie personal control over the manner of death, professional medical assistance, and the avoidance of unnecessary and severe physical suffering—combined.

. . . Justice Harlan's dissenting opinion in *Poe v. Ullman* . . . (1961), offers some support for such a claim. In that opinion, Justice Harlan referred to the "liberty" that the Fourteenth Amendment protects as including "a freedom from all substantial arbitrary impositions and purposeless restraints" and also as recognizing that "certain interests require particularly careful scrutiny of the state needs asserted to justify their abridgment." . . . The "certain interests" to which Justice Harlan referred may well be similar (perhaps identical) to the rights, liberties, or interests that the Court today, as in the past, regards as "fundamental." . . .

Justice Harlan concluded that marital privacy was such a "special interest." He found in the Constitution a right of "privacy of the home"—with the home, the bedroom, and "intimate details of the marital relation" at its heart—by examining the protection that the law had earlier provided for related, but not identical, interests described by such words as "privacy," "home," and "family." . . . The respondents here essentially ask us to do the same. They argue that one can find a "right to die with dignity" by examining the protection the law has provided for related, but not identical, interests relating to personal dignity, medical treatment, and freedom from state inflicted pain. . . .

I do not believe, however, that this Court need or now should decide whether or a not such a right is "fundamental." That is because, in my view, the avoidance of severe physical pain (connected with death) would have to comprise an essential part of any successful claim and because, as Justice O'Connor points out, the laws before us do not force a dying person to undergo that kind of pain. . . . Rather, the laws of New York and of Washington do not prohibit doctors from providing patients with drugs sufficient to control pain despite the risk that those drugs themselves will kill. . . . And under these circumstances the laws of New York and Washington would overcome any remaining significant interests and would be justified, regardless.

Medical technology, we are repeatedly told, makes the administration of pain relieving drugs sufficient, except for a very few individuals for whom the ineffectiveness of pain control medicines can mean, not pain, but the need for sedation which can end in a coma. . . . We are also told that there are many instances in which patients do not receive the palliative care that, in principle, is available, . . . but that is so for institutional reasons or inadequacies or obstacles, which would seem possible to overcome, and which do not include a prohibitive set of laws. . . .

This legal circumstance means that the state laws before us do not infringe directly upon the (assumed) central interest (what I have called the core of the interest in dying with dignity) as, by way of contrast, the state anticontraceptive laws at issue in *Poe* did interfere with the central interest there at stake—by bringing the State's police powers to bear upon the marital bedroom.

Were the legal circumstances different—for example, were state law to prevent the provision of palliative care, including the administration of drugs as needed to avoid pain at the end of life—then the law's impact upon serious and otherwise unavoidable physical pain (accompanying death) would be more directly at issue. And as Justice O'Connor suggests, the Court might have to revisit its conclusions in these cases.

12

EQUAL PROTECTION AND THE ANTIDISCRIMINATION PRINCIPLE

Chapter Outline

Introduction

Levels of Judicial Scrutiny in Equal Protection Cases

The Struggle for Racial Equality

The Affirmative Action Controversy

Gender-Based Discrimination

Other Forms of Discrimination

The Ongoing Problem of Private Discrimination

Conclusion

Key Terms

For Further Reading

Internet Resources

The Civil Rights Cases (1883)

Plessy v. Ferguson (1896)

Brown v. Board of Education I (1954)

Brown v. Board of Education II (1955)

Loving v. Virginia (1967)

Swann v. Charlotte-Mecklenburg Board of Education (1971)

Missouri v. Jenkins (1995)

Adarand Constructors, Inc. v. Peña (1995)

Frontiero v. Richardson (1973)

United States v. Virginia (1996)

Romer v. Evans (1996)

Our constitution is color-blind, and neither knows nor tolerates classes among citizens. In respect of civil rights all are equal before the law.

—JUSTICE JOHN M. HARLAN (THE ELDER), DISSENTING IN *PLESSY V. FERGUSON* (1896)

The unhappy persistence of both the practice and the lingering effects of racial discrimination against minority groups in this country is an unfortunate reality, and government is not disqualified from acting in response to it.

—JUSTICE SANDRA DAY O'CONNOR, ANNOUNCING THE JUDGMENT OF THE COURT IN *ADARAND CONSTRUCTORS, INC. V. PEÑA* (1995)

INTRODUCTION

One of the philosophical foundations of American democracy is the idea that all individuals are equal before the law. This ideal is expressed both in the Declaration of Independence and in the Equal Protection Clause of the Fourteenth Amendment, which provides that no state shall "deny to any person within its jurisdiction the equal protection of the laws." The Equal Protection Clause prohibits states from denying any person or class of persons the same protection and rights that the law extends to other similarly situated persons or classes of persons.

Like other rights guaranteed by the post–Civil War Amendments, the Equal Protection Clause was motivated in large part by a desire to protect the civil rights of African-Americans recently freed from slavery. However, the text of the Clause makes no mention of race; rather, it refers to any person within the jurisdiction of a state. Although the Supreme Court attempted initially to limit the scope of the Equal Protection Clause to discrimination claims

John M. Harlan (the elder):
Associate Justice, 1877–1911

brought by African-Americans (see *The Slaughter-House Cases* [1873] and *Strauder v. West Virginia* [1880]), the Clause has developed into a broad prohibition against unreasonable governmental discrimination directed at any identifiable group.

In the late nineteenth century, the Supreme Court declared that the word "person" in the **Equal Protection Clause** included corporations (see *Santa Clara County v. Southern Pacific Railroad Company* [1886]). Occasionally, the clause was employed as a basis for invalidating discriminatory business regulation (see *Yick Wo v. Hopkins* [1886]). In the modern era, the Equal Protection Clause has been invoked successfully to challenge discrimination against racial and ethnic minorities, as well as discrimination against women, the poor, illegitimate children, the mentally retarded, illegal aliens, and, most recently, gays and lesbians. Under the so-called **New Equal Protection,** the Supreme Court has used the Equal Protection Clause to scrutinize closely any state law or practice that discriminates among groups in their enjoyment of **fundamental rights.** Without question, the scope of the Equal Protection Clause has been expanded far beyond the expectations of its authors. Along with the Due Process Clause of the Fourteenth Amendment, the Equal Protection Clause has become the principal basis for challenging the constitutionality of a broad range of state laws, actions, and policies.

The Equal Protection "Component" of the Fifth Amendment

Because the Fourteenth Amendment applies only to the states and because the Bill of Rights contains no explicit equal protection provision, does it follow that the national government is under no constitutional obligation to provide equal protection of the laws? The Supreme Court has answered this question emphatically in the negative, "finding" an "equal protection component" in the Due Process Clause of the Fifth Amendment. The Court has concluded that the values underlying the equal protection guarantee are embraced within the broad definition of due process of law (see *Bolling v. Sharpe* [1954]). Since the Fourteenth Amendment contains a Due Process Clause virtually identical to that found in the Fifth Amendment, one might conclude that the Equal Protection Clause of the Fourteenth Amendment is superfluous. Although this may be true in a formal, logical sense, the Equal Protection Clause was the historic basis for judicial scrutiny of governmental policies challenged as discriminatory. In the absence of the Equal Protection Clause, such scrutiny would have been more difficult to justify.

LEVELS OF JUDICIAL SCRUTINY IN EQUAL PROTECTION CASES

Although the adoption and early development of the Equal Protection Clause must be understood in the context of the historic struggle for racial equality in this country, courts have over the years entertained a variety of equal protection claims going well beyond issues of racial discrimination. The Supreme Court has developed a set of standards for judging the constitutionality of policies that are challenged on equal protection grounds.

The Rational Basis Test

State and federal laws are replete with discriminations, or classifications, of various kinds. Yet very few of these classifications are considered constitutionally offensive. For example, a state law that requires a person to possess a license to practice psychiatry discriminates against those persons who are unable to meet the qualifications necessary to obtain a license. Yet few would question the reasonableness of such discrimination. Similarly, when the state limits the driving privilege to persons sixteen and older, it is engaging in age discrimination. But, again, few would challenge the reasonableness of such discrimination.

The traditional test employed by courts in judging challenged legislative classifications is the **rational basis test** (first articulated by the Supreme Court in *Gulf, Colorado & Santa Fe Railway Company v. Ellis* [1897]). Under this deferential approach, the burden is on the party challenging the statute to show that (1) the purpose of the challenged discrimination is an illegitimate state objective and (2) the means employed by the state are not rationally related to the achievement of its objective. Thus, for example, the state law requiring psychiatrists to be licensed reflects a legitimate state interest in protecting the public health and safety and is rationally related to that end. The rational basis test remains the primary test for determining the constitutionality of classifications that impinge on economic interests.

As noted in previous chapters, during the age of conservative activism (1890 to 1937), the Supreme Court emphasized the protection of private property against government regulation and redistribution. Although the Equal Protection Clause played a limited role in this protection, the Court relied more heavily on the Due Process Clauses of the Fifth and Fourteenth Amendments. In the wake of the constitutional revolution of 1937, the locus of Supreme Court activism moved away from the protection of economic individualism. Instead, the post–New Deal Court focused its attention on civil rights and liberties, especially the rights of traditionally disadvantaged minorities. In a famous footnote to his opinion in *United States v. Carolene Products Company* (1938), Justice Harlan Fiske Stone stated that "prejudice against discrete and insular minorities may be a special condition, which tends seriously to curtail the operation of those political processes ordinarily to be relied upon to protect minorities and . . . may call for a more searching judicial scrutiny."

The Court's desire to protect **discrete and insular minorities** who lack political clout in Congress and/or the state legislatures resulted in numerous controversial decisions concerning the rights of the accused, prisoners, aliens (legal and illegal), persons with disabilities, and unorthodox religious sects. The Equal Protection Clause figured prominently in this process. In expanding the scope of the Equal Protection Clause, the Court developed a style of analysis that to a great extent superseded the traditional rational basis test.

The Suspect Classification Doctrine

Korematsu v. United States (1944) provided the first real indication that the Court was embarking on a new approach to the Equal Protection Clause. In *Korematsu,* the Court upheld the constitutionality of the "relocation" of Japanese-Americans living on the West Coast during the Second World War (for further discussion and excerpts from the opinions, see Chapter 3). In his majority opinion, Justice Hugo Black stated that all legal restrictions which curtail the civil rights of a single group are immediately suspect. That is not to say that all such restrictions are unconstitutional. It is to say that courts must subject them to the most rigid scrutiny. Pressing public necessity may sometimes justify the existence of such restrictions; racial antagonism never can.

It is now widely recognized that no compelling justification supported the relocation order. However, the majority in *Korematsu* apparently did not have full access to information, later made public, clearly indicating that the relocation order stemmed more from racial prejudice than from military necessity.

Although on its face the *Korematsu* decision was hardly a victory for civil rights, it marked the inception of the **suspect classification doctrine,** which holds that certain kinds of discrimination are inherently suspect and therefore must be subjected to **strict judicial scrutiny.** Included among those laws that are inherently suspect are those that classify persons based on race, religion, or ethnicity, as well as those that impinge on fundamental rights.

Operationally speaking, strict judicial scrutiny means that the ordinary **presumption of constitutionality** is reversed; the government carries the **burden of proof** that its challenged policy is constitutional. To carry that burden, government must show that its policy is necessary to the achievement of a **compelling interest.** Although these tests are far from precise, the compelling interest test is generally understood to be far more stringent than the traditional rational basis test. Using the suspect classification doctrine, the Court has invalidated, explicitly or implicitly, virtually all public policies that overtly discriminate among persons on the basis of their race (see, for example, *Loving v. Virginia* [1967]). In the Court's view, it is virtually impossible for government to have a compelling interest that would require or justify racial or ethnic discrimination.

Judging the Disparate Impact of Facially Neutral Policies

The suspect classification doctrine applies only to policies that overtly discriminate on the basis of race, religion, or ethnicity. What standard should be applied to judge policies that are neutral on their face but have disparate impacts on people of different races? In *Washington v. Davis* (1976), the Supreme Court considered a challenge to the practice of requiring applicants to the District of Columbia police department to pass a verbal skills test that was used widely in the federal civil service. African-American applicants were approximately four times as likely to fail this test as were white applicants. The Court rejected the argument that the testing requirement should be subjected to strict scrutiny under the suspect classification doctrine. Writing for the Court, Justice Byron White said:

> A rule that a statute designed to serve neutral ends is nevertheless invalid, absent compelling justification, if in practice it benefits or burdens one race more than another would be far-reaching and would raise serious questions about, and perhaps invalidate, a whole range of tax, welfare, public service, regulatory and licensing statutes. . . .

Under *Washington v. Davis* and similar decisions, a policy that is racially neutral on its face but has a **disparate impact** on people of different races will be upheld unless plaintiffs can show that it was adopted to serve a racially discriminatory purpose.

Heightened Scrutiny

To complicate matters further, the Supreme Court has developed still another level of equal protection review, falling somewhere between the rational basis test and the suspect classification doctrine. This approach, often described as **heightened scrutiny,** has been applied most prominently, but not exclusively, to gender discrimination claims. Under this approach, government must show that a challenged policy bears a "substantial" relationship to an "important" government interest. How exactly this test differs from either the less stringent rational basis test or the more stringent compelling interest test is difficult to articulate.

Thus, there are currently three tiers of review for judging equal protection claims. Shortly before his retirement in 1991, Justice Thurgood Marshall suggested that the Court adopt a "sliding scale" that would embrace a "spectrum of standards" of review. Others on the Court have been put off by what they regard as needless doctrinal complexity. Justice John Paul Stevens, for example, has argued for a return to the rational basis standard, which he believes to be adequate to invalidate all invidious forms of discrimination. Others on the Court, most notably Chief Justice Rehnquist, are dissatisfied with the modern Court's special solicitude for the claims of discrete and insular minorities. Given the conservative character of the contemporary Supreme Court, we can anticipate significant doctrinal changes in the Court's equal protection jurisprudence.

TO SUMMARIZE

- The Supreme Court has developed three tiers of review for determining whether challenged policies violate the Equal Protection Clause.
- The most lenient approach is the rational basis test. In this test, the burden is on the party challenging the policy to show that its purpose is illegitimate and/or that the means employed are not rationally related to the achievement of the government's objective.
- The Court employs "strict scrutiny" in judging policies that discriminate on the basis of race, religion, or national origin, classifications that are deemed to be "inherently suspect." In such cases the burden is on the government to show that its challenged policy is narrowly tailored to the achievement of a compelling governmental interest.
- In cases involving claims of gender discrimination and in certain other areas, the Court employs "heightened scrutiny" in which government must show that a challenged policy bears a "substantial" relationship to an "important" government interest.

THE STRUGGLE FOR RACIAL EQUALITY

Although the Equal Protection Clause is now recognized as a broad shield against arbitrary governmental action, little doubt exists that the Fourteenth Amendment was adopted primarily to protect the rights of the newly freed former slaves. Specifically, the Fourteenth Amendment was designed to provide constitutional authority for newly enacted federal civil rights legislation aimed at ending discrimination against African-Americans. Section 5 of the Fourteenth Amendment gives Congress the power to enforce, "by appropriate legislation," the abstract promises of the Equal Protection Clause and other provisions of the amendment.

Federal Civil Rights Statutes Enacted during Reconstruction

During the Reconstruction Era, Congress passed four major civil rights acts. Some provisions of these statutes remain important components of contemporary civil rights law.

THE CIVIL RIGHTS ACT OF 1866. This act provided that citizens of all races have the same rights to make and enforce contracts, to sue and give evidence in the courts, and to own, purchase, sell, rent, and inherit real and personal property. For modern counterparts, see 42 U.S. Code, Sections 1981 and 1982.

THE CIVIL RIGHTS ACT OF 1870. Also known as the Ku Klux Klan Act, this statute made it a federal crime to conspire to "injure, oppress, threaten or intimidate any citizen in the free exercise of any right or privilege secured to him by the Constitution or laws of the United States." For modern counterpart, see 18 U.S. Code, Section, 241. The statute also criminalized any act under color of state law that subjects persons to deprivations of constitutional rights. See 18 U.S. Code, Section 242.

THE CIVIL RIGHTS ACT OF 1871. This statute made individuals acting under color of state law personally liable for acts violating the constitutional rights of others. Civil actions under this statute are commonly referred to as "Section 1983 actions" because the act is codified at 42 U.S. Code, Section 1983. The 1871 act also permitted civil suits against those conspiring to violate the civil rights of others (codified at 42 U.S. Code, Section 1985).

THE CIVIL RIGHTS ACT OF 1875. This statute forbade denial of equal rights and privileges by places of public accommodation. It was declared invalid as applied to privately owned public accommodations in *The Civil Rights Cases* (1883). Access to public accommodations was ultimately achieved under Title II of the Civil Rights Act of 1964.

Early Interpretations of the Equal Protection Clause

Shortly before the Fourteenth Amendment was ratified, Congress passed the **Civil Rights Act of 1866,** which, among other things, protected the right of African-Americans to inherit, own, and convey property. In the wake of the Civil War, many of the Southern states had adopted **Black Codes,** which denied such basic economic rights to former slaves. Under the new Civil Rights Act, violation of these rights was made a federal offense where it could be shown that the violator was acting "under color of state law." Apparently having some reservations about the constitutionality of this law, Congress rushed to adopt the Fourteenth Amendment, believing that the Equal Protection Clause of Section 1 together with the enforcement provision of Section 5 would provide an adequate constitutional basis for far-ranging civil rights legislation.

The Civil Rights Cases of 1883

While the modern Supreme Court recognizes broad congressional power under the Fourteenth Amendment, the Supreme Court's early view of congressional authority in the field of civil rights was much more restrictive. In adopting the **Civil Rights Act of 1875,** Congress made a serious attempt to eradicate racial discrimination in **places of public accommodation,** including hotels, taverns, restaurants, theaters, and "public conveyances." In *The Civil Rights Cases* (1883), the Supreme Court struck down the key provisions of this act, ruling that the Fourteenth Amendment limited congressional action to the prohibition of official, state-sponsored discrimination as distinct from discrimination practiced by privately owned places of public accommodation. The Supreme Court's decision in *The Civil*

The "colored entrance" to a movie theater during the era of segregation

Rights Cases may have been motivated by a desire to promote reconciliation between North and South and between the federal and state governments. Unfortunately, any such reconciliation was achieved at the expense of African-Americans.

Adoption of Jim Crow Laws

Not only did the Court's decision in *The Civil Rights Cases* preserve widespread practices of racial discrimination in restaurants, hotels, and the like, it was also regarded as a green light for the passage of legislation mandating strict racial segregation. The so-called **Jim Crow laws** adopted in the aftermath of *The Civil Rights Cases* required segregation in virtually every area of public life. They required blacks and whites to attend separate schools, to use separate parks, to ride in separate railroad cars, and even to be buried in separate cemeteries. Perhaps the most ludicrous of the many Jim Crow laws required white and black witnesses in court to take their oaths on separate Bibles!

The Separate but Equal Doctrine

In *Plessy v. Ferguson* (1896), the Supreme Court upheld racial segregation in the context of public transportation. The Court's ruling provided a rationale for government-mandated segregation on a broad scale. At issue in *Plessy* was an

1890 Louisiana law requiring passenger trains operating within the state to provide "equal but separate" accommodations for the "white and colored races." Homer Plessy, who was considered "colored" under Louisiana law because one of his great grandparents was black, was ordered to leave a railroad car reserved for whites. Plessy, who intended to challenge the constitutionality of the law, refused to vacate his seat and was arrested. Dividing 7 to 1 (Justice David Brewer not participating), the Court sustained the Louisiana statute. Writing for the majority, Justice Henry Billings Brown asserted that "in the nature of things, [the Fourteenth Amendment] could not have been intended to abolish distinctions based upon color, or to enforce social, as distinguished from political, equality, or a commingling of the two races upon terms unsatisfactory to either."

In one of the most widely quoted opinions in American constitutional law, Justice John M. Harlan (the elder) dissented vehemently. For Justice Harlan, ironically a former Kentucky slave owner, the "arbitrary separation of citizens on the basis of race" was tantamount to imposing a "badge of servitude" on the Negro race. He asserted that "our Constitution is color-blind, and neither knows nor tolerates classes among citizens."

The **separate but equal doctrine** approved in *Plessy* remained the authoritative interpretation of the Equal Protection Clause for fifty-eight years. Ultimately, of course, it was repudiated by the Supreme Court in *Brown v. Board of Education of Topeka* (1954). The **state action doctrine** announced in *The Civil Rights Cases* remains authoritative to this day, and not until the 1960s was Congress willing or able to prohibit discrimination in places of public accommodation. When Congress did finally act in passing the **Civil Rights Act of 1964,** it chose to rely primarily on its broad powers under the Commerce Clause, rather than on Section 5 of the Fourteenth Amendment (see Chapter 2).

The net effect of *The Civil Rights Cases* and *Plessy v. Ferguson* was to defer the dream of legal and political equality for African-Americans for nearly a century after ratification of the Fourteenth Amendment. During this period, racial discrimination was simply a way of life for many Americans, both black and white. In the 1990s, although considerable progress toward racial equality has been achieved, racial discrimination and hatred have by no means disappeared from American society.

The Decline of *De jure* Racial Segregation

The Court's decision in *Plessy v. Ferguson* rested on two obvious fictions: (1) that racial segregation conveyed no negative statement about the status of African-Americans and (2) that separate accommodations and facilities for blacks were in fact equal to those reserved for whites. Blacks, and no doubt whites as well, knew better. As time went by, it became increasingly obvious to the Supreme Court that the separate but equal doctrine was a mere rationalization for relegating African-Americans to second-class citizenship.

In a series of cases decided between 1938 and 1950, the Supreme Court chipped away at the separate but equal doctrine, as applied to higher education, without repudiating the doctrine altogether. In *Missouri ex rel. Gaines v. Canada* (1938), the Court mandated the admission of a qualified African-American resident of Missouri to the state university law school. The Court held that a state could not escape its obligation by making provisions for its African-American students to attend out-of-state law schools. The Supreme Court reaffirmed its holding in *Gaines* a decade later in *Sipuel v. Oklahoma Board of Regents* (1948). Two years later, in *McLaurin v.*

Thurgood Marshall: Associate Justice, 1967–1991

Oklahoma State Regents (1950), the Court disallowed an attempt by the University of Oklahoma to segregate a black graduate student from his white colleagues after he was admitted pursuant to a court order. In class, the student, McLaurin, was required to sit in a row of desks restricted to blacks. In the cafeteria, he was required to eat alone at a particular table. He was restricted to a designated table in the library. He was even prohibited from visiting his professors during their regular office hours in order to minimize his interactions with white students. In the Court's view, this isolation significantly detracted from McLaurin's educational experience and thus could not be justified under the separate but equal doctrine.

In *Sweatt v. Painter* (1950), the Court considered an attempt by the state of Texas to provide a separate law school for African-Americans. The Court found that the newly created law school at the Texas College for Negroes was substantially inferior, in terms of both measurable and intangible factors, to the white-only law school at the University of Texas.

Desegregation

By the early 1950s, it was clear that the Supreme Court would no longer tolerate the provision of demonstrably inferior educational services or facilities to African-Americans under the aegis of the separate but equal doctrine. But considerable uncertainty remained, both within and outside the Court, as to whether the justices would, or should, abandon the *Plessy* doctrine altogether. The NAACP mounted a major challenge to segregated public schools, instituting lawsuits in four states and the District of Columbia. These cases were first argued before the Supreme Court in 1952, but because of the political magnitude of the issue presented, the Court directed that the cases be reargued in 1953. Before the second round of oral argument, Chief Justice Fred M. Vinson died and was succeeded by Earl Warren.

The *Brown* Decision

Finally, on May 17, 1954, the uncertainty regarding segregated public schools came to an end when the Court handed down its landmark decision in *Brown v. Board of Education.* In one of the most important decisions in its history, the Court unanimously struck down racial segregation in the public schools of Kansas, South Carolina, Delaware, and Virginia. Speaking for the Court in *Brown,* Chief Justice Warren declared that "in the field of public education, the doctrine of 'separate but equal' has no place. Separate educational facilities are inherently unequal." Thus, in a concise and forceful opinion, the Warren Court abandoned a long-standing constitutional precedent and precipitated a revolution in public education.

In a companion case, *Bolling v. Sharpe,* the Court held that the operation of segregated schools by the District of Columbia violated the Due Process Clause of the Fifth Amendment. Here, as noted at the beginning of this chapter, the Court recognized an "equal protection component" in the Fifth Amendment due process requirement, indicating that uniform antidiscrimination mandates were to be applied to the federal government as well as the states.

Implementation of *Brown*

The *Brown* decision of 1954 left open the question of how and when desegregation would have to be achieved. In a follow-up decision in 1955 (referred to as *Brown* II), the Court blunted the revolutionary potential of the original decision by adopting a formula calling for implementation of **desegregation** with **"all deliberate speed."** Recognizing that compliance would be more difficult to achieve in the South than in other sections of the country, the Court left it up to federal district judges to apply this formula, taking into account the particular circumstances characterizing race relations within their respective jurisdictions. This approach ensured great diversity in the implementation of *Brown* I and invited the use of delaying tactics by state and local officials. Despite its concern for the difficulties public officials would face in bringing about desegregation, the Court was reviled in many quarters for "meddling" in state and local affairs. Some of the Court's harsher critics went so far as to call for the impeachment of Chief Justice Warren.

Some of the more extreme critics of school desegregation called for militant noncompliance with the Court's directive. John Kasper, a well-known white supremacist and self-styled protege of the fascist poet Ezra Pound, went around the country preaching the use of violence and intimidation to prevent black students from entering formerly all-white public schools. In the late summer of 1956, Kasper went to Clinton, Tennessee, where he succeeded in fomenting violent resistance to court-ordered integration of Clinton High School. In late August, Kasper was ordered by federal judge Robert Taylor "to cease hindering, obstructing, or in any wise interfering" with court-ordered integration. Kasper persisted in his efforts, and Clinton experienced a turbulent fall replete with riots, beatings, death threats directed at various school officials, and harassment of African-American students. After the National Guard was called in to restore order, Kasper was arrested and convicted for violating the federal court injunction. Ultimately, peace returned to Clinton, and desegregation proceeded apace.

The Little Rock Crisis

In one of the best known and most dramatic efforts to resist the Supreme Court's desegregation decisions, Arkansas Governor Orval Faubus called out the National Guard in 1957 to prevent nine African-American students from entering Little Rock Central High School. The guard was soon withdrawn, but an angry mob of whites continued to harass the black students. President Dwight D. Eisenhower, who had expressed serious reservations about the *Brown* decision, nevertheless intervened with federal troops to quell the violence and enforce the court-ordered integration. In *Cooper v. Aaron* (1958), the Court delivered a sharp rebuke to Arkansas officials who had attempted to frustrate the Court's mandate (see Chapter 1). Would the Court's language in *Cooper v. Aaron* have been so strong in the absence of Eisenhower's intervention in Little Rock?

The Court Repudiates "All Deliberate Speed"

In efforts less dramatic than what transpired in Little Rock, state and local governments intent on avoiding desegregation adopted a strategy of "legislate and litigate" that delayed universal compliance with *Brown* for well over a decade. But in *Alexander v. Holmes County* (1969), after many years of delay, the Supreme Court finally abandoned the permissive "all deliberate speed" policy and ordered desegregation "at once."

A scene from the Little Rock School desegregation crisis, September 1957

The Busing Controversy

As previously noted, the Supreme Court's *Brown* II decision left the implementation of school desegregation largely to the discretion of federal district judges. Of the various measures that these judges employed in dismantling "dual" school systems, "forced busing" was by far the most controversial. In *Swann v. Charlotte-Mecklenburg Board of Education* (1971), the Supreme Court unanimously approved the use of **court-ordered busing** to achieve the goal of desegregation. In 1973, the Court turned its attention to school desegregation outside the South. In *Keyes v. Denver School District,* the Court, with only Justice Rehnquist dissenting, found *de jure* **discrimination** where a series of administrative decisions in the 1960s had helped to maintain racially segregated public schools in the city of Denver. Thus, in *Keyes,* as in *Swann,* the Supreme Court upheld a busing plan imposed by a federal district court.

As court-ordered busing became more pervasive, it erupted into a major political issue. In the 1972 presidential campaign, candidate George Wallace exploited the busing issue quite successfully, goading incumbent Richard Nixon into taking a stronger antibusing posture than he had previously maintained. Perhaps as a reaction to widespread criticism of *Swann* and *Keyes,* as well as anti-busing rumblings in Congress, the Supreme Court backed away from busing in the case of *Milliken v. Bradley* (1974). *Milliken* involved a challenge to a court-ordered desegregation plan for greater Detroit that involved busing students across school district lines within the metropolitan area. Although *Milliken* by no means overturned *Swann* and *Keyes,* a 5-to-4 majority of the justices held that court-ordered busing of students across school district lines is permissible only if all affected districts had been guilty of past discriminatory practices. By thus limiting interdistrict busing plans, the Supreme Court placed substantial limits on this approach to school desegregation in metropolitan areas.

To the proponents of racial busing, the decision in *Milliken* was an unfortunate retreat from the Court's long-standing commitment to integration. For others, *Milliken* was a welcome concession to public opinion, which was generally negative toward busing. Clearly, the effect of the *Milliken* decision was to defuse much of the harsh criticism that had previously been directed at the Court over the busing issue. Nevertheless, interdistrict busing schemes continued to be ordered by federal judges where interdistrict violations were uncovered. In the unfortunate case of Boston, interdistrict busing in 1974 produced intense hostility and violence.

The use of busing to achieve desegregation continues to this day, although it is not as pervasive as it was in the early seventies. Indeed, African-American intellectuals and educators no longer uniformly support busing. Some reject what they regard as a racist implication that black children cannot improve themselves without exposure to white children. Clearly, the political and intellectual impetus behind racial busing has diminished dramatically. Consequently, busing is no longer a salient political issue. The Supreme Court continues to hear cases in this area, but the major thrust of current litigation is toward the termination, rather than the continued implementation, of busing and related desegregation plans. In a significant 1991 decision, *Board of Education v. Dowell,* the Court granted federal district courts clear authority to terminate desegregation orders provided that two conditions are met: (1) The local school board in question has complied in good faith with the desegregation decree and (2) all vestiges of prior discrimination have been effectively removed. The *Dowell* decision left many questions unanswered, but the Court made it clear that judicial supervision of school desegregation is, after all, temporary in nature.

In *Freeman v. Pitts* (1992) the Supreme Court amplified its decision in *Dowell* by permitting a federal district court that for many years had supervised desegregation of the DeKalb County, Georgia, schools to relinquish supervision over certain aspects of school administration. The Court held that district judges have discretion to relinquish supervision of school systems where racial imbalances stemming from *de jure* segregation have disappeared, even if schools remain "racially identifiable" due to demographic factors. Under the approach taken in *Dowell* and *Freeman,* local school districts that show good-faith efforts to comply with court-mandated desegregation plans will eventually regain full control of their school systems.

Magnet Schools

Clarence Thomas:
Associate Justice, 1991–

In *Missouri v. Jenkins* (1995) the Supreme Court reviewed a federal district judge's efforts to desegregate the Kansas City school system. Splitting 5 to 4, the Supreme Court invalidated the judge's order, finding it to be excessive and abusive of the district court's remedial powers. The Court also instructed the lower court to review the rest of its remedial orders under the stricter level of scrutiny articulated in *Freeman v. Pitts* (1992). Writing for the Court, Chief Justice Rehnquist reminded the district court "that its end purpose is not only 'to remedy the violation' to the extent practicable, but also 'to restore state and local authorities to the control of a school system that is operating in compliance with the Constitution.' "

In her concurring opinion in *Jenkins,* Justice O'Connor emphasized the narrowness of the Court's holding. In contrast, Justice Thomas's twenty-seven-page concurring opinion launched a broadside against desegregation jurisprudence: "Given that desegregation has not produced the predicted leaps forward in black educational achievement, there is no reason to think that black students cannot learn as well when surrounded by members of their own race as when they are in an integrated environment." Thomas also attacked the "virtually unlimited" power of federal district judges to craft desegregation remedies: "Federal courts simply cannot gather sufficient information to render an effective decree, have limited resources to induce compliance, and cannot seek political and public support for their remedies. When we presume to have the institutional ability to set effective educational, budgetary, or administrative policy, we transform the least dangerous branch into the most dangerous one."

Dissenting in *Jenkins,* Justice Souter noted that state and local officials "intentionally created this segregated system of education, and subsequently failed to correct it. . . ." Clearly, in Souter's view, officials "defaulted in their obligation to uphold the Constitution." In remedying the violation, the district court must be accorded broad latitude. It must be "authorized to remedy all conditions flowing directly from the constitutional violations committed by state or local officials, including the educational deficits that result from a segregated school system. . . ." Justice Souter was joined in this view by Justices Ginsburg, Breyer, and Stevens. In her separate dissent, Justice Ginsburg sounded a cautionary note: "Given the deep, inglorious history of segregation in Missouri, to curtail desegregation at this time and in this manner is an action at once too swift and too soon."

TO SUMMARIZE

- Although the Equal Protection Clause is now recognized as a broad shield against arbitrary governmental action, little doubt exists that the Fourteenth Amendment was adopted primarily to protect the rights of the newly freed former slaves.
- The Supreme Court was slow to take up the cause of civil rights, and in early cases refused to use the Fourteenth Amendment to invalidate racial discrimination and segregation. The Warren Court, most notably in *Brown v. Board of Education* (1954), made civil rights a major priority and in so doing wrought major changes in American politics and society.
- Section 5 of the Fourteenth Amendment gives Congress the power to enforce, "by appropriate legislation," the abstract promises of the Equal Protection Clause and other provisions of the amendment. In the wake of the Civil War, Congress adopted a number of important civil rights statutes. In the modern era, Congress has continued to rely on Section 5 of the Fourteenth Amendment in legislating in the civil rights field.
- *Brown v. Board of Education* was the beginning of a process of desegregating public schools, a process that involved considerable resistance from supporters of segregation and numerous legal controversies over busing of students and federal judicial supervision of many public school systems.

THE AFFIRMATIVE ACTION CONTROVERSY

The furor over court-ordered busing that occurred during the 1970s had largely subsided by the late 1980s. But as usually happens in American politics, a new ongoing controversy emerged to take its place. The controversy involves **affirmative action,** which is a broad term referring to a variety of efforts designed to assist members of traditionally disfavored minority groups. The affirmative action concept is manifested in three major areas of distributive policy: employment, government contracts, and higher education. Affirmative action actually emerged through executive orders handed down during the Kennedy, Johnson, and Nixon administrations of the 1960s and early 1970s. Initially, it was limited to the requirement that federal government contractors make increased efforts to recruit minority employees. Thereafter, state higher education programs were subjected to affirmative action guidelines as a condition of accepting federal subsidies. Soon federal and state courts were adopting **race-conscious remedies** (for example, racial busing) in resolving desegregation lawsuits. Eventually, what began as little more than a public exhortation became a series of goals, quotas, and timetables designed to integrate African-Americans, Hispanics, Native Americans, and other traditionally disfavored minorities into the economic and educational mainstream.

Although the ultimate objective of affirmative action was, and is, universally applauded, the means of achieving it—quotas, formulas, and ratios based on immutable racial characteristics—are distasteful to many and appear downright unjust to others. To many critics, affirmative action represents an unfortunate degeneration of the noble ideal of equality of opportunity into "statistical parity." For some legal critics, affirmative action is a violation of the color-blind Constitution idealized by Justice Harlan's dissent in *Plessy v. Ferguson*. Still others, some of them members of nonpreferred ethnic minorities, object to affirmative action not on principle but because they have not been given preferred status. Yet, the many defenders of affirmative action characterize it as the only practicable means of realizing the American dream for those who have been traditionally locked out.

Competing Models of Justice

Affirmative action is problematic legally because it involves two competing models of racial justice. One theory views race discrimination and its appropriate remedies in terms of identifiable groups. Under this theory, all individuals properly belonging to a traditionally disfavored minority are entitled to partake of a remedy. The competing individualistic theory holds that remedies are to be provided only to those individuals who can show that they have been the targets of invidious discrimination. The conflict can also be viewed as one between contemporary politics and traditional principles of law. In the contemporary pluralistic political process, we are accustomed to thinking in terms of group interests. However, our system of law rests on a foundation of individualism and does not easily accommodate the concept of **group rights.**

Naturally, people on all sides of the affirmative action controversy looked to the Supreme Court for a settlement of the issue. The Supreme Court initially avoided the constitutionality of affirmative action when it decided *DeFunis v. Odegaard* (1974), holding that the question presented in this case was moot.

The *Bakke* and *Fullilove* Cases

Eventually, however, the Supreme Court did hand down a ruling on affirmative action, but *Regents of the University of California v. Bakke* (1978) could hardly be regarded as a definitive resolution of the issue. Alan Bakke, a thirty-seven-year-old white male engineer, brought suit to challenge the affirmative action policy of the medical school at the University of California at Davis (Cal-Davis). Bakke had been denied admission to the medical school, although his objective indicators (that is, Medical College Admission Test score and grade point average) were better than those of several of the sixteen minority students admitted under a **set-aside** policy. The California Supreme Court found this to be a violation of equal protection and ordered Bakke to be admitted to the medical school. Seeking a more authoritative resolution of the issue, the university appealed. Bakke ultimately won the appeal, completed his medical school program, and is now a practicing anesthesiologist.

In a fragmented decision, the Court voted 5 to 4 to invalidate the Cal-Davis quota system and admit Alan Bakke to medical school. However, also by a 5-to-4 margin, the Court endorsed affirmative action in the abstract, by recognizing race as a legitimate criterion of admission to medical school. According to Justice Lewis Powell's controlling opinion in *Bakke,* the state has a compelling interest in achieving diversity in its medical school, and this interest justifies the use of race as one of several criteria of admission. However, the use of a rigid quota system

> tells applicants who are not Negro, Asian or Chicano that they are totally excluded from a specific percentage of the seats in an entering class. No matter how strong their qualifications, quantitative and extracurricular, including their own potential for contribution to educational diversity, they are never afforded the chance to compete with applicants from the preferred groups for the special admissions seats.

For Justice Powell, this was the fatal flaw in the Cal-Davis affirmative action plan. Powell's brethren were less equivocal. Four members of the Court—Burger, Stewart, Rehnquist, and Stevens—would have declared the entire policy to be in violation of the Civil Rights Act, which, in their judgment, requires government to observe a standard of color-blindness. On the other hand, Justices Brennan, Marshall, White, and Blackmun found no statutory or constitutional violation in the minority "set-aside" policy. According to Justice William Brennan, "[g]overnment may take race into account when it acts not to demean or insult any racial group, but to remedy disadvantages cast on minorities by past racial prejudice. . . ."

An equally equivocal endorsement of affirmative action was provided by the Supreme Court in *Fullilove v. Klutznick* (1980). In *Fullilove,* the Court upheld a federal public works program that provided a 10 percent set-aside of federal funds for "minority business enterprises." Because this case involved an act of Congress, rather than state action, the set-aside policy was challenged as a violation of the equal protection component of the Fifth Amendment Due Process Clause. The Supreme Court upheld the minority set-aside by a vote of 6 to 3. Unfortunately, as in *Bakke,* the Court was unable to produce a majority opinion. Chief Justice Warren Burger's plurality opinion stressed Congress's broad powers under Section 5 of the Fourteenth Amendment but stopped far short of providing a wholesale endorsement of affirmative action. In a concurring opinion Justice Brennan echoed the strong proaffirmative action position he had taken in *Bakke:*

> [The] principles outlawing the irrelevant or pernicious use of race [are] inapposite to racial classifications that provide benefits to minorities for the purpose of remedying the present effects of past racial discrimination. Such classifications may disadvantage some whites, but whites as a class lack the "traditional indicia of suspectness: the class is not saddled with such disabilities, or subjected to such a history of purposeful unequal treatment, or relegated to such a position of political powerlessness as to command extraordinary protection from the majoritarian political process."

Justice Stewart, joined by Justice Rehnquist, cited Justice Harlan's *Plessy* dissent as a barrier to any sort of race preferences, while Justice Stevens's dissenting opinion focused on Congress's failure to demonstrate that remedial preferences were being bestowed on a truly disadvantaged class. The Court's failure to produce majority opinions in *Bakke* and *Fullilove* compounded the uncertainties surrounding the myriad affirmative action policies in effect by the early 1980s.

The Rehnquist Court Curtails Affirmative Action

In the wake of *Bakke* and *Fullilove,* the Supreme Court continued to grapple with the affirmative action issue, most notably through a series of decisions interpreting the federal civil rights statutes. In general, the Court continued to support various affirmative action programs (see, for example, *Steelworkers v. Weber* [1979], *Sheet Metal Workers v. Equal Employment Opportunity Commission* [1986], *Firefighters v. Cleveland* [1986], and *Johnson v. Transportation Agency of Santa Clara* [1987]).

Despite its apparent acceptance of affirmative action, the Court placed limits on the scope of affirmative action policies, for example, by refusing to allow affirmative action objectives to override seniority in determining layoffs (see *Memphis Firefighters v. Stotts* [1984]). The Court also held that, if their interests are adversely affected, white employees may challenge the legality of affirmative action plans that are established under **consent decrees,** even if they were not parties to the original litigation (*Martin v. Wilks* [1989]).

The biggest change in the perspective of the Court in this area came in *City of Richmond v. J. A. Croson Company* (1989) when the Rehnquist Court dealt a serious blow to affirmative action. In 1983, the Richmond City Council passed an ordinance requiring that construction companies awarded city contracts in turn award at least 30 percent of their subcontracts to minority-owned business enterprises. A plumbing contractor, the J. A. Croson Company, sued the city in federal court, arguing that the set-aside was unconstitutional. The federal district court upheld the ordinance, relying heavily on the Supreme Court's earlier decision in *Fullilove v. Klutznick.* The Court of Appeals reversed, however, and the city of Richmond asked the Supreme Court to review the case.

The personnel on the High Court in 1989 had changed significantly since *Fullilove,* of course. Justice Stewart had been replaced by Justice Sandra Day O'Connor in 1981. Justice Antonin Scalia had joined the Court after Chief Justice Burger retired, and Justice Rehnquist became chief justice in 1986. Justice Anthony Kennedy joined the Court in 1988 after the retirement of Justice Powell. These personnel changes produced a shift in the ideological character of the Court, moving it substantially to the right. It was no surprise, therefore, that the Court, voting 6 to 3, struck down the Richmond set-aside plan. Writing for the Court, Justice O'Connor noted that "[t]he Richmond Plan denies certain citizens the opportunity to compete for a fixed percentage of public contracts based solely upon their race." After reviewing the relevant history and facts, Justice O'Connor concluded that

> the city has failed to demonstrate a compelling interest in apportioning public contracting opportunities on the basis of race. To accept Richmond's claim that past societal discrimination alone can serve as the basis for rigid racial preferences would be to open the door to competing claims for "remedial relief" for every disadvantaged group. The dream of a Nation of equal citizens in a society where race is irrelevant to personal opportunity and achievement would be lost in a mosaic of shifting preferences based on inherently unmeasurable claims of past wrongs. . . .

In a bitter dissent, Justice Marshall (joined by Justices Brennan and Blackmun) characterized the decision as a "deliberate and giant step backward" and "a full-scale retreat from the Court's long-standing solicitude to race-conscious remedial efforts. . . ." Marshall predicted that the decision would "inevitably discourage or prevent governmental entities, particularly States and localities, from acting to rectify the scourge of past discrimination."

In her *Croson* opinion, Justice O'Connor attempted to distinguish the Richmond set-aside plan from the congressional program that the Court had approved in *Fullilove v. Klutznick*. O'Connor emphasized the broad powers of Congress under Section 5 of the Fourteenth Amendment, indicating that municipalities lack equally broad powers. Many critics of the *Croson* decision found this distinction unpersuasive. Students reading *Croson* and *Fullilove* should consider whether the two cases can in fact be distinguished from one another.

It is interesting to speculate as to how the Supreme Court would have decided *Fullilove* if that case had come to the Court in 1989, instead of 1980. As the Court became even more conservative with the departures of Justices Marshall and Brennan and the arrival of Justices Souter and Thomas, many commentators thought that the *Croson* case was the beginning of a process of dismantling affirmative action policies.

Those who believed that affirmative action was on the way out were surprised when the Supreme Court decided *Metro Broadcasting v. Federal Communications Commission* (FCC) in 1990. In *Metro Broadcasting* the Court upheld an FCC affirmative action policy designed to foster increased minority participation in the broadcasting industry. From a jurisprudential point of view, the significance of *Metro Broadcasting* was the distinction the Court drew between state and local affirmative action programs on the one hand and federal affirmative action programs on the other. Relying on *Fullilove v. Klutznick,* the Court said in effect that federal affirmative action programs were entitled to a greater presumption of validity. The Court said that federal affirmative action programs are "constitutionally permissible to the extent that they serve important governmental objectives within the power of Congress and are substantially related to achievement of those objectives." Obviously, this was a more lenient approach than the Court took in the *Croson* case.

Five years later the Court repudiated *Metro Broadcasting* and the approach it embodied. In *Adarand Constructors, Inc. v. Peña* (1995), the Court held that one standard of review should govern all affirmative action programs, whether local, state, or federal.

The *Adarand* case dealt with federal highway contracts. Under a policy of the U.S. Department of Transportation, general contractors were given a financial incentive to hire subcontractors controlled by "socially and economically disadvantaged individuals." Even though it submitted a lower bid, Adarand Constructors was passed over as a subcontractor on a federal highway project in favor of a company that received preferred status under the affirmative action policy. Adarand unsuccessfully argued in the lower courts that federal affirmative action programs should be subjected to the same standard applied to state and local programs.

In a 5-to-4 decision, the Supreme Court sent the case back to the trial court for reconsideration. Writing for the Court, Justice O'Connor held that "all racial classifications, imposed by whatever federal, state, or local governmental actor, must be analyzed by a reviewing court under strict scrutiny. In other words, such classifications are constitutional only if they are narrowly tailored measures that further compelling governmental interests." But O'Connor also recognized that, given sufficient justification, a racial preference might be sustained: "The unhappy persistence of both the practice and the lingering effects of racial discrimination against minority groups in this country is an unfortunate reality, and government is not disqualified from acting in response to it." Dissenting, Justice Stevens argued that "[i]nvidious discrimination is an engine of oppression, subjugating a disfavored group to enhance or maintain the power of the majority. Remedial race-based preferences reflect the opposite impulse: a desire to foster equality in society. No sensible conception of the Government's constitutional obligation to 'govern impartially,' should ignore this distinction. . . ."

In their separate concurring opinions, Justices Scalia and Thomas stated their unequivocal opposition to affirmative action. Their position did not prevail in *Adarand*, but it could command a majority in some future case. For the present, the *Adarand* decision does not sound the death knell for affirmative action, but clearly increases the likelihood that federal affirmative action programs will be challenged and invalidated.

The *Hopwood* Case

In *Hopwood v. Texas* (1995) the Fifth U.S. Circuit Court of Appeals struck down an affirmative action program at the University of Texas law school. In an effort to obtain an entering class consisting of at least 10 percent Mexican-Americans and 5 percent blacks, the law school established lower test-score standards and created a separate admissions process for black and Mexican-American applicants. The court of appeals ruled that this system violated the rights of four unsuccessful white applicants. In a move that startled many observers, the court went further and held that the Supreme Court's landmark 1978 *Bakke* decision was no longer good law. In *Hopwood*, the Fifth Circuit court flatly stated that "the law school may not use race as a factor in law school admissions." This decision created a firestorm of controversy among civil rights groups and within higher education. Many commentators hoped and expected that the Supreme Court would grant certiorari. The Clinton administration, the District of Columbia, and nine states filed *amicus curiae* briefs in support of Texas's cert petition. But the Supreme Court was unmoved, denying cert on the closing day of the 1995 term. Two of the Court's more liberal members, Justices Ginsburg and Souter, produced a brief opinion stating that although affirmative action "is an issue of great national importance," the case presented no live controversy because the program that motivated the lawsuit to begin with had been discontinued. The denial of cert left the *Hopwood* decision intact, but *Hopwood* applies only within the three states (Texas, Louisiana, and Mississippi) that comprise the Fifth Circuit. This created an unusual legal situation in that while institutions of higher education in the Fifth Circuit are barred from using race as a criterion in their admissions, other colleges and universities across the country are under court order to do exactly that! Eventually, the Supreme Court will be compelled to take up this matter in order to standardize the law on this controversial issue.

Proposition 209

Buoyed by recent federal judicial decisions, opponents of affirmative action in California in 1996 succeeded in passing an amendment to the state constitution banning race and gender preferences in hiring and educational admissions. Proposition 209 provides that state and local government agencies in California may not discriminate against or grant preferential treatment to any individual or group on the basis of race, sex, color, ethnicity, or national origin. Within days after Proposition 209 was adopted by popular referendum, opponents went to federal court and obtained an injunction against its enforcement. But the federal district court eventually upheld the measure, as did the Ninth Circuit Court of Appeals. The Coalition for Economic Equity, which brought the suit, backed by civil rights groups across the country, asked the Supreme Court to grant review. But, as in the *Hopwood* case, the Court denied cert, at least in part because the controversy remained abstract (see *Coalition for Economic Equity v. Wilson* [1997]).

The Court's refusal to grant review in both *Hopwood* and the Proposition 209 case frustrated affirmative action supporters and opponents alike. But the Court was merely exercising self-restraint in not deciding an issue before it was necessary to do so. Eventually, however, the Court will have to confront these issues squarely. When it does, the outcome will depend, as always, on who is on the Court at the time. In 1998, it is fair to say that the Court's predisposition toward affirmative action is decidedly negative.

The Ongoing Problem of Racial Discrimination

Students will readily recall the enormous violence and destruction that ravaged areas of Los Angeles in early May 1992. The catalyst for the riot was the acquittal of several city police officers accused of brutality in the beating of African-American motorist Rodney King, who had been stopped by police for an automobile violation. The acquittal and subsequent riot sent shock waves through the American political and legal systems. People of all races questioned whether, nearly forty years after *Brown v. Board of Education,* the nation had made significant progress toward the constitutional ideal of racial justice. In the early 1990s, the terrible problems of America's inner cities, the disproportionate "representation" of African-Americans in the nation's prisons, and the persistence of racial animosity ensure that race will continue to be a serious political and legal problem for many years to come. For the Supreme Court in particular, the issue of racial equality remains a difficult challenge.

TO SUMMARIZE

- Affirmative action is a broad term referring to a variety of efforts designed to assist members of traditionally disfavored minority groups. It is manifested in three major areas of distributive policy: employment, government contracts, and higher education.
- The affirmative action concept emerged in the 1960s, and by the 1970s it was a major topic of litigation chiefly initiated by those who challenged it as "reverse discrimination."
- The Burger Court sought middle ground in the affirmative action area, approving the basic concept but rejecting its more rigid applications.
- The Rehnquist Court has taken a more negative view of affirmative action but has not repudiated the concept altogether.

GENDER-BASED DISCRIMINATION

Women are hardly a "discrete and insular minority." In fact, they comprise a majority of the adult population. Nevertheless, women have been historically subjected to considerable legal discrimination. Some of this discrimination was ostensibly benign, reflecting the paternalism of a patriarchal society. Not only were women once thought unfit to vote or hold public office, they were also regarded as in need of special protection from a cruel world. Thus, some **gender-based classifications** actually benefited females and burdened males. For example, a number of states and the federal government for a time maintained minimum-wage requirements for women but not for men. Most graphically, women have traditionally been exempted from compulsory military service.

Until very recently, the Supreme Court refused to recognize even the most blatant forms of sex discrimination as constitutionally offensive. In *Bradwell v. Illinois* (1873), the Court upheld an Illinois law that prohibited women from practicing law. Similarly, in *Minor v. Happersett* (1875), the Court held that women had no constitutional right to vote. Even as late as 1948, the Court upheld a Michigan law that prohibited women from serving as bartenders (see *Goesaert v. Cleary*). These decisions reflected broader societal attitudes that relegated women, much like African-Americans, to a position of social inferiority and second-class citizenship.

The Second World War did much to change the social status of women. Women in great numbers left the home and entered the industrial workplace, often assuming jobs many thought they were incapable of handling. By the 1970s, women had begun to compete with men for managerial and professional positions. Although women are still on average paid less than men, even for equal work, society has come to accept women in the workplace. Society is also learning to accept women in political roles: in Congress, in state legislatures, as mayors, governors, presidential candidates, and as justices of the Supreme Court. Naturally, the changing role of women is accompanied by demands for legal equality.

Congressional Responses to Demands for Sexual Equality

Congress responded to growing demands for legal equality between the sexes by passing the Equal Pay Act of 1963, the 1972 Amendments to Title VII of the Civil Rights Act

During the 1970s, women's rights became a major constitutional issue

of 1964, and Title IX of the Federal Education Act of 1972. The first and second of these statutes were aimed at eliminating sex discrimination in the workplace. The third authorized the withholding of federal funds from educational institutions that engaged in sex discrimination. These statutes have been an important source of civil rights for women and have given rise to a number of significant Supreme Court decisions. For example, in *Meritor Savings Bank v. Vinson* (1986), the Court held that Title VII of the Civil Rights Act of 1964 bars **sexual harassment** on the job.

The Equal Rights Amendment

In 1972, Congress attempted to broaden legal protection of women's rights by adopting a constitutional amendment that read as follows:

Section 1. Equality of rights under the law shall not be denied or abridged by the United States or by any State on account of sex.

Section 2. The Congress shall have the power to enforce, by appropriate legislation, the provisions of this article.

Section 3. This amendment shall take effect two years after the date of ratification.

Like all constitutional amendments, the **Equal Rights Amendment** (ERA) had to be ratified by at least three-fourths of the states to become part of the Constitution. Initially, the ERA met with much enthusiasm and little controversy in the state legislatures. By 1976, it had been ratified by thirty-five of the necessary thirty-eight states. However, in the late 1970s, opposition to the ERA crystallized in those states that had yet to ratify. Although Congress extended the period for ratification until 1982, the amendment ultimately failed to win approval by the requisite number of states.

Judicial Scrutiny of Gender-Based Discrimination

The demise of the Equal Rights Amendment left constitutional interpretation in the field of sex discrimination largely in the domain of the Fourteenth Amendment. In the early 1970s, it appeared that the Supreme Court was going to add sex to the list of "suspect classifications" under the Fourteenth Amendment. In *Reed v. Reed* (1971), the Court struck down a provision of the Idaho Probate Code that required probate judges to prefer males to females in appointing administrators of estates. Writing for the majority in *Reed,* Chief Justice Burger noted that "to give a mandatory preference to members of either sex over members of the other . . . is to make the very kind of arbitrary legislative choice forbidden by the Equal Protection Clause."

In *Frontiero v. Richardson* (1973), the Supreme Court divided 8 to 1 (Justice Rehnquist dissenting) in upholding Lt. Sharron Frontiero's claim that the Air Force violated the equal protection component of the Fifth Amendment in requiring women, but not men, to demonstrate that their spouses were in fact dependents for the purpose of receiving medical and dental benefits. While the Court was receptive to the equal protection claim, it was unable to achieve majority support for the proposition that sex is a suspect classification. Expressing the views of four members of the Court, Justice Brennan's plurality opinion was unequivocal in declaring gender-based discrimination to be inherently suspect and thus presumptively unconstitutional:

. . . [S]ince sex, like race and national origin, is an immutable characteristic determined solely by the accident of birth, the imposition of special disabilities upon the members of a particular sex because of their sex would seem to violate "the basic concept of our system that legal burdens should bear some relationship to individual responsibility. . . ."

The remaining four members of the majority were not prepared to go so far. In an opinion concurring in the judgment only, Justice Powell wrote that "[i]t is unnecessary for the Court in this case to characterize sex as a suspect classification, with all of the far-reaching implications of such a holding."

Heightened Scrutiny

As yet, the Court has not officially recognized sex discrimination as inherently suspect, but it has nevertheless invalidated a number of gender-based policies under a "heightened scrutiny" or "intermediate scrutiny" approach. For example, in *Weinberger v. Wiesenfeld* (1975), the Court unanimously voided a provision of the Social Security Act that authorized survivors' benefits for the widows of deceased workers but withheld them for men in the same situation. Similarly, in *Califano v. Goldfarb* (1977), a sharply divided Court struck down another Social Security requirement that widowers, but not widows, had to demonstrate their financial dependence on their deceased spouses as a condition for obtaining survivors' benefits.

In *Craig v. Boren* (1976), the Court articulated a test for judging gender-based policies under the intermediate standard of review. According to this test, a gender-based policy must be substantially related to an important government objective. Presumably, this test is stricter than the rational basis test but less strict than the compelling state interest test.

In *Craig v. Boren,* the Court struck down an Oklahoma law that forbade the sale of "3.2 beer" to females under the age of eighteen and males under twenty-one. Oklahoma attempted to justify the statute as a means of promoting its interest in traffic safety, citing data that were purported to show that men in the eighteen to twenty-one age bracket were more likely to be arrested for drunk driving than were women in the same age bracket. Unpersuaded by the statistical evidence, the Court held that the state had failed to demonstrate a substantial relationship between its sexually discriminatory policy and its admittedly important interest in traffic safety. In a sharp dissent, Justice Rehnquist challenged the new intermediate standard of equal protection review. In Rehnquist's view, the terms "important objective" and "substantial relation" were so " . . . elastic as to invite subjective judicial preferences or prejudices." Despite this criticism, the Court has maintained the intermediate standard of review for gender-based policies.

In *Orr v. Orr* (1979), the Court considered the question of differential alimony requirements for men and women. The Alabama law in question required divorced men, under certain circumstances, to make alimony payments to their ex-wives but exempted women in the same circumstances from paying alimony to their ex-husbands. Somewhat disingenuously, the state argued that its gender-based alimony policy was designed to compensate women for economic discrimination produced by the institution of marriage. The Court accepted the state's asserted interest as both legitimate and important but rejected the argument that its alimony policy was substantially related to the achievement of this objective. Writing for the Court, Justice Brennan asserted that

Alabama's alleged compensatory purpose may be effectuated without placing burdens solely on husbands. Progress toward fulfillment of such a purpose would not be hampered, and it would cost the state nothing more, if it were to treat men and women equally by making alimony burdens independent of sex. . . . Thus, "[t]he [wives] who benefit from the disparate treatment are those who were . . . nondependent on their husbands. . . ." They are precisely those who are not "needy spouses" and who are the "least likely to have been victims of discrimination" by the institution of marriage.

The preceding sample of cases is not meant to suggest that the Supreme Court's sex-discrimination decisions have uniformly cut in one direction. On the contrary, the flexible approach to sex discrimination employed by the Court has resulted in a number of decisions upholding challenged gender-based policies. For example, in *Kahn v. Shevin* (1974), the Court let stand a Florida statute that gave property tax exemptions to widows but not widowers. According to Justice William O. Douglas's majority opinion, the distinction was

> reasonably designed to further the state policy of cushioning the financial impact of spousal loss upon the sex for which that loss imposes a disproportionately heavy burden. . . . The financial difficulties confronting the lone woman in Florida or any other state exceed those facing the man.

The same year, in *Geduldig v. Aiello* (1974), the Court upheld a state health insurance policy that excluded pregnancy from the list of disabilities for which a state employee could be compensated. In approving the policy, the Court concluded that it did not discriminate

> against any definable group or class in terms of the aggregate risk protection derived by the group or class from the program. There is no risk from which men are protected and women are not. Likewise, there is no risk from which women are protected and men are not.

Not surprisingly, a number of observers took issue with the Court's assumption that a state's refusal to extend its disability policy to include pregnancy was **gender neutral.**

One of the most controversial issues in the area of sex discrimination is the role that women should play in military service. Opponents of the Equal Rights Amendment argued that adoption of the amendment would result in women being drafted into combat, a prospect that many people still find unacceptable. In *Rostker v. Goldberg* (1981), the Supreme Court considered the constitutionality of the male-only draft registration law. Emphasizing its traditional deference to Congress in the area of military affairs, the Court upheld the challenged policy by a vote of 6 to 3. Writing for the majority, Justice Rehnquist asserted that exclusion of women from the draft "was not an 'accidental by-product of a traditional way of thinking about women.'" According to Justice Rehnquist, men and women "are simply not similarly situated for purposes of a draft or registration for a draft." No doubt many women and men would challenge Rehnquist's assumption, especially in light of the expanded role women played in the war against Iraq in early 1991. It is difficult to say with any precision what principles have guided the Court's treatment of sex discrimination cases under the intermediate scrutiny approach. Perhaps each decision rests on each justice's intuitive sense of whether the challenged discrimination is "benign" or "invidious." As Justice Oliver Wendell Holmes, Jr., pointed out in his dissent in *Lochner v. New York* (1905), judicial decisions often "depend on a judgment or intuition more subtle than any articulate major premise." What Holmes was suggesting was that judicial decision making is preeminently political behavior: that any exercise in legal methodology is subordinate to the assertion of judicial values. While this position can be overstated, one cannot examine the history of American constitutional decision making and deny the essential validity of Holmes's observation.

Sex Discrimination by Educational Institutions

In perhaps the most significant of its sex discrimination decisions, the Burger Court voted 5 to 4 to require the Mississippi University for Women (MUW) to admit a male student to its nursing school (*MUW v. Hogan* [1982]). Joe Hogan was a registered nurse working in Columbus, the city where MUW is located. Lacking a bachelor's degree, he applied for admission to the MUW nursing program and was denied solely on account of sex, although the school did inform him that he could register on a noncredit basis. Rather than quit his job to enroll in another state institution, Hogan filed suit. The state of Mississippi argued that operating a school solely for women compensated for sex discrimination in the past. Additionally, the state argued that the presence of men would detract from the performance of female students. Writing for the Supreme Court, Justice O'Connor gave both of the state's arguments short shrift. Justice O'Connor rejected the "compensation" argument as contrived since the state had made no showing that women had historically lacked opportunities in the field of nursing. O'Connor then pointed out that the state's argument that male students would adversely affect the performance of females was undermined by the university's willingness to accept male students as auditors. In O'Connor's view, the principal effect of the female-only nursing program was to "perpetuate the stereotyped view of nursing as an exclusively women's job."

In a strongly worded dissent, Justice Powell asserted that the Court's decision adversely affected the opportunities of women by forbidding the "States from providing women with an opportunity to choose the type of university they prefer." Powell further suggested that the Court's decision

> bows deeply to conformity. Left without honor . . . is an element of diversity that has characterized much of American education and enriched much of American life.

The *Hogan* decision addressed the question of whether state-operated professional schools could limit enrollment to one sex. It did not address the broader question of whether publicly operated or supported educational institutions generally may constitutionally impose such restrictions. Of course, the only two state-supported institutions of higher education limiting enrollment to members of one sex were military schools—the Citadel in Charleston, South Carolina, and Virginia Military Institute (VMI) in Blacksburg. In the wake of the *Hogan* decision, young women seeking admission to these institutions brought suit in federal court. Ultimately, they prevailed.

In one of the most widely anticipated decisions of the 1990s, *United States v. Virginia* (1996), the Supreme Court struck down VMI's male-only admissions policy. In so doing, the Court closed the book on a case that had been in litigation for nearly six years. The suit had been brought by the Justice Department, after a complaint was filed by a female high school student who wanted to go to VMI but was barred from doing so by the Institute's prohibition against admitting women.

In a 7-to-1 decision, the Supreme Court, speaking through Justice Ginsburg, ruled that the state of Virginia had "fallen far short of establishing the 'exceedingly persuasive justification,' that must be the solid base for any gender-defined classification. . . ." Although the Court rejected the argument advanced by the Clinton

Ruth Bader Ginsburg: Associate Justice, 1993–

administration that sex discrimination should be subjected to the same "strict scrutiny" the courts apply to race discrimination, Justice Ginsburg's opinion suggested that the current Court has increased the level of scrutiny applied to policies that treat men and women differently. According to Ginsburg, the Court should apply a "skeptical scrutiny" under which government must demonstrate an "exceedingly persuasive justification" for any gender discrimination. "The justification must be genuine, not hypothesized or invented *post hoc* in response to litigation," said Ginsburg. Moreover, it must not rely on "overbroad generalizations about the different talents, capacities, or preferences of males and females."

Although technically applicable only to the VMI case, the decision in *United States v. Virginia* affected the resolution of a similar widely publicized case involving the Citadel in South Carolina. In fact, within days after the VMI decision was announced, the Citadel's governing board voted unanimously to eliminate sex as a criterion for admission, ending a 154-year tradition of admitting only men.

The sweeping character of the Court's opinion seemed to imply that it would be extremely difficult for any state to defend any single-sex educational institution. Chief Justice Rehnquist, who concurred in the judgment only, adopted a more restrained position. For Rehnquist, the state had failed in its obligation to provide equal protection because it had not demonstrated any serious effort to provide comparable opportunities to women who were interested in the kind of "citizen-soldier" training that men receive at VMI. According to Rehnquist, it was "not the 'exclusion of women' that violate[d] the Equal Protection Clause, but the maintenance of an all-men school without providing any—much less a comparable—institution for women." Rehnquist's opinion left open the possibility that single-sex public higher education might, under certain circumstances, pass constitutional muster. Of course, Rehnquist's concurrence is just one person's opinion. Six justices representing the Court's liberal and moderate blocs clearly wanted to make a stronger and a more definitive statement.

In another of his scathing dissents, Justice Scalia asserted that the majority's "amorphous 'exceedingly persuasive justification' phrase" was an unwarranted departure from the "heightened scrutiny" test used by the Court in gender-discrimination cases. Scalia concluded by lamenting the fact that, in his view, "single-sex public education is functionally dead." Scalia expressed his regret that the Court had, in his view, "shut down an institution that has served the people of the commonwealth of Virginia with pride and distinction for over a century and a half." He ended by observing that "I do not think any of us, women included, will be better off for its destruction."

Not surprisingly, Justice Scalia's sentiments were shared by students, faculty, and administrators at VMI. Major General Josiah Bunting III, the superintendent of VMI, described the Court's decision as a "savage disappointment." Of course, women's rights groups hailed the decision as a major victory.

Gender Equity in Collegiate Athletics

Intercollegiate athletics, once the sole province of men, has witnessed considerable change in recent years. Under the rubric of **gender equity,** state colleges and universities have been putting more resources into women's athletic programs. Still, there are some who believe that forbidding women to participate in male-only athletic programs at state institutions constitutes invidious discrimination. Is the separate but equal doctrine appropriate when considering collegiate athletics? Suppose a female student wants to play football at a state university. Since the university does not have a women's football program, does the Equal Protection Clause require the university to let the woman try out for the men's team? While some may feel that such issues trivialize the Constitution, these matters tend to be far from trivial in the minds of plaintiffs.

TO SUMMARIZE

- Since the 1970s, the Supreme Court has recognized that the Equal Protection Clause imposes significant restrictions on official discrimination on the basis of gender.
- The failure of the effort to ratify the Equal Rights Amendment left the issue of gender discrimination solely within the province of the Equal Protection Clause as interpreted by the courts.
- The Court has applied an intermediate standard of review in judging classifications based on gender, often finding that such classifications merely perpetuate sex-based stereotypes.
- The Court's most important decisions in this area have focused on discrimination against women in the military and in public institutions of higher education.

OTHER FORMS OF DISCRIMINATION

By the late 1990s, the only suspect classifications that have been identified by the Supreme Court are those based on race, national origin, and religious affiliation. As previously noted, gender-based classifications, which are the subject of much current controversy, have not been added to the inventory of suspect classifications. Rather, sex discrimination, along with several other types of discrimination, occupies a middle tier in what has become a complex, multitiered approach to judging challenged classifications.

Illegitimacy

Although laws discriminating against persons based on **illegitimacy** have not been declared to be inherently suspect, blatant instances of this type of discrimination have been invalidated. For example, in *Weber v. Aetna Casualty and Surety Company* (1972), the Supreme Court struck down a Louisiana law barring illegitimate offspring from collecting death benefits under workers' compensation. And in *Jimenez v. Weinberger* (1974), the Court invalidated a federal provision that denied welfare benefits to the illegitimate dependent children of disabled persons. However, in a case reminiscent of the landmark sex discrimination case *Reed v. Reed*, the Court upheld a law subordinating illegitimate offspring to other relatives in determining intestate succession (*Labine v. Vincent* [1971]). And in *Lalli v. Lalli* (1978), the Court upheld a law allowing illegitimate children to inherit from their intestate fathers only if paternity had been judicially determined during the lifetime of the deceased.

More recently, in *Michael H. v. Gerald D.* (1989), the Court upheld a California statute that created a legal presumption that a child born to a married woman living with her husband is the product of that marriage, thus making it more difficult for natural fathers of children who are the product of extramarital affairs to establish paternity. While clear principles are difficult to discern in this area, the Court has not hesitated to invalidate laws it perceives to be based solely on prejudice against illegitimate children. At the same time, however, it has recognized the primacy of the nuclear family and the social undesirability of producing children outside of wedlock.

Persons with Disabilities

Although persons with disabilities can be viewed as constituting a "discrete and insular minority," policies and practices that discriminate against such persons have not been recognized as "inherently suspect" under the Fourteenth Amendment. Nor has the Supreme Court yet held that the Constitution imposes an obligation on government to equalize physical access for persons with handicaps to government buildings or other physical facilities. Arguably, a government's failure to provide a wheelchair ramp at a place where votes are cast could be viewed as an unreasonable burden on the exercise of a "fundamental right." Congress has attempted to increase access to the polls for persons with handicaps through passage of the Voting Accessibility Act of 1984. For the most part Congress, not the Supreme Court, has taken the lead in recognizing the rights of persons with handicaps. With the passage of Title V of the Rehabilitation Act of 1973, the Education for all Handicapped Children Act of 1975, and especially the **Americans with Disabilities Act** of 1990, Congress has attempted to remove barriers confronting persons with disabilities in such areas as employment, education, and public transportation. Some commentators have criticized the Supreme Court for narrowly interpreting legislation in this field, thus constraining the rights of persons with disabilities. Others believe Congress and the courts have gone too far in this area, creating difficult problems for local governments, schools systems, and businesses.

Certainly the Supreme Court has not been completely insensitive to the rights of individuals with handicaps. For example, in *Cleburne v. Cleburne Living Center* (1985), the Court struck down a zoning law that had been applied to prohibit a home for persons with mental retardation from operating in a residential neighborhood. Justice White's majority opinion not only rejected the argument that retardation is a suspect classification but also rejected the lower court's characterization of retardation as "quasi-suspect." Opting for the traditional standard of review, Justice White nevertheless found no rational basis for the city's decision. The *Cleburne* case demonstrates that the rational basis standard is not necessarily synonymous with judicial deference.

Residency and Alienage

The Fifth and Fourteenth Amendments do not protect citizens alone from arbitrary or unjust government actions. Rather, the amendments use the broader term "persons." The Supreme Court has stressed the text of the Fourteenth Amendment in striking down a number of state laws that differentiate between residents and nonresidents or between citizens and aliens. For example, in *Shapiro v. Thompson* (1969), the Supreme Court struck down a series of laws that imposed one-year waiting periods on new state residents seeking welfare benefits. Then, in *Sugarman v. Dougall* (1973), the Court struck down a New York law that denied civil service jobs to aliens. In 1976, the Court extended this ruling to invalidate similar federal civil service restrictions *(Hampton v. Mow Sun Wong).*

In a controversial 1982 decision, the Supreme Court went so far as to invalidate discrimination against the children of illegal aliens. In *Plyler v. Doe,* the Court voted 5 to 4 to strike down a Texas law that denied free public education to the children of illegal immigrants. Using "heightened scrutiny," Justice Brennan found no "substantial interest" of the state to justify the denial of educational benefits to the children of illegal aliens. Dissenting sharply, Chief Justice Burger complained that "if ever a court was guilty of an unabashedly result-oriented approach, this case is a prime example." The Court's decisions in *Shapiro v. Thompson* and *Plyler v. Doe* involved not merely the distinction between residents and nonresidents or between legal residents and illegal aliens, they also implicated the underlying issue of poverty.

Wealth, Poverty, and Equal Protection

Discrimination based on wealth has never been held to be inherently suspect, although some justices on the Supreme Court have indicated a desire to do so. However, the Court has often invalidated forms of economic discrimination that prevent individuals from exercising their constitutional rights. Wealth-based discriminations that burden fundamental rights have been subjected to strict judicial scrutiny; those that do not involve fundamental rights have been judged by the traditional rational basis test. For example, in the case of *Shapiro v. Thompson,* described in the last section, the Court found that the state residency requirement infringed the fundamental right of interstate travel. Similarly, in *Harper v. Virginia State Board of Elections* (1966), the Supreme Court invalidated a state's poll tax as a denial of equal protection. Certainly the imposition of a tax on voting can be seen as a burden on the exercise of a fundamental right (see Chapter 13).

In *Gideon v. Wainwright* (1963), the Court, relying on the Sixth Amendment right to counsel, required states to appoint counsel for indigent defendants accused of felonies. On the same day, in *Douglas v. California,* the Court required states to provide counsel to indigent defendants seeking appellate review in state courts. These wealth-discrimination rulings of the Warren Court were closely related to the maintenance of procedural due process in the context of criminal prosecutions (see Chapter 10).

To what extent does the Equal Protection Clause require the equalization of services or benefits provided by state and local governments? Can a city's provision of public goods, such as roads, sewage systems, parks, and recreational facilities, vary according to neighborhood property tax revenues? The answer depends on whether such discriminations involve fundamental rights or "interests." But which interests are "fundamental"? Is education a fundamental right?

The Controversy over Public School Funding

In *San Antonio v. Rodriguez* (1973), the Court considered a challenge to the Texas system of financing public schools primarily through local property taxes. The Texas system, which is similar to that employed in most states, resulted in dramatically different amounts of money being spent among the state's school districts. In reviewing the Texas system of school funding, a sharply divided Court employed the traditional rational basis test, refusing to recognize wealth as a suspect classification. Using this approach, the Court found no constitutional violation. According to Justice Powell's majority opinion, the school finance system

> allegedly discriminates against a large, diverse, and amorphous class, unified only by the common factor of residence in districts which happen to have less taxable wealth than other districts. The system of alleged discrimination and the class it defines have none of the traditional indicia of suspectness; the class is not saddled with such disabilities, or subjected to such history of purposeful unequal treatment, or relegated to such a position of political powerlessness as to command extraordinary protection from the majoritarian political process.

Justice Marshall protested vehemently in *Rodriguez,* arguing that education was a "fundamental interest" and that "poverty" was indeed a "suspect classification." According to Justice Marshall,

> [the] Court has never suggested that because some "adequate" level of benefits is provided to all, discrimination in the provision of services is therefore constitutionally excusable. The Equal Protection Clause is not addressed to the minimal sufficiency but to the unjustifiable inequalities of state action.

The Supreme Court's interpretation of the Fourteenth Amendment in Rodriguez in no way prevents state courts from adopting a contrary view of the relevant provisions of their state constitutions. Indeed, the California Supreme Court did so in *Serrano v. Priest* (1971). Since then, more than twenty state supreme courts have followed suit in holding that disparities in funding among school districts violate state constitutional requirements of equal protection. This trend nicely illustrates the principle of **judicial federalism,** under which state courts are free to interpret their state laws in a way that provides additional rights beyond those secured by federal law. At a time in which the U.S. Supreme Court is dominated by conservatives, advocates of civil rights and liberties may find state tribunals receptive to claims that would be rejected by the federal courts.

Restriction of Abortion Funding for Indigent Women

Another controversial issue reaching the Burger Court under the aegis of the New Equal Protection was the dispute over legislative efforts to cut off government funds to support abortions. In *Maher v. Roe* (1977), the Court upheld the constitutionality of a Connecticut policy withholding Medicaid payments for nonessential abortions. Writing for a majority of six justices, Justice Powell opined that

> [a]n indigent woman desiring an abortion does not come within the limited category of disadvantaged classes so recognized by our cases. Nor does the fact that the impact of the regulation falls upon those who cannot pay lead to a different conclusion. In a sense, every denial of welfare to an indigent creates a wealth classification as compared to nonindigents who are able to pay for the desired goods or services. But this Court has never held that financial need alone identifies a suspect class for purposes of Equal Protection analysis.

Subsequently, in *Harris v. McRae* (1980), the Court upheld the **Hyde Amendment,** a federal law that severely limited the use of federal funds to support abortions for indigent women. Writing for the sharply divided bench, Justice Stewart observed that

> [t]he Hyde Amendment, like the Connecticut welfare regulation at issue in *Maher,* places no governmental obstacle in the path of a woman who chooses to terminate her pregnancy, but rather, by means of unequal subsidization of abortion and other medical services, encourages alternative activity deemed in the public interest. The present case does differ factually from *Maher* insofar as that case involved a failure to fund nontherapeutic abortions, whereas the Hyde Amendment withholds funding of certain medically necessary abortions.

Nevertheless, Justice Stewart concluded that

> [h]ere as in *Maher,* the principal impact of the Hyde Amendment falls on the indigent. But that fact does not itself render the funding restriction constitutionally invalid, for this Court has held repeatedly that poverty, standing alone, is not a suspect classification. . . .

Dissenting, Justice Marshall chastised the majority for its insensitivity to the plight of the poor, saying that "[t]here is another world 'out there,' the existence of which the Court . . . either chooses to ignore or refuses to recognize." In Marshall's view, "it is only by blinding itself to that other world" that the Court could uphold the Hyde Amendment. (This issue is also addressed in Chapter 11.)

Possible Interpretations of Economic Equal Protection

Although most commentators have associated an expansion of the Equal Protection Clause to protect economic interests with liberal, redistributive policy objectives, such a broadening of equal protection might well turn out to be a double-edged sword. If a more conservative Supreme Court were to make "wealth," as distinct from "poverty," a suspect classification, then government presumably would have to show a compelling interest to justify progressive taxation, subsidies, and a host of redistributive policies. Just as the Due Process Clause was once used to frustrate progressivism, populism, and the New Deal, so the Equal Protection Clause could conceivably be employed by a more conservative Supreme Court to attack the welfare state.

As we have pointed out repeatedly in this book, constitutional language, such as "due process" and "equal protection," is sufficiently broad to embrace various potential applications. Indeed, socialists could "find" in the Equal Protection Clause a requirement that government equalize material conditions in society. Similarly, the Takings Clause of the Fifth Amendment could be cited to provide a constitutional justification for the nationalization of private industries. This is not to say that the Constitution has no plain or obvious meanings, which it surely does. It is only to say that certain language in the Constitution, such as the Equal Protection Clause, is written broadly enough to allow for various, even opposing, interpretations. The constitutional values that are actualized through decision making depend greatly on the political ideologies of the justices who happen to be on the Court and on the broader political culture within which the Court functions.

Discrimination on the Basis of Sexual Orientation

While some states and cities have enacted laws protecting homosexuals against discrimination in housing, employment, and the like, there is no such protection under federal civil rights laws. Moreover, the federal courts have had little to say about "gay rights" in terms of the equal protection requirements of the Constitution.

One question of gay rights that came to the fore during the 1980s was the military's policy of discharging persons who admitted to being homosexual. In *Watkins v. U.S. Army* (1988), the U.S. Court of Appeals for the Ninth Circuit invalidated this policy. Writing for the court, Judge Norris concluded that "the Army's regulations violate the constitutional guarantee of equal protection of the laws because they discriminate against persons of homosexual orientation, a suspect class, and because the regulations are not necessary to promote a legitimate compelling governmental interest." On *en banc* rehearing the Court of Appeals affirmed the judgment but did so on nonconstitutional grounds, finding it "unnecessary to reach the constitutional issues. . . ." The Supreme Court denied certiorari, thus leaving open the constitutional question as to whether the military's ban on homosexuals violates constitutional equal protection standards. Shortly after his election to the presidency in November 1992, Bill Clinton announced that he intended to issue an executive order abolishing the military's ban on homosexuals. But a firestorm of controversy caused Clinton to back down. Instead, Clinton issued an order instituting a "don't ask, don't tell" policy in the military. Although this approach has alleviated some of the conflict over gays in the military, gay rights activists have continued to press the issue in the courts. As yet, the Supreme Court has not addressed the question.

In 1996, however, the Court did take up the issue of gay rights in a case involving an unusual legal measure. In what may turn out to be a pivotal decision in this area, the Court in *Romer v. Evans* struck down Colorado's controversial Amendment 2, which banned state and local government from providing various legal protections for gays and lesbians. Writing for a majority of six, Justice Kennedy concluded that "Amendment 2 . . . in making a general announcement that gays and lesbians shall not have any particular protections from the law, inflicts on them immediate, continuing, and real injuries that outrun and belie any legitimate justifications that may be claimed for it." In dissent, Justice Scalia argued that Amendment 2 "is not the manifestation of a 'bare . . . desire to harm' homosexuals, but is rather a modest attempt by seemingly tolerant Coloradans to preserve traditional sexual mores against the efforts of a politically powerful minority to revise those mores through use of the laws." Scalia attacked the reasoning of the majority, saying that the Court's opinion "has no foundation in American constitutional law, and barely pretends to." But the Court concluded that "it is not within our constitutional tradition to enact laws of this sort." Justice Kennedy opined that "a law declaring that in general it shall be more difficult for one group of citizens than for all others to seek aid from the government is itself a denial of equal protection of the laws in the most literal sense."

The *Romer* decision halts a movement in which communities around the country sought to copy the Colorado amendment. Law professor Susan Bloch of Georgetown University has observed that the Colorado amendment was "the most vulnerable to constitutional challenge" because it represented "the essence of what it is to deny people equal protection of the law." Justice Kennedy seemed to make the same point in the majority opinion, asserting that Amendment 2 was unconstitutional because "it identifies persons by a single trait and then denies them equal protection across the board." This suggests that Kennedy, as well as the other moderate members of the Court, might have been more sympathetic to a measure that merely outlawed preferential treatment for gays and lesbians. It may be that the Court will be called upon to rule on other, perhaps narrower, versions of Amendment 2 in the future. Of course, other gay rights issues remain on the Supreme Court's horizon, including same-sex marriage and the "gays in the military" controversy. Intense partisans on both sides of the gay rights debate will be watching closely as the Supreme Court navigates its way through this cultural minefield.

TO SUMMARIZE

- The Supreme Court has recognized constitutional issues of discrimination in a number of other areas, including classifications based on wealth, residency, alienage, illegitimacy, age, and disability. To the extent that discriminatory practices in these areas impinge on fundamental rights, the Court has subjected them to strict scrutiny. Otherwise, the court has employed the rational basis test or in some instances heightened scrutiny.
- The Court has taken a decidedly conservative approach in dealing with the issue of discrimination against the poor. The Court has, for example, refused to invalidate local systems of public school finance alleged to disadvantage poor students and has upheld restrictions on public funding of nontherapeutic abortions for indigent women.
- One of the most controversial issues in the equal protection area involves discrimination against gays and lesbians. The Supreme Court has recently indicated its willingness to scrutinize public policies in this area.

THE ONGOING PROBLEM OF PRIVATE DISCRIMINATION

The repudiation of the separate but equal doctrine in *Brown* and subsequent decisions led to the virtual disappearance of *de jure* racial segregation, that is, segregation required or created by law or public policy. Yet, ***de facto* segregation** in housing, employment, and education nevertheless still exists to a great extent, as a function of both social norms and economic disparities. As the Supreme Court held as far back as 1883 (see *The Civil Rights Cases*), segregation that is purely *de facto* is beyond the purview of the Equal Protection Clause per se. Many forms of *de facto* segregation, however, may be within the remedial power of both state and federal statutes. For example, under the Fair Housing Act of 1968, Congress prohibited racial discrimination in the rental or sale of homes where the transaction is handled by a licensed agent. The questions surrounding such attempts at eradicating *de facto* discrimination are by no means closed.

As we previously noted, the Supreme Court in 1883 drew a sharp distinction between racial discrimination that is purely private in character and that which is supported by state action. Without formally overruling *The Civil Rights Cases*, the Court has blurred this distinction as applied to racial discrimination. Nevertheless, the Court has shown no inclination to abandon the state action doctrine. For example, in the case of a racially restrictive private club's refusal to serve the African-American guest of a white member, the Court determined that the mere grant of a liquor license did not convert the club's discriminatory policy into state action under the Fourteenth Amendment (*Moose Lodge v. Irvis* [1972]). A decade earlier, in *Burton v. Wilmington Parking Authority* (1961), the Court had found state action when a state agency leased property to a restaurant that refused to serve African-Americans. Legalistically, whether there is state action in support of discrimination depends on whether there is a "close nexus" between the functions of the state and the private discrimination. More realistically, it probably depends on whether circumstances foster a perception that the state approves of the discrimination at issue.

Blacks attempt to order lunch at a "whites only" lunch counter

Restrictive Covenants

A classic form of private discrimination was the **restrictive covenant** in which a group of homeowners agreed not to sell or rent their homes to African-Americans, Jews, and other disfavored minorities. Under the decision in *The Civil Rights Cases,* this purely private form of racial discrimination was deemed to be beyond the purview of the Equal Protection Clause. However, in *Shelley v. Kraemer* (1948), the Supreme Court held such covenants to be unenforceable in state courts, because any such enforcement would amount to state action in contravention of the Fourteenth Amendment. Arguably, for a state court to enforce such an agreement would foster a public perception that the state approves of racially restrictive covenants. On the other hand, it would be a mistake to conclude that the mere judicial enforcement of every private agreement necessarily constitutes state action for purposes of the Fourteenth Amendment. In fact, ordinary contracts and other private transactions are generally not brought within the limitations of the Fourteenth Amendment merely because they are enforced in court. *Shelley v. Kraemer* seems to stand for the proposition that questions of private racial discrimination constitute a unique category.

Although restrictive covenants are no longer judicially enforceable, racial restrictions are still written into many deeds, a fact that aroused considerable public attention during the 1986 Senate confirmation hearings on the elevation of William Rehnquist to be chief justice. In the course of these hearings, it was revealed that the deed to a piece of property owned by Rehnquist himself contained a restrictive covenant.

Finally, it should be noted that although the decision in *The Civil Rights Cases* has not been overruled, Congress has employed its broad powers, chiefly under the

Commerce Clause (Article I, Section 8) to prohibit racial discrimination by places of public accommodation whose operations affect interstate commerce (see Chapter 2). In *Heart of Atlanta Motel v. United States* (1964), the Supreme Court upheld Title II of the 1964 Civil Rights Act, thus allowing Congress to accomplish under its commerce power what the Court in 1883 prevented it from doing under the Fourteenth Amendment.

State Powers to Prohibit Private Discrimination

Historically, the state governments were anything but leaders in the struggle for civil rights. Yet today, many states have civil rights or **human rights statutes.** An emerging constitutional issue is the extent to which states can act affirmatively to foster integration. Can a state adopt legislation that outlaws racial discrimination in the places of public accommodation perceived as not currently subject to federal civil rights laws? Can the states require "quasi-public" organizations, such as the Rotary Club, the Kiwanis, or the Jaycees, to admit women? What about private social clubs? Can the states require racially or religiously exclusive country clubs to admit those their membership policies currently exclude? Here, we have a classic confrontation between the state's legitimate interest in eradicating invidious discrimination and the freedom of association protected by the First and Fourteenth Amendments. In the landmark decision *Roberts v. United States Jaycees* (1984) (discussed and reprinted in Chapter 8), the Court upheld a Minnesota human rights law requiring a civic organization to accept women as full members, despite the organization's reliance on the First Amendment. For Justice Brennan, the state's interest in eradicating discrimination was more compelling than the Jaycees' claim to free association. However, Justice O'Connor was careful to point out that the Jaycees behaved more like a commercial enterprise than a political organization or a private club. Justice O'Connor's concurrence left open the question of whether "less public" entities are subject to state intervention.

The principle articulated in the *Jaycees* decision has been followed fairly consistently by the Supreme Court. For example, in 1987, the Court unanimously extended this principle to encompass the Rotary Club as well *(Rotary International v. Rotary Club of Duarte)*. Likewise, in 1988, a unanimous Court relied on *Roberts v. Jaycees* in upholding a New York City ordinance that required certain all-male social clubs to admit women *(New York Club Association v. City of New York)*.

On the other hand, the Court has shown that it is not interested in completely eviscerating the First Amendment right of free association to achieve the goal of ending discrimination. In *Hurley v. Irish-American Gay, Lesbian and Bisexual Group of Boston* (1995), the Court held that the state of Massachusetts could not prohibit a private organization from excluding a gay rights group from its annual St. Patrick's Day parade (see Chapter 8). A state court had ruled that gay groups could not be excluded under Massachusetts' **public accommodations statute.** The Supreme Court reversed, holding that the state could not compel the parade's organizers to promote a message of which they disapproved. Some commentators suggested that the Court's decision might reflect animus toward gays and lesbians and wondered whether the decision would have been the same had the parade's organizers sought to exclude women or African-Americans. Others argued that the Court had struck a blow for freedom from state coercion.

TO SUMMARIZE

- The Supreme Court held long ago that the prohibitions of the Fourteenth Amendment extend only to discrimination fostered by government. Thus, to challenge a particular discriminatory practice under the Equal Protection Clause, a plaintiff must demonstrate that there is "state action" in support of the challenged practice.
- The existence of state action in support of discrimination depends on whether there is a "close nexus" between the functions of the state and the challenged discriminatory practice.
- Discrimination that is purely *de facto* or private in nature is beyond the reach of the Fourteenth Amendment. However, such discrimination may violate federal, state, and local laws, such as the laws prohibiting discrimination by places of public accommodation.

CONCLUSION

In a brief introductory essay such as this, it is impossible to discuss all the important issues of equal protection, both actual and potential. After more than two decades of the New Equal Protection, it is clear that any government policy that differentiates among identifiable groups poses a potential equal protection problem. For example, as longevity of the American population increases and more people stay on the job beyond the traditional age of retirement, discrimination against the elderly is becoming a more prominent equal protection issue. Another issue on the horizon is whether laws forbidding single-sex marriage unreasonably discriminate against homosexuals.

In spite of recent changes in the ideological makeup of the Supreme Court, there exists an elaborate framework of statutes and judicial decisions reflecting a strong national commitment to the antidiscrimination principle. Some observers may view recent limitations on affirmative action programs and disengagement of the federal courts from supervision of public school desegregation as departures from this commitment. The antidiscrimination principle, however, is far broader than specific remedial measures adopted to address immediate problems. The fundamental commitment to this principle is likely to outlast ephemeral changes in the political landscape.

Politically, one of the most important applications of the Equal Protection Clause has been to the historic problem of legislative malapportionment. This problem, along with other issues related to the themes of representation and political participation, is examined in Chapter 13.

KEY TERMS

Equal Protection Clause	strict judicial scrutiny	Black Codes	desegregation
New Equal Protection	presumption of	Civil Rights Act of 1875	all deliberate speed
fundamental rights	constitutionality	places of public	court-ordered busing
rational basis test	burden of proof	accommodation	*de jure* discrimination
discrete and insular	compelling interest	Jim Crow laws	affirmative action
minorities	disparate impact	separate but equal doctrine	race-conscious remedies
suspect classification	heightened scrutiny	state action doctrine	group rights
doctrine	Civil Rights Act of 1866	Civil Rights Act of 1964	set-aside

consent decrees	gender neutral	judicial federalism	human rights statutes
gender-based classifications	gender equity	Hyde Amendment	public accommodations
sexual harassment	illegitimacy	*de facto* segregation	statute
Equal Rights Amendment	Americans with Disabilities Act	restrictive covenant	

FOR FURTHER READING

Baer, Judith. *Equality Under the Constitution: Reclaiming the Fourteenth Amendment.* Ithaca, N.Y.: Cornell University Press, 1983.

Berger, Raoul. *Government by Judiciary: The Transformation of the Fourteenth Amendment.* Cambridge, Mass.: Harvard University Press, 1977.

Finch, Minnie. *The NAACP: Its Fight for Justice.* Metuchen, N.J.: Scarecrow Press, 1981.

Franklin, John Hope. *From Slavery to Freedom: A History of Negro Americans.* New York: Knopf, 1980.

Ginsberg, Ruth. *Constitutional Aspects of Sex-Based Discrimination.* St. Paul, Minn.: West, 1974.

Glazer, Nathan. *Affirmative Discrimination: Ethnic Inequality and Public Policy.* New York: Basic Books, 1975.

Graham, Hugh Davis. *The Civil Rights Era: Origins and Development of a National Policy.* New York: Oxford University Press, 1990.

Kennedy, Randall. *Race, Crime and the Law.* New York: Pantheon Books, 1997.

Kluger, Richard. *Simple Justice.* New York: Vintage Books, 1975.

O'Connor, Karen. *Women's Organizations' Use of the Courts.* Lexington, Mass.: Lexington Books, 1980.

Orfield, Gary. *Must We Bus?* Washington, D.C.: Brookings Institute, 1978.

Peltason, Jack W. *58 Lonely Men: Southern Federal Judges and School Desegregation.* Urbana, Ill.: University of Illinois Press, 1961.

Rhode, Deborah. *Justice and Gender.* Cambridge, Mass.: Harvard University Press, 1989.

Rossum, Ralph. *Reverse Discrimination: The Constitutional Debate.* New York: Dekker, 1980.

Scheingold, Stuart. *The Politics of Rights.* New Haven: Yale University Press, 1974.

Schwartz, Bernard (ed). *The Fourteenth Amendment.* New York: New York University Press, 1970.

Sindler, Allan P. *Bakke, DeFunis and Minority Admissions.* New York: Longman, 1978.

Thomas, William R. *The Burger Court and Civil Liberties* (rev. ed). Brunswick, Ohio: Kings Court Communications, 1979.

Wasby, Stephen L., Anthony A. D'Amato, and Rosemary Metrailer. *Desegregation from Brown to Alexander: An Exploration of Supreme Court Strategies.* Carbondale, Ill.: Southern Illinois University Press, 1977.

Wilkinson, J. Harvie III. *From Brown to Bakke: The Supreme Court and School Integration: 1954–1978.* New York: Oxford University Press, 1981.

Wolters, Raymond. *The Burden of Brown: Thirty Years of School Desegregation.* Knoxville, Tenn.: University of Tennessee Press, 1984.

Woodward, C. Vann. *The Strange Career of Jim Crow.* New York: Oxford University Press, 1968.

Yarbrough, Tinsley (ed). *The Reagan Administration and Human Rights.* New York: Praeger, 1985.

INTERNET RESOURCES

Name of Resource	Description	URL (circa 1998)
NAACP	The oldest and best known organization devoted to promoting civil rights for African Americans	http://www.naacp.org/
National Organization for Women	The leading interest group in the movement for women's rights	http://www.now.org/
The National Gay and Lesbian Task Force (NGLTF)	A leading gay rights organization	http://www.ngltf.org/
Eagle Forum	Phyllis Shlafly's organization—a conservative alternative to feminism	http://www.accessus.net/~eagle/

Case

THE CIVIL RIGHTS CASES

109 U.S. 3; 3 S.Ct. 18; 27 L.Ed. 835 (1883)
Vote: 8–1

In this landmark opinion, the Court holds that private discrimination is, in and of itself, beyond the purview of the Fourteenth amendment.

Mr. Justice Bradley delivered the opinion of the Court:

These cases are all founded on the . . . "Civil Rights Act," passed March 1, 1875. . . . Two of the cases . . . are indictments for denying to persons of color the accommodations and privileges of an inn or hotel; two of them, . . . for denying to individuals the privileges and accommodations of a theater. . . . The case of Robinson and wife against the Memphis & Charleston Railroad Company was an action . . . to recover the penalty of $500 given by the second section of the act; and the gravamen was the refusal by the conductor of the railroad company to allow the wife to ride in the ladies' car, [because] she was a person of African descent.

The sections of the law referred to provide as follows:

Sec. 1. That all persons within . . . United States shall be entitled to the full and equal enjoyment of the accommodations, advantages, facilities, and privileges of inns, public conveyances on land or water, theaters, and other places of public amusement; subject only to the conditions and limitations established by law, and applicable alike to citizens of every race and color, regardless of any previous condition of servitude.

Sec. 2. That any person who shall violate the foregoing section . . . shall, for every such offense, forfeit and pay the sum of $500 to the person aggrieved [and] be deemed guilty of a misdemeanor, and upon conviction thereof shall be fined not less than $500 nor more than $1,000, or shall be imprisoned not less than 30 days nor more than one year. . . .

The first section of the Fourteenth Amendment . . . declares that "no state shall make or enforce any law which shall abridge the privileges or immunities of citizens of the United States; nor shall any state deprive any person of life, liberty, or property without due process of law; nor deny to any person within its jurisdiction, the equal protection of the laws." It is state action of a particular character that is prohibited. Individual invasion of individual rights is not the subject-matter of the amendment. . . . It nullifies and makes void all state legislation, and state action of every kind, which impairs the privileges and immunities of citizens of the United States, or which injures them in life, liberty, or property without due process of law, or which denies to any of them the equal protection of the laws. . . . [T]he last section of the amendment invests Congress with power to enforce it by appropriate legislation. To enforce what? To enforce the prohibition. To adopt appropriate legislation for correcting the effects of such prohibited state law and state acts, and thus to render them effectually null, void, and innocuous. . . . It does not invest Congress with power to legislate upon subjects which are within the domain of state legislation. . . . It does not authorize Congress to create a code of municipal law for the regulation of private rights; but to provide modes of redress against the operation of state laws, and the action of state officers, executive or judicial, when these are subversive of the fundamental rights specified in the amendment. . . .

An inspection of the law shows that it makes no reference whatever to any supposed or apprehended violation of the Fourteenth Amendment on the part of the states. . . . It proceeds ex directo to declare that certain acts committed by individuals shall be deemed offenses, and shall be prosecuted and punished by proceedings in the courts of the United States. It does not profess to be corrective of any constitutional wrong committed by the states. . . . [I]t steps into the domain of local jurisprudence, and lays down rules for the conduct of individuals in society towards each other . . . without referring in any manner to any supposed action of the state or its authorities.

If this legislation is appropriate for enforcing the prohibitions of the amendment, it is difficult to see where it is to stop. Why may not Congress, with equal show of authority, enact a code of laws for the enforcement and vindication of all rights of life, liberty, and property? If it is supposable that the states may deprive persons of life, liberty, and property without due process of law (and the amendment itself does suppose this), why should not Congress proceed at once to prescribe due process of law for the protection of every one of these fundamental rights, in every possible case, as well as to prescribe equal privileges in inns, public conveyances, and theaters. The truth is that the implication of a power to legislate in this manner is based upon the assumption that if the states are forbidden to legislate or act in a particular way on a particular subject, and power is conferred upon Congress to enforce the prohibition, this gives Congress power to legislate generally upon that subject, and not merely power to provide modes of redress against such state legislation or action. The assumption is certainly unsound. It is repugnant to the Tenth Amendment. . . .

. . . [C]ivil rights, such as are guarantied by the Constitution against state aggression, cannot be impaired by the wrongful acts of individuals, unsupported by state authority in the shape of laws, customs, or judicial or executive proceedings. The wrongful act of an individual, unsupported by any such authority, is simply a private wrong, or a crime of that individual. . . . An individual cannot deprive a man of his right to vote, to hold property, to buy and to sell, to sue in the courts, or to be a witness or a juror; he may, by force or fraud, interfere with the enjoyment of the right in a particular case; . . . but unless protected in these wrongful acts by some shield of state law or state authority, he cannot destroy or injure the right; he will only render himself amenable to satisfaction or punishment; and amenable therefore to the laws of the state where the wrongful acts are committed. Hence, in all those cases where the Constitution seeks to protect the rights of the citizen against discriminative and unjust laws of the state by prohibiting such laws, it is not individual offenses, but abrogation and denial of rights, which it denounces, and for which it clothes the Congress with power to provide a remedy. This abrogation and denial of rights, for which the states alone were or could be responsible, was the great seminal and fundamental wrong which was intended to be remedied. . . .

Of course, these remarks do not apply to those cases in which Congress is clothed with direct and plenary powers of legislation over the whole subject, accompanied with an express or implied denial of such power to the states, as in the regulation of commerce with foreign nations, among the several states, and with the Indian tribes, the coining of money, the establishment of post-offices and post-roads, the declaring of war, etc. In these cases Congress has power to pass laws for regulating the subjects specified, in every detail, and the conduct and transactions of individuals in respect thereof. . . .

But the power of Congress to adopt direct and primary, as distinguished from corrective, legislation on the subject in hand, is sought, in the second place, from the Thirteenth Amendment, which . . . declares "that neither slavery, nor involuntary servitude, except as a punishment for crime, whereof the party shall have been duly convicted, shall exist within the United States, or any place subject to their jurisdiction;" and it gives Congress power to enforce the amendment by appropriate legislation. . . .

. . . [I]t is assumed that the power vested in Congress to enforce the article by appropriate legislation, clothes Congress with power to pass all laws necessary and proper for abolishing all badges and incidents of slavery in the United States; and upon this assumption it is claimed that this is sufficient authority for declaring by law that all persons shall have equal accommodations and privileges in all inns, public conveyances, and places of public amusement; the argument being that the denial of such equal accommodations and privileges is in itself a subjection to a species of servitude within the meaning of the amendment. . . .

. . . [T]he civil rights bill of 1866, passed in view of the Thirteenth Amendment, before the Fourteenth was adopted, understood to wipe out these burdens and disabilities, the necessary incidents of slavery, constituting its substance and visible form; and to secure to all citizens of every race and color, and without regard to previous servitude, those fundamental rights which are the essence of civil freedom, namely, the same right to make and enforce contracts, to sue, be parties, give evidence, and to inherit, purchase, lease, sell, and convey property, as is enjoyed by white citizens. Whether this legislation was fully authorized by the Thirteenth Amendment alone, without the support which it afterwards received from the Fourteenth Amendment, after the adoption of which it was re-enacted with some additions, it is not necessary to inquire. It is referred to for the purpose of showing that at that time (in 1866) Congress did not assume, under the authority given by the Thirteenth Amendment, to adjust what may be called the social rights of men and races in the community; but only to declare and vindicate those fundamental rights which appertain to the essence of citizenship, and the enjoyment or deprivation of which constitutes the essential distinction between freedom and slavery.

. . . Many wrongs may be obnoxious to the prohibitions of the Fourteenth Amendment which are not, in any just sense, incidents or elements of slavery. Such, for example, would be the taking of private property without due process of law; or allowing persons who have committed certain crimes (horse-stealing, for example) to be seized and hung by the posse comitatus without regular trial; or denying to any person, or class of persons, the right to pursue any peaceful avocations allowed to others. What is called class legislation would belong to this category, and would be obnoxious to the prohibitions of the Fourteenth Amendment, but would not necessarily be so to the Thirteenth, when not involving the idea of any subjection of one man to another. . . . Can the act of a mere individual, the owner of the inn, the public conveyance, or place of amusement, refusing the accommodation, be justly regarded as imposing any badge of slavery or servitude upon the applicant, or only as inflicting an ordinary civil injury. . . ? [S]uch an act of refusal has nothing to do with slavery or involuntary servitude, . . . if it is violative of any right of the party, his redress is to be sought under the laws of the state; or, if those laws are adverse to his rights and do not protect him, his remedy will be found in the corrective legislation which Congress has adopted, or may adopt, for counter-acting the effect of state laws, or state action, prohibited by the Fourteenth Amendment. It would be running the slavery argument into the ground to make it apply to every act of discrimination which a person may see fit to make as to the guests he will entertain, or as to the people he will take into his coach or cab or car, or admit to his concert or theater, or deal with in other matters of intercourse or business. Innkeepers and public carriers, by the laws of all the states, so far as we are aware, are bound, to the extent of their facilities, to furnish proper accommodation to all unobjectionable persons who in good faith apply for them. If the laws themselves make any unjust discrimination, amenable to the prohibitions of the Fourteenth Amendment, Congress has full power to afford a remedy under that amendment and in accordance with it.

. . . There were thousands of free colored people in this country before the abolition of slavery, enjoying all the essential rights of life, liberty, and property the same as white citizens; yet no one, at that time, thought that it was any invasion of their personal status as freemen because they were not admitted to all the privileges enjoyed by white citizens, or because they were subjected to discriminations in the enjoyment of accommodations in inns, public conveyances, and places of amusement. Mere discriminations on account of race or color were not regarded as badges of slavery. . . .

On the whole, we are of the opinion that no countenance of authority for the passage of the law in question can be found in either the Thirteenth or Fourteenth Amendment of the Constitution; and no other ground of authority for its passage being suggested, it must necessarily be declared void. . . .

Mr. Justice Harlan, dissenting.

The opinion in these cases proceeds, as it seems to me, upon grounds entirely too narrow and artificial. The substance and spirit of the recent amendments of the Constitution have been sacrificed by a subtle and ingenious verbal criticism. . . .

The Thirteenth Amendment, my brethren concede, did something more than to prohibit slavery as an institution, resting upon distinctions of race, and upheld by positive law. They admit that it established and decreed universal civil freedom throughout the United States. But did the freedom thus established involve nothing more . . . than to forbid one man from owning another as property? . . . I do not contend that the Thirteenth Amendment invests Congress with authority, by legislation, to regulate the entire body of the civil rights which citizens enjoy, or may enjoy, in the several states. But I do hold that since slavery . . . was the moving or principal cause of the adoption of that amendment, and since that institution rested wholly upon the inferiority, as a race, of those held in bondage, their freedom necessarily involved immunity from, and protection against, all discrimination against them, because of their race, in respect of such civil rights as belong to freemen of other races. Congress, therefore, under its express power to enforce that amendment, by appropriate legislation, may enact laws to protect that people against the deprivation, on account of their race, of any civil rights enjoyed by other freemen in the same state; and such legislation may be of a direct and primary character, operating upon states, their officers and agents, and also upon, at least, such individuals and corporations as exercise public functions and wield power and authority under the State. . . .

I am of the opinion that . . . discrimination practised by corporations and individuals in the exercise of their public or quasi-public functions is a badge of servitude, the imposition of which Congress may prevent under its power through appropriate legislation, to enforce the Thirteenth Amendment. . . .

It remains now to consider these cases with reference to the power Congress has possessed since the adoption of the Fourteenth Amendment. . . .

The first clause of the first section—"all persons born or naturalized in the United States, and subject to the jurisdiction thereof, are citizens of the United States, and of the state wherein they reside"—is of a distinctly affirmative character. In its application to the colored race, previously liberated, it created and granted, as well citizenship of the United States, as citizenship of the state in which they respectively resided. . . . Further, they were brought, by this supreme act of the nation, within the direct operation of the provision of the Constitution which declares that "the citizens of each state shall be entitled to all privileges and immunities of citizens in the several states." . . .

The citizenship thus acquired by that race, in virtue of an affirmative grant by the nation, may be protected, not alone by the judicial branch of the government, but by congressional legislation of a primary direct character; this, because the power of Congress is not restricted to the enforcement of prohibitions upon state laws or state action. It is, in terms distinct and positive, to enforce "the provisions of this article" of amendment; not simply those of a prohibitive character, but the provisions—all of the provisions—affirmative and prohibitive, of the amendment. . . .

But what was secured to colored citizens of the United States—as between them and their respective states— by the grant to them of state citizenship? With what rights, privileges, or immunities did this grant from the nation invest them? There is one, if there be no others— exemption from race discrimination in respect of any civil right belonging to citizens of the white race in the same state. . . . It is fundamental in American citizenship that, in respect of such rights, there shall be no discrimination by the state, or its officers, or by individuals, or corporations exercising public functions or authority, against any citizen because of his race or previous condition of servitude.

. . . [T]o hold that the amendment remits that right to the states for their protection, primarily, and stays the hands of the nation, until it is assailed by state laws or state proceedings, is to adjudge that the amendment, so far from enlarging the powers of Congress—

as we have heretofore said it did—not only curtails them, but reverses the policy which the general government has pursued from its very organization. Such an interpretation of the amendment is a denial to Congress of the power, by appropriate legislation, to enforce one of its provisions. In view of the circumstances under which the recent amendments were incorporated into the Constitution, and especially in view of the peculiar character of the new rights they created and secured, it ought not to be presumed that the general government has abdicated its authority, by national legislation, direct and primary in its character, to guard and protect privileges and immunities secured by that instrument. . . . It was perfectly well known that the great danger to the equal enjoyment by citizens of their rights, as citizens, was to be apprehended, not altogether from unfriendly state legislation, but from the hostile action of corporations and individuals in the states. And it is to be presumed that it was intended, by [the Fourteenth Amendment] to clothe Congress with power and authority to meet that danger. . . .

It is said that any interpretation of the Fourteenth Amendment different from that adopted by the court, would authorize Congress to enact a municipal code for all the states, covering every matter affecting the life, liberty, and property of the citizens of the several states. Not so. Prior to the adoption of that amendment the constitutions of the several states, without, perhaps, an exception, secured all persons against deprivation of life, liberty, or property, otherwise than by due process of law, and, in some form, recognized the right of all persons to the equal protection of the laws. These rights, therefore, existed before that amendment was proposed or adopted. . . .

Case

PLESSY V. FERGUSON

163 U.S. 537; 16 S.Ct. 1138; 41 L.Ed. 256 (1896)
Vote: 7–1

A Louisiana law passed in 1890 required all passenger trains in the state to have "equal but separate accommodations for the white, and colored races." Homer Plessy, claiming that he "was seven-eighths Caucasian and one-eighth African blood; that the

mixture of colored blood was not discernible in him; and that he was entitled to every right . . . of the white race," was arrested after refusing to vacate a seat in a car that was reserved for white passengers. Plessy's attack on the statute's constitutionality was unsuccessful in the Louisiana courts. He appealed.

Mr. Justice Brown . . . delivered the opinion of the Court.

. . . That [the statute] does not conflict with the Thirteenth Amendment, which abolished slavery and involuntary servitude, except as a punishment for crime, is too clear for argument. Slavery implies involuntary servitude,—a state of bondage; the ownership of mankind as a chattel, or, at least, the control of the labor and services of one man for the benefit of another, and the absence of a legal right to the disposal of his own person, property, and services. This amendment . . . was regarded by the statesmen of that day as insufficient to protect the colored race from certain laws which had been enacted in the Southern states, imposing upon the colored race onerous disabilities and burdens, and curtailing their rights in the pursuit of life, liberty, and property to such an extent that their freedom was of little value; and . . . the Fourteenth Amendment was devised to meet this exigency. . . .

The object of the amendment was undoubtedly to enforce the absolute equality of the two races before the law, but, in the nature of things, it could not have been intended to abolish distinctions based upon color, or to enforce social, as distinguished from political, equality, or a commingling of the two races upon terms unsatisfactory to either. Laws permitting, and even requiring, their separation, in places where they are liable to be brought into contact . . . have been generally, if not universally, recognized as within the competency of the state legislatures in the exercise of their police power. The most common instance of this is connected with the establishment of separate schools for white and colored children, which have been [upheld] even by courts of states where the political rights of the colored race have been longest and most earnestly enforced.

One of the earliest of these cases is that of *Roberts v. City of Boston,* . . . (1849). "The great principle," said Chief Justice Shaw, "advanced by the learned and eloquent advocate for the plaintiff (Mr. Charles Sumner), is that, by the constitution and laws of Massachusetts, all persons, without distinction of age or sex, birth, or color, origin or condition, are equal before the law. . . . But, when this great principle comes to be applied to the actual and various conditions of persons in society, it will not warrant the assertion that men and women are legally clothed with the same civil and political powers, and that children and adults are legally to have the same functions and be subject to the same treatment; but only that the rights of all, as they are settled and regulated by law, are equally entitled to the paternal consideration and protection of the law for their maintenance and security." Similar laws have been enacted by Congress under its general power of legislation over the District of Columbia, as well as by the legislatures of many of the

states, and have been generally, if not uniformly, sustained by the courts. . . .

Laws forbidding the intermarriage of the two races may be said in a technical sense to interfere with the freedom of contract, and yet have been universally recognized as within the police power of the state. . . .

The distinction between laws interfering with the political equality of the negro and those requiring the separation of the two races in schools, theaters, and railway carriages has been frequently drawn by this court.

[It is suggested] that the same argument that will justify the state legislature in requiring railways to provide separate accommodations for the two races will also authorize them to require separate cars to be provided for people whose hair is of a certain color, or who are aliens, or who belong to certain nationalities, or to enact laws requiring colored people to walk upon one side of the street, and white people upon the other, or requiring white men's houses to be painted white, and colored men's black, or their vehicles or business signs to be of different colors, upon the theory that one side of the street is as good as the other, or that a house or vehicle of one color is as good as one of another color. The reply to all this is that every exercise of the police power must be reasonable, and extend only to such laws as are enacted in good faith for the promotion of the public good, and not for the annoyance or oppression of a particular class. . . .

So far, then, as a conflict with the Fourteenth Amendment is concerned, the case reduces itself to the question whether the statute of Louisiana is a reasonable regulation, and with respect to this there must necessarily be a large discretion on the part of the legislature. In determining the question of reasonableness, it is at liberty to act with reference to the established usages, customs, and traditions of the people, and with a view to the promotion of their comfort, and the preservation of the public peace and good order. Gauged by this standard, we cannot say [that this law] is unreasonable, or more obnoxious to the Fourteenth Amendment than the acts of Congress requiring separate schools for colored children in the District of Columbia, the constitutionality of which does not seem to have been questioned, or the corresponding acts of state legislatures.

We consider the underlying fallacy of the plaintiff's argument to consist in the assumption that the enforced separation of the two races stamps the colored race with a badge of inferiority. If this be so, it is not by reason of anything found in the act, but solely because the colored race chooses to put that construction upon it. The argument necessarily assumes that if, as has been more than once the case, and is not unlikely to be so again, the colored race should become the dominant power in the state legislature, and should enact a law in precisely similar terms, it would thereby relegate the white race to an inferior position. We imagine that the white race, at least, would not acquiesce in this assumption. The argument also assumes that social prejudices may be overcome by legislation, and that equal rights cannot be secured to the negro except by an enforced commingling of the two races. We cannot accept this proposition. If the two races are to meet upon terms of social equality, it must be the result of natural affinities, a mutual appreciation of each other's merits, and a voluntary consent of individuals. . . . Legislation is powerless to eradicate racial instincts, or to abolish distinctions based upon physical differences, and the attempt to do so can only result in accentuating the difficulties of the present situation. If the civil and political rights of both races be equal, one cannot be inferior to the other civilly or politically. If one race be inferior to the other socially, the Constitution of the United States cannot put them upon the same plane. . . .

Affirmed.

Mr. Justice Brewer did not . . . participate in the decision of this case.

Mr. Justice Harlan dissenting.

. . . In respect of civil rights, common to all citizens, the Constitution of the United States does not, I think, permit any public authority to know the race of those entitled to be protected in the enjoyment of such rights. Every true man has pride of race, and under appropriate circumstances, when the rights of others, his equals before the law, are not to be affected, it is his privilege to express such pride and to take such action based upon it as to him seems proper. But I deny that any legislative body or judicial tribunal may have regard to the race of citizens when the civil rights of those citizens are involved. Indeed, such legislation as that here in question is inconsistent not only with that equality of rights which pertains to citizenship, national and state, but with the personal liberty enjoyed by every one within the United States.

The Thirteenth Amendment does not permit the withholding or the deprivation of any right necessarily inhering in freedom. It not only struck down the institution of slavery as previously existing in the United States, but it prevents the imposition of any burdens or disabilities that constitute badges of slavery or servitude. . . . It was followed by the Fourteenth [and Fifteenth] amendment[s], which added greatly to the dignity and glory of American citizenship, and to the security of personal liberty. . . .

It was said in argument that the statute of Louisiana does not discriminate against either race, but prescribes a rule applicable alike to white and colored citizens. But this argument does not meet the difficulty. Everyone knows that the statute in question had its origin in the purpose, not so much to exclude white persons from railroad cars occupied by blacks, as to exclude colored people from coaches occupied by or assigned to white persons. . . . No one would be so wanting in candor as to assert the contrary. The fundamental objection, therefore, to the statute, is that it interferes with the personal freedom of citizens. "Personal liberty," it has been well said, "consists in the power of locomotion, of changing situation, or removing one's person to whatsoever places one's own inclination may direct, without imprisonment or restraint, unless by due course of law." . . . If a white man and a black man choose to occupy the same public conveyance on a public highway, it is their right to do so; and no government, proceeding alone on grounds of race, can prevent it without infringing the personal liberty of each.

. . . If a state can prescribe, as a rule of civil conduct, that whites and blacks shall not travel as passengers in the same railroad coach, why . . . may it not require sheriffs to assign whites to one side of a court room, and blacks to the other? And why may it not also prohibit the commingling of the two races in the galleries of legislative halls or in public assemblages convened for the consideration of the political questions of the day? [W]hy may not the state require the separation in railroad coaches of native and naturalized citizens of the United States, or of Protestants and Roman Catholics? . . .

The white race deems itself to be the dominant race in this country. And so it is, in prestige, in achievements, in education, in wealth, and in power. So, I doubt not, it will continue to be for all time, if it remains true to its great heritage, and holds fast to the principles of constitutional liberty. But in view of the Constitution, in the eye of the law, there is in this country no superior, dominant, ruling class of citizens. There is no caste here. Our Constitution is color-blind, and neither knows nor tolerates classes among citizens. . . .

In my opinion, the judgment this day rendered will, in time, prove to be quite as pernicious as the decision made by this tribunal in the Dred Scott Case . . . that the descendants of Africans who were imported into this country, and sold as slaves, were not included nor intended to be included under the word "citizens" in the Constitution; . . . that, at the time of the adoption of the Constitution, they were "considered as a subordinate and inferior class of beings, who had been subjugated by the dominant race, and, whether emancipated or not, yet remained subject to their authority, and had not rights or privileges but such as those who held the power and the government might choose to grant them." . . . The recent amendments of the Constitution, it was supposed, has eradicated these principles from our institutions. But it seems that we have yet, in some of the states, a dominant race—a superior class of citizens—which assumes to regulate the enjoyment of civil rights, common to all citizens, upon the basis of race. The present decision . . . will encourage the belief that it is possible by means of state enactments, to defeat the beneficent purposes which the people of the United States had in view when they adopted the recent amendments of the Constitution. . . . What can more certainly arouse race hate, what more certainly create and perpetuate a feeling of distrust between these races, than state enactments which, in fact, proceed on the ground that colored citizens are so inferior and degraded that they cannot be allowed to sit in public coaches occupied by white citizens? . . . This question is not met by the suggestion that social equality cannot exist between the white and black races in this country . . . for social equality no more exists between two races when traveling in a passenger coach or a public highway than when members of the same races sit by each other in a street car or in the jury box, or stand or sit with each other in a political assembly. . . .

If evils will result from the comminglings of the two races upon public highways established for the benefit of all, they will be infinitely less than those that will surely come from state legislation regulating the enjoyment of civil rights upon the basis of race. We boast of the freedom enjoyed by our people above all other peoples. But it is difficult to reconcile that boast with a state of the law which, practically, puts the brand of servitude and degradation upon a large class of our fellow citizens—our equals before the law. The thin disguise of "equal" accommodations for passengers in railroad coaches will not mislead any one, nor atone for the wrong this day done. . . .

I do not deem it necessary to review the decisions of state courts to which reference was made in argument. Some, and the most important, of them, are wholly inapplicable, because rendered prior to the adoption of the last amendments of the Constitution. . . . Others were made at a time when public opinion, in many localities, was dominated by the institution of slavery; when it would not have been safe to do justice to the black man; and when, so far as the rights of blacks were concerned, race prejudice was, practically, the supreme law of the land. Those decisions cannot be guides in the era introduced by the recent amendments of the supreme law, which established universal civil freedom. . . .

Case

Brown v. Board of Education of Topeka I

347 U.S. 483; 74 S.Ct. 686; 98 L.Ed. 873 (1954)
Vote: 9–0

In what has been dubbed "the case of the century," the Supreme Court invalidates compulsory racial segregation in the public schools.

Mr. Chief Justice Warren delivered the opinion of the Court:

These cases come to us from the States of Kansas, South Carolina, Virginia, and Delaware. They are premised on different facts and different local conditions, but a common legal question justifies their consideration in this consolidated opinion.

In each of the cases, minors of the Negro race, through their legal representatives, seek the aid of the courts in obtaining admission to the public schools of their community on a nonsegregated basis. In each instance, they had been denied admission to schools attended by white children under laws requiring or permitting segregation according to race. This segregation was alleged to deprive the plaintiffs of the equal protection of the laws under the Fourteenth Amendment. In each of the cases other than the Delaware case, a three-judge federal district court denied relief to the plaintiffs on the so-called "separate but equal" doctrine announced by this Court in *Plessy v. Ferguson.* . . . Under that doctrine, equality of treatment is accorded when the races are provided substantially equal facilities, even though these facilities be separate. In the Delaware case, the Supreme Court of Delaware adhered to that doctrine, but ordered that the plaintiffs be admitted to the white schools because of their superiority to the Negro schools. . . .

Because of the obvious importance of the question presented, the Court took jurisdiction. Argument was heard in the 1952 Term, and reargument was heard this Term on certain questions propounded by the Court.

Reargument was largely devoted to the circumstances surrounding the adoption of the Fourteenth Amendment in 1868. It covered exhaustively consideration of the Amendment in Congress, ratification by the states, then existing practices in racial segregation, and the views of proponents and opponents of the Amendment. This discussion and our own investigation convince us that, although these sources cast some light, it is not enough to resolve the problem with which we are faced. At best, they are inconclusive. The most avid proponents of the post–War Amendments undoubtedly intended them to remove all legal distinctions among "all persons born or naturalized in the United States." Their opponents, just as certainly, were antagonistic to both the letter and the spirit of the Amendments and wished them to have the most limited effect. What others in Congress and the state legislatures had in mind cannot be determined with any degree of certainty.

An additional reason for the inconclusive nature of the Amendment's history, with respect to segregated schools, is the status of public education at that time. In the South, the movement toward free common schools, supported by general taxation, had not yet taken hold. Education of white children was largely in the hands of private groups. Education of Negroes was almost non-existent, and practically all of the race were illiterate. In fact, any education of Negroes was forbidden by law in some states. Today, in contrast, many Negroes have achieved outstanding success in the arts and sciences as well as in the business and professional world. It is true that public education had already advanced further in the North, but the effect of the Amendment on Northern States was generally ignored in the congressional debates. Even in the North, the conditions of public education did not approximate those existing today. The curriculum was rudimentary; ungraded schools were common in rural areas; the school term was but three months a year in many states; and compulsory school attendance was virtually unknown. As a consequence, it is not surprising that there should be so little in the history

of the Fourteenth Amendment relating to its intended effect on public education.

In the first cases in this Court construing the Fourteenth Amendment, decided shortly after its adoption, the Court interpreted it as proscribing all state-imposed discriminations against the Negro race. The doctrine of "separate but equal" did not make its appearance in this Court until 1896 in the case of *Plessy v. Ferguson,* . . . involving not education but transportation. American courts have since labored with the doctrine for over half a century. In this Court, there have been six cases involving the "separate but equal" doctrine in the field of public education. In *Cumming v. County Board of Education,* . . . and *Gong Lum v. Rice,* . . . the validity of the doctrine itself was not challenged. In more recent cases, all on the graduate school level, inequality was found in that specific benefits enjoyed by white students were denied to Negro students of the same educational qualifications. . . . In none of these cases was it necessary to reexamine the doctrine to grant relief to the Negro plaintiff. And in *Sweatt v. Painter,* . . . the Court expressly reserved decision on the question whether *Plessy v. Ferguson* should be held inapplicable to public education.

In the instant cases, that question is directly presented. Here, unlike *Sweatt v. Painter,* there are findings below that the Negro and white schools involved have been equalized, or are being equalized, with respect to buildings, curricula, qualifications and salaries of teachers, and other "tangible" factors. Our decision, therefore, cannot turn on merely a comparison of these tangible factors in the Negro and white schools involved in each of the cases. We must look instead to the effect of segregation itself on public education.

In approaching this problem, we cannot turn the clock back to 1868 when the Amendment was adopted, or even to 1896 when *Plessy v. Ferguson* was written. We must consider public education in the light of its full development and its present place in American life throughout the Nation. Only in this way can it be determined if segregation in public schools deprives these plaintiffs of the equal protection of the laws.

Today, education is perhaps the most important function of state and local governments. Compulsory school attendance laws and the great expenditures for education both demonstrate our recognition of the importance of education to our democratic society. It is required in the performance of our most basic public responsibilities, even service in the armed forces. It is the very foundation of good citizenship. Today it is a principal instrument in awakening the child to cultural values, in preparing him for later professional training, and in helping him to adjust normally to his environment. In these days, it is doubtful that any child may reasonably be expected to succeed in life if he is denied the opportunity of an education. Such an opportunity, where the state has undertaken to provide it, is a right which must be made available to all on equal terms.

We come then to the question presented: Does segregation of children in public schools solely on the basis of race, even though the physical facilities and other "tangible" factors may be equal, deprive the children of the minority group of equal educational opportunities? We believe that it does.

In *Sweatt v. Painter,* in finding that a segregated law school for Negroes could not provide them equal educational opportunities, this Court relied in large part on "those qualities which are incapable of objective measurement but which make for greatness in a law school." In *McLaurin v. Oklahoma State Regents,* . . . the Court, in requiring that a Negro admitted to a white graduate school be treated like all other students, again resorted to intangible considerations: " . . . his ability to study, to engage in discussions and exchange views with other students, and, in general, to learn his profession." Such considerations apply with added force to children in grade and high schools. To separate them from others of similar age and qualifications solely because of their race generates a feeling of inferiority as to their status in the community that may affect their hearts and minds in a way unlikely ever to be undone. The effect of this separation on their educational opportunities was well stated by a finding in the Kansas case by a court which nevertheless felt compelled to rule against the Negro plaintiffs.

Segregation of white and colored children in public schools has a detrimental effect upon the colored children. The impact is greater when it has the sanction of the law; for the policy of separating the races is usually interpreted as denoting the inferiority of the Negro group. A sense of inferiority affects the motivation of a child to learn. Segregation with the sanction of law, therefore, has a tendency to retard the educational and mental development of Negro children and to deprive them of some of the benefits they would receive in a racially integrated school system.

Whatever may have been the extent of psychological knowledge at the time of *Plessy v. Ferguson,* this finding is amply supported by modern authority. Any language in *Plessy v. Ferguson* contrary to this finding is rejected.

We conclude that in the field of public education the doctrine of "separate but equal" has no place. Separate educational facilities are inherently unequal. Therefore, we hold that the plaintiffs and others similarly situated for whom the actions have been brought are, by reason of the segregation complained of, deprived of the equal protection of the laws guaranteed by the Fourteenth Amendment. This disposition makes unnecessary any discussion whether such segregation also violates the Due Process Clause of the Fourteenth Amendment.

Because these are class actions, because of the wide applicability of this decision, and because of the great variety of local conditions, the formulation of decrees in these cases presents problems of considerable complexity. On reargument, the consideration of appropriate relief was necessarily subordinated to the primary question—the constitutionality of segregation in public education. We have now announced that such segregation is a denial of the equal protection of the laws. In order that we may have the full assistance of the parties in formulating decrees, the cases will be restored to the docket, and the parties are requested to present further argument. . . .

It is so ordered.

Case

BROWN V. BOARD OF EDUCATION OF TOPEKA II

349 U.S. 294; 75 S.Ct. 753; 99 L.Ed. 1083 (1955)
Vote: 9–0

Here the Court considers how its holding in Brown I *should be implemented by the lower federal courts.*

Mr. Chief Justice Warren delivered the opinion of the Court.

These cases were decided on May 17, 1954. The opinions of that date, declaring the fundamental principle that racial discrimination in public education is unconstitutional, are incorporated herein by reference. All provisions of federal, state, or local law requiring or permitting such discrimination must yield to this principle. There remains for consideration the manner in which relief is to be accorded.

Because these cases arose under different local conditions and their disposition will involve a variety of local problems, we requested further argument on the question of relief. In view of the nationwide importance of the decision, we invited the Attorney General of the United States and the Attorneys General of all states requiring or permitting racial discrimination in public education to present their views on that question. The parties, the United States, and the States of Florida, North Carolina, Arkansas, Oklahoma, Maryland, and Texas filed briefs and participated in the oral argument.

These presentations were informative and helpful to the Court in its consideration of the complexities arising from the transition to a system of public education freed of racial discrimination. The presentations also demonstrated that substantial steps to eliminate racial discrimination in public schools have already been taken, not only in some of the communities in which these cases arose, but in some of the states appearing as *amici curiae,* and in other states as well. Substantial progress has been made in the District of Columbia and in the communities in Kansas and Delaware involved in this litigation. The defendants in the cases coming to us from South Carolina and Virginia are awaiting the decision of this Court concerning relief.

Full implementation of these constitutional principles may require solution of varied local school problems. School authorities have the primary responsibility for elucidating, assessing, and solving these problems; courts will have to consider whether the action of school authorities constitutes good faith implementation of the governing constitutional principles. Because of their proximity to local conditions and the possible need for further hearings, the courts which originally heard these cases can best perform this judicial appraisal. Accordingly, we believe it appropriate to remand the cases to those courts.

In fashioning and effectuating the decrees, the courts will be guided by equitable principles. Traditionally, equity has been characterized by a practical flexibility in shaping its remedies and by a facility for adjusting and reconciling public and private needs. These cases call for the exercise of these traditional attributes of equity power. At stake is the personal interest of the plaintiffs in admission to public schools as soon as practicable on a nondiscriminatory basis. To effectuate this interest may call for elimination of a variety of obstacles in making the transition to school systems operated in accordance with the constitutional principles set forth in our May 17, 1954, decision. Courts of equity may properly take into account the public interest in the elimination of such obstacles in a systematic and effective manner. But it should go without saying that the vitality of these constitutional principles cannot be allowed to yield simply because of disagreement with them.

While giving weight to these public and private considerations, the courts will require that the defendants make a prompt and reasonable start toward full compliance with our May 17, 1954, ruling. Once such a start has been made, the courts may find that additional time is necessary to carry out the ruling in an effective manner. The burden rests upon the defendants to establish that such time is necessary in the public interest and is consistent with good faith compliance at the earliest practicable date. To that end, the courts may consider problems related to administration, arising from the physical condition of the school plant, the school transportation system, personnel, revision of school districts and attendance areas into compact units to achieve a system of determining admission to the public schools on a nonracial basis, and revision of local laws and regulations which may be necessary in solving the foregoing problems. They will also consider the adequacy of any plans the defendants may propose to meet these problems and to effectuate a transition to a racially nondiscriminatory school system. During this period of transition, the courts will retain jurisdiction of these cases.

The judgments below, except that in the Delaware case, are accordingly reversed and remanded to the District courts to take such proceedings and enter such orders and decrees consistent with this opinion as are necessary and proper to admit to public schools on a racially nondiscriminatory basis with all deliberate speed the parties to these cases. The judgment in the Delaware case—ordering the immediate admission of the plaintiffs to schools previously attended only by white children—is affirmed on the basis of the principles stated in our May 17, 1954, opinion, but the case is remanded to the Supreme Court of Delaware for such further proceedings as that court may deem necessary in light of this opinion.

It is so ordered.

Case

LOVING V. VIRGINIA

388 U.S. 1; 87 S.Ct. 1817; 18 L.Ed. 2d. 1010 (1967)
Vote: 9–0

Here the Court reviews a Virginia law prohibiting interracial marriage.

Mr. Chief Justice Warren delivered the opinion of the Court.

This case presents a constitutional question never addressed by this Court: whether a statutory scheme adopted by the State of Virginia to prevent marriages between persons solely on the basis of racial classifications violates the . . . Fourteenth Amendment. For reasons which seem to us to reflect the central meaning of those constitutional commands, we conclude that these statutes cannot stand consistently with the Fourteenth Amendment.

In June 1958, two residents of Virginia, Mildred Jeter, a Negro woman, and Richard Loving, a white man, were married in the District of Columbia pursuant to its laws. Shortly after their marriage, the Lovings returned to Virginia and established their marital abode in Caroline County. At the October Term, 1958, of the Circuit Court of Caroline County, a grand jury issued an indictment charging the Lovings and violating Virginia's ban on interracial marriages. On January 6, 1959, the Lovings pleaded guilty to the charge and were sentenced to one year in jail; however the trial judge suspended the sentence for a period of 25 years on the condition that the Lovings leave the State and not return to Virginia together for 25 years, stating that:

> Almighty God created the races white, black, yellow, malay, and red, and he placed them on separate continents. And but for the interference with his arrangements there would be no cause for such marriages. The fact that he separated the races shows that he did not intend for the races to mix.

After their convictions the Lovings took up residence in the District of Columbia. On November 6, 1963, they filed a motion in the state trial court to vacate the judgment and set aside the sentence on the ground that the statutes which they had violated were repugnant to the Fourteenth Amendment. The motion not having been decided by October 28, 1964, the Lovings instituted a class action in the United States District Court for the Eastern District of Virginia requesting that a three-judge court be convened to declare the Virginia antimiscegenation statutes unconstitutional and to enjoin state officials from enforcing their convictions. On January 22, 1965, the state trial judge denied the motion to vacate the sentences, and the Lovings perfected an appeal to the Supreme Court of Appeals of Virginia. On February 11, 1965, the three-judge District Court continued the case to allow the Lovings to present their constitutional claims to the highest state court.

The [Virginia] Supreme Court of Appeals upheld the constitutionality of the antimiscegenation statutes and, after modifying the sentence, affirmed the convictions. The Lovings appealed this decision, and we noted probable jurisdiction on December 12, 1966. The two statutes under which appellants were convicted and sentenced are part of a comprehensive statutory scheme aimed at prohibiting and punishing interracial marriages. The Lovings were convicted of violating Sec. 20-58 of the Virginia Code:

> Leaving State to Evade Law. If any white person and colored person shall go out of this State, for the purpose of being married, and with the intention of returning, and be married out of it, and afterwards return to and reside in it, cohabiting as man and wife, they shall be punished as provided in Section 20-59, and the marriage shall be governed by the same law as if it had been solemnized in this State. The fact of their cohabitation here as man and wife shall be evidence of their marriage.

Section 20-59, which defines the penalty for miscegenation, provides:

> Punishment for Marriage. If any white person intermarry with a colored person, or any colored person intermarry with a white person, he shall be guilty of a felony and shall be punished by confinement in the penitentiary for not less than one nor more than five years.

Other central provisions in the Virginia statutory scheme are Section 20-57, which automatically voids all marriages between "a white person and a colored person" without any judicial proceeding, and Sections 20-54 and 1-14 which, respectively, define "white persons" and "colored persons and Indians" for purposes of the statutory prohibitions. The Lovings have never disputed in course of this litigation that Mrs. Loving is a "colored person" or that Mr. Loving is a "white person" within the meanings given those terms by the Virginia statutes.

Virginia is now one of 16 States which prohibit and punish marriages on the basis of racial classifications. Penalties for miscegenation arose as an incident to slavery and have been common in Virginia since the colonial period. The present statutory scheme dates from the adoption of the Racial Integrity Act of 1924, passed during the period of extreme nativism which followed the end of the First World War. The central features of this Act, and current Virginia law, are the absolute prohibition of a "white person" marrying other than another "white person," a prohibition against issuing marriage licenses until the issuing official is satisfied that the applicants' statements as to their race are correct, certificates of "racial composition" to be kept by both local and state registrars, and the carrying forward of earlier prohibitions against racial intermarriage. . . .

In upholding the constitutionality of these provisions in the decision below, the Supreme Court of Appeals of Virginia referred to its 1955 decision in *Naim v. Naim,* . . . as stating the reasons supporting the validity of these laws. In *Naim,* the state court concluded that the State's legitimate purposes were "to preserve the racial integrity of its citizens," and to prevent "the corruption of blood," "a mongrel breed of citizens," and "the obliteration of racial pride," obviously an endorsement of the doctrine of White Supremacy. The court also reasoned that marriage has traditionally been subject to state regulation without federal intervention, and, consequently, the regulation of marriage should be left to exclusive state control by the Tenth Amendment.

While the state court is no doubt correct in asserting that marriage is a social relation subject to the State's police power, . . . the State does not contend in its argument before this Court that its powers to regulate marriage are unlimited notwithstanding the commands of the Fourteenth Amendment. Nor could it do so in light of *Meyer v. State of Nebraska* . . . (1923) and *Skinner v. State of Oklahoma* . . . (1942). Instead, the State argues that the meaning of the Equal Protection Clause, as illuminated by the statements of the Framers, is only that state penal laws containing an interracial element as part of the definition of the offense must apply equally to whites and Negroes in the sense that members of each race are punished to the same degree. Thus, the State contends that, because its miscegenation statutes punish equally both the white and the Negro participants in an interracial marriage, these statutes, despite their reliance on racial classifications do not constitute an invidious discrimination based upon race. The second argument advanced by the State assumes the validity of its equal application theory. The argument is that, if the Equal Protection Clause does not outlaw miscegenation statutes because of their reliance on racial classifications, the question of constitutionality would thus become whether there was any rational basis for a State to treat interracial marriages differently from other marriages. On this question, the State argues, the scientific evidence is substantially in doubt and, consequently, this Court should defer to the wisdom of the state legislature in adopting its policy of discouraging interracial marriages.

Because we reject the notion that the mere "equal application" of a statute containing racial classification is enough to remove the classifications from the Fourteenth Amendment's proscription of all invidious racial discriminations, we do not accept the State's contention that these statutes should be upheld if there is any possible basis for concluding that they serve a rational purpose. The mere fact of equal application does not mean that our analysis of this statute should follow the approach we have taken in cases involving no racial discrimination where the Equal Protection Clause has been arrayed against a statute discriminating between the kinds of advertising which may be displayed on trucks in New York City, . . . or an exemption in Ohio's ad valorem tax for merchandise owned by a non-resident in a storage warehouse. . . . In these cases, involving distinctions not drawn according to race, the Court has merely asked whether there is any rational foundation for the discriminations, and has deferred to the wisdom of the state legislatures. In the case at bar, however, we deal with statutes containing racial classifications, and the fact of equal application does not immunize the statute from the very heavy burden of justification which the Fourteenth Amendment has traditionally required of state statutes drawn according to race.

The State argues that statements in the Thirty-ninth Congress about the time of the passage of the Fourteenth Amendment indicate that the Framers did not intend the Amendment to make unconstitutional state miscegenation laws. Many of the statements alluded to by the State concern the debates over the Freemen's Bureau Bill, which President Johnson vetoed, and the Civil Rights Act of 1966, enacted over his veto. While these statements have some relevance to the intention of Congress in submitting the Fourteenth Amendment, it must be understood that they pertained to the passage of specific statutes and not to the broader, organic purpose of a constitutional amendment. As for the various statements directly concerning the Fourteenth Amendment, we have said in connection with a related problem, that although these historical sources "cast some light" they are not sufficient to resolve the problem; "[a]t best, they are inconclusive. The most avid proponents of the post–War Amendments undoubtedly intended them to remove all legal distinctions among 'all persons born or naturalized in the United States.' Their opponents, just as certainly, were antagonistic to both the letter and the spirit of the Amendments and wished them to have the most limited effect." . . . We have rejected the proposition that the debates in the Thirty-ninth Congress or in the state legislatures which ratified the Fourteenth Amendment supported the theory advanced by the State, that the requirement of equal protection of the laws is satisfied by penal laws defining offenses based on racial classifications so long as white and Negro participants in the offense were similarly punished. . . .

The State finds support for its "equal application" theory in the decision of the Court in *Pace v. Alabama* . . . (1882). In that case, the Court upheld a conviction under an Alabama statute forbidding adultery or fornication between a white person and a Negro which imposed a greater penalty than that of a statute proscribing similar conduct by members of the same race. The Court reasoned that the statute could not be said to discriminate against Negroes because the punishment for each participant in the offense was the same. However, as recently as the 1964 Term, in rejecting the reasoning of that case, we stated "Pace represents a limited view of the Equal Protection Clause which has not withstood analysis in the subsequent decisions of this Court." . . . As we there demonstrated, the Equal Protection Clause requires the consideration of whether the classifications drawn by any statute constitute an arbitrary and invidious discrimination. The clear and central purpose of the Fourteenth Amendment was to eliminate all official state sources of invidious racial discrimination in the States. . . .

There can be no question but that Virginia's miscegenation statutes rest solely upon distinctions drawn according to race. The statutes proscribe generally accepted conduct if engaged in by members of different races. Over the years, this Court has consistently repudiated "[d]istinctions between citizens solely because of their ancestry" as being "odious to a free people whose institutions are founded upon the doctrine of equality." . . . At the very least, the Equal Protection Clause demands that racial classifications, especially suspect in criminal statutes, be subjected to the "most rigid scrutiny," . . . and, if they are ever to be upheld, they must be shown to be necessary to the accomplishment of some permissible state objective, independent of the racial discrimination which it was the object of the Fourteenth Amendment to eliminate. Indeed, two members of this Court have already stated that they "cannot conceive of a valid legislative purpose . . . which makes the color of a person's skin the test of whether his conduct is a criminal offense." . . .

There is patently no legitimate overriding purpose independent of invidious racial discrimination which justifies this classification. The fact that Virginia only prohibits interracial marriages involving white persons demonstrates that the racial classifications must stand on their own justification, as measures designed to maintain White Supremacy. We have consistently denied the constitutionality of measures which restrict the rights of citizens on account of race. There can be no doubt that restricting the freedom to marry solely because of racial classification violates the central meaning of the Equal Protection Clause. . . .

These convictions must be reversed. It is so ordered.

Mr. Justice Stewart, concurring. . . .

Case

SWANN V. CHARLOTTE-MECKLENBURG BOARD OF EDUCATION

402 U.S. 1; 91 S.Ct. 1267; 28 L.Ed. 2d. 554 (1971)
Vote: 9–0

In Charlotte-Mecklenburg, North Carolina, the nation's forty-third largest school district, the board of education devised a desegregation plan in order to comply with the Supreme Court's ruling in the Brown *case. The U.S. district court, however, rejected the board's plan as not producing sufficient racial integration at the elementary level. Instead, the district court accepted a plan prepared by an outside expert that called for, among other things, racial quotas, alteration of attendance zones, and busing of students. In this case, the Supreme Court considers the permissibility of such measures.*

Mr. Chief Justice Burger delivered the opinion of the Court.

. . . The central issue in this case is that of student assignment, and there are essentially four problem areas: (1) to what extent racial balance or racial quotas may be used as an implement in a remedial order to correct a previously segregated system; (2) whether every all-Negro and all-white school must be eliminated as an indispensable part of a remedial process of desegregation; (3) what are the limits, if any, on the rearrangement of school districts and attendance zones, as a remedial measure; and (4) what are the limits, if any, on the use of transportation facilities to correct state-enforced racial school segregation.

(1) Racial Balance or Racial Quotas.

The constant theme and thrust of every holding from *Brown* I (1954) to date is that state-enforced separation of races in public schools is discrimination that violates the Equal Protection clause. The remedy commanded was to dismantle dual school systems.

We are concerned in these cases with the elimination of the discrimination inherent in the dual school systems, not with myriad factors of human existence which can cause discrimination in a multitude of ways on racial, religious, or ethnic grounds. The target of the cases from *Brown* I to the present was the dual school system. The elimination of racial discrimination in public schools is a large task and one that should not be retarded by efforts to achieve broader purposes lying beyond the jurisdiction of school authorities. One vehicle can carry only a limited amount of baggage. . . .

Our objective in dealing with the issues presented by these cases is to see that school authorities exclude no pupil or a racial minority from any school, directly or indirectly, on account of race; it does not and cannot embrace all the problems of racial prejudice, even when those problems contribute to disproportionate racial concentrations in some schools.

In this case it is urged that the District Court has imposed a racial balance requirement of 71 percent—29 percent on individual schools. . . . If we were to read the holding of the District Court to require, as a matter of substantive constitutional right, any particular degree of racial balance or mixing, that approach would be disapproved and we would be obliged to reverse. The constitutional command to desegregate schools does not mean that every school in every community must always reflect the racial composition of the school system as a whole. . . .

. . . The use made of mathematical ratios was no more than a starting point in the process of shaping a remedy, rather than an inflexible requirement. From that starting point the District Court proceeded to frame a decree that was within its discretionary powers, an equitable remedy for the particular circumstances. As we said in *Green [v. County School Board]* a school authority's remedial plan or a district court's remedial decree is to be judged by its effectiveness. Awareness of the racial composition of the whole school system is likely to be a useful starting point in shaping a remedy to correct past constitutional violations. In sum, the very limited use made of mathematical ratios was within the equitable remedial discretion of the District Court.

(2) One-Race Schools.

The record in this case reveals the familiar phenomenon that in metropolitan areas minority groups are often found concentrated in one part of the city. In some circumstances certain schools may remain all or largely of one race until new schools can be provided or neighborhood patterns change. Schools all or predominately of one race in a district of mixed population will require close scrutiny to determine that school assignments are not part of state-enforced segregation.

In light of the above, it should be clear that the existence of some small number of one-race, or virtually one-race, schools within a district is not in and of itself the mark of a system which still practices segregation by a law. . . . Where the school authority's proposed plan for conversion from a dual to a unitary system contemplates the continued existence of some schools that are all or predominately of one race, they have the burden of showing that such school assignments are genuinely nondiscriminatory. The court should scrutinize such schools, and the burden upon the school authorities will be to satisfy the court that their racial composition is not the result of present or past discriminatory action on their part.

An optional minority-to-minority transfer provision has long been recognized as a useful part of every desegregation plan. Provision for optional transfer of those in the majority racial group of a particular school to other schools where they will be in the minority is an indispensable remedy for those students willing to transfer to other schools in order to lessen the impact on them of the state-imposed stigma of segregation. In order to be effective, such a transfer arrangement must grant the transferring student free transportation and space must be made available in the school to which he desires to move. . . . The court orders in this and the companion Davis case now provide such an option.

(3) Remedial Altering of Attendance Zones.

The maps submitted in these cases graphically demonstrate that one of the principal tools employed by school planners and by courts to break up the dual school system has been a frank—and sometimes drastic—gerrymandering of school districts and attendance zones. An additional step was pairing, "clustering," or "grouping" of schools with attendance assignments made deliberately to accomplish the transfer of Negro students out of formerly segregated Negro schools and transfer of white students to formerly all-Negro schools. More often than not, these zones are neither compact nor contiguous; indeed they may be on opposite ends of the city. As in interim corrective measure, this cannot be said to be beyond the broad remedial powers of a court.

Absent a constitutional violation there would be no basis for judicially ordering assignment of students on a racial basis. All things being equal, with no history of discrimination, it might well be desirable to assign pupils to schools nearest their homes. But all things are not equal in a system that has been deliberately constructed and maintained to enforce racial segregation. . . .

No fixed or even substantially fixed guidelines can be established as to how far a court can go, but it must be recognized that there are limits. The objective is to dismantle the dual school system. "Racially neutral" assignment plans proposed by school authorities to a district court may be inadequate; such plans may fail to counteract the continuing effects of past school segregation resulting from discriminatory location of school sites or distortion of school size in order to achieve or maintain an artificial racial separation. When school authorities present a district court with a "loaded game board," affirmative action in the form of remedial altering of attendance zones is proper to achieve truly nondiscriminatory assignments. In short, an assignment plan is not acceptable simply because it appears to be neutral. . . .

We hold that the pairing and grouping of noncontiguous school zones is a permissible tool and such action is to be considered in light of the objectives sought. . . .

(4) Transportation of Students.

The scope of permissible transportation of students as an implement of a remedial decree has never been defined by this Court and by the very nature of the problem it cannot be defined with precision. . . .

The importance of bus transportation as a normal and accepted tool of educational policy is readily discernible in this and the companion case. The Charlotte school authorities did not purport to assign students on the basis of geographically drawn zones until 1965 and then they allowed almost unlimited transfer privileges. The District Court's conclusion that assignment of children to the school nearest their home serving their grade would not produce an effective dismantling of the dual system is supported by the record.

Thus the remedial techniques used in the District Court's order were within that court's power to provide equitable relief; implementation of the decree is well within the capacity of the school authority.

The decree provided that the buses used to implement the plan would operate on direct routes. Students would be picked up at schools near their homes and transported to the schools they were to attend. The trips for elementary school pupils average about seven miles and the District Court found that they would take "not over 35 minutes at the most." This system compares favorably with the transportation plan previously operated in Charlotte under which each day 23,600 students on all grade levels were transported an average of 15 miles one way for an average trip requiring over an hour. In these circumstances, we find no basis for holding that the local school authorities may not be required to employ bus transportation as one tool of school desegregation. Desegregation plans cannot be limited to the walk-in school. . . .

. . . At some point, these school authorities and others like them should have achieved full compliance with this Court's decision in *Brown* I. The systems will then be "unitary" in the sense required by our decisions in *Green [v. County School Board]* and *Alexander [v. Holmes County Board of Education]*.

It does not follow that the communities served by such systems will remain demographically stable, for in a growing, mobile society, few will do so. Neither school authorities nor district courts are constitutionally required to make year-by-year adjustments of the racial composition of student bodies once the affirmative duty to desegregate has been accomplished and racial discrimination through official action is eliminated from the system. This does not mean that federal courts are without power to deal with future problems; but in the absence of a showing that either the school authorities or some other agency of the State has deliberately attempted to fix or alter demographic patterns to affect the racial composition of the schools, further intervention by a district court should not be necessary. . . .

It is so ordered.

Case

MISSOURI V. JENKINS

515 U.S. 70, 115 S.Ct. 2038, 132 L.Ed. 2d. 63 (1995)
Vote: 5–4

As of 1995, this case involving the Kansas City Metropolitan School District (KCMSD) had been in litigation for more than seventeen years. In 1977, a federal district court found that "prior to 1954 'Missouri mandated segregated schools for black and white children' " and that, since then, Kansas City school authorities "had failed in their affirmative obligations to eliminate the vestiges of the State's dual school system. . . . " The court then issued a series of remedial orders that necessitated dramatic funding increases in order to establish "magnet schools" to attract whites from the suburbs. The court also ordered salary increases for approximately 5,000 school employees at a cost of more than $200 million since 1987. Here the Supreme Court reviews the permissibility of the district court's mandates.

Chief Justice Rehnquist delivered the opinion of the Court.

. . . Almost 25 years ago, in *Swann v. Charlotte-Mecklenburg Bd. of Ed.* . . . (1971), we dealt with the authority of a district court to fashion remedies for a school district that had been segregated in law in violation of the Equal Protection Clause of the Fourteenth Amendment. Although recognizing the discretion that must necessarily adhere in a district court in fashioning a remedy, we also recognized the limits on such remedial power. . . .

Three years later, in *Milliken v. Bradley* I . . . (1974), we held that a District Court had exceeded its authority in fashioning interdistrict relief where the surrounding school districts had not themselves been guilty of any constitutional violation. . . . We said that a desegregation remedy "is necessarily designed, as all remedies are, to restore the victims of discriminatory conduct to the position they would have occupied in the absence of such conduct." . . . "[W]ithout an interdistrict violation and interdistrict effect, there is no constitutional wrong calling for an interdistrict remedy." . . . We also rejected "[t]he suggestion . . . that schools which have a majority of Negro students are not 'desegregated,' whatever the makeup of the school

district's population and however neutrally the district lines have been drawn and administered." . . .

Three years later, in *Milliken* II [1977], we articulated a three part framework derived from our prior cases to guide district courts in the exercise of their remedial authority. "In the first place, like other equitable remedies, the nature of the desegregation remedy is to be determined by the nature and scope of the constitutional violation. . . . Second, the decree must indeed be remedial in nature, that is, it must be designed as nearly as possible 'to restore the victims of discriminatory conduct to the position they would have occupied in the absence of such conduct.' . . . Third, the federal courts in devising a remedy must take into account the interests of state and local authorities in managing their own affairs, consistent with the Constitution." . . .

We added that the "principle that the nature and scope of the remedy are to be determined by the violation means simply that federal court decrees must directly address and relate to the constitutional violation itself." . . . In applying these principles, we have identified "student assignments, . . . 'faculty, staff, transportation, extracurricular activities and facilities,'" as the most important indicia of a racially segregated school system. . . .

Because "federal supervision of local school systems was intended as a temporary measure to remedy past discrimination," . . . we also have considered the showing that must be made by a school district operating under a desegregation order for complete or partial relief from that order.

. . . The ultimate inquiry is "whether the [constitutional violator] ha[s] complied in good faith with the desegregation decree since it was entered, and whether the vestiges of past discrimination ha[ve] been eliminated to the extent practicable." . . .

Proper analysis of the District Court's orders challenged here, then, must rest upon their serving as proper means to the end of restoring the victims of discriminatory conduct to the position they would have occupied in the absence of that conduct and their eventual restoration of "state and local authorities to the control of a school system that is operating in compliance with the Constitution." . . . We turn to that analysis.

The State argues that the order approving salary increases is beyond the District Court's authority because it was crafted to serve an "interdistrict goal," in spite of the fact that the constitutional violation in this case is "intradistrict" in nature. . . . The proper response to an intradistrict violation is an intradistrict remedy, . . . that serves to eliminate the racial identity of the schools within the effected school district by eliminating, as far as practicable, the vestiges of *de jure* segregation in all facets of their operations. . . .

Here, the District Court has found, and the Court of Appeals has affirmed, that this case involved no interdistrict constitutional violation that would support interdistrict relief. . . . Thus, the proper response by the District Court should have been to eliminate to the extent practicable the vestiges of prior *de jure* segregation within the KCMSD: a system wide reduction in student achievement and the existence of 25 racially identifiable schools with a population of over 90% black students. . . .

The District Court and Court of Appeals, however, have felt that because the KCMSD's enrollment remained 68.3% black, a purely intradistrict remedy would be insufficient. . . . But, as noted in *Milliken* I, supra, we have rejected the suggestion "that schools which have a majority of Negro students are not 'desegregated' whatever the racial makeup of the school district's population and however neutrally the district lines have been drawn and administered." . . .

Instead of seeking to remove the racial identity of the various schools within the KCMSD, the District Court has set out on a program to create a school district that was equal to or superior to the surrounding SSD's. Its remedy has focused on "desegregative attractiveness," coupled with "suburban comparability." Examination of the District Court's reliance on "desegregative attractiveness" and "suburban comparability" is instructive for our ultimate resolution of the salary order issue.

The purpose of desegregative attractiveness has been not only to remedy the system wide reduction in student achievement, but also to attract nonminority students not presently enrolled in the KCMSD. This remedy has included an elaborate program of capital improvements, course enrichment, and extracurricular enhancement not simply in the formerly identifiable black schools, but in schools throughout the district. The District Court's remedial orders have converted every senior high school, every middle school, and one half of the elementary schools in the KCMSD into "magnet" schools. The District Court's remedial order has all but made the KCMSD itself into a magnet district.

We previously have approved of intradistrict desegregation remedies involving magnet schools. . . . Magnet schools have the advantage of encouraging voluntary movement of students within a school district in a pattern that aids desegregation on a voluntary basis, without requiring extensive busing and redrawing of district boundary lines. . . . As a component in an intradistrict remedy, magnet schools also are attractive because they promote desegregation while limiting the withdrawal of white student enrollment that may result from mandatory student reassignment. . . .

The District Court's remedial plan in this case, however, is not designed solely to redistribute the students within the KCMSD in order to eliminate racially identifiable schools within the KCMSD. Instead, its purpose is to attract nonminority students from outside the KCMSD schools. But this interdistrict goal is beyond the scope of the intradistrict violation identified by the District Court. In effect, the District Court has devised a remedy to accomplish indirectly what it admittedly lacks the remedial authority to mandate directly: the interdistrict transfer of students. . . .

In *Milliken* I we determined that a desegregation remedy that would require mandatory interdistrict reassignment of students throughout the Detroit metropolitan area was an impermissible interdistrict response to the intradistrict violation identified. . . . In that case, the lower courts had ordered an interdistrict remedy because " 'any less comprehensive a solution than a metropolitan area plan would result in an all black school system immediately surrounded by practically all white suburban school systems, with an overwhelmingly white majority population in the total metropolitan area.' " . . . We held that before a district court could order an interdistrict remedy, there must be a showing that "racially discriminatory acts of the state or local school districts, or of a single school district have been a substantial cause of interdistrict segregation." . . . Because the record "contain[ed] evidence of *de jure* segregated conditions only in the Detroit Schools" and there had been "no showing of significant violation by the 53 outlying school districts and no evidence of interdistrict violation or effect," we reversed the District Court's grant of interdistrict relief. . . .

What we meant in *Milliken* I by an interdistrict violation was a violation that caused segregation between adjoining districts. Nothing in *Milliken* I suggests that the District Court in that case could have circumvented the limits on its remedial authority by requiring the State of Michigan, a constitutional violator, to implement a magnet program designed to achieve the same interdistrict transfer of students that we held was beyond its remedial authority. Here, the District Court has done just that: created a magnet district of the KCMSD in order to serve the interdistrict goal of attracting nonminority students from the surrounding SSD's and redistributing them within the KCMSD. The District Court's pursuit of "desegregative attractiveness" is beyond the scope of its broad remedial authority. . . .

. . . A district court seeking to remedy an intradistrict violation that has not "directly caused" significant interdistrict effects, . . . exceeds its remedial authority if it orders a remedy with an interdistrict purpose. This conclusion follows directly from . . . the bedrock principle that "federal court decrees exceed appropriate limits if they are aimed at eliminating a condition that does not violate the Constitution or does not flow from such a violation." . . . In *Milliken* II, we also emphasized that "federal courts in devising a remedy must take into account the interests of state and local authorities in managing their own affairs, consistent with the Constitution." . . .

The District Court's pursuit of "desegregative attractiveness" cannot be reconciled with our cases placing limitations on a district court's remedial authority. It is certainly theoretically possible that the greater the expenditure per pupil within the KCMSD, the more likely it is that some unknowable number of nonminority students not presently attending schools in the KCMSD will choose to enroll in those schools. Under this reasoning, however, every increased expenditure, whether it be for teachers, noninstructional employees, books, or buildings, will make the KCMSD in some way more attractive, and thereby perhaps induce nonminority students to enroll in its schools. But this rationale is not susceptible to any objective limitation. . . . This case provides numerous examples demonstrating the limitless authority of the District Court operating under this rationale. . . . In short, desegregative attractiveness has been used "as the hook on which to hang numerous policy choices about improving the quality of education in general within the KCMSD." . . .

Nor are there limits to the duration of the District Court's involvement. The expenditures per pupil in the KCMSD currently far exceed those in the neighboring SSD's. 19 F. 3d, at 399 (Beam, J., dissenting from denial of rehearing *en banc*) (per pupil costs within the SSD's, excluding capital costs, range from $2,854 to $5,956; per pupil costs within the KCMSD, excluding capital costs, are $9,412); Brief for Respondent KCMSD *et al.* 18, n. 5 (arguing that per pupil costs in the KCMSD, excluding capital costs, are $7,665.18). Sixteen years after this litigation began, the District Court recognized that the KCMSD has yet to offer a viable method of financing the "wonderful school system being built." . . . Each additional program ordered by the District Court—and fi-

nanced by the State—to increase the "desegregative attractiveness" of the school district makes the KCMSD more and more dependent on additional funding from the State; in turn, the greater the KCMSD's dependence on state funding, the greater its reliance on continued supervision by the District Court. But our cases recognize that local autonomy of school districts is a vital national tradition, . . . and that a district court must strive to restore state and local authorities to the control of a school system operating in compliance with the Constitution. . . .

The District Court's pursuit of the goal of "desegregative attractiveness" results in so many imponderables and is so far removed from the task of eliminating the racial identifiability of the schools within the KCMSD that we believe it is beyond the admittedly broad discretion of the District Court. In this posture, we conclude that the District Court's order of salary increases, which was "grounded in remedying the vestiges of segregation by improving the desegregative attractiveness of the KCMSD," App. to Pet. for Cert. A-90, is simply too far removed from an acceptable implementation of a permissible means to remedy previous legally mandated segregation. . . .

Similar considerations lead us to conclude that the District Court's order requiring the State to continue to fund the quality education programs because student achievement levels were still "at or below national norms at many grade levels" cannot be sustained. The State does not seek from this Court a declaration of partial unitary status with respect to the quality education programs. . . . It challenges the requirement of indefinite funding of a quality education program until national norms are met, based on the assumption that while a mandate for significant educational improvement, both in teaching and in facilities, may have been justified originally, its indefinite extension is not. . . .

In reconsidering this order, the District Court should apply our three part test from [1992] *Freeman v. Pitts.* . . . The District Court should consider that the State's role with respect to the quality education programs has been limited to the funding, not the implementation, of those programs. As all the parties agree that improved achievement on test scores is not necessarily required for the State to achieve partial unitary status as to the quality education programs, the District Court should sharply limit, if not dispense with, its reliance on this factor. . . . Just as demographic changes independent of *de jure* segregation will affect the racial composition of student assignments, . . . so too will numerous external factors beyond the control of the

KCMSD and the State affect minority student achievement. So long as these external factors are not the result of segregation, they do not figure in the remedial calculus. . . . Insistence upon academic goals unrelated to the effects of legal segregation unwarrantably postpones the day when the KCMSD will be able to operate on its own.

The District Court also should consider that many goals of its quality education plan already have been attained: the KCMSD now is equipped with "facilities and opportunities not available anywhere else in the country." . . . It may be that in education, just as it may be in economics, a "rising tide lifts all boats," but the remedial quality education program should be tailored to remedy the injuries suffered by the victims of prior *de jure* segregation. . . . Minority students in kindergarten through grade 7 in the KCMSD always have attended AAA rated schools; minority students in the KCMSD that previously attended schools rated below AAA have since received remedial education programs for a period of up to seven years.

On remand, the District Court must bear in mind that its end purpose is not only "to remedy the violation" to the extent practicable, but also "to restore state and local authorities to the control of a school system that is operating in compliance with the Constitution." . . .

The judgment of the Court of Appeals is reversed.

Justice O'Connor, concurring.

. . . School desegregation remedies are intended, "as all remedies are, to restore the victims of discriminatory conduct to the position they would have occupied in the absence of such conduct." . . . In the paradigmatic case of an interdistrict violation, where district boundaries are drawn on the basis of race, a regional remedy is appropriate to ensure integration across district lines. So too where surrounding districts contribute to the constitutional violation by affirmative acts intended to segregate the races. . . . *Milliken* I of course permits interdistrict remedies in these instances of interdistrict violations. Beyond that, interdistrict remedies are also proper where "there has been a constitutional violation within one district that produces a significant segregative effect in another district." . . . Such segregative effect may be present where a predominantly black district accepts black children from adjacent districts, . . . or perhaps even where the fact of intradistrict segregation actually causes whites to flee the district, . . . for example, to avoid discriminatorily underfunded schools— and such actions produce regional segregation along district lines. In those cases, where a purely intradistrict violation has caused a significant interdistrict segrega-

tive effect, certain interdistrict remedies may be appropriate. Where, however, the segregative effects of a district's constitutional violation are contained within that district's boundaries, there is no justification for a remedy that is interdistrict in nature and scope.

Here, where the District Court found that KCMSD students attended schools separated by their race and that facilities have "literally rotted," . . . the district court of course should order restorations and remedies that would place previously segregated black KCMSD students at par with their white KCMSD counterparts. The District Court went further, however, and ordered certain improvements to KCMSD as a whole, including schools that were not previously segregated; these district wide remedies may also be justified (the State does not argue the point here) in light of the finding that segregation caused "a system wide reduction in student achievement in the schools of the KCMSD." . . . Such remedies obviously may benefit some who did not suffer under—and, indeed, may have even profited from—past segregation. There is no categorical constitutional prohibition on non victims enjoying the collateral, incidental benefits of a remedial plan designed "to restore the victims of discriminatory conduct to the position they would have occupied in the absence of such conduct." . . . Thus, if restoring KCMSD to unitary status would attract whites into the school district, such a reversal of the white exodus would be of no legal consequence.

What the District Court did in this case, however, and how it transgressed the constitutional bounds of its remedial powers, is to make desegregative attractiveness the underlying goal of its remedy for the specific purpose of reversing the trend of white flight. However troubling that trend may be, remedying it is within the District Court's authority only if it is "directly caused by the constitutional violation." . . . The Court and the dissent attempt to reconcile the different statements by the lower courts as to whether white flight was caused by segregation or desegregation. . . . One fact, however, is uncontroverted. When the District Court found that KCMSD was racially segregated, the constitutional violation from which all remedies flow in this case, it also found that there was neither an interdistrict violation nor significant interdistrict segregative effects. . . . Whether the white exodus that has resulted in a school district that is 68% black was caused by the District Court's remedial orders or by natural, if unfortunate, demographic forces, we have it directly from the District Court that the segregative effects of KCMSD's constitutional violation did not transcend its geographical boundaries. In light of that finding, the District Court cannot order remedies seeking to rectify regional demographic trends that go beyond the nature and scope of the constitutional violation.

This case, like other school desegregation litigation, is concerned with "the elimination of the discrimination inherent in the dual school systems, not with myriad factors of human existence which can cause discrimination in a multitude of ways on racial, religious, or ethnic grounds." . . . Those myriad factors are not readily corrected by judicial intervention, but are best addressed by the representative branches; time and again, we have recognized the ample authority legislatures possess to combat racial injustice. . . .

Courts, however, are different. The necessary restrictions on our jurisdiction and authority contained in Article III of the Constitution limit the judiciary's institutional capacity to prescribe palliatives for societal ills. The unfortunate fact of racial imbalance and bias in our society, however pervasive or invidious, does not admit of judicial intervention absent a constitutional violation. . . .

In this case, it may be the "myriad factors of human existence," . . . that have prompted the white exodus from KCMSD, and the District Court cannot justify its transgression of the above constitutional principles simply by invoking desegregative attractiveness. The Court today discusses desegregative attractiveness only insofar as it supports the salary increase order under review, . . . and properly refrains from addressing the propriety of all the remedies that the District Court has ordered, revised, and extended in the 18-year history of this case. These remedies may also be improper to the extent that they serve the same goals of desegregative attractiveness and suburban comparability that we hold today to be impermissible, and, conversely, the District Court may be able to justify some remedies without reliance on these goals. But these are questions that the Court rightly leaves to be answered on remand. For now, it is enough to affirm the principle that "the nature of the desegregation remedy is to be determined by the nature and scope of the constitutional violation." . . .

For these reasons, I join the opinion of the Court.

Justice Thomas, concurring.

It never ceases to amaze me that the courts are so willing to assume that anything that is predominantly black must be inferior. Instead of focusing on remedying the harm done to those black schoolchildren injured by segregation, the District Court here sought to convert the Kansas City, Missouri, School District (KCMSD) into a "magnet district" that would reverse the "white flight"

caused by desegregation. In this respect, I join the Court's decision concerning the two remedial issues presented for review. I write separately, however, to add a few thoughts with respect to the overall course of this litigation. In order to evaluate the scope of the remedy, we must understand the scope of the constitutional violation and the nature of the remedial powers of the federal courts.

Two threads in our jurisprudence have produced this unfortunate situation, in which a District Court has taken it upon itself to experiment with the education of the KCMSD's black youth. First, the court has read our cases to support the theory that black students suffer an unspecified psychological harm from segregation that retards their mental and educational development. This approach not only relies upon questionable social science research rather than constitutional principle, but it also rests on an assumption of black inferiority. Second, we have permitted the federal courts to exercise virtually unlimited equitable powers to remedy this alleged constitutional violation. The exercise of this authority has trampled upon principles of federalism and the separation of powers and has freed courts to pursue other agendas unrelated to the narrow purpose of precisely remedying a constitutional harm.

The mere fact that a school is black does not mean that it is the product of a constitutional violation. A "racial imbalance does not itself establish a violation of the Constitution." . . . Instead, in order to find unconstitutional segregation, we require that plaintiffs "prove all of the essential elements of *de jure* segregation—that is, stated simply, a current condition of segregation resulting from intentional state action directed specifically to the [allegedly segregated] schools." . . .

In the present case, the District Court inferred a continuing constitutional violation from two primary facts: the existence of *de jure* segregation in the KCMSD prior to 1954, and the existence of *de facto* segregation today. The District Court found that in 1954, the KCMSD operated 16 segregated schools for black students, and that in 1974 39 schools in the district were more than 90% black. Desegregation efforts reduced this figure somewhat, but the District Court stressed that 24 schools remained "racially isolated," that is, more than 90% black, in 1983–1984. . . . For the District Court, it followed that the KCMSD had not dismantled the dual system entirely. . . . The District Court also concluded that because of the KCMSD's failure to "become integrated on a system wide basis," the dual system still exerted "lingering effects" upon KCMSD black students, whose "general attitude of inferiority" produced "low achievement . . .

which ultimately limits employment opportunities and causes poverty." . . .

Without more, the District Court's findings could not have supported a finding of liability against the state. It should by now be clear that the existence of one race schools is not by itself an indication that the State is practicing segregation. . . . The continuing "racial isolation" of schools after *de jure* segregation has ended may well reflect voluntary housing choices or other private decisions. Here, for instance, the demography of the entire KCMSD has changed considerably since 1954. Though blacks accounted for only 18.9% of KCMSD's enrollment in 1954, by 1983–1984 the school district was 67.7% black. . . . That certain schools are overwhelmingly black in a district that is now more than two thirds black is hardly a sure sign of intentional state action. . . .

Even if segregation were present, we must remember that a deserving end does not justify all possible means. The desire to reform a school district, or any other institution, cannot so captivate the Judiciary that it forgets its constitutionally mandated role. Usurpation of the traditionally local control over education not only takes the judiciary beyond its proper sphere, it also deprives the States and their elected officials of their constitutional powers. At some point, we must recognize that the judiciary is not omniscient, and that all problems do not require a remedy of constitutional proportions.

Justice Souter, with whom *Justice Stevens, Justice Ginsburg,* and *Justice Breyer* join, dissenting.

. . . On its face, the Court's opinion projects an appealing pragmatism in seeming to cut through the details of many facts by applying a rule of law that can claim both precedential support and intuitive sense, that there is error in imposing an interdistrict remedy to cure a merely intradistrict violation. Since the District Court has consistently described the violation here as solely intradistrict, and since the object of the magnet schools under its plan includes attracting students into the district from other districts, the Court's result seems to follow with the necessity of logic, against which arguments about detail or calls for fair warning may not carry great weight.

The attractiveness of the Court's analysis disappears, however, as soon as we recognize two things. First, the District Court did not mean by an "intradistrict violation" what the Court apparently means by it today. The District Court meant that the violation within the KCMSD had not led to segregation outside of it, and that no other school districts had played a part in the violation. It did not mean that the violation had not produced effects of any sort beyond the district. Indeed, the record that we have indicates that the District Court understood that the violation here did produce effects spanning district borders and leading to greater segregation within the KCMSD, the reversal of which the District Court sought to accomplish by establishing magnet schools. Insofar as the Court assumes that this was not so in fact, there is at least enough in the record to cast serious doubt on its assumption. Second, the Court violates existing case law even on its own apparent view of the facts, that the segregation violation within the KCMSD produced no proven effects, segregative or otherwise, outside it. Assuming this to be true, the Court's decision that the rule against interdistrict remedies for intradistrict violations applies to this case, solely because the remedy here is meant to produce effects outside the district in which the violation occurred, is flatly contrary to established precedent. . . .

I respectfully dissent.

Justice Ginsburg, dissenting. . . .

Case

ADARAND CONSTRUCTORS, INC. V. PEÑA

515 U.S. 200, 115 S.Ct. 2097, 132 L.Ed. 2d. 158 (1995)
Vote: 5–4

In this case the Court reexamines the controversial issue of affirmative action in the context of the federal government's practice of providing financial incentives to contractors to hire minority subcontractors.

Justice O'Connor announced the judgment of the Court. . . .

Petitioner Adarand Constructors, Inc., claims that the Federal Government's practice of giving general contractors on government projects a financial incentive to hire subcontractors controlled by "socially and economically disadvantaged individuals," and in particular, the Government's use of race-based presumptions in identifying such individuals, violates the equal protection component of the Fifth Amendment's Due Process Clause. The Court of Appeals rejected Adarand's claim. We conclude, however, that courts should analyze cases of this kind under a different standard of review than the one the Court of Appeals applied. We therefore vacate the Court of Appeals' judgment and remand the case for further proceedings. . . .

In 1989, the Central Federal Lands Highway Division (CFLHD), which is part of the United States Department of Transportation (DOT), awarded the prime contract for a highway construction project in Colorado to Mountain Gravel & Construction Company. Mountain Gravel then solicited bids from subcontractors for the guardrail portion of the contract. Adarand, a Colorado-based highway construction company specializing in guardrail work, submitted the low bid. . . . Gonzales Construction Company also submitted a bid.

The prime contract's terms provide that Mountain Gravel would receive additional compensation if it hired subcontractors certified as small businesses controlled by "socially and economically disadvantaged individuals," . . . Gonzales is certified as such a business; Adarand is not. Mountain Gravel awarded the subcontract to Gonzales, despite Adarand's low bid, and Mountain Gravel's Chief Estimator has submitted an affidavit stating that Mountain Gravel would have accepted Adarand's bid, had it not been for the additional payment it received by hiring Gonzales instead. . . . Federal law requires that a subcontracting clause similar to the one used here must appear in most federal agency contracts, and it also requires the clause to state that "[t]he contractor shall presume that socially and economically disadvantaged individuals include Black Americans, Hispanic Americans, Native Americans, Asian Pacific Americans, and other minorities, or any other individual found to be disadvantaged by the [Small Business] Administration pursuant to section 8(a) of the Small Business Act." . . . Adarand claims that the presumption set forth in that statute discriminates on the basis of race in violation of the Federal Government's Fifth Amendment obligation not to deny anyone equal protection of the laws. . . .

The Government urges that "[t]he Subcontracting Compensation Clause program is . . . a program based on disadvantage, not on race," and thus that it is subject only to "the most relaxed judicial scrutiny." . . . To the extent that the statutes and regulations involved in this case are race neutral, we agree. The Government concedes, however, that "the race-based rebuttable presumption used in some certification determinations under the Subcontracting Compensation Clause" is subject to some heightened level of scrutiny. . . . The parties disagree as to what that level should be. . . .

. . . [T]he Court's cases through *[Richmond v. J. A. Croson Co.]* had established three general propositions with respect to governmental racial classifications. First, skepticism: " '[a]ny preference based on racial or ethnic criteria must necessarily receive a most searching examination.' " . . . Second, consistency: "the standard of review under the Equal Protection Clause is not dependent on the race of those burdened or benefited by a particular classification." . . . And third, congruence: "[e]qual protection analysis in the Fifth Amendment area is the same as that under the Fourteenth Amendment." . . . Taken together, these three propositions lead to the conclusion that any person, of whatever race, has the right to demand that any governmental actor subject to the Constitution justify any racial classification subjecting that person to unequal treatment under the strictest judicial scrutiny. . . .

A year later, however, the Court took a surprising turn. *Metro Broadcasting, Inc. v. FCC* . . . (1990) involved a Fifth Amendment challenge to two race-based policies of the Federal Communications Commission. In *Metro Broadcasting,* the Court repudiated the long-held notion that "it would be unthinkable that the same Constitution would impose a lesser duty on the Federal Government" than it does on a State to afford equal protection of the laws. . . . It did so by holding that "benign" federal racial classifications need only satisfy intermediate scrutiny, even though *Croson* had recently concluded that such classifications enacted by a State must satisfy strict scrutiny. "[B]enign" federal racial classifications, the Court said, "even if those measures are not 're-medial' in the sense of being designed to compensate victims of past governmental or societal discrimination are constitutionally permissible to the extent that they serve important governmental objectives within the power of Congress and are substantially related to achievement of those objectives." . . . The Court did not explain how to tell whether a racial classification should be deemed "benign," other than to express "confiden[ce] that an 'examination of the legislative scheme and its history' will separate benign measures from other types of racial classifications." . . .

Applying this test, the Court first noted that the FCC policies at issue did not serve as a remedy for past discrimination. . . . Proceeding on the assumption that the policies were nonetheless "benign," it concluded that they served the "important governmental objective" of "enhancing broadcast diversity," . . . and that they were

795 EQUAL PROTECTION AND THE ANTIDISCRIMINATION PRINCIPLE

"substantially related" to that objective. . . . It therefore upheld the policies.

By adopting intermediate scrutiny as the standard of review for congressionally mandated "benign" racial classifications, *Metro Broadcasting* departed from prior cases in two significant respects. First, it turned its back on *Croson's* explanation of why strict scrutiny of all governmental racial classifications is essential. . . .

Second, *Metro Broadcasting* squarely rejected one of the three propositions established by the Court's earlier equal protection cases, namely, congruence between the standards applicable to federal and state racial classifications, and in so doing also undermined the other two— skepticism of all racial classifications, and consistency of treatment irrespective of the race of the burdened or benefited group. . . . Under *Metro Broadcasting*, certain racial classifications ("benign" ones enacted by the Federal Government) should be treated less skeptically than others; and the race of the benefited group is critical to the determination of which standard of review to apply. *Metro Broadcasting* was thus a significant departure from much of what had come before it.

The three propositions undermined by *Metro Broadcasting* all derive from the basic principle that the Fifth and Fourteenth Amendments to the Constitution protect persons, not groups. It follows from that principle that all governmental action based on race—a group classification long recognized as "in most circumstances irrelevant and therefore prohibited," . . . should be subjected to detailed judicial inquiry to ensure that the personal right to equal protection of the laws has not been infringed. These ideas have long been central to this Court's understanding of equal protection, and holding "benign" state and federal racial classifications to different standards does not square with them. "[A] free people whose institutions are founded upon the doctrine of equality," . . . should tolerate no retreat from the principle that government may treat people differently because of their race only for the most compelling reasons. Accordingly, we hold today that all racial classifications, imposed by whatever federal, state, or local governmental actor, must be analyzed by a reviewing court under strict scrutiny. In other words, such classifications are constitutional only if they are narrowly tailored measures that further compelling governmental interests. To the extent that *Metro Broadcasting* is inconsistent with that holding, it is overruled. . . .

"Although adherence to precedent is not rigidly required in constitutional cases, any departure from the doctrine of *stare decisis* demands special justifica-

tion." . . . In deciding whether this case presents such justification, we recall Justice Frankfurter's admonition that "*stare decisis* is a principle of policy and not a mechanical formula of adherence to the latest decision, however recent and questionable, when such adherence involves collision with a prior doctrine more embracing in its scope, intrinsically sounder, and verified by experience." . . . Remaining true to an "intrinsically sounder" doctrine established in prior cases better serves the values of *stare decisis* than would following a more recently decided case inconsistent with the decisions that came before it; the latter course would simply compound the recent error and would likely make the unjustified break from previously established doctrine complete. In such a situation, "special justification" exists to depart from the recently decided case.

As we have explained, *Metro Broadcasting* undermined important principles of this Court's equal protection jurisprudence, established in a line of cases stretching back over fifty years. . . . Those principles together stood for an "embracing" and "intrinsically soun[d]" understanding of equal protection "verified by experience," namely, that the Constitution imposes upon federal, state, and local governmental actors the same obligation to respect the personal right to equal protection of the laws. . . .

Some have questioned the importance of debating the proper standard of review of race-based legislation. . . . But we agree . . . that, "[b]ecause racial characteristics so seldom provide a relevant basis for disparate treatment, and because classifications based on race are potentially so harmful to the entire body politic, it is especially important that the reasons for any such classification be clearly identified and unquestionably legitimate," and that "[r]acial classifications are simply too pernicious to permit any but the most exact connection between justification and classification." . . . We think that requiring strict scrutiny is the best way to ensure that courts will consistently give racial classifications that kind of detailed examination, both as to ends and as to means. . . . Any retreat from the most searching judicial inquiry can only increase the risk of another such error occurring in the future.

Finally, we wish to dispel the notion that strict scrutiny is "strict in theory, but fatal in fact." . . . The unhappy persistence of both the practice and the lingering effects of racial discrimination against minority groups in this country is an unfortunate reality, and government is not disqualified from acting in response to it. As recently as 1987, for example, every Justice of this Court agreed that the Alabama Department of Public Safety's "pervasive, systematic, and obstinate discriminatory conduct" justified a narrowly tailored race-based remedy. . . . When race-based action is necessary to further a compelling interest, such action is within constitutional constraints if it satisfies the "narrow tailoring" test this Court has set out in previous cases. . . .

Because our decision today alters the playing field in some important respects, we think it best to remand the case to the lower courts for further consideration in light of the principles we have announced. The Court of Appeals, following *Metro Broadcasting* and *Fullilove,* analyzed the case in terms of intermediate scrutiny. It upheld the challenged statutes and regulations because it found them to be "narrowly tailored to achieve [their] significant governmental purpose of providing subcontracting opportunities for small disadvantaged business enterprises." . . . The Court of Appeals did not decide the question whether the interests served by the use of subcontractor compensation clauses are properly described as "compelling." It also did not address the question of narrow tailoring in terms of our strict scrutiny cases, by asking, for example, whether there was "any consideration of the use of race-neutral means to increase minority business participation" in government contracting, . . . whether the program was appropriately limited such that it "will not last longer than the discriminatory effects it is designed to eliminate." . . .

Moreover, unresolved questions remain concerning the details of the complex regulatory regimes implicated by the use of subcontractor compensation clauses. . . . The question whether any of the ways in which the Government uses subcontractor compensation clauses can survive strict scrutiny, and any relevance distinctions such as these may have to that question, should be addressed in the first instance by the lower courts.

Accordingly, the judgment of the Court of Appeals is vacated, and the case is remanded for further proceedings consistent with this opinion. . . .

Justice Scalia, concurring in part and concurring in the judgment.

I join the opinion of the Court, except . . . insofar as it may be inconsistent with the following: In my view, government can never have a "compelling interest" in discriminating on the basis of race in order to "make up" for past racial discrimination in the opposite direction. . . . Individuals who have been wronged by unlawful racial discrimination should be made whole; but under our Constitution there can be no such thing as either a cred-

itor or a debtor race. That concept is alien to the Constitution's focus upon the individual . . . and its rejection of dispositions based on race. . . . To pursue the concept of racial entitlement—even for the most admirable and benign of purposes—is to reinforce and preserve for future mischief the way of thinking that produced race slavery, race privilege and race hatred. In the eyes of government, we are just one race here. It is American.

It is unlikely, if not impossible, that the challenged program would survive under this understanding of strict scrutiny, but I am content to leave that to be decided on remand.

Justice Thomas, concurring in part and concurring in the judgment.

I agree with the majority's conclusion that strict scrutiny applies to all government classifications based on race. I write separately, however, to express my disagreement with the premise underlying Justice Stevens' and Justice Ginsburg's dissents: that there is a racial paternalism exception to the principle of equal protection. I believe that there is a "moral [and] constitutional equivalence" . . . between laws designed to subjugate a race and those that distribute benefits on the basis of race in order to foster some current notion of equality. Government cannot make us equal; it can only recognize, respect, and protect us as equal before the law.

That these programs may have been motivated, in part, by good intentions cannot provide refuge from the principle that under our Constitution, the government may not make distinctions on the basis of race. As far as the Constitution is concerned, it is irrelevant whether a government's racial classifications are drawn by those who wish to oppress a race or by those who have a sincere desire to help those thought to be disadvantaged. There can be no doubt that the paternalism that appears to lie at the heart of this program is at war with the principle of inherent equality that underlies and infuses our Constitution. . . .

These programs not only raise grave constitutional questions, they also undermine the moral basis of the equal protection principle. Purchased at the price of immeasurable human suffering, the equal protection principle reflects our Nation's understanding that such classifications ultimately have a destructive impact on the individual and our society. Unquestionably, "[i]nvidious [racial] discrimination is an engine of oppression." . . . It is also true that "[r]emedial" racial preferences may reflect "a desire to foster equality in society." . . . But there can be no doubt that racial paternalism and its unintended consequences can be as poisonous and pernicious as any other form of discrimination. So-called "benign" discrimination teaches many that because of chronic and apparently immutable handicaps, minorities cannot compete with them without their patronizing indulgence. Inevitably, such programs engender attitudes of superiority or, alternatively, provoke resentment among those who believe that they have been wronged by the government's use of race. These programs stamp minorities with a badge of inferiority and may cause them to develop dependencies or to adopt an attitude that they are "entitled" to preferences. . . .

In my mind, government-sponsored racial discrimination based on benign prejudice is just as noxious as discrimination inspired by malicious prejudice. In each instance, it is racial discrimination, plain and simple. . . .

Justice Stevens, with whom ***Justice Ginsburg*** joins, dissenting:

. . . This is the third time in the Court's entire history that it has considered the constitutionality of a federal affirmative-action program. On each of the two prior occasions, the first in 1980, . . . and the second in 1990, . . . the Court upheld the program. Today the Court explicitly overrules *Metro Broadcasting* . . . and undermines *Fullilove* [*v. Klutznick* (1980)] by recasting the standard on which it rested and by calling even its holding into question. . . . By way of explanation, Justice O'Connor advises the federal agencies and private parties that have made countless decisions in reliance on those cases that "we do not depart from the fabric of the law; we restore it." A skeptical observer might ask whether this pronouncement is a faithful application of the doctrine of *stare decisis*. . . .

The Court's holding in *Fullilove* surely governs the result in this case. The Public Works Employment Act of 1977 . . . which this Court upheld in *Fullilove,* is different in several critical respects from the portions of the Small Business Act (SBA) . . . and the Surface Transportation and Uniform Relocation Assistance Act of 1987 (STURAA) . . . challenged in this case. Each of those differences makes the current program designed to provide assistance to disadvantaged business enterprises (DBE's) significantly less objectionable than the 1977 categorical grant of $400 million in exchange for a 10% set-aside in public contracts to "a class of investors defined solely by racial characteristics." . . . In no meaningful respect is the current scheme more objectionable than the 1977 Act. Thus, if the 1977 Act was constitutional, then so must be the SBA and STURAA. Indeed,

even if my dissenting views in *Fullilove* had prevailed, this program would be valid.

Unlike the 1977 Act, the present statutory scheme does not make race the sole criterion of eligibility for participation in the program. Race does give rise to a rebuttable presumption of social disadvantage which, at least under STURAA, gives rise to a second rebuttable presumption of economic disadvantage. . . . But a small business may qualify as a DBE, by showing that it is both socially and economically disadvantaged, even if it receives neither of these presumptions. . . . Thus, the current preference is more inclusive than the 1977 Act because it does not make race a necessary qualification.

More importantly, race is not a sufficient qualification. Whereas a millionaire with a long history of financial successes, who was a member of numerous social clubs and trade associations, would have qualified for a preference under the 1977 Act merely because he was an Asian American or an African American, . . . neither the SBA nor STURAA creates any such anomaly. The DBE program excludes members of minority races who are not, in fact, socially or economically disadvantaged. . . . The presumption of social disadvantage reflects the unfortunate fact that irrational racial prejudice—along with its lingering effects—still survives. The presumption of economic disadvantage embodies a recognition that success in the private sector of the economy is often attributable, in part, to social skills and relationships. Unlike the 1977 set-asides, the current preference is designed to overcome the social and economic disadvantages that are often associated with racial characteristics. If, in a particular case, these disadvantages are not present, the presumptions can be rebutted. . . . The program is thus designed to allow race to play a part in the decisional process only when there is a meaningful basis for assuming its relevance. . . .

The current program contains another forward-looking component that the 1977 set-asides did not share. Section 8(a) of the SBA provides for periodic review of the status of DBE's, . . . and DBE status can be challenged by a competitor at any time under any of the routes to certification. . . . Such review prevents ineligible firms from taking part in the program solely because of their minority ownership, even when those firms were once disadvantaged but have since become successful. The emphasis on review also indicates the Administration's anticipation that after their presumed disadvantages have been overcome, firms will "graduate" into a status in which they will be able to compete for business, including prime contracts, on an equal basis. . . . As with other phases of the statutory policy of encouraging the formation and growth of small business enterprises, this program is intended to facilitate entry and increase competition in the free market.

Significantly, the current program, unlike the 1977 set-aside, does not establish any requirement—numerical or otherwise—that a general contractor must hire DBE subcontractors. The program we upheld in *Fullilove* required that 10% of the federal grant for every federally funded project be expended on minority business enterprises. In contrast, the current program contains no quota. Although it provides monetary incentives to general contractors to hire DBE subcontractors, it does not require them to hire DBE's, and they do not lose their contracts if they fail to do so. The importance of this incentive to general contractors (who always seek to offer the lowest bid) should not be underestimated; but the preference here is far less rigid, and thus more narrowly tailored, than the 1977 Act. . . .

Finally, the record shows a dramatic contrast between the sparse deliberations that preceded the 1977 Act, . . . and the extensive hearings conducted in several Congresses before the current program was developed. However we might evaluate the benefits and costs—both fiscal and social—of this or any other affirmative-action program, our obligation to give deference to Congress' policy choices is much more demanding in this case than it was in *Fullilove.* If the 1977 program of race-based set-asides satisfied the strict scrutiny dictated by Justice Powell's vision of the Constitution—a vision the Court expressly endorses today—it must follow as night follows the day that the Court of Appeals' judgment upholding this more carefully crafted program should be affirmed. . . .

My skeptical scrutiny of the Court's opinion leaves me in dissent. The majority's concept of "consistency" ignores a difference, fundamental to the idea of equal protection, between oppression and assistance. The majority's concept of "congruence" ignores a difference, fundamental to our constitutional system, between the Federal Government and the States. And the majority's concept of *stare decisis* ignores the force of binding precedent. I would affirm the judgment of the Court of Appeals.

Justice Souter, with whom ***Justice Ginsburg*** and ***Justice Breyer*** join, dissenting. . . .

Justice Ginsburg, with whom ***Justice Breyer*** joins, dissenting.

. . . The statutes and regulations at issue, as the Court indicates, were adopted by the political branches in response to an "unfortunate reality": "[t]he unhappy persistence of both the practice and the lingering effects of racial discrimination against minority groups in this country." . . . The United States suffers from those lingering effects because, for most of our Nation's history, the idea that "we are just one race" . . . was not embraced. For generations, our lawmakers and judges were unprepared to say that there is in this land no superior race, no race inferior to any other. . . .

Not until *Loving v. Virginia* . . . (1967), which held unconstitutional Virginia's ban on interracial marriages, could one say with security that the Constitution and this Court would abide no measure "designed to maintain White Supremacy." . . .

The divisions in this difficult case should not obscure the Court's recognition of the persistence of racial inequality and a majority's acknowledgment of Congress' authority to act affirmatively, not only to end discrimination, but also to counteract discrimination's lingering effects. . . . Those effects, reflective of a system of racial caste only recently ended, are evident in our workplaces, markets, and neighborhoods. Job applicants with identical resumes, qualifications, and interview styles still experience different receptions, depending on their race. White and African-American consumers still encounter different deals. People of color looking for housing still face discriminatory treatment by landlords, real estate agents, and mortgage lenders. Minority entrepreneurs sometimes fail to gain contracts though they are the low bidders, and they are sometimes refused work even after winning contracts. Bias both conscious and unconscious, reflecting traditional and unexamined habits of thought, keeps up barriers that must come down if equal opportunity and nondiscrimination are ever genuinely to become this country's law and practice.

Given this history and its practical consequences, Congress surely can conclude that a carefully designed affirmative action program may help to realize, finally, the "equal protection of the laws" the Fourteenth Amendment has promised since 1868. . . .

While I would not disturb the programs challenged in this case, and would leave their improvement to the political branches, I see today's decision as one that allows our precedent to evolve, still to be informed by and responsive to changing conditions.

Case

FRONTIERO V. RICHARDSON

411 U.S. 677; 93 S.Ct. 1764; 36 L.Ed. 2d. 583 (1973)
Vote: 8–1

In this landmark case, the Court considers the appropriate standard of equal protection review in cases alleging gender discrimination by the government.

Mr. Justice Brennan announced the judgment of the Court and an opinion in which **Mr. Justice Douglas, Mr. Justice White,** and **Mr. Justice Marshall** join.

The question before us concerns the right of a female member of the uniformed services to claim her spouse as a "dependent" for the purposes of obtaining increased quarters allowances and medical and dental benefits . . . on an equal footing with male members. Under [the statutes at issue], a serviceman may claim his wife as a "dependent" without regard to whether she is in fact dependent upon him for any part of her support. A servicewoman, on the other hand, may not claim her husband as a "dependent" under these programs unless he is in fact dependent upon her for over one-half of his support. . . . Thus, the question for decision is whether this difference in treatment constitutes an unconstitutional discrimination against servicewomen in violation of the [equal protection component] of the Fifth Amendment. A three-judge District Court for the Middle District of Alabama, one judge dissenting, rejected this contention and sustained the constitutionality of the provisions of the statutes making this distinction. . . . We noted probable jurisdiction. . . . We reverse. . . .

In an effort to attract career personnel through reenlistment, Congress established . . . a scheme for the provision of fringe benefits to members of the uniformed services on a competitive basis with business and industry. . . . [A] member of the uniformed services with dependents is entitled to an increased "basic allowance for quarters" and . . . a member's dependents are provided comprehensive medical and dental care.

Appellant Sharron Frontiero, a lieutenant in the United States Air Force, sought increased quarters allowance, and housing and medical benefits for her husband, appellant Joseph Frontiero, on the ground that he was her "dependent." Although such benefits would automatically have been granted with respect to the wife of a male member of the uniformed services, appellant's

application was denied because she failed to demonstrate that her husband was dependent on her for more than one-half of his support. Appellants then commenced this suit, contending that, by making this distinction, the statutes unreasonably discriminate on the basis of sex in violation of the Due Process Clause of the Fifth Amendment. In essence, appellants asserted that the discriminatory impact of the statutes is two-fold: first, as a procedural matter, a female member is required to demonstrate her spouse's dependency, while no such burden is imposed upon male members; and second, as a substantive matter, a male member who does not provide more than one-half of his wife's support receives benefits, while a similarly situated female member is denied such benefits. Appellants therefore sought a permanent injunction against the continued enforcement of these statutes and an order directing the appellees to provide Lieutenant Frontiero with the same housing and medical benefits that a similarly situated male member would receive.

Although the legislative history of these statutes sheds virtually no light on the purposes underlying the differential treatment accorded male and female members, a majority of the three-judge District Court surmised that Congress might reasonably have concluded that, since the husband in our society is generally the "breadwinner" in the family—and the wife typically the "dependent" partner—"it would be more economical to require married female members claiming husbands to prove actual dependency than to extend the presumption of dependency to such members." . . . Indeed, given the fact that approximately 99% of all members of the uniformed services are male, the District Court speculated that such differential treatment might conceivably lead to a "considerable saving of administrative expense and manpower." . . .

At the outset, appellants contend that classifications based upon sex, like classifications based upon race, alienage, and national origin, are inherently suspect and must therefore be subjected to close judicial scrutiny. We agree and, indeed, find at least implicit support for such an approach in our unanimous decision only last Term in *Reed v. Reed*. . . .

In *Reed,* the Court considered the constitutionality of an Idaho statute providing that, when two individuals are otherwise equally entitled to appointment as administrator of an estate, the male applicant must be preferred to the female. Appellant, the mother of the deceased, and appellee, the father, filed competing petitions for appointment as administrator of their son's estate. Since the parties, as parents of the deceased, were members of the same entitlement class, the statutory preference was invoked and the father's petition was therefore granted. Appellant claimed that this statute, by giving a mandatory preference to males over females without regard to their individual qualifications, violated the Equal Protection Clause of the Fourteenth Amendment.

The Court noted that the Idaho statute "provides that different treatment be accorded to the applicants on the basis of their sex; it thus establishes a classification subject to scrutiny under the Equal Protection Clause." . . . Under "traditional" equal protection analysis, a legislative classification must be sustained unless it is "patently arbitrary" and bears no rational relationship to a legitimate governmental interest. . . .

In an effort to meet this standard, appellee contended that the statutory scheme was a reasonable measure designed to reduce the workload on probate courts by eliminating one class of contests. Moreover, appellee argued that the mandatory preference for male applicants was in itself reasonable since "men [are] as a rule more conversant with business affairs than . . . women." Indeed, appellee maintained that "it is a matter of common knowledge, that women still are not engaged in politics, the professions, business or industry to the extent that men are." And the Idaho Supreme Court, in upholding the constitutionality of this statute, suggested that the Idaho Legislature might reasonably have "concluded that in general men are better qualified to act as an administrator than are women."

Despite these contentions, however, the Court held the statutory preference for male applicants unconstitutional. In reaching this result, the Court implicitly rejected appellee's apparently rational explanation of the statutory scheme, and concluded that, by ignoring the individual qualifications of particular applicants, the challenged statute provided "dissimilar treatment for men and women who are . . . similarly situated." . . . The Court therefore held that, even though the State's interest in achieving administrative efficiency "is not without some legitimacy," . . . "[t]o give a mandatory preference to members of either sex over members of the other, merely to accomplish the elimination of hearings on the merits, is to make the very kind of arbitrary legislative choice forbidden by the [Constitution]. . . ." . . . This departure from "traditional" rational basis analysis with respect to sex-based classifications is clearly justified.

There can be no doubt that our Nation has had a long and unfortunate history of sex discrimination. Traditionally, such discrimination was rationalized by an attitude of "romantic paternalism" which, in practical effect, put women not on a pedestal, but in a cage. Indeed, this paternalistic attitude became so firmly rooted in our national consciousness that, exactly 100 years ago, a distinguished member of this Court was about to proclaim:

> Man is, or should be, woman's protector and defender. The natural and proper timidity and delicacy which belongs to the female sex evidently unfits it for many of the occupations of civil life. The constitution of the family organizations, which is founded in the divine ordinance, as well as in the nature of things, indicates the domestic sphere as that which properly belongs to the domain and functions of womanhood. The harmony, not to say identity, of interests and views which belong, or should belong, to the family institution is repugnant to the ideas of a woman adopting a distinct and independent career from that of her husband. . . . The paramount destiny and mission of woman are to fulfill the noble and benign offices of wife and mother. This is the law of the Creator. . . .

As a result of notions such as these, our statute books gradually became laden with gross, stereotypical distinctions between the sexes and, indeed, throughout much of the 19th century the position of women in our society was, in many respects, comparable to that of blacks under the pre–Civil War slave codes. Neither slaves nor women could hold office, serve on juries, or bring suit in their own names, and married women traditionally were denied the legal capacity to hold or convey property or to serve as legal guardians of their own children. . . . And although blacks were guaranteed the right to vote in 1870, women were denied even that right—which is itself "preservative of other basic civil and political rights"—until adoption of the Nineteenth Amendment half a century later.

It is true, of course, that the position of women in America has improved markedly in recent decades. Nevertheless, it can hardly be doubted that, in part because of the high visibility of the sex characteristic, women still face pervasive, although at times more subtle, discrimination in our educational institutions, on the job market and, perhaps most conspicuously, in the political arena. . . .

Moreover, since sex, like race and national origin, is an immutable characteristic determined solely by the accident of birth, the imposition of special disabilities upon the members of a particular sex because of their sex would seem to violate "the basic concept of our system that legal burdens should bear some relationship to individual responsibility. . . ." . . . And what differentiates sex from such nonsuspect statutes as intelligence or physical disability, and aligns it with the recognized suspect criteria, is that the sex characteristic frequently bears no relation to ability to perform or contribute to society. As a result, statutory distinctions between the sexes often have the effect of invidiously relegating the entire class of females to inferior legal status without regard to the actual capabilities of its individual members.

We might also note that, over the past decade, Congress has itself manifested an increasing sensitivity to sex-based classifications. In Title VII of the Civil Rights Act of 1964, for example, Congress expressly declared that no employer, labor union, or other organization subject to the provisions of the Act shall discriminate against any individual on the basis of "race, color, religion, sex, or national origin." Similarly, the Equal Pay Act of 1963 provides that no employer covered by the Act "shall discriminate . . . between employees on the basis of sex." And Section 1 of the Equal Rights Amendment, passed by Congress on March 22, 1972, and submitted to the legislatures of the States for ratification, declares that "[e]quality of rights under the law shall not be denied or abridged by the United States or by any State on account of sex." Thus, Congress has itself concluded that classifications based upon sex are inherently invidious, and this conclusion of a coequal branch of government is not without significance to the question presently under consideration. . . .

With these considerations in mind, we can only conclude that classifications based upon sex, like classifications based upon race, alienage, or national origin, are inherently suspect, and must therefore be subjected to strict judicial scrutiny. Applying the analysis mandated by that stricter standard of review, it is clear that the statutory scheme now before us is constitutionally invalid.

The sole basis of the classification established in the challenged statutes is the sex of the individuals involved. Thus . . . a female member of the uniformed services seeking to obtain housing and medical benefits for her spouse must prove his dependency in fact, whereas no such burden is imposed upon male members. In addition, the statutes operate so as to deny benefits to a female member, such as appellant Sharron Frontiero, who provides less than one-half of her spouse's support, while at the same time granting such benefits to a male member who likewise provides less than one-half of his spouse's support. Thus to this extent at least, it may fairly be said

that these statutes command "dissimilar treatment for men and women who are . . . similarly situated." . . .

Moreover, the Government concedes that the differential treatment accorded men and women under these statutes serves no purpose other than mere "administrative convenience." In essence, the Government maintains that, as an empirical matter, wives in our society frequently are dependent upon their husbands, while husbands rarely are dependent upon their wives. Thus, the Government argues that Congress might reasonably have concluded that it would be both cheaper and easier simply conclusively to presume that wives of male members are financially dependent upon their husbands, while burdening female members with the task of establishing dependency in fact.

The Government offers no concrete evidence, however, tending to support its view that such differential treatment in fact saves the Government any money. In order to satisfy the demands of strict judicial scrutiny, the Government must demonstrate, for example, that it is actually cheaper to grant increased benefits with respect to all male members, than it is to determine which male members are in fact entitled to such benefits and to grant increased benefits only to those members whose wives actually meet the dependency requirement. Here, however, there is substantial evidence that, if put to the test, many of the wives of male members would fail to qualify for benefits. And in light of the fact that the dependency determination with respect to the husbands of female members is presently made solely on the basis of affidavits, rather than through the more costly hearing process, the Government's explanation of the statutory scheme is, to say the least, questionable.

In any case, our prior decisions make clear that, although efficacious administration of governmental programs is not without some importance, "the Constitution recognizes higher values than speed and efficiency." . . . And when we enter the realm of "strict judicial scrutiny," there can be no doubt that "administrative convenience" is not a shibboleth, the mere recitation of which dictates constitutionality. . . . On the contrary, any statutory scheme which draws a sharp line between the sexes, solely for the purpose of achieving administrative convenience, necessarily commands "dissimilar treatment for men and women who are . . . similarly situated," and therefore involves the "very kind of arbitrary legislative choice forbidden by the [Constitution]. . . ." . . . We therefore conclude that, by according differential treatment to male and female members of the uniformed services for the sole purpose of achieving administrative convenience, the challenged statutes violate the Due Process Clause of the Fifth Amendment insofar as they require a female member to prove the dependency of her husband.

Reversed.

Mr. Justice Powell, with whom the **Chief Justice** and **Mr. Justice Blackmun** join, concurring in the judgment.

I agree that the challenged statutes constitute an unconstitutional discrimination against service women in violation of the Due Process Clause of the Fifth Amendment, but I cannot join the opinion of Mr. Justice Brennan, which would hold that all classifications based upon sex, "like classifications based upon race, alienage, and national origin," are "inherently suspect and must therefore be subjected to close judicial scrutiny." . . . It is unnecessary for the Court in this case to characterize sex as a suspect classification, with all of the far-reaching implications of such a holding. . . . In my view, we can and should decide this case on the authority of *Reed* and reserve for the future any expansion of its rationale.

There is another, and I find compelling, reason for deferring a general categorizing of sex classifications as invoking the strictest test of judicial scrutiny. The Equal Rights Amendment, which if adopted will resolve the substance of this precise question, has been approved by the Congress and submitted for ratifica-tion by the States. If this Amendment is duly adopted, it will represent the will of the people accomplished in the manner prescribed by the Constitution. By acting prematurely and unnecessarily, as I view it, the Court has assumed a decisional responsibility at the very time when state legislatures, functioning within the traditional democratic process, are debating the proposed Amendment. It seems to me that this reaching out to pre-empt by judicial action a major political decision which is currently in process of resolution does not reflect appropriate respect for duly prescribed legislative processes.

There are times when this Court, under our system, cannot avoid a constitutional decision on issues which normally should be resolved by the elected representatives of the people. But democratic institutions are weakened, and confidence in the restraint of the Court is impaired, when we appear unnecessarily to decide sensitive issues of broad social and political importance at the very time they are under consideration within the prescribed constitutional processes.

Mr. Justice Stewart concurs in the judgment, agreeing that the statutes before us work an invidious discrimination in violation of the Constitution. . . .

Mr. Justice Rehnquist dissents.

Case

UNITED STATES V. VIRGINIA

518 U.S. 515, 116 S.Ct. 2264, 135 L.Ed. 2d. 735 (1996)
Vote: 7–1

In this case the Court considers the male-only admissions policy of Virginia Military Institute. Justice Ruth Ginsburg, who as an attorney argued a number of important gender discrimination cases before the High Court, authors the majority opinion.

Justice Ginsburg delivered the opinion of the Court.

Virginia's public institutions of higher learning include an incomparable military college, Virginia Military Institute (VMI). The United States maintains that the Constitution's equal protection guarantee precludes Virginia from reserving exclusively to men the unique educational opportunities VMI affords. We agree.

Founded in 1839, VMI is today the sole single-sex school among Virginia's 15 public institutions of higher learning. VMI's distinctive mission is to produce "citizen-soldiers," men prepared for leadership in civilian life and in military service. VMI pursues this mission through pervasive training of a kind not available anywhere else in Virginia. Assigning prime place to character development, VMI uses an "adversative method" modeled on English public schools and once characteristic of military instruction. VMI constantly endeavors to instill physical and mental discipline in its cadets and impart to them a strong moral code. The school's graduates leave VMI with heightened comprehension of their capacity to deal with duress and stress, and a large sense of accomplishment for completing the hazardous course.

VMI has notably succeeded in its mission to produce leaders; among its alumni are military generals, Members of Congress, and business executives. The school's alumni overwhelmingly perceive that their VMI training helped them to realize their personal goals. VMI's endowment reflects the loyalty of its graduates; VMI has the largest per-student endowment of all undergraduate institutions in the Nation.

Neither the goal of producing citizen-soldiers nor VMI's implementing methodology is inherently unsuitable to women. And the school's impressive record in producing leaders has made admission desirable to some women. Nevertheless, Virginia has elected to preserve exclusively for men the advantages and opportunities a VMI education affords.

From its establishment in 1839 as one of the Nation's first state military colleges, . . . VMI has remained financially supported by Virginia and "subject to the control of the [Virginia] General Assembly." . . . The first southern college to teach engineering and industrial chemistry, . . . VMI once provided teachers for the State's schools. . . . Civil War strife threatened the school's vitality, but a resourceful superintendent regained legislative support by highlighting "VMI's great potential[,] through its technical know-how," to advance Virginia's postwar recovery. . . .

VMI today enrolls about 1,300 men as cadets. Its academic offerings in the liberal arts, sciences, and engineering are also available at other public colleges and universities in Virginia. But VMI's mission is special. It is the mission of the school " 'to produce educated and honorable men, prepared for the varied work of civil life, imbued with love of learning, confident in the functions and attitudes of leadership, possessing a high sense of public service, advocates of the American democracy and free enterprise system, and ready as citizen-soldiers to defend their country in time of national peril.' " . . .

In contrast to the federal service academies, institutions maintained "to prepare cadets for career service in the armed forces," VMI's program "is directed at preparation for both military and civilian life"; "[o]nly about 15% of VMI cadets enter career military service." . . .

VMI produces its "citizen-soldiers" through "an adversative, or doubting, model of education" which features "[p]hysical rigor, mental stress, absolute equality of treatment, absence of privacy, minute regulation of behavior, and indoctrination in desirable values." . . . As one Commandant of Cadets described it, the adversative method "dissects the young student," and makes him aware of his "limits and capabilities," so that he knows "how far he can go with his anger, . . . how much he can take under stress, . . . exactly what he can do when he is physically exhausted." . . .

VMI cadets live in spartan barracks where surveillance is constant and privacy nonexistent; they wear uniforms, eat together in the mess hall, and regularly participate in drills. . . . Entering students are incessantly exposed to the rat line, "an extreme form of the adversative model," comparable in intensity to Marine Corps boot camp. . . . Tormenting and punishing, the rat line bonds new cadets to their fellow sufferers and, when they have completed the 7-month experience, to their former tormentors. . . .

VMI's "adversative model" is further characterized by a hierarchical "class system" of privileges and responsibilities, a "dyke system" for assigning a senior class mentor to each entering class "rat," and a stringently enforced "honor code," which prescribes that a cadet " 'does not lie, cheat, steal nor tolerate those who do.' " . . .

VMI attracts some applicants because of its reputation as an extraordinarily challenging military school, and "because its alumni are exceptionally close to the school." . . . "[W]omen have no opportunity anywhere to gain the benefits of [the system of education at VMI]." . . .

In 1990, prompted by a complaint filed with the Attorney General by a female high-school student seeking admission to VMI, the United States sued the Commonwealth of Virginia and VMI, alleging that VMI's exclusively male admission policy violated the Equal Protection Clause of the Fourteenth Amendment. . . .

The cross-petitions in this case present two ultimate issues. First, does Virginia's exclusion of women from the educational opportunities provided by VMI—extraordinary opportunities for military training and civilian leadership development—deny to women "capable of all of the individual activities required of VMI cadets," . . . the equal protection of the laws guaranteed by the Fourteenth Amendment? Second, if VMI's "unique" situation—as Virginia's sole single-sex public institution of higher education—offends the Constitution's equal protection principle, what is the remedial requirement?

. . . Parties who seek to defend gender-based government action must demonstrate an "exceedingly persuasive justification" for that action. . . .

Measuring the record in this case against the review standard just described, we conclude that Virginia has shown no "exceedingly persuasive justification" for excluding all women from the citizen-soldier training afforded by VMI. . . .

Single-sex education affords pedagogical benefits to at least some students, Virginia emphasizes, and that reality is uncontested in this litigation. Similarly, it is not disputed that diversity among public educational institutions can serve the public good. But Virginia has not shown that VMI was established, or has been maintained, with a view to diversifying, by its categorical exclusion of women, educational opportunities within the State. In cases of this genre, our precedent instructs that "benign" justifications proffered in defense of categorical exclusions will not be accepted automatically; a tenable justification must describe actual state purposes, not rationalizations for actions in fact differently grounded. . . .

Mississippi Univ. for Women is immediately in point. There the State asserted, in justification of its exclusion of men from a nursing school, that it was engaging in "educational affirmative action" by "compensat[ing] for discrimination against women." . . . Undertaking a "searching analysis," . . . the Court found no close resemblance between "the alleged objective" and "the actual purpose underlying the discriminatory classification." . . . Pursuing a similar inquiry here, we reach the same conclusion.

Neither recent nor distant history bears out Virginia's alleged pursuit of diversity through single-sex educational options. In 1839, when the State established VMI, a range of educational opportunities for men and women was scarcely contemplated. Higher education at the time was considered dangerous for women; reflecting widely held views about women's proper place, the Nation's first universities and colleges—for example, Harvard in Massachusetts, William and Mary in Virginia—admitted only men. . . . VMI was not at all novel in this respect: In admitting no women, VMI followed the lead of the State's flagship school, the University of Virginia, founded in 1819.

"[N]o struggle for the admission of women to a state university," a historian has recounted, "was longer drawn out, or developed more bitterness, than that at the University of Virginia." . . . In 1879, the State Senate resolved to look into the possibility of higher education for women, recognizing that Virginia " 'has never, at any period of her history,' " provided for the higher education of her daughters, though she " 'has liberally provided for the higher education of her sons.' " . . . Despite this recognition, no new opportunities were instantly open to women.

Virginia eventually provided for several women's seminaries and colleges. Farmville Female Seminary became a public institution in 1884. . . . Two women's schools, Mary Washington College and James Madison University, were founded in 1908; another, Radford University, was founded in 1910. . . . By the mid-1970's, all four schools had become coeducational. . . .

Debate concerning women's admission as undergraduates at the main university continued well past the century's midpoint. Familiar arguments were rehearsed. If women were admitted, it was feared, they "would encroach on the rights of men; there would be new problems of government, perhaps scandals; the old honor system would have to be changed; standards would be lowered to those of other coeducational schools; and the glorious reputation of the university, as a school for men, would be trailed in the dust." . . .

Ultimately, in 1970, "the most prestigious institution of higher education in Virginia," the University of Virginia, introduced coeducation and, in 1972, began to admit women on an equal basis with men. . . . A three-judge Federal District Court confirmed: "Virginia may not now deny to women, on the basis of sex, educational opportunities at the Charlottesville campus that are not afforded in other institutions operated by the [S]tate." . . .

Virginia describes the current absence of public single-sex higher education for women as "an historical anomaly." . . . But the historical record indicates action more deliberate than anomalous: First, protection of women against higher education; next, schools for women far from equal in resources and stature to schools for men; finally, conversion of the separate schools to coeducation. The state legislature, prior to the advent of this controversy, had repealed "[a]ll Virginia statutes requiring individual institutions to admit only men or women." . . . And in 1990, an official commission, "legislatively established to chart the future goals of higher education in Virginia," reaffirmed the policy "of affording broad access" while maintaining "autonomy and diversity." . . . Significantly, the Commission reported: " 'Because colleges and universities provide opportunities for students to develop values and learn from role models, it is extremely important that they deal with faculty, staff, and students without regard to sex, race, or ethnic origin.' " . . .

This statement, the Court of Appeals observed, "is the only explicit one that we have found in the record in which the Commonwealth has expressed itself with respect to gender distinctions." . . .

Our 1982 decision in *Mississippi Univ. for Women* prompted VMI to reexamine its male-only admission policy. . . . Virginia relies on that reexamination as a legitimate basis for maintaining VMI's single-sex character. . . . A Mission Study Committee, appointed by the VMI Board of Visitors, studied the problem from October 1983 until May 1986, and in that month counseled against "change of VMI status as a single-sex college." . . . Whatever internal purpose the Mission Study Committee served—and however well-meaning the framers of the report—we can hardly extract from that effort any state policy evenhandedly to advance diverse educational options. As the District Court observed, the Committee's analysis "primarily focuse[d] on anticipated difficulties in attracting females to VMI," and the report, overall, supplied "very little indication of how th[e] conclusion was reached." . . .

In sum, we find no persuasive evidence in this record that VMI's male-only admission policy "is in furtherance of a state policy of 'diversity.' " . . . No such policy, the Fourth Circuit observed, can be discerned from the movement of all other public colleges and universities in Virginia away from single-sex education. . . . That court also questioned "how one institution with autonomy, but with no authority over any other state institution, can give effect to a state policy of diversity among institutions." . . . A purpose genuinely to advance an array of educational options, as the Court of Appeals recognized, is not served by VMI's historic and constant plan—a plan to "affor[d] a unique educational benefit only to males." . . . However "liberally" this plan serves the State's sons, it makes no provision whatever for her daughters. That is not equal protection.

Virginia next argues that VMI's adversative method of training provides educational benefits that cannot be made available, unmodified, to women. Alterations to accommodate women would necessarily be "radical," so "drastic," Virginia asserts, as to transform, indeed "destroy," VMI's program. . . . Neither sex would be favored by the transformation, Virginia maintains: Men would be deprived of the unique opportunity currently available to them; women would not gain that opportunity because their participation would "eliminat[e] the very aspects of [the] program that distinguish [VMI] from . . . other institutions of higher education in Virginia." . . .

. . . It may be assumed, for purposes of this decision, that most women would not choose VMI's adversative method. . . . [I]t is also probable that "many men would not want to be educated in such an environment." . . . (On that point, even our dissenting colleague might agree.) Education, to be sure, is not a "one size fits all" business. The issue, however, is not whether "women—or men—should be forced to attend VMI"; rather, the question is whether the State can constitutionally deny to women who have the will and capacity, the training and attendant opportunities that VMI uniquely affords. . . .

The notion that admission of women would downgrade VMI's stature, destroy the adversative system and, with it, even the school, is a judgment hardly proved, a prediction hardly different from other "self-fulfilling prophec[ies]," . . . once routinely used to deny rights or opportunities. When women first sought admission to the bar and access to legal education, concerns of the same order were expressed. . . .

Women's successful entry into the federal military academies, and their participation in the Nation's military forces, indicate that Virginia's fears for the future of VMI may not be solidly grounded. The State's justification for excluding all women from "citizen-soldier" training for which some are qualified, in any event, cannot rank as "exceedingly persuasive," as we have explained and applied that standard.

Virginia and VMI trained their argument on "means" rather than "end," and thus misperceived our precedent. Single-sex education at VMI serves an "important governmental objective," they maintained, and exclusion of women is not only "substantially related," it is essential to that objective. By this notably circular argument, the "straightforward" test *Mississippi Univ. for Women* described, . . . was bent and bowed.

The State's misunderstanding . . . is apparent from VMI's mission: to produce "citizen-soldiers," individuals " 'imbued with love of learning, confident in the functions and attitudes of leadership, possessing a high sense of public service, advocates of the American democracy and free enterprise system, and ready . . . to defend their country in time of national peril.' " . . .

Surely that goal is great enough to accommodate women, who today count as citizens in our American democracy equal in stature to men. Just as surely, the State's great goal is not substantially advanced by women's categorical exclusion, in total disregard of their individual merit, from the State's premier "citizen-soldier" corps. Virginia, in sum, "has fallen far short of establishing the 'exceedingly persuasive justification,' " . . . that must be the solid base for any gender-defined classification. . . .

A generation ago, "the authorities controlling Virginia higher education," despite long established tradition, agreed "to innovate and favorably entertain[ed] the [then] relatively new idea that there must be no discrimination by sex in offering educational opportunity." . . . Commencing in 1970, Virginia opened to women "educational opportunities at the Charlottesville campus that [were] not afforded in other [State-operated] institutions." . . . A federal court approved the State's innovation, emphasizing that the University of Virginia "offer[ed] courses of instruction . . . not available elsewhere." . . . The court further noted: "[T]here exists at Charlottesville a 'prestige' factor [not paralleled in] other Virginia educational institutions." . . .

VMI, too, offers an educational opportunity no other Virginia institution provides, and the school's "prestige"—associated with its success in developing "citizen-soldiers"—is unequaled. . . . Women seeking and fit for a VMI-quality education cannot be offered anything less, under the State's obligation to afford them genuinely equal protection. . . .

Justice Thomas took no part in the consideration or decision of this case.

Chief Justice Rehnquist, concurring in the judgment.

The Court holds first that Virginia violates the Equal Protection Clause by maintaining the Virginia Military Institute's (VMI's) all-male admissions policy, and second, that establishing the Virginia Women's Institute for Leadership (VWIL) program does not remedy that violation. While I agree with these conclusions, I disagree with the Court's analysis and so I write separately.

Two decades ago in *Craig v. Boren*, . . . we announced that "[t]o withstand constitutional challenge, . . . classifications by gender must serve important governmental objectives and must be substantially related to achievement of those objectives." We have adhered to that standard of scrutiny ever since. . . . While the majority adheres to this test today, . . . it also says that the State must demonstrate an " 'exceedingly persuasive justification' " to support a gender-based classification. . . . It is unfortunate that the Court thereby introduces an element of uncertainty respecting the appropriate test.

While terms like "important governmental objective" and "substantially related" are hardly models of precision, they have more content and specificity than does the phrase "exceedingly persuasive justification." That phrase is best confined, as it was first used, as an observation on the difficulty of meeting the applicable test, not as a formulation of the test itself. . . . To avoid introducing potential confusion, I would have adhered more closely to our traditional, "firmly established," . . . standard that a gender-based classification "must bear a close and substantial relationship to important governmental objectives." . . .

Our cases dealing with gender discrimination also require that the proffered purpose for the challenged law be the actual purpose. . . . It is on this ground that the Court rejects the first of two justifications Virginia offers for VMI's single-sex admissions policy, namely, the goal of diversity among its public educational institutions. While I ultimately agree that the State has not carried

the day with this justification, I disagree with the Court's method of analyzing the issue. . . .

Before this Court, Virginia has sought to justify VMI's single-sex admissions policy primarily on the basis that diversity in education is desirable, and that while most of the public institutions of higher learning in the State are coeducational, there should also be room for single-sex institutions. I agree with the Court that there is scant evidence in the record that this was the real reason that Virginia decided to maintain VMI as men only. . . . But, unlike the majority, I would consider only evidence that postdates our decision in *[Mississippi University for Women v.] Hogan,* and would draw no negative inferences from the State's actions before that time. I think that after *Hogan,* the State was entitled to reconsider its policy with respect to VMI, and to not have earlier justifications, or lack thereof, held against it.

Even if diversity in educational opportunity were the State's actual objective, the State's position would still be problematic. The difficulty with its position is that the diversity benefited only one sex; there was single-sex public education available for men at VMI, but no corresponding single-sex public education available for women. When *Hogan* placed Virginia on notice that VMI's admissions policy possibly was unconstitutional, VMI could have dealt with the problem by admitting women; but its governing body felt strongly that the admission of women would have seriously harmed the institution's educational approach. Was there something else the State could have done to avoid an equal protection violation? Since the State did nothing, we do not have to definitively answer that question. . . .

. . . The private women's colleges are treated by the State exactly as all other private schools are treated, which includes the provision of tuition-assistance grants to Virginia residents. Virginia gives no special support to the women's single-sex education. But obviously, the same is not true for men's education. Had the State provided the kind of support for the private women's schools that it provides for VMI, this may have been a very different case. For in so doing, the State would have demonstrated that its interest in providing a single-sex education for men, was to some measure matched by an interest in providing the same opportunity for women.

Virginia offers a second justification for the single-sex admissions policy: maintenance of the adversative method. I agree with the Court that this justification does not serve an important governmental objective. A State does not have substantial interest in the adversative methodology unless it is pedagogically beneficial.

While considerable evidence shows that a single-sex education is pedagogically beneficial for some students, . . . and hence a State may have a valid interest in promoting that methodology, there is no similar evidence in the record that an adversative method is pedagogically beneficial or is any more likely to produce character traits than other methodologies.

The Court defines the constitutional violation in this case as "the categorical exclusion of women from an extraordinary educational opportunity afforded to men." . . . By defining the violation in this way, and by emphasizing that a remedy for a constitutional violation must place the victims of discrimination in " 'the position they would have occupied in the absence of [discrimination],' " . . . the Court necessarily implies that the only adequate remedy would be the admission of women to the all-male institution. As the foregoing discussion suggests, I would not define the violation in this way; it is not the "exclusion of women" that violates the Equal Protection Clause, but the maintenance of an all-men school without providing any—much less a comparable—institution for women.

Accordingly, the remedy should not necessarily require either the admission of women to VMI, or the creation of a VMI clone for women. An adequate remedy in my opinion might be a demonstration by Virginia that its interest in educating men in a single-sex environment is matched by its interest in educating women in a single-sex institution. To demonstrate such, the State does not need to create two institutions with the same number of faculty Ph.D.'s, similar SAT scores, or comparable athletic fields. . . . Nor would it necessarily require that the women's institution offer the same curriculum as the men's; one could be strong in computer science, the other could be strong in liberal arts. It would be a sufficient remedy, I think, if the two institutions offered the same quality of education and were of the same overall caliber.

If a state decides to create single-sex programs, the state would, I expect, consider the public's interest and demand in designing curricula. And rightfully so. But the state should avoid assuming demand based on stereotypes; it must not assume a priori, without evidence, that there would be no interest in a women's school of civil engineering, or in a men's school of nursing.

In the end, the women's institution Virginia proposes, VWIL, fails as a remedy, because it is distinctly inferior to the existing men's institution and will continue to be for the foreseeable future. VWIL simply is not, in any sense, the institution that VMI is. In particular, VWIL is a program appended to a private college, not a self-standing institution; and VWIL is substantially underfunded as compared to VMI. I therefore ultimately agree with the Court that Virginia has not provided an adequate remedy. . . .

Justice Scalia, dissenting.

Today the Court shuts down an institution that has served the people of the Commonwealth of Virginia with pride and distinction for over a century and a half. To achieve that desired result, it rejects (contrary to our established practice) the factual findings of two courts below, sweeps aside the precedents of this Court, and ignores the history of our people. As to facts: it explicitly rejects the finding that there exist "gender-based developmental differences" supporting Virginia's restriction of the "adversative" method to only a men's institution, and the finding that the all-male composition of the Virginia Military Institute (VMI) is essential to that institution's character. As to precedent: it drastically revises our established standards for reviewing sex-based classifications. And as to history: it counts for nothing the long tradition, enduring down to the present, of men's military colleges supported by both States and the Federal Government. . . .

Much of the Court's opinion is devoted to deprecating the closed-mindedness of our forebears with regard to women's education, and even with regard to the treatment of women in areas that have nothing to do with education. Closed-minded they were—as every age is, including our own, with regard to matters it cannot guess, because it simply does not consider them debatable. The virtue of a democratic system with a First Amendment is that it readily enables the people, over time, to be persuaded that what they took for granted is not so, and to change their laws accordingly. That system is destroyed if the smug assurances of each age are removed from the democratic process and written into the Constitution. So to counterbalance the Court's criticism of our ancestors, let me say a word in their praise: they left us free to change. The same cannot be said of this most illiberal Court, which has embarked on a course of inscribing one after another of the current preferences of the society (and in some cases only the counter-majoritarian preferences of the society's law-trained elite) into our Basic Law. Today it enshrines the notion that no substantial educational value is to be served by an all-men's military academy—so that the decision by the people of Virginia to maintain such an institution denies equal protection to women who cannot attend that institution but can attend others. Since it is entirely clear that the Constitution of the United States—the old one—takes no sides in this educational debate, I dissent. . . .

To reject the Court's disposition today . . . it is only necessary to apply honestly the test the Court has been applying to sex-based classifications for the past two decades. . . .

Although the Court in two places recites the test as stated in *Hogan,* . . . which asks whether the State has demonstrated "that the classification serves important governmental objectives and that the discriminatory means employed are substantially related to the achievement of those objectives," . . . the Court never answers the question presented in anything resembling that form. When it engages in analysis, the Court instead prefers the phrase "exceedingly persuasive justification" from *Hogan.* The Court's nine invocations of that phrase, . . . and even its fanciful description of that imponderable as "the core instruction" of the Court's decisions in *J. E. B. v. Alabama ex rel. T. B.* . . . (1994), and *Hogan,* . . . would be unobjectionable if the Court acknowledged that whether a "justification" is "exceedingly persuasive" must be assessed by asking "[whether] the classification serves important governmental objectives and [whether] the discriminatory means employed are substantially related to the achievement of those objectives." Instead, however, the Court proceeds to interpret "exceedingly persuasive justification" in a fashion that contradicts the reasoning of *Hogan* and our other precedents.

That is essential to the Court's result, which can only be achieved by establishing that intermediate scrutiny is not survived if there are some women interested in attending VMI, capable of undertaking its activities, and able to meet its physical demands. . . .

Only the amorphous "exceedingly persuasive justification" phrase, and not the standard elaboration of intermediate scrutiny, can be made to yield this conclusion that VMI's single-sex composition is unconstitutional because there exist several women (or, one would have to conclude under the Court's reasoning, a single woman) willing and able to undertake VMI's program. Intermediate scrutiny has never required a least-restrictive-means analysis, but only a "substantial relation" between the classification and the state interests that it serves. Thus, in *Califano v. Webster* . . . (1977) (per curiam), we upheld a congressional statute that provided higher Social Security benefits for women than for men. We reasoned that "women . . . as such have been unfairly hindered from earning as much as men," but we did not require proof that each woman so benefited had suffered discrimination or that each disadvantaged man had not; it

was sufficient that even under the former congressional scheme "women on the average received lower retirement benefits than men." . . . The reasoning in our other intermediate-scrutiny cases has similarly required only a substantial relation between end and means, not a perfect fit. In *Rostker v. Goldberg,* . . . (1981), we held that selective-service registration could constitutionally exclude women, because even "assuming that a small number of women could be drafted for noncombat roles, Congress simply did not consider it worth the added burdens of including women in draft and registration plans." . . . In *Metro Broadcasting, Inc. v. FCC* . . . (1990), overruled on other grounds, *Adarand Constructors, Inc. v. Pena* . . . (1995), we held that a classification need not be accurate "in every case" to survive intermediate scrutiny so long as, "in the aggregate," it advances the underlying objective. There is simply no support in our cases for the notion that a sex-based classification is invalid unless it relates to characteristics that hold true in every instance.

Not content to execute a *de facto* abandonment of the intermediate scrutiny that has been our standard for sex-based classifications for some two decades, the Court purports to reserve the question whether, even in principle, a higher standard (i.e., strict scrutiny) should apply. "The Court has," it says, "thus far reserved most stringent judicial scrutiny for classifications based on race or national origin . . . ," . . . and it describes our earlier cases as having done no more than decline to "equat[e] gender classifications, for all purposes, to classifications based on race or national origin." . . . The wonderful thing about these statements is that they are not actually false—just as it would not be actually false to say that "our cases have thus far reserved the 'beyond a reasonable doubt' standard of proof for criminal cases," or that "we have not equated tort actions, for all purposes, to criminal prosecutions." But the statements are misleading, insofar as they suggest that we have not already categorically held strict scrutiny to be inapplicable to sex-based classifications. . . . And the statements are irresponsible, insofar as they are calculated to destabilize current law. Our task is to clarify the law—not to muddy the waters, and not to exact over-compliance by intimidation. The States and the Federal Government are entitled to know before they act the standard to which they will be held, rather than be compelled to guess about the outcome of Supreme Court peek-a-boo.

The Court's intimations are particularly out of place because it is perfectly clear that, if the question of the applicable standard of review for sex-based classifications were to be regarded as an appropriate subject for reconsideration, the stronger argument would be not for elevating the standard to strict scrutiny, but for reducing it to rational-basis review. The latter certainly has a firmer foundation in our past jurisprudence: Whereas no majority of the Court has ever applied strict scrutiny in a case involving sex-based classifications, we routinely applied rational-basis review until the 1970's. . . . And of course normal, rational-basis review of sex-based classifications would be much more in accord with the genesis of heightened standards of judicial review, the famous footnote in *United States v. Carolene Products Co.* . . . (1938), which said (intimatingly) that we did not have to inquire in the case at hand "whether prejudice against discrete and insular minorities may be a special condition, which tends seriously to curtail the operation of those political processes ordinarily to be relied upon to protect minorities, and which may call for a correspondingly more searching judicial inquiry." . . .

It is hard to consider women a "discrete and insular minorit[y]" unable to employ the "political processes ordinarily to be relied upon," when they constitute a majority of the electorate. And the suggestion that they are incapable of exerting that political power smacks of the same paternalism that the Court so roundly condemns. . . . Moreover, a long list of legislation proves the proposition false. . . .

With this explanation of how the Court has succeeded in making its analysis seem orthodox—and indeed, if intimations are to be believed, even overly generous to VMI—I now proceed to describe how the analysis should have been conducted. The question to be answered, I repeat, is whether the exclusion of women from VMI is "substantially related to an important governmental objective."

It is beyond question that Virginia has an important state interest in providing effective college education for its citizens. That single-sex instruction is an approach substantially related to that interest should be evident enough from the long and continuing history in this country of men's and women's colleges. But beyond that, as the Court of Appeals here stated: "That single-gender education at the college level is beneficial to both sexes is a fact established in this case." . . .

The evidence establishing that fact was overwhelming—indeed, "virtually uncontradicted" in the words of the court that received the evidence. . . . As an initial matter, Virginia demonstrated at trial that "[a] substantial body of contemporary scholarship and research supports the proposition that, although males and females have significant areas of

developmental overlap, they also have differing developmental needs that are deep-seated." . . . While no one questioned that for many students a coeducational environment was nonetheless not inappropriate, that could not obscure the demonstrated benefits of single-sex colleges. . . .

"[I]n the light of this very substantial authority favoring single-sex education," the District Court concluded that "the VMI Board's decision to maintain an all-male institution is fully justified even without taking into consideration the other unique features of VMI's teaching and training." . . . This finding alone, which even this Court cannot dispute, . . . should be sufficient to demonstrate the constitutionality of VMI's all-male composition.

But besides its single-sex constitution, VMI is different from other colleges in another way. It employs a "distinctive educational method," sometimes referred to as the "adversative, or doubting, model of education." . . . "Physical rigor, mental stress, absolute equality of treatment, absence of privacy, minute regulation of behavior, and indoctrination in desirable values are the salient attributes of the VMI educational experience." . . . No one contends that this method is appropriate for all individuals; education is not a "one size fits all" business. Just as a State may wish to support junior colleges, vocational institutes, or a law school that emphasizes case practice instead of classroom study, so too a State's decision to maintain within its system one school that provides the adversative method is "substantially related" to its goal of good education. Moreover, it was uncontested that "if the state were to establish a women's VMI-type [i.e., adversative] program, the program would attract an insufficient number of participants to make the program work," . . . and it was found by the District Court that if Virginia were to include women in VMI, the school "would eventually find it necessary to drop the adversative system altogether." . . . Thus, Virginia's options were an adversative method that excludes women or no adversative method at all.

There can be no serious dispute that . . . single-sex education and a distinctive educational method "represent legitimate contributions to diversity in the Virginia higher education system." . . . As a theoretical matter, Virginia's educational interest would have been best served (insofar as the two factors we have mentioned are concerned) by six different types of public colleges—an all-men's, an all-women's, and a coeducational college run in the "adversative method," and an all-men's, an all-women's, and a coeducational college run in the "traditional method." But as a practical matter, of course, Virginia's financial resources, like any State's, are not limitless, and the Commonwealth must select among the available options. Virginia thus has decided to fund, in addition to some 14 coeducational 4-year colleges, one college that is run as an all-male school on the adversarial model: the Virginia Military Institute.

Virginia did not make this determination regarding the make-up of its public college system on the unrealistic assumption that no other colleges exist. Substantial evidence in the District Court demonstrated that the Commonwealth has long proceeded on the principle that " '[h]igher education resources should be viewed as a whole—public and private' "—because such an approach enhances diversity and because " 'it is academic and economic waste to permit unwarranted duplication.' " . . . It is thus significant that, whereas there are "four all-female private [colleges] in Virginia," there is only "one private all-male college," which "indicates that the private sector is providing for th[e] [former] form of education to a much greater extent that it provides for all-male education." . . . In these circumstances, Virginia's election to fund one public all-male institution and one on the adversarial model—and to concentrate its resources in a single entity that serves both these interests in diversity—is substantially related to the State's important educational interests.

The Court today has no adequate response to this clear demonstration of the conclusion produced by application of intermediate scrutiny. Rather, it relies on a series of contentions that are irrelevant or erroneous as a matter of law, foreclosed by the record in this case, or both. . . .

Under the constitutional principles announced and applied today, single-sex public education is unconstitutional. By going through the motions of applying a balancing test—asking whether the State has adduced an "exceedingly persuasive justification" for its sex-based classification—the Court creates the illusion that government officials in some future case will have a clear shot at justifying some sort of single-sex public education. Indeed, the Court seeks to create even a greater illusion than that: It purports to have said nothing of relevance to other public schools at all. "We address specifically and only an educational opportunity recognized . . . as 'unique'. . . ." . . .

The Supreme Court of the United States does not sit to announce "unique" dispositions. Its principal function is to establish precedent—that is, to set forth principles of law that every court in America must follow. As we said only this Term, we expect both ourselves and lower courts to adhere to the "rationale upon which the Court based the results of its earlier decisions." . . . That is the principal reason we publish our opinions.

And the rationale of today's decision is sweeping: for sex-based classifications, a redefinition of intermediate scrutiny that makes it indistinguishable from strict scrutiny. . . . Indeed, the Court indicates that if any program restricted to one sex is "uniqu[e]," it must be opened to members of the opposite sex "who have the will and capacity" to participate in it. . . . I suggest that the single-sex program that will not be capable of being characterized as "unique" is not only unique but nonexistent.

In any event, regardless of whether the Court's rationale leaves some small amount of room for lawyers to argue, it ensures that single-sex public education is functionally dead. The costs of litigating the constitutionality of a single-sex education program, and the risks of ultimately losing that litigation, are simply too high to be embraced by public officials. Any person with standing to challenge any sex-based classification can haul the State into federal court and compel it to establish by evidence (presumably in the form of expert testimony) that there is an "exceedingly persuasive justification" for the classification. Should the courts happen to interpret that vacuous phrase as establishing a standard that is not utterly impossible of achievement, there is considerable risk that whether the standard has been met will not be determined on the basis of the record evidence—indeed, that will necessarily be the approach of any court that seeks to walk the path the Court has trod today. No state official in his right mind will buy such a high-cost, high-risk lawsuit by commencing a single-sex program. The enemies of single-sex education have won; by persuading only seven Justices (five would have been enough) that their view of the world is enshrined in the Constitution, they have effectively imposed that view on all 50 States. . . .

Case

ROMER V. EVANS

517 U.S. 620, 116 S.Ct. 1620, 134 L.Ed. 2d. 855 (1996)
Vote: 6–3

Here the Court addresses the issue of gay rights in the context of a state constitutional amendment disallowing minority status, preferred treatment, or claims of discrimination on the basis of homosexual or lesbian orientation.

Justice Kennedy delivered the opinion of the Court.

. . . The enactment challenged in this case is an amendment to the Constitution of the State of Colorado, adopted in a 1992 statewide referendum. The parties and the state courts refer to it as "Amendment 2," its designation when submitted to the voters. The impetus for the amendment and the contentious campaign that preceded its adoption came in large part from ordinances that had been passed in various Colorado municipalities. For example, the cities of Aspen and Boulder and the City and County of Denver each had enacted ordinances which banned discrimination in many transactions and activities, including housing, employment, education, public accommodations, and health and welfare services. . . . What gave rise to the statewide controversy was the protection the ordinances afforded to persons discriminated against by reason of their sexual orientation. . . . Amendment 2 repeals these ordinances to the extent they prohibit discrimination on the basis of "homosexual, lesbian or bisexual orientation, conduct, practices or relationships." . . .

Yet Amendment 2, in explicit terms, does more than repeal or rescind these provisions. It prohibits all legislative, executive or judicial action at any level of state or local government designed to protect the named class, a class we shall refer to as homosexual persons or gays and lesbians. The amendment reads:

> No Protected Status Based on Homosexual, Lesbian, or Bisexual Orientation. Neither the State of Colorado, through any of its branches or departments, nor any of its agencies, political subdivisions, municipalities or school districts, shall enact, adopt or enforce any statute, regulation, ordinance or policy whereby homosexual, lesbian or bisexual orientation, conduct, practices or relationships shall constitute or otherwise be the basis of or entitle any person or class of persons to have or claim any minority status, quota preferences, protected status or claim of discrimination. This Section of the Constitution shall be in all respects self-executing. . . .

Soon after Amendment 2 was adopted, this litigation to declare its invalidity and enjoin its enforcement was commenced in the District Court for the City and County of Denver. . . .

The trial court granted a preliminary injunction to stay enforcement of Amendment 2, and an appeal was taken to the Supreme Court of Colorado. Sustaining the interim injunction and remanding the case for further proceedings, the State Supreme Court held that Amendment 2 was subject to strict scrutiny under the Fourteenth Amendment because it infringed the fundamental right of gays and lesbians to participate in the political process. . . . To reach this conclusion, the state court relied on our voting rights cases . . . and on our precedents involving discriminatory restructuring of governmental decision making. . . . On remand, the State advanced various arguments in an effort to show that Amendment 2 was narrowly tailored to serve compelling interests, but the trial court found none sufficient. It enjoined enforcement of Amendment 2, and the Supreme Court of Colorado, in a second opinion, affirmed the ruling. . . . We granted certiorari and now affirm the judgment, but on a rationale different from that adopted by the State Supreme Court.

The State's principal argument in defense of Amendment 2 is that it puts gays and lesbians in the same position as all other persons. So, the State says, the measure does no more than deny homosexuals special rights. This reading of the amendment's language is implausible. We rely not upon our own interpretation of the amendment but upon the authoritative construction of Colorado's Supreme Court. The state court, deeming it unnecessary to determine the full extent of the amendment's reach, found it invalid even on a modest reading of its implications. . . .

Sweeping and comprehensive is the change in legal status effected by this law. So much is evident from the ordinances that the Colorado Supreme Court declared would be void by operation of Amendment 2. Homosexuals, by state decree, are put in a solitary class with respect to transactions and relations in both the private and governmental spheres. The amendment withdraws from homosexuals, but no others, specific legal protection from the injuries caused by discrimination, and it forbids reinstatement of these laws and policies.

The change that Amendment 2 works in the legal status of gays and lesbians in the private sphere is far-reaching, both on its own terms and when considered in light of the structure and operation of modern anti-discrimination laws. That structure is well illustrated by contemporary statutes and ordinances prohibiting discrimination by providers of public accommodations. "At common law, innkeepers, smiths, and others who 'made profession of a public employment,' were prohibited from refusing, without good reason, to serve a customer." . . . The duty was a general one and did not specify protection for particular groups. The common law rules, however, proved insufficient in many instances, and it was settled early that the Fourteenth Amendment did not give Congress a general power to prohibit discrimination in public accommodations. . . . In consequence, most States have chosen to counter discrimination by enacting detailed statutory schemes. . . .

Colorado's state and municipal laws typify this emerging tradition of statutory protection and follow a consistent pattern. The laws first enumerate the persons or entities subject to a duty not to discriminate. The list goes well beyond the entities covered by the common law. The Boulder ordinance, for example, has a comprehensive definition of entities deemed places of "public accommodation." They include "any place of business engaged in any sales to the general public and any place that offers services, facilities, privileges, or advantages to the general public or that receives financial support through solicitation of the general public or through governmental subsidy of any kind." . . . The Denver ordinance is of similar breadth, applying, for example, to hotels, restaurants, hospitals, dental clinics, theaters, banks, common carriers, travel and insurance agencies, and "shops and stores dealing with goods or services of any kind." . . .

These statutes and ordinances also depart from the common law by enumerating the groups or persons within their ambit of protection. Enumeration is the essential device used to make the duty not to discriminate concrete and to provide guidance for those who must comply. In following this approach, Colorado's state and local governments have not limited anti-discrimination laws to groups that have so far been given the protection of heightened equal protection scrutiny under our cases. . . . Rather, they set forth an extensive catalogue of traits which cannot be the basis for discrimination, including age, military status, marital status, pregnancy, parenthood, custody of a minor child, political affiliation, physical or mental disability of an individual or of his or her associates—and, in recent times, sexual orientation. . . .

Amendment 2 bars homosexuals from securing protection against the injuries that these public-accommodations laws address. That in itself is a severe consequence, but there is more. Amendment 2, in addition, nullifies specific legal protections for this targeted class in all transactions in housing, sale of real estate, insurance, health and welfare services, private education, and employment. . . .

Not confined to the private sphere, Amendment 2 also operates to repeal and forbid all laws or policies providing specific protection for gays or lesbians from discrimination by every level of Colorado government. The State Supreme Court cited two examples of protections in the governmental sphere that are now rescinded and may not be reintroduced. The first is Colorado Executive Order D0035 (1990), which forbids employment discrimination against " 'all state employees, classified and exempt' on the basis of sexual orientation." . . . Also repealed, and now forbidden, are "various provisions prohibiting discrimination based on sexual orientation at state colleges." . . . The repeal of these measures and the prohibition against their future reenactment demonstrates that Amendment 2 has the same force and effect in Colorado's governmental sector as it does elsewhere and that it applies to policies as well as ordinary legislation.

Amendment 2's reach may not be limited to specific laws passed for the benefit of gays and lesbians. It is a fair, if not necessary, inference from the broad language of the amendment that it deprives gays and lesbians even of the protection of general laws and policies that prohibit arbitrary discrimination in governmental and private settings. . . . At some point in the systematic administration of these laws, an official must determine whether homosexuality is an arbitrary and thus forbidden basis for decision. Yet a decision to that effect would itself amount to a policy prohibiting discrimination on the basis of homosexuality, and so would appear to be no more valid under Amendment 2 than the specific prohibitions against discrimination the state court held invalid.

If this consequence follows from Amendment 2, as its broad language suggests, it would compound the constitutional difficulties the law creates. The state court did not decide whether the amendment has this effect, however, and neither need we. In the course of rejecting the argument that Amendment 2 is intended to conserve resources to fight discrimination against suspect classes, the Colorado Supreme Court made the limited observation that the amendment is not intended to affect many anti-discrimination laws protecting non-suspect classes. . . . In our view that does not resolve the issue. In any event, even if, as we doubt, homosexuals could find some safe harbor in laws of general application, we cannot accept the view that Amendment 2's prohibition on specific legal protections does no more than deprive homosexuals of special rights. To the contrary, the amendment imposes a special disability upon those persons alone. Homosexuals are forbidden the safeguards that others enjoy or may seek without constraint. They can obtain specific protection against discrimination only by enlisting the citizenry of Colorado to amend the state constitution or perhaps, on the State's view, by trying to pass helpful laws of general applicability. This is so no matter how local or discrete the harm, no matter how public and widespread the injury. We find nothing special in the protections Amendment 2 withholds. These are protections taken for granted by most people either because they already have them or do not need them; these are protections against exclusion from an almost limitless number of transactions and endeavors that constitute ordinary civic life in a free society.

The Fourteenth Amendment's promise that no person shall be denied the equal protection of the laws must co-exist with the practical necessity that most legislation classifies for one purpose or another, with resulting disadvantage to various groups or persons. . . . We have attempted to reconcile the principle with the reality by stating that, if a law neither burdens a fundamental right nor targets a suspect class, we will uphold the legislative classification so long as it bears a rational relation to some legitimate end. . . .

Amendment 2 fails, indeed defies, even this conventional inquiry. First, the amendment has the peculiar property of imposing a broad and undifferentiated disability on a single named group, an exceptional and, as we shall explain, invalid form of legislation. Second, its sheer breadth is so discontinuous with the reasons offered for it that the amendment seems inexplicable by anything but animus toward the class that it affects; it lacks a rational relationship to legitimate state interests.

Taking the first point, even in the ordinary equal protection case calling for the most deferential of standards, we insist on knowing the relation between the classification adopted and the object to be attained. The search for the link between classification and objective gives substance to the Equal Protection Clause; it provides guidance and discipline for the legislature, which is entitled to know what sorts of laws it can pass; and it marks the limits of our own authority. In the ordinary case, a law will be sustained if it can be said to advance a legitimate government interest, even if the law seems unwise or works to the disadvantage of a particular group, or if the rationale for it seems tenuous. . . . The laws challenged in the cases just cited were narrow enough in scope and grounded in a sufficient factual context for us

to ascertain that there existed some relation between the classification and the purpose it served. By requiring that the classification bear a rational relationship to an independent and legitimate legislative end, we ensure that classifications are not drawn for the purpose of disadvantaging the group burdened by the law. . . .

Amendment 2 confounds this normal process of judicial review. It is at once too narrow and too broad. It identifies persons by a single trait and then denies them protection across the board. The resulting disqualification of a class of persons from the right to seek specific protection from the law is unprecedented in our jurisprudence. The absence of precedent for Amendment 2 is itself instructive; "[d]iscriminations of an unusual character especially suggest careful consideration to determine whether they are obnoxious to the constitutional provision." . . .

It is not within our constitutional tradition to enact laws of this sort. Central both to the idea of the rule of law and to our own Constitution's guarantee of equal protection is the principle that government and each of its parts remain open on impartial terms to all who seek its assistance. "Equal protection of the laws is not achieved through indiscriminate imposition of inequalities." . . . Respect for this principle explains why laws singling out a certain class of citizens for disfavored legal status or general hardships are rare. A law declaring that in general it shall be more difficult for one group of citizens than for all others to seek aid from the government is itself a denial of equal protection of the laws in the most literal sense. "The guaranty of 'equal protection of the laws is a pledge of the protection of equal laws.'" . . .

. . . A second and related point is that laws of the kind now before us raise the inevitable inference that the disadvantage imposed is born of animosity toward the class of persons affected. "[I]f the constitutional conception of 'equal protection of the laws' means anything, it must at the very least mean that a bare . . . desire to harm a politically unpopular group cannot constitute a legitimate governmental interest." . . . Even laws enacted for broad and ambitious purposes often can be explained by reference to legitimate public policies which justify the incidental disadvantages they impose on certain persons. Amendment 2, however, in making a general announcement that gays and lesbians shall not have any particular protections from the law, inflicts on them immediate, continuing, and real injuries that outrun and belie any legitimate justifications that may be claimed for it. We conclude that, in addition to the far-reaching deficiencies of Amendment 2 that we have noted, the principles it offends, in another sense, are conventional and venerable;

a law must bear a rational relationship to a legitimate governmental purpose, . . . and Amendment 2 does not.

The primary rationale the State offers for Amendment 2 is respect for other citizens' freedom of association, and in particular the liberties of landlords or employers who have personal or religious objections to homosexuality. Colorado also cites its interest in conserving resources to fight discrimination against other groups. The breadth of the Amendment is so far removed from these particular justifications that we find it impossible to credit them. We cannot say that Amendment 2 is directed to any identifiable legitimate purpose or discrete objective. It is a status-based enactment divorced from any factual context from which we could discern a relationship to legitimate state interests; it is a classification of persons undertaken for its own sake, something the Equal Protection Clause does not permit. "[C]lass legislation . . . . [is] obnoxious to the prohibitions of the Fourteenth Amendment. . . ." . . .

We must conclude that Amendment 2 classifies homosexuals not to further a proper legislative end but to make them unequal to everyone else. This Colorado cannot do. A State cannot so deem a class of persons a stranger to its laws. Amendment 2 violates the Equal Protection Clause, and the judgment of the Supreme Court of Colorado is affirmed. . . .

Justice Scalia, with whom the **Chief Justice** and **Justice Thomas** join, dissenting.

The Court has mistaken a Kulturkampf for a fit of spite. The constitutional amendment before us here is not the manifestation of a "bare . . . desire to harm" homosexuals, . . . but is rather a modest attempt by seemingly tolerant Coloradans to preserve traditional sexual mores against the efforts of a politically powerful minority to revise those mores through use of the laws. That objective, and the means chosen to achieve it, are not only unimpeachable under any constitutional doctrine hitherto pronounced (hence the opinion's heavy reliance upon principles of righteousness rather than judicial holdings); they have been specifically approved by the Congress of the United States and by this Court.

In holding that homosexuality cannot be singled out for disfavorable treatment, the Court contradicts a decision, unchallenged here, pronounced only 10 years ago, see *Bowers v. Hardwick* . . . (1986), and places the prestige of this institution behind the proposition that opposition to homosexuality is as reprehensible as racial or religious bias. Whether it is or not is precisely the cultural debate that gave rise to the Colorado constitutional amendment (and to the preferen-

tial laws against which the amendment was directed). Since the Constitution of the United States says nothing about this subject, it is left to be resolved by normal democratic means, including the democratic adoption of provisions in state constitutions. This Court has no business imposing upon all Americans the resolution favored by the elite class from which the Members of this institution are selected, pronouncing that "animosity" toward homosexuality . . . is evil. I vigorously dissent. . . .

. . . The Court's opinion contains grim, disapproving hints that Coloradans have been guilty of "animus" or "animosity" toward homosexuality, as though that has been established as Unamerican. Of course it is our moral heritage that one should not hate any human being or class of human beings. But I had thought that one could consider certain conduct reprehensible—murder, for example, or polygamy, or cruelty to animals—and could exhibit even "animus" toward such conduct. Surely that is the only sort of "animus" at issue here: moral disapproval of homosexual conduct, the same sort of moral disapproval that produced the centuries-old criminal laws that we held constitutional in *Bowers*. The Colorado amendment does not, to speak entirely precisely, prohibit giving favored status to people who are homosexuals; they can be favored for many reasons—for example, because they are senior citizens or members of racial minorities. But it prohibits giving them favored status because of their homosexual conduct—that is, it prohibits favored status for homosexuality.

But though Coloradans are, as I say, entitled to be hostile toward homosexual conduct, the fact is that the degree of hostility reflected by Amendment 2 is the smallest conceivable. The Court's portrayal of Coloradans as a society fallen victim to pointless, hate-filled "gay-bashing" is so false as to be comical. Colorado not only is one of the 25 States that have repealed their antisodomy laws, but was among the first to do so. . . . But the society that eliminates criminal punishment for homosexual acts does not necessarily abandon the view that homosexuality is morally wrong and socially harmful; often, abolition simply reflects the view that enforcement of such criminal laws involves unseemly intrusion into the intimate lives of citizens. . . .

There is a problem, however, which arises when criminal sanction of homosexuality is eliminated but moral and social disapprobation of homosexuality is meant to be retained. The Court cannot be unaware of that problem; it is evident in many cities of the country, and occasionally bubbles to the surface of the news, in heated political disputes over such matters as the introduction into local schools of books teaching that homosexuality is an optional and fully acceptable "alternate life style." The problem (a problem, that is, for those who wish to retain social disapprobation of homosexuality) is that, because those who engage in homosexual conduct tend to reside in disproportionate numbers in certain communities, . . . and of course care about homosexual-rights issues much more ardently than the public at large, they possess political power much greater than their numbers, both locally and statewide. Quite understandably, they devote this political power to achieving not merely a grudging social toleration, but full social acceptance, of homosexuality. . . .

By the time Coloradans were asked to vote on Amendment 2, their exposure to homosexuals' quest for social endorsement was not limited to newspaper accounts of happenings in places such as New York, Los Angeles, San Francisco, and Key West. Three Colorado cities—Aspen, Boulder, and Denver—had enacted ordinances that listed "sexual orientation" as an impermissible ground for discrimination, equating the moral disapproval of homosexual conduct with racial and religious bigotry. . . . The phenomenon had even appeared statewide: the Governor of Colorado had signed an executive order pronouncing that "in the State of Colorado we recognize the diversity in our pluralistic society and strive to bring an end to discrimination in any form," and directing state agency-heads to "ensure non-discrimination" in hiring and promotion based on, among other things, "sexual orientation." . . . I do not mean to be critical of these legislative successes; homosexuals are as entitled to use the legal system for reinforcement of their moral sentiments as are the rest of society. But they are subject to being countered by lawful, democratic countermeasures as well.

That is where Amendment 2 came in. It sought to counter both the geographic concentration and the disproportionate political power of homosexuals by (1) resolving the controversy at the statewide level, and (2) making the election a single-issue contest for both sides. It put directly, to all the citizens of the State, the question: Should homosexuality be given special protection? They answered no. The Court today asserts that this most democratic of procedures is unconstitutional. Lacking any cases to establish that facially absurd proposition, it simply asserts that it must be unconstitutional, because it has never happened before. . . .

I would not myself indulge in . . . official praise for heterosexual monogamy, because I think it no business of the courts (as opposed to the political branches) to take sides in this culture war. But the Court today has done so, not only by inventing a novel and extravagant consti-

tutional doctrine to take the victory away from traditional forces, but even by verbally disparaging as bigotry adherence to traditional attitudes. To suggest, for example, that this constitutional amendment springs from nothing more than "a bare . . . desire to harm a politically unpopular group," . . . is nothing short of insulting. (It is also nothing short of preposterous to call "politically unpopular" a group which enjoys enormous influence in American media and politics, and which, as the trial court here noted, though composing no more than 4% of the population had the support of 46% of the voters on Amendment 2. . . .)

When the Court takes sides in the culture wars, it tends to be with the knights rather than the villains—and more specifically with the Templars, reflecting the views and values of the lawyer class from which the Court's Members are drawn. How that class feels about homosexuality will be evident to anyone who wishes to interview job applicants at virtually any of the Nation's law schools. The interviewer may refuse to offer a job because the applicant is a Republican; because he is an adulterer; because he went to the wrong prep school or belongs to the wrong country club; because he eats snails; because he is a womanizer; because she wears real-animal fur; or even because he hates the Chicago Cubs. But if the interviewer should wish not to be an associate or partner of an applicant because he disapproves of the applicant's homosexuality, then he will have violated the pledge which the Association of American Law Schools requires all its member-schools to exact from job interviewers: "assurance of the employer's willingness" to hire homosexuals. . . . This law-school view of what "prejudices" must be stamped out may be contrasted with the more plebeian attitudes that apparently still prevail in the United States Congress, which has been unresponsive to repeated attempts to extend to homosexuals the protections of federal civil rights laws . . . and which took the pains to exclude them specifically from the Americans With Disabilities Act of 1990. . . .

Today's opinion has no foundation in American constitutional law, and barely pretends to. The people of Colorado have adopted an entirely reasonable provision which does not even disfavor homosexuals in any substantive sense, but merely denies them preferential treatment. Amendment 2 is designed to prevent piecemeal deterioration of the sexual morality favored by a majority of Coloradans, and is not only an appropriate means to that legitimate end, but a means that Americans have employed before. Striking it down is an act, not of judicial judgment, but of political will. I dissent.

13

ELECTIONS, REPRESENTATION, AND VOTING RIGHTS

Chapter Outline

Introduction

Racial Discrimination in Voting Rights

The Reapportionment Decisions

Political Parties and Electoral Fairness

The Problem of Campaign Finance

Conclusion

Key Terms

For Further Reading

Internet Resources

Smith v. Allwright (1944)

Gomillion v. Lightfoot (1960)

Mobile v. Bolden (1980)

Rogers v. Lodge (1982)

Shaw v. Hunt (1995)

Reynolds v. Sims (1964)

Karcher v. Daggett (1983)

Undoubtedly, the right of suffrage is a fundamental matter in a free and democratic society. Especially since the right to exercise the franchise in a free and unimpaired manner is preservative of other basic civil and political rights, any alleged infringement of the right of citizens to vote must be carefully and meticulously scrutinized.

—CHIEF JUSTICE EARL WARREN, WRITING FOR THE COURT IN *REYNOLDS V. SIMS* (1964)

INTRODUCTION

The right to vote is essential to **representative democracy,** that form of government in which policy decisions are made by representatives chosen in periodic competitive elections. Because democracy is based on the principle of **political equality,** a genuine democracy entails **universal suffrage,** which is the right of all law-abiding adult citizens to vote. Of course, the right to vote is meaningless if elections are rigged or susceptible to fraud. Nor is the right to vote as meaningful if one is compelled to vote, as is the case in some countries. Ideally, then, the right to vote involves voluntary participation in **free and fair elections.**

From a constitutional standpoint, voting is among the most important rights that citizens possess. As the Supreme Court recognized in *Yick Wo v. Hopkins* (1886), voting is "a fundamental political right, because [it is] preservative of all rights." Like free speech, voting has important instrumental value as a means of ensuring the continuing viability of constitutional democracy in this country. Of course, voting is by no means a sufficient guarantee of liberty. Indeed, it may foster the **tyranny of the majority,** which is precisely what the framers of the American Constitution wanted to prevent.

Although the United States today is a democratic country, the term "democracy" was an anathema to many of the framers of the Constitution. They accepted the notion of **popular sovereignty** in the abstract, but they certainly did not believe that every question of policy was to be subjected to majority rule. Many of the delegates to the Constitutional Convention of 1787 shared Alexander Hamilton's view that democracy was little more than legitimized mob rule, an ever-present danger to personal security, liberty, and property. The framers thus sought to establish a **constitutional republic,** in which public policy would be made by elected representatives within limits delineated in the Constitution. As we have noted in previous chapters, the Constitution was adopted to place certain values above the political fray, in order to protect individual rights from the tyranny of transient majorities. With its several elitist elements and many limitations on majority rule, the framers' Constitution can be seen as rather undemocratic. But two centuries of history have witnessed the democratization of the Constitution. What was conceived as a constitutional *republic* has become a constitutional *democracy.*

The Democratization of America

It should be remembered that property qualifications for voting still existed in 1787 and that the franchise was granted originally only to white males. With the advent of Jacksonian democracy in the 1830s, property qualifications rapidly diminished and were virtually nonexistent by the time of the Civil War. The Fifteenth Amendment, adopted in 1870, theoretically extended the franchise to African-Americans, although another century of struggle was necessary to realize the promise of the Amendment. The Nineteenth Amendment, ratified in 1920, removed sex as a qualification for voting. In addition to women's suffrage, another accomplishment of the progressive movement was passage of the Seventeenth Amendment in 1913, providing for the direct election of U.S. senators. The Twenty-fourth Amendment, ratified in 1964, abolished **poll taxes** as prerequisites for voting in federal elections. Finally, the minimum voting age was lowered to eighteen with the adoption of the Twenty-sixth Amendment in 1971. Thus, through two centuries of political change highlighted by historic amendments, the U.S. Constitution has undergone a democratic transformation.

Despite theories of the "ruling class" and the "power elite," which portray power as concentrated in a few hands, most observers would agree that political influence is more widely dispersed in the United States than in most other countries. Through mass media, political parties, interest group activity, and public demonstrations, the American people have numerous opportunities to make their demands and preferences known to their political leaders. And, of course, many of these leaders are accountable to the public through regular, competitive elections. The American people elect an astonishing array of public officials from the president all the way down to local school board members. Unfortunately, however, election practices, and even the laws governing elections, have not always reflected a serious commitment to the ideal of political equality.

Policing the Democratic Process

What happens when the majority decides to strip the minority of certain rights, even to exclude it from political participation? In a political system based solely on majority rule, there would be no remedy for the minority group. The problem is far from hypothetical. History resounds with instances of majorities oppressing minorities. Even in the United States, the "people's representatives" have passed laws isolating minority groups, diluting their right to vote, and even excluding them from the political process altogether. Such sordid conduct underscores the need for limitations on legislative power, especially in the area of voting rights. Those constitutional amendments safeguarding the right to vote and to organize politically are essential to a minority group's ability to protect itself from a hostile majority. Equally important, however, is the role that courts have played in ensuring that minorities are not locked out of the political process. Indeed, one of the paradoxes of American democracy is that the U.S. Supreme Court, a fundamentally elitist institution, has played a major part in the progressive democratization of the country. Through its exercise of judicial review, the Court, especially during the first half of the twentieth century, struck down a number of laws restricting the right to vote. More recently, it has upheld and thus reinforced the constitutional legitimacy of statutes, such as the Voting Rights Act of 1965, designed to safeguard and expand the franchise.

Justice Harlan Fiske Stone's famous footnote in *United States v. Carolene Products* (1938) recognized potential problems that could result from efforts to limit political participation, including "restrictions upon the right to vote," "restraints upon the dissemination of information," "interferences with political organizations," and "prohibition[s] of peaceable assembly." Stone asserted that "prejudice against discrete and insular minorities may be a special condition, which tends seriously to curtail the operation of those political processes ordinarily to be relied upon to protect minorities. . . ." Accordingly, claims brought by groups that have been locked out of the political process call for a "more searching judicial inquiry."

RACIAL DISCRIMINATION IN VOTING RIGHTS

As previously noted, the ratification of the Fifteenth Amendment in 1870 did not result in the immediate enfranchisement of most African-Americans. In some areas, public officials blatantly refused to honor the mandates of the Fifteenth Amendment. In other areas, groups such as the Ku Klux Klan resorted to terrorism to prevent African-Americans from exercising their newly won right to vote. The Supreme Court initially aided such resistance by limiting congressional power to enforce the Fifteenth Amendment. In *United States v. Reese* (1876), the Court struck down the Enforcement Act of 1870, by which Congress attempted to protect the right of blacks to vote in state elections. By 1884, the Court changed course and recognized Congress's power to enforce the Fifteenth Amendment (see *Ex parte Yarbrough*). By this time, however, Congress was not particularly concerned with the rights of African-Americans. Nevertheless, once it became clear that the Court would permit the federal government to secure blacks' voting rights, states bent on maintaining African-Americans in a position of second-class citizenship resorted to disingenuous methods designed to exclude them from the political process.

Grandfather Clauses

Perhaps the most blatant official means of preventing black Americans from exercising their newly granted constitutional right to vote was the **grandfather clause.** First enacted by Mississippi in 1890, this device soon spread throughout Southern and border states. Oklahoma's version, adopted as an amendment to the state constitution in 1910, was typical in that it required literacy tests for all voters whose ancestors had not been entitled to vote prior to 1866. The overall effect of grandfather clauses was to subject almost all potential black voters to literacy tests arbitrarily administered by white officials, while exempting numerous illiterate whites from this requirement.

Largely in response to invidious discrimination of this kind, the National Association for the Advancement of Colored People (NAACP) was formed in the early twentieth century. The first of many legal victories won by the NAACP came in 1915 when the Supreme Court struck down the Oklahoma grandfather clause (*Guinn v. United States*). Undaunted, the Oklahoma legislature in 1916 adopted a new law aimed at keeping African-Americans from the polls. This statute granted permanent voting registration to all persons who had voted in 1914, when the grandfather clause was still in effect. All other persons were required to register to vote during a twelve-day period or be permanently disqualified from voting. The Supreme Court ultimately invalidated this blatant subterfuge as well (see *Lane v. Wilson* [1939]).

The White Primary

After the demise of the grandfather clause, Southern states resorted to the equally infamous **white primary.** This device was an extremely effective means of keeping African-Americans from exercising their right to vote in any meaningful sense. Until the 1960s, the "solid South" maintained a virtual one-party political system. Thus, in all but a few areas, nomination by the Democratic Party was tantamount to election. In fact, Republicans seldom bothered to run in the general elections. In order to keep African-Americans out of the political process, the Democratic Party in many states adopted a rule excluding them from party membership. Concomitantly, state legislatures closed the primaries to everyone except party members. The Supreme Court had previously ruled that political parties were private organizations, not part of the government election apparatus (see *Newberry v. United States* [1921]). Consequently, through the white primary device, blacks were effectively disenfranchised but, arguably, not by official state action.

In a series of cases from the late 1920s through the early 1950s, the Supreme Court grappled with the white primary issue. In two early decisions, it effectively barred formal state endorsement of the white primary (see *Nixon v. Herndon* [1927] and *Nixon v. Condon* [1932]). However, in *Grovey v. Townsend* (1935), the Supreme Court upheld a Texas white primary based not on legislative enactment but exclusively on a resolution adopted by the state Democratic Party. The Court's decision in *Grovey* thus reinforced the prevailing legal view that political parties were merely private organizations beyond the purview of the Constitution. In *United States v. Classic* (1941), however, the Court moved away from this highly artificial view of party primaries. The *Classic* case involved the question of whether the federal government could regulate party primaries in order to prevent election fraud. In upholding this exercise of congressional power, the Court overruled *Newberry* and undercut the logic of *Grovey v. Townsend*. In *Smith v. Allwright* (1944), the Court struck down the white primary as violative of the Fifteenth Amendment, thus overruling the *Grovey* decision. Writing for the Court, Justice Stanley Reed expressed a pragmatic view of the concept of state action:

> This grant to the people of the opportunity for choice is not to be nullified by a State through casting its electoral process in a form which permits a private organization

to practice racial discrimination in the election. Constitutional rights would be of little value if they could be thus indirectly denied.

In an attempt to circumvent the Supreme Court's ruling in *Smith v. Allwright,* Texas Democrats established the "Jaybird Democratic Association," from which African-Americans were excluded. The Jaybirds held "preprimary" elections in which candidates for the Democratic primaries were selected. This shabby attempt at further evasion of constitutional requirements was invalidated by the Supreme Court (*Terry v. Adams* [1953]). In *Terry,* the Court observed that under the preprimary scheme, both the primary and the general election were little more than "perfunctory ratifiers" of the Jaybirds' choices for elected officials.

Literacy Tests

The eradication of grandfather clauses and white primaries was insufficient to integrate African-Americans into the political process, because die-hard racism manifested itself in alternative exclusionary tactics. For example, many states relied on **literacy tests** that, despite superficial neutrality, were administered in a highly discriminatory manner. Quite frequently, white people were not required to take the tests, even if their literacy was questionable. However, since the Constitution had left the determination of voting qualifications to the states and since these tests were on their face racially neutral, the Supreme Court refused to strike them down. In *Lassiter v. Northampton County Board of Education* (1959), the Court explicitly upheld the use of literacy tests. Writing for the Court, Justice William O. Douglas reasoned that "in our society where newspapers, periodicals, books and other printed matter canvass and debate campaign issues, a State might conclude that only those who are literate should exercise the franchise." Ultimately, literacy tests as devices of racial discrimination were done away with, not by the Supreme Court but by Congress through the landmark Voting Rights Act of 1965.

Poll Taxes

Another less common but equally effective means of keeping African-Americans from voting was the poll tax. At the time the Constitution was adopted, poll taxes were widely used as a legitimate means of raising revenue. During the 1780s, however, poll taxes did not significantly hamper voting because only white property owners were entitled to vote anyway! By the mid-nineteenth century, poll taxes had virtually disappeared. Around 1900, a number of states resurrected the poll tax for the obvious purpose of preventing African-Americans from voting. The tax generally amounted to two dollars per election—quite sufficient to deter many blacks, as well as poor whites, from exercising the franchise. On its face, however, the poll tax was racially neutral, and the Supreme Court initially refused to strike it down (see *Breedlove v. Suttles* [1937]). Eventually, however, the poll tax was thoroughly repudiated. In 1964, the poll tax was abolished in federal elections through adoption of the Twenty-fourth Amendment. Three years later, in *Harper v. Virginia Board of Elections* (1966), the Supreme Court held that poll taxes in state elections violated the Fourteenth Amendment. Writing for the Court, Justice Douglas emphasized the arbitrariness of the tax:

> To introduce wealth, or payment of a fee as a measure of a voter's qualifications is to introduce a capricious or irrelevant factor. . . . Wealth, like race, creed, or color, is not germane to one's ability to participate intelligently in the electoral process.

Racial Gerrymandering

Perhaps the most outrageous attempt to disenfranchise African-American voters occurred in Tuskegee, Alabama, in 1957. At the city's behest, the all-white Alabama legislature dramatically altered the boundaries of Tuskegee from a square to a twenty-eight-sided figure (see Figure 13.1). The purpose of the **gerrymander** was obvious in that all but five of the city's four hundred black voters were placed outside the city limits, while no white voters were displaced. A number of the "former residents" of Tuskegee brought suit in federal court, seeking a declaratory judgment that the **racial gerrymandering** measure was unconstitutional and an injunction to prohibit its enforcement. The U.S. District Court for the Middle District of Alabama dismissed the case for lack of jurisdiction, stating that it had "no control over, no supervision over, and no power to change any boundaries of a municipal corporation fixed by a duly convened legislative body. . . ." The Court of Appeals for the Fifth Circuit agreed. But the Supreme Court reversed the lower courts and reinstated the complaint, saying that the "petitioners are entitled to prove their allegations at trial." Speaking for a unanimous bench, Justice Felix Frankfurter stated that if the plaintiffs' allegations were proven, it would be "difficult to appreciate what stands in the way of adjudging [the redistricting measure] invalid . . ." (*Gomillion v. Lightfoot* [1960]). Indeed, plaintiffs prevailed at trial, and the gerrymander was invalidated.

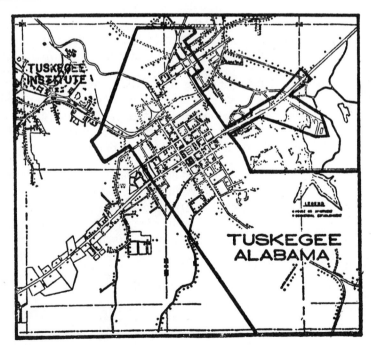

The entire area of the square comprised the city prior to Act 140. The irregular black-bordered figure within the square represents the post-enactment city.

Appendix to Opinion of the Court in *Gomillion v. Lightfoot* (1960)

FIGURE 13.1
Tuskegee, Alabama, Before and After the Racial Gerrymander

Earl Warren: Chief Justice,
1953–1969

The Voting Rights Act of 1965

A 1961 report of the U.S. Commission on Civil Rights documented the pervasiveness of voting discrimination in the South. According to the report, fewer than 10 percent of eligible African-Americans were registered to vote in at least 129 counties in ten Southern states. In counties where blacks comprised a majority of the population, the average level of black registration was only 3 percent. As the Civil Rights movement of the early 1960s galvanized the nation's conscience, the demand for federal action grew. The federal government responded with the Civil Rights Act of 1964 and the **Voting Rights Act of 1965,** both of which were pushed through Congress under the skillful leadership of President Lyndon B. Johnson.

The Voting Rights Act employed a rough index of discrimination to apply the scrutiny of the federal government to those states that had historically been most recalcitrant in refusing to allow African-Americans to vote: Alabama, Georgia, Louisiana, Mississippi, South Carolina, and Virginia. Specifically, the act waived accumulated poll taxes and abolished literacy tests and similar devices in those areas to which the statute applied. The act also required the aforementioned states to obtain **preclearance** from the U.S. Department of Justice before making changes in their electoral systems. Not surprisingly, this historic and far-reaching act was challenged on the ground that Congress had exceeded its power to enforce the Fifteenth Amendment. The Supreme Court, although recognizing the Voting Rights Act as "inventive," upheld the law (see *South Carolina v. Katzenbach* [1966]). Writing for a nearly unanimous Court (only Justice Hugo Black partially dissented), Chief Justice Earl Warren expressed optimism about the Voting Rights Act:

> Hopefully, millions of non-white Americans will now be able to participate for the first time on an equal basis in the government under which they live. We may finally look forward to the day when truly "the right of citizens of the United States to vote shall not be denied or abridged by the United States or by any State on account of race, color or previous condition of servitude."

Despite its strong endorsement by the Warren Court and subsequent extension by Congress, the Voting Rights Act remained controversial. Of particular concern to many were the strict preclearance requirements of Section 5, under which designated states are required to submit proposed changes in election laws to the Justice Department for approval. Equally controversial is Section 2, which allows plaintiffs in any jurisdiction to challenge electoral schemes that impermissibly dilute the voting strength of minority groups. These provisions led many conservatives to oppose renewal of the Voting Rights Act in 1982.

The Reagan administration, more conservative than its Democratic and Republican predecessors in the field of civil rights, initially opposed the extension of the act without major changes in these controversial provisions. However, bipartisan support in Congress for extending the act forced the administration to back down. The act was renewed and strengthened in 1982. Although some civil rights activists argue that the Voting Rights Act has not been enforced vigorously enough, one must recognize the very real impact that it has had on minority political participation. Enforcement of the Voting Rights Act has resulted in substantially higher levels of voter registration among African-Americans, particularly in the Deep South. Accordingly, many politicians who formerly made overt appeals to white supremacy tempered their racist rhetoric in order to draw support from new black voters. Perhaps the best example of this metamorphosis was Alabama Governor George Wallace who, in the face of the Civil Rights movement of the 1960s, maintained a strong segregationist stance. In the late 1970s and early 1980s, Wallace dropped the racist rhetoric in order to appeal to newly enfranchised African-Americans who might be tempted to vote Republican. Another excellent example of this political realism is seen in the long career of Republican Senator Strom Thurmond of South Carolina. In 1948, when he was the Democratic governor of the state, Thurmond ran for president on the strongly segregationist Dixiecrat ticket. With the enfranchisement of African-Americans, however, Thurmond began actively soliciting (and often receiving) their support in his U.S. Senate races.

At-Large Elections

As African-Americans began to register and vote in greater numbers, black politicians made substantial gains, especially at the local level. Seeking to thwart the growing influence of black voters, a number of white-dominated cities and counties adopted basic structural changes in their systems of representation. Because the overt racial gerrymander had been declared unconstitutional in *Gomillion v. Lightfoot* (1960), these communities converted to **at-large elections** in which local candidates ran for office on a citywide or countywide basis. This election method was by no means novel in the United States, but its use as a deliberate means of limiting the political clout of African-American voters raised new constitutional issues. At-large systems of voting were often coupled with the annexation of predominantly white suburban areas, thereby further diluting black voting power. Since the 1970s, many of these at-large and annexation schemes have been challenged in court as unlawful attempts to undermine the voting strength of minority groups.

The Supreme Court Rules on At-Large Elections

In 1980, the Supreme Court handed down a ruling on the constitutionality of at-large elections (*Mobile v. Bolden*). Since 1911, the city of Mobile, Alabama, had used at-large elections to choose its three-member city commission. At the time the lawsuit was filed, more than 35 percent of the residents of Mobile were African-American. Despite several attempts, however, no African-American had ever been elected to the city commission. Plaintiffs argued that the at-large system was unconstitutional because it had the effect of unfairly diluting the voting strength of racial minorities. The U.S. District Court for the Southern District of Alabama agreed, as did the Fifth Circuit Court of Appeals. The Supreme Court reversed, holding that there must be a showing of a discriminatory intent on the part of public officials in order to warrant a finding that the Constitution has been violated. Dissenting vehemently, Justice Thurgood Marshall asserted that "[s]uch judicial deference to official decision making has no place under the Fifteenth Amendment." Marshall went on to accuse the Court of being "an accessory to the perpetuation of racial discrimination."

In spite of, or perhaps in response to Justice Marshall's accusatory rhetoric in *Mobile v. Bolden,* the Supreme Court in 1982 demonstrated that the "intentional discrimination" standard can in fact be met. In *Rogers v. Lodge,* the Court, voting

How Can Courts Determine Whether Changes in Voting Systems Are Motivated by an Intention to Dilute the Voting Strength of the Minority?

An excerpt from Justice O'Connor's Opinion of the Court in *Reno v. Bossier Parish School Board* (1997)

. . . [A]ssessing a jurisdiction's motivation in enacting voting changes is a complex task requiring a "sensitive inquiry into such circumstantial and direct evidence as may be available."

The "important starting point" for assessing discriminatory intent . . . is "the impact of the official action whether it 'bears more heavily on one race than an-

other.' " . . . [This] "impact" might include a plan's retrogressive effect and . . . its dilutive impact. Other considerations relevant to the purpose inquiry include, among other things, "the historical background of the [jurisdiction's] decision"; "[t]he specific sequence of events leading up to the challenged decision"; "[d]epartures from the normal procedural sequence"; and "[t]he legislative or administrative history, especially . . . [any] contemporary statements by members of the decisionmaking body." . . .

6 to 3, struck down an at-large election scheme in Burke County, Georgia, on the basis of the standard handed down in the *Mobile* case. In this case, the Court reasserted a commitment to the Fifteenth Amendment that some critics found lacking in *Mobile v. Bolden.*

The Effects Test under the 1982 Voting Rights Act Amendments

In its 1982 extension of the Voting Rights Act, Congress amended Section 2 to allow plaintiffs to prevail in voting dilution cases on the basis of an **effects test,** rather than on the **intent standard** of *Mobile v. Bolden.* In other words, Congress accomplished through statute what the Supreme Court refused to do under the Fifteenth Amendment. Thus, *Mobile v. Bolden* is essentially irrelevant to a group of minority plaintiffs seeking to challenge an election scheme. It matters not to plaintiffs whether they prevail under a provision of the federal Constitution or under Section 2 of the Voting Rights Act. Here is an important lesson for students of the American legal system: Civil rights law is by no means the exclusive province of courts and constitutions. Legislatures may act to enhance civil rights through their power to adopt ordinary legislation.

The Problem of Racially Proportionate Representation

The voting dilution cases raise the serious question of proportionate representation (not to be confused with *proportional* representation existing under some parliamentary systems). A scheme of proportionate representation would require citizens to be represented by individuals possessing specific racial, sexual, religious, occupational, or other characteristics in proportion to their occurrence in the population. Thus, under a scheme of racial proportionate representation, African-Americans in Mobile (see *Mobile v. Bolden,* discussed earlier) would be "entitled" to one seat on the city commission. Indeed, ostensibly because of its opposition to racially proportionate representation, the Reagan administration consistently opposed the effects standard in voting rights litigation, whether brought under the Fifteenth Amendment or Section 2 of the Voting Rights Act.

The Supreme Court has said repeatedly that the Constitution does not require or permit proportionate representation. Few would disagree with the Court on this point of theory. The problem is of a more practical nature. Suppose a federal district judge finds that a city's system of at-large elections was established for the single purpose of diluting the voting strength of African-Americans. Clearly, the court may order the city to set up a system of single-member districts, but how should those districts be drawn? Should the court impose a scheme that virtually ensures proportionate representation of African-Americans on the city council? Would such a **race-conscious remedy** be constitutionally acceptable? In fact, what usually happens in voting rights cases is that both the plaintiff and the defendant submit remedial plans and the court attempts to fashion an equitable compromise. The final remedy that emerges will almost certainly enhance the electoral prospects for African-American candidates but may not ensure proportionate representation.

Challenges to Judicial Election Systems

When Congress extended the Voting Rights Act in 1982, it changed the statutory language in a way that eventually proved to be highly significant. Instead of applying only to elections of "legislators," the act now refers to "representatives." This suggests the applicability of Voting Rights Act challenges to nonlegislative elections, but which elections? In a controversial 6-to-3 decision, the Supreme Court held in 1991 that plaintiffs may challenge judicial election systems under Section 2 of the Voting Rights Act. In *Chisom v. Roemer,* the Court decided that the statutory term "representatives" includes elected judges. The *Chisom* case is one of myriad examples of important civil rights policies being determined through statutory, as opposed to constitutional, interpretation. Students of constitutional law must realize that much of the important law of civil rights stems not from judicial interpretation of the Fourteenth and Fifteenth Amendments but from the broad-gauged statutes passed under Congress's power to enforce the guarantees of those Amendments.

Chisom v. Roemer involved a challenge to Louisiana's system for electing judges to the state supreme court. Under that system, five of the seven state supreme court judges were elected from single-member districts; the remaining two jurists were elected at large from a sixth district that included predominantly black Orleans Parish and several other parishes where African-Americans were in the minority. Plaintiffs in the case argued that this scheme had the effect of diluting the voting strength of blacks in New Orleans. Had Orleans Parish been set up as a separate single-member district, an African-American candidate would have had a greater chance of being elected to the state supreme court. Under the existing system, no black had ever been elected to Louisiana's highest tribunal, despite a number of attempts. After a bench trial, the U.S. district court concluded that there had been no violation of the Voting Rights Act under the standard set forth in the landmark case of *Thornburgh v. Gingles* (1986). On appeal, the Fifth Circuit Court of Appeals concluded that the Voting Rights Act did not apply to judicial elections, holding that the district court should have dismissed the complaint altogether. On certiorari, the Supreme Court reversed, declaring that "[w]hen each of several members of a court must be a resident of a different district, and must be elected by the voters of that district, it seems both reasonable and realistic to characterize the winners as representatives of that district." The Supreme Court expressed no opinion on the merits of the plaintiffs' case. It merely remanded the case to the Fifth Circuit Court of Appeals for further consideration.

In a related case, the Supreme Court decided that Section 2 of the Voting Rights Act applies also to the election of state trial judges. In *Houston Lawyers' Association v. Attorney General of Texas* (1991), the Court said that "[i]f a State decides to elect its trial judges, . . . those elections must be conducted in compliance with the Voting Rights Act." Since at least half the states still use elections to select some or all of their judges, the Court's decisions in *Chisom v. Roemer* and *Houston Lawyers' Association* have plowed a fertile field for litigation. It remains to be seen whether plaintiffs will be successful in mounting challenges to judicial elections. However, one can be sure that the Supreme Court will be revisiting this new area of voting rights law.

The Rehnquist Court Restricts Race-Conscious Redistricting

In a decision carrying great potential to affect litigation under the Voting Rights Act of 1965, the Court ruled that strangely shaped legislative districts designed to produce African-American electoral majorities are subject to challenge under the Equal Protection Clause of the Fourteenth Amendment. In *Shaw v. Reno* (1993), white voters had sued to challenge the "racial gerrymandering" that led to the creation of the unusually shaped 12th Congressional District of North Carolina. A three-judge panel in the federal district court dismissed the suit for failure to state a cause of action for which relief is available under the Fourteenth Amendment. On appeal, the Supreme Court reversed by a vote of 5 to 4. Writing for the Court, Justice O'Connor observed that "[w]hen a district is created solely to effectuate the perceived common interests of one racial group, elected officials are more likely to believe that their primary obligation is to represent only the members of that group, rather than their constituency as a whole." In O'Connor's view, such an effect would be "altogether antithetical to our system of representative democracy." In dissent, Justice White argued that

> the notion that North Carolina's plan, under which whites remain a voting majority in a disproportionate number of congressional districts, and pursuant to which the State has sent its first black representatives since Reconstruction to the United States Congress, might have violated appellants' constitutional rights is both a fiction and a departure from settled equal protection principles.

In *Shaw v. Reno,* the Supreme Court stopped short of invalidating the North Carolina plan, leaving that determination to the lower federal courts. On remand, the district court in North Carolina upheld the redistricting plan on the ground that the plan was narrowly tailored to further the state's compelling interests in complying with the Voting Rights Act of 1965. Not surprisingly, the Supreme Court granted cert and the case returned to the High Bench.

In *Shaw v. Hunt* (1996), the Supreme Court struck down the North Carolina plan. Writing for the majority of five, Chief Justice Rehnquist took issue with the District Court's conclusion that the plan was justified as a means of meeting the state's responsibilities under the Voting Rights Act. Among other things, this statute protects minorities from **vote dilution.** In Rehnquist's view, vote dilution suffered by African-American voting in congressional elections throughout North Carolina is " . . . not remedied by creating a safe majority-black district somewhere else in the State."

The real thrust of the Court's opinion appears to have been a repudiation of the Justice Department's policy of maximizing the number of majority-black districts. Rehnquist asserted that "this maximization policy is not properly grounded in Section 5 [of the Voting Rights Act] and the Department's authority thereunder." In a stinging dissent, Justice Stevens observed that "[t]here is no small irony in the fact that the Court's decision to intrude into the State's districting process comes in response to a lawsuit brought on behalf of white voters who have suffered no history of exclusion from North Carolina's political process, and whose only claims of harm are at best rooted in speculative and stereotypical assumptions about the kind of representation they are likely to receive from the candidates that their neighbors have chosen."

In a similar case, *Bush v. Vera* (1996), the Court invalidated a Texas redistricting plan that created three minority-majority districts. Writing for a plurality, Justice O'Connor observed that the "districts' shapes are bizarre, and their utter disregard of city limits, local election precincts, and voter tabulation district lines has caused a severe disruption of traditional forms of political activity and created administrative headaches for local election officials." O'Connor noted that the "appellants adduced evidence that incumbency protection played a role in determining the bizarre district lines" but concluded, as had the district court, that "the districts' shapes are unexplainable on grounds other than race and, as such, are the product of presumptively unconstitutional racial gerrymandering is inescapably corroborated by the evidence." Justices Stevens, Souter, Ginsburg, and Breyer dissented, as they did in *Shaw v. Hunt.*

TO SUMMARIZE:

- In spite of the ratification of the Fifteenth Amendment in 1870, African-Americans did not achieve full voting rights until implementation of the Voting Rights Act of 1965.
- States intent on inhibiting electoral participation by blacks developed a variety of mechanisms, including grandfather clauses, white primaries, literacy tests, racial gerrymanders, and poll taxes. All of these efforts to frustrate political participation by African-Americans were eventually invalidated either by Supreme Court decisions, federal statutes, or amendments to the U.S. Constitution.
- Federal courts have continued to scrutinize changes in state and local electoral systems, using both the Voting Rights Act of 1965, as amended, and the Fourteenth and Fifteenth Amendments to the U.S. Constitution. Many such changes have been challenged by minority groups on the ground that they impermissibly dilute minority influence.
- In recent years, the Rehnquist Court has shifted the focus of judicial scrutiny away from efforts to dilute the voting power of minorities and toward efforts to increase the political influence of African-Americans through the race-conscious redrawing of district lines.

THE REAPPORTIONMENT DECISIONS

Questions of inequality with respect to voting rights are by no means limited to the issue of racial discrimination. For many years, one of the most intractable and pervasive forms of inequality was that of legislative **malapportionment.**

Representation in the U.S. House of Representatives, in all fifty state legislatures, and in most local governments is apportioned on the basis of population. Representatives in state legislatures and in the U.S. House are elected from single-member districts (although a few states are allotted only one representative who of course is elected statewide). Malapportionment exists to the extent that the number of voters comprising such districts is unequal. Malapportionment can come about in two ways. It has generally occurred as a function of natural population shifts due to urbanization and interstate migration. It has also come about through gerrymandering, where district lines are intentionally drawn to create inequalities for political purposes.

Historically, malapportionment of the state legislatures and the U.S. House favored rural over urban interests. In many states, it was not uncommon for urban districts to be ten times as populous as rural districts, thus diluting the value of urban votes by a factor of ten. A particularly egregious example of malapportionment was provided by Georgia's "county unit system" (declared unconstitutional by the Supreme Court in *Gray v. Sanders* [1963]). Under that scheme, Fulton County (comprising much of metropolitan Atlanta) with a population of more than half a million was entitled to three seats in the state House of Representatives. Echols County in rural South Georgia, with a 1960 population of only 1,876, was entitled to one representative. Thus, the discrepancy in representation was more than a hundred to one in favor of Echols County!

Even though apportionment discrepancies throughout the United States were great and growing, it was unrealistic to expect elected officials (many of whom benefited from the status quo) to address the problem. Yet most Americans seemed to assume that this problem, like so many others, had a legal solution. Accordingly, voters from grossly underrepresented urban areas turned for relief to the federal courts, citing, among other things, the Equal Protection Clause of the Fourteenth Amendment. In *Colegrove v. Green* (1946), the Supreme Court invoked the political questions doctrine to foreclose judicial relief, at least from the federal bench. Writing for a plurality of the Court, Justice Frankfurter warned of the dangers of entering the "political thicket" of malapportionment:

> It is hostile to a democratic system to involve the judiciary in the politics of the people. . . . The remedy for unfairness in districting is to secure state legislatures that will apportion properly, or to invoke the ample powers of Congress.

The Reapportionment Revolution

Between 1946 and 1962, groups representing urban interests tried, without much success, to secure **reapportionment** through the state legislatures and through the ballot box. Beginning in 1962, however, the Supreme Court produced a series of decisions on reapportionment that would permanently alter the American political landscape and draw the Court into a firestorm of criticism.

In *Baker v. Carr* (1962), the Supreme Court opened the doors of the federal courthouse to plaintiffs pressing reapportionment claims. The Court reversed its previous position and declared malapportionment to be justiciable (see Chapter 4). Shortly thereafter, the Court declared malapportionment in its various contexts unconstitutional (see Table 13.1). Reapportionment, wrote Chief Justice Warren in *Reynolds v. Sims* (1964), would have to follow the principle of "one person, one vote." In *Reynolds,* the Court held that "the Equal Protection Clause requires that a State make an honest and good faith effort to construct districts, in both houses of its legislature, as nearly of equal population as is practicable."

TABLE 13.1   Major Supreme Court Decisions Extending Reapportionment

Case	Year	Target of Reapportionment
Gray v. Sanders	1963	Georgia "county unit" system of apportioning state legislature
Wesberry v. Sanders	1964	Congressional districts
Reynolds v. Sims	1964	All state legislatures
Lucas v. Colorado 44th General Assembly	1964	State legislative apportionment based on constitutional provisions
Avery v. Midland County	1968	Local governing bodies
Hadley v. Junior College District	1970	School boards

Not surprisingly, many observers soon began to wonder just how strict the Court would be in requiring population equality among legislative districts. In *Reynolds,* Chief Justice Warren had observed that "it is a practical impossibility to arrange legislative districts so that each one has an identical number of residents, or citizens, or voters. Mathematical exactness is hardly a workable constitutional requirement. . . ."

In 1969, the Court provided an indication of just how strict it intended to be when it struck down an apportionment scheme for congressional districts in Missouri. The plan invalidated by the Court in *Kirkpatrick v. Preisler* involved a 6 percent population deviation between the smallest and the largest districts and only a 1.8 percent average deviation from the ideal district population. Many praised the Court for its rigorous application of the one-person, one-vote principle. Others decried the Court's meddling in the technicalities of legislative apportionment. Regardless of the position one takes on this issue, the importance of the Court's reapportionment decisions can hardly be overstated. Indeed, on a number of occasions, Chief Justice Warren himself pointed without hesitation to the reapportionment decisions as his principal contribution to constitutional law.

Reapportionment Under the Burger Court

For the most part, the Supreme Court under Chief Justice Warren Burger maintained the Warren Court's strong commitment to the one-person, one-vote principle. The counterrevolution many critics feared from a more conservative Court did not materialize, at least not in the realm of apportionment cases. The Burger Court, however, did allow state legislatures more leeway in determining state legislative boundaries than in drawing congressional district lines. The Court made it clear that, in scrutinizing state districts, it was willing to entertain "legitimate considerations incident to the effectuation of a rational state policy." Thus, in *Brown v. Thomson* (1983), the Court upheld an apportionment scheme for the Wyoming legislature based on county lines, even though the scheme had a population deviation of nearly 90 percent between the largest and the smallest districts. On the very same day, in *Karcher v. Daggett,* the Court invalidated a New Jersey scheme for congressional districts where the maximum deviation was less than 1 percent! The majority agreed with the federal district court that the plan was "not a good-faith effort to achieve population equality using the best available census data."

The 1990 Census and Congressional Reapportionment

Although state legislatures are responsible for drawing the boundaries of congressional districts, the Constitution empowers Congress to determine the number of representatives that each state shall have. Every ten years, after completion of the census, Congress reallocates congressional seats among the states. Article I, Section 2, of the Constitution imposes three restrictions on the exercise of Congress's discretion in this area: (1) Every state is guaranteed at least one congressional seat; (2) district lines may not cross state borders; and (3) no district shall include fewer than thirty thousand persons.

In 1941, Congress enacted a law specifying that "the method of equal proportions" would be used to ascertain the number of congressional seats to which each state would be entitled. Applying this method to the results of the 1990 census, Congress determined that Montana would lose one of its two congressional seats. After reapportionment, the average population of congressional districts was 572,466, while Montana's population was 803,655. Montana's single district was thus 231,189 persons larger than the average district. Had Montana retained two districts, each would have been 170,638 persons smaller than the average district. Because the loss of a congressional seat means the decline of influence in Congress and the electoral college, Montana promptly filed suit to challenge the allocation. Relying on *Wesberry v. Sanders* (1964) and *Kirkpatrick v. Preisler* (1969), the state argued that the greater discrepancy between actual and ideal district size by its loss of a seat violated the principle of one person, one vote. A three-judge district court issued a summary judgment upholding Montana's claim and declaring the 1941 statute unconstitutional. On direct appeal, the Supreme Court unanimously reversed (see *Department of Commerce v. Montana* [1992]). Writing for the Court, Justice John Paul Stevens concluded that Congress had ample power to adopt the method of least proportions or any other reasonable method as long as it is applied consistently after each census. The *Montana* decision suggests that the contemporary Supreme Court is willing to accord far more latitude to Congress than to state legislatures in the field of reapportionment.

Assessing the Reapportionment Decisions

The Supreme Court's reapportionment decisions have been sharply criticized by conservative scholars and by some politicians. In the mid-1960s, a widely publicized effort to overrule the reapportionment decisions through constitutional amendment was spearheaded by Senate Minority Leader Everett Dirksen (R–Illinois). Despite auspicious beginnings, the Dirksen Amendment proved to be a flash in the pan. It soon became clear that the American people fundamentally approved of the reapportionment decisions, irrespective of the strident attacks by many elected officials. A Gallup Poll conducted shortly after *Reynolds v. Sims* was decided found that 47 percent approved of the decision, 30 percent disapproved, and 23 percent expressed no opinion. Apparently the one-person, one-vote principle appealed to the American people's sense of fair play.

While many observers believe that the Supreme Court's school prayer and desegregation decisions were somewhat damaging to its prestige and credibility, the reapportionment decisions seem to have had the opposite effect. Thus, while the continuing debate over the proper role of the Court is important, the Court's legitimacy does not depend so much on fastidious adherence to legal principles, procedures, and traditions as it does on public support for the substance of the Court's decisions. One of the great ironies of American democracy (and perhaps its greatest strength) is that the judicial elite must from time to time interfere with the people's elected representatives for the purpose of maintaining the norm of political equality.

For some jurisprudential thinkers, such as John Hart Ely, the primary utility of and justification for judicial review is to maintain the integrity of the democratic process. Certainly the reapportionment decisions make sense from this perspective. It is noteworthy that the reapportionment decisions, although much reviled by incumbent politicians, were met with a far greater degree of compliance than, for example, the school prayer decisions. The strong public support for reapportionment as a policy was undoubtedly a critical factor promoting legislative compliance. The clarity of the Supreme Court's one-person, one-vote mandate likewise facilitated implementation of reapportionment. Finally, the obvious nature of noncompliance probably had a substantial effect on legislative willingness to abide by the Court's decisions.

TO SUMMARIZE:

- By the mid-twentieth century, malapportionment of legislative bodies at all levels of government had become a serious problem, one that state legislatures were unwilling to address. After refusing an invitation to enter this "political thicket" in the mid-1940s, the Supreme Court in *Baker v. Carr* (1962) precipitated a revolution in American politics by determining that malapportionment was a justiciable issue under the Equal Protection Clause of the Fourteenth Amendment.
- In *Reynolds v. Sims* (1964) and related cases, the Court applied the principle of "one person, one vote" to legislative districts at all levels of government. As a result, reapportionment today is a regularly recurring feature of American politics.

POLITICAL PARTIES AND ELECTORAL FAIRNESS

Although the framers of the Constitution neither desired nor anticipated the development of political parties, by 1800 a two-party system had taken root in the young republic. While particular political parties have come and gone since then, the two-party system remains an established feature of the political order. Most political scientists regard the two-party system as a source of desirable political stability.

The merits of the two-party system aside, there is surely a constitutional right for disaffected voters to form new parties or support independent candidates who challenge the established order. Despite ideological disagreements, the two established parties tend to collaborate in suppressing competition by rival third parties and independent candidates. State legislatures frequently adopt laws making it difficult, if not impossible, for third parties to get candidates on the ballot. Unrealistic filing deadlines and petition requirements are often employed to frustrate the electoral ambitions of third-party and independent candidates.

In 1980, independent presidential candidate John Anderson filed suit in federal court to challenge Ohio's March filing deadline for the November general elections. In *Anderson v. Celebrezze* (1983), Anderson received a favorable ruling from the Supreme Court, which declared the Ohio regulation to be excessively burdensome on the efforts of independent candidates. Anderson's belated legal victory, however, did not altogether eliminate problems that third-party and independent candidates encounter when attempting to get their names on the ballot, as both David Duke and Ross Perot discovered during their 1992 presidential campaigns.

Partisan Gerrymandering

Historically, one of the weapons of interparty competition has been the gerrymander, the intentional drawing of district lines for political purposes. Although legislative apportionment must proceed on the principle of one person, one vote and must not be based on race discrimination, there remains the prospect that the party in power in the state legislature will redraw district lines so as to minimize the likelihood that the opposing party will gain seats in the next election. The process of reapportionment, which occurs after each decennial census, thus provides an opportunity for the party holding the majority of seats in the legislature to further strengthen its position. Until recently, this **partisan gerrymandering** was thought to be constitutionally unassailable.

In a significant 1986 decision, however, the Supreme Court upheld the justiciability of cases challenging partisan gerrymandering. In *Davis v. Bandemer* (1986), the Court ruled that Indiana Democrats could challenge a 1981 reapportionment plan adopted by the Republican-controlled state legislature. A plurality of four justices maintained, however, that to prevail in such cases, plaintiffs would have to make "a threshold showing of discriminatory vote dilution. . . ." In a concurring opinion reminiscent of Justice Frankfurter's plea for judicial restraint in *Colegrove v. Green,* Justice Sandra Day O'Connor lamented the Court's "far-reaching step into the 'political thicket' " and predicted dire consequences. According to Justice O'Connor, a former state legislator,

> [t]o turn these matters over to the federal judiciary is to inject the courts into the most heated partisan issues. It is predictable that the courts will respond by moving away from the nebulous standard a plurality of the Court fashions today and toward some form of proportional representation.

The consequences of federal court involvement in partisan gerrymandering will certainly be closely examined by lawyers, scholars, and politicians. Whether *Davis v. Bandemer* represents a permanent entry into the field remains to be seen. As yet, few significant developments have taken place in this area.

TO SUMMARIZE:

- Although the Supreme Court has on occasion invalidated restrictions on candidates' access to the ballot, such restrictions still pose a formidable obstacle to independent or third-party candidates.
- The Court has held that partisan gerrymandering is a justiciable issue, but has provided little guidance to lower federal courts in this area.

THE PROBLEM OF CAMPAIGN FINANCE

Reformers have long advocated measures designed to remove what they see as the corrupting influence of money in the political process. In particular, reformers have proposed limitations on campaign spending, restrictions on campaign contributions, and various degrees of **public financing** of campaigns. The most extreme proposals call for eliminating private funding altogether and providing all candidates equal amounts of public money with which to conduct their campaigns.

In the midst of the Watergate scandal, Congress attempted to tackle the thorny problem of **campaign finance.** Among other things, the **Federal Election Campaign Act Amendments of 1974** limited campaign spending by candidates in federal elections and limited individual contributions to such candidates. In *Buckley v. Valeo* (1976), both of these limitations were challenged as infringements of political expression as protected by the First Amendment. In a convoluted and fragmented set of opinions, the Supreme Court struck down the spending limits but upheld the limits on individual contributions. The Court also upheld provisions providing for public funding of campaigns and the limits on expenditures that accompanied the acceptance of public funds. Subsequently, in *Federal Election Commission v. National Conservative Political Action Committee* (1985), the Court said that such limits cannot be applied to persons or parties who spend money in support of a candidate who accepts public funds. Such so-called "soft money" expenditures have played an important and controversial role in recent presidential and congressional campaigns. However, unless and until the Supreme Court abandons the position that spending money in a political campaign is a form of political expression protected by the First Amendment, there is little that can be done to control such expenditures. Of course, not all reformers, and certainly not all political scientists agree that limiting spending and contributions has a salutary effect on the system. Many would argue that such limits tend to benefit incumbents, who already enjoy a number of advantages. However, most would agree that current laws requiring full disclosure of contributions and expenditures are both necessary and proper. Certainly, the Supreme Court has never held or implied that such laws violate the First Amendment or any other constitutional provision.

TO SUMMARIZE:

- Congress has attempted to regulate campaign finance, most notably through the Federal Election Campaign Act Amendments of 1974. In *Buckley v. Valeo* (1976), the Supreme Court struck down spending limits imposed on candidates but upheld the limits imposed on individual contributions. The Court recognized that campaign spending is a form of political expression protected by the First Amendment.

CONCLUSION

The fundamental question of whether courts of law ought to have the power to invalidate legislative and executive acts has long since been put to rest. Yet there remains substantial controversy over the appropriate role of courts in applying the tenets of the Constitution to challenged legislation. Many are troubled by substantive due process decisions in which the Supreme Court has invalidated legislative policies on the basis of arguably dubious principles, such as liberty of contract and the right of privacy, nowhere mentioned in the Constitution. While the appropriate role of the Supreme Court in addressing substantive issues of policy is debatable, there is little disagreement about the legitimacy of the Court's role in maintaining the integrity of the democratic process.

Applying a standard of strict scrutiny, the Supreme Court since *Baker v. Carr* (1962) and *Reynolds v. Sims* (1964) has had a significant impact with respect to representation and voting rights. The Court's major decisions in this area reflect three fundamental principles: First, suffrage must be universally available; second, all votes must count equally; and, third, elections must offer the voter a choice among candidates and parties. Although politicians may resent the Court's "meddling" with the political process, the principles underlying the Court's decisions are essential to the realization of constitutional democracy.

Attempts by legislative majorities to close the channels of political participation to disfavored groups of citizens, whether they are city dwellers, ethnic minorities, or rival political parties, are antithetical to the ideals underlying our system of representative government. Guarding the ideal of political equality is thus without question one of the most important obligations of the Supreme Court. Like its concern for separation of powers, checks and balances, and freedom of expression, the Court's protection of voting rights is critical to the preservation of constitutional democracy in the United States.

KEY TERMS

representative democracy
political equality
universal suffrage
free and fair elections
tyranny of the majority
popular sovereignty
constitutional republic

poll taxes
grandfather clause
white primary
literacy tests
gerrymander
racial gerrymandering
Voting Rights Act of 1965

preclearance
at-large elections
effects test
intent standard
race-conscious remedy
vote dilution
malapportionment

reapportionment
partisan gerrymandering
public financing
campaign finance
Federal Election Campaign
    Act Amendments of 1974

FOR FURTHER READING

Baker, Gordon E. *The Reapportionment Revolution.* New York: Random House, 1966.

Ball, Howard. *The Warren Court's Conceptions of Democracy: An Evaluation of the Supreme Court's Apportionment Cases.* Rutherford, N.J.: Fairleigh Dickinson University Press, 1971.

Berger, Raoul. *Government by Judiciary: The Transformation of the Fourteenth Amendment.* Cambridge, Mass.: Harvard University Press, 1977.

Bullock, Charles S., and Kathryn S. Butler. "Voting Rights." *In* Tinsley E. Yarbrough, (ed.), *The Reagan Administration and Human Rights.* New York: Praeger, 1985.

Cortner, Richard C. *The Reapportionment Cases.* Knoxville, Tenn.: University of Tennessee Press, 1970.

Davidson, Chandler, and Bernard Grofman (eds.). *Quiet Revolution in the South: The Impact of the Voting Rights Act 1965–1990.* Princeton, N.J.: Princeton University Press, 1994.

Dixon, Robert G., Jr. *Democratic Representation: Reapportionment in Law and Politics.* New York: Oxford University Press, 1968.

Ely, John Hart. *Democracy and Distrust.* Cambridge, Mass.: Harvard University Press, 1980.

Grofman, Bernard. *Political Gerrymandering and the Courts.* New York: Agathon Press, 1990.

Hamilton, Howard D. (ed.). *Legislative Reapportionment: Key to Power.* New York: Harper and Row, 1964.

Hanson, Royce. *The Political Thicket: Reapportionment and Constitutional Democracy.* Englewood Cliffs, N.J.: Prentice Hall, 1966.

Mendelson, Wallace. *Discrimination.* Englewood Cliffs, N.J.: Prentice Hall, 1962.

Norrell, Robert J. *Reaping the Whirlwind: The Civil Rights Movement in Tuskegee* (rev. ed.). Chapel Hill, N.C.: University of North Carolina Press, 1998.

Polsby, Nelson W. (ed.). *Reapportionment in the 1970s.* Berkeley, Calif.: University of California Press, 1971.

Taper, Bernard. *Gomillion v. Lightfoot: Apartheid in Alabama.* New York: McGraw-Hill, 1967.

United States Commission on Civil Rights. *1961 Report.* Washington, D.C.: U.S. Government Printing Office, 1961.

INTERNET RESOURCES		
Name of Resource	**Description**	**URL (circa 1998)**
Center for Voting and Democracy	Organization interested in the impact of different voting systems on voter turnout, representation, accountability, and the influence of money on elections	http://www.igc.org/cvd/
Rock the Vote	An organization devoted to encouraging young people to participate in the political process	http://www.rockthevote.org/
Ballot Access News	A nonpartisan on-line newsletter reporting on the problems associated with ballot access for independent and third-party candidates	http://www.ballot-access.org/
Voting Rights Review	Newsletter published by the Southern Regional Council, a civil rights organization based in Atlanta	http://www.src.w1.com/vrr.htm
ACLU Voting Rights Project	Effort by the ACLU to promote its vision of voting rights and political equality	http://www.aclu.org/issues/voting/hmvr.html

Case

SMITH V. ALLWRIGHT

321 U.S. 649; 64 S.Ct. 757; 88 L.Ed. 987 (1944)
Vote: 8–1

In 1927, the Texas legislature passed a law that authorized political parties to set qualifications for party membership. Pursuant to this law, the state Democratic Party, at its convention in May 1932, adopted the following resolution: "Be it resolved that all white citizens of the State of Texas who are qualified to vote under the Constitution and laws of the State shall be eligible to membership in the Democratic Party and, as such, entitled to participate in its deliberations." Lonnie Smith, a black resident of Texas, sued S. E. Allwright, an election judge, for refusing to allow him to vote in a Democratic primary at which candidates for state and national office were to be nominated. Through the efforts of the National Association for the Advancement of Colored People, this case ultimately reached the U.S. Supreme Court. Thurgood Marshall, as counsel for the NAACP, participated in the argument of the case on behalf of Smith.

Mr. Justice Reed delivered the opinion of the Court.

. . . Texas is free to conduct her elections and limit her electorate as she may deem wise, save only as her action may be affected by the prohibitions of the United States Constitution or in conflict with powers delegated to and exercised by the National Government. The Fourteenth Amendment forbids a State from making or enforcing any law which abridges the privileges or immunities of citizens of the United States and the Fifteenth Amendment specifically interdicts any denial or abridgement by a State of the right of citizens to vote on account of color. Respondents appeared in the District Court and the Circuit Court of Appeals and defended on the ground that the Democratic Party of Texas is a voluntary organization with members banded together for the purpose of selecting individuals of the group representing the common political beliefs as candidates in the general election. As such a voluntary organization, it was claimed, the Democratic Party is free to select its own membership and limit to whites participation in the party primary. Such action, the answer asserted, does not violate the Fourteenth, Fifteenth or Seventeenth Amendments as officers of government cannot be chosen at primaries and the Amendments are applicable only to general elections where governmental officers are actually elected. . . .

Since *Grovey v. Townsend* and prior to the present suit, no case from Texas involving primary elections has been before this Court. We did decide, however, *United States v. Classic.* . . . We there held that Section 4 of Article I of the Constitution authorized Congress to regulate primary as well as general elections, "where the primary is by law made an integral part of the election machinery." . . . Consequently, in the *Classic* case, we upheld the applicability to frauds in a

Louisiana primary of Sections 19 and 20 of the Criminal Code. . . . *Classic* bears upon *Grovey v. Townsend* not because exclusion of Negroes from primaries is any more or less state action by reason of the unitary character of the electoral process but because the recognition of the place of the primary in the electoral scheme makes clear that state delegation to a party of the power to fix the qualifications of primary elections is delegation of a state function that may make the party's action the action of the State. When *Grovey v. Townsend* was written, the Court looked upon the denial of a vote in a primary as a mere refusal by a party of party membership. . . . As the Louisiana statutes for holding primaries are similar to those of Texas, our ruling in *Classic* as to the unitary character of the electoral process calls for a reexamination as to whether or not the exclusion of Negroes from a Texas party primary was state action. . . .

It may now be taken as a postulate that the right to vote in such a primary for the nomination of candidates without discrimination by the State, like the right to vote in a general election, is a right secured by the Constitution. . . . By the terms of the Fifteenth Amendment that right may not be abridged by any State on account of race. Under our Constitution the great privilege of the ballot may not be denied a man by the State because of his color.

We are thus brought to an examination of the qualifications for Democratic primary electors in Texas, to determine whether state action or private action has excluded Negroes from participation. Despite Texas' decision that the exclusion is produced by private or party action . . . federal courts must for themselves appraise the facts leading to that conclusion. It is only by the performance of this obligation that a final and uniform interpretation can be given to the Constitution, the "supreme Law of the Land." . . .

Primary elections are conducted by the party under state statutory authority. The county executive committee selects precinct election officials and the county, district or state executive committees, respectively, canvass the returns. These party committees or the state convention certify the party's candidates to the appropriate officers for inclusion on the official ballot for the general election. No name which has not been so certified may appear upon the ballot for the general election as a candidate of a political party. No other name may be printed on the ballot which has not been placed in nomination by qualified voters who must take oath that they did not participate in a primary for the selection of a candidate for the office for which the nomination is made.

The state courts are given exclusive original jurisdiction of contested elections and of *mandamus* proceedings to compel party officers to perform their statutory duties.

We think that this statutory system for the selection of party nominees for inclusion on the general election ballot makes the party which is required to follow these legislative directions an agency of the State in so far as it determines the participants in a primary election. The party takes its character as a state agency from the duties imposed upon it by state statutes; the duties do not become matters of private law because they are performed by a political party. The plan of the Texas primary follows substantially that of Louisiana, with the exception that in Louisiana the State pays the cost of the primary while Texas assesses the cost against candidates. In numerous instances, the Texas statutes fix or limit the fees to be charged. Whether paid directly by the State or through state requirements, it is state action which compels. When primaries become a part of the machinery for choosing officials, state and national, as they have here, the same tests to determine the character of discrimination or abridgement should be applied to the primary as are applied to the general election. If the State requires a certain electoral procedure, prescribes a general election ballot made up of party nominees so chosen and limits the choice of the electorate in general elections for state offices, practically speaking, to those whose names appear on such a ballot, it endorses, adopts and enforces the discrimination against Negroes, practiced by a party entrusted by Texas law with the determination of the qualifications of participants in the primary. This is state action within the meaning of the Fifteenth Amendment. . . .

The United States is a constitutional democracy. Its organic law grants to all citizens a right to participate in the choice of elected officials without restriction by any State because of race. This grant to the people of the opportunity for choice is not to be nullified by a State through casting its electoral process in a form which permits a private organization to practice racial discrimination in the election. Constitutional rights would be of little value if they could be thus indirectly denied. . . .

. . . In reaching this conclusion we are not unmindful of the desirability of continuity of decision in constitutional questions. However, when convinced of former error, this Court has never felt constrained to follow precedent. In constitutional questions, where correction depends upon amendment and not upon legislative action this Court throughout its history has freely exercised its power to reexamine the basis of its constitutional decisions. This has long been accepted practice, and this practice has continued to this day. This is particularly true when the decision believed erroneous is the application of a constitutional principle rather than an interpretation of the Constitution to extract the principle itself. Here we are applying, contrary to the recent decision in *Grovey v. Townsend,* the well-established principle of the Fifteenth Amendment, forbidding the abridgement by a State of a citizen's right to vote. *Grovey v. Townsend* is overruled.

Mr. Justice Frankfurter concurs in the result.

Mr. Justice Roberts [dissenting]:

. . . I have expressed my views with respect to the present policy of the court freely to disregard and to overrule considered decisions and the rules of law announced in them. This tendency, it seems to me, indicates an intolerance for what those who have composed this court in the past have conscientiously and deliberately concluded, and involves an assumption that knowledge and wisdom reside in us which was denied to our predecessors. I shall not repeat what I there said for I consider it fully applicable to the instant decision, which but points the moral anew. . . .

The reason for my concern is that the instant decision, overruling that announced about nine years ago, tends to bring adjudications of this tribunal into the same class as a restricted railroad ticket, good for this day and train only. I have no assurance, in view of current decisions, that the opinion announced today may not shortly be repudiated and overruled by justices who deem they have new light on the subject. In the present term the court has overruled three cases.

In the present case, . . . the court below relied, as it was bound to, upon our previous decision. As that court points out, the statutes of Texas have not been altered since *Grovey v. Townsend* was decided. The same resolution is involved as was drawn in question in *Grovey v. Townsend.* Not a fact differentiates that case from this except the names of the parties.

It is suggested that *Grovey v. Townsend* was overruled *sub silentio* in *United States v. Classic.* . . . If so, the situation is even worse than that exhibited by the outright repudiation of an earlier decision, for it is the fact that, in the *Classic* case, *Grovey v. Townsend* was distinguished in brief and argument by the Government without suggestion that it was wrongly decided, and was relied on by the appellee, not as a controlling decision, but by way of analogy. The case is not mentioned in either of the opinions in the *Classic* case. Again and again it is said in the opinion of the court in that case that the voter who was denied the right to vote was a fully qualified voter. In other words, there was no question of his being a person entitled under state law to vote in the primary. The offense charged was the fraudulent denial of his conceded right by an election officer because of his race. Here the question is altogether different. It is whether, in a Democratic primary, he who tendered his vote was a member of the Democratic Party. . . .

It is regrettable that in an era marked by doubt and confusion, an era whose greater need is steadfastness of thought and purpose, this court, which has been looked to as exhibiting consistency in adjudication, and a steadiness which would hold the balance even in the face of temporary ebbs and flows of opinion, should now itself become the breeder of fresh doubt and confusion in the public mind as to the stability of our institutions.

Case

GOMILLION V. LIGHTFOOT

364 U.S. 339; 81 S.Ct. 125; 5 L.Ed. 2d. 110 (1960)
Vote: 9–0

Here the Court confronts a blatant attempt to disenfranchise minority voters by gerrymandering the boundaries of a city.

Mr. Justice Frankfurter delivered the opinion of the Court.

This litigation challenges the validity, under the United States Constitution, of Local Act No. 140, passed by the Legislature of Alabama in 1957, redefining the boundaries of the City of Tuskegee. Petitioners, Negro citizens of Alabama who were, at the time of this redistricting measure, residents of the City of Tuskegee, brought an action in the United States District Court for the Middle District of Alabama for a declaratory judgment that Act 140 is unconstitutional, and for an injunction to restrain the Mayor and officers of Tuskegee and the officials of Macon County, Alabama, from enforcing the Act against them and other Negroes similarly situated. Petitioners' claim is that enforcement of the statute, which alters the shape of Tuskegee from a square to an uncouth twenty-eight-sided figure, will constitute a discrimination against them in violation of the Due Process and Equal Protection Clauses of the Fourteenth Amendment to the Constitution and will deny them the right to vote in defiance of the Fifteenth Amendment.

The respondents moved for dismissal of the action for failure to state a claim upon which relief could be granted and for lack of jurisdiction of the District Court. The court granted the motion, stating, "This court has no control over, no supervision over, and no power to change any boundaries of municipal corporations fixed by a duly convened and elected legislative body, acting for the people for the State of Alabama." . . . On appeal, the Court of Appeals for the Fifth Circuit affirmed the judgment, one judge dissenting. . . . We brought the case here since serious questions were raised concerning the power of a State over its municipalities in relation to the Fourteenth and Fifteenth Amendments. . . . The essential inevitable effect of this redefinition of Tuskegee's boundaries is to remove from the city all save only four or five of its 400 Negro voters while not removing a single white voter or resident. The result of the Act is to deprive the Negro petitioners discriminatorily of the benefits of residence in Tuskegee, including, *inter alia,* the right to vote in municipal elections.

These allegations, if proven, would abundantly establish that Act 140 was not an ordinary geographic redistricting measure even within familiar abuses of gerrymandering. If these allegations upon a trial remained uncontradicted or unqualified, the conclusion would be irresistible, tantamount for all practical purposes to a mathematical demonstration, that the legislation is solely concerned with segregating white and colored voters by fencing Negro citizens out of town so as to deprive them of their preexisting municipal vote.

It is difficult to appreciate what stands in the way of adjudging a statute having this inevitable effect invalid in light of the principles by which this Court must judge, and uniformly has judged, statutes that, howsoever speciously defined, obviously discriminate against colored citizens. "The [Fifteenth] Amendment nullified sophisticated as well as simple-minded modes of discrimination." . . .

The complaint amply alleges a claim of racial discrimination. Against this claim the respondents have never suggested, either in their brief or in oral argument, any countervailing municipal function which Act 140 is designed to serve. The respondents invoke generalities expressing the State's unrestricted power—unlimited, that is, by the United States Constitution—to establish, destroy, or reorganize by contraction or expansion its political subdivisions, to wit, cities, counties, and other local units. We freely recognize the breadth and importance of this aspect of the State's political power. To exalt this power into an absolute is to misconceive the reach and rule of this Court's decisions. . . .

. . . The Court has never acknowledged that the States have power to do as they will with municipal corporations regardless of consequences. Legislative control of municipalities, no less than other state power, lies within the scope of relevant limitations imposed by the United States Constitution. . . .

. . . Such power, extensive though it is, is met and overcome by the Fifteenth Amendment to the Constitution of the United States, which forbids a State from passing any law which deprives a citizen of his vote because of his race. The opposite conclusion, urged upon us by respondents, would sanction the achievement by a State of any impairment of voting rights whatever so long as it was cloaked in the garb of the realignment of political subdivisions. "It is inconceivable that guaranties embedded in the Constitution of the United States may thus be manipulated out of existence." . . .

When a State exercises power wholly within the domain of state interest, it is insulated from federal judicial review. But such insulation is not carried over when state power is used as an instrument for circumventing a federally protected right. This principle has had many applications. It has long been recognized in cases which have prohibited a State from exploiting a power acknowledged to be absolute in an isolated context to justify the imposition of an "unconstitutional condition." What the Court has said in those cases is equally applicable here, viz., that "Act generally lawful may become unlawful when done to accomplish an unlawful end, . . . and a constitutional power cannot be used by way of condition to attain an unconstitutional result." The petitioners are entitled to prove their allegations at trial.

For these reasons, the principal conclusions of the District Court and the Court of Appeals are clearly erroneous and the decision below must be

Reversed.

Mr. Justice Douglas, [concurring]. . . .

Mr. Justice Whittaker, concurring.

I concur in the Court's judgment, but not in the whole of its opinion. It seems to me that the decision should be rested not on the Fifteenth Amendment, but rather on the equal Protection Clause of the Fourteenth Amendment to the Constitution. I am doubtful that the averments of the complaint, taken for present purposes to be true, show a purpose by Act No. 140 to abridge petitioners' "right . . . to vote," in the Fifteenth Amendment sense. It seems to me that the "right . . . to vote" that is guaranteed by the Fifteenth Amendment is but the same right to vote as is enjoyed by all others within the same election precinct, ward or other political division. And, inasmuch as no one has the right to vote in a political division, or in a local election concerning only an area in which he does not reside, it would seem to follow that one's right to vote in Division A is not abridged by a redistricting that places his residence in Division B if he there enjoys the same voting privileges as all others in that Division, even though the redistricting was done by the State for the purposes of placing a racial group of citizens in Division B rather than A.

But it does seem clear to me that accomplishment of a State's purpose—to use the Court's phrase—of "fencing Negro citizens out of" Division A and into Division B is an unlawful segregation of races of citizens, in violation of the Equal Protection Clause of the Fourteenth Amendment, . . . and, as stated, I would think the decision should be rested on that ground. . . .

Case

MOBILE V. BOLDEN

446 U.S. 55; 100 S.Ct. 1490; 64 L.Ed. 2d. 47 (1980)
Vote: 6–3

In this case, the Supreme Court considers a challenge to at-large local elections based on the Voting Rights Act of 1965 and the Fifteenth Amendment.

Mr. Justice Stewart announced the judgment of the court and delivered an opinion, in which the **Chief Justice, Mr. Justice Powell,** and **Mr. Justice Rehnquist** joined.

The City of Mobile, Ala., has since 1911 been governed by a City Commission consisting of three members elected by the voters of the city at large. The question in this case is whether this at-large system of municipal elections violates the rights of Mobile's Negro voters in contravention of federal statutory or constitutional law.

The appellees brought this suit in the Federal District Court for the Southern District of Alabama as a class action on behalf of all Negro citizens of Mobile. Named as defendants were the city and its three incumbent Commissioners, who are the appellants before this Court. The complaint alleged that the practice of electing the City Commissioners at large unfairly diluted the voting strength of Negroes in violation of [Section] 2 of the Voting Rights Act of 1965, of the Fourteenth Amendment, and of the Fifteenth Amendment. Following a bench trial, the District Court found that the constitutional rights of the appellees had been violated, entered a judgment in their favor, and ordered that the City Commission be disestablished and replaced by a municipal government consisting of a Mayor and a City Council with members elected from single-member districts. . . . The Court of Appeals affirmed the judgment in its entirety. . . .

In Alabama, the form of municipal government a city may adopt is governed by state law. Until 1911, cities not covered by specific legislation were limited to governing themselves through a mayor and city council. In that year, the Alabama Legislature authorized every large municipality to adopt a commission form of government. Mobile established its City Commission in the same year, and has maintained that basic system of municipal government ever since.

Three Commissioners jointly exercise all legislative, executive, and administrative power in the municipality. They are required after election to designate one of their number as Mayor, a largely ceremonial office, but no formal provision is made for allocating specific executive or administrative duties among the three. As required by the state law enacted in 1911, each candidate for the Mobile City Commission runs for election in the city at large for a term of four years in one of three numbered posts, and may be elected only by a majority of the total vote. This is the same basic electoral system that is followed by literally thousands of municipalities and other local governmental units throughout the Nation.

Although required by general principles of judicial administration to do so, . . . neither the District Court nor the Court of Appeals addressed the complaint's statutory claim—that the Mobile electoral system violates [Section] 2 of the Voting Rights Act of 1965. Even a cursory examination of that claim, however, clearly discloses that it adds nothing to the appellees' complaint.

Section 2 of the Voting Rights Act provides:

No voting qualification or prerequisite to voting, or standard, practice, or procedure shall be imposed or applied by any State or political subdivision to deny or abridge the right of any citizen of the United States to vote on account of race or color. . . .

Assuming, for present purposes, that there exists a private right of action to enforce this statutory provision, it is apparent that the language of [Section] 2 no more than elaborates upon that of the Fifteenth Amendment, and the sparse legislative history of [Section] 2 makes clear that it was intended to have an effect no different from that of the Fifteenth Amendment itself.

Section 2 was an uncontroversial provision in proposed legislation whose other provisions engendered protracted dispute. The House Report on the bill simply recited that [Section] 2 "grants . . . a right to be free from enactment or enforcement of voting qualifications . . . or practices which deny or abridge the right to vote on account of race or color." . . . The view that this section simply restated the prohibitions already contained in the Fifteenth Amendment was expressed without contradiction during the Senate hearings. Senator Dirksen indicated at one point that all States, whether or not covered by the preclearance provisions of [Section] 5 of the proposed legislation, were prohibited from discriminating against Negro voters by [Section] 2, which he termed "almost a rephrasing of the 15th [A]mendment." Attorney General Katzenbach agreed. . . .

In view of the section's language and its sparse but clear legislative history, it is evident that this statutory provision adds nothing to the appellees' Fifteenth Amendment claim. We turn, therefore, to a consideration of the validity of the judgment of the Court of Appeals with respect to the Fifteenth Amendment.

The Court's early decision under the Fifteenth Amendment established that it imposes but one limitation on the powers of the States. It forbids them to discriminate against Negroes in matters having to do with voting. . . . The Amendment's command and effect are wholly negative. "The Fifteenth Amendment does not confer the right of suffrage upon any one," but has "invested the citizens of the United States with a new constitutional right which is within the protecting power of Congress. That right is exemption from discrimination in the exercise of the elective franchise on account of race, color, or previous condition of servitude." . . .

Our decisions, moreover, have made clear that action by a State that is racially neutral on its face violates the Fifteenth Amendment only if motivated by a discriminatory purpose. . . .

The Court's more recent decisions confirm the principle that racially discriminatory motivation is a necessary ingredient of a Fifteenth Amendment violation. . . .

While other of the Court's Fifteenth Amendment decisions have dealt with different issues, none has questioned the necessity of showing purposeful discrimination in order to show a Fifteenth Amendment violation. The cases of *Smith v. Allwright* . . . [1944] and *Terry v. Adams* . . . [1953] for example, dealt with the question whether a State was so involved with racially discriminatory voting practices as to invoke the Amendment's protection. . . .

The answer to the appellees' argument is that, as the District Court expressly found, their freedom to vote has not been denied or abridged by anyone. The Fifteenth Amendment does not entail the right to have Negro candidates elected, and neither *Smith v. Allwright* nor *Terry v. Adams* contains any implication to the contrary. That Amendment prohibits only purposefully discriminatory denial or abridgment by government of the freedom to vote "on account of race, color, or previous condition of servitude." Having found that Negroes in Mobile "register and vote without hindrance," . . . the District Court and Court of Appeals were in error in believing that the appellants invaded the protection of that Amendment in the present case.

The Court of Appeals also agreed with the District Court that Mobile's at-large electoral system violates the Equal Protection Clause of the Fourteenth Amendment. There remains for consideration, therefore, the validity of its judgment on that score.

The claim that at-large electoral schemes unconstitutionally deny to some persons the equal protection of the laws has been advanced in numerous cases before this Court. That contention has been raised most often with regard to multimember constituencies within a state legislative apportionment system. The constitutional objection to multimember districts is not and cannot be that, as such, they depart from apportionment on a population basis in violation of *Reynolds v. Sims* [1964] and its progeny. Rather the focus in such cases has been on the lack of representation multimember districts afford various elements of the voting population in a system of representative legislative democracy. "Criticism [of multimember districts] is rooted in their winner-take-all aspects, their tendency to submerge minorities . . . , a general preference for legislatures reflecting community interests as closely as possible and disenchantment with political parties and elections as devices to settle policy differences between contending interests." . . .

Despite repeated constitutional attacks upon multimember legislative districts, the Court has consistently held that they are not unconstitutional *per se*. . . . We have recognized, however, that such legislative apportionments could violate the Fourteenth Amendment if their purpose were invidiously to minimize or cancel out the voting potential of racial or ethnic minorities. . . . To prove such a purpose it is not enough to show that the group allegedly discriminated against has not elected representatives in proportion to its numbers. . . .

The judgment is reversed, and the case is remanded to the Court of Appeals for further proceedings.

Mr. Justice Blackmun, concurring in the result.

Assuming that proof of intent is a prerequisite to appellees' prevailing on their constitutional claim of vote dilution, I am inclined to agree with Mr. Justice White that, in this case, "the findings of the District Court amply support an inference of purposeful discrimination." . . . I concur in the Court's judgment of reversal, however, because I believe that the relief afforded appellees by the District Court was not commensurate with the sound exercise of judicial discretion.

It seems to me that the city of Mobile, and its citizenry, have a substantial interest in maintaining the commission form of government that has been in effect there for nearly 70 years. The District Court recognized that its remedial order, changing the form of the city's government to a mayor–council system, "raised serious constitutional issues." . . . Nonetheless, the court was "unable to see how the impermissibly unconstitutional dilution can be effectively corrected by any other approach." . . .

Contrary to the District Court, I do not believe that, in order to remedy the unconstitutional vote dilution it found, it was necessary to convert Mobile's city government to a mayor–council system. In my view, the District Court should have at least considered alternative remedial orders that would have maintained some of the basic elements of the commission system Mobile long ago had selected. . . .

Mr. Justice Stevens, concurring in the judgment. . . .

Mr. Justice Brennan, dissenting. . . .

Mr. Justice White, dissenting. . . .

Mr. Justice Marshall, dissenting.

. . . The plurality concludes that our prior decisions establish the principle that proof of discriminatory intent is a necessary element of a Fifteenth Amendment claim. In contrast, I continue to adhere to my conclusion . . . that "[t]he Court's decisions relating to the relevance of purpose-and/or-effect analysis in testing the constitutionality of legislative enactments are somewhat less than a seamless web." . . . [A]t various times the Court's decisions have seemed to adopt three inconsistent approaches: (1) that purpose alone is the test for unconstitutionality; (2) that effect alone is the test; and (3) that purpose or effect, either alone or in combination, is sufficient to show unconstitutionality. . . . In my view, our Fifteenth Amendment jurisprudence on the necessity of proof of discriminatory purpose is no less unsettled than was our approach to the importance of such proof in Fourteenth Amendment racial discrimination cases prior to *Washington v. Davis* . . . (1976). What is called for in the present cases is a fresh consideration—similar to our inquiry in *Washington v. Davis* with regard to Fourteenth Amendment discrimination claims—of whether proof of discriminatory purpose is necessary to establish a claim under the Fifteenth Amendment. . . .

. . . [I]t is beyond dispute that a standard based solely upon the motives of official decision makers creates significant problems of proof for plaintiffs and forces the inquiring court to undertake an unguided, tortuous look into the minds of officials in the hope of guessing why certain policies were adopted and others rejected. . . . An approach based on motivation creates the risk that officials will be able to adopt policies that are the products of discriminatory intent so long as they sufficiently mask their motives through the use of subtlety and illusion. . . .

I continue to believe, then, that under the Fifteenth Amendment an "[e]valuation of the purpose of a legislative enactment is just too ambiguous a task to be the sole tool of constitutional analysis. . . . [A] demonstration of effect ordinarily should suffice. If, of course, purpose may conclusively be shown, it too should be sufficient to demonstrate a statute's unconstitutionality." . . . The plurality's refusal in this case even to consider this approach bespeaks an indifference to the plight of minorities who, through no fault of their own, have suffered diminution of the right preservative of all other rights.

The American approach to government is premised on the theory that, when citizens have the unfettered right to vote, public officials will make decisions by the democratic accommodation of competing beliefs, not by deference to the mandates of the powerful. The American approach to civil rights is premised on the complementary theory that the unfettered right to vote is preservative of all other rights. The theoretical foundations for these approaches are shattered where, as in the present cases, the right to vote is granted in form, but denied in substance.

It is time to realize that manipulating doctrines and drawing improper distinctions under the Fourteenth and Fifteenth Amendments, as well as under Congress'
remedial legislation enforcing those Amendments, make this Court an accessory to the perpetuation of racial discrimination. The plurality's requirement of proof of intentional discrimination, so inappropriate in today's cases, may represent an attempt to bury the legitimate concerns of the minority beneath the soil of a doctrine almost as impermeable as it is spacious. If so, the superficial tranquility created by such measures can be but short-lived. If this Court refuses to honor our long-recognized principle that the Constitution "nullifies sophisticated as well as simple-minded modes of discrimination," . . . it cannot expect the victims of discrimination to respect political channels of seeking redress. I dissent.

Case

ROGERS V. LODGE

458 U.S. 613; 102 S.Ct. 3272; 73 L.Ed. 2d. 1012 (1982)
Vote: 6–3

Here the Court considers whether an at-large voting system in Burke County, Georgia, violates the constitutional rights of African-American voters in the County.

Justice White delivered the opinion of the Court.

. . . Burke County is a large, predominantly rural county located in eastern Georgia. Eight hundred and thirty-one square miles in area, it is approximately two-thirds the size of the State of Rhode Island. According to the 1980 census, Burke County had a total population of 19,349, of whom 10,385, or 53.6%, were black. The average age of blacks living there is lower than the average age of whites and therefore whites constitute a slight majority of the voting age population. As of 1978, 6,373 persons were registered to vote in Burke County, of whom 38% were black.

The Burke County Board of Commissioners governs the county. It was created in 1911, . . . and consists of five members elected at large to concurrent 4-year terms by all qualified voters in the county. The county has never been divided into districts, either for the purpose of imposing a residency requirement on candidates or for the purpose of requiring candidates to be elected by voters residing in a district. In order to be nominated or elected, a candidate must receive a majority of the votes
cast in the primary or general election, and a runoff must be held if no candidate receives a majority in the first primary or general election. . . . Each candidate must run for a specific seat on the Board, and a voter may vote only once for any candidate. No Negro has been elected to the Burke County Board of Commissioners.

Appellees, eight black citizens of Burke County, filed this suit in 1976 in the United States District Court for the Southern District of Georgia. The suit was brought on behalf of all black citizens in Burke County. The class was certified in 1977. The complaint alleged that the county's system of at-large elections violates appellees' First, Thirteenth, Fourteenth and Fifteenth Amendment rights . . . by diluting the voting power of black citizens. Following a bench trial at which both sides introduced extensive evidence, the court issued an order on September 29, 1978, stating that appellees were entitled to prevail and ordering that Burke County be divided into five districts for purposes of electing County Commissioners. . . .

The Court of Appeals affirmed. . . . It stated that while the proceedings in the District Court took place prior to the decision in *Mobile v. Bolden,* . . . the District Court correctly anticipated *Mobile* and required appellees to prove that the at-large voting system was maintained for a discriminatory purpose. . . . The Court of Appeals also held that the District Court's findings were not clearly erroneous, and that its conclusion that the at-large system was maintained for invidious purpose was "virtually mandated by the overwhelming proof." . . . We noted probable jurisdiction, and now affirm. . . .

II

At-large voting schemes and multimember districts tend to minimize the voting strength of minority groups by permitting the political majority to elect all representatives of the district. A distinct minority, whether it be a racial, ethnic, economic, or political group, may be unable to elect any representatives if the political unit is divided into single-member districts. The minority's voting power in a multimember district is particularly diluted when bloc voting occurs and ballots are cast along strict majority—minority lines. While multimember districts have been challenged for "their winner-take-all aspects, their tendency to submerge minorities and to over-represent the winning party," . . . this Court has repeatedly held that they are not unconstitutional *per se*. . . . The Court has recognized, however, that multimember districts violate the Fourteenth Amendment if "conceived or operated as purposeful devices to further racial discrimination" by minimizing, canceling out or diluting the voting strength of racial elements in the voting population. . . . Cases charging that multimember districts unconstitutionally dilute the voting strength of racial minorities are thus subject to the standard of proof generally applicable to Equal Protection Clause cases. . . . In order for the Equal Protection Clause to be violated, "the invidious quality of a law claimed to be racially discriminatory must ultimately be traced to a racially discriminatory purpose."

Arlington Heights [*v. Metropolitan Housing Development Corp.*] . . . and *Washington v. Davis* . . . both rejected the notion that a law is invalid under the Equal Protection Clause simply because it may affect a greater proportion of one race than another. However, both cases recognized that discriminatory intent need not be proved by direct evidence. "Necessarily, an invidious discriminatory purpose may often be inferred from the totality of the relevant facts, including the fact, if it is true, that the law bears more heavily on one race than another." . . . Thus determining the existence of a discriminatory purpose "demands a sensitive inquiry into such circumstantial and direct evidence of intent as may be available." . . .

In *Mobile v. Bolden*, the Court was called upon to apply these principles to the at-large election system in Mobile, Ala. Mobile is governed by three commissioners who exercise all legislative, executive, and administrative power in the municipality. . . . Each candidate for the City Commission runs for one of three numbered posts in an at-large election and can only be elected by a majority vote. . . . Plaintiffs brought a class action on behalf of all Negro citizens of Mobile alleging that the at-large scheme diluted their voting strength in violation of several statutory and constitutional provisions. The District Court concluded that the at-large system "violates the constitutional rights of the plaintiffs by improperly restricting their access to the political process," . . . and ordered that the commission form of government be replaced by a mayor and a nine-member City Council elected from single-member districts. . . . The Court of Appeals affirmed. . . . This Court reversed.

Justice Stewart, writing for himself and three other Justices, noted that to prevail in their contention that the at-large voting system violates the Equal Protection Clause of the Fourteenth Amendment, plaintiffs had to prove the system was " 'conceived or operated as [a] purposeful devic[e] to further racial . . . discrimination.' " . . . Such a requirement "is simply one aspect of the basic principle that only if there is purposeful discrimination can there be a violation of the Equal Protection Clause of the Fourteenth Amendment." . . .

The plurality went on to conclude that the District Court had failed to comply with this standard. The District Court had analyzed plaintiffs' claims in light of the standard which had been set forth in *Zimmer v. McKeithen*. . . . *Zimmer* set out a list of factors . . . that a court should consider in assessing the constitutionality of at-large and multimember district voting schemes. Under *Zimmer*, voting dilution is established "upon proof of the existence of an aggregate of these factors." . . .

The plurality in *Mobile* was of the view that *Zimmer* was "decided upon the misunderstanding that it is not necessary to show a discriminatory purpose in order to prove a violation of the Equal Protection Clause—that proof of a discriminatory effect is sufficient." . . . The plurality observed that while "the presence of the indicia relied on in *Zimmer* may afford some evidence or a discriminatory purpose," the mere existence of those criteria is not a substitute for a finding of discriminatory purpose. . . . The District Court's standard in *Mobile* was likewise flawed. Finally, the plurality concluded that the evidence on which the lower courts had relied was "insufficient to prove an unconstitutionally discriminatory purpose in the present case." . . . Justice Stevens rejected the intentional discrimination standard but concluded that the proof failed to satisfy the legal standard that in his view was the applicable rule. He therefore concurred in the judgment of reversal. . . .

Because the District Court in the present case employed the evidentiary factors outlined in *Zimmer*, it is urged that its judgment is infirm for the same reasons that led to the reversal in *Mobile*. We do not agree. First, and fundamentally, we are unconvinced that the District Court in this case applied the wrong legal standard.

The District Court . . . demonstrated its understanding by observing that a determination of discriminatory intent is "a requisite to a finding of unconstitutional vote dilution" under the Fourteenth Amendments. . . . Furthermore, while recognizing that the evidentiary factors identified in *Zimmer* were to be considered, the District Court was aware that it was "not limited in its determination only to the *Zimmer* factors" but could consider other relevant factors as well. . . . The District Court then proceeded to deal with what it considered to be the relevant proof and concluded that the at-large scheme of electing commissioners, "although racially neutral when adopted, is being maintained for invidious purposes." . . . That system "while neutral in origin . . . has been subverted to invidious purposes." . . .

III

. . . The District court found that blacks have always made up a substantial majority of the population in Burke County, . . . but that they are a distinct minority of the registered voters. . . . There was also overwhelming evidence of bloc voting along racial lines. Hence, although there had been black candidates, no black had ever been elected to the Burke County Commission. These facts bear heavily on the issue of purposeful discrimination. Voting along racial lines allows those elected to ignore black interests without fear of political consequences, and without bloc voting the minority candidates would not lose elections solely because of their race. Because it is sensible to expect that at least some blacks would have been elected in Burke County, the fact that none have ever been elected is important evidence of purposeful exclusion. . . .

Under our cases, however, such facts are insufficient in themselves to prove purposeful discrimination absent other evidence such as proof that blacks have less opportunity to participate in the political processes and to elect candidates of their choice. . . . Both the District Court and the Court of Appeals thought the supporting proof in this case was sufficient to support an inference of intentional discrimination. . . .

The District Court began by determining the impact of past discrimination on the ability of blacks to participate effectively in the political process. Past discrimination was found to contribute to low black voter registration because prior to the Voting Rights Act of 1965, blacks had been denied access to the political process by means such as literacy tests, poll taxes, and white primaries. The result was that "Black suffrage in Burke County was virtually non-existent." . . . Black voter registration in Burke County has increased following the Voting Rights Act to the point that some 38% of blacks eligible to vote are registered to do so. . . . On that basis the District Court inferred that "past discrimination has had an adverse effect on black voter registration which lingers to this date." . . . Past discrimination against blacks in education also had the same effect. Not only did Burke County schools discriminate against blacks as recently as 1969, but also some schools still remain essentially segregated and blacks as a group have completed less formal education than whites. . . .

The District Court found further evidence of exclusion from the political process. Past discrimination had prevented blacks from effectively participating in Democratic Party affairs and in primary elections. Until this lawsuit was filed, there had never been a black member of the County Executive Committee of the Democratic Party. There were also property ownership requirements that made it difficult for blacks to serve as chief registrar in the county. There had been discrimination in the selection of grand jurors, the hiring of county employees, and in the appointments to boards and committees which oversee the county government. . . . The District Court thus concluded that historical discrimination had restricted the present opportunity of blacks effectively to participate in the political process. Evidence of historical discrimination is relevant to drawing an inference of purposeful discrimination, particularly in cases such as this one where the evidence shows that discriminatory practices were commonly utilized, that they were abandoned when enjoined by courts or made illegal by civil rights legislation, and that they were replaced by laws and practices which, though neutral on their face, serve to maintain the status quo.

Extensive evidence was cited by the District Court to support its finding that elected officials of Burke County have been unresponsive and insensitive to the needs of the black community, which increases the likelihood that the political process was not equally open to blacks. This evidence ranged from the effects of past discrimination which still haunt the county courthouse to the infrequent appointment of blacks to county boards and committees; the overtly discriminatory pattern of paving county roads; the reluctance of the county to remedy black complaints, which forced blacks to take legal action to obtain school and grand jury desegregation; and the role played by the County Commissioners in the incorporation of an all-white private school to which they donated public funds for the purchase of band uniforms. . . .

The District Court also considered the depressed socio-economic status of Burke County blacks. It found that proportionately more blacks than whites have incomes below the poverty level. . . . Nearly 53% of all black families living in Burke County had incomes equal to or less than three-fourths of a poverty-level income. . . . Not only have blacks completed less formal education than whites, but also the education they have received "was qualitatively inferior to a marked degree." . . . Blacks tend to receive less pay than whites, even for similar work, and they tend to be employed in menial jobs more often than whites. . . . Seventy-three percent of houses occupied by blacks lacked all or some plumbing facilities; only 16% of white-occupied houses suffered the same deficiency. . . . The District Court concluded that the depressed socioeconomic status of blacks results in part from "the lingering effects of past discrimination. . . ."

Although finding that the state policy behind the at-large electoral system in Burke County was "neutral in origin," the District Court concluded that the policy "has been subverted to invidious purposes." . . . As a practical matter, maintenance of the state statute providing for at-large elections in Burke County is determined by Burke County's state representatives, for the legislature defers to their wishes on matters of purely local application. The court found that Burke County's state representatives "have retained a system which has minimized the ability of Burke County Blacks to participate in the political system." . . .

The trial court considered, in addition, several factors which this Court has indicated enhance the tendency of multimember districts to minimize the voting strength of racial minorities. . . . It found that the sheer geographic size of the county, which is nearly two-thirds the size of Rhode Island, "has made it more difficult for blacks to get to polling places or to campaign for office." The court concluded, as a matter of law, that the size of the county tends to impair the access of blacks to the political process. The majority vote requirement was found "to submerge the will of the minority" and thus "deny the minority's access to the system." . . . The court also found the requirements that candidates run for specific seats, enhances appellees' lack of access because it prevents a cohesive political group from concentrating on a single candidate. Because Burke County has no resi-

dency requirement, "[a]ll candidates could reside in Waynesboro, or in '[lily]-white' neighborhoods. To that extent, the denial of access becomes enhanced." . . .

None of the District Court's findings underlying its ultimate finding of intentional discrimination appears to us to be clearly erroneous; and as we have said, we decline to overturn the essential finding of the District Court, agreed to by the Court of Appeals, that the at-large system in Burke County has been maintained for the purpose of denying blacks equal access to the political processes in the county. As in *White v. Regester,* . . . the District Court's findings were "sufficient to sustain [its] judgment . . . and, on this record, we have no reason to disturb them."

We also find no reason to overturn the relief ordered by the District Court. Neither the District Court nor the Court of Appeals discerned any special circumstances that would militate against utilizing single-member districts. Where "a constitutional violation has been found, the remedy is tailored to cure the 'condition that offends the Constitution.' " . . .

The judgment of the Court of Appeals is affirmed.

Justice Powell, with whom **Justice Rehnquist** joins, dissenting.

. . . *Mobile v. Bolden* . . . establishes that an at-large voting system must be upheld against constitutional attack unless maintained for a discriminatory purpose. In *Mobile* we reversed a finding of unconstitutional vote dilution because the lower courts had relied on factors insufficient as a matter of law to establish discriminatory intent. . . . The District Court and Court of Appeals in this case based their findings of unconstitutional discrimination on the same factors held insufficient in *Mobile.* Yet the Court now finds their conclusion unexceptionable. The *Mobile* plurality also affirmed that the concept of "intent" was no mere fiction, and held that the District Court had erred in "its failure to identify the state officials whose intent it considered relevant." . . . Although the courts below did not answer that question in this case, the Court today affirms their decision.

Whatever the wisdom of *Mobile,* the Court's opinion cannot be reconciled persuasively with that case. There are some variances in the largely sociological evidence presented in the two cases. But *Mobile* held that this kind of evidence was not enough. Such evidence, we found in *Mobile,* did not merely fall short, but "fell far short[,] of showing that [an at-large electoral scheme was] 'conceived or operated [as a] purposeful devic[e] to further racial . . . discrimination.' " . . . Because I believe that *Mobile* controls this case, I dissent. . . .

Justice Stevens, dissenting.

Our legacy of racial discrimination has left its scars on Burke County, Georgia. The record in this case amply supports the conclusion that the governing officials of Burke County have repeatedly denied black citizens rights guaranteed by the Fourteenth and Fifteenth Amendments to the Federal Constitution. No one could legitimately question the validity of remedial measures, whether legislative or judicial, designed to prohibit discriminatory conduct by public officials and to guarantee that black citizens are effectively afforded the rights to register and to vote. Public roads may not be paved only in areas in which white citizens live; black citizens may not be denied employment opportunities in country government; segregated schools may not be maintained.

Nor, in my opinion, could there be any doubt about the constitutionality of an amendment to the Voting Rights Act that would require Burke County and other covered jurisdictions to abandon specific kinds of at-large voting schemes that perpetuate the effects of past discrimination. . . .

The Court's decision today, however, is not based on either its own conception of sound policy or any statutory command. The decision rests entirely on the Court's interpretation of the requirements of the Federal Constitution. Despite my sympathetic appraisal of the Court's laudable goals, I am unable to agree with its approach to the constitutional issue that is presented. In my opinion, this case raises questions that encompass more than the immediate plight of disadvantaged black citizens. I believe the Court errs by holding the structure of the local governmental unit unconstitutional without identifying an acceptable, judicially manageable standard for adjudicating cases of this kind. . . .

Ever since I joined the Court, I have been concerned about the Court's emphasis on subjective intent as a criterion for constitutional adjudication. Although that criterion is often regarded as a restraint on the exercise of judicial power, it may in fact provide judges with a tool for exercising power that otherwise would be confined to the legislature. My principal concern with the subjective-intent standard, however, is unrelated to the quantum of power it confers upon the judiciary. It is based on the quality of that power. For in the long run constitutional adjudication that is premised on a case-by-case appraisal of the subjective intent of local decision-makers cannot possibly satisfy the requirement of impartial administration of the law that is embodied in the Equal Protection Clause of the Fourteenth Amendment.

The facts of this case illustrate the ephemeral character of a constitutional standard that focuses on subjective intent. When the suit was filed in 1976, approximately 58 percent of the population of Burke County was black and approximately 42 percent was white. Because black citizens had been denied access to the political process—through means that have since been outlawed by the Voting Rights Act of 1965—and because there had been insufficient time to enable the registration of black voters to overcome the history of past injustice, the majority of registered voters in the county were white. The at-large electoral system therefore served, as a result of the presence of bloc voting, to maintain white control of the local government. Whether it would have continued to do so would have depended on a mix of at least three different factors—the continuing increase in voter registration among blacks, the continuing exodus of black residents from the county, and the extent to which racial block voting continued to dominate local politics.

If those elected officials in control of the political machinery had formed the judgment that these factors created a likelihood that a bloc of black voters was about to achieve sufficient strength to elect an entirely new administration, they might have decided to abandon the at-large system and substitute five single-member districts with the boundary lines drawn to provide a white majority in three districts and a black majority in only two. Under the Court's intent standard, such a change presumably would violate the Fourteenth Amendment. It is ironic that the remedy ordered by the District fits that pattern precisely. . . .

Case

SHAW V. HUNT

517 U.S. 899; 116 S.Ct. 1894; 135 L.Ed. 2d. 207 (1996)
Vote: 5–4

In Shaw v. Reno . . . *(1993)* (Shaw I), *the Supreme Court held that a group of white plaintiffs could challenge the race-conscious redistricting of their state's congressional districts. On remand, the federal district court upheld the redistricting plan. Here the Supreme Court reviews that decision. The relevant facts are summarized in Chief Justice Rehnquist's majority opinion.*

Chief Justice Rehnquist delivered the opinion of the Court.

. . . After the 1990 census, North Carolina's congressional delegation increased from 11 to 12 members. The State General Assembly adopted a reapportionment plan, Chapter 601, that included one majority-black district, District 1, located in the northeastern region of the State. . . . The legislature then submitted the plan to the Attorney General of the United States for preclearance under Section 5 of the Voting Rights Act of 1965. . . . The Assistant Attorney General for Civil Rights, acting on the Attorney General's behalf, objected to the proposed plan because it failed "to give effect to black and Native American voting strength" in "the south-central to southeastern part of the state" and opined that the State's reasons for not creating a second majority-minority district appeared "to be pretextual." . . . Duly chastened, the legislature revised its districting scheme to include a second majority-black district. . . . The new plan, Chapter 7, located the minority district, District 12, in the north-central or Piedmont region, not in the south-central or south-eastern region identified in the Justice Department's objection letter. The Attorney General nonetheless precleared the revised plan.

By anyone's measure, the boundary lines of Districts 1 and 12 are unconventional. A map portrays the districts' deviance far better than words . . . but our prior opinion describes them as follows:

The first of the two majority-black districts . . . is somewhat hook shaped. Centered in the northeast portion of the State, it moves southward until it tapers to a narrow band; then, with finger-like extensions, it reaches far into the southern-most part of the State near the South Carolina border. . . .

The second majority-black district, District 12, is even more unusually shaped. It is approximately 160 miles long and, for much of its length, no wider than the [Interstate]-85 corridor. It winds in snake-like fashion through tobacco country, financial centers, and manufacturing areas "until it gobbles in enough enclaves of black neighborhoods." . . .

Five North Carolinians commenced the present action in the United States District Court for the Eastern District of North Carolina against various state officials. Following our reversal of the District Court's dismissal of their complaint in *Shaw I*, the District Court allowed a number of individuals to intervene, 11 on behalf of the plaintiffs and 22 for the defendants. After a 6-day trial, the District Court unanimously found "that the Plan's lines were deliberately drawn to produce one or more districts of a certain racial composition." . . . A majority of the court held that the plan was constitutional, nonetheless, because it was narrowly tailored to further the State's compelling interests in complying with Sections 2 and 5 of the Voting Rights Act. . . . The dissenting judge disagreed with that portion of the judgment. We noted probable jurisdiction. . . .

We explained in *Miller v. Johnson* [1995] that a racially gerrymandered districting scheme, like all laws that classify citizens on the basis of race, is constitutionally suspect. . . . This is true whether or not the reason for the racial classification is benign or the purpose remedial. . . . Applying traditional equal protection principles in the voting-rights context is "a most delicate task," . . . however, because a legislature may be conscious of the voters' races without using race as a basis for assigning voters to districts. . . . The constitutional wrong occurs when race becomes the "dominant and controlling" consideration. . . .

The plaintiff bears the burden of proving the race-based motive and may do so either through "circumstantial evidence of a district's shape and demographics" or through "more direct evidence going to legislative purpose." . . . After a detailed account of the process that led to enactment of the challenged plan, the District Court found that the General Assembly of North Carolina "deliberately drew" District 12 so that it would have an effective voting majority of black citizens. . . .

Appellees urge upon us their view that this finding is not phrased in the same language that we used in our opinion in *Miller v. Johnson*, . . . where we said that a plaintiff must show "that race was the predominant factor motivating the legislature's decision to place a significant number of voters within or without a particular district." . . .

The District Court, of course, did not have the benefit of our opinion in *Miller* at the time it wrote its opinion. While it would have been preferable for the court to have analyzed the case in terms of the standard laid down in *Miller*, that was not possible. This circumstance has no consequence here because we think that the District Court's findings, read in the light of the evidence that it had before it, comport with the *Miller* standard.

First, the District Court had evidence of the district's shape and demographics. The court observed "the obvious fact" that the district's shape is "highly irregular and geographically non-compact by any objective standard that can be conceived." . . . In fact, the serpentine district has been dubbed the least geographically compact district in the Nation. . . .

The District Court also had direct evidence of the legislature's objective. The State's submission for preclearance expressly acknowledged that the Chapter 7's "overriding purpose was to comply with the dictates of the Attorney General's December 18, 1991 letter and to create two congressional districts with effective black voting majorities." . . . This admission was confirmed by Gerry Cohen, the plan's principal draftsman, who testified that creating two majority-black districts was the "principal reason" for Districts 1 and 12. . . . Indeed, appellees in their first appearance before the District Court "formally concede[d] that the state legislature deliberately created the two districts in a way to assure black-vote majorities," . . . and that concession again was credited by the District Court on remand. . . . Here, as in *Miller*, "we fail to see how the District Court could have reached any conclusion other than that race was the predominant factor in drawing [the challenged district]." . . .

In his dissent, Justice Stevens argues that strict scrutiny does not apply where a State "respects" or "compl[ies] with traditional districting principles." . . . That, however, is not the standard announced and applied in *Miller*, where we held that strict scrutiny applies when race is the "predominant" consideration in drawing the district lines such that "the legislature subordinate[s] race-neutral districting principles . . . to racial considerations." . . . The *Miller* standard is quite different from the one that Justice Stevens advances, as an examination of the dissent's reasoning demonstrates. The dissent explains that "two race-neutral, traditional districting criteria" were at work in determining the shape and placement of District 12, and from this suggests that strict scrutiny should not apply. . . . We do not quarrel with the dissent's claims that, in shaping District 12, the State effectuated its interest in creating one rural and one urban district, and that partisan politicking was actively at work in the districting process. That the legislature addressed these interests does not in any way refute the fact that race was the legislature's predominant consideration. Race was the criterion that, in the State's view, could not be compromised; respecting communities of interest and protecting Democratic incumbents came into play only after the race-based decision had been made.

Racial classifications are antithetical to the Fourteenth Amendment, whose "central purpose" was "to eliminate racial discrimination emanating from official sources in the States." . . . While appreciating that a racial classification causes "fundamental injury" to the "individual rights of a person," . . . we have recognized that, under certain circumstances, drawing racial distinctions is permissible where a governmental body is pursuing a "compelling state interest." A State, however, is constrained in how it may pursue that end: "[T]he means chosen to accomplish the State's asserted purpose must be specifically and narrowly framed to accomplish that purpose." . . . North Carolina, therefore, must show not only that its redistricting plan was in pursuit of a compelling state interest, but also that "its districting legislation is narrowly tailored to achieve [that] compelling interest." . . .

Appellees point to three separate compelling interests to sustain District 12: to eradicate the effects of past and present discrimination; to comply with Section 5 of the Voting Rights Act; and to comply with Section 2 of that Act. We address each in turn.

A State's interest in remedying the effects of past or present racial discrimination may in the proper case justify a government's use of racial distinctions. . . . For that interest to rise to the level of a compelling state interest, it must satisfy two conditions. First, the discrimination must be " 'identified discrimination.' " . . . "While the States and their subdivisions may take remedial action when they possess evidence" of past or present discrimination, "they must identify that discrimination, public or private, with some specificity before they may use race-conscious relief." . . . A generalized assertion of past discrimination in a particular industry or region is not adequate because it "provides no guidance for a legislative body to determine the precise scope of the injury it seeks to remedy." . . . Accordingly, an effort to alleviate the effects of societal discrimination is not a compelling interest. . . . Second, the institution that makes the racial distinction must have had a "strong basis in evidence" to conclude that remedial action was necessary, "before it embarks on an affirmative-action program." . . .

In this case, the District Court found that an interest in ameliorating past discrimination did not actually precipitate the use of race in the redistricting plan. While some legislators invoked the State's history of discrimination as an argument for creating a second majority-black district, the court found that these members did not have enough voting power to have caused the creation of the second district on that basis alone. . . .

Appellees, to support their claim that the plan was drawn to remedy past discrimination, rely on passages from two reports prepared for this litigation by a historian and a social scientist. . . . Obviously these reports, both dated March 1994, were not before the General Assembly when it enacted Chapter 7. And there is little to suggest that the legislature considered the historical events and social-science data that the reports recount, beyond what individual members may have recalled from personal experience. We certainly cannot say on the basis of these reports that the District Court's findings on this point were clearly erroneous.

Appellees devote most of their efforts to arguing that the race-based redistricting was constitutionally justified by the State's duty to comply with the Voting Rights Act. The District Court agreed and held that compliance with Sections 2 and 5 of the Act could be, and in this case was, a compelling state interest. . . . In *Miller,* we expressly left open the question whether under the proper circumstances compliance with the Voting Rights Act, on its own, could be a compelling interest. . . . Here once again we do not reach that question because we find that creating an additional majority-black district was not required under a correct reading of Section 5 and that District 12, as drawn, is not a remedy narrowly tailored to the State's professed interest in avoiding Section 2 liability.

With respect to Section 5 of the Voting Rights Act, we believe our decision in *Miller* forecloses the argument, adopted by the District Court, that failure to engage in the race-based districting would have violated that section. In *Miller,* we considered an equal protection challenge to Georgia's Eleventh Congressional District. As appellees do here, Georgia contended that its redistricting plan was necessary to meet the Justice Department's preclearance demands. The Justice Department had interposed an objection to a prior plan that created only two majority-minority districts. We held that the challenged congressional plan was not required by a correct reading of Section 5 and therefore compliance with that law could not justify race-based districting. . . .

We believe the same conclusion must be drawn here. North Carolina's first plan, Chapter 601, indisputably was ameliorative, having created the first majority-black district in recent history. Thus, that plan, "even if [it] fall[s] short of what might be accomplished in terms of increasing minority representation," . . . "cannot violate Section 5 unless the new apportionment itself so discriminates on the basis of race or color as to violate the Constitution." . . .

As in *Miller,* the United States relies on the purpose prong of Section 5 to explain the Department's preclearance objections, alleging that North Carolina, for pretextual reasons, did not create a second majority-minority district. . . . We again find the Government's position . . . . The General Assembly, in its submission filed with Chapter 601, explained why it did not create a second minority district; among its goals were "to keep precincts whole, to avoid dividing counties into more than two districts, and to give black voters a fair amount of influence by creating at least one district that was majority black in voter registration and by creating a substantial number of other districts in which black voters would exercise a significant influence over the choice of congressmen." . . . The submission also explained in detail the disadvantages of other proposed plans. . . . A memorandum, sent to the Department of Justice on behalf of the legislators in charge of the redistricting process, provided still further reasons for the State's decision not to draw two minority districts as urged by various interested parties. . . . We have recognized that a "State's policy of adhering to other districting principles instead of creating as many majority-minority districts as possible does not support an inference that the plan 'so discriminates on the basis of race or color as to violate the Constitution,' and thus cannot provide any basis under Section 5 for the Justice Department's objection." . . .

It appears that the Justice Department was pursuing in North Carolina the same policy of maximizing the number of majority-black districts that it pursued in Georgia. . . . The two States underwent the preclearance processes during the same time period and the objection letters they received from the Civil Rights Division were substantially alike. . . . A North Carolina legislator recalled being told by the Assistant Attorney General that "you have twenty-two percent black people in this State, you must have as close to twenty-two percent black

Congressmen, or black Congressional Districts in this State." . . . We explained in *Miller* that this maximization policy is not properly grounded in Section 5 and the Department's authority thereunder. . . . We again reject the Department's expansive interpretation of Section 5. . . .

With respect to Section 2, appellees contend, and the District Court found, that failure to enact a plan with a second majority-black district would have left the State vulnerable to a lawsuit under this section. Our precedent establishes that a plaintiff may allege a Section 2 violation in a single-member district if the manipulation of districting lines fragments politically cohesive minority voters among several districts or packs them into one district or a small number of districts, and thereby dilutes the voting strength of members of the minority population. . . . To prevail on such a claim, a plaintiff must prove that the minority group "is sufficiently large and geographically compact to constitute a majority in a single-member district"; that the minority group "is politically cohesive"; and that "the white majority votes sufficiently as a bloc to enable it . . . usually to defeat the minority's preferred candidate." . . . A court must also consider all other relevant circumstances and must ultimately find based on the totality of those circumstances that members of a protected class "have less opportunity than other members of the electorate to participate in the political process and to elect representatives of their choice." . . .

We assume, *arguendo,* for the purpose of resolving this case, that compliance with Section 2 could be a compelling interest, and we likewise assume, *arguendo,* that the General Assembly believed a second majority-minority district was needed in order not to violate Section 2, and that the legislature at the time it acted had a strong basis in evidence to support that conclusion. We hold that even with the benefit of these assumptions, the North Carolina plan does not survive strict scrutiny because the remedy—the creation of District 12—is not narrowly tailored to the asserted end.

Although we have not always provided precise guidance on how closely the means (the racial classification) must serve the end (the justification or compelling interest), we have always expected that the legislative action would substantially address, if not achieve, the avowed purpose. . . . Where, as here, we assume avoidance of Section 2 liability to be a compelling state interest, we think that the racial classification would have to realize that goal; the legislative action must, at a minimum, remedy the anticipated violation or achieve compliance to be narrowly tailored.

District 12 could not remedy any potential Section 2 violation. As discussed above, a plaintiff must show that the minority group is "geographically compact" to establish Section 2 liability. No one looking at District 12 could reasonably suggest that the district contains a "geographically compact" population of any race. . . . Therefore where that district sits, "there neither has been a wrong nor can be a remedy." . . .

Appellees do not defend District 12 by arguing that the district is geographically compact, however. Rather they contend, and a majority of the District Court agreed, . . . that once a legislature has a strong basis in evidence for concluding that a Section 2 violation exists in the State, it may draw a majority-minority district anywhere, even if the district is in no way coincident with the compact *Gingles* district, as long as racially polarized voting exists where the district is ultimately drawn. . . .

We find this position singularly unpersuasive. We do not see how a district so drawn would avoid Section 2 liability. If a Section 2 violation is proven for a particular area, it flows from the fact that individuals in this area "have less opportunity than other members of the electorate to participate in the political process and to elect representatives of their choice." . . . The vote dilution injuries suffered by these persons are not remedied by creating a safe majority-black district somewhere else in the State. For example, if a geographically compact, cohesive minority population lives in south-central to southeastern North Carolina, as the Justice Department's objection letter suggested, District 12 which spans the Piedmont Crescent would not address that Section 2 violation. The black voters of the south-central to southeastern region would still be suffering precisely the same injury that they suffered before District 12 was drawn. District 12 would not address the professed interest of relieving the vote dilution, much less be narrowly tailored to accomplish the goal.

Arguing, as appellees do and the District Court did, that the State may draw the district anywhere derives from a misconception of the vote-dilution claim. To accept that the district may be placed anywhere implies that the claim, and hence the coordinate right to an undiluted vote (to cast a ballot equal among voters), belongs to the minority as a group and not to its individual members. It does not. . . .

The United States submits that District 12 does, in fact, incorporate a "substantial portio[n]" of the concentration of minority voters that would have given rise to a Section 2 claim. . . . Specifically, the Government claims that "District 12 . . . contains the heavy concentration of

African Americans in Mecklenburg County, the same urban component included in the second minority opportunity district in some of the alternative plans." . . . The portion of District 12 that lies in Mecklenburg County covers not more than 20% of the district. . . . We do not think that this degree of incorporation could mean that District 12 substantially addresses the Section 2 violation. We hold, therefore, that District 12 is not narrowly tailored to the State's asserted interest in complying with Section 2 of the Voting Rights Act. . . .

Justice Stevens, with whom **Justice Ginsburg** and **Justice Breyer** join . . . , dissenting.

As I have explained on prior occasions, I am convinced that the Court's aggressive supervision of state action designed to accommodate the political concerns of historically disadvantaged minority groups is seriously misguided. A majority's attempt to enable the minority to participate more effectively in the process of democratic government should not be viewed with the same hostility that is appropriate for oppressive and exclusionary abuses of political power. . . . But even if we accept the Court's refusal to recognize any distinction between two vastly different kinds of situations, we should affirm the judgment of the District Court in this case.

As the Court analyzes the case, it raises three distinct questions: (1) Should North Carolina's decision to create two congressional districts in which a majority of the voters are African-American be subject to strict constitutional scrutiny?; (2) If so, did North Carolina have a compelling interest in creating such districts?; and (3) If so, was the creation of those districts "narrowly tailored" to further the asserted compelling interest? The Court inadequately explains its answer to the first question, and it avoids answering the second because it concludes that its answer to the third disposes of the case. In my estimation, the Court's disposition of all three questions is most unsatisfactory. . . .

. . . As I understand the *Miller* [v. *Johnson* (1995)] test . . . , state legislatures may take racial and ethnic characteristics of voters into account when they are drawing district boundaries without triggering strict scrutiny so long as race is not the "predominant" consideration guiding their deliberations. . . . To show that race has been "predominant," a plaintiff must show that "the legislature subordinated traditional race-neutral districting principles . . . to racial considerations" in drawing that district. . . .

In holding that the present record shows race to have been the "predominant" consideration in the

creation of District 12, the Court relies on two pieces of evidence: the State's admission that its "overriding" purpose was to " 'create two congressional districts with effective black voting majorities,' " . . . and the " 'geographically non-compact' " shape of District 12. . . . In my view, this evidence does not suffice to trigger strict scrutiny under the "demanding" test that *Miller* establishes. . . .

North Carolina's admission reveals that it intended to create a second majority-minority district. That says nothing about whether it subordinated traditional districting principles in drawing District 12. States which conclude that federal law requires majority-minority districts have little choice but to give "overriding" weight to that concern. . . .

District 12's noncompact appearance also fails to show that North Carolina engaged in suspect race-based districting. There is no federal statutory or constitutional requirement that state electoral boundaries conform to any particular ideal of geographic compactness. In addition, although the North Carolina Constitution requires electoral districts for state elective office to be contiguous, it does not require them to be geographically compact. . . . Given that numerous States have written geographical compactness requirements into their state constitutions, North Carolina's omission on this score is noteworthy. . . . It reveals that North Carolina's creation of a geographically noncompact district does not itself mark a deviation from any prevailing state districting principle. Thus, while the serpentine character of District 12 may give rise to an inference that traditional districting principles were subordinated to race in determining its boundaries, it cannot fairly be said to prove that conclusion in light of the clear evidence demonstrating race-neutral explanations for the district's tortured shape. . . .

There is a more fundamental flaw in the majority's conclusion that racial concerns predominantly explain the creation of District 12. The evidence of shape and intent relied on by the majority cannot overcome the basic fact that North Carolina did not have to draw Districts 1 and 12 in order to comply with the Justice Department's finding that federal law required the creation of two majority-minority districts. That goal could have been more straightforwardly accomplished by simply adopting the Attorney General's recommendation to draw a geographically compact district in the southeastern portion of the State in addition to the majority-minority district that had already been drawn in the northeastern and Piedmont regions. . . .

That the legislature chose to draw Districts 1 and 12 instead surely suggests that something more than the desire to create a majority-minority district took precedence. For that reason, this case would seem to present a version of the very hypothetical that the principal opinion in Bush suggests should pose no constitutional problem—"an otherwise compact majority-minority district that is misshapen by nonracial, political manipulation." . . .

Here, no evidence suggests that race played any role in the legislature's decision to choose the winding contours of District 12 over the more cartographically pleasant boundaries proposed by the Attorney General. Rather, the record reveals that two race-neutral, traditional districting criteria determined District 12's shape: the interest in ensuring that incumbents would remain residents of the districts they have previously represented; and the interest in placing predominantly rural voters in one district and predominantly urban voters in another. . . .

Unlike most States, North Carolina has not given its chief executive any power to veto enactments of its legislature. Thus, even though the voters had elected a Republican Governor, the Democratic majority in the legislature was in control of the districting process. It was the Democrats who first decided to adopt the 11-white-district plan that arguably would have violated Section 2 of the Voting Rights Act and gave rise to the Attorney General's objection under Section 5. It was also the Democrats who rejected Republican Party maps which contained two majority-minority districts because they created too many districts in which a majority of the residents were registered Republicans. . . .

If race rather than incumbency protection had been the dominant consideration, it seems highly unlikely that the Democrats would have drawn this bizarre district rather than accepting more compact options that were clearly available. If race, rather than politics, had been the "predominant" consideration for the Democrats, they could have accepted the Republican Plan, thereby satisfying the Attorney General and avoiding any significant risk of liability as well as the attack mounted by the plaintiffs in this case. Instead, as the detailed findings of the District Court demonstrate, the legislature deliberately crafted a districting plan that would accommodate the needs of Democratic incumbents. . . .

If the Democrats remain in control of the districting process after the remand in this case, it will be interesting to see whether they will be willing to sacrifice one or more Democratic-majority districts in order to create at least two districts with effective minority voting majorities. My review of the history revealed in the findings of

the District Court persuades me that political considerations will probably take priority over racial considerations in the immediate future, just as they surely did during the process of rejecting the Republican plan and ultimately adopting the plan challenged in this case.

A deliberate effort to consolidate urban voters in one district and rural voters in another also explains District 12's highly irregular shape. Before District 12 had been drawn, members of the public as well as legislators had urged that "the observance of distinctive urban and rural communities of interest should be a prime consideration in the general redistricting process." . . . As a result, the legislature was naturally attracted to a plan that, although less than aesthetically pleasing, included both District 12, which links the State's major urban centers, and District 1, which has a population that predominantly lives in cities with populations of less than 20,000. . . .

Moreover, the record reveals that District 12's lines were drawn in order to unite an African-American community whose political tradition was quite distinct from the one that defines African-American voters in the Coastal Plain, which District 1 surrounds. . . . Indeed, two other majority-minority-district plans with less torturous boundaries were thought unsatisfactory precisely because they did not unite communities of interest. . . . Significantly, the irregular contours of District 12 track the State's main interstate highway and are located entirely within the culturally distinct Piedmont Crescent region. . . . Clearly, then, District 12 was drawn around a community "defined by actual shared interests" rather than racial demography. . . .

In light of the majority's decision not to remand for proper application of the *Miller* test, I do not understand how it can condemn the drawing of District 12 given these two race-neutral justifications for its shape. To be sure, in choosing a district that snakes rather than sits, North Carolina did not put a premium on geographical compactness. But I do not understand why that should matter in light of the evidence which shows that other race-neutral districting considerations were determinative.

As the foregoing discussion illustrates, legislative decisions are often the product of compromise and mixed motives. For that reason, I have always been skeptical about the value of motivational analysis as a basis for constitutional adjudication. . . . I am particularly skeptical of such an inquiry in a case of this type, as mixed motivations would seem to be endemic to the endeavor of political districting. . . .

The majority's analysis of the "compelling interest" issue nicely demonstrates the problem with parsing legislative motive in this context. The majority posits that the legislature's compelling interest in drawing District 12 was its desire to avoid liability under Section 2 of the Voting Rights Act. Yet it addresses the question whether North Carolina had a compelling interest only because it first concludes that a racial purpose dominated the State's districting effort.

It seems to me that if the State's true purpose were to serve its compelling interest in staving off costly litigation by complying with federal law, then it cannot be correct to say that a racially discriminatory purpose controlled its line-drawing. A more accurate conclusion would be that the State took race into account only to the extent necessary to meet the requirements of a carefully thought out federal statute. . . . The majority's implicit equation of the intentional consideration of race in order to comply with the Voting Rights Act with intentional racial discrimination reveals the inadequacy of the framework it adopts for considering the constitutionality of race-based districting.

However, even if I were to assume that strict scrutiny applies, and thus that it makes sense to consider the question, I would not share the majority's hesitancy in concluding that North Carolina had a "compelling interest" in drawing District 12. In my view, the record identifies not merely one, but at least three acceptable reasons that may have motivated legislators to favor the creation of two such districts. Those three reasons easily satisfy the judicially created requirement that the state legislature's decision be supported by a "compelling state interest," particularly in a case in which the alleged injury to the disadvantaged class—i.e., the majority of voters who are white—is so tenuous.

First, some legislators felt that the sorry history of race relations in North Carolina in past decades was a sufficient reason for making it easier for more black leaders to participate in the legislative process and to represent the State in the Congress of the United States. . . . Even if that history does not provide the kind of precise guidance that will justify certain specific affirmative action programs in particular industries, . . . it surely provides an adequate basis for a decision to facilitate the election of representatives of the previously disadvantaged minority.

As a class, state legislators are far more likely to be familiar with the role that race plays in electoral politics than they are with the role that it plays in hiring decisions within discrete industries. Moreover, given the North Carolina Legislature's own recent experience with voting rights litigation, . . . as well as the fact that 40 of the State's districts are so-called covered jurisdictions which the Attorney General directly monitors as a result of prior discriminatory practices, . . . there is less reason to assume that the state legislative judgments under review here are based on unwarranted generalizations than may be true in other contexts. Thus, even if a desire to correct past discrimination did not itself drive the legislative decision to draw two majority-minority districts, it plainly constituted a legitimate and significant additional factor supporting the decision to do so. . . .

Second, regardless of whether Section 5 of the Act was actually violated, I believe the State's interest in avoiding the litigation that would have been necessary to overcome the Attorney General's objection to the original plan provides an acceptable reason for creating a second majority-minority district. It is entirely proper for a State whose past practices have subjected it to the pre-clearance obligation set forth in Section 5 to presume that the Attorney General's construction of the Act is correct, and to take corrective action rather than challenging him in Court.

Moreover, even if the State's interest in avoiding a court challenge that might have succeeded does not constitute a sufficient justification for its decision to draw a majority-minority district, the State plainly had an interest in complying with a finding by the Attorney General that it reasonably believed could not have been successfully challenged in court. The majority disagrees, relying on our analysis in *Miller v. Johnson*. . . .

In *Miller,* the Court concluded that Georgia had simply acceded to the Attorney General's unreasonable construction of Section 5 without performing any independent assessment of its validity. . . . By contrast, the District Court here found as a factual matter that the legislature's independent assessment of the reasons for the Attorney General's denial of preclearance led it to the reasonable conclusion that its 11-white district plan would violate the purpose prong of Section 5. . . . As a result, I do not accept the Court's conclusion that it was unreasonable for the State to believe that its decision to draw 1 majority-minority district out of 12 would have been subject to a successful attack under the purpose prong of Section 5. . . .

I acknowledge that when North Carolina sought preclearance it asserted nondiscriminatory reasons for deciding not to draw a second majority-minority district. . . . On careful reflection, however, the legislature concluded that those reasons would not likely suffice in a federal action to challenge the Attorney General's ruling. The District Court found that conclusion to be reasonable. . . . I am mystified as to why this finding does not deserve our acceptance. Nor do I understand the Court's willingness to credit the State's declarations of nondiscriminatory purpose in this context, . . . in light of its unwillingness to accept any of North Carolina's race-neutral explanations for its decision to draw District 12. . . .

Third, regardless of the possible outcome of litigation alleging that Section 2 of the Voting Rights Act would be violated by a plan that ensured the election of white legislators in 11 of the State's 12 congressional districts, the interest in avoiding the expense and unpleasantness of such litigation was certainly legitimate and substantial. That the legislature reasonably feared the possibility of a successful Section 2 challenge cannot be credibly denied.

In the course of the redistricting debate, numerous maps had been presented showing that blacks could constitute more than 50 percent of the population in two districts. . . . The District Court found that these plans had demonstrated that "the state's African-American population was sufficiently large and geographically compact to constitute a majority in two congressional districts." . . .

Moreover, the Attorney General denied preclearance on the ground that North Carolina could have created a second majority-minority district that was, under any reasonable standard, geographically compact. . . . Maps prepared by the plaintiff-intervenors for this litigation conclusively demonstrate that two compact, majority-minority districts could indeed have been drawn. . . .

Even if many of the maps proposing two majority-African-American districts were not particularly compact, the legislature reasonably concluded that a federal court might have determined that some of them could have provided the basis for a viable vote dilution suit pursuant to *Thornburg v. Gingles.* . . . That conclusion is particularly reasonable in light of the fact that *Gingles* was a case fresh in the minds of many of North Carolina's state legislators. . . . There, the State challenged the plaintiffs' Section 2 claim by pointing to the oddly configured lines that defined their proposed majority-minority districts. . . . As we know, North Carolina's defense to Section 2 liability proved unsuccessful in that instance, even though the district court acknowledged that the "single-member district specifically suggested by the plaintiffs as a viable one is obviously not a model of aesthetic tidiness." . . .

Finally, even if the record shows that African-American voters would not have comprised more than 50 percent of the population in any plan containing two compact, majority-minority districts, the record reveals that it would have been possible to have drawn a map containing one compact district in which African-Americans would have comprised more than 50 percent of the population and another compact district in which African-Americans, by reason of the large presence of Native Americans, would have by far constituted the largest racial group. . . . Given our recent emphasis on considering the totality of the circumstances in Section 2 cases, we are in no position to rebuke a State for concluding that a 40-plus percent African-American district could provide a defense to a viable *Gingles* challenge as surely as could one with a 50.1 percent African-American population. . . .

Although the Court assumes that North Carolina had a compelling interest in "avoiding liability" under Section 2, . . . it avoids conclusively resolving that question because it holds that District 12 was not a "narrowly tailored" means of achieving that end. The majority reaches this conclusion by determining that District 12 did not "remedy" any potential violation of Section 2 that may have occurred. . . .

In my judgment, if a State's new plan successfully avoids the potential litigation entirely, there is no reason why it must also take the form of a "remedy" for an unproven violation. Thus, the fact that no Section 2 violation has been proven in the territory that comprises District 12 does not show that the district fails to serve a compelling state interest. It shows only that a federal court, which is constrained by Article III, would not have had the power to require North Carolina to draw that district. It is axiomatic that a State should have more authority to institute a districting plan than would a federal court. . . .

That District 12 will protect North Carolina from liability seems clear. The record gives no indication that any of the potential Section 2 claimants is interested in challenging the plan that contains District 12. Moreover, as a legal matter, North Carolina is in a stronger position to defend against a Section 2 lawsuit with District 12 than without it. . . .

. . . [T]he Court today rejects North Carolina's plan because it does not provide the precise remedy that might have been ordered by a federal court, even though it satisfies potential plaintiffs, furthers such race-neutral legislative ends as incumbency protection and the preservation of distinct communities of interest, and essentially serves to insulate the State from a successful statutory challenge. There is no small irony in the fact that the Court's decision to intrude into the State's districting process comes in response to a lawsuit brought on behalf of white voters who have suffered no history of exclusion from North Carolina's political process, and whose only claims of harm are at best rooted in speculative and stereotypical assumptions about the kind of representation they are likely to receive from the candidates that their neighbors have chosen.

It is, of course, irrelevant whether we, as judges, deem it wise policy to create majority-minority districts as a means of assuring fair and effective representation to minority voters. We have a duty to respect Congress' considered judgment that such a policy may serve to effectuate the ends of the constitutional Amendment that it is charged with enforcing. We should also respect North Carolina's conscientious effort to conform to that congressional determination. Absent some demonstration that voters are being denied fair and effective representation as a result of their race, I find no basis for this Court's intervention into a process by which federal and state actors, both black and white, are jointly attempting to resolve difficult questions of politics and race that have long plagued North Carolina. Nor do I see how our constitutional tradition can countenance the suggestion that a State may draw unsightly lines to favor farmers or city dwellers, but not to create districts that benefit the very group whose history inspired the Amendment that the Voting Rights Act was designed to implement. . . .

Justice Souter, with whom **Justice Ginsburg** and **Justice Breyer** join, dissenting. . . .

Case

Reynolds v. Sims

377 U.S. 533; 84 S.Ct. 1362; 12 L.Ed. 2d. 506 (1964)
Vote: 8–1

Prior to this lawsuit, the apportionment scheme for the Alabama legislature created a thirty-five-member senate elected from districts whose population varied from 15,417 to 634,864 and a house of representatives with 106 members elected from districts whose populations varied from 6,731 to 104,767. Registered voters from two urban counties brought this lawsuit challenging the constitutionality of the existing apportionment. The U.S. district court ruled for the plaintiffs and ordered a temporary reapportionment plan. On appeal, the Supreme Court affirmed the lower court's decision.

Mr. Chief Justice Warren delivered the opinion of the Court.

. . . A predominant consideration in determining whether a State's legislative apportionment scheme constitutes an invidious discrimination violative of rights asserted under the Equal Protection Clause is that the rights allegedly impaired are individual and personal in nature. . . . [T]he judicial focus must be concentrated upon ascertaining whether there has been any discrimination against certain of the State's citizens which constitutes an impermissible impairment of their constitutionally protected right to vote. . . . Undoubtedly, the right of suffrage is a fundamental matter in a free and democratic society. Especially since the right to exercise the franchise in a free and unimpaired manner is preservative of other basic civil and political rights, any alleged infringement of the right of citizens to vote must be carefully and meticulously scrutinized. . . .

Legislators represent people, not trees or acres. Legislators are elected by voters, not farms or cities or economic interests. As long as ours is a representative form of government, and our legislatures are those instruments of government elected directly by and directly representative of the people, the right to elect legislators in a free and unimpaired fashion is a bedrock of our political system. It could hardly be gainsaid that a constitutional claim had been asserted by an allegation that certain otherwise qualified voters had been entirely prohibited from voting for members of their state legislature. And, if a State should provide that the votes of citizens in one part of the State should be given two times, or five times, or 10 times the weight of votes of citizens in another part of the State, it could hardly be contended that the right to vote of those residing in the disfavored area had not been effectively diluted. It would appear extraordinary to suggest that a State could be constitutionally permitted to enact a law providing that certain of the State's voters could vote two, five, or 10 times for their legislative representatives, while voters living elsewhere could vote only once. And it is inconceivable that a state law to the effect that, in counting votes for legislators, the votes of citizens in one part of the State would be multiplied by two, five, or 10, while the votes of persons in another area would be counted only at face value, could be constitutionally sustainable. Of course, the effect of state legislative districting schemes which give the same number of representatives to unequal numbers of constituents is identical. Overweighting and overvaluation of the votes of those living here has the certain effect of dilution and under valuation of the votes of those living there. The resulting discrimination against those individual voters living in disfavored areas is easily demonstrable mathematically. Their right to vote is simply not the same right to vote as that of those living in a favored part of the State. Two, five, or 10 of them must vote before the effect of their voting is equivalent to that of their favored neighbor. Weighting the votes of citizens differently, by any method or means, merely because of where they happen to reside, hardly seems justifiable. . . .

State legislatures are, historically, the fountainhead of representative government in this country. . . . Most citizens can achieve [full and effective] participation only as qualified voters through the election of legislators to represent them. Full and effective participation by all citizens in state government requires, therefore, that each citizen have an equally effective voice in the election of members of his state legislature. Modern and viable state government needs, and the Constitution demands, no less.

Logically, in a society ostensibly grounded on representative government, it would seem reasonable that a majority of the people of a State could elect a majority of that State's legislators. To conclude differently, and to sanction minority control of state legislature bodies, would appear to deny majority rights in a way that far surpasses any possible denial of minority rights that might otherwise be thought to result. Since legislatures are responsible for enacting laws by which all citizens are to be governed, they should be bodies which are collectively responsive to the popular will. And the concept of equal protection has been traditionally viewed as requiring the uniform treatment of persons standing in the same relation to the governmental action questioned or challenged. With respect to the allocation of legislative representation, all voters, as citizens of a State, stand in the same relation regardless of where they live. Any suggested criteria for the differentiation of citizens are insufficient to justify any discrimination, as to the weight of their votes, unless relevant to the permissible purposes of legislative apportionment. Since the achieving of fair and effective representation for all citizens is concededly the basic aim of legislative apportionment, we conclude that the Equal Protection Clause guarantees

the opportunity for equal participation by all voters in the election of state legislators. Diluting the weight of votes because of place of residence impairs basic constitutional rights under the Fourteenth Amendment just as much as invidious discriminations based upon factors such as race . . . or economic status. . . . Our constitutional system amply provides for the protection of minorities by means other than giving them majority control of state legislatures. And the democratic ideals of equality and majority rule, which have served this Nation so well in the past, are hardly of any less significance for the present and the future.

We are told that the matter of apportioning representation in a state legislature is a complex and many-faceted one. We are advised that States can rationally consider factors other than population in apportioning legislative representation. We are admonished not to restrict the power of the States to impose differing views as to political philosophy on their citizens. We are cautioned about the dangers of entering into political thickets and mathematical quagmires. Our answer is this: a denial of constitutionally protected rights demands judicial protection; our oath and our office require no less of us.

To the extent that a citizen's right to vote is debased, he is that much less a citizen. The fact that an individual lives here or there is not a legitimate reason for overweighting or diluting the efficacy of his vote. The complexions of societies and civilizations change, often with amazing rapidity. A nation once primarily rural in character becomes predominantly urban. Representation schemes once fair and equitable become archaic and outdated. But the basic principle of representative government remains, and must remain, unchanged—the weight of a citizen's vote cannot be made to depend on where he lives. Population is, of necessity, the starting point for consideration and the controlling criterion for judgment in legislative apportionment controversies. A citizen, a qualified voter, is no more nor no less so because he lives in the city or on the farm. This is the clear and strong command of our Constitution's Equal Protection Clause. This is an essential part of the concept of a government of laws and not men. This is at the heart of Lincoln's vision of "government of the people, by the people, [and] for the people." The Equal Protection Clause demands no less than substantially equal state legislative representation for all citizens, of all places as well as of all races. . . .

By holding that as a federal constitutional requisite both houses of a state legislature must be apportioned on a population basis, we mean that the Equal Protection

Clause requires that a State make an honest and good faith effort to construct districts, in both houses of its legislature, as nearly of equal population as is practicable. We realize that it is a practical impossibility to arrange legislative districts so that each one has an identical number of residents, or citizens, or voters. Mathematical exactness or precision is hardly a workable constitutional requirement. . . .

. . . So long as the divergences from a strict population standard are based on legitimate considerations incident to the effectuation of a rational state policy, some deviations from the equal-population principle are constitutionally permissible with respect to the apportionment of seats in either or both of the two houses of a bicameral state legislature. But neither history alone, nor economic or other sorts of group interests, are permissible factors in attempting to justify disparities from population-based representation. Citizens, not history or economic interests, cast votes. Considerations of area alone provide an insufficient justification for deviations from the equal-population principle. Again, people, not land or trees or pastures, vote. Modern developments and improvements in transportation and communications make rather hollow, in the mid-1960's, most claims that deviations from population-based representation can validly be based solely on geographical considerations. Arguments for allowing such deviations in order to insure effective representation for sparsely settled areas and to prevent legislative districts from becoming so large that the availability of access of citizens to their representatives is impaired are today, for the most part, unconvincing.

A consideration that appears to be of more substance in justifying some deviations from population-based representation in state legislatures is that of insuring some voice to political subdivisions, as political subdivisions. . . . In many States much of the legislature's activity involves the enactment of so-called local legislation, directed only to the concerns of particular political subdivisions. And a State may legitimately desire to construct districts along political subdivision lines to deter the possibilities of gerrymandering. But if, even as a result of a clearly rational state policy of according some legislative representation to political subdivisions, population is submerged as the controlling consideration in the apportionment of seats in the particular legislative body, then the right of all of the State's citizens to cast an effective and adequately weighted vote would be unconstitutionally impaired. . . .

Mr. Justice Clark, concurring. . . .

Mr. Justice Stewart, concurring. . . .

Mr. Justice Harlan, dissenting:

. . . The Court's constitutional discussion . . . is remarkable . . . for its failure to address itself at all to the Fourteenth Amendment as a whole or to the legislative history of the Amendment pertinent to the matter at hand. Stripped of aphorisms, the Court's argument boils down to the assertion that appellee's right to vote has been invidiously "debased" or "diluted" by systems of apportionment which entitle them to vote for fewer legislators than other voters, an assertion which is tied to the Equal Protection Clause only by the constitutionally frail tautology that "equal" means "equal."

Had the Court paused to probe more deeply into the matter, it would have found that the Equal Protection Clause was never intended to inhibit the States in choosing any democratic method they pleased for the apportionment of their legislatures. . . .

The history of the adoption of the Fourteenth Amendment provides conclusive evidence that neither those who proposed nor those who ratified the Amendment believed that the Equal Protection Clause limited the power of the States to apportion their legislatures as they saw fit. Moreover, the history demonstrates that the intention to leave this power undisturbed was deliberate and was widely believed to be essential to the adoption of the Amendment. . . .

Although the Court—necessarily, as I believe—provides only generalities in elaboration of its main thesis, its opinion nevertheless fully demonstrates how far removed these problems are from fields of judicial competence. Recognizing that "indiscriminate districting" is an invitation to "partisan gerrymandering," . . . the Court nevertheless excludes virtually every basis for the formation of electoral districts other than "indiscriminate districting." In one or another of today's opinions, the Court declares it unconstitutional for a State to give effective consideration to any of the following in establishing legislative districts:

1. history;
2. "economic or other sorts of group interests";
3. area;
4. geographical considerations;
5. a desire "to insure effective representation for sparsely settled areas";
6. "availability of access of citizens to their representatives";
7. theories of bicameralism (except those approved by the Court);

8. occupation;

9. "an attempt to balance urban and rural power,"

10. the preference of a majority of voters in the State.

So far as presently appears, the only factor which a State may consider, apart from numbers, is political subdivisions. But even "a clearly rational state policy" recognizing this factor is unconstitutional if "population is submerged as the controlling consideration. . . ."

I know of no principle of logic or practical or theoretical politics, still less any constitutional principle, which establishes all or any of these exclusions. Certain it is that the Court's opinion does not establish them. So far as the Court says anything at all on this score, it says

only that "legislators represent people, not trees or acres," . . . that "citizens, not history or economic interests, cast votes," . . . that "people, not land or trees or pastures, vote." . . . All this may be conceded. But it is surely equally obvious, and, in the context of elections, more meaningful to note that people are not ciphers and that legislators can represent their electors only by speaking for their interests—economic, social, political—many of which do reflect the place where the electors live. The Court does not establish, or indeed even attempt to make a case for the proposition that conflicting interests within a State can only be adjusted by disregarding them when voters are grouped for purposes of representation. . . .

Case

KARCHER V. DAGGETT

462 U.S. 725; 103 S.Ct. 2653; 77 L.Ed. 2d. 133 (1983)
Vote: 5–4

The guiding principle is "one person, one vote," but as a practical matter it is impossible to make legislative districts exactly equal in population. How much deviation from absolute equality is permissible? Here the Court addresses this question in the context of a 1982 reapportionment plan for New Jersey's congressional districts.

Justice Brennan delivered the opinion of the Court.

. . . A three-judge District Court declared New Jersey's 1982 reapportionment plan unconstitutional on the authority of *Kirkpatrick v. Preisler* . . . (1969) and *White v. Weiser* (1973), . . . because the population deviations among districts, although small, were not the result of a good-faith effort to achieve population equality. . . .

After the results of the 1980 decennial census had been tabulated, the Clerk of the United States House of Representatives notified the governor of New Jersey that the number of Representatives to which the State was entitled had decreased from 15 to 14. Accordingly, the New Jersey Legislature was required to reapportion the State's congressional districts. The State's 199th Legislature passed two reapportionment bills. One was vetoed by the Governor, and the second, although signed into law, occasioned significant dissatisfaction

among those who felt it diluted minority voting strength in the city of Newark. . . . In response, the 200th Legislature returned to the problem of apportioning congressional districts when it convened in January 1982, and it swiftly passed a bill (S-711) introduced by Senator Feldman, President pro tem of the State Senate, which created the apportionment plan at issue in this case. The bill was signed by the Governor on January 19, 1982. . . .

Like every plan considered by the legislature, the Feldman Plan contained 14 districts, with an average population per district (as determined by the 1980 census) of 526,059. Each district did not have the same population. On the average, each district differed from the "ideal" figure by 0.1384%, or about 726 people. The largest district, the Fourth District, which includes Trenton, had a population of 527,472, and the smallest, the Sixth District, embracing most of Middlesex County, a population of 523,798. The difference between them was 3,674 people, or 0.6984% of the average district. The populations of the other districts also varied. The Ninth District, including most of Bergen County, in the northeastern corner of the State, had a population of 527,349, while the population of the Third District, along the Atlantic shore, was only 524,825. . . .

The legislature had before it other plans with appreciably smaller population deviations between the largest and smallest districts. The one receiving the most attention in the District Court was designed by Dr. Ernest Reock, a political science professor at Rutgers University and Director of the Bureau of Government Research. A version of the

Reock Plan introduced in the 200th Legislature by Assemblyman Hardwick had a maximum population difference of 2,375, or 0.4514% of the average figure. . . .

Almost immediately after the Feldman Plan became law, a group of individuals with varying interests, including all incumbent Republican Members of Congress from New Jersey, sought a declaration that the apportionment plan violated Article I, Section 2, of the Constitution and an injunction against proceeding with the primary election for United States Representatives under the plan. . . .

Shortly thereafter, the District Court issued an opinion and order declaring the Feldman Plan unconstitutional. Denying the motions for summary judgment and resolving the case on the record as a whole, the District Court held that the population variances in the Feldman Plan were not "unavoidable despite a good-faith effort to achieve absolute equality." . . . The court rejected appellants' argument that a deviation lower than the statistical imprecision of the decennial census was "the functional equivalent of mathematical equality." . . . It also held that appellants had failed to show that the population variances were justified by the legislature's purported goals of preserving minority voting strength and anticipating shifts in population. . . . The District Court enjoined appellants from conducting primary or general elections under the Feldman Plan, but that order was stayed pending appeal to this Court. . . .

Article I, Section 2, establishes a "high standard of justice and common sense" for the apportionment of congressional districts: "equal representation for equal numbers of people." . . . Precise mathematical equality, however, may be impossible to achieve in an imperfect world; therefore the "equal representation" standard is enforced only to the extent of requiring that districts be apportioned to achieve population equality "as nearly as is practicable." . . . As we explained further in *Kirkpatrick v. Preisler*:

> [T]he "as nearly as practicable" standard requires that the State make a good-faith effort to achieve precise mathematical equality. . . . Unless population variances among congressional districts are shown to have resulted despite such effort, the State must justify each variance, no matter how small. . . .

Article I, Section 2, therefore, "permits only the limited population variances which are unavoidable despite a good-faith effort to achieve absolute equality, or for which justification is shown." . . .

Thus two basic questions shape litigation over population deviations in state legislation apportioning congressional districts. First, the court must consider whether the population differences among districts could have been reduced or eliminated altogether by a good-faith effort to draw districts of equal population. Parties challenging apportionment legislation must bear the burden of proof on this issue, and if they fail to show that the differences could have been avoided the apportionment scheme must be upheld. If, however, the plaintiffs can establish that the population differences were not the result of a good-faith effort to achieve equality, the State must bear the burden of proving that each significant variance between districts was necessary to achieve some legitimate goal. . . .

Appellants' principal argument in this case is addressed to the first question described above. They contend that the Feldman Plan should be regarded per se as the product of a good-faith effort to achieve population equality because the maximum population deviation among districts is smaller than the predictable undercount in available census data. . . .

Kirkpatrick squarely rejected a nearly identical argument. "The whole thrust of the 'as nearly as practicable' approach is inconsistent with adoption of fixed numerical standards which excuse population variances without regard to the circumstances of each particular case." . . . Adopting any standard other than population equality, using the best census data available, . . . would subtly erode the Constitution's ideal of equal representation. If state legislators knew that a certain *de minimis* level of population differences was acceptable, they would doubtless strive to achieve that level rather than equality. . . .

Furthermore, choosing a different standard would import a high degree of arbitrariness into the process of reviewing apportionment plans. . . . In this case, appellants argue that a maximum deviation of approximately 0.7% should be considered *de minimis*. If we accept that argument, how are we to regard deviations of 0.8%, 0.9%, 1%, or 1.1%?

Any standard, including absolute equality, involves a certain artificiality. As appellants point out, even the census data are not perfect, and the well-known restlessness of the American people means that population counts for particular localities are outdated long before they are completed. Yet problems with the data at hand apply equally to any population-based standard we could choose. As between two standards—equality or something less than equality—only the former reflects the aspirations of Article I, Section 2. [Accepting the] population deviations in this case would mean to reject the basic premise of *Kirkpatrick* and *Wesberry* [*v. Sanders*]. We decline appellants' invitation to go that far. The unusual rigor of their standard has been noted several times. Because of that rigor, we have required that absolute population equality be the paramount objective of apportionment only in the case of congressional districts, for which the command of Article I, Section 2 as regards the National Legislature outweighs the local interests that a State may deem relevant in apportioning districts for representatives to state and local legislatures. . . . The principle of population equality for congressional districts has not proved unjust or socially or economically harmful in experience. . . . If anything, this standard should cause less difficulty now for state legislatures than it did when we adopted it in *Wesberry.* The rapid advances in computer technology and education during the last two decades make it relatively simple to draw contiguous districts of equal population and at the same time to further whatever secondary goals the State has. Finally, to abandon unnecessarily a clear and oft-confirmed constitutional interpretation would impair our authority in other cases, . . . would implicitly open the door to a plethora of requests that we reexamine other rules that some may consider burdensome, and would prejudice those who have relied upon the rule of law in seeking an equipopulous congressional apportionment in New Jersey. . . . We thus reaffirm that there are no *de minimis* population variations, which could practicably be avoided, but which nonetheless meet the standard of Article I, Section 2, without justification.

The sole difference between appellants' theory and the argument we rejected in *Kirkpatrick* is that appellants have proposed a *de minimis* line that gives the illusion of rationality and predictability: the "inevitable statistical imprecision of the census." They argue: "Where, as here, the deviation from ideal district size is less than the known imprecision of the census figures, that variation is the functional equivalent of zero." . . . There are two problems with this approach. First, appellants concentrate on the extent to which the census systematically undercounts actual population—a figure which is not known precisely and which, even if it were known, would not be relevant to this case. Second, the mere existence of statistical imprecisions does not make small deviations among districts the functional equivalent of equality. . . .

The census may systematically undercount population, and the rate of undercounting may vary from place to place. Those facts, however, do not render meaningless the differences in population between congressional districts, as determined by uncorrected census counts. To the contrary, the census data provide the only reliable—albeit less than perfect—indication of the districts' "real" relative population levels. Even if one cannot say with certainty that one district is larger than another merely because it has a higher census count, one can say with certainty that the district with a larger census count is more likely to be larger than the other district than it is to be smaller or the same size. That certainty is sufficient for decision-making. . . . Furthermore, because the census count represents the "best population data available," . . . it is the only basis for good-faith attempts to achieve population equality. Attempts to explain population deviations on the basis of flaws in census data must be supported with a precision not achieved here. . . .

Given that the census-based population deviations in the Feldman Plan reflect real differences among the districts, it is clear that they could have been avoided or significantly reduced with a good-faith effort to achieve population equality. For that reason alone, it would be inappropriate to accept the Feldman Plan as "functionally equivalent" to a plan with districts of equal population.

The District Court found that several other plans introduced in the 200th Legislature had smaller maximum deviations than the Feldman Plan. . . . Appellants object that the alternative plans considered by the District Court were not comparable to the Feldman Plan because their political characters differed profoundly. . . . We have never denied that apportionment is a political process, or that state legislatures could pursue legitimate secondary objectives as long as those objectives were consistent with a good-faith effort to achieve population equality at the same time. Nevertheless, the claim that political considerations require population differences among congressional districts belongs more properly to the second level of judicial inquiry in these cases, . . . in which the State bears the burden of justifying the differences with particularity.

In any event, it was unnecessary for the District Court to rest its finding on the existence of alternative plans with radically different political effects. As in *Kirkpatrick,* "resort to the simple device of transferring entire political subdivisions of known population between contiguous districts would have produced districts much closer to numerical equality." . . . Starting with the Feldman Plan itself and the census data available to the legislature at the time it was enacted, . . . one can reduce the maximum population deviation of the plan merely by shifting a handful of municipalities from one district to another. . . .

Thus the District Court did not err in finding that the plaintiffs had met their burden of showing that the Feldman Plan did not come as nearly as practicable to population equality. . . .

By itself, the foregoing discussion does not establish that the Feldman Plan is unconstitutional. Rather, appellees' success in proving that the Feldman Plan was not the product of a good-faith effort to achieve population equality means only that the burden shifted to the State to prove that the population deviations in its plan were necessary to achieve some legitimate state objective. *White v. Weiser* demonstrates that we are willing to defer to state legislative policies, so long as they are consistent with constitutional norms, even if they require small differences in the population of congressional districts. . . . Any number of consistently applied legislative policies might justify some variance, including, for instance, making districts compact, respecting municipal boundaries, preserving the cores of prior districts, and avoiding contests between incumbent Representatives. As long as the criteria are nondiscriminatory, . . . these are all legitimate objectives that on a proper showing could justify minor population deviations. . . .

The State must, however, show with some specificity that a particular objective required the specific deviations in its plan, rather than simply relying on general assertions. The showing required to justify population deviations is flexible, depending on the size of the deviations, the importance of the State's interests, the consistency with which the plan as a whole reflects those interests, and the availability of alternatives that might substantially vindicate those interests yet approximate population equality more closely. By necessity, whether deviations are justified requires case-by-case attention to these factors. . . .

The District Court properly applied the two-part test of *Kirkpatrick v. Preisler* to New Jersey's 1982 apportionment of districts for the United States House of Representatives. It correctly held that the population deviations in the plan were not functionally equal as a matter of law, and it found that the plan was not a good-faith effort to achieve population equality using the best available census data. It also correctly rejected appellants' attempt to justify the population deviations as not supported by the evidence. The judgment of the District Court, therefore, is affirmed.

Justice Stevens, concurring. . . .

Justice White, with whom the *Chief Justice, Justice Powell,* and *Justice Rehnquist* join, dissenting.

. . . "[T]he achieving of fair and effective representation for all citizens is concededly the basic aim of legislative apportionment." . . . One must suspend credulity to believe that the Court's draconian response to a trifling 0.6984% maximum deviation promotes "fair and effective representation" for the people of New Jersey. . . .

There can be little question but that the variances in the New Jersey plan are "statistically insignificant." Although the Government strives to make the decennial census as accurate as humanly possible, the Census Bureau has never intimated that the results are a perfect count of the American population. The Bureau itself estimates the inexactitude in the taking of the 1970 census at 2.3%, a figure which is considerably larger than the 0.6984% maximum variance in the New Jersey plan, and which dwarfs the 0.2470% difference between the maximum deviations of the selected plan and the leading alternative plan. . . . Because the amount of undercounting differs from district to district, there is no point for a court of law to act under an unproved assumption that such tiny differences between redistricting plans reflect actual differences in population. . . .

Even if the 0.6984% deviation here is not encompassed within the scope of the statistical imprecision of the census, it is minuscule when compared with the variations among the districts inherent in translating census numbers into citizens' votes. First, the census "is more of an event than a process." . . . "It measures population at only a single instant in time. District populations are constantly changing, often at different rates in either direction, up or down." As the Court admits, "the well-known restlessness of the American people means that population counts for particular localities are outdated long before they are completed." . . . Second, far larger differences among districts are introduced because a substantial percentage of the total population is too young to register or is disqualified by alienage. Third, census figures cannot account for the proportion of all those otherwise eligible individuals who fail to register. The differences in the number of eligible voters per district for these reasons overwhelm the minimal variations attributable to the districting plan itself.

Accepting that the census, and the districting plans which are based upon it, cannot be perfect represents no backsliding in our commitment to assuring fair and equal representation in the election of Congress. I agree with the views of Judge Gibbons, who dissented in the District

Court, that Kirkpatrick should not be read as a "prohibition against toleration of *de minimis* population variances which have no statistically relevant effect on relative representation." A plus–minus deviation of 0.6984% surely falls within this category.

If today's decision simply produced an unjustified standard with little practical import, it would be bad enough. Unfortunately, I fear that the Court's insistence that "there are no *de minimis* population variations, which could practicably be avoided, but which nonetheless meet the standard of Article I, Section 2, without justification," . . . invites further litigation of virtually every congressional redistricting plan in the Nation. At least 12 States which have completed redistricting on the basis of the 1980 census have adopted plans with a higher deviation than that presented here, and 4 others have deviations quite similar to New Jersey's. Of course, under the Court's rationale, even Rhode Island's plan—whose two districts have a deviation of 0.02% or about 95 people—would be subject to constitutional attack.

In all such cases, state legislatures will be hard pressed to justify their preference for the selected plan. A good-faith effort to achieve population equality is not enough if the population variances are not "unavoidable." The court must consider whether the population differences could have been further "reduced or eliminated altogether." . . . With the assistance of computers, there will generally be a plan with an even more minimal deviation from the mathematical ideal. Then, "the State must bear the burden of proving that each significant variance between districts was necessary to achieve some legitimate goal." . . . As this case illustrates, literally any variance between districts will be considered "significant." . . .

Yet no one can seriously contend that such an inflexible insistence upon mathematical exactness will serve to promote "fair and effective representation." The more likely result of today's extension of *Kirkpatrick* is to move closer to fulfilling Justice Fortas' prophecy that "a legislature might have to ignore the boundaries of common sense, running the congressional district line down the middle of the corridor of an apartment house or even dividing the residents of a single-family house between two districts." . . . Such sterile and mechanistic application only brings the principle of "one man, one vote" into disrepute. . . .

Justice Powell, dissenting. . . .

Appendix A

THE CONSTITUTION OF THE UNITED STATES OF AMERICA

We the People of the United States, in Order to form a more perfect Union, establish Justice, insure domestic Tranquility, provide for the common defence, promote the general Welfare, and secure the Blessings of Liberty to ourselves and our Posterity, do ordain and establish this Constitution for the United States of America.

Article I

Section 1

All legislative Powers herein granted shall be vested in a Congress of the United States, which shall consist of a Senate and House of Representatives.

Section 2

(1) The House of Representatives shall be composed of Members chosen every second Year by the People of the several States, and the Electors in each State shall have the Qualifications requisite for Electors of the most numerous Branch of the State Legislature.

(2) No Person shall be a Representative who shall not have attained to the age of twenty-five Years, and been seven Years a Citizen of the United States, and who shall not, when elected, be an Inhabitant of that State in which he shall be chosen.

(3) Representatives and direct Taxes shall be apportioned among the several States which may be included within this Union, according to their respective Numbers, which shall be determined by adding to the whole Number of free Persons, including those bound to Service for a Term of Years, and excluding Indians not taxed, three fifths of all other Persons. The actual Enumeration shall be made within three Years after the first Meeting of the Congress of the United States, and within every subsequent Term of ten Years, in such Manner as they shall by Law direct. The Number of Representatives shall not exceed one for every thirty Thousand, but each State shall have at Least one Representative; and until such enumeration shall be made,

the State of New Hampshire shall be entitled to chuse three, Massachusetts eight, Rhode Island and Providence Plantations one, Connecticut five, New York six, New Jersey four, Pennsylvania eight, Delaware one, Maryland six, Virginia ten, North Carolina five, South Carolina five, and Georgia three.

(4) When vacancies happen in the Representation from any State, the Executive Authority thereof shall issue Writs of Election to fill such Vacancies.

(5) The House of Representatives shall chuse their Speaker and other Officers; and shall have the sole Power of Impeachment.

Section 3

(1) The Senate of the United States shall be composed of two Senators from each State, chosen by the Legislature thereof, for six Years; and each Senator shall have one Vote.

(2) Immediately after they shall be assembled in Consequence of the first Election, they shall be divided as equally as may be into three Classes. The Seats of the Senators of the first Class shall be vacated at the Expiration of the second Year, of the second Class at the Expiration of the fourth Year, and of the third Class at the Expiration of the sixth Year, so that one third may be chosen every second Year; and if Vacancies happen by Resignation, or otherwise, during the Recess of the Legislature of any State, the Executive thereof may make temporary Appointments until the next Meeting of the Legislature, which shall then fill such Vacancies.

(3) No Person shall be a Senator who shall not have attained, to the Age of thirty Years, and been nine Years a Citizen of the United States, and who shall not, when elected, be an Inhabitant of that State for which he shall be chosen.

(4) The Vice President of the United States shall be President of the Senate, but shall have no Vote, unless they be equally divided.

(5) The Senate shall chuse their other Officers, and also a President pro tempore, in the Absence of the Vice President, or when he shall exercise the Office of the President of the United States.

(6) The Senate shall have the sole Power to try all Impeachments. When sitting for that Purpose, they shall be on Oath or Affirmation. When the President of the United States is tried, the Chief Justice shall preside: And no Person shall be convicted without the Concurrence of two thirds of the Members present.

(7) Judgment in Cases of Impeachment shall not extend further than to removal from Office, and disqualification to hold and enjoy any Office of honor, Trust or Profit under the United States: but the Party convicted shall nevertheless be liable and subject to Indictment, Trial, Judgment and Punishment, according to Law.

Section 4

(1) The Times, Places and Manner of holding Elections for Senators and Representatives, shall be prescribed in each State by the Legislature thereof; but the Congress may at any time by Law make or alter such Regulations, except as to the Places of chusing Senators.

(2) The Congress shall assemble at least once in every Year, and such Meeting shall be on the first Monday in December, unless they shall by Law appoint a different Day.

Section 5

(1) Each House shall be the Judge of the Elections, Returns and Qualifications of its own Members, and a Majority of each shall constitute a Quorum to do Business; but a smaller Number may adjourn from day to day, and may be authorized to compel the Attendance of absent Members, in such Manner, and under such Penalties as each House may provide.

(2) Each House may determine the Rules of its Proceedings, punish its Members for disorderly Behaviour, and, with the Concurrence of two thirds, expel a Member.

(3) Each House shall keep a Journal of its Proceedings, and from time to time publish the same, excepting such Parts as may in their Judgment require Secrecy; and the Yeas and Nays of the Members of either House on any question shall, at the Desire of one fifth of those Present, be entered on the Journal.

(4) Neither House, during the Session of Congress, shall, without the Consent of the other, adjourn for more than three days, nor to any other Place than that in which the two Houses shall be sitting.

Section 6

(1) The Senators and Representatives shall receive a Compensation for their Services, to be ascertained by Law, and paid out of the Treasury of the United States. They shall in all Cases, except Treason, Felony and Breach of the Peace, be privileged from Arrest during their Attendance at the Session of their respective Houses, and in going to and returning from the same; and for any Speech or Debate in either House, they shall not be questioned in any other Place.

(2) No Senator or Representative shall, during the Time for which he was elected, be appointed to any civil Office under the Authority of the United States, which shall have been created, or the Emoluments whereof shall have been increased during such time; and no Person holding any Office under the United States, shall be a Member of either House during his Continuance in Office.

Section 7

(1) All Bills for raising Revenue shall originate in the House of Representatives; but the Senate may propose or concur with Amendments as on other Bills.

(2) Every Bill which shall have passed the House of Representatives and the Senate, shall, before it become a Law, be presented to the President of the United States; If he approve he shall sign it, but if not he shall return it, with his Objections to that House in which it shall have originated, who shall enter the Objections at large on their Journal, and proceed to reconsider it. If after such Reconsideration two thirds of that House shall agree to pass the Bill, it shall be sent, together with the Objections, to the other House, by which it shall likewise be reconsidered, and if approved by two thirds of that House, it shall become a Law. But in all such Cases the Votes of both Houses shall be determined by Yeas and Nays, and the Names of the Persons voting for and against the Bill shall be entered on the Journal of each House respectively. If any Bill shall not be returned by the President within ten Days (Sunday excepted) after it shall have been presented to him, the Same shall be a Law, in like Manner as if he had signed it, unless the Congress by their Adjournment prevent its Return, in which Case it shall not be a Law.

(3) Every Order, Resolution, or Vote to which the Concurrence of the Senate and House of Representatives may be necessary (except on a question of Adjournment) shall be presented to the President of the United States; and before the Same shall take Effect, shall be approved by him, or being disapproved by him, shall be repassed by two thirds of the Senate and House of Representatives, according to the Rules and Limitations prescribed in the Case of a Bill.

Section 8

(1) The Congress shall have Power To lay and collect Taxes, Duties, Imposts and Excises, to pay the Debts and provide for the common Defence and general Welfare of the United States; but all Duties, Imposts and Excises shall be uniform throughout the United States;

(2) To borrow Money on the credit of the United States;

(3) To regulate Commerce with foreign Nations, and among the several States, and with the Indian Tribes;

(4) To establish an uniform Rule of Naturalization, and uniform Laws on the subject of Bankruptcies throughout the United States;

(5) To coin Money, regulate the Value thereof, and of foreign Coin, and to fix the Standard of Weights and Measures;

(6) To provide for the Punishment of counterfeiting the Securities and current Coin of the United States;

(7) To establish Post Offices and post Roads;

(8) To promote the Progress of Science and useful Arts, by securing for limited Times to Authors and Inventors the exclusive Right to their respective Writings and Discoveries;

(9) To constitute Tribunals inferior to the supreme Court;

(10) To define and punish Piracies and Felonies committed on the high Seas, and Offenses against the Law of Nations;

(11) To declare War, grant Letters of Marque and Reprisal, and make Rules concerning Captures on Land and Water;

(12) To raise and support Armies, but no Appropriation of Money to that Use shall be for a longer Term than two Years;

(13) To provide and maintain a Navy;

(14) To make Rules for the Government and Regulation of the land and naval Forces;

(15) To provide for calling forth the Militia to execute the Laws of the Union, suppress Insurrections and repel Invasions;

(16) To provide for organizing, arming, and disciplining the Militia, and for governing such Part of them as may be employed in the Service of the United States, reserving to the States respectively, the Appointment of the Officers, and the Authority of training the Militia according to the discipline prescribed by Congress;

(17) To exercise exclusive Legislation in all Cases whatsoever, over such District (not exceeding ten Miles square) as may, by Cession of particular States, and the Acceptance of Congress, become the Seat of the Government of the United States, and to exercise like Authority over all Places purchased by the Consent of the Legislature of the State in which the Same shall be, for the Erection of Forts, Magazines, Arsenals, dock-Yards, and other needful Buildings;—And

(18) To make all Laws which shall be necessary and proper for carrying into Execution the foregoing Powers, and all other Powers vested by this Constitution in the Government of the United States, or in any Department or Officer thereof.

Section 9

(1) The Migration or Importation of such Persons as any of the States now existing shall think proper to admit, shall not be prohibited by the Congress prior to the Year one thousand eight hundred and eight, but a Tax or Duty may be imposed on such Importation, not exceeding ten dollars for each Person.

(2) The Privilege of the Writ of Habeas Corpus shall not be suspended unless when in Cases of Rebellion or Invasion the public Safety may require it.

(3) No Bill of Attainder or ex post facto Law shall be passed.

(4) No Capitation, or other direct, Tax shall be laid, unless in Proportion to the Census or Enumeration herein before directed to be taken.

(5) No Tax or Duty shall be laid on Articles exported from any State.

(6) No Preference shall be given by any Regulation of Commerce or Revenue to the Ports of one State over those of another; nor shall Vessels bound to, or from, one State, be obliged to enter, clear or pay Duties in another.

(7) No Money shall be drawn from the Treasury, but in Consequence of Appropriations made by Law; and a regular Statement and Account of the Receipts and Expenditures of all public Money shall be published from time to time.

(8) No Title of Nobility shall be granted by the United States: And no Person holding any Office of Profit or Trust under them, shall, without the Consent of the Congress, accept of any present, Emolument, Office, or Title, of any kind whatever, from any King, Prince or foreign State.

Section 10

(1) No State shall enter into any Treaty, Alliance, or Confederation; grant Letters of Marque and Reprisal; coin Money; emit Bills of Credit; make any Thing but gold and silver Coin a Tender in Payment of Debts; pass any Bill of Attainder, ex post facto Law, or Law impairing the Obligation of Contracts, or grant any Title of Nobility.

(2) No State shall, without the Consent of Congress, lay any Imposts or Duties on Imports or Exports, except what may be absolutely necessary for executing its inspection Laws: and the net Produce of all Duties and Imposts, laid by any State on Imports or Exports, shall be for the Use of the Treasury of the United States; and all such Laws shall be subject to the Revision and Control of the Congress.

(3) No State shall, without the Consent of Congress, lay any Duty of Tonnage, keep Troops, or Ships of War in time of Peace, enter into any Agreement or Compact with another State, or with a foreign Power, or engage in War, unless actually invaded, or in such imminent Danger as will not admit of Delay.

Article II

Section 1

(1) The executive Power shall be vested in a President of the United States of America. He shall hold his Office during the Term of four Years, and, together with the Vice President, chosen for the same Term, be elected, as follows:

(2) Each State shall appoint, in such Manner as the Legislature thereof may direct, a Number of Electors, equal to the whole Number of Senators and Representatives to which the State may be entitled in the Congress: but no Senator or Representative, or Person holding an Office of Trust or Profit under the United States, shall be appointed an Elector.

(3) The Electors shall meet in their respective States, and vote by Ballot for two Persons, of whom one at least shall not be an Inhabitant of the same State with themselves. And they shall make a List of all the Persons voted for, and of the Number of Votes for each; which List they shall sign and certify, and transmit sealed to the Seat of the Government of the United States, directed to the President of the Senate. The President of the Senate shall, in the presence of the Senate and House of Representatives, open all

the Certificates, and the Votes shall then be counted. The Person having the greatest Number of Votes shall be the President, if such Number be a Majority of the whole Number of Electors appointed; and if there be more than one who have such Majority, and have an equal Number of Votes, then the House of Representatives shall immediately chuse by Ballot one of them for President; and if no Person have a Majority, then from the five highest on the List the said House shall in like Manner chuse the President. But in chusing the President, the Votes shall be taken by States, the Representation from each State having one Vote; a quorum for this Purpose shall consist of a Member or Members from two thirds of the States, and a Majority of all the States shall be necessary to a Choice. In every Case, after the Choice of the President, the Person having the greatest Number of Votes of the Electors shall be the Vice President. But if there should remain two or more who have equal Votes, the Senate shall chuse from them by Ballot the Vice President.

(4) The Congress may determine the Time of chusing the Electors, and the Day on which they shall give their Votes; which Day shall be the same throughout the United States.

(5) No Person except a natural born Citizen, or a Citizen of the United States, at the time of the Adoption of this Constitution, shall be eligible to the Office of President; neither shall any Person be eligible to that Office who shall not have attained to the Age of thirty five Years, and been fourteen Years a Resident within the United States.

(6) In Case of the Removal of the President from Office, or of his Death, Resignation, or Inability to discharge the Powers and Duties of the said Office, the Same shall devolve on the Vice President, and the Congress may by Law provide for the Case of Removal, Death, Resignation or Inability, both of the President and Vice President, declaring what Officer shall then act as President, and such Officer shall act accordingly, until the Disability be removed, or a President shall be elected.

(7) The President shall, at stated Times, receive for his Services, a Compensation, which shall neither be increased nor diminished during the Period for which he shall have been elected, and he shall not receive within that Period any other Emolument from the United States, or any of them.

(8) Before he enter on the Execution of his Office, he shall take the following Oath or Affirmation:—"I do solemnly swear (or affirm) that I will faithfully execute the Office of President of the United States, and will to the best of my Ability, preserve, protect and defend the Constitution of the United States."

Section 2

(1) The President shall be Commander in Chief of the Army and Navy of the United States, and of the Militia of the several States, when called into the actual Service of the United States; he may require the Opinion, in writing, of the principal Officer in each of the executive Departments, upon any Subject relating to the Duties of their respective Offices, and he shall have Power to grant Reprieves and Pardons for Offenses against the United States, except in Cases of Impeachment.

(2) He shall have Power, by and with the Advice and Consent of the Senate, to make Treaties, provided two thirds of the Senators present concur; and he shall nominate, and by and with the Advice and Consent of the Senate, shall appoint Ambassadors, other public Ministers and Consuls, Judges of the supreme Court, and all other Officers of the United States, whose Appointments are not herein otherwise provided for, and which shall be established by Law: but the Congress may by Law vest the Appointment of such inferior Officers, as they think proper, in the President alone, in the Courts of Law, or in the Heads of Departments.

(3) The President shall have Power to fill up all Vacancies that may happen during the Recess of the Senate, by granting Commissions which shall expire at the End of their next Session.

Section 3

He shall from time to time give to the Congress Information of the State of the Union, and recommend to their Consideration such Measures as he shall judge necessary and expedient; he may, on extraordinary Occasions, convene both Houses, or either of them, and in Case of Disagreement between them, with Respect to the Time of Adjournment, he may adjourn them to such Time as he shall think proper; he shall receive Ambassadors and other public Ministers; he shall take Care that the Laws be faithfully executed, and shall Commission all the Officers of the United States.

Section 4

The President, Vice President and all Civil Officers of the United States, shall be removed from Office on Impeachment for, and Conviction of, Treason, Bribery, or other high Crimes and Misdemeanors.

Article III

Section 1

The judicial Power of the United States, shall be vested in one supreme Court, and in such inferior Courts as the Congress may from time to time ordain and establish. The Judges, both of the supreme and inferior Courts, shall hold their Offices during good Behaviour, and shall, at stated Times, receive for their Services, a Compensation, which shall not be diminished during their Continuance in Office.

Section 2

(1) The judicial Power shall extend to all Cases, in Law and Equity, arising under this Constitution, the Laws of the United States, and Treaties made, or which shall be made, under their Authority;—to all Cases affecting Ambassadors, other public Ministers and Consuls;—to all Cases of admiralty and maritime Jurisdiction;—to Controversies to which the United States shall be a party;—to Controversies be-

tween two or more States;—between a State and Citizens of another State;—between Citizens of different States;—between Citizens of the same State claiming Lands under Grants of different States, and between a State, or the Citizens thereof, and foreign States, Citizens or Subjects.

(2) In all Cases affecting Ambassadors, other public Ministers and Consuls, and those in which a State shall be Party, the supreme Court shall have original Jurisdiction. In all the other Cases before mentioned, the supreme Court shall have appellate Jurisdiction, both as to Law and Fact, with such Exceptions, and under such Regulations as the Congress shall make.

(3) The Trial of all Crimes, except in Cases of Impeachment, shall be by Jury; and such Trial shall be held in the State where the said Crimes shall have been committed; but when not committed within any State, the Trial shall be at such Place or Places as the Congress may by Law have directed.

Section 3

(1) Treason against the United States, shall consist only in levying War against them, or in adhering to their Enemies, giving them Aid and Comfort. No Person shall be convicted of Treason unless on the Testimony of two Witnesses to the same overt Act, or on Confession in open Court.

(2) The Congress shall have Power to declare the Punishment of Treason, but no Attainder of Treason shall work Corruption of Blood, or Forfeiture except during the Life of the Person attainted.

Article IV

Section 1

Full Faith and Credit shall be given in each State to the public Acts, Records, and judicial Proceedings of every other State. And the Congress may by general Laws prescribe the Manner in which such Acts, Records and Proceedings shall be proved, and the Effect thereof.

Section 2

(1) The Citizens of each State shall be entitled to all privileges and Immunities of Citizens in the several States.

(2) A Person charged in any State with Treason, Felony, or other Crime, who shall flee from Justice, and be found in another State, shall on Demand of the executive Authority of the State from which he fled, be delivered up, to be removed to the State having Jurisdiction of the Crime.

(3) No Person held to Service of Labour in one State, under the Laws thereof, escaping into another, shall, in Consequence of any Law or Regulation therein, be discharged from such Service or Labour, but shall be delivered up on Claim of the Party to whom such Service or Labour may be due.

Section 3

(1) New States may be admitted by the Congress into this Union; but no new State shall be formed or erected within the Jurisdiction of any other State; nor any State be formed by the Junction of two or more States, or Parts of States, without the Consent of the Legislatures of the States concerned as well as of the Congress.

(2) The Congress shall have power to dispose of and make all needful Rules and Regulations respecting the Territory or other Property belonging to the United States; and nothing in this Constitution shall be so construed as to Prejudice any Claims of the United States, or of any particular State.

Section 4

The United States shall guarantee to every State in this Union a Republican Form of Government, and shall protect each of them against Invasion; and on Application of the Legislature, or of the Executive (when the Legislature cannot be convened) against domestic Violence.

Article V

The Congress, whenever two thirds of both Houses shall deem it necessary, shall propose Amendments to this Constitution, or, on the Application of the Legislatures of two thirds of the several States, shall call a Convention for proposing Amendments, which, in either Case, shall be valid to all Intents and Purposes, as Part of this Constitution, when ratified by the Legislatures of three fourths of the several States, or by Conventions in three fourths thereof, as the one or the other Mode of Ratification may be proposed by the Congress; Provided that no Amendment which may be made prior to the Year One thousand eight hundred and eight shall in any Manner affect the first and fourth Clauses in the Ninth Section of the first Article; and that no State, without its Consent, shall be deprived of its equal Suffrage in the Senate.

Article VI

(1) All Debts contracted and Engagements entered into, before the Adoption of this Constitution, shall be as valid against the United States under this Constitution, as under the Confederation.

(2) This Constitution, and the Laws of the United States which shall be made in Pursuance thereof; and all Treaties made, or which shall be made, under the Authority of the United States, shall be the supreme Law of the Land; and the Judges in every State shall be bound thereby, any Thing in the Constitution or Laws of any State to the Contrary notwithstanding.

(3) The Senators and Representatives before mentioned, and the Members of the several State Legislatures, and all executive and judicial Officers, both of the United States and of the several States, shall be bound by Oath or Affirmation, to support this Constitution; but no religious Test shall ever be required as a Qualification to any Office or public Trust under the United States.

Article VII

The Ratification of the Conventions of nine States, shall be sufficient for the Establishment of this Constitution between the States so ratifying the Same.

Articles in Addition to, and Amendment of, the Constitution of the United States of America, Proposed by Congress, and Ratified by the Several States, Pursuant to the Fifth Article of the Original Constitution

Amendments I – X   Bill of Rights

Amendment I (1791)

Congress shall make no law respecting an establishment of religion, or prohibiting the free exercise thereof; or abridging the freedom of speech, or of the press; or the right of the people peaceably to assemble, and to petition the Government for a redress of grievances.

Amendment II (1791)

A well regulated Militia, being necessary to the security of a free state, the right of the people to keep and bear Arms, shall not be infringed.

Amendment III (1791)

No Soldier shall, in time of peace be quartered in any house, without the consent of the Owner, nor in time of war, but in a manner to be prescribed by law.

Amendment IV (1791)

The right of the people to be secure in their persons, houses, papers, and effects, against unreasonable searches and seizures, shall not be violated, and no Warrants shall issue, but upon probable cause, supported by Oath or affirmation, and particularly describing the place to be searched, and the persons or things to be seized.

Amendment V (1791)

No person shall be held to answer for a capital, or otherwise infamous crime, unless on a presentment or indictment of a Grand Jury, except in cases arising in the land or naval forces, or in the Militia, when in actual service in time of War or public danger; nor shall any person be subject for the same offence to be twice put in jeopardy of life or limb; nor shall be compelled in any criminal case to be a witness against himself, nor be deprived of life, liberty, or property, without due process of law; nor shall private property be taken for public use, without just compensation.

Amendment VI (1791)

In all criminal prosecutions, the accused shall enjoy the right to a speedy and public trial, by an impartial jury of the State and district wherein the crime shall have been committed, which district shall have been previously ascertained by law, and to be informed of the nature and cause of the accusation; to be confronted with the witnesses against him; to have compulsory process for obtaining witnesses in his favor, and to have the Assistance of Counsel for his defence.

Amendment VII (1791)

In Suits at common law, where the value in controversy shall exceed twenty dollars, the right of trial by jury shall be preserved, and no fact tried by a jury, shall be otherwise reexamined in any Court of the United States, than according to the rules of the common law.

Amendment VIII (1791)

Excessive bail shall not be required, nor excessive fines imposed, nor cruel and unusual punishments inflicted.

Amendment IX (1791)

The enumeration in the Constitution, of certain rights, shall not be construed to deny or disparage others retained by the people.

Amendment X (1791)

The powers not delegated to the United States by the Constitution, nor prohibited by it to the States, are reserved to the States respectively, or to the people.

Amendment XI (1798)

The Judicial power of the United States shall not be construed to extend to any suit in law or equity, commenced or prosecuted against one of the United States by Citizens of another State, or by Citizens or Subjects of any Foreign State.

Amendment XII (1804)

The Electors shall meet in their respective states and vote by ballot for President and Vice-President, one of whom, at least, shall not be an inhabitant of the same state with themselves; they shall name in their ballots the person voted for as President, and in distinct ballots the person voted for as Vice-President, and they shall make distinct lists of all persons voted for as President, and of all persons voted for as Vice-President, and of the number of votes for each, which lists they shall sign and certify, and transmit sealed to the seat of the government of the United States, directed to the President of the Senate;—The President of the Senate shall, in the presence of the Senate and House of Representatives, open all the certificates and the votes shall then be counted;—The person having the greatest number of votes for President, shall be the President, if such number be a majority of the whole number of Electors appointed; and if no person have such majority, then from the persons having the highest numbers not exceeding three on the list of those voted for as President, the House of Representatives shall choose immediately, by ballot, the President. But in choosing the President, the votes shall be taken by states, the representation from each state having one vote; a quorum for this purpose shall consist of a member or members from two-thirds of the states, and a majority of all the states shall be necessary to a choice. And if the House of Representatives shall not choose a President whenever the right of choice shall devolve upon them, before the fourth day of March next following, then the Vice-President shall act as President, as in the case of the death or other constitutional disability of the President—The person having the greatest number of votes as Vice-President, shall be the Vice-President, if such number be a majority of the whole number of Electors appointed, and if no person have a majority, then from the two highest numbers on the list, the Senate shall choose the Vice-President; A quorum for the purpose shall consist of two-thirds of the whole number of Senators, and a majority of the whole number shall be necessary to a choice. But no person constitutionally ineligible to the office of President shall be eligible to that of Vice-President of the United States.

Amendment XIII (1865)

Section 1
Neither slavery nor involuntary servitude, except as a punishment for crime whereof the party shall have been duly convicted, shall exist within the United States, or any place subject to their jurisdiction.

Section 2
Congress shall have power to enforce this article by appropriate legislation.

Amendment XIV (1868)

Section 1
All persons born or naturalized in the United States and subject to the jurisdiction thereof, are citizens of the United States and of the State wherein they reside. No State shall make or enforce any law which shall abridge the privileges or immunities of citizens of the United States; nor shall any State deprive any person of life, liberty, or property, without due process of law; nor deny to any person within its jurisdiction the equal protection of the laws.

Section 2
Representatives shall be apportioned among the several States according to their respective numbers, counting the whole number of persons in each State, excluding Indians not taxed. But when the right to vote at any election for the choice of electors for President and Vice-President of the United States, Representatives in Congress, the Executive and Judicial officers of a State, or the members of the Legislature thereof, is denied to any of the male inhabitants of such State, being twenty-one years of age, and citizens of the United States, or in any way abridged, except for participation in rebellion, or other crime, the basis of representation therein shall be reduced in the proportion which the number of such male citizens shall bear to the whole number of male citizens twenty-one years of age in such State.

Section 3
No person shall be a Senator or Representative in Congress, or elector of President and Vice-President, or hold any office, civil or military, under the United States, or under any State, who, having previously taken an oath, as a member of Congress, or as an officer of the United States, or as a member of any State legislature, or as an executive or judicial officer of any State, to support the Constitution of the United States, shall have engaged in insurrection or rebellion against the same, or given aid or comfort to the enemies thereof. But Congress may by a vote of two-thirds of each House, remove such disability.

Section 4
The validity of the public debt of the United States, authorized by law, including debts incurred for payment of pensions and bounties for services in suppressing insurrection or rebellion, shall not be questioned. But neither the United States nor any State shall assume or pay any debt or obligation incurred in aid of insurrection or rebellion against the United States, or any claim for the loss or emancipation of any slave; but all such debts, obligations and claims shall be held illegal and void.

Section 5
The Congress shall have power to enforce, by appropriate legislation, the provisions of this article.

Amendment XV (1870)

Section 1
The right of citizens of the United States to vote shall not be denied or abridged by the United States or by any State on account of race, color, or previous condition of servitude.

Section 2
The Congress shall have power to enforce this article by appropriate legislation.

Amendment XVI (1913)

The Congress shall have power to lay and collect taxes on incomes, from whatever source derived, without apportionment among the several States, and without regard to any census or enumeration.

Amendment XVII (1913)

The Senate of the United States shall be composed of two Senators from each State, elected by the people thereof, for six years; and each Senator shall have one vote. The electors in each State shall have the qualifications requisite for electors of the most numerous branch of the State legislatures.

When vacancies happen in the representation of any State in the Senate, the executive authority of such State shall issue writs of election to fill such vacancies: Provided, That the legislature of any State may empower the executive thereof to make temporary appointments until the people fill the vacancies by election as the legislature may direct.

This amendment shall not be so construed as to affect the election or term of any Senator chosen before it becomes valid as part of the Constitution.

Amendment XVIII (1919)

Section 1
After one year from the ratification of this article the manufacture, sale, or transportation of intoxicating liquors within, the importation thereof into, or the exportation thereof from the United States and all territory subject to the jurisdiction thereof for beverage purposes is hereby prohibited.

Section 2
The Congress and the several States shall have concurrent power to enforce this article by appropriate legislation.

Section 3
This article shall be inoperative unless it shall have been ratified as an amendment to the Constitution by the legisla-

tures of the several States, as provided in the Constitution, within seven years from the date of the submission hereof to the States by the Congress.

Amendment XIX (1920)

The right of citizens of the United States to vote shall not be denied or abridged by the United States or by any State on account of sex.

Congress shall have power to enforce this article by appropriate legislation.

Amendment XX (1933)

Section 1
The terms of the President and Vice President shall end at noon on the 20th day of January, and the terms of Senators and Representatives at noon on the 3d day of January, of the years in which such terms would have ended if this article had not been ratified; and the terms of their successors shall then begin.

Section 2
The Congress shall assemble at least once in every year, and such meeting shall begin at noon on the 3d day of January, unless they shall by law appoint a different day.

Section 3
If, at the time fixed for the beginning of the term of the President, the President elect shall have died, the Vice President elect shall become President. If a President shall not have been chosen before the time fixed for the beginning of his term, or if the President elect shall have failed to qualify, then the Vice President elect shall act as President until a President shall have qualified; and the Congress may by law provide for the case wherein neither a President elect nor a Vice President elect shall have qualified, declaring who shall then act as President, or the manner in which one who is to act shall be selected, and such person shall act accordingly until a President or Vice President shall have qualified.

Section 4
The Congress may by law provide for the case of the death of any of the persons from whom the House of Representatives may choose a President whenever the right of choice shall have devolved upon them, and for the case of the death of any of the persons from whom the Senate may choose a Vice President whenever the right of choice shall have devolved upon them.

Section 5
Sections 1 and 2 shall take effect on the 15th day of October following the ratification of this article.

Section 6

This article shall be inoperative unless it shall have been ratified as an amendment to the Constitution by the legislatures of three-fourths of the several States within seven years from the date of its submission.

Amendment XXI (1933)

Section 1

The eighteenth article of amendment to the Constitution of the United States is hereby repealed.

Section 2

The transportation or importation into any State, Territory or possession of the United States for delivery or use therein of intoxicating liquors, in violation of the laws thereof, is hereby prohibited.

Section 3

This article shall be inoperative unless it shall have been ratified as an amendment to the Constitution by conventions in the several States, as provided in the Constitution, within seven years from the date of the submission hereof to the States by the Congress.

Amendment XXII (1951)

Section 1

No person shall be elected to the office of the President more than twice, and no person who has held the office of President, or acted as President, for more than two years of a term to which some other person was elected President shall be elected to the office of the President more than once. But this Article shall not apply to any person holding the office of President when this Article was proposed by the Congress, and shall not prevent any person who may be holding the office of President, or acting as President, during the term within which this Article becomes operative from holding the office of President or acting as President during the remainder of such term.

Section 2

This Article shall be inoperative unless it shall have been ratified as an amendment to the Constitution by the legislatures of three-fourths of the several States within seven years from the date of its submission to the States by the Congress.

Amendment XXIII (1961)

Section 1

The District constituting the seat of Government of the United States shall appoint in such manner as the Congress may direct:

A number of electors of President and Vice President equal to the whole number of Senators and Representatives in Congress to which the District would be entitled if it were a State, but in no event more than the least populous State; they shall be in addition to those appointed by the States, but they shall be considered, for the purposes of the election of President and Vice President, to be electors appointed by a State; and they shall meet in the District and perform such duties as provided by the twelfth article of amendment.

Section 2

The Congress shall have power to enforce this article by appropriate legislation.

Amendment XXIV (1964)

Section 1

The right of citizens of the United States to vote in any primary or other election for President or Vice President, for electors for President or Vice President, or for Senator or Representative in Congress, shall not be denied or abridged by the United States or any State by reason of failure to pay any poll tax or other tax.

Section 2

The Congress shall have power to enforce this article by appropriate legislation.

Amendment XXV (1967)

Section 1

In case of the removal of the President from office or of his death or resignation, the Vice President shall become President.

Section 2

Whenever there is a vacancy in the office of the Vice President, the President shall nominate a Vice President who shall take office upon confirmation by a majority vote of both Houses of Congress.

Section 3

Whenever the President transmits to the President pro tempore of the Senate and the Speaker of the House of Representatives his written declaration that he is unable to discharge the powers and duties of his office, and until he transmits to them a written declaration to the contrary, such powers and duties shall be discharged by the Vice President as Acting President.

Section 4

Whenever the Vice President and a majority of either the principal officers of the executive departments or of such other body as Congress may by law provide, transmit to the President pro tempore of the Senate and the Speaker of the House of Representatives their written declaration that the President is unable to discharge the powers and duties of his office, the Vice President shall immediately assume the powers and duties of the office as Acting President.

Thereafter, when the President transmits to the President pro tempore of the Senate and the Speaker of the House of Representatives his written declaration that no inability exists, he shall resume the powers and duties of his office unless the Vice President and a majority of either the principal officers of the executive department or of such other body as Congress may by law provide, transmit within four days to the President pro tempore of the Senate and the Speaker of the House of Representatives their written declaration that the President is unable to discharge the powers and duties of his office. Thereupon Congress shall decide the issue, assembling within forty-eight hours for that purpose if not in session. If the Congress, within twenty-one days after receipt of the latter written declaration, or, if Congress is not in session, within twenty-one days after Congress is required to assemble, determines by two-thirds vote of both Houses that the President is unable

to discharge the powers and duties of his office, the Vice President shall continue to discharge the same as Acting President; otherwise, the President shall resume the powers and duties of his office.

Amendment XXVI (1971)

Section 1
The right of citizens of the United States, who are eighteen years of age or older, to vote shall not be denied or abridged by the United States or by any State on account of age.

Section 2
The Congress shall have power to enforce this article by appropriate legislation.

Amendment XXVII (1992)

No law, varying the compensation for the services of the Senators and Representatives, shall take effect, until an election of Representatives shall have intervened.

CHRONOLOGY OF JUSTICES OF THE UNITED STATES SUPREME COURT

Year of Court as Constituted	Chief Justice	Associate Justices							
1789	Jay	Rutledge, J.	Cushing	Wilson	Blair				
1790–91	Jay	Rutledge, J.	Cushing	Wilson	Blair	Iredell			
1792	Jay	Johnson, T.	Cushing	Wilson	Blair	Iredell			
1793–94	Jay	Paterson	Cushing	Wilson	Blair	Iredell			
1795	Rutledge, J.	Paterson	Cushing	Wilson	Blair	Iredell			
1796–97	Ellsworth	Paterson	Cushing	Wilson	Chase, S.	Iredell			
1798–99	Ellsworth	Paterson	Cushing	Washington	Chase, S.	Iredell			
1800	Ellsworth	Paterson	Cushing	Washington	Chase, S.	Moore			
1801–03	Marshall, J.	Paterson	Cushing	Washington	Chase, S.	Moore			
1804–05	Marshall, J.	Paterson	Cushing	Washington	Chase, S.	Johnson, W.			
1806	Marshall, J.	Livingston	Cushing	Washington	Chase, S.	Johnson, W.			
1807–10	Marshall, J.	Livingston	Cushing	Washington	Chase, S.	Johnson, W.	Todd		
1811–12	Marshall, J.	Livingston	Story	Washington	Duvall	Johnson, W.	Todd		
1813–25	Marshall, J.	Thompson	Story	Washington	Duvall	Johnson, W.	Todd		
1826–28	Marshall, J.	Thompson	Story	Washington	Duvall	Johnson, W.	Trimble		
1829	Marshall, J.	Thompson	Story	Washington	Duvall	Johnson, W.	McLean		
1830–34	Marshall, J.	Thompson	Story	Baldwin	Duvall	Johnson, W.	McLean		
1835	Marshall, J.	Thompson	Story	Baldwin	Duvall	Wayne	McLean		
1836	Taney	Thompson	Story	Baldwin	Barbour	Wayne	McLean		
1837–40	Taney	Thompson	Story	Baldwin	Barbour	Wayne	McLean	Catron	McKinley
1841–44	Taney	Thompson	Story	Baldwin	Daniel	Wayne	McLean	Catron	McKinley
1845	Taney	Nelson	Woodbury	(vacant)	Daniel	Wayne	McLean	Catron	McKinley
1846–50	Taney	Nelson	Woodbury	Grier	Daniel	Wayne	McLean	Catron	McKinley
1851–52	Taney	Nelson	Curtis	Grier	Daniel	Wayne	McLean	Catron	McKinley
1853–57	Taney	Nelson	Curtis	Grier	Daniel	Wayne	McLean	Catron	Campbell
1858–60	Taney	Nelson	Clifford	Grier	Daniel	Wayne	McLean	Catron	Campbell

*Congress ended the use of a ten-person Court in this year.

Year of Court as Constituted	Chief Justice	Associate Justices								
1861	Taney	Nelson	Clifford	Grier	(vacant)	Wayne	McLean	Catron	Campbell	
1862	Taney	Nelson	Clifford	Grier	Miller	Wayne	Swayne	Catron	Davis	
1863	Taney	Nelson	Clifford	Grier	Miller	Wayne	Swayne	Catron	Davis	Field
1864–65	Chase, S. P.	Nelson	Clifford	Grier	Miller	Wayne	Swayne	Catron	Davis	Field
1866–67	Chase, S. P.	Nelson	Clifford	Grier	Miller	Wayne	Swayne	(ended)*	Davis	Field
1868–69	Chase, S. P.	Nelson	Clifford	Grier	Miller	(vacant)	Swayne		Davis	Field
1870–71	Chase, S. P.	Nelson	Clifford	Strong	Miller	Bradley	Swayne		Davis	Field
1872–73	Chase, S. P.	Hunt	Clifford	Strong	Miller	Bradley	Swayne		Davis	Field
1874–76	Waite	Hunt	Clifford	Strong	Miller	Bradley	Swayne		Davis	Field
1877–79	Waite	Hunt	Clifford	Strong	Miller	Bradley	Swayne		Harlan	Field
1880	Waite	Hunt	Clifford	Woods	Miller	Bradley	Swayne		Harlan	Field
1881	Waite	Hunt	Gray	Woods	Miller	Bradley	Matthews		Harlan	Field
1882–87	Waite	Blatchford	Gray	Woods	Miller	Bradley	Matthews		Harlan	Field
1888	Fuller	Blatchford	Gray	Lamar, L.	Miller	Bradley	Matthews		Harlan	Field
1889	Fuller	Blatchford	Gray	Lamar, L.	Miller	Bradley	Brewer		Harlan	Field
1890–91	Fuller	Blatchford	Gray	Lamar, L.	Brown	Bradley	Brewer		Harlan	Field
1892	Fuller	Blatchford	Gray	Lamar, L.	Brown	Shiras	Brewer		Harlan	Field
1893	Fuller	Blatchford	Gray	Jackson, H.	Brown	Shiras	Brewer		Harlan	Field
1894	Fuller	White	Gray	Jackson, H.	Brown	Shiras	Brewer		Harlan	Field
1895–97	Fuller	White	Gray	Peckham	Brown	Shiras	Brewer		Harlan	Field
1898–1901	Fuller	White	Gray	Peckham	Brown	Shiras	Brewer		Harlan	McKenna
1902	Fuller	White	Holmes	Peckham	Brown	Shiras	Brewer		Harlan	McKenna
1903–05	Fuller	White	Holmes	Peckham	Brown	Day	Brewer		Harlan	McKenna
1906–08	Fuller	White	Holmes	Peckham	Moody	Day	Brewer		Harlan	McKenna
1909	Fuller	White	Holmes	Lurton	Moody	Day	Brewer		Harlan	McKenna
1910–11	White, E.	Van Devanter	Holmes	Lurton	Lamar, J.	Day	Hughes		Harlan	McKenna
1912–13	White, E.	Van Devanter	Holmes	Lurton	Lamar, J.	Day	Hughes		Pitney	McKenna
1914–15	White, E.	Van Devanter	Holmes	McReynolds	Lamar, J.	Day	Hughes		Pitney	McKenna
1916–20	White, E.	Van Devanter	Holmes	McReynolds	Brandeis	Day	Clarke		Pitney	McKenna
1921	Taft	Van Devanter	Holmes	McReynolds	Brandeis	Day	Clarke		Pitney	McKenna
1922	Taft	VanDevanter	Holmes	McReynolds	Brandeis	Butler	Sutherland		Pitney	McKenna
1923–24	Taft	Van Devanter	Holmes	McReynolds	Brandeis	Butler	Sutherland		Sanford	McKenna

Year of Court as Constituted	Chief Justice	Associate Justices							
1925–29	Taft	Van Devanter	Holmes	McReynolds	Brandeis	Butler	Sutherland	Sanford	Stone
1930–31	Hughes	Van Devanter	Holmes	McReynolds	Brandeis	Butler	Sutherland	Roberts	Stone
1932–36	Hughes	Van Devanter	Cardozo	McReynolds	Brandeis	Butler	Sutherland	Roberts	Stone
1937	Hughes	Black	Cardozo	McReynolds	Brandeis	Butler	Sutherland	Roberts	Stone
1938	Hughes	Black	Cardozo	McReynolds	Brandeis	Butler	Reed	Roberts	Stone
1939	Hughes	Black	Frankfurter	McReynolds	Douglas	Butler	Reed	Roberts	Stone
1940	Hughes	Black	Frankfurter	McReynolds	Douglas	Murphy	Reed	Roberts	Stone
1941–42	Stone	Black	Frankfurter	Byrnes	Douglas	Murphy	Reed	Roberts	Jackson, R.
1943–44	Stone	Black	Frankfurter	Rutledge, W.	Douglas	Murphy	Reed	Roberts	Jackson, R.
1945	Stone	Black	Frankfurter	Rutledge, W.	Douglas	Murphy	Reed	Burton	Jackson, R.
1946–48	Vinson	Black	Frankfurter	Rutledge, W.	Douglas	Murphy	Reed	Burton	Jackson, R.
1949–52	Vinson	Black	Frankfurter	Minton	Douglas	Clark	Reed	Burton	Jackson, R.
1953–54	Warren	Black	Frankfurter	Minton	Douglas	Clark	Reed	Burton	Jackson, R.
1955	Warren	Black	Frankfurter	Minton	Douglas	Clark	Reed	Burton	Harlan
1956	Warren	Black	Frankfurter	Brennan	Douglas	Clark	Reed	Burton	Harlan
1957	Warren	Black	Frankfurter	Brennan	Douglas	Clark	Whittaker	Burton	Harlan
1958–61	Warren	Black	Frankfurter	Brennan	Douglas	Clark	Whittaker	Stewart	Harlan
1962–65	Warren	Black	Goldberg	Brennan	Douglas	Clark	White, B.	Stewart	Harlan
1965–67	Warren	Black	Fortas	Brennan	Douglas	Clark	White, B.	Stewart	Harlan
1967–69	Warren	Black	Fortas	Brennan	Douglas	Marshall, T.	White, B.	Stewart	Harlan
1969	Burger	Black	Fortas	Brennan	Douglas	Marshall, T.	White, B.	Stewart	Harlan
1969–70	Burger	Black	(vacant)	Brennan	Douglas	Marshall, T.	White, B.	Stewart	Harlan
1970–71	Burger	Black	Blackmun	Brennan	Douglas	Marshall, T.	White, B.	Stewart	Harlan
1972–75	Burger	Powell	Blackmun	Brennan	Douglas	Marshall, T.	White, B.	Stewart	Rehnquist
1975–81	Burger	Powell	Blackmun	Brennan	Stevens	Marshall, T.	White, B.	Stewart	Rehnquist
1981–86	Burger	Powell	Blackmun	Brennan	Stevens	Marshall, T.	White, B.	O'Connor	Rehnquist
1986–87	Rehnquist	Powell	Blackmun	Brennan	Stevens	Marshall, T.	White, B.	O'Connor	Scalia
1987–90	Rehnquist	Kennedy	Blackmun	Brennan	Stevens	Marshall, T.	White, B.	O'Connor	Scalia
1990–91	Rehnquist	Kennedy	Blackmun	Souter	Stevens	Marshall, T.	White, B.	O'Connor	Scalia
1991–93	Rehnquist	Kennedy	Blackmun	Souter	Stevens	Thomas	White, B.	O'Connor	Scalia
1993–94	Rehnquist	Kennedy	Blackmun	Souter	Stevens	Thomas	Ginsburg	O'Connor	Scalia
1994–	Rehnquist	Kennedy	Breyer	Souter	Stevens	Thomas	Ginsburg	O'Connor	Scalia

Appendix C

SUPREME COURT JUSTICES

by Appointing President,
State Appointed From, and
Political Party

President/Justices Appointed	State Appointed from	Political Party
Washington		
John Jay (1745–1829)*	N.Y.	Federalist
John Rutledge (1739–1800)	S.C.	Federalist
William Cushing (1732–1810)	Mass.	Federalist
James Wilson (1724–1798)	Pa.	Federalist
John Blair (1732–1800)	Va.	Federalist
James Iredell (1751–1799)	N.C.	Federalist
Thomas Johnson (1732–1819)	Md.	Federalist
William Paterson (1745–1806)	N.J.	Federalist
Samuel Chase (1741–1811)	Md.	Federalist
Oliver Ellsworth (1745–1807)	Conn.	Federalist
Adams, J.		
Bushrod Washington (1762–1829)	Va.	Federalist
Alfred Moore (1755–1810)	N.C.	Federalist
John Marshall (1755–1835)	Va.	Federalist
Jefferson		
William Johnson (1771–1834)	S.C.	Democratic—Republican
Henry Livingston (1757–1823)	N.Y.	Democratic—Republican
Thomas Todd (1765–1826)	Va.	Democratic—Republican
Madison		
Gabriel Duvall (1752–1844)	Md.	Democratic—Republican
Joseph Story (1779–1845)	Mass.	Democratic—Republican

C-1

President/Justices Appointed	State Appointed from	Political Party
Monroe		
Smith Thompson (1768–1843)	N.Y.	Democratic—Republican
Adams, J. Q.		
Robert Trimble (1776–1828)	Ky.	Democratic—Republican
Jackson		
John McLean (1785–1861)	Ohio	Democrat (later Rep.)
Henry Baldwin (1780–1844)	Penn.	Democrat
James M. Wayne (1790–1867)	Ga.	Democrat
Roger B. Taney (1777–1864)	Va.	Democrat
Philip P. Barbour (1783–1841)	Va.	Democrat
Van Buren		
John Catron (1778–1865)	Tenn.	Democrat
John McKinley (1780–1852)	Ala.	Democrat
Peter V. Daniel (1784–1860)	Va.	Democrat
Tyler		
Samuel Nelson (1792–1873)	N.Y.	Democrat
Polk		
Levi Woodbury (1789–1851)	N.H.	Democrat
Robert C. Grier (1794–1870)	Pa.	Democrat
Fillmore		
Benjamin R. Curtis (1809–1874)	Mass.	Whig
Pierce		
John A. Campbell (1811–1889)	Ala.	Democrat
Buchanan		
Nathan Clifford (1803–1881)	Maine	Democrat
Lincoln		
Noah H. Swayne (1804–1884)	Ohio	Republican
Samuel F. Miller (1816–1890)	Iowa	Republican
David Davis (1815–1886)	Ill.	Republican (later Dem.)
Stephen J. Field (1816–1899)	Calif.	Democrat
Salmon P. Chase (1808–1873)	Ohio	Republican
Grant		
William Strong (1808–1895)	Pa.	Republican
Joseph P. Bradley (1813–1892)	N.J.	Republican
Ward Hunt (1810–1886)	N.Y.	Republican
Morrison Waite (1816–1888)	Ohio	Republican

President/Justices Appointed	State Appointed from	Political Party
Hayes		
John M. Harlan (1833–1911)	Ky.	Republican
William B. Woods (1824–1887)	Ga.	Republican
Garfield		
Stanley Matthews (1824–1889)	Ohio	Republican
Arthur		
Horace Gray (1828–1902)	Mass.	Republican
Samuel Blatchford (1820–1893)	N.Y.	Republican
Cleveland		
Lucius Q. C. Lamar (1825–1893)	Miss.	Democrat
Melville W. Fuller (1833–1910)	Ill.	Democrat
Harrison		
David J. Brewer (1837–1910)	Kans.	Republican
Henry B. Brown (1836–1913)	Mich.	Republican
George Shiras, Jr. (1832–1924)	Pa.	Republican
Howell E. Jackson (1832–1895)	Tenn.	Democrat
Cleveland		
Edward D. White (1845–1921)	La.	Democrat
Rufus W. Peckham (1838–1909)	N.Y.	Democrat
McKinley		
Joseph McKenna (1843–1926)	Calif.	Republican
Roosevelt, T.		
Oliver W. Holmes (1841–1935)	Mass.	Republican
William R. Day (1849–1923)	Ohio	Republican
William H. Moody (1853–1917)	Mass.	Republican
Taft		
Horace H. Lurton (1844–1914)	Tenn.	Democrat
Charles E. Hughes (1862–1948)	N.Y.	Republican
Willis Van Devanter (1859–1941)	Wyo.	Republican
Joseph R. Lamar (1857–1916)	Ga.	Democrat
Mahlon Pitney (1858–1924)	N.J.	Republican
Wilson		
James C. McReynolds (1862–1946)	Tenn.	Democrat
Louis D. Brandeis (1856–1941)	Mass.	Independent
John H. Clarke (1857–1945)	Ohio	Democrat

President/Justices Appointed	State Appointed from	Political Party
Harding		
William H. Taft (1857–1930)	Conn.	Republican
George Sutherland (1862–1942)	Utah	Republican
Pierce Butler (1866–1939)	Minn.	Democrat
Edward T. Sanford (1865–1930)	Tenn.	Republican
Coolidge		
Harlan F. Stone (1872–1946)	N.Y.	Republican
Hoover		
Owen J. Roberts (1875–1955)	Pa.	Republican
Benjamin N. Cardozo (1870–1938)	N.Y.	Democrat
Roosevelt, F. D.		
Hugo L. Black (1886–1971)	Ala.	Democrat
Stanley F. Reed (1884–1980)	Ky.	Democrat
Felix Frankfurter (1882–1965)	Mass.	Independent
William O. Douglas (1898–1980)	Conn.	Democrat
Frank Murphy (1890–1949)	Mich.	Democrat
James F. Byrnes (1879–1972)	S.C.	Democrat
Robert H. Jackson (1892–1954)	N.Y.	Democrat
Wiley B. Rutledge (1894–1949)	Iowa	Democrat
Truman		
Harold H. Burton (1888–1964)	Ohio	Republican
Fred M. Vinson (1890–1953)	Ky.	Democrat
Tom C. Clark (1899–1977)	Texas	Democrat
Sherman Minton (1890–1965)	Ind.	Democrat
Eisenhower		
Earl Warren (1891–1974)	Calif.	Republican
John M. Harlan (1899–1971)	N.Y.	Republican

President/Justices Appointed	State Appointed from	Political Party
William J. Brennan (b. 1906)	N.J.	Democrat
Charles E. Whittaker (1901–1973)	Mo.	Republican
Potter Stewart (1915–1986)	Ohio	Republican
Kennedy		
Byron R. White (b. 1917)	Colo.	Democrat
Arthur J. Goldberg (b. 1908)	Ill.	Democrat
Johnson, L. B.		
Abe Fortas (1910–1982)	Tenn.	Democrat
Thurgood Marshall (b. 1908)	N.Y.	Democrat
Nixon		
Warren E. Burger (b. 1907)	Minn.	Republican
Harry R. Blackmun (b. 1908)	Minn.	Republican
Lewis F. Powell, Jr. (b. 1907)	Va.	Democrat
William H. Rehnquist (b. 1924)	Ariz.	Republican
Ford		
John Paul Stevens (b. 1920)	Ill.	Republican
Reagan		
Sandra Day O'Connor (b. 1930)	Ariz.	Republican
Antonin Scalia (b. 1936)	N.J.	Republican
Anthony M. Kennedy (b. 1936)	Calif.	Republican
Bush		
David Souter (b. 1939)	N.H.	Republican
Clarence Thomas (b. 1948)	Va.	Republican
Clinton		
Ruth Bader Ginsburg (b. 1933)	Washington, D.C.	Democrat
Stephen G. Breyer (b. 1938)	Mass.	Democrat

*Dates in parentheses indicate birth and death dates.

GLOSSARY

a fortiori   With greater force of reason.

abate   To do away with or lessen the impact of, as in abatement of a nuisance.

abortion   The intentional termination of a pregnancy through destruction of the fetus.

abrogate   To annul, destroy, or cancel.

abstention   The doctrine under which the U.S. Supreme Court and other federal courts do not decide on, or interfere with, state cases even when empowered to do so. This doctrine is typically invoked when a case can be decided on the basis of state law.

accessory   A person who aids in the commission of a crime.

accessory after the fact   A person who with knowledge that a crime has been committed conceals or protects the offender.

accessory before the fact   A person who aids or assists another in commission of an offense.

accomplice   A person who voluntarily unites with another in commission of an offense.

accusatorial system   A system of criminal justice in which the prosecution bears the burden of proving the defendant's guilt.

acquittal   A judicial finding that a defendant is not guilty of a crime with which he or she has been charged.

act of omission   The failure to perform an act required by law.

actual damages   Money awarded to a plaintiff in a civil suit to compensate for injuries to that party's rights.

actual imprisonment standard   The standard governing the applicability of the federal constitutional right of an indigent person to have counsel appointed in a misdemeanor case. In order for the right to be violated, the indigent defendant must actually be sentenced to jail time after having been tried without appointed counsel.

actual malice   The deliberate intention to cause harm or injury.

actual possession   Possession of something with the possessor having immediate control.

actus reus   A "wrongful act" that, combined with other necessary elements of crime, constitutes criminal liability.

ad hoc   "For this." For a special purpose.

ad hoc **balancing**   An effort by a court to balance competing interests in the context of the unique facts of a given case. In constitutional law, this term is used most frequently in connection with the adjudication of First Amendment issues.

ad litem   For the lawsuit; pending the lawsuit, as in "guardian *ad litem.*"

ad valorem   "According to the value." Referring to a tax or duty guaranteed according to the assessed value of the matter taxed.

adjudication   The formal process by which courts decide cases.

adjudicatory hearing   A proceeding in juvenile court to determine whether a juvenile has committed an act of delinquency.

administrative law   The body of law dealing with the structure, authority, policies, and procedures of administrative and regulatory agencies.

Administrative Procedure Act   1946 Act of Congress specifying rule making and adjudicatory procedures for federal agencies.

administrative searches   Searches of premises by a government official to determine compliance with health and safety regulations.

adultery   Voluntary sexual intercourse where at least one of the parties is married to someone other than the sexual partner.

adversary proceeding   A legal action involving parties with adverse or opposing interests. A basic aspect of the American legal system, the adversary proceeding provides the framework within which most constitutional cases are decided. For an exception to this generalization, see *ex parte.*

adversary system   A system of justice involving conflicting parties where the role of the judge is to remain neutral.

advisory opinion   A judicial opinion, not involving adverse parties in a "case or controversy," that is given at the request of the legislature or the executive. It has been a long-standing policy of the U.S. Supreme Court not to render advisory opinions.

affiant   A person who makes an affidavit.

affidavit   A person's voluntary sworn declaration attesting to a set of facts.

affirm   To uphold, ratify, or approve.

affirmative action   A program under which women and/or persons of particular minority groups are granted special consideration in employment, government contracts, and/or admission to programs of higher education.

aggravating circumstances   Factors attending the commission of a crime that make the crime or its consequences worse.

aggravating factors   See **aggravating circumstances.**

aiding and abetting   Assisting in or otherwise facilitating the commission of a crime.

alibi   Defense to a criminal charge that places the defendant at some place other than the scene of the crime at the time the crime occurred.

allegation   Assertion or claim made by a party to a legal action.

amendment   A modification, addition, or deletion.

Americans with Disabilities Act   1990 federal statute forbidding discrimination on grounds of disability and guaranteeing access for the handicapped to public buildings.

amici   "Friends," usually in reference to "friends of the Court." See **amicus curiae.**

amicus curiae   "Friend of the court." An individual or organization allowed to take part in a judicial proceeding, not as one of the adversaries, but as a party interested in the outcome. Usually an *amicus curiae* files a brief in support of one side or the other but occasionally takes a more active part in the argument of the case.

amnesty   A blanket pardon issued to a large group of lawbreakers.

anonymous tip   Information from an unknown source concerning alleged criminal activity.

answer brief   The appellee's written response to the appellant's law brief filed in an appellate court.

anticipatory search warrant   A search warrant issued based on an affidavit that at a future time evidence of a crime will be at a specific place.

appeal   Review by a higher court of a lower court decision.

appeal by right   An appeal brought to a higher court as a matter of right under federal or state law.

appellant   A person who takes an appeal to a higher court.

appellate courts   Judicial tribunals that review decisions from lower tribunals.

appellate jurisdiction   The legal authority of a court of law to hear an appeal from or otherwise review a decision by a lower court.

appellee   The party against whom a case is appealed to a higher court.

appointment power   The power of the president to appoint, with the consent of the Senate, judges, ambassadors, and high-level executive officials.

apportionment   The allocation of representatives among a set of legislative districts.

arguendo   For the sake of argument.

arraignment   An appearance before a court of law for the purpose of pleading to a criminal charge.

arrest   To take someone into custody or otherwise deprive that person of freedom of movement.

arrest warrant   A document issued by a magistrate or judge directing that a named person be taken into custody for allegedly having committed an offense.

arrestee   A person who is arrested.

Article I, Section 8   Key section of the Constitution outlining the powers of Congress.

Articles of Confederation   The constitution under which the United States was governed between 1781 and 1789.

assault   The attempt or threat to inflict bodily injury upon another person.

assign   To transfer or grant a legal right.

assignee   One to whom a legal right is transferred.

assignments of error   A written presentation to an appellate court identifying the points the appellant claims constitute errors made by the lower tribunal.

asylum   Sanctuary; a place of refuge.

at bar   Before the court, as in "the case at bar."

at-large election   An election in which a number of officials are chosen to represent the district, as opposed to an arrangement under which each of the officials represents one smaller district or ward.

attempt   An intent to commit a crime coupled with an act taken toward committing the offense.

attorney general   The highest legal officer of a state or of the United States.

attorney–client privilege   The right of a person (client) not to testify about matters discussed in confidence with an attorney in the course of the attorney's representation.

automobile exception   The warrantless search of a vehicle by police who have probable cause to search but because of exigent circumstances it is impracticable to secure a warrant.

automobile search   The search of an automobile by police, usually performed without a warrant.

bad tendency test   A restrictive interpretation of the First Amendment under which government may prohibit expression having a tendency to cause people to break the law.

bail The conditional release from custody of a person charged with a crime pending adjudication of the case.

battery The unlawful use of force against another person that entails some injury or offensive touching.

bench trial A trial before a judge rather than a jury.

bench warrant An arrest warrant issued by a judge.

benevolent neutrality An approach to interpreting the Establishment Clause of the First Amendment that holds that government can and should take a benevolent posture toward religion while at the same time being officially neutral on such matters.

beyond a reasonable doubt The standard of proof that is constitutionally required to be introduced before a defendant can be found guilty of a crime or before a juvenile can be adjudicated a delinquent.

bicameralism The characteristic of having two houses or chambers. The U.S. Congress is a bicameral body in that it has a Senate and a House of Representatives.

bifurcated trial A capital trial with separate phases for determining guilt and punishment.

bigamy The crime of being married to more than one person at the same time.

bill of attainder A legislative act imposing punishment on a party without the benefit of a judicial proceeding.

Bill of Rights The first ten amendments to the U.S. Constitution, ratified in 1791, concerned primarily with individual rights and liberties.

Black Codes Statutes enacted in Southern states after the Civil War denying African-Americans a number of basic rights.

bloc A group of decision makers in a collegial body who usually vote the same way. In judicial politics, the term refers to groups of judges or justices on appellate courts who usually vote together.

bona fide "In good faith"; without the attempt to defraud or deceive.

border search A search of persons entering the borders of the United States.

bounty hunter A person paid a fee or commission to capture a defendant who had fled a jurisdiction to escape punishment.

Brady Bill Legislation passed by Congress in 1993 requiring a five-day waiting period before the purchase of a handgun during which time a background check is conducted on the buyer.

Brandeis brief Pioneered by attorney Louis D. Brandeis in 1908, this type of appellate brief emphasizes empirical evidence of the social or economic impact of law, as distinguished from a conventional brief that focuses solely on legal analysis.

breach of contract The violation of a provision in a legally enforceable agreement that gives the damaged party the right to recourse in a court of law.

breach of the peace The crime of disturbing the public tranquility and order. A generic term encompassing disorderly conduct, riot, etc.

brief In the judicial process, a document submitted by counsel setting forth legal arguments germane to a particular case; in the study of constitutional law, a summary of a given case, reviewing the essential facts, issues, holdings, and reasoning of the court.

burden of persuasion The legal responsibility of a party to convince a court of the correctness of a position asserted.

burden of production of evidence The obligation of a party to produce some evidence in support of a proposition asserted.

burden of proof The requirement to introduce evidence to prove an alleged fact or set of facts.

bureaucracy Any large, complex, hierarchical organization staffed by appointed officials.

business affected with a public interest A nineteenth century doctrine holding that certain businesses are more closely associated with the public interest and are therefore more subject to government regulation.

cabinet The collective term for the heads of the executive departments of the federal government, such as the secretary of state, the attorney general, and the secretary of defense.

capias "That you take." A general term for various court orders requiring that some named person be taken into custody.

capital offense A crime punishable by death.

capital punishment The death penalty.

capitalist economy An economy based on private ownership and free enterprise.

carnal knowledge Sexual intercourse.

case A legal dispute between adverse parties to be resolved by a court of law.

case law Law derived from judicial decisions, also known as decisional law.

case or controversy requirement Article III of the U.S. Constitution extends the federal judicial power to actual cases or controversies, not to hypothetical or abstract questions of law.

case reporter A series of books reprinting the decisions of a given court or set of courts. For example, the decisions of the U.S. Courts of Appeals are reported in the *Federal Reporter,* published by West Publishing Company.

castle doctrine "A man's home is his castle." At common law, the right to use whatever force is necessary to protect one's dwelling and its inhabitants from an unlawful entry or attack.

causation An act that produces an event or an effect.

cause A synonym for case. See also **probable cause, show cause.**

caveat emptor   "Let the buyer beware." Common-law maxim requiring the consumer to judge the quality of a product before making a purchase.

censorship   Broadly defined, any restriction imposed by the government on speech, publication, or other form of expression.

certification   A procedure under which a lower court requests a decision by a higher court on specified questions in a case, pending a final decision by the lower court.

certiorari   "To be informed." A petition similar to an appeal, but it may be granted or refused at the discretion of the appellate court.

certiorari, writ of   An order from a higher court to a lower court directing that the record of a particular case be sent up for review. See also **certiorari.**

challenge for cause   Objection to a prospective juror on some specified ground (e.g., a close relationship to a party to the case).

change of venue   The removal of a legal proceeding, usually a trial, to a new location.

checks and balances   Refers to constitutional powers granted each branch of government to prevent one branch from dominating the others.

child benefit theory   The doctrine that government assistance to religious schools can be justified if the effect is to benefit the child rather than to promote religion.

chilling effect   The effect of discouraging persons from exercising their rights.

circumstantial evidence   Indirect evidence from which the existence of certain facts may be inferred.

citation   (1) A summons to appear in court, often used in traffic violations. (2) A reference to a statute or court decision, often designating a publication where the law or decision appears.

civil action   A lawsuit brought to enforce private rights and to remedy violations thereof.

civil case   See **civil action.**

civil infractions   Noncriminal violation of a law, often referring to minor traffic violations.

civil law   (1) The law relating to rights and obligations of parties. (2) The body of law, based essentially on Roman law, that exists in most non-English-speaking nations.

civil liberties   The freedoms protected by the Constitution and statutes, for example, freedom of speech, religion, and assembly.

civil rights   Legal protection against invidious discrimination in citizens' exercise of the rights of life, liberty, and property. The right to equality before the law and equal treatment by government.

Civil Rights Act of 1866   Federal civil rights law passed after the Civil War aimed at eliminating the discriminatory Black Codes enacted by Southern states.

Civil Rights Act of 1875   Federal civil rights law aimed at ending racial discrimination by places of public accommodation. Declared unconstitutional in 1883.

Civil Rights Act of 1964   Landmark civil rights statute aimed at ending racial discrimination in employment and by places of public accommodation.

Civil Rights movement   The social movement beginning in the 1950s aimed at securing civil rights for African-Americans.

civil service   The system under which government employees are selected and retained based on merit, rather than political patronage.

civil suit   See **civil action.**

Civil War Amendments   Reference to the Thirteenth, Fourteenth, and Fifteenth Amendments to the U.S. Constitution.

claim of right   A contention that an item was taken in a good-faith belief that it belonged to the taker; sometimes asserted as a defense to a charge of larceny or theft.

class action   A lawsuit brought by one or more parties on behalf of themselves and others similarly situated.

classical conservatism   Traditional conservatism stressing preservation of order and maintenance of traditional values.

clear and convincing evidence standard   An evidentiary standard that is higher than the standard of "preponderance of the evidence" applied in civil cases, but lower than the standard of "beyond a reasonable doubt" applied in criminal cases. For example, under the new federal standard for the affirmative defense of insanity, the defendant must establish the defense of insanity by "clear and convincing evidence."

clear and present danger doctrine   The doctrine that the First Amendment protects expression up to the point that it poses a clear and present danger of bringing about some substantive evil that government has a right to prevent.

clear and probable danger test   A somewhat more restrictive First Amendment test than clear and present danger. The test is "whether the gravity of the 'evil,' discounted by its improbability, justifies such invasion of speech as is necessary to avoid the danger."

clemency   A grant of mercy by an executive official commuting a sentence or pardoning a criminal.

closing arguments   Arguments presented at trial by counsel at the conclusion of the presentation of evidence.

closure of pretrial proceedings   Decision by a judge to close proceedings prior to trial of a criminal case in order to protect the defendant's right to a fair trial.

code   A systematic collection of laws.

coercive federalism   Reference to the fact that the federal government often uses federal grants to coerce states into adopting policies the federal government cannot directly mandate.

collateral attack   The attempt to defeat the outcome of a judicial proceeding by challenging it in another court.

collateral estoppel   A rule barring the making of a claim in one judicial proceeding that has been adjudicated in another, earlier proceeding.

comity   Courtesy, respect, civility. A matter of good will and tradition, rather than of right. Particularly important in a federal system where one jurisdiction is bound to respect the judgments of another.

commander in chief   Refers to the president's authority to command the armed forces of the country.

commercial speech   Commercial advertising, now viewed as entitled to some protection under the First Amendment.

common law   A body of law that develops primarily through judicial decisions, rather than legislative enactments. The common law is not a fixed system but an ever-changing body of rules and principles articulated by judges and applied to changing needs and circumstances. See also **English Common law.**

community control   A sentence imposed on a person found guilty of a crime that requires that the offender be placed in an individualized program of noninstitutional confinement.

community service   A sentence requiring that the criminal perform some specific service to the community for some specified period of time.

community standards   Standards of decency which may vary from community to community.

commutation   A form of clemency that lessens the punishment for a person convicted of a crime.

comparative proportionality review   A judicial examination to determine whether the sentence imposed in a given criminal case is proportionate to sentences imposed in similar cases.

compelling government interest   A government interest sufficiently strong that it overrides the fundamental rights of persons adversely affected by government action or policy.

compelling interest   An interest or justification of the highest order.

competency   The state of being legally fit to give testimony or stand trial.

complicity   A person's voluntary participation with another person in commission of a crime or wrongful act.

comprehensive planning   A guide for the orderly development of a community, usually implemented by enactment of zoning ordinances.

compulsory process   The requirement that witnesses appear and testify in court or before a legislative committee. See also **subpoena.**

compulsory self-incrimination   The requirement that an individual give testimony leading to his or her own criminal conviction. Forbidden by the U.S. Constitution, Amendment V.

compulsory sterilization   Requiring an individual to undergo procedures that render him or her unable to conceive children.

concurrent jurisdiction   Jurisdiction that is shared by different courts of law.

concurrent powers   Powers exercised jointly by the state and federal governments.

concurrent resolution   An act expressing the will of both houses of the legislature but lacking a mechanism through which to enforce that will on parties outside the legislature.

concurrent sentencing   The practice in which a trial court imposes separate sentences that may be served at the same time.

concurring in the judgment   An agreement by a judge or justice in the judgment of an appellate court without necessarily agreeing to the court's reasoning processes.

concurring opinion   An opinion by a judge or justice agreeing with the decision of the court. A concurring opinion may or may not agree with the rationale adopted by the court in reaching its decision (see **Opinion of the Court**).

conditions of probation   A set of rules that must be observed by a person placed on probation.

conference   As applied to the appellate courts, a private meeting of judges to decide a case or to determine whether to grant review in a case.

confidential informant   An informant known to the police but whose identity is held in confidence.

conscientious objector   One who opposes military service on religious or moral grounds.

consecutive sentencing   The practice in which a trial court imposes a sentence or sentences to be served following completion of a prior sentence or sentences.

consent   Voluntarily yielding to the will or desire of another person.

consent decree   A court-enforced agreement reached by mutual consent of parties in a civil case or administrative proceeding.

consent to a search   The act of a person voluntarily permitting police to conduct a search of person or property.

conspiracy   The crime of two or more persons planning to commit a specific criminal act.

constitutional case   A judicial proceeding involving an issue of constitutional law.

constitutional law   The fundamental and supreme law of the land defining the structure and powers of government and the rights of individuals vis-à-vis government.

constitutional right of privacy   The right to make choices in matters of intimate personal concern without interference by government.

constitutional supremacy   The doctrine that the Constitution is the supreme law of the land and that all actions and policies of government must be consistent with it.

constitutional theory   (1) Broad term referring to theories about the Constitution generally, or particular theories about particular provisions of the Constitution. (2) In the area of the presidency, the theory that the president can exercise only those powers specifically granted by Article II.

construction   Interpretation.

contemnor   A person found to be in contempt of court.

contempt   An action that embarrasses, hinders, obstructs, or is calculated to lessen the dignity of a judicial or legislative body.

contempt of Congress   Any action that embarrasses, hinders, obstructs, or is calculated to lessen the dignity of Congress.

contempt of court   Any action that embarrasses, hinders, obstructs, or is calculated to lessen the dignity of a court of law.

content-neutral   Refers to a time, place, or manner regulation that is enforced without regard to the content of expression.

continuance   Delay of a judicial proceeding on the motion of one of the parties.

contraband   Any property that is inherently illegal to produce or possess.

Contract Clause   Provision of Article I, Section 10, forbidding states from impairing the obligations of contracts.

contracts   Legally binding agreements between or among specific parties.

contractual immunity   A grant by a prosecutor with approval of court that makes a witness immune from prosecution for the witness' testimony.

controlled substance   A drug designated by law as contraband.

convening authorities   The military authorities with jurisdiction to convene a court-martial for trial of persons subject to the Uniform Code of Military Justice.

conversion   The unlawful assumption of the rights of ownership to someone else's property.

cooperative federalism   A modern approach to American federalism in which powers and functions are shared among national, state, and local authorities.

corporal punishment   Punishment that inflicts pain or injury on a person's body.

corpus delicti   "The body of the crime." The material thing upon which a crime has been committed (e.g., a burned-out building in a case of arson).

corrections system   The system of prisons, jails, and other penal and correctional institutions.

corroboration   Evidence that strengthens or validates evidence already given.

counsel   A lawyer who represents a party.

Court of Appeals for the Armed Forces   A court consisting of five civilian judges that reviews sentences affecting a general or flag officer or imposing the death penalty as well as cases certified for review by the judge advocate general of a branch of service. May grant review of convictions and sentences on petitions by service members.

court of general jurisdiction   A trial court with broad authority to hear and decide a wide range of civil and criminal cases.

court of last resort   The highest court in a judicial system, the last resort for deciding appeals.

court of limited jurisdiction   A trial court with narrow authority to hear and decide cases, typically misdemeanors and/or small claims.

court system   A set of trial and appellate courts established to resolve legal disputes in a particular jurisdiction.

court-martial   A military tribunal convened by a commander of a military unit to try a person subject to the Uniform Code of Military Justice who is accused of violating a provision of that code.

court-ordered busing   Refers to court orders requiring that public school students be transported to different schools to alleviate racial segregation.

courts of general jurisdiction   Courts that conduct trials in felony and major misdemeanor cases. Also refers to courts that have jurisdiction to hear civil as well as criminal cases.

courts of limited jurisdiction   Courts that handle pretrial matters and conduct trials in minor misdemeanor cases.

creation science   The idea that there are scientific reasons to believe in creationism as opposed to evolution.

criminal   Pertaining to crime; a person convicted of a crime.

criminal action   A judicial proceeding initiated by government against a person charged with the commission of a crime.

criminal case   A judicial proceeding in which a person is accused of a crime.

criminal conspiracy   See **conspiracy.**

criminal contempt   Punishment imposed by a judge against a person who violates a court order or otherwise intentionally interferes with the administration of the court.

criminal intent   A necessary element of a crime—the evil intent associated with the criminal act.

criminal law   The law defining crimes and punishments.

criminal negligence   A failure to exercise the degree of caution or care necessary to avoid being charged with a crime.

criminal procedure   The rules of law governing the procedures by which crimes are investigated, prosecuted, adjudicated, and punished.

criminal prosecution   Legal action brought against a person accused of a crime.

criminal responsibility Refers to the set of doctrines under which individuals are held accountable for criminal conduct.

criminal syndicalism The crime of advocating violence as a means to accomplish political change (archaic).

criminology The study of the nature of, causes of, and means of dealing with crime.

critical pretrial stages Significant procedural steps that occur preliminary to a criminal trial. A defendant has the right to counsel at these critical stages.

cross-examination The process of interrogating a witness who has testified on direct examination by asking the witness questions concerning testimony given. Cross-examination is designed to bring out any bias or inconsistencies in the witness's testimony.

cruel and unusual punishments Degrading punishment that shocks the moral standards of the community, e.g., torturing or physically beating a prisoner.

culpability Guilt.

curtilage At common law, the enclosed space surrounding a dwelling house; in modern codes this space has been extended to encompass other buildings.

custodial interrogation Questioning by the police of a suspect in custody.

damages Monetary compensation awarded by a court to a person who has suffered injuries or losses to person or property as a result of someone else's conduct.

de facto "In fact"; as a matter of fact.

de facto segregation Racial segregation that exists in fact even though it is not required by law.

de jure In law; as a matter of law.

de jure discrimination Discrimination that results from law, whether on its face or as applied.

de minimis Minimal, trifling, trivial.

de novo Anew; for a second time.

deadlocked jury A jury where the jurors cannot agree on a verdict.

deadly force The degree of force that may result in the death of the person against whom the force is applied.

death penalty Capital punishment; a sentence to death for the commission of a crime.

death-qualified jury A trial jury composed of persons who do not entertain scruples against imposing a death sentence.

decision on the merits A judicial decision that reaches the subject matter of a case.

decisional law Law declared by appellate courts in their written decisions and opinions.

declaratory judgment A judicial ruling conclusively declaring the rights, duties, or status of the parties but imposing no additional order, restriction, or requirement on them.

defamation A tort involving the injury to one's reputation by the malicious or reckless dissemination of a falsehood.

defendant A person charged with a crime or against whom a civil action is brought.

defense A defendant's stated reasons of law or fact as to why the prosecution or plaintiff should not prevail.

defense attorneys Lawyers who represent defendants in criminal cases.

definite sentencing Legislatively determined sentencing with no discretion given to judges or corrections officials to individualize punishment.

delegation of legislative power A legislative act authorizing an administrative or regulatory agency to promulgate rules and regulations having the force of law.

delinquency petition A written document alleging that a juvenile has committed an offense and asking the court to hold an adjudicatory hearing to determine the merits of the petition.

demurrer An action of a defendant admitting to a set of alleged facts but nevertheless challenging the legal sufficiency of a complaint or criminal charge.

Department of Justice The department of the federal government that is headed by the attorney general and staffed by U.S. attorneys.

deposition The recorded sworn testimony of a witness; not given in open court.

derivative evidence Evidence that is derived from or obtained only as a result of other evidence.

desegregation Efforts to eliminate de jure or de facto racial segregation.

detention Holding someone in custody.

detention hearing A proceeding held to determine whether a juvenile charged with an offense should be detained pending an adjudicatory hearing.

determinate sentence Variation on definite sentencing whereby a judge fixes the term of incarceration within statutory limits.

determinate sentencing The process of sentencing whereby the judge sets a fixed term of years within statutory parameters and the offender must serve that term without possibility of early release.

deterrence Prevention of criminal activity by punishing criminals so that others will not engage in such activity.

dicta See **obiter dicta.**

diplomatic immunity A privilege to be free from arrest and prosecution granted under international law to diplomats, their staffs, and household members.

direct contempt An obstructive or insulting act committed by a person in the immediate presence of the court.

direct evidence Evidence that applies directly to proof of a fact or proposition. For example, a witness who testifies to having seen an act done or heard a statement made is giving direct evidence.

direct filing   A term often used in reference to a prosecutor filing an information charging a juvenile with an offense rather than filing a petition in juvenile court to declare the juvenile delinquent for having committed an offense.

direct–indirect test   A test once used by the Supreme Court in its Commerce Clause jurisprudence. Under this test, a statute was valid only if the targeted activity had a direct impact on interstate commerce.

directed verdict   A verdict rendered by a jury upon direction of the presiding judge.

discrete and insular minorities   Minority groups that are locked out of the political process.

discretion   The power of public officials to act in certain situations according to their own judgment rather than relying on set rules or procedures.

discretionary review   Form of appellate court review of lower court decisions that is not mandatory but occurs at the discretion of the appellate court. See also **certiorari.**

discuss list   The list of petitions for certiorari that are deemed worthy of discussion in conference.

dismissal   A judicial order terminating a case.

disorderly conduct   Illegal behavior that disturbs the public peace or order.

disparate impact   A facially neutral law or policy that has a differential impact on members of different races or genders.

disposition   The final settlement of a case.

dissent   An appellate judge's formal vote against the judgment of the court in a given case.

dissenting opinion   A written opinion by a judge or justice setting forth reasons for disagreeing with a particular decision of the court.

distinction between manufacturing and commerce An important element of the Supreme Court's Commerce Clause jurisprudence in the late nineteenth and early twentieth century. The distinction between manufacturing, or production, on the one hand, and commerce, or distribution, on the other hand, served to limit the reach of Congress's power under the Commerce Clause.

distributive articles   Articles I, II, and III of the U.S. Constitution, delineating the powers and functions of the legislative, executive, and judicial branches, respectively, of the national government.

diversity jurisdiction   The authority of a federal court to entertain a civil suit in which the parties are citizens of different states and the amount in controversy exceeds fifty thousand dollars.

diversity of citizenship action   A federal civil suit in which the parties are citizens of different states and the amount in controversy exceeds seventy-five thousand dollars.

diversity of citizenship jurisdiction   The authority of federal courts to hear lawsuits in which the parties are citizens of different states and the amount in controversy exceeds seventy-five thousand dollars.

docket   The set of cases pending before a court of law.

doctor-assisted suicide   Administration by a physician of lethal drugs or gas to a terminally ill patient in order to produce death.

doctrine   A legal principle or rule developed through judicial decisions.

doctrine of abstention   The doctrine that federal courts should refrain from interfering with state judicial processes.

doctrine of harmless error   The doctrine that holds that an error committed by a lower tribunal shall be deemed harmless and thus no ground for reversal of the lower tribunal's judgment. To be considered harmless, an error of constitutional magnitude must be found by the appellate court to be "harmless beyond any reasonable doubt."

doctrine of incorporation   The doctrine under which provisions of the Bill of Rights are held to be incorporated within the Due Process Clause of the Fourteenth Amendment and are thereby made applicable to actions of the state and local governments.

doctrine of original intent   The doctrine that the Constitution is to be understood in terms of the intentions of the framers.

doctrine of overbreadth   This doctrine enables a person to make a facial challenge to a law on the ground that the law might be applied in the future against activities protected by the First Amendment.

doctrine of saving construction   The doctrine under which courts adopt an interpretation of a statute saves the statute from being declared unconstitutional.

doctrine of strict necessity   The doctrine under which courts engage in judicial review only when strictly necessary to the settlement of a case.

double jeopardy   The condition of being prosecuted a second time for the same offense.

drug courier profile   A controversial law enforcement practice of identifying possible drug smugglers by relying on a set of characteristics and patterns of behavior believed to typify persons who smuggle drugs.

drug paraphernalia   Items closely associated with the use of illegal drugs.

drug testing   The practice of subjecting employees to urine tests to determine whether they are using illegal substances.

dual federalism   A concept of federalism in which the national and state governments exercise authority within separate, self-contained areas of public policy and public administration.

Due Process Clause   Refers to clauses in both the Fifth and Fourteenth Amendments that prohibit government from taking a person's life, liberty, or property without due process of law.

Due Process Clause of the Fourteenth Amendment The provision of the Fourteenth Amendment that prohibits states from taking a person's life, liberty, or property without due process of law.

due process of law Procedural and substantive rights of citizens against government actions that threaten the denial of life, liberty, or property.

duress The use of illegal confinement or threats of harm to coerce someone to do something he or she would not do otherwise.

duty An obligation that a person has by law or contract.

easement A right of use over the property of another. This term frequently refers to a right-of-way across privately owned land.

ecclesiastical Pertaining to religious laws or institutions.

economic due process Refers to the doctrine under which the Supreme Court in the late nineteenth and early twentieth centuries used the Due Process Clauses of the Fifth and Fourteenth Amendments to protect free enterprise from government intervention.

economic freedom Another term for free enterprise, that is, the ability to conduct one's business without interference by government.

economic protectionism An attempt by one state to protect its domestic economy from outside competition.

Eighth Amendment The provisions of the Bill of Rights prohibiting excessive bail, excessive fines, and cruel and unusual punishments.

electoral college The body of electors chosen by the voters of each state and the District of Columbia for the purpose of formally electing the president and vice-president of the United States. The number of electors (538) is equivalent to the total number of representatives and senators to which each state is entitled, plus three electors from the District of Columbia.

electronic eavesdropping Covert listening to or recording of a person's conversations by electronic means.

electronic media Electronic means of mass communication, including television, radio, and the Internet.

Eleventh Amendment An amendment to the U.S. Constitution prohibiting federal courts from hearing suits brought by a citizen of one state against the government of another state.

emergency search A warrantless search performed during an emergency, such as a fire or potential explosion.

eminent domain The power of government, or of individuals and corporations authorized to perform public functions, to take private property for public use.

en banc "In the bench." Refers to a session of a court, usually an appellate court, in which all judges assigned to the court participate.

en banc rehearing A rehearing in an appellate court in which all or a majority of the judges participate.

enabling legislation As applied to public law, a statute authorizing the creation of a government program or agency and defining the functions and powers thereof.

enforcement power under the Fourteenth Amendment Refers to Congress's authority, recognized by Section 5 of the Fourteenth Amendment, to legislate in furtherance of the substantive provisions of the amendment.

English common law A system of legal rules and principles recognized and developed by English judges prior to the colonization of America and accepted as a basic aspect of the American legal system.

entrapment The act of government agents in inducing someone to commit a crime that the person otherwise would not be disposed to commit.

enumerated powers Powers specified in the text of the federal and state constitutions.

equal access Refers to policies that permit religious and secular groups the same access to public buildings for purposes of meetings.

Equal Protection Clause Clause contained in Section 1 of the Fourteenth Amendment prohibiting states from denying to persons within their jurisdictions the equal protection of the laws.

equal protection of the laws Constitutional requirement that the government not engage in prohibited forms of discrimination against persons under its jurisdiction.

Equal Rights Amendment Failed attempt to amend the Constitution to guarantee equal rights for women.

equality A condition in which persons hold the same status with respect to a particular criterion such as wealth, standing, power, etc.

equity Historically, a system of rules, remedies, customs, and principles developed in England to supplement the harsh common law by emphasizing the concept of fairness. In addition, because the common law served only to recompense after injury, equity was devised to prevent injuries that could not be repaired or recompensed after the fact. While American judges continue to distinguish between law and equity, these systems of rights and remedies are, for the most part, administered by the same courts.

error correction Refers to the function of appellate courts in correcting more or less routine errors committed by lower courts.

error, writ of An order issued by an appellate court for the purpose of correcting an error revealed in the record of a lower court proceeding.

escape Unlawfully fleeing to avoid arrest or confinement.

Establishment Clause Clause contained in the First Amendment prohibiting Congress from enacting laws "respecting an establishment of religion."

establishment of religion   Official government support of religion or religious institutions. Prohibited by the First Amendment. See also **separation of church and state.**

et al.   "And others."

euthanasia   Mercy killing.

evanescent evidence   Evidence that will likely disappear if not immediately seized.

evidence   Testimony, writings, or material objects offered in proof of an alleged fact or proposition.

evidentiary   Pertaining to the rules of evidence or the evidence in a particular case.

evidentiary hearing   A hearing on the admissibility of evidence into a civil or criminal trial.

evidentiary presumption   Establishment of one fact allows inference of another fact or circumstance.

evolving standards of decency   Doctrine that holds that what constitutes cruel and unusual punishment must be determined in light of changing social standards of acceptable government conduct.

ex officio   By virtue of the office.

ex parte   Refers to a proceeding in which only one party is involved or represented.

ex post facto   "After the fact."

ex post facto **law**   A retroactive law that criminalizes actions that were innocent at the time they were taken or increases punishment for a criminal act after it was committed.

ex proprio vigore   By its own force.

ex rel.   "On the relation or information of." Usually designating the name of a person on whose behalf the government is bringing legal action against another party.

ex vi termini   By definition; from the very meaning of the term or expression used.

excessive bail   Where a court requires a defendant to post an unreasonably large amount or imposes unreasonable conditions as a prerequisite for a defendant to be released before trial. The Eighth Amendment to the U.S. Constitution prohibits courts from requiring "excessive bail."

excessive fines   Fines that are deemed to be greater than is appropriate for the punishment of a particular crime.

exclusionary rule   Judicial doctrine forbidding the use of evidence in a criminal trial where the evidence was obtained in violation of the defendant's constitutional rights.

exculpatory   Tending to exonerate a person of allegations of wrongdoing.

exculpatory information   That which exonerates or tends to exonerate a person from fault or guilt.

excusable homicide   A death caused by accident or misfortune.

executive agreement   An agreement between the United States and one or more foreign countries entered into by the president without ratification by the Senate.

executive order   An order by a president or governor directing some particular action to be taken.

executive privilege   The right of the president to withhold certain information from Congress or a court of law.

exhaustion of remedies   The requirement that a party seeking review by a court first exhaust all legal options for resolution of the issue by nonjudicial authorities or lower courts.

exigent circumstances   Situations that demand unusual or immediate action.

expert witness   A witness with specialized knowledge or training called to testify in his or her field of expertise.

expressive conduct   Conduct undertaken to express a message.

expressive religious conduct   Conduct undertaken to express a religious message.

extradition   The surrender of a person by one jurisdiction to another for the purpose of criminal prosecution.

facial attack   A legal attack on the constitutionality of a law as it is written, as opposed to how it is applied in practice.

facial neutrality   Pertains to a law that on its face does not discriminate between or among classes of persons.

facial validity   The quality of being legitimate or permissible on its face. A law may nevertheless be invalid as applied in a given case.

fair hearing   A hearing in a court of law that conforms to standards of procedural justice.

fair notice   The requirement stemming from due process that government provide adequate notice to a person before it deprives that person of life, liberty, or property.

fair trial doctrine   The doctrine that, under the Fourteenth Amendment, states are required to provide fair trials to persons accused of crimes.

Federal Bureau of Investigation   The primary agency charged with investigating violations of federal criminal laws.

federal bureaucracy   The collective term for the myriad departments, agencies, and bureaus of the federal government.

federal courts   The courts operated by the U.S. government.

federal habeas corpus review   Review of a state criminal trial by a federal district court on a writ of habeas corpus after the defendant has been convicted, incarcerated, and has exhausted appellate remedies in the state courts.

federal preemption   The doctrine that federal law preempts states from enforcing regulations in areas necessarily occupied solely by the federal government.

federal question   An issue arising under the U.S. Constitution or a federal statute, executive order, regulation, or treaty.

federal question jurisdiction   The authority of federal courts to decide issues of national law.

Federal Register   The publication containing all regulations proposed and promulgated by federal agencies.

Federal Rules of Appellate Procedure   Rules governing the practice of law in the U.S. Courts of Appeals.

federal system   A political system in which sovereignty is shared by national and regional governments.

federalism   The constitutional distribution of government power and responsibility between the national government and the states.

fee simple   Ownership of real property; the highest interest in real estate the law will permit.

felony   A serious crime for which a person may be incarcerated for more than one year.

felony murder   A homicide committed during the course of committing another felony other than murder (e.g., armed robbery). The felonious act substitutes for malice aforethought ordinarily required in murder.

field sobriety test   A test administered by police to persons suspected of driving while intoxicated. Usually consists of requiring the suspect to demonstrate the ability to perform such physical acts as touching one's finger to nose or walking backwards.

Fifteenth Amendment   Amendment to the U.S. Constitution ratified in 1870 that prohibits states from denying the right to vote on account of race.

Fifth Amendment   Provisions of the Bill of Rights providing for due process of law and prohibiting compulsory self-incrimination.

Fifth Amendment Due Process Clause   The clause of the Fifth Amendment that forbids the federal government from depriving persons of life, liberty, or property without due process of law.

fighting words   Utterances that are inherently likely to provoke a violent response from the audience.

fighting words doctrine   The First Amendment doctrine that holds that certain utterances are not constitutionally protected as free speech if they are inherently likely to provoke a violent response from the audience.

First Amendment   Provisions of the Bill of Rights protecting freedom of religion and freedom of expression.

First Amendment absolutism   The idea that the First Amendment prohibits any and all attempts by government to regulate the content of expression.

first appearance   An initial judicial proceeding at which the defendant is informed of the charges, and the right to counsel, and a determination is made as to bail.

first-degree murder   The highest degree of unlawful homicide usually defined as "an unlawful act committed with the premeditated intent to take the life of a human being."

force   The element of compulsion in such crimes against persons as rape and robbery.

forcible rape   Rape, as defined by common law, i.e., sexual intercourse with a female, other than the offender's wife, by force and against the will of the victim.

forensic experts   Persons qualified in the application of scientific knowledge to legal principles, usually applied to those who participate in discourse or who testify in court.

forensic methods   The application of scientific knowledge to legal principles.

foreperson   The person selected by fellow jurors to chair deliberations and report the jury's verdict.

forfeiture   Sacrifice of ownership or some right (usually property) as a penalty.

forgery   The crime of making a false written instrument or materially altering a written instrument (e.g., a check, promissory note, or college transcript) with the intent to defraud.

fornication   Sexual intercourse between unmarried persons; an offense in some jurisdictions.

Fourteenth Amendment   Amendment to the U.S. Constitution, ratified in 1868, prohibiting states from depriving persons in their jurisdiction of due process of law.

Fourth Amendment   Amendment within the Bill of Rights prohibiting unreasonable searches and seizures.

fraud   Intentional deception or distortion in order to gain something of value.

Free Exercise Clause   Clause in the First Amendment prohibiting Congress from abridging the free exercise of religion.

free exercise of religion   The constitutional right to be free from government coercion or restraint with respect to religious beliefs and practices. Guaranteed by the First Amendment.

free marketplace of ideas   The idea that expression should be unrestricted so that ideas can be traded freely in society much as goods are freely exchanged in the marketplace.

freedom of assembly   The right of people to peaceably assemble in a public place.

freedom of association   Implicitly protected by the First Amendment, the right of people to associate freely without unwarranted interference by government.

freedom of expression   A summary term embracing freedom of speech and freedom of the press as well as symbolic speech and expressive conduct.

Freedom of Information Act   Federal statute providing citizens a broad right of access to government information.

freedom of religion   The First Amendment right to free exercise of one's religion.

freedom of speech   The right to speak or express oneself freely without unreasonable interference by government.

freedom of the press   The right to publish newspapers, magazines, and other print media free from prior restraint or sanctions by the government.

frivolous appeals   An appeal wholly lacking in legal merit.

fruit of the poisonous tree doctrine   The doctrine that evidence derived from illegally obtained and thus inadmissible evidence is tainted and therefore likewise inadmissible.

Full Faith and Credit Clause   The constitutional requirement (Article IV, Section 1) that states recognize and give effect to the records and legal proceedings of other states.

full opinion decision   An appellate judicial decision rendered with one or more written opinions expressing the views of the judges in the case.

fundamental constitutional rights   Those constitutional rights that have been declared to be fundamental by the courts. Includes First Amendment freedoms, the right to vote, and the right to privacy.

fundamental error   An error in a judicial proceeding that adversely affects the substantial rights of the accused.

fundamental rights   Those rights, whether or not explicitly stated in the Constitution, deemed to be basic and essential to a person's liberty and dignity.

gag order   An order by a judge prohibiting certain parties from speaking publicly or privately about a particular case.

gambling   Operating or playing a game for money in the expectation of gaining more than the amount played.

gay rights   Summary term referring to the idea that persons should be permitted to engage in private homosexual conduct and be free from discrimination based on their sexual orientation.

gender-based classifications   Laws that discriminate on the basis of gender.

gender-based peremptory challenges   A challenge to a prospective juror's competency to serve based solely on the prospective juror's gender.

gender equity   Idea that women should receive equal benefits conferred by government.

gender-neutral   A law or practice that applies equally to males and females, i.e., nondiscriminatory. For example, rape laws traditionally proscribed acts by a male against a female while newer sexual battery laws proscribe acts by or against a person of either gender. Thus they are gender-neutral.

general court-martial   A court-martial composed of three or more military members and a military judge or a military judge alone with jurisdiction to try the most serious offenses under the Uniform Code of Military Justice.

general objection   An objection raised against a witness's testimony or introduction of evidence when the objecting party does not recite a specific ground for the objection.

general warrant   A search or arrest warrant that is not particular as to the person to be arrested or the property to be seized.

gerrymandering   The intentional manipulation of legislative districts for political purposes.

good-faith exception   An exception to the exclusionary rule that bars use of evidence obtained by a search warrant found to be invalid. The exception allows use of the evidence if the police relied in good faith on the search warrant, even though the warrant is subsequently held to be invalid.

good-time credit   Credit toward early release from prison based on good behavior during confinement (often referred to as "gain time").

grand jury   A group of twelve to twenty-three citizens convened to hear evidence in criminal cases to determine whether indictment is warranted.

grandfather clause   In its modern, general sense, any legal provision protecting someone from losing a right or benefit as a result of a change in policy. In its historic sense, a legal provision limiting the right to vote to persons whose ancestors held the right to vote prior to passage of the Fifteenth Amendment in 1870.

group rights   Rights that people have by virtue of membership in a group, as distinct from purely individual rights.

habeas corpus   "You have the body." See **habeas corpus, writ of.**

habeas corpus, writ of   A judicial order issued to an official holding someone in custody, requiring the official to bring the prisoner to court for the purpose of allowing the court to determine whether that person is being held legally.

habitual offender   One who has been repeatedly convicted of crimes.

habitual offender statute   A law that imposes an additional punishment on a criminal who has previously been convicted of crimes.

handwriting exemplar   A sample of a suspect's handwriting.

hard-core pornography   Pornography that is extremely graphic in its depiction of sexual conduct.

harmless error   A procedural or substantive error that does not affect the outcome of a judicial proceeding.

harmless error analysis   Judicial determination as to whether a particular procedural error requires reversal of a lower court's judgment.

harmless error doctrine   The doctrine that minor or harmless errors during a trial do not require reversal of the lower court's judgment by an appellate court.

hate crimes   Crimes in which the victim is selected on the basis of race, religion, or ethnicity.

hate speech   Offensive speech directed at members of racial, religious, or ethnic minorities.

hearing   A public proceeding in a court of law, legislature, or administrative body for the purpose of ascertaining facts and deciding matters of law or policy.

hearsay evidence   Statements made by someone other than a witness offered in evidence at a trial or hearing to prove the truth of the matter asserted.

heightened scrutiny   The requirement that government justify a challenged policy by showing that it is substantially necessary to the achievement of an important objective.

high crimes and misdemeanors   Offenses for which an official of the federal government may be impeached and removed from office by Congress.

holding   The legal principle drawn from a judicial decision.

homicide   The killing of a human being.

hot pursuit   (1) The right of police to cross jurisdictional lines to apprehend a suspect or criminal. (2) The Fourth Amendment doctrine allowing warrantless searches and arrests where police pursue a fleeing suspect into a protected area.

house arrest   A sentencing alternative to incarceration where the offender is allowed to leave home only for employment and approved community service activities.

human rights statutes   State laws protecting people from discrimination in a variety of forms.

hung jury   A trial jury unable to reach a verdict.

Hyde Amendment   Prohibition on the use of federal welfare funds to pay for nontherapeutic abortions.

hypothetical question   A question based on an assumed set of facts. Hypothetical questions may be asked of expert witnesses in criminal trials.

illegitimacy   The condition of being born out of wedlock.

imminent lawless action   Unlawful conduct that is about to take place and which is inevitable unless there is intervention by the authorities.

imminently dangerous or outrageous conduct   The type of action that, when resulting in someone's death, usually characterizes second-degree murder.

immunity   Exemption from civil suit or prosecution. See also **transactional immunity** and **use immunity.**

impeachment   (1) A legislative act bringing a charge against a public official that, if proven in a legislative trial, will cause his or her removal from public office. (2) Impugning the credibility of a witness by introducing contradictory evidence or proving his or her bad character.

implied consent   An agreement or acquiescence manifested by a person's actions or inaction.

implied consent statutes   A law providing that by accepting a license a driver arrested for a traffic offense consents to urine, blood, and breath tests to determine blood alcohol content.

implied powers   Governmental powers not stated in but implied by the Constitution.

implied powers, doctrine of   A basic doctrine of American constitutional law derived from the Necessary and Proper Clause of Article I, Section 8. Under this doctrine, Congress is not limited to exercising those powers specifically enumerated in Article I but rather may exercise powers reasonably related to the fulfillment of its broad constitutional powers and responsibilities.

Imports-Exports Clause   Article I, Section 10, Clause 2 of the Constitution, restricting state power to tax imports and exports.

impoundment   (1) Action by a president in refusing to allow expenditures approved by Congress. (2) In criminal law, the seizure and holding of a vehicle or other property by the police.

in camera   "In a chamber." In private. Refers to a judicial proceeding or conference from which the public is excluded.

in forma pauperis   "In the manner of a pauper." Waiver of filing costs and other fees associated with judicial proceedings to allow an indigent person to proceed.

in loco parentis   "In the place of the parent(s)."

in personam   Refers to legal actions brought against a person, as distinct from actions against property (see *in rem*).

in propria persona   "In one's proper person." Referring to the proper person to bring a legal action or make a motion before a court of law.

in re   "In the matter of."

in rem   Refers to legal actions brought against things rather than persons.

incapacitation   Making it impossible for someone to do something.

incapacity   An inability, legal or actual, to act.

incarceration   Imprisonment.

incest   Sexual intercourse with a close blood relative or, in some cases, a person related by affinity.

inchoate offenses   Offenses preparatory to committing other crimes. Inchoate offenses include attempt, conspiracy, and solicitation.

incite   To provoke or set in motion.

inciting a riot   The crime of instigating or provoking a riot.

incorporation, doctrine of   The doctrine under which most provisions of the Bill of Rights have been extended to limit state action by way of the Due Process Clause of the Fourteenth Amendment. Specific protections of the Bill of Rights are said to be incorporated within the Fourteenth Amendment's broad restrictions on the states.

inculpatory   Tending to incriminate.

indefinite sentence   Form of criminal sentencing whereby a judge imposes a term of incarceration within statutory parameters, and corrections officials determine actual time served through parole or other means.

independent agencies   Federal agencies located outside the major cabinet-level departments.

independent counsel   A special prosecutor appointed to investigate and, if warranted, prosecute official misconduct.

independent source doctrine   The doctrine that permits evidence to be admitted at trial as long as it was obtained independently from illegally obtained evidence.

independent state grounds   The doctrine that an individual's claim to a right or benefit not supported by federal law will nevertheless be recognized by a federal court if a state court has found that the claimed right or benefit rests on a valid provision of state law.

indeterminate sentence   A prison sentence for an indefinite time, but within stipulated parameters, that allows correction officials to determine the prisoner's release date.

indeterminate sentencing   Form of criminal sentencing where criminals are sentenced to prison for indeterminate periods until corrections officials determine that rehabilitation has been accomplished.

indictment   A formal document handed down by a grand jury accusing one or more persons of the commission of a crime or crimes.

indigency   Poverty; inability to afford legal representation.

indigent defendants   Defendants who cannot afford to retain private legal counsel and are therefore entitled to be represented by a public defender or a court-appointed lawyer.

indirect contempt   An act committed outside the presence of the court that insults the court or obstructs a judicial proceeding.

ineffective representation   Representation by an attorney who is incompetent or less than reasonably effective.

inevitable discovery doctrine   The doctrine that holds that evidence derived from inadmissible evidence is admissible if it inevitably would have been discovered independently by lawful means.

inflammatory remarks   Remarks by counsel during a trial designed to excite the passions of the jury.

information   A document filed by a prosecutor charging one or more persons with commission of crime.

infra   "Below."

inherent executive power   The powers of the president that flow from the nature of the office rather than from specific provisions of Article II.

inherent power   The power existing in an agency, institution, or individual by definition of the office.

inherently suspect   A law, policy, or classification that is, from a constitutional standpoint, questionable on its face.

initial appearance   After arrest, the first appearance of the accused before a judge or magistrate.

injunction   A judicial order requiring a person to do, or to refrain from doing, a designated thing.

inmate   One who is confined in a jail or prison.

insanity   A degree of mental illness that negates the legal capacity or responsibility of the affected person.

insanity defense   A defense that seeks to exonerate the accused by showing that he or she was insane at the time of the crime and thus not legally responsible.

insufficient evidence   Evidence that falls short of establishing that required by law, usually referring to evidence that does not legally establish an offense or a defense.

intelligible principle standard   The doctrine that states that, in delegating power to the executive branch, Congress must provide a clear statement of policy to guide executive discretion.

intent   A state of mind in which a person seeks to accomplish a given result through a course of action.

inter alia   "Among other things."

intergovernmental tax immunity   The doctrine that federal and state governments may not levy taxes on one another.

intermediate appellate courts   Appellate courts positioned below the supreme or highest appellate court. Their primary function is to decide routine appeals not deserving review by the Supreme Court.

intermediate appellate courts   Judicial tribunals consisting of three or more judges that review decisions of trial courts but which are subordinate to the final appellate tribunals.

intermediate scrutiny   See **heightened scrutiny.**

interposition   The archaic doctrine holding that when the federal government attempts to act unlawfully on an object within the domain of the state governments, a state may interpose itself between the federal government and the object of the federal government's action.

interpretivism   The theory of constitutional interpretation holding that judges should confine themselves to the plain meaning of the text, the intentions of the framers, and/or the historical meaning of the document.

interrogation   Questioning of a suspect by police or questioning of a witness by counsel.

interrogatories   Written questions put to a witness.

interstate agreements   Formal agreements or compacts between or among states.

interstate commerce   Commercial activity potentially extending beyond the boundaries of a state.

Interstate Commerce Act of 1887   Landmark act of Congress establishing the Interstate Commerce Commission.

interstate compacts Agreements between or among state governments, somewhat analogous to treaties.

intoxication A state of drunkenness resulting from the use of alcoholic beverages or drugs.

invalidate Annul, negate, set aside.

invasion of privacy A tort involving the unreasonable or unwarranted intrusion on the privacy of an individual.

inventory search An exception to the warrant requirement that allows police who legally impound a vehicle to conduct a routine inventory of the contents of the vehicle.

investigatory detention Brief detention of suspects by a police officer who has reasonable suspicion that criminal activity is afoot. See also **stop-and-frisk.**

invidious Arousing animosity, envy, or resentment.

ipse dixit "He himself said it." An assertion resting on the authority of an individual.

ipso facto "By the mere fact"; by the fact itself.

irreparable injury An injury for which the award of money may not be adequate compensation and that may require the issuance of an injunction to fulfill the requirements of justice.

irresistible impulse A desire that cannot be resisted due to impairment of the will by mental disease.

item veto The power of the chief executive to veto one or more parts of a bill without rejecting the bill in its entirety.

Jim Crow laws Laws originating in the 19th century requiring various forms of racial segregation.

joinder Coupling two or more criminal prosecutions.

joinder and severance of parties The uniting or severing of two or more parties charged with a crime or crimes.

joinder of offenses The uniting for trial in one case of different charges or counts alleged in an information or indictment.

joint resolution An act expressing the will of both houses of Congress in attempting to impose duties or limitations on parties outside the Congress. Joint resolutions must be presented to the president for signature or veto.

judgment A judicial determination as to the claims made by parties to a lawsuit. In a criminal case, the court's formal declaration to the accused regarding the legal consequences of a determination of guilt.

judgment of acquittal In a nonjury trial: a judge's order exonerating a defendant based on a finding that the defendant is not guilty. In a case heard by a jury finding a defendant guilty: a judge's order exonerating a defendant on the ground that the evidence was not legally sufficient to support the jury's finding of guilt.

judicial activism Defined variously, but the underlying philosophy is that judges should exercise power vigorously. See also **judicial restraint.**

judicial behavior The way judges make decisions; the academic study thereof.

judicial conference A meeting of judges to deliberate on the disposition of a case.

judicial federalism The constitutional relationship between federal and state courts of law.

judicial notice The act of a court recognizing, without proof, the existence of certain facts that are commonly known. Such facts are often brought to the court's attention through the use of a calendar or almanac.

judicial restraint Defined variously, but the underlying philosophy is that judges should exercise power cautiously and show deference to precedent to the decisions of other branches of government. See also **judicial activism.**

judicial review Generally, the review of any issue by a court of law. In American constitutional law, judicial review refers to the authority of a court to invalidate acts of government on constitutional grounds.

Judiciary Act of 1789 Landmark statute establishing the federal courts system.

juris privati "The private law," including such areas as torts, contracts, and property.

jurisdiction "To speak the law." The geographical area within which, the subject matter with respect to which, and the persons over whom a court can properly exercise its power.

jurist A person who is skilled or well versed in the law; term often applied to lawyers and judges.

jury A group of citizens convened for the purpose of deciding factual questions relevant to a civil or criminal case.

jury instructions A judge's explanation of the law applicable to a case being heard by a jury.

jury nullification The fact of a jury disregarding the court's instructions and rendering a verdict on basis of consciences of the jurors.

jury pardon An action taken by a jury, despite the quality of the evidence, acquitting a defendant or convicting the defendant of a lesser crime than charged.

jury selection The process of selecting prospective jurors at random from lists of persons representative of the community.

jury trial A judicial proceeding to determine a defendant's guilt or innocence conducted before a body of persons sworn to render a verdict based on the law and the evidence presented.

just compensation The constitutional requirement that a party whose property is taken by government under the power of eminent domain be justly compensated for the loss.

Just Compensation Clause Clause found in the Fifth Amendment requiring the federal government to provide owners reasonable and fair compensation when taking their property for a public use.

justiciability The quality of appropriateness for judicial decision. A justiciable dispute is one that can be effectively decided by a court of law.

justifiable homicide   Killing another in self-defense or defense of others when there is serious danger of death or great bodily harm to self or others, or when authorized by law.

justifiable use of force   The necessary and reasonable use of force by a person in self-defense, defense of another, or defense of property.

justification   A valid reason for one's actions.

juvenile   A person who has not yet attained the age of legal majority.

juvenile court   A judicial tribunal having jurisdiction over minors defined as juveniles who are alleged to be status offenders or to have committed acts of delinquency.

juvenile delinquency   Actions of a juvenile in violation of the criminal law.

juvenile delinquency hearing   Hearing in which a juvenile court determines whether a juvenile should be found to be delinquent. Analogous to a criminal trial in the adult justice system.

knock-and-announce rule   The provision under federal and most state laws that requires a law enforcement officer to first knock and announce his or her presence and purpose before entering a person's home to serve a search warrant.

knowing and intelligent waiver   A waiver of rights that is made with an awareness of the consequences.

laissez-faire capitalism   The theory holding that a capitalist economy functions best when government refrains from interfering with the marketplace.

law clerk   A judge's staff attorney.

lawmaking function   One of the principal functions of an appellate court, often referred to as the law development function.

leading questions   A question that suggests an answer. Leading questions are permitted at a criminal trial on cross-examination of witnesses and in other limited instances.

least restrictive means test   A judicial inquiry as to whether a particular policy that is being challenged as an infringement of some fundamental right is the least burdensome means of achieving the government's objective.

legislation   Law enacted by a lawmaking body.

legislative veto   A statutory provision under which a legislative body is permitted to overrule a decision of an executive agency.

legislature   An elected lawmaking body such as the Congress of the United States or a state assembly.

Lemon test   Three-part test set forth in *Lemon v. Kurtzman* (1971). To pass muster under the Establishment Clause, a law must have a secular purpose, not have the principal effect of advancing or inhibiting religion, and avoid excessive entanglement between government and religious institutions.

lex non scripta   "The unwritten law" or common law.

liability   A broad legal term connoting debt, responsibility, or obligation. The condition of being bound to pay a debt, obligation, or judgment. This responsibility can be either civil or criminal.

libel   The tort of defamation through published material. See **defamation.**

libertarianism   A philosophy that stresses individual freedom as the highest good.

liberty   The absence of restraint.

liberty of contract   The freedom to enter into contracts without undue interference from government.

limiting doctrines   Doctrines by which courts may refuse to render a decision on the merits in a case. See abstention, exhaustion of remedies, political questions doctrine, mootness, standing.

line-item veto   Executive act nullifying certain portions of a bill.

lineup   A police identification procedure where a suspect is included in a lineup with other persons who are exhibited to a victim.

literacy test   A test of reading and/or writing skills, often given as a prerequisite to employment. At one time, literacy tests were required by many states as preconditions for voting in elections.

litigant   A party to, or participant in, a legal action.

local aspects of interstate commerce   Regulations of interstate commerce imposed by local governments in response to unique local conditions such as the shape of a harbor.

loitering   Standing around idly, "hanging around."

loss of civil rights   Forfeiture of certain rights, such as voting, as a result of a criminal conviction.

lottery   A drawing in which prizes are distributed to winners selected by lot from among those who have participated by paying a consideration.

magistrate   A judge with minor or limited authority.

Magna Charta   The "Great Charter" signed by King John in 1215 guaranteeing the legal rights of English subjects. Generally considered the foundation of Anglo-American constitutionalism.

majority opinion   An appellate court opinion joined in by a majority of the judges who heard the appeal.

mala in se   "Evil in itself." Refers to crimes like murder that are universally condemned.

mala prohibita   "Prohibited evil." Refers to crimes that are wrong primarily because the law declares them to be wrong.

malfeasance   Misconduct that adversely affects the performance of official duties.

malice aforethought   The mental predetermination to commit an illegal act.

mandamus, writ of "We command." A judicial order commanding a public official or an organization to perform a specified duty.

mandate A command or order.

mandatory minimum sentence A sentence in which the minimum duration of incarceration is specified by law.

mandatory sentencing Sentencing practice in which trial courts are constrained by law to impose prison terms of certain minimum duration.

manifest necessity That is which clearly or obviously necessary or essential.

market participant exception The doctrine that states may impose regulations that inhibit competition by out-of-state competitors where the state is itself a participant in the market.

material Important, relevant, necessary.

memorandum decision A judicial decision rendered without a supporting Opinion of the Court.

mens rea "Guilty mind," criminal intent.

militia Historically, a military force composed of all able-bodied citizens, in service only during time of war, rebellion, or emergency.

minimal scrutiny The most lenient form of judicial review of policies challenged as violations of civil rights and liberties.

Miranda **warning** Based on the Supreme Court's decision in *Miranda v. Arizona* (1966), this warning is given by police to individuals who are taken into custody before they are interrogated. The warning informs persons in custody that they have the right to remain silent and to have a lawyer present during questioning, and that anything they say can and will be used against them in a court of law.

misappropriation Wrongful taking or diversion of funds or other property.

miscarriage of justice Decision of a court that is inconsistent with the substantial rights of a party to the case.

misdemeanor A minor crime usually punishable by a fine or confinement for less than one year.

misrepresentation An untrue statement of fact made to deceive or mislead.

mistake of fact Unconscious ignorance of a fact or belief in the existence of something that does not exist.

mistake of law An erroneous opinion of legal principles applied to a set of facts.

mistrial A trial that is terminated due to misconduct, procedural error, or a "hung jury" (one that is unable to reach a verdict).

mitigating circumstances Circumstances or factors that tend to lessen culpability.

mitigating factors See **mitigating circumstances.**

mitigation Reduction or alleviation, usually of punishment.

mockery of justice test Judicial test for determining whether a defendant was provided adequate representation. The question is whether performance by counsel constituted a mockery of justice.

modern administrative state Refers to the highly bureaucratized federal government that emerged in the twentieth century.

moment of silence Policy under which public school students are required to observe a minute of silence at the beginning of the school day.

monetary fines Sums of money offenders are required to pay as punishment for the commission of crimes.

monogamy The practice of having only one spouse, as distinct from bigamy or polygamy.

moot A point that no longer has any practical significance; academic.

mootness Refers to a question that does not involve rights currently at issue in, or pertinent to, the outcome of a case.

moral individualism The doctrine that individuals, not society or government, should make moral choices.

motion An application to a court to obtain a particular ruling or order.

motion for a new trial A formal request made to a trial court to hold a new trial in a particular case that has already been adjudicated.

motion for rehearing A formal request made to a court of law to convene another hearing in a case in which the court has already ruled.

motion to dismiss A formal request to a trial court to dismiss the criminal charges against the defendant.

motive A person's conscious reason for acting.

myth of legality The belief that judicial decisions are a function of legal rules, procedures, and principles rather than the ideological leanings of policy preferences of judges.

narrowly tailored Refers to a policy that is carefully designed to achieve its intended goal with a minimal negative impact on civil liberties.

narrowness doctrine The doctrine that judicial decisions should be framed in the narrowest possible terms or based on the narrowest possible grounds.

national supremacy The doctrine that holds that when state and federal authority collide, the federal authority must prevail.

natural law Principles of human conduct believed to be ordained by God or nature, existing prior to and superseding human law.

natural rights Rights believed to be inherent in human beings, the existence of which is not dependent on their recognition by government. In classical liberalism, natural rights are "life, liberty, and property." As recognized by the

Declaration of Independence, they are "life, liberty, and the pursuit of happiness."

negligence   The failure to exercise ordinary care or caution.

neutral and detached officer   A judge or magistrate, one without an interest in the outcome of a case.

New Equal Protection   A modern interpretation of the Equal Protection Clause of the Fourteenth Amendment under which policies that impinge on fundamental rights or discriminate on the basis of suspect classifications are presumed invalid by the courts.

new federalism   Refers to a variety of efforts in recent decades to revitalize the role of the states in the federal system or return power to them.

new property   Refers to a person's interest in government benefits or entitlements.

Nineteenth Amendment   Amendment to the U.S. Constitution, adopted in 1920, which prohibits the denial of voting rights on account of gender.

Ninth Amendment   Amendment contained within the Bill of Rights that recognizes rights retained by the people even though they are not specifically enumerated in the Constitution.

no contest plea   A plea to a criminal charge that, although it is not an admission of guilt, generally has the same effect as a plea of guilty.

nolo contendere   "I will not contest it." Refers to a plea of no contest in a criminal case.

nondeadly force   Force that does not result in death.

nondelegation doctrine   The doctrine that Congress may not delegate its legislative authority to the Executive Branch.

noninterpretivism   A term referring to a variety of theories of constitutional interpretation the common property of which is the rejection of interpretivism. See **interpretivism.**

nonunanimous verdicts   Jury verdicts rendered by a less-than-unanimous vote of the jurors.

notary public   A person empowered by law to administer oaths, to certify things as true, and to perform various minor official acts.

notice of appeal   Document filed with an appellate court notifying the court of an appeal from a judgment of a lower court.

nuisance   An unlawful or unreasonable use of a person's property that results in an injury to another or to the public.

nullification   The act of rendering something invalid; the process by which something may be invalidated. Historically, a doctrine under which states claimed the right to nullify actions of the national government.

obiter dicta   "Something said in passing." Incidental statements in a judicial opinion that are not binding and are unnecessary to support the decision.

objective test   A legal test based on external circumstances rather than the perceptions or intentions of an individual actor.

obscenity   Explicit sexual material that is patently offensive, appeals to a prurient or unnatural interest in sex, and lacks serious scientific, artistic, or literary content.

obstruction of justice   The crime of impeding or preventing law enforcement or the administration of justice.

open fields doctrine   The doctrine that the Fourth Amendment does not apply to the open fields around a home, even if these open fields are private property.

open public trial   A trial that is held in public and is open to spectators.

opening statement   A prosecutor's or defense lawyer's initial statement to the judge or jury in a trial.

opinion   A written statement accompanying a judicial decision, authored by one or more judges, supporting or dissenting from that decision.

opinion concurring in the judgment   A judicial opinion in which the author agrees with the decision of the court, but for reasons other than those stated in the court's principal opinion.

opinion evidence   Testimony in which the witness expresses an opinion, as distinct from knowledge of specific facts.

Opinion of the Court   An opinion announcing both the decision of the court and its supporting rationale. The opinion can either be a majority opinion or a unanimous opinion.

oral argument   A hearing before an appellate court in which counsel for the parties appear for the purpose of making statements and answering questions from the bench.

ordinance   An enactment of a local governing body such as a city council or commission.

organized crime   Syndicates involved in racketeering and other criminal activities.

original intent, doctrine of   The doctrine holding that the Constitution should be interpreted and applied according to the intentions of its framers, insofar as those intentions can be determined.

original jurisdiction   The authority of a court of law to hear a case in the first instance.

original package doctrine   Archaic doctrine under which states were prohibited from imposing taxes on imported goods that, although they were no longer in the stream of commerce, remained in their original packages.

originalism   The doctrine that courts must preserve the original meaning of the Constitution.

overbreadth doctrine   First Amendment doctrine that holds that a law is invalid if it can be applied to punish people for engaging in constitutionally protected expression.

overrule   To reverse or annul by subsequent action.

oversight   Refers to the responsibility of a legislative body to monitor the activities of government agencies it created.

oversight hearings   Formal hearings conducted for the purpose of monitoring actions by government agencies.

panel   A set of jurors or judges assigned to hear a case.

pardon   An executive action that mitigates or sets aside punishment for a crime.

parens patriae   "The parent of the country." Refers to the role of the state as guardian of minors or other legally disabled persons.

parochial legislation   Legislation that favors narrow, localized interests.

parole   The conditional early release from prison.

parole revocation hearing   An administrative hearing held for the purpose of determining whether an offender's parole should be revoked.

partisan gerrymandering   The intentional manipulation of legislative district lines in order to provide one political party a competitive advantage over another.

party   A person taking part in a legal transaction. This term includes plaintiffs and defendants in lawsuits but has a far broader legal connotation. In politics, an organization established for the principal purpose of recruiting and nominating candidates for public office.

pat-down search   A manual search of the exterior of a suspect's outer garments.

patently offensive   Plainly or obviously offensive, disgusting.

penal   Of or pertaining to punishment.

pendency of the appeal   The period after an appeal is filed but before the appeal is adjudicated.

penitentiary   A prison.

penology   The study or practice of prison management.

penumbra   An implied right or power emanating from an enumerated right or power.

per curiam   "By the court." Refers to an opinion attributed to a court collectively, usually not identified with the name of any particular member of the court.

per se   "By itself"; in itself.

peremptory challenge   An objection to the selection of a prospective juror in which the attorney making the challenge is not required to state the reason for the objection.

petit jury   A trial jury, usually composed of either six or twelve persons.

petition   A written request, usually addressed to a court, asking for a specified action. Sometimes the term indicates written requests in an *ex parte* proceeding, where there is no adverse party. In some jurisdictions, the term refers to the first pleading in a lawsuit.

petition   A formal written request addressed to a court of law.

petitioner   A person who brings a petition before a court of law.

petty (petit) offenses   Minor crimes for which fines or short jail terms are the only prescribed modes of punishment.

picketing   Carrying of signs to protest in the public forum.

places of public accommodation   Businesses that open their doors to the general public.

plain view   Readily visible to the naked eye.

plain view doctrine   The Fourth Amendment doctrine under which a police officer may seize evidence of crime that is readily visible to the officer's naked eye as long as the officer is legally in the place where the evidence becomes visible.

plaintiff   The party initiating legal action; the complaining party.

plea bargain   An agreement between a defendant and a prosecutor whereby the defendant agrees to plead guilty in exchange for some concession (e.g., a reduction in the number of charges brought).

plea of guilty   A formal answer to a criminal charge in which the accused acknowledges guilt and waives the right to trial.

plea of not guilty   A formal answer to a criminal charge in which the accused denies guilt and thus exercises the right to a trial.

plenary   Full, complete. Often used with reference to the nature and extent of governmental powers enumerated in the federal Constitution.

plenary review   Full, complete review by an appellate court.

pluralism   A social or political system in which diverse groups compete for status or power; the theory that the role of government is to serve as broker among competing interest groups.

plurality opinion   An opinion that states the judgment of the Court but that does not have the endorsement of a majority of justices.

pocket veto   The power of a chief executive to effectively veto legislation by not acting on a bill passed within ten days prior to adjournment of a legislative session.

police deception   Intentional deception by police in order to elicit incriminating statements from a suspect.

police interrogation   Questioning by the police of a suspect in custody.

police power   The power of government to legislate to protect public health, safety, welfare, and morality.

police powers of the states   The powers of state governments to enact laws to further the public health, safety, welfare, and morality.

political dissent   Organized or public opposition to the government.

political question   Refers to a question that a court believes to be appropriate for decision by the legislative or the executive branch of government and thus improper for judicial decision making.

political questions doctrine   The doctrine that holds that courts should avoid ruling on a **political question.**

poll tax   A tax that must be paid before a person is permitted to vote in an election.

polling the jury   Practice in which trial judge asks each member of the jury to affirm that he or she supports the jury's verdict.

polygamy   Plural marriage; having more than one spouse.

polygraph evidence   Results of lie detector tests (generally inadmissible into evidence).

popular sovereignty   The idea that political authority is vested ultimately not in the rulers but in the people they rule.

pornography   Material that appeals to the sexual impulse or appetite.

postconviction relief   Term applied to various mechanisms a defendant may use to challenge a conviction after other routes of appeal have been exhausted.

power of contempt   The authority of a court of law to punish someone who insults the court or flouts its authority.

power to investigate   Refers to the power of a legislative body to conduct hearings and subpoena witnesses in order to investigate an issue or area over which it has legislative authority.

power to regulate interstate commerce   Refers to the power of Congress, and to a lesser extent, the powers of state and local governments, to enact laws and regulations affecting commerce involving more than one state.

precedent   A judicial decision cited as authority controlling or influencing the outcome of a similar case.

preemption   In constitutional law, the doctrine under which a field of public policy, previously open to action by the states, is brought by the U.S. Congress within the primary or exclusive control of the national government.

preferred freedoms doctrine   The doctrine that certain freedoms, in particular those protected by the First Amendment, occupy a preferred position in relation to other freedoms.

prejudicial error   An error at trial that substantially affects the interests of the accused.

preliminary hearing   A hearing held to determine whether there is sufficient evidence to hold an accused for trial.

preliminary injunction   An injunction issued pending a trial on the merits of the case.

preparatory conduct   Actions taken in order to prepare to commit a crime.

preponderance of evidence   Evidence that has greater weight than countervailing evidence.

presentment   The requirement that legislation be sent to the chief executive for signature or veto; also, a synonym for indictment.

presidential immunity   The barrier against bringing a civil suit against the president for any of his official actions.

presidential pardon   Action by the president pardoning one or more persons for the commission of a crime.

presidential power to make foreign policy   Refers to the president's broad authority to set policy as it relates to international relations and foreign affairs.

presidential war powers   Refers to the president's authority as commander-in-chief.

presumption   (1) An inference drawn by reasoning. (2) A rule of law subject to rebuttal.

presumption of constitutionality   The doctrine of constitutional law holding that laws are presumed to be constitutional with the burden of proof resting on the plaintiff to demonstrate otherwise.

presumption of innocence   In a criminal trial, the accused is presumed innocent until proven guilty.

presumption of validity   See **presumption of constitutionality.**

preterm conference   The Supreme Court's conference held prior to the beginning of its annual term in which the Court disposes of numerous petitions for certiorari.

pretextual stop   An incident in which police stop a suspicious vehicle on the pretext of a motor vehicle infraction.

pretrial detention   The holding of a defendant in custody prior to trial.

pretrial discovery   The process by which the defense and prosecution interrogate witnesses for the opposing party and gain access to the evidence possessed by the opposing party prior to trial.

pretrial diversion program   A program in which a first-time offender is afforded the opportunity to avoid a criminal conviction by participating in some specified treatment, counseling or community service.

pretrial motion   Any of a variety of motions made by counsel prior to the inception of a trial.

pretrial publicity   Media coverage of a case that has the potential to deprive a defendant of the right to a fair trial by an impartial jury.

pretrial release   The release of a defendant pending trial.

preventive detention   Holding a suspect in custody before trial to prevent escape or other wrongdoing.

prima facie   At first glance; on the face of it. Referring to a point that will be considered true if uncontested or unrefuted.

principals   Persons whose conduct involves direct participation in a crime.

prior restraint   An official act preventing publication of a particular work.

prisoners' rights   Refers to the set of rights that prisoners retain or attempt to assert through litigation.

private property   Property held by individuals or corporations, not by the public generally.

privilege   In general, an activity in which a person may engage without interference. The term is often used interchangeably with "right" in American constitutional law, with reference to the Privileges and Immunities Clauses of Article IV and the Fourteenth Amendment of the U.S. Constitution.

privileges   Rights extended to persons by virtue of law.

Privileges and Immunities Clause   (1) Article IV, Section 2, Clause 1, of the Constitution, providing that "citizens of each state shall be entitled to all privileges and immunities of citizens in the several states." (2) Similar provision contained in Section 1 of the Fourteenth Amendment.

pro bono   "For the good." Performing service without compensation.

pro forma   Merely for the sake of form.

pro se   On one's own behalf.

***pro se* defense**   Representing oneself in a criminal case.

probable cause   Knowledge of specific facts providing reasonable grounds for believing that criminal activity is afoot.

probable cause hearing   A hearing held in a court to make a formal determination on an issue of probable cause.

probation   Conditional release of a convicted criminal in lieu of incarceration.

probative   Tending to prove the truth or falsehood of a proposition.

procedural criminal law   The branch of the criminal law that deals with the processes by which crimes are investigated, prosecuted and punished.

procedural due process   Set of procedures designed to ensure fairness in a judicial or administrative proceeding.

procedural law   The law regulating governmental procedure (e.g., rules of criminal procedure).

profanity   Vulgar, coarse, or filthy language; irreverence toward sacred things.

prohibition, writ of   An appellate court order preventing a lower court from exercising its jurisdiction in a particular case.

promissory estoppel   The doctrine of contract law under which a promise that induces action on the part of the promisee may be legally enforceable.

pronouncement of sentence   Formal announcement of a criminal punishment by a trial judge.

proof beyond a reasonable doubt   The standard of proof in a criminal trial or a juvenile delinquency hearing.

proper forum   The correct court or other institution in which to press a particular claim.

property rights   Refers to the bundle of rights that exist relative to private ownership and control of property.

proportional representation   An electoral system in which the percentage of votes received by a given political party entitles that party to the same percentage of seats in the legislature.

proportionality   The degree to which a particular punishment matches the seriousness of a crime or matches the penalty other offenders have received for the same crime.

proportionate representation   The idea that certain groups should be represented by ensuring that the legislature is composed according to the proportion of such groups in society.

proscribe   To forbid; prohibit.

prosecution   Initiation and conduct of a criminal case.

prosecutor   A public official empowered to initiate criminal charges and conduct prosecutions.

prosecutorial discretion   The leeway afforded prosecutors in deciding whether or not to bring charges and to engage in plea bargaining.

prosecutorial immunity   A prosecutor's legal shield against civil suits stemming from his or her official actions.

provocation   Refers to conduct that prompts another person to react through criminal conduct.

proximate cause   The cause that is nearest a given effect in a causal relationship.

prurient interest   An excessive or unnatural interest in sex.

public accommodations statute   A law prohibiting various forms of discrimination by businesses that open their doors to the general public.

public defender   An attorney responsible for defending indigent persons charged with crimes.

public drunkenness   The offense of appearing in public while intoxicated.

public figures   Public officials or persons who are in the public eye.

public forum   A public space generally acknowledged as appropriate for public assemblies or expressions of views.

public law   General classification of law consisting of constitutional law, administrative law, international law, and criminal law.

public safety exception   Exception to the requirement that police officers promptly inform suspects taken into custody of their rights to remain silent and have an attorney present during questioning. Under the public safety exception, police may ask suspects questions motivated by a desire to protect public safety without jeopardizing the admissibility of suspects' answers to those questions or subsequent statements.

punitive damages   A sum of money awarded to the plaintiff in a civil case as a means of punishing the defendant for wrongful conduct.

punitive isolation   Solitary confinement of a person who is incarcerated.

pure speech   Communication that is purely spoken.

putting witnesses under the rule   Placing witnesses under the rule that requires them to remain outside the courtroom except when testifying.

qua   As; in the character or capacity of.

quash   To vacate or annul.

quasi-judicial authority   Refers to the authority of certain regulatory or administrative agencies to make determinations with respect to the rights of private parties under their jurisdiction.

race-conscious remedies   Remedies to racial injustices that specifically take race into account.

racially based peremptory challenges   Peremptory challenges to prospective jurors which are based solely on racial animus or racial stereotypes.

rational basis test   The test of the validity of a statute inquiring whether it is rationally related to a legitimate government objective.

real property   Land and buildings permanently attached thereto.

reapportionment   The redrawing of legislative district lines so as to remedy malapportionment.

reasonable doubt   The doubt that a reasonable person could have with respect to the veracity of a given proposition after hearing the evidence.

reasonable expectation of privacy   A person's reasonable expectation that his or her activities in a certain place are private; society's expectations with regard to whether activities in certain places are private.

reasonable force   The maximum degree of force that is necessary to accomplish a lawful purpose.

reasonable suspicion   A reasonable person's suspicion that criminal activity is afoot.

reasoning   The logic of a legal argument or judicial opinion.

rebuttal witnesses   Witnesses called to dispute the testimony of the opposing party's witnesses.

reciprocal immunity   See **intergovernmental tax immunity.**

recognizance   An obligation to appear in a court of law at a given time.

recusal   A decision of a judge to withdraw from a case, usually due to bias or personal interest in the outcome.

recuse   To disqualify oneself from hearing a court case.

redeeming social importance   Value to society that redeems an otherwise worthless instance of expression.

referendum   An election in which voters decide a question of public policy.

regulation   A legally binding rule or order prescribed by a controlling authority. The term is generally used with respect to the rules promulgated by administrative and regulatory agencies.

regulation   A rule or order prescribed by controlling authority.

rehabilitation   Restoring someone or something to its former status; a justification for punishment emphasizing reform rather than retribution.

release on personal recognizance   Pretrial release of a defendant based solely on the defendant's promise to appear for future court dates.

released time programs   Public school programs in which students are permitted to leave school grounds to attend religious exercises.

relevant evidence   Evidence tending to prove or disprove an alleged fact.

Religion Clauses of the First Amendment   The Establishment Clause and Free Exercise Clause of the First Amendment.

Religious Freedom Restoration Act (RFRA)   Act of Congress designed to enhance religious freedom vis-à-vis government; declared unconstitutional by the Supreme Court in 1997.

religious speech   Expression of a religious nature.

religious tests   Tests to determine whether individuals hold "appropriate" religious convictions.

remand   To send back, as from a higher court to a lower court, for the latter to take specified action in a case or to follow proceedings designated by the higher court.

remedy   The means by which a right is enforced or a wrong is redressed.

removal power   The power of the president to remove officials in executive departments and agencies.

rendition   The act of one state in surrendering a fugitive to another state.

Rendition Clause   Clause of Article IV, Section 2, of the Constitution requiring states to surrender fugitives to other states upon proper request.

repeal   A legislative act removing a law from the statute books.

reply brief   A brief submitted in response to an appellee's answer brief.

reporters   Books containing judicial decisions and accompanying opinions.

representative government   Form of government in which officials responsible for making policy are elected by the people in periodic free elections.

reprimands   Minor punitive actions taken by military commanders for various infractions committed by military servicepersons.

res judicata   "A thing decided." A matter decided by a judgment, connoting the firmness and finality of the judgment as it affects the parties to the lawsuit. *Res judicata* has the general effect of bringing litigation on a contested point to an end.

res nova   "New thing." A new issue or case.

resentencing   Refers to a new sentencing hearing ordered by an appellate court.

reserved powers   Powers reserved to the states or the people under the Tenth Amendment.

resolution   A legislative act expressing the will of one or both houses of the legislature. Unlike a statute, a resolution has no enforcement clause. See also **concurrent resolution** and **joint resolution.**

respondent   A person asked to respond to a lawsuit or writ.

restitution   The act of compensating someone for losses suffered.

restrictive covenant   An agreement among property holders restricting the use of property or prohibiting the rental or sale of it to certain parties.

retribution   Something demanded in payment for a debt; in criminal law, the demand that a criminal pay his or her debt to society.

retroactive   Changing the legal status or character of past events or transactions.

reverse   To set aside a decision on appeal.

review   An examination by an appellate court of a lower court's decision.

revocation   The withdrawal of some right or power (e.g., the revocation of parole).

RICO Act   The Racketeer Influenced Corrupt Organizations Act.

rider   An attachment of a small provision to a contract, document, or bill.

right   Anything to which a person has a just and valid claim.

right of confrontation   The right to cross-examine witnesses for the opposing party in a criminal case.

right of cross-examination   See **right of confrontation.**

right of privacy   Constitutional right to engage in intimate personal conduct or make fundamental life decisions without interference by the state.

right to a speedy trial   Constitutional right to have an open public trial conducted without unreasonable delay.

right to appeal   Statutory right to appeal decisions of lower courts in certain circumstances.

right to be let alone   Another term for the right of privacy.

right to counsel   (1) The right to retain an attorney to represent oneself in court. (2) The right of an indigent person to have an attorney provided at public expense.

right to die   Controversial "right" to terminate one's own life under certain circumstances.

right to keep and bear arms   Right to possess certain weapons, protected against federal infringement by the Second Amendment to the U.S. Constitution.

right to refuse medical treatment   The right of a patient or patient's surrogate in some instances to refuse to allow doctors to perform medical treatment.

right to vote   The right of an individual to cast a vote in an election.

riot   A public disturbance involving acts of violence, usually by three or more persons.

ripeness   Readiness for review by a court of law. An issue is "ripe for review" in the Supreme Court when a case presents adverse parties who have exhausted all other avenues of appeal.

ripeness doctrine   The doctrine under which courts consider only those questions that are deemed to be "ripe for review."

roadblocks   Barriers set up by police to stop motorists.

robbery   The crime of taking money or property from a person against that person's will by means of force.

rule making   The power of a court or agency to promulgate rules; the process through which rules are promulgated.

rule of four   U.S. Supreme Court rule whereby the Court grants certiorari only on the agreement of at least four justices.

rule of law   The idea that law, not the discretion of officials, should govern public affairs.

rules of procedure   Rules promulgated by courts governing civil, criminal, and appellate procedure.

sanction   Penalty or other mechanism of enforcement.

saving construction, doctrine of   The doctrine that, given two plausible interpretations of a statute, a court will adopt the interpretation that prevents the statute from being declared unconstitutional.

scarcity theory   Theory holding that government can and should regulate access to the public airwaves as these are scarce commodities.

school prayer   Refers to various activities of a religious nature in the public schools.

school prayer decisions   Collective term for the Supreme Court's decisions of the 1960s prohibiting various activities of a religious nature in the public schools.

scientific evidence   Evidence obtained through scientific and technological innovations.

Scopes trial   Sensational criminal trial held in Dayton, Tennessee, in 1925 in which John Scopes, a high school biology teacher, was convicted under a state law (now defunct) prohibiting the teaching of evolution.

search and seizure   Refers to the police search for and/or seizure of contraband or other evidence of crime.

search based on consent   See **consent to a search.**

search incident to a lawful arrest   Search of a person placed under arrest and the area within the arrestee's grasp and control.

search warrant   A court order authorizing a search of a specified area for a specified purpose.

secession   Action by a state formally withdrawing from the Union.

Second Amendment   Amendment contained within the Bill of Rights guaranteeing the "right to keep and bear arms."

Section 1983 action   A federal lawsuit brought under 42 U.S. Code Section 1983 to redress violations of civil and/or constitutional rights.

secular government   Government that is not affiliated with or controlled by religious authorities.

secular humanism   The philosophy that man, not God, is the source of standards of right and wrong.

sedition   The crime of inciting insurrection or attempting to overthrow the government.

seditious speech   Expression aimed at inciting insurrection or overthrow of the government.

seduction   The common-law crime of inducing a woman of previously chaste character to have sexual intercourse outside of wedlock on the promise of marriage.

seizure   Action of police in taking possession or control of property or persons.

selective incorporation   Doctrine under which selected provisions comprising most of the Bill of Rights are deemed applicable to the states by way of the Fourteenth Amendment.

selective prosecution   Singling out defendants for prosecution on the basis of race, religion, or other impermissible classifications.

self-representation   See *pro se* **defense.**

sentence   The official pronouncement of punishment in a criminal case.

sentencing guidelines   Legislative guidelines mandating that sentencing conform to guidelines absent a compelling reason for departing from them.

sentencing hearing   A hearing held by a trial court prior to the pronouncement of sentence.

separate but equal doctrine   A now defunct doctrine that permitted racial segregation as long as equal facilities or accommodations were provided.

separation of church and state   First Amendment doctrine that holds that there must be a "wall of separation" between religion and government.

separation of powers   Constitutional assignment of legislative, executive, and judicial powers to different branches of government.

sequestration   Holding jurors incommunicado during trial.

seriatim   Serially, individually.

set aside   Affirmative action policies that reserve a certain proportion of government contracts for minority businesses.

Seventh Amendment   Amendment contained within the Bill of Rights guaranteeing the right to a jury trial in federal civil suits.

severability   The doctrine under which courts will declare invalid only the offending provision of a statute and allow the other provisions to remain in effect.

severability clause   A clause found in a statute indicating that if any particular provision of the law is invalidated, the other provisions remain in effect.

sexual harassment   Offensive interaction of a sexual nature in the workplace.

Sherman Antitrust Act of 1890   A federal statute prohibiting any contract, combination or conspiracy in restraint of trade. The act is designed to protect and preserve a system of free and open competition. Its scope is broad and reaches individuals and entities in profit and nonprofit activities as well as local governments and educational institutions.

show cause   A court order requiring a party to appear and present a legal justification for a particular act.

showup   An event in which a crime victim is taken to see a suspect to make an identification.

silver platter doctrine   Doctrine under which federal and state authorities could share illegally obtained evidence before the exclusionary rule was made applicable to all jurisdictions.

similar fact evidence   Refers to evidence of facts similar to the facts in the crime charged. The test of admissibility is whether such evidence is relevant and has a probative value in establishing a material issue. Under some limited circumstances, evidence of other crimes or conduct similar to that charged against the defendant may be admitted in evidence in a criminal prosecution.

sine qua non   "Without which not." A necessary or indispensable condition or prerequisite.

Sixth Amendment   Amendment contained within the Bill of Rights guaranteeing the right to counsel and the right to trial by jury in criminal cases.

slander   The tort of defaming someone's character through verbal statements.

small claims   Minor civil suits.

sobriety checkpoints   Roadblocks set up for the purpose of administering field sobriety tests to motorists who appear to be intoxicated.

social contract   The theory that government is the product of agreement among rational individuals to subordinate themselves to collective authority in exchange for security of life, liberty, and property.

social Darwinism   The theory that society improves through unrestricted competition and the "survival of the fittest."

sodomy   Oral or anal sex between persons, or sex between a person and an animal (the latter is often referred to as bestiality).

solicitation   (1) The crime of offering someone money or other thing of value in order to persuade that person to commit a crime. (2) An active effort on the part of an attorney or other professional to obtain business.

sovereign immunity   A common law doctrine under which the sovereign may be sued only with its consent.

special prosecutor   A prosecutor appointed specifically to investigate a particular episode and, if criminal activity is found, to prosecute those involved.

specific performance   A court-imposed requirement that a party perform obligations incurred under a contract.

Speech or Debate Clause   Provision of Article I, Section 6, protecting members of Congress from arrest or interference with their official duties.

speedy and public trial   An open and public criminal trial held without unreasonable delay.

spending power   The power of the legislature to spend public money for public purposes.

standby counsel   An attorney appointed to assist an indigent defendant who elects to represent himself or herself at trial.

standing   The right to initiate a legal action or challenge based on the fact that one has suffered or is likely to suffer a real and substantial injury.

stare decisis   "To stand by decided matters." The principle that past decisions should stand as precedents for future decisions. This principle, which stands for the proposition that precedents are binding on later decisions, is said to be followed less rigorously in constitutional law than in other branches of the law.

state action, doctrine of   The doctrine that limits constitutional prohibitions to official government or government-sponsored action, as opposed to action that is merely private in character.

state power to regulate interstate commerce   The limited power of a state government to make and enforce rules affecting commerce that transcends the state.

state's attorney   A state prosecutor.

states' rights   The constitutional rights and powers reserved to state governments under the Tenth Amendment. Historically, the philosophy that states should be accorded broad latitude within the American federal system.

status offenses   Noncriminal conduct on the part of juveniles that may subject juveniles to the authority.

statute   A generally applicable law enacted by a legislature.

statute of limitations   A law proscribing prosecutions for specific crimes after specified periods of time.

statutory construction   The official interpretation of a statute rendered by a court of law.

statutory rape   The strict-liability offense of having sexual intercourse with a minor.

stay   To postpone, hold off, or stop the execution of a judgment.

stay of execution   An order suspending the enforcement of a judgment of a court.

stewardship theory   The theory that the president, being steward of the country, may exercise any and all powers he deems necessary to that end, unless they are specifically prohibited by the Constitution.

stop-and-frisk   An encounter between a police officer and a suspect during which the latter is temporarily detained and subjected to a "pat-down" search for weapons.

stream of commerce doctrine   First articulated by Justice Holmes in 1905, this doctrine permitted federal regulation of commerce that is no longer of an interstate nature.

strict judicial scrutiny   Judicial review of government action or policy in which the ordinary presumption of constitutionality is reversed.

strict liability offenses   Offenses that do not require proof of the defendant's intent.

strict necessity, doctrine of   The doctrine that a court should consider a constitutional question only when strictly necessary to resolve the case at bar.

strict neutrality   Refers to the doctrine that government must be strictly neutral on matters of religion.

strict scrutiny   The most demanding level of judicial review in cases involving alleged infringements of civil rights or liberties.

strip searches   Searches of suspects' or prisoners' private parts.

sua sponte   "Of its own will." Voluntarily, without coercion or suggestion.

subjective test   A legal test based on the perceptions or intentions of an individual actor, rather than external circumstances.

subpoena   "Under penalty." A judicial order requiring a person to appear in court in connection with a designated proceeding.

subpoena duces tecum   "Under penalty you shall bring with you." A judicial order requiring a party to bring certain described records, papers, books, or documents to court.

substantial federal question A significant legal question pertaining to the U.S. Constitution, a federal statute, treaty, regulation, or judicial interpretation of any of the foregoing.

substantial step A significant step toward completion of an intended result.

substantive criminal law That branch of the criminal law that defines criminal offenses and defenses and specifies criminal punishments.

substantive due process Doctrine that due process clauses of the Fifth and Fourteenth Amendments to the United States Constitution require legislation to be fair and reasonable in content as well as application.

substantive law That part of the law that creates rights and proscribes wrongs.

sui juris Under law.

summary decisions Decisions made by appellate courts without the submission of briefs or oral arguments.

summary judgment A decision rendered without extended argument where no material legal question is presented in a case.

summary justice Trial held by court of limited jurisdiction without benefit of a jury.

summary trial A bench trial of a minor misdemeanor.

summons A court order requiring a person to appear in court to answer a criminal charge.

Sunday closing laws Laws, now largely defunct, prohibiting business from opening on Sundays.

supervisory power The power of the Supreme Court to supervise the lower federal courts.

suppression doctrine See **exclusionary rule.**

supra "Above."

Supremacy Clause Provision of Article VI of the U.S. Constitution making that document, and all federal legislation consistent with it, the "supreme law of the land."

suspect classification doctrine The doctrine that laws classifying people according to race, ethnicity, and religion are inherently suspect and subjected to strict judicial scrutiny.

suspended sentence Trial court's decision to place a defendant on probation or under community control instead of imposing an announced sentence on the condition that the original sentence may be imposed if the defendant violates the conditions of the suspended sentence.

sustain To uphold.

symbolic speech An activity that expresses a point of view or message symbolically, rather than through pure speech.

taking Refers to government action taking private property or depriving owner the use and control thereof.

tax exemptions Rules under which certain organizations or individuals are not required to pay certain taxes.

taxing power The power of government to levy taxes.

taxpayer suits Suits brought by taxpayers to challenge certain government actions. Taxpayer suits as such are prohibited in the federal courts in that one does not acquire standing merely by virtue of paying taxes to support policies of which one does not approve.

Tenth Amendment Amendment to the Constitution reserving to the states powers not delegated to the federal government.

Terry stop See **stop-and-frisk.**

testimony Evidence given by a witness who has sworn to tell the truth.

Third Amendment Amendment found in the Bill of Rights prohibiting the military from quartering soldiers in citizens' homes without their consent.

third party A person not directly connected with a legal proceeding but potentially affected by its outcome.

third-party consent Consent, usually to a search, given by a person on behalf of another. For example, a college roommate who allows the police to search his or her roommate's effects.

Thirteenth Amendment Amendment to the U.S. Constitution ratified in 1865 formally abolishing slavery.

time, place, and manner doctrine First Amendment doctrine holding that government may impose reasonable limitations on the time, place, and manner of expressive activities.

time, place, and manner regulations Reasonable government regulations as to the time, place, and manner of expressive activities protected by the Constitution.

tolling Ceasing. For example, one who conceals self from the authorities generally causes a "tolling" of the statutes of limitation on prosecution of a crime.

tort A wrong or injury other than a breach of contract for which the remedy is a civil suit for damages.

totality of circumstances The entire collection of relevant facts in a particular case.

transactional immunity A grant of immunity applying to offenses to which a witness's testimony relates.

transcript A written record of a trial or hearing.

treason The crime of attempting by overt acts to overthrow the government, or of betraying the government to a foreign power.

treaty A legally binding agreement between one or more countries. In the United States, treaties are negotiated by the president but must be ratified by the Senate.

trespass An unlawful interference with one's person or property.

trial A judicial proceeding held for the purpose of making factual and legal determinations.

trial by jury   A trial in which the verdict is determined not by the court but by a jury of the defendant's peers.

trial courts   Courts whose primary function is the conduct of civil and/or criminal trials.

trial *de novo*   "A new trial." Refers to trial court review of convictions for minor offenses by courts of limited jurisdiction by conducting a new trial instead of merely reviewing the record of the initial trial.

trial jury   A fixed number of citizens, usually six or twelve, selected according to law and sworn to hear the evidence presented at a trial and to render a verdict based on the law and the evidence.

tribunal   A court of law.

trimester framework   The framework established in *Roe v. Wade* (1973) governing the validity of laws regulating abortion in the three stages of pregnancy.

true bill   An indictment handed down by a grand jury.

trustee   A person entrusted to handle the affairs of another.

trusty   A prisoner entrusted with authority to supervise other prisoners in exchange for certain privileges and status.

tuition tax credits   Vouchers that taxpayers may "spend" at schools of their choice, be they public or private.

Twenty-fifth Amendment   Amendment ratified in 1967 dealing with issues of presidential disability and removal.

Twenty-first Amendment   The Amendment ratified in 1933 repealing the unpopular Eighteenth Amendment (1919) that established "Prohibition."

Twenty-second Amendment   Amendment ratified in 1951 limiting presidents to two terms in office.

Twenty-sixth Amendment   Amendment ratified in 1971 lowering the voting age in federal and state elections to eighteen.

two-party system   A political system, such as that of the United States, organized around two major competing political parties.

two-witness rule   A requirement that to prove a defendant guilty of perjury the prosecution must prove the falsity of the defendant's statements either by two witnesses or by one witness and corroborating documents or circumstances.

ultra vires   Beyond the scope of a prescribed authority.

umpire of the federal system   Refers to the Supreme Court's role in refereeing disputes between the national government and the states.

unalienable rights   Rights that are vested in individuals by birth, not granted by government.

unanimity rule   A decision rule requiring a unanimous vote.

unconstitutional as applied   Declaration by a court of law that a statute is invalid insofar as it is enforced in some particular context.

unconstitutional *per se*   A statute that is unconstitutional under any given circumstances.

unconventional religious practices   Practices outside the religious mainstream.

Uniform Code of Military Justice (UCMJ)   A code of laws enacted by Congress that govern military servicepersons and defines the procedural and evidentiary requirements in military law and the substantive criminal offenses and punishments.

unitary system   A political system in which all power is vested in one central government.

United States attorneys   Attorneys appointed by the president with consent of the U.S. Senate to prosecute federal crimes in a specific geographical area of the United States.

United States Court of Appeals for the Armed Forces   See **Court of Appeals for the Armed Forces.**

United States Courts of Appeals   The intermediate appellate courts of appeals in the federal system that sit in geographical areas of the United States and in which panels of appellate judges hear appeals in civil and criminal cases primarily from the U.S. District Courts.

United States District Court   The principal trial courts in the federal system that sit in ninety-four districts where usually one judge hears proceedings and trials in civil and criminal cases.

United States Sentencing Commission   A federal body that proposes guideline sentences for defendants convicted of federal crimes.

United States Supreme Court   The highest court in the United States consisting of nine justices that has jurisdiction to review, by appeal or writ of certiorari, the decisions of lower federal courts and many decisions of the highest courts of each state.

universal suffrage   The requirement that all citizens (at least all competent adults not guilty of serious crimes) be eligible to vote in elections.

unlawful assembly   A group of individuals, usually five or more, assembled to commit an unlawful act or to commit a lawful act in an unlawful manner.

unreasonable searches and seizures   Searches that violate the Fourth Amendment to the Constitution.

use immunity   A grant of immunity that forbids prosecutors from using immunized testimony as evidence in criminal prosecutions.

vacate   To annul, set aside, or rescind.

vagrancy   The crime of going about without visible means of support (virtually archaic).

vagueness doctrine   Doctrine of constitutional law holding unconstitutional (as a violation of due process) legislation that fails to clearly inform the person what is required or proscribed.

venire   The set of persons summoned for jury duty. The actual jury is selected from the venire. See ***voir dire.***

venue   The location of a trial or hearing.

verdict The formal decision rendered by a jury in a civil or criminal trial.

vested rights Rights acquired by the passage of time.

veto The power of a chief executive to block adoption of a law by refusing to sign the legislation.

viability That point in pregnancy where the fetus is able to survive outside the womb.

victim impact evidence Evidence relating to the physical, economic, and psychological impact that a crime has on the victim or victim's family.

victimless crimes Crimes in which no particular person appears or claims to be injured, such as prostitution or gambling.

voice exemplar A sample of a person's voice; usually taken by police for the purpose of identifying a suspect.

void-for-vagueness doctrine See **vagueness doctrine.**

voir dire "To speak the truth." The process by which prospective jurors are questioned by counsel and/or the court before being selected to serve on a jury.

voluntariness of confessions The quality of a confession having been freely given.

voting blocs Groups of individuals who usually vote together.

Voting Rights Act of 1965 Landmark federal legislation protecting voters from racial discrimination.

waiver The intentional and voluntary relinquishment of a right, or conduct from which such relinquishment may be inferred.

waiver of juvenile court jurisdiction A relinquishment by a juvenile court to allow prosecution of a juvenile in an adult court.

waiver of *Miranda* rights A known relinquishment of the right against self-incrimination provided by the Fifth Amendment to the U.S. Constitution.

War Powers Resolution 1973 act of Congress purporting to limit a president's authority to commit troops to a combat situation abroad.

warrant A court order authorizing a search, seizure, or arrest.

warrant requirement The Fourth Amendment's "preference" that searches be based on warrants issued by judges or magistrates.

warrantless arrest An arrest made by police who do not possess an arrest warrant.

warrantless search A search made by police who do not possess a search warrant.

weight of the evidence The balance or preponderance of the evidence. Weight of the evidence is to be distinguished from "legal sufficiency of the evidence" which is the concern of an appellate court.

well-regulated militia Body of citizens organized for military service but subject to government regulation.

white primary Historically, a primary election in which participation was limited to whites.

wiretap order A court order permitting electronic surveillance for a limited period.

wiretapping The use of highly sensitive electronic devices designed to intercept electronic communications.

writ An order issued by a court of law requiring the performance of some specific act.

writ of certiorari See **certiorari, writ of.**

writ of error See **error, writ of.**

writ of habeas corpus See **habeas corpus, writ of.**

writ of mandamus See **mandamus, writ of.**

writ of prohibition See **prohibition, writ of.**

writs of assistance Ancient writs issuing from the Court of Exchequer in England granting sheriffs broad powers of search and seizure for the purpose of assisting in the collection of debts owed to the Crown.

yellow dog contracts Contracts making the right to work conditioned upon the employee's agreement not to join a labor union (defunct).

zoning Laws regulating the use of land.

TABLE OF CASES

Principal cases are in bold type. Non-principal cases are in roman type. References are to pages.

44 Liquormart, Inc. v. Rhode Island, 517 U.S. 484, 116 S.Ct. 1495, 134 L.Ed.2d 711 (1996), 463, **508**

Abington School Dist. v. Schempp, 374 U.S. 203, 83 S.Ct. 1560, 10 L.Ed.2d 844 (1963), 536, 540, **564**

Abrams v. United States, 250 U.S. 616, 40 S.Ct. 17, 63 L.Ed. 1173 (1919), 436, 438

Adair v. United States, 208 U.S. 161, 28 S.Ct. 277, 52 L.Ed. 436 (1908), 387

Adamson v. California, 323 U.S. 46, 67 S.Ct. 1672, 91 L.Ed. 1903 (1947), 349, **365,** 371, 375, 710

Adarand Constructors v. Peña, 515 U.S. 200, 115 S.Ct. 2097, 132 L.Ed.2d 158 (1995), 753, **793,** 808

Adderley v. Florida, 385 U.S. 39, 87 S.Ct. 242, 17 L.Ed.2d 149 (1966), 455, **505**

Adkins v. Children's Hospital, 261 U.S. 525, 543 S.Ct. 394, 67 L.Ed. 785 (1923), 387, 389, 390, 391, 392, **415,** 420, 421, 422, 423, 424

Agostini v. Felton, 521 U.S. —, 117 S.Ct. 1997, 138 L.Ed.2d 391 (1997), 533, 536, **573**

Aguilar v. Felton, 473 U.S. 402, 105 S.Ct. 3232, 87 L.Ed.2d 290 (1985), 535, 536, 573, 574, 575

Aguilar v. Texas, 375 U.S. 812, 84 S.Ct. 86, 11 L.Ed.2d 48 (1963), 589, 590

Akron v. Akron Center for Reproductive Health, 462 U.S. 416, 103 S.Ct. 2481, 76 L.Ed.2d 687 (1983), 684, 689, 723

Alabama v. White, 496 U.S. 325, 110 S.Ct. 412, 110 L.Ed.2d 301 (1990), 590, 593

Alberts v. California, 354 U.S. 476, 77 S.Ct. 1304 (1957), 451

Albertson, State v., 93 Idaho 640, 470 P.2d 300 (Idaho 1970), 694

Alexander v. County Bd. of Educ., 396 U.S. 19, 90 S.Ct. 29, 24 L.Ed.2d 19 (1969), 746, 787

Allegheny, County of, v. American Civil Liberties Union (ACLU), 492 U.S. 573, 109 S.Ct. 3086, 106 L.Ed.2d 472 (1989), 541

Allgeyer v. Louisiana, 165 U.S. 578, 17 S.Ct. 427, 41 L.Ed. 832 (1897), 385

Allied Structural Steel Co. v. Spannaus, 438 U.S. 234, 98 S.Ct. 2716, 57 L.Ed.2d 727 (1978), 381

American Communications Ass'n v. Douds, 339 U.S. 382, 70 S.Ct. 674, 94 L.Ed. 925 (1950), 336

Anderson v. Celebrezze, 460 U.S. 780, 103 S.Ct. 1564, 75 L.Ed.2d 547 (1983), 831

Apodaca v. Oregon, 406 U.S. 404, 92 S.Ct. 1628, 32 L.Ed.2d 184 (1972), 611

Ardery v. State, 56 Ind. 328 (1877), 492

Argersinger v. Hamlin, 407 U.S. 25, 92 S.Ct. 2006, 32 L.Ed.2d 530 (1972), 605

Arizona v. Fulminante, 499 U.S. 279, 111 S.Ct. 1246, 113 L.Ed.2d 302 (1991), 602, 622

Arkansas v. Sanders, 442 U.S. 753, 99 S.Ct. 2586, 61 L.Ed.2d 235 (1979), 591, 592

Arlington Heights v. Metropolitan Housing Dev. Corp., 429 U.S. 252, 97 S.Ct. 555, 50 L.Ed.2d 450 (1977), 843

Ashcraft v. Tennessee, 322 U.S. 143, 64 S.Ct. 921, 88 L.Ed. 1192 (1944), 600

Austin v. United States, 509 U.S. 602, 113 S.Ct. 2801, 125 L.Ed.2d 488 (1993), 343, 614

Baker v. Carr, 369 U.S. 186, 82 S.Ct. 691, 7 L.Ed.2d 663 (1962), 828, 831, 834

Ballew v. Georgia, 435 U.S. 223, 98 S.Ct. 1029, 55 L.Ed.2d 234 (1978), 611

Barnes v. Glen Theatre, Inc., 501 U.S. 560, 111 S.Ct. 2456, 115 L.Ed.2d 504 (1991), 447, **487,** 676

Barron v. Baltimore, 32 U.S. 243, 8 L.Ed. 672 (1833), 348, **359,** 393

Barry, Guardianship of Andrew, 445 So.2d 365 (Fla.App. 2 Dist. 1984), 694, 695

Bates v. State Bar of Ariz., 433 U.S. 350, 97 S.Ct. 2691, 53 L.Ed.2d 810 (1977), 463

Batson v. Kentucky, 476 U.S. 79, 106 S.Ct. 1712, 90 L.Ed.2d 69 (1986), 612, **656**

Baxter v. Palmigiano, 425 U.S. 308, 96 S.Ct. 1551, 47 L.Ed.2d 810 (1976), 616

Bedford Cut Stone Co. v. Journeymen Stone Cutters' Ass'n, 274 U.S. 37, 47 S.Ct. 522, 71 L.Ed. 916 (1927), 388

Belle Terre v. Boraas, 416 U.S. 1, 94 S.Ct. 1536, 39 L.Ed.2d 797 (1974), 690, 691

Bellotti v. Baird, 443 U.S. 622, 99 S.Ct. 3035, 61 L.Ed.2d 797 (1979), 684

Benton v. Maryland, 395 U.S. 784, 89 S.Ct. 2056, 23 L.Ed.2d 707 (1969), 350, 613

Berman v. Parker, 348 U.S. 26, 75 S.Ct. 98, 98 L.Ed.2d 27 (1954), 424-425

Betts v. Brady, 316 U.S. 455, 62 S.Ct. 1252, 86 L.Ed. 1595 (1942), 654, 655, 656

Bigelow v. Virginia, 421 U.S. 809, 95 S.Ct. 2222, 44 L.Ed.2d 600 (1975), 508

Bivens v. Six Unknown Named Federal Narcotics Agents, 403 U.S. 388, 91 S.Ct. 1999, 29 L.Ed.2d 619 (1971), 596, 597

Bland, United States v., 283 U.S. 636, 51 S.Ct. 569, 75 L.Ed. 1319 (1931), 530

Blockberger v. United States, 284 U.S. 299, 52 S.Ct. 180, 76 L.Ed. 306 (1932), 665

Board of Airport Comm'rs v. Jews for Jesus, 482 U.S. 569, 107 S.Ct. 2568, 96 L.Ed.2d 500 (1987), 457

Board of Educ. v. Allen, 389 U.S. 1031, 88 S.Ct. 767, 19 L.Ed.2d 819 (1968), 534

Board of Educ. v. Dowell, 498 U.S. 237, 111 S.Ct. 630, 112 L.Ed.2d 715 (1991), 748

Board of Educ. v. Mergens, 496 U.S. 226, 110 S.Ct. 2356, 110 L.Ed.2d 191 (1990), 535

Bob Jones Univ. v. United States, 461 U.S. 574, 103 S.Ct. 2017, 76 L.Ed.2d 157 (1983), 542

Boerne, City of, v. Flores, — U.S. —, 117 S.Ct. 2157, 138 L.Ed.2d 624 (1997), 528

Bolling v. Sharpe, 347 U.S. 497, 74 S.Ct. 693, 98 L.Ed. 884, 53 O.O. 331 (1954), 738, 745

Booth v. Maryland, 482 U.S. 496, 107 S.Ct. 2529, 96 L.Ed.2d 440 (1987), 620, 671, 673, 674

Bordenkircher v. Hayes, 434 U.S. 357, 98 S.Ct. 663, 54 L.Ed.2d 604 (1978), 608

Bouvia v. Superior Court, 179 Cal.App.3d 1127, 225 Cal.Rptr. 297 (Cal.App. 2 Dist. 1986), 695

Bowers v. Hardwick, 478 U.S. 186, 106 S.Ct. 2841, 92 L.Ed.2d 140 (1986), 488, 692, 693, **727,** 814

Boyd v. United States, 116 U.S. 616, 6 S.Ct. 524, 29 L.Ed. 746 (1886), 587, 594, 634, 710

Boykin v. Alabama, 395 U.S. 238, 89 S.Ct. 1709, 23 L.Ed.2d 274 (1969), 608

Bradwell v. Illinois, 83 U.S. 130, 2 L.Ed. 442 (1872), 756

Bram v. United States, 168 U.S. 532, 18 S.Ct. 183, 42 L.Ed. 568 (1897), 600

Brandenburg v. Ohio, 395 U.S. 444, 89 S.Ct. 1827, 23 L.Ed.2d 430, 48 O.O.2d 320 (1969), 441, **478**

Branti v. Finkel, 445 U.S. 507, 100 S.Ct. 1287, 63 L.Ed.2d 574 (1980), 465

Brecht v. Abrahamson, 507 U.S. 619, 113 S.Ct. 1710, 123 L.Ed.2d 353 (1993), 623

Breed v. Jones, 421 U.S. 519, 95 S.Ct. 1779, 44 L.Ed.2d 346 (1975), 625

Breedlove v. Suttles, 302 U.S. 277, 58 S.Ct. 205, 82 L.Ed. 252 (1937), 352, 353, 820

Brinegar v. United States, 338 U.S. 160, 69 S.Ct. 1302, 93 L.Ed. 1879 (1949), 589

Brown v. Allen, 344 U.S. 443, 73 S.Ct. 397, 97 L.Ed. 469 (1953), 622

Brown v. Board of Educ. of Topeka (Brown I), 347 U.S. 483, 74 S.Ct. 686, 98 L.Ed. 873 (1954), 345, 744, 745, 749, 755, 768, **779,** 786, 787

Brown v. Board of Educ. of Topeka (Brown II), 349 U.S. 294, 75 S.Ct. 753, 99 L.Ed. 1083 (1955), 746, 747, **781**

Brown v. Pena, 441 F.Supp. 1382 (D.C. Fla. 1977), 525

Brown v. Thomson, 462 U.S. 835, 103 S.Ct. 2690, 77 L.Ed.2d 214 (1983), 829

Brown, United States v., 381 U.S. 437, 85 S.Ct. 1707, 14 L.Ed.2d 484 (1965), 336

Bryant v. Zimmerman, 278 U.S. 63, 49 S.Ct. 61, 73 L.Ed. 184 (1928), 467

Buck v. Bell, 274 U.S. 200, 47 S.Ct. 584, 71 L.Ed. 1000 (1927), 679, **702**

Buckley v. Valeo, 424 U.S. 1, 96 S.Ct. 612, 46 L.Ed.2d 659 (1976), 833

Bunting v. Oregon, 243 U.S. 426, 37 S.Ct. 435, 61 L.Ed. 830 (1917), 387, 418, 419

Burch v. Louisiana, 441 U.S. 130, 99 S.Ct. 1623, 60 L.Ed.2d 96 (1979), 611

Burton v. Wilmington Parking Auth., 365 U.S. 715, 81 S.Ct. 856, 6 L.Ed.2d 45 (1961), 768

Bush v. Vera, 517 U.S. 952, 116 S.Ct. 1941, 135 L.Ed.2d 248 (1996), 827

Butler v. Michigan, 352 U.S. 380, 77 S.Ct. 524, 1 L.Ed.2d 412 (1957), 499

Butler, United States v., 297 U.S. 1, 56 S.Ct. 213, 80 L.Ed. 477 (1936), 389

Byars v. United States, 273 U.S. 28, 47 S.Ct. 248, 71 L.Ed. 520 (1927), 636

Calandra, United States v., 414 U.S. 338, 94 S.Ct. 613, 38 L.Ed.2d 561, 66 O.O.2d 320 (1974), 596, 642, 643

Calder v. Bull, 3 U.S. 386, 1 L.Ed. 648 (1798), 335, 377, 379, 614

Califano v. Goldfarb, 430 U.S. 199, 97 S.Ct. 1021, 51 L.Ed.2d 270 (1977), 758

Califano v. Webster, 430 U.S. 313, 97 S.Ct. 1192, 51 L.Ed.2d 360 (1977), 808

California v. Acevedo, 500 U.S. 565, 111 S.Ct. 1982, 114 L.Ed.2d 619 (1991), 592

California v. LaRue, 409 U.S. 109, 93 S.Ct. 390, 34 L.Ed.2d 342 (1972), 487

Cantwell v. Connecticut, 310 U.S. 296, 60 S.Ct. 900, 84 L.Ed. 1213 (1940), 349, 522, 524, 556

Carey v. Population Servs., 431 U.S. 678, 97 S.Ct. 2010, 52 L.Ed.2d 675 (1977), 727

Carolene Prods., United States v., 304 U.S. 144, 58 S.Ct. 778, 82 L.Ed. 1234 (1938), 739, 809, 818

Carroll v. United States, 60 Ct. Cl. 1032 (Ct. Cl. 1925), 591

Cartler v. Carter Coal Co., 298 U.S. 238, 56 S.Ct. 855, 80 L.Ed. 1160 (1936), 389-390

Central Hudson Gas & Elec. Corp. v. Public Serv. Comm'n of N.Y., 447 U.S. 557, 100 S.Ct. 2343, 65 L.Ed.2d 341 (1980), 462, 509, 510, 511

Chandler v. Florida, 449 U.S. 560, 101 S.Ct. 802, 66 L.Ed.2d 740 (1981), 610

Chandler v. Miller, 520 U.S. 305, 117 S.Ct. 1295, 137 L.Ed.2d 513 (1997), 340

Chaplinsky v. New Hampshire, 315 U.S. 568, 62 S.Ct. 766, 86 L.Ed. 1031 (1942), 441, 442, 443, 448

Chapman v. California, 386 U.S. 18, 87 S.Ct. 824, 17 L.Ed.2d 705 (1967), 622

Charles River Bridge Co. v. Warren Bridge Co., 36 U.S. 420, 9 L.Ed. 773 (1837), 380, 381, 382, **401**

Charles Wolff Packing Co. v. Court of Industrial Relations, 262 U.S. 522, 43 S.Ct. 630, 67 L.Ed. 1103 (1923), 387

Chas. C. Steward Machine Co. v. Davis, 301 U.S. 548, 57 S.Ct. 883, 81 L.Ed. 1279 (1937), 391

Chicago, Burlington & Quincy R.R. Co. v. Chicago, 166 U.S. 226, 17 S.Ct. 581, 41 L.Ed. 979 (1897), 348, **363,** 393

Chicago, Milwaukee, & St. Paul R.R. Co. v. Minnesota, 123 U.S. 418, 10 S.Ct. 462, 33 L.Ed. 970 (1890), 385

Chimel v. California, 395 U.S. 752, 89 S.Ct. 2034, 23 L.Ed.2d 685 (1969), 591

Chisholm v. Roemer, 501 U.S. 380, 111 S.Ct. 775, 112 L.Ed.2d 838 (1991), 825

Church of the Lukumi Babalu Aye, Inc. v. City of Hialeah, 508 U.S. 520, 113 S.Ct. 2217, 124 L.Ed.2d 472 (1993), 528-529, **558**

City of (see name of city)

Civil Rights Cases, The, 109 U.S. 3, 3 S.Ct. 18, 27 L.Ed. 835 (1883), 347, 742, 768, 769, **773**

Clark v. Community for Creative Non-Violence, 468 U.S. 288, 1-4 S.Ct. 3065, 82 L.Ed.2d 221 (1984), 488

Classic, United States v., 313 U.S. 299, 61 S.Ct. 1031, 85 L.Ed. 1368 (1941), 819, 835, 836, 837

Cleburne v. Cleburne Living Center, 473 U.S. 432, 105 S.Ct. 3249, 87 L.Ed.2d 313 (1985), 763

Coalition for Economic Equity v. Wilson, — U.S. —, 118 S.Ct. 17, 138 L.Ed.2d 1049 (1997), 754

Cohen v. California, 403 U.S. 15, 91 S.Ct. 1780, 29 L.Ed.2d 284 (1971), 442, 443, 444, **480**

Coker v. Georgia, 433 U.S. 584, 97 S.Ct. 2861, 53 L.Ed.2d 982 (1977), 619, 621

Colegrove v. Green, 328 U.S. 549, 66 S.Ct. 1198, 90 L.Ed.2d 1432 (1946), 828, 832

Colgrove v. Battin, 413 U.S. 149, 93 S.Ct. 2449, 37 L.Ed.2d 522 (1973), 342

Committee for Public Educ. v. Nyquist, 413 U.S. 756, 93 S.Ct. 2955, 37 L.Ed.2d 948 (1973), 543

Committee to Defend Reproductive Rights v. Myers, 172 Cal.Rptr. 866, 625 P2d 779 (Cal. 1981), 686

Communist Party v. Subversive Activities Control Bd., 367 U.S. 1, 81 S.Ct. 1357, 6 L.Ed.2d 625 (1961), 440

Communist Party of Indiana v. Whitcomb, 414 U.S. 441, 94 S.Ct. 656, 38 L.Ed.2d 635 (1974), 441

Coolidge v. New Hampshire, 403 U.S. 43, 91 S.Ct. 2022, 29 L.Ed.2d 564 (1971), 589, 591

Coppage v. Kansas, 236 U.S. 1, 35 S.Ct. 240, 59 L.Ed. 441 (1915), 387, 392, 424

Corfield v. Coryell, 6 Fed. Cas. 546 (C.C. Pa. 1823), 408

County of (see name of county)

Cox v. Louisiana, 379 U.S. 559, 85 S.Ct. 476, 113 L.Ed.2d 487 (1965), 455, 505

Cox Broadcasting v. Cohn, 402 U.S. 469, 95 S.Ct. 1029, 43 L.Ed.2d 328 (1975), 450

Craig v. Boren, 429 U.S. 190, 97 S.Ct. 451, 50 L.Ed.2d 397 (1976), 758, 806

Crandall v. Nevada, 73 U.S. 35, 18 L.Ed. 745 (1868), 409

Cruikshank, United States v., 92 U.S. 542, 23 L.Ed. 588 (1875), 338

Cruz v. Beto, 405 U.S. 319, 92 S.Ct. 1079, 31 L.Ed.2d 263 (1972), 616

Cruzan v. Missouri Health Dept., 497 U.S. 261, 110 S.Ct. 2841, 111 L.Ed.2d 224 (1990), 696, 731, 733

Cumming v. County Bd. of Educ., 175 U.S. 528, 205 S.Ct. 197, 44 L.Ed. 262 (1899), 780

Cummings v. Missouri, 71 U.S. 277, 18 L.Ed. 356 (1866), 335

Curtis Publishing Co. v. Butts, 388 U.S. 130, 87 S.Ct. 1975, 18 L.Ed.2d 1094 (1967), 449

Curtis v. Loether, 415 U.S. 189, 94 S.Ct. 1005, 39 L.Ed.2d 260 (1974), 342

Darby, United States v., 312 U.S. 100, 61 S.Ct. 451, 85 L.Ed. 609 (1941), 391

Dartmouth College v. Woodward, 17 U.S. 518, 4 L.Ed. 629 (1819), 379, 382, **399**

Davis v. Bandemer, 478 U.S. 109, 106 S.Ct. 2797, 92 L.Ed.2d 85 (1986), 832

Davis v. Beason, 133 U.S. 333, 10 S.Ct. 299, 33 L.Ed. 637 (1890), 523

Defore, People v., 242 N.Y. 13, 150 N.E. 585 (1926), 636–637

DeFunis v. Odegaard, 416 U.S. 312, 94 S.Ct. 1704, 40 L.Ed.2d 164 (1974), 750

Dennis v. United States, 341 U.S. 494, 71 S.Ct. 857, 95 L.Ed. 1137 (1951), 439, 440

Denver Area Educational Telecommunications Consortium v. Federal Communications Comm'n, 518 U.S. 727, 116 S.Ct. 2374, 135 L.Ed.2d 888 (1996), 461

Department of Commerce v. Montana, 503 U.S. 442, 112 S.Ct. 1415, 118 L.Ed.2d 87 (1992), 830

Department of Revenue of Mont. v. Kurth Ranch, 511 U.S. 767, 114 S.Ct. 1937, 128 L.Ed.2d 767 (1994), 614

DeShaney v. Winnebago Social Servs., 489 U.S. 189, 109 S.Ct. 998, 103 L.Ed.2d 249 (1989), 347, **357**

Doe v. Commonwealth's Attorney, 425 U.S. 985, 96 S.Ct. 2192, 48 L.Ed.2d 810 (1976), 691, 727

Dolan v. City of Tigard, 512 U.S. 374, 114 S.Ct. 2309, 129 L.Ed.2d 304 (1994), 395, 396, **426**

Doran v. Salem Inn, 422 U.S. 922, 95 S.Ct. 2561, 45 L.Ed.2d 648 (1975), 446, 447, 487

Douglas v. California, 372 U.S. 353, 83 S.Ct. 814, 9 L.Ed.2d 811 (1963), 604, 764

Douglas v. City of Jeanette, 319 U.S. 157, 63 S.Ct. 877, 87 L.Ed. 1324 (1943), 525

Dred Scott v. Sanford, 60 U.S. 393, 15 L.Ed. 691 (1857), 345, 381

Dring v. Missouri, 107 U.S. 221, 2 S.Ct. 443, 27 L.Ed. 506 (1883), 335

Duncan v. Louisiana, 391 U.S. 145, 88 S.Ct. 1444, 20 L.Ed.2d 491 (1968), 349, **372,** 609

Duplex Printing Co. v. Deering, 254 U.S. 443, 41 S.Ct. 172, 65 L.Ed. 349 (1921), 388

Duquesne Light Co. v. Barasch, 488 U.S. 299, 109 S.Ct. 609, 102 L.Ed.2d 646 (1989), 396

Eddings v. Oklahoma, 455 U.S. 104, 102 S.Ct. 869, 71 L.Ed.2d 1 (1982), 625

Edge Broadcasting, United States v., 509 U.S. 418, 113 S.Ct. 2696, 125 L.Ed.2d 345 (1993), 510

Edmondson v. Leesville Concrete Co., 500 U.S. 614, 111 S.Ct. 2077, 114 L.Ed.2d 660 (1991), 612

Edwards v. Aguillard, 482 U.S. 578, 107 S.Ct. 2573, 96 L.Ed.2d 510 (1987), 538, **570**

Edwards v. South Carolina, 372 U.S. 229, 83 S.Ct. 680, 9 L.Ed.2d 697 (1963), 455, **503,** 505

Edwards v. United States, 358 U.S. 847, 79 S.Ct. 74, 3 L.Ed.2d 82 (1958), 605

Eichman, United States v., 496 U.S. 310, 110 S.Ct. 2404, 110 L.Ed.2d 287 (1990), 446

Eisenstadt v. Baird, 405 U.S. 438, 92 S.Ct. 1029, 31 L.Ed.2d 349 (1972), 681, 691, 727

Employment Div., Oregon Dept. of Human Resources v. Smith, 494 U.S. 872, 110 S.Ct. 1595, 108 L.Ed.2d 876 (1990), 526, 527, 528, 529, 544, **553,** 561

Engel v. Vitale, 370 U.S. 421, 82 S.Ct. 1261, 8 L.Ed.2d 601, 20 O.O.2d 328 (1962), 536

Engle v. Isaac, 456 U.S. 107, 102 S.Ct. 1558, 71 L.Ed.2d 783 (1982), 623

Epperson v. Arkansas, 393 U.S. 97, 89 S.Ct. 266, 21 L.Ed.2d 228 (1968), 538, 571, 572

Escobedo v. Illinois, 378 U.S. 478, 84 S.Ct. 1758, 12 L.Ed.2d 977, 32 O.O.2d 31 (1964), 600, 604, 644

Everson v. Board of Educ., 330 U.S. 1, 67 S.Ct. 504, 91 L.Ed. 711 (1947), 349, 522, 532, 534, **562,** 569

Ex parte (see name of party)

Faretta v. California, 422 U.S. 806, 95 S.Ct. 2525, 45 L.Ed.2d 562 (1975), 605

Fay v. Noia, 372 U.S. 391, 83 S.Ct. 822, 9 L.Ed.2d 837, 24 O.O.2d 12 (1963), 334, 622

Federal Communications Comm'n v. League of Women Voters, 468 U.S. 364, 104 S.Ct. 3106, 82 L.Ed.2d 278 (1984), 461

Federal Communications Comm'n v. Pacifica Found., 438 U.S. 726, 98 S.Ct. 3026, 57 L.Ed.2d 1973 (1978), 460, **496,** 500

Federal Election Comm'n v. National Conservative Political Action Comm., 470 U.S. 480, 105 S.Ct. 1459, 84 L.Ed.2d 455 (1985), 833

Feiner v. New York, 340 U.S. 315, 71 S.Ct. 303, 95 L.Ed. 295 (1951), 504

Felker v. Turpin, 518 U.S. 1051, 116 S.Ct. 2333, 135 L.Ed.2d 827 (1996), 624

Ferguson v. Skrupa, 372 U.S. 726, 83 S.Ct. 1028, 10 L.Ed.2d 93 (1963), 392, **423**

Firefighters v. Cleveland, 478 U.S. 510, 106 S.Ct. 3063, 92 L.Ed.2d 405 (1986), 752

First English Evangelical Lutheran Church v. County of Los Angeles, 482 U.S. 304, 107 S.Ct. 2378, 96 L.Ed.2d 250 (1987), 385

Fiske v. Kansas, 274 U.S. 380, 47 S.Ct. 655, 71 L.Ed. 1108 (1927), 349, 437

Fletcher v. Peck, 10 U.S. 87, 3 L.Ed. 162 (1810), 379

Florida v. Bostick, 501 U.S. 429, 111 S.Ct. 2382, 115 L.Ed.2d 389 (1991), 591

Florida Star, The, v. B.J.F., 491 U.S. 524, 109 S.Ct. 2603, 105 L.Ed.2d 443 (1989), 450

Ford v. Wainwright, 477 U.S. 399, 106 S.Ct. 2595, 91 L.Ed.2d 335 (1986), 619

Freeman v. Pitts, 503 U.S. 467, 112 S.Ct. 1430, 118 L.Ed.2d 108 (1992), 748, 790

Frontiero v. Richardson, 411 U.S. 677, 93 S.Ct. 1764, 36 L.Ed.2d 583 (1973), 757, **799**

Fullilove v. Klutznick, 448 U.S. 448, 100 S.Ct. 2758, 65 L.Ed.2d 902 (1980), 751, 752, 753, 796, 797

Furman v. Georgia, 408 U.S. 238, 92 S.Ct. 2726, 33 L.Ed.2d 346 (1972), 617, 619, **665,** 670, 671

Gannett v. DePasquale, 443 U.S. 368, 99 S.Ct. 2898, 61 L.Ed.2d 608 (1979), 610

Garland, Ex parte, 71 U.S. 333, 18 L.Ed. 366 (1866), 335

Gault, In re, 387 U.S. 1, 87 S.Ct. 1428, 18 L.Ed.2d 527, 40 O.O. 378 (1967), 346, 625

Geduldig v. Aiello, 417 U.S. 484, 94 S.Ct. 2485, 41 L.Ed.2d 256 (1974), 759

Georgia v. McCollum, 505 U.S. 42, 112 S.Ct. 2348, 120 L.Ed.2d 33 (1992), 612

Gerstein v. Pugh, 420 U.S. 103, 95 S.Ct. 854, 43 L.Ed.2d 54 (1975), 599

Gertz v. Robert Welch, Inc., 418 U.S. 323, 94 S.Ct. 2997, 41 L.Ed.2d 789 (1974), 449

Gideon v. Wainwright, 372 U.S. 335, 83 S.Ct. 792, 9 L.Ed.2d 799, 23 O.O. 258 (1963), 341, 604, 605, 606, 625, **654,** 764

Ginsberg v. New York, 390 U.S. 629, 88 S.Ct. 1274, 20 L.Ed.2d 195 (1968), 497, 500

Gitlow v. New York, 268 U.S. 652, 45 S.Ct. 625, 69 L.Ed. 1138 (1925), 349, 431, 437, 438

Goesaert v. Cleary, 335 U.S. 464, 69 S.Ct. 198, 93 L.Ed. 163 (1948), 756

Goldman v. Weinberger, 475 U.S. 503, 106 S.Ct. 1310, 89 L.Ed.2d 478 (1986), 530

Gomillion v. Lightfoot, 364 U.S. 339, 81 S.Ct. 125, 5 L.Ed.2d 110 (1960), 821, 823, **837**

Gong Lum v. Rice, 275 U.S. 78, 48 S.Ct. 91, 72 L.Ed. 172 (1927), 780

Grace, United States v., 461 U.S. 171, 103 S.Ct. 1702, 75 L.Ed.2d 736 (1983), 457

Grand Rapids School Dist. v. Ball, 473 U.S. 373, 105 S.Ct. 3216, 87 L.Ed.2d 267 (1985), 535, 536, 573, 574, 575

Gray v. Sanders, 372 U.S. 368, 83 S.Ct. 801, 9 L.Ed.2d 821 (1963), 828

Green v. County School Bd., 391 U.S. 430, 88 S.Ct. 1689, 20 L.Ed.2d 716 (1968), 786, 787

Gregg v. Georgia, 428 U.S. 153, 96 S.Ct. 2909, 49 L.Ed.2d 859 (1976), 617, 619, **670**

Griswold v. Connecticut, 381 U.S. 479, 85 S.Ct. 1678, 14 L.Ed.2d 510 (1965), 344, 346, 677, 679, 680, 681, 682, 692, 698, **709,** 724, 727, 730

Grovey v. Townsend, 295 U.S. 45, 55 S.Ct. 622, 79 L.Ed. 1292 (1935), 819, 835, 836, 837

Guinn v. United States, 238 U.S. 347, 35 S.Ct. 926, 59 L.Ed. 1340 (1915), 819

Gulf, Colorado & Santa Fe Ry. Co. v. Ellis, 165 U.S. 150, 17 S.Ct. 255, 41 L.Ed. 666 (1897), 739

Hamilton v. Regents of the Univ. of Cal., 293 U.S. 245, 55 S.Ct. 197, 79 L.Ed. 343 (1934), 522

Hamilton, In the Matter of, 657 S.W.2d 425 (Tenn.App. 1983), 531

Hampton v. Mow Sun Wong, 426 U.S. 88, 96 S.Ct. 1895, 48 L.Ed.2d 495 (1976), 764

Hardenbaugh v. New York, 454 U.S. 958, 102 S.Ct. 496, 70 L.Ed.2d 374 (1981), 542

Harmelin v. Michigan, 501 U.S. 957, 111 S.Ct. 2680, 115 L.Ed.2d 836 (1991), 615

Harper v. Virginia State Bd. of Elections, 383 U.S. 663, 86 S.Ct. 1079, 16 L.Ed.2d 169 (1966), 353, 764, 820

Harris v. McRae, 448 U.S. 297, 100 S.Ct. 2671, 65 L.Ed.2d 784 (1980), 686, 765

Harris v. New York, 401 U.S. 222, 91 S.Ct. 643, 28 L.Ed.2d 1 (1971), 601

Harris, United States v., 216 F.2d 690 (5th Cir. 1954), 464

Hawaii Housing Auth. v. Midkiff, 467 U.S. 229, 104 S.Ct. 2321, 81 L.Ed.2d 186 (1984), 394, **424**

Hazelwood School Dist. v. Juhlmeier, 484 U.S. 260, 108 S.Ct. 562, 98 L.Ed.2d 592 (1988), 435

Heart of Atlanta Motel v. United States, 379 U.S. 241, 85 S.Ct. 348, 13 L.Ed.2d 258 (1964), 770

Heffron v. International Soc'y for Krishna Consciousness (ISKCON), 452 U.S. 640, 101 S.Ct. 2559, 69 L.Ed.2d 298 (1981), 458, 525

Herndon v. Lowry, 301 U.S. 242, 57 S.Ct. 732, 81 L.Ed. 1066 (1937), 439

Herrera v. Collins, 506 U.S. 390, 113 S.Ct. 853, 122 L.Ed.2d 203 (1993), 623

Hess v. Indiana, 414 U.S. 105, 94 S.Ct. 326, 38 L.Ed.2d 303 (1973), 441

Hobbie v. Unemployment Appeals Div., 480 U.S. 136, 107 S.Ct. 1046, 94 L.Ed.2d 190 (1987), 526, 553

Holden v. Hardy, 169 U.S. 366, 18 S.Ct. 383, 42 L.Ed. 780 (1989), 385, 412, 421

Holt v. Sarver, 300 F.Supp. 825 (D.C.Ark. 1969), 616

Home Building & Loan Ass'n v. Blaisdell, 290 U.S. 398, 54 S.Ct. 231, 78 L.Ed. 413 (1934), 381, 382, 388, **404**

Hopwood v. Texas, 518 U.S. 1033, 116 S.Ct. 2581, 135 L.Ed.2d 1095 (1995), 754, 755

Houston Lawyers' Ass'n v. Attorney General of Tex., 501 U.S. 419, 111 S.Ct. 2376, 115 L.Ed.2d 379 (1991), 825–826

Hudson v. McMillian, 503 U.S. 1, 112 S.Ct. 995, 117 L.Ed.2d 156 (1992), 616

Hudson v. Palmer, 468 U.S. 517, 104 S.Ct. 3194, 82 L.Ed.2d 393 (1984), 616

Hurley v. Irish-American Gay, Lesbian & Bisexual Group of Boston, 515 U.S. 557, 115 S.Ct. 2338, 132 L.Ed.2d 487 (1995), 468, **515,** 770

Hurtado v. California, 110 U.S. 516, 4 S.Ct. 111, 28 L.Ed. 232 (1884), 348, **359, 655**

Hustler Magazine v. Falwell, 485 U.S. 46, 108 S.Ct. 876, 99 L.Ed.2d 41 (1988), 449

Hutto v. Finney, 437 U.S. 678, 98 S.Ct. 2565, 57 L.Ed.2d 522 (1978), 616

Illinois v. Gates, 462 U.S. 213, 103 S.Ct. 2317, 76 L.Ed.2d 527 (1983), 589, 590

In re (see name of party)

Jackson v. United States, 393 U.S. 899, 89 S.Ct. 75, 21 L.Ed.2d 192 (1968), 608

Jacobellis v. Ohio, 378 U.S. 184, 84 S.Ct. 1676, 12 L.Ed.2d 793, 28 O.O.2d 101 (1964), 452

Jacobson v. Massachusetts, 197 U.S. 11, 25 S.Ct. 358, 49 L.Ed. 643 (1905), 678, 679, **699**

Janis, United States v., 428 U.S. 433, 96 S.Ct. 3021, 49 L.Ed.2d 1046 (1976), 596

Jay Burns Baking Co. v. Bryan, 264 U.S. 504, 44 S.Ct. 412, 68 L.Ed. 813 (1924), 424

J. E. B. v. Alabama ex rel. T. B., 511 U.S. 127, 114 S.Ct. 1419, 128 L.Ed.2d 89 (1994), 612, 808

Jenkins v. Georgia, 418 U.S. 153, 94 S.Ct. 2750, 41 L.Ed.2d 642 (1974), 452

Jimenez v. Weinberger, 417 U.S. 628, 94 S.Ct. 2496, 41 L.Ed.2d 363 (1974), 762

Johnson v. Louisiana, 406 U.S. 356, 92 S.Ct. 1620, 32 L.Ed.2d 152 (1972), 611

Johnson v. Transportation Agency of Santa Clara, 480 U.S. 616, 107 S.Ct. 1442, 94 L.Ed.2d 615 (1987), 752

Kahn v. Shevin, 416 U.S. 351, 94 S.Ct. 1734, 40 L.Ed.2d 189 (1974), 759

Kam, State v., 69 Haw. 483, 748 P.2d 372 (Haw. 1988), 355

Kansas v. Hendricks, — U.S. —, 117 S.Ct. 2072, 138 L.Ed.2d 501 (1997), 614, **661**

Karcher v. Daggett, 462 U.S. 725, 103 S.Ct. 2653, 77 L.Ed.2d 133 (1983), 829, **858**

Katz v. United States, 389 U.S. 347, 88 S.Ct. 507, 19 L.Ed.2d 576 (1967), 340, 588, **631,** 677

Keeney v. Tamayo-Reyes, 504 U.S. 1, 112 S.Ct. 1715, 118 L.Ed.2d 318 (1992), 623

Ker v. California, 374 U.S. 23, 83 S.Ct. 1623, 17 L.Ed.2d 726, 24 O.O.2d 201 (1963), 598

Keyes v. Denver School Dist., 413 U.S. 189, 93 S.Ct. 2686, 37 L.Ed.2d 548 (1973), 747

Keystone Bituminous Coal Ass'n v. DeBenedictis, 480 U.S. 470, 107 S.Ct. 1232, 94 L.Ed.2d 472 (1987), 394

Kirkpatrick v. Preisler, 394 U.S. 526, 89 S.Ct. 1225, 22 L.Ed.2d 519 (1969), 829, 858, 859, 860, 861

Kiryas Joel School Dist. v. Grumet, 512 U.S. 687, 114 S.Ct. 2481, 129 L.Ed.2d 546 (1994), 536

Koon, United States v., 34 F.3d 1416 (9th Cir. 1994), 613

Korematsu v. United States, 323 U.S. 214, 65 S.Ct. 193, 89 L.Ed. 194 (1944), 354, 739

Kovacs v. Cooper, 336 U.S. 77, 69 S.Ct. 448, 93 L.Ed. 513 (1949), 458

Kuhlmann v. Wilson, 477 U.S. 436, 106 S.Ct. 2616, 91 L.Ed.2d 364 (1986), 623

Labine v. Vincent, 401 U.S. 532, 91 S.Ct. 1017, 28 L.Ed.2d 288 (1971), 762

Lalli v. Lalli, 439 U.S. 259, 99 S.Ct. 518, 58 L.Ed.2d 503 (1978), 762

Lane v. Wilson, 307 U.S. 268, 59 S.Ct. 872, 83 L.Ed. 1281 (1939), 819

Lassiter v. Northampton County Bd. of Educ., 360 U.S. 45, 79 S.Ct. 985, 3 L.Ed.2d 1072 (1959), 820

Lee v. International Soc'y for Krishna Consciousness, 505 U.S. 830, 112 S.Ct. 2709, 120 L.Ed.2d 669 (1992), 457

Lee v. Wesiman, 505 U.S. 577, 112 S.Ct. 2649, 120 L.Ed.2d 467 (1992), 537

Lemon v. Kurtzman, 403 U.S. 602, 91 S.Ct. 2105, 29 L.Ed.2d 745 (1971), 533, 534, 535, 536, 540, 541, 567, 570, 573, 576, 578

Leon, United States v., 468 U.S. 897, 104 S.Ct. 3405, 82 L.Ed.2d 677 (1984), 596, 597, **639**

Lewis v. United States, 445 U.S. 55, 100 S.Ct. 915, 63 L.Ed.2d 198 (1980), 339

Lloyd Corp. v. Tanner, 407 U.S. 551, 92 S.Ct. 2219, 33 L.Ed.2d 131 (1972), 457

Locher v. New York, 198 U.S. 45, 49 L.Ed. 937 (1905), 346, 385, 387, 391, 392, **411,** 418, 419, 424, 678, 709, 719, 759

Lockhart v. McCree, 476 U.S. 162, 106 S.Ct. 1758, 90 L.Ed.2d 137 (1986), 619

Loewe v. Lawlor, 208 U.S. 274, 28 S.Ct. 301, 52 L.Ed. 488 (1908), 388

Lovett, United States v., 328 U.S. 303, 66 S.Ct. 1073, 90 L.Ed. 1252 (1946), 335

Loving v. Virginia, 388 U.S. 1, 87 S.Ct. 1817, 18 L.Ed.2d 1010 (1967), 740, **783,** 798

Lynch v. Donnelly, 465 U.S. 668, 104 S.Ct. 1355, 79 L.Ed.2d 604 (1984), 541, 544, **579**

Lyons v. Oklahoma, 322 U.S. 596, 64 S.Ct. 1208, 88 L.Ed. 1481 (1944), 600

Madsen v. Women's Health Center, 512 U.S. 753, 114 S.Ct. 2516, 129 L.Ed.2d 593 (1994), 456

Maher v. Roe, 432 U.S. 464, 97 S.Ct. 2376, 53 L.Ed.2d 484 (1977), 685, 686, 765, 766

Malley v. Briggs, 475 U.S. 335, 106 S.Ct. 1092, 89 L.Ed.2d 271 (1986), 597, 598

Malloy v. Hogan, 378 U.S. 1, 84 S.Ct. 1489, 12 L.Ed.2d 653 (1964), 600

Mapp v. Ohio, 367 U.S. 643, 81 S.Ct. 1684, 6 L.Ed.2d 1081, 16 O.O.2d 384 (1961), 595, 596, 598, 600, 625, **635,** 643, 710

Marbury v. Madison, 5 U.S. 137, 2 L.Ed. 60 (1803), 681

Marsh v. Chambers, 463 U.S. 783, 103 S.Ct. 3330, 77 L.Ed.2d 1019 (1983), 533, 540, 541, **576**

Martin v. Wilks, 490 U.S. 755, 109 S.Ct. 2180, 104 L.Ed.2d 835 (1989), 752

Maryland v. Wilson, 518 U.S. 1053, 117 S.Ct. 34, 135 L.Ed.2d 1126 (1997), 594

Massachusetts v. Sheppard, 468 U.S. 981, 104 S.Ct. 3424, 82 L.Ed.2d 737 (1984), 596, 597

Massachusetts v. Upton, 466 U.S. 727, 104 S.Ct. 2085, 80 L.Ed.2d 721 (1984) , 590

Massachusetts Bd. of Retirement v. Murgia, 427 U.S. 307, 96 S.Ct. 2562, 49 L.Ed.2d 520 (1976), 354

Matter of (see name of party)

McCardle, Ex parte, 74 U.S. 506, 19 L.Ed. 264 (1869), 622

McCleskey v. Kemp, 481 U.S. 279, 107 S.Ct. 1756, 95 L.Ed.2d 262 (1987), 620

McCleskey v. Zant, — U.S. —, 111 S.Ct. 1454, 113 L.Ed.2d 517 (1991), 334

McCollum v. Board of Educ., 333 U.S. 203, 68 S.Ct. 461, 92 L.Ed. 649 (1948), 534

McDaniel v. Paty, 435 U.S. 618, 98 S.Ct. 1322, 55 L.Ed.2d 593 (1978), 524

McGowan v. Maryland, 366 U.S. 420, 81 S.Ct. 1101, 6 L.Ed.2d 393 (1961), 540, 582

McKane v. Durston, 153 U.S. 684, 14 S.Ct. 913, 38 L.Ed. 867 (1894), 621

McKeiver v. Pennsylvania, 403 U.S. 528, 91 S.Ct. 1976, 29 L.Ed.2d 647 (1971), 625

McLaurin v. Oklahoma State Regents, 339 U.S. 637, 70 S.Ct. 851, 94 L.Ed. 1149 (1950), 744–745, 781

M'Culloch v. Maryland, 17 U.S. 316, 4 L.Ed.2d 579 (1819), 542

Meek v. Pittenger, 421 U.S. 349, 95 S.Ct. 1753, 44 L.Ed.2d 217 (1975), 534

Memoirs v. Massachusetts, 383 U.S. 413, 86 S.Ct. 975, 16 L.Ed.2d 1 (1966), 452, 494

Memphis Firefighters v. Stotts, 467 U.S. 561, 104 S.Ct. 2576, 81 L.Ed.2d 483 (1984), 752

Meritor Savings Bank v. Vinson, 477 U.S. 57, 106 S.Ct. 2399, 91 L.Ed.2d 49 (1986), 757

Metro Broadcasting v. Federal Communications Comm'n (FCC) 497, U.S. 547, 110 S.Ct. 2997, 111 L.Ed.2d 445 (1990), 753, 794, 795, 796, 797, 808

Meyer v. Nebraska, 262 U.S. 390, 43 S.Ct. 625, 67 L.Ed. 1042 (1923), 437, 532, 678, 679, 681, **701,** 709, 784

Michael H. v. Gerald D., 491 U.S. 110, 109 S.Ct. 2333, 105 L.Ed.2d 91 (9189), 763

Michigan v. Tyler, 436 U.S. 499, 98 S.Ct. 1942, 56 L.Ed.2d 486 (1978), 591

Miller v. California, 413 U.S. 15, 93 S.Ct. 2607, 37 L.Ed.2d 419 (1973), 452, 454, **493,** 501

Miller v. Johnson, 515 U.S. 900, 115 S.Ct. 2475, 132 L.Ed.2d 762 (1995), 847-853

Miller, United States v., 307 U.S. 174, 59 S.Ct. 816, 83 L.Ed. 1206 (1939), 339

Millikin v. Bradley (Millikin I), 418 U.S. 717, 94 S.Ct. 3112, 41 L.Ed.2d 1069 (1974), 747, 788, 789, 791

Millikin v. Bradley (Millikin II), 433 U.S. 267, 97 S.Ct. 2749, 53 L.Ed.2d 745 (1977), 788, 790

Minersville School Dist. v. Gobitis, 310 U.S. 586, 60 S.Ct. 1010, 84 L.Ed. 1375 (1940), 444, 529, 545, 546

Minnesota v. Dickerson, 508 U.S. 366, 113 S.Ct. 2130, 124 L.Ed.2d 3334 (1993), 592

Minnesota v. Hershberger, 495 U.S. 901, 110 S.Ct. 1918, 109 L.Ed.2d 282 (1990), 531

Minor v. Happersett, 88 U.S. 162, 22 L.Ed. 627 (1875), 352, 756

Miranda v. Arizona, 384 U.S. 436, 86 S.Ct. 1602, 16 L.Ed.2d 694 (1966), 600, 601, 603, 604, 625, **644,** 647, 648, 649, 650

Mississippi Univ. for Women v. Hogan, 458 U.S. 718, 102 S.Ct. 3331, 73 L.Ed.2d 1090 (1982), 760, 804, 805, 806, 808

Missouri v. Jenkins, 515 U.S. 70, 115 S.Ct. 2038, 132 L.Ed.2d 63 (1995), 748, **788**

Missouri ex rel. Gaines v. Canada, 305 U.S. 337, 59 S.Ct. 232, 83 L.Ed. 208 (1938), 744

Missouri Pac. R.R. Co. v. Nebraska, 164 U.S. 403, 17 S.Ct. 130, 41 L.Ed. 489 (1896), 425

Mobile v. Bolden, 446 U.S. 55, 100 S.Ct. 1490, 64 L.Ed.2d 47 (1980), 823, 824, **839,** 842, 843, 844, 845

Moe v. Secretary of Administration, 382 Mass. 629, 417 N.E.2d 387 (Mass. 1981), 686

Montoya de Hernandez, United States v., 473 U.S. 531, 105 S.Ct. 3304, 87 L.Ed.2d 381 (1985), 593

Moore v. City of East Cleveland, 431 U.S. 494, 97 S.Ct. 1932, 52 L.Ed.2d 531 (1977), 691, 728, 730

Moose Lodge v. Irvis, 407 U.S. 163, 92 S.Ct. 1965, 32 L.Ed.2d 627 (1972), 768

Moran v. Burbine, 475 U.S. 412, 106 S.Ct. 1135, 89 L.Ed.2d 410 (1986), 602

Morehead v. New York ex rel. Tipaldo, 298 U.S. 587, 56 S.Ct. 918, 80 L.Ed. 1347 (1936), 389, 390, 391, 420, 421, 423

Morey v. Doud, 354 U.S. 457, 77 S.Ct. 1344, 1 L.Ed.2d 1485 (1957), 393

Mozert v. Hawkins County Public Schools, 484 U.S. 1066, 108 S.Ct. 1029, 98 L.Ed.2d 993 (1988), 539

Mueller v. Allen, 463 U.S. 388, 103 S.Ct. 3062, 77 L.Ed.2d 721 (1983), 543

Mugler v. Kansas, 123 U.S. 623, 8 S.Ct. 273, 31 L.Ed. 205 (1887), 385

Mulford v. Smith, 307 U.S. 38, 59 S.Ct. 648, 83 L.Ed. 1092 (1939), 391

Muller v. Oregon, 208 U.S. 412, 28 S.Ct. 324, 52 L.Ed. 551 (1908), 386, 416, 419, 421

Munn v. Illinois, 94 U.S. 113, 24 L.Ed. 77 (1876), 384, 389

Murdock v. Pennsylvania, 319 U.S. 105, 63 S.Ct. 870, 87 L.Ed. 1292)(1943), 432, 525

Murray v. Curlett, 374 U.S. 203, 83 S.Ct. 1560, 10 L.Ed.2d 844 (1963) , 536

Naim v. Naim, 350 U.S. 891, 76 S.Ct. 151, 100 L.Ed. 784 (1955), 784

National Ass'n for the Advancement of Colored People v. Alabama, 357 U.S. 449, 78 S.Ct. 1163, 2 L.Ed.2d 1488 (1958), 467, 709

National Ass'n for the Advancement of Colored People v. Claiborne Hardware Co., 458 U.S. 886, 102 S.Ct. 3409, 73 L.Ed.2d 1215 (1982), 441

National Endowment for the Arts v. Finley, WL 33299 (U.S.) (June 25, 1998), 466, **512**

National Labor Relations Bd. v. Jones & Laughlin Steel Corp., 301 U.S. 1, 57 S.Ct. 615, 81 L.Ed. 893 (1937), 391

National Treasury Employees Union v. Von Raab, 489 U.S. 656, 109 S.Ct. 1384, 103 L.Ed.2d 685 (1989), 340

National Treasury Employees Union, United States v., 513 U.S. 454, 115 S.Ct. 1003, 130 L.Ed.2d 964 (1995), 465

Near v. Minnesota, 283 U.S. 697, 51 S.Ct. 625, 75 L.Ed. 1357 (1931), 349, 433, **470,** 474, 476

Nebbia v. New York, 291 U.S. 502, 54 S.Ct. 505, 78 L.Ed. 940 (1934), 384, 388, 389, 396

Nebraska Press Ass'n v. Stuart, 427 U.S. 539, 96 S.Ct. 2791, 49 L.Ed.2d 683 (1976), 609

Newberry v. United States, 256 U.S. 232, 41 S.Ct. 469, 65 L.Ed. 913 (1921), 819

New York v. Ferber, 458 U.S. 747, 102 S.Ct. 3348, 73 L.Ed.2d 1113 (1982), 354, 453

New York v. Quarles, 467 U.S. 649, 104 S.Ct. 2626, 81 L.Ed.2d 550 (1984), 601, **647**

New York Club Ass'n v. City of New York, 487 U.S. 1, 108 S.Ct. 225, 101 L.Ed.2d 1 (1988), 520, 770

New York Times v. Sullivan, 376 U.S. 254, 84 S.Ct. 710, 11 L.Ed.2d 686 (1964), 448, 449, 450, 451, **490**

New York Times Co. v. United States (The Pentagon Papers Case), 403 U.S. 713, 91 S.Ct. 2140, 29 L.Ed.2d 822 (1971), 434, **473**

Niemotko v. Maryland, 340 U.S. 268, 71 S.Ct. 328, 95 L.Ed. 280 (1951), 525

Nix v. Williams, 467 U.S. 431, 104 S.Ct. 2501, 81 L.Ed.2d 377 (1984), 602

Nixon v. Administrator of General Servs., 433 U.S. 425, 97 S.Ct. 2777, 53 L.Ed.2d 867 (1977), 336

Nixon v. Condon, 286 U.S. 73, 52 S.Ct. 484, 76 L.Ed. 984 (1932), 819

Nixon v. Herndon, 273 U.S. 536, 47 S.Ct. 446, 71 L.Ed. 759 (1927), 819

Nollan v. California Coastal Comm'n, 483 U.S. 825, 107 S.Ct. 3141, 97 L.Ed.2d 677 (1987), 395, 396, 426, 427

Noto v. United States, 367 U.S. 290, 81 S.Ct. 1517, 6 L.Ed.2d 836 (1961), 440, 479

O'Brien, United States v., 391 U.S. 367, 88 S.Ct. 1673, 20 L.Ed.2d 672 (1968), 444, 483, 484, 488, 489

Ogden v. Saunders, 25 U.S. 212, 6 L.Ed. 606 (1827), 380

Ohio v. Robinette, 519 U.S. 33, 117 S.Ct. 417, 136 L.Ed.2d 347 (1996), 591

Old Dominion Co. v. United States, 269 U.S. 55, 46 S.Ct. 39, 76 L.Ed. 162 (1925), 425

Oliver v. United States, 466 U.S. 170, 104 S.Ct. 1735, 80 L.Ed.2d 214 (1984), 588

Olmstead v. United States, 277 U.S. 438, 48 S.Ct. 564, 72 L.Ed. 944 (1928), 587, **628,** 631, 638, 677

O'Neil v. Vermont, 144 U.S. 323, 12 S.Ct. 693, 36 L.Ed. 450 (1892), 615

Oregon v. Mathiason, 429 U.S. 492, 97 S.Ct. 711, 50 L.Ed.2d 714 (1977), 602

Oregon v. Mitchell, 400 U.S. 112, 91 S.Ct. 260, 27 L.Ed.2d 272 (1970), 353

Orr v. Orr, 440 U.S. 268, 99 S.Ct. 1102, 59 L.Ed.2d 306 (1979), 758

Osborne v. Ohio, 495 U.S. 103, 110 S.Ct. 1691, 109 L.Ed.2d 98 (1990), 453

Pace v. Alabama, 106 U.S. 583, 1 S.Ct. 637, 27 L.Ed. 207 (1882), 785

Palko v. Connecticut, 302 U.S. 319, 58 S.Ct. 149, 82 L.Ed. 288 (1937), 349, 350, **364,** 431, 613, 728

Payne v. Tennessee, 501 U.S. 808, 111 S.Ct. 2597, 115 L.Ed.2d 720 (1991), 620, **671**

Pennell v. City of San Jose, 485 U.S. 1, 108 S.Ct. 849, 99 L.Ed.2d 1 (1988), 396

Pennsylvania v. Finley, 481 U.S. 551, 107 S.Ct. 1990, 95 L.Ed.2d 539 (1987), 604

Pennsylvania Coal Co. v. Mahon, 260 U.S. 393, 43 S.Ct. 158, 67 L.Ed. 322 (1922), 394

Penny v. Lynaugh, 492 U.S. 302, 109 S.Ct. 2934, 106 L.Ed.2d 256 (1989), 619

Perry Educational Ass'n v. Perry Local Educators' Ass'n, 460 U.S. 37, 103 S.Ct. 948, 74 L.Ed.2d 794 (1983), 457

Pickering v. Board of Educ., 391 U.S. 563, 88 S.Ct. 1731, 20 L.Ed.2d 811 (1968), 465

Pierce v. Society of Sisters, 268 U.S. 510, 45 S.Ct. 571, 69 L.Ed. 1070 (1925), 437, 549, 678, 679, 681, 709

Planned Parenthood v. Ashcroft, 462 U.S. 476, 103 S.Ct. 2517, 76 L.Ed.2d 733 (1983), 355, 684

Planned Parenthood v. Casey, 505 U.S. 833, 112 S.Ct. 2791, 12 L.Ed.2d 674 (1992), 688, 690, **719,** 731, 733

Planned Parenthood of Central Mo. v. Danforth, 428 U.S. 52, 96 S.Ct. 2831, 49 L.Ed.2d 788 (1976), 864, 723, 724

Plessy v. Ferguson, 163 U.S. 537, 16 S.Ct. 1138, 41 L.Ed. 256 (1896), 743, 744, 745, 750, 751, **776,** 779, 780, 781

Plyler v. Doe, 457 U.S. 202, 102 S.Ct. 2382, 72 L.Ed.2d 786 (1982), 764

Poe v. Ullman, 367 U.S. 497, 81 S.Ct. 1752, 6 L.Ed.2d 989 (1961), 679, 691, **703,** 712, 735, 736

Pope v. Illinois, 481 U.S. 497, 107 S.Ct. 1918, 95 L.Ed.2d 439 (1987), 452

Posadas de Puerto Rico Assocs. v. Tourism Co., 478 U.S. 328, 106 S.Ct. 2968, 92 L.Ed.2d 266 (1986), 463, 510

Powell v. Alabama, 287 U.S. 45, 53 S.Ct. 55, 77 L.Ed. 158 (1932), 603, 605, **651,** 655

Powers v. Ohio, 499 U.S. 400, 111 S.Ct. 1364, 113 L.Ed.2d 411 (1991), 612

Preseault v. Interstate Commerce Comm'n, 494 U.S. 1, 110 S.Ct. 914, 108 L.Ed.2d 1 (1990), 396

Price v. Johnson, 334 U.S. 266, 68 S.Ct. 1049, 92 L.Ed. 1356 (1948), 615

Prince v. Massachusetts, 321 U.S. 158, 64 S.Ct. 438, 88 L.Ed. 645 (1944), 531

Printz v. United States, 521 U.S. —, 117 S.Ct. 2365, 138 L.Ed.2d 914 (1997), 339

Proctor v. California, 512 U.S. 967, 114 S.Ct. 2630, 129 L.Ed.2d 750 (1994), 620

Procunier v. Martinez, 416 U.S. 396, 94 S.Ct. 1800, 40 L.Ed.2d 224, 71 O.O.2d 139 (1974), 616

Progressive, United States v., 467 F.Supp. 990 (D.C.Wis. 1979), 435

Proprietors of the Stourbridge Canal v. Wheely, 109 E.R. 1336 (Court of King's Bench 1831), 401

Prudential Ins. Co. v. Cheek, 259 U.S. 530, 42 S.Ct. 516, 66 L.Ed. 1044 (1922), 437

PruneYard Shopping Center v. Robins, 447 U.S. 74, 100 S.Ct. 2035, 64 L.Ed.2d 741 (1980), 396, 457

Purkett v. Elem, 515 U.S. 1170, 115 S.Ct. 2635, 132 L.Ed.2d 874 (1995), 612

Quinlan, In re, 70 N.J. 10, 355 A.2d 647 (N.J. 1976), 695

Rankin v. McPherson, 483 U.S. 378, 107 S.Ct. 2891, 97 L.Ed.2d 315 (1987), 465

Ravin v. State, 537 P.2d 494 (Alaska 1975), 693

R.A.V. v. St. Paul, 505 U.S. 377, 112 S.Ct. 2538, 120 L.Ed.2d 305 (1992), 442, 443, 444

Red Lion Broadcasting Co. v. FCC, 395 U.S. 367, 89 S.Ct. 1794, 23 L.Ed.2d 371 (1969), 500

Reed v. Reed, 404 U.S. 71, 92 S.Ct. 251, 30 L.Ed.2d 225 (1971), 757, 762, 799, 802

Reese, United States v., 92 U.S. 214, 23 L.Ed. 563 (1875), 818

Regents of the Univ. of Cal. v. Bakke, 438 U.S. 265, 98 S.Ct. 2733, 57 L.Ed.2d 750 (1978), 750, 754

Regina v. Hicklin, L.R. 3 Q.B. 360 (1868), 451

Reno v. American Civil Liberties Union (ACLU), — U.S. —, 117 S.Ct. 2329, 138 L.Ed.2d 874 (1997), 453, 461, **500**

Renton v. Playtime Theatres, Inc., 475 U.S. 41, 106 S.Ct. 925, 89 L.Ed.2d 29 (1986), 459, 500

Reynolds v. Sims, 377 U.S. 533, 84 S.Ct. 1362, 12 L.Ed.2d 506 (1964), 828, 830, 831, 834, 840, **855**

Reynolds v. United States, 98 U.S. 145, 25 L.Ed. 244 (1878), 526, 527

Ribnic v. McBridge, 277 U.S. 350, 48 S.Ct. 545, 72 L.Ed. 913 (1928), 384

Richards v. Wisconsin, 520 U.S. 385, 117 S.Ct. 1416, 137 L.Ed.2d 615 (1997), 590

Richmond, City of, v. J. A. Croson Co., 488 U.S. 469, 109 S.Ct. 706, 102 L.Ed.2d 854 (1989), 752, 794, 795

Richmond Newspapers v. Virginia, 448 U.S. 555, 100 S.Ct. 2814, 65 L.Ed.2d 973 (1980), 610

Right to Choose v. Byrne, 91 N.J. 287, 450 A.2d 925 (N.J. 1982), 686

Riley v. Garrett, 219 Ga. 345, 133 S.E.2d 367 (1963), 729, 730

Riverside, County of, v. McLaughlin, 500 U.S. 44, 111 S.Ct. 1661, 114 L.Ed.2d 49 (1991), 599

Roberts v. City of Boston, 5 Cush. 198 (Mass. 1849), 777

Roberts v. United States Jaycees, 468 U.S. 609, 104 S.Ct. 3244, 82 L.Ed.2d 462 (1984), 468, 770

Robinson v. California, 370 U.S. 660, 82 S.Ct. 1417, 8 L.Ed.2d 758 (1962), 615

Rochin v. California, 342 U.S. 165, 72 S.Ct. 205, 96 L.Ed. 183 (1952), 346, 349, **369**

Roe v. Wade, 410 U.S. 113, 93 S.Ct. 705, 35 L.Ed.2d 147 (1973), 347, 354, 675, 676, 682, 683, 684, 686, 687, 689, 690, 692, **714,** 720, 721, 722, 724, 725, 726, 727

Rogers v. Lodge, 458 U.S. 613, 102 S.Ct. 3272, 73 L.Ed.2d 1012 (1982), 823, **842**

Romer v. Evans, 517 U.S. 620, 116 S.Ct. 1620, 134 L.Ed.2d 855 (1996), 693, 767, **811**

Rosenberger v. University of Virginia, 515 U.S. 819, 115 S.Ct. 2510, 132 L.Ed.2d 700 (1995), 539

Ross, United States v., 456 U.S. 798, 102 S.Ct. 2157, 72 L.Ed.2d 572 (1982), 591-592

Rostker v. Goldberg, 453 U.S. 57, 101 S.Ct. 2646, 69 L.Ed.2d 478 (1981), 530, 759, 808

Rotary Int'l v. Rotary Club of Duarte, 481 U.S. 537, 107 S.Ct. 1940, 95 L.Ed.2d 474 (1987), 468, 770

Roth v. United States, 354 U.S. 476, 77 S.Ct. 1304, 1 L.Ed.2d 1498, 14 O.O.2d 331 (1957), 451, 494, 495, 499

Rubin v. Coors Brewing Co., 514 U.S. 476, 115 S.Ct. 1585, 131 L.Ed.2d 532 (1995), 508

Rummel v. Estelle, 445 U.S. 263, 100 S.Ct. 1133, 63 L.Ed.2d 382 (1980), 615

Rust v. Sullivan, 500 U.S. 173, 111 S.Ct. 1759, 114 L.Ed.2d 233 (1991), 465, 466, 688

Saia v. New York, 334 U.S. 558, 68 S.Ct. 1148, 92 L.Ed. 1574 (1948), 458

Salerno, United States v., 481 U.S. 739, 107 S.Ct. 2095, 95 L.Ed.2d 697 (1987), 343, 607

San Antonio v. Rodriguez, 411 U.S. 1, 93 S.Ct. 1278, 36 L.Ed.2d 16 (1973), 764

Sanders v. United States, 375 U.S. 844, 84 S.Ct. 95, 11 L.Ed.2d 7 (1963), 622, 623

Santa Clara County v. Southern Pac. R.R., 118 U.S. 394, 6 S.Ct. 1132, 30 L.Ed. 118 (1886), 385, 738

Santobello v. New York, 404 U.S. 257, 92 S.Ct. 495, 30 L.Ed.2d 427 (1971), 608

Scales v. United States, 367 U.S. 203, 81 S.Ct. 1469, 6 L.Ed.2d 782 (1961), 440, 467

Schad v. Borough of Mount Ephraim, 452 U.S. 61, 101 S.Ct. 2176, 68 L.Ed.2d 671 (1981), 487

Schall v. Martin, 467 U.S. 253, 104 S.Ct. 2403, 81 L.Ed.2d 207 (1984), 625

Schenck v. Pro-Choice Network, 519 U.S. 357, 117 S.Ct. 855, 137 L.Ed.2d 1 (1997), 457

Schenck v. United States, 249 U.S. 47, 39 S.Ct. 247, 63 L.Ed. 470 (1919), 436, 438, **477**

Schmerber v. California, 384 U.S. 757, 86 S.Ct. 1826, 16 L.Ed.2d 908 (1966), 591

Schneckloth v. Bustamonte, 412 U.S. 218, 93 S.Ct. 2041, 36 L.Ed.2d 854 (1973), 591

Scott v. Illinois, 440 U.S. 367, 99 S.Ct. 1158, 59 L.Ed.2d 383 (1979), 605

Seeger, United States v., 380 U.S. 163, 85 S.Ct. 850, 13 L.Ed.2d 733 (1965), 523, 524, 530

Serrano v. Priest, 96 Cal.Rptr. 601, 487 P.2d 1241 (Cal. 1971), 765

Shapiro v. Thompson, 394 U.S. 618, 89 S.Ct. 1322, 22 L.Ed.2d 600 (1969), 354, 763

Shaw v. Hunt, 517 U.S. 899, 116 S.Ct. 1894, 135 L.Ed.2d 207 (1995), 826, **847**

Shaw v. Reno, 509 U.S. 630, 113 S.Ct. 2816, 125 L.Ed.2d 511 (1993), 826, 847

Sheet Metal Workers v. Equal Employment Opportunity Comm'n, 478 U.S. 421, 106 S.Ct. 3019, 82 L.Ed.2d 344 (1986), 752

Shelley v. Kraemer, 334 U.S. 1, 68 S.Ct. 836, 92 L.Ed. 1161 (1948), 769

Sheppard v. Maxwell, 384 U.S. 333, 86 S.Ct. 1507, 16 L.Ed.2d 600, 35 O.O.2d 431 (1966), 609

Sherbert v. Verner, 374 U.S. 398, 83 S.Ct. 1790, 10 L.Ed.2d 965 (1963), 526, 553, 554, 556

Sipuel v. Oklahoma Bd. of Regents, 199 Okl. 586, 190 P.2d 437 (Okl.1948), 744

Skinner v. Oklahoma, 316 U.S. 535, 62 S.Ct. 1110, 86 L.Ed. 1655 (1942), 679, 784

Skinner v. Railway Labor Executives Ass'n, 489 U.S. 602, 109 S.Ct. 1402, 103 L.Ed.2d 639 (1989), 340

Slaughterhouse Cases, The, 83 U.S. 36, 21 L.Ed. 394 (1873), 366, 383, **407**, 738

Smith v. Allwright, 321 U.S. 649, 64 S.Ct. 757, 88 L.Ed. 987 (1944), 347, 819, **835,** 840

Smith v. Board of School Comm'rs of Mobile County, 827 F.2d 684 (11th Cir. 1987), 539

Sokolow, United States v., 490 U.S. 1, 109 S.Ct. 1581, 104 L.Ed.2d 1 (1989), 593

Solem v. Helm, 463 U.S. 277, 103 S.Ct. 3001, 77 L.Ed.2d 637 (1983), 615

South Carolina v. Gathers, 490 U.S. 805, 109 S.Ct. 2207, 104 L.Ed.2d 876 (1989), 620, 671, 673

South Carolina v. Katzenbach, 383 U.S. 301, 86 S.Ct. 803, 15 L.Ed.2d 769 (1966), 822

Southeastern Promotions, Ltd. v. Conrad, 420 U.S. 546, 95 S.Ct. 1239, 43 L.Ed.2d 448 (1975), 500

Spinelli v. United States, 393 U.S. 410, 89 S.Ct. 584, 21 L.Ed.2d 637 (1969), 589, 590

Stack v. Boyle, 342 U.S. 1, 72 S.Ct. 1, 96 L.Ed. 3 (1951), 343, 606

Stanford v. Kentucky, 492 U.S. 361, 109 S.Ct. 2969, 106 L.Ed.2d 306 (1989), 626

Stanford v. Texas, 380 U.S. 926, 85 S.Ct. 879, 13 L.Ed.2d 813 (1965), 589

Stanley v. Georgia, 394 U.S. 557, 89 S.Ct. 1243, 22 L.Ed.2d 542 (1969), 453, 692, 728

State v. (see opposing party)

State ex rel. v. (see opposing party and relator)

State of (see name of state)

Steelworkers v. Weber, 443 U.S. 193, 99 S.Ct. 2721, 61 L.Ed.2d 480 (1979), 752

Stone v. Graham, 449 U.S. 39, 101 S.Ct. 192, 66 L.Ed.2d 199 (1980), 537

Stone v. Mississippi, 101 U.S. 814, 25 L.Ed. 1079 (1879), 381

Stone v. Powell, 428 U.S. 465, 96 S.Ct. 3037, 49 L.Ed.2d 1067 (1976), 334, 623

Straight v. Wainwright, 475 U.S. 1099, 106 S.Ct. 1502, 89 L.Ed.2d 903 (1986), 623

Strauder v. West Virginia, 100 U.S. 303, 25 L.Ed. 664 (1879), 611, 656, 657, 738

Street v. New York, 394 U.S. 576, 89 S.Ct. 1354, 22 L.Ed.2d 572 (1969), 445

Strickland v. Washington, 466 U.S. 668, 104 S.Ct. 2052, 80 L.Ed.2d 674 (1984), 605

Sturges v. Crowninshield, 17 U.S. 122, 4 L.Ed. 529 (1819), 380

Superintendent of Belchertown State School v. Saikewicz, 373 Mass. 728, 370 N.E.2d 417 (Mass. 1977), 694, 695

Swain v. Alabama, 382 U.S. 944, 86 S.Ct. 399, 15 L.Ed.2d 353 (1965), 611, 656, 657, 658, 659, 660

Swann v. Charlotte-Mecklenburg Bd. of Educ., 402 U.S. 1, 91 S.Ct. 1267, 28 L.Ed.2d 554 (1971), 747, **785, 788**

Swann, State ex rel., v. Pack, 527 S.W.2d 99 (Tenn. 1975), 526

Sweatt v. Painter, 339 U.S. 629, 70 S.Ct. 848, 94 L.Ed. 1114 (1950), 745, 780, 781

Tennessee v. Garner, 471 U.S. 1, 105 S.Ct. 1694, 85 L.Ed.2d 1 (1985), 598

Terry v. Adams, 345 U.S. 461, 73 S.Ct. 809, 97 L.Ed. 1152 (1953), 820, 840

Terry v. Ohio, 392 U.S. 1, 88 S.Ct. 1868, 20 L.Ed.2d 889, 44 O.O.2d 383 (1968), 592, 593

Texas v. Johnson, 491 U.S. 397, 109 S.Ct. 2533, 105 L.Ed.2d 342 (1989), 441, 446, **483**

Thomas v. Review Bd., 450 U.S. 707, 101 S.Ct. 1425, 67 L.Ed.2d 624 (1981), 526, 553

Thomas v. Unions Carbide, 473 U.S. 568, 105 S.Ct. 3325, 87 L.Ed.2d 409 (1985), 342

Thompson v. Aldredge, 187 Ga. 467, 200 S.E. 799 (1939), 729

Thompson v. Oklahoma, 487 U.S. 815, 108 S.Ct. 2687, 101 L.Ed.2d 702 (1988), 626

Thompson v. Utah, 170 U.S. 343, 18 S.Ct. 620, 42 L.Ed. 1061 (1898), 335

Thornburgh v. American College of Obstetricians & Gynecologists, 476 U.S. 747, 106 S.Ct. 2169, 90 L.Ed.2d 779 (1986), 686, 689, 723

Thornburgh v. Gingles, 478 U.S. 30, 106 S.Ct. 2732, 92 L.Ed.2d 25 (1986), 825, 850, 854

Time, Inc. v. Firestone, 424 U.S. 448, 96 S.Ct. 958, 47 L.Ed.2d 154 (1976), 449

Time, Inc. v. Hill, 385 U.S. 374, 87 S.Ct. 534, 17 L.Ed.2d 456 (1967), 450

Tinker v. Des Moines Independent Community School Dist., 383 U.S. 503, 89 S.Ct. 733, 21 L.Ed.2d 731, 49 O.O.2d 222 (1969), 435, 444

Torasco v. Watkins, 367 U.S. 488, 81 S.Ct. 1680, 6 L.Ed.2d 982 (1961), 524

Townsend v. Sain, 372 U.S. 293, 83 S.Ct. 745, 9 L.Ed.2d 770 (1963), 623

Trop v. Dulles, 356 U.S. 86, 78 S.Ct. 590, 2 L.Ed.2d 630 (1958), 343, 617

Truax v. Raich, 239 U.S. 33, 36 S.Ct. 7, 60 L.Ed. 131 (1915), 393

Tuilaepa v. California, 512 U.S. 967, 114 S.Ct. 2630, 129 L.Ed.2d 750 (1994), 620

T. W., In re, 551 So.2d 1186 (Fla. 1989), 355, 690

Twining v. New Jersey, 211 U.S. 78, 78 S.Ct. 127, 53 L.Ed.2d 97 (1980), 365, 366, 368

Tyson v. Banton, 273 U.S. 418, 47 S.Ct. 426, 71 L.Ed. 718 (1927), 384

United States v. (see opposing party)

United States Civil Serv. Comm'n v. National Ass'n of Letter Carriers, AFL-CIO, 413 U.S. 548, 93 S.Ct. 2880, 37 L.Ed.2d 796 (1973), 464-465

United States Trust Co. v. New Jersey, 431 U.S. 1, 97 S.Ct. 1505, 52 L.Ed.2d 92 (1977), 381

Virginia, United States v., 518 U.S. 515, 116 S.Ct. 2264, 135 L.Ed.2d 735 (1996), **802**

Virginia, United States v., 766 F.Supp. 1407 (W.D.Va. 1991), 760

Virginia Bd. of Pharmacy v. Virginia Citizens Consumer Council, 425 U.S. 748, 96 S.Ct. 1817, 48 L.Ed.2d 346 (1976), 462, 508, 509, 511

Wallace v. Jaffree, 472 U.S. 38, 105 S.Ct. 2479, 86 L.Ed.2d 29 (1985), 537, **567**

Waller v. Georgia, 467 U.S. 39, 104 S.Ct. 2210, 81 L.Ed.2d 31 (1984), 610

Walton v. Arizona, 497 U.S. 639, 110 S.Ct. 3047, 111 L.Ed.2d 511 (1990), 620

Walz v. Tax Comm'n, 397 U.S. 664, 90 S.Ct. 1409, 25 L.Ed.2d 697 (1970), 542, 577, **583**

Warden v. Hayden, 387 U.S. 294, 87 S.Ct. 1642, 18 L.Ed.2d 782 (1967), 591

Washington v. Davis, 426 U.S. 229, 96 S.Ct. 2040, 48 L.Ed.2d 597 (1976), 740, 841, 843

Washington v. Glucksberg, 521 U.S. —, 117 S.Ct. 2258, 138 L.Ed.2d (1997), 697, **731**

Watkins v. U.S. Army, 847 F.2d 1329 (9th Cir. 1988), 767

Weber v. Aetna Casualty & Surety Co., 406 U.S. 164, 92 S.Ct. 1400, 31 L.Ed.2d 768 (1972), 762

Webster v. Reproductive Health Servs., 492 U.S. 490, 109 S.Ct. 3040, 106 L.Ed.2d 410 (1989), 687, 688, 725

Weeks v. United States, 232 U.S. 383, 34 S.Ct. 341, 58 L.Ed. 652 (1914), 594, 595, 598, **633,** 636, 639

Weinberger v. Wiesenfeld, 420 U.S. 636, 95 S.Ct. 1225, 43 L.Ed.2d 514 (1975), 758

Welch, United States ex rel. TVA v., 327 U.S. 546, 66 S.Ct. 715, 90 L.Ed. 843 (1946), 425

Wesberry v. Sanders, 376 U.S. 1, 84 S.Ct. 526, 11 L.Ed.2d 481 (1964), 830, 860

West Coast Hotel Co. v. Parrish, 300 U.S. 379, 57 S.Ct. 578, 81 L.Ed. 703 (1937), 300 U.S. 379, 57 S.Ct. 578, 81 L.Ed. 703 (1937), 390, 391, 392, **420**

West Virginia State Bd. of Educ. v. Barnette, 319 U.S. 624, 63 S.Ct. 1178, 87 L.Ed. 1628 (1943), 444, 529, **545**

White v. Weiser, 412 U.S. 783, 93 S.Ct. 2348, 37 L.Ed.2d 335 (1973), 858, 861

Whitney v. California, 274 U.S. 357, 47 S.Ct. 641, 71 L.Ed. 1095 (1927), 438, 441, 478, 479

Widmar v. Vincent, 454 U.S. 263, 102 S.Ct. 269, 70 L.Ed.2d 440 (1981), 535, 544

Williams v. Florida, 399 U.S. 78, 90 S.Ct. 1893, 26 L.Ed.2d 446, 53 O.O.2d 55 (1970), 610, 611

Winfield v. Division of PariMutuel Wagering, 477 So.2d 544 (Fla. 1985), 690

Winters v. New York, 333 U.S. 507, 68 S.Ct. 665, 92 L.Ed. 840 (1948), 488

Wisconsin v. Mitchell, 508 U.S. 476, 113 S.Ct. 2194, 124 L.Ed.2d 436 (1993), 443

Wisconsin v. Yoder, 406 U.S. 205, 92 S.Ct. 1526, 32 L.Ed.2d 15 (1972), 531, **548,** 556, 557

Wolf v. Colorado, 338 U.S. 25, 69 S.Ct. 1359, 93 L.Ed. 1782 (1949), 595, 597, 636, 638, 639, 643

Wong Sun v. United States, 371 U.S. 471, 83 S.Ct. 407, 9 L.Ed.2d 441 (1963), 601

Wooley v. Maynard, 430 U.S. 705, 97 S.Ct. 1428, 51 L.Ed.2d 752 (1977), 530

Wynehamer v. New York, 13 N.Y. 378 (1856), 382

Yarbrough, Ex parte, 110 U.S. 651, 4 S.Ct. 152, 28 L.Ed. 274 (1884), 818

Yates v. United States, 354 U.S. 298, 77 S.Ct. 1064, 1 L.Ed.2d 1356 (1957), 440

Yick Wo v. Hopkins, 118 U.S. 356, 6 S.Ct. 1064, 30 L.Ed. 220 (1886), 393, 738, 816

Zimmer v. McKeithen, 485 F.2d 1297 (5th Cir. 1973), 843, 844

Zorach v. Clauson, 343 U.S. 306, 72 S.Ct. 679, 96 L.Ed. 954 (1952), 534, 542

INDEX

Abortion
  conflict over, 682–90
  eroding support for, on Supreme
    Court, 686–88
  and privacy rights, 347, 675–76
  pro-life demonstrations against,
    456–57
  public funding restrictions, 684–86,
    765–66
  regulation of, 684
  restricting counseling on, 465–66
  restricting information about, 688
  and state constitutions, 690
  support for, on Supreme Court,
    683–84, 688–89
Abrams, Jacob, 436–37
Accommodation, 541
Actual malice, 448–49
Adams, John, enforcement of Sedition
  Act, 431
Adderley, Harriet Louise, 455
Ad hoc balancing, 440
Advertising, commercial, 462–64
Affirmative action, 749–55
Age of Conservative Activism, 378
Aggravating factors, 619
Agricultural Adjustment Act, 391
Airport, as public forum, 457
Alcoholic beverages, commercial
  advertising of, 463
Alienage, and discrimination, 763–64
"All deliberate speed," 746
American Bar Association, 384
American Civil Liberties Union
  (ACLU), 688, 693
American Express Company, 393
Americans with Disabilities Act
  (ADA), 763
Amish, 531–32

Anderson, John, 831
Animal sacrifices, and religious liberty,
  528–29
Anonymous informants, 589–90
Anonymous tips, detention of
  automobile based on, 593
Anthony, Susan B., 352
Anti-Federalists, 337, 431
Antiterrorism and Effective Death
  Penalty Act, 335, 624
Appeal and postconviction relief,
  621–25
Appeals by right, 621–22
Appointed counsel, effectiveness of,
  605
Arms, right to keep and bear, 338
Arraignment, 606
Arrest
  probable cause hearing, 599
  use of force by police during, 598
Arrest warrant, 598–99
Assembly, freedom of, 338, 430, 454,
  459–60
  anti-abortion demonstrations,
    456–57
  civil rights demonstrations, 455–56
  and time, place, and manner
    regulations, 458
  and zoning regulations, 458–59
  See also Expressive freedom
Association, freedom of, 430, 466–67
  gay rights versus, 468
  political, 467
  and problem of discrimination,
    467–68, 770
  See also Expressive freedom
At-large elections, 823–24
Attorneys, advertising and solicitation
  by, 463–64

Automobile detention
  based on anonymous tips, 593
  requiring people to exit car during,
    593–94
Automobile searches, 591–92

Bad tendency test, 436–39
Bail
  excessive, 343, 606
  and pretrial detention, 606–7
Bail Reform Act, 607
Bakke, Alan, 750–51
Barry, Andrew, 694
Benevolent neutrality, 541
Bill of Rights
  adoption and ratification of, 333
  civil rights and liberties in, 337–45
  criminal justice protections in,
    586–87
  incorporation of, 348
  privacy rights in, 680–81
  See also specific amendments
Bills of attainder, 335–36, 587
Birth control, and privacy rights, 344,
  679–82
Black, Galen, 527, 528
Black, Hugo
  on civil rights demonstrations, 456
  on clear and probable danger, 440
  on economic due process, 392
  on education, 534
  on First Amendment, 432
  on incorporation of Bill of Rights,
    349–50
  on Ninth Amendment, 344
  on obscenity, 452
  on police interrogation, 600
  on political association, 467

on privacy rights, 675, 681
on school prayer, 536
on suspect classification doctrine, 739–40
on voting rights, 822
Black Codes, 742
Blackmun, Harry A.
on abortion, 683, 687–88, 689
on affirmative action, 751, 752
on capital punishment, 620
on commercial speech, 462
on gay rights, 692
on gender-based peremptory challenges, 612
on juvenile justice, 625
on nude dancing, 447
on plea bargaining, 608
on religious freedom, 527, 528, 541
on state action, 347
on takings issue, 395
Blackstone, William, 433
Bloch, Susan, 767
Bob Jones University, 543
Bork, Robert H., 675, 687
Bradley, Joseph L., 383
Brady Bill, 339
Brandeis, Louis D.
on clear and present danger test, 437, 438, 439
on economic due process, 386–87, 390
on privacy rights, 588, 677–78
Brandeis brief, 387
Brennan, William
on affirmative action, 751, 752, 753
on automobile detention, 593
on child pornography, 453
on death penalty, 617, 619
on flag burning, 446
on gender-based discrimination, 757, 758–59
on good-faith exception, 596–97
on informants, 590
on political association, 467, 468
on press freedom, 435
on privacy rights, 682, 691
on private discrimination, 770
on prurient interest test, 451
on religious liberty, 527, 528, 535, 538, 540
residency and alienage, 764
on Seventh Amendment, 342
on speech restrictions, 461
on takings issue, 395
on zoning regulations, 459

Brewer, David J., 385, 744
Breyer, Stephen G.
on aid to parochial schools, 536
on desegregation, 749
ideology of, 396, 689
on indecent programming on cable television, 461
on race-conscious redistricting, 827
on religious expression in public schools, 539
on sexual predators, 614
Brown, Henry Billings, 744
Brown, Stanley Oscar, 524
Bryan, William Jennings, 538
Buck, Carrie, 679
Bundy, Ted, 606
Bunting, Josiah, III, 761
Burden of proof, 740
Burger, Warren E.
on abortion, 686, 765
on affirmative action, 751, 752
on compulsory school attendance, 531
on death penalty, 619
on exclusionary rule, 596–97
on Fourth Amendment, 340
on gender-based discrimination, 757, 760
on habeas corpus, 334, 622, 623
on imminent lawless action, 441
on informants, 589
on obscenity, 452
on press freedom, 610
on reapportionment, 829
on religious liberty, 540, 541, 542
on residency and alienage, 764
on right to counsel, 605
on self-incrimination, 601
Burton, Harold, 534
Bush, George, and abortion issue, 466, 688
Business affected with a public interest, 384
Busing controversy, 747–49
Butler, Pierce, 389, 390

Cable television, "indecent" programming on, 460–61
Cable Television Consumer Protection and Competition Act, 461
Campaign finance, problem of, 832–33
Cantwell, Newton, 524
Capital punishment, 617–21
of juveniles, 625–26

Cardozo, Benjamin N., 349, 390, 431–32
Carlin, George, 460
Censorship, 349, 432. *See also* Prior restraint
Chafee, Zechariah, Jr., 438
Change of venue, 609
Charles River Bridge Company, 380–81
Chase, Samuel, 335, 377, 379
Child benefit theory, 534
Child labor, 388
Child pornography, 453
Chilling effect, 431
Christmas displays, on public property, 541
Church
separation of state and, 532–34
tax exemptions for, 541–43
See also Religious liberty
Citadel, 760, 761
Civic duties, and religious liberty, 529–31
Civil forfeitures, 343, 614
Civil Rights Act of 1866, 742
Civil Rights Act of 1964, 756–57, 822
Civil rights and liberties, 332–33, 356
in Bill of Rights, 337–45
in Fourteenth Amendment, 345–51
in original Constitution, 333–37
standards of review in, 353–55
in state constitutions, 355
and voting rights, 351–53
Civil rights demonstrations, 455–56
Civil suits, 342
to enforce Fourth Amendment, 597–98
See also Libel
Clark, Tom, 523, 595
Clarke, John H., 437
Classical conservatism, 676
Clear and present danger test, 436
Clear and probable danger test, 439–40
Clinton, Bill
and affirmative action, 754
and Antiterrorism and Effective Death Penalty Act, 624
and "don't ask, don't tell" policy, 767
and gender-based discrimination, 760–61
Supreme Court appointments of, 396
Coalition for Economic Equity, 754
Coffee, Linda, 682

Cohen, Paul Robert, 442
Cold War, 439
Collegiate athletics, gender equity in, 761–62
Commercial speech, 462–64
Communications Decency Act, 453
Community standards, 452
Compelling government interest, 354, 526
Compelling interest, 683, 740
Compulsory school attendance, 531–32
Compulsory self-incrimination, protection against, 340, 349, 600
Compulsory sterilization, 679
Confessions of guilt, 599–603
Confidential and anonymous informants, 589–90
Congress. *See* U.S. Congress
Conkling, Roscoe, 384–85
Connecticut birth control controversy, 679–81
Conscientious objectors, 523
Consent decrees, 752
Consent searches, 591
Constitution, U.S. *See specific amendments and clauses*
Constitutional democracy, 817
Constitutional republic, 817
Content neutrality, and freedom of assembly, 458
Contraceptives. *See* Birth control
Contract Clause, 336–37, 378–79, 382
  later developments, 381
  Marshall Court decisions, 379–80
  Taney Court decisions, 380–81
Contracts, 376
Cooley, Thomas M., 382–83
Counsel
  appointed, effectiveness of, 605
  right to, 341, 603–6
Court-ordered busing, 747
Cox, B. Elton, 455
Creationism–evolution conflict, 538–39
Criminal justice, 626–27
  appeal and postconviction relief, 621–25
  arrest, 598–99
  bail and pretrial detention, 606–7
  death penalty, 617
  exclusionary rule, 594–97, 598
  incarceration and prisoners' rights, 615–17
  jury trials, 609–13

  juvenile, 625–26
  plea bargaining, 607–8
  police interrogation and confessions of guilt, 599–603
  protection against double jeopardy, 613–15
  relevant constitutional provisions, 586–87
  right to counsel, 603–6
  search and seizure, 587–94
Criminal syndicalism, 440
Cruel and unusual punishments, 343, 615, 618
Cruzan, Nancy, 696
Custodial interrogation, 599

Darrow, Clarence, 538
Dartmouth College, 379–80
Day, William R., 594–95
Death penalty, 617–21
  for juveniles, 625–26
Debt adjusting, 392
De facto segregation, 768
Defamation, 432, 448–51
De jure racial segregation, decline of, 744–45
Democracy, representative, 816
Democratic Party, white primary, 819–20
Democratic process, policing, 817–18
Dennis, Eugene, 439
Depression, 381, 388
Desegregation, 745–49
Dirksen, Everett, 830
Dirksen Amendment, 830
Disabled persons, discrimination against, 763
Discrete and insular minorities, 616, 739
Discretionary review, 622
Discrimination, 737–38
  based on sexual orientation, 766–68
  of disabled persons, 763
  and freedom of association, 467–68
  gender-based, 354, 468, 755–62
  and illegitimacy, 762–63
  private, 768–71
  against religious expression, 539
  and residency and alienage, 763–64
  wealth-based, 764
  See also Racial discrimination
Disparate impact, of racially neutral policies, 740
Doctor-assisted suicide, 696–97

Double jeopardy
  and Fifth Amendment, 340, 349, 350
  protection against, 613–15
Douglas, William O.
  on birth control, 679–80, 681
  and First Amendment freedom, 440
  on gender-based discrimination, 759
  on incorporation of Bill of Rights, 349, 350
  on obscenity, 452
  on political association, 467
  on poll taxes, 820
  on religious liberty, 525, 535, 542
Drug courier profile, 591
Drug Enforcement Administration (DEA), 593
Drugs, recreational, private use of, 693–94
Drug testing, 340
Due Process Clause
  in Fifth Amendment, 341
    and affirmative action, 751
    and death penalty, 617
    and freedom of association, 467
    and privacy rights, 677
    and segregation, 745
    substantive interpretation of, 678
  in Fourteenth Amendment, 346
    and clear and present danger, 437, 439
    and death penalty, 617
    and freedom of association, 467
    and incorporation of Bill of Rights, 522, 587, 595, 604, 605
    and prior restraint, 433
    and privacy rights, 677
    and property rights, 348–49
    substantive interpretation of, 678
Due process of law
  economic, 382–92
  procedural, 346
  substantive, 346, 381, 382–83, 387, 388, 391, 678
Duke, David, 832

Easement, 395
Eckhardt, Christopher, 444
Economic due process
  corporate influence on, 384–85
  decline of, 388–92
  early Supreme Court resistance to, 383–84
  heyday of, 386–88

maturation of, 385–86
and origins of substantive due
process, 382–83
Economic equal protection, 764–66
Economic freedom, 376, 397–98
and Contract Clause, 378–82
and economic due process, 382–92
in age of conservative activism, 378
modern judicial perspectives on,
378
Economic regulation
and equal protection, 393
Supreme Court's contemporary
position on, 392
Editorializing on public television and
radio, 461–62
Education
and affirmative action, 750–51, 754
compulsory school attendance,
531–32
desegregation in, 745–49
and evolution-creationism conflict,
538–39
and gender-based discrimination,
760–62
and press freedom, 435
public school funding controversy,
764–65
religion and, 534–40, 541–43. See
also School prayer
segregation in, 744–45
and symbolic speech, 444–45
tuition tax credits, 543
Education for all Handicapped
Children Act, 763
Effects test, 824
Eighth Amendment, 343
incorporation of, 350, 351
and pretrial detention, 606–7
protection against cruel and
unusual punishments, 615, 616,
619, 626
and victim impact evidence, 620
Eisenhower, Dwight D., and school
desegregation, 746
Elections, 833–34
at-large, 823–24
and campaign finance, 832–33
free and fair, 816
judicial, challenges to systems of,
825–26
partisan gerrymandering, 832
and political parties, 831–32
and racial gerrymandering, 821,
826–27

See also Voting rights
Electronic media, and First
Amendment, 460–62
Ely, John Hart, 831
Emergency searches, 591
Eminent domain, 340, 394, 395
Enforcement Act of 1870, 818
Epperson, Susan, 538
Epstein, Richard, 397
Equal access policies, 534–35
Equal Pay Act, 756
Equal protection, 737–38
for disabled persons, 763
economic, 764–66
and economic regulation, 393
Fifth Amendment component of,
738
gender-based discrimination,
755–62
and illegitimacy, 762–63
levels of judicial scrutiny, 738–41
racial equality struggle (see Racial
equality, struggle for)
and residency and alienage, 763–64
See also Discrimination
Equal Protection Clause, 345, 393,
737–38
and compulsory sterilization, 679
and peremptory challenges, 612
and race-conscious redistricting,
826
and reapportionment, 828
See also Equal protection
Equal Rights Amendment (ERA), 757,
759
Error correction, 622
Establishment Clause, 338
incorporation of, 349, 522
interpretations of, 532–34
and religious liberty, 539, 541, 542
and religious tests, 334
Ethics in Government Act, 465
Euthanasia, and privacy rights, 675
Euthanasia. See Right to die
Evanescent evidence, 591
Evangelical Lutheran Church, 395
Evolution-creationism conflict,
538–39
Excessive Bail Clause, 606
Excessive Fines Clause, 343
Exclusionary rule, 594–95, 598
Burger Court's curtailing of, 596–97
Warren Court's expansion of,
595–96
Exigent circumstances, 590

Ex post facto laws, 335, 587
Expressive freedom, 338
and ad hoc balancing, 440
and bad tendency test, 436–39
and clear and present danger test,
436
and clear and probable danger test,
439–40
and commercial speech, 462–64
and electronic media, 460–62
and imminent lawless action,
440–41
interpretive foundations of, 430–33
private control of property versus,
396
of public employees and
beneficiaries, 464–66
in public forum, 454–60
and symbolic speech, 444–48
Expressive religious conduct, 524

Fair Housing Act, 342, 768
Fair Labor Standards Act, 391
Fair trial doctrine, 609
Falwell, Jerry, libel suit against
Hustler, 449–50
Faubas, Orval, 746
Federal Anti-Drug Abuse Act, 621
Federal Communications Commission
(FCC), 460–61
Federal Crime Bill, 621
Federal death penalty, 621
Federal Education Act, Title IX, 757
Federal Election Campaign Act
Amendments, 833
Federal Flag Protection Act, 446
Federal Lobbying Act, 464–65
Federalism, judicial, 765
Federalist Papers, The, 431
Fee simple, 394
Field, Stephen J., 383, 384, 523
Fifteenth Amendment, 351–52, 817,
818
Fifth Amendment, 340–41
Double Jeopardy Clause, 340, 349,
350, 613–15
equal protection component of, 738,
757
Just Compensation Clause, 340,
348–49, 393–97
Self-Incrimination Clause, 340, 349,
600
See also Due Process Clause
Fighting words, 432, 442

Fines, excessive, 343, 614
Firestone, Dorothy, 449
First Amendment, 338, 348, 430
    and campaign finance, 833
    and electronic media, 460–62
    and privacy rights, 677 (*see also*
        Privacy rights)
    scope of, 432–33
    See also Establishment Clause;
        Expressive freedom; Free
        Exercise Clause; Religious liberty
First Amendment absolutism, 432
Flag burning, and symbolic speech,
    445–46
Flag salute controversy, 444, 529–30
Forfeitures, civil, 343, 614
Fortas, Abe, 445, 538
Fourteenth Amendment, 345–51, 390,
    741
    and affirmative action, 751, 753
    and civil rights demonstrations, 455
    and discrimination of disabled
        persons, 763
    and gender-based discrimination,
        757
    incorporation of Bill of Rights,
        348–51, 587
        Fourth Amendment, 595
        Religion Clauses, 522, 534
        right to counsel, 605
        Sixth Amendment, 604
    and peremptory challenges, 611
    and poll taxes, 820
    and privacy rights, 346–47, 677
    and public school funding, 765
    and racial equality, 741, 742, 744
    ratification of, 382
    and restrictive covenants, 769
    and state action, 347
    See also Due Process Clause; Equal
        Protection Clause
Fourth Amendment, 340
    civil suits to enforce, 597–98
    exclusionary rule, 594–97
    good faith exception, 596–97
    search and seizure under, 587–99,
        677
Frankfurter, Felix
    on birth control, 679
    on clear and probable danger test,
        440
    on exclusionary rule, 595
    on flag salute, 529
    and Fourth Amendment, 597
    on partisan gerrymandering, 832

    on racial gerrymandering, 821
    on reapportionment, 828
    on religious education, 534
Free Exercise Clause, 338, 524
    and freedom of association, 467
    incorporation of, 349, 522
    parens patriae versus, 531
    and tax exemptions, 541, 542
    and unconventional religious
        practices, 525, 526, 527
Free marketplace of ideas, 438
Frohnmeyer, John, 466
Frontiero, Sharon, 757
Fruit of the poisonous tree doctrine,
    601, 602
Fuller, Melville W., 385
Fulminante, Oreste, 602, 603
Fundamentalists, 538–39
Fundamental rights, 347, 526, 683

Gag orders, 609
Gay rights
    and discrimination based on sexual
        orientation, 766–68
    freedom of association versus, 468
    and privacy rights, 675, 691–93
Gender-based discrimination, 755–56
    in collegiate athletics, 761–62
    congressional responses to sexual
        equality demands, 756
    by educational institutions, 760–61
    and Equal Rights Amendment, 757
    freedom of association versus, 468
    and intermediate scrutiny, 354
    judicial scrutiny of, 757–60
Gender-based peremptory challenges,
    612
General warrants, 589
Gerrymandering
    partisan, 832
    racial, 821, 826–27
Ginsburg, Ruth Bader
    on affirmative action, 754
    on aid to religious schools, 536
    on gender-based discrimination,
        760, 761
    ideology of, 396, 689
    on race-conscious redistricting, 827
    on religious liberty, 539
    on school desegregation, 749
    on sexual predators, 614
    on takings issue, 395
Gitlow, Benjamin, 437–38
Good faith exception, 596–97

Government contractors, First
    Amendment rights of, 465
Grandfather clauses, 352, 818–19
Grand jury, indictment from, 340
Great Depression, 381, 388, 390, 391
Griswold, Estelle, 680
Group rights, 750
Guilt, confessions of, 599–603

Habeas corpus, writ of, 334–35
    federal review of state criminal
        cases, 622–24
Habitual offender, 615
Hamilton, Alexander
    on Bill of Rights, 337
    on democracy, 817
Hand, Learned, 440
Handicapped persons, discrimination
    against, 763
Hardwick, Michael, 692
Harlan, John Marshall
    on *ad hoc* balancing, 440
    on affirmative action, 750, 751
    on birth control, 680–81
    on corporate influence, 385
    on economic due process, 386
    on exclusionary rule, 595
    on fighting words exception, 442
    on flag burning, 445–46
    on gay rights, 691
    on privacy rights, 588, 677
    on profanity, 443
    on separate but equal
        doctrine, 744
    on substantive due process, 678
Harmless error analysis, 603
Harmless errors, 622
Hate speech, 442–43
Hayes, Paul, 608
Health and Human Services,
    Department of, 465, 688
Hearing
    fair, provided in Fourteenth
        Amendment, 346
    probable cause, 599
Heightened scrutiny, 741
    of gender-based discrimination,
        758–60
Helmet laws, and privacy rights, 694
"Helms Amendment," 461
Hinckley, John, 465
Hogan, Joe, 760
Holmes, Oliver Wendell, Jr.
    on birth control, 679

on clear and present danger test, 436, 437, 438, 439

on economic due process, 386, 388, 391

on heightened scrutiny, 759

on imminent lawless action standard, 441

on takings issue, 394

Homosexuality

and gay rights, 468, 675, 691–93

discrimination based on, 766–68

Hot pursuit, 591

House Un-American Activities Committee, 335

Hughes, Charles Evans

on Contract Clause, 381

on economic due process, 390–91

on prior restraint, 433

Human rights statutes, 770

Hung jury, 613

Hustler (magazine), libel suit against, 449–50

Hyde Amendment, 686, 765, 766

Illegitimacy, and discrimination, 762–63

Imminent lawless action, 440–41

Incarceration, and prisoners' rights, 615–17

Incorporation, doctrine of, 348–51

Indictment, 340

Individual rights, modern concern for, 398. *See also* Civil rights and liberties

Inevitable discovery exception, 602

Informants, confidential and anonymous, 589–90

Intent standard, 824

Intermediate scrutiny, 354

Internal Revenue Service (IRS), 543

Internal Security Act, 439–40

International Society for Krishna Consciousness (ISKCON), 458–59

Internet

and First Amendment protections, 432, 462

"indecency" on, 461

pornography on, 453

Interrogation. *See* Police interrogation

Interstate Commerce Commission (ICC), 396

Investigatory detention, 592–94

Iredell, James, 378

Jackson, Robert H.

on clear and probable danger test, 440

on flag salute controversy, 444, 529

on police interrogation, 600

on religious schools, 534

J. A. Croson Company, 752

Jaybird Democratic Association, 820

Jaycees, 468, 770

Jefferson, Thomas

on Bill of Rights, 337–38

and freedom of speech, 431

Jehovah's Witnesses

and flag saluting, 444, 529

and *parens patriae,* 531

religious solicitation by, 524–25

Jim Crow laws, 743

Johnson, Gregory, 446

Johnson, Lyndon B.

and affirmative action, 749

and voting rights, 822

Johnson, William, 379

Judicial activism, 378

Judicial election systems, challenges to, 825–26

Judicial federalism, 765

Judicial restraint, 616

Judicial scrutiny

heightened, 741, 758–60

of gender-based discrimination, 757–60

levels of, in equal protection cases, 738–41

Judiciary Act of 1789, 621

Juries

exclusion of minorities from, 611–12

size of, 342, 610–11

Jury trial, 341, 609–10, 612–13

exclusion of minorities from juries, 611–12

jury size, 610–11

pretrial publicity problems, 609–10

unanimity principle, 611

Just Compensation Clause, 340, 348–49, 393–97

Justice Department, 822

Justices. *See specific Supreme Court justices*

Juvenile justice, 625–26

Juveniles, capital punishment of, 625–26

Kasper, John, 756

Katz, Charles, 588

Kennedy, Anthony

on abortion, 687, 689

on affirmative action, 752

on aid to religious schools, 536

on anti-abortion demonstrations, 457

on attorney advertising and solicitation, 464

on capital punishment, 620

on discrimination based on sexual orientation, 767

on flag burning, 446

on government contractors, 465

on religious liberty, 528–29

on sexual predators, 614

Kennedy, John F., and affirmative action, 749

Kevorkian, Jack, 695

King, Rodney, 613, 755

Knock-and-announce requirement, 590

Knowing and intelligent waiver, 608

Kolbert, Kathryn, 688

Ku Klux Klan, 338, 441, 467, 818

Laissez-faire capitalism, 378, 380, 386

Least restrictive means test, 461

"Left Wing Manifesto," 437

Lemon test, 533

Libel, 432, 448–51

actual malice, 448–49

invasions of privacy, 450

and public figures, 449–50

Libertarianism, 676

Liberty, 333. *See also* Civil rights and liberties

Liberty of contract, 346, 385

Life imprisonment, mandatory, 615

Life magazine, 450

Lincoln, Abraham, 334, 431

Literacy tests, 352, 820

Little Rock crisis, 746

Living arrangements, and privacy rights, 690–91

Locke, John, 332, 377

Madison, James

and Bill of Rights, 338, 522, 587

on Ninth Amendment, 343

Madsen, Judy, 456

Magistrate, neutral and detached, 589

Magnet schools, 748–49

Malapportionment, 827–28
Malice, actual, 448–49
Mandatory life imprisonment, 615
Marital privacy, 682
Marshall, John
 on Contract Clause, 379–80
 and incorporation of Bill of Rights,
  348
Marshall, Thurgood
 on affirmative action, 751, 752, 753
 on at-large elections, 823
 on automobile searches, 592
 on child pornography, 453
 on death penalty, 617–18, 619, 620
 on habeas corpus, 623
 on heightened scrutiny, 741
 on informants, 593
 on nude dancing, 447
 on privacy rights, 691
 on public school funding, 765, 766
 on religious liberty, 527, 528
 on Seventh Amendment, 342
 on speech rights of public
  employees, 465
 on unanimity principle, 611
Matthews, Stanley, 385, 393
McCarthyism, 439
McCleskey, Warren, 623
McCorvey, Norma. *See* Roe, Jane
McPherson, Ardith, 465
McReynolds, James C., 389
McVeigh, Timothy, 621
Medical treatment, right to refuse,
 531, 694–97
"Mercy killing." *See* Right to die
Meredith, James, 445
Military service, and religious liberty,
 530
Militia, well-regulated, 339
Miller test, 452
Miller, Samuel F., 383
Minimal scrutiny, 354
Minimum wage laws, 390–91
Minorities, exclusion from juries, 611
Miranda warnings, 601
 inevitable discovery exception, 602
 public safety exception, 601
Mississippi University for Women
 (MUW), 760
Mistrials, 613–14
Mitigating circumstances, 620
Mockery of justice test, 605
Moment of silence, 537
"Monkey Trial," 538
Moral individualism, 676

Mormon polygamy case, 526
Murphy, Frank, 597

Narrowly tailored laws, 354
National Association for the
 Advancement of Colored People
 (NAACP), 467, 819
National Endowment for the Arts
 (NEA), funding controversy, 466
National Prohibition Act, 588
Native American Church, and use of
 peyote, 526
Natural rights, 333, 377
Necessary and Proper Clause, 337
Nineteenth Amendment, 352, 387,
 817
Ninth Amendment, 343–44, 677, 678
Nixon, Richard M.
 and affirmative action, 749
 and busing controversy, 747
 presidential papers of, 336
Nude performances, as symbolic
 speech, 446–48

O'Brien, David Paul, 444
Obscenity, 432, 454
 child pornography, 453
 "indecent" television and radio
  programming, 460–61
 Internet pornography, 453
 Miller test, 452
 prurient interest test, 451–52
O'Connor, Sandra Day
 on abortion, 686, 687, 689
 on affirmative action, 752, 753
 on aid to religious schools, 536
 on attorney advertising and
  solicitation, 464
 on capital punishment of juveniles,
  626
 on desegregation, 748
 on gender-based discrimination, 760
 on partisan gerrymandering, 832
 on private discrimination, 770
 on probable cause hearing, 599
 on race-conscious redistricting, 826,
  827
 on religious liberty, 527, 539
 on sexual predators, 614
 on takings issue, 394
Old Order Amish, 531–32
Olmstead Roy, 587–88
Open fields, 588

Operation Rescue, 456
Otis, James, 587

Pacifica Foundation, 460
Parens patriae
 and juvenile justice, 625
 religious liberty versus, 531–32
Partisan gerrymandering, 832
Pat-down search, 592
Patently offensive material, 452
Patriotic rituals, and religious liberty,
 529–31
Peckham, Rufus, 385–86
Pentagon papers case, 434
Peremptory challenge, 612
Perot, Ross, 832
Peter, Forest, 523
Peyote, use of, in Native American
 Church, 526–28
Pichardo, Ernesto, 528
Picketing, 432
Planned Parenthood, 680
Plea bargaining, 607–8
Plessy, Homer, 744
Police, use of force by, 598
Police deception, 602–3
Police interrogation, 599–600
 deception in, 602–3
 Miranda warnings, 601–2
Police powers, 376, 380, 381, 382,
 385–86, 394
Political association, freedom of, 467
Political equality, 816
Political parties
 and electoral fairness, 831–32
 partisan gerrymandering, 832
 white primary, 819–20
Poll taxes, 352–53, 817, 820
Polygamy, and religious liberty, 526
Popular sovereignty, 817
Pornography
 child, 453
 hard-core, 451, 452
 on Internet, 453
Poverty, and discrimination, 764–66
Powell, Lewis
 on abortion, 687
 on affirmative action, 751, 752
 on commercial advertising, 462–63
 on gay rights, 693
 on gender-based discrimination,
  758, 760
 on public school funding, 765
Preate, Ernest, Jr., 688

Preclearance, 822
Preferred freedoms, 388, 431–32
Presidential Recordings and Materials
    Preservation Act, 336
Press
    broadcast media
        editorializing on public television
            and radio, 461–62
        "indecent" television and radio
            programming, 460–61
    commercial advertising, 462–64
    freedom of, 338, 430 (*see also*
        Expressive freedom)
        imminent lawless action versus,
            441
        incorporation of, 431
        as preferred freedom, 432
        libel, 448–51
        obscenity, 451–54
        pretrial publicity, problem of,
            609–10
        rule against prior restraint, 433–35
Presumption of constitutionality, 354,
    740
Pretrial detention, 343, 606–7
Pretrial proceedings, closure of, 610
Pretrial publicity, problem of, 609–10
Pretrial release, 343
Prior restraint, prohibition of, 433–35
Prisoners, rights of, 615–17
Privacy rights, 675–76, 697–98
    abortion controversy, 682–90
    constitutional basis for, 675, 677–79
    Fourteenth Amendment basis for,
        346–47
    and gay rights, 691–93
    and helmet and seat belt laws, 694
    invasions of, 450
    and living arrangements, 690–91
    philosophical foundations for,
        676–77
    procreation and birth control,
        679–82
    reasonable expectations of, 587–88
    and recreational drug use, 693–94
    refusal of medical treatment and
        right to die, 694–97
    and victimless crimes, 693–94
Private discrimination, 768–71
Privileges and Immunities Clause, 383
Probable cause, 587, 588–89
Probable cause hearing, 599
Procedural due process, 346
Procreation, and privacy rights,
    679–82

Proctor, William, 620
Profanity, 432, 443, 460
Progressive, The, 435
Property
    forfeiture of, 343
    private, 376. *See also* Property
        rights
Property rights, 376, 397–98
    and Contract Clause, 378–82
    and economic due process, 382–92
    equal protection and economic
        regulation, 393
    evolving judicial perspectives on,
        377–78
    Fifth Amendment protection of,
        340, 377
    freedom of expression versus, 396
    and takings issue, 393–97
Proportionate representation, 824–25
Proposition 209 (California), 754–55
Protestantism, fundamentalist, 538–39
PruneYard Shopping Center, 396
Prurient interest test, 451–52
Public accommodations statute, 770.
    See also Association, freedom of
Public education. *See* Education
Public employees and beneficiaries,
    rights of, 464–66
Public forum, expressive activities in,
    454–60
Public office, prohibition of religious
    tests for, 334
Public persons, libel suits brought by,
    449–50
Public property, Christmas displays
    on, 541
Public safety exception to, 601
Public television and radio,
    editorializing on, 461–62
Public Use Clause, 394
Punishments, cruel and unusual, 343
Punitive isolation, 616
Pure speech, 432

Quarles, Benjamin, 601
Quinlan, Karen, 695

Race-conscious remedies, 750, 825,
    826–27
Racial discrimination
    and busing controversy, 747
    Jim Crow laws, 743
    ongoing problem of, 755

in public accommodations, 770–71
in religious schools, 542–43
and suspect classification doctrine,
    739–40
in voting rights, 818
    at-large elections, 823–24
    challenges to judicial election
        systems, 825–26
    grandfather clauses, 818–19
    literacy tests, 820
    poll taxes, 820
    racial gerrymandering, 821,
        826–27
    white primary, 819–20
Racial equality, struggle for, 741
    affirmative action, 749–55
    de jure racial segregation, decline
        of, 744–45
    desegregation, 745–49
    Equal Protection Clause, 742–43
    Jim Crow laws, 743
    separate but equal doctrine, 743–44
Racial gerrymandering, 821, 826–27
Racial segregation. *See* Segregation
Radio
    "indecent" programming on, 460–61
    public, editorializing on, 461–62
Rational basis test, 354, 739
Reagan, Ronald
    and abortion, 465, 687
    assassination attempt on, 465
    on school prayer, 537
    on tuition tax credits, 543
    on Voting Rights Act, 822
Reapportionment, 827–31
Reasonable doubt standard, 611
Reasonable suspicion, 592
Recreational drugs, private use of, 693
Redeeming social importance, 452
Reed, Stanley, 819–20
Rehabilitation Act, 763
Rehnquist, William
    on abortion, 687, 689
    on affirmative action, 751, 752–55
    on aid to religious schools, 536
    on anti-abortion demonstrations,
        456–57
    on bail and pretrial detention, 607
    on child pornography, 453
    on civil forfeitures, 614
    on commercial advertising, 463
    on death penalty, 620
    on First Amendment freedoms, 432
    on flag burning, 446
    on Fourth Amendment, 340

on gender-based discrimination, 758, 759, 761

on good-faith exception, 597

on habeas corpus review, 334, 622, 624

on heightened scrutiny, 741

on imminent lawless action standard, 441

on "indecent" television programming, 461

on informants, 589–90

on juvenile justice, 625

on nude dancing, 447

on probable cause hearing, 599

on public figures, 449, 450

on race-conscious redistricting, 826–27

on religious liberty, 530

on restrictive covenants, 769

on right to counsel, 605

on right to die, 696, 697

on school desegregation, 747, 748

on speech rights of public employees, 465

on state action, 347

takings issue under, 395–96

on tuition tax credits, 543

on unanimity principle, 611

Released-time programs, 534–35

Religion, defining, 522–24

Religion Clauses, 338, 522. *See also* Establishment Clause; Free Exercise Clause

Religious beliefs, governmental affirmations of, 540–41

Religious Freedom Restoration Act (RFRA), 528

Religious liberty, 521–22, 544

defining religion, 522–24

and door-to-door solicitation, 524–25

and drug use, 526

and education, 534–40

evolution-creationism conflict, 538–39

parens patriae versus, 531–32

and patriotic rituals and civic duties, 529–31

school prayer controversy, 522, 536–38, 542

separation of church and state, 532–34

and tax exemptions, 541–43

time, place, and manner regulations, 525

unconventional practices, 525–29

Religious practices, unconventional, 525–29

Religious schools

child benefit theory, 534

government assistance for, 535–36

racial discrimination in, 542–43

tax exemptions for, 541–43

Religious speech, 524–25

Religious tests, prohibition of, for public office, 334

Representation. *See* Elections; Voting rights

Representative democracy, 816

Residency, and discrimination, 763–64

Restrictive covenants, 769–70

Revolutionary Age, The, 438

Right to die, and privacy rights, 694–97

Roberts, Owen J., 388, 390

Roe, Jane, 682

Roosevelt, Franklin D., court-packing plan, 390

Rotary Club, 770

Rutledge, Wiley, 534

Sanford, Edward T., 387, 437, 438, 439

Santeria, 528–29

Sarivola, Anthony, 602–3

Scalia, Antonin

on abortion, 687, 689

on affirmative action, 752, 754

on aid to religious schools, 536

on anti-abortion demonstrations, 457

on flag burning, 446

on gay rights, 693, 767

on gender-based discrimination, 761

on hate speech, 442

on "indecent" television programming, 461

on nude dancing, 447

on prisoners' rights, 616

on privacy rights, 676–77

on probable cause hearing, 599

on religious liberty, 527

on sexual predators, 614

on speech rights of public employees and contractors, 465

on takings issue, 395

Scarcity theory, 460

Schenck, Charles T., 436

School attendance, compulsory, 531–32

School prayer, 522, 536–38, 542

School Prayer Amendment, 537

Schools. *See* Education; Religious schools

Scopes, John T., 538

Scopes trial, 538

Search and seizure, 587

automobile searches, 591–92

confidential and anonymous informants, 589–90

investigatory detention, 592–94

knock-and-announce requirement, 590

probable cause, 588–89

reasonable expectations of privacy, 587–88

stop and frisk, 592

unreasonable, protection against, 340

warrantless searches, 590–91

warrant requirement, 589

Search based on consent, 591

Search incidental to a lawful arrest, 591

Search warrants, 589, 590

Seat belt laws, and privacy rights, 694

Second Amendment, 338–39, 350

Secular humanism, 539

Sedition Act, 431

Seditious speech, 432

Seeger, Daniel, 523

Segregation

de facto, 768

de jure, decline of, 744–45

protests against, 455–56

separate but equal doctrine, 743–44

Seigan, Bernard, 397

Selective incorporation, 348–51

Self-incrimination, compulsory, protection against, 340, 349, 600

Self-representation, 605–6

Separate but equal doctrine, 743

Set-aside policy, 750, 752–53

Seventeenth Amendment, 817

Seventh Amendment, 341–42, 350, 609

Severability doctrine, 53–54

Sex discrimination. *See* Gender-based discrimination

Sexual harassment, 757

Sexual orientation, discrimination based on, 766–68

Sexual predators, confinement in mental institutions, 614

Sheppard, Sam, 609

Silver platter doctrine, 595
Sixth Amendment, 341
    right to counsel, 603–6
    right to jury trials, 351, 609, 610
Slavery, Fourteenth Amendment on, 345
Smith, Alfred, 527, 528
Smith Act, 439–40, 467
Social contract theory, 377
Social Darwinism, 385
Socialist party, 437–38
Sodomy laws, 691–93
Solicitation, by attorneys, 463–64
Souter, David
    on abortion, 689
    on aid to religious schools, 536, 539
    on desegregation, 749, 753, 754
    on gay rights, 468
    on nude dancing, 447
    on race-conscious redistricting, 827
    on sexual predators, 614
    on takings issue, 395
South Boston Allied War Veterans
    Council, 468
Speech
    commercial, 462–64
    fighting words, 432, 442
    freedom of, 338, 430 (see also
        Expressive freedom)
        and clear and present danger
            test, 440
        and imminent lawless action, 441
        incorporation of, 431
        as preferred freedom, 432
    hate, 442–43
    and obscenity, 451–54
    profanity, 443
    of public employees and
        beneficiaries, 464–66
    pure, 432
    religious, 524
    seditious, 432
    symbolic, 444–48
Spencer, Herbert, 385
Stanton, Elizabeth Cady, 352
Starr, Kenneth W., 688
State action doctrine, 744
    and Fourteenth Amendment, 347
State constitutions, civil rights and
    liberties in, 355
States
    criminal cases, federal habeas
        corpus review of, 622–23
    powers of
        police powers, 380, 381, 382,
            385–86

to prohibit private discrimination,
    770
Sterilization, compulsory, 679
Stevens, John Paul
    on abortion, 689
    on affirmative action, 751, 753
    on aid to religious schools, 536
    on automobile detention, 614
    on automobile searches, 592, 593
    on child pornography, 453
    on commercial advertising, 463
    on flag burning, 446
    on gay rights, 692
    on heightened scrutiny, 741
    on "indecent" radio programming, 461
    on Internet pornography, 453
    on nude dancing, 447
    on prurient interest test, 452
    on race-conscious redistricting,
        826–27
    on reapportionment, 830
    on religious liberty, 539
    on school desegregation, 749
    on speech rights of public
        employees, 465
    on takings issue, 395
Stewart, Potter
    on abortion, 686, 765–66
    on affirmative action, 751, 752
    on civil rights demonstrations, 455
    on Contract Clause, 381
    on death penalty, 618, 619
    on Ninth Amendment, 344
    on pretrial publicity, 610
    on privacy rights, 588
    on prurient interest test, 452
    on school prayer, 536
    on warrantless searches, 591
Stone, Harlan Fiske
    on economic due process, 390
    on political participation, 818
    on rational basis test, 739
Stop and frisk, 592
Street, Sidney, 445, 446
Strict judicial scrutiny, 354, 740
Strict neutrality, 540
Student newspapers, and prior
    restraint, 435
Subjective voluntariness, 600
Subpoena, 341
Substantive due process, 346, 381
    origins of, 382–83
    and privacy rights, 678
    as restriction on economic
        legislation, 387, 388, 391

Suffrage, universal, 816
Suicide
    doctor-assisted, 696–97
    right to, 695
Sullivan, L. B., 449
Sumner, William Graham, 385
Sunday closing laws, 540
Supervisory power, 595
Suspect classification doctrine,
    739–40
Sutherland, George, 387, 389, 391,
    603–4
Symbolic speech
    flag burning, 445–46
    flag salute controversy, 444
    nude performances as, 446–48
    in Vietnam era, 444–45

Taft, William Howard
    on economic due process, 387, 391
    on privacy rights, 588
Takings issue, and property rights,
    393–97, 766
Taney, Roger B.
    on Contract Clause, 380–81
Taxation
    exemptions, and religious liberty,
        541–43
    poll taxes, 352–53, 817, 820
Taylor, Robert, 746
Television
    "indecent" programming on, 460–61
    public, editorializing on, 461–62
Tenth Amendment, 344
Third Amendment, 340, 350, 677
Thirteenth Amendment, 345, 436
Thomas, Clarence
    on abortion, 689
    on affirmative action, 753, 754
    on aid to religious schools, 536
    on anti-abortion demonstrations,
        457
    on commercial advertising, 463
    on "indecent" television
        programming, 461
    on prisoners' rights, 616
    on school desegregation, 748–49
    on search warrants, 590
    on sexual predators, 614
    on speech rights of public
        employees and contractors, 465
Thurmond, Strom, 823
Time, place, and manner regulations,
    458, 525

Tin Drum, The, 453
Tinker, John, 444
Tinker, Mary Beth, 444
Totality of circumstances, 589
Treason, circumscribing crime of, 333–34
Trial by jury. *See* Jury trial
Trimester framework, 686
Tuition tax credits, 543
Twenty-first Amendment, 463
Twenty-fourth Amendment, 352–53, 817
Twenty-sixth Amendment, 353, 817
Tyranny of the majority, 816, 817

Unalienable rights, 332
Unanimity rule, 611
United States, democratization of, 817
U.S. Congress
    modification of federal habeas corpus procedure, 624
    reapportionment laws, 830
U.S. Constitution. *See specific amendments and clauses*
U.S. Supreme Court
    corporate influence on, 384–85
    and economic due process, early resistance to, 383–84
    rule against prior restraint, 433–35
Universal Military Training and Service Act, 523

Vagueness, as challenge to capital punishment statutes, 620
Van Devanter, Willis, 389
Venue, change of, 609
Verdicts, nonunanimous, 611
Vested rights, 381
Viability, 683
Victim impact statements, 620
Victimless crimes, and privacy rights, 693–94
Vietnam War, and symbolic speech, 444–45
Vinson, Fred M., 440, 745
Violent Crime Control and Law Enforcement Act, 621
Virginia Military Institute (VMI), 760–61
Vote dilution, 826
Voting Accessibility Act, 763
Voting age, 353

Voting rights, 816, 833–34
    Fifteenth Amendment on, 351–52
    Nineteenth Amendment on, 352
    racial discrimination in, 818
        at-large elections, 823–24
        challenges to judicial election systems, 825–26
        grandfather clauses, 818–19
        literacy tests, 820
        poll taxes, 820
        racial gerrymandering, 821, 826–27
        white primary, 819–20
    racially proportionate representation, problem of, 824–25
    and reapportionment, 827–31
    Twenty-fourth Amendment on, 352–53
    Twenty-sixth Amendment on, 353
Voting Rights Act of 1965, 345–46
    impact of, 352, 822–23
    and literacy tests, 820
Voting Rights Act of 1982
    and challenges to judicial election systems, 825–26
    effects test under, 824

Wade, Henry, 682
Waite, Morrison R., 384, 385, 526
Wallace, George, 747, 823
Walz, Frederick, 542
Warrant
    arrest, 598–99
    general, 589
    search, 589, 590
Warrantless arrest, 599
Warrantless searches, 590–91
    of automobiles, 591–92
    stop and frisk, 592
Warrant requirement, 588, 589
Warren, Earl
    on civil rights demonstrations, 456
    on compelling government interest, 526
    on criminal rights, 349, 604
    on cruel and unusual punishment, 343, 617
    on exclusionary rule, 595–96
    on flag burning, 446
    on habeas corpus review, 334, 622, 623
    on imminent lawless action standard, 441

on obscenity, 452
on political association, 467
on reapportionment, 828, 829
on school desegregation, 745
on Sunday closing laws, 540
on symbolic speech, 444
on voting rights, 822
on wealth-based discrimination, 764
on wiretapping, 340
Wealth-based discrimination, 764–66
Weddington, Sarah, 682
White, Byron
    on abortion, 687, 688, 689
    on affirmative action, 751
    on aid to religious schools, 535, 536
    on automobile detention, 593
    on birth control, 680–81
    on death penalty, 619
    on discrimination against disabled persons, 763
    on gay rights, 692, 693
    on jury size, 610
    on nude dancing, 447
    on obscenity, 452
    on police deception, 602
    on press freedom, 435
    on race-conscious redistricting, 826
    on racially neutral policies, 740
    on speech rights of public employees, 465
    on unanimity principle, 611
    on zoning regulations, 458
White, Vanessa, 593
White primary, 352, 819–20
Whitney, Charlotte Anita, 438–39
Wilson, Woodrow, 352
Wiretapping, 340, 588
Women
    indigent, abortion funding restrictions for, 765–66
    right to vote, 352, 387, 817
    See also Abortion; Gender-based discrimination
World Wide Web (WWW), 453
Writ of habeas corpus, 334–35
    federal review of state criminal cases, 622–24

Yellow dog contracts, 387

Zoning regulations, and freedom of assembly, 458